November 2–6, 2015
Cancun, Mexico

**Association for
Computing Machinery**

Advancing Computing as a Science & Profession

MSWiM'15

Proceedings of the 18th ACM International Conference on

Modeling, Analysis and Simulation of Wireless and Mobile Systems

Sponsored by:
ACM SIGSIM

**Association for
Computing Machinery**

Advancing Computing as a Science & Profession

The Association for Computing Machinery
2 Penn Plaza, Suite 701
New York, New York 10121-0701

Notice to Past Authors of ACM-Published Articles
ACM intends to create a complete electronic archive of all articles and/or other material previously published by ACM. If you have written a work that has been previously published by ACM in any journal or conference proceedings prior to 1978, or any SIG Newsletter at any time, and you do NOT want this work to appear in the ACM Digital Library, please inform permissions@acm.org, stating the title of the work, the author(s), and where and when published.

ISBN: 978-1-4503-3762-5   **ACM Order No:** 617151

Additional copies may be ordered prepaid from:

ACM Order Department
PO Box 30777
New York, NY 10087-0777, USA

Phone: 1-800-342-6626 (USA and Canada)
+1-212-626-0500 (Global)
Fax: +1-212-944-1318
E-mail: acmhelp@acm.org
Hours of Operation: 8:30 am – 4:30 pm ET

Printed in the USA

General Chairs' Welcome Message

Welcome to the 18th ACM International Conference on Modelling, Analysis and Simulation of Wireless and Mobile Systems (MSWiM), held this year in astonishing Cancun, Mexico. Resting on the southeast of Mexico, Cancun is well known for its great weather, beautiful "cenotes" (sinkholes), white sand, and heavenly beaches. Cancun serves as an important archeological spot hosting part of the ancient Mayan civilization, and is still considered the gateway to "El Mundo Maya" (the Mayan World). The ruins of this world can be found in the neighborhoods of Cancun, such as Tulum or Chichen Itza, a UNESCO World Heritage site.

MSWiM has established itself over the years as a leading venue where some of the best research in the area of performance evaluation of wireless and mobile systems is presented, and this is no exception.

Putting together a high-quality conference like MSWiM is an enormous undertaking that requires a great team effort. We thank Falko Dressler, Antonio F. Loureiro, and Brahim Bensaou for putting together the technical program, from the Call for Papers to the final program selection and its schedule. We also acknowledge the volunteer efforts of TPC members and external reviewers whose expertise and hard work culminated in selecting excellent papers. This year, MSWiM presents strong poster and demonstration sessions, managed by Robson E. De Grande, the Poster Sessions Chair, and Laura-Marie Feeney, the Demo Session Chair. Finally, the technical program includes two distinguished keynotes addresses by outstanding experts, Prof. Mario Gerla (UCLA USA) and Dr. Pablo Vidales (IBM, Mexico).

To recognize excellence in research work in the field of Wireless Communications and Mobile Networking from academia and industry, the ***Reginald G. Fessenden Award*** has been established and is granted to a distinguished researcher for the remarkable contributions that have been in the area. In 2014, the award was presented to Professor Ian F. Akyildiz in recognition of his pioneering contributions for modeling and analysis of cellular and multihop wireless communications systems. The winner for this year will be announced at the MSWiM 2015 banquet dinner.

Four symposia will be held this year along with the main conference program, covering several specializations within mobile and wireless systems. The four symposia are: MobiWAC, PE-WASUN, DIVANET and Q2SWinet. Over the years, these symposia have become successful and quite competitive in their own right.

We also wish to express our gratitude to those who have managed the many practical details of the event. These individuals include Mirela Notare as the Publicity Chair; and Carolina Medina-Ramirez, Miguel Lopez-Guerrero, and Enrique Rodríguez-de-la-Colina for overseeing the local arrangements. We also express our appreciation to the MSWiM Steering Committee for their guidance and support, which helped us to bring together an exceptional conference program this year. Last but not least, we wish to thank our main sponsor, ACM SIGSIM.

We are very pleased to welcome you to MSWiM 2015 and beautiful Cancun. We are certain that you will find this year's event full of stimulating ideas and discussions.

J. J. Garcia-Luna-Aceves
University of California,
Santa Cruz, USA

Graciela Román Alonso
Universidad Autónoma Metropolitana,
Iztapalapa, Mexico

Technical Program Chairs' Welcome

The technical program of the 18th ACM International Conference on Modeling, Analysis and Simulation of Wireless and Mobile Systems (MSWiM), held in 2015 in Cancun, Mexico, continues to build upon the high standards set by previous editions of the conference.

In 2015, the call for papers attracted 142 registered papers in all areas of mobile and wireless systems. The submitted papers came from 36 countries. Members of the Technical Program Committee are affiliated to universities and industry in 17 countries spread over five continents, reflecting the truly international profile of MSWiM. The five most commonly listed topics for submissions to MSWiM'15 were:

- Performance evaluation and modeling
- Wireless network algorithms and protocols
- Wireless mesh networks, mobile ad hoc networks, Vehicular networks
- Algorithms and protocols for energy efficiency and power control
- Analytical models

The submissions included a large number of papers of very high quality making the selection process difficult and competitive. In the end, we selected 34 regular papers, which correspond to an acceptance rate of approximately 24%. An additional 12 short papers were recommended for the program owing to their quality and contribution.

Among the regular papers, the following three papers were shortlisted as candidates for the best paper award:

- *"5G mmWave Module for the ns-3 Network Simulation,"* Marco Mezzavilla, Sourjya Dutta, Menglei Zhang, Mustafa Akdeniz, and Sundeep Rangan;
- *"Data Dependency based Parallel Simulation of Wireless Networks,"* Mirko Stoffers, Torsten Sehy, James Gross, and Klaus Wehrle;
- *"Minimizing Access Delay for M2M Traffic in Multi-RAT HetNets,"* Prajwal Osti, Samuli Aalto, and Pasi Lassila.

The winner among these three papers will be announced at the conference banquet, and will be reported in the proceedings of MSWiM 2016. At this point, we take the opportunity to congratulate the winners of the best paper award for MSWiM 2015:

- *"Impact of Node Mobility on Single-Hop Cluster Overlap in Vehicular Ad Hoc Networks,"* authored by Khadige Abboud and Weihua Zhuang.

TPC Co-Chairs

Falko Dressler
University of Paderborn, Germany

Brahim Bensaou
Hong Kong University of Science and Technology, Hong Kong

Antonio F. Loureiro
Federal University of Minas Gerais, Brazil

Table of Contents

Session 5: Delay Tolerant and Opportunistic Networks

Session 6: Wireless Sensor Networks (I)

Session 7: Cellular Networks and Mobility Management

Session 8: Cognitive Radio Networks (II)

Session 9: Wireless Networks

Session 10: Performance Evaluation

Session 11: Modeling and Simulation

Session 12: Network Coding and Data Forwarding

MSWiM 2015 Conference Organization

General Co-Chairs: J. J. Garcia-Luna-Aceves *(University of California, USA)*
Graciela Román Alonso *(Universidad Autónoma Metropolitana, Mexico)*

Program Chair: Falko Dressler *(University of Paderborn, Germany)*

Vice Program Co-Chairs: Brahim Bensaou *(Hong Kong University of Science and Technology, Hong Kong)*
Antonio F. Loureiro *(Federal University of Minas Gerais, Brazil)*

Workshop Co-Chairs: Melike Erol-Kantarci *(Clarkson University, USA)*
Sung Bum Hong *(Jackson State University, USA)*

Poster Chair: Robson E. De Grande *(DIVA Strategic Research Network, Canada)*

Demo/Tools Chair: Laura Marie Feeney *(Swedish Institute of Computer Science, Sweden)*

Tutorials Co-Chairs: Periklis Chatzimisios *(Alexander TEI of Thessaloniki, Greece)*
Enrique R. De la Colina *(Universidad Autónoma Metropolitana, Mexico)*

Publicity Chair: Mirela. A. M. Notare *(FAERO/AeroTD – Faculdade de Tecnologia em Transporte Aéreo, Brazil)*

PhD Forum Chair: Bjorn Landfeldt *(Lund University, Sweden)*

Local Arrangements Co-Chairs: Carolina Medina-Ramirez *(Universidad Autónoma Metropolitana, Mexico)*
Miguel Lopez-Guerrero *(Universidad Autónoma Metropolitana, Mexico)*

Steering Committee: Azzedine Boukerche *(University of Ottawa, Canada)*
Sajal K. Das *(University of Texas at Arlington, USA)*
Lorenzo Donatiello *(Università di Bologna, Bologna, Italy)*
Jason Yi-Bing Lin *(National Chiao-Tung University, Taiwan)*
William C.Y. Lee *(AirTouch Inc., USA)*
Simon Taylor *(Brunel University, UK)*
Robson E. De Grande *(DIVA Strategic Research Network, Canada)*

Program Committee:
Antonio A.F. Loureiro *(Federal University of Minas Gerais, Brazil)*
Adam Wolisz *(Technische Universität Berlin, Germany)*
Andrea Passarella *(IIT-CNR, Italy)*
Andreas Willig *(University of Canterbury, New Zealand)*
Angel Cuevas *(Universidad Carlos III de Madrid, Spain)*
Azzedine Boukerche *(University of Ottawa, Canada)*
Bjorn Landfeldt *(Lund University)*
Brahim Bensaou *(The Hong Kong University of Science and Technology, Hong Kong)*
Carla-Fabiana Chiasserini *(Politecnico di Torino, Italy)*
Cheng Li *(Memorial University of Newfoundland, Canada)*
David Eckhoff *(University of Erlangen, Germany)*
Dirk Staehle *(Docomo Euro-Labs, Germany)*
Ehab Elmallah *(University of Alberta, Canada)*
Enzo Mingozzi *(University of Pisa, Italy)*
Falko Dressler *(University of Innsbruck, Austria)*
Francesco Lo Presti *(Universita' di Roma Tor Vergata, Italy)*
Holger Karl *(University of Paderborn, Germany)*
Hongyi Wu *(University of Louisiana at Lafayette, USA)*
Hossam Hassanein *(Queen's University, Canada)*
Isabel Wagner *(University of Hull, UK)*
Isabelle Guérin Lassous *(Université Claude Bernard Lyon 1 - LIP, France)*
Jalel Ben-Othman *(University of Paris 13, France)*
James Gross *(Royal Institute of Technology (KTH), Sweden)*
JJ Garcia-Luna-Aceves *(University of California at Santa Cruz, USA)*
Juan-Carlos Cano *(Universidad Politecnica de Valencia, Spain)*
Klaus Wehrle *(RWTH Aachen University, Germany)*
Lorenzo Donatiello *(Università di Bologna, Italy)*
Luciano Bononi *(University of Bologna, Italy)*
Martina Zitterbart *(Karlsruhe Institute of Technology, Germany)*
Matthias Wählisch *(Freie Universität Berlin)*
Mineo Takai *(University of California, Los Angeles, USA)*
Mónica Aguilar Igartua *(Universitat Politècnica de Catalunya, Spain)*
Raffaele Bruno *(IIT-CNR, Italy)*
Ravi Prakash *(University of Texas at Dallas)*
Renato Lo Cigno *(University of Trento, Italy)*
Roberto Beraldi *(Università di Roma, Italy)*
Robson De Grande *(DIVA Strategic Research Network, Canada)*
Sotiris Nikoletseas *(University of Patras, Greece)*
Stephan Eidenbenz *(Los Alamos National Laboratory, USA)*
Terence D. Todd *(McMaster University, Canada)*
Torsten Braun *(University of Bern, Switzerland)*
Violet Syrotiuk *(Arizona State University, USA)*
Zygmunt Haas *(Cornell University, USA)*

MSWiM 2015 Sponsor & Supporter

Sponsor:

Supporter:

AVANET Services, Autonomous Vehicles and the Mobile Cloud

Mario Gerla
Department of Computer Science
University of California
Los Angeles, CA 90095, USA
http://web.cs.ucla.edu/ gerla/

ABSTRACT

As vehicles will soon become network connected, new vehicle applications are emerging, from navigation safety to location aware content distribution, urban surveillance and intelligent transport. Autonomous vehicles stand out as important players, with plenty of sensors, memory and processing power. The richness of on-board resources and the diversity of applications set the Vehicular ad Hoc Network (VANET) apart from conventional MANETs and introduce new challenges in the services they provide. First, it becomes apparent that safe navigation in a future with autonomous car platoons, say, will demand efficient, low latency V2V. Moreover, other applications (eg, surveillance, traffic management, etc) will require a degree of coordination not possible with the conventional Internet Cloud. To this end, low latency cooperation can be best supported by a Mobile Computing Cloud (MCC), where vehicles use V2V to propagate computation results, share resources and provide mobile services. This talk will revisit VANET applications and will propose a Vehicular Cloud platform along with representative mobile service examples.

Categories and Subject Descriptors

C.2.1 [**Computer-Communication Networks**]: Network Architecture and Design—Wireless communication; C.2.3 [**Computer-Communication Networks**]: [Network Operations—Network management]

Keywords

Networking; Vehicular Networks; Mobile Cloud Computing

Bio

Dr. Mario Gerla is a Professor in the Computer Science Dept at UCLA. He holds an Engineering degree from Politecnico di Milano, Italy and the Ph.D. degree from UCLA. At UCLA, he was part of the team that developed the early ARPANET protocols under the guidance of Prof. Leonard Kleinrock. He joined the UCLA Faculty in 1976. At UCLA he has designed network protocols including ad hoc wireless clustering, multicast (ODMRP and CODE-Cast) and Internet transport (TCP Westwood). He has lead the ONR MINUTEMAN project, designing the next generation scalable airborne Internet for tactical and homeland defense scenarios. His team is developing a Campus Vehicular Testbed. Parallel research activities are wireless medical monitoring using smart phones and cognitive radios in urban environments. He is active in the organization of conferences and workshops, including MedHocNet and WONS. He serves on the IEEE TON Scientific Advisory Board. He became IEEE Fellow in 2002, was recently recognized with the MILCOM Technical Contribution Award in 2011, the IEEE Ad Hoc and Sensor Network Society Achievement Award in 2011 and the ACM Sigmobile Outstanding Contribution Award in 2015.

MSWiM'15, November 2–6, 2015, Cancun, Mexico.
ACM 978-1-4503-3762-5/15/11.
DOI: http://dx.doi.org/10.1145/2811587.2811633 .

Unleashing the True Power of Mobile Systems: Big Data and Analytics

Pablo Vidales
IBM
Mexico
pablo.vidales@cantab.net

ABSTRACT

Mobile systems have continuously evolved in the last years. However, user demand really smart phones that will assist them in daily activities. The new developments in processing and analyzing data are a new chance to make a quantum jump in mobile systems. Every two years the available data duplicates and in combination with existing machine learning and unstructured data analysis closed doors have been open. Today we can really personalized mobile applications to meet the specific needs of each customer, we have more than enough data to develop true context aware mobile solutions; it is just a matter of connecting the dots. This keynote will explore the challenge and opportunities that Big Data and Advanced Analytics are facing, and will present some examples of how we can combine the power of processing and analyzing unstructured and structure data to unleash the true power of mobile systems.

Categories and Subject Descriptors

E.m [**Data**]: [Miscellaneous]; H.3.1 [**Information Storage and Retrieval**]: [Content Analysis and Indexing]

Keywords

Advanced Analytics; Big Data; Mobile Computing

Bio

Dr. Pablo Vidales has a two Bachelor in Science degrees, one in Computer Science and one in Telecommunications from ITAM, Mexico. He got his Master Degree in the University of Cambridge in 2002 and his PhD in 2005. Then, he moved to Berlin, where he did a 2-year Postdoc and continue working for the Deustche Telekom R&D Labs in the area of mobile and distributed systems. During his time in Germany, Dr. Vidales also studied the Executive Program on Strategy and Innovation in the MIT Sloan Business School. Currently he is Associate Professor in ITAM and has taught courses on Mobile Communications and Innovation & Strategy in several academic institutions including TEC de Monterey Campus Puebla, Ibero Campus Puebla and IPADE. Dr. Vidales has co-authored over 70 scientific papers in international conferences and journals and has recently achieved more than 1,000 references to his work. He is also co-inventor in more than 12 granted patents in the area of mobile communications. In 1999, Dr. Vidales founded Letsmap, a startup in the area of mobile services and he also co-founded two spin offs from Deutsche Telekom in the same field. He came back to Mexico in 2010 and since then he has been working in executive positions, leading technology innovation transformational programs for the following companies: T-Systems, Grupo Nacional Provincial, as CIO in RSA Seguros and since May 2014 he took a new challenges as the Executive Lead for LATAM in Advanced Analytics, collaborating with IBM. Pablo is passionate about Innovation and blue sky technology, and in how this can be applied in the private industry to improve our lives. He believes that big data and analytics will unleash the true power of mobile systems.

MSWiM'15, November 2–6, 2015, Cancun, Mexico.
ACM 978-1-4503-3762-5/15/11.
DOI: http://dx.doi.org/10.1145/2811587.2823534 .

Deep Inspection of the Noise in WiFi Time-of-Flight Echo Techniques

Domenico Giustiniano
IMDEA Networks Institute
Madrid, Spain

Theodoros Bourchas
ETH Zurich
Zurich, Switzerland

Maciej Bednarek
ETH Zurich
Zurich, Switzerland

Vincent Lenders
armasuisse
Thun, Switzerland

ABSTRACT

Time-of-flight (ToF) echo techniques have been proposed to estimate the distance between a local and a target station using regular WiFi radio devices. As of today, there is little understanding of the noise sources from ToF measurements. We conduct extensive experimental tests based on a customized WiFi echo technique implementation residing in the core of the 802.11 MAC processor and a high-resolution signal analysis of the WiFi traffic captured with a wideband oscilloscope. We discern the root of the error components in WiFi echo technique measurements and statistically characterize the offset noise added by the target station. Our measurements provide key insights to model the sources of noise and guidance for the design of robust distance estimators.

Categories and Subject Descriptors

C.2.1 [**Computer-Communication Networks**]: Network Architecture and Design—*Wireless Communication*

Keywords

Indoor localization; 802.11; Time of Flight; Measurement noise; Analysis; Implementation; Evaluation

1. INTRODUCTION

Location-based services have recently experienced a huge growth of interest to support entertainment, social media, rescue, advertisement, sport and navigation applications. This unprecedented interest is witnessed by huge commercial and scientific efforts to provide a pin-point indoor positioning system. Following this trend, WiFi Positioning Systems (WPS) based on the signal strength have achieved wide commercial success to complement GPS in indoor and urban canyon environments, even despite being proved to be error-prone and offering limited performance figures [1].

In order to alleviate this problem, solutions such as [2–12] have attempted to use the time-of-flight (ToF) principle to devise an echo technique for ranging measurements that leverages the existing 802.11 protocol. While WiFi echo techniques may offer a cost-effective alternative to estimate the distance, they suffer from severe noise, which may lead to low accuracy and precision of the estimate, particularly when the time to collect samples is limited by the mobility of the target user.

The goal of this work is to dissect the current limitations of WiFi echo techniques. We conduct an in-depth experimental inspection with a customized WiFi echo technique operating in the core of the 802.11 MAC state machine. With controlled tests in the laboratory, we then extract and characterize the offset originated by commercial 802.11 radio chipsets operating as target stations. We study the statistical error distribution of the ToF and characterize how it affects the ranging accuracy and precision. In particular, we aim to answer the following key questions related to timing information extracted for 802.11 ranging:

- How deterministic and predictable are the time offsets for ranging measurements using regular IEEE 802.11 chipsets?
- What are the dominating sources of unpredictiveness in the offset noise?
- How do different IEEE 802.11 chipsets and different physical modulations behave in terms of timing accuracy and precision?
- How stable are the device's offsets over time and according to the network traffic conditions?

Our statistical analysis concludes that the chipset-dependent offset noise at the target station and the additional quantization error of the WiFi clock for timing measurements at the local station are the dominant sources of noise. We provide guidance to discern which features must be taken into account in order to design a robust estimator of the distance.

The rest of this paper is organized as follows. Section 2 introduces the principles of WiFi echo techniques. Our experimental platform is described in Section 3. In Section 4, we investigate the accuracy and the precision of the WiFi echo technique using our platform. We then introduce the setup we use to measure the error of the target station in Section 5 and present our main insights in Section 6. In Section 7, we provide statistical evidence that the target station introduces significant error in ranging measurements, and we finally discuss the implications and conclusions in Section 8.

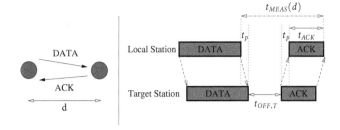

Figure 1: WiFi ToF echo technique. The local station measures $t_{MEAS}(d)$ and computes the distance to the target station. $t_{OFF,T}$ is originated at the target station, and it depends on the 802.11 SIFS time. Not shown in the figure, $t_{OFF,L}$ appears from quantization errors at the local station and errors in the operation of starting and stopping the timer.

2. TOF LOCALIZATION

While traditional echo techniques like radar systems are based on uncoded RF signals and their reflections, WiFi echo techniques use regular frames of communication. These approaches exploit the fact that frames propagate in the air as electromagnetic waves, and thus their propagation times linearly depend on the distance traveled. Echo techniques were first introduced by [3] to resolve the absence (or low precision) of clock synchronization in WiFi chipsets, and then extended by [4–6]. The most recent and promising approaches in the field rely on regular 802.11 DATA frames for the echo requests and on ACK control frames for the echo replies [7, 8, 10]. The distance estimation procedure of these techniques is visualized in Fig. 1. A local station measures the time $t_{MEAS}(d)$ elapsed from the instant that the DATA frame has been transmitted to the instant that the ACK has been received. Depending on the implementation, the local station may either wait until the ACK is completely received or it may stop its timer as soon as it detects the signal energy of the ACK. In this work, we make use of the first approach. Waiting until the ACK has been completely received has the advantage of reducing the time estimation uncertainty for very weak and very strong signal-to-noise ratios inherent in approaches which rely on energy detection [7, 13, 14]. The measurement time is therefore given by

$$t_{MEAS}(d) = 2 * t_P(d) + t_{ACK} + t_{OFF}, \qquad (1)$$

where $t_P(d)$ is the signal propagation time between the local and target station, t_{ACK} indicates the duration of the ACK frame and t_{OFF} is an offset given by

$$t_{OFF} = t_{OFF,T} + t_{OFF,L}, \qquad (2)$$

where $t_{OFF,T}$ and $t_{OFF,L}$ are the target and local offsets caused by the two stations, respectively. $t_{OFF,T}$ originates from hardware processing delays at the target station. It reflects the Short InterFrame Space (SIFS) time according to a tolerance level defined in the 802.11 standard [15]. $t_{OFF,L}$ originates from hardware and software processing delays at the local station. The distance between the local station and the target station is then inferred as

$$\hat{d} = \frac{c}{2} \cdot (t_{MEAS}(d) - t_{ACK} - t_{OFF}), \qquad (3)$$

where c is the speed of light.

3. PLATFORM FOR RANGING MEASUREMENTS

In this section, we present the experimental platform for the ToF echo technique ranging measurements. For cost reasons, an important requirement in the design of the platform is that it must work with commercial off-the-shelf chipsets, such that it can be integrated in legacy networks with a software upgrade. Our implementation meets this requirement, since we rely on a customized software of a low-cost Wi-Fi chipset, with a cost per unit of less than six dollars.

In order to alleviate any source of instability, WiFi echo techniques have to work as close as possible to the radio hardware, and should ideally be integrated in the 802.11 MAC state machine such that the ranging computation is independent of the main CPU processes running in the local and target stations. Our experimental platform is based on the open source openFWWF firmware code for Broadcom chipsets and written in assembler [16]. $t_{MEAS}(d)$ is measured by monitoring two events, the end of the DATA transmission and the end of the ACK reception. The timing of the WiFi echo technique is defined by the General Purpose Timer (GPT), that operates in the wireless chipset at the resolution of the internal clock (88 MHz in our chipset). The GPT is launched in the MAC state machine of the firmware just after the 802.11 processor sets up the COND_TX_DONE condition register (a frame has been sent) which indicates that the timer starts to count clock cycles. The firmware does other operations as required by the 802.11 protocol. Once the ACK frame has been received (or the ACK timeout has elapsed), the COND_RX_COMPLETE register gets updated and the timer gets stopped. The value is saved as the number of clock cycles elapsed since the end of the DATA transmission.

The 802.11b implementation is affected by a quantization error of one clock cycle, equal to a resolution of approximately 11 ns. The 802.11g mode has instead a quantization error of 4 clock cycles, caused by the internal circuit design. Given the speed of light $c = 300\,\text{m}/\mu s$ and the factor 2 of eq. (3), an error of 20 ns corresponds to a distance error of 3 m. Hence, we have a resolution of approximately 1.7 m for 802.11b and 6.4 m for 802.11g[1]. In addition to this, the operation of starting and stopping the timer may introduce an error of one clock cycle in the ToF measurement.

4. RANGING ACCURACY AND PRECISION

Before digging into the detailed offset noise analysis, we first look in this section at the general distance estimation uncertainty that arises with a firmware-based ToF approach as described in the previous section. The uncertainty in distance estimation has two components, the accuracy (the degree of closeness to the true value) and the precision (the degree of certainty of the accuracy). In this section, we provide the results for these metrics. Unless specified otherwise, we use an estimator of the distance based on the median in order to provide estimates which are robust to non-Gaussian distributions of the offset noise components. In addition, outliers in the measurements are filtered out applying the Thompson Tau technique, a statistical method for deciding

---

[1]Other chipsets, such as the Atheros used by [7], have a distance resolution of 3.4 m for both 802.11b and 802.11g modulation schemes.

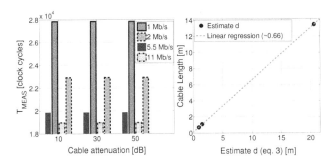

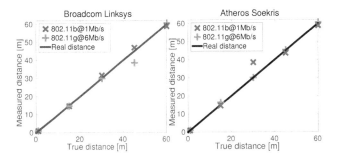

Figure 2: On the left, bar plot of the cable tests (short cable). The measurement at a given distance is independent of the signal strength between the two stations. On the right, plot of the cable length versus the estimate distance. It shows that the estimated distance d increases linearly with the cable length (scaling factor of 0.66 due to cable refractive index).

Figure 3: The indoor tests show that most of the ranging measurements have an accuracy below 2 m. Samples have been gathered for different 802.11 modes and different data rates. The distance is estimated calculating the median out of 10000 samples per test.

whether to keep or discard samples based on the expected value and the expected deviation of the sequence of samples.

4.1 Accuracy

We first measure the distance accuracy using an access point (AP) as local station and a laptop as remote station. Both stations are equipped with a Broadcom AirForce54G BCM4318 802.11 chipset and run the customized firmware for ToF ranging as presented in Section 3. In order to avoid any environmental effects, we connect the two stations using coaxial cables. The cables are of length 0.7 m (short), 1.1 m (medium) and 13.5 m (long), and are based on the standard RG-58. We produced different gain amplifier and signal strength values by introducing different attenuators before the cable of 10, 30 and 50 dB. For each test, we send a total of 10^4 frames and we fix the PHY rate to 1, 2, 5.5, or 11 Mb/s.

On the left of Fig. 2, we report the results for a fixed cable length of 0.7 m. From the bar plot, we draw the conclusion that the results are independent of the signal strength between the two stations, which confirms our expectations (cf. Section 2) that the timing triggered at the end of the ACK reduces the uncertainty for very weak and very strong signal-to-noise ratios with respect to approaches such as [7]. We then measure the estimated distance as a function of the cable length. An example is given on the right of Fig. 2 for the tests at 11 Mb/s. Given that the results are independent of the signal strength, we include at each distance all the measurements with different attenuators and compute the average. We find that the estimated distance increases linearly with the cable length. Note also that we measure a slope coefficient of ≈ 0.66 rather than one, as expected from the refractive index of our coaxial cables.

We then perform tests using a large number of samples sent over antennas in a long corridor with local and target stations in line-of-sight channel conditions where we expect that most of the ranging samples use the direct path between the two stations. This measurement is performed to get a rough feeling on the accuracy that our WiFi echo technique implementation can achieve. We place the local station measuring the ToF ranges and two types of target stations with different 802.11 chipsets at few selected distances (1, 15, 30,

45, 60 m), and collect measurements in order to compute $\hat{d}$ according to eq. (3). At each distance, we gather around 10^4 samples by flooding the channel. We then convert the clock difference between the reference value at 1 m and the median at each distance from clock cycles to meters (one clock cycle corresponds to ≈ 1.7 m) and compute median ranging values of gathered samples.

Figure 3 shows the accuracy by comparing the measured distance with the expected one for the 802.11b modulation at 1 Mb/s and 6 Mb/s. We do not report tests we conducted at other 802.11b and 802.11g PHY rates since they have similar results to the one illustrated here. The results in Figure 3 show that most of the measurements report an accuracy below 2 m. The measurement at 30 m with the Atheros Soekris is likely affected by multipath, which tends to cause an overestimation of the distance. Note also that, using an estimator based on the median, the accuracy is a step function of the distance, with steps equal to 1.7 m for 802.11b. The steps increase to 5.1 – 6.4 m for 802.11g, according to the 802.11g quantization noise and the noise caused by starting and stopping the timers. For instance, the measurement at 45 m with Broadcom Linksys 802.11g is affected by the lower clock resolution of 802.11g timing measurements.

4.2 Precision

We study the 95% confidence interval (CI) of the median as an indicator of the precision of the estimate. Fig. 4 depicts the 95% CI as a function of the number of collected samples for both 802.11 modes at 60 m. Since the measurements are affected by the clock resolution of the WiFi echo technique, we observe step functions. The figure shows that, in order to reach higher precision than 2 m, we need from 80 up to more than 600 samples. Besides the high uncertainty of the measured median for small number of samples, we further observe some fluctuation of the precision in some of the tests - even for large sets of samples. While some multipath in the measurement may be one of the reasons, 802.11g is further affected by the coarser grained clock resolution using OFDM modulation of our firmware. Similar results have been encountered at other distances.

As a result of this investigation, it is evident that the quantization error of $t_{OFF,L}$ plays an important role. However, it is less clear what are the other sources of offset noise. As

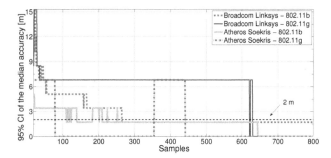

Figure 4: Precision of the estimate as a function of the number of samples for the Broadcom Linksys and Atheros Soekris, operating in 802.11b and 802.11g modes. The distance between the local and target station is 60 m.

such, in the next sections, we first study and quantify how much the target station contributes to the low precision of the distance measured for relatively small number of samples.

5. METHODOLOGY TO EVALUATE THE TARGET OFFSET

To discern the individual sources of offset noise, we present in this section a methodology that we have developed to independently study the offset at the target station $t_{OFF,T}$. Measuring the target offset in practice is quite challenging because we have to remove the channel noise as much as possible and make sure that our measurement system does not add any significant source of noise itself. To this end, we have developed a sophisticated measurement system using a high performing oscilloscope.

5.1 Measurement setup

We measure $t_{OFF,T}$ by monitoring the actual distribution of the PHY SIFS time over the wireless channel. In the rest of this paper, we interchangeably use the term $t_{OFF,T}$ and PHY SIFS time. One constraint of the methodology to monitor PHY SIFS time is that we must assure that the captured DATA/ACK time series have a resolution of at least the main 802.11 clock, so that a direct comparison with $t_{MEAS}(d)$ is viable. One approach could be to access the pins of the baseband signal with an oscilloscope. However, these pins are chipset dependent, and mostly available in older WiFi chipsets. Besides, measurements of the baseband signal would exclude the noise that is generated in the radio front-end.

We therefore employ the setup shown in Fig. 5 that allows us to collect DATA/ACK traffic over the air by measuring the PHY idle time. It consists of:

(i) Traffic monitoring: An Infiniium 90000A Oscilloscope is used to capture signal samples at a rate of 10 GSamples/sec and store data of 20 MB/50 MB per trace, which results in several GBs of total traces collected. A horn antenna is plugged to the I/O port of the oscilloscope and operates as baseband filter in the 2.4 GHz band.

(ii) Local station: Atheros Soekris, configured as access point (AP).

(iii) Target station: One among a) Broadcom Linksys with the Broadcom AirForce54G BCM4318 802.11 chipset

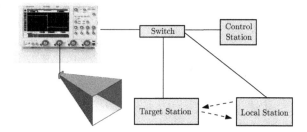

Figure 5: The experimental setup to investigate $t_{OFF,T}$ (PHY SIFS).

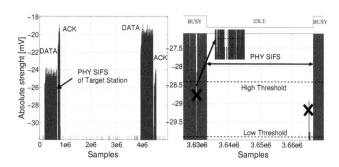

Figure 6: Two traces gathered with the Infiniium 90000A. Figure on the left: the local station sends a ping request and the target answers with a ping reply. We are interested in the distribution of the PHY SIFS ($t_{OFF,T}$) at the target station, acknowledging the reception of the DATA frame (ping request) with an ACK frame. Figure on the right: the Schmitt trigger avoids false detections of busy and idle state, indicated with crosses in the figure. We then compute $t_{OFF,T}$, how long the channel is idle at the target station between the DATA and the ACK.

b) Atheros Soekris with Atheros AR9220 802.11 chipset
c) Samsung GALAXY Nexus smartphone, with Broadcom BCM4335 chipset.

(iv) Control station: a laptop connected to both the oscilloscope and the local station (and the target station, in case of the Broadcom Linksys and the Atheros Soekris). It is used to issue commands to the oscilloscope and to copy the data traces collected by the oscilloscope. The laptop further configures the local and target station, setting the PHY data rate, the number of frames per second (fps) and the frame size. A commodity switch is used to connect through Ethernet cables the oscilloscope, the local station, the target station and the control station.

We place the local station and the target station at a distance of one meter and send ping echo requests from the local to the target station. Traces are collected using both the 802.11b 1 Mb/s and the 802.11g 6 Mb/s PHY rates. Simultaneously, the control station enforces the oscilloscope through a python script to capture traces at a fixed time interval and store them in the control station's hard disk. We collect from 134 to 400 samples per setup. In addition, the target station is in close proximity to the horn antenna, so that its radio signals are immediately captured by the oscilloscope, and the effect of reflections is minimized. Once the

Table 1: Statistical analysis of PHY SIFS time.

	Atheros Soe.	Broadcom Lin.	Broadcom Sam.	Atheros Soe.	Broadcom Lin.	Broadcom Samsung
Mode	802.11b	802.11b	802.11b	802.11g	802.11g	802.11g - display ON, display OFF
Number of samples	310	296	146	350	400	189 − 134
Median (μs)	10.209	10.326	11.581	16.173	16.816	16.190 − 16.200
CI of median (μs)	[10.206 − 10.211]	[10.319 − 10.335]	[11.464 − 11.801]	[16.170 − 16.176]	[16.805 − 16.823]	[16.183 − 16.194] − [16.193 − 16.207]
Standard Deviation (ns)	12.4	47.7	340.2	13.4	34.8	17.4 − 17.1
Skewness	−0.102	0.186	−0.188	0.017	0.078	0.568 − 0.161
Normality Hypothesis	rejected	not rejected	rejected	rejected	rejected	rejected (dis. ON) - not rejected (dis. OFF)

traces are collected, we downsample them by a factor of five to reduce the computational burden of the data processing. An example of trace is shown on the left of Fig. 6. We are interested in the PHY idle time between the DATA received by the target station and the ACK sent back. Note that we do not process the PHY SIFS of the local station, since the value measured by the oscilloscope may not reflect the one observed by the local station (given that it is not in close proximity).

5.2 Inferring the PHY SIFS time

Since the analysis is conducted based on the traces of the oscilloscope, we have to discriminate the PHY SIFS of the target station (first DATA/ACK observed in the left of Fig. 6) from the one of the local station (second DATA/ACK observed in the left of Fig. 6). The target station is in close proximity to the horn antenna and its measured power is higher than the one of the traffic sent by the local station. Hence, we can infer which station transmitted the frame by monitoring the power level. We further double check this fact by slightly moving one between the local and the target station, and observing the power level's changes in the oscilloscope.

The second problem is to convert the traces from the raw data into busy and idle channel states as needed to sense the presence (busy channel) or absence (idle channel) of a frame on the medium. In addition, the conversion should be robust against any false detection of state change, due to spikes of noise, which would affect the accuracy of the observed PHY SIFS. We therefore apply a Schmitt trigger filter over smoothed samples with exponential weighted moving average and forgetting factor α equal to 0.9. In order to have a common baseline, we apply the same high threshold for the Schmitt trigger, 1.5 dB over the noise (low) threshold, for all the tests. An example of trace is illustrated on the right of Fig. 6. Once the idle and busy state have been determined as above, we finally derive the idle time between the DATA and the ACK based on the delimiters of the busy-to-idle and idle-to-busy transitions, and finally remove outliers in the measurements using again the Thompson Tau technique.

6. EVALUATION OF THE TARGET OFFSET

In this section, we explore the results we obtain with the setup presented in the previous section. Our evaluation shows that:

- The statistical distribution of the PHY SIFS time is chipset (and partially modulation) dependent, and the distribution may or may not pass the normality test according to the specific chipset/ modulation/ traffic rate configuration.

- The median of the PHY SIFS is affected by the number of samples considered for computation (error of up to 10 − 20 ns) and by the selection of the frame rate at the local station (the dispersion increases with the frame rate).
- Tests using a smartphone with display on and off show that the median PHY SIFS varies by 10 ns as a result of the power saving state of the device.
- We find that some chipset/modulation introduces an unacceptable level of degradation of the PHY SIFS.

While the errors above may seem small, their impact on the WiFi ToF echo technique is not negligible. Hence, we remark (cf. Section 3) that an error of 20 ns is mapped to a distance error of 3 m.

6.1 Analysis of PHY SIFS and impact on WiFi echo technique

Table 1 reports a summary of the median and the CI of the median (confidence level 95%) of each test. A first general conclusion we can draw is that the 802.11b (802.11g) PHY SIFS time does not have the nominal value of 10 μs (16 μs) [15] but we observe a systematic error[2]. This result is expected, since the 802.11 standard tolerates up to 1 μs of error of the SIFS time with respect to the nominal value [15]. While in the 802.11g Atheros Soekris and the 802.11g Broadcom Samsung, this bias is approximately 0.17 − 0.2 μs, the 802.11g Broadcom Linksys has a higher bias of approximately 0.8 μs, still in the range tolerated by the standard. On the other hand, the 802.11b Broadcom Samsung does not respect the 802.11 standard (bias of 1.58 μs). Concluding, we can state that the median PHY SIFS time is chipset and modulation dependent, which indicates that this value must be measured/calibrated per chipset and modulation in order to perform ToF-based distance estimation.

Another result can be observed comparing statistically the 802.11g PHY SIFS for Broadcom Samsung in the two cases when the display is switched on and off. When the display is switched off, the smartphone transmits frames periodically in a burst. The reported median varies by 10 ns, which entails a variation of the estimated ToF distance of 1.5 m. We hope that the next generation of WLAN chipsets will reduce this error, allowing to provide an estimate of the distance regardless of the smartphone's power state.

6.2 Evolution of the median of PHY SIFS

Figure 7 displays the evolution of the median of the PHY SIFS over the collected samples for the Atheros Soekris and

---

[2]Note that the 802.11g SIFS observed at MAC layer is 10 μs, for backward compatibility with the 802.11b standard [15]. This is achieved with 6-μs virtual SIFS extension.

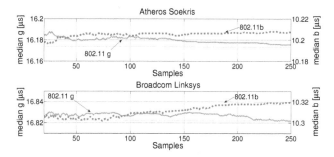

Figure 7: Evolution of the median of PHY SIFS. Median g (median b) indicates the median for 802.11g (802.11b). The median deviates by 10–20 ns with respect to the values reported after the very few samples, which would tend to reduce the accuracy of the WiFi echo technique for small number of samples.

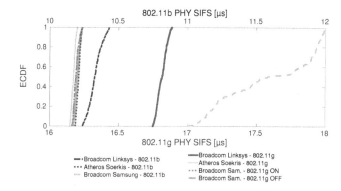

Figure 8: The experiments show that the ECDF of the PHY SIFS is chipset and (partially) modulation dependent. The dispersion is an undesired effect for the WiFi ToF echo technique.

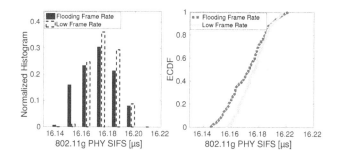

Figure 9: Impact of frame rate. Histogram (on the left) and ECDF (on the right). The dispersion increases with the frame rate.

the Broadcom Linksys. The plot clearly shows that the value reported after a few samples for the four scenarios differs from the one measured over several samples by less than 10 ns. A slightly higher variation is encountered for 802.11b Broadcom Linksys. These variations would affect the median accuracy of the WiFi ToF echo technique by up to 1.5 m (higher for 802.11b Broadcom Linksys) when a small number of samples are collected for the estimation.

6.3 PHY SIFS distribution

We then study the distribution of the PHY SIFS time varying the chipset and the modulation. The empirical cumulative distribution function (ECDF) for the three target stations is plotted in Fig. 8. We observe different types of distributions but none of them provides a constant bias over multiple samples: While for the Atheros chipset and the 802.11g Broadcom Samsung we observe a high density of values around the median value, the Broadcom Linksys exhibits a wider deviation of the values. Since the Broadcom chipset in the Linksys is older than the others, this may indicate the tendency towards smaller dispersion of the target noise in newer chipsets, with a standard deviation that is reduced by a factor of at least 3, as shown in Table 1. However, this is not always the case: in 802.11b Broadcom Samsung, the very large dispersion of the PHY SIFS samples ($\approx 1\,\mu s$) is unacceptable to reliably estimate the distance. We further observe that in most of the experiments there is little skewness, with up to 0.18 in most of the cases. Only for the 802.11g Broadcom Samsung with display on, we measure a higher (right) skewness of 0.56.

We then evaluate whether any of the configurations of chipset and modulation is normal by means of both the Lilliefors and Anderson-Darling tests. We find that some of the distributions do not reject the normality hypothesis for a significant level of 0.05 (802.11b Broadcom Linksys with a p-value of 0.43, and 802.11g Broadcom Samsung with display off with a p-value of 0.31). However, all the other configurations of chipset and modulation reject the normality hypothesis.

6.4 Impact of number of frames per second

We evaluate how the number of frames per second affects $t_{OFF,T}$ at the target station. To this end, we compare the

results of 802.11g Atheros Soekris of previous section with a test where we send 10 fps as opposed to flooding. For ease of representation, we group PHY SIFS samples in bins, with a bin size equal to the 802.11 clock rate, and plot the normalized histogram on the left of Fig 9. On the right of Fig 9, we further show the ECDF for the same tests.

The resulting median for the low frame rate is 16.177 μs (95% CI equal to [16.174–16.179]), which is close to the results observed in Table 1 for the flooding frame rate. We further observe a reduction of the standard deviation from 13.4 to 9.9 ns, which would tend to increase the precision of the WiFi echo technique, at the cost of requiring longer time to collect the same number of samples as for the flooding rate.

With regard to the normality test, it is remarkable that the distribution for the low frame rate does not reject the hypothesis test with a significant level of 0.05 and a p-value of 0.09. This is in contrast to the distribution for the flooding rate. This suggests that the high load of the chipset at the target station for the flooding rate does impact the normality of the distribution. However, normality of the PHY SIFS distribution is not guaranteed at the low rate. For instance, tests with the 802.11b Atheros Soekris (not shown in the figure) do reject the normality hypothesis also at the low transmission rate.

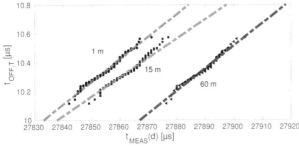

(a) Broadcom Linksys.

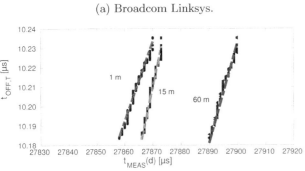

(b) Atheros Soekris.

Figure 10: Quantile-quantile plots. The tests show that $t_{MEAS}(d)$ and $t_{OFF,T}$ come from very similar distributions. It follows that the distribution of the error observed at the local station is mostly caused by the noise of the target offset.

7. ANALYSIS OF TARGET VS LOCAL OFFSET NOISE

In this section, we aim to understand the relative importance of the error of the target offset with respect to the noise in the $t_{MEAS}(d)$ samples, locally reported by the WiFi echo technique. Our goal is to quantify how much of the low precision we have for small number of samples (Section 4.2) is originated by $t_{OFF,T}$ or may come from the local offset $t_{OFF,L}$.

7.1 Quantile-quantile plots for $t_{OFF,T}$ and $t_{MEAS}(d)$

We compare the distribution of $t_{OFF,T}$ with the one of $t_{MEAS}(d)$ using the method of the quantile-quantile plot. For $t_{MEAS}(d)$, we show the samples collected at $d = 1\,\text{m}$, $d = 15\,\text{m}$, and $d = 60\,\text{m}$. Regarding $t_{OFF,T}$, we use the PHY SIFS samples collected with the experimental setup presented in Section 5.1. Results for the Broadcom Linksys and the Atheros Soekris for 802.11b modulation at $1\,\text{Mb/s}$ are summarized in Fig. 10. (Similar results can be found in other configurations.) We observe a linear pattern in all the tests, which indicates that $t_{OFF,T}$ and $t_{MEAS}(d)$ have a very similar distribution.

7.2 Confidence interval of the target offset and precision of the WiFi echo technique

On the left of Fig. 11, we display the 95% CI of the median $t_{OFF,T}$. We observe that the CI for the Broadcom Linksys is larger than the one from the Atheros Soekris. For a target error of less than $2\,\text{m}$, we require around $45 - 50$ samples for the Atheros Soekris, while the Broadcom Linksys does not reach a precision higher than $2\,\text{m}$ in the measurement

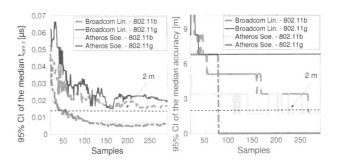

Figure 11: On the left: 95% confidence interval of the median $t_{OFF,T}$ (PHY SIFS time) as a function of the number of samples for the Broadcom Linksys and the Atheros Soekris. The results are in agreement with the precision of the distance measured at the local station (Fig. 4), and reported for ease of comparison on the right, which is further affected by quantization error and timing error in the operation of start and stop of the timer.

set (despite being close to it). Besides, comparing these results with the the 95% CI of the median distance accuracy reported on the right of Fig. 11, we find an agreement between the CI of the median $t_{OFF,T}$ and of the median distance accuracy (measured with eq. (3)). However, in general, we observe further degradation of the CI for the median distance accuracy. As already stressed in Section 4, aside from some multipath in the experimental tests, the origin of this additional noise are the quantization error and the noise of starting and stopping the timer at the local station.

From the results on the left of Fig. 11, we also note that, for a given chipset, the CI follows a similar trend for the 802.11b and 802.11g modulation. Not shown in the figure, the 802.11g Samsung Broadcom has a performance in the middle between the other two platforms, while the Samsung Broadcom 802.11b has, by far, the worst 95% CI of the median.

Comparing the results on the left and on the right of Fig. 11, when higher WiFi clock rates for timing measurements are available at the local station, as for our 802.11b experiments, we see that the convergence rate of the CI of the median distance accuracy is still relatively slow, and hence, even higher WiFi clocks are desired. Concluding, the interplay of the noise of the $t_{OFF,T}$ and the quantization error of $t_{OFF,L}$ strongly limit the precision of the distance measurement. It is remarkable that both sources of noise are originated by intrinsic limitations of the underlying hardware, rather than by any software component of the WiFi ToF echo technique.

8. DISCUSSION AND CONCLUSION

We have demonstrated that, with the recent evolution of WiFi echo techniques, the estimation of the distance between WiFi devices is not bounded by any software implementation, but rather by the intrinsic limitations of the underlying hardware. This problem adversely affects the application of WiFi echo techniques for tracking the distance and position of mobile devices. Our in-depth statistical analysis and evaluation with a customized experimental platform for ToF ranging measurements and independent tools to investigate the origins of noise has dismantled the different components that are limiting the performance figures of current ranging solutions. We have identified and statistically characterized the offset noise of the target station. We have further shown that, together with the quantization error of the main WiFi clock, the target offset is a main source of noise in environments with modest multipath. Given that Fig. 8 shows a target offset's dispersion in the order of $50-200$ ns in most of the chipsets, this dispersion will strongly impact the distance estimation even in harsh environments with large multipath (e.g. 3 m of multipath errors would add a delay of 20 ns to the WiFi echo technique measurement). This would prevent from using standard methods to estimate the distance in harsh multipath environments.

While the quantization error of the local station may be alleviated by newer WiFi chipsets operating on wideband channels (such as the 160 MHz clock of 802.11ac), the variability of the target offset implies that some level of intervention of the target station would be needed to increase the precision of the measurement, such as the 802.11v amendment which would allow location-related timing information to be shared between local and target stations. However, as of today, there is very limited support of 802.11v features in chipsets and drivers. As a result of our investigation, the estimation of the distance must currently be based on a statistical analysis of the noise. Considering that estimators relying on the Gaussian noise assumption of the target device would be suboptimal, robust statistics would be necessary here. The chipset-dependent statistical distribution of the target offset implies that different approaches are used by vendors to implement the SIFS time specification of the standard. Luckily, vendors do not usually exploit all the available dispersion allowed by the standard itself. However, we are far from a very precise ACK generation of the target station to incoming DATA frames.

Acknowledgments

We are grateful to Francesco Gringoli for sharing his open-FWWF code and supporting the project with his enlightening comments. We further thank Srdjan Capkun and Aanjhan Ranganathan from the Information Security Laboratory at ETH Zurich, who let us have access to the Infiniium 90000A oscilloscope. This work has been funded in part by the European Commission in the framework of the H2020-ICT-2014-2 project Flex5Gware (Grant agreement no. 671563) and in part by Ministerio de Economía y Competitividad grant TEC2014-55713-R.

9. REFERENCES

[1] D. Lymberopoulos, J. Liu, X. Yang, R. R. Choudhury, V. Handziski, and S. Sen, "A realistic evaluation and comparison of indoor location technologies: Experiences and lessons learned," in *Proceedings of the 14th International Conference on Information Processing in Sensor Networks*, ser. IPSN '15. New York, NY, USA: ACM, 2015, pp. 178–189.

[2] X. Li, K. Pahlavan, M. Latva-aho, and M. Ylianttila, "Comparison of indoor geolocation methods in dsss and ofdm wireless lan systems," in *IEEE Fall VTC 2000*, vol. 6, 2000, pp. 3015–3020 vol.6.

[3] D. McCrady, L. Doyle, H. Forstrom, T. Dempsey, and M. Martorana, "Mobile ranging using low-accuracy clocks," *Microwave Theory and Techniques, IEEE Transactions on*, vol. 48, no. 6, pp. 951–958, 2000.

[4] A. Günther and C. Hoene, "Measuring round trip times to determine the distance between wlan nodes," in *Proceedings of the 4th IFIP-TC6 international conference on Networking Technologies, Services, and Protocols; Performance of Computer and Communication Networks; Mobile and Wireless Communication Systems*, ser. NETWORKING'05. Berlin, Heidelberg: Springer-Verlag, 2005, pp. 768–779.

[5] M. Ciurana, F. Barcelo-Arroyo, and F. Izquierdo, "A ranging system with ieee 802.11 data frames," in *Radio and Wireless Symposium, 2007 IEEE*, 2007, pp. 133–136.

[6] S. A. Golden and S. S. Bateman, "Sensor measurements for Wi-Fi location with emphasis on time-of-arrival ranging," *IEEE Trans. Mobile Comput.*, vol. 6, no. 10, pp. 1185–1198, Oct. 2007.

[7] D. Giustiniano and S. Mangold, "Caesar: Carrier sense-based ranging in off-the-shelf 802.11 wireless lan," in *Proceedings of the Seventh COnference on Emerging Networking EXperiments and Technologies*, ser. CoNEXT '11. New York, NY, USA: ACM, 2011, pp. 10:1–10:12.

[8] A. Marcaletti, M. Rea, D. Giustiniano, V. Lenders, and A. Fakhreddine, "Filtering noisy 802.11 time-of-flight ranging measurements," in *Proceedings of the 10th ACM International on Conference on Emerging Networking Experiments and Technologies*, ser. CoNEXT '14. New York, NY, USA: ACM, 2014, pp. 13–20.

[9] P. Gallo, D. Garlisi, F. Giuliano, F. Gringoli, and I. Tinnirello, "WMPS: A positioning system for localizing legacy 802.11 devices," in *Transactions on Smart Processing and Computing*, October 2012.

[10] A. T. Mariakakis, S. Sen, J. Lee, and K.-H. Kim, "Sail: Single access point-based indoor localization," in *Proceedings of the 12th Annual International Conference on Mobile Systems, Applications, and Services*, ser. MobiSys '14. New York, NY, USA: ACM, 2014, pp. 315–328.

[11] L. Sun, S. Sen, and D. Koutsonikolas, "Bringing mobility-awareness to wlans using phy layer information," in *Proceedings of the 10th ACM International on Conference on Emerging Networking Experiments and Technologies*, ser. CoNEXT '14. New York, NY, USA: ACM, 2014, pp. 53–66.

[12] D. Vasisht, S. Kumar, and D. Katabi, "Sub-nanosecond time of flight on commercial wi-fi cards," *arXiv preprint arXiv:1505.03446*, 2015.

[13] P. Gallo, S. Mangione, and G. Tarantino, "Widar: Bistatic wi-fi detection and ranging for off-the-shelf devices," in *2013 IEEE World of Wireless, Mobile and Multimedia Networks (WoWMoM)*, June 2013, pp. 1–6.

[14] S. Sen, D. Kim, S. Laroche, K.-H. Kim, and J. Lee, "Bringing cupid indoor positioning system to practice," in *Proceedings of the 24th International Conference on World Wide Web*. International World Wide Web Conferences Steering Committee, 2015, pp. 938–948.

[15] "IEEE standard for information technology–telecommunications and information exchange between systems local and metropolitan area networks–specific requirements part 11: Wireless LAN medium access control (MAC) and physical layer (PHY) specifications," pp. 1–2793, 2012.

[16] openFWWF, "Open firmware for wi-fi networks," http://www.ing.unibs.it/openfwwf/.

Delay Analysis for Wireless Fading Channels with Finite Blocklength Channel Coding

Sebastian Schiessl
schiessl@kth.se

James Gross
james.gross@ee.kth.se

Hussein Al-Zubaidy
hzubaidy@kth.se

School of Electrical Engineering
KTH Royal Institute of Technology
100 44 Stockholm, Sweden

ABSTRACT

Upcoming low-latency machine-to-machine (M2M) applications are currently attracting a significant amount of interest from the wireless networking research community. The design challenge with respect to such future applications is to allow wireless networks to operate extremely reliably at very short deadlines for rather small packets. To date, it is unclear how to design wireless networks efficiently for such novel requirements. One reason is that existing performance models for wireless networks often assume that the rate of the channel code is equal to the Shannon capacity. However, this model does not hold anymore when the packet size and thus blocklength of the channel code is small. Although it is known [1] that finite blocklength has a major impact on the physical layer performance, we lack higher-layer performance models which account in particular for the queueing effects under the finite blocklength regime.

A recently developed methodology [2] provides probabilistic higher-layer delay bounds for fading channels when assuming transmission at the Shannon capacity limit. Based on this novel approach, we develop service process characterizations for fading channels with finite blocklength channel coding, leading to novel probabilistic delay bounds that can give a fundamental insight into the capabilities and limitations of wireless networks when facing low-latency M2M applications. In particular, we show that the Shannon capacity model significantly overestimates the delay performance for such applications, which would lead to insufficient resource allocations. Finally, based on our (validated) analytical model, we study various important parameter trade-offs highlighting the sensitivity of the delay distribution under the finite blocklength regime.

Categories and Subject Descriptors

C.2.1 [**Computer-Communication Networks**]: Network Architecture and Design - Wireless communication

MSWiM'15, November 2–6, 2015, Cancun, Mexico.
© 2015 ACM. ISBN 978-1-4503-3762-5/15/11 ...$15.00.
DOI: http://dx.doi.org/10.1145/2811587.2811596.

Keywords

Finite blocklength regime; stochastic network calculus; quality of service; queueing systems; fading channels

1. INTRODUCTION

While state-of-the-art wireless systems have mostly been designed for human users, it is expected that next generation systems will be strongly utilized by so-called machine-to-machine communications (M2M). In such applications, automated distributed processes communicate over wireless networks and thus require quite different network features than typical human-related applications. Despite these new requirements, wireless systems offer many advantages for M2M applications, such as reduced cabling cost, increased flexibility, and higher robustness [3]. Thus, M2M applications for traffic safety, the smart electricity grid, or in the context of industrial automation systems are currently of high interest in the domain of 5G cellular networks [4] .

One of the biggest distinguishing factors between M2M and human-related applications are the requirements with respect to the delay. For instance, in factory automation there are often closed-loop control systems, where sensors, controllers, and actuators must exchange information with cycle times (i.e. delays) of 5 ms and below while requiring reliability levels of $1 - 10^{-5}$ and higher (with respect to the deadline). Despite these tough requirements, packet sizes for these applications are typically rather small, i.e. only a few bytes need to be transmitted per datagram. Thus, the academic and industrial research community faces the question how wireless networks can be designed to support such novel application types, also referred to as *low-latency* applications.

This turns out to be a difficult question. Despite the huge interest, we lack a solid theoretical base for modeling the performance of such systems due to the short time spans and small packet sizes involved. Many existing performance models assume that channel coding can provide error-free transmissions in a noisy channel, and that those codes offer a data rate equal to the Shannon capacity. However, this model only holds in the limit of channel codes with infinite blocklength. In low-latency applications with small packet sizes and small blocklengths, there is always a probability that transmissions fail due to noise. Furthermore, for high reliability, data must be encoded at a rate which is significantly lower than the Shannon capacity. Regarding the pure physical layer behavior, Polyanskiy et al. [1]

derived an information-theoretic performance model of the finite blocklength regime, which quantifies these effects.

In order to characterize the possibilities and limitations of wireless networks with respect to low-latency M2M applications, such finite-blocklength performance models need to be extended up to the application layer, where queueing effects are taken into account. One factor that causes queueing is channel fading, which means that the signal strength and thus the data rate of a wireless channel changes randomly over time. In general, it is difficult to analyze the queueing performance of fading channels due to the difficulty of finding a stochastic characterization of the random data rate. When the physical layer model also considers finite blocklength effects, the analysis at the application layer becomes even more challenging.

In this paper, we address this fundamental challenge. Al-Zubaidy et al. [2] recently provided a methodology for wireless network performance analysis in fading channels with the Shannon capacity model. By applying stochastic network calculus in a transform domain, they were able to derive probabilistic delay bounds in closed form. Based on this novel approach, we provide a performance model for wireless systems that operate at finite blocklength. In particular, the core contributions of this paper are:

- We derive probabilistic delay bounds for wireless systems that use channel coding at finite blocklength.

- We provide a fast and efficient method to compute the bounds for Rayleigh fading channels. The computation requires solving an integral, which we accomplished through several series expansions, leading to an infinite number of infinite sums. However, we demonstrate that the series converges very quickly for reasonable channel parameters.

- We validate the analytical delay bounds by simulations.

- Our results quantify the performance difference between the Shannon capacity model and the finite blocklength model in [1]. We show that finite blocklength effects can be significant and must be taken into account, in particular for low-latency M2M applications.

The rest of the paper is structured as follows: In Section 2 we discuss related work. In Section 3 we present the basic assumptions and the problem formulation of our work, while in Section 4 we present a brief review of stochastic network calculus. Our main analytical contribution follows in Section 5, while we validate this work and present further numerical results in Section 6. Finally, we conclude our work in Section 7.

2. RELATED WORK

The characterization of channel codes at finite blocklength by Polyanskiy et al. [1] has renewed the research interest in this area. Most notably, Yang et. al [5] performed studies for finite blocklength coding in fading channels. They analyzed systems where the transmitter does not adapt the rate according to the instantaneous SNR of the channel and computed the maximum achievable rate for a certain error probability. It was found that for many fading distributions,

including Rayleigh, the difference between the infinite and the finite blocklength model is very small. In another work [6], they investigated the tradeoff between transmit diversity and the cost of learning the channel. However, none of these results apply to our scenario where the rate is always adapted to the current SNR of the channel. Furthermore, they do not consider queueing effects. Wu and Jindal [7] considered queueing effects in a simple ARQ system but did not address the delay.

Performance analysis of wireless networks in fading channels has often been based on discrete/finite-state channel models such as the Gilbert-Elliott channel or finite-state Markov channels (FSMC), e.g. [8, 9]. However, such discrete models cannot provide exact solutions when the fading channels show a continuous distribution of the SNR.

The $(\min, \times)$ network calculus approach developed in [2] was used for transmit power minimization for process automation under delay constraints [10]. However, the service was characterized by the infinite blocklength Shannon capacity model.

Finite blocklength effects in wireless networks were studied by Gursoy [11], who applied the effective capacity framework [12] to fading channels at finite blocklength and proved that there is a unique optimal tradeoff between the rate and the error probability. This work is the closest to our work. It was extended to the scenario where a codeword is distributed across multiple coherence blocks [13]. The downside of the effective capacity framework is that it provides results only for constant arrivals and that it analyzes the tail of the delay distribution, meaning that it works only for relatively large delays [12]. Furthermore, the authors in [11] provided no analytical method to compute the effective capacity at finite blocklength, which means that numerical integration is necessary.

Apart from the work by Gursoy, only a few authors have worked on the higher-layer analysis of wireless networks in the finite blocklength regime. Zhang et al. [14] provide a network calculus analysis of an AWGN channel without fading. However, they ignored that the error rate is no longer zero and assumed a deterministic service curve.

3. SYSTEM MODEL

We consider data transmission between a data source, (e.g. a sensor in an industrial automation system) to another device (e.g. a control unit) over a wireless channel. A discrete-time model is used, i.e. time is divided into time slots with duration T. In each time slot i, the source generates a_i data bits and stores them in a queue. Then the queued data bits are transmitted over the wireless channel.

3.1 Wireless Channel Model

The wireless link is modeled as a single-antenna Rayleigh fading channel, where the signal-to-noise ratio (SNR) at the receiver varies over time. We assume a block-fading model where the SNR γ_i remains constant during each time slot and varies independently from one time slot to the other. Hence, the SNR values in different time slots are independent and identically distributed (i.i.d.) with exponential distribution:

$$f(\gamma_i) = \frac{1}{\bar{\gamma}} e^{-\frac{\gamma_i}{\bar{\gamma}}}, \tag{1}$$

where $\bar{\gamma}$ is the average SNR at the receiver, which depends on the transmit power at the source, among other parameters. In each slot, the system transmits N symbols, which consist of n symbols for data transmission and n_h symbols for headers and channel estimation, as well as for feedback and acknowledgments from the receiver. The system thus occupies a bandwidth of N/T [Hz].

In each time slot i, the transmitter uses a channel code of length n and rate R_i to encode the first nR_i bits in the queue and then transmits the codeword to the receiver. The receiver replies with an acknowledgment, which is assumed to be instantaneous and error-free. Furthermore, we assume that the transmitter has perfect estimates of the instantaneous SNR γ_i and adapts the coding rate R_i according to γ_i. A standard rate model that is often applied in wireless networking research, including in [2], assumes that the achievable rate R_i in bits per (complex-valued) symbol is equal to the Shannon capacity of the channel, and no errors occur:

$$R_{i,\text{Shannon}} = \log_2(1 + \gamma_i). \tag{2}$$

We will refer to the standard rate model as *Shannon model*. The Shannon capacity is an upper bound for codes which only holds when the blocklength n tends to infinity.

At finite blocklength, there is always a probability $\epsilon > 0$ that a transmission error occurs. This error probability can be reduced by decreasing the rate of the code. It was shown by Polyanskiy et al. [1, Thm. 54] that for an AWGN channel with SNR γ_i at a blocklength n and error probability ϵ, the achievable rate in bits per symbol can be closely approximated by

$$R_i(n, \epsilon) \approx \log_2(1 + \gamma_i) - \sqrt{\frac{V}{n}} Q^{-1}(\epsilon) \log_2 e, \tag{3}$$

where γ_i is the instantaneous SNR of the channel, $Q^{-1}(x)$ the inverse of the Gaussian Q-function, and the channel dispersion V is given as[1]

$$V = 1 - \frac{1}{(1 + \gamma_i)^2}. \tag{4}$$

The achievable rate expression in Eq. (3) is a tight approximation for an information-theoretic bound. Even though current coding and modulation schemes cannot yet fully achieve this rate, this model provides a much better description than a simple Shannon model. A comparison between the information-theoretic bounds and current LDPC channel codes can be found in [1]. Furthermore, it was also proven that Eq. (3) closely approximates the converse bound, which means that even the best future coding schemes cannot exceed this rate.

At very low SNR γ_i, the expression for $R_i(n, \epsilon)$ can become negative. Therefore, the achievable rate must be lower-bounded by zero:

$$R_i^*(n, \epsilon) = \max\left(R_i(n, \epsilon), 0\right). \tag{5}$$

We assume in the following that there exist codes with blocklength n and error probability ϵ that achieve the rate $R_i^*(n, \epsilon)$ exactly. The throughput in time slot i is $n \cdot R_i^*(n, \epsilon)$ bits if no transmission error occurs.

---

[1]We use a different notation than [1] and put $\log_2 e$ as a separate factor in Eq. (3).

3.2 Queueing Model

For the system-level analysis of a wireless communication network, we use the same stochastic system-theoretic model as in [2]. The a_i data bits that are generated at the source correspond to the arrival process of the queueing system during time slot i. The departure process d_i describes the number of bits that arrives successfully at the destination. The departures depend both on the number of bits waiting in the queue and on the service offered by the wireless link. The service process s_i is equal to $nR_i^*(n, \epsilon)$ when the transmission is successful and a positive acknowledgment is received. When there is a transmission error, we set s_i to zero. This means that the bits remain in the queue; they will be transmitted again in future time slots. Therefore, all data will eventually be transmitted to the destination and the queueing system is lossless. The wireless link transmits the data from the queue in FIFO (first-in first-out) fashion.

In order to derive delay bounds, we need to define the cumulative arrival, service and departure processes in the time interval $[\tau, t)$:

$$A(\tau, t) = \sum_{i=\tau}^{t-1} a_i, \qquad S(\tau, t) = \sum_{i=\tau}^{t-1} s_i, \qquad D(\tau, t) = \sum_{i=\tau}^{t-1} d_i.$$

The delay $W(t)$ at time t describes the number of time slots it takes for an information bit arriving at time t to be received at the destination. It is defined as

$$W(t) \triangleq \inf\left\{u > 0: \quad A(0, t) \leq D(0, t + u)\right\}. \tag{6}$$

3.3 Problem Statement

We are interested in finding a probabilistic bound on the delay $W(t)$. Thus, we define a target delay $\hat{w}$. The probability that the delay is larger than $\hat{w}$, i.e. that some data bits are not received within a certain deadline, is denoted by the delay violation probability $p_\text{v}(\hat{w})$

$$p_\text{v}(\hat{w}) = \mathbb{P}\left\{W(t) > \hat{w}\right\}. \tag{7}$$

We assume that a system is reliable when only a very small percentage $p_\text{v}(\hat{w})$ of bits is received after the deadline $\hat{w}$. Our main goal in this work is to find an estimate for the delay violation probability $p_\text{v}(\hat{w})$ when the rate of the channel code is given by the finite blocklength model. Furthermore, we investigate how the proposed model can be used to aid the design of communication systems that operate at low delay.

4. STOCHASTIC NETWORK CALCULUS

In this section, we provide an overview of the results derived in [2], where stochastic network calculus in a transform domain was used to derive an upper bound for the delay. Even for coding at infinite blocklength, the major problem in deriving stochastic performance bounds for fading channels is the nonlinear mapping of SNR to achievable rate as $R = \log_2(1 + \text{SNR})$. While the probability distribution for the SNR is usually given in a simple form as in Eq. (1), the statistics of the rate cannot be stated in a simple closed form. This problem remains when the achievable rate approximation $R^*(n, \epsilon)$ for finite blocklengths is used because the mapping is essentially still logarithmic except for some penalty term.

15

4.1 Network Calculus in the SNR Domain

The authors in [2] solved this problem for infinite block-length by analyzing the system in the exponential domain, also referred to as *SNR domain*. Instead of describing the cumulative service and arrival $S(\tau,t)$ and $A(\tau,t)$ in the bit domain, they are converted to the SNR domain as follows:

$$\mathcal{A}(\tau,t) = e^{A(\tau,t)}, \quad \mathcal{S}(\tau,t) = e^{S(\tau,t)}. \tag{8}$$

The arrivals can then be interpreted as a series of power or SNR demands on the system. Due to the exponential function, the cumulative arrival and service processes are now multiplicative instead of additive:

$$\mathcal{A}(\tau,t) = \prod_{i=\tau}^{t-1} e^{a_i}, \quad \mathcal{S}(\tau,t) = \prod_{i=\tau}^{t-1} e^{s_i}. \tag{9}$$

As s_i is usually a logarithmic function of the SNR, switching to the SNR domain (i.e. taking the exponential function) eliminates the logarithm. Then, closed-form statistical analysis becomes possible through stochastic network calculus.

Stochastic network calculus allows the description and analysis of queueing systems through simple linear input-output relations. In the bit domain it is based on a $(\min,+)$ dioid algebra on $(\mathbb{R} \cup \{+\infty\})$ where the standard addition is replaced by the minimum (or infimum) and the standard multiplication replaced by addition. Similar to the convolution and deconvolution in standard algebra, there are definitions for convolution and deconvolution operators in $(\min,+)$ algebra. The convolution and deconvolution operators in $(\min,+)$-algebra are often used for performance evaluation. The reader is referred to [2] for more information.

In the SNR domain network calculus, the arrival, service and departure processes become multiplicative instead of additive. This requires using a $(\min,\times)$-algebra instead of $(\min,+)$ where $\times$ denotes the standard multiplication. The non-commutative convolution and deconvolution operators are defined as

$$\mathcal{X} \otimes \mathcal{Y}(\tau,t) \triangleq \inf_{\tau \leq u \leq t} \{\mathcal{X}(\tau,u) \cdot \mathcal{Y}(u,t)\}, \tag{10}$$

$$\mathcal{X} \oslash \mathcal{Y}(\tau,t) \triangleq \sup_{u \leq \tau} \left\{ \frac{\mathcal{X}(u,t)}{\mathcal{Y}(u,\tau)} \right\}. \tag{11}$$

Many of the input-output relationships of the queueing system can be expressed using these operators. The delay can be bounded as follows [2]:

$$W(t) \leq \inf \{u \geq 0 : \mathcal{A} \oslash \mathcal{S}(t+u,t) \leq 1\}, \tag{12}$$

which means that the delay violation probability $p_v(w) = \mathbb{P}\{W(t) > w\}$ can be bounded as [2]:

$$p_v(w) \leq \mathbb{P}\{\mathcal{A} \oslash \mathcal{S}(t+w,t) > 1\}. \tag{13}$$

This bound cannot be computed directly. However, it can be upper-bounded again by using the Mellin transform. The Mellin transform $\mathcal{M}_{\mathcal{X}}(s)$ of a nonnegative random variable $\mathcal{X}$ is defined as [2]

$$\mathcal{M}_{\mathcal{X}}(s) \triangleq \mathbb{E}\left[\mathcal{X}^{s-1}\right]. \tag{14}$$

We denote the Mellin transform of a bivariate process $\mathcal{X}(\tau,t)$ as $\mathcal{M}_{\mathcal{X}}(s,\tau,t)$ and choose values for $s \in \mathbb{R}$.

The Mellin transform is used to formulate the moment bound, which is given for $a > 0$ and $s > 0$ as [2]

$$\mathbb{P}(\mathcal{X} \geq a) \leq a^{-s}\mathcal{M}_{\mathcal{X}}(1+s). \tag{15}$$

The moment bound follows directly from Markov's inequality as $\mathbb{P}(\mathcal{X} \geq a) = \mathbb{P}(\mathcal{X}^s \geq a^s)$ for any $s > 0$. The moment bound with $a = 1$ on Eq. (13) results in

$$p_v(w) \leq \mathcal{M}_{\mathcal{A} \oslash \mathcal{S}}(1+s, t+w, t). \tag{16}$$

The Mellin transform of the $(\min,\times)$-deconvolution of two processes can be upper-bounded for $s > 0$ [2]:

$$\mathcal{M}_{\mathcal{A} \oslash \mathcal{S}}(1+s,\tau,t) \leq \sum_{u=0}^{\tau} \mathcal{M}_{\mathcal{A}}(1+s,u,t) \cdot \mathcal{M}_{\mathcal{S}}(1-s,u,\tau). \tag{17}$$

Therefore, a bound on $p_v(w)$ can be computed from the Mellin transforms of the arrival and service processes.

4.2 Mellin Transform of the Arrival Process

Analogue to [2] we focus on $(\sigma(s),\rho(s))$-bounded arrivals where the log-moment generating function (log-MGF) of the cumulative arrivals in the bit domain is bounded by

$$\frac{1}{s}\log \mathbb{E}\left[e^{sA(\tau,t)}\right] \leq \rho(s) \cdot (t-\tau) + \sigma(s). \tag{18}$$

To simplify notation, we restrict the following analysis to values (σ,ρ) that are independent of s, which is true for constant arrivals. Using Eqs. (18) and (8), the Mellin transform of the SNR-domain arrival process can be upper-bounded:

$$\mathcal{M}_{\mathcal{A}}(s,\tau,t) = \mathbb{E}\left[\mathcal{A}(\tau,t)^{s-1}\right] \leq e^{(s-1)(\rho \cdot (t-\tau)+\sigma)}. \tag{19}$$

4.3 Mellin Transform of the Service Process

When the service, i.e. the achievable rate in time slot i can be written as $s_i = n \cdot \log_2 g(\gamma_i) = \frac{n}{\ln 2} \cdot \ln g(\gamma_i)$, and when the s_i of different time slots are i.i.d. (independent and identically distributed), then the Mellin transform of the cumulative service $\mathcal{M}_{\mathcal{S}}(s,\tau,t)$ can be computed from the Mellin transform of $g(\gamma_i)$, which will be derived in Sec. 5:

$$\mathcal{M}_{\mathcal{S}}(s,\tau,t) = \mathbb{E}\left[\left(\prod_{i=\tau}^{t-1} g(\gamma_i)^{\frac{n}{\ln 2}}\right)^{s-1}\right]$$
$$= \mathbb{E}\left[g(\gamma_i)^{\frac{n(s-1)}{\ln 2}}\right]^{t-\tau} = \left(\mathcal{M}_{g(\gamma_i)}\left(1+\frac{n(s-1)}{\ln 2}\right)\right)^{t-\tau}. \tag{20}$$

4.4 Delay Bound

When the Mellin transforms of the arrival and service processes are known, one can combine Eq. (17) with Eq. (16), which must hold for all $s \in \mathbb{R}^+$, to compute a bound on the delay violation probability $p_v(w)$:

$$p_v(w) \leq \inf_{s>0} \{K(s,t+w,t)\}. \tag{21}$$

where $K(s,t+w,t)$ is defined as

$$K(s,t+w,t) \triangleq \sum_{u=0}^{t} \mathcal{M}_{\mathcal{A}}(1+s,u,t) \cdot \mathcal{M}_{\mathcal{S}}(1-s,u,t+w). \tag{22}$$

Note: $K(s,t+w,t)$ is essentially the right side of Eq. (17), except that the upper limit of the sum was changed from $t+w$ to t. This change was proven in [2].

When using the bounded arrival model in (19), the service model in (20), and

$$Y(s) \triangleq \mathcal{M}_{g(\gamma_i)}\left(1 - \frac{n}{\ln 2}s\right),$$

then $K(s, t+w, t)$ can be computed as

$$K(s, t+w, t) \leq \sum_{u=0}^{t} e^{\sigma s} (e^{\rho s})^{t-u} \cdot Y(s)^{t+w-u}$$

$$= e^{\sigma s} Y(s)^w \sum_{v=0}^{t} (e^{\rho s} Y(s))^v$$

$$= e^{\sigma s} Y(s)^w \frac{1 - (e^{\rho s} Y(s))^{t+1}}{1 - e^{\rho s} Y(s)}.$$

The queueing system is stable if

$$e^{\rho s} Y(s) < 1. \tag{23}$$

In a stable queueing system, we can obtain a bound on the function $K(s, t+w, t)$ by letting $t \to \infty$:

$$K(s, t+w, t) \leq e^{\sigma s} Y(s)^w \frac{1}{1 - e^{\rho s} Y(s)}. \tag{24}$$

5. SERVICE CHARACTERIZATION IN THE FINITE BLOCKLENGTH REGIME

When using stochastic network calculus, the computation of delay bounds requires the computation of the Mellin transform of e^{s_i}, i.e. the service process in the SNR domain. We assume in the following that s_i follows the finite blocklength model.

At finite blocklength, there is always a chance that errors will occur. The error probability is denoted as ϵ. In Sec. 5.1, we will show how to compute the Mellin transform of the service process when transmission errors occur.

Apart from the chance that errors occur, coding at finite blocklength also causes a rate loss, which depends on the instantaneous SNR γ_i and makes the computation of the Mellin transform difficult. In Sec. 5.3, we show how to approximate the Mellin transform by approximating the rate loss as a constant. In Sec. 5.4, we compute the Mellin transform through a number of series expansions, which allows approximation of the Mellin transform with arbitrary accuracy.

5.1 Characterization of Transmission Errors

In Sec. 4.3, we showed that if the offered service in the bit domain is given as $s_i = n \cdot \log_2 g(\gamma_i)$, then the Mellin transform of the cumulative service $\mathcal{S}(\tau, t)$ in the SNR domain can be computed from the Mellin transform of $g(\gamma_i)$. However, when coding at finite blocklength there is always a chance that an error occurs. In case of error, the offered service s_i is zero. The service model needs to be modified to describe transmission errors. We use the Bernoulli random variable $Z_i \in \{\text{error}, \text{success}\}$ to describe the error event. Then, the service in the bit domain depends on two random variables:

$$s_i = \begin{cases} n \log_2 h(\gamma_i) & \text{if } Z_i = \text{success} \\ 0 & \text{if } Z_i = \text{error} \end{cases}, \tag{25}$$

where $h(\gamma_i)$ will be specified later. Now, the service can be written as $s_i = n \cdot \log_2 g(\gamma_i, Z_i)$ with

$$g(\gamma_i, Z_i) \triangleq \begin{cases} h(\gamma_i) & \text{if } Z_i = \text{success} \\ 1 & \text{if } Z_i = \text{error} \end{cases}. \tag{26}$$

In general, the two random variables γ_i and Z_i might not be independent. However, in this work we restrict the anal-

ysis to constant values[2] of the error probability ϵ. When the transmitter chooses a code with rate $R^*(n, \epsilon)$ according to (5), then the rate of this code depends on the SNR γ_i but the error probability of this code is always ϵ. Therefore, the error event Z_i is also independent of γ_i, and the Mellin transform of $g(\gamma_i, Z_i)$ can be computed as

$$\mathcal{M}_{g(\gamma_i, z_i)}(s) = \mathbb{E}_{\gamma_i, Z_i} \left[g(\gamma_i, Z_i)^{s-1} \right]$$

$$= (1 - \epsilon) \cdot \mathbb{E}_{\gamma_i} \left[h(\gamma_i)^{s-1} \right] + \epsilon$$

$$= (1 - \epsilon) \cdot \mathcal{M}_{h(\gamma_i)}(s) + \epsilon. \tag{27}$$

We already know from Eq. (20) that the Mellin transform of the SNR-domain service process $\mathcal{S}(\tau, t)$ can be computed from the Mellin transform of the $g()$-function, which holds also when the $g()$-function has two arguments. Now, Eq. (27) showed that the Mellin transform of the $g()$-function can in turn be easily computed from $\mathcal{M}_{h(\gamma_i)}(s)$, which we will derive in the following sections.

5.2 Service at Finite Blocklength

When the blocklength n and the error probability ϵ are fixed, the achievable rate is given by Eq. (5):

$$R_i^*(n, \epsilon) = \max \left(\log_2(1 + \gamma_i) - \sqrt{\frac{V}{n}} Q^{-1}(\epsilon) \log_2 e, 0 \right).$$

We define the constant

$$P = \sqrt{\frac{1}{n}} Q^{-1}(\epsilon) \tag{28}$$

and rewrite Eq. (5):

$$R_i^*(n, \epsilon) = \max \left(\log_2 \left(\frac{1 + \gamma_i}{e^{\sqrt{V} P}} \right), 0 \right).$$

Now, define

$$h(\gamma_i) \triangleq \max \left(\frac{1 + \gamma_i}{e^{\sqrt{V} P}}, 1 \right). \tag{29}$$

In case the transmission is successful, the service is given as $s_i = nR_i^*(n, \epsilon) = n \log_2 h(\gamma_i)$. In case of error, the service is zero. The Mellin transform of $h(\gamma_i)$ is however difficult to obtain because the channel dispersion V given in Eq. (4) depends on the SNR γ_i.

5.3 Approximation for High SNR Values

Our first approach to find the Mellin transform of $h(\gamma_i)$ approximates the channel dispersion as constant, which is accurate at high SNR values. Note that the second term of the channel dispersion V approaches zero when the SNR is high. Thus, at high SNR we can approximate the channel dispersion as

$$V = 1 - \frac{1}{(1 + \gamma_i)^2} \approx 1. \tag{30}$$

The penalty term $\sqrt{V} P$ becomes equal to the constant P.

---

[2] Note that varying ϵ with SNR, e.g. allowing more errors when the channel is bad, might result in better performance. Investigating this effect is left for future work.

For Rayleigh fading channels, γ_i is distributed according to Eq. (1) and the Mellin transform of $h(\gamma_i)$ is approximately

$$\mathcal{M}_{h(\gamma_i)}(s) \approx \mathbb{E}\left[\left(\max\left(\frac{1+\gamma_i}{e^P}, 1\right)\right)^{s-1}\right]$$

$$= \int_0^{e^P-1} \frac{1}{\bar{\gamma}} e^{-\frac{\gamma_i}{\bar{\gamma}}} d\gamma_i + \int_{e^P-1}^{\infty} \left(\frac{1+\gamma_i}{e^P}\right)^{s-1} \frac{1}{\bar{\gamma}} e^{-\frac{\gamma_i}{\bar{\gamma}}} d\gamma_i.$$

The first integral is simply the cumulative distribution function of the SNR. Denote the second integral as $B_0(s)$:

$$
\begin{aligned}
B_0(s) &= \int_{e^P-1}^{\infty} \left(\frac{1+\gamma_i}{e^P}\right)^{s-1} \frac{1}{\bar{\gamma}} e^{-\frac{\gamma_i}{\bar{\gamma}}} d\gamma_i \\
&= e^{\frac{1}{\bar{\gamma}}} \left(\frac{\bar{\gamma}}{e^P}\right)^{s-1} \int_{e^P}^{\infty} \left(\frac{u}{\bar{\gamma}}\right)^{s-1} \frac{1}{\bar{\gamma}} e^{-\frac{u}{\bar{\gamma}}} du \\
&= e^{\frac{1}{\bar{\gamma}}} \left(\frac{\bar{\gamma}}{e^P}\right)^{s-1} \int_{\frac{e^P}{\bar{\gamma}}}^{\infty} q^{s-1} e^{-q} dq \\
&= e^{\frac{1}{\bar{\gamma}}} \left(\frac{\bar{\gamma}}{e^P}\right)^{s-1} \Gamma\left(s, \frac{e^P}{\bar{\gamma}}\right),
\end{aligned}
\tag{31}
$$

where $\Gamma(s,x)$ denotes the upper incomplete gamma function:

$$\Gamma(s,x) = \int_x^{\infty} q^{s-1} e^{-q} dq. \tag{32}$$

The Mellin transform of $h(\gamma_i)$ is then

$$\mathcal{M}_{h(\gamma_i)}(s) \approx 1 - e^{-\frac{e^P-1}{\bar{\gamma}}} + B_0(s). \tag{33}$$

Observe that if we allow $P = 0$, we obtain the Mellin transform of the service process with the infinite blocklength model, which is given in [2].

5.4 Extension to all SNR Values

In order to extend the previous result to lower SNR values, a series expansion for the square root channel dispersion $\sqrt{V}$ is used, which is based on the following expansion of $\sqrt{1-x}$ for $-1 \le x \le 1$ (Formula 1.110 in [15]):

$$
\begin{aligned}
\sqrt{1-x} &= 1 + \sum_{j=1}^{\infty} \binom{1/2}{j} (-x)^j \\
&= 1 - \frac{x}{2} - \frac{x^2}{8} - \frac{x^3}{16} \cdots
\end{aligned}
$$

With the definition[3]

$$b_j \triangleq \left| \binom{1/2}{j} \right| = \left| \frac{\left(\frac{1}{2}\right)\left(\frac{1}{2}-1\right) \cdots \left(\frac{1}{2}-j+1\right)}{j!} \right|,$$

one can write $\sqrt{V}$ as

$$\sqrt{V} = \sqrt{1 - \frac{1}{(1+\gamma_i)^2}} = 1 - \sum_{j=1}^{\infty} \frac{b_j}{(1+\gamma_i)^{2j}}. \tag{34}$$

The convergence of the series in Eq. (34) to the actual value is illustrated in Fig. 1. If all terms of the infinite series in (34) are ignored, then $\sqrt{V}$ is approximated to 1. This corresponds to the approximation for high SNR as discussed in the previous section. In order to get a better approximation, the terms in the infinite sum need to be included. It

---

[3]The signs of the binomial coefficient and $(-x)^j$ are always opposite

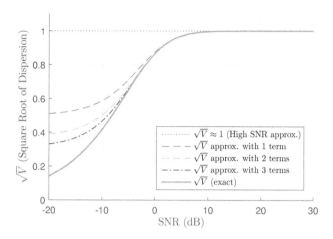

Figure 1: Approximation for $\sqrt{V}$ when the series in Eq. (34) is limited

can be seen that three terms in the sum already lead to a very tight approximation when the instantaneous SNR γ_i is above -10 dB.

A useful property is that when the series is approximated by a limited number of terms, the approximation is always larger than the actual value. The rate is reduced by a term that is linear in $\sqrt{V}$, so the approximation always underestimates the achievable rate. Therefore, the approximation leads to higher delays, and creates a valid upper bound on the delay.

The series expansion is used to compute the Mellin transform of $h(\gamma_i)$ given in (29). First, we must find the point where the maximum in $h(\gamma_i)$ becomes greater than 1. When the high SNR approximation was used, this point was easily found at $\gamma_i^* = e^P - 1$. Now, we suggest to do a simple line search. Near this point, the achievable rate is close to 0, and thus any inaccuracies will only have minor impact on the result. We assume that the point is found at $\gamma_i^* = e^{P'} - 1$ for some value P'.

Then, the Mellin transform of $h(\gamma_i)$ is:

$$\mathcal{M}_{h(\gamma_i)}(s) = \int_0^{e^{P'}-1} \frac{1}{\bar{\gamma}} e^{-\frac{\gamma_i}{\bar{\gamma}}} d\gamma_i + B(s)$$

with

$$
\begin{aligned}
B(s) &= \int_{e^{P'}-1}^{\infty} \left(\frac{1+\gamma_i}{e^{\sqrt{V}P}}\right)^{s-1} \frac{1}{\bar{\gamma}} e^{-\frac{\gamma_i}{\bar{\gamma}}} d\gamma_i \\
&= \int_{e^{P'}-1}^{\infty} \left(\frac{1+\gamma_i}{e^P} e^{\sum_{j=1}^{\infty} \frac{b_j P}{(1+\gamma_i)^{2j}}}\right)^{s-1} \frac{1}{\bar{\gamma}} e^{-\frac{\gamma_i}{\bar{\gamma}}} d\gamma_i \\
&= \int_{e^{P'}-1}^{\infty} \left(\frac{1+\gamma_i}{e^P}\right)^{s-1} \prod_{j=1}^{\infty} e^{\frac{b_j P(s-1)}{(1+\gamma_i)^{2j}}} \frac{1}{\bar{\gamma}} e^{-\frac{\gamma_i}{\bar{\gamma}}} d\gamma_i, \quad (35)
\end{aligned}
$$

where we used the power series of Eq. (34). Now, for each factor in the infinite product, the series expansion of the exponential function is applied, and the factors that do not depend on γ_i are denoted as $c_{j,k}$:

$$e^{\frac{b_j P \cdot (s-1)}{(1+\gamma_i)^{2j}}} = \sum_{k_j=0}^{\infty} \frac{1}{k_j!} \left(\frac{b_j P \cdot (s-1)}{(1+\gamma_i)^{2j}}\right)^{k_j} = \sum_{k_j=0}^{\infty} \frac{c_{j,k_j}}{(1+\gamma_i)^{2jk_j}}. \tag{36}$$

In addition, define the variables

$$h_{j,k} \triangleq \frac{c_{j,k}}{\bar{\gamma}^{2\cdot j \cdot k}} = \frac{1}{k!} \cdot \left(\frac{b_j P \cdot (s-1)}{\bar{\gamma}^{2\cdot j}} \right)^k, \qquad (37)$$

$$\mu \triangleq \left(\frac{\bar{\gamma}}{e^P} \right)^{s-1} \cdot e^{\frac{1}{\bar{\gamma}}}. \qquad (38)$$

To see how the integral can be solved, first assume that the product in $B(s)$ includes only the first factor $j = 1$. Call this integral $B_1(s)$:

$$B_1(s) = \int_{e^{P'}-1}^{\infty} \left(\frac{1+\gamma_i}{e^P} \right)^{s-1} e^{\frac{b_1 P(s-1)}{(1+\gamma_i)^2}} \frac{1}{\bar{\gamma}} e^{-\frac{\gamma_i}{\bar{\gamma}}} d\gamma_i$$

$$= \sum_{k_1=0}^{\infty} c_{1,k_1} \int_{e^{P'}-1}^{\infty} \left(\frac{1+\gamma_i}{e^P} \right)^{s-1} \frac{1}{(1+\gamma_i)^{2\cdot 1 \cdot k_1}} \cdot \frac{1}{\bar{\gamma}} e^{-\frac{\gamma_i}{\bar{\gamma}}} d\gamma_i$$

$$= \sum_{k_1=0}^{\infty} \frac{c_{1,k_1}}{\bar{\gamma}^{2\cdot 1 \cdot k_1}} \cdot \left(\frac{\bar{\gamma}}{e^P} \right)^{s-1} \int_{e^{P'}-1}^{\infty} \left(\frac{1+\gamma_i}{\bar{\gamma}} \right)^{s-1-2k_1} \frac{1}{\bar{\gamma}} e^{-\frac{\gamma_i}{\bar{\gamma}}} d\gamma_i$$

$$= \sum_{k_1=0}^{\infty} h_{1,k_1} \cdot \left(\frac{\bar{\gamma}}{e^P} \right)^{s-1} \cdot e^{\frac{1}{\bar{\gamma}}} \int_{\frac{e^{P'}}{\bar{\gamma}}}^{\infty} q^{s-1-2k_1} e^{-q} dq$$

$$= \sum_{k_1=0}^{\infty} h_{1,k_1} \cdot \mu \cdot \Gamma\left(s - 2 \cdot 1 \cdot k_1, \frac{e^{P'}}{\bar{\gamma}} \right).$$

When the first J factors $(j = 1, \dots, J)$ in Eq. (35) are used, and each factor is expanded according to Eq. (36), then there are J sums, and each term includes the factor

$$\prod_{j=1}^{J} \frac{c_{j,k_j}}{(1+\gamma_i)^{2jk_j}} = \left(\frac{\bar{\gamma}}{1+\gamma_i} \right)^{\sum_{j=1}^{J} 2jk_j} \prod_{j=1}^{J} h_{j,k_j}. \qquad (39)$$

Then, similar to the computation of $B_1(s)$, the integral $B_J(s)$ can be computed as

$$B_J(s) = \sum_{k_J=0}^{\infty} \cdots \sum_{k_1=0}^{\infty} \mu \cdot \Gamma\left(s - \sum_{j=1}^{J} 2jk_j, \frac{e^{P'}}{\bar{\gamma}} \right) \cdot \prod_{j=1}^{J} h_{j,k_j}. \qquad (40)$$

To obtain $B(s)$, let J go to infinity. $B(s)$ contains an infinite number of infinite sums. For practical SNR values, it is however sufficient to compute only very few terms, as the value of the incomplete gamma function decreases very quickly with j and k_j. We suggest to include only terms with $\sum_{j=1}^{\infty} 2jk_j \leq L$, e.g. $L = 10$, which allows fast calculations but still gives tight approximations for reasonable SNR values. Note that the computation of the incomplete gamma function $\Gamma(s, x)$ needs itself a numerical approximation. However, when computing $B_J(s)$, $\Gamma(s, x)$ needs to be computed only for the first term through this numerical approximation. The other terms can be computed much faster by using the recurrence relation, e.g. [16, Eq. 6.5.21].

6. NUMERICAL RESULTS

In this section, we evaluate the bounds on the delay violation probability numerically and compare it to simulation results. Unless stated otherwise, we use a blocklength of $N = 168$ symbols and set the length of one time slot to 1

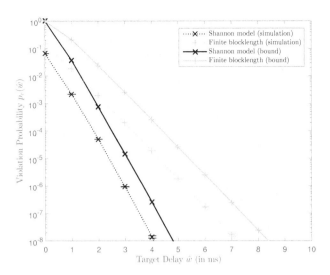

Figure 2: Simulation results and delay bounds for average SNR $\bar{\gamma} = 2$ dB, with arrivals $a = 24$ bits. $T = 1$ ms, $n = 168$. The optimal error probability was found at $\epsilon = 0.0138$. 10^{11} simulations were performed.

ms. The choice of 168 symbols is inspired by the size of a resource block in an LTE system, which contains $12 \cdot 7 = 84$ symbols and lasts 0.5 ms [17]. We assume that the channel stays constant for 1 ms, i.e. two LTE resource blocks, and then changes to a different value. Furthermore, for most of our results the n_h overhead symbols are ignored. Thus, the number of symbols for the channel code n is also 168.

For the arrivals, e.g. data generated at a sensor, we assume a constant and periodic process where in each time slot a packet of size a bits arrives into the queue. The Mellin transform of the arrival process is then given by (19), which is satisfied with equality, with $\rho(s) = a$ and $\sigma(s) = 0$.

The simulations use the same channel model as used by the analysis, i.e. the coding rate is assumed to be equal to information-theoretic bound in Eq. (3) for finite blocklengths.

6.1 Validity of the Bounds

For an average SNR of 2 dB, Fig. 2 shows the delay violation probability $p_v(\hat{w})$ for different target delays $\hat{w}$. In each time slot, $a = 24$ bits were generated at the source. When the effects of coding at finite blocklength are taken into account, the delay increases significantly. The analytical bounds that were obtained with the Shannon capacity model would underestimate the actual delays.

Fig. 3 shows a similar effect at an average SNR of 10 dB with $a = 240$ bits arriving in each time slot. Here, the differences between the Shannon model and the finite blocklength model are smaller than in Fig. 2. This result is reasonable: at high SNR, the absolute rate penalty of finite blocklength codes is nearly constant. Thus, with higher SNR and higher rate, the relative penalty becomes smaller.

The analytical bounds are extremely useful for predicting the system performance even though there is a difference between the analytical bounds and the simulation results. The difference was also observed in [2] and [18] and seems to be unrelated to the finite blocklength model. Despite the difference, the slope of exponential decay of the delay violation

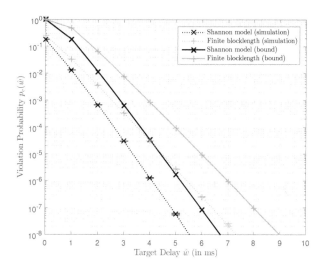

Figure 3: Simulation results and delay bounds for average SNR $\bar{\gamma} = 10$ dB, with arrivals $a = 240$ bits. $T = 1$ ms, $n = 168$. The optimal error probability was found at $\epsilon = 0.0046$. 10^{11} simulations were performed.

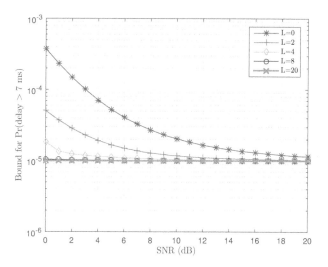

Figure 4: Delay bounds for finite blocklength $n = 168$ with different approximations for the integral $B(s)$. At each SNR, the packet size a was chosen such that the delay bound with the tightest approximation $L = 20$ is at $p_v(\hat{w}) = 10^{-5}$ for a target delay $\hat{w} = 7$ ms.

probability matches with the simulation results. In addition, the horizontal distance between analytical and simulation results is small. When the bounds predict a delay of e.g. 8 ms for a certain delay violation probability, the actual delay is e.g. 6 or 7 ms. Most importantly, the analytical results provide upper bounds for the delay violation probability, so a system that achieves the rate $R(n, \epsilon)$ will perform better than those bounds. When allocating resources, we would rather allocate a bit more resources than necessary and get a system that performs better than required.

To compute the delay bounds efficiently, we must use an approximation for the integral $B(s)$, which uses the infinite sum in Eq. (40) where only terms with $\sum_{j=1}^{\infty} 2jk_j \leq L$ are considered. The resulting delay bounds for different values of L are shown in Fig. 4 for different SNR values. At each SNR, the maximum possible size a of the arriving packets was chosen such that the best approximation with $L = 20$ still satisfies the delay requirements $\hat{w} = 7$ ms, $p_v(\hat{w}) \leq 10^{-5}$. When using fewer approximation terms, the delay bounds become more loose. Those bounds are still valid upper bounds, but they do not estimate the actual performance of the system well. It can also be seen that very few terms are sufficient. For the selected parameters, we find that the approximation with $L = 8$ is already very accurate. At high SNR, even simpler approximations are acceptable.

6.2 Resource Allocation

An analytical method can help a system in deciding how much bandwidth and resources must be allocated to a certain application. When dimensioning a system, we require that $p_v(\hat{w})$ must be smaller than some target delay violation probability $\hat{p}$. Thus, the delay requirements are represented by the tuple $(\hat{w}, \hat{p})$.

In Fig. 5 we show the minimum average SNR at the receiver for different requirements on the delay. We set a fixed target delay violation probability of $\hat{p} = 10^{-5}$, but we vary

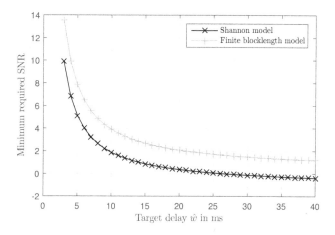

Figure 5: Minimum SNR for different requirements on the delay. For each target delay $\hat{w}$, we required $p_v(\hat{w}) \leq 10^{-5}$. $n = 168$, $a = 120$ bits.

the target delay $\hat{w}$ at which the system must satisfy this target. In each time slot $T = 1$ ms, a packet with $a = 120$ arrives. When the system demands very small delays $\hat{w}$, the required SNR increases, so the transmitter should choose a higher transmit power. For very small target delays, the difference between the Shannon model and the finite blocklength model is more than 3dB. This is a significant difference that must be taken into account when allocating resources.

Instead of allocating more resources to the system, perhaps there is a way to reduce the demand on the system. In the example of a sensor that generates data, one could perhaps reduce the accuracy of the sensor readings in order to meet the delay requirements. This is shown in Fig. 6 for different SNR values and fixed delay requirements of $\hat{w} = 7$ ms and $\hat{p} = 10^{-5}$. Here, the Shannon model would again overestimate the performance of the system.

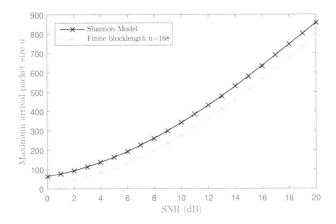

Figure 6: Maximum packet size a (in bits) of the arrival traffic for different SNR. $n = 168$, $T = 1$ ms. Delay requirements: $\hat{w} = 7$ ms and $\hat{p} = 10^{-5}$.

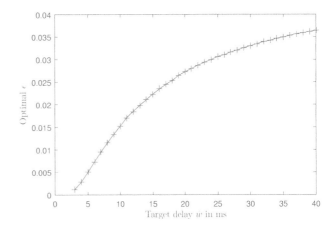

Figure 8: Optimal ϵ for the parameters in Fig. 5

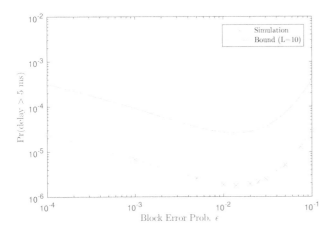

Figure 7: The delay violation probability $p_v(\hat{w})$ for $\hat{w} = 5$ ms depends on the the block error probability ϵ. Parameters: $\bar{\gamma} = 2$ dB, $T = 1$ ms, $n = 168$, $a = 24$ bits. $2 \cdot 10^{10}$ simulations were performed.

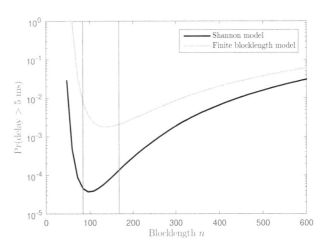

Figure 9: Delay violation probability at $\hat{w} = 5$ ms for different blocklengths. $\bar{\gamma} = 10$ dB, $a = 150$ bits, $n_h = 84$ symbols. The blue lines are located at $n = 84$ and $n = 168$.

6.3 Optimal Error Probability

When coding at finite blocklength, there is always a probability ϵ that the data cannot be decoded at the receiver. Fig. 7 shows that the analytical delay bounds can be used to find an optimal value for ϵ. For a blocklength $n = 168$, SNR 2 dB and $a = 24$ bits arriving in every time slot, the optimum is at $\epsilon = 0.0138$. For higher values of ϵ, too many transmissions are lost, and the delay increases. For smaller values of ϵ, the system chooses very small transmission rates, such that the queue cannot be served fast enough and the delay also increases. Our simulation results confirm that the analytical bounds can be used to find the value of ϵ leads to the best performance.

In all results presented so far, we have chosen the optimum value for ϵ. Fig. 8 shows the optimal values that were used for the analysis in Fig. 5. It shows that when the delay requirements are very strict (small $\hat{w}$), the system should operate at a very small error probability ϵ and thus at very low rate. When larger delays are acceptable, then the system performs best when it uses higher rate and accepts a higher probability of error.

6.4 Optimizing the Blocklength

In a fading channel, the instantaneous SNR varies randomly over time. If this instantaneous value remains too small for some time, then only very little data can be transmitted, and the data experiences a long delay. By making the channel variations faster, it becomes less likely to experience a long delay. Although a system cannot influence directly how fast the channel changes, it can employ frequency hopping. The SNR values of channels at sufficiently different frequencies can be assumed to be independent.

Without the impact of finite blocklength effects and without any overhead from metadata, channel estimation and feedbacks, a queueing system should change the channel as quickly as possible, i.e. change the frequency as often as possible. This is no longer true when the overhead and the effects of finite blocklength are taken into account. In that case, varying the channel too quickly creates a lot of overhead. On the other hand, the channel still needs to change often enough to avoid long delays. How quickly should it change?

In the following example, we assume that the channel remains constant for a long time, but after each transmission of duration T, frequency hopping is employed so that the SNR changes to a different and independent value. As in the previous examples, we assume that it takes 1 ms to transmit $12 \cdot 14 = 168$ symbols. However, we change the number of symbols n in multiples of 12. We assume that the overhead is always $n_h = 84$ symbols. Thus, the duration T of one time slot is now assumed to be $\frac{n+n_h}{168}$ ms.

Fig. 9 shows the delay violation probabilities for a target delay of 5 ms for different blocklengths. When considering the Shannon model, the best performance is obtained for a blocklength of $n = 96$ symbols. Thus, it would be best to transmit $84 + 96$ symbols, so $T = 1.07$ ms, and then hop to a different frequency. In contrast to that, when finite blocklength effects are considered, the optimal blocklength is at 132 symbols, so the system should transmit a block of $84 + 132$ symbols ($T = 1.29$ ms). The difference might increase further when the system is only allowed to change the duration in multiples of 0.5 ms, as visualized by the vertical blue lines. Then the system would choose $T = 1$ ms with the Shannon model but $T = 1.5$ms with the finite blocklength model.

7. CONCLUSION

In this work, we use a stochastic network calculus approach to compute probabilistic delay bounds for delay sensitive wireless systems in terms of the fading channel parameters. We provide a service characterization for the underlying fading channel in the finite blocklength regime. We then use a recently developed $(\min, \times)$ network calculus methodology to compute the desired bounds. The finite blocklength channel model leads to analytical challenges that we overcome by using multiple series expansions which converge quite rapidly. We use simulations to validate the obtained delay bounds. Our analysis shows that the infinite blocklength assumption can significantly overestimate the performance of a system that operates at finite blocklength, especially at low SNR. Thus, low-latency M2M applications require more power or bandwidth than a simpler analysis with infinite blocklength models would predict.

The obtained results can be used for network dimensioning and parameters optimization. In future work, the obtained results can be extended to multi-hop settings with cross traffic and variable arrival traffic. Further research may also investigate less idealized channel models with effects like time-correlated fading, imperfect channel state information, or lost acknowledgment packets.

8. REFERENCES

[1] Y. Polyanskiy, H. V. Poor, and S. Verdú, "Channel coding rate in the finite blocklength regime," *IEEE Trans. Inf. Theory*, vol. 56, pp. 2307–2359, May 2010.

[2] H. Al-Zubaidy, J. Liebeherr, and A. Burchard, "Network-Layer Performance Analysis of Multihop Fading Channels," *IEEE/ACM Trans. Netw.*, Oct. 2014. to appear. Online: http://dx.doi.org/10.1109/TNET.2014.2360675.

[3] J. Akerberg, M. Gidlund, and M. Bjorkman, "Future research challenges in wireless sensor and actuator networks targeting industrial automation," in *Proc. IEEE Int. Conf. on Industrial Informatics (INDIN)*, vol. 9, pp. 410–415, Jul. 2011.

[4] A. Osseiran, F. Boccardi, V. Braun, *et al.*, "Scenarios for 5G mobile and wireless communications: the vision of the METIS project," *IEEE Commun. Mag.*, vol. 52, pp. 26–35, May 2014.

[5] W. Yang, G. Durisi, T. Koch, and Y. Polyanskiy, "Quasi-Static Multiple-Antenna Fading Channels at Finite Blocklength," *IEEE Trans. Inf. Theory*, vol. 60, pp. 4232–4243, Jul. 2014.

[6] W. Yang, G. Durisi, T. Koch, and Y. Polyanskiy, "Diversity versus channel knowledge at finite block-length," in *Proc. IEEE Information Theory Workshop (ITW)*, pp. 572–576, Sep. 2012.

[7] P. Wu and N. Jindal, "Coding versus ARQ in fading channels: how reliable should the PHY be?," *IEEE Trans. Commun.*, vol. 59, pp. 3363–3374, Dec. 2011.

[8] J. G. Kim and M. M. Krunz, "Bandwidth allocation in wireless networks with guaranteed packet-loss performance," *IEEE/ACM Trans. Netw.*, vol. 8, pp. 337–349, Jun. 2000.

[9] M. Hassan, M. M. Krunz, and I. Matta, "Markov-based channel characterization for tractable performance analysis in wireless packet networks," *IEEE Trans. Wireless Commun.*, vol. 3, pp. 821–831, May 2004.

[10] Petreska, Neda and Al-Zubaidy, Hussein and Gross, James, "Power minimization for industrial wireless networks under statistical delay constraints," in *Proc. Int. Teletraffic Congr. (ITC)*, pp. 1–9, 2014.

[11] M. C. Gursoy, "Throughput analysis of buffer-constrained wireless systems in the finite blocklength regime," *EURASIP Journal on Wireless Communications and Networking*, Dec. 2013.

[12] D. Wu and R. Negi, "Effective capacity: a wireless link model for support of quality of service," *IEEE Trans. Wireless Commun.*, vol. 2, pp. 630–643, Jul. 2003.

[13] D. Qiao, M. C. Gursoy, and S. Velipasalar, "Channel coding over multiple coherence blocks with queueing constraints," in *Proc. IEEE Int. Conf. on Communications (ICC)*, pp. 1–5, Jun. 2011.

[14] Y. Zhang and Y. Jiang, "Performance of data transmission over a gaussian channel with dispersion," in *Proc. Int. Symp. on Wireless Communication Systems (ISWCS)*, pp. 721–725, VDE, Aug. 2012.

[15] I. Gradshteyn and I. Ryzhik, *Table of Integrals, Series, and Products*. Elsevier, 7th ed., 2007.

[16] M. Abramowitz and I. A. Stegun, *Handbook of mathematical functions*. Courier Corporation, 1964.

[17] S. Sesia, M. Baker, and I. Toufik, *LTE-The UMTS Long Term Evolution: From Theory to Practice*. John Wiley & Sons, 2011.

[18] N. Petreska, H. Al-Zubaidy, R. Knorr, and J. Gross, "On the Recursive Nature of End-to-End Delay Bound for Heterogenous Networks," in *IEEE Int. Conf. on Communications (ICC)*, Jun. 2015. Online: http://www.researchgate.net/publication/275648083.

Mechanisms for Multi-Packet Reception Protocols in Multi-Hop Networks

Ke Li
Computing Science
Department
University of Alberta
Edmonton, Canada
kli4@ualberta.ca

Ioanis Nikolaidis
Computing Science
Department
University of Alberta
Edmonton, Canada
nikolaidis@ualberta.ca

Janelle Harms
Computing Science
Department
University of Alberta
Edmonton, Canada
janelleh@ualberta.ca

ABSTRACT

We consider multi-hop wireless networks composed of nodes with transceivers capable of multi-packet transmission and reception (MPT/MPR). Legacy MAC protocols based on CSMA/CA are overly restrictive in the interest of avoiding collisions, and are unable to exploit the MPR capability of receivers. We demonstrate how a combination of mechanisms, based on well-known techniques, such as Additive Increase Multiplicative Decrease (AIMD), and the back–pressure (BP) principle, can be used to effectively control medium access in multi-hop MPT/MPR networks. The AIMD component is used to regulate the size of "bundles" of simultaneously transmitted packets, while back–pressure provides the basis for prioritizing, locally, which flows' packets should be transmitted in a bundle. We study the performance of the proposed protocol, AB-MAC, under three different models of node coordination in static wireless multi-hop MPT/MPR networks. We find that, under various scenarios and for the same capacity resources, AB-MAC's throughput performance surpasses that of IEEE 802.11b.

Categories and Subject Descriptors

C.2.2 [**Computer-Communication Networks**]: Network Protocols—*Protocol architecture*

Keywords

MAC protocol; multi-packet reception; multi-hop networks; additive-increase multiplicative-decrease; backpressure

1. INTRODUCTION

As wireless communication has become the dominant mode of communication in everyday life, the demands for faster wireless communication networks have escalated. To address these demands, advanced techniques at the physical layer such as multiple-input and multiple-output (MIMO)

MSWiM'15, November 2–6, 2015, Cancun, Mexico.
© 2015 ACM. ISBN 978-1-4503-3762-5/15/11 ...$15.00.
DOI: http://dx.doi.org/10.1145/2811587.2811618.

transceivers, multi-user detection (MUD), advanced modulation, etc., have contributed towards making multi-packet transmission (MPT) and multi-packet reception (MPR) a possibility [9]. The main advantage of MPR is that it allows multiple packets to be received concurrently, whereas traditional receivers would consider such an event a collision. Conceivably, this advantage should lead to improved protocol performance except for the fact that medium-access control (MAC) protocols have to be specifically designed to exploit the MPR property. However, the MPR capability alone cannot linearly scale the performance of multi-hop networks and the multi-packet transmission (MPT) techniques are suggested to be applied to further improve the system performance [6, 7]. The need for MPT capability in a multi-hop system should be intuitively clear. For example, consider a node that only relays traffic. Even if the node has MPR capability, it cannot utilize it effectively if it cannot transmit at the same rate, because in the long run the input and output rates of traffic traversing the node should match.

We have previously proposed and analyzed [4, 5] the AIMD-MAC algorithm (based on an Additive Increase Multiplicative Decrease principle) for a single-hop scenario where a number of nodes compete for a single channel to communicate to one MPR receiver. In [6] we studied the MPT/MPR multi-hop wireless network from a centralized viewpoint to construct a global schedule. In this paper, we consider the problem of what mechanisms should be included in a distributed MAC protocol to effectively exploit the MPT/MPR capabilities of transceivers. We base our design on AIMD combined with a backpressure-based (BP) [8, 11] mechanism, and we call the family of protocols AB-MAC.

We note that, whereas in legacy protocols we resort to backoff mechanisms to avoid collisions by regulating the number of slots a node should defer its transmission, in the case of MPT/MPR networks, we would also need to estimate the *number* of packets a node should concurrently transmit when allowed to do so by a control mechanism (backoff-based or otherwise). In AIMD-MAC [4], we remarked that by having every node adaptively adjust its access probability (AP) (i.e. the probability it will attempt a transmission in the next slot) according to the transmission outcome (success/failure) history, the nodes can reach an "agreement" to efficiently and fairly use the channel. In this paper, we extend the concept of AIMD-MAC to multi-hop scenarios.

We emphasize that the MPT/MPR channel model is distinctly different from the multi-channel model [10, 12] in that, in MPT/MPR channels, the nodes in transmission range can hear each other because they are not separated by channels. Therefore, for any transmitter, all the receivers (within transmission range of the considered transmitter) are exposed to the signal sent by the transmitter. Whether the concurrent transmissions can be successfully decoded at the desired receiver is decided by the total number of packets arriving at the receiver and its MPR capacity limit. We define the MPR limit to be K_R, i.e., up to K_R transmissions can be concurrently received. If the concurrently received transmissions exceed K_R then the decoding of all those transmissions is assumed to have failed, i.e., the MPR is assumed to behave in an all-or-nothing manner. Symmetrically, we define the MPT property to be governed by a limit K_T.

We endow every node with its own access probability, AP, regardless of the number of flows crossing the node. The adjustment of AP reflects the MPR limits of its receivers. Specifically, we use AP to compute the number of packets a node should concurrently transmit in the next slot (which could be zero), and we call this the *transmission quota* of the node. We also name the packets sent concurrently by a node, a *bundle*. We will answer the question of how to allocate transmission quota to the flows crossing the nodes and how to create the transmission bundles. To this end, we adopt the strategy of backpressure, BP, according to which only flows with positive differential backlog between successive hops can be assigned transmission quota. Furthermore, in order to fairly treat the flows, the transmission quota distribution process prioritizes the most poorly treated flow based on local flow information.

In Section 2 we present the component mechanisms that, collectively, define the AB-MAC protocol. In Section 3 we introduce additional assumptions regarding the coordination (or lack thereof) between nodes, and provide corresponding simulation-based performance results. Finally, Section 4 provides conclusions and plans for future work.

2. AB-MAC

In this section we describe the AB-MAC mechanisms: (a) exchange of local information, (b) AP computation and, (c), distribution of transmission quota.

2.1 Local Information Exchange

We consider a multi-hop wireless network, where nodes keep track of the flows traversing through them and maintain information about the next hop for each flow. To update its own AP, a node requires the neighbors' latest reception status as well as the backlog information at the next hop for each flow that traverses the node (in order to calculate the differential backlog). This local information is exchanged in two ways: (1) end-of-reception acknowledgments emanating from neighboring nodes and (2) piggybacked local flow status. To update the AP, the node needs the recent reception status of its immediate neighbors. Thus, at the end of a reception, each and every receiver broadcasts an acknowledgement to signify the status of the reception. The local flow status is piggybacked in the header of regular data packets and exchanged between neighbors as part of the regular packet exchanges.

The main mechanism for status updates is the end-of-reception acknowledgement. At the end of a reception, a receiver broadcasts its reception status via a binary acknowledgement (success/failure) to indicate whether it has been able to successfully decode the concurrently received transmissions (i.e., if $\leq K_R$) or not. We will use the term ACK (NAK) to indicate success or failure, noting that ACK is different from its legacy meaning in CSMA/CA because we assume it does not include any packet information. The purpose of ACK is to inform all its neighbors of the latest reception status seen by the receiver. The ACK is assumed to be of short and constant length regardless of the number of packets decoded by the receiver. A NAK, on the other hand, is a similar message indicating that the receiver could not successfully decode the concurrently received transmissions ($> K_R$).

The reception of concurrent ACK/NAKs follows the same MPR model as for the data packets: if the total number of ACK/NAKs is less than or equal to K_R, the ACK/NAKs can be decoded by the node; otherwise, the ACK/NAKs will collide and cannot be decoded. Due to the half-duplex property, at the end of slot, if a node is sending ACK/NAKs, it cannot receive the ACK/NAKs from other nodes. Since a node needs to broadcast ACK/NAK at the end of a receiving slot, only nodes which are in transmitting or idle state can receive the ACK/NAKs from others at the end of that slot.

To keep track of the transmission status, every node maintains three sets:

- **intended-receivers**: A set containing all intended receivers of the bundle of packets transmitted by the node in the current slot. If the node does not transmit at the slot, this set is empty.

- **receive-ACK-from**: A set containing the transmitters of all the successfully decoded ACKs at the end of slot.

- **receive-NAK-from**: A set containing the transmitters of all the successfully decoded NAKs at the end of slot.

Note that for any node, the intersection of receive-ACK-from and receive-NAK-from is empty because a receiver cannot indicate both success and failure at the end of the same slot. The set receive-ACK-from (receive-NAK-from) does not necessarily belong to the set intended-receivers because a node can receive ACK/NAK from a node which was not its intended receiver. In subsection 2.2, we will discuss how to use the received ACK/NAKs to update the AP.

Additionally, the neighbors exchange local flow status by piggybacking in the header of a data packet the backlog information $Q_n^{(f)}$ (queue occupancy) at that node for a flow together with the id, f, of that flow. Since multiple flows traverse node n, a round-robin scheme is used to send in turns the backlog of the list of flows (ordered in some fashion) traversing the node. Additionally the node sends, again in the header, the current degree information, d_n, i.e., the current number of its one-hop neighbors. While the round-robin sending of backlog updates means that the backlog information is not necessarily up-to-date, we remark that due to the MPT/MPR multiple data packets and, hence, header information piggybacking backlog updates are usually transmitted together. We will show in the simulations of a 100 node network (Section 3) that even when the number of flows is greater than the value of K_R, our schemes still outperform the benchmark, *i.e.*, the impact of delayed status updates due to the round-robin piggybacking appears to be insignificant.

Each node maintains a flow table for all the flows crossing the node, containing the local and the collected flow status from its neighbors from piggybacked information in the headers of received data packets. For each flow f, the node stores its own local backlog information $Q_n^{(f)}$, and the next hop's, n_f', backlog information, $Q_{n_f'}^{(f)}$, as received piggybacked in headers. The node also calculates the differential backlog $\psi_n^{(f)}$ of each flow as $\psi_n^{(f)} = Q_n^{(f)} - Q_{n_f'}^{(f)}$. Finally, we keep track of $\mathcal{T}_n^{(f)}$, the total packets node n has transmitted so far for flow f, which is used to decide the priority levels of the potential flows when distributing the transmission quota.

2.2 AP Computation

The basic idea of the AIMD approach is to decrease the value of AP multiplicatively after a collision; otherwise, increase the AP additively. The increments probe for the channel capacity limit while the reduction decreases the chance of collisions. We introduce the all-receiver-considered AIMD (ARC-AIMD) strategy to update the APs.

2.2.1 The ARC-AIMD Method

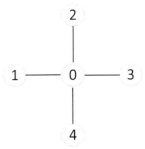

Figure 1: Example topology for ARC-AIMD.

Fig. 1 shows an example topology to explain the ARC-AIMD method. Since a node's transmission will not only be heard by the desired receiver but all the nodes in transmission range, to adjust the AP of a node n, it is useful to take into consideration the latest reception status of all the neighbors of node n. For example, in Fig. 1, if any neighbor of node 0 (e.g., node 1) just experienced a failed reception, the AP of node 0 should be multiplicatively decreased because the transmission from node 0 can be heard by node 1; on the other hand, if all the intended receivers of node 0 respond by an ACK at the end of slot, node 0 should increase the AP additively to probe for higher transmission opportunities.

For a node n_o, denote the three sets intended-receivers, receive-ACK-from and receive-NAK-from by $\boldsymbol{n}_I(n_o)$, $\boldsymbol{n}_A(n_o)$ and $\boldsymbol{n}_N(n_o)$, respectively. At the end of a non-receiving slot (receiving nodes need to broadcast ACK/NAK and hence cannot receive at the same time), a node n_o can receive ACK/NAKs from its neighbors. With the latest reception status of the neighbors, n_o can decide whether it should increase or decrease its AP (i.e., p_{n_o}) following the ARC-AIMD algorithm (Fig. 2). Note that if $|\boldsymbol{n}_A(n_o)| + |\boldsymbol{n}_N(n_o)| > K_R$, the acknowledgement arriving at n_o exceeds the reception capacity limit and cannot be decoded by n_o.

Each packet transmission from n_o can have three possible dispositions at the intended receiver n_r: (i) the packet is suc-

cessfully decoded by the receiver n_r; (ii) the packet collides (received packets $> K_R$) with other arriving packets at the receiver n_r (named the 2nd-hop collision at n_r) and (iii) n_r is in transmitting state and ignores the packet (named the 1st-hop collision at n_r, i.e. a side-effect of half-duplex operation). The successful reception (case i) can be confirmed by an ACK from n_r and a 2nd-hop collision (case ii) can be confirmed by a NAK from n_r. If n_r does not respond by neither an ACK nor NAK, it implies that a 1st-hop collision occurs at n_r because n_r ignores the packets while transmitting and will not broadcast any acknowledgement after a transmission. Normally, if $\boldsymbol{n}_I(n_o) \setminus (\boldsymbol{n}_A(n_o) \cup \boldsymbol{n}_N(n_o))$ is not empty, a 1st-hop collision occurs in at least one of n_o's intended receivers.

```
ARC-AIMD ($\boldsymbol{n}_I(n_o)$, $\boldsymbol{n}_A(n_o)$, $\boldsymbol{n}_N(n_o)$)
1    if (($|\boldsymbol{n}_I(n_o)| > 0$) and
        (($|\boldsymbol{n}_N(n_o)| > 0$) or
         ($|\boldsymbol{n}_A(n_o)| + |\boldsymbol{n}_N(n_o)| > K_R$) or
         ($|\boldsymbol{n}_I(n_o) \setminus (\boldsymbol{n}_A(n_o) \cup \boldsymbol{n}_N(n_o))| > 0$)))
2        $p_{n_o} = \max\{p_{n_o} \times \beta, \alpha\}$;
3    else
4        $p_{n_o} = \min\{p_{n_o} + \alpha, 1.0\}$;
5    end
6    return $p_{n_o}$;
```

Figure 2: The ARC-AIMD algorithm.

In the ARC-AIMD algorithm, n_o multiplicatively decreases the AP by the decreasing factor β ($0 < \beta < 1$) after a transmission (i.e., when $|\boldsymbol{n}_I(n_o)| > 0$) if one of the three conditions holds: 1) n_o receives NAKs (i.e., $|\boldsymbol{n}_N(n_o)| > 0$), 2) ACK/NAKs collide at n_o (i.e., $\boldsymbol{n}_A(n_o)| + |\boldsymbol{n}_N(n_o)| > K_R$), or, 3) a 1st-hop collision happens in at least one of n_o's intended receivers (i.e., $|\boldsymbol{n}_I(n_o) \setminus (\boldsymbol{n}_A(n_o) \cup \boldsymbol{n}_N(n_o))| > 0$). These three conditions include all the possible causes for which n_o does not receive ACKs from all its intended neighbors. Decreasing the AP under these conditions guarantees that n_o will only keep transmitting to a node n_r if n_o has confirmation that n_r can decode the packets from n_o. If n_o receives a NAK, it means at one of n_o's neighbor, the arriving packets (including the packets from n_o) exceed the MPR capacity limit. Since the packets transmitted from n_o can be heard by all its neighbors, n_o should decrease its AP to prevent future collisions at this neighbor even if this neighbor was not one of n_o's intended receivers. On the other hand, if none of these conditions holds or n_o did not transmit, it means that either n_o has received the ACKs from all of its intended receivers or n_o has no impact on the channel at the current slot. In either case, n_o increases the AP by the minimum AP α ($0 < \alpha < 1$) and hence probes for more transmission opportunities.

A question is what should be the values of α and β used to regulate AIMD dynamics. These depend on the density of the network and the value of K_T and K_R. Based on our earlier work on AIMD-MAC [5], we recognized that the equilibrium point of the AP, denoted by $\tilde{p}$, can be computed as $\alpha/(1 - \beta)$. If $\tilde{p}$ is close to the optimal AP, denoted by p^*, the APs of the nodes tend to oscillate around p^*, which can lead to the desirable performance in the long run. Unfortunately, even for the single-hop scenario, we do not have a closed formula to compute p^*. Therefore, in order to appropriately set α and β for AB-MAC in a multi-hop network, we apply a heuristic approach. Namely, we approximate p^* by the value of K_R/d_n where d_n are the 1-hop neighbors of the receiver node, n. This approximation can be interpreted as follows: the reception capability of the receiver should be evenly distributed across all nodes competing for the resource where the resource is seen to be the receiver's receive capacity. Note that the p^* loses its meaning as probability when $K_R > d_n$ and it is then set to 1, since all neighbors could potentially transmit and their transmissions successfully decoded. In a multi-hop scenario, however, any node n_o may have multiple potential receivers, each with different degree. Hence, the problem is, which node's degree should be chosen as the one to provide the best performing AP, $p^*_{n_o}$, for n_o.

A conservative approach, which we adopt, is to select the largest degree over all the active neighbors. Formally, $p^*_{n_o}$ is approximated by Eq. 1 where $\mathcal{D}_{n_o} = \max\{d_n | n \in \boldsymbol{n}_1(n_o)\}$ where $\boldsymbol{n}_1(n_o)$ denotes the 1-hop neighbors of n_o. K_T and K_R are the transmission and reception capacity limits.

$$p^*_{n_o} \approx \frac{K_R}{\mathcal{D}_{n_o} K_T} \qquad (1)$$

To allow the APs to oscillate around the approximated $p^*_{n_o}$, combining $\tilde{p} = \alpha/(1-\beta)$ and Eq. 1 leads to the relationship between α and β represented by Eq. 2. Eq. 2 implies that the nodes with busy neighbors (*i.e.*, nodes with high degree) will have a lower equilibrium point and therefore lower value of AP.

$$\frac{\alpha}{1-\beta} = \frac{K_R}{\mathcal{D}_{n_o} K_T} \qquad (2)$$

With Eq. 2, if we know the value of α, the value of β can be computed accordingly. As mentioned earlier, the AP is increased by α to probe for the channel capacity limit. Thus, the value of α determines how fast a node will reach the channel capacity limit. We set an integer parameter τ to configure the value of α as shown in Eq. 3. We will show in the next subsection that τ is the number of increment operations needed for a node to be able to transmit one more packet. From Eq. 2 and 3, the value of β is expressed by Eq. 4.

$$\alpha = \frac{1}{\tau K_T} \qquad (3)$$

$$\beta = 1 - \frac{\mathcal{D}_{n_o}}{\tau K_R} \qquad (4)$$

Hence, in total, AB-MAC has three parameters K_T, K_R and τ to jointly decide the value of α and β. The value of AP is a fraction between 0 and 1. Next, we illustrate how to convert the fraction into an integer, which consequently expresses the upper-bound of the number of packets a node can simultaneously transmit in a bundle.

2.3 Transmission Quota Distribution

A first constraint imposed by AB-MAC is that a node is not allowed to transmit in two successive slots, *i.e.*, only after a reception or idle slot, can a node transmit. This transmission constraint ensures that every node has a chance to listen after its transmission so that it can extract the latest flow status from the data packets received from its neighbors. Note that in a multi-hop flow traversing a path of nodes equipped with half-duplex radios, the relays should alternate between transmitting and receiving states over time

such that the flow can traverse smoothly from the source to the destination. The constraint however limits the throughput of single-hop flows which we consider it a reasonable sacrifice to make for a predominantly multi-hop communication system.

Knowing the value of p_{n_o}, the number of packets n_o can transmit in the next slot is computed by Eq. 5. Γ_{n_o} is referred to as the ***transmission quota*** of node n_o. $\mathcal{X}$ is equal to 1 with probability $(K_T \times p_{n_o} - \lfloor K_T \times p_{n_o} \rfloor)$ and is equal to 0 with probability $(1 - (K_T \times p_{n_o} - \lfloor K_T \times p_{n_o} \rfloor))$. Since p_{n_o} is multiplied by K_T when computing the transmission quota, if $p_{n_o} \leq (1 - 1/K_T)$, after τ consecutive increasing operations, Γ_{n_o} will be increased by 1.

$$\Gamma_{n_o} = \lfloor K_T \times p_{n_o} \rfloor + \mathcal{X} \qquad (5)$$

The next question is, how to distribute the Γ_{n_o} packets among all the flows crossing n_o. We adopt the strategy suggested by the BP algorithm [8] which only selects the flows with positive differential backlog as the potential flows to be assigned the transmission quota. This BP method prevents upstream nodes from starving the downstream nodes and therefore relieves the intra-flow contention problem. Additionally, every flow records the number of packets it has sent out by updating $\mathcal{T}^{(f)}_{n_o}$. The potential flows are then sorted in increasing order of $\mathcal{T}^{(f)}_{n_o}$. $\mathcal{T}^{(f)}_{n_o}$ reflects the amount of channel resource flow f has used at node n_o, thus, by prioritizing the most poorly treated flow (*i.e.*, the one at the head of the sorted potential flows), we can prioritize the most poorly treated flow at node n_o. The TQD algorithm (Fig. 3) formally describes the procedure to distribute the transmission quota Γ_{n_o} to the flows crossing n_o, denoted by $\boldsymbol{f}_{n_o}$.

TQD $(\Gamma_{n_o}, \boldsymbol{f}_{n_o})$
1    $t^{(f)}_{n_o} = 0$ for any flow $f \in \boldsymbol{f}_{n_o}$;
2   **while** $\Gamma_{n_o} > 0$
3   Update $\psi^{(f)}_{n_o}$ by Eq. 6;
4   Compute $\boldsymbol{f}^*_{n_o}$ according to Eq. 7;
5   **if** $\boldsymbol{f}^*_{n_o} \neq \emptyset$
6   Update $\mathcal{T}^{(f)}_{n_o}$ for any $f \in \boldsymbol{f}^*_{n_o}$ by Eq. 8;
7          $f^*_{n_o} = \arg\min_{f \in \boldsymbol{f}^*_{n_o}} \left(\mathcal{T}^{(f)}_{n_o} \right)$. Break ties arbitrarily.
8          $t^{(f^*_{n_o})}_{n_o} = t^{(f^*_{n_o})}_{n_o} + 1$;
9          $\Gamma_{n_o} = \Gamma_{n_o} - 1$;
10         $\boldsymbol{f}^*_{n_o} = \emptyset$;
11   **else**
12   **break**;
13   **end**
14   **end**
15   **return** $\boldsymbol{t}_{n_o}$;

Figure 3: The transmission quota distribution (TQD) algorithm.

$$\psi^{(f)}_{n_o} = \psi^{(f)}_{n_o} - 2t^{(f)}_{n_o} \qquad (6)$$

$$\boldsymbol{f}^*_{n_o} = \{f | \psi^{(f)}_{n_o} > 0 \land f \in \boldsymbol{f}_{n_o}\} \qquad (7)$$

$$\mathcal{T}^{(f)}_{n_o} = \mathcal{T}^{(f)}_{n_o} + t^{(f)}_{n_o} \qquad (8)$$

$t^{(f)}_{n_o}$ represents the number of packets flow f should transmit from n_o and it is set to 0 initially. $\boldsymbol{t}_{n_o}$ represents the set of transmission quotas for all the flows traversing n_o and is returned by TQD. If Γ_{n_o} is less than one, the procedure terminates. Otherwise, at line 3, the differential backlog $\psi_{n_o}^{(f)}$ is updated by Eq. 6. If n_o transmitted $t_{n_o}^{(f)}$ packets for flow f, the downstream node will increase the backlog by $t_{n_o}^{(f)}$ packets, if it is not the destination of flow f. Thus, $\psi_{n_o}^{(f)}$ should be decreased by $2t_{n_o}^{(f)}$.

The potential flow set $\boldsymbol{f}_{n_o}^*$ contains the flows which can transmit according to Eq. 7. If there does not exist such a flow, the procedure terminates. Note that the flows with empty backlog cannot have a positive differential backlog, therefore, those empty flows will not consume transmission quota. $\mathfrak{T}_{n_o}^{(f)}$ is the total number of packet n_o has transmitted for flow f. It is updated at line 6 by counting in the newly determined value of $t_{n_o}^{(f)}$ (Eq. 8). The flow with the minimum $\mathfrak{T}_{n_o}^{(f)}$ is selected (denoted by $f_{n_o}^*$) at line 7 and its transmission quota (i.e., $t_{n_o}^{(f_{n_o}^*)}$) is increased by one (line 8). Accordingly, the total transmission quota Γ_{n_o} is decreased by one (line 9). At this point, one unit of the transmission quota is assigned to a flow and the candidate flow set $\boldsymbol{f}_{n_o}^*$ is cleared (line 10) before the next round of quota distribution starts. Each iteration of the TQD algorithm allows the most poorly treated potential flow to transmit one more packet. The procedure repeats until either Γ_{n_o} is zero or there are no more potential flows satisfying Eq. 7. The complete AB-MAC algorithm is shown in Fig. 4.

AB-MAC (K_T, K_R, τ, I)
1   Update $\boldsymbol{n}_I(n_o)$, $\boldsymbol{n}_A(n_o)$, $\boldsymbol{n}_N(n_o)$ and the flow table;
2   p_{n_o}=ARC-AIMD($\boldsymbol{n}_I(n_o)$, $\boldsymbol{n}_A(n_o)$, $\boldsymbol{n}_N(n_o)$);
3   Generate random number x, $x \in unif[0, 1]$;
4   **if** ((n_o did not transmit) **or**
               $(|\boldsymbol{n}_I(n_o) \setminus (\boldsymbol{n}_A(n_o) \cup \boldsymbol{n}_N(n_o))| > 0$ **and** $x < 0.5$))
5   Compute the transmission quota Γ_{n_o} by Eq. 5;
6    $\boldsymbol{t}_{n_o}$ = TQD(Γ_{n_o}, $\boldsymbol{f}_{n_o}$);
7    $\mathbf{P} = \emptyset$;
8   **for each** $f \in \boldsymbol{f}_{n_o}$
9   **while** $t_{n_o}^{(f)} > 0$
10   Select one packet $\mathcal{P}$ from flow f;
11          $t_{n_o}^{(f)} = t_{n_o}^{(f)} - 1$;
12          $I = I \mod (|\boldsymbol{f}_{n_o}|) + 1$;
13   Select the I-th flow's info to piggyback;
14   Add the header to packet $\mathcal{P}$ and $\mathbf{P} = \{\mathbf{P}, \mathcal{P}\}$;
15   **end**
16   **end**
17 **end**

Figure 4: The AB-MAC algorithm at node n_o.

Fig. 4 describes the AB-MAC algorithm at node n_o, which runs at the end of each slot and computes the content of the ready-to-transmit queue $\mathbf{P}$ for the following slot. If $\mathbf{P}$ is not empty, n_o will encapsulate all the packets in $\mathbf{P}$ and transmit at the next slot. The first step is to update the three sets $\boldsymbol{n}_I(n_o)$, $\boldsymbol{n}_A(n_o)$ and $\boldsymbol{n}_N(n_o)$ and the flow table based on the most recently received piggybacked information and ACK/NAKs. p_{n_o} is then updated using the ARC-AIMD algorithm.

At the beginning of this subsection we explained that in multi-hop flows, a node should not transmit in two consecutive slots so that it can accomplish two things 1) receive updated local information of its neighbors and 2) give a chance for next hop to transmit to accomplish multi-hop forwarding. Thus, if n_o does not transmit at the current slot, it can transmit in the next slot as shown by the first condition of line 4. The purpose of the second condition is to alleviate the 1st-hop collisions. A 1st-hop collision occurs because the intended receiver is transmitting in the same slot. For example, if both n_o and its intended receiver n_r transmits at the odd-indexed slots, n_r can never decode the packets from n_o. We alleviate this problem by flipping a coin when a 1st-hop collision is detected at one of n_o's intended receivers. If $|\boldsymbol{n}_I(n_o) \setminus (\boldsymbol{n}_A(n_o) \cup \boldsymbol{n}_N(n_o))| > 0$ holds (i.e., 1st-hop collision occurs), n_o generates a normally distributed value x between 0 and 1. If $x < 0.5$, n_o can transmit in two consecutive slots, which indeed swaps n_o's transmitting slot from odd to even or from even to odd.

The transmission quota Γ_{n_o} is computed by Eq. 5 and distributed according to TQD. The ready-to-transmit queue $\mathbf{P}$ is initially empty. To implement the round-robin flow selection, the last parameter of AB-MAC I points to the flow (in the flow table) to be included in the header. I is set initially to 0 and updated at line 12. n_o selects the data packets as assigned by TQD and encodes the status of one flow (indicated by I) in the header of each packet. The prepared packet is added to $\mathbf{P}$.

3.   PERFORMANCE EVALUATION

In this section, we evaluate the throughput performance of the AB-MAC mechanisms using simulation. We consider a network where 100 nodes are randomly placed in a 1600 by 1600 square. The interference range is set to be equal to the transmission range, which is 200 distance units. Two nodes within transmission range are in one-hop distance of each other and are connected by a solid line in Fig. 5.

We compare the aggregate end-to-end throughput of AB-MAC against that of IEEE 802.11b distributed coordination function (DCF) [3]. DCF is implemented based on the *WiFi* model of the ns-3 simulator [1] with link rate (b) of 1Mbps. In order to present a clear comparison, the PHY layer is simplified by assuming zero propagation delay and the physical layer convergence protocol (PLCP) header and preamble overheads are omitted. AB-MAC is simulated on MPT/MPR channels where $K_T = 5$ and $K_R >= K_T$. In order to present a fair comparison, the link rate of AB-MAC is set to 0.2Mbps, which is $1/K_T$ of the link rate of DCF. The data packets (including the headers of the higher-layer control protocols and the payload) for both AB-MAC and DCF are set to 1500 bytes. The length of a slot is equal to $1500 \times 8 \times 10^6/b$ seconds. The third parameter of AB-MAC is τ. Following our earlier observations in experiments with the AIMD methods [4, 5], we set τ to be 10 slots.

To explore the performance of the three mechanism of AB-MAC, we apply them in scenarios with varying levels of medium access coordination. In the first scenario, there is no coordination to avoid contention when nodes decide to transmit. We model small variations in start time due to clock drift and propagation delay in distributed systems by randomly staggering transmission over four virtual slots. This enables carrier sensing to have some effect, however multiple neighbouring nodes may transmit at the same time. It is possible that a transmitter's intended receiver will be transmitting; resulting in the receiver being unable to receive the packet. This we call a first-hop collision. We call this virtual slot scenario, *the mini-slot scheme.*

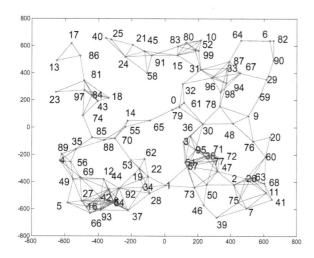

Figure 5: The 100 node random topology.

The second coordination scheme assumes that nodes coordinate within their immediate neighbourhood so that only one node will transmit among the neighbours. A receiver may still receive from multiple nodes due to hidden terminal. However, in MPT/MPR networks, multiple concurrent transmissions do not necessarily lead to collision if the receiver can handle all the arriving packets. For this simulation, the choice of which of the ready nodes should transmit within a neighbourhood is random. This is called *the random scheme*. The random scheme prevents the 1st-hop collisions from happening because the transmitter and its receiver will not transmit at the same slot. Nonetheless, it is worth noting that the random scheme is not necessarily a benefit for MPT/MPR networks because it can stop concurrent transmissions that could have been accommodated by the intended receiver of the transmitters.

The third scheme is similar to the random scheme but it selects the node in a neighbourhood with the largest ready-to-transmit queue. This is called *the prioritized scheme*. If the channel contention procedure prioritizes the contending nodes with large backlog, it can maximize the overall channel utilization efficiency and hence improve the system performance.

In Fig. 6(a) (mini-slot scheme), Fig. 6(b) (random scheme) and Fig. 6(c) (prioritized scheme) the aggregate throughput of 20 flows in the network is given for different arrival rates. Each flow has the same arrival rate at the source. We simulate AB-MAC on MPT/MPR channels where $K_T = 5$ and K_R varies from 5, 6, ... ,10 to 1000. Note that $K_R = 1000$ is a means to express "infinite" receiving capacity. We compare with IEEE 802.11 DCF with and without the RTS/CTS mechanism. Every data point is the mean of 10 runs lasting 10 seconds. The error bars are one standard deviation wide and are smaller than the line markers in the figure.

In Fig. 6(a), Fig. 6(b), and Fig. 6(c), the experiments show that the throughput of AB-MAC increases with the nodes' coordination level. In Fig. 6(a), the case where the contending nodes do not coordinate during channel access, DCF with RTS/CTS outperforms AB-MAC even when K_R is unlimited. When the MPR capacity is not a constraint, the performance is mostly affected by the 1st-hop collisions

where the intended receiver is transmitting in the same slot as the transmitter. The failed transmissions caused by the 1st-hop collisions significantly affect the aggregate throughput and degrade the performance of AB-MAC under light traffic. However, when the traffic is heavier, the protocol reduces transmission based on the limited MPR capacity and the AB-MAC outperforms DCF, which collapses in saturated dense networks. If these 1st-hop collisions are eliminated by coordination, we can see that in the random scheme, in Fig. 6(b), even under light traffic AB-MAC can outperform DCF. Also, the aggregate throughput of AB-MAC is increased compared to the mini-slot scheme. If further coordination is allowed to prioritize the heavily loaded contending nodes, the overall performance can be greatly improved as we can see in the prioritized scheme in Fig. 6(c).

Fig. 6(a), Fig. 6(b), and Fig. 6(c), illustrate the performance of AB-MAC under both light and heavy traffic load, suggesting that it is capable of mitigating certain problems inherent in using CSMA/CA over the same channel capacity, such as the asymmetric information problem [2] and intra-flow interference problems. The experiments also show the dramatic difference in performance depending on the existence (and the extent) of coordination among nodes.

In the mini-slot scheme, contending nodes do not coordinate and thus AB-MAC exhibits the worst performance which can even be outperformed by DCF under light traffic, although the situation turns in favor of AB-MAC at heavier traffic. Once the 1st-hop collisions are resolved, as in the case of the random scheme, AB-MAC can outperform DCF in any scenario. The tighter coordination, as captured in the prioritized scheme, not only outperforms DCF but exploits the available capacity better than the random scheme, by giving priority to nodes with larger ready-to-transmit queue backlogs. Finally, there are limits to the performance of AB-MAC as we can see by the fact that, for increasing load, AB-MAC eventually reaches a plateau of throughput. This plateau is a function of the topology of the network, because once K_R becomes practically infinite, the throughput depends on K_T and the degree of the nodes.

4. CONCLUSION

In this paper, we propose the AB-MAC algorithm to regulate transmissions of multi-hop flows in MPT/MPR wireless networks. The AB-MAC algorithm consists of three major components: 1) exchange of local information, 2) computation of local access probabilities using AIMD and 3) distribution of transmission quota across flows using a backpressure–based algorithm. Regulating the access probability mitigates several problems inherent in using RTS/CTS CSMA/CA and is a convenient basis to compute the transmission quota for each node. AIMD takes care of deciding if a node is eligible to transmit; while the BP method can alleviate the intra-flow contention and prevent the upstream nodes from monopolizing the channel.

The AB-MAC protocol is evaluated using simulation under three medium access coordination schemes: a scheme that does not coordinate transmissions at all, thus allowing 1st-hop collisions; a scheme that randomly chooses one node to transmit among a set of neighbours, and a scheme that chooses the ready node with the largest backlog queue to transmit. These schemes exhibit increasing levels of node coordination during channel access, leading to correspond-

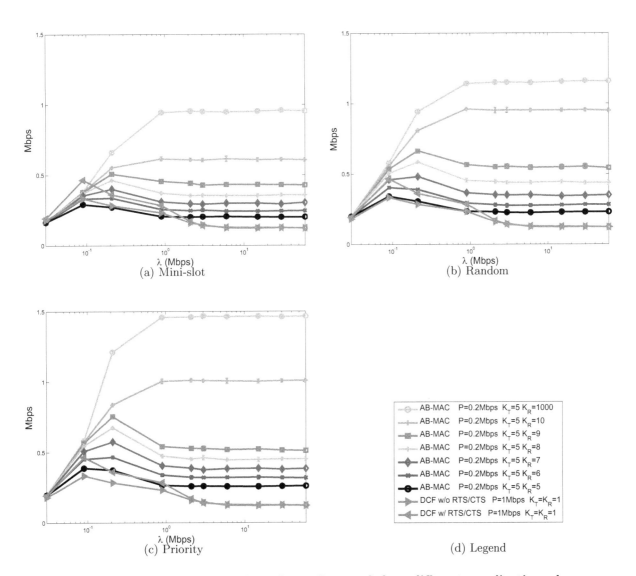

Figure 6: The aggregate throughput for 20 flows and three different coordination schemes.

ingly better performance. Simulation results show that DCF cannot effectively resolve collisions in networks with many flows, AB-MAC is adaptive in various scenarios. Generally, increasing the value of K_R can improve the overall performance of AB-MAC. The random coordination scheme and the prioritized scheme show different directions in which the performance of AB-MAC can be further improved.

5. REFERENCES

[1] http://code.nsnam.org/ns-3-dev/.

[2] V. Bharghavan, A. Demers, S. Shenker, and L. Zhang. MACAW: A media access protocol for wireless LAN's. *SIGCOMM Comput. Commun. Rev.*, 24(4):212–225, October 1994.

[3] IEEE Committee. IEEE standard for information technology-telecommunications and information exchange between systems-local and metropolitan area networks-specific requirements - part 11: Wireless LAN medium access control (MAC) and physical layer (PHY) specifications. *IEEE Std 802.11-2007 (Revision of IEEE Std 802.11-1999)*, pages C1–1184, 12 2007.

[4] K. Li, M. Ghanbarinejad, I. Nikolaidis, and C. Schlegel. Additive-increase multiplicative-decrease mac protocol with multi-packet reception. In Vassilis Tsaoussidis, AndreasJ. Kassler, Yevgeni Koucheryavy, and Abdelhamid Mellouk, editors, *Wired/Wireless Internet Communication*, volume 7889 of *Lecture Notes in Computer Science*, pages 15–28. Springer Berlin Heidelberg, 2013.

[5] K. Li, I. Nikolaidis, and J. Harms. The analysis of the additive-increase multiplicative-decrease MAC protocol. In *Proceedings of the 10th Annual Conference on Wireless On-Demand Network Systems and Services (WONS)*, pages 122–124, Banff, Alberta, Canada, 2013.

[6] K. Li, I. Nikolaidis, and J. Harms. On the potential of mpt/mpr wireless networks. In *Local Computer Networks (LCN), 2014 IEEE 39th Conference on*, pages 46–54, Sept 2014.

[7] T. Mortimer and J. Harms. A MAC protocol for multihop RP-CDMA ad hoc wireless networks. In *Communications (ICC), 2012 IEEE International Conference on*, pages 424–429, 2012.

[8] M.J. Neely, E. Modiano, and C. Li. Fairness and optimal stochastic control for heterogeneous networks. *Networking, IEEE/ACM Transactions on*, 16(2):396–409, April 2008.

[9] C. Schlegel and A. Grant. *Coordinated multiuser communications*. Springer, New York, 2006.

[10] J. So and N. H. Vaidya. Multi-channel MAC for ad hoc networks: Handling multi-channel hidden terminals using a single transceiver. In *Proceedings of the 5th ACM International Symposium on Mobile Ad Hoc Networking and Computing*, MobiHoc '04, pages 222–233, New York, NY, USA, 2004. ACM.

[11] L. Tassiulas and A. Ephremides. Stability properties of constrained queueing systems and scheduling policies for maximum throughput in multihop radio networks. *Automatic Control, IEEE Transactions on*, 37(12):1936–1948, Dec 1992.

[12] S. Wu, C. Lin, Y. Tseng, and J. Sheu. A new multi-channel MAC protocol with on-demand channel assignment for multi-hop mobile ad hoc networks. In *Parallel Architectures, Algorithms and Networks, 2000. I-SPAN 2000. Proceedings. International Symposium on*, pages 232–237, 2000.

Traversal Strategies for Wireless Power Transfer in Mobile Ad-Hoc Networks*

Constantinos Marios Angelopoulos
Computer Science Department
University of Geneva, Switzerland
Marios.Angelopoulos@unige.ch

Julia Buwaya
Computer Science Department
University of Geneva, Switzerland
Julia.Buwaya@unige.ch

Orestis Evangelatos
Computer Science Department
University of Geneva, Switzerland
Orestis.Evangelatos@unige.ch

José Rolim
Computer Science Department
University of Geneva, Switzerland
Jose.Rolim@unige.ch

ABSTRACT

We investigate the problem of wireless power transfer in mobile ad-hoc networks. In particular we investigate which traversal strategy should a Mobile Charger follow in order to efficiently recharge agents that are randomly and dynamically moving inside an area of interest. We first formally define this problem as the Charger Traversal Decision Problem and prove its computational hardness. We then define a weighting function which evaluates several network parameters in order to prioritize the nodes during the charging process. Based on this function we define three traversal strategies for the MC; a global-knowledge strategy that uses an Integer Linear Program to optimize its trajectory; a global-knowledge strategy which tessellates the network area and prioritizes the charging process over each tile; a local-knowledge strategy that uses local network information collected and ferried distributively by the moving agents. We also evaluate two naive zero-knowledge strategies; a space-filling deterministic one in which the MC systematically sweeps the network area and a randomized one in which the MC performs a blind random walk. We evaluate these strategies both in homogeneous and heterogeneous agent distributions and for various network sizes with respect to number of alive nodes over time, energy distribution among the nodes over time and charging efficiency over distance traveled. Our findings indicate that in small networks network agnostic strategies are sufficient. However, as the network scales the use of local distributed network information achieves good performance-overhead trade-offs.

Categories and Subject Descriptors

C.2.1 [**Network Architecture and Design**]: Distributed Networks, Network Communications, Wireless Communication

---

*This work was partially supported by EU/FIRE IoT Lab project - STREP ICT-610477 and by the SNSF Swiss Sense Synergy project - CRSII2-154458.

General Terms

Algorithms, Experimentation, Performance

1. INTRODUCTION

In principle, the theoretical and technological know-how regarding wireless power transfer has been known since the beginning of the previous century. However, only recently the corresponding technology has become mature enough so as to be used in practice and to be commercialized. In particular, in [12] it has been shown that through strongly coupled magnetic resonances, the efficiency of transferring 60 watts of power over a distance in excess of 2 meters is as high as 40%. Industrial research has also demonstrated that it is possible to improve transferring 60 watts of power over a distance of up to two to three feet with efficiency of 75% [9]. As the technology constantly improves, commercial products utilizing wireless power transfer have been available on the market such as those in [2] and [1]. The potential of this technology has led to the establishment of corresponding industrial standardization bodies such as the Rezence Alliance for Wireless Power [3] and the Wireless Power Consortium (WPC) [4] that seek to maximize the use of the wireless power transfer.

In parallel, significant research effort is conducted in the context of this technological advance. In the field of ad-hoc networks, a new paradigm has emerged; the Wireless Rechargeable Sensor Networks (WRSN). In WRSNs sensor motes are equipped with fast rechargeable batteries [10] and with specialized hardware components called wireless power receivers. There also exist special mobile entities called Mobile Chargers (MC), that are able to wirelessly transfer power to the sensor motes while traversing the network area. The existence of the MCs enables the detailed and efficient energy management of the network while it also renders obsolete the need of complex and computationally intense energy management algorithms that infer significant computational and communication overhead to the network. However, as hand-held mobile devices demonstrate high acceptance rates by the general public, we believe that research efforts in Wireless Power Transfer should not be restricted only to WRSNs but should also address mobile ad-hoc networks in general.

The Problem. We consider a set of mobile agents deployed in an area of interest. The agents abstract moving people that carry portable autonomous devices, such as smartphones, smart-watches or sensor motes, that are capable of wirelessly receiving power and fast charging their batteries. The type of motion of the agents is considered to be diverse and unpredictable. Finally, we consider

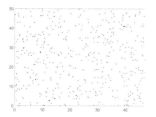 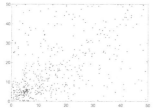

(a) Snapshot of a homogeneous agent distribution under the RWMM model.

(b) Snapshot of a heterogeneous agent distribution under the extended with social hotspots RWMM model.

Figure 1: Example snapshots of homogeneous and heterogeneous agent distributions.

a single, special purpose mobile entity, called the Mobile Charger (MC), that traverses the networking area of interest and is capable of wirelessly recharging devices that lie in its vicinity.

The problem we study is which traversal strategy should the Mobile Charger follow in order to efficiently recharge the moving agents of the network. We focus on the process of efficiently transferring energy from the MC to the network and therefore the strategies we design and evaluate are agnostic to any underlying, energy consuming tasks.

Remarks. We note that, although the wireless charging problem might look similar to other related research problems (such as aggressive data collection via mobile sinks), it admits special features that necessitate a direct approach, while the optimization of concrete trade-offs and the fine-tuning of design alternatives that arise in wireless charging necessitate the distinct investigation of special protocol design parameters. Finally, we note that Mobile Charger optimization problems are (inherently) computationally hard e.g. in [5] we have formulated the wireless charging problem as the Charger Dispatch Decision Problem - CDDP, and showed that it is NP-complete (via reduction from the Geometric Travelling Salesman Problem, G-TSP; see e.g. [7], p. 212).

Our Contribution. This paper is, to the best of our knowledge, the first one to directly address the traversal strategy of a MC in large scale mobile ad-hoc networks. Our contribution can be summarized as follows: a) We formally define the Charger Traversal Decision Problem (CTDP) and prove its computational hardness. b) We identify four network parameters that affect the MC in choosing its trajectory; the energy needs of the nodes, their energy dissipation rates, their mobility level and their distance from the MC. We define a corresponding weighting function used to prioritise the nodes during the charging process. c) Based on this weighting function, we design three traversal strategies for the MC; a global-knowledge strategy that uses an Integer Linear Program, to compute the MC's trajectory, a global-knowledge strategy that tessellates the network area and prioritizes each tile based on its aggregated weight, and a local-knowledge strategy that uses local network information collected an ferried distributively by the moving agents. d) We evaluate the designed strategies along with two naive zero-knowledge ones; one space-filling deterministic strategy and one in which the MC performs a blind random walk. In our evaluation we use several performance metrics and simulate various network sizes and densities. Our findings indicate that in small networks network agnostic strategies are sufficient. However, as the network scales the use of local distributed network information achieves good performance-overhead trade-offs.

2. RELATED WORK AND COMPARISON

There has been much research effort in WRSNs; in particular for the case where the charged entities (e.g. sensors) are *static*. In [6, 19] authors study the cases where a Mobile Charger traverses the network area where a set of static sensors is deployed. In each work, authors focus on some particular aspect of the network (e.g. on the ratio of the MC's vacation time over the cycle time) and provide methods in order to compute corresponding optimal charging tours. In [13], the authors formulate an energy-constrained wireless charging problem, which maximizes the number of sensors wirelessly charged by a Mobile Charger. The paper proposes heuristic solutions based on the meta-heuristics of Particle Swarm Optimization. However, the model assumes the charger has an extensive knowledge on the network and the performance evaluation is limited to simulations of small-scale networks.

In a previous work of our group in [5], the authors study the impact of the charging process to the network lifetime for selected routing protocols. They propose a mobile charging protocol that locally adapts the circular trajectory of the Mobile Charger to the energy dissipation rate of each sub-region of the network. They compare this protocol against several other trajectories via a detailed experimental evaluation. The derived findings demonstrate performance gains, but are *limited to uniform network deployments*, in contrast to our approach in this paper which also considers heterogeneous node distributions.

Alternative versions of the problem have also attracted important research attention. In [20, 17, 14] the authors consider the wireless recharging problem, using multiple mobile chargers. In this case, several other interesting aspects emerge, such as the minimum number of chargers that suffice to cover the network area, inter-charger coordination, etc.

Few research efforts have also taken into consideration settings in which the charged entities are *mobile*. In [11] authors study the throughput of an energy-constrained mobile network where MCs recharge the battery of each mobile node. However, they do not focus on the traversal of the MC *per se* as they consider it to perform only a random walk. Also, they assume a naive mobility model for the mobile nodes (they assume identically distributed random processes). In [8] authors consider a small scale network of mobile robots in which the MC needs to rendezvous with the robots in order to recharge them. Authors provide a centralized solution while considering direct-contact charging technologies.

Although these efforts successfully identify and address fundamental aspects of wireless power transfer in ad-hoc networks, they significantly differ from our approach in this paper. They mostly consider networks with low dynamics, where the sensor motes are static or small scale networks. Also, motivated by the characteristics of the wireless power transfer via conductive charging technologies that operate efficiently in very small distances (in the order of few centimeters), in most of the previous efforts the charging model considered is point-to-point. On the contrary, we envision a wireless power transfer scheme that is based on *inductive charging*; i.e. the MC is able to simultaneously charge devices that lie inside its charging radius by creating an electromagnetic field.

3. THE MODEL

In our model we consider two types of entities: the set of n mobile agents $\mathcal{A} = \{A_i \mid i : 1 \leq i \leq n\}$, that abstracts autonomous devices carried by people (such as smartphones, smart-watches and sensor motes) and a *Mobile Charger* (MC) which is a special purpose entity capable of wirelessly transferring power to devices located in its vicinity while traversing the network area Ω. We discuss below the mobility and energy aspects of our model.

3.1 Mobility Models

We consider a planar area of interest Ω in which the set of mobile agents $\mathcal{A}$ is initially uniformly at random deployed. The speed at which each agent traverses the network is modelled as a random variable following the Poisson distribution. The corresponding mean value s_i capturing the *average speed* of agent A_i is drawn uniformly at random from a set of four indicative values corresponding to four distinct mobility levels $\mathcal{M}_x^i$ ($x \in \{work; walk; bic; veh\}$). Each mobility level captures a different kind of activity such as moving in an office environment, walking, riding the bicycle and moving by using a vehicle. As a result, a diverse population of agents is created in terms of mobility in Ω. In order to model the particular *type of motion* of each A_i we use two mobility models, each one leading to a different agent distribution over Ω.

The Random Walk Mobility Model - RWMM. According to this model, the agents are initially deployed uniformly at random inside Ω. Then each agent A_i performs a random walk independently of the other agents. The motion of each agent in this model consists of consecutive movements of a constant time duration Δt. We refer to these intervals as rounds. In particular, each agent A_i given its current position and its mobility level $\mathcal{M}_x^i$, moves to a new location by randomly choosing a *direction* in which to travel from $[0, 2\pi]$; if the agent lies close to the borders of Ω, then the interval is properly adjusted so as the agents to always remain inside Ω. From a broad point of view, this model over time results in a uniform distribution of agents over Ω, while at the same time local minima and maxima emerge in the density of the agents.

Although similar mobility models to the RWMM (e.g. the well-known Random Waypoint Model) have been proven not so efficient in capturing particular characteristics of human mobility (note we assume that agents abstract people carrying electronic devices), we choose to use this model for its simplicity that helps us focus and high-light the qualitative characteristics of each traversal strategy during the evaluation process.

The extended Random Walk Mobility Model - eRWMM. To better address the intrinsic social aspects of human mobility, we take into consideration the notion of *social attraction*. Social attraction comes from the field of social network theory and is broadly used in mobility models for Mobile Social Networks [15]. In particular, it is used in *community-based* mobility models in order to capture in a more realistic way the aspects of human mobility [16]. Social attractivity is defined as the aggregate attraction among the agents as well as towards physical locations inside the area of interest. Real-life examples would include the commercial mall of a city or a cafeteria in a university campus.

Towards more heterogeneous and dynamic placements, we expand the RWMM by adding *social hotspots* inside area Ω, that attract the agents during their network traversal. More specifically, in this extended model each agent randomly chooses a new direction in $[0, 2\pi]$ not uniformly but with a bias factor b towards the hotspots. The value of b affects the impact of the hotspot on the network; higher values result to denser hotspots and thus in more heterogeneous agent distributions in Ω. Figure 1(a) depicts a snapshot of a network following the RWMM model while Figure 1(b) depicts a network following the eRWMM model.

3.2 Energy Model

We denote with E_i^t the amount of energy reserves of agent A_i on time t and with E_{max} the maximum amount of energy each agent may have; i.e. when an agent is *fully charged*. Initially each agent is assumed to be fully charged; i.e. $E_i^0 = E_{max}, \forall A_i \in \mathcal{A}$. We also assume that the amount of energy each agent A_i dissipates during a time interval Δt, i.e. a round, follows a Poisson distribution with mean value λ_i. For each agent, λ_i is constant and is chosen uniformly at random from $[\lambda_{min}, \lambda_{max}]$. Intuitively, small values of λ_i correspond to users that mainly perform light activities with their devices (e.g. taking pictures or chatting), while larger values correspond to users that tend to perform more intense activities (e.g. high definition video streaming or GPS navigation).

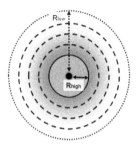

Figure 2: Graphical representation of the charging zones around the Mobile Charger. Over all zones, the efficiency of the power transfer reduces sub-quadratically to the distance from the Mobile Charger. However, for distance $d \le R_{high}$ (central zone) the efficiency of charging is sufficiently high for the MC to fully charge agents in a single round. In distances $d > R_{low}$, efficiency is so low, that effectively no charging takes place.

3.3 Charging Model

We assume that the Mobile Charger uses inductive charging technology thus being able to wirelessly transmit energy in an omnidirectional way and to simultaneously recharge multiple devices that lie in its vicinity. We identify two *charging zones* around the MC (Fig. 2). The first one extents up to a radius R_{high} around the MC. Inside this zone the charging process is conducted at such a high efficiency that the corresponding agents can be fully charged during a single round. The second zone lies in distances greater than R_{high} and smaller than R_{low}. In this zone although the devices are being charged, this happens with a lower efficiency and therefore an agent may end-up being only partially recharged after a single round (depending of course on its residual energy at the beginning of the round). For distances greater than R_{low}, although energy is still emitted, we assume that charging efficiency is so low that effectively no charging takes place.

Based on the specifications of commercially available wireless chargers (such as those in [2]), we assume that the amount of energy each agent receives and eventually stores in its battery per round is reversely proportional to the square of its euclidean distance from the MC. In fact, in order to estimate the amount of the received power, industrial manufacturers make use of the Friis transmission equation. Figure 3 shows the theoretical received power rates from the specifications of a 3 Watt Powercast transmitter [2]. In fact, the actual power that can be received by the battery of the receiver is about 50% less than the power its antenna receives in distances up to 6 meters and more than 70% less in distances further than that. This is due to the RF-to-DC energy conversion efficiency.

We consider the energy reserves of the MC to be significantly bigger than those of the agents' or to be easily and continuously replenished during network traversal; e.g. via energy harvesting from the environment (like solar panels) or via more conventional means such as having the charger draw energy from the vehicle it is at-

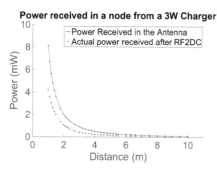

Figure 3: Received power using a 3 Watt Powercast charger (transmitter).

tached on. Therefore, in this work we consider the energy reserves of the MC to be infinite.

4. THE CHARGER TRAVERSAL DECISION PROBLEM

Based on the model presented in the latter section, we formally define the Charger Traversal Decision Problem and proof its NP-completeness.

DEFINITION 1 (CTDP). *Suppose that we are given a set $\{A_i \mid i = 1, ..., n\}$ of mobile agents with positions (x_i^t, y_i^t) at times $t = 0, ..., T$. We assume that at initial time $t = 0$ all agents are charged up to their maximum energy level of E_{max} energy units. The energy dissipation units EU_i^t in time windows $[t - 1, t]$ are known for all agents and times $t = 1, ..., T$. Furthermore, we are given a mobile charger MC which charges all agents in its range up to radius R_{high} in one time unit up to their maximum energy level. All agents with distances greater than R_{high} up to R_{low} are charged following a rule such that the amount of energy units received by an agent is reversely proportional to the square of its distance from the MC. The additional amount of energy units the agent eventually stores is limited such that the maximum energy level of the agent is not exceeded. The Charger Traversal Decision Problem (CTDP) is to determine whether there is a feasible schedule for the MC to visit points in the plane such that no agent falls below sufficient energy level at any time.*

THEOREM 1. *The CTDP is $\mathcal{NP}$-complete.*

PROOF. Given a schedule S of the MC visiting positions in the plane, we can verify whether all agents have sufficient energy at all times in polynomial time. Let E_i^t denote the residual energy of agent A_i at time t. For all times $t > 0$, we compute the euclidean distances d_i^t of the agents to the MC. Let $E_i^{rec}(d_i^t)$ denote the additional energy units an agent A_i receives reversely proportional to the square of its distance d_i^t. From d_i^t we can infer the residual energy of agent i which equals to $E_i^{t-1} - EU_i^t$, if $d_i^t > R_{low}$; equals to the $\max\{E_{max}, E_i^{t-1} - EU_i^t + E_i^{rec}(d_i^t)\}$, if $R_{low} \geq d_i^t > R_{high}$; or else equals to E_{max}. Note that the value of $E_i^{rec}(d_i^t)$ can be computed in polynomial time in d_i^t. Therefore CTDP $\in \mathcal{NP}$.

Now consider the subclass of CTDP problem instances where the positions of the agents are static; i.e. there exists x_i, y_i such that $x_i^t = x_i$ and $y_i^t = y_i$ for all $i = 1, ..., n$ and $t = 0, ..., T$. Let us denote this subclass by CTDP^{stat}. To proof completeness, we reduce the Charger Dispatch Decision Problem (CDDP), introduced and proven to be $\mathcal{NP}$-complete in [5], to the CTDP^{stat} in polynomial time. In the CDDP, we are given a set of sensors S with a maximum energy deposit of discrete energy units and information of distances between every two sensors in the form of a distance matrix.

These sensor motes are the agents in our corresponding CTDP^{stat} instance. Now in the CDDP, for every sensor $s \in S$, we have a list L_s of pairs (t_s^j, e_s^j), $j \geq 1$ in which t_s^j corresponds to the time that the j-th message of s was generated and e_s^j to the energy that the sensor used to transmit it. In the corresponding CTDP^{stat}, we consider these values by setting the energy dissipation units of the agents as $EU_s^t = \sum_{j:t_s^j=t} e_s^j$ (i.e., we are summing up the transmission energy of node s for messages send at time t_s^j). In the CDDP, a charger which can charge a sensor in one time unit to its initial (maximum) energy is given. In order to create the same setting, we increase distances between nodes by a constant factor such that the smallest distance between two nodes is larger that R_{low}. In this way, the corresponding charger in the CTDP^{stat} can charge at most one node per time unit as well. The CDDP is to determine whether there is a feasible schedule for the charger to visit the sensors so that no message is lost due to insufficient energy. This corresponds to the decision problem of the CTDP^{stat} for the created instance. An answer to the CTDP^{stat} would provide an answer to the CDDP, hence the CTDP^{stat} is $\mathcal{NP}$-complete. As all instances of the CTDP^{stat} are in the CTDP, thus the CTDP is $\mathcal{NP}$-complete. $\square$

Note that the CTDP and CDDP differ particularly in the mobility of agents and in the charging range enabling the MC in the CTDP to charge several agents at the same time. In addition, in the CTDP we consider energy dissipation of agents independently of their precedent actions while in the CDDP energy is considered in relation to message transmission.

Distinguishing our work from previous related works, in this paper we focus on the investigation of tackling the mobility of nodes in an ad-hoc network while recharging it. In real-life settings a MC would have limited local knowledge about the decentralized mobile ad-hoc network it traverses; i.e. the charger will only have information on agents it encounters and no exact information on future events. Therefore, our goal is to define traversal strategies that are applicable in such local knowledge online settings.

Ensuing from the CTDP, let us consider the associated NP-hard problem of optimizing the network life time in terms of maximizing the number of agents alive over time. We go directly over to its online problem with global information about the agents and their attributes at the current time only. Further investigation of the offline version of the problem in order to obtain an upper bound for the results of the online optimization is not presented here due to lack of space. In fact, we intent to provide such a solution in our future work. However, we note that experimental results extracted from our detailed simulation study demonstrate that our online heuristics have sufficiently high performance (see subsection 7). In addition, the consideration of the online problem offers valuable insights on optimization aspects when information on the future positions of agents is missing. This insight is then used to define a distributed local knowledge strategy which also has to act online.

5. THE WEIGHTING FUNCTION

As the MC traverses the network area, it needs a way to prioritize the agents in terms of visiting them for recharging. This prioritization will take into consideration several network aspects that affect the evolution of the network over time. For mobile ad-hoc networks we identify these aspects to be:

1. the *energy need* $E_i^{need} := E_{max} - E_i$ (with E_i indicating residual energy) of each agent A_i

2. the mean energy *dissipation* rate λ_i of each agent A_i

3. the *mobility* level $\mathcal{M}_{x(i)}^i$ of each agent A_i

4. the euclidean *distance* d_i of each agent A_i from the MC

However, each one of these aspects is measured in different units and has different ranges. Therefore, the *Weighting Function* (see below) considers their normalized values. We multiply by the factor 100 in order to simplify arithmetics as these values will be used as basis for exponents (see below).

- we normalize the *energy needs* over the maximum energy an agent may store; i.e. $\bar{E}_i^{need} := \frac{E_{max} - E_i}{E_{max}} \cdot 100$

- we normalize the *dissipation rates* over λ_{max}; i.e. $\bar{\lambda}_i := \frac{\lambda_i}{\lambda_{max}} \cdot 100$

- we normalize the *mobility levels* over the maximum mobility level $\mathcal{M}_{max}$; i.e. $\bar{\mathcal{M}}_{x(i)}^i := \frac{\mathcal{M}_{x(i)}^i}{\mathcal{M}_{max}} \cdot 100$

- we normalize the *distances* over the maximum distance possible in the network area d_{max} (e.g. if Ω is a rectangle then d_{max} is its diagonal); i.e. $\bar{d}_i := \frac{d_i}{d_{max}} \cdot 100$

Given these normalized values, the MC will assign a weight to each agent via a *Weighting Function* W^* whose generic form is defined as:

$$W^* : \mathcal{A} \to \mathbb{R}_0^+; \quad W_i^* \mapsto (\bar{E}_i^{need})^\alpha (\bar{\lambda}_i)^\beta (\bar{\mathcal{M}}_{x(i)}^i)^\gamma (\bar{d}_i)^\delta \quad (1)$$

The higher the weight assigned to an agent, the higher priority it will have during the charging traversal of the MC. The use of the exponents enables us to fine-tune the significance of each network aspect by adjusting the value of the corresponding exponent. The monotony of W_i^* with respect to each network aspect will help us define the sign of each exponent. In this context we denote that

1. the higher the current *energy need* $\bar{E}_i^{need}$ of agent, A_i the higher the value of W_i^*

2. the higher the mean energy *dissipation* $\bar{\lambda}_i$, the higher W_i^*

3. the higher the *mobility* level $\bar{\mathcal{M}}_{x(i)}^i$ of agent A_i, the smaller W_i^*

4. the higher the distance $\bar{d}_i$ of A_i, the smaller the value of W_i^*.

While the rationale for relations 1 and 2 is intuitively straight forward, rules 3 and 4 capture the abilities of the MC to react in a timely manner to spatio-temporal dynamics of the network. In the online problem even if the MC has global knowledge, we assume that it cannot infer the exact future positions of the agents; instead the MC has to make decisions based on a "snap shot" of the network at the current time. Rule 3 supports the idea that the smaller the mobility level of an agent the more likely that in the near future the agent will still be in close vicinity to its current positions. Hence, the incentive for the charger to start travelling towards the direction of such an agent is to be successful in actually reaching the agent and charging it. A similar motivation can be used to reason on rule 4 concerning the distance of an agent to the charger; the closer an agent is, the more likely that the MC will reach the agent in the near future.

In the light of the previous discussion the final generic form of the *Weighting Function* (assuming that all exponents are positive) is:

$$W : \mathcal{A} \to \mathbb{R}_0^+; \quad W_i \mapsto \frac{(\bar{E}_i^{need})^\alpha (\bar{\lambda}_i)^\beta}{(\bar{\mathcal{M}}_{x(i)}^i)^\gamma (\bar{d}_i)^\delta} \quad (2)$$

As mentioned before, the exponents in the generic form of W enable us to investigate the relationship and importance of individual attributes with respect to the charging process. In order to define the exact numerical values for each exponent, in this paper we adopt the One-Factor-At-A-Time (OFAT) methodological approach (see

e.g. [18]); i.e. varying the value of the exponent of one of the attributes at the time, while fixing the others to a base value in order to evaluate the impacts on the performance of the MC.

Experimental findings indicate that the uniform consideration of all network aspects (i.e., all exponents equal to one) already lead to good results in our MC traversal strategies (see details in section 7). Fine tuning via more sophisticated methods would only further increase the already high efficiency of the proposed traversal strategies.

6. TRAVERSAL STRATEGIES FOR THE MOBILE CHARGER

We now discuss five traversal strategies for the Mobile Charger that are qualitatively different in terms of the assumed level of knowledge that the MC has on the network. The first one is a zero-knowledge deterministic space-filling strategy. The second one is a zero-knowledge randomized strategy. The third and fourth ones are online, complete-knowledge centralized strategies integrating the node *Weighting Function* defined above. The last strategy is a reactive one that is based on local network information gathered by the agents in a distributed way.

In terms of network knowledge, complete-knowledge strategies are the most powerful strategies for the MC. At any given moment, the MC is aware of the exact distribution of the agents over the area Ω and is therefore able to choose its trajectory accordingly towards maximizing the number of nodes alive over time while considering the delay between the time of computing positions and the arrival time of the MC in the online setting. Such recharging schemes have the strong assumption that the agents are able to periodically propagate data regarding their position and energy needs to the MC; e.g. over the Internet. The MC is assumed to have the required computational power in order to be able to perform the necessary calculations.

6.1 The Space-filling Strategy (SPF)

This zero-knowledge deterministic traversal strategy consists in having the MC to systematically sweep the network area in such a way that no overlaps occur. In particular, according to this strategy the MC is moving along the one dimension of Ω until it reaches its border. Then, it takes a U-turn shifted by a distance of $2R_{low}$ along the second direction. When the entire network area has been covered the process is repeated. This traversal strategy guarantees that eventually all network sub-regions will be covered by the MC and in uniform agent distributions it is expected to have a satisfactory performance. However, in heterogeneous distributions where big numbers of agents are located in confined sub-regions (i.e. the social hotspots) significant latencies in inter-charging times are expected.

6.2 The Random Walk Strategy (RAND)

This is a zero-knowledge randomized traversal strategy for the MC. Given its current position, the MC chooses the direction of its next move uniformly at random from $[0, 2\pi]$ and the distance to be covered uniformly at random from $[0, 2R_{low}]$. This strategy assumes zero-knowledge on the network and the distribution of the agents. Therefore, like the SPF, it is characterized by the absence of any overhead as the agents maintain a passive role, simply waiting to encounter the MC in order to be recharged. Moreover, this strategy probabilistically guarantees that eventually all the sub-regions of the network will be visited by the MC, although it may infer long waiting periods for the agents among consecutive charges, particularly for highly heterogeneous topologies.

6.3 Global Knowledge ILP Strategy (GK-ILP)

Initially the Mobile Charger is placed at a random position in the network area Ω. At each round, given the current positions of all the agents in Ω and the current values of their network attributes (i.e. $E_i^{\overline{need}}, \bar{\lambda}_i, \bar{\mathcal{M}}_{(x)}^i, \bar{d}_i$), the MC is able to compute the exact location it should visit (or move towards to) at the current time. The MC could do so by finding the center of the circle of radius R_{low} which encircles the agents that cumulatively have the highest node weights with respect to the *Weighting Function*. By the design of the *Weighting Function*, the cumulation of the node weights correctly prioritizes the various areas with respect to demand for being charged. The corresponding non-linear problem formulation is as follows:

$$\max_{x,y,\beta_i,d_i} \quad \sum_i W_i\beta_i \tag{3a}$$

$$d_i = (\,(x_i - x)^2 + (y_i - y)^2\,)^{1/2} \quad \forall i \tag{3b}$$

$$R_{low} + (1 - \beta_i) \cdot \mathbf{M} \geq d_i \quad \forall i \tag{3c}$$

$$\beta_i \in \{0, 1\} \quad \forall i \tag{3d}$$

In the problem formulation the i's are the indices of the agents $A_i \in \mathcal{A}$, W_i indicate their weights, β_i are binary decision variables, d_i the distance of the agents to the MC at position (x, y), x_i and y_i are the position coordinates of the agents, and $\mathbf{M}$ is a very large constant. In (3b) we compute the distances of the agents to the MC. In (3c) we make sure that if $\beta_i = 1$ (i.e., if the weight of agent A_i is considered in the objective function) then $R_{low} \geq d_i$.

To create an ILP, we approximate d_i. Instead of a circle with radius R_{low}, we look for a rectangle whose sides are at most of length R_{low} and whose center (x, y) is the position of the MC:

$$\max_{x,y,\beta_i,d_i} \quad \sum_i W_i\beta_i \tag{4a}$$

$$d_i \geq |x_i - x| \quad \forall i \tag{4b}$$

$$d_i \geq |y_i - y| \quad \forall i \tag{4c}$$

$$R_{low} + (1 - \beta_i) \cdot \mathbf{M} \geq d_i \quad \forall i \tag{4d}$$

$$\beta_i \in \{0, 1\} \quad \forall i \tag{4e}$$

In the later equations the constraints (4b) can be replaced by linear equations $d_i \geq x_i - x$ and $d_i \geq -(x_i - x)$. Corresponding replacements can be made for (4c) resulting in an ILP. By solving this ILP, the MC is able to identify the rectangle that maximizes demands and move towards its center. The MC is updating its directions using the ILP with updated information at each time step.

Note that even for relatively big and dense network instances the ILP can be solved in reasonable amount of time.

6.4 Global Knowledge Tessellation Strategy (GK-TS)

In this traversal strategy the MC is initially deployed at a random position inside the network area Ω. First, the MC virtually tessellates the network area in square tiles of the same size. In order to minimize overlaps in the charging areas the pivot of the tessellation is chosen to be equal to $2R_{low}$. Then on each round, given the current positions of all the agents in the Ω and the current values of their attributes, the MC assigns weights to each agent via the *Weighting Function* and computes the aggregated weight for each tile by summing the weights of the agents located in that tile. Finally, the MC chooses to move towards the center of the tile with the highest cumulative weight.

6.5 The Reactive Local Knowledge Strategy (RLK)

This is a local knowledge traversal strategy that exploits local information collected distributively. The agents overtake an active role in collecting local network information and informing the MC on the current demands of their neighbourhood (we assume that R_{low} and the communication range of the agents, although not equal, are of the same order). This way the MC is able to identify and serve stressed areas of the network as well as to react to changes of the network topology under a more realistic and efficient distributed scheme.

More specifically, each agent periodically collects information regarding the network attribute values of its neighbouring agents; i.e. each agent poles its one-hop neighbours on their energy needs, their average energy dissipation rate and their mobility levels. Then this information is used to assign to each neighbour a weight via a modified *Weighting Function* that does not take in consideration the distance to the MC. This is due to the fact that the agent is unaware of the actual location of the MC. Instead, the agent associates the assigned weights to its current position for future reference. The modified *Weighting Function* applied by an agent in the GK-TS strategy:

$$\bar{W} : \bar{A} \to \mathbb{R}_0^+; \quad \bar{W}_i \mapsto \frac{E_i^{\overline{need}} \bar{\lambda}_i}{\bar{\mathcal{M}}_{x(i)}^i} \tag{5}$$

Eventually, the agent stores in its memory and ferries a tuple consisting of the cumulative weight of its current neighbourhood and the coordinates of the position where this weight was measured. As each agent is moving inside the network area, the quality (in terms of accuracy) of the measurements degrade over time due to the dynamics of the network, such as the mobility of the agents. In order to address this issue we introduce the following ageing mechanism. At every round each agent updates the carried tuples by multiplying the stored aggregated weight with a constant $q \in [0, 1]$. Therefore, after T rounds the corresponding value will have been multiplied by a factor of q^T and will be a percentage of the initial weight. The lower the value of q is set, the more aggressive the reduction over time of the weight stored in the tuple.

On another aspect, as the agent traverses the network, it periodically collects local network information and stores them in tuples in its memory. As new tuples are being created, at each round the agent re-evaluates the already existing ones and compares them to the new tuples. Low weight entries are replaced by higher weight entries once the storage space limit of the agent has been reached. An agent carries stored tuples and opportunistically delivers it to the MC once it encounters it.

Table 1: Structure of the tuple each agent maintains.

tuple.x	% X coordinates of the measurement location
tuple.y	% Y coordinates of the measurement location
tuple.weight	% Modified weight of the measured location

The MC is initially placed at a randomly chosen position inside Ω. As the MC traverses the network, it receives and saves tuples from each agent it encounters. Then, the MC uses the information provided in order to solve the ILP introduced in the later subsection thus adjusting its trajectory correspondingly at each time step.

The presented reactive, local knowledge traversal strategy introduces a communication overhead to the network as the agents need to exchange information with each other. However, this overhead is rather small, thus not yielding significant energy consumption for the agents. Further, we note that information regarding network areas with high agent density and/or high energy needs (such as social hotspots) will be carried by the agents for a longer time period and will traverse a longer distance into the network. Finally, the distributed nature of this strategy makes it scalable and applicable in more realistic settings.

7. PERFORMANCE EVALUATION

7.1 Simulation Set-up

We evaluate the performance of the five traversal strategies by conducting extensive simulation studies in Matlab 2015. We conduct simulations with three different sizes for Ω; a) 50×50, b) 100×100 and c) 150×150 where in each setting 100 agents are deployed. We make this choice as it provide us with qualitatively different sizes and densities of the network in which the agents are distributed enabling us to better study the performance of each heuristic. In terms of speed of movement, we set the mean agent speed for each mobility level to be (all numbers are in space units over time units) $M_{work} = 2$; $M_{walk} = 4$; $M_{bic} = 8$; $M_{veh} = 16$ and the speed of the MC $MC_{sp} = 10$. Mobility levels are assigned to the agents u.a.r., thus leading each one to correspond to approximately 25% of the population. We also set the maximum and initial energy for each agent to be $E_{max} = 3000$ units of Energy. At each round of simulation, the amount of energy that each agent dissipates follows a Poisson distribution whose mean value for each agent is chosen independently and u.a.r. in [20, 80] units of Energy. We study both homogeneous and heterogeneous placements. In the heterogeneous placements three social hotspots are considered each on in different network subregion with a bias factor of: 0.45; 0.15; 0.15 accordingly. Note that the agents are *attracted* towards the hotspots; they do not move directly to them. For each setting we simulate the network for 500 rounds. Each simulation is repeated for 60 iterations and we compute the mean values for each metric; results demonstrate strong concentration around the mean (evaluated via the standard error over the mean).

7.2 Preliminary Evaluation of the Weighting Function

Before running the simulations for the evaluation of each strategy we turn to the task of finding appropriate parameter settings for the attribute exponents in the *Weighting Function* introduced in section 5. We employ the simple One-Factor-At-A-Time (OFAT) methodology: varying the parameter values of the exponent of one of the attributes while fixing the others to a base value in order to evaluate the impacts on the simulation outputs (see e.g. [18]). OFAT has the advantage of being relatively easily conducted and, as it will turn out, over relatively few trials will provide settings which result in sufficiently high performance. We will leave a more sophisticated analysis of the exponent parameter settings for future work claiming that this would only ameliorate the our findings. For the evaluation of the exponents we measure the performance of varying parameter settings when employing the *Global Knowledge ILP Strategy* as this strategy employs the base version of the *Weighting Function* and in terms of adjusting the traversal strategy of the MC may, out of all of the presented strategies, best exploit the added value of *Weighting Function*.

We first evaluated different values for the E^{need} exponent with values ranging from 1 to 10 (keeping the other exponents at 0). Figure 4 a) shows the percentage of alive nodes over the number of rounds for different exponents of E^{need} in a 50x50 area with a homogeneous agent distribution. We observe that the more we in-

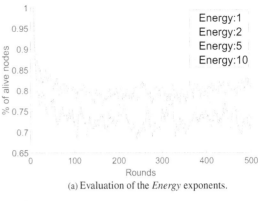

(a) Evaluation of the *Energy* exponents.

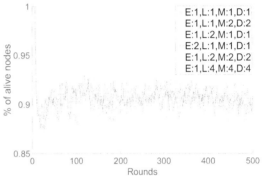

(b) Evaluation of all the exponents of the *Weighting Function*.

Figure 4: Evaluation of exponents using the *GLK-ILP* strategy

crease the value of the E^{need} exponent the less alive nodes we have in the area. Similar results are achieved for 100x100 and 150x150. This can be explained by how the *Weighting Function* assigns values with respect to the exponents: the higher the exponent of E^{need} is, the higher the weight distance between two agents, even if their actual energy needs are similar. For instance, for value 10, consider two nodes: one with energy need equal to 2 and one with energy need 2.5. These would end up in receiving weights 1024 vs. 9537. In a network with several nodes the MC integrating the *Weighting Function* with high exponents might focus too much on some few individual nodes.

As E^{need} is the indicative factor for a the survivability of an agent, we conducted tests for evaluating the exponents of pairs of $\{E^{need}\} \times$ *Dissipation, Mobility, Distance*. Similarly to the tests on using only the E^{need} exponent, the results were changing with respect to changes of the E^{need} exponent only. As such we run tests for evaluating all the exponents by keeping the E^{need} exponent at 1. The results can be seen in figure 4 b). Considering the relatively high performance, we used for our strategies evaluation the exponents in a uniform manner (i.e. all exponents equal to 1).

7.3 Evaluation of traversal strategies

7.3.1 Evaluation Metrics

Number of alive agents. In this metric we examine the percentage of alive agents each traversal strategy is able to achieve in a given amount of rounds. We note here that a fully charged agent with highest possible dissipation rate in the absence of the MC will die in 12 rounds. This metric is a good indicator of whether a strategy manages to provide energy to the network where and when is needed.

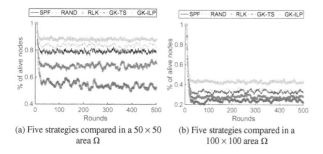

(a) Five strategies compared in a 50×50 area Ω

(b) Five strategies compared in a 100×100 area Ω

Figure 5: Percentage of alive nodes over 500 Rounds in homogeneous setting

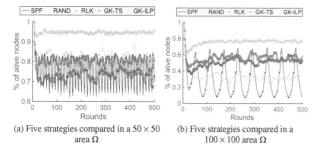

(a) Five strategies compared in a 50×50 area Ω

(b) Five strategies compared in a 100×100 area Ω

Figure 6: Percentage of alive nodes over 500 Rounds in heterogeneous setting

Energy Distribution. In this metric we examine the energy distribution to the agents by the MC in percentiles over time. In particular, we tessellate the percentage of agents that have residual energy in the ranges of: [0%-20%),[20%-40%),[40%-80%),[80%-100%]. We take some samples of the network in terms of energy distribution and we examine the % of the agents that lie in each of the ranges.

Distance Coverage. In this metric we examine the cumulative distance covered by the MC in the network. This metric although it is not directly correlated with the operation of the network itself, it can lead to useful conclusions regarding the charging process and the efficiency of the route that the MC is following. In addition, this metric is associated to relevant movement costs of the MC.

7.3.2 Findings

Homogeneous Agent Distribution. Figure 5 depicts the percentage of alive nodes (*survivability of the network*) in an homogeneous agent distribution for a (a) 50×50 and (b) 100×100 area Ω. We observe in the subfigure (a) that the *GK-ILP* strategy outperforms the other ones, as expected. This is due to the knowledge the Mobile Charger has and its ability to best exploit the *Weighting Function*. The second best strategy is the *Random Walk* of the Mobile Charger and this is due to the nature of the homogeneous area and the fact that the random walk probabilistically will eventually visit the entire area. Comparing the *RAND* to the *Space-Filling* strategy, it distributes "more evenly" the probabilities of visiting all the subareas. The *SPF* strategy comes third since the MC is sweeping the network and thus some sub-areas are left without being charged until the MC will revisit them in the next iteration. The *GLK-TS* performs even worse. This may be explained by the limitation of the positions the MC can visit when this strategy is applied, i.e. it may only visit the centres of the tiles of the tessellation. In the case where nodes are positioned towards the edges of the tiles, the MC will not have the chance to fully charge these

nodes in one round. We observe that in the homogeneous set-up, the *RLK* strategy has the poorest performance: the MC has limited information about the agents and they are equally distributed over the area Ω. We observe that in all settings of 50×50, 100×100 and 150×150, the strategies follow the same trend. The differences of the strategies in comparison to the topologies lie in the absolute values of % of alive nodes they are able to achieve. In a bigger area with the same MC the distances are longer thus the MC does not have enough speed and sufficient time to keep a high % of overall alive nodes.

Figure 7 shows the energy distribution in percentiles in the homogeneous 100×100 area. In general we observe that the performance of all the strategies is stable over time. We note also that even though the *GK-ILP* performance in terms of number of alive nodes is much better than the other strategies, its energy distribution percentiles are only slightly better. The *SFP*, *RAND* and *GK-ILP* have relatively high values for nodes with energy levels higher than 40%.

Heterogeneous Agent Distribution. Figure 6 depicts the % of alive nodes in an heterogeneous agent distribution for a (a) 50×50 area Ω and (b) 100×100 area Ω. In the heterogeneous setting the *GLK-ILP* strategy is again clearly the best in all topologies, as expected. In the 50×50 area the *GK-TS* and the *RAND* have almost identical behaviour but in the 100×100 area the *RAND* performs much worse. This is explained as follows: since the distribution of the agents in the area is done in a heterogeneous manner and there are three hotspots, when the overall area is small, the MC manages to cover a sufficient area thus charging a relative high number of agents. On the contrary, when the area is relatively big, the random walk of the MC does not manage to cover sufficiently neither the whole area nor the hotspots. The *RLK* strategy in the 50×50 area performs weaker again, even though much better in relation to all of the other strategies and much better than the *SPF* strategy in terms of maintaining the agents alive. However in a larger area, its performance increases quite significantly, i.e. in the 100×100 area the *RLK* strategy performs similarly well as the *GK-TS* although it is only employing local knowledge collected while traversing the network. At the same setting the performances of both zero-knowledge strategies, *SPF* and *RAND*, drop significantly. Lastly we observe that the *SPF* strategy maintains the least number of agents alive in both topologies and specifically it is following a "wave charging" every time it is passing through the hotspots.

Figure 8 shows the energy distribution in percentiles in the homogeneous 100×100 area. We observe that the *GK-ILP* manages to both keep a high number of nodes alive and hold a relatively even distribution over them. The *RAND* has a performance similar to the homogeneous setting but compared to the non-naive strategies, it performs much better. Moreover, we observe that similarly to the performance of the number of alive nodes, the *RAND* and *GK-TS* perform equally good; i.e. both being successful in keeping a relatively high number of nodes at high energy levels.

Table 2: Cumulative distance (Units of Space) covered by the MC in 500 Rounds in 100×100 area Ω.

Strategy	Homogeneous	Heterogeneous
SPF	10800	10800
RAND	12000	12000
RLK	4271	2982
GLK-TS	6553	5387
GLK-ILP	10692	8933

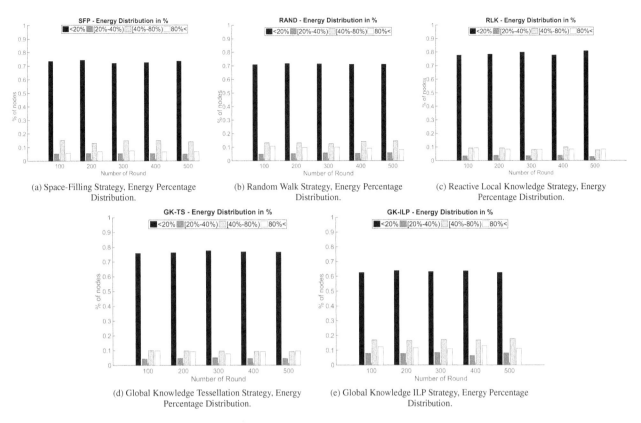

(a) Space-Filling Strategy, Energy Percentage Distribution.

(b) Random Walk Strategy, Energy Percentage Distribution.

(c) Reactive Local Knowledge Strategy, Energy Percentage Distribution.

(d) Global Knowledge Tessellation Strategy, Energy Percentage Distribution.

(e) Global Knowledge ILP Strategy, Energy Percentage Distribution.

Figure 7: **Energy Percentage Distribution in homogeneous setting in a** 100×100 **area** Ω.

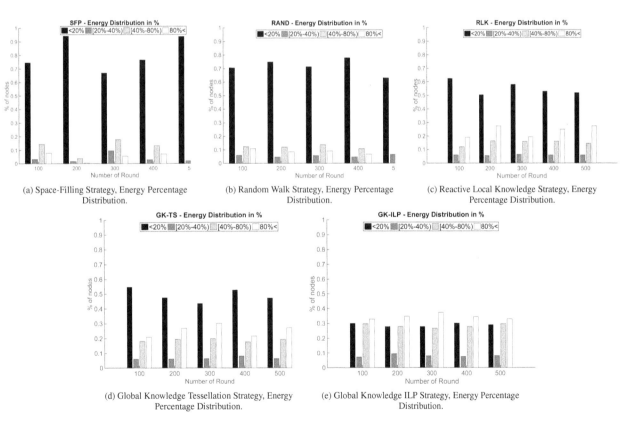

(a) Space-Filling Strategy, Energy Percentage Distribution.

(b) Random Walk Strategy, Energy Percentage Distribution.

(c) Reactive Local Knowledge Strategy, Energy Percentage Distribution.

(d) Global Knowledge Tessellation Strategy, Energy Percentage Distribution.

(e) Global Knowledge ILP Strategy, Energy Percentage Distribution.

Figure 8: **Energy Distribution Metric in heterogeneous setting in a** 100×100 **area** Ω

7.3.3 General Findings

Conclusively, for a homogeneous distribution of agents, our simulation results suggest that when the knowledge of the MC is limited, as in most real world applications for mobile ad-hoc networks, it may be advisable to employ a naive, low-cost *Random Walk* strategy. In the heterogeneous setting, experimental results suggest an outstanding suitability of our local knowledge *RLK* strategy when the area of interest is relatively large. In addition, table 2 shows the cumulative distance travelled by the MC in a 100×100 area Ω over 500 Rounds in homogeneous and heterogeneous setting. We observe that the MC, in our *RLK* strategy and in the heterogeneous setting, is travelling the least distance. This is a significant result given that the *RLK* performs also very well in terms of keeping the a high number of agents alive.

8. CONCLUSIONS

In this work we addressed the Wireless Recharge Problem in mobile ad-hoc networks characterized by diverse and unpredictable spatio-temporal dynamics. First, we defined the charging model and then utilized the notion of social attraction in order to better capture human mobility in our mobility model. We evaluated the performance of five qualitatively different traversal strategies for the MC; a zero-knowledge deterministic space-filling strategy, a zero-knowledge randomized strategy, two complete-knowledge centralized strategies and a local distributed knowledge reactive strategy. Our findings indicate that in homogeneous topologies the added value of the network information is degraded. However, in heterogeneous topologies strategies utilizing local network knowledge can outperform more powerful schemes if they efficiently exploit their knowledge.

In future research we aim at investigating more diverse topologies of the network area, more accurate mobility models as well as coordination schemes among multiple Mobile Chargers. In fact, our aim will be to efficiently coordinate the Mobile Chargers so as their effect on the network to be at least super-linear with respect to their number. Finally, we will also employ more detailed evaluation methods for further fine tuning the *Weighting Function*.

9. REFERENCES

[1] Murata manufacturing. http://www.murata.com/, retrieved Feb. 2015.

[2] Powercast. http://www.powercastco.com/, retrieved Feb. 2015.

[3] Rezence alliance for wireless power. http://www.rezence.com/, retrieved Feb. 2015.

[4] The wireless power consortium. http://www.wirelesspowerconsortium.com/, retrieved Feb. 2015.

[5] C. M. Angelopoulos, S. Nikoletseas, T. P. Raptis, C. Raptopoulos, and F. Vasilakis. Efficient energy management in wireless rechargeable sensor networks. In *ACM International Conference on Modeling, Analysis and Simulation of Wireless and Mobile Systems, (MSWiM)*, 2012.

[6] L. Fu, P. Cheng, Y. Gu, J. Chen, and T. He. Optimal charging in wireless rechargeable sensor networks. *IEEE Transactions on Vehicular Technology Society*, DOI 10.1109/TVT.2015.2391119, 2015.

[7] M. R. Garey and D. S. Johnson. *Computers and intractability*. W. H. Freeman and Company, 1979.

[8] L. He, P. Cheng, Y. Gu, J. Pan, T. Zhu, and C. Liu. Mobile-to-mobile energy replenishment in mission-critical robotic sensor networks. *Proceedings - IEEE INFOCOM*, pages 1195–1203, 2014.

[9] Intel. Wireless resonant energy link (wrel) demo. http://software.intel.com/en-us/videos/wireless-resonant-energy-link-wrel-demo/, retrieved Feb. 2015.

[10] B. Kang and G. Ceder. Battery materials for ultrafast charging and discharging. In *Nature 458, pp.190-193*, 2009.

[11] S.-W. Ko, S. M. Yu, and S.-L. Kim. The Capacity of Energy-Constrained Mobile Networks with Wireless Power Transfer. *IEEE Communications Letters*, 17(3):529–532, 2013.

[12] A. Kurs, A. Karalis, R. Moffatt, J. D. Joannopoulos, P. Fisher, and M. Soljacic. Wireless power transfer via strongly coupled magnetic resonances. *Science*, 317:83, 2007.

[13] K. Li, H. Luan, and C.-C. Shen. Qi-ferry: Energy-constrained wireless charging in wireless sensor networks. In *IEEE Wireless Communications and Networking Conference,(WCNC)*, 2012.

[14] A. Madhja, S. Nikoletseas, and T. P. Raptis. Distributed wireless power transfer in sensor networks with multiple mobile chargers. *Elsevier Computer Networks*, 80:89–108, 2015.

[15] M. Musolesi, S. Hailes, and C. Mascolo. An ad hoc mobility model founded on social network theory. In *ACM International Conference on Modeling, Analysis and Simulation of Wireless and Mobile Systems, (MSWiM)*, pages 20–24, 2004.

[16] N. Vastardis and K. Yang. An enhanced community-based mobility model for distributed mobile social networks. *J. Ambient Intelligence and Humanized Computing*, 5(1):65–75, 2014.

[17] C. Wang, J. Li, F. Ye, and Y. Yang. Multi-vehicle coordination for wireless energy replenishment in sensor networks. In *International Parallel and Distributed Processing Symposium, (IPDPS)*, 2013.

[18] C. J. Wu and M. S. Hamada. *Experiments: planning, analysis, and optimization*, volume 552. John Wiley & Sons, 2011.

[19] L. Xie, Y. Shi, Y. T. Hou, and H. D. Sherali. Making sensor networks immortal: An energy-renewal approach with wireless power transfer. *IEEE/ACM TRANSACTIONS ON NETWORKING*, DOI: 10.1109/TNET.2012.2185831, 2012.

[20] S. Zhang, J. Wu, and S. Lu. Collaborative mobile charging for sensor networks. In *IEEE International Conference on Mobile Ad hoc and Sensor Systems, (MASS)*, 2012.

The Geometry-Based Statistical Modeling of MIMO Mobile-to-Mobile Channels Revisited

Carlos A. Gutiérrez
cagutierrez@ieee.org

José T. Gutiérrez-Mena
j.g.gutierrez@ieee.org

José M. Luna-Rivera
mlr@fciencias.uaslp.mx

Daniel U. Campos-Delgado
ducd@fciencias.uaslp.mx

Universidad Autonoma de San Luis Potosi
Av. Dr. Salvador Nava Martínez S/N, Zona Universitaria
San Luis Potosi 78290, Mexico

ABSTRACT

In this paper, we discuss a problem in the formulation of geometry-based statistical models for multiple-input multiple-output (MIMO) mobile-to-mobile (M2M) fading channels that have been proposed under the plane wave propagation (PWP) assumption. The problem is caused by an oversimplification of the PWP model in the characterization of the channel complex envelope (CCE). This modeling imprecision has led to impose an unnecessary restriction on the size of the antenna arrays to warrant the mathematical tractability of the geometrical PWP channel models. The results presented in previous papers for relevant channel statistics, such as the space-time cross-correlation function (ST-CCF), are not invalidated if the problem is corrected. On the contrary, a thorough description of the physical process of PWP reduces the number of approximations required to obtain such results, extending in consequence their validity to a wider range of propagation scenarios.

Categories and Subject Descriptors

C.2.1 [**Computer-Communication Networks**]: Network Architecture and Design—*Wireless Communication*; I.6.5 [**Simulation and Modeling**]: Model Development—*Modeling methodologies*; G.3 [**Probability and Statistics**]: Stochastic processes

General Terms

Theory

Keywords

Fading channels; mobile-to-mobile communications; plane wave model; radiowave propagation; spherical wave model; vehicular communications.

MSWiM'15, November 2–6, 2015, Cancun, Mexico.
ⓒ 2015 ACM. ISBN 978-1-4503-3762-5/15/11 ...$15.00.
DOI: http://dx.doi.org/10.1145/2811587.2811615.

1. INTRODUCTION

The geometry-based statistical modeling (GBSM) approach is a widely accepted framework for the characterization of MIMO-M2M fading channels. The relevance of this approach is evident by the number of geometrical channel models that have been proposed in recent years (e.g., see [2–4,7,8] and the references therein). These models can be classified as spherical wave propagation (SWP) models [4,6,7] and PWP models [2,3,8]. In the framework of the SWP, the angle of departure (AOD) and angle of arrival (AOA) of the received signals are determined by the instantaneous relative position between the wave source and the observer. The AODs and AOAs are therefore time-dependent (space-variant) quantities. This feature makes the SWP models well-suited for characterizing non-stationary channels, but renders the derivation of closed-form expressions for important channel statistics, such as the ST-CCF and cross-power spectrum (CPS), a cumbersome task. The PWP models, on the other hand, are more mathematically tractable. These models owe their simplicity to the fact that the AOD/AOA of a plane wave is constant at any observation point along the wavefront's path [1, Fig. 1]. This planar approximation of the spherical nature of radiowave propagation is valid over small local areas (spanning a few tens of wavelengths), as long as the source and destination are far enough from each other (see [1] for an in-depth discussion on the validity of the PWP model).

A highlight of the geometry-based statistical PWP models is that they lend themselves for the derivation of compact analytic expressions for the ST-CCF and CPS of MIMO-M2M channels. However, such expressions are computed in the state of the art by assuming the size of the antenna arrays to be much smaller than the distance from the mobile stations to their local scatterers [2, 3, 8]. This consideration is necessary to approximate the path lengths of the received scattered waves—which are modeled in the literature by sums of Euclidean distances—by simple sums of trigonometric functions [2,3,8]. In this paper, we show that the need for invoking the aforementioned assumption stems from an oversimplification of the PWP model in the formulation of the MIMO-M2M CCE. We demonstrate that the correction of this imprecision does not invalidate the results presented in previous papers for the ST-CCF and CPS of MIMO-M2M channels. On the contrary, it simplifies the computation of such results, and allows to extend their validity to a wider range of scenarios.

The remainder of the paper is organized as follows: An overview of the current approach to the GBSM of MIMO-M2M PWP channels is presented in Section 2. The principles of the GBSM for SWP and PWP channels are revisited in Section 3. The problem in the formulation of the geometric PWP models for MIMO-M2M channels is discussed in Section 4. Finally, the conclusions are given in Section 5.

Notation: The complex conjugate and the absolute value operations are denoted by $(\cdot)^*$ and $|\cdot|$, respectively. Vectors are written in bold-face. The transpose operation is denoted by $(\cdot)^\dagger$, $\arg\{\cdot\}$ indicates the angle of a (two-dimensional) vector, $\|\cdot\|$ stands for the Euclidean norm, and the scalar product between two vectors $\mathbf{z}_1$ and $\mathbf{z}_2$ is represented as $\langle \mathbf{z}_1, \mathbf{z}_2 \rangle$. The operator $E\{\cdot\}$ designates the statistical expectation.

2. OVERVIEW OF THE GBSM OF MIMO-M2M PWP CHANNELS

2.1 Mathematical Models and Definitions

We consider a MIMO communication system with N_T transmit antennas and N_R receive antennas. For simplicity, we restrict our discussion to the GBSM of small-scale frequency-nonselective channels, and we assume that each echo of the transmitted signal interacts with exactly one scatterer before impinging on the receive antennas. Under these conditions, the complex envelope of the MIMO-M2M channel is modeled in the state of the art according to the definition below [2,3,8].

DEFINITION 1. *Suppose that the signal radiated by the n-th transmit antenna reaches the m-th receive antenna via single-bounce interaction with K ($K \in \{1,2,3,\ldots\}$) fixed scatterers. Suppose also that the transmitted signal and the scattered waves are vertically polarized. If the far-field condition holds, and if the received signal echoes have similar path lengths, then the CCE $h_{m,n}(t)$ connecting the n-th transmit antenna with the m-th receive antenna can be modeled by the superposition of K homogeneous plane waves as*

$$h_{m,n}(t) \triangleq \sum_{k=1}^{K} g_k \exp\big\{ j\big[\theta_k + \xi_{n,k}^T + \xi_{k,m}^R \\ -2\pi t \big(f_k^T + f_k^R\big)\big]\big\} \tag{1}$$

where $j \triangleq \sqrt{-1}$, g_k and θ_k stand for the gain and phase shift introduced by the k-th scatterer, respectively, while $\xi_{n,k}^T$ and $\xi_{k,m}^R$ are phase rotations related to the distance traveled by the k-th scattered wave. These terms are defined as $\xi_{n,k}^T \triangleq k_0 \zeta_{n,k}^T$, and $\xi_{k,m}^R \triangleq k_0 \zeta_{k,m}^R$, where $k_0 \triangleq 2\pi/\lambda$ is the wavenumber, λ denotes the wavelength, $\zeta_{n,k}^T$ is the (Euclidean) distance from the n-th transmit antenna to the k-th scatterer at time $t = 0$, and $\zeta_{k,m}^R$ is the distance from the k-th scatterer to the m-th receive antenna also at $t = 0$. The Doppler frequencies f_k^T and f_k^R are given as $f_k^T \triangleq f_{max}^T \cos(\alpha_k^T - \gamma_T)$ and $f_k^R \triangleq f_{max}^R \cos(\alpha_k^R - \gamma_R)$, where $f_{max}^T \triangleq \nu_T/\lambda$ and $f_{max}^R \triangleq \nu_R/\lambda$ are the maximum Doppler shifts due to the movement of the transmitter and the receiver, respectively, ν_T is the speed of the transmitter, and ν_R is the speed of the receiver. The angles γ_T and γ_R indicate the direction in azimuth at which the transmitter and the receiver

are moving, respectively. In turn, α_k^T and α_k^R are the AOD and AOA in azimuth of the k-th multipath component.

Definition 1 can be extended to frequency-selective (time-dispersive) channels, multiple-bounce scattering scenarios, three-dimensional propagation, fading channels with specular or line-of-sight components, and polarized channels [2, 3,8]. However, the simple model in (1) suffices to illustrate and analyze the problem that motives this communication.

2.2 Characterization of the Channel Model by GBSM

The gains g_k introduced in (1) are modeled in the literature as constant quantities equal to $g_k = \sqrt{1/K}$, $\forall k$, or as independent and identically distributed (i.i.d.) positive random variables with an average power $E\{|g_k|^2\} = 1/K$, $\forall k$. In turn, the phases θ_k are characterized by i.i.d. random variables, each having a uniform distribution over $[-\pi, \pi)$ [2,3,8]. The phase shifts $\xi_{n,k}^T$ and $\xi_{k,m}^R$, or more precisely, the path lengths $\zeta_{n,k}^T$ and $\zeta_{k,m}^R$, are modeled with reference to a given geometrical model of the propagation environment, such as the one depicted in Fig. 1. In this figure, white dots represent antenna elements, while effective scatterers are represented by black dots. We suppose that the terminals at both link ends are equipped with uniform linear antenna arrays. The size of the transmit antenna array is $\delta_T = (N_T - 1)\Delta_T$, where Δ_T indicates the separation between adjacent antennas. Analogously, $\delta_R = (N_R - 1)\Delta_R$ designates the size of the receive antenna array, where Δ_R is the distance between contiguous antennas. The origin of the coordinate system in Fig. 1 is denoted by $\mathcal{O} = [0,0]^\dagger$, and is defined by the center location of the transmit antenna array at time $t = 0$. On the other hand, $\mathcal{O}' = [D,0]^\dagger$ designates the center location of the receive antenna array at $t = 0$, where D is the distance between the fixed reference points $\mathcal{O}$ and $\mathcal{O}'$.

Vector $\mathbf{p}_{n,k}^T(t)$ indicates the position of the k-th scatterer relative to the n-th transmit antenna at time t, and $\mathbf{p}_{k,m}^R(t)$ describes the position of the m-th receive antenna as seen from the k-th scatterer at time t. These vectors are equal to:

$$\mathbf{p}_{n,k}^T(t) = \mathbf{s}_k^T - \mathbf{a}_n^T - t \cdot \mathbf{v}_T \tag{2a}$$

$$\mathbf{p}_{k,m}^R(t) = \mathbf{a}_m^R + t \cdot \mathbf{v}_R - \mathbf{s}_k^R \tag{2b}$$

In these equations, $\mathbf{v}_T \triangleq \nu_T [\cos(\gamma_T), \sin(\gamma_T)]^\dagger$ and $\mathbf{v}_R \triangleq \nu_R [\cos(\gamma_R), \sin(\gamma_R)]^\dagger$ are the velocity vectors of the transmitter and the receiver. Vectors $\mathbf{a}_n^T \triangleq A_n^T [\cos(\varphi_T), \sin(\varphi_T)]^\dagger$ and $\mathbf{a}_m^R \triangleq A_m^R [\cos(\varphi_R), \sin(\varphi_R)]^\dagger$ describe the location of the n-th transmit antenna and the m-th receive antenna, as seen from the center of the corresponding antenna arrays at any time instant. The rotation angles in azimuth of the transmit and receive antenna arrays are denoted by φ_T and φ_R, respectively, whereas $A_n^T = \frac{\Delta_T}{2}(2n - N_T - 1)$, and $A_m^R = \frac{\Delta_R}{2}(2m - N_R - 1)$. The position of the k-th scatterer relative to $\mathcal{O}$ and $\mathcal{O}'$ at time $t = 0$ is denoted by $\mathbf{s}_k^T \triangleq d_k^T [\cos(\alpha_k^T), \sin(\alpha_k^T)]^\dagger$ and $\mathbf{s}_k^R \triangleq d_k^R [\cos(\alpha_k^R), \sin(\alpha_k^R)]^\dagger$, respectively. The parameters of $\mathbf{s}_k^T$ and $\mathbf{s}_k^R$ are defined on the grounds of the geometry of the scattering scenario as constant quantities, random variables, or a mixture of both [2,3,8].

Note that the symbols used to denote the angles of $\mathbf{s}_k^T$ and $\mathbf{s}_k^R$ are the same as those introduced in Definition 1 to des-

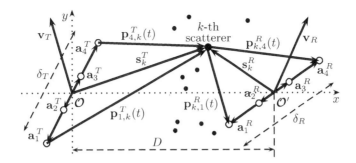

Figure 1: The reference 2D scattering propagation scenario at time $t = 0$.

ignate the AODs and AOAs of the received scattered waves. This is a notational convention that implies collinearity between the wavevector $\mathbf{w}_{n,m}^T$ of the k-th transmitted wave and $\mathbf{s}_k^T$, and between the wavevector $\mathbf{w}_{k,m}^R$ of the k-th received scattered wave and $\mathbf{s}_k^R$ [2, 3, 8]. However, these vectors do not need to be collinear. To prevent ambiguities, we shall associate α_k^T and α_k^R with the position vectors $\mathbf{s}_k^T$ and $\mathbf{s}_k^R$, while the AOD and AOA of the k-th plane wave traveling from the n-th transmit antenna to the k-th receive antenna will be denoted in general by $\phi_{n,k}^T$ and $\phi_{k,m}^R$, respectively, in such a way that:

$$\mathbf{w}_{n,k}^T \triangleq k_0 \left[\cos(\phi_{n,k}^T), \sin(\phi_{n,k}^T) \right]^{\dagger} \tag{3a}$$

$$\mathbf{w}_{k,m}^R \triangleq k_0 \left[\cos(\phi_{k,m}^R + \pi), \sin(\phi_{k,m}^R + \pi) \right]^{\dagger} \tag{3b}$$

The reader should keep in mind that the relationships

$$\phi_{n,k}^T = \alpha_k^T, \quad \forall n, k \tag{4a}$$

$$\phi_{k,m}^R = \alpha_k^R, \quad \forall m, k, \tag{4b}$$

are assumed to hold in the context of Definition 1. From (2), we find that the Euclidean distances $\zeta_{n,k}^T = \|\mathbf{p}_{n,k}^T(0)\|$ and $\zeta_{k,m}^R = \|\mathbf{p}_{k,m}^R(0)\|$ are equal to:

$$\zeta_{n,k}^T = d_k^T \sqrt{1 + \left(\frac{A_n^T}{d_k^T} \right)^2 - \frac{2A_n^T}{d_k^T} \cos\left(\alpha_k^T - \varphi_T \right)} \tag{5a}$$

$$\zeta_{k,m}^R = d_k^R \sqrt{1 + \left(\frac{A_m^R}{d_k^R} \right)^2 - \frac{2A_m^R}{d_k^R} \cos\left(\alpha_k^R - \varphi_R \right)}. \tag{5b}$$

2.3 Cross-Correlation Properties of the CCE

The computation of the channel ST-CCF $r_{m,n;p,q}(t_1, t_2) \triangleq E\{h_{m,n}^*(t_1)\, h_{p,q}(t_2)\}$ of any pair of channel gains $h_{m,n}(t)$ and $h_{p,q}(t)$ varies depending on the nature (deterministic or random) of the parameters of $\mathbf{s}_k^T$ and $\mathbf{s}_k^R$. However, the state-of-the-art solutions to this parameterization problem, while diverse, produce basically the same results. In the particular case of single-bounce scattering, and assuming local scattering around the receiver, these solutions lead to [8, Eq. (27)]:

$$r_{m,n;p,q}(t_1, t_2) = r_{m,n;p,q}(\tau)$$

$$= \int_{-\pi}^{\pi} \exp\left\{ jk_0 \left[\zeta_p^R(\alpha) - \zeta_m^R(\alpha) + \zeta_q^T(\alpha_T) \right. \right.$$

$$\left. - \zeta_n^T(\alpha_T) \right] - j2\pi\tau \left[f_{\max}^T \cos(\alpha_T - \gamma_T) \right.$$

$$\left. \left. + f_{\max}^R \cos(\alpha - \gamma_R) \right] \right\} p_\alpha^R(\alpha) d\alpha \tag{6}$$

where $r_{m,n;p,q}(\tau) \triangleq E\{h_{m,n}^*(t)\, h_{p,q}(t + \tau)\}$, $p_\alpha^R(\alpha)$ is the probability density function (PDF) of the AOA, and α_T solves

$$\sin(\alpha_T) = \frac{\mathcal{G}_S^R(\alpha)}{D} \sin(\alpha - \alpha_T). \tag{7}$$

The function $\mathcal{G}_S^R(\cdot)$ defines the distance d_k^R from $\mathcal{O}'$ to the local scatterers in terms of the AOA and the geometry of the scattering scenario, while $\zeta_n^T(\cdot)$ and $\zeta_m^R(\cdot)$ give the Euclidean distances in (5) in terms of the differential AODs α_T and AOAs α, respectively. An expression similar as (6), although given in terms of the AOD, is obtained if the scatterers are concentrated around the transmitter [8].

In general, (6) has to be solved by applying numerical integration techniques, because the derivation of a closed-form solution is hindered by two factors: The transcendental equation relating the AODs and the AOAs (see (7)), and the sum of square-root terms ζ_p^R, ζ_q^T, ζ_m^R, and ζ_n^T in the integrand's exponent. The first factor is an issue only in case of single-bounce scattering, because the AODs and AOAs can be modeled independently to each other under multiple-bounce scattering conditions. To circumvent the problem, the distance between mobile stations is assumed to be much greater than the distance from the stations to their local scatterers, in such a way that

$$D \gg \min\{d_k^T, d_k^R\}, \quad k = 1, \ldots, K. \tag{8}$$

The solution of (7) can thereby be approximated as

$$\alpha_T \approx \frac{\mathcal{G}_S^R(\alpha)}{D} \sin(\alpha), \quad D \gg \mathcal{G}_S^R(\alpha). \tag{9}$$

The second factor, on the other hand, is common to all geometrical PWP models for MIMO-M2M channels, regardless of the number of bounces experienced by the scattered waves. To bypass the limitations due to this factor, the distance from the mobile stations to their local scatterers is assumed much greater than the size of the antenna arrays, i.e.,

$$\min\{d_k^T, d_k^R\} \gg \max\{\delta_T, \delta_R\}, \quad k = 1, \ldots, K. \tag{10}$$

The distances in (5) can then be approximated as [2, 3, 8]

$$\zeta_{n,k}^T \approx d_k^T - A_n^T \cos\left(\alpha_k^T - \varphi_T \right) \tag{11a}$$

$$\zeta_{k,m}^R \approx d_k^R - A_m^R \cos\left(\alpha_k^R - \varphi_R \right). \tag{11b}$$

To the best of the authors' knowledge, all closed-form expressions proposed for the channel ST-CCF on the basis of the GBSM approach have been derived by assuming the fulfillment of (8) and (10). In the case of the channel model in (1), these inequalities allow to approximate (6) by

$$
r_{m,n;p,q}(\tau) \approx \int_{-\pi}^{\pi} \exp \left\{ jk_0 \left[\Lambda_{m,p}^R \cos(\alpha - \varphi_R) \right. \right.
$$
$$
+ \Lambda_{n,q}^T \left(\cos(\varphi_T) + \frac{\mathcal{G}_S^R(\alpha)}{D} \sin(\alpha) \sin(\varphi_T) \right) \right]
$$
$$
- j2\pi\tau \left[f_{\max}^R \cos(\alpha - \gamma_R) + f_{\max}^T \left(\cos(\gamma_T) \right. \right.
$$
$$
\left. \left. \left. + \frac{\mathcal{G}_S^R(\alpha)}{D} \sin(\alpha) \sin(\gamma_T) \right) \right] \right\} p_\alpha^R(\alpha) d\alpha \qquad (12)
$$

where $\Lambda_{n,q}^T = A_n^T - A_q^T$, and $\Lambda_{m,p}^R = A_m^R - A_p^R$. The equation above can be solved in a closed form if the function $\mathcal{G}_S^R(\cdot)$ and the circular PDF $p_\alpha^R(\alpha)$ allow to express the integral in (12) in terms of a standard function (e.g., see [8, Eq. (32)]).

3. SPHERICAL AND PLANE WAVE PROPAGATION MODELING OF MIMO-M2M CHANNELS

3.1 Generic Model of the CCE

A weak aspect of the inequalities in (8) and (10) is that the "much greater" condition is not well specified. In fact, no rule-of-thumb has been established so far as to how small should be the antenna arrays, or how far should be the mobile stations from each other and from their corresponding local scatterers. The purpose of this paper is not to answer these questions, but to demonstrate that (10) is not a necessary condition to warrant the tractability of the channel ST-CCF. In fact, we will show in the following section that the need for assuming the fulfillment of (10) stems from an oversimplification of the PWP model in the formulation of (1). The veracity of these statements is readily apparent from the fundamental differences between the SWP and PWP models. We give an overview of such differences by introducing a generic definition of the CCE.

DEFINITION 2. *Under the conditions stated at the beginning of Definition 1, the CCE $h_{m,n}(t)$ can be modeled as*

$$
h_{m,n}(t) \triangleq \sum_{k=1}^{K} g_k \exp \left\{ j \left[\theta_k + \vartheta_{n,k}^T(t) + \vartheta_{k,m}^R(t) \right] \right\} \quad (13)
$$

where g_k and θ_k are defined as in (1), while $\vartheta_{n,k}^T(t)$ and $\vartheta_{k,m}^R(t)$ account for the rotation of the wave's phase due to the traveled distance at any given time instant t; $\vartheta_{n,k}^T(t)$ is associated with the path from the n-th transmit antenna to the k-th scatterer, and $\vartheta_{k,m}^R(t)$ with the path from the k-th scatterer to the m-th receive antenna.

3.2 SWP Modeling of MIMO-M2M Channels

Definition 2 is valid for both SWP and PWP. In the SWP framework, the wavefront reaches a given observation point by traveling over a path with a length equal to the instantaneous separation (or radial distance) between the source and the observer. Thus, $\vartheta_{n,k}^T(t)$ and $\vartheta_{k,m}^R(t)$ can be written as

$$
\vartheta_{n,k}^T(t) = k_0 \|\mathbf{p}_{n,k}^T(t)\| \qquad (14a)
$$
$$
\vartheta_{k,m}^R(t) = k_0 \|\mathbf{p}_{k,m}^R(t)\| \qquad (14b)
$$

Substituting (2) into (14), we find that

$$
\vartheta_{n,k}^T(t) = \xi_{n,k}^T - 2\pi t f_{\max}^T \cos(\phi_{n,k}^T(t) - \gamma_T) \quad (15a)
$$
$$
\vartheta_{k,m}^R(t) = \xi_{k,m}^R - 2\pi t f_{\max}^R \cos(\phi_{k,m}^R(t) - \gamma_R) \quad (15b)
$$

where $\phi_{n,k}^T(t) = \arg\{\mathbf{p}_{n,k}^T(t)\}$ and $\phi_{k,m}^R(t) = \arg\{\mathbf{p}_{k,m}^R(t)\}$ are the AOD and AOA of the k-th incident spherical wave. Note that (4) is not meaningful in the SWP framework. Also, in this context, the spatial variation of $h_{m,n}(t)$ are determined by $\xi_{n,k}^T$ and $\xi_{k,m}^R$, while the temporal variations depend on time-variant AODs and AOAs. (cf. [1,4,6,7]).

3.3 PWP Modeling of MIMO-M2M Channels

In the framework of PWP, on the other hand, the path length of a traveling wave is approximated by the scalar projection of the vector $\mathbf{p}(t)$ describing the observer's position relative to the source's location at time t onto the unit vector $\mathbf{u}$ pointing at the direction of propagation [5, Ch. 3]. The time-variant phase shifts $\vartheta_{n,k}^T(t)$ and $\vartheta_{k,m}^R(t)$ are thereby given as:

$$
\vartheta_{n,k}^T(t) = \langle \mathbf{p}_{n,k}^T(t), \mathbf{w}_{n,k}^T \rangle \qquad (16a)
$$
$$
\vartheta_{k,m}^R(t) = \langle \mathbf{p}_{k,m}^R(t), \mathbf{w}_{k,m}^R \rangle \qquad (16b)
$$

where $\mathbf{w}_{n,k}^T$ and $\mathbf{w}_{k,m}^R$ are the wavevector defined in (3). From (2), (3), and (16), we find:

$$
\vartheta_{n,k}^T(t) = \langle \mathbf{s}_k^T - \mathbf{a}_n^T, \mathbf{w}_{n,k}^T \rangle - t\langle \mathbf{v}_T, \mathbf{w}_{n,k}^T \rangle \quad (17a)
$$
$$
= \xi_{n,k}^T \cos\left(\arg\{\mathbf{p}_{n,k}^T(0)\} - \phi_{n,k}^T \right)
$$
$$
- 2\pi t f_{\max}^T \cos(\phi_{n,k}^T - \gamma_T) \quad (17b)
$$
$$
\vartheta_{k,m}^R(t) = \langle \mathbf{a}_m^R - \mathbf{s}_k^R, \mathbf{w}_{k,m}^R \rangle + t\langle \mathbf{v}_R, \mathbf{w}_{k,m}^R \rangle \quad (17c)
$$
$$
= \xi_{k,m}^R \cos\left(\arg\{\mathbf{p}_{k,m}^R(0)\} - \phi_{k,m}^R \right)
$$
$$
- 2\pi t f_{\max}^R \cos(\phi_{k,m}^R - \gamma_R). \quad (17d)
$$

In this case, the spatial variations of $h_{m,n}(t)$ are not only determined by $\xi_{n,k}^T$ and $\xi_{k,m}^R$, they also depend on the angles of vectors $\mathbf{p}_{n,k}^T(0)$ and $\mathbf{p}_{k,m}^R(0)$, while the temporal variations are determined by time-invariant AODs and AOAs.

4. THE GBSM OF MIMO-M2M FADING CHANNELS REVISITED

From the previous section, it follows that the definition of $h_{m,n}(t)$ given by (1) is consistent with the PWP model provided that there exists AODs $\phi_{n,k}^T$ and AOAs $\phi_{k,m}^R$ that solve the system of nonlinear equations that results by comparing (1) with (13) and (17)—(17a) and (17c):

$$
\langle \mathbf{s}_k^T - \mathbf{a}_n^T, \mathbf{w}_{n,k}^T \rangle = \xi_{n,k}^T \qquad (18a)
$$
$$
\langle \mathbf{v}_T, \mathbf{w}_{n,k}^T \rangle = 2\pi f_k^T \qquad (18b)
$$
$$
\langle \mathbf{a}_m^R - \mathbf{s}_k^R, \mathbf{w}_{k,m}^R \rangle = \xi_{k,m}^R \qquad (18c)
$$
$$
\langle \mathbf{v}_R, \mathbf{w}_{k,m}^R \rangle = -2\pi f_k^R. \qquad (18d)
$$

If $N_T > 1$ and $N_R > 1$, the equations in (18) can simultaneously be solved for all n, m, and k, if and only if (see the Appendix):

$$
\phi_{n,k}^T = \alpha_k^T = \varphi_T \qquad (19a)
$$
$$
\phi_{k,m}^R = \alpha_k^R = \varphi_R \qquad (19b)
$$

and

$$
\varphi_T = \begin{cases} \pi + \varphi_R, & \text{if } D = d_k^T + d_k^R \\ \varphi_R, & \text{if } D < d_k^T + d_k^R \end{cases} \quad (19c)
$$

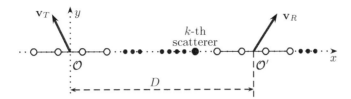

Figure 2: Scattering scenario for the equivalence of Definitions 1 and 2.

where $\phi_{n,k}^T, \phi_{k,m}^R \in [-\pi, \pi)$. This result shows that Definition 1 is consistent with the PWP model only for the rather artificial scenario sketched in Fig. 2, where the antenna arrays and the scatterers are perfectly aligned. We further observe that the solutions of (18a) and (18c) are given by

$$\phi_{n,k}^T = \arg\{\mathbf{p}_{n,k}^T(0)\}$$
$$\phi_{k,m}^R = \arg\{\mathbf{p}_{k,m}^R(0)\}$$

whereas the solutions of (18b) and (18d) are given by

$$\phi_{n,k}^T = 2\gamma_T - \alpha_T \text{ (or } \phi_{n,k}^T = \alpha_k^T)$$
$$\phi_{k,m}^R = 2\gamma_R - \alpha_R \text{ (or } \phi_{k,m}^R = \alpha_k^R)$$

respectively. This implies that the spatial and the temporal variations of the CCE model in (1) are modeled with respect to different sets of AODs and AOAs. Specifically, the spatial variations are characterized by assuming that the wavevectors $\mathbf{w}_{n,k}^T$ and $\mathbf{w}_{k,m}^R$ point in the same direction as vectors $\mathbf{p}_{n,k}^T(0)$ and $\mathbf{p}_{k,m}^R(0)$, respectively, while the temporal variations are modeled by considering that the direction of $\mathbf{w}_{n,k}^T$ and $\mathbf{w}_{k,m}^R$ is the same as that of $\mathbf{s}_k^T$ and $-\mathbf{s}_k^R$ (cf. (17b) and (17d)).

The fact that the spatial and the temporal variations of $h_{m,n}(t)$ are not modeled with respect to the same set of AODs and AOAs reveals an oversimplification of the PWP model. This modeling imprecision leads to an inconsistency whenever the AODs and AOAs are not given as in (19). However, the inconsistency can be presumed resolved if the inequality in (10) holds, i.e., if the Euclidean distances $\zeta_{n,k}^T$ and $\zeta_{k,m}^R$ are given as in (11). Under this condition, the solution of (18) can be approximated by (4), regardless of the geometry of the scattering scenario. This inequality is thus necessary not only to facilitate the analysis of the correlation properties of the CCE model in (1), but also to ensure the theoretical soundness of the channel models proposed on the grounds of Definition 1.

Even though the inconsistency discussed above is solved if (10) is fulfilled, the problem can be avoided from the outset if the CCE is characterized in strict accordance with the PWP, i.e., if $h_{m,n}(t)$ is characterized by following (13) and (16). In fact, the assumption of (10) proves unnecessary if the PWP model is thoroughly applied. Note that if the AODs and AOAs are given as in (4), then, from (17a) and (17c), we find that the time-variant phases of the PWP model are equal to:

$$\vartheta_{n,k}^T(t) = k_0 \left[d_k^T - A_n^T \cos(\alpha_k^T - \varphi_T) \right] - 2\pi f_k^T t \quad (20\text{a})$$

$$\vartheta_{k,m}^R(t) = k_0 \left[d_k^R - A_m^R \cos(\alpha_k^R - \varphi_R) \right] - 2\pi f_k^R t \quad (20\text{b})$$

The enforcement of (10) is thus pointless, since the purpose of this consideration is to approximate the time-variant

phase rotations $\xi_{n,k}^T - 2\pi f_{\max}^T t$ and $\xi_{k,m}^R - 2\pi f_{\max}^R t$ by the right-hand side of (20), as indicated by (11).

Now, following any of the state-of-the-art approaches for the parameterization of $\mathbf{s}_k^T$ and $\mathbf{s}_k^R$, and assuming that the local scatterers are distributed around the receiver, we find that the ST-CCF of the CCE defined by (13) and (20) equals:

$$r_{m,n;p,q}(\tau) = \int_{-\pi}^{\pi} \exp\left\{ jk_0 \left[\Lambda_{n,q}^T \cos(\alpha_T - \varphi_T) \right.\right.$$
$$\left. + \Lambda_{m,p}^R \cos(\alpha - \varphi_R) \right] - j2\pi\tau \left[f_{\max}^T \cos(\alpha_T - \gamma_T) \right.$$
$$\left.\left. + f_{\max}^R \cos(\alpha - \gamma_R) \right] \right\} p_\alpha^R(\alpha) d\alpha \quad (21)$$

where

$$\alpha_T = \arctan\left(\frac{\mathcal{G}_S^R(\alpha) \sin(\alpha)}{\mathcal{G}_S^R(\alpha) \cos(\alpha) + D} \right). \quad (22)$$

If (8) holds, in such a way that $\mathcal{G}_S^R(\alpha) \ll D$, $\forall \alpha$, then the solution of (22) is given by $\alpha_T \approx (\mathcal{G}_S^R(\alpha)/D) \sin(\alpha)$. Thereby, (21) can be approximated by (12). This shows that the approximate closed-form expressions of the ST-CCF that have been derived on the grounds of (12) are also valid by following (13) and (16). However, in this latter context, such approximate expressions are not constrained by (10). They are therefore valid also in presence of near scatterers. Similar conclusions can be drawn if the local scatterers are distributed around the transmitter, or if the received waves undergo multiple bounce-scattering.

The fact that the enforcement of (10) is an unnecessary consideration is further evidenced by measured data analyzed in [9], where a good match between measurements and simulations was obtained, even though the antennas spacing was as large as 0.36m, the nearest scatterers were 4.5m away, and the distance between transmitter and receiver was 300m. Thus, it proves more relevant to investigate how far should be the scatterers from the transmit and receive stations to determine whether the PWP model can be used, instead of evaluating how large should be the antenna arrays to fulfill the inequality in (10). This problem can be dealt with by following the methods proposed in [1], where the transition between the PWP model and the more realistic SWP model is investigated.

5. SUMMARY AND CONCLUSIONS

The motivation in modeling the CCE of MIMO-M2M fading channels as in Definition 1 is unclear. However, the discussion presented throughout this paper shows that this approach does not offer any advantage over the plain application of the PWP model. On the contrary, the former solution makes the modeling task considerably more involved. Even though the assumption of (10) provides an effective patch to the problems caused by the oversimplification of the PWP model, we believe that the modeling imprecisions discussed in this paper should be avoided to promote consistency and prevent misunderstanding.

6. ACKNOWLEDGEMENTS

This work was financed in part by the Mexican Ministry of Education (SEP) and by the Mexican Council for Science and Technology (CONACYT) through the SEP-CONACYT Basic Research Program: Project reference #236188.

7. REFERENCES

[1] F. Bøhagen, P. Orten, and G. E. Øien. On spherical vs. plane wave modeling of line-of-sight MIMO channels. *IEEE Trans. Commun.*, 57(3):841–849, May 2009.

[2] X. Cheng, Q. Yao, M. Wen, C.-X. Wang, L.-Y. Song, and B.-L. Jiao. Wideband channel modeling and intercarrier interference cancellation for vehicle-to-vehicle communication systems. *IEEE J. Sel. Areas Commun.*, 31(9):434–448, Sept. 2013.

[3] M. T. Dao, V. A. Nguyen, Y. T. Im, S. O. Park, and G. Yoon. 3D polarized channel modeling and performance comparison of MIMO antenna configurations with different polarizations. *IEEE Trans. Antennas Propag.*, 59(7):2672–2682, June 2011.

[4] J. Karedal, F. Tufvesson, N. Czink, A. Paier, C. Dumard, T. Zemen, C. Mecklenbräuker, and A. F. Molisch. A geometry-based stochastic MIMO model for vehicle-to-vehicle communications. *IEEE Trans. Wireless Commun.*, 8(7):3646–3657, 2009.

[5] C. A. Levis, J. T. Johnson, and F. L. Teixeira. *Radiowave Propagation: Physics and Applications.* John Wiley and Sons, New Jersey, 2010.

[6] F. M. Schubert, M. L. Jakobsen, and B. H. Fleury. Non-stationary propagation model for scattering volumes with application to the rural LMS channel. *IEEE Trans. Antennas Propag.*, 61(5):2817–2828, 2013.

[7] M. Walter, D. Shutin, and U.-C. Fiebig. Delay-dependent Doppler probability density functions for vehicle-to-vehicle scatter channels. *IEEE Trans. Antennas Propag.*, 62(4):2238–2249, Apr. 2014.

[8] A. G. Zajić and G. L. Stüber. Space-time correlated mobile-to-mobile channels: Modelling and simulation. *IEEE Trans. Veh. Technol.*, 57(2):715–726, Mar. 2008.

[9] A. G. Zajić, G. L. Stüber, T. G. Pratt, and S. T. Nguyen. Wideband MIMO mobile-to-mobile channels: Geometry-based statistical modeling with experimental verification. *IEEE Trans. Veh. Technol.*, 58(2):517–534, Feb. 2009.

APPENDIX

The system of equations in (18) can be rewritten as:

$$\langle \overline{\mathbf{p}}_{n,k}^T(0), \overline{\mathbf{w}}_{n,k}^T \rangle = 1 \tag{23a}$$

$$\langle \mathbf{v}_T, \overline{\mathbf{w}}_{n,k}^T \rangle = \langle \mathbf{v}_T, \bar{\mathbf{s}}_k^T \rangle \tag{23b}$$

$$\langle \overline{\mathbf{p}}_{k,m}^R(0), \overline{\mathbf{w}}_{k,m}^R \rangle = 1 \tag{23c}$$

$$\langle \mathbf{v}_R, \overline{\mathbf{w}}_{k,m}^R \rangle = \langle \mathbf{v}_R, \bar{\mathbf{s}}_k^R \rangle \tag{23d}$$

where the overline indicates that the vector's magnitude has been normalized. By direct evaluation, one can verify that (19) is a sufficient condition for the solution of these systems. To show that (19) is also a necessary condition, let us consider first the system of equations given by (23a) and (23b). Equation (23a) has a unique solution given by $\overline{\mathbf{w}}_{n,k}^T = \overline{\mathbf{p}}_{n,k}^T(0)$, implying that $\phi_{n,k}^T = \arg\{\mathbf{p}_{n,k}^T(0)\}$, $\forall n, k$ (subject to $\phi_{n,k}^T \in [-\pi, \pi)$). With this in mind, we can rewrite (23b) as

$$\langle \mathbf{v}_T, \overline{\mathbf{p}}_{n,k}^T(0) \rangle = \langle \mathbf{v}_T, \bar{\mathbf{s}}_k^T \rangle. \tag{24}$$

This equation has two possible solutions: $\arg\{\mathbf{p}_{n,k}^T(0)\} = \alpha_k^T$, and $\arg\{\mathbf{p}_{n,k}^T(0)\} = 2\gamma_T - \alpha_k^T$. Both solutions imply that the transmit antennas are located on a line that passes through the coordinates of $\mathbf{s}_k^T$. However, only the first solution is meaningful, because it considers a line crossing the origin, while the second solution does not. Thus, (23a) and (23b) can be solved simultaneously for all n, k only if $\phi_{n,k}^T = \alpha_k^T = \varphi_R$, where $\tan\{\varphi_R\}$ is the slope of the line on which the transmit antennas lie. Analogously, it can be shown that $\phi_{k,m}^R = \alpha_k^R = \varphi_R$ is a sufficient and a necessary condition for the solution of (23c) and (23d).

Now, if (19a) and (19b) hold, and the scatterers lie somewhere between the transmit and receive antenna arrays, in such a way that $D = d_k^T + d_k^R$, then the traveling waves should be forward-scattered to reach the receive antennas, meaning that $\alpha_k^T = \pi + \alpha_k^R$, and therefore $\varphi_T = \pi + \varphi_R$. Under a similar reasoning, we can conclude that if the scatterers are not located between the antenna arrays, in such a way that $D < d_k^T + d_k^R$, then the incident waves should be back-scattered to reach the receiver. Hence, $\alpha_k^T = \alpha_k^R$, and therefore $\varphi_T = \varphi_R$.

Filling the Gaps of Vehicular Mobility Traces

Fabrício A. Silva
Federal University of Minas
Gerais
Belo Horizonte, Brazil
fabricio.asilva@dcc.ufmg.br

Clayson Celes
Federal University of Minas
Gerais
Belo Horizonte, Brazil
claysonceles@dcc.ufmg.br

Azzedine Boukerche
University of Ottawa
Ottawa, Canada
boukerch@site.uottawa.ca

Linnyer B. Ruiz
State University of Maringá
Maringá, Brazil
linnyer@gmail.com

Antonio A. F. Loureiro
Federal University of Minas
Gerais
Belo Horizonte, Brazil
loureiro@dcc.ufmg.br

ABSTRACT

Simulation is the approach most adopted to evaluate Vehicular Ad hoc Network (VANET) and Delay-Tolerant Network (DTN) solutions. Furthermore, the results' reliability depends fundamentally on mobility models used to represent the real network topology with high fidelity. Usually, simulation tools use mobility traces to build the corresponding network topology based on existing contacts established between mobile nodes. However, the traces' quality, in terms of spatial and temporal granularity, is a key factor that affects directly the network topology and, consequently, the evaluation results. In this work, we show that highly adopted existing real vehicular mobility traces present gaps, and propose a solution to fill those gaps, leading to more fine-grained traces. We propose and evaluate a cluster-based solution using clustering algorithms to fill the gaps. We apply our solution to calibrate three existing, widely adopted taxi traces. The results reveal that indeed the gaps lead to network topologies that differ from reality, affecting directly the performance of the evaluation results. To contribute to the research community, the calibrated traces are publicly available to other researchers that can adopt them to improve their evaluation results.

Categories and Subject Descriptors

C.2.4 [**Computer-Communication Networks**]: Distributed Systems

General Terms

Design, Algorithms, Performance

MSWiM'15, November 2–6, 2015, Cancun, Mexico.
© 2015 ACM. ISBN 978-1-4503-3762-5/15/11 ...$15.00.
DOI: http://dx.doi.org/10.1145/2811587.2811612.

Keywords

vehicular mobility traces; filling the gaps; calibration; vehicular ad-hoc networks; performance evaluation;

1. INTRODUCTION

Simulation is the approach most adopted to evaluate Vehicular Ad hoc Network (VANET) solutions [10, 17]. Their performance evaluation is an important challenge faced by researchers, given the particular characteristics of this type of ad hoc network, such as a highly dynamic and large-scale topology. The conduction of real experiments using ordinary vehicles is a very expensive and time-consuming approach, particularly when a large-scale evaluation is required. In addition, there is no publicly available, large-scale testbed. Moreover, it is unlikely that a large-scale testbed will be available in the near future due to involved deployment and maintenance costs. Simulation, on the other hand, is a cost-effective, large-scale approach widely adopted by researchers. However, the reliability of the simulation results depends on appropriate and accurate vehicular mobility models to represent the network topology with high fidelity.

The adopted vehicular mobility model plays an important role on the reliability of the simulation results [7, 8, 11, 18]. Existing simulation tools use mobility models to build scenarios where vehicles move and communicate with each other. The mobility model is responsible for determining the position of vehicles at each instant, which is used to build the network topology. In other words, unrealistic mobility models lead to unrealistic network topologies, and, consequently, unreliable evaluation results, as demonstrated by Baumann et al. [2]. Therefore, it is very important to adopt realistic vehicular mobility models when evaluating VANET solutions.

Vehicular mobility traces typically describe the position of vehicles over time and are used to bring realism to simulation tools. With the advance of GPS-enabled devices, real traces collected by vehicles during their daily routine are publicly available in the literature [3, 23, 26]. These real traces are very useful to the evaluation process, since they define movements of real vehicles and are used in different scenarios, as discussed in the next section. However, their quality, in terms of spatial and temporal granularity, is a key factor that affects the network topology and, consequently, the evaluation results. The existence of spatial and temporal gaps (i.e., long periods or distances between two consecutive entries of a vehicle in the trace) lead to network topologies that differ from reality. In fact, the traces we analyzed present spatial and temporal gaps that affect the simulation results presented in the literature. Hence, it turns out that finding and eliminating such gaps to build a high-fidelity mobility model is a key aspect to guarantee reliability of the results. Nevertheless, this problem is not tackled appropriately in the literature, since most solutions focus on finding a high-level path between two sparse points (i.e., a gap), instead of building a fine-grained trajectory. In this study, we find and fill existing gaps appropriately, leading to calibrated fine-grained traces.

In this work, we contribute to the research community by finding and eliminating gaps of vehicular mobility traces. First, we demonstrate the existence of gaps in the publicly available traces, which must then be calibrated to eliminate such gaps. Given that, we propose and evaluate a cluster-based solution to fill the gaps, following the methodology proposed in [25]. Our solution relies on the existing trajectory points, obtained from the trace itself, that are organized into clusters to represent anchor points used in the calibration. Therefore, our approach is flexible to be adopted in different real traces, since there is no need for looking at a map nor any further information. In fact, we demonstrate that by applying our solution to calibrate three existing, widely adopted taxi traces. We consider taxi traces in our study because they are real, publicly available, and widely adopted in the literature. However, our solution is general enough to be applied to any vehicular mobility trace. The results reveal that indeed the gaps lead to different network topology graphs, affecting directly the results of the performance evaluation. To cooperate with the research community, we made the calibrated traces publicly available at [29].

The remainder of this work is organized as follows. In Section 2, we present the studies found in the literature that are related to ours. Next, in Section 3, we describe the real traces used in our work and analyze the existence of gaps that need to be filled. In Section 4, we present a calibration solution to fill the gaps. We present the calibration results in Section 5. Finally, we conclude our study and present some future work in Section 6.

2. RELATED WORK

The demand for real vehicular mobility traces has increased significantly in the last decade because of the interest of the research community in VANETs and Delay-Tolerant Networks (DTNs). This demand has led some research groups to install GPS-enabled devices on taxis and collect their routes, which are then organized and made publicly available. Currently, there are publicly taxi mobility traces from San Francisco, USA [23, 24], Rome, Italy [1, 3], Shanghai [26] and Beijing [30], China.

The public availability of such traces has led the research community to question how to model vehicles and their connectivity. To this end, some studies started characterizing the mobility traces. In [1], the authors characterize the taxi trace from Rome and analyze an epidemic dissemination protocol using this trace as the mobility model. The studies presented in [4, 6, 13] characterize the network topology and connectivity metrics of the taxi trace from San Francisco. Furthermore, the taxi trace of Shanghai is used to

study mobility patterns [15, 16, 19, 31] and network topology and connectivity metrics [14, 32, 33]. Similarly, the trace from Beijing is also explored in mobility characterization studies [9, 30].

Those characterization and analyzes lead to important findings about mobility patterns, helping defining novel solutions related to communication and dissemination protocols for VANETs and DTNs. However, most VANET and DTN performance evaluations rely on vehicle contacts. It turns out that the network graph representing those contacts is built based on the mobility traces, which may present gaps in space and time (see Section 4.1). Furthermore, such gaps lead to missing contacts and, consequently, an incomplete graph representing the network topology that does not represent correctly the real contacts among vehicles.

There are only a few studies analyzing how meaningful a network topology obtained from a trace is, and, when necessary, proposing calibrating algorithms to improve it. In [12], the authors focus on extrapolating people trajectories based on sparse collected points. To this end, the authors assume users have a daily routine, and exploit their historical trajectories to infer unknown ones. The assumption of the existence of daily routines does not apply to taxis that move according to user demands. Furthermore, the inferred trajectory is not represented by a high number of points, which is required to build the network topology.

In [20], the authors propose a probabilistic model to infer the path a mobile user follows given two position points. The path is represented by the roads in the map that the user probably traveled to move from the origin point to the destination one. Since the path does not present any point representing a high-granularity trajectory of a mobile user, it is not feasible to build a contact graph with this solution. Therefore, it is not useful to evaluate the performance of VANETs and DTNs.

In [13], the authors interpolate adjacent points with the objective of finding an intermediary point between them. To this end, it averages samples one minute backward and forward to estimate the position of a mobile entity in a given period. This simple approach works when the mobile entity travels following a straight line. However, it fails when the entity turns its direction at an intersection, a very common mobility pattern when it comes to vehicles.

In [25], the authors propose a methodology composed of two components, adopted in this work, to calibrate trajectories: a reference system and a calibration method. The reference system is built from a set of anchor points independent of the trajectory. The calibration method uses the reference system to find points to be inserted along the trajectory, making it more complete. The authors evaluate and present results of different strategies of their methodology. However, the following drawbacks motivate us to develop the current work. First, the detailed algorithm to build a reference system is not presented. Also, their calibration method ignores the relationship between anchor points in the reference system, leading to an inaccurate calibration. In addition, the taxi trace mentioned and used in their work is not described; in other words, it is not possible to reproduce their results. Finally, the calibrated trace is not publicly available.

Our current work complements [25] by proposing and describing algorithms to calibrate incomplete trajectory data, and by making calibrated traces available to the research community. Furthermore, our calibration method performs better than [25], since it considers the relationships between the points in the reference system. Therefore, researchers can easily reproduce our results, apply our solution to other traces, and download the already calibrated traces from three cities located in different parts of the world. Moreover, we envision a significant improvement on the performance evaluation results of VANET and DTN solutions.

3. THE MOBILITY TRACES

The vehicular mobility traces available in the literature can be classified as synthetic or real. The synthetic traces are built by mobility generator tools based on particular characteristics of the city, such as population, neighborhood (i.e., residential, commercial, industrial), among other aspects collected by the city managers. The most known synthetic mobility traces are from Cologne [28] and Zurich [22]. Since synthetic traces present a high granularity in terms of space and time, there is no need to fill their gaps.

The real mobility traces are the ones generated by real vehicles equipped with GPS-enabled devices. Usually, the real mobility traces represent the mobility of taxis, since it is easier to deploy and maintain this kind of experiment in vehicles of this category than in ordinary vehicles. Among the existing real mobility traces in the literature, we selected three to be used in this work: Rome, San Francisco, and Shanghai. The selection was motivated by the high demand for such traces and their geographical locations that represent three different parts of the world, namely Europe, North America, and Asia.

Each trace comes from a different source and presents a different format. To facilitate their adoption and use, we formatted all entries as tuples $\langle id, timestamp, lat, long \rangle$, where id is the vehicle unique identifier, $timestamp$ is the date and time of the entry in the format $yyyy\text{-}mm\text{-}dd\ HH{:}MM{:}ss$, and lat and $long$ are the latitude and longitude, respectively, in the WGS84 coordinate system format. In the following, we describe the main details of each trace.

3.1 Rome

The trace of Rome [1, 3] contains the position of taxi cabs working during the entire month of February, 2014. Each taxi driver has a device running Android and is equipped with a GPS receiver that periodically retrieves its position and sends it to a central server. Positions with a precision error higher than 20 m were ignored. This trace contains, for the entire month, a total of 21,817,851 position entries coming from 316 taxis. On average, each vehicle contributes with 69,040 positions for the whole collection period. However, few vehicles contribute with higher values up to 118,500, while others contribute with values as low as 19, for example.

3.2 San Francisco

The trace of San Francisco [23, 24] contains position entries of 536 taxis working during the month of May, 2008. Each taxi has a GPS receiver installed in it, and sends location information (identifier, timestamp, latitude, longitude) periodically to a central server. This trace contains, for the entire month, a total of 11,219,955 position entries. Each taxi contributes, on average, with around 20,930 entries. A very few of them contribute with significant lower values, while others contribute with higher measures up to 49,370.

3.3 Shanghai

The trace from Shanghai [15, 26] presents positions of 4,316 taxis from February to April of 2007[1]. However, we could find publicly available only the data from one single day of February, containing 6,075,587 position entries. Similar to the other cases, the taxis were equipped with GPS-enabled devices, which sent their position information periodically to a server. On average, each vehicle collected around 1,408 entries for the only day publicly available. Few vehicles contribute with lower values, while others contribute with higher values, up to 7,011.

4. CALIBRATION SOLUTION

In this section, we describe our solution to fill the gaps between consecutive points far enough from each other, causing the topology graph of the network to be incomplete. First, we show how distant in space the entries of the traces are. Next, we present our solution to fill such gaps and, consequently, improve the quality of the traces.

4.1 Measuring the gaps

The completeness of the topology graph is a key factor in the performance evaluation of VANET and DTN solutions. In fact, contacts among vehicles or mobile devices that occurred in reality, but were not considered due to gaps in the traces, affect the evaluation, since data exchange depends on the contacts. To measure how expressive the gaps in the existing traces are, we evaluate the distance between every two consecutive entries, as discussed in the following.

Figure 1 depicts the Complementary Cumulative Distribution Function (CCDF) of the distances between every two consecutive points for Rome (Figure 1(a)), San Francisco (Figure 1(b)) and Shanghai (Figure 1(c)). As indicated by the third quartile (blue vertical line), 25% of two consecutive points are 66.7 m, 446.7 m, and 163.3 m apart for Rome, San Francisco, and Shanghai, respectively. Considering those gaps and assuming a transmission range of 100 m [5], many existing contacts will be missed when the network topology graph is built from the trace.

In addition to spatial gaps, temporal gaps should also be considered since they also lead to missing contacts. For example, two vehicles not moving (or moving very slowly) close to each other, will be in contact for a period of time. If the trace lacks these points for the entire period, the contacts will not be considered in the topology graph, since it is not possible to know whether or not the vehicles were close enough to be in contact in a particular period.

To evaluate the existence of temporal gaps, we also measured the intervals between two consecutive points of the three traces, and it was possible to note that 25% of the intervals between two consecutive points are longer than 15 s, 62 s, and 63 s, for Rome, San Francisco, and Shanghai, respectively. Given the highly dynamic aspect of VANETs and DTNs, such long intervals between two consecutive points will cause gaps in the induced topology and many existing contacts will be missed.

Given that, we conclude that the existing vehicular mobility traces indeed present spatial and temporal gaps, which may lead to incorrect representation of the network topology for performance evaluation. In addition, we observe that

---

[1]These data were obtained from Wireless and Sensor networks Lab (WnSN), Shanghai Jiao Tong University.

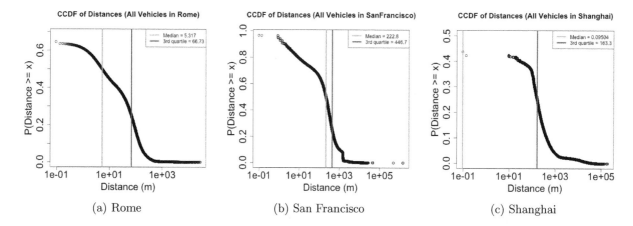

(a) Rome	(b) San Francisco	(c) Shanghai

Figure 1: Complementary Cumulative Distribution Function (CCDF) of the distances between two adjacent points. These plots reveal that a significant number of entries present a distance between points that could affect the network topology.

linear interpolation is not an attractive technique for filling the gaps, since it would lead to points outside the roads. To solve this problem, in the next section we present a cluster-based solution to fill the existing gaps.

4.2 Filling the gaps

Our approach for filling the gaps in vehicular mobility traces is divided into two stages. The first one extracts a reference system from the vehicles's historical GPS trajectory dataset. The second stage applies a calibration method, using a subset of anchor points of the previously built reference system. In the following, we describe both steps.

4.2.1 Cluster-based Reference System

The reference system consists of a set of points resulting from a clustering process that uses historical trajectories. Each point, called centroid, represents a cluster of GPS points close together recorded by all vehicles in the trace. Given that those GPS points represent real trajectories, it is reasonable to assume that each centroid is a potential location for a new point in a trajectory. In other words, it is very likely that a centroid represents a correct point in a road where vehicles travel through. Here, we adopt the K-Means clustering method [21] for partitioning the data into K clusters according to the density of GPS points and, then, we obtain the centroid point of each cluster to form the reference system.

Algorithm 1 - Reference System based on Clustering

Input: The historical of vehicles trajectories (raw data) and number of clusters (K)

Output: Reference System ($RefSys$), a set of centroid points.

1: **procedure** CLUSTERINGGPSPOINTS
2:     $Clusters \leftarrow applyClustering(raw\_data, K)$
3:     $RefSys \leftarrow getCentroids(Clusters)$
4: **end procedure**

Algorithm 1 shows the basic steps to obtain the reference system. Initially, the K-means method partitions the data into K groups according to the density of points (Line 2).

Then, we obtain the centroid of each group and add to the reference system (Line 3).

A particular problem when using K-Means is the identification of an appropriate value of K. Thus, to overcome this problem, we applied the elbow method [27], which finds the minimum value of K that seems to give the smallest error. In other words, if we increase the value K, the error will not decrease significantly, meaning it is not worth to do so. Regarding the computational complexity, the running time of K-Means clustering method is given as $O(nkdi)$, where n is the number of samples, d is the number of dimensions (two dimensions in our case, namely latitude and longitude), k is the number of clusters, and i is the number of iterations needed until the convergence of the clustering process is reached.

4.2.2 Calibration Method

In this stage, we perform the calibration following a geometric-based approach, which is an improvement of the base method described in [25]. More specifically, when we found a gap in a trajectory T, we obtain the reference system of the region and, then, select the centroid points between the endpoints of the gaps to the trajectory T.

The calibration method receives as input the following parameters: T is a set of n consecutive points with spatio-temporal information; $RefSys$ is the reference system obtained from the Algorithm 1; min_d and max_d are the limits to consider the existence of a spatial gap, and $time\_d$ is the threshold to consider a temporal gap. As result, we have a new trajectory T' with the original points from T and a set of calibrated points added to fill the existing gaps in T.

Algorithm 2 describes the calibration method. For each sequence of two points in T, we check if there is a gap between them according to input parameters (Lines 4–8). If this is the case, we perform the calibration. Initially, we detect the set of centroid points from the reference system near the corresponding gap. For this, the *bounding_box* function finds the point half-way (midpoint) between the two endpoints of the gap and returns the circle with center in this midpoint (Line 9). Then, we obtain all centroid points from the reference system with coordinates inside the circle and store them in C (Line 10). Next, we iteratively find the nearest point $a^* \in C$ to the centroid that satisfies the angular condition (Lines 14–15). The angular condition (Line 15) guarantees that only centroids in the same direction of the trajectory are considered, to avoid the selection of points in the opposite direction. If true, insert a^* in L between p_p and p_n. Next, remove a^* from C and repeat this last sequence of steps while C is not empty (Lines 13–23). Finally, we insert the calibrated points of L into T'.

The algorithm described in [25] does not consider the relationship between the points inserted in the gaps. In our solution, presented in Algorithm 2, we consider the relationship for choosing each new centroid based on the distance from the last selected centroid (Line 14).

Algorithm 2 - Calibration Method

Input: Trajectory ($T = [P_1, P_2, ..., P_n]$), Reference System ($RefSys$), minimum spatial distance (min_d), maximum spatial distance (max_d) and temporal distance (time_d)
Output: A calibrated trajectory (T') without gaps.

1: **procedure** CALIBRATE
2:    $T' \leftarrow T[1]$
3:    **for** $i = 2$ to $length(T)$ **do**
4:       $p_p \leftarrow T[i-1]$ $\triangleright$ p_p is the previous point
5:       $p_n \leftarrow T[i]$ $\triangleright$ p_n is the next point
6:       $d \leftarrow distance(p_p, p_n)$
7:       $t \leftarrow interval(p_p, p_n)$
8:       **if** d in $[min\_d, max\_d]$ and $t \leq time\_d$ **then**
9:          $bb\_coord \leftarrow bounding\_box(p_p, p_n)$
10:        $C \leftarrow subset(RefSys, bb\_coord)$
11:        Initialize an empty list L
12:        $a' \leftarrow p_p$
13:        **while** TRUE **do**
14:          $a^* = \arg\min_{a \in C} d(a, a')$
15:          **if** $\angle(\overrightarrow{a'a^*}, \overrightarrow{p_p p_n}) < \frac{\pi}{2}$ **then**
16:            Add a^* to L
17:            $a' = a^*$
18:          **end if**
19:          Remove a^* from C
20:          **if** C is empty **then**
21:            break
22:          **end if**
23:        **end while**
24:        Insert the centroids in L into T'
25:       **else**
26:        Insert p_n in T'
27:       **end if**
28:    **end for**
29:    return T'
30: **end procedure**

Besides inserting the calibrated points because of the spatial gap, it is important to obtain their timestamp to accurately represent the trajectory. Thus, before adding a^* to L (Line 16), we compute an estimated time for temporal occurrence of the centroid a^* using Equation 1 [25], where $d(\cdot, \cdot)$ is the distance between two coordinates:

$$a^* \cdot t = p_p \cdot t + \frac{(p_n \cdot t - p_p \cdot t) \cdot d(p_p, a^*) \cdot \left| \overrightarrow{p_p a^*} \cdot \overrightarrow{p_p p_n} \right|}{d(p_p, p_n) \cdot \left| \overrightarrow{p_p a^*} \right| \cdot \left| \overrightarrow{p_p p_n} \right|} \quad (1)$$

Regarding the computational complexity, the running time of Algorithm 2 depends of the length of T and the

Metric	Trace	Original	Calibrated
	Rome	7	3
No. Clusters	San Francisco	2	1
	Shanghai	297	141
Avg.	Rome	4.3	3.1
Eccentricity	San Francisco	3.5	2.0
	Shanghai	16.37	16.09
Avg.	Rome	2.4	1.9
Path Length	San Francisco	2.3	1.4
	Shanghai	4.20	2.92

Table 1: Graph properties of original and calibrated traces. The calibrated traces present different complex network metric values than the original one.

number of centroid points in C for each calibrated gap. As N_c is the average number of centroids for a gap and N_T is the length of the trajectory, it follows that the complexity is $O(N_T \cdot N_c^2)$. Given that the number of centroids is not high because of the adopted elbow method, and that this is an offline process that aims to calibrate the traces only once, we consider very reasonable this complexity.

5. CALIBRATION RESULTS

In this section, we assess the performance of our calibration solution by applying it to the mobility traces from Rome, San Francisco, and Shanghai. To this end, we apply algorithm 1 to build the reference system for each scenario, and algorithm 2 to calibrate them. We consider as gap when two consecutive points are more than 50 m and less than 500 m apart. In addition, the interval between two consecutive points must be lower than 1200 s. Otherwise, it is considered as a break period of the driver, and not as a gap. The input parameters for algorithm 2 were then set as $min\_d = 50m$, $max\_d = 500m$ and $time\_d = 1200s$.

First, we compare our calibration method to the one described in [25]. Figure 2 illustrates an example of one gap, where red points represent the endpoints of the gap (i.e., the original points) and the blue points are new ones added by the calibration method. Our calibration method fills the gap more accurately, since the previous added anchor point (i.e., centroid) is considered as reference to the selection of the next one. In contrast, the original solution does not consider the relationship among the anchors to be selected. This demonstrates one of the contributions of our solution, as already discussed, which is the improvement of the calibration method.

To assess the impact of filling the gaps in the network topology, we compare some network topology metrics of the original and calibrated traces. The objective is to show that the gaps in the original trace are responsible for a network topology that differs from reality. To this end, we pick a random sample of an entire weekday from each of the original traces, apply our calibration method to them, and build the topology graphs for the original and the calibrated traces. It is important to mention that our goal here is to focus on analyzing how the network topology built from the original trace differs from the calibrated one, and not explaining their mobility patterns.

Figure 3 illustrates the CCDF of the vehicles' degree, which is the number of contacts a vehicle had during the entire period. In this case, the degree is the number of other

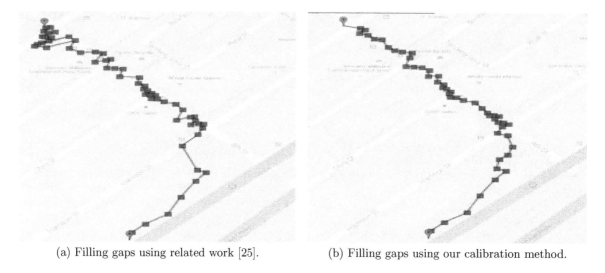

(a) Filling gaps using related work [25].   (b) Filling gaps using our calibration method.

Figure 2: Comparing our calibration method with [25].

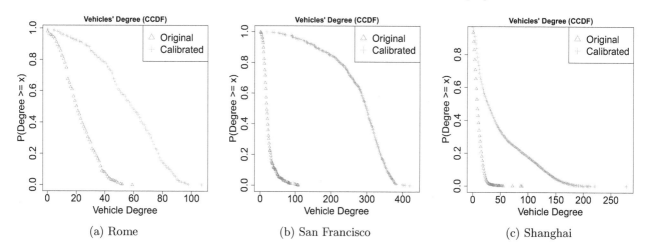

(a) Rome   (b) San Francisco   (c) Shanghai

Figure 3: CCDF of vehicles' degree. Notice that a significant number of contacts are lost due to the gaps in the original traces.

vehicles that a particular vehicle had contact with during the entire evaluation period. A contact exists when two vehicles are less than 100 m apart from each other. Because of the existing gaps, some contacts that occur in reality may not be represented by the traces. In fact, it is remarkable the amount of contacts lost due to the existing gaps. As stated earlier, the missing contacts lead to unrealistic topology and, consequently, inaccurate results.

The betweenness of a vehicle counts the number of shortest paths from all other vehicles to all others that pass through it. This is an important metric, since a vehicle with a high betweenness is expected to have a higher influence in the dissemination of messages in the network. Therefore, the betweenness is relevant to the performance evaluation, since it represents the importance of vehicles to the network topology. For example, the betweenness could be used to select the most appropriate vehicle to carry and forward packets. As expected, the gaps also lead to differences in centrality metrics such as betweenness, as depicted in Figure 4. We can observe that vehicles in the calibrated traces present, on average, lower betweenness values for Rome and San Francisco, and about the same for Shanghai.

The same is observed for other structural properties of the topology graphs, such as average nearest neighbor degree, as illustrated in Figure 5. For all scenarios, it is possible to see that vehicles are connected to other vehicles presenting higher degree in the calibrated traces. This is also due to the fact that not all contacts that occur are represented in the original traces. Again, this metric affects the performance evaluation, since it interferes on the communication among vehicles.

To conclude, we have also measured other graph properties, namely the number of clusters formed in the graph, the average eccentricity of vehicles, and the average path length of vehicles. These results, presented in Table 1, also demonstrate that the original traces with gaps differ from reality.

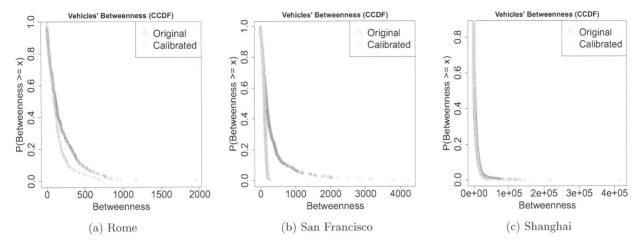

(a) Rome   (b) San Francisco   (c) Shanghai

Figure 4: The vehicles' betweenness is, in general, lower for the calibrated traces.

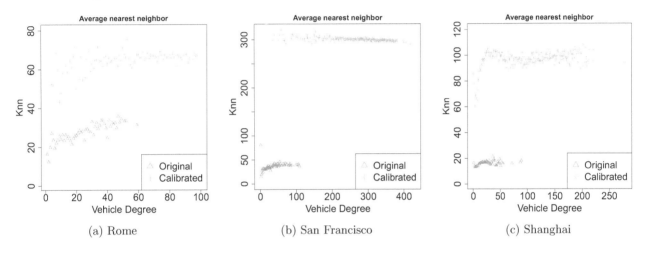

(a) Rome   (b) San Francisco   (c) Shanghai

Figure 5: The average nearest neighbor is also higher for the calibrated traces.

6. CONCLUSION AND FUTURE WORK

In this work, we showed that existing real vehicular mobility traces present temporal and spatial gaps. These gaps lead to network topologies that differ from reality and, consequently, to an unreliable performance evaluation. To tackle this problem, we proposed and evaluated a solution to find and fill the gaps by adopting a cluster-based reference system and a calibration method. The results revealed that our approach was able to fill properly the gaps, and that indeed the network topologies built from the calibrated traces differ significantly from the original ones. To contribute with the research community, we made the calibrated traces from three different cities publicly available.

As future work, we plan to fine-tune the calibration solution to avoid adding calibrated points outside roads caused by GPS errors in the traces. Furthermore, it is important to evaluate other clustering algorithms, as well as other strategies to build the reference system.

7. ACKNOWLEDGEMENT

This work is supported by NSERC, Canada Research Chair Program and NSERC-DIVA Strategic Research Network, by CNPq under grant 573.738/2008-4 (INCT NA-MITEC), and by CAPES under grant 99999.002061/2014-07.

8. REFERENCES

[1] R. Amici, M. Bonola, L. Bracciale, A. Rabuffi, P. Loreti, and G. Bianchi. Performance assessment of an epidemic protocol in VANET using real traces. In *Int'l Conference on Selected Topics in Mobile and Wireless Networking*, volume 40, pages 92–99, 2014.

[2] R. Baumann, S. Heimlicher, and M. May. Towards Realistic Mobility Models for Vehicular Ad-hoc Networks. In *IEEE Mobile Networking for Vehicular Environments*, pages 73–78, 2007.

[3] L. Bracciale, M. Bonola, P. Loreti, G. Bianchi, R. Amici, and A. Rabuffi. CRAWDAD data set roma/taxi (v. 2014-07-17). Downloaded from http://crawdad.org/roma/taxi/, July 2014.

[4] Y. Chen, M. Xu, Y. Gu, P. Li, and X. Cheng. Understanding topology evolving of vanets from taxi traces. *Advanced Science and Technology Letters*, 42(Mobile and Wireless):13–17, 2013.

[5] L. Cheng, B. Henty, D. Stancil, F. Bai, and P. Mudalige. Mobile vehicle-to-vehicle narrow-band

channel measurement and characterization of the 5.9 ghz dedicated short range communication (dsrc) frequency band. *IEEE Journal on Selected Areas in Communications*, 25(8):1501–1516, 2007.

[6] A. Cornejo, C. Newport, S. Gollakota, J. Rao, and T. J. Giuli. Prioritized gossip in vehicular networks. *Ad Hoc Networks*, 11(1):397–409, 2013.

[7] M. Fiore and J. Härri. The networking shape of vehicular mobility. In *Proc. of the 9th ACM international symposium on Mobile ad hoc networking and computing*, pages 261–272. ACM, 2008.

[8] M. Fiore, J. Harri, F. Filali, and C. Bonnet. Understanding vehicular mobility in network simulation. In *IEEE Internatonal Conference on Mobile Adhoc and Sensor Systems*, pages 1–6, 2007.

[9] M. Gao, T. Zhu, X. Wan, and Q. Wang. Analysis of travel time patterns in urban using taxi gps data. In *IEEE International Conference on Green Computing and Communications*, pages 512–517, 2013.

[10] A. Grzybek, M. Seredynski, G. Danoy, and P. Bouvry. Aspects and trends in realistic VANET simulations. In *IEEE International Symposium on a World of Wireless, Mobile and Multimedia Networks (WoWMoM)*, pages 1–6, June 2012.

[11] J. Harri, F. Filali, and C. Bonnet. Mobility models for vehicular ad hoc networks: a survey and taxonomy. *IEEE Communications Surveys & Tutorials*, 11(4):19–41, 2009.

[12] A. Hess and J. Ott. Extrapolating sparse large-scale gps traces for contact evaluation. In *ACM Workshop on HotPlanet*, pages 39–44, 2013.

[13] M. A. Hoque, X. Hong, and B. Dixon. Efficient multi-hop connectivity analysis in urban vehicular networks. *Vehicular Communications*, 1(2):78–90, 2014.

[14] X. Hou, Y. Li, D. Jin, D. Wu, and S. Chen. Modeling the impact of mobility on the connectivity of vehicular networks in large-scale urban environment. *IEEE Transactions on Vehicular Technology*, (99), 2015.

[15] H. Huang, D. Zhang, Y. Zhu, M. Li, and M.-Y. Wu. A metropolitan taxi mobility model from real gps traces. *Journal of Universal Computer Science*, 18(9):1072–1092, 2012.

[16] H. Huang, Y. Zhu, X. Li, M. Li, and M.-Y. Wu. Meta: A mobility model of metropolitan taxis extracted from gps traces. In *IEEE Wireless Communications and Networking Conference (WCNC)*, pages 1–6, 2010.

[17] S. Joerer, F. Dressler, and C. Sommer. Comparing apples and oranges? In *ACM International Workshop on Vehicular Inter-networking, Systems and Applications*, pages 27–32, New York, USA, 2012.

[18] A. Kesting, M. Treiber, , and D. Helbing. Connectivity statistics of store-and-forward intervehicle communication. *IEEE Transactions on Intelligent Transportation Systems*, 11(1):172–181, March 2010.

[19] C.-H. Lee, J. Kwak, and D. Y. Eun. Characterizing link connectivity for opportunistic mobile networking: Does mobility suffice? In *IEEE INFOCOM*, pages 2076–2084, 2013.

[20] M. Li, A. Ahmed, and A. J. Smola. Inferring movement trajectories from gps snippets. In *International Conference on Web Search and Data Mining (WSDM)*, 2015.

[21] S. Lloyd. Least squares quantization in pcm. *IEEE Trans. Inf. Theor.*, 28(2):129–137, Sept. 2006.

[22] V. Naumov, R. Baumann, and T. Gross. An evaluation of inter-vehicle ad hoc networks based on realistic vehicular traces. In *The 7th ACM International Symposium on Mobile Ad Hoc Networking and Computing (MobiHoc)*, pages 108–119, New York, NY, USA, May 2006.

[23] M. Piorkowski, N. Sarafijanovic-Djukic, and M. Grossglauser. CRAWDAD data set epfl/mobility (v. 2009-02-24). Downloaded from http://crawdad.org/epfl/mobility/, Feb. 2009.

[24] M. Piorkowski, N. Sarafijanovoc-Djukic, and M. Grossglauser. A Parsimonious Model of Mobile Partitioned Networks with Clustering. In *The First International Conference on COMmunication Systems and NETworkS (COMSNETS)*, January 2009.

[25] H. Su, K. Zheng, J. Huang, H. Wang, and X. Zhou. Calibrating trajectory data for spatio-temporal similarity analysis. *The International Journal on Very Large Data Bases (VLDB)*, 24(1):93–116, 2015.

[26] SUVnet. Shanghai data trace. Online (available at http://wirelesslab.sjtu.edu.cn/taxi_trace_data.html).

[27] R. L. Thorndike. Who belongs in the family? *Psychometrika*, 18(4):267–276, 1953.

[28] S. Uppoor, O. Trullols-Cruces, M. Fiore, and J. M. Barcelo-Ordinas. Generation and Analysis of a Large-Scale Urban Vehicular Mobility Dataset. *IEEE Transactions on Mobile Computing*, 13(5), 2014.

[29] Wisemap. Urban mobility. Available at www.wisemap.dcc.ufmg.br/urbanmobility, May 2015.

[30] C. Xia, D. Liang, H. Wang, M. Luo, and W. Lv. Characterization and modeling in large-scale urban DTNs. In *IEEE 37th Conference on Local Computer Networks (LCN)*, pages 352–359, 2012.

[31] L. Zhang, M. Ahmadi, J. Pan, and L. Chang. Metropolitan-scale taxicab mobility modeling. In *IEEE Global Communications Conference (GLOBECOM)*, pages 5404–5409, 2012.

[32] D. Zhao, H. Ma, L. Liu, and X.-Y. Li. Opportunistic coverage for urban vehicular sensing. *Computer Communications*, 60:71–85, 2015.

[33] H. Zhu, M. Li, S. Member, L. Fu, and G. Xue. Impact of Traffic Influxes: Revealing Exponential Intercontact Time in Urban VANETs. *IEEE Transactions on Parallel and Distributed Systems*, 22(8):1258–1266, 2011.

Rendezvous in Cognitive Radio Ad-Hoc Networks with Channel Ranking

Md Akbar Hossain [*]
School of Computer and
Mathematical Sciences
Auckland University of Technology (AUT)
Auckland, New Zealand
akbar.hossain@aut.ac.nz

Nurul I Sarkar
School of Computer and
Mathematical Sciences
Auckland University of Technology (AUT)
Auckland, New Zealand
nurul.sarkar@aut.ac.nz

ABSTRACT

In distributed cognitive radio (CR) networks, rendezvous (RDV) is one of the most critical issues. Due to the dynamic radio environment, achieving RDV on a predetermined common control channel (CCC) is a challenging task. Channel hopping (CH) provides an effective method to guarantee RDV in cognitive radio ad-hoc networks (CRAHNs). Most of the existing CH schemes utilize the channel quantity as an input to the family of mathematical concepts such as prime number theory, Chinese remainder theory (CRT), quorum system and combinatorial block design to achieve RDV. However, RDV on a channel is rather influenced by channel quality or CR user's preference on which it wants to achieve RDV on available channels. Based on this philosophy, a channel rank based torus quorum CH RDV protocol (TQCH) is proposed which finds a commonly available channel between a pair of CR nodes. We formulate the channel ranking as a linear optimisation problem based on the channel availability under collision constraints. A detailed mathematical formulation is derived to estimate the degree of overlap in terms of expected quorum overlap size. Simulation results show that the proposed TQCH scheme outperforms than that of other CH schemes in terms of average time-to-rendezvous (ATTR) and the degree of overlap in asymmetric channel scenario.

Categories and Subject Descriptors

C.2 [**COMPUTER-COMMUNICATION NETWORKS**]: Miscellaneous; C.2.2 [**Network Protocols**]: Metrics—*Applications (SMTP, FTP, etc.), Protocol architecture, Protocol verification*

---

[*]Md Akbar is corresponding author

MSWiM'15, November 2–6, 2015, Cancun, Mexico.
© 2015 ACM. ISBN 978-1-4503-3762-5/15/11 ...$15.00.
DOI: http://dx.doi.org/10.1145/2811587.2811607.

Keywords

Rendezvous; Torus Quorum; Cognitive Radio; Channel Ranking

1. INTRODUCTION

The increasing demand for new wireless services and applications, as well as the increasing demand for higher capacity wireless networks, the wireless networks become highly heterogeneous, with mobile devices consisting of multiple radio interfaces. In this context, CR approach is one of the most promising concepts to realize DSA which facilitate the flexible usage of radio spectrum by changing its transmission parameters based on interaction with the multichannel wireless environment[13]. In multi-channel wireless ad-hoc environment, RDV is the first key step for CR users to be able to communicate each other. RDV in CRAHNs is analogous to control channel establishment in traditional multi-channel wireless ad-hoc networks. To achieve RDV, a CCC is often used as a common platform to exchange control information. The CCC based RDV protocols are studied in [16, 12, 17, 7] to exchange the common available channel list and control information. Unfortunately these protocols do not suite with CRAHNs because of (i) unable to protect incumbent users (ii) channel saturation and Single point failure problem (iii) complex and expensive to maintain both global and local CCC and (iv) control channel jamming issue. To overcome the shortcoming of CCC based RDV, node ID based CH protocols are proposed in [3, 15, 10]. These protocols exploits the frequency diversity and generate a CH sequence by using a set of (channel, node ID) pairs. However, in order to achieve RDV, a designed CH sequence should have two fundamental characteristics [4]: Guaranteed time to rendezvous (TTR) i.e. overlap between sender and degree of overlap in a hopping period. Permutation is one of the methods which integrate these desired properties in the CH sequence [6]. A protocol based on similar concept is presented in [9], where a sequential CH sequence is designed in both frequency and time domain. However, RDV only achieved if both CR users observe same set of channels. Unfortunately, the channel availability of CR nodes are tightly coupled with their geographic locations and sensing capability. The authors in [11] proposed jump-stay based CH algorithm for both symmetric and asymmetric models without exploiting the time synchronization. Due to random channel mapping TTR grows dramatically with the number of available channels. Hence, the timeslots assignment on a given channel is not uniform and is a function of the LUs' activity [5]. The robustness against LUs' activity can be achieved by profiling (ranking) the available channels based on local channel sensing information. Only two CH sequences; AMRCC [5] and gQ-RDV [14] can be found in the existing literatures that consider channel quality to design CH sequence. Both of these protocols can guarantee RDV with symmetric channel information however; there is no guarantee that they can achieve RDV on each available common channel with asymmetric channel information.

In this paper, we propose an asymmetric asynchronous channel hopping scheme which utilize the torus quorum concept together with channel ranking information called torus quorum channel hopping (TQCH). Our approach utilizes the mathematical concept of extended torus quorum systems with rotation closure property to generate CH sequences that enable RDV on multiple channels. Moreover, the TQCH scheme integrates the channel sensing information to assign the quorums (i.e. timeslots). The main contributions of our work are as follows:

- A Channel ranking based CH scheme called TQCH for asymmetric and asynchronous pairwise RDV in CRAHNs is proposed.

- We integrate the physical layer channel information to design the CH sequence. We analyse the channel ranking as a linear optimisation problem and sort the channel based on average channel availability times and collision probability.

- An adaptive channel access strategy is proposed to protect the incumbent PU users.

- A detail mathematical formulation is derived to calculate the expected quorum overlap size for the proposed TQCH protocol.

The rest of the paper is organized as follows: In section 2, we define the RDV problem in CRAHNs. In section 3 a channel occupancy model is analysed using a Markov model. A detail description of channel hopping sequence generation is presented in section 4 which includes torus grid formation, channel mapping and an adaptive CH strategy in case of sudden PU reappearance. Channel ranking is presented in section 5. A detailed mathematical formulation to estimate the expected quorum overlap size of TQCH protocol is described in section 6. Simulation is performed to measure the performance of TQCH protocol in section 7. Results show that, CH sequence with channel ranking can guarantee to achieve RDV on number of available channels. We conclude our work in section 8.

2. PROBLEM DEFINITION

Rendezvous in CRAHNs is corresponds to the telephone coordination game [2], where two players are placed in two separate rooms each with n telephone lines. There is a one-to-one matching between the lines in two rooms, and players can use matched lines to connect each other; the matching is not known to either of the players. In every round each player can select a line in his room and see whether it connects with the line chosen by another user, provided that users do not have any prior agreement of choosing a line. The goal is to design a strategy for players to get connected

while minimizing the number of trail rounds. The same coordination game can be applied in CRAHNs to describe the RDV problem with few additional constraints.

In CR ad-hoc networks, each CR node performs primary user detection process to exploit unoccupied channels in its vicinity. An assumption is often made that there is a common set of available channels known to all CR nodes. But this information is to be independently obtained by individual radios by channel sensing. It is unlikely that two independently sensed sets of vacant frequencies will be identical. Let consider, there are $P \geq 2$ CR users in the network, who share the set of available licensed channels, such as $(0, X[0]), (1, X[1]), ..., (T-1, X[T-1])$ and $(0, Y[0]), (1, Y[1]), ..., (T-1, Y[T-1])$. Hence, RDV sequences must have overlapped property in order to ensure any pair of nodes can establish communication. Fig. 1 illustrates the overlapping property of different RDV sequences where user A and B achieve RDV at time slot 2 and user B and User C in time slot $T-1$. Having fairness among RDV channels is another most important requirement of any RDV sequences. Otherwise, the control channel bottleneck problem would rise due to same channel assignment in most of the time slots in CH sequence. Furthermore, in an asynchronous system node may starts its channel hopping at different times, which impose shift RDV requirements on CH sequences which is shown in the bottom part of Fig. 1, where user C and User D achieve RDV at time slot 3 for user C but at time slot 2 for user D. Therefore, the apparent randomness of the hopping sequence is not an essential requirement for RDV purposes rather deterministic hopping patterns turn out to be entirely sufficient for the purpose of achieving frequency RDV in cognitive radio networks (CRNs).

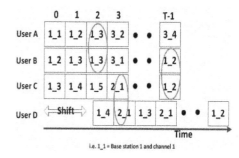

Figure 1: Illustration of rendezvous in CRAHNs

3. SYSTEM MODEL

According to the definition of CR, channel that is currently used for data transmission or RDV process by any CR users would become unavailable if PU reappear on that particular channel. Therefore, it is important to take into consideration of PU reappearance during the hopping period or RDV period of CR users. We use Continuous Time Markov Chain (CTMC) to model the PU user activity as shown in Fig. 2. We assume that, there are N CR users operating in $L = f_1, f_2, f_3, ..., f_m$ licensed channels if they are not occupied by PUs. The service request of both PUs and CR users modeled as a Poisson process with rate λ_P and $\lambda_{CR}S^{-1}$ and is terminated with rate μ_p and μ_{CR}. Moreover, we assume that a channel cannot be used by more than one user simultaneously. Therefore each channel can be in one of the states shown in Fig. 2: Idle state, PU state and CR state. An idle state indicates that channel is not being used by any users at this time instant. The channel state will move from idle to PU or CR state if it is used by any PUs or CR_i. In CRN, the PU has a license to operate in the channel and should not be interfered with CR transmission. Hence, the channel state will move from CR state to PU state but it is not possible to have a transition from PU to CR state. Let $x = 0, P, CR_1, CR_2, ...CR_N$ be the $(N + 2)$ element space vector of for the CTMC model and Q is the transition matrix specified in equation 1.

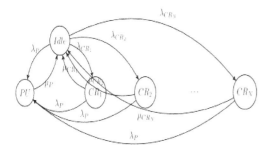

Figure 2: Channel state transition diagram

Let $\pi^m(t) = [\pi_1^m(t), \pi_2^m(t), \pi_3^m(t), ..., \pi_N^m(t), \pi_P^m(t)]$ be the steady state distribution for channel m. The ith element of $\pi^m(t)$ is given by $\pi_i^m(t) = P[x(t) = i], \forall i \in X$. To analyse the steady state behavior, it is assumed that channel are in ON condition for long time to achieve the steady state values. Hence the steady state probability of state i can be written as $\pi^m = \lim_{t\to\infty} \pi_i^m(t)$. Now, the steady state probability vector π can be obtained by solving following steady state equations 2 and 3:

$$\sum_i \pi_i^m \mathbf{Q}_{ij}^m = 0; \forall j \tag{2}$$

$$\sum_{\forall i \in X} \pi_i^m = 1 \tag{3}$$

where, $\mathbf{Q}_{ij}^m$ is the product of the rate to leave state i and the probability of transition to state j form state i which is the rate of transition from i to j. By using Eqn. 2 and 3, a system of linear equation can be derived in Eqn.(4-6) as follows:

$$\pi_0^m (\lambda_1^m + \lambda_2^m + \lambda_3^m + ... + \lambda_N^m + \lambda_P^m) + \pi_1^m \mu_1^m + \pi_2^m \mu_2^m +$$
$$+ \pi_3^m \mu_3^m + ... + \pi_N^m \mu_N^m + \pi_P^m \mu_P^m = 0 \tag{4}$$

$$\pi_0^m \lambda_i^m - \pi_0^m (\mu_i^m + \lambda_i^m) = 0, (1 \le i \le N) \tag{5}$$

$$(\pi_1^m + \pi_2^m + \pi_3^m + ... + \pi_N^m) \lambda_P^m - \pi_P^m \mu_P^m = 0 \tag{6}$$

After a series of arithmetic manipulation π_i^m can be written as:

$$\pi_i^m = \frac{\lambda_i^m}{(\mu_i^m + \lambda_P^m)} \pi_0^m; where \; \pi_0^m = \frac{\mu_P^m}{(\mu_P^m + \lambda_P^m)\left(1 + \sum_{i=1}^N \frac{\lambda_i^m}{(\mu_i^m + \lambda_P^m)}\right)} \pi_P^m = \frac{\lambda_P^m}{(\mu_P^m + \lambda_P^m)}$$

Hence, the design challenge of CH algorithm is to generate hopping sequence which can guarantee to achieve RDV within finite time, if they (CR users) have at least one common channel. In addition to that, CH algorithm is able to avoid or reduce RDV collisions among CR users and regenerate the sequence with PUs activity.

4. CHANNEL HOPPING SEQUENCE GENERATION

In this section, we propose a systematic approach to generate channel hopping sequence based on the quorum system for a RDV in CRAHNs without the assumption of global clock synchronization. In our proposal, we integrate the channel heterogeneity (symmetric and asymmetric channel information) between CR users, channel status variation due to PUs activity and collision among CR users. The sequence is used by each node to decide the order in which the available channels are to be visited. The proposed approach is called channel ranking based Channel Hopping (**TQCH**) system, can be used for implementing RDV protocols in DSA networks that are robust against link breakage caused by the appearance of incumbent user signals.In this section, we provide a brief introduction of quorum systems and its properties.

Definition 1: Quorum System: Let us assume a finite universal set $S = \{0, 1, ...n - 1\}$ of n elements, where n also represents the cycle length. A quorum system Q under universal set S is a collection of non-empty subsets of S, provided that it satisfies the intersection property: $\forall X, Y \in Q : X \bigcap Y \neq 0$. For example $Q = \{\{a, b\}, \{a, c\}, \{b, c\}\}$ is a quorum system under $S = \{a, b, c\}$. The fundamental idea of the CH scheme in CRAHNs is design hopping sequences so that two different nodes can achieve RDV which is analogous to quorum system where two subsets have at least one intersection. A CH sequence determines the order with which a node visits all available channels. We represent a CH sequence u of period T as a set of channel indexes: $u = \{u_0, u_1, ..., u_i, ..., u_{(T-1)}\}$,where $u_i \in [0, N-1]$ represents the channel index of sequence u in the ith timeslot of a CH period. Given two CH sequences of period T, u and v,if $\exists i \in [0, T-1]$ s.t. $u_i = v_i = h$, where $h \in [0, N-1]$, we say that u and v RDV in the ith time slot on channel h. The ith time slot is called the RDV slot and channel h is called the RDV channel between u and v. Given N channels, let $C(u, v)$ denote the number of rendezvous channels between two CH sequences u and v, and $C(u, v) \in [0, N]$.

Definition 2: Torus Grid Quorum System: A torus grid of size $h \times w$ consists of a rectangular array of h rows and w columns, in which for $1 \le i \le h - 1$, row i is followed by row $i + 1$, and row h is followed by row 1 using wraparound. Similarly, for $1 \le j \le w - 1$, column j is followed by column $j + 1$, and column w is followed by column 1 using wraparound. A torus quorum in an $h \times w$ torus grid is a set of $h + \left\lfloor \frac{w}{2} \right\rfloor$ timeslots, consisting of one entire column (say, $column_j$), plus one slot out of each of the $\left\lfloor \frac{w}{2} \right\rfloor$ column following row i and column $j + 1$ using end wraparound. We call the column portion of a quorum its head, and the portion consisting of one slot from each $\left\lfloor \frac{w}{2} \right\rfloor$ succeeding columns the quorum's tail. In our proposal, we assigned three tails instead of one in the former approach to achieve the RDV in best channels. Hence, it becomes a torus quorum in an hw torus grid is a set of $h + 3 \times \left\lfloor \frac{w}{2} \right\rfloor$ timeslots as quorum size.

4.1 Grid Formation and Quorum Selection

In this section, we present the torus quorum based channel hopping algorithm. Our algorithm generates a CH sequence based on available channel information to use for data transmission. At the very first stage upon joining in the network, a CR node will perform periodic sensing and ranked the available channel based on PU activity. Using this channel information, a CR node will generate a torus grid of $h \times w$ where $w = 2 \times h - 1$ dimension as shown in Fig. 3. Here h represents the number of available channels observed by a CR suer. Each number inside the grid represents a time slot. When a CR node receives a packet from an upper layer, it will generate a torus grid quorum as shown in Fig. 3 and select a column based on channel ranking list and three associated diagonals (2 positive and and 1 negative diagonal) is described in algorithm 1.

Now, let us consider the number of available channels,$avail_{CH} = 5$ i.e. $h = 5$. Also assumed that channels are ranked (i.e.5/4/2/1/3) based on QoS. The channel ranking procedure is presented in sec-

$$\mathbf{Q} = \begin{bmatrix} -(\lambda_1 + \lambda_2 + \cdots + \lambda_N + \lambda_P) & \lambda_1 & \lambda_2 & \cdots & \lambda_N & \lambda_P \\ \mu_1 & -(\mu_1 + \lambda_P) & 0 & \cdots & 0 & \lambda_P \\ \mu_2 & 0 & -(\mu_2 + \lambda_P) & \cdots & 0 & \lambda_P \\ \vdots & \vdots & \vdots & \ddots & \vdots & \\ \mu_N & 0 & 0 & \cdots & -(\mu_1 + \lambda_P) & \lambda_P \\ \mu_P & 0 & 0 & \cdots & 0 & -\lambda_P \end{bmatrix} \qquad (1)$$

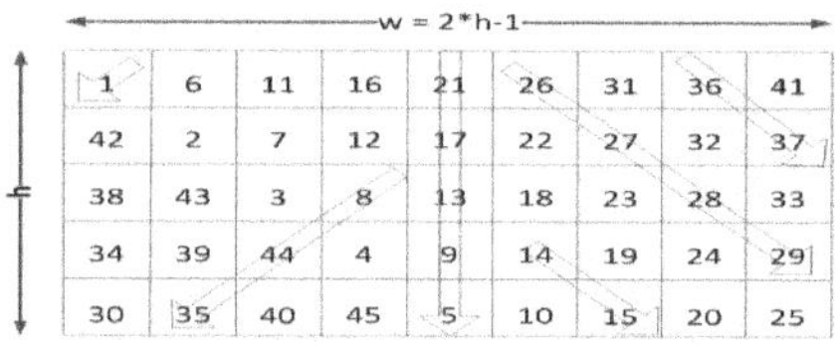

Figure 3: Time slot assignment and quorum selection in torus grid structure

tion 8. Hence, a CR node will generate 5×9 torus grid and assign the timeslots as per line 7 of the algorithm 1 which is shown in Fig. 3. The complete CH sequence is generated by line 4 of the algorithm 1. The column and three diagonals are shown by arrows in fig. 3. The idea is to assign more time slots for the best channel and decrease gradually. We also assume, it is highly probable that neighboring nodes experience similar channel quality indicator (CQI) across the channels which implies high correlation among their channel ranking tables and, consequently, between their hopping sequences.

4.2 Channel Mapping

At any time CR node has data to send, it first discovers the intended receiver. Under the discovery process or RDV process CR transmitting node performs radio scanning to gather available channel information. The channel information might be different for intended transmitter and receiver due to fading and geographical location. However, they should have at least one common channel to establish communication. In this context, both sender and receiver node will create an array of $h \times w$ elements, where h is the number of available channels of each CR user and $w = 2 * h - 1$. Suppose, we have 5 channels available which would become 5×9 grid having 45 elements. Each of the grid elements is treated as time slots starting from 1 to 45. Each node maps its channels according to CQI which is not necessarily be same for sender and receiver. CQI includes signal to noise ratio (ratio), Bit Error Rate (BER) or channel utilization (not frequently used by licensed users). Channel ranking procedure is discussed in section 5. Let us consider CR_X has channel lists as per CQI, $C5/C3/C1/C2/C4$, C5 (channel 5) is best, and C3 is second best and so on. CR_Y might have the channel lists $C5/C1/C4/C3/C2$. The idea of the proposed protocol is to spend more time on the best channel and decreases accordingly. At first the best channel is mapped to chosen quorum with highest quorum size. The CR node will choose the column according to the channel index as it is described in line 6 of algorithm 2 and 3-diagonal branches as per algorithm 1. The resulting time slots are assigned to the best channel. In our example node X and Y will both choose the same time slots for C5 as it is the best channel for both of them which are 1,5,8,9,13,14,15,17,21,26,27,28,29,35,36,37,44.

Each time when a set element is chosen, a torus grid is cut to a sub-grid, together with the already mapped channel. Such as, 1, 5, 8, 9, 13, 14, 15, 17, 21, 26, 27, 28, 29, 35, 36, 37, 44 total 17 timeslots will be cut out from the grid and form a new grid which would become 4×7 grid with 28 timeslots in it. The interesting part is, every time the new sub-grid would be another grid with rest of channel numbers. This is the inherent property of our proposed torus protocol and is valid for 3 or more than 3 channels available. Otherwise, a CR node will select the timeslots analogous to the row-column based quorum selection.Therefore, two nodes

---

Algorithm 1 Torus Grid Formation

Input: (i) Number of available channels, m;

(ii) Transmission flag, $Flag_{Tx}$;

(iii) Rescan period, T_{out};

Output:
Grid with 3 diagonals (2 positive and 1 negative).

Begin
1: **while** $mod(t, T_{out}) = 0$ **do**
2: $\quad [Avail_{CH}]$; {Available Channel Set}
3: $\quad$ Rank($[Avail_{CH}]$) $= [CH_{List}]$
4: $\quad h = \mid Avail_{CH} \mid$
5: $\quad w = 2 \times h - 1$
6: $\quad$ Generate $h \times w$ Torus Grid
7: $\quad T_{slots}(r, c) = ((r \times avail_{CH}) - ((avail_{CH} - 1) * c))\%(avail_{CH} \times (2 * avail_{CH} - 1));$ {Timeslots assignment in the torus grid}
8: **end while**
9: **while** packets arrive **do**
10: $\quad q \leftarrow q + 1$
11: $\quad m \in [1 : w]$
12: $\quad$ **for** $Diag = 1 : 3$ **do**
13: $\qquad$ **for** $i = \lfloor \frac{w}{2} \rfloor$ **do**
14: $\qquad\quad 1_{Diag}(i) = [r((i) \bmod h); c((m + i) \bmod W)]$
15: $\qquad\quad$ **if** r is ODD **then**
16: $\qquad\qquad 2_{Diag}(i) = [r(h - 2 + i) \bmod h); c((m + i) \bmod W)]$
17: $\qquad\qquad 3_{Diag}(i) = [r(\lfloor \frac{h}{2} \rfloor + i) \bmod h); c((m + i) \bmod W)]$
18: $\qquad\quad$ **else if** r is $EVEN$ **then**
19: $\qquad\qquad 2_{Diag}(i) = [r(h - 2 + i) \bmod h); c((m + i) \bmod W)]$
20: $\qquad\qquad 3_{Diag}(i) = [r(\lfloor \frac{h}{2} \rfloor + i) \bmod h); c((m + i) \bmod W)]$
21: $\qquad\quad$ **end if**
22: $\qquad$ **end for**
23: $\quad$ **end for**
24: **end while**
End

---

having same best channel will always meet thanks to rotation closure property of torus quorum system. To introduce the asynchronous scenario, we assume CR_X clock is $K < n(n = h \times w)$ times ahead to clock CR_Y but the time slots are aligned. It is very easy to prove that still CR_X and CR_Y can achieved RDV within bounded time due to rotation closure property of the torus quorum system.

Definition 3:Rotation Closure Property (RCP): For a quorum H in a quorum system Q under $U = \{0, ..., n - 1\}$ and a non-negative integer $i \in \{1, 2, ..., n - 1\}$, we define $rotate(H, i) = \{(j + i) \bmod n \mid j \in H\}$. A quorum system Q is said to have the rotation closure property if $\forall H', H \in q, i \in \{1, 2, ...n - 1\}$: $H' \bigcap H \neq 0$.

For instance, the quorum system $Q = \{\{0, 1\}, \{0, 2\}, \{0, 2\}\}$ under $U = \{0, 1, 2\}$ satisfies RCP. However, the quorum system $Q' = \{\{0, 1\}, \{0, 2\}, \{0, 3\}, \{1, 2, 3\}\}$ under $U = \{0, 1, 2\}$ has no RCP since $\{0, 1\} \bigcap rotate(\{0, 3\}, 3) = 0$.

Theorem 1: A torus quorum system satisfies the rotation closure property. *Proof:* Let Q be a torus formed by a $h \times w$ array and $H \in Q$ be a quorum containing column c. By the definition of torus quorum, H also contains another 3 branches of $\lfloor \frac{h}{2} \rfloor$ elements. Each of the branches consists of $\lfloor \frac{h}{2} \rfloor$ elements, each from

Algorithm 2 Channel Mapping

Input: (i) Available channel $avail_{CH}$;

    (ii) Channel index CH_i;

    (iii) Channel list, CH_{List};

Output(i) Channel map CH_{map};

    (ii) Channel timeslots CH_{t_slots};

Begin

1: **for** map = 1:$avail_{CH} - 2$ **do**

2:     $CH_{t\_slots} = Grid(:,(CH_{List}(map) mod(2 * avail_{CH} - 1)))$

3:     $Algorithm1$

4:     $GRID(CH_{t\_slots}) = [\ ]$

5:     **if** $avail_{CH} = 2$ **then**

6:         $CH_{t\_slots} = [Grid(:,CH_i mod(length(column)))'$
                        $Grid(CH_i mod(length(row)),:)]$

7:         $GRID(CH_{t\_slots}) = [\ ]$

8:     **else**

9:         $CH_{t\_slots} = Grid(CH_{t\_slots})$

10:    **end if**

11: **end for**

End

Number of Channel = 5							
1	6	11	16	21	26	31	36	41
42	2	7	12	17	22	27	32	37
38	43	3	8	13	18	23	28	33
34	39	44	4	9	14	19	24	29
30	35	40	45	5	10	15	20	25

Number of Channel = 4						
2	3	4	6	7	10	11
12	16	18	19	20	26	27
28	29	30	31	32	33	34
38	39	40	41	42	43	45

Number of Channel = 3				
3	4	7	11	12
16	18	26	28	29
32	34	38	40	43

Number of Channel = 2		
4	12	16
18	32	40

Number of Channel = 1	
4	16

Figure 4: Channel assignment at different time slots according to algorithm 2

one of the $\left\lfloor \frac{h}{2} \right\rfloor$ succeeding columns of c and wrap around. Hence it is obvious, $rotate(H,i)$ still has the torus quorum structure for an arbitrary i. That means that it follows the rotation closure property $\forall H', H \in q, i \in \{1, 2, ...n - 1\} : H' \bigcap H \neq 0$. Suppose $H = \{1, 5, 8, 9 13, 14, 15, 17, 21, 26, 27, 28, 29, 35, 36, 37, 44\}$ is quorum under $Q = 1 : 45$ and $H' = rotate(H, 2) = \{1, 3, 7, 9, 10, 11, 15, 16, 19, 23, 28, 29, 30, 31, 37, 38, 39\}$ which follows the rotation closure property as $H' \bigcap H = \{1, 9, 15, 28, 29, 37\}$

4.3 An Adaptive CH Strategy

Before joining in the network, a CR node starts channel sensing and create channel list according to channel ranking. Using the algorithm1, the CR node will generate CH sequence. In this research, we have considered two radio transceivers architecture: a) Rendezvous Radio (RDV-Radio) and b) Data Radio (D-Radio). RDV-Radio is used for established and maintain RDV for data communication including control information exchange. A CR node uses the data radio for data transmission. During the network set up phase, A CR node selects the channel from CH sequence and sense using D-Radio. If the channel is sensed idle for a distributed coordination function inter-frame space (DIFS) interval, implying that currently there are no ongoing transmissions over the channel, the CR node initiates a request-to-send (RTS) transmission using RDV-Radio. If no clear-to-send (CTS) is received after a short inter-frame space (SIFS) interval, it continues channel hopping. Notice that it is also possible that the transmitted RTS/CTS is lost in the error-prone wireless channel or due to hidden terminal problems in a multi-hop network. If

the channel condition between a CR pairs is below threshold, it is preferable not to start data transmission in the first place. In addition, with multiple channels operating in parallel, the collision probability on any of these channels is greatly reduced. Therefore, when a CR node sends an RTS but receives no CTS after an SIFS, most likely, the corresponding destination does not access the same channel at this moment. Thus, the CR node should switch to a different channel. If CTS is received after an SIFS, which means that the corresponding destination also accesses the channel at this time, after the successful handshake, the CR node starts data transmissions to its destination using D-Radio. If the channel is sensed busy, which implies that the current channel is occupied by other CR node pairs, the CR node will modify the channel hopping sequence by replacing the busy channel with the last RDV channel. If there is no RDV achieved so far, the busy channel will replaced by the best channel from channel list for rest of the hopping sequence. The Fig. 6 presented below illustrate the channel access strategy.

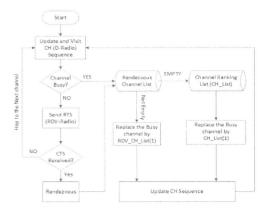

Figure 5: Channel hopping update

Assume we have channel sequence

2	2	4	4	4	1	1	3	3	4	2

At any time of RDV process channel 1 becomes busy. Then the busy channel would be replaced by channel 2 assuming CR established RDV in channel 2 in previous cycle. Therefore, the updated CH sequence would be:

2	2	4	4	4	2	2	3	3	4	2

Otherwise, the busy channel will replace by the channel in the top of the channel ranking list. Assuming channel 4 is in the top of channel rank.

2	2	4	4	4	4	4	3	3	4	2

5. CHANNEL RANKING

In this paper, we consider channel sorting problem as convex combination of linear optimization problem as described in [1]. The objective of the optimization problem is to maximize a weighted sum of the channel average availability times and channel sojourn times. As we described in section 4.2, channel mapping is fundamentally based on channel rank. Maximum timeslots are assigned to the channel with higher rank or high weighted channel. Probability of collision with PUs and other SUs are considered as the constraints of this optimization problem. Equation 7 described the constraints of the optimization problem for our torus quorum structure. The left side of equation 2 has four parts; one for the column and rest of the part for three different diagonals. $p_u(1,s)$ is the probability that the channel will

move from the idle state (i.e. state 1) to state s in quorum slot u. $1 - p_u(1, s)$ is the probability that the channel state will not change during slot u. $\prod (1 - p_u(1, s))$ is the probability that the channel state will not change during any of the quorum slots of a particular quorum. $1 - \prod (1 - p_u(1, s))$ is the probability that the channel state will change (i.e., will no longer stay idle) during at least one of the slots that belong to a particular quorum. Hence, $1 - \prod (1 - p_u(1, s))$ is the prob. of collision with a PU (when $s = 2$) or another SU (when s = 3). Now, note that channel sensing occurs at the beginning of a grid. Taking into account the processing time for assigning the probabilities and assigning the channels, this sensing can be used for the next grid, not the current grid. This is why n is added to each index. That means whenever a quorum starts, its channel has been already assigned during the previous quorum. In our work, n is considered as an individual total timeslots rather considering as a global system parameter like in [1]. Here n is the length of RDV cycle or number of timeslots which is depends on no. of available channels. In asymmetric channel scenario, node would experiences different no. of channels and has different cycle length. Hence, channel sorting would also different due to collision probability. To perform channel sorting, we consider the average availability times of a channel in the idle state and maximize it with weighted sum of $w_m(0 \leq w_m \geq 1)$ for each channel. This is the objective function of the linear programming problem presented in Eqn. 7.
LP1:

$$w = \underset{(w_1, w_2, \ldots, w_L)}{\text{maximize}} \{ \mathbf{C(w)} \overset{\text{def}}{=} \sum_{m=1}^{L} \pi_1^{(m)} w_m \}$$

subject to

$$\left[1 - \prod_{i=1}^{h} \left(1 - p_{(n+mi)T}^{(m)}(1, S) \right) \prod_{i=1}^{\lfloor \frac{w}{2} \rfloor} (1 -$$

$$p_{(n + (x(1+i) \bmod h).y((m+i) \bmod w))}^{(m)}(1, s)) \prod_{i=1}^{\lfloor \frac{w}{2} \rfloor} (1 -$$

$$p_{(n + (x(1+i) \bmod h).y((m-i) \bmod w))}^{(m)}(1, s)) \prod_{i=1}^{\lfloor \frac{w}{2} \rfloor} (1 -$$

$$p_{(n + (x(\lfloor \frac{h}{2} \rfloor + i) \bmod h).y((m+i) \bmod w))}^{(m)}(1, s)) \right] w_m < \lambda_s^{(m)} col(n)$$

$$\forall s \{K, P\}, \forall m \in \{1, 2, \ldots, L\}, K \in \{1, 2, 3, \ldots, N\}$$

$$\sum_{m=1}^{L} w_m = 1; 0 \leq w_m \leq 1, \forall m \in \{1, 2, \ldots, L\}$$

$$(7)$$

Table 1: Channel Ranking

Channel	CH1	CH2	CH3	CH4	CH5	CH6	CH7	CH8
π_1^m	0.657	0.700	0.482	0.742	0.378	0.396	0.254	0.211
CHANNEL RANK								
Rank	1	2	3	4	5	6	7	8
Channel	CH4	CH2	CH1	CH3	CH6	CH5	CH7	CH8

6. EXPECTED QUORUM OVERLAP SIZE (EQOS) OF TQCH SEQUENCE

Suppose Q and Q' are the torus quorum system formed according to quorum formation rule describe in section 4.1, where Q contains all elements of column C and Q' contains all elements of column C'. We define d, the distance between C and C', is $min((C' - C) \bmod w, (C - C') \bmod w)$. It is noted that in the following analysis, let $E(h, i, j)$ be the expected number of the

common members of two independently chosen subsets of a set of h elements, where the first and the second subsets, respectively contain i and j elements. By the knowledge of combinatorics and applied probability, we can derive that $E(h, i, j) = (i \times j)/h^2$ when i and j are equal in size. For asymmetric scenario, where the number of elements are not chosen from the same universal set, $E(h, k, i, j)$ is the expected number of elements common to both samples. If we assume that $H = 1, 2,, h$ and $K = 1, 2,, k$, and if i elements are chosen (uniformly and without replacement) from H and j elements are chosen (uniformly and without replacement) from K, then $E(h, k, i, j) = (i \times j \ min(h, k))/(h \times k) = (i \times j)/(max(h, k))$ this is obtained by adding, for each $n \in 1, 2,, min(h, k)$, the probability that n is chosen in both samples. Let $K_r = \lceil \frac{K}{2} \rceil$, $K_l = \lfloor \frac{K}{2} \rfloor$, $K_r' = \lceil \frac{K'}{2} \rceil$, $K_l' = \lfloor \frac{K'}{2} \rfloor$, $W_r = \lceil \frac{W}{2} \rceil$, $W_l = \lfloor \frac{W}{2} \rfloor$, $W_r' = \lceil \frac{W'}{2} \rceil$, $W_l' = \lfloor \frac{W'}{2} \rfloor - 1$. According to the proposal of torus quorum system $K = 3$, hence $K_r = K_r' = 2$ and $K_l = K_l' = 1$.

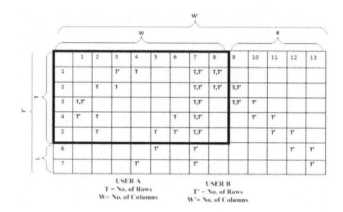

Figure 6: Torus quorum system

- *Case 1:* $d = 0$; this means user A and user B on the same column; $L = 0$; $R = 0$, which reflects that user A and B have same number channels in the channel list. The expected overlap size between Q_A and Q_B is

$$O_1 = T + E(T, K_r, K_r').W_r + E(T, K_l, K_l').W_l \quad (8)$$

- *Case 2:* $d = 0; L \geq 1, R \geq 1$; this means user A and user B have asymmetric channel information but they are not on the same column; Hence the expected quorum overlap size is $L = 0$; $R = 0$, which reflects that user A and B have same number channels in the channel list. The expected overlap size between Q_A and Q_B is
$$O_2 = min(T, T') + E(T, T', K_r, K_r').W_r + E(T, T', K_l, K_l') \\ \cdot W_l$$
$$(9)$$

- *Case 3(1):* $1 \leq d \leq W_r$; here $d = (C' - C) \bmod W$; $L = 0$, $R = 0$.The overlap of quorums have size of:
$$O_{31} = (d-1).E(T, K_r, K_r') + (W_r - d).E(T, K_r, K_r') + \\ d.E(T, K_l, K_r') + (W_l - d)E(T, K_l, K_r') + K_l' + K_r$$
$$(10)$$

- *Case 3(2):* $1 \leq d < W_r$; here $d = (C' - C) \bmod W$; $L = 0$, $R = 0$.The overlap of quorums have size of:
$$O_{32} = (d-1).E(T, K_l, K_r') + (W_r - d).E(T, K_r, K_r') + \\ d.E(T, K_r, K_l') + (W_l - d)E(T, K_l, K_l') + K_l + K_r'$$
$$(11)$$

- *Case 4(1):* $1 : n < d$; here $d = (C' - C) \bmod W$; $n = T - T', L \geq 1$, $R \geq 1$.The overlap size is:
$$O_{41} = (d-1).E(T, T', K_r, K_l') + (W_r - d).E(T, T', K_r, K_r') + \\ d.E(T, T', K_l, K_r') + (W_l - d)E(T, T', K_l, K_l') + K_l' + K_r$$
$$(12)$$

- *Case 4(2):1 : $n < d$; here $d = (C' - C) \bmod W$; $n = T - T', L \geq 1, R \geq 1$.The overlap size is:*
  $O_{42} = (d-1).E(\overline{T}, T', K_l, K_r') + (W_r - d).E(T, T', K_r, K_r') +$
  $\qquad d.E(T, T', K_r, K_l') + (W_l - d)E(T, T', K_l, K_l') + K_l + K_r'$
  $$(13)$$

- *Case 4(3):1 : $n < d$; here $d = (C - C') \bmod W$; $n = T - T', L \geq 1, R \geq 1$.Assume C' is outside of W but inside W'. The overlap size is:*
  $O_{43} = (d-1).E(T, T', K_r, K_l') + (W_r' - d).E(T, T', K_r, K_r') +$
  $\qquad d.E(T, T', K_l, K_r') + (W_l' - d)E(T, T', K_l, K_l') + K_l'$
  $$(14)$$

- *Case 5(1):$n \leq d < W_r$; here $d = (C' - C) \bmod W$; $n = T - T', L \geq 1, R \geq 1$. The overlap size is:*
  $O_{51} = (d-1).E(\overline{T}, T', K_l, K_r') + (W_r - d).E(T, T', K_r, K_r') +$
  $\qquad d.E(T, T', K_r, K_l') + (W_l - d)E(T, T', K_l, K_l') + K_r$
  $$(15)$$

- *Case 5(2):$n \leq d < W_r$; here $d = (C - C') \bmod W$; $n = T - T', L \geq 1, R \geq 1$. The overlap size is:*
  $O_{52} = (d-1).E(\overline{T}, T', K_l, K_l') + (W_r - d).E(T, T', K_r, K_r') +$
  $\qquad d.E(T, T', K_r, K_l') + (W_l - d)E(T, T', K_r, K_l') + K_l + K_r'$
  $$(16)$$

- *Case 5(3):$n \leq d < W_r$; here $d = (C' - C) \bmod W$; $n = T - T', L \geq 1, R \geq 1$.Assume C' is outside of W but inside W'. The overlap size is:*
  $O_{53} = (d-1).E(T, T', K_r, K_l') + (W_r' - d).E(T, T', K_r, K_r') +$
  $\qquad d.E(T, T', K_l, K_r') + (W_l' - d)E(T, T', K_l, K_l') + K_r$
  $$(17)$$

- *Case 6(1):$d = W_r$ and W is **ODD**, here $d = (C' - C) \bmod W$; $L = 0, R = 0$. The overlap size is:*
  $O_{61} = (W_r - 1).E(T, K_r, K_l') + W_r.E(T, K_l, K_r') + K_r + K_l'$
  $$(18)$$

- *Case 6(2):$d = W_r$ and W is **ODD**, here $d = (C - C') \bmod W$; $L = 0, R = 0$. The overlap size is:*
  $O_{62} = (W_r - 1).E(T, K_l, K_r') + W_r.E(T, K_r, K_l') + K_r' + K_l$
  $$(19)$$

- *Case 7(1):$d = W_r$ and W is **ODD**, here $d = (C' - C) \bmod W$; $L \leq 1, R \leq 1$. Assume C' is outside of W but inside W'. The overlap size is:*
  $O_{71} = (d-1).E(T, T', K_r, K_l') + d.E(T, T', K_l, K_r') +$
  $\qquad (W_l' - d)E(T, T', K_l, K_l') + K_l$
  $$(20)$$

- *Case 7(2):$d = W_r$ and W is **ODD**, here $d = (C - C') \bmod W$; $L \leq 1, R \leq 1$. Assume C' is outside of W but inside W'. The overlap size is:*
  $O_{72} = (W_r - 1).E(T, T', K_l, K_r') + W_r.E(T, T', K_r, K_l') +$
  $\qquad K_r' + K_l$
  $$(21)$$

- *Case 8:$d = W_r$ and W is **EVEN**, here $d = (C - C') \bmod W = (C' - C) \bmod W$; $L = 0, R = 0$. W and W' both are even. The overlap size is:*
  $O_8 = (W_r - 1).E(T, K_r, K_l') + E(T, K_l, K_r') + K_r + K_l'$
  $$(22)$$

- *Case 9(1):$d = W_r$ and W is **EVEN**, here $d = (C - C') \bmod W = (C' - C) \bmod W$; $L \leq 1, R \leq 1$. Assume C' is outside of W but inside W'. The overlap size is:*
  $O_{91} = (d-1).E(T, T', K_r, K_l') + (W_r - d).E(T, T', K_r,$
  $\qquad K_r') + d.E(T, T', K_l, K_r') + (W_l' - d)E(T, T', K_l, K_l')$
  $\qquad + K_l$
  $$(23)$$

- *Case 9(2):$d = W_r$ and W is **EVEN**, here $d = (C - C') \bmod W = (C' - C) \bmod W$; $L \leq 1, R \leq 1$. The overlap size is:*
  $O_{92} = (W_r - 1).(E(T, T', K_r, K_l') + E(T, T', K_l, K_r')) + K_r$
  $$(24)$$

- *Case 10(1):$W_r < d < W_r'$;here $d = (C' - C) \bmod W$ and $n = T - T'$ $L \leq 1, R \leq 1$. The overlap size is:*
  $O_{101} = (d-1).E(T, T', K_r, K_l') + d.E(T, T', K_r, K_r') +$
  $\qquad (W_l' - d)E(T, T', K_l, K_l') + K_l'$
  $$(25)$$

- *Case 10(2):$W_r < d < W_r'$;here $d = (C - C') \bmod W$ and $n = T - T'$ $L \leq 1, R \leq 1$. This is the similar case as mentioned in $5(2)$.*

- *Case 11:$d = W_r'$ and W is **ODD**, here $d = (C'-C) \bmod W'$; $L \leq 1, R \leq 1$. The overlap size is:*
  $O_{11} = (W_r' - 1).(E(T, T', K_r, K_l') + W_r'E(T, T', K_l, K_r')) +$
  $\qquad K_l'$
  $$(26)$$

- *Case 12:$d = W_r'$ and W is **EVEN**, here $d = (C'-C) \bmod W'$; $L \leq 1, R \leq 1$. The overlap size is:*
  $O_{12} = (W_r' - 1).(E(T, T', K_r, K_l') + E(T, T', K_l, K_r'))$
  $$(27)$$

There are W occurrences for each of these cases mentioned above. W, W' are possible permutations of Q and Q'. Therefore, the expected overlap size of two torus quorum system can be written as: For symmetric scenario:

$$\frac{W \cdot O_1 + W \cdot \sum_{d=1}^{W_r - 1}[O_{31}(d) + O_{32}(d)] + W \cdot (O_{61} + O_{62})}{W^2}$$

$$(W \text{ is } ODD)$$

$$= \frac{O_1 + W \cdot \sum_{d=1}^{W_r - 1}[O_{31}(d) + O_{32}(d)] + (O_{61} + O_{62})}{W}$$

$$= \frac{W \cdot O_1 + W \cdot \sum_{d=1}^{W_r - 1}[O_{31}(d) + O_{32}(d)] + W \cdot O_8}{W^2} \quad (28)$$

$$(W \text{ is } EVEN)$$

$$= \frac{O_1 + W \cdot \sum_{d=1}^{W_r - 1}[O_{31}(d) + O_{32}(d)] + O_8}{W}$$

For asymmetric Scenario: When W and W' are ODD

$$\frac{W \cdot O_2 + W \cdot \sum_{d=1}^{n-1}[O_{41}(d) + O_{42}(d)] + W \cdot \sum_{d=n}^{W_r - 1}[O_{51}(d) + O_{52}(d) + O_{53}(d)] + W \cdot (O_{71} + O_{72}) + W \cdot (O_{10} + O_{11})}{W \cdot W'}$$

$$= \frac{O_2 + \sum_{d=1}^{n-1}[O_{41}(d) + O_{42}(d)] + \sum_{d=n}^{W_r - 1}[O_{51}(d) + O_{52}(d) + O_{53}(d)] + O_{71} + O_{72} + O_{10} + O_{11}}{W'} \quad (29)$$

When W and W' are EVEN

$$\frac{W \cdot O_2 + W \cdot \sum_{d=1}^{n-1}[O_{41}(d) + O_{42}(d)] + W \cdot \sum_{d=n}^{W_r - 1}[O_{51}(d) + O_{52}(d) + O_{53}(d)] + W \cdot (O_{91} + O_{92}) + W \cdot (O_{10} + O_{12})}{W \cdot W'}$$

$$= \frac{O_2 + \sum_{d=1}^{n-1}[O_{41}(d) + O_{42}(d)] + \sum_{d=n}^{W_r - 1}[O_{51}(d) + O_{52}(d) + O_{53}(d)] + O_{91} + O_{92} + O_{10} + O_{12}}{W'} \quad (30)$$

7. PERFORMANCE EVALUATION

A MATLAB based simulation is built to evaluate the performance of the TQCH protocol. A networked with varying CR nodes is considered with number of available licensed channels varied from 2 to 50 in an 500mŒ500m area where each of the nodes have the equal transmission radius of 100m. In this work secondary channels are not considered. Hence the CR users operate only in licensed band. All the results shown in this section are averaged over 10000 iterations. The simulation covers both symmetric and asymmetric models with channel ranking starts from zero (zero means channels between users A and B is completely out of order) to 1 (1 means CR users A and B have same channel ranking list). Each PU is randomly assigned a channel when a new packet needs to be transmitted and packet arrivals follow the Poisson distribution with exponentially distributed inter-arrival time.

7.1 Impact of Channel Ordering/Ranking

Figure 7 shows the impact of channel ordering on the network performance in terms of ATTR (fig. 7a) and degree of overlap (fig. 7b). In order to compare the performance, the representative protocols in this category are AMRCC [5] and gQ-RDV [14] which considered channel ranking in CH sequence design. We observed that in all protocols, the ATTR increases gradually with decreasing channel ranking. However a rapid growth of ATTR is observed when channel ranking is completely out of order. The ATTR for TQCH is shows mostly similar performance like gQ-RDV. But TQCH shows more than 50% improvement in worst case scenario when $\alpha = 0$. The performance of basic AMRCC and enhance AMRCC is mostly dominated by pseudo random assignment of timeslots. Moreover, in enhance AMRCC the length of CH sequence is increases exponentially with the number of channels which further increases the ATTR. Fig. 7b shows the degree overlapping or the number of intersection of two sequences in a hopping sequence period with channel order for $\gamma = 0.8$. Here $\gamma(0 < \gamma < 1)$ defines the degree of asymmetry of channel sizes between 2 CR users [8]. Number of RDV per cycle is depends on cycle size, which is design choice of each protocols. Hence, to compare the performance of different protocols we define normalized degree of overlap per 100 timeslots. As we expected, all the protocols shows increasing curve with the degree of channel order. However, TQCH performs better than the other protocols in all different channel ranks. Significant performance enhancement can be observed when specially in the worst case scenarios where channel order is below 60%. This is the inherent property of TQCH protocol design, where two Torus quorums with 3 branches are spread evenly over the trunks of the quorum's structure and detect each other more often compare to gQ-RDV. Random quorum distribution is considered in both AMRCC protocols which suffer to reach the RDV as channel order decreases.

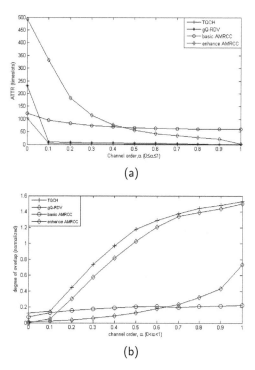

(a)

(b)

Figure 7: Comparison of Average TTR and degree of overlap under different channel ranking: (a) ATTR (b) Degree of overlap

7.2 Impact of number of Channels

Figure 8 depicts the impact of number of channels on the network performance which includes ATTR and degree of overlap. We assume that maximum 40 channels are available in the sys-

tem and two CR users observe channels with 60% similar channel ranking. Fig. 8a shows that the ATTR for all protocols increases with the number of channel. However, mostly similar ATTR performance is observed when the number of channel in the system is smaller. This is due to the dependency of RDV cycle length on number of available channels observed by a CR node in CH sequence design. Our proposed TQCH protocol performs better compare to all other protocols as it can facilitate higher number of overlaps in a given RDV cycle. The ATTR of TQCH protocol is 1.174 timeslots with 22 channels while it is 54% higher for gQ-RDV and this difference is increasing with the number of channels. Fig. 8b provides the detail reasoning for ATTR differences between different protocols. According to the definition of ATTR, (presented in section **??**) it can only be minimized by increasing the number of RDV which is also illustrates in fig. 8b. For instance, when there are 22 channels in the system, the degree of overlap achieved by TQCH is 91.1 while it is 81.1, 5.88 and 4 for gQ-RDV, basic-AMRCC and enhance-AMRCC respectively. In all CH based RDV techniques, RDV cycle length is increased with number of available channels, which incurs higher ATTR and lower normalized degree of overlaps. Therefore, one of the design aspects is hopped on channels more often which can provide higher QoS and distribute the channels over the RDV cycle.

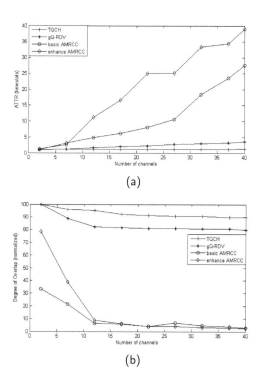

(a)

(b)

Figure 8: Comparison of Average TTR and degree of overlap with increasing number of channels: (a) ATTR (b) Degree of overlap

7.3 Impact of Asymmetry

Under the asymmetric model, different users may have different cardinality of the available channel set which is defined by degree of asymmetry, β, where $\beta = \frac{|C\_A|}{|C\_B|}$; $| C\_A |$ and $| C\_B |$ is the cardinality of available channel set of user A and B. In this scenario, we compare the average ATTR and degree of overlap of TQCHCH and gQ-RDV. Basic AMRCC and enhance AMRCC algorithms are excluded in this analysis as they doesn't support asymmetric channel view. Fig. 9a exhibits the ATTR of TQCH, gQ-RDV for $\beta = 0.8$ and $\beta = 0.6$. For both cases, the number of common channels between users is fixed as 4. However, at each run the common channels are selected randomly from the available channel set. Based on fig. 9a, the ATTR of both protocols increases with degree of asymmetry, as node has to spend more times on the channels out of RDV facility. Our TQCH protocol performs better than gQ-RDV. For instance, when the number of available channels is 50, the ATTR of TQCH is 52% and 60% less than gQ-RDV at $\beta = 0.8$ and $\beta = 0.6$. Moreover, it becomes severe when increases the number of available channels. The same statistics has collected for 80 channels and shows that it reaches 76% and 68% for $\beta = 0.8$ and $\beta = 0.6$. Fig. 9b illustrates the comparison of degree of overlap between TQCH and gQ-RDV protocols. It shows that with the increase of degree of asymmetry number of overlap is increased. However, both of the protocols experienced decreasing trend with number of channels for the same degree of asymmetry.

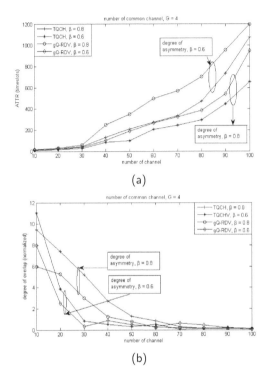

(a)

(b)

Figure 9: Comparison of Average TTR and degree of overlap under asymmetric scenario: (a) ATTR (b) Degree of overlap

8. CONCLUSION

In this paper, a systematic approach of CH design is presented considering asymmetric channel information. The fundamental concept of the TQCH sequence is based on quorum system with an extension of torus structure. The special feature of this protocol is that it integrates the channel ranking information to achieve RDV. It shows that CH sequence with channel ranking can significantly improve the performance in terms of ATTR and degree of overlap. A detailed mathematical formulation is presented to quantify the degree of overlap for TQCH and gQ-RDV protocols. It also shows that RDV can be achieved in bounded time on all common channels without the requirement of time synchronization. This protocol can also applicable for symmetric scenario without any modification. Simulation results have shown that our CH scheme is highly resilient to dynamic channels in CRAHNs. Further extension of our work would deal with multihop communication in CRAHNs.

9. ACKNOWLEDGMENTS

This work is supported in part by School of Computer and Mathematical Sciences, Auckland University of Technology.

10. REFERENCES

[1] M. J. Abdel Rahman, H. Rahbari, and M. Krunz. Adaptive frequency hopping algorithms for multicast rendezvous in dsa networks. In *IEEE International Symposium on Dynamic Spectrum Access Networks (DYSPAN)*, pages 517–528. IEEE, 2012.

[2] S. Alpern and M. Pikounis. The telephone coordination game. *GAME THEORY AND APPLICATIONS*, 5:2000, 1998.

[3] P. Bahl, R. Chandra, and J. Dunagan. Ssch:slotted seeded channel hopping for capacity improvement in ieee 802.11 ad-hoc wireless networks. In *Proceedings of the 10th annual international conference on Mobile computing and networking*, pages 216–230. ACM, 2004.

[4] K. Bian, J.-M. Park, and R. Chen. Control channel establishment in cognitive radio networks using channel hopping. *IEEE Journal on Selected Areas in Communications*, 29(4):689 –703, April 2011.

[5] C. Cormio and K. R. Chowdhury. Common control channel design for cognitive radio wireless ad hoc networks using adaptive frequency hopping. *Ad Hoc Network*, 8(4):430–438, June 2010.

[6] L. DaSilva and I. Guerreiro. Sequence-based rendezvous for dynamic spectrum access. In *3rd IEEE Symposium on Dynamic Spectrum Access Networks*, pages 1–7. IEEE, 2008.

[7] J. Jia, Q. Zhang, and X. Shen. Hc-mac: A hardware-constrained cognitive mac for efficient spectrum management. *IEEE Journal on Selected Areas in Communications*, 26(1):106–117, 2008.

[8] J.-R. Jiang. Expected quorum overlap sizes of quorum systems for asynchronous power-saving in mobile ad hoc networks. *Computer Networks*, 52(17):3296–3306, 2008.

[9] Y. Kondareddy and P. Agrawal. Synchronized mac protocol for multi-hop cognitive radio networks. In *IEEE International Conference on Communications*, pages 3198–3202. IEEE, 2008.

[10] H. Liu, Z. Lin, X. Chu, and Y.-W. Leung. Ring-walk based channel-hopping algorithms with guaranteed rendezvous for cognitive radio networks. In *IEEE/ACM International Conference on Cyber, Physical and Social Computing*, pages 755 –760, Dec. 2010.

[11] H. Liu, Z. Lin, X. Chu, and Y.-W. Leung. Jump-stay rendezvous algorithm for cognitive radio networks. *IEEE Transactions onParallel and Distributed Systems*, 23(10):1867–1881, Oct 2012.

[12] L. Ma, X. Han, and C. Shen. Dynamic open spectrum sharing mac protocol for wireless ad hoc networks. In *First IEEE International Symposium on Dynamic Spectrum Access Networks*, pages 203–213. IEEE, 2005.

[13] I. Mitola, J. and J. Maguire, G.Q. Cognitive radio: making software radios more personal. *IEEE Personal Communications*, 6(4):13 –18, Aug 1999.

[14] S. Romaszko and P. Mähönen. Quorum-based channel allocation with asymmetric channel view in cognitive radio networks. In *Proceedings of the 6th ACM Workshop on Performance Monitoring and Measurement of Heterogeneous Wireless and Wired Networks*, PM2HW2N '11, pages 67–74, New York, NY, USA, 2011. ACM.

[15] W. So, J. Walrand, J. Mo, et al. Mcmac: A parallel rendezvous multi-channel mac protocol. In *IEEE Wireless Communications and Networking Conference*, pages 334–339. IEEE, 2007.

[16] S. Wu, C. Lin, Y. Tseng, and J. Sheu. A new multi-channel mac protocol with on-demand channel assignment for multi-hop mobile ad hoc networks. In *IEEE International Symposium on Parallel Architectures, Algorithms and Networks*, pages 232–237. IEEE, 2000.

[17] S. Yoo, H. Nan, and T. Hyon. Dcr-mac: Distributed cognitive radio mac protocol for wireless ad hoc networks. *Wireless Communications and Mobile Computing*, 9(5):631–653, 2009.

Optimal Rendezvous Strategies for Different Environments in Cognitive Radio Networks

Haisheng Tan
Jinan University
Guangdong, China

Jiajun Yu
Tsinghua University
Beijing, China

Hongyu Liang
Facebook Inc.
USA

Rui Wang[*]
SUSTC
Guangdong, China

Zhenhua Han
SUSTC
Guangdong, China

ABSTRACT

In Cognitive Radio Networks (CRNs), a fundamental operation for the secondary users (SUs) is to establish communication through choosing a common available channel at the same time slot, which is referred to as rendezvous. In this paper, we study fast rendezvous for two SUs.

The channel availability for SUs is subject to temporal and spatial variation. Moreover, in a distributed system, one user is oblivious of the other user's channel status. Therefore, a fast rendezvous is not trivial. Recently, a number of rendezvous strategies have been proposed for different system settings, but rarely have they taken the temporal variation of the channels into account. In this work, we first derive a time-adaptive strategy with optimal expected time-to-rendezvous (TTR) for synchronous systems in stable environments, where channel availability is assumed to be static over time. Next, in dynamic environments, which better represent temporally dynamic channel availability in CRNs, we first derive optimal strategies for two special cases, and then prove that our strategy is still asymptotically optimal in general dynamic cases.

Numerous simulations are conducted to demonstrate the performance of our strategies, and validate the theoretical analysis. The impacts of different parameters on the TTR are also investigated, such as the number of channels, the channel open possibilities, the extent of the environment being dynamic, and the existence of an intruder.

Categories and Subject Descriptors

C.2.1 [**Network Architecture and Design**]: Wireless communication

---

*Contact him at wang.r@sustc.edu.cn.

Keywords

Rendezvous; Cognitive Radio Networks

1. INTRODUCTION

1.1 Background

The number of wireless devices has skyrocketed over the last decade, which exasperates the scarcity of spectral resources. Cognitive Radio (CR) realizes the unlicensed devices (called *secondary users, SUs*) to utilize the temporarily unused licensed spectrums without interfering with the licensed devices (called *primary users, PUs*). CR is a promising technology to alleviate the spectrum shortage problem, and Cognitive Radio Network (CRN) is considered the next generation of communication networks.

In a CRN, each SU has the ability to detect current open (or available) channels at its site, i.e., channels that are not occupied by PUs. Due to dynamic come and go of PUs, the available channels to SUs have the following characteristics: 1) *Spatial Variation*: SUs at different locations may have different available channels; and 2) *Temporal Variation*: the available channels of a SU may change over time.

Spectrum assignment is to allocate available channels to SUs to improve network performance, such as connectivity, spectrum utilization, network throughput and fairness [11, 13, 18, 19]. Spectrum assignment is one of the most challenging problems in CRNs. One fundamental action in spectrum assignment is referred to as the *rendezvous* problem of which the simplest form can be stated as:

For two secondary users, Alice and Bob, how do they establish a connection through choosing a common available channel at the same time slot?

We call the approach they adopt for choosing a channel at each round as *a rendezvous strategy*. A strategy attaining a fast time-to-rendezvous (TTR) is not trivial due to the following facts: 1) the local available channels for Alice and Bob are asymmetric; 2) in a distributed system, one SU only knows his/her local channel status but not the other's; 3) the local channel availability may change during the rendezvous; and 4) in asynchronous systems, rendezvous is even more complicated as one does not know the time of the other SU or how many tries the other SU has made.

1.2 Related Work

1.2.1 Basic Rendezvous Problem and its Variants

In the basic form of the Rendezvous problem (also called the telephone coordination game [2]), two players are placed in two separated rooms each with n one-to-one connected telephone lines. In every round each player can select a line in his room and see whether it is connected with the line chosen by the other player. The goal is to design a strategy for the players to get connected while minimizing the number of trial rounds. It is not hard to see that the optimal strategy takes $n/2$ rounds in expectation, which is achievable by letting the first player choose a random line and keep using it, and letting the second try the lines in a random order. However, this strategy only works when the players can correctly determine who is the first player, which may not be possible in distributed applications. Thus, a player-independent strategy is desired. Anderson and Weber [3] presented such a strategy using at most $0.829n$ rounds in expectation, where each player will repeat either to keep on choosing one line or randomly choosing a line different from his last choice with some probabilities. There are many other well-studied variants of the traditional rendezvous problem, e.g., [1] and the references therein.

1.2.2 Rendezvous in CRNs

In contrast to the basic version, rendezvous in CRNs happens in an asymmetric dynamic scenario, where each user may have different and time-variant sets of available channels. There are quite many research outputs related to rendezvous (in some places, it is also called discovery problem), such as the coordination problem studied in [7]. Here, we only focus on the rendezvous strategies mostly related to this work. One group of these strategies makes use of a dedicated channel, called a Common Control Channel (CCC), to exchange information between users for rendezvous (e.g., [6, 10, 20]). However, assuming a CCC might not be practical as the channel could be occupied by some PUs, and it also introduces an easy attack point. *Blind rendezvous* without any centralized controller or a dedicated CCC is therefore preferred (in this paper, unless specified otherwise, rendezvous stands for this blind case). A main group of these rendezvous strategies adopts the channel-hopping (CH) technique, where SUs hop among their available channels based on a hopping sequence to achieve rendezvous (e.g., [8, 12, 15]). Specifically, Quorum Systems are frequently adopted for rendezvous in CRNs(e.g., [14, 16]). Besides, in paper [4], Azar et. al. proposed an strategy using geometric distribution for asynchronous systems, and proved it to be optimal when there are a large number of channels. Essential details of their strategy will be covered in Section 3.1. Although most of the above work have considered the spatial variation of the channels, i.e., users in different locations may have different sets of available channels, they are limited to stable (channel) environments where the channel availabilities are static over time. Recently, rendezvous is also considered in heterogeneous CRNs, where the sensing ability of SUs might be different(e.g. [16, 17, 5, 9]).

Seldom of the above research takes the temporal variation of channels into account. In this work, we will study both the stable and the dynamic environment in asynchronous and synchronous systems. We hope this work may inspire further research on the temporally dynamic version of the rendezvous problem.

1.3 Our Results

In this paper, we investigate the rendezvous problem for two SUs and derive optimal strategies for different system settings. For the sake of theoretical analysis, we assume each channel of Alice and Bob has an available probability of p_a and p_b respectively, and denote the total number of channels as n. Note that at any time one SU is only aware of its own available channels but not the other's. Our results are summarized as follows:

- For a synchronous stable environment, we derive a time-adaptive strategy that guarantees successful rendezvous at the first common channel, say channel m, within at most m rounds. The expected TTR of our strategy is $\frac{2-\max(p_a,p_b)}{\min(p_a,p_b)}$ when $n \to +\infty$, which is a 2-approximation to the optimal.

- Our main effort is devoted to the dynamic environments where the available channels of SUs change over time, which better reflect the nature of temporal variation in CRNs. We first define two special cases, the semi-stable and the independent dynamic cases (refer to Section 4). For the synchronous semi-stable case, we derive an optimal strategy based on the one used in the synchronous stable environment. For the independent dynamic environment, we derive a simple stationary strategy and prove that it is exactly optimal no matter whether there is a common clock or not. When $n \to +\infty$, its expected TTR is $\frac{1}{p_a} + \frac{1}{p_b} - 1$. Then, we model the channel availability in the general dynamic environment as a Markov process. When neither of the environments of two SUs is stable nor semi-stable, we prove the expected TTR of our strategy is $O\left(\ln\left(\frac{1}{\min(p_a,p_b)}\right) \cdot \left(\frac{1}{p_a} + \frac{1}{p_b} - 1\right)\right)$, which is asymptotically optimal.

- Our simulations validate the above theoretical analysis and demonstrate the efficiency of our strategies when there are a small number of channels. Besides, we reveal the impacts of different parameters on the TTR, such as the number of channels, the channel open possibilities, the extent to which the environment being dynamic, and the existence of an intruder.

Paper Organization: In Section 2, we formally define our model and problems studied. We investigate the rendezvous problem in stable environments in Section 3. The different cases in dynamic environments are studied in Sections 4. Section 5 gives the simulation results and discussions. The whole paper is concluded in Section 6 with future works.

2. PROBLEM DEFINITION

We consider a pair of secondary nodes, called Alice and Bob, which need to establish a connection. There are totally n channels with ID's from 1 to n. A binary vector $A^t = \{A_1^t, A_2^t, \ldots, A_n^t\}$ indicates whether a channel is open for Alice at time t, e.g., if channel i is open at time t, $A_i^t = 1$; otherwise, $A_i^t = 0$. Vector B^t is similarly defined for Bob. Through spectrum sensing, both Alice and Bob can know their local available channels. However, as in a distributed

Table 1: Definitions of the symbols

Symbol	Definition
n	the total number of channels
A_i^t or B_i^t	availability of channel i for Alice or Bob at t
$\mathcal{S}_a$ or $\mathcal{S}_b$	the strategy of Alice or Bob
$\mathcal{S}_a^t(i)$ or $\mathcal{S}_b^t(i)$	the probability that Alice or Bob chooses channel i at time slot t
ϕ_t	the flag indicating whether a rendezvous is achieved successfully at time t
TTR	the time-to-rendezvous

system, Alice and Bob are oblivious of B^t and A^t, respectively. In addition, there is no information (i.e., the node IDs) to break the symmetry of the two nodes.

We investigate both *synchronous* and *asynchronous* distributed systems in *stable* and *dynamic* environments. In a synchronous system, Alice and Bob will have a common clock, whereas in an asynchronous system, they do not know each other's clock. As mentioned before, in a stable environment, the channel availability will be static over time, while in a dynamic environment, the channel status may change over time. We assume at least one common channel exists in the channel environment, or otherwise the rendezvous can never happen [1]. Within a round (time slot), each node will try to achieve rendezvous once.

In CRNs, one node might wake up and start trying rendezvous earlier than the other. These tries will definitely fail. Thus, we count the TTR from the starting point when both Alice and Bob have waken up. Based on the symbols in Table 1, the possibility for a successful rendezvous at t is $Pr[\phi_t = 1|\{A_i^t\}, \{B_i^t\}] = \sum_{i=1}^n A_i^t B_i^t \mathcal{S}_a^t(i)\mathcal{S}_b^t(i)$. The TTR is the first instant when Alice and Bob choose a common channel simultaneously: $TTR = \min\{t : \phi_t = 1\}$. Our goal is to derive strategies for Alice and Bob that minimize $E[TTR]$, the expectation of TTR.

For convenience of analysis, at any round we assume each channel i of Alice has a probability of p_a to be open ($0 < p_a \leq 1$) independently. That is to say, for Alice, in the dynamic environment, without the knowledge of the channel status in previous slots, $Pr[A_i^t = 1] = p_a, \forall t \geq 1$; in the stable environment, each channel will open with probability of p_a at the first time slot and never change status subsequently. p_b is similarly defined for Bob.

3. STABLE ENVIRONMENT

3.1 Strategy for Asynchronous Systems

In an asynchronous system, as there is no common clock, neither of Alice and Bob know the time of the other player nor how many time slots the other player has tried for rendezvous. Therefore, a strategy adaptive to time is meaningless, and stationary strategies are required. In [4], the authors proposed a stationary strategy based on geometric distributions shown as Strategy A.

Its expected TTR is $O(\frac{1}{p_a p_b})$ when $n \to +\infty$, which is proved to be essentially optimal as the TTR of any stationary strategy is $\Omega(\frac{1}{p_a p_b})$. They also claimed a lower bound of the expected TTR as $\frac{1}{\min(p_a, p_b)}$, which holds for any strate-

---

Strategy A [4]:

At each round,

$\mathcal{S}_a$: Alice chooses her i-th open channel ($i \geq 1$) with possibility of $\frac{p_b}{6}(1 - \frac{p_b}{6})^{i-1}$.

$\mathcal{S}_b$: Bob chooses his i-th open channel ($i \geq 1$) with possibility of $\frac{p_a}{6}(1 - \frac{p_a}{6})^{i-1}$.

---

gies in the stable environments. The proof is trivial. Alice is oblivious of Bob's channel status. Therefore, on the side of Alice, the rendezvous possibility at a round is no more than p_b. A similar result holds for Bob. Then, at each round, the rendezvous probability can not exceed $\min(p_a, p_b)$.

However, a main weakness of Strategy A is that Alice (Bob) has to have the knowledge of p_b (p_a) [2], which might be not feasible in practice. Next, we will extend their work and present our simple optimal strategy in synchronous stable environments which guarantees a fast rendezvous and is applicable for finite channels.

3.2 Strategy for Synchronous Systems

In a synchronous system, although one user can not know the other user's channel status, he/she is aware of the time of the other user. Therefore, we can derive non-stationary strategies that are adaptive to time:

Strategy B:

In the i-th round ($i \geq 1$),

$\mathcal{S}_a$: Alice chooses her first local open channel from channel i to channel n; that is, she chooses channel $a^* = \min\{a \mid A_a^i = 1; i \leq a \leq n\}$.

$\mathcal{S}_b$: Bob chooses his first local open channel from channel i to channel n; that is, he chooses channel $b^* = \min\{b \mid B_b^i = 1; i \leq b \leq n\}$.

EXAMPLE 1. Set $n = 8$. As it is a stable environment, suppose the channel statuses of Alice and Bob are $A^t = \{0, 0, 1, 0, 1, 1, 0, 1\}$ and $B^t = \{0, 1, 0, 0, 0, 1, 1, 1\}$ for all time t. According to Strategy B, from round 1 to 6, Alice will sequentially choose channel $\{3, 3, 3, 5, 5, 6\}$, while Bob chooses $\{2, 2, 6, 6, 6, 6\}$. So, they achieve rendezvous at round 6.

An example is shown in Example 1. Although one user knows only his/her own available channels, Strategy B can smartly guarantee a novel *waiting-to-meeting* scheme: the one who reaches the first common open channel will stick to it until the other reaches that same channel. Therefore, we have this theorem:

THEOREM 2. *Suppose the first common open channel of Alice and Bob is channel m. With Strategy B, they will definitely achieve rendezvous on m with no more than m rounds in synchronous stable environments.*

Next, we prove the optimality of our strategy.

THEOREM 3. *In the synchronous stable environment, when $n \to +\infty$, the expected TTR of Strategy B satisfies $E[TTR] \leq \frac{2 - \max(p_a, p_b)}{\min(p_a, p_b)}$, which is a 2-approximation to the optimal.*

PROOF. At i-th round, if Alice chooses channel $i+k$ where $0 \leq k \leq n - i$, it means that channels $i, i+1, \ldots, i+k-1$

---

[1] In dynamic environments, there could be no common channel at some time slots.

[2] The authors also considered a third party, called Eve, which is treated as an intruder in Section 5.2.4.

67

are all closed and that channel $i + k$ is open. In addition, as in a stable environment, the channel status at the i-th round is the same as that in the first round. Therefore, the probability that Alice chooses channel $i+k$ on the i-th round is $P_{i,k}^a = (1 - p_a)^k p_a$. Similarly, Bob chooses channel $i + k$ with probability $P_{i,k}^b = (1 - p_b)^k p_b$. Thus, on the i-th round, the rendezvous probability is

$$
\begin{aligned}
Pr[\phi_i = 1] &= \sum_{k=0}^{n-i} P_{i,k}^a P_{i,k}^b = p_a p_b \sum_{k=0}^{n-i} (1 - p_a)^k (1 - p_b)^k \\
&= p_a p_b \cdot \frac{1 - ((1 - p_a)(1 - p_b))^{n-i+1}}{1 - (1 - p_a)(1 - p_b)} \quad (1) \\
&= \frac{p_a p_b}{p_a + p_b - p_a p_b}, \quad \text{when } n \to +\infty. \quad (2)
\end{aligned}
$$

According to Eqn (2), when $n \to +\infty$, the rendezvous possibility of each round converges to a constant[3]. Without loss of generality, we set $p_a \leq p_b$. We can estimate the expected TTR as $E[TTR] = \frac{p_a + p_b - p_a p_b}{p_a p_b} = \frac{p_a(1 - p_b) + p_b}{p_a p_b} \leq \frac{p_b(1 - p_b) + p_b}{p_a p_b} = \frac{2 - p_b}{p_a} < \frac{1}{\min(p_a, p_b)} \times 2$. Further, a trivial lower bound of $E(TTR)$ is $\frac{1}{\min(p_a, p_b)}$ [4]. Thus, Strategy B is a 2-approximation to the optimal. $\square$

4. DYNAMIC ENVIRONMENT

As mentioned before, the channel availability for SUs actually is dynamic in time. In this section, we study rendezvous for SUs in dynamic environments by starting with special cases and then investigating the general cases.

4.1 Special Case 1: semi-stable environment

In the first special case, for Alice and Bob, once a channel is open (closed) at one time slot, it will definitely change its status to close (open) at the next time slot. We call this case the *semi-stable environment*. One common property between semi-stable and stable environments is that, once the status of a channel at a time slot is known, we can correctly compute its status at any other time.

In a semi-stable environment, if we only consider the odd or even rounds, it is equivalent to a stable environment. Therefore, if there is no common clock, Strategy A using geometric distribution is still essentially optimal, since its expected TTR is at most twice the time in a stable environment. Similarly, when there is a common clock, we can modify Strategy B a bit and get Strategy $\widetilde{B}$, as follows:

Strategy $\widetilde{B}$:

In the i-th round ($i \geq 1$),

$\mathcal{S}_a$: Alice chooses her first local open channel from channel $\lceil \frac{i}{2} \rceil$ to n; that is, she chooses channel $a^* = \min\{a \mid A_a^i = 1; \lceil \frac{i}{2} \rceil \leq a \leq n\}$.

$\mathcal{S}_b$: Bob chooses his first local open channel from channel $\lceil \frac{i}{2} \rceil$ to n; that is, he chooses channel $b^* = \min\{b \mid B_b^i = 1; \lceil \frac{i}{2} \rceil \leq b \leq n\}$.

Strategy $\widetilde{B}$ is still based on the waiting-to-meeting scheme. Its expected TTR is at most twice the time of Strategy B

---
[3]In fact, we can see from Eqn (1) that, even when n is a small finite integer, e.g. $n = 20$, ϕ_i is still close to the derived constant. Simulations will demonstrate the efficiency of our strategy when there are finite channels.

in a stable environment. Therefore, the following corollary is straightforward.

COROLLARY 4. *In a semi-stable environment, when $n \to +\infty$, 1) Strategy A achieves essentially optimal expected T-TR in asynchronous systems; and 2) Strategy $\widetilde{B}$ is 4-approximation in synchronous systems.*

4.2 Special Case 2: independent dynamic environment

We come to another extreme special case, where for Alice and Bob, a channel is open at time t is independent from the status of the same channel at time t' for any $t' < t$. Thus, we call this case the *independent dynamic environment*. Recall that we assume at each round a channel of Alice (Bob) has a probability of p_a (p_b) to be open.

In an independent dynamic environment, we give the following simple stationary strategy, called Strategy C: at each round, Alice chooses her first local open channel, and Bob does similarly. Note that Strategy C does not need a common clock. In addition, Strategy C can not be applicable to stable environments, since Alice and Bob can never achieve rendezvous successfully when the first open channels of them are not common, even if there are other common channels. Similarly, it can not be used in a semi-stable case.

For channel i, Alice will select it only if it is open and all the channels before it are closed. At any time slot, for Alice, all her channel status will be refreshed with open possibility of p_a. Therefore, at any time slot, Alice select channel i with probability of $p_a(1 - p_a)^{i-1}$. A similar conclusion can be achieved for Bob. Further, at any round, the rendezvous probability of Alice and Bob on channel i is $p_a p_b (1 - p_a)^{i-1} (1 - p_b)^{i-1}$. Thus, the following theorem can be easily obtained.

THEOREM 5. *At any round t, the rendezvous probability of Strategy C is*

$$
Pr[\phi_t = 1] = \sum_{i=1}^{n} p_a p_b (1 - p_a)^{i-1} (1 - p_b)^{i-1}, \quad (3)
$$

which is actually independent of t. When $n \to +\infty$, the expected TTR is $E[TTR] = \frac{1}{Pr[\phi_t=1]} = \frac{1}{p_a} + \frac{1}{p_b} - 1$.

Further, the following theorem infers that our strategy is exactly the optimal one.

THEOREM 6. *In an independent dynamic case, no matter whether there is a common clock or not, the rendezvous of any strategy at any time slot t satisfies $Pr[\phi_t = 1] \leq \sum_{i=1}^{n} p_a p_b (1 - p_a)^{i-1} (1 - p_b)^{i-1}$.*

PROOF. For any strategy, it is reasonable without loss of generality to assume that Alice and Bob will always make a try by choosing an open channel per round. At time t, the probability that Alice and Bob chooses channel i is denoted as $\mathcal{S}_a^t(i)$ and $\mathcal{S}_b^t(i)$ respectively. We have at any time t, $\sum_{i=1}^{n} \mathcal{S}_a^t(i) = \sum_{i=1}^{n} \mathcal{S}_b^t(i) = 1$. The probability that they can achieve rendezvous at time t is $Pr[\phi_t = 1] = \sum_{i=1}^{n} \mathcal{S}_a^t(i) \mathcal{S}_b^t(i)$. Set $\{i_1, i_2, \ldots, i_n\}$ as a permutation of numbers from 1 to n such that $\mathcal{S}_a^t(i_1) \geq \mathcal{S}_a^t(i_2) \geq \cdots \geq \mathcal{S}_a^t(i_n)$. Similarly, $\{j_1, j_2, \ldots, j_n\}$ is set such that $\mathcal{S}_b^t(j_1) \geq \mathcal{S}_b^t(j_2) \geq \cdots \geq \mathcal{S}_b^t(j_n)$. By Abel's Inequality (or simple mathematical manipulations), we have $Pr[\phi_t = 1] =$

$\sum_{i=1}^{n} \mathcal{S}_a^t(i) \mathcal{S}_b^t(i) \leq \sum_{k=1}^{n} \mathcal{S}_a^t(i_k) \mathcal{S}_b^t(j_k)$. At each round, each channel of Alice has an open probability of p_a, so $\mathcal{S}_a^t(i_1) \leq p_a$. Set $\mathcal{S}_a^t(i_1) = p_a - \epsilon$ ($\epsilon \geq 0$), and $\sum_{k=2}^{n} \epsilon_k = \epsilon$ ($\forall 2 \leq k \leq n, \epsilon_k \geq 0$). Then, we have

$$
\begin{aligned}
Pr[\phi_t = 1] &\leq \sum_{k=1}^{n} \mathcal{S}_a^t(i_k) \mathcal{S}_b^t(j_k) \\
&= (p_a - \epsilon) \mathcal{S}_b^t(j_1) + \sum_{k=2}^{n} \mathcal{S}_a^t(i_k) \mathcal{S}_b^t(j_k) \\
&= (p_a - \sum_{k=2}^{n} \epsilon_k) \mathcal{S}_b^t(j_1) + \sum_{k=2}^{n} \mathcal{S}_a^t(i_k) \mathcal{S}_b^t(j_k) \\
&\leq p_a \mathcal{S}_b^t(j_1) + \sum_{k=2}^{n} (\mathcal{S}_a^t(i_k) - \epsilon_k) \mathcal{S}_b^t(j_k). \quad (4)
\end{aligned}
$$

The last step above is due to $\mathcal{S}_b^t(j_1) \geq \mathcal{S}_b^t(j_k)$ ($k \geq 2$).

According to Eqn (4), to maximize the rendezvous probability for a round, we should set $\epsilon_k = 0$ ($k \geq 2$). So we have $\epsilon = 0$ and $\mathcal{S}_a^t(i_1) = p_a$. Hence, to get the largest rendezvous probability, we have to set $\mathcal{S}_a^t(i_1)$ maximal. Due to a similar argument, for Alice, $\mathcal{S}_a^t(i_2)$ should be maximized on the premise that $\mathcal{S}_a^t(i_1)$ is set to be maximal. That is to say, once channel i_1 is open, we choose channel i_1; otherwise, we choose i_2 as long as it is open. Inductively, to achieve the largest rendezvous probability, all $\mathcal{S}_a^t(i_k)$ ($k \geq 2$) must be maximized with the premise that $\mathcal{S}_a^t(i_1,), \mathcal{S}_a^t(i_2), ..., \mathcal{S}_a^t(i_{k-1})$ are set to be maximal. Therefore, we can set $\mathcal{S}_a^t(i_k) = p_a(1 - p_a)^{k-1}$ when $k \geq 1$. We have the results for Bob similarly as $\mathcal{S}_b^t(i_k) = p_b(1 - p_b)^{k-1}$ when $k \geq 1$. Eqn (4) can be further written as $Pr[\phi_t = 1] = \sum_{i=1}^{n} \mathcal{S}_a^t(i) \mathcal{S}_b^t(i) \leq \sum_{k=1}^{n} \mathcal{S}_a^t(i_k) \mathcal{S}_b^t(j_k) \leq \sum_{i=1}^{n} p_a p_b (1 - p_a)^{i-1} (1 - p_b)^{i-1}$. $\square$

Based on Theorem 5 and Theorem 6, the following corollary is straightforward.

COROLLARY 7. *In the independent dynamic environment, no matter whether there is a common clock or not, Strategy C is optimal to achieve the minimum expected TTR.*

4.3 General Cases in Dynamic Environment

We model the channel availability in general dynamic environments as a Markov process. At any time slot $t \geq 2$, for Alice, a channel that is open at time $t - 1$ will become closed with probability a_0, and a channel that is closed at $t - 1$ will be open with probability a_1. b_0 and b_1 are similarly defined for Bob. As we assume at each round a channel of Alice (Bob) has a probability of p_a (p_b) to be open, it is easy to obtain $p_a(1 - a_0) + (1 - p_a)a_1 = p_a$ and $p_a a_0 + (1 - p_a)(1 - a_1) = 1 - p_a$. Therefore, a_0 and a_1 should satisfy $a_0 = a_1 = 0$, or $\frac{a_0}{a_1} = \frac{1 - p_a}{p_a}$ where $0 < a_0, a_1 \leq 1$. Here, we can define a parameter λ_a and set $a_0 = \lambda_a(1 - p_a)$, $a_1 = \lambda_a p_a$. where $0 \leq \lambda_a \leq \min(\frac{1}{p_a}, \frac{1}{1-p_a}) \leq 2$.

We call λ_a and λ_b the *environment dynamic factor* of Alice and Bob, repectively. We have $0 \leq \lambda_b \leq \min(\frac{1}{p_b}, \frac{1}{1-p_b}) \leq 2$, and $b_0 = \lambda_b(1 - p_b)$, $b_1 = \lambda_b p_b$. Now, we can see the parameters p_a and p_b reflect the channel open probabilities at a round, and λ_a and λ_b reflect the dynamic of channel availability over rounds. Moreover, the stable environment discussed in Section 3 is actually a special case when $\lambda_a = \lambda_b = 0$. The semi-stable environment is $\lambda_a = \lambda_b = 2$, and the independent dynamic environment is $\lambda_a = \lambda_b = 1$.

The closer to 1 the dynamic factor, the more dynamic the environment. We regard the environment dynamic factors as constants, which is reasonable in real applications.

As Alice and Bob do not know the channel status of each other, the expected TTR for a dynamic environment also satisfies $E[TTR] = \Omega(\frac{1}{\min(p_a, p_b)})$. The following theorem gives an asymptotically matching upper bound of the TTR by analyzing the performance of Strategy C in general dynamic environments when neither of the environment at Alice and Bob is stable or semi-stable, i.e., $\lambda_a, \lambda_b \notin \{0, 2\}$. Its proof is deferred to Appendix A due to space limitations.

THEOREM 8. *When $n \to +\infty$, the expected TTR of Strategy C in the dynamic environments where $\lambda_a, \lambda_b \notin \{0, 2\}$ is $O\left(\ln\left(\frac{1}{\min(p_a, p_b)}\right) \cdot \left(\frac{1}{p_a} + \frac{1}{p_b} - 1\right)\right)$, which is optimal up to a logarithmic factor $\ln(\frac{1}{\min(p_a, p_b)})$.*

5. SIMULATION

In this section, we will carry out numerous simulations to demonstrate the efficiency of our strategies in different system settings, which validate our theoretical analysis. We also try to exploit the impacts of different parameters on performance of the strategies, such as the number of channels n, the channel open possibilities p_a and p_b, the environment dynamic factors λ_a and λ_b, and the intruder.

Our simulation includes 4 different strategies, Strategy A, B, C, and random, which means SUs choose an open channel randomly at each round. For simplicity, we set $\lambda_a = \lambda_b = \lambda$ and $p_a = p_b = p$. For each set of the parameters n, p and λ, we run simulations a large number of times for each strategy, and take the average TTR as $E(TTR)$. To make sure there is at least one common channel in stable environments, we check each case generated and drop the ones of no common channels. For dynamic environments, we allow no common channels temporarily in some time slots.

According to the real applications, we set $n \in [20, 100]$ and mostly focus on $n \in \{20, 30, 50\}$. Moreover, we simulate more extensively the cases with a large p, i.e., $p \geq 0.6$, because 1) it is assumed that the channels in white spaces have a high probability to open for SUs; and 2) it will guarantee there are common channels with a high probability when n is relatively small.

5.1 Performance of the Strategies

We first describe the performance of the 4 different strategies. Table 2 shows the results with different settings of n, λ and p. Recall that Strategy C is not applicable to stable environments ($\lambda = 0$) (Refer to Section 4.2).

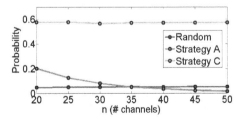

Figure 1: The probability of strategies with $E(TTR) \geq 3n$ in stable environments ($p = 0.6$).

69

Table 2: Performance of the Strategies

Setting $n=20$	Strategy	$p=0.6$	$p=0.75$	$p=0.9$	Setting $n=50$	Strategy	$p=0.6$	$p=0.75$	$p=0.9$
$\lambda=0$	Random	21.095	20.492	20.090	$\lambda=0$	Random	50.227	50.430	50.518
	A	39.877	21.490	14.087		A	34.466	21.196	14.006
	B	**2.599**	**1.716**	**1.214**		B	**2.585**	**1.705**	**1.224**
$\lambda=0.1$	Random	20.421	19.843	19.793	$\lambda=0.1$	Random	49.552	49.555	50.544
	A	35.566	20.715	13.750		A	32.206	20.627	14.158
	B	**2.534**	**1.697**	**1.228**		B	**2.531**	**1.694**	**1.222**
	C	9.111	5.564	2.999		C	8.956	5.808	2.864
$\lambda=1$	Random	20.052	20.068	19.988	$\lambda=1$	Random	49.616	49.239	49.072
	A	35.180	21.022	13.899		A	32.379	20.191	13.833
	B	2.311	1.681	1.223		B	2.311	1.672	1.236
	C	**2.308**	**1.677**	**1.217**		C	**2.299**	**1.658**	**1.222**

Note: As an example, the first entry 21.095 means that, when $n = 20$, $\lambda = 0$ and $p = 0.6$, the expected TTR of the random strategy is 21.095 rounds.

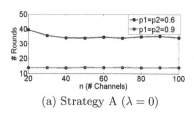
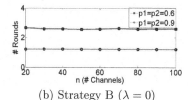
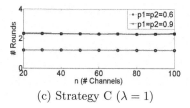

(a) Strategy A ($\lambda = 0$) (b) Strategy B ($\lambda = 0$) (c) Strategy C ($\lambda = 1$)

Figure 2: Performance of strategies with different numbers of channels.

We can find that our Strategy B can achieve a fast rendezvous and significantly outperforms the random strategy (Random) and Strategy A in stable environments ($\lambda = 0$). However, recall that Strategy B needs a common clock. In independent dynamic environments ($\lambda = 1$), Strategy C is optimal which validates our theoretical analysis.

Another fact is that, although Strategy A is proved to be optimal in asynchronous stable environments [4], it performs poorly in dynamic environments compared with C which does not need a common clock either, even when λ is as small as 0.1.

In addition, in stable environments, Strategy A may have a bad performance, worse than the random, when n is small (e.g., $n = 20$). It is due to the property of the geometric distribution used in Strategy A. We study the the probabilities of $E(TTR) \geq 3n$ for Strategies A, C and Random[4]. Figure 1 shows the results, which validates that A can not handle cases well when there are only a small number of open channels at Alice and Bob. Moreover, Strategy C always has a high failure probability, which coincides with the fact that Strategy C is not applicable to stable environments.

5.2 Impacts of different parameters

Now, we perform analyses to examine the impacts of different parameters: (1) the channel number n; (2) the channel open probability p; (3) the environment dynamic factor λ; and (4) a third party: an intruder.

5.2.1 The channel number n

We first examine how the channel number n influences the performance. Figure 2 shows the results with different settings of n when $p_a = p_b = p \in \{0.6, 0.9\}$. We can see with relatively large channel open possibilities, the performance is insensitive to n. Only Strategy A becomes worse when $n \leq 30$, which is caused by the properties of geometry distribution. In addition, for a larger p, the influence of n is smaller. It is reasonable because with a large p there has been plenty of common channels even with a small n.

5.2.2 The channel open probabilities p_a and p_b

Figure 3 shows the performance of A, B and C with different channel open probabilities. We can see with the increasing of the open probability, the expected TTR for Strategies A, B and C have a clear decreasing trend, which coincides with our theoretical results stating that the expected time is a reciprocal function of the channel open probability.

5.2.3 The environment dynamic factor

Table 2 has already shown that Strategy C achieves the best performance in independent dynamic environments ($\lambda = 1$). Here, we quantitatively examine how the environment dynamic factor λ will affect Strategy C. Figure 4 illustrates the performance of Strategy C when $\lambda \in [0.05, 1.2]$[5]. We can see the more dynamic the environment is (the closer λ approaches to 1), the better Strategy C performs. It is also straightforward that with larger p, the influence of λ is smaller as there are plenty of open channels.

5.2.4 A third party: an intruder

A third party, i.e., an intruder, may block some channels between Alice and Bob. We assume an intruder opens each channel with probability of q and does not change the blocked channels over time. One user does not know a closed

---

[4]We do not investigate B here as it guarantees a fast rendezvous with no more than n rounds in stable synchronous environments.

[5]Recall that for $p_a = p_b = p$, $0 \leq \lambda \leq \frac{1}{\min(p, 1-p)}$ (Section 4).

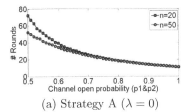

(a) Strategy A ($\lambda = 0$)

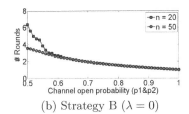

(b) Strategy B ($\lambda = 0$)

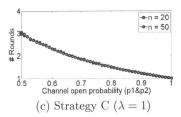

(c) Strategy C ($\lambda = 1$)

Figure 3: Performance of strategies with different channel open probabilities.

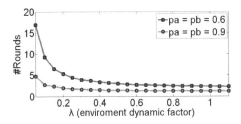

Figure 4: Performance of Strategy C with different environment dynamic factors ($n = 30$).

channel at his side is due to the existence of the intruder or PUs. Therefore, for the theoretical analysis of rendezvous strategies, this case is equivalent to the environment where there are only Alice and Bob with channel open probabilities of $p_a q$ and $p_b q$, respectively.

Here, we will examine the influence of an intruder in experiments, and Figure 5 illustrates the results. We can find that 1) The larger the channel open probability is, the smaller influence the intruder causes, which is straightforward; and 2) the existence of an intruder has the largest influence to Strategy A, which is due to the property of geometry distribution used in A.

6. CONCLUSION

In this paper we study the rendezvous problem in cognitive radio networks. For different system settings, such as asynchronous or synchronous systems in stable or dynamic environments, we derive various strategies and prove their optimality in time-to-rendezvous. Simulations have been carried out to demonstrate the efficiency of our strategies. The impacts of different parameters on the TTR are also investigated. In our current work, each secondary user can only access one channel at a time slot. Designing optimal rendezvous strategies for SUs that can access multiple (continuous) channels at a time is an interesting extension of this work. In addition, to achieve rendezvous among more than two nodes, where there are additional challenges such as the interference between simultaneously transmitting nodes, is also an exciting direction of the future work.

7. ACKNOWLEDGMENTS

This work was supported in part by Natural Science Foundation of Guangdong Province Grant 2014A030310172, the National Natural Science Foundation of China Grant 61401192, and the Fundamental Research Funds for the Central Universities in China.

APPENDIX
A. PROOF OF THEOREM 5

PROOF. We first explain why the argument for the independent dynamic environment is not applicable to the general cases. Take Alice as an example. Given that channel i of Alice is open at time t, it will have a probability of $a_0 = \lambda_a(1 - p_a)$ to change to close at time $t + 1$. Hence, the open probability of channel i at time $t + 1$ is $1 - \lambda_a(1 - p_a)$, which in general may not be equal to p_a. Consequently, the events of a channel being open in different time slots are not independent, which makes the previous argument fail when applying to the general cases.

In order to analyze the performance of Strategy C, our idea is to find some special time slots such that, restricted on these slots alone, the environment becomes close to the independent dynamic environment for which a tight upper bound on the TTR has already been obtained. We then argue that such "closeness" can guarantee a similar time upper bound, which gives the desired result.

Let R be a parameter to be specified later. We restrict Strategy C on the $(jR + 1)$-th rounds for all non-negative integers j, or equivalently, consider a new strategy C' which is identical to C on the $(jR + 1)$-th rounds, but in other rounds both Alice and Bob do nothing, i.e., not trying to connect with each other. Obviously the TTR of C' is at least as large as that of Strategy C. Hence, a proper upper bound on the TTR of C' will suffice for our purpose.

For $i \in \{1, 2, \dots, n\}$ and $K, M \geq 1$, let $\mathcal{P}_i^{K+M}$ denote the probability that channel i is open for Alice at round $K + M$ given A_i^K, i.e., the availability of channel i for Alice at round K. Let $\mathcal{P}_i^K := A_i^K$. (Rigorously speaking A_i^k is a random variable which takes value 0 or 1. Nonetheless, as shown in the following, the actual value of A_i^K does not affect the result. Thus we treat A_i^K as a constant.) Recalling that $a_0 = \lambda_a(1 - p_a)$ and $a_1 = \lambda_a p_a$, it is clear that for any integer $M \geq 0$,

$$\begin{aligned} \mathcal{P}_i^{K+M+1} &= (1 - \lambda_a(1 - p_a))\mathcal{P}_i^{K+M} + \lambda_a p_a(1 - \mathcal{P}_i^{K+M}) \\ &= (1 - \lambda_a)\mathcal{P}_i^{K+M} + \lambda_a p_a. \end{aligned}$$

Rearranging terms gives that for any $M \geq 0$,

$$\mathcal{P}_i^{K+M+1} - p_a = (1 - \lambda_a)(\mathcal{P}_i^{K+M} - p_a),$$

from which it follows that

$$\mathcal{P}_i^{K+R} - p_a = (1 - \lambda_a)^R(\mathcal{P}_i^K - p_a) = (1 - \lambda_a)^R(A_i^K - p_a). \tag{5}$$

Noting that $(A_i^K - p_a)$ is a constant independent of R and that $|1 - \lambda_a| < 1$, we have

$$\mathcal{P}_i^{K+R} - p_a \to 0 \quad \text{as } R \to +\infty.$$

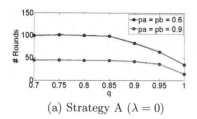

(a) Strategy A ($\lambda = 0$)

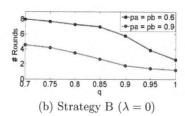

(b) Strategy B ($\lambda = 0$)

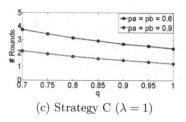

(c) Strategy C ($\lambda = 1$)

Figure 5: Performance of strategies with existence of an intruder (n=30).

Therefore, for any $j \geq 1$, the open probability for channel i at round $K + jR$ given its status at round K can be arbitrarily close to p_a, provided that R is sufficiently large (which can always be guaranteed when $n \to +\infty$). So the events that channel i is open for Alice at round $jR + 1$, for all $j \geq 0$, are "approximately" independent from each other. More precisely, by choosing

$$R = \max\left\{ \frac{\ln(1/(0.001p_a))}{\ln(1/|1-\lambda_a|)}, \frac{\ln(1/(0.001p_b))}{\ln(1/|1-\lambda_b|)} \right\},$$

we can obtain from Eqn (5) that $|\mathcal{P}_i^{K+R} - p_a| \leq 0.001p_a$, which implies that $0.999p_a \leq \mathcal{P}_i^{K+R} \leq 1.001p_a$. (Here the constant 0.001 is just an illustration; it can be arbitrarily small.) Similar results also hold for Bob.

Then, in the $(jR + 1)$-th round for each $j \geq 1$, the probability that Alice and Bob both find channel i is at least $(0.999/1.001)^2 \sum_{i=1}^{n}(1.001p_a(1-1.001p_a)^{i-1}) \times (1.001p_b(1-1.001p_b)^{i-1})$, which can be regarded as $(0.999/1.001)^2$ times the probability in Eqn (3) with p_a and p_b replaced with $1.001p_a$ and $1.001p_b$ respectively. Then, by routine probability calculations similar to Theorem 5, the expected TTR is at most $\left(\frac{1.001}{0.999}\right)^2 \times \left(\frac{1}{1.001p_a} + \frac{1}{1.001p_b} - 1\right) = O\left(\frac{1}{p_a} + \frac{1}{p_b} - 1\right)$. Finally note that, since only the $(jR + 1)$-th rounds are considered, the actually upper bound on the expected TTR should be R times the previous bound. By our choice we have $R = O\left(\ln(1/\min(p_a, p_b))\right)$, as the environment dynamic factors are regarded as constants. $\square$

B. REFERENCES

[1] S. Alpern and S. Gal. The theory of search games and rendezvous. *International Series in Operations Research & Management Science*, 2003. Kluwer Academic Publishers.

[2] S. Alpern and M. Pikounis. The telephone coordination game. *Game theory and applications.* L.A. Petrosjan and V.V. Mazalov (Eds.), Nova Science Publishers Incorporated, Huntington, New York, USA.

[3] E. J. Anderson and R. R. Weber. The rendezvous problem on discrete locations. *J. Appl. Probab.,* 27(4):839–851, 1990.

[4] Y. Azar1, O. Gurel-Gurevich, E. Lubetzky and T. Moscibroda. Optimal discovery strategies in white space networks. In *ESA*, 2011.

[5] L. Chen, K. Bian, L. Chen, C. Liu, J.-M. J. Park, and X. Li. A group-theoretic framework for rendezvous in heterogeneous cognitive radio networks. In *Mobihoc,* 2014.

[6] C. Cordeiro, K. Challapali, D. Birru and N. Sai Shankar. IEEE 802.22: the first worldwide wireless standard based on cognitive radios. *J. of Communications,* 1(1):38–47, 2006.

[7] V. Gardellin, S. K. Das and L. Lenzini Coordination problem in cognitive wireless mesh networks. *Pervasive and Mobile Computing,* 9(1): 18–34, 2013.

[8] R. Gandhi, C.-C. Wang, Y.C. Hu. Fast rendezvous for multiple clients for cognitive radios using coordinated channel hopping. In *SECON,* 2012.

[9] Z. Gu, Q.-S Hua and W. Dai. Fully distributed algorithms for blind rendezvous in cognitive radio networks. In *Mobihoc,* 2014.

[10] J. Jia, Q. Zhang and X. Shen. HC-MAC: a hardware-constrained cognitive MAC for efficient spectrum management. *IEEE J. on Selected Areas in Communications,* 26(1):106–117, 2008.

[11] H. Liang, T. Lou, H. Tan, Y. Wang, and D. Yu, On the complexity of connectivity in cognitive radio networks through spectrum assignment. *Journal of Combinatorial Optimization,* 2013.

[12] Z. Lin, H. Liu, X. Chu and Y.-W. Leung. Jump-stay based channelhopping algorithm with guaranteed rendezvous for cognitive radio networks. In *INFOCOM,* 2011.

[13] W. Ren, Q. Zhao and A. Swami. Power control in cognitive radio networks: How to cross a multi-lane highway. *IEEE J. on Selected Areas in Communications,* 27(7):1283–1296, 2009.

[14] S. Romaszko, D. Denkovski, V. Pavlovska and L. Gavrilovska. Asynchronous Rendezvous Protocol for Cognitive Radio Ad Hoc Networks. In *Ad Hoc Networks,* Vol. 111, pp. 135–148, 2013

[15] N. C. Theis, R. W. Thomas, and L. A. DaSilva. Rendezvous for cognitive radios. *IEEE Trans. on Mobile Computing,* 10(2):216–227, 2011.

[16] C.-C. Wu and S.-H. Wu. On bridging the gap between homogeneous and heterogeneous rendezvous schemes for cognitive radios. In *Mobihoc,* 2013.

[17] S.-H. Wu, C.-C. Wu, W.-K. Hon and K. G. Shin. Rendezvous for heterogeneous spectrum-agile devices. In *INFOCOM,* 2014.

[18] C. Xu and J. Huang. Spatial spectrum access game: nash equilibria and distributed learning. In *Mobihoc,* 2012.

[19] Y. Yuan, P. Bahl, R. Chandra, T. Moscibroda and Y. Wu. Allocating dynamic time-spectrum blocks in cognitive radio networks. In *Mobicom,* 2007.

[20] J. Zhao, H. Zheng and G.-H. Yang. Distributed coordination in dynamic spectrum allocation networks. In *DySpan,* 2005.

RFT: Identifying Suitable Neighbors for Concurrent Transmissions in Point-to-Point Communications

Jin Zhang[1][3], Andreas Reinhardt[2], Wen Hu[1][3], Salil S. Kanhere[1]
[1]The University of New South Wales, Australia
Email: {jinzhang,salilk}@cse.unsw.edu.au, wen.hu@unsw.edu.au
[2]Technische Universität Clausthal, Germany, Email: reinhardt@ieee.org
[3]CSIRO Digital Productivity Flagship, Australia, Email: wen.hu@csiro.au

ABSTRACT

Point-to-point traffic has emerged as a widely used communications paradigm for cyber-physical systems and wireless sensor networks in industrial settings. However, existing point-to-point communication protocols often entail substantial overhead to find and maintain reliable routes. In recent research, protocols that rely on the phenomenon of constructive interference have thus emerged. They allow to quickly, efficiently, and reliably flood packets to the entire network. As all nodes in the network need to (re-)broadcast all packets in such protocols by design, substantial energy is consumed by nodes that do not even contribute to the actual point-to-point transmission. We propose a novel point-to-point communication protocol, called RFT, which attempts to discover the most reliable route between a source and a destination. To achieve this objective, RFT selects the minimum number of participating nodes required to ensure reliable communications while allowing all other devices in the network to sleep. During data transmissions, the nodes on the direct route as well as all helper nodes broadcast the data packets and exploit the benefits of constructive interference in order to reduce end-to-end latency.

Nodes which are neither part of the direct route nor helpers go to sleep mode, which helps to reduce network energy consumption significantly. Our extensive evaluation in a real sensor network testbed shows that RFT can reduce network energy consumption by up to 82.5% compared to a state-of-the-art approach whilst achieving a similar end-to-end transmission reliability.

Categories and Subject Descriptors

C.2.2 [**Computer-Communication Networks**]: Network Protocols

Keywords

Wireless sensor networks; constructive interference; energy-efficiency

1. INTRODUCTION

An increasing number of real-world Wireless Sensor Network (WSN) deployments rely on point-to-point communications between sensors or actuators.

Especially in factory environments, sensor nodes often need to directly relay control information to actuator nodes.

For example, in [19], wireless temperature and pressure sensors are attached to pipes and need to report their readings to specific actuators (e.g., valves or sinks) within certain time bounds for reasons of safety and productivity. The emerging Internet of Things (IoT) technology features heterogeneous devices, which makes reliable and energy efficient point-to-point communications even more important in the future.

Existing data transmission protocols that support point-to-point traffic (such as [16, 15, 20]) require sensor nodes to maintain network state information (e.g., link quality estimations, routing and neighbor table entries, etc) and to be compliant with a specific channel access protocol, both of which involve significant control overhead.

In contrast, recent works based on synchronized transmissions ([8, 7]) have shown that a significant amount of energy can be saved by eliminating this overhead while achieving very high end-to-end transmission reliabilities. To this end, techniques like constructive interference and the exploitation of the capture effect (introduced in detail in Section 3) are being widely used.

The work presented in [8] and [7] introduces and implements these techniques for network-wide flooding in WSNs. However, flooding data to all devices is unnecessary for point-to-point communications, as it leads to significant energy consumption. Sparkle [22] is one solution to address this issue by exploiting the capture effect to identify a set of paths between a source and a destination, and by allowing nodes which are not part of any path to switch to sleep mode. However, the capture effect is unable to guarantee the link quality of the identified paths. In order to maintain transmission reliability, Sparkle combines multiple paths for data transmission and identifies alternative paths if packet loss is experienced. However, how to select the optimal number of good quality paths in Sparkle is not a trivial question to answer. This is because the discovery of additional paths which may potentially improve end-to-end transmission reliability incurs overheads. This overhead can be particularly profound when the radio environment is noisy.

We address this challenge by proposing a novel protocol called the *Reinforcement* protocol or *RFT* for short. In-

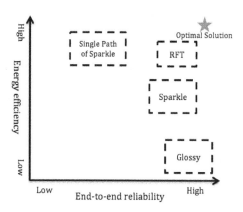

Figure 1: Design space for efficient point-to-point communication protocols based on synchronized transmissions.

stead of searching for new paths whenever the path reliability drops unexpectedly, paths identified by RFT are immediately reinforced by means of helper nodes that assist in maintaining high reliability. Like the aforementioned solutions, RFT relies on constructive interference in data transmissions to achieve a high transmission reliability. Its operation is similar to Sparkle, although differing in one major regard: RFT exploits both capture effect and link quality control to identify a *single* path between a source and a destination, and at the same time RFT also automatically identifies a set of neighboring nodes along the path, which assist in forwarding data by exploiting constructive interference. This novel neighbor selection algorithm, which we call *NeighborFinder*, is unique to RFT and essential to achieve its high path reliability.

Fig. 1 shows the design space for efficient point-to-point communication protocols based on synchronized transmissions that strive for both high energy efficiency and high reliability. Existing solutions such as Glossy [8] and Low Power Wireless Bus [7] are reliable but consume a significant amount of energy. Sparkle, if identifying only one path, is energy efficient but also unreliable. In turn, when Sparkle combines a set of paths it is more reliable but no longer as energy efficient. RFT tries to strike a balance (i.e., find a "sweet spot") between reliability and energy efficiency.

The contributions of this paper include:

1. We propose RFT, an energy efficient and reliable communication protocol for point-to-point transmissions in WSNs. RFT exploits the capture effect and constructive interference in order to reduce the communication overhead and achieve a high end-to-end transmission reliability while also keeping its energy demand low.

2. RFT introduces a new path identification method which combines capture effect and link quality control techniques to find reliable paths. To this end RFT features the NeighborFinder algorithm, which leverages the capture effect to efficiently identify the best suited helper nodes by assigning different transmission power levels. These helper nodes *reinforce* data transmissions along the primary path by exploiting constructive interference. We demonstrate that this strategy has a

fast converge time (one to two second only in our evaluation) and is energy efficient.

3. We implement RFT and conduct extensive evaluations on the Indriya WSN testbed [3]. The results show that RFT achieves up to 82.5% energy savings compared to the state-of-the-art approach (Sparkle) while maintaining similar Packet Reception Rates (PRRs) in a range of different settings.

The remainder of the paper is organized as follows. Section 2 summarizes related work. Subsequently, we revisit the technical background in constructive interference and capture effect in Section 3. We provide the overview of RFT in Section 4, which is followed by its detailed description in Section 5. We evaluate RFT extensively in a large scale real-world WSN testbed in Section 6, and conclude in Section 7.

2. RELATED WORK

Pioneering work in [8] proposed the Glossy architecture, which exploits constructive interference in WSNs and provides low latency, highly reliable and microsecond-level network synchronization by flooding the network. LWB [7] is based on Glossy and proposes a universal data bus that efficiently supports many-to-many traffic patterns by network-wide flooding. Another approach, P^3 [2], exploits constructive interference and multiple channels to establish a packet pipeline and achieves an end-to-end throughput close to the theoretical capacity bound. RushNet [13] exploits transmission power differences and capture effect to achieve high throughput for both realtime and delay-tolerant traffic in saturated networks. Chaos [11] uses capture effect to implement an all-to-all data sharing primitive for WSNs. Chaos also exploits in-network processing/aggregation to further increase communication efficiency. In contrast to the aforementioned protocols, RFT has been designed to improve the communication efficiency for point-to-point communications in WSNs. To be specific, RFT uses capture effect to identify a reliable primary path between a source and a destination. Additionally, nodes in the immediate neighborhood of the primary relays are identified as helpers. The primary relays together with the helpers use constructive interference to increase the transmission reliability.

Protocols have also been proposed to utilize constructive interference for point-to-point communications. For example, PEASST [10] combines the Lower-Power Probing (LPP) presented in Koala [15] with the concept behind Glossy to support multiple traffic flows. It selectively wake up nodes and utilizes Glossy to deliver data. However, PEASST requires that nodes perform Clear Channel Assessment (CCA) checks to detect potential other concurrent transmissions and back off when needed, which incurs extra overhead and latency and has the potential to decrease transmission reliability. Forwarder Selection [1] uses a node's hop count as the metric to measure the distance between a source and a destination. It selects a set of nodes that do not increase hop count as relay nodes. Forwarder Selection uses part of the network for data delivery and can reduce energy consumption by approximately 30% compared to Glossy [8]. Sparkle [22] aims to further cut down network energy consumption. For this purpose, it relies on the capture effect to identify relay nodes that receive packets with the highest Signal to Noise Ratio (SNR) and thus increase the transmission reliability. Sparkle spends much energy on the path identification. RFT improves the path discovery process by identifying potential helper nodes, which will be used to increase the reliability of data transmissions based on constructive interference. Other neighbor selection methods have been exploited for improving network throughput and energy consumption [9]. However, methods based on exchanging beacons and acknowledgments in order to identify neighbors no doubt lead to a significant communication burden. The NeighborFinder algorithm in RFT, in contrast, requires measurably less communication overhead.

3. TECHNICAL BACKGROUND

In this section we provide the overview of two physical layer phenomena, constructive interference and capture effect, which play a key role in our work.

3.1 Constructive Interference

Constructive interference occurs when two or more *identical* packets are being transmitted at the same time and arrive at a receiver within at most $0.5\,\mu s$ of each other. The concurrent transmission of packets increases the strength of the superimposed signal, and thus the decoding probability at the receiver. Concurrent transmissions were traditionally considered harmful because of the resulting risk of packet collisions [14]. However, Glossy [8] has successfully shown that concurrent transmissions could in fact be helpful and increase transmission reliability. Although Glossy can perform network-wide flooding of identical packets fast and reliably, later work showed that the positive effect of concurrent transmissions does not scale linearly as the number of concurrent transmitters increases [4]. Furthermore, network energy consumption will increase proportionally to the number of active nodes. Therefore, RFT activates a *limited* number of helper nodes at each hop in the point-to-point routing path to increase data packet transmission reliability by exploiting constructive interference while also achieving energy efficiency.

3.2 Capture Effect

Another physical layer phenomenon related to concurrent transmissions is capture effect [12], which enables a node to correctly receive the packet with the highest signal strength when multiple simultaneous transmissions are being detected at the same time. Reference [6] shows that capture effect performs best if the strongest signal is at least $3\,dB$ more powerful than the sum of all other signals. One of the key differences between capture effect and constructive interference is that *the packets being transmitted simultaneously can be different for the capture effect to take place*, whereas they need to be identical in case of constructive interference. Furthermore, the strongest signal needs to arrive within a more relaxed bound of $160\,\mu s$ (vs. $0.5\,\mu s$ for constructive interference) after the first (weaker) signal arrives. RFT exploits capture effect for the identification of *the primary* routing path. In summary, RFT exploits the capture effect for path and helper node identification, as well as constructive interference of the relay nodes and helper nodes along the path to increase data transmission reliability and energy efficiency.

4. THE RFT PROTOCOL

In this section we will describe the architecture of RFT. As outlined in Fig. 2, RFT initially identifies a single path

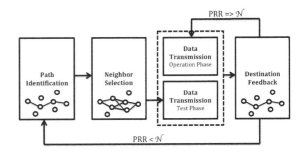

Figure 2: The structure of RFT. See Section 5.1 and 5.2 for the details of Path Identification and Neighbor Selection modules, respectively.

between a source and a destination. Once the path has been established, the second operational phase selects neighbors (helpers) along the identified path in order to reinforce it and cater to the reliability requirement. Moreover, RFT features a Destination Feedback module to constantly observe the end-to-end Packet Reception Rate (PRR) and adapt to the changing path reliability if necessary.

Please note that RFT's Path Identification module attempts to select a single "best" path between a source and a destination. Since our focus is on ensuring reliability, a node is selected as a relay only if the Received Signal Strength Indicator (RSSI, which is a popular hardware proxy for SNR [17]) of received packets is higher than a pre-defined threshold $\mathcal{H}$. In summary, the end-to-end path is composed of individual hops that exhibit RSSI values in excess of the threshold $\mathcal{H}$.

The Neighbor Selection module is responsible for selecting suitable neighboring nodes for each relay node along the path identified earlier as helper nodes using the NeighborFinder algorithm. The main novelty in NeighborFinder is the combination of a transmission power adjustment with the exploitation of the capture effect to find helper nodes. All nodes on the point-to-point path, i.e., intermediate nodes, identify a number of helper nodes locally by adjusting transmission power levels of their neighbors. Based on the link quality of every hop in the identified path, the intermediate nodes define the number of helper nodes automatically. Helper nodes in this paper are limited to the one-hop neighbors of the intermediate nodes, which are able to receive and forward data packets concurrently with intermediate nodes at the same hop distance. The concurrent packet transmissions from intermediate and helper nodes are thus being used to increase the link quality and improve the reliability by leveraging constructive interference.

The actual Data Transmission module follows a two-stage design and is comprised of the test stage and the operation stage. Every newly identified path is first tested for a short period in the test stage. RFT will use the identified path for a longer period during the operation stage, provided it is reliable (i.e., if the end-to-end PRR is equal or above a predefined threshold $\mathcal{N}$). On the other hand, if the path is unreliable (i.e., if the PRR is smaller than $\mathcal{N}$), RFT will trigger the Path Identification module again to find a better path. The threshold $\mathcal{N}$ is 90% in our implementation. Triggering the Path Identification module is implemented within the scope of the Destination Feedback module. As the radio transceivers of all the nodes in the network are turned on concurrently, the destination node disseminates the stage transition decision to the whole network quickly using Glossy.

By leveraging constructive interference, a fine-grained (e.g., on the order of microseconds) network time synchronization is also catered for. Similar to LWB [7], RFT floods a synchronization packet in the network every second. For the actual data transmissions, RFT employs a static Time Division Multiple Access (TDMA) mechanism with equal-sized time slots. During data transmissions, most of the nodes in the network (i.e., all devices apart from source, destination, nodes on the identified path, and helpers) turn off their radio transceivers in order to lower their energy consumption. Moreover, the TDMA mechanism inherently enables RFT to support multiple data flows. When required, a coordinator node can schedule data flows in different time slots or using different channels in the same slots. Without loss of generality, however, we focus on finding a reliable path for one data flow in this paper.

5. RFT: DETAILED MECHANISMS

In this section we will provide more details of the major RFT modules, as visualized in Fig. 2.

5.1 Path Identification

As introduced in Section 2, Sparkle proposes a method to establish a routing path between a source and a destination based on the capture effect. While this is efficient, the identified path may be unreliable and potentially experience high packet losses (experimental results for PRR values collected in testbed experiments are shown in Table 1).

The detailed Path Identification protocol is described as follows. Initially, RFT uses Glossy to synchronize all nodes in the network. In practice, the source broadcasts a path identification packet containing two vectors for node identifiers and RSSI samples. The *node ID* vector is used to store the identifiers of all nodes which have relayed the packet. The RSSI value vector is being used to log the link quality of every hop. The motes allocate statically two arrays with ten entries for the vectors, although this size allocation can easily be adapted to the expected network diameter and path length.

Before transmitting the path identification packet, the source adds its own ID into the node ID vector before the broadcast. Following the broadcast by the source node, each node that receives a path identification packet will analyze the RSSI value of the packet. If the RSSI is higher than threshold $\mathcal{H}$, the node will add its own ID and the RSSI value to the node ID and RSSI value vectors, respectively, before re-broadcasting the packet. Otherwise, it will drop the packet.

Once the first identification packet has arrived at the destination, the stored node IDs are chosen as the identified path. Since paths with weak wireless links (i.e., low RSSI values) have been dropped by the intermediate nodes in previous step, this first arrival path also consists of strong wireless links only. Based on the RSSI vector in the received path identification packet, the required number of helper nodes for each intermediate hop along the path is determined, as explained in Section 6. Finally, the newly established path is *activated*, i.e., the nodes are notified of their role and prompted to identify helpers in order to reinforce the link quality of that path. To this end, the destination floods an *activation packet*, which includes the nodes along the se-

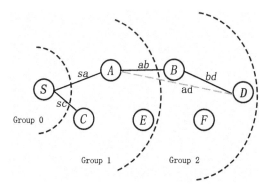

Figure 3: Example of Path Identification.

lected path and the number of required helper nodes at each hop. The chosen nodes listed in the activation packet will mark themselves as relay nodes and initiate the neighbor selection to reinforce that path, as will be discussed in detail in Section 5.2.

Since the path identification packets, which carry node ID and RSSI values of intermediate nodes, are *different* for different paths, the path discovery process can exploit the *capture effect*. Fig. 3 shows an simple example of path identification process. The nodes in the figure are grouped into three categories. The node in Group 0 (i.e., source node S), can directly communicate with the nodes in Group 1 (i.e., A, C, and E), and vice versa. Similarly, the nodes in Group 1 can directly communicate amongst each other as well with all nodes in Groups 0 and 2, and so on. After node S has broadcast the Path Identification packet, all nodes in Group 1 will rebroadcast the packet *simultaneously* after adding their own IDs and RSSI values. As outlined before, constructive interference is inherently disabled due to the differing packet contents, however the capture effect will still ensure only the strongest links are eventually considered. Although the Path Identification packet received directly from Node A arrives destination Node D the first, Node D will drop the packet because its RSSI value is smaller than the predefined threshold $\mathcal{H}$, which implies that a segment of the Path $S \rightarrow A \rightarrow D$, e.g., $A \rightarrow D$, is a weak wireless link. Instead, Node D will select the Path Identification packet from Node B (received shortly after the first Path Identification packet) and choose Path $S \rightarrow A \rightarrow B \rightarrow D$ as the data transmission path.

After the Path Identification process has completed, the selected path may still contain unreliable links, whose RSSI value barely exceeds $\mathcal{H}$. To this end, RFT features a Neighbor Selection module to find a number of helper nodes to improve the reliability of wireless transmissions via constructive interference, which will be introduced next. Prior work [18, 21] has closely examined the relationship between the PRR and RSSI in a WSN. Based on their findings, RFT relies on the following three RSSI ranges to classify link qualities:

- Good Connectivity: As the RSSI varies between -76 dBm and -82 dBm, the PRR gradually drops from 100% to 85%. The link quality is mostly robust here.

- Grey Zone: When the RSSI varies between -83 dBm and -90 dBm, the PRR generally exhibits a decreasing trend with some significant variations. This region corresponds to variable link quality.

- Poor Connectivity: When the RSSI is lower than $-90\,dBm$, the link quality is very poor with the PRR almost equal to zero.

The RSSI threshold $\mathcal{H}$ is used to control the link qualities in the path identification process. As shown by [18] and [21], when receiving packets with RSSI values below $-90\,dBm$ the underlying links are likely to provide poor connectivity. At the same time, $\mathcal{H}$ should not be defined within the good connectivity zone, as otherwise many redundant nodes may be identified. We thus examine the selection of $\mathcal{H}$ in more detail in Section 6.4, and choose a value of $-90dBm$ unless noted otherwise.

Corresponding to the aforementioned distinct RSSI zones, we use the observations for configuring the number of potential helpers needed in RFT described. We establish a mapping between the RSSI and the number of helper nodes as follows: (i) one helper for RSSI values between $-76\,dBm$ and $-82\,dBm$; (ii) two helpers in grey zone connections, i.e., between $-83\,dBm$ and $-90\,dBm$; (iii) four helpers for bad connections with RSSI values below $-90\,dBm$. RFT thus seeks to adapt the number helper nodes in accordance with the link quality, in an effort to maintain high reliability. Please note that these settings have been specified for the Tmote sky nodes deployed in the testbed; while RFT is suitable for operation on other hardware, the values need to be adapted according to the specifications and capabilities of the underlying hardware.

5.2 Neighbor Selection

After the Path Identification has completed, all relay nodes have knowledge about the number of helpers needed, disseminated through the activation packet. The actual identification and selection of the determined number of neighbors, i.e., the NeighborFinder algorithm, follows in this step. One precondition needs to hold for the relay and helper nodes, namely the relay node and the helpers for this relay should have the same previous and next hop nodes. Only when helpers are located at the same depth, all relays and helpers at the given category can receive and forward packets simultaneously and thus enable the benefits of constructive interference. Moreover, the ideal helpers should be connected with exactly three nodes: The local and two adjacent intermediate nodes from the previous and next hop (which could also be the source or destination nodes). Only these neighbors can be the qualified concurrent transmitters for the relay nodes and strengthen the signal through the application of constructive interference.

To enable finding such helpers, all one-hop neighbors of only relay nodes in the path need to set up and maintain a Neighbor table and RSSI table to learn about potential relays in their one-hop neighborhood and the quality of the corresponding links, respectively. The hop counts of identified path are normally less than ten in our implementation, so the two tables predefine ten entries for relay nodes, which does not incur a large overhead in terms of packet sizes or node memory. RFT thus locally establishes and stores a Neighbor table and RSSI table and bases the identification of additional helpers on the information stored therein.

We detail the operation of the NeighborFinder algorithm next. Since nodes may have tens of neighbors in dense deployments (e.g., the Indriya testbed [3] used in our evaluations), the chance of collisions is high, reducing a node's chance to correctly decode a packet if all its neighbors simul-

taneously broadcast different packets using the same transmission power level. The reason for being unable to properly decode the packet is simple: The highest signal will not be $3\,dB$ higher than the sum of the others [6]. In order to still identify helpers despite the potentially dense nature of WSNs, NeighborFinder applies three steps to establish the neighbor table, as shown in Fig. 4.

We provide more detail about the three main procedures of NeighborFinder as follows. The first step is the neighbor table establishment, for which all relays sequentially broadcast a Notice packet in different time slots to their one-hop neighbors. The sequential nature of these messages is ensured by the TDMA mechanism of RFT. Upon reception of this packet, the neighbors insert this relay node as an entry into their neighbor table and log the corresponding RSSI value in their RSSI table. Thus all one-hop neighbors of the identified path have established a local table which stores the identifiers and RSSI values of their one-hop neighbors. The two tables are subsequently used for the computation of TX power levels in the following neighbor selection process step.

For the actual neighbor selection process, each relay node iteratively broadcasts notification packets, requesting one helper node at a time. Every one-hop neighbor then sends back its ID. By ensuring that all responses are being transmitted at the same time, the capture effect is again being exploited to identify the strongest signal and thus the best-suited neighbor. However, responses to the notification messages are not all transmitted at the same power level, but potential helper nodes use a modified TX power setting (cf. Fig. 4), which depends on their connectivity to other relays along the initially identified path. On the one hand, our decision in favor of TX power control thus significantly reduces the risk of potential collisions due to the shorter radio range. On the other hand, neighbors with reliable connections to multiple relays transmit at a higher power. This way, well-connected neighbors increase their chances of being selected as helpers.

The mapping that transforms the entries in the Neighbor and RSSI tables into their assigned transmission power level works as follows. The RSSI value of each entry is mapped to a TX power level $\mathbf{P'}$ based on the average signal strength R of the received notification packets of the nodes along the initially determined path. For values of R in the grey zone (i.e., between $-83\,dBm$ to $-90\,dBm$) the default TX power level $\mathbf{P}$ is decreased by a value of Δ. In the poor connectivity range (i.e., for R below $-90\,dBm$), double the value of Δ is subtracted from T in order to assign them even less weight for a potential helper role. If the neighbor node is only connected to two of three relay nodes, the mapped TX power levels are further reduced, as shown in Fig. 4. In the end multiple TX power levels $\mathbf{P'}$ are averaged to $\overline{\mathbf{P'}}$ as the modified TX power. Once all neighbors determine their TX powers $\overline{\mathbf{P'}}$ based on their Neighbor and RSSI tables, they concurrently transmit their IDs using this TX power setting. The path identification process finds one helper at a time, and relay nodes will repeat this process until the number of helpers satisfies the requirements defined by the Path Identification module.

The final step is the helper activation. The selected neighbors are informed of their status as helper nodes and activated in the following data transmission period. Fig. 5 shows a typical procedure highlighting how the relay node B iden-

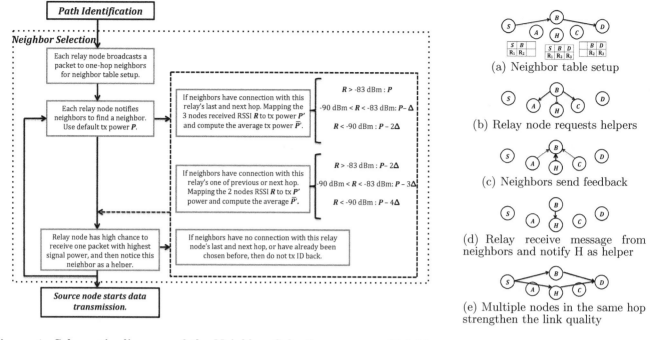

Figure 4: Schematic diagram of the Neighbor Selection process. Neighbors change their TX power based on the entries in their neighbor and RSSI tables. In our implementation, the value of Δ has been set to $5\,dBm$.

(a) Neighbor table setup

(b) Relay node requests helpers

(c) Neighbors send feedback

(d) Relay receive message from neighbors and notify H as helper

(e) Multiple nodes in the same hop strengthen the link quality

Figure 5: Example of the Neighbor Selection process.

tifies the helper H, which has reliable links with S, B, and D.

All three steps are very fast and only need few transmission slots. One time slot t contains one reception and one transmission based on Glossy [8]. In our implementation, the duration of one slot has been set to 0.1 second. The radio chip will be turned off once nodes have transmitted packets in each slot. Hence other duration settings are possible and no energy is being wasted when longer slots are being used.

It is worth mentioning that we have also considered neighbors which are connected to two relays, such as nodes A and C in Fig. 5. We decrease the TX power of this kind of nodes by multiple Δ when computing $\overline{\mathbf{P'}}$, because they are not ideal helper nodes. But if no ideal helpers exist like H in Fig. 5, the relative low $\overline{\mathbf{P'}}$ still gives such nodes A or C opportunities to be identified as relay nodes. These nodes are beneficial as cooperators in some situations. All values used in Fig. 4 are based on the TI CC2420 transceiver, and can be easily applied to other hardware with different RSSI thresholds.

NeighborFinder algorithm is a general method for efficiently selecting neighboring nodes, which is useful for other variant protocols, that focusing on energy balancing issues as an example. Multiple methods of TX power mapping may be applied for selecting specific neighbors, for instance, the ones with more remaining battery energy, or the ones with less allocated transmission tasks, etc.. In comparison to traditional methods like [9], which require multiple unicasts and piggybacking messages algorithms, NeighborFinder enables nodes to efficiently identify the best suited neighbors within very short time. This is shown in Fig. 5 that just 3 concurrent transmissions (b) (c) (d) are needed for identifying a neighbor.

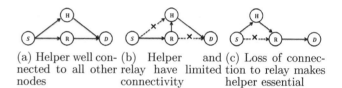

(a) Helper well connected to all other nodes
(b) Helper and relay have limited connectivity
(c) Loss of connection to relay makes helper essential

Figure 6: Potential roles of helper nodes.

5.3 Benefits of Helpers

This section studies the benefits of RFT theoretically. In particular, we are focusing on the benefits to the end-to-end reliability achieved by the addition of helper nodes. We consider the simplified network structure in Fig. 6 to this end. Node R stands for one identified relay and H for a potential helper node.

When the relay selects a potential neighbor to help forward data packets, three potential situations may occur. The most ideal situation is shown in Fig. 6(a), in which both of the helper and the relay can receive the packets from S and route these packets to D. Note that the link of the second hop (i.e., from R and H to D) entirely depends on the positive effects of constructive interference. In Fig. 6(b), the relay can no longer forward data to D directly, but as relay and helper can communicate with each other, the data can still be routed using one additional hop. Note that a similar scenario is also possible when the links S to R and H to D suffer from low reliability. Finally, the scenario depicted in Fig. 6(c) shows a situation in which the helper can only set up connections with two out of three nodes, leading to a similar result as in the previous setting. Please note that the last two cases will increase the hop count by one, which can be illustrated in the experiment results (Fig. 7).

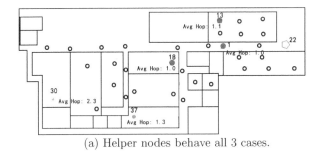

(a) Helper nodes behave all 3 cases.

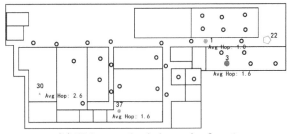

(b) Helper nodes behave the first 2 cases.

Figure 7: Average hop counts of the helpers and relays in two instances. Blue squares represent helper nodes, red circles are used to depict relay nodes. Nodes shown as empty black circles have never participated in any data transmission.

In order to assess the occurrence likelihood of the situations depicted in Fig. 6, we have empirically determined their occurrences on the Indriya testbed. Fig. 7 shows the average hop count distances of the identified helpers and relays in two experiments. Helpers are mostly located at the same distance as their corresponding relays, which means they concurrently transmit packets and exploit constructive interference to improve the end-to-end reliability. Since we impose the restrictions on the link qualities when finding the path at first, the relays and helpers can always receive packets simultaneously, like the ideal case shown in Fig. 6(a). The helpers in some hops have shorter distance than the relays. In Fig. 7(a) the relay node (node index 37) has the average hop count 1.3 and helper nodes have 1.0. This observation confirms that the situation visualized in Fig. 6(c) may indeed happen, although with low probability.

6. EVALUATION

In this section we evaluate the performance of RFT by conducting extensive experiments. All experiments were conducted on the Indriya testbed [3], which comprises of a network of over 100 TelosB sensor nodes deployed on multiple floors of a university building. The presence of human activity and co-located WiFi networks in the testbed surroundings creates a realistic radio environment for our experiments. We had access to 100 nodes during our experiments.

6.1 Experiment Setup

RFT is implemented in Contiki OS [5]. The processing duration at each node is set to be 1,700 MCU clock cycles, which corresponds to a processing time of 0.4 ms. It is sufficient for executing the neighbor table setup and making reactive changes to the transmission power in RFT (as described in Section 5.2). The subsequent tasks such as the path selection and the computation of the number of helpers are executed after the nodes turn off their radio. This allows RFT to reduce its overall energy consumption.

We have also implemented the state-of-the-art point-to-point communication protocol Sparkle [22] as a benchmark. We use similar durations of test phase and the operation phases in Sparkle and RFT. To ensure that we have a multi-hop network topology in our experiments, the default transmission power of the TelosB nodes was set to $\mathbf{P} = $ -3 dBm. Each experiment lasts over half hour, and more than ten thousand data packets are transmitted by the source node in

Table 1: The comparison of the end-to-end packet reception ratio of RFT(Single Path) and RFT

	PRR (%)	Variance
Single Path (RFT)	93.04	4.53
RFT	97.32	2.03

each experiment. Each experiment is furthermore repeated at least 5 times at different times of the day (morning, afternoon, and night) to allow us to test the performance under different radio conditions. In both protocols (i.e. Sparkle and RFT), the data transmission rate is 9 packets per second. We set the PRR requirement threshold $\mathcal{N}$ is 90% which is same with Sparkle.

Metrics: We consider the following four key performance metrics: (a) Latency is the total time for a data packet to make its way from the source node to the destination node; (b) Energy consumption refers to the energy expended in the entire network for transmission and reception of *both data and control* packets. The energy consumption at a node is estimated based on the *radio-on time* or *radio duty cycle* of the node. The radio-on time is measured in software using Energest provided by Contiki OS; and (c) Packet Reception Rate (PRR), i.e., the percentage of packets received at the destination.

6.2 Impact of Helpers

We first evaluate the impact of neighbor selection modules. We let RFT find the path without using the neighbor selection process, denoted as Single Path (RFT). Subsequently, we have executed the full-fledged version of RFT using the threshold $\mathcal{H}$ to find helper nodes to further increase the reliability. We compare Single Path (RFT) and RFT to evaluate the benefits of the helper nodes in RFT. Table 1 shows how the neighbor selection mechanism helps RFT to be more robust than the single path version; it achieves approximately 4% higher PRR values as well as a smaller PRR variance. After examining the experiment logs, Single Path (RFT) occasionally chose relatively weak links whose RSSI values were insignificantly higher than the threshold $\mathcal{H}$. On the contrary, RFT exploited the helper nodes via *constructive interference* to increase wireless transmission reliability and was able to achieve the high PRR consistently.

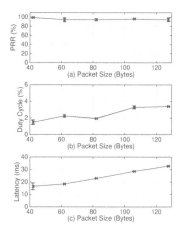

Figure 8: Impact of packet size on PRR, duty cycles, and latency.

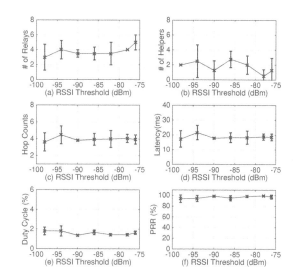

Figure 9: The impact of the RSSI threshold ($\mathcal{H}$).

6.3 Impact of Packet Size

Next we investigate the impact of the packet size on the performance of RFT. Large packets increase the duration of the transmissions, which makes them easier to be interfered. We vary the packet size from 42 to 128 bytes, and Fig. 8 shows that the average PRR is more than 97% for all packet sizes and the packet sizes have insignificant impact upon PRR because RFT exploits *constructive interference* to increase wireless transmission reliability. The radio duty cycle of the network and the end-to-end transmission latency increase with an increase in the packet size because it takes longer time to transmit larger size packets.

6.4 Impact of RSSI Threshold $\mathcal{H}$

We vary the $\mathcal{H}$ value between $-98\,dBm$ and $-76\,dBm$ to investigate its impact on RFT. Fig. 9(a) shows that RFT chooses more nodes as relay nodes as $\mathcal{H}$ increases because more nodes are needed to form an end-to-end transmission path. However, Fig. 9(b) shows that RFT choose smaller numbers of helper nodes with high $\mathcal{H}$ values because the identified data transmission paths have fewer number of weak wireless links and fewer number helper nodes are needed for RFT. In summary, a higher $\mathcal{H}$ value requires more relay nodes but fewer helper nodes; on the contrary, a lower $\mathcal{H}$ value requires fewer relay nodes but more helper nodes. As a result, Fig 9(c) to (f) show that the values of $\mathcal{H}$ does not have significant impact on network performance metrics.

6.5 Impact of Δ Value

We examine how the RSSI delta settings in the RFT Neighbor Selection module affects the effectiveness of identifying neighbors as helper nodes. After the nodes have set up their neighbor tables and RSSI tables as described in Section 5.2, they will vary their TX powers in order to let the relay nodes identify one best neighbor by means of the *capture effect*. The value of Δ is used to reduce the transmit power (cf. the protocol shown in Fig. 4). Fig. 10(c) shows that RFT can find more helper nodes by using a larger value of Δ; however, this has insignificant impact on PRR (Fig. 10(a)) and the radio duty cycle (Fig. 10(b)) because RFT is able to find reliable data transmission paths with a

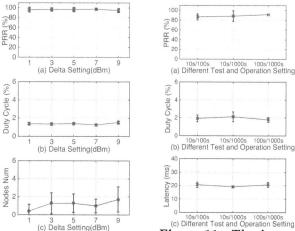

Figure 10: Impact of the Δ setting.

Figure 11: The impact of test and operation phase durations.

small number of helper nodes. Therefore, we set $\Delta = 5$ for the rest of the paper.

6.6 Impact of Test and Operation Phase Durations

Herein, we investigate how the duration of the test and operation phases affect the performance of RFT. We evaluate three settings: $10\,s$ / $100\,s$ (i.e., 10 s for test phase and 100 s for operation phase), $10\,s$ / $1000\,s$, and the default value of $100\,s$ / $1000\,s$. Results are shown in Fig. 11.

Fig. 11(a) shows that the PRR of RFT remains comparably steady, although a slight trend towards a better performance for longer test phase durations can be seen. Moreover, as observed from Fig. 11(b), the node duty cycle is consistently low for all settings, including when the test phase is rather short (10s). Recall that RFT may be required to find an alternate path at the end of the test phase if the current path is unreliable. A low duty cycle suggests that the overhead incurred due to any potential updates to the primary path and subsequent neighbor selection is negligi-

Table 2: Comparison of end-to-end PRR of Single Path (Sparkle) and Single Path (RFT)

	PRR (%)	Variance
Single Path (Sparkle)	90.73	14.48
Single Path (RFT)	93.04	4.53

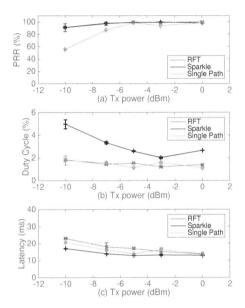

Figure 12: Impact of transmit power (network diameter), comparing RFT, Sparkle, and Single Path (Sparkle).

ble. This result reinforces the energy efficient operation of RFT.

6.7 Comparison of RFT and Sparkle

We finally compare RFT against Sparkle, which proposes a similar approach to achieve point-to-point communications. We compare the two protocols in two aspects: the effectiveness of path finding method and further test the full function both protocols.

6.7.1 Evaluating the Primary Path

Both RFT and Sparkle use the capture effect to find paths between the source and destination. Their primary difference during path identification is that RFT just identify one primary path and also additionally ensures that each hop along the selected path is reliable (by ensuring that the RSSI of each link is above a threshold $\mathcal{H}$).

In the first instance, we evaluate the benefit of this link quality control employed by RFT during path identification. For this we compare the end-to-end PRR for the primary path identified by RFT (referred to as Single Path (RFT)) with that for a single path as identified by Sparkle (referred to as Single Path (Sparkle)). Table 2 illustrates that Single Path (RFT) not only achieves higher reliability but also exhibits lower variance than Single Path (Sparkle). This demonstrates that the additional per-hop quality control employed in RFT achieves better reliability.

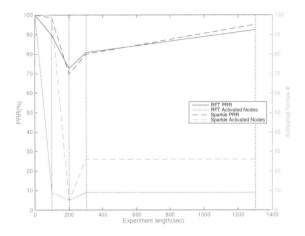

Figure 13: A experiment of RFT and Sparkle

6.7.2 Comprehensive Comparison

Next, we compare the performance of RFT and Sparkle in full function. We firstly test the two protocols under different network diameters. With a larger network diameter, the paths are expected to be longer (i.e. include more hops) which in turn may impact the reliability. To change the network diameter, we vary the transmission power of the TelosB nodes from $-10\,dBm$ to $0\,dBm$. The corresponding resultant network diameters ranges from 4 to 7. We also include Single Path (Sparkle) in our comparisons.

Fig. 12 shows that both RFT and Sparkle achieve high reliability, with more than 90% PRR for different network sizes. However, observe that the duty cycle (and thus energy consumption) for RFT is significantly lower than that achieved by Sparkle. In fact, the duty cycle for RFT is as low as a single path version of Sparkle. It demonstrates the efficiency of the neighbor selection module which increases the path reliability by additional neighbors without taking much extra time. The trade-off is that RFT incurs a slightly higher latency than RFT. The reason is that RFT requires a short data processing period for neighbor table setup and reactive transmission power changes as mentioned in Section 6.1. Also observe that lower TX power settings (i.e., a larger network diameter) leads to longer paths and thus increased latency and duty cycle with a slightly lower PRR for both protocols. Fig. 13 shows one run experiment of RFT and Sparkle for comparing their performance. RFT activates less nodes and maintain the end-to-end reliability over the satisfactory 90% level $\mathcal{N}$ at the end of experiment. Even after the interference introduced at $t = 200\,s$, RFT re-identifies new paths and increase the reliability. The vertical dashed lines show the state transitions in Sparkle and represent multiple work cycles in RFT (cf. Fig. 2).

In the experiments above, we tested the performance of Sparkle and RFT for a single source-destination pair. Next, we compare the performance of these two protocols for multiple source-destination pairs which span different nodes in the testbed. This allows us to observe if the above results can be generalized. We conducted 11 different experiments, each of which uses a different source-destination pair in the testbed. We also explicitly compare the energy consumption for forwarding control traffic and data traffic for both protocols. The energy consumption is estimated by radio-on times that clearly detail the used energy. As observed from

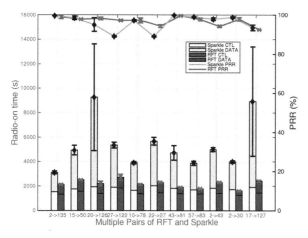

Figure 14: Packet Reception Rate and energy consumption for multiple source-destination pairs.

Fig. 14, both RFT and Sparkle achieve similar PRR values across most source-destination pairs. However, as illustrated in Fig. 14, RFT incurs significant lower energy expenditure than Sparkle; in the best case scenario (node 17→127), the overall energy consumption for RFT is 82.5% lower. When just regarding the data transmission phase, the energy consumption of RFT reduces by an even larger degree, with savings of 91.5%. Averaged over all 11 source-destination pairs, RFT achieves 55.6% energy savings as compared to Sparkle, and an average 75.6% energy savings when only considering the actual data transmissions without any control overhead. Moreover, Sparkle also exhibits a higher variation in the energy demand between experiments. This can be attributed to the fact that Sparkle frequently switches between its different operating modes (e.g., flooding, using the two most frequently used paths, and using one hundred paths). The mode switches compensate for the unsteadiness of paths, although their presence is also reflected in the significantly higher energy consumption overhead. When Sparkle switches to other operating modes such as flooding or using multiple paths then a greater number of nodes are involved in forwarding traffic. However, in RFT the link quality control and helper nodes are able to maintain the high end-to-end reliability and keep energy efficiency.

7. CONCLUSION

We have presented the RFT protocol, a lightweight and fast communication protocol for point-to-point traffic in low-power wireless sensor networks. Recent works have demonstrated the feasibility and benefits of concurrent transmissions, which leverage constructive interference and the capture effect to increase the reliability of point-to-point data traffic. While state-of-art approaches utilize many redundant nodes to achieve high reliability, they commonly also incur a high energy requirement. RFT limits the number of concurrently active devices by identifying reliable relay nodes and applying its NeighborFinder algorithm to reinforce the reliability of those links through additional neighbors. Our thorough testbed evaluations have confirmed that the consolidated paths achieve higher end-to-end reliability and energy efficiency. In comparison to the state-of-the-art Sparkle protocol, RFT can lead to energy savings of up to 82.5% while maintaining a high end-to-end reliability across all scenarios.

8. REFERENCES

[1] D. Carlson, M. Chang, A. Terzis, Y. Chen, and O. Gnawali. Forwarder selection in multi-transmitter networks. In *DCOSS*, pages 1–10, 2013.

[2] M. Doddavenkatappa and M. C. Chan. P3: A practical packet pipeline using synchronous transmissions for wireless sensor networks. In *IPSN*, pages 203–214, 2014.

[3] M. Doddavenkatappa, M. C. Chan, and A. L. Ananda. Indriya: A low-cost, 3D wireless sensor network testbed. In *TridentCom*, pages 302–316, 2012.

[4] M. Doddavenkatappa, M. C. Chan, and B. Leong. Splash: Fast data dissemination with constructive interference in wireless sensor networks. In *NSDI*, pages 269–282, 2013.

[5] A. Dunkels. The contiki operating system. Online: http://www.sics.se/adam/contiki, 2006.

[6] P. Dutta, S. Dawson-Haggerty, Y. Chen, C.-J. M. Liang, and A. Terzis. Design and evaluation of a versatile and efficient receiver-initiated link layer for low-power wireless. In *SenSys*, pages 1–14, 2010.

[7] F. Ferrari, M. Zimmerling, L. Mottola, and L. Thiele. Low-power wireless bus. In *SenSys*, pages 1–14, 2012.

[8] F. Ferrari, M. Zimmerling, L. Thiele, and O. Saukh. Efficient network flooding and time synchronization with glossy. In *IPSN*, pages 73–84, 2011.

[9] J. Jeong, D. Culler, and J.-H. Oh. Empirical analysis of transmission power control algorithms for wireless sensor networks. In *INSS*, pages 27–34. IEEE, 2007.

[10] J. Jeong, J. Park, H. Jeong, J. Jun, C.-J. M. Liang, and J. Ko. Low-power and topology-free data transfer protocol with synchronous packet transmissions. In *SECON*, 2014.

[11] O. Landsiedel, F. Ferrari, and M. Zimmerling. Chaos: Versatile and efficient all-to-all data sharing and in-network processing at scale. In *SenSys*, pages 1–14, 2013.

[12] K. Leentvaar and J. Flint. The capture effect in fm receivers. *IEEE Transactions on Communications*, 24(5):531–539, 1976.

[13] C.-J. M. Liang, K. Chen, N. B. Priyantha, J. Liu, and F. Zhao. RushNet: Practical traffic prioritization for saturated wireless sensor networks. In *SenSys*, pages 105–118, 2014.

[14] R. Maheshwari, S. Jain, and S. R. Das. A measurement study of interference modeling and scheduling in low-power wireless networks. In *SenSys*, pages 141–154. ACM, 2008.

[15] R. Musaloiu-E, C.-J. Liang, and A. Terzis. Koala: Ultra-low power data retrieval in wireless sensor networks. In *IPSN*, pages 421–432, 2008.

[16] J. Ortiz, C. R. Baker, D. Moon, R. Fonseca, and I. Stoica. Beacon location service: A location service for point-to-point routing in wireless sensor networks. In *IPSN*, pages 166–175, 2007.

[17] M. Petrova, J. Riihijarvi, P. Mahonen, and S. Labella. Performance study of ieee 802.15. 4 using measurements and simulations. In *WCNC*, volume 1, pages 487–492. IEEE, 2006.

[18] K. Srinivasan and P. Levis. RSSI is under appreciated. In *EmNets*, 2006.

[19] P. Suriyachai, J. Brown, and U. Roedig. Time-critical data delivery in wireless sensor networks. In *DCOSS*, pages 216–229, 2010.

[20] T. Winter. RPL: IPv6 routing protocol for low-power and lossy networks. RFC 6550, 2012.

[21] Y. Wu, J. A. Stankovic, T. He, and S. Lin. Realistic and efficient multi-channel communications in wireless sensor networks. In *INFOCOM*, 2008.

[22] D. Yuan, M. Riecker, and M. Hollick. Making 'glossy' networks sparkle: Exploiting concurrent transmissions for energy efficient, reliable, ultra-low latency communication in wireless control networks. In *EWSN*, pages 133–149, 2014.

Broadcast Strategies in Wireless Body Area Networks

Wafa BADREDDINE
UPMC Sorbonne Universités,
LIP6-CNRS UMR 7606,
France
wafa.badreddine@lip6.fr

Claude CHAUDET
Institut Mines-Telecom
Telecom ParisTech
CNRS LTCI UMR 5141
claude.chaudet@telecom-paristech.fr

Federico PETRUZZI
UPMC Sorbonne Universités,
LIP6-CNRS UMR 7606,
France
federico.petruzzi@lip6.fr

Maria POTOP-BUTUCARU
UPMC Sorbonne Universités,
LIP6-CNRS UMR 7606,
France
maria.potop-butucaru@lip6.fr

ABSTRACT

The rapid advances in sensors and ultra-low power wireless communication has enabled a new generation of wireless sensor networks: Wireless Body Area Networks (WBAN). To the best of our knowledge the current paper is the first to address broadcast in WBAN. We first analyze several broadcast strategies inspired from the area of Delay Tolerant Networks (DTN). The proposed strategies are evaluated via the OMNET++ simulator that we enriched with realistic human body mobility models and channel models issued from the recent research on biomedical and health informatics. Contrary to the common expectation, our results show that existing research in DTN cannot be transposed without significant modifications in WBANs area. That is, existing broadcast strategies for DTNs do not perform well with human body mobility. However, our extensive simulations give valuable insights and directions for designing efficient broadcast in WBAN. Furthermore, we propose a novel broadcast strategy that outperforms the existing ones in terms of end-to-end delay, network coverage and energy consumption.

1. INTRODUCTION

Wireless Body Area Networks (WBAN) open an interdisciplinary area within Wireless Sensor Networks (WSN) research, in which sensors are used to monitor, collect and transmit medical signs and other measurements of body parameters. The intelligent sensors can be integrated into clothes (wearable WBANs), or placed directly on or inside a body. If typical applications target personalized, predictive, preventive and participatory healthcare, WBANs also have interesting applications in military, security, sports and gaming fields. Healthcare workers, for instance, are really in demand of systems that permit a continuous monitoring of elderly people or patients to support them in their daily life. WBANs history is just at its beginning, and many news and improvements are expected in near future.

Body area networks differ from typical large-scale wireless sensor networks in many aspects: the size of the network is limited to a dozen of nodes, in-network mobility follows the body movements and the wireless channel has its specificities. Links have, in general, a very short range and a quality that varies with the wearer's posture, but remains low in the general case. Indeed, the transmission power is kept low, which improves devices autonomy and reduces wearers electromagnetic exposition. Consequently, the effects of body absorption, reflections and interference cannot be neglected and it is difficult to maintain a direct link (one-hop) between a data collection point and all WBAN nodes. Multi-hop communication represent a viable alternative, but multi-hop communication protocols proposed in literature are not optimized for this specific mobility pattern. Adapted algorithms could easily take advantage of the particular connection changes pattern to limit control traffic, preserving bandwidth, energy and limiting radio emissions. Delay-Tolerant Networks protocols seem particularly relevant in this context, as they are designed to tackle the intermittent connectivity, thanks to their store-and-forward philosophy. However, they usually either suppose a perfectly known mobility as in interplanetary networks, or a fully random mobility. WBANs mobility exhibit a certain regularity that could be utilized, with a certain degree of randomness.

In this paper, we concentrate on the sole *broadcasting* problem. We analyze the behavior of various broadcast strategies adapted from DTN literature and propose an alternative strategy from the analysis of the strengths and weaknesses of the different approaches. We compare network coverage, completion delay and required transmissions of 5 different algorithms over real human body mobility traces.

The paper is organized as follow: Section 2 presents the broadcast problem. Section 3 introduces relevant related works and presents various broadcast strategies, including an original contribution, that we have compared through simulation in Section 4. Section 4 first describes the limitations of the channel models used so far in OMNET++, then describes the realistic channel model we implemented and finally presents and analyzes the evaluation results from

MSWiM'15, November 2-6, 2015, Cancun, Mexico
© 2015 ACM. ISBN 978-1-4503-3762-5/15/11 ...$15.00.
DOI: http://dx.doi.org/10.1145/2811587.2811611.

various broadcast strategies in terms of end-to-end delay, energy and node coverage.

2. BACKGROUND

In the past decade, several routing protocols have been proposed for different types of multi-hop networks (ad-hoc, sensors, vehicular or DTN). Most of these protocols rely on the periodical update of a cost function, the algorithm seeking for the minimal cost paths across the network. The cost function can be based on any network-related parameter (delay, number of hops, congestion, stability, QoS parameters, etc.), system-related parameter (e.g. battery level, temperature or available memory), or application level (e.g. security or measured data). The algorithm can rely on a local vision of the network, each node selects locally the path that exhibits the smallest cost to reach the destination, or it computes following a global optimization process that tries to minimize the total, network-wide, cost. Multiple metrics can be combined, generally through a linear combination (weighted sum). In most cases, in-network mobility is handled by updating frequently the measured parameters and the cost, and by selecting dynamically the best path. Human body mobility, however, has a quasi-periodical behavior that could be exploited. Links appear and disappear quickly, in a quasi-regular pattern and learning this pattern, its regularities and its deviations, could influence the protocol design, reducing the frequency of cost updates. Such patterns were already utilized in the area of interplanetary networks (IPN), which leaded to standard proposals in the DTN field. However, on-body wireless channel is far less reliable and less predictable than the satellite-to-satellite link and mobility has a periodical component but is never perfectly regular. Therefore even though DTN paradigms are clearly of interest, adaptations are necessary.

3. BROADCAST STRATEGIES

Based on the amount of knowledge that is available, the broadcast algorithms for DTN are divided in two big families [2]: dissemination (a.k.a. flooding) algorithms and forwarding (a.k.a. knowledge) algorithms. Flooding consists in disseminating every message to every node in the network. This strategy is adopted when no knowledge on the networks is available. Flooding maximizes the probability that a message is successfully transferred to its destination(s) by replicating multiple copies of the message, hoping that one will succeed in reaching its destination.

While providing near-optimal performance regarding delay, the primary limitation of these protocols is their energy consumption and their overhead due to excessive packet transmissions. Blind flooding algorithms generate numerous useless transmissions, while more intelligent algorithms usually rely on the knowledge of the nodes movement to predict spatio-temporal connectivity. The more precisely the mobility pattern is characterized, the more optimized the dissemination will be. However, acquiring this information also has a cost and there is a subtle balance to find between duplicate data packets and control messages.

3.1 Related works

Optimizing flooding in wireless multihop networks has been a constant concern over the past decades. In their seminal paper [14], Ni et al. the broadcast storm problem in mobile ad-hoc networks: blind flooding generates numerous transmissions all over the network in the same time frame, causing collisions, increased contention and redundant transmissions. Ni et al. analyze different strategies to alleviate this effect. Each node can simply condition its retransmission to a constant probability, or take a forwarding decision based on the number of copies received during a certain time frame, on the distance between the source and the destination or on the location of the nodes if it is available. They also examine the effect of partitioning the network in 1-hops clusters, the cluster heads forming a dominating set among the network. The dominating sets-based approaches will be the source of numerous contributions, but is not really relevant in WBANs, as the size and diameter of the network remains very limited.

Many works have explored the probabilistic flooding approach, starting from Haas et al. [4], who identify the existence of a threshold on the forwarding probability below which probabilistic flooding fails. Sasson et al., in [17] will push the analysis further using percolation theory to find the threshold that triggers such phase transition on random graphs. These works are not directly applicable to WBANs, as the mobility pattern is very different and non-homogeneous, but they show that the networks shape and dynamics have an influence on the optimal forwarding probability.

However, even with a probabilistic transmission, a node may receive multiple instances of the same message from various paths. Vahdat et al., in [19], introduce epidemic routing. They suppose that a MANET is formed by multiple mobile clusters that eventually meet. Inside a cluster, they disseminate information through basic flooding and when two nodes belonging to different clusters meet, they exchange a summary vector containing the messages ID they already possess. They then exchange only the missing messages that will reach new clusters this way. Considering that the nodes were divided in connected groups without any guarantee from global connectivity was a first step towards delay-tolerant networks.

When connection is intermittent, unicast routing towards a single destination cannot be based simply on a classical shortest path algorithm like link-state routing. Indeed, the time required to collect all links information is too high compared to the links intermittency. That's why several papers such as [9, 6] propose and evaluate mobility-aware shortest path algorithms. Besides the chosen strategies, these contributions confirmed that the transmissions efficiency increases with the knowledge of the mobility pattern. In other words, knowing how nodes move allows to reduce the number of unnecessary transmissions and the delivery delay.

In [5], the authors compared various strategies for controlling flooding in delay tolerant networks. They compare basic probabilities approaches with time-to-live approaches in terms of number of hops or time stamps and with explicit notification when the destination has received the message. Further more, [18] proposes an interesting flooding-forwarding strategy, **Spray and Wait**. The spray phase (flooding) is as follows: for every message originating at a source node, copies are initially spread and forwarded by the source and possibly other nodes receiving a copy to distinct relays. In the wait phase (forwarding), if the destination is not found in the spraying phase, each node carrying a message copy performs a direct transmission (will forward the message only to its destination). A variant of this algorithm is *Spray and Focus*. The forwarding requirement is to have some knowledge of the network, called in this article as "utility function" that represent how much the node is useful to reach the destination. The authors of [3] propose another strategy to optimize broadcasting in DTN: the *k-neighbor* broadcast scheme, in which a packet is retransmitted if and only if the number of neighbors present exceed a threshold, K, and if at least one of these neighbors did not receive the message yet. Even if the implementation is different, we find back here the concepts behind epidemic routing and the notion of not systematically transmitting a packet to reduce the number of transmission. The simulation-based evaluation shows a good performance and study the influence of the threshold on the number of neighbors, K. Yet, this threshold is the same all across the network.

In the past decade, several routing protocols have been proposed for WBANs that can be classified with respect to their aims in different categories [10, 11]: temperature based routing protocols, cross layer, cost-effective routing protocols, QoS-based routing protocols. Most of these proposals are not suitable when sensors are external (on the body and not in the body). DTN like solutions [1] and many other WBAN proposals (such as EDSR [12]) do not take into account the mobility of the human-body: during the transmissions of the message over the path already computed, disconnections can happen causing failures.

The authors of [16] study the case of unicast routing under the assumption that postural changes provoke network disconnections. They propose a store-and-forward approach and use a probabilistic proactive routing approach, defining stochastic links costs. They show through simulation and experiments that taking into account the particular mobility of the body improves transmission delay when compared to a traditional probabilistic algorithm for DTN. The same authors present in [15] an adaptation of their algorithm taking into account location-aware networks: a node forwards packets if this action results in bringing the data closer (physically) to the destination.

3.2 Old and new broadcast strategies

This excerpt from the literature shows that there is room for optimizing the flooding procedure by taking into account the specific mobility pattern. When a node receives a flooded packet, it needs to take a decision whether to forward it or not, to which of its neighbors and when. However, acquiring the necessary information on the nodes mobility is not free. It either requires a precise nodes localization mechanism, which is typically achieved by measuring round-trip time of flights between couple of nodes in IR-UWB body area networks, or requires to rely on hello messages to learn connections/disconnection patterns. In both cases the improvement realized by the mobility pattern characterization could be lost by the necessary control traffic. That's why we wished to compare various strategies with different levels of knowledge, in a scenario that is representative of a real WBAN.

More specifically, we will compare the following strategies:

- *Plain flooding* in which nodes retransmit every new packet they receive. Each packet will be retransmitted once and only once by each node in the network.

- *Pruned flooding* in which nodes retransmit each packet to K peers chosen randomly.

- *Probabilistic flooding (P=0.5)* in which nodes retransmit packets according to a constant probability. For simulations, we set this probability to 0.5.

- *Probabilistic flooding (P=P/2)* in which nodes retransmit packets with a probability decreasing as the number of retransmissions increase. The first instance of the packet is retransmitted with probability 1, then with probability 0.5 at the next hop, then 0.25, etc.

- *Tabu flooding* in which a vector is added in the packet indicating which nodes in the network already received the same message. Consequently each node retransmits only to the nodes not yet covered.

- *EBP (Efficient broadcast protocol)*, adapted to WBAN from by [3]. In this protocol nodes retransmit a packet only when they are surrounded by at least K neighbors and if at least one of these neighbors has not received the packet yet. While in [3] the threshold value (K) is fixed and uniform across the network, we adapt its value to the WBAN environment, setting a higher value for the gateway and a lower one for the peripheral nodes who are less likely to encounter uncovered nodes. In our implementation the K value is set to 3 for the gateway (chest), to 1 for the ankle and the wrist (peripheral nodes) and to 2 for the other nodes.

- **MBP (Mixed Broadcast Protocol)**, our novel protocol described below.

The simulation results we detail in Section 4 allowed us to come out with an interesting set of conclusions:

- Regarding the completion delay, i.e. the time required to reach all the nodes, both dissemination (flooding-based approaches) and knowledge-based (EPB-like) protocols spend more time to cover the peripheral nodes (which represent about 20 % of the network) compared to the rest of the network.

- When looking at the volume of control traffic, using an EBP-like protocol makes the number of unnecessary retransmissions increase, due to an increased volume of control packets in the network to discover neighbors.

- For flooding, it is very important to set a good TTL value. However the relative typically small WBAN dimension limits the problem of the flooding algorithms that, with very large networks, makes the retransmissions uncontrollable.

- Probabilistic flooding is not efficient unless related to some knowledge on the network.

- EBP using a relatively high threshold on the number of neighbors required to transmit (K) works well only if the Hello-interval is short enough to have a "realistic" representation of the network. Otherwise, with large Hello-interval the simulation performances of high K

values are similar to the $K = 1$ case: only the last Hello message received is reliable, while the other neighbors saved in the neighbor-table could be obsolete.

- Knowledge-based algorithms include control messages such as request and reply besides the neighborhood discovery messages. This approach does not work in the BAN scenario because it may happen that during the communication (exchange of control messages) to "take decision" the connection disappear. Moreover this increases further transmissions, receptions, and related problems such as collisions.

These conclusions guided us to define a novel protocol *Mixed Broadcast Protocol* (**MBP**) by combining the "dissemination" and "knowledge" approaches. The protocol is divided into two phases: the broadcast begins as the plain flooding algorithm. Each node that receives the packet checks the number of hops (NH) this message has traveled since its emission, and compares it with a threshold Δ:

- As long as $NH < \Delta$, it forwards the packet, using simple flooding, simply transmitting the packet to all neighbors in its range.

- When $NH = \Delta$, the node waits during a time T to receive up to Q acknowledgments.

  - if it receives a number of acknowledgments greater or equal than Q, the node stops the flooding.

  - if it fails to receive Q acknowledgments, it retransmits the packet.

- When $NH > \Delta$, the node applies the same strategy as when $NH = \Delta$, but it sends in addition an acknowledgment to the node it received the packet from.

In the simulation detailed in the next section, the values of Q for each node are set equal to the K parameter of EBP.

4. SIMULATION SETTINGS AND RESULTS

In order to test the algorithms described above in the specific WBAN scenario, we implemented them under the Omnet++ simulator. Indeed, Omnet++ includes a set of modules that specifically model the lower network layers of WSN and WBAN through the Mixim project [8]. It includes a set of propagation models, electronics and power consumption models and medium access control protocols.

The MoBAN framework for Omnet++ adds mobility models for WBANs of 12 nodes in 4 different postures. Unfortunately studying in deep the MoBAN code, we discovered that it mainly focuses on the mobility resulting from the change of position, rather than describing coherent and continuous movements. Besides, it models the movement of each node with respect to the centroid of the body and the signal attenuation between couples of nodes is approximated with a simple propagation formula that is not accurate enough to model low-power on-body transmission. It does not model absorption and reflection effects due to the body, alterations due to the presence of clothes and eventually interference from other technologies at the same frequency since 2.4 GHz is a crowded band.

4.1 Channel model

We therefore decided to implement a realistic channel model published in [13] over the physical layer implementation provided by the Mixim framework. This channel model results from a dynamic simulation using the Finite Difference Time Domain method of an on-body 2.45 GHz channel between 7 nodes, that belong to the same WBAN and positioned on the navel, chest, head, upper arm, ankle, thigh and wrist of a body, using small directional antennas modeled as if they were 1.5cm away from the body. The nodes positions are calculated in 7 postures: walking, running, sitting down, lying down, wearing a jacket, sleeping and run weakly, represented on Fig. 1 that are modeled at a resolution of 30 positions (frames) per second. Channel attenuation is calculated between each couple of nodes for each of these positions as the average attenuation (in dB) and the standard deviation (in dBm).

4.2 Simulation Settings

Above the channel model described in the previous section, we used standard protocol implementations provided by the Mixim framework. In particular, we used, for the medium access control layer, the IEEE 802.15.4 implementation. The sensitivity levels, header length of the packets and other basic information and parameters are taken from the 802.15.4 standards.

Each data point is the average of 50 simulations run with different seeds. The simulations are performed with only one packet transmission from the gateway. The transmission power is set at the minimum limit level (-60 dBm) that allows an intermittent communication given the channel attenuation and the receiver sensitivity (-100 dBm). With this value of transmission power, we guarantee that at each time t of the simulation, we have a connected network and at the same time we ensure a limited energy consumption.

4.3 Simulation results

4.3.1 Percentage of network covered

We first compare the percentage of network covered during the broadcast. Figures 2 and 3 show its variations for each algorithm in function of the TTL set for the packets, which is the only parameter present in all the considered algorithms.

The "Flooding" represents the reference oblivious flooding in which nodes always retransmit a packet until its time-to-leave counter reaches 0, regardless of the past. In the case of pruned flooding, K represents the number of peers a node chooses randomly to forward the message to. For EBP, I represents the interval between two successive Hello messages emitted by each node.

With K=3 for the gateway, after just one transmission with a high probability half of the nodes are covered. Nevertheless, the percentage of EBP slightly decreases as the *Hello interval* increases from $I = 0.25$ to $I = 0.5$.

A notable difference lies in the fact that EBP stops automatically the broadcast when the network is covered, while the classical flooding algorithms (Figure 2) have to wait until the TTL of all packets reaches 0.

The plain flooding and tabu flooding coverage starts to increase with the TLL and stabilize rapidly. Since a few number of transmissions is allowed, both algorithms stop even when the network is not fully covered. As it is very hard for these two algorithms to reach a full coverage, the notions of

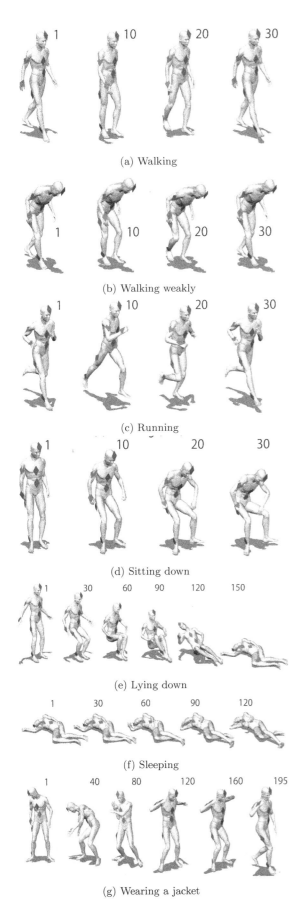

(a) Walking

(b) Walking weakly

(c) Running

(d) Sitting down

(e) Lying down

(f) Sleeping

(g) Wearing a jacket

Figure 1: Postures used in [13] to model the WBAN channel (Pictures source: [13])

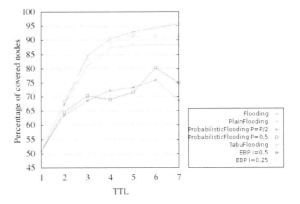

Figure 2: Percentage of covered nodes (first group)

completion delay and the required amount of transmissions to cover the whole network are meaningless. Therefore these algorithms will be left out of the subsequent evaluations.

The Probabilistic Flooding with decreasing probability (P=P/2) achieves the same coverage as the constant probability version with P=0.5. Nevertheless, all flooding algorithms are not efficient, as they require a larger amount of transmissions than EBP or limited flooding approaches.

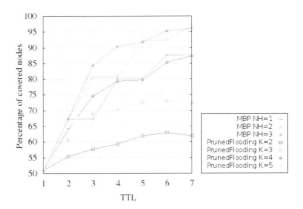

Figure 3: Percentage of covered nodes (Second group)

Let us, now examine limited flooding strategies such as pruned flooding. Figure 3 shows that the number of allowed transmissions has a direct effect on the coverage probability. With $K = 2$, it is impossible to cover the whole network.

Finally, MBP, has a coverage slightly lower than Flooding.

Figure 4 represents the network coverage percentage in the different postures. While the classical flooding and MBP results are practically independent from the posture, the EBP algorithm presents a lower coverage in the "static" positions as sleep and weak. Indeed, in these postures the low mobility produces longer disconnections and the strong constraint on the number of neighbors that need to be present for EBP to allow forwarding represents a limitation. The Pruned and Probabilistic Flooding have higher variations among the postures due to their probabilistic nature.

4.3.2 Completion Delay

Figure 5 represents the average End-to-End delay, i.e. the average time required to reach a node. As expected, the oblivious version of the flooding algorithm has the best per-

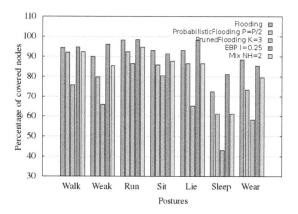

Figure 4: Percentage of covered nodes per posture

formance due to the huge amount of packets circulating in the networks. The adaptive probabilistic flooding (P=P/2) exhibits a slightly higher delay due to the decreasing amount of retransmissions with respect to the Flooding.

The delay achieved by EBP is strictly dependent from the Hello interval: when this interval is short, for instance 0.25s, each time the connections in the model change, the nodes send a new hello message, resulting in a precise acquisition of the node mobility.

Pruned Flooding completion delay is directly related to the value of parameter K: the higher the K, the lower the delay. In particular in the case $K = 2$ and $K = 3$, the algorithm spends a lot of time to cover the whole network. This is due to the low number of nodes that receive the packet transmitted from each sender.

MBP presents better performances in term of End-to-End delay than EBP and pruned flooding, even if a node delays packet retransmission after T time.

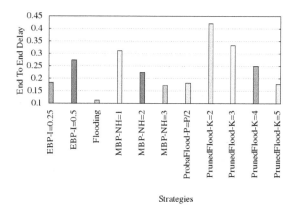

Figure 5: End-to-End delay comparison

Figure 6 details the End-to-End delay per node. We can notice that all algorithms behave similarly: most of the time is spent covering the peripheral nodes of the network (ankle). Peripheral nodes are highly mobile and located at a greater distance from the other ones. As a result, even if an algorithm is able to cover the central part of the network in a very short time, it then has to wait for a connection opportunity with the last nodes.

Figure 7 represents completion delay for different postures. EBP seems to perform better in the high mobility

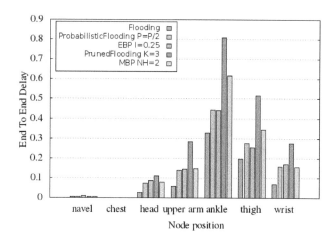

Figure 6: End-to-End Delay per node

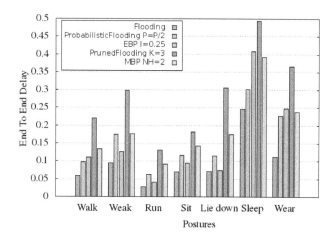

Figure 7: End-to-End delay per posture

postures, a peak is noticed in sleep position. In other hand, MBP is less affected by the mobility than EBP and Pruned flooding.

4.3.3 Number of transmissions and receptions

The number of transmissions and receptions is a key parameter for these networks. The number of transmissions reflects the channel load and also gives an indication on the amount of electro-magnetic energy that will be absorbed by the body. Adding the number of receptions gives an indication on the energy consumption of the different nodes in the network and hence on the devices autonomy, their capability to rely on a reduced size battery or even to harvest energy.

Figure 8 compares these totals for different algorithms. Flooding pays its good completion delay and coverage performance, as it exhibits the highest energy consumption. It is the only algorithm that has no limitation on the number of transmissions besides the TTL. The adaptive Probabilistic Flooding (P=P/2) has a better performance than the classical flooding, because the probability decrease limits the number of transmissions as the packet travels deeper in the network. The energy consumed by Pruned Flooding depends on the parameter K: while for the end-to-end delay and coverage the algorithm performs well with high K (4), in

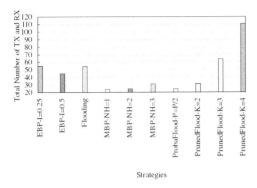

Figure 8: Number of transmissions and receptions

this case a visible reduction of transmissions and receptions is obtained only with lower values (2 or 3).

The number of transmissions made by EBP is not really lower than the other algorithms. In fact, EBP strongly relies on the transmission of "hello messages" that cannot be neglected, collision causes lots of dropped packets. However it is important to note here that these results only account for data packets transmissions and receptions.

MBP does not suffer from the same issue, even if control messages such as acknowledgments are also necessary. As acknowledgments are only sent when a packet is effectively forwarded, the control traffic is directly related to the network activity. MBP performance therefore mostly depends on the NH parameter and lowering this value results in a better energy efficiency.

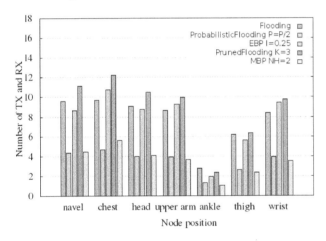

Figure 9: Number of transmissions and receptions per node

Figure 9 shows the individual number of Tx and Rx of each node. The gateway node is definitively the one with higher number in all cases. Its position at the center of the network allows it to send and receive from more neighbors. On the contrary the node on the ankle is the one with lower number of Tx and Rx because standing in the periphery has few occasions of communication with the rest of the network. Besides, when the message reaches this node, its TTL will already be reduced and it generally has no uncovered neighbor as far as knowledge-based algorithms are concerned.

Probabilistic Flooding (P=P/2) performs better than the other algorithms. Indeed, the central nodes happen to transmit more than the others, but their neighbors will limit their

transmission probability immediately, resulting in a lower number of receptions. This algorithm therefore better distributes the consumption across the network.

One of the main weaknesses of the flooding algorithms that their performance strongly depends on the TTL. Increasing the TTL lets the total amount of transmissions and receptions rise very quickly. This issue is partially solved in the adaptive Probabilistic Flooding (P=P/2): the probability decrease works as an automatic brake, drastically reducing the transmission probability.

MBP uses the information from the ACK to stop the transmissions. However the amount of transmissions and receptions increases since MBP schedules a retransmission if less than Q acknowledgements are received.

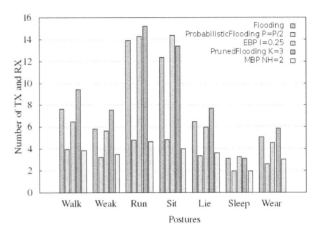

Figure 10: Number of transmissions and receptions per posture

Figure 10 represents the number of transmissions and receptions in function of the posture. We can notice, on this graph, a similar behavior between the "flooding" and "knowledge-based" algorithms. The two strategies MBP and the probabilistic flooding are able to reduce the number of transmission especially in the "static" postures. We can say that MBP is almost independent from the postures.

5. CONCLUSIONS AND DISCUSSIONS

In this paper we evaluated through simulation the performance of several DTN-inspired broadcast strategies in a WBAN context. Our simulations, realized with the Omnet++ simulator, the Mixim framework and a WBAN channel model proposed in the literature, allowed us to compare flooding-like strategies that forward packets blindly and differ mostly by how their stopping criterion with a representative knowledge-based algorithm, EBP, which relies on the knowledge of the neighborhood of each node and its evolutions. The simulations realized over a 7 nodes network in 7 types of movements allow a fine characterization of the compromise that exists between the capacity to flood the whole network quickly and the cost induced by this performance. Simulations also allowed us to identify some less intuitive behaviors: for all strategies, most of the time is spent trying to reach leaf nodes, which makes us think that the key lies in adaptive algorithms that are able to mix different strategies.

We described a novel protocol that relies on such an adaptive approach. MBP, for Mixed Broadcast Protocol, applies a more aggressive strategy in the center of the network, where connections are more stable, and becomes more cautious at the border of the network, where a blind transmission has a good chance of success. As future works, we will try to adapt this work to the context of IR-UWB transmissions, which is a promising technology for WBAN. Another future work would be a detailed study of existing channel models [20] and a comparison with the channel model. Furthermore, another interesting future direction would be to consider collisions among multiple WBANs [21, 7].

6. REFERENCES

[1] N. T. Antonio Manuel Ortiz, Nedal Ababneh and J. Morrison. Adaptive routing for multihop IEEE 802.15.6 wireless body area networks. In *20th International Conference on Software, Telecommunications and Computer Networks, SoftCOM 2012 , Split, Croatia, September 11-13,2012*, pages 1–5, 2012.

[2] J. K. S. Evan P. C. Jones, Lily Li and P. A. S. Ward. Practical routing in delay-tolerant networks. *IEEE Trans. Mob. Comput.*, 6(8):943–959, 2007.

[3] A. Goundan, E. Coe, and C. Raghavendra. Efficient broadcasting in delay tolerant networks. In *IEEE Global Telecommunications Conference (GLOBECOM)*, New Orleans, LA, USA, Nov. 2008.

[4] Z. Haas, J. Y. Halpern, and L. Li. Gossip-based ad hoc routing. In *21st Annual Joint Conference of the IEEE Computer and Communications Societies (Infocom)*, New York, USA, June 2002.

[5] K. A. Harras, K. C. Almeroth, and E. M. Belding-Royer. Delay tolerant mobile networks (dtmns): Controlled flooding in sparse mobile networks. In *4th IFIP-TC6 international conference on Networking Technologies, Services, and Protocols (Networking)*, Waterloo, Canada, May 2005.

[6] S. Jain, K. Fall, and R. Patra. Routing in a delay tolerant network. In *2004 conference on Applications, technologies, architectures, and protocols for computer communications (Sigcomm '04)*, Oct. 2004.

[7] B. K.-P. Koh and P.-Y. Kong. Performance study on zigbee-based wireless personal area networks for real-time health monitoring. volume vol. 28, pages 537–540, Aug 2006.

[8] A. Köpke, M. Swigulski, K. Wessel, D. Willkomm, P. K. Haneveld, T. Parker, O. Visser, H. S. Lichte, and S. Valentin. Simulating wireless and mobile networks in omnet++ – the mixim vision. In *1st International Workshop on OMNeT++ (hosted by SIMUTools 2008)*, Marseill, France, Mar. 2008.

[9] S. Merugu, M. H. Ammar, and E. W. Zegura. Routing in space and time in networks with predictable mobility. Technical Report GIT-CC-04-07, Georgia Institute of Technology, 2004.

[10] S. Movassaghi, M. Abolhasan, and J. Lipman. A review of routing protocols in wireless body area networks. *JNW*, 8(3):559–575, 2013.

[11] S. Movassaghi, M. Abolhasan, J. Lipman, D. Smith, and A. Jamalipour. Wireless body area networks: A survey. *IEEE Communications Surveys and Tutorials*, 16(3):1658–1686, 2014.

[12] Ms.Venkateswari.R and D. Rani.S. Design of an energy efficient and delay tolerant routing protocol for wireless body area network. In *International Journal on Computer Science and Engineering (IJCSE)*.

[13] J.-i. Naganawa, K. Wangchuk, M. Kim, T. Aoyagi, and J.-i. Takada. Simulation-based scenario-specific channel modeling for wban cooperative transmission schemes. *IEEE Journal of Biomedical and Health Informatics*, PP(99), May 2014.

[14] S.-Y. Ni, Y.-C. Tseng, Y.-S. Chen, and J.-P. Sheu. The broadcast storm problem in a mobile ad hoc network. In *5th annual ACM/IEEE international conference on Mobile computing and networking (MobiCom)*, Seattle, WA, USA, Aug. 1999.

[15] M. Quwaider and S. Biswas. On-body packet routing algorithms for body sensor networks. In *First International Conference on Networks and Communications (NETCOM '09)*, Chennai, India, Dec. 2009.

[16] M. Quwaider and S. Biswas. Probabilistic routing in on-body sensor networks with postural disconnections. In *7th ACM international symposium on Mobility management and wireless access (MobiWAC '09)*, Tenerife, Spain, Oct. 2009.

[17] Y. Sasson, D. Cavin, and A. Schiper. Probabilistic broadcast for flooding in wireless mobile ad hoc networks. In *Wireless Communications and Networking (WCNC)*, New Orleans, LA, USA, Mar. 2003.

[18] T. Spyropoulos, K. Psounis, and C. S. Raghavendra. Spray and wait: An efficient routing scheme for intermittently connected mobile networks. In *Proceedings of the 2005 ACM SIGCOMM Workshop on Delay-tolerant Networking*, WDTN '05, pages 252–259, 2005.

[19] A. Vahdat and D. Becker. Epidemic routing for partially connected ad hoc networks. Technical Report CS-2000-06, Department of Computer Science, Duke University, Apr. 2000.

[20] H. Viittala, M. Hamalainen, J. Iinatti, and A. Taparugssanagorn. Different experimental wban channel models and ieee802.15.6 models: Comparison and effects. In *Applied Sciences in Biomedical and Communication Technologies,2009.ISABEL 2009. 2nd International Symposium on*, pages 1–5, Nov 2009.

[21] T. R. Youssef Iraqi and P. Kong. Prevention of collisions among two wireless personal area networks. In *7th IFIP Wireless and Mobile Networking Conference, WMNC 2014, Vilamoura, Portugal, May 20-22, 2014.* pages 1–7.

A Resilient Dynamic Gateway Selection Algorithm Based on Quality Aware Metrics for Smart Grids

Vitor Hugo Okabayashi
Federal Fluminense University
vhugo@ic.uff.br

Igor Ribeiro
Federal Fluminense University
iribeiro@ic.uff.br

Diego Passos
Federal Fluminense University
dpassos@ic.uff.br

Célio Albuquerque
Federal Fluminense University
celio@ic.uff.br

ABSTRACT

Smart Grid represents the evolution of the current electrical power system. It is designed to meet the challenge of increasing demands for energy by fully integrating the electrical power grid with data communication networks. One of the main challenges faced by this kind of network is to fulfill reliability and resilience requirements in order to meet various types of services and applications. Wireless mesh networks can provide scalability and resilience to this communication network, but there are issues that need to be addressed before it can be used in practical smart grids. One of these issues relates to the robustness of the network when it faces gateway failures. In this situation, communication to smart meters may be unavailable for a considerable amount of time, which is prohibitive for many types of applications. In this sense, we present DDSA, an algorithm for dynamic selection of gateways in a multihoming smart grid network. The algorithm uses a probabilistic approach for choosing gateways, prioritizing those with the most reliable paths. Results indicate that DDSA increases network robustness and resilience in the presence of gateway failures compared to existing algorithms for dynamic gateway selection.

Categories and Subject Descriptors

C.2 [**COMPUTER-COMMUNICATION NETWORKS**]: General

Keywords

Smart Grids; Advanced Metering Infrastructure; AMI; Reliability

1. INTRODUCTION

The current electrical power system architecture does not meet the future demands of energy consumption, presenting

MSWiM'15, November 2–6, 2015, Cancun, Mexico.
© 2015 ACM. ISBN 978-1-4503-3762-5/15/11 ...$15.00.
DOI: http://dx.doi.org/10.1145/2811587.2811613.

a number of shortcomings such as: low and deficient communication and reliability problems [9]. Smart Grids represent an evolution of the existing electrical power system and aims at solving these inefficiencies, departing from the current model of one-way flow and deploying a two-way flow for energy and communication [9, 19]. A two-way communication network is essential for smart grids, supporting the sending of commands and the gathering of information from components and sensors in real time, allowing monitoring, maintenance and control [12].

The Advanced Metering Infrastructure (AMI) is a fundamental component of a smart grid, and it is the first step in its deployment [1, 17, 18]. The AMI is basically composed of smart meters, which collect data such as energy consumption of the equipment inside a residence and Data Aggregation Points (DAPs) that act as gateways to forward data from smart meters to the utility's headend and commands from the headend to the smart meters. In order for a smart grid to work properly, the AMI communication network must meet some strict requirements regarding its reliability, latency and response time to each application [12].

Communication in smart grids may use available wired or wireless technologies that support the exchange of information between components of the AMI [6, 24]. Different types of technologies can be used: cellular technology [22], ZigBee [22], RF Mesh [15], IEEE 802.11-based Wireless Mesh Networks (WMN) [2] and Power Line Communication (PLC) [16]. PLC is a promising wired technology, but it has limitations. In case of failures, such as physical disruption of power lines, it would not be possible to maintain communication between AMI components [11]. Wireless networks offer more benefits than wired networks, such as lower cost, ease of deployment and signal availability in large areas [22].

Among all wireless technologies, WMN has advantages compared to single-hop infrastructured network architectures since it communicates in a multi-hop fashion, what extends the coverage of the network and allows communication with alternative paths in case of failures [8,15]. However, the WMN must be adapted to the communication requirements of AMI. Typically, an AMI is composed of a communication network connecting smart meters within a given neighborhood to a specific single DAP. Each DAP is connected to the utility's headend through the network's backbone.

In this architecture, in case of DAP failure, the associated smart meters become temporarily disconnected from the utility's headend, therefore failing to meet AMI's availability and reliability requirements. To overcome this problem, we propose the Dynamic DAP Selection Algorithm (DDSA). Assuming that each meter can reach multiple DAPs through one or more hops, DDSA maintains a set of reachable DAPs that provides the best path metrics. When a smart meter needs to send a packet, DDSA randomly selects one DAP from the list and route the packet through this selected DAP. The main goal of DDSA is to allow smart meters to use multiple DAPs, therefore increasing network's robustness and resiliency.

The contributions of this paper are three-fold:

- Proposal of DDSA, an algorithm that improves the resiliency and robustness of an AMI network in the presence of DAP failures;

- Mathematical analysis of an algorithm that always selects the DAP to which the routing metric is the best possible. Throughout this paper, we call this algorithm Best_ETX;

- Mathematical model of DDSA and its comparison against the Best_ETX algorithm.

The remaining of this paper is organized as follows. Section 2 presents the related works. Section 3 provides a mathematical analysis of the Best-ETX algorithm in a scenario with a DAP failure. In Section 4 we present the proposed DDSA algorithm. In addition, a mathematical model of DDSA configured with the ETX routing metric is presented and compared against the Best-ETX model. Simulation results are discussed in Section 5, and Section 6 concludes the paper and presents future works.

2. RELATED WORK

One class of proposals uses a single DAP to implement AMI networks [11, 15]. The work in [11] proposes the use of WMN where multiple domains of mesh networks are connected by a WiMAX backbone. This architecture provides redundant paths between smart meters mitigating problems like broken routes due to node failure increasing their resilience. However, this work considers only one DAP acting as gateway in each WMN domain. If it becomes unavailable, there will be no communication between smart meters and the headend. This is the same problem studied by [15] where the WMN consists of smart meters, routers and collectors. The smart meters communicate with routers or directly to collectors, and the latter controls up to 25,000 smart meters and routers on a single network.

The second class of proposals uses multiple DAPs in the AMI network [5, 10, 14]. The work in [5] makes use of multiple gateways to increase WMN resilience because in addition to providing redundant paths, it also provides gateway redundancy. This approach is applied to WMN that serves as the backbone for Internet access but uses only the gateway with the best path.

The works in [14] and [10] are designed to meet the requirements of AMI networks and make use of multiple DAPs for communication between smart meters and headend, modifying the HWMP protocol (Hybrid Wireless Mesh Protocol). Although the work in [10] solves some deficiencies of the HWMP protocol, it still suffers from other problems such as route instability and loops. According to the authors, this is a characteristic of the distributed backpressure system adopted by them. However, neither of them has evaluated the protocol behavior in an environment with DAP failures nor allowed transmission rate adaptation, which increases the problem of route instability. They use a base protocol that has scalability problems due to the congestion caused by control messages [3] making it difficult to use in AMI.

Our proposal, DDSA, makes use of multiple DAPs for communication between smart meters and the utility's headend and differs from [14] and [10] because it is designed to improve performance in environments with DAP failures. DDSA is independent from the routing protocol. Moreover, it can be implemented in a protocol that best suits the implementation of the AMI.

3. MOTIVATION

In the Advanced Metering Infrastructure, all smart meters must be able to communicate with at least one DAP. The AMI imposes strong requirements on the communication network in terms of reliability and latency. However, due to the unstable nature of the wireless networks and to the fact that the network equipment is deployed in public venues (and, thus are vulnerable to accidents, attacks and natural disasters), it is imperative to employ a routing protocol robust enough to maintain good performance even in case of DAP failures.

Ideally, in a WMN-based AMI, smart meters can reach multiple DAPs directly or through multi-hop paths. However, typical WMN routing protocols select a single DAP (i.e., the closest one according to the routing metric). If the selected DAP fails, the associated smart meters become disconnected. The amount of time in which the smart meters will remain disconnected depends on the time the metric takes to reflect the failure and the time needed for the route update to propagate throughout the network.

To better understand the implications of a DAP failure in the Smart Grid, lets consider the scenario in which smart meter A (called node A henceforth) directly reaches DAPs B and C through links $(A-B)$ and $(A-C)$, respectively. To improve performance, it is important to use a routing metric that considers the path quality. Hence, in this example we use the Expected Transmission Count (ETX) as the routing metric.

The ETX of a link represents the expected number of link layer transmissions until a packet is successfully delivered to the destination. In fact, ETX only considers a packet to be successfully delivered through a link if it has been received by the destination and the corresponding acknowledgment from the destination is also correctly received by the source. From the perspective of node A, the ETX in the link $(A-B)$ in a given time t can be calculated according to Equation 1, where $d_f(t)^{A \rightarrow B}$ is the probability the packet is successfully received by its destination (forward direction) and $d_r(t)^{B \rightarrow A}$ is the probability the ack is successfully received by the source (reverse direction).

$$ETX(t)^{A-B} = \frac{1}{d_f(t)^{A \rightarrow B} \cdot d_r(t)^{B \rightarrow A}} \qquad (1)$$

In order to calculate the ETX metric, nodes A and B send probe packets every T seconds. They keep track of all probes received during the current time window W, which can contain at most $\frac{W}{T}$ probes. Consequently, each node can easily calculate the probability of successful delivery of a packet in the reverse path. Specifically, node A can calculate

$d_r(t)^{B \to A}$ using Equation 2, where $C_B(t)$ is the number of probes node A correctly received from DAP B in the current time window. However, node A does not know how many of its probes to DAP B were successfully received. Therefore, node A must retrieve this information from DAP B in order to calculate $d_f(t)^{A \to B}$. Hence, every probe sent from DAP B to node A contains the number of probes sent from A and received by DAP B in the current time window.

$$d_r(t)^{B \to A} = \frac{C_B(t)}{\frac{W}{T}} \qquad (2)$$

Now, lets consider that when node A needs to send some data to the utility's headend, it always selects the DAP that provides the path with the best (lowest) ETX metric among all reachable DAPs. From now on we call this algorithm Best_ETX. Suppose that at time t_0, $ETX(t_0)^{A-B} < ETX(t_0)^{A-C}$. Consequently, all packets sent by node A to the utility's headend are routed through DAP B. Moreover, the delivery probability of the link $(A - B)$ is given by $\frac{1}{ETX(t_0)^{A-B}}$. In order to make the analysis simpler, we assume $ETX(t)^{A-C} = ETX(t_0)^{A-C}, \forall t$.

Now, suppose that at time t_f DAP B fails and stops working. Consequently, DAP B stops sending probes, making it impossible for node A to correctly learn new values of $d_f(t)^{A \to B}$. Hence, we consider $d_f(t)^{A \to B} = d_f(t_f)^{A \to B}$ for $t \geq t_f$[1]. In addition, because node A stops receiving probes from DAP B, the value of $C_B(t)$ decreases with time. In fact, after every T seconds, the ETX time window W shifts one position to the right. At this time, if the leftmost probe of W sent by DAP B has been correctly received by node A, $C_B(t)$ is reduced by one. However, if the leftmost probe in W sent by DAP B has not been correctly received by node A, $C_B(t)$ remains the same. Approximating each entry of the ETX time window by its expected value, we obtain Equation 3.

$$C_B(t) = C_B(t_f) - \frac{C_B(t_f)}{\frac{W}{T}} \cdot \frac{(t - t_f)}{T}, t > t_f \qquad (3)$$

After W seconds, the ETX window of the link $(A - B)$ will become completely empty. At this time, which we call t_{end}, $d_r(t_{end})^{B \to A} = 0$ and, consequently, $ETX(t_{end})^{A-B} = \infty$. Hence, after time t_{end}, the link $A - B$ is considered broken and node A will have no alternative but to route packets through DAP C. Notice, however, that DAP C will be chosen by node A before t_{end}, namely at time t_{eq}, where $t_f < t_{eq} < t_{end}$ and $ETX(t_{eq})^{A-B} = ETX(t_{eq})^{A-C} = ETX(t_0)^{A-C}$.

$$Prob_{etx}(t) = \begin{cases} \frac{1}{ETX(t_f)^{A-B}} & t \leq t_f \\ 0 & t_f < t < t_{eq} \\ \frac{1}{ETX(t_f)^{A-C}} & t \geq t_{eq} \end{cases} \qquad (4)$$

Equation 4 summarizes the behavior of Best_ETX algorithm in the previous example scenario in terms of packet delivery probability between node A and its chosen DAP. It can

---

[1]In fact, routing protocols often associate an validity property to $d_r(t)^{B \to A}$ and $d_f(t)^{A \to B}$ in such a way that if the current value of $d_r(t)^{B \to A}$ or $d_f(t)^{A \to B}$ is older than the validity property, the value is discarded. However, for our purposes, we consider that all calculations performed in this section occur in a time frame shorter than any validity property.

be observed that before the recovery time $T_{rec} = (t_{eq} - t_f)$ the delivery probability is zero. Since availability is very important for AMI applications, T_{rec} provides a good measure of the network performance in case of DAP failures. Notice that T_{rec} can be derived by applying Equation 3 to Equations 2 and 1, as shown in Equation 5.

$$T_{rec} = W \cdot \left(1 - \frac{ETX(t_f)^{A-B}}{ETX(t_f)^{A-C}}\right), t > t_f \qquad (5)$$

Consider the following numerical example. Let $d_f(t_f)^{A \to B} = d_r(t_f)^{B \to A} = 0.9$ and $d_f^{A \to C} = d_r^{C \to A} = 0.6$. Therefore, we have $ETX(t_f)^{A-B} = 1.23$ and $ETX(t_f)^{A-C} = 2.78$. Every node sends one probe per second ($T = 1s$) and is configured with $W = 100s$. Suppose that DAP B fails at time $t_f = 20s$. Applying these parameters to Equation 5 results that no packets sent by node A are received by any DAP for approximately $56s$. Considering that some AMI applications have latency restrictions of about $2s$ [13], this scenario becomes undesirable.

In fact, this scenario is an optimistic one. Consider now that node A is connected to DAPs B and C through multiple hops. In this case, when DAP B fails, the changes in the ETX metric are not directly perceived by node A. Instead, this information must be propagated back by the routing protocol as a route update. Hence, in a multihop scenario, the recovery time T_{rec} can be much greater than the value calculated through Equation 5.

4. THE DYNAMIC DAP SELECTION ALGORITHM (DDSA)

The idea behind the Dynamic DAP Selection Algorithm (DDSA) is to leverage the existence of multiple DAPs to improve network resilience in case of failures. A naive approach could lead to a simplistic solution in which the sending node replicates all packets and sends a copy to each reachable DAP. In this case, the delivery probability would be, in principle, maximized. However, since typical wireless technologies employed in WMN (such as 802.11) are contention-based, flooding all packets to all DAPs could result in an excessive number of collisions, increasing latency and degrading network performance.

As an alternative solution, the sending node could probabilistically choose a destination DAP each time it needs to send a packet. However, the efficiency of this solution depends highly on the way in which probabilities are assigned to DAPs. For example, if we suppose that the probabilities are uniformly distributed over all DAPs, then all of them would be equally likely to be selected, regardless of their respective path quality. In other words, if DAP A presents the best possible path metric and all other DAPs present the worst possible path metric, the sending node would select the best DAP with probability $\frac{1}{N}$, while the worst DAPs would be selected with probability $\frac{(N-1)}{N}$. Clearly, this approach is very inefficient. We can therefore conclude that the assignment of probabilities to DAPs must consider the path metric in order to give higher probabilities to better DAPs. Therefore, we argue that the routing metric must be quality aware and must handle varying link rates.

The proposed Dynamic DAP Selection Algorithm (DDSA) is based on a randomized algorithm triggered by two events: *Topology Update* and *Send Data*.

4.1 Topology Update

When routing information is updated in smart meter m_i, DDSA recalculates the selection probability for all reachable DAPs. This task can be accomplished in two different ways depending on the behavior of the routing metric being used. If the routing metric assigns higher values to better quality links, the selection probability of DAP d_j is given by Equation 6. On the other hand, if the routing metric assigns lower values to better quality links, Equation 7 is used instead. In both equations, $M(m_i, d_k)$ represents the cost of the best path from smart meter m_i to DAP d_k and N is the number of reachable DAPs. Consequently, when smart meter m_i needs to send a data packet, it chooses DAP d_k with probability $P(m_i, d_k)$.

$$P(m_i, d_j) = \frac{M(m_i, d_j)}{\sum\limits_{k=1}^{N} M(m_i, d_k)} \qquad (6)$$

The selection probability assignment process provided by equations 6 and 7 allows us to select better DAPs more often. However, in some cases, the value $M(m_i, d_j)$ for some DAP d_j may be too low (or too high), what makes DAP d_j useless in practice. Even so, some packets would still be sent to DAP d_j because the selection probability $P(m_i, d_j)$ is not zero. This problem can reduce the overall delivery probability of DDSA.

$$P(m_i, d_j) = \frac{1/M(m_i, d_j)}{\sum\limits_{k=1}^{N} 1/M(m_i, d_k)} \qquad (7)$$

Algorithm 1: Exclude DAP with Cost Below Threshold.

1 $d_{best} \leftarrow find\_best\_dap()$
3 $\gamma \leftarrow \alpha \times P(m_i, d_{best}) \leftarrow get\_selection\_probability(m_i, d_{best})$
4 $discarded \leftarrow FALSE$
5 **for** each DAP d_k **do**
6      $P(m_i, d_k) \leftarrow get\_selection\_probability(m_i, d_k)$
7   **if** $P(m_i, d_k) < \gamma$ **then**
8         $P(m_i, d_k) \leftarrow 0$
9         $discarded \leftarrow TRUE$
10   **end**
11 **end**
12 **if** $discarded$ **then**
13     $recalculate\_selection\_probabilities()$
14 **end**

To overcome this problem, DDSA executes Algorithm 1, which discards all DAPs d_k whose $P(m_i, d_k)$ is below a threshold. First, the algorithm finds the DAP d_{best} such that $M(m_i, d_{best})$ has the best value considering all other reachable DAPs (line 1). Next, the algorithm retrieves the selection probability for DAP d_{best} (line 2). This process is straightforward because DDSA has already calculated and stored the selection probability to all reachable DAPs.

In the next step, Algorithm 1 calculates the value of the threshold γ (line 3). In order to do so, the user must con-

figure the value of parameter $\alpha \in [0, 1]$. This choice must be done carefully, because higher values of α result in the use of better DAPs at the price of reducing resilience in case of DAP failures. Then, the algorithm discards all DAPs d_k such that $P(m_i, d_k) < \gamma$ (lines 5 through 11). Finally, if any DAP was discarded, then the selection probability for all remaining DAPs must be recalculated (line 13). Notice that recalculate the selection probabilities means to calculate the summation in the denominator of Equation 6 or Equation 7 considering every DAP d_k that was not excluded by the Algorithm 1.

4.2 Send Data

The Send Data event is triggered whenever a smart meter needs to send information to the utility's headend. DDSA keeps a table containing the assigned selection probability for all reachable DAPs. Consequently, when smart meter m_i needs to send a packet, it chooses DAP d_k with probability $P(m_i, d_k)$. Note that if the DAP d_k was excluded by Algorithm 1, it will never be selected because $P(m_i, d_k) = 0$.

Algorithm 2: DAP Selection

1 $Prob\_Sum \leftarrow 0$
2 $rand \leftarrow randomUniform(0, 1)$
3 **for** each DAP d_k **do**
4      $P(m_i, d_k) \leftarrow get\_selection\_probability(m_i, d_k)$
5      $Prob\_Sum \leftarrow Prob\_Sum + P(m_i, d_k)$
6   **if** $Prob\_Sum >= rand$ **then**
7         $Selected\_DAP \leftarrow d_k$ **break**
8   **end**
9 **end**
10 **return** $Selected\_DAP$

Algorithm 2 shows the steps of the DAP selection process. First, the algorithm randomly chooses a value between 0 and 1 (line 2). Next, for each reachable DAP d_k, the algorithm retrieves de probability $P(m_i, d_k)$ and sums it to variable $Prob\_Sum$ (lines 4 and 5). These steps are repeated until $Prob\_Sum$ is greater than or equal to the selected value $rand$, in which case the current DAP is chosen as the gateway for this specific application message (lines 6 through 8). It's worth mentioning that the list of DAPs is not sorted by cost nor by selection probability, which could influence the result of the DAP selection process.

4.3 Comparing DDSA with Best_ETX

Before we move to Section 5, let's analyze how DDSA compares to Best_ETX in the scenario explained in Section 3. In this analysis, we assume that DDSA operates using the ETX metric. Because greater values of ETX indicate worse links, we must use Equation 7 to calculate the selection probability, resulting in Equation 8. Note that, as already said, we consider $ETX(t)^{A-C} = ETX(t_f)^{A-C}, \forall t$.

$$P(t)^{A-B} = \frac{ETX(t_f)^{A-C}}{ETX(t_f)^{A-C} + ETX(t)^{A-B}} \qquad (8)$$

Before time t_f, when DAP B fails, node A sends packets to DAP B with probability $P(t)^{A-B}$ and to DAP C with probability $P(t)^{A-C}$. Once a packet is destined to DAP B, it is correctly delivered with probability $\frac{1}{ETX(t_f)^{A-B}}$. Similarly, once a packet is destined to DAP C, it is correctly delivered with probability $\frac{1}{ETX(t_f)^{A-C}}$. When DAP B fails, all packets sent to it are lost. However, some packets are still destined to DAP C and some of them are correctly delivered. After W time units from time t_f ($t_{rec} = t_f + W$), we get $ETX(t_{rec})^{A-B} = \infty$. Consequently, DAP B's selection probability becomes zero. From this time onward, all packets start to be routed through DAP C. Equation 9 summarizes this scenario in terms of the delivery probability of a packet.

$$Prob(t)_{ddsa} = \begin{cases} P(t)^{A-B} \cdot \frac{1}{ETX(t_f)^{A-B}} + \\ P(t)^{A-C} \cdot \frac{1}{ETX(t_f)^{A-C}} & t \leq t_f \\ P(t)^{A-C} \cdot \frac{1}{ETX(t_f)^{A-C}} & t_f < t < t_{rec} \\ \frac{1}{ETX(t_f)^{A-C}} & t \geq (t_{rec}) \end{cases}$$
(9)

Notice, however, that in a typical WMN, a link-layer protocol such as 802.11 MAC will provide up to M retransmissions of unicast frames, resulting in higher delivery probabilities, according to Equation 10, where $Prob(t)$ is the probability a packet is correctly received in time t.

$$Prob_{retrans}(t) = 1 - (1 - Prob(t))^M$$
(10)

Table 1: Parameters of the numerical example.

W	100 s
T	1
$ETX(t_f)^{A-B}$	1.23
$ETX(t_f)^{A-C}$	2.78
t_f	20 s

In order to compare the behaviors of Best_ETX and DDSA, we will use the same parameters used in the numerical example in Section 3. These parameters are summarized in Table 1. After calculating $Prob_{etx}(t)$ (Equation 4) and $Prob_{ddsa}$ (Equation 9(t)), we applied the results to parameter $Prob(t)$ in Equation 10 and defined $M = 4$ (the default value for 'large' frames in the 802.11 MAC).

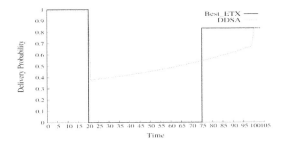

Figure 1: Example Scenario.

In Figure 1 we can observe that before DAP B fails (time $20s$) the delivery probabilities for both Best_ETX and DDSA are close to 100%. In fact, Best_ETX provides a slightly greater delivery probability than DDSA. When DAP B fails, the delivery probability considering Best_ETX falls instantly to zero and maintains this value until time $75s$, when

$ETX(75)^{A-B} = ETX(75)^{A-C}$. On the other hand, DDSA presents a much better behavior. At time 20s the delivery probability falls rapidly to approximately 40% and continually grows until time 100s.

Before DAP B fails, most of the packets were being sent to it. Consequently, when it failed, all these packets were lost, what made the delivery probability instantly drop. After that, as the ETX to DAP B increases, its selection probability decreases, what causes more packets to be addressed do DAP C instead of DAP B. At time 75s, the delivery probability considering Best_ETX instantly grows to approximately 83%, which corresponds to the inverse of the ETX to DAP C, and maintains this value since forth. However, because DDSA keeps sending some packets to DAP B, its delivery probability continues to increase, but remains below the delivery probability of Best_ETX until time 100s.

Finally, at time 100s the ETX to DAP B reaches infinity and its selection probability drops to zero. From this point onward the curves of Best_ETX and DDSA are coincident. Clearly, the DDSA algorithm provides better robustness in the presence of DAP failures, delivering more packets in average in the presence of DAP failures.

5. PERFORMANCE EVALUATION

5.1 Simulation Environment

In order to evaluate the performance of DDSA in the AMI layer of a smart grid, we set up the simulation environment shown in Figure 2 in the ns-2 simulator [21]. In this topology, there are thirty six smart meters arranged in a grid and three DAPs. All the nodes are supposed to operate in a suburban external scenario, which was simulated using the shadowing propagation model according to [20].

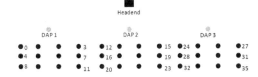

Figure 2: Scenario used in the simulation.

To simulate the exchange of information between smart meters and DAPs in a typical AMI application, a Constant Bit Rate (CBR) UDP traffic was used with fixed packet size of 400B at a rate of 1 packet at 3 seconds. Although UDP does not provide reliable transmission of data, it has some advantages over TCP, such as its lower latency, which is important for many smart grid applications. On the other hand, typical AMI applications require a high degree of reliability, which is not provided by UDP. To solve this problem, we employed a protocol at the application layer running on top of UDP that implements its own transport service suitable for AMI traffic [7]. This protocol uses a proactive retransmission strategy in which, for each generated data packet, 10 replicas are transmitted simultaneously. If any of the replicas reaches one of the DAPs, the original packet is considered to be successfully delivered. Therefore, the results regarding packet delivery rate reported in this section are calculated considering the point of view of the application layer.

As already explained, the type of routing metric used is an important factor in the DDSA performance. Consequently, in the simulations presented in this section, the routing protocol OLSR [4] was used in conjunction with the routing metric MARA [23], which estimates the path delay and performs rate adaptation. The smart meters start to send data at time 150s and at time 300s DAP 2 fails. We performed ten simulation rounds, each lasting for 650 seconds and configured with a different seed. Finally, all averages are presented with their respective 95% confidence intervals.

Lets consider now the influence of the parameter α in our simulation scenario. We evaluated two configurations of DDSA, one with a low value of α (30%) and the other with a high value of α (80%). In addition, we also compared the results from DDSA against the algorithm proposed by [5], which we call Multi-DAP henceforth. This algorithm dynamically selects the best DAP according to its path routing metric at the time the data packet is transmitted by its source node. The evaluated configurations are summarized in the following list.

(1) DDSA with $\alpha = 0.3$ referred to as DDSA-30%;

(2) DDSA with $\alpha = 0.8$ referred to as DDSA-80%; and

(3) Multi-DAP.

5.2 Simulation Results

Figure 3(a) shows the packet delivery ratio for all nodes as a function of time, considering the average of the latest 60 seconds. It is noticeable that the performance of DDSA-30% is higher than the other proposals after the occurrence of a DAP failure. At time 363s DDSA-30% sustains a delivery ratio of 93%, while DDSA-80% reaches 73% and Multi-DAP only 67%, what shows that DDSA-30% is less affected by the failure of the DAP 2. Particularly, Figure 3(b) shows that after the failure of DAP 2 (time 363s), DDSA-30% provides 80% of packet delivery ratio, while DDSA-30% and Multi-DAP provide only 23% and 5%, respectively, considering the central region of the network (nodes 12 to 23).

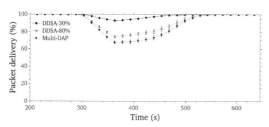

(a) Packet delivery for all nodes

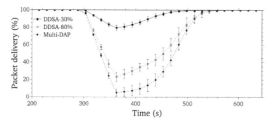

(b) Packet delivery for nodes 12-23

Figure 3: Packet delivery rates as a function of time.
From the graphics in Figure 3, we can conclude two important facts. First, the design choice of distributing packets among DAPs (instead of choosing a single DAP) makes the

data collection more robust and resilient in face of failures. Second, the value of α is crucial in the performance of the algorithm. The choice of its value represents an important trade-off, where lower values increase the reliability of the network, but also make the algorithm choose DAPs with lower quality paths. On the other hand, choosing higher values of α makes the algorithm choose DAPs with the best path qualities, but also reduces the network reliability in case of DAP failures, which can be observed by the results achieved by DDSA-80%.

To better understand how the behavior of DDSA differs from the behavior of Multi-DAP in terms of DAP selection, Figure 4 shows the choices made by node 16 using the three evaluated proposals during one round of simulation (same seed). With Multi-DAP, Before DAP 2 fails, node 16 sent all packets to DAP 2 because it has the best quality path. However, when DAP 2 fails (at 300 seconds), node 16 takes 123 seconds to employ an alternative DAP. During this period, all packets sent by note 16 are lost, what is illustrated by the gap in Figure 4(c). On the other hand, even before the failure, DDSA-30% already distributed traffic more evenly between DAPs. Consequently, when DAP 2 fails, node 16 is able to shortly recover sending its packets to DAPs 1 and 3. This behavior can be noted in Figure 4(a), where no gaps can be observed.

When we increase the value of α, the DAPs with the worse path metrics are excluded. Since in our simulation scenario there are only three available DAPs, we noticed that nodes in the center of the network (i.e., closer to DAP 2) would frequently discard DAPs 1 and 3 when $\alpha = 80\%$. That can be seen in Figure 4(b) by the existence of a gap similar to that of Figure 4(c), although shorter. After about 66 seconds, node 16 realizes that the new metric to DAP 2, although still better than the metric to the two other DAPs, is not low enough to causes DAP 1 to be excluded (refer to line 3 of Algorithm 1). From this point onward, the probability of DDSA selecting DAP 1 increases as the metric to DAP 2 decreases. Eventually, DAP 1 becomes the best DAP and DAP 2 is excluded.

The behavior of node 16 gave us a good insight regarding the performance of the DDSA algorithm and the impact of the value of α. However, this behavior depends on the position of the node in the grid. Consequently, Figure 5 expands the analysis done in Figure 4 including all nodes (smart meters). Note that DDSA-30% (Fig. 5(a)) has a much more balanced DAP selection than the other proposals. For nodes in the central region of the network, with DDSA-30%, the lowest usage percentage is 16.4%. For Multi-DAP (Fig. 5(c)), six nodes (nodes 12, 15, 16, 19, 20, 23) only use two DAPs. Except by nodes 13 and 14, in DDSA-30% all usage percentages in the central region are below 41.6% for DAP 2 (the preferable DAP for that region). For DDSA-80%, all values are above 40.2% and for Multi-DAP they are above 45.7% for DAP 2. This demonstrates that DDSA-30% distributes packets more evenly among DAPs in the central region of the network, improving the resilience against DAP failures.

Figure 6 shows the unavailability period τ for each node with respect to the utility's headend, i.e., the sum of the periods during which each node could not reach the headend through any DAP. It is clear that the long gap to deliver new packets is not unique for node 16. This behavior is repeated for other nodes in the central region of the network as well.

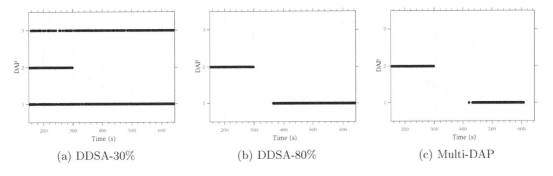

(a) DDSA-30%   (b) DDSA-80%   (c) Multi-DAP

Figure 4: Packets received by DAP from node 16.

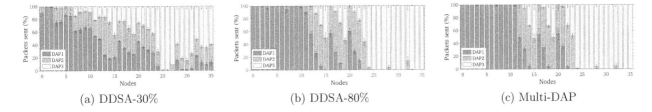

(a) DDSA-30%   (b) DDSA-80%   (c) Multi-DAP

Figure 5: Percentage of DAP usage by each node.

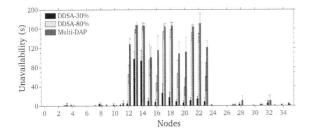

Figure 6: Unavailability Period.

For DDSA-80% and Multi-DAP, these nodes suffered long periods of unavailability, while DDSA-30% sustained lower values of τ.

Nodes 13 and 14 are the closest ones to the failed DAP 2, thus suffering more influence of this failure (because their path cost to DAP 2 is much lower than the cost to other DAPs). Except for these nodes, the average unavailability period τ_{avg} for the DDSA-30% is 4.2 seconds and the maximum unavailability period τ_{max} is 26.2 seconds. For DDSA-80%, τ_{avg} is 29.5 seconds and τ_{max} is 158.8 seconds, and for Multi-DAP τ_{avg} is 40.7 seconds and τ_{max} is 166.4 seconds.

6. CONCLUSION AND FUTURE WORK

This work presented DDSA, a dynamic DAP selection algorithm to increase the reliability and resilience of AMI applications through the use of multiple DAPs in Smart Grids where the nodes are connected by a Wireless Mesh Network. In this kind of network, the DAP has an important role in the exchange of information between the smart meter and the utility's headend, because all traffic flows through it. A failure in a DAP inhibits the exchange of information on the AMI network, so alternative routes through other DAPs should be used after failure to allow the communication to happen.

First, we motivated our proposal through a mathematical analysis of the behavior of an algorithm that always selects the DAP with the best ETX metric (Best_ETX) in face of DAP failures. We shown that the selection of a single DAP, the one that presents the best metric, is problematic in case of DAP failures, causing some affected nodes to be disconnected from the utility's headend for a long period of time, reducing the delivery ratio of the overall system. In the case of Best_ETX, we provided an equation that can be used to calculate how long a node remains disconnected from the utility's headend in case of a DAP failure. After presenting the details of DDSA, we also developed a mathematical model of the algorithm, considering its use in conjunction with the ETX metric. We then compared this model with Best_ETX algorithm and showed that DDSA presents a better reliability, providing a higher overall delivery ratio.

Finally, we performed simulations to evaluate the performance of DDSA in face of DAP failures. We compared three different configurations: the DDSA algorithm with the parameter $\alpha = 0.3$, the same algorithm but with $\alpha = 0.8$ and an algorithm that always selects the DAP with the best metric (Multi-DAP). Comparing these configurations, our conclusions are two-fold:

1. DDSA improves the network reliability when a DAP fails compared to the Multi-DAP algorithm;

2. Lower values of α increase the robustness of the network, but also causes the selection of worse DAPs, what can negatively influence other network parameters, such as latency.

For future work we intend to conduct a deeper analysis of the impact of the α parameter in order to properly adjust it to provide good resilience while sustaining acceptable levels of performance. In addition, We intend to investigate the usage of a dynamic α, which automatically adapts to the ongoing network conditions. In addition, we expect to analyze the impact of other routing metrics on the performance of DDSA.

7. ACKNOWLEDGMENTS

This research was supported in part by grants from CNPq, CAPES, FAPERJ and CELESC/ANEEL (Brazil).

8. REFERENCES

[1] C. Bennett and D. Highfill. Networking AMI smart meters. In *IEEE Energy 2030 Conference.*, 2008.

[2] M. Campista, P. Esposito, I. Moraes, L. Costa, O. Duarte, D. Passos, C. de Albuquerque, D. Saade, and M. Rubinstein. Routing metrics and protocols for wireless mesh networks. *IEEE Network*, 22(1):6–12, 2008.

[3] R. Carrano, L. Magalhães, D. Saade, and C. Albuquerque. IEEE 802.11s multihop MAC: A Tutorial. *IEEE Communications Surveys & Tutorials*, 13(1):52–67, 2011.

[4] T. Clausen, P. Jacquet, C. Adjih, A. Laouiti, P. Minet, P. Muhlethaler, A. Qayyum, L. Viennot, et al. Optimized link state routing protocol (OLSR). *RFC 3626, Oct.*, 2003.

[5] C. da Silva, D. Passos, J. Duarte, I. Moraes, and C. Albuquerque. Dyntun: A tool for providing multihoming support in wireless mesh networks. In *International Information and Telecommunication Technologies Symposium*, 2010.

[6] G. Deconinck. An evaluation of two-way communication means for advanced metering in flanders (belgium). In *IEEE Instrumentation and Measurement Technology Conference Proceedings.*, 2008.

[7] D. M. F. Baker. Internet protocols for the smart grid. Rfc 6272, Cisco Systems, 2011.

[8] X. Fang, S. Misra, G. Xue, and D. Yang. Smart grid - the new and improved power grid: A Survey. *IEEE Communications Surveys & Tutorials*, 14(4):944–980, 2012.

[9] H. Farhangi. The path of the smart grid. *IEEE Power and Energy Magazine*, 8(1):18–28, 2010.

[10] H. Gharavi and B. Hu. Multigate communication network for smart grid. *Proceedings of the IEEE*, 99(6):1028–1045, 2011.

[11] V. Gungor and F. Lambert. A survey on communication networks for electric system automation. *Computer Networks: The International Journal of Computer and Telecommunications Networking*, 50(7):877–897, 2006.

[12] V. C. Gungor, D. Sahin, T. Kocak, S. Ergut, C. Buccella, C. Cecati, and G. P. Hancke. Smart grid technologies: Communication technologies and standards. *IEEE Transactions on Industrial Informatics*, 7(4):529–539, Nov 2011.

[13] V. C. Gungor, D. Sahin, T. Kocak, S. Ergut, C. Buccella, C. Cecati, and G. P. Hancke. A survey on smart grid potential applications and communication requirements. *IEEE Transactions on Industrial Informatics*, 9(1):28–42, Feb 2013.

[14] J. Kim, D. Kim, K. Lim, Y. Ko, and S. Lee. Improving the reliability of IEEE 802.11s based wireless mesh networks for smart grid systems. *Journal of Communications and Networks*, 14(6):629–639, Dec 2012.

[15] B. Lichtensteiger, B. Bjelajac, C. Muller, and C. Wietfeld. RF Mesh systems for smart metering: System architecture and performance. In *IEEE International Conference on Smart Grid Communications*, 2010.

[16] J. Liu, B. Zhao, J. Wang, Y. Zhu, and J. Hu. Application of power line communication in smart power consumption. In *IEEE International Symposium on Power Line Communications and Its Applications*, 2010.

[17] W. Luan, D. Sharp, and S. Lancashire. Smart grid communication network capacity planning for power utilities. In *IEEE PES Transmission and Distribution Conference and Exposition*, April 2010.

[18] R. Mohassel, A. Fung, F. Mohammadi, and K. Raahemifar. A survey on advanced metering infrastructure and its application in smart grids. In *Proceedings of the 27th Canadian Conference on Electrical and Computer Engineering (CCECE)*, pages 1–8, Toronto, ON, CAN, 2014. IEEE.

[19] K. Moslehi and R. Kumar. A reliability perspective of the smart grid. *IEEE Transactions on Smart Grid*, 1(1), 2010.

[20] NIST. NISTIR 7761 - Guidelines for assessing wireless standards for smart grid applications, 2011.

[21] NS-2. The network simulator - ns-2, 2013.

[22] P. Parikh, M. Kanabar, and T. Sidhu. Opportunities and challenges of wireless communication technologies for smart grid applications. In *IEEE Power and Energy Society General Meeting*, 2010.

[23] D. Passos and C. Albuquerque. A joint approach to routing metrics and rate adaptation in wireless mesh networks. *IEEE/ACM Transactions on Networking*, 20(4):999–1009, Aug 2012.

[24] N. Saputro, K. Akkaya, and S. Uludag. A survey of routing protocols for smart grid communications. *Computer Networks: The International Journal of Computer and Telecommunications Networking*, 56(11):2742 – 2771, 2012.

Modeling Multi-path TCP Throughput with Coupled Congestion Control and Flow Control

Qingfang Liu, Ke Xu
TNLIST,Tsinghua University
Beijing, P.R.China
liuqf13@gmail.com
xuke@mail.tsinghua.edu.cn

Haiyang Wang
University of Minnesota
Duluth, America
haiyang@d.umn.edu

Lei Xu
Tsinghua University
Beijing, P.R.China
xl_7@sina.com

ABSTRACT

Multi-Path Transmission Control Protocol (MPTCP) is e-merging as a dominant paradigm that enables users to u-tilize multiple Network Interface Controllers (NICs) simultaneously. Due to the complexity of its protocol design, the steady-state performance of MPTCP still remains large-ly unclear through model analysis. This introduces severe challenges to quantitatively study the efficiency, fairness and stability of existing MPTCP implementations. In this paper, we for the first time investigate the modeling of coupled congestion control and flow control algorithms in MPTCP. By proposing a closed-form throughput model, we reveal the relationship between MPTCP throughput and subflow characters, such as Round Trip Time (RTT), packet loss rate and receive buffer size. The extensive NS2-based evaluation indicates that the proposed model can be applied to understand the throughput of MPTCP in various situations. In particular, when MPTCP subflows have similar RTTs, the average Error Rate (ER) of the proposed model is less than 8%. Even in the situation where huge RTT difference exists between subflows, the model can still behave well with average ER less than 10%.

Categories and Subject Descriptors

C.4 [**Performance of Systems**]: Modeling techniques

Keywords

Throughput Modeling; Multi-path TCP; Coupled Congestion Control; Flow Control;

1. INTRODUCTION

Recent advances in mobile computing have turned the idea of multi-homing into a reality. To better utilize multiple Network Interface Controllers (NICs), Multi-path TCP (MPTCP) extension [2] has been widely suggested in recent years. This design enables the simultaneous use of several interfaces by a modification of TCP and presents a regular

MSWiM'15, November 02–06, 2015, Cancun, Mexico.
ⓒ 2015 ACM. ISBN 978-1-4503-3762-5/15/11 ...$15.00.
DOI: http://dx.doi.org/10.1145/2811587.2811590.

TCP interface to the application layer, while in fact transmitting data across several subflows. MPTCP brings better end-to-end throughput, higher connection reliability and s-moother failure recovery. The MPTCP implementation in Linux Kernel [6] has recently broke the record of the fastest TCP connection with a speed of 51.8 Gbit/second. On the other hand, MPTCP is not only compatible with regular TCP but also transparent to application layer and various middlewares in network. Enticed by these salient features of MPTCP, industry leaders such as Apple and Samsung are implementing this revolutionary protocol into their latest iOS and Android systems. For example, the MPTCP implementation in Apple's iOS7 has been adopted in September 2013 to optimize the delay-sensitive traffic generated by Siri. MPTCP implementations on Amazon's EC2, different Android-based handsets (i.e., Samsung Galaxy S2/S3), the largest multi-homing experimental platform NorNet [4] and Citrix's Netscaler are also available to end users.

Despite its increasing popularity, the development of MP-TCP throughput models is still in the premature stage, which introduces severe challenges to quantitatively study the efficiency and fairness of existing MPTCP implementations. And the performance of its most important components, such as the congestion control and flow control algorithms, is still hard to understand through theoretical analysis. In order not to unfairly take up too much bandwidth resource when coexisting with regular TCP on bottlenecks, MPTCP uses coupled congestion control algorithm to control its ag-gregate aggressiveness. The coupling between MPTCP sub-flows' congestion control unavoidably introduces significant challenges to model its aggregate throughput. Moreover, a connection-level receive buffer must be used in MPTCP to accommodate out-of-order packets, i.e., all MPTCP sub-flows share one receive buffer. Thus the subflow with large delay may block the transmission on other subflows due to the limit of available receive buffer size. So the influence of flow control also cannot be ignored in the modeling of MPTCP throughput.

In this paper, we take our first step towards the modeling of MPTCP steady-state throughput by addressing the above two big challenges. Our end-point objective is to derive a model to precisely predict the aggregate throughput of MPTCP in terms of packet loss rate, RTT and receive buffer size. Since math is just a tool rather than a language, this paper provides a step-by-step modeling process to reduce the complexity of the analysis. First, we only focus on the modeling of coupled congestion control algorithm. In this case, we try to find the average increase rate of the congestion window size in order to get one subflow's throughput. Then, based on the simple model derived in this case, we further analyse the influence of receive buffer size by computing the time proportion one subflow blocked by other subflows under the influence of flow control. Finally, MPTCP integrated throughput model is derived and carefully fitted by extensive NS2-based simulations. The results indicate that the proposed model can precisely predict the throughput of MPTCP connections in various situations. In particular, when MPTCP subflows have similar RTTs, the average Error Rate (ER) of the proposed model is less than 8%. Even in the situation where huge RTT difference exists between subflows, the model can still get an average ER less than 10%.

The remainder of the paper is organized as follows. Section 2 reviews the related work. Section 3 presents the background of MPTCP. Section 4 and 5 describe the detailed modeling process of congestion control and flow control, respectively. Section 6 validates the accuracy of our model. Finally, Section 7 concludes the paper.

2. RELATED WORK

TCP plays an important role in today's Internet protocol suite. In the late 90s, Mathis et al. [5] proposed a simple yet efficient model to understand the throughput of long-lived TCP connections. Following this pioneer study, Padhye et al. [7] developed an enhanced approach to capture the behavior of fast retransmit mechanism and the timeout mechanism. Dunaytsev et al. [1] extended this model with a more accurate examination of fast retransmit/fast recovery dynamics and slow start phases after timeout.

To better utilize the multiple NICs simultaneously, one TCP-based approach, most notably MPTCP [2], has been widely suggested in the past few years. The IETF working group has proposed a series of MPTCP standards such as architectural design [2], detailed operation design [3], congestion control [9], performance effect on applications and API [12]. As a drop-in replacement for TCP, tradeoffs between the aggressiveness of a MPTCP flow and the fairness compared to regular TCP flows must be considered when designing and implementing MPTCP congestion control algorithm. Four congestion control algorithms with different coupling degrees are proposed by Raiciu and Wischik et al. in [10] in 2009. Then they validate these algorithms for multi-homed servers, data centers and mobile clients in [13]. The result shows that the algorithm compensating for dissimilar RTTs behaves well and finally is standardized by IETF in [9]. In this paper, we only focus on the congestion control algorithm standardized in [9], which will be described in detail in Section 3.

The delay performance of MPTCP is thoroughly studied in [8], however, the development of MPTCP throughput models is still in the premature stage. A discrete packet throughput model based on Markov processes is presented in [14], but a explicit formula of throughput is not included. A simple throughput formula (1) for MPTCP is proposed in [13], which introduces deviation as our simulation results indicate. p_j and RTT_j in (1) represent the packet loss rate and RTT of subflow j, respectively. Different from these existing studies, we for the first time provide a comprehensive analysis of MPTCP coupled congestion control and flow control algorithms. Our end-point objective is to precisely predict the aggregate throughput of MPTCP in terms of packet loss rate, RTT and receive buffer size.

$$TP = \max(\frac{1}{RTT_j} * \sqrt{\frac{2}{p_j}}) \qquad (1)$$

3. BACKGROUND

MPTCP splits a single TCP connection into multiple subflows and transmits data simultaneously on these subflows. Considering the reality that MPTCP subflows may coexist with regular TCPs on bottlenecks, MPTCP should have a new congestion control algorithm so that it won't unfairly take up too much bandwidth resource. We call the algorithm standardized in RFC 6356 [9] as coupled congestion control algorithm, because the evolution of CWND on different subflows are correlated with each other as we will show.

Each subflow in MPTCP maintains a congestion control state (e.g., CWND and ssthresh) of itself and runs coupled congestion control algorithm. This algorithm mainly makes some modifications of congestion avoidance phase in regular TCP: when subflow j receives an ACK, the increase of its CWND is shown in (2) in unit of packet.

$$min(\frac{\alpha}{cw_{total}}, \frac{1}{cw_j}) \qquad (2)$$

Here, cw_{total} represents the total CWND of all MPTCP subflows at that time and cw_j denotes the current CWND on subflow j. The increase shown in (2) ensures any MPTCP subflow can not be more aggressive than a regular TCP flow in the same condition. α in (2) represents the aggressiveness of the MPTCP flow and the value of α is shown in (3). From (2) and (3), we can find that the evolution of CWND on one subflow depends on the states of all subflows.

$$\alpha = cw_{total} * \frac{max(\frac{cw_i}{RTT_i^2})}{(\sum \frac{cw_i}{RTT_i})^2} \qquad (3)$$

The fast recovery phase in MPTCP is the same as regular TCP. But when timeout events occur, things are different. The packet causing this timeout event will be retransmitted both on original subflow j and another subflow k. The latter packet arrived at the receiver will be ignored by the receiver. No matter on which subflow the sender receives the ACK for the retransmitted packet, subflow j will recover from the timeout event and enter slow start phase.

Flow control is another important part in MPTCP. In order to ensure in-order delivery, MPTCP must use the connection-level receive buffer [2]. Packets from all subflows are placed in the common receive buffer until they are in-order and can be read by the up-layer application. All subflows in MPTCP share common receive buffer, so the packets transmitted on high-delay paths may block the transmissions on other subflows, which makes flow control important in this paper.

4. MODELING MPTCP COUPLED CONGESTION CONTROL ALGORITHM

In this section, we only focus on the modeling of MPTCP congestion control algorithm, so we assume that the receive buffer is infinite in order to clear the influence of flow control. The influence of flow control will be analysed in Section 5. Section 4.1 lists all assumptions. Then we try to derive the model in three steps, including the modeling of one congestion avoidance in Section 4.2, the modeling of timeouts in Section 4.3 and the integrated model in Section 4.4.

4.1 Assumptions

Here, we summarize all assumptions used in modeling MPTCP congestion control algorithm, regarding the end points and networks. Most of our assumptions are similar to a prior TCP modeling work [7].

4.1.1 Assumptions of sender and receiver

We assume that both the sender and the receiver enable MPTCP defined by RFC 6182 [2] at the transport layer. As our model focuses on MPTCP steady-state throughput, we assume that the application has an infinite amount of data to transmit. For simplicity, the sender will send fixed-sized packets as long as the sliding window allows (i.e., one MSS in most cases). Similar to other bulk data transfer model [1,7,11], the three-way handshakes will be ignored because it makes little difference for long-term MPTCP throughput.

4.1.2 Assumptions of networks

Moreover, we model MPTCP behavior in terms of "round", as proposed in [7]. A round starts with the transmission of a window of packets and ends with receiving the first ACK for one of these packets. The length of a round equals to the RTT of that subflow. The same as [7], we also assume that packet loss is correlated within a round, i.e., if one packet is lost then the subsequent packets in that round are also lost. But the packet losses in different rounds are independent. This assumption seems awkward, however it is an effort to capture the influence of loss burst. We assume that ACKs are never lost as the size of ACK packets is small relatively to data packets.

4.2 Modeling Triple Duplicate ACKs

In this subsection, we assume that all losses are detected by triple duplicate ACKs, i.e., timeout events never occur in this subsection. Under this assumption, one congestion avoidance phase can be seen as a cycle during a MPTCP subflow's lifetime. The expected throughput in a cycle can be used to express MPTCP steady-state throughput.

Because of the difference of MPTCP implementations in different end systems, the receiver may send one cumulative ACK for different number of data packets. Let b denote the number of packets acknowledged by one ACK packet. On subflow j, in a round without packet loss, the sender will receive cw_j/b ACKs. As the increase of CWND when receiving an ACK is shown in (2), the increase of subflow j's CWND after a round without packet loss will be

$$\frac{cw_j}{b} * min(\frac{\alpha}{cw_{total}}, \frac{1}{cw_j}) = \frac{1}{b} * min(\frac{\alpha * cw_j}{cw_{total}}, 1) \quad (4)$$

Let m_j denote the number of rounds when the increase of subflow j's CWND cumulated to one in unit of packet. Obviously, m_j is the reciprocal of (4) as shown in (5).

$$m_j = b * max(\frac{cw_{total}}{\alpha * cw_j}, 1) \quad (5)$$

The increase of CWND when receiving an ACK and the decrease of CWND when detecting a packet loss must be balanced out in equilibrium. It means the ACK-receiving rate multiplying the increase of CWND per ACK equals to

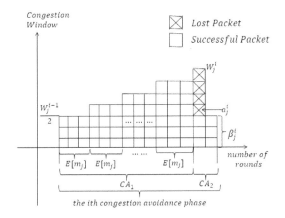

Figure 1: the ith congestion avoidance phase.

the packet-loss detection rate multiplying the decrease of CWND per loss, so we have:

$$(\frac{cw_j}{RTT_j}(1-p_j)) * min(\frac{\alpha}{cw_{total}}, \frac{1}{cw_j}) = (\frac{cw_j}{RTT_j}p_j) * \frac{cw_j}{2} \quad (6)$$

From (6), we can get the mathematical expectation of m_j in (7). One main difference between a TCP flow and an MPTCP subflow lies in the increase rate of CWND in congestion avoidance phase. In regular TCP, in a round without packet loss, the increase of CWND is $1/b$, which is a constant number. But as shown in (4), the value in an MPTCP subflow depends on all MPTCP subflows' states. However, as we focus on long-term MPTCP performance, the CWND in the congestion avoidance phase can be regarded as smoothly increasing one in unit of packet every $E[m_j]$ rounds.

$$E[m_j] = \frac{2 * b * (1 - p_j)}{p_j * E[cw_j]^2} \quad (7)$$

Fig. 1 shows the packet transmission process in the ith congestion avoidance phase on subflow j. A bare square represents one successful packet transmission while the X-marked square represents the lost packet. A column in Fig. 1 represents the packets sent during one round. As assumed, after the first packet numbered a_j^i lost, the subsequent packets in that round are also lost. Then in the last round, before detecting the packet loss by triple duplicate ACKs , β_j^i packets are sent. We denote the value of CWND at the end of the ith congestion avoidance phase by W_j^i. Let Z_j^{CA} represent the time length of a congestion avoidance phase, and Y_j^{CA} represent the number of packets sent during Z_j^{CA}. The expected throughput TP_j can be derived from (8). Then we focus on the derivation of Y_j^{CA} and Z_j^{CA}.

$$TP_j = \frac{E[Y_j^{CA}]}{E[Z_j^{CA}]} \quad (8)$$

For packet loss rate p_j, the number of packets successfully transmitted between two losses is roughly $1/p_j$, i.e., $E[a_j] = 1/p_j$. From Fig. 1, we can find that after the first lost packet a_j^i, $W_j^i - 1$ more packets are sent in the ith congestion avoidance phase. We can get the expected number of packets sent $E[Y_j^{CA}]$ in (9).

$$E[Y_j^{CA}] = E[a_j] + E[W_j] - 1 = \frac{1 - p_j}{p_j} + E[W_j] \quad (9)$$

Table 1: $Y_j^{CA_2}$ and $Z_j^{CA_2}$ in different cases

First loss in which round	Value of $Y_j^{CA_2}$	Value of $Z_j^{CA_2}$
$h-1$	$\frac{E[W_j]}{2}$	RTT_j
h	$E[W_j] + \frac{E[W_j]}{2}$	$2*RTT_j$
...	...	...
$h + E[m_j] - 2$	$(E[m_j]-1)E[W_j] + \frac{E[W_j]}{2}$	$E[m_j]*RTT_j$

Observing Fig. 1, we can find that the expected number of rounds whose CWND is W_j^i is not $E[m_j]$ in equilibrium, while the expected number of rounds whose CWND is $W_j^i - 1$ should be $E[m_j]$. So we split the congestion avoidance phase into two portions: the first portion whose CWND from $W_j^{i-1}/2$ changing to $W_j^i - 1$ is denoted by CA_1; and the rest portion is denoted by CA_2. In portion CA_1, CWND of subflow j increases one every $E[m_j]$ rounds, so the number of packets sent ($Y_j^{CA_1}$) and time length ($Z_j^{CA_1}$) of CA_1 can be easily derived as follows:

$$Y_j^{CA_1} = (\frac{W_j^{i-1}}{2} + W_j^i - 1)(W_j^i - 1 - \frac{W_j^{i-1}}{2} + 1)\frac{1}{2}*E[m_j] \quad (10)$$

$$Z_j^{CA_1} = (W_j^i - 1 - \frac{W_j^{i-1}}{2} + 1)*E[m_j]*RTT_j \quad (11)$$

As for the CA_2 portion, we also let the number of packets been sent in the last round in a congestion avoidance phase be uniformly distributed from 0 to W_j^i, i.e., $E[\beta_j] = E[W_j]/2$, the same process as in [7]. For the convenience of description, let the first round whose CWND is W_j^i to be the hth round. Then the number of packets sent in CA_2 ($Y_j^{CA_2}$) and the time length of CA_2 ($Z_j^{CA_2}$) are shown in Table 1. There are totally $E[m_j]$ cases. The first packet loss occurs randomly in a round, so these $E[m_j]$ cases should have the same probability to occur. Thus we can easily get the expected value of $Y_j^{CA_2}$ and $Z_j^{CA_2}$ as follows:

$$E[Y_j^{CA_2}] = \frac{E[W_j]*E[m_j]}{2} \quad (12)$$

$$E[Z_j^{CA_2}] = \frac{(E[m_j]+1)*RTT_j}{2} \quad (13)$$

Plus (10) and (12), (11) and (13), we can get $E[Y_j^{CA}]$ and $E[Z_j^{CA}]$ as follows:

$$E[Y_j^{CA}] = (\frac{3*E[W_j]^2}{4} + \frac{E[W_j]}{2})*\frac{E[m_j]}{2} \quad (14)$$

$$E[Z_j^{CA}] = \frac{[(E[W_j]+1)*E[m_j]+1]*RTT_j}{2} \quad (15)$$

$E[cw_j]$ in (7) represents the average congestion window size on subflow j, while $E[W_j]$ represents the expected congestion window size at the end of a congestion avoidance phase. Let t present the ratio of $E[cw_j]$ to $E[W_j]$, i.e., $E[cw_j] = t*E[W_j]$. To get the value of parameter t, we consider the scenario that only one path is available in the MPTCP connection. In this case, the value of α in (3) should

be 1, and the increase of CWND after one round without packet loss as shown in (4) should be $1/b$. This is exactly the same as the regular TCP. That is, when there is only one path available in an MPTCP connection, MPTCP will turn back to regular TCP. So we try to find the value of t in the scenario of regular TCP. At equilibrium, the increase and decrease of CWND must be balanced out in TCP, so we have (16). Thus, we can get $E[cw] = \sqrt{2*(1-p)/p}$ in regular TCP.

$$(1-p)*\frac{1}{cw} = p*\frac{cw}{2} \quad (16)$$

Based on [7], the expected value of CWND at the end of a congestion avoidance phase is shown in (17). Hence the ratio t defined above in regular TCP approximately equals to $\sqrt{3*b/4}$. The difference of congestion avoidance phase between MPTCP and TCP in equilibrium mainly lies in the growing rate of CWND, which makes no difference to t. So we can assign $\sqrt{3*b/4}$ to t on subflow j.

$$E[W] = \sqrt{\frac{8}{3bp}} + o(1/\sqrt{p}) \quad (17)$$

Then based on (7), (9) and (14), we can get the expression of $E[W_j]$ as follow:

$$E[W_j] = \frac{1}{2}*[-\frac{(4t^2-3b)*(1-p_j)}{4t^2 p_j} + \sqrt{[\frac{(4t^2-3b)*(1-p_j)}{4t^2 p_j}]^2 + \frac{2b*(1-p_j)}{t^2 p_j}}] \quad (18)$$

Then we can get the expected throughput of subflow j in (19) when only considering the packet loss detected by triple duplicate ACKs events, where $E[W_j]$ is shown in (18).

$$E[TP_j] = \frac{E[Y_j^{CA}]}{E[Z_j^{CA}]} = \frac{\frac{1-p_j}{p_j} + E[W_j]}{\frac{(E[W_j]+1)*E[m_j]+1}{2}*RTT_j} \quad (19)$$

4.3 Modeling Timeout Event

When one packet is lost but there are insufficient ACKs to trigger a triple duplicate ACKs event, the sender will wait for a timeout event and then retransmit the lost packet. MPTCP specifications in RFC 6182 [2] and RFC 6824 [3] suggest that the lost packet should be retransmitted both on the original subflow j and a different subflow k. If a path fails and causes this timeout event, retransmitting the lost packet on a different subflow k can obviously improve the user experience. The original subflow j still need to retransmit the lost packet in order to preserve the subflow integrity. The latter packet arrived at the receiver will be ignored as suggested in RFC 6824. No matter on which subflow the retransmitted packet is acknowledged, the original subflow j will recover from the lost and enter the slow start phase. Taking timeout event into consideration, a cycle during a MPTCP subflow's lifetime should include a timeout phase, a slow start phase and a sequence of congestion avoidance phase. In this subsection, we focus on the modeling of timeout phase and slow start phase.

The time, when the receiver successfully receives the lost packet, depends on the arriving of the retransmitted packets both on these two subflows. So there are two cases shown in Fig. 2. Let T_{detect} denote the time from the end of the round in which the lost packet first sent to the expiring of RTO

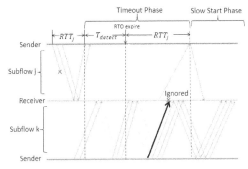

(a) The retransmitted packet first arrives on the original subflow

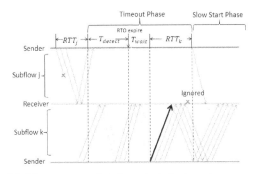

(b) The retransmitted packet first arrives on a different subflow

Figure 2: Detailed representations of timeout phase.

timer on subflow j. Thus, $T_{detect} = RTO_j - RTT_j$. After T_{detect}, the sender realized that the packet is lost and then try to retransmit the lost packet. The packet retransmitted on the original subflow j can be retransmitted right now (i.e., the yellow line in Fig. 2), but on subflow k, it may wait some time until the sliding window of subflow k allows one packet to be sent. We denote the time by T_{wait}. The packet transmission state on subflow k is independent with subflow j, so T_{wait} should be uniformly distributed from 0 to RTT_k, i.e., $E[T_{wait}] = RTT_k/2$. Fig. 2(a) represents the case where the lost packet retransmitted on subflow j first arrives at the receiver. In this case, the time length of a timeout phase should be $T_{detect} + RTT_j$. While in Fig. 2(b) where the lost packet retransmitted on subflow k first arrives at the receiver, the time should be $T_{detect} + E[T_{wait}] + RTT_k$. As a result, we use (20) to model the average time of a timeout phase (i.e., $E[Z_j^{TO}]$).

$$E[Z_j^{TO}] = \min(T_{detect} + RTT_j, T_{detect} + E[T_{wait}] + RTT_k)$$
$$= \min(RTO_j, RTO_j - RTT_j + \frac{3 * E[RTT_k]}{2}) \quad (20)$$

In the timeout phase, the original subflow j needs to retransmit the lost packet although the packet may be ignored at the receiver, so only one packet is sent in a timeout phase, i.e., $Y_j^{TO} = 1$. The packet retransmitted on subflow k is contained in the number of packet sent on subflow k. As for the choice of subflow k, we use a simple strategy that the subflow with the smallest packet loss rate has the biggest possibility

to be chosen. So we have

$$E[RTT_k] = \sum_{k=1, k \neq j}^{k=N} \frac{1/p_k}{\sum_{l=1, l \neq j}^{l=N} 1/p_l} * RTT_k \quad (21)$$

After the timeout phase, subflow j enters slow start phase, which is exactly the same as regular TCP. The CWND will grow exponentially in slow start phase until it reaches slow start threshold (i.e., ssthresh). Using the simple mathematical analysis, we can get the number of packets sent (Y_j^{SS}) and time length of slow start phase (Z_j^{SS}) as follows:

$$Y_j^{SS} = \sum_{i=1}^{\log_2 ssthresh+1} 2^{i-1} = 2 * ssthresh - 1 \quad (22)$$

$$Z_j^{SS} = (\log_2 ssthresh + 1) * RTT_j \quad (23)$$

4.4 Integrated Throughput Model

Now we try to derive the integrated throughput model for MPTCP considering the packet loss detected by triple duplicate ACKs and by timeout events. Considering these two events, the ith cycle on subflow j (S_j^i) should include a timeout phase, a slow start phase and a sequence of congestion avoidance phase. Let Q_j be the probability that one congestion avoidance phase ends with a timeout event. That is, one congestion avoidance phase is followed by timeout phase with the probability of Q_j. Then the expected throughput on subflow j can be modeled as follows:

$$E[TP_j] = \frac{Q_j * (E[Y_j^{TO}] + E[Y_j^{SS}]) + E[Y_j^{CA}]}{Q_j * (E[Z_j^{TO}] + E[Z_j^{SS}]) + E[Z_j^{CA}]} \quad (24)$$

Only Q_j is unknown in (24). In order to get Q_j, we find that packet loss first occurs in the penultimate round in a congestion avoidance phase (see Fig. 1). And if in the penultimate round, the congestion window is less than three and one of the packet is lost, even though the packets sent in the last round all successfully arrive at receiver, there are less than three duplicate ACKs the sender will receive, so timeout event will occur. If in the penultimate round, the CWND is no less than three, only less than three packets arrived at the receiver in the last round will trigger the timeout event. So the same as illustrated in [7], we can also get the value of Q_j in (25) with $E[W_j]$ expressed in (18).

$$Q_j = \min(1, \frac{3}{E[W_j]}) \quad (25)$$

So considering packet loss detected both by triple duplicate ACKs and timeout events, the expected throughput of subflow j should be as follows:

$$E[TP_j] = \frac{Q_j * 2 * ssthresh + \frac{1-p_j}{p_j} + E[W_j]}{Q_j * ((\log_2 ssthresh + 1) * RTT_j + E[Z_j^{TO}]) + E[Z_j^{CA}]} \quad (26)$$

where $E[Z_j^{CA}]$, $E[W_j]$, $E[Z_j^{TO}]$, $E[RTT_k]$ and Q_j are shown in (15), (18), (20), (21), (25), respectively.

Taking no account of flow control, MPTCP aggregate throughput can be expressed as in (27). Here MPTCP has N subflows and TP_j is shown in (26).

$$E[TP] = \sum_{j=1}^{j=N} E[TP_j] \quad (27)$$

5. MODELING MPTCP FLOW CONTROL ALGORITHM

In this section, we try to capture the influence of receive buffer size (denoted by L_{Buf}) to MPTCP throughput. To simplify the derivation process, we only consider the events when transmission stops due to the available receive buffer size decreasing to zero. Let $P(j, i)$ denote the time proportion when traffic on subflow j is not blocked by the packets transmitted on subflow i, and $P(j, *)$ denote the time proportion subflow j is not blocked by all other subflows. Then MPTCP aggregate throughput should be (28) with $E[TP_j]$ in (26). We first study a simple situation where there are only two subflows in MPTCP and then extend the model to adapt to multiple subflows.

$$E[TP] = \sum_{j=1}^{j=N} P(j, *) * E[TP_j] \quad (28)$$

5.1 Two subflows

Without loss of generality, let $l = \frac{RTT_1}{RTT_2} \geq 1$, i.e, subflow 1 has larger RTT. After the packet D_1 transmitted on subflow 1 and before it arrives at the receiver, there are n_2 packets arriving at the receiver on subflow 2. If $n_2 \geq L_{Buf}$, subflow 2 will stop its transmission due to limit of receive buffer. Let r denote the number of rounds that subflow 2 can fill up the receive buffer, which can be derived from (29). If the time length for packet D_1 to successfully arrive at the receiver is larger than $r * RTT_2$, the transmission on subflow 2 will be blocked.

$$r * E[cw_2] = L_{Buf} \quad (29)$$

There are three cases happened to one packet transmitted on subflow 1: successfully transmitted to the receiver with probability $1 - p_1$, dropping and causing a triple duplicate ACKs event with probability $p_1 * (1 - Q_1)$ or causing a timeout event with probability $p_1 * Q_1$. Depending on the value of l, transmission stopping on subflow 2 may occur in each of these three cases.

- With probability $1 - p_1$, packet D_1 can successfully arrive at the receiver after $\frac{RTT_1}{2}$. If $\frac{RTT_1}{2} \geq r * RTT_2$, even though the packet successfully arrives at the receiver, it will still cause subflow 2 to stop its transmission. We define $(a)^+ = a$ when $a < 1$ and $(a)^+ = 1$ when $a \geq 1$. So we can get (30).

$$P_{case1}(2, 1) = (1 - p_1)\left(\frac{r * RTT_2}{\frac{RTT_1}{2}}\right)^+ = (1 - p_1)\left(\frac{2r}{l}\right)^+ \quad (30)$$

- If $l < 2r$, then the transmission of not-lost packet on subflow 1 will not cause subflow 2 to stop its transmission. But if the packet is lost when it is first transmitted, then a triple duplicate ACKs event may occur with probability $p_1 * (1 - Q_1)$. The time length from the lost packet first transmitted to the retransmitted packet successfully arrives at the receiver is around $\frac{3 * RTT_1}{2}$: RTT_1 to get triple duplicate ACKs and $\frac{RTT_1}{2}$ for the retransmitted packet to reach the receiver. If the time is large than $r * RTT_2$, subflow 2 still can be blocked. So we can get (31).

$$P_{case2}(2, 1) = p_1 * (1 - Q_1) * \left(\frac{2r}{3l}\right)^+ \quad (31)$$

- If $l < \frac{2r}{3}$, triple duplicate ACKs can't block transmission on subflow 2, but timeout event can make it possible. The time length to successfully transmit the timeout packet is around $RTO_1 + E[RTT_k]$. So we can get (32).

$$P_{case3}(2, 1) = p_1 * Q_1 * \left(\frac{r * RTT_2}{RTO_1 + E[RTT_k]}\right)^+ \quad (32)$$

Then we can get the value of $P(2, *)$ which equals to $P(2, 1)$ here in (33). $P(1, 2)$ can be derived in the same manner, thus we can get MPTCP throughput from (28).

$$P(2, 1) = P_{case1}(2, 1) + P_{case2}(2, 1) + P_{case3}(2, 1) \quad (33)$$

5.2 Multiple Subflows

When MPTCP has N subflows and their RTTs satisfy (34), we can get the throughput model by extending the above two paths model.

$$RTT_1 : RTT_2 : ... : RTT_N = l_1 : l_2 : ... : l_N \quad (34)$$

When deriving $P(j, i)$, we first redefine the value of r in (35) for the reason that the receive buffer is filled up with the effort of all subflows except subflow i. Let $l = \frac{RTT_i}{RTT_j} = \frac{l_i}{l_j}$. Then extending the formula (33), $P(j, i)$ should be (36).

$$r * \left(\sum_{k=1, k \neq i}^{k=N} \frac{l_j}{l_k} * E[cw_j]\right) = L_{Buf} \quad (35)$$

$$P(j, i) = (1 - p_i) * \left(\frac{2r}{l}\right)^+ + p_i * (1 - Q_i) * \left(\frac{2r}{3l}\right)^+ \\ + p_i * Q_i * \left(\frac{r * RTT_j}{RTO_i + E[RTT_k]}\right)^+ \quad (36)$$

Then we can get $P(j, *)$ by (37) and substituting it into (28) we can get the throughput of a MPTCP connection considering the receive buffer restriction. When the RTT difference between MPTCP subflows is small enough that one subflow never blocked by others, (28) will return back to (27).

$$P(j, *) = 1 - \sum_{i=1, i \neq j}^{i=N} \left[(1 - P(j, i)) * \prod_{k \neq i, k \neq j} P(j, k)\right] \quad (37)$$

The throughput model (28) is non-trivial: First, (28) helps to quantitatively study the efficiency and TCP-friendliness of MPTCP implementations; Second, (28) quantizes the influence of large-delay paths, from which MPTCP can make a optimization to provide best performance to users. For example, using a slowest path to transfer data may reduce the integrated throughput, so it is prudent for MPTCP to use this path only for backup rather than data transmission.

6. SIMULATION

In this section, we try to validate the precision of our model and compare it with the simple model (1). We perform MPTCP bulk data transfer simulations on NS2 simulator. To quantify the accuracy of the proposed model, we define a metric named Error Rate (ER) in (38) to reveal the degree of absolute deviation between the model and the simulation results. Here, TP_{model} represents throughput value deriving from the model and $TP_{simulation}$ represents the simulation

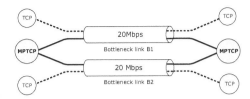

(a) Each of two subflows shares bottlenecks with one TCP flow

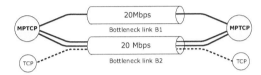

(b) Two of three subflows share bottlenecks with a TCP flow

Figure 3: Two typical network topologies.

results. The smaller value of ER means the better throughput model.

$$ER = \frac{|TP_{model} - TP_{simulation}|}{TP_{simulation}} * 100\% \qquad (38)$$

6.1 Network Topologies and Basic Setup

Before discussing the simulation results, we first present two network topologies and the basic setup used in our NS2 simulations. Specifically, Fig. 3 shows two simple but typical network topologies used in our simulations. We use a pair of MPTCP-capable sources (colored gray in Fig. 3) to transfer data through two or three paths simultaneously. These MPTCP subflows coexists with regular TCP flows in two different topologies. In each topology, there exists two bottleneck link B_1 and B_2. In topology 4-(a), MPTCP has two subflows and each subflow shares bottleneck capacity with a TCP flow respectively. In topology 4-(b), there are three MPTCP subflows with two of the three sharing bottlenecks with a TCP flow. We refer to the tcp traffic as "background" flows while MPTCP traffic being monitored as "foreground" flows.

We set the capacity of bottleneck link B_1 and B_2 fixed at 20 Mbps while the other links (omitted from Fig. 3) have a high bandwidth of 100 Mbps. The queue size at bottlenecks is fixed at 100 packets and DropTail queue management policy is used when buffer overflows at the bottlenecks. The packet drop rate and propagation delays of the access link are varied to simulate the desired RTT and packet loss rate between the sources. To get a steady state of MPTCP performance, both the foreground and background flows have a long duration of 300 seconds. We set the receive buffer for the MPTCP flow to be 100 packets with a fixed packet size of 592 bytes. The Round-Robin packet scheduling policy is used in the MPTCP implementation code. We test the performance of our model when MPTCP subflows have similar or dissimilar properties with each other.

6.2 Similar Properties Simulation Results

In this section, we change the properties of all MPTCP subflows simultaneously, i.e., in each experiment, all sub-

flows have similar properties. First, we keep the packet loss rate of all MPTCP subflows unchanged at 4%, and vary RTT from 12ms to 80ms. We compare the precision of our model with (1). Fig. 4(a) and 4(b) show the results for the above two topologies with the average ER of our model to be 2.99% and 1.6%, respectively. The formula (1) over predicts the MPTCP performance especially when the RTT is small. The average ERs of (1) are 45.46% and 30.02% for these two topologies, respectively. Our model behaves well over a wider range of RTTs in this scenario. Specially, our model can improve the precision for an order of magnitude compared to (1).

Then we keep the RTT unchanged at 20ms, and vary the packet loss rate for all subflows from 0.5% to 15%. The results are shown in Fig. 5. The average ER of our model for these two topologies are 7.62% and 7.96%, respectively. But the (1) introduces high average ER of 1.43 and 92.17%, respectively. Particularly, when packet loss rate grows, the ER of (1) also increases obviously. From Fig. 4 and 5, we can find that (1) applies to network conditions with small packet loss rate and relatively large RTT, while our model behaves well over a wide range of RTT and packet loss rate.

6.3 Dissimilar Properties Simulation Results

In this section, we try to validate the proposed model when the RTTs are different between MPTCP subflows, and show the influence of receive buffer size. Here, we fix the packet loss rate for all subflows at 4%, and only change the propagation delays of the bottleneck link B_1 to get the desired RTT changing from 20ms to 2s. To better see the influence of receive buffer size, we set the receive buffer size to be 100 and 50 packets in different experiments. The results are shown in Fig. 6(a) and 6(b). In topology 4-(a), the average ERs of our model for receive buffer of 100 and 50 packets are 7.41% and 7.05%, respectively. In topology 4-(b), the average ERs are 9.65% and 9.15%, respectively. Though a little performance degradation, our model can still give a satisfactory prediction, even in the situation where the RTT of slow path larger than $100x$ of the fast path.

From the comparisons above, we can find that our throughput model of MPTCP can precisely predict the throughput of MPTCP in several different scenarios. With similar properties of MPTCP subflows, the average ER of our proposed model is smaller than 8%. If differences exist between MPTCP subflows, our model can still predict the throughput with the average ER of 10%. Using WiFi and 3G interfaces simultaneously on smart phones or tablets, the differences of RTT always exist on MPTCP subflows. As the simulation result shows, our model can behave well with satisfactory small ER.

7. CONCLUSION

This paper presents a detailed model for MPTCP steady-state throughput in terms of packet loss rate, RTT and receive buffer size. The proposed model takes into account not only the behavior of MPTCP coupled congestion control algorithm in the presence of triple duplicate ACKs and timeout events, but also the influence of flow control. Two challenges in deriving the model are addressed in this paper, including the dependence between subflows and the influence of flow control. We validate the proposed model through extensive NS2-based simulations. The results indicate that our model can precisely predict MPTCP through-

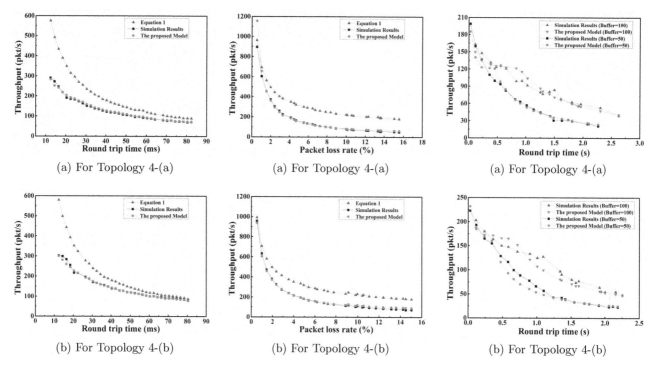

(a) For Topology 4-(a)   (a) For Topology 4-(a)   (a) For Topology 4-(a)

(b) For Topology 4-(b)   (b) For Topology 4-(b)   (b) For Topology 4-(b)

Figure 4: RTT for all subflows synchronously changes.   **Figure 5: Packet loss rate for all subflows synchronously changes.**   **Figure 6: RTT differs between subflows.**

put over a wide range of packet loss rate and RTT. Even in the situations where the RTT difference exists between MPTCP subflows, our model can still behave well.

8. ACKNOWLEDGEMENT

This work has been supported in part by NSFC Project (61170292, 61472212), National Science and Technology Major Project (2015ZX03003004), 973 Project of China (2012C-B315803), 863 Project of China (2013AA013302, 2015AA01-5601), EU MARIE CURIE ACTIONS EVANS (PIRSES-GA-2013-610524) and multidisciplinary fund of Tsinghua National Laboratory for Information Science and Technology.

9. REFERENCES

[1] R. Dunaytsev, Y. Koucheryavy, and J. Harju. The pftk-model revised. *Computer communications*, 29(13):2671–2679, 2006.

[2] A. Ford, C. Raiciu, M. Handley, S. Barre, and J. Iyengar. Architectural guidelines for multipath tcp development. *Internet Engineering Task Force, RFC6182, March*, 2011.

[3] A. Ford, C. Raiciu, M. Handley, and O. Bonaventure. Tcp extensions for multipath operation with multiple addresses. *Internet Engineering Task Force, RFC6824,January*, 2013.

[4] E. G. Gran, T. Dreibholz, and A. Kvalbein. Nornet core–a multi-homed research testbed. *Computer Networks*, 61:75–87, 2014.

[5] M. Mathis, J. Semke, J. Mahdavi, and T. Ott. The macroscopic behavior of the tcp congestion avoidance algorithm. *ACM SIGCOMM Computer Communication Review*, 27(3):67–82, 1997.

[6] C. Paasch, S. Barríe, et al. Multipath tcp in the linux kernel. http:www.multipath-tcp.org.

[7] J. Padhye, V. Firoiu, D. F. Towsley, and J. F. Kurose. Modeling tcp reno performance: a simple model and its empirical validation. *IEEE/ACM Transactions on Networking (ToN)*, 8(2):133–145, 2000.

[8] S.-Y. Park, C. Joo, Y. Park, and S. Bank. Impact of traffic splitting on the delay performance of mptcp. In *Communications (ICC), 2014 IEEE International Conference on*, pages 1204–1209. IEEE, 2014.

[9] C. Raiciu, M. Handley, and D. Wischik. Coupled congestion control for multipath transport protocols. *Internet Engineering Task Force, RFC6356, October*, 2011.

[10] C. Raiciu, D. Wischik, and M. Handley. Practical congestion control for multipath transport protocols. *University College London, London/United Kingdom, Tech. Rep*, 2009.

[11] C. B. Samios and M. K. Vernon. Modeling the throughput of tcp vegas. In *ACM SIGMETRICS Performance Evaluation Review*, volume 31, pages 71–81. ACM, 2003.

[12] M. Scharf and A. Ford. Multipath tcp (mptcp) application interface considerations. *Internet Engineering Task Force, RFC6897, March*, 2013.

[13] D. Wischik, C. Raiciu, A. Greenhalgh, and M. Handley. Design, implementation and evaluation of congestion control for multipath tcp. In *NSDI*, volume 11, pages 8–18, 2011.

[14] M. Xu and Z. Zhang. Markov modeling of mptcp's coupled congestion control. *Journal of Tsinghua University Science and Technology*, 52(9):1281–1285, 2012.

Two-way Communications in Cognitive Personal Area Networks

Md. Mizanur Rahman
Ryerson University
Toronto, ON, Canada

Jelena Mišić
Ryerson University
Toronto, ON, Canada

Vojislav B. Mišić
Ryerson University
Toronto, ON, Canada

ABSTRACT

We describe a low-overhead two-way bridging scheme for cognitive personal area networks (CPANs) and analyze its performance through probabilistic analysis and renewal theory. We show that the CPANs are indeed decoupled in terms of synchronization, but the performance of both local and non-local traffic in either CPAN depends on the traffic intensity in both CPANs, as well as on the portion of traffic targeting non-local destinations.

1. INTRODUCTION

Opportunistic spectrum access allows for more efficient spectrum sharing between licensed or primary users (PUs) and non-licensed, cognitive-capable secondary users (SUs) [2, 3]. To establish effective communications, SU devices or nodes forms a Cognitive Personal Area Network (CPAN) under the control of a dedicated coordinator node. The coordinator allocates bandwidth to individual nodes upon request and makes decisions about switching channels, often done in a rapid, frequency-hopping manner [4] to avoid interference to and from PU transmissions. Channel switching decisions are typically made on the basis of spectrum sensing [5, 7], aided by static information about transmitter locations, frequencies, and hours of operation where such information is available [1]. Overseeing spectrum sensing through allocating sensing tasks to nodes and collecting the results of their sensing is thus another important task for the CPAN coordinator.

Multi-hop opportunistic spectrum access networks are beginning to attract research attention [6, 14] with performance of data transfers being among the most important research challenges[10, 12]. In our earlier work [15], we have considered unidirectional data transfer in a network formed by two channel-hopping CPANs that use the transmission tax-based MAC protocol [9] and a dedicated bridge node that switched back and forth between CPANs to deliver data from the source to the destination CPAN. However, the analysis was done under a number of assumptions: first, that CPAN superframes are synchronized so that they begin and finish at the same time; second, that the bridge switched from one to the other CPAN in each superframe; finally, that bridge transmissions were given higher priority by scheduling them early in the superframe.

MSWiM'15, November 2–6, 2015, Cancun, Mexico.
© 2015 ACM. ISBN 978-1-4503-3762-5/15/11 ...$15.00.
DOI: http://dx.doi.org/10.1145/2811587.2811617.

In this paper, we relax these constraints to arrive at a more flexible arrangement. First, the CPANs superframes may be skewed in time by an arbitrary period. Second, the bridge switches between the CPANs without any predefined arrangement, which results in increased fairness for all nodes and does not require any fixed scheduling points for the bridge. Last but not least, we assume that the bridge carries bidirectional traffic, which is more feasible in practice. We model the operation of the resulting two-hop network using probabilistic analysis and renewal theory and obtain the probability distributions of CPAN and bridge cycle times, as well as of end-to-end delays for both local and non-local (i.e., intra- and inter-CPAN) traffic.

The rest of the paper is structured as follows: Section 2 describes the CPAN environment and the operation of the bidirectional bridge. Section 3 presents the probabilistic model of bridging algorithm with transmission, sensing and reception by ordinary nodes. Access delay for both intra-CPAN and inter-CPAN traffic is discussed in Section 4. Results of the performance analysis are presented and discussed in Section 5. Section 6 concludes the paper with stating future work.

2. CPAN AND BRIDGE OPERATION

The CPAN operates under the control of a dedicated coordinator node. Time is divided into constant size superframes, the beginning and end of which are denoted with a leading and a trailing beacon frame, respectively, sent by the coordinator. Portions of the superframe sub-frames are devoted to beacon transmissions, data transmissions, reporting of sensing results, and sending bandwidth requests and other administrative activities.

The nodes (including the bridge) apply for bandwidth in the reservation sub-frame. Requests are sorted according to the round-robin principle, beginning with the lowest node ID that is larger than the last scheduled ID in previous superframe. The coordinator announces the pending transmissions in the leading beacon. Therefore, any given node—bridge included—from a given CPAN must wait a random time interval with respect to the leading beacon before it can begin its transmission.

A node is allowed to request transmission only for the packets that were in its buffer at the time of the request; packets that arrive to the node during the transmission of earlier requested packets will be serviced in one of the subsequent CPAN service cycles. By the same token, the bridge also requests transmission in any given CPAN only for the inter-CPAN packets which it has received from the other CPAN. Therefore, this scheduling scheme can be modeled as a gated exhaustive policy with vacations [16].

Upon finishing the data transmission, the node has to wait for another random time period in order to synchronize with beacon. This time period, from the end of transmission to the next leading

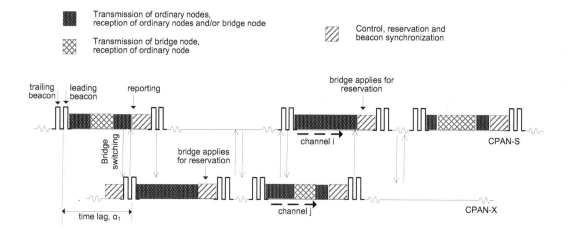

Figure 1: Bridge switching algorithm for two-way traffic

beacon (and, thus, includes the control and reservation sub-frames), is referred to as beacon synchronization.

The leading beacon also contains announcements of the sensing duty. Namely, upon successful packet transmission nodes have to 'pay' by sensing some of the channels in the working band. The nodes then submit the sensing results to the coordinator during the dedicated sub-frame. The duration of the sensing period is determined as the product of the sensing penalty coefficient k_p and the number of packets transmitted since the last round of sensing duty. Performing sensing duty is a prerequisite for time slot allocation for packet transmission.

The coordinator uses sensing results to build and update the free channel table. It uses this table to select the next-hop channel – i.e., the working channel for the next superframe – among the channels least likely to be busy during that time [13]. The next-hop channel is announced in the trailing beacon, together with a number of backup channels which are used to attempt recovery in case of collision with a primary user transmission [11].

In this setup, inter-CPAN traffic is routed through the shared bridge node which collects the data from one CPAN and delivers it to the other and vice versa, as shown in the Fig. 1. To this end, the bridge hops back and forth between the CPANs without predefined rendezvous times. In each of the CPANs, the bridge must request bandwidth in order to deliver data packets and report its presence to the corresponding CPAN coordinator in order to receive data packets. However, the bridge is not present in either CPAN all the time, which means there is a risk that it might not learn about the next-hop channel and thus be unable to return to the corresponding CPAN due to dynamic channel hopping. Synchronization can be maintained if the bridge listens to every trailing beacon so as to learn about the corresponding next-hop channel. The bridge must also listen to the leading beacon in the CPAN it is currently associated with in order to be able to send and receive data. Obviously the overhead of these actions is considerable, which is why the bridge is not required to perform sensing duty.

Transmission requests are serviced in the round-robin fashion, i.e., nodes with lower ID get access before a node with higher ID. If any of the requests cannot be accommodated in the current superframe, it will be deferred to the next one. This applies to the transmissions of ordinary nodes, as well as to those that involve the bridge, both as the source and as the destination. In the latter case, the coordinator can allocate bandwidth to inter-CPAN traffic (for which the bridge is the recipient) only if the bridge is present in the

CPAN, which is why the bridge needs to report its presence to the coordinator. Note that the bridge, once it begins its data packet exchange with nodes in a given CPAN, will stay in that CPAN for as many superframes as necessary, not counting the visits to the other CPAN in order to listen to the trailing beacons.

3. MODELING THE MAC ALGORITHM

We consider a network with two CPANs, hereafter referred to as CPAN-S and CPAN-X, having M_S and M_X nodes, respectively, which includes the coordinator node for each CPAN, as well as a shared node which serves as the bridge between the CPANs. Time is measured in unit slots while the duration of each superframe is s_f slots. Since CPANs are formed at different times and may experience collisions with PU transmissions and subsequent recovery on different channels, their superframes are not aligned with each other. The time lag between the starting points of their respective superframes is α_1 unit slots, where α_1 is a random value that is uniformly distributed over one superframe. We assume that data packets have a constant size of k_d slots with an additional slot used for acknowledgments, for a total of $k_d + 1$ slots per packet. Let λ_S and λ_X denote the packet arrival rate per node for CPAN-S and CPAN-X, respectively, assuming Poisson arrivals of data packets. We also assume that a fraction P_{ic} of the traffic generated by each node is actually inter-CPAN traffic (i.e., the destination is in the other CPAN), hence the arrival rates for the inter-CPAN traffic will be $\lambda_{bSX} = P_{ic}(M_S - 2)\lambda_S$ and $\lambda_{bXS} = P_{ic}(M_X - 2)\lambda_X$, for traffic from CPAN-S to CPAN-X and vice versa, respectively.

The timing diagram in Fig. 2 depicts the general CPAN service cycle, as well as the operation of an arbitrary ordinary node and the bridge node. A CPAN service cycle is defined as the time period between two successive transmissions of the same node. Due to traffic variability and sensing policy, CPAN service cycle is a random variable that can span a number of superframes.

Modeling the service period. The probability generating function (PGF) for constant packet size k_d with additional acknowledgement is $b(z) = z^{k_d+1}$, with the mean value of $\bar{b} = k_d + 1$. The Laplace-Stieltjes transform (LST) of packet time, $b^*(s) = e^{-s(k_d+1)}$, can be obtained by replacing variable z with e^{-s}. Therefore, the offered load per node is $\rho_S = \lambda_S \bar{b}$ and $\rho_X = \lambda_X \bar{b}$ for CPAN-S and CPAN-X, respectively.

The distribution of the number of packets that arrive at the ordinary node buffer between two successive transmission requests

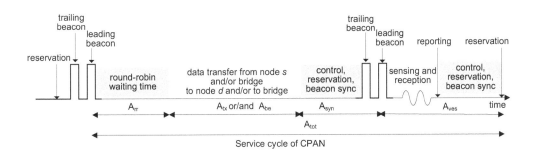

Figure 2: Pertaining to packet arrivals during a service cycle.

can be represented by the PGF of $\beta_S(z) = \sum_{k1=1}^{\infty} \beta_{Sk1} z^{k1}$ and $\beta_X(z) = \sum_{k2=1}^{\infty} \beta_{Xk2} z^{k2}$ for CPAN-S and CPAN-X, respectively. The β_{Sk1} and β_{Xk2} represent the mass probabilities that $k1$ and $k2$ denote the number of packets found in the buffer when an ordinary node applies for bandwidth, in the CPAN-S and CPAN-X, respectively. Therefore, mean number of packets to be transmitted in a single cycle of CPAN-S and CPAN-X are $\overline{\beta_S} = \beta_S'(1) = \sum_{k1=1}^{\infty} k1\beta_{Sk1}$ and $\overline{\beta_X} = \beta_X'(1) = \sum_{k2=1}^{\infty} k2\beta_{Xk2}$, respectively.

The probability distribution of the duration of transmission (service) period for CPAN-S and CPAN-X can be represented by the PGF $S_S(z) = \beta_S(b(z))$ and $S_X(z) = \beta_X(b(z))$, respectively, as this duration depends on the number of packets that arrive during two successive transmission requests and the duration of each packet sent between the two. Therefore, the LSTs of the duration of ordinary node service periods are $S_S^*(s) = \beta_S(b(e^{-s})) = \beta_S(b^*(s))$ and $S_X^*(s) = \beta_X(b(e^{-s})) = \beta_X(b^*(s))$; their mean values are $\overline{S_S} = \overline{\beta_S}b$ and $\overline{S_X} = \overline{\beta_X}b$, for CPAN-S and CPAN-X, respectively.

CPAN service cycle. The CPAN service cycle time is the time between two successive transmission opportunities for a given node. This time varies depending on the number of nodes and bridge transmission time.

The PGF for the CPAN-S service cycle time can be represented by

$$C_{Scyc}(z) = ((1 - \rho_S) + \rho_S S_S(z))^{M_S - 2} b_{exXS}(z) \quad (1)$$

where $b_{exXS}(z)$ is the PGF for the duration of bridge exchange in CPAN-S which depends on the number of packets the bridge has received from CPAN-X. The LST of this CPAN-S service cycle time is

$$C_{Scyc}^*(s) = ((1 - \rho_S) + \rho_S S_S^*(s))^{M_S - 2} b_{exXS}^*(s). \quad (2)$$

with mean value of $\overline{C_{Scyc}} = -C_{Scyc}^{*'}(0)$.

By the same token the PGF for the CPAN-X service cycle time is

$$C_{Xcyc}(z) = ((1 - \rho_X) + \rho_X S_X(z))^{M_X - 2} b_{exSX}(z) \quad (3)$$

where $b_{exSX}(z)$ is the PGF for the duration of bridge exchange in CPAN-X, the LST of which is

$$C_{Xcyc}^*(s) = ((1 - \rho_X) + \rho_X S_X^*(s))^{M_X - 2} b_{exSX}^*(s) \quad (4)$$

with mean value of $\overline{C_{Xcyc}} = -C_{Xcyc}^{*'}(0)$.

Bridge cycle time. Bridge cycle time is the time between two successive bridge transmissions in any given CPAN; this time depends on a number of phases as shown in the Fig. 1.

After transmitting inter-CPAN packets collected from CPAN-X in the CPAN-S, the bridge stays in the remaining superframe to receive inter-CPAN packets and to synchronize with beacons. The time from transmitting packet(s) in the current superframe to the next beacon may be considered as residual time, using the terms of renewal theory [16] where residual time is the time interval from an arbitrary moment in a renewal cycle to the beginning of the new renewal cycle, and its LST is

$$s_{f+}^*(s) = \frac{1 - e^{-ss_f}}{ss_f} \quad (5)$$

with the mean value of $\overline{s_{f+}} = -s_{f+}^{*'}(0)$.

Then, the bridge switches over to the CPAN-X to apply for bandwidth. However, it has to wait for α_1 (i.e., the time lag between superframes of CPAN-S and CPAN-X) before it can place the bandwidth request.

Due to the round robin service discipline, upon placing bandwidth request, the bridge has to wait while nodes with lower IDs are being serviced in the CPAN-X. The time from the beginning of a new superframe to an arbitrary point in that superframe may be considered as elapsed time, using the terms of renewal theory [16] where elapsed time is the time interval from the beginning of the new renewal cycle to an arbitrary moment in that cycle, and its LST is

$$C_{Xcyc-}^*(s) = \frac{1 - C_{Xcyc}^*(s)}{s\overline{C_{Xcyc}}} \quad (6)$$

with the mean value of $\overline{C_{Xcyc-}} = \frac{C_{Xcyc}^{(2)}}{2\overline{C_{Xcyc}}}$.

During its allocated transmission time, the bridge sends all packets it has received from CPAN-S. The PGF of this exchange time is $b_{exSX}(z)$ with mean value $\overline{b_{exSX}}$. Note that this exchange may last for several superframes.

Once the transmission is over, the bridge has to remain in CPAN-X for an additional time in order to receive packets for destinations in CPAN-S and synchronize with the beacons; the PGF of this time is $s_{f+}^*(s)$.

The bridge then switches back to the CPAN-S in order to deliver those packets. Due to the time lag between superframes, the bridge must wait to place the bandwidth request. The PGF of that time is $s_f - \alpha_1$ to CPAN-X.

Finally, after applying for bandwidth, the bridge waits for another round-robin waiting time in the CPAN-S; the LST of this time is

$$C_{Scyc-}^*(s) = \frac{1 - C_{Scyc}^*(s)}{s\overline{C_{Scyc}}} \quad (7)$$

with the mean value of $\overline{C_{Scyc-}} = \frac{C_{Scyc}^{(2)}}{2\overline{C_{Scyc}}}$.

Therefore, the total bridge cycle time for CPAN-S is

$$B_{Scyc} = \overline{s_{f+}} + \alpha_1 + \overline{C_{Xcyc-}} + \overline{b_{exSX}} + \overline{s_{f+}} + (s_f - \alpha_1) + \overline{C_{Scyc-}}. \quad (8)$$

The corresponding PGF is

$$B_{Scyc}(z) = z^{(2\overline{s_{f+}} + s_f)} C_{Xcyc-}(z) b_{exSX}(z) C_{Scyc-}(z) \quad (9)$$

with the LST of

$$B_{Scyc}^*(s) = B_{Scyc}(e^{-s}) \quad (10)$$

$$= e^{-s(2\overline{s_{f+}} + s_f)} C_{Xcyc-}^*(s) b_{exSX}^*(s) C_{Scyc-}^*(s). \quad (11)$$

During this time, the number of packets collected in CPAN-X for destinations in the other CPAN can be described with the PGF of

$$Qb_S(z) = B_{Scyc}^*(\lambda_{bSX} - \lambda_{bSX} z) \quad (12)$$

Since each packet needs a service time of $b(z)$, the PGF for the duration of the bridge exchange in the CPAN-X is

$$b_{exSX}(z) = Qb_S(b(z)) \quad (13)$$

and the LST of bridge transmission is

$$b_{exSX}^*(s) = b_{exSX}(e^{-s}) \quad (14)$$

The probability distribution of the duration of bridge exchange in the CPAN-X can also be represented as a series:

$$b_{exSX}(z) = \sum_{k=0}^{k_{max}} d_k z^k \quad (15)$$

where d_k represents the mass probability that the bridge exchange takes k slots. The mass probabilities in (15) can be obtained by expanding (13) into power series on variable z.

By the same token, the bridge cycle time for CPAN-X is

$$B_{Xcyc} = \overline{s_{f+}} + (s_f - \alpha_1) + \overline{C_{Scyc-}} + \overline{b_{ex-XS}} + \overline{s_{f+}} + \alpha_1 + \overline{C_{XScyc-}} \quad (16)$$

The PGF for the bridge cycle time in CPAN-X is

$$B_{Xcyc}(z) = z^{(2\overline{s_{f+}} + s_f)} C_{Scyc-}(z) b_{exXS}(z) C_{Xcyc-}(z) \quad (17)$$

The probability distribution of the duration of bridge exchange in CPAN-S can be found in an analogous manner.

Using (14), we can define the PGF for the number of packet arrivals to an ordinary node buffer during the bridge transmission as

$$A_{be}(z) = b_{exSX}^*(\lambda_X - \lambda_X z). \quad (18)$$

However, for a given CPAN, a target node may not experience bridge transmission delay in every superframe as the bridge transmission takes place once per bridge cycle period which can last several superframes. Probability that the bridge transmission takes place in the current superframe is $\frac{s_f}{B_{Xcyc}}$. Therefore, the final PGF for the number of packet arrivals to an ordinary node buffer during the bridge transmission can be defined as

$$A_{be_p}(z) = \frac{s_f}{B_{Xcyc}} A_{be}(z) = \frac{s_f}{B_{Xcyc}} b_{exSX}^*(\lambda_X - \lambda_X z). \quad (19)$$

Round-robin waiting time. As explained above, round-robin waiting time is the time a node has to wait while nodes with lower IDs are being serviced. Using (6), we can define the PGF of the number of packet arrivals during the round-robin waiting time as

$$A_{rr}(z) = C_{Xcyc-}^*(\lambda_X - \lambda_X z). \quad (20)$$

The number of packet arrivals during the transmission (service period) can be described by the PGF

$$A_{tx}(z) = S_X^*(\lambda_X - \lambda_X z). \quad (21)$$

Delay due to beacon synchronization. The time from transmitting packet(s) in the current superframe to the next control sub-frame (at which time a node can submit the sensing report to the coordinator) may be considered as residual time of a superframe. Hence, the PGF for the number of packet arrivals during this time is

$$A_{syn}(z) = s_{f+}^*(\lambda_X - \lambda_X z). \quad (22)$$

Duration of sensing. The coordinator assigns sensing duty to the nodes that have transmitted their packets, and the duration of this duty, expressed in superframes, is the product of sensing penalty, k_p and the number of packets transmitted in the service period of the corresponding CPAN (k_1 for CPAN-S-S, $k2$ for CPAN-X). Thus, the distribution of time spent in sensing can be represented by the PGF $V_X(z) = \sum_{k2=1}^{\infty} \beta_{Xk2} z^{k_p s_f k2} = \beta_X(z^{k_p s_f})$ and its mean value is $\overline{V_X} = k_p s_f \overline{\beta_X}$. The corresponding LST of the single sensing period is $V_X^*(s) = \sum_{k2=1}^{\infty} \beta_{Xk2} e^{-k_p s_f k2}$. The number of packets that arrive during the sensing period can be obtained by replacing s with $\lambda_X - \lambda_X z$ in the last equation,

$$A_{Xvc}(z) = V_X^*(\lambda_X - \lambda_X z). \quad (23)$$

Impact of packet reception during sensing. As explained above, reception preempts sensing in the sense that a node has to take a break from ongoing sensing duty in order to receive packets. Packet reception may take place in one or more superframes, but the node still has to finish its sensing duty before placing a new transmission request. As the result, the sensing period will be effectively expanded due to reception. To model this effect, we need to find the probability of packet reception during the sensing period.

Each of the nodes in the CPAN-X generates intra-CPAN (local) traffic at a rate of $\frac{\lambda_X(1 - P_{ic})}{M_X - 2}$, assuming uniform distribution of destination nodes. Probability of having no packets for a given target node during a sensing period is $P_{nrs} = e^{-\frac{\lambda_X(1-P_{ic})}{M_X-2}\overline{V_X}}$, and the PGF for extended sensing period due to reception is $V_{Xes}(z) = P_{nrs} + (1 - P_{nrs})z^{s_f}$.

However, a node in the CPAN-X receives intra-CPAN traffic at a rate of $\frac{\lambda_X}{M_X-2}$, and inter-CPAN packets at a rate of $\frac{\lambda_{bSX}}{M_X-2}$. Probability of having no packets during the sensing period is $P_{nrd} = e^{-\frac{\lambda_{bSX}}{M_X-2}\overline{B_{Xcyc}}} e^{-\frac{\lambda_X}{M_X-2}\overline{V_X}}$. Therefore, the PGF for extended sensing period in the CPAN-X due to reception is $V_{Xes}(z) = P_{nrd} + (1 - P_{nrd})z^{s_f}$. The number of packets that arrive during this extended sensing period can be described by the PGF of $A_{Xves}(z) = V_{Xes}(\lambda_X - \lambda_X z)$.

Time between successive transmission requests. The PGF for the number of packets arrivals to a node in the CPAN-X during the interval between two successive bandwidth requests is

$$Q_X(z) = A_{be_p}(z) A_{rr}(z) A_{tx}(z) A_{syn}(z) A_{Xves}(z) = \sum_{k2=0}^{\infty} q_{Xk2} z^{k2}. \quad (24)$$

If the node finishes sensing and has no packets in its buffer, it will continue with sensing duty, which occurs with the probability of $q_{X0} = Q_X(0)$. The distribution of the number of packets that arrive at the ordinary node buffer between two successive transmission requests can be described by the PGF of

$$\beta_X(z) = \frac{Q_X(z) - q_{X0}}{1 - q_{X0}} \quad (25)$$

110

and its mean value is $\overline{\beta_X} = \overline{A_{be_p}} + \overline{A_{rr}} + \overline{A_{tx}} + \overline{A_{syn}} + \overline{A_{Xves}}$. Probability distribution of the total sensing period is

$$V_{Xtot}(z) = \frac{V_{Xes}(1 - q_{X0})}{1 - V_{Xes}q_{X0}}. \tag{26}$$

Equations from (1) to (26) and the corresponding equations from CPAN-S which can be derived in an analogous manner can be solved together as a system with unknowns β_{Sk1} and β_{Xk2} for $k1 = k2 = 1..n_c$, if we limit the number of terms in each PGF or LST to n_c.

4. PACKET ACCESS DELAY

Intra-CPAN packet delay. Let us assume that an ordinary node in the CPAN-X already has L^* intra-CPAN packets at the moment it applies for bandwidth. Let us also assume that A_i packets arrive to the node while it is transmitting the ith packet. Thus after transmitting the nth packet in the transmission (service) period, the buffer has $L_n = L^* + A_{rr} + A_1 + A_2 + ... + A_n - n$ packets, and the PGF of the number of packets left after n^{th} departing packet can be obtained as

$$L_n(z) = \frac{A_{rr}(z)A(z)^n \sum_{k=n}^{\infty} \beta_{Xk}z^k}{z^n \sum_{k=n}^{\infty} \beta_{Xk}} \tag{27}$$

The PGF of the number of packets left in the buffer after any departing packet can be deduced from the last equation and the single packet serving time $b^*(\lambda - \lambda z)$ as

$$\begin{aligned} L(z) &= \sum_{n=1}^{\infty} \frac{\sum_{k=n}^{\infty} \beta_{Xk}}{\overline{\beta_X}} L_n(z) \\ &= A_{rr}(z)\frac{(\beta_X[b^*(\lambda_X - \lambda_X z)] - \beta_X(z))b^*(\lambda_X - \lambda_X z)}{\overline{\beta_X}[b^*(\lambda_X - \lambda_X z) - z]} \end{aligned} \tag{28}$$

Packets are serviced in FIFO order and the number of packets left after a departing packet is equal to the number of packets that arrived during the departing packet was in the system. Probability distribution of the packet waiting time can be obtained from

$$L(z) = T_a^*(\lambda_X - \lambda_X z) = W^*(\lambda_X - \lambda_X z)b^*(\lambda_X - \lambda_X z) \tag{29}$$

and the corresponding LST of intra-CPAN packet waiting time is

$$W^*(s) = A_{rr}(1 - \frac{s}{\lambda_X})\frac{\lambda_X\left(\beta_X[b^*(s)] - \beta_X(1 - \frac{s}{\lambda_X})\right)}{\overline{\beta_X}[\lambda_X b^*(s) - \lambda_X + s]} \tag{30}$$

with the mean value of $\overline{W} = \frac{dW^*}{ds}|_{s=0} = \frac{(1+\rho_X)\beta_X^{(2)}(1)}{2\lambda_X\overline{\beta_X}}$.

Inter-CPAN packet delay. We note that an inter-CPAN packet undergoes no less than five different phases from its arrival to the CPAN-S to the reception by the CPAN-X node and vice versa, as shown in Fig. 1.

First, the packet waits to be transmitted to the bridge. This time, commonly referred to as access delay, W_a, is equal to the residual time of bridge cycle period, $W_a^*(s) = \frac{1 - B_{Scyc}^*(s)}{s\overline{B}_{Scyc}}$, with mean value of $\overline{W}_a = -W_a^{*'}(0)$.

Second, the packet waits until bridge finishes receiving all of the inter-CPAN packets from the CPAN-S and synchronizes with the beacon, which lasts for the remaining superframe duration, $W_{syn}^*(s) = \frac{1 - e^{-ss_f}}{ss_f}$, with mean value of $\overline{W}_{syn} = -W_{syn}^{*'}(0)$.

Third, the bridge switches to CPAN-X to apply for bandwidth. Due to time lag α_1 between CPAN-S and CPAN-X, the bridge waits for $W_{ab} = \alpha_1$ before applying for bandwidth in the CPAN-X.

Fourth, bridge waits for its turn to transmit in CPAN-X for round-robin waiting time. The delay observed by an inter-CPAN packet may thus be considered to be the elapsed time of the duration of CPAN-X cycle time, $W_{rr}^*(s) = \frac{1 - C_{Xcyc}^*(s)}{s\overline{C}_{Xcyc}}$, with mean value of $\overline{W}_{rr} = -W_{rr}^{*'}(0)$.

Finally, the bridge stays in CPAN-X to deliver its packets to target node. Since packets are randomly positioned within the bridge queue, the delay experienced by a bridge packet in the CPAN-X is the elapsed time of the duration of bridge transmission: $W_{bt}^*(s) = \frac{1 - b_{exSX}^*(s)}{s\overline{b}_{exSX}}$, the mean value of which is $\overline{W}_{bt} = -W_{bt}^{*'}(0)$.

Therefore, mean end-to-end delay for an inter-CPAN packet from CPAN-S to CPAN-X can be obtained as $\overline{W}_a + \overline{W}_{syn} + W_{ab} + \overline{W}_{rr} + \overline{W}_{bt}$.

The mean end-to-end delay for an inter-CPAN packet from CPAN-X to CPAN-S can be found in an analogous manner, except that the bridge waits $W_{ab} = s_f - \alpha_1$ before applying for bandwidth in CPAN-S.

5. PERFORMANCE ANALYSIS

To evaluate the performance of the proposed scheme, we have solved the system of equations presented above using Maple 16 from Maplesoft, Inc. [8]. The number of nodes for CPAN-S is $M_S = 14$ and CPAN-X is $M_X = 10$; these numbers include the coordinator in each CPAN and a shared bridge node. We have assumed that both CPANs use $N = 19$ channels, each with an independent primary source. Packet size is assumed to be constant at $k_d = 10$ unit slots, while the size of the superframe s_f is set to 130 time units, 30 of which are allocated for the control and reservation purposes. Packet arrival rate was varied from $\lambda_S = 0.001$ to $\lambda_S = 0.006$ while the fraction of inter-CPAN traffic was set to P_{ic} 0.2, in both CPANs. Sensing penalty was set to $k_p = 0.6$ while the time lag α_1 was initially set to $0.5s_f = 65$ time units.

Fig. 3 shows the performance of ordinary node operations: mean number of packet arrivals to an ordinary node between successive transmissions by that same node and mean service cycle time – i..e, the time needed to service all nodes in a CPAN.

As expected, the number of packet arrivals increases with the increase in the traffic intensity of the local CPAN. However, the number of packet arrivals also increases with the increase in traffic intensity of the other CPAN, which is due to the fact that the duration of bridge exchange of a given CPAN depends on the traffic intensity in the other CPAN. As the result, bridge exchanges last longer and more packets arrive to the node during that time. As it can be seen, mean number of packet arrivals begins at approximately equal values in both CPANs, but the maximum value is higher in CPAN-X, Fig. 3(c), than in CPAN-S, Fig. 3(a). This is caused by the higher number of inter-CPAN packets sent from CPAN-S which has more nodes; this translates into longer bridge exchanges in CPAN-X and, consequently, longer intervals between successive packet transmissions.

Regarding the service cycle, we observe that higher traffic intensity translates into higher number of packets and, by extension, into longer service cycle period. Higher traffic intensity also means that the volume of inter-CPAN traffic will be higher and bridge transmissions will last longer, which should also contribute to the extension of the service cycle. Due to the interdependency of the CPANs introduced by the bridge, mean service cycle time also increases for higher traffic intensity in the other CPAN.

Fig. 4 shows the parameters of bridge operations: mean duration of a bridge exchange and mean bridge cycle period. Mean duration of bridge cycle period depends on the duration of the bridge ex-

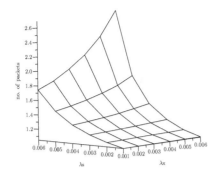

(a) Mean number of packet arrivals in CPAN-S.

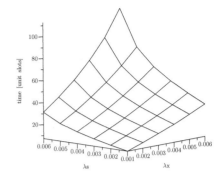

(b) Mean service cycle time in CPAN-S.

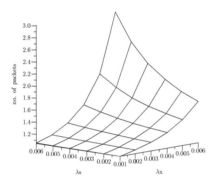

(c) Mean number of packet arrivals in CPAN-X.

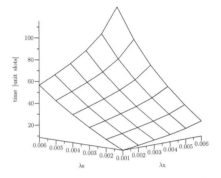

(d) Mean service cycle time in CPAN-X.

Figure 3: Mean number of packet arrivals to an ordinary node between two successive transmissions (left column) and mean service cycle time (right column).

change in both CPANs, as well as on the round-robin waiting time. As can be seen, mean bridge cycle period increases at higher traffic intensity, with longer values observed in CPAN-S which has more nodes and, consequently, generates more inter-CPAN traffic. This leads to an increase of the bridge cycle in CPAN-X and extends the waiting time for traffic in that CPAN, both local and non-local, which in turn contributes to the increase of bridge cycle in CPAN-S.

Regarding bridge exchange, the higher number of nodes in CPAN-S means that a higher number of inter-CPAN packets are generated there. To deliver those packets to their destinations in CPAN-X, the bridge exchange must last longer in CPAN-X, as can be seen by comparing the diagram in Fig. 4(c) with the one in Fig. 4(a).

Fig. 5 shows the mean packet waiting times or delays, first for intra-CPAN (local) traffic in each CPAN, then for inter-CPAN (non-local) traffic. Of course, the intra-CPAN packet waiting time increases with traffic intensity in that CPAN. However, the intra-CPAN packet waiting time strongly depends on both the round-robin waiting time and the duration of bridge exchange in the current CPAN. The round-robin waiting time is affected by the CPAN traffic intensity, but also by the duration of bridge exchange which, in turn, depends on the traffic intensity in the other CPAN. Thus, the intra-CPAN packet waiting time for a given CPAN increases

for higher traffic intensity in either CPAN. Longer waiting times observed in CPAN-X, Fig. 5(b), compared to those in CPAN-S, the Fig. 5(a), are due to the longer duration of bridge exchanges in the former.

Figs. 5(c) and 5(d) show the delay for inter-CPAN packet in the direction from CPAN-S to CPAN-X, and from CPAN-X to CPAN-S, respectively. This delay is mainly dependent on the bridge cycle period which, in turn, depends on the number of nodes in both CPANs and the packet arrival rate. This causes the bridge to carry more packets which affects bridge delivery (in the target CPAN) more than bridge collection (in the source CPAN). As the result, inter-CPAN delays turn out to be longer for traffic from CPAN-S to CPAN-X, Fig. 5(c), than for traffic going in the opposite direction, Fig. 5(d).

Our final experiment concerns the mean end-to-end delay for inter-CPAN packet as the function of the time lag between CPAN superframes when packet arrival rates in both CPANs are set to $\lambda_S = \lambda_X = 0.003$. In this scenario, the delay is affected by the time lag only, in the phase where the bridge is waiting to apply for bandwidth in the destination CPAN, while all other components of the end-to-end delay remain unchanged. Therefore, end-to-end delay for inter-CPAN packets increases almost linearly with the in-

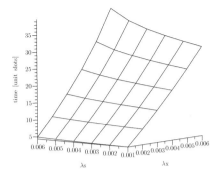

(a) Mean bridge exchange in CPAN-S.

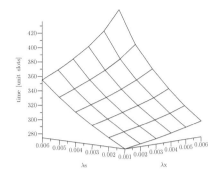

(b) Mean bridge cycle period in CPAN-S.

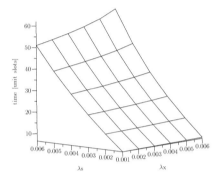

(c) Mean bridge exchange in CPAN-X.

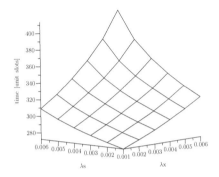

(d) Mean bridge cycle period in CPAN-X.

Figure 4: Mean duration of bridge exchange and mean bridge cycle period.

crease of time lag, α_1 in case of the traffic from CPAN-S to CPAN-X, or $s_f - \alpha_1$, in the case of the traffic from CPAN-X to CPAN-S. This dependency is easily observed in Fig. 5(e). The crossover point where the two delays have equal values is not in the middle of the range for α_1 on account of the difference in the number of nodes (and the resulting traffic) in the two CPANs.

6. CONCLUSION AND FUTURE WORK

We have discussed a simple yet effective scheme for bridging between two cognitive personal area networks (CPANs). The main feature of the proposed bridging scheme is that the bridge is free to remain in a given CPAN as long as it takes to deliver all the data originating from the other CPAN and to collect all the data to be delivered there, without a predefined schedule which means that CPANs need not be synchronized with each other. Through probabilistic analysis and renewal theory, we have obtained complete probability distribution for service cycle time, bridge cycle time, and end-to-end packet delays for both intra- and inter-CPAN traffic. Experiments have confirmed the validity of the scheme, but they have also shown that the CPANs are not fully decoupled, as the performance of one of the CPANs depends on local as well as non-local traffic intensity.

Our future work will focus on incorporating the impact of collisions with primary users in our analysis, including possible CPAN

recovery through the use of backup channels. We also plan to extend the scheme to networks consisting of three or more CPANs, where a number of bridges can coexist and carry the inter-CPAN traffic by visiting CPANs in sequence. The application of the proposed scheme to traditional as well as delay-tolerant networks will also be studied.

7. REFERENCES

[1] DARPA. The XG vision. Request for comments, Jan. 2004.

[2] Spectrum policy task force report. Technical Report FCC 02-155, Federal Communications Commission, Nov. 2002.

[3] C. Jiang, Y. Chen, K. R. Liu, and Y. Ren. Renewal-theoretical dynamic spectrum access in cognitive radio network with unknown primary behavior. *Selected Areas in Communications, IEEE Journal on*, 31(3):406–416, 2013.

[4] P. K. Lee. Joint frequency hopping and adaptive spectrum exploitation. In *IEEE Military Communications Conference MILCOM2001*, volume 1, pages 566–570, Washington, DC, Oct. 2001.

[5] Y.-E. Lin, K.-H. Liu, and H.-Y. Hsieh. On using interference-aware spectrum sensing for dynamic spectrum access in cognitive radio networks. *Mobile Computing, IEEE Transactions on*, 12(3):461–474, 2013.

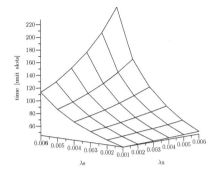
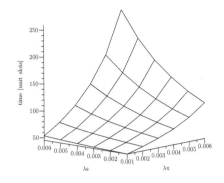

(a) Mean intra-CPAN traffic delay in CPAN-S.   (b) Mean intra-CPAN traffic delay in CPAN-X

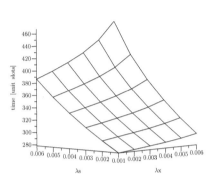
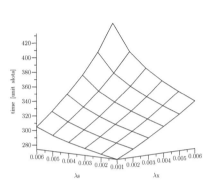
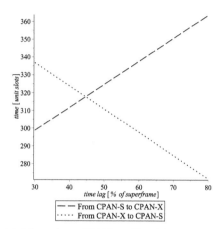

(c) Mean inter-CPAN traffic delay from CPAN-S to CPAN-X.   (d) Mean inter-CPAN traffic delay from CPAN-X to CPAN-S.   (e) Mean inter-CPAN traffic delay as the function of time lag between superframes.

Figure 5: Mean end-to-end delay.

[6] Y. Liu, L. X. Cai, and X. Shen. Spectrum-aware opportunistic routing in multi-hop cognitive radio networks. *Selected Areas in Communications, IEEE Journal on*, 30(10):1958–1968, 2012.

[7] J. Mišić and V. B. Mišić. Performance of cooperative sensing at the MAC level: Error minimization through differential sensing. *IEEE Transactions on Vehicular Technology*, 58(5):2457–2470, June 2009.

[8] Maplesoft, Inc. *Maple 16*. Waterloo, ON, Canada, 2013.

[9] J. Mišić and V. B. Mišić. Simple and efficient MAC for cognitive wireless personal area networks. In *Proc. Global Telecommunications Conference GLOBECOM'09*, Honolulu, HI, Nov. 2009.

[10] Z. Cai, Y. Duan, and A. G. Bourgeois. Delay efficient opportunistic routing in asynchronous multi-channel cognitive radio networks. *Journal of Combinatorial Optimization*, 29(4), 815–835, 2013.

[11] J. Mišić and V. B. Mišić. Recovery in channel-hopping cognitive networks under random primary user activity. *IEEE Transactions on Vehicular Technology*, 63(5):2392–2406, June 2014.

[12] W. Li, X. Cheng, T. Jing, and X. Xing. Cooperative multi-hop relaying via network formation games in cognitive radio networks. In *INFOCOM, 2013 Proceedings IEEE*, pages 971–979. IEEE, 2013.

[13] J. Mišić, V. B. Mišić, and M. S. I. Khan. On the selection of working channels in a channel-hopping cognitive PAN. In *9th Int. Wireless Communications and Mobile Computing Conf. (IWCMC 2013)*, Cagliari, Sardinia, Italy, July 2013.

[14] M. Pan, P. Li, Y. Song, Y. Fang, and P. Lin. Spectrum clouds: A session based spectrum trading system for multi-hop cognitive radio networks. In *INFOCOM, 2012 Proceedings IEEE*, pages 1557–1565. IEEE, 2012.

[15] M. M. Rahman, J. Mišić, and V. B. Mišić. Performance of bridging in cognitive wireless personal area networks. In *IEEE Conference on Wireless Communications and Networking Conference (WCNC 2015)*, New Orleans, LA, The USA, Mar. 2015.

[16] H. Takagi. *Queueing Analysis*, volume 1: Vacation and Priority Systems. North-Holland, Amsterdam, The Netherlands, 1991.

Two Hops or More:
On Hop-Limited Search in Opportunistic Networks

Suzan Bayhan
University of Helsinki
Finland
bayhan@hiit.fi

Esa Hyytiä
Aalto University
Finland
esa@netlab.tkk.fi

Jussi Kangasharju
University of Helsinki
Finland
jakangas@cs.helsinki.fi

Jörg Ott
Aalto University
Finland
jo@netlab.tkk.fi

ABSTRACT

While there is a drastic shift from host-centric networking to content-centric networking, how to locate and retrieve the relevant content efficiently, especially in a mobile network, is still an open question. Mobile devices host increasing volume of data which could be shared with the nearby nodes in a multi-hop fashion. However, searching for content in this resource-restricted setting is not trivial due to the lack of a content index, as well as, desire for keeping the search cost low. In this paper, we analyze a lightweight search scheme, *hop-limited search*, that forwards the search messages only till a maximum number of hops, and requires no prior knowledge about the network. We highlight the effect of the hop limit on both search performance (i.e., success ratio and delay) and associated cost along with the interplay between content availability, tolerated waiting time, network density, and mobility. Our analysis, using the real mobility traces, as well as synthetic models, shows that the most substantial benefit is achieved at the first few hops and that after several hops the extra gain diminishes as a function of content availability and tolerated delay. We also observe that the *return path* taken by a response is on average longer than the *forward path* of the query and that the search cost increases only marginally after several hops due to the small network diameter.

Categories and Subject Descriptors

C.2.1 [**Computer-Communication Networks**]: Network Architecture and Design–Store and forward networks.

Keywords

Mobile opportunistic networks, opportunistic search, hop neighborhood.

1. INTRODUCTION

Mobile devices can establish opportunistic networks—a flavour of Delay-tolerant Networks (DTNs) [9]—among each

MsWiM'15, November 02–06, 2015, Cancun, Mexico.
© 2015 ACM. ISBN 978-1-4503-3762-5/15/11...$15.00.
DOI: http://dx.doi.org/10.1145/2811587.2811592.

other in a self-organising manner and facilitate communication without the need for network infrastructure. The capabilities of today's smart mobile devices yield substantial computing and storage resources and means for creating, viewing, archiving, manipulating, and sharing content. In addition, content downloaded from Internet is recommended to be cached at the handset [24]. This yields a huge reserve of data stored in mobile devices, which users may be willing to share. While this is typically done using Internet-based services, opportunistic networks enable content sharing among users in close proximity of each other.

In this paper, we focus on a human-centric DTN, where nodes search for information stored in some of the nodes. The nodes lack a global view of the network, i.e., there is no service that could index the stored content and assist a searching node in finding content (or indicate that the sought information does not exist). This means that operations are decentralized and, as mobile nodes have resource constraints (e.g., energy), we need to control the spread of the messages when searching. One such control mechanism is imposing the maximum number of hops a message can travel. We call a search scheme that limits the message's path to maximum h hops as h-hop search. *Hop-limited search* [17, 27] is of our interest as it is a lightweight scheme that does not require intensive information collection about the nodes or the content items. However, determining the optimal h is not straightforward. Although a large h tends to increase replication, it also increases the chance of finding the desirable target (content or searching node), thereby decreasing replication.

While many works in the literature apply hop limitations [6, 27], mostly two-hop such as [2], to the designed routing protocols, the motivation behind setting a particular hop value is not clear. In [4], we analyze the effect of hop limit on the routing performance by modelling the optimal hop limited routing as *all hops optimal path* problem [15]. However, opportunistic search necessitates considering the availability of the sought content as well as routing of the response to the searching node. In our previous work [17], we analytically modelled the search utility and derived the optimal hop count for a linear network, e.g., search flows through a single path and response messages follow the same path. In this paper, we provide an elaborate analysis of hop-limited search in a mobile opportunistic network considering the search success, completion time, and the cost.

Search is a two-phase process. We refer to the first phase in which query is routed towards the content providers as *forward path* and the second phase in which response is routed towards the searching node as *return path*. First, we present an analysis on the forward path via an analytical model. We show the interplay between tolerated waiting time (how long the searching node can wait for the forward path), content availability, and the hop count providing the maximum search success ratio for a specific setting. Next, we verify our analysis of the forward path and elaborate also on the return path via simulations.

Our results suggest the following:

- Generally speaking, search performance increases with increasing h especially for scarcely available content. However, the highest improvement is often achieved at the second hop. After that, the improvements become smaller and practically diminish when $h > 5$.

- We observe that return path requires on average longer hops/time compared to the forward path, which may imply that optimal settings for the forward path does not yield the optimal performance on the return path.

- We show that the search cost first increases and after several hops ($h \approx 4$) it tends to stabilise. This is due to the small diameter of the network; even if h is large letting the nodes replicate a message to other nodes, each node gets informed about the search status quickly so that replication of obsolete messages is stopped.

The rest of the paper is organised as follows. Section 2 introduces the considered system model followed by Section 3 introducing the hop-limited search. Section 4 numerically analyzes the forward path, while Section 5 focuses on the whole search process. Section 6 overviews the related work and highlights the points that distinguish our work from the others. Finally, Section 7 concludes the paper.

2. SYSTEM MODEL

We consider a mobile opportunistic network of N nodes as in Fig. 1. Nodes move according to a mobility model which results in i.i.d. meeting rates between any two nodes. We use the following terminology:

Searching node (n_s) is a node that initiates the search for a content item. We assume that content items are equally likely to be sought, i.e., uniform *content popularity*. In reality, content items have diverse popularities; e.g., YouTube video popularity follows a Zipf distribution [13]. We choose uniform distribution to avoid a bias toward the "easy" searches.

Tagged node is a node that holds a copy of the sought content. Only a fraction α of the nodes are tagged, where α is referred to as the *content availability*. Although it is expected that search dynamics such as caching changes α, we assume that it does not change over time. The sets of all and tagged nodes are denoted by $\mathcal{N}$ and $\mathcal{M}$, and their sizes N and M, respectively. The number of tagged nodes is $M = \alpha N$. Every node is equally likely to be a tagged node.

Forward path and return path: In the first step of the search, a query is disseminated in the network to find a tagged node. In case the first step is completed, a response generated by a content provider is routed back towards n_s in the second step. We refer to the former as the *forward* or *query path* and to the latter as the *return* or *response path*.

Tolerated waiting time (T) is the maximum duration to find the content (excluding the return path). Note that total tolerated waiting time is $2T$ if we assume the same delay restriction for the return path.

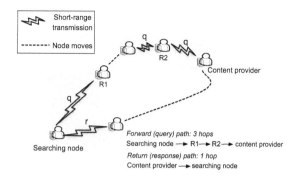

Figure 1: Network model, forward and return paths.

3. HOP-LIMITED SEARCH

To describe the basic operation of hop-limited search, assume that n_s creates a query that includes information about its search at time $t = 0$. When n_s encounters another node that does not have this query, n_s replicates the query to it to reach a tagged node faster. A node acquiring a copy of the message becomes a *discovered node*. The discovered node also starts to search and replicate the query to *undiscovered nodes*. Each message contains a header, referred to as *hop count*, representing the number of nodes that forwarded this message so far. Messages at n_s are 0-hop messages; those received directly from n_s are 1-hop messages. We refer to a search scheme as h-hop search if a search message can travel at most h hops. Hence, when a node has h-hop message, it does not forward it further. We also call a node with a i-hop message as the i-hop node for that particular message. In h-hop search, when an i-hop and j-hop node meet (without loss of generality we assume $i < j \leq h$), the state of j-hop node is updated to $(i+1)$-hop if $j > i+1$. The forward path completes when a copy of the query reaches a tagged node.

3.1 Search Success Ratio

Let us first consider a search scheme that does not put any hop limitation but instead limits the total number of replications on the forward path and the return path to K and K', respectively. For a content item with availability α, we can calculate the forward success ratio of this search scheme as[1]:

$$\text{Forward success ratio} = 1 - (1-\alpha)^K. \quad (1)$$

Similarly, we calculate the search success ratio, i.e., both steps are completed, as:

$$P_s = \sum_{k=1}^{K} Pr\{\text{k content providers are discovered}\}$$
$$\times Pr\{\text{at least one of k responses reaches } n_s\}.$$

We can expand the above formulation which leads to:

$$P_s = \sum_{k=1}^{K} \binom{K}{k} \alpha^k (1-\alpha)^{K-k} \left(1 - (1 - \frac{K'}{N-1})^k\right). \quad (2)$$

Let $\gamma = \frac{K'}{N-1}$, i.e., the probability that a response reaches n_s. After replacing γ into (2), we apply some manipulations by the help of binomial theorem: that is $(x+y)^n =$

---

[1]Please see Appendix in [5] for detailed derivations.

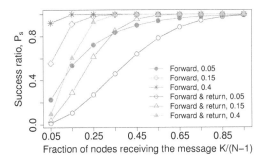

Figure 2: **Search success with increasing degree of replication** K **for** $\alpha = \{0.05, 0.15, 0.40\}$.

$\sum_{k=0}^{n} x^k y^{n-k}$. Then, we find the search success as:

$$P_s = 1 - (1 - \alpha\gamma)^K. \quad (3)$$

Fig. 2 plots the success ratio with increasing fraction of nodes that receive the message. We plot the success of both the forward path and the total search under various content availability values. The results are for equal number of replications for the forward and return path, i.e., $K' = K$. The figure shows that to ensure a desirable level of success, search has to cover certain fraction of nodes, which depends on the content availability. In hop-limited search, there is no explicit restriction on number of replications K, but rather it is implicitly set by h and T. This result brings us to the question of how search coverage in the number of nodes changes with h and T.

Let $\mathcal{N}_h(t)$ be the set of discovered nodes excluding n_s at time t and $N_h(t) = |\mathcal{N}_h(t)|$ its size. Faloutsos *et al.* [10] define N_h for a static graph as node neighborhood within h hops. Similarly, we define $N_h(T)$ as the number of nodes that can be reached from a source node less than or equal to h hops under time limitation T. Let $P_h(T)$ denote the *forward path success ratio* defined as the probability that a query reaches one of the tagged nodes in a given time period T under h-hop limitation. For a search that seeks a content item with availability α, we approximate $P_h(T)$ as follows:

$$
\begin{aligned}
P_h(T) &= \sum_{n=1}^{N} P\{N_h(T) = n\} \cdot (1 - (1-\alpha)^n) \\
&= 1 - E[(1-\alpha)^{N_h(T)}] \\
&\approx 1 - (1-\alpha)^{E[N_h(T)]}. \quad (4)
\end{aligned}
$$

Note that (4) provides an upper bound for $P_h(T)$ and will only be used to understand the effect of h and T. In numerical evaluations, we relax all the simplifications (e.g., i.i.d meeting rates) and experiment using real mobility traces. Given (4), our problem reduces to discovering how $E[N_h(T)]$ changes with h and T. However, as observed in [12], each meeting may not lead to a new node being discovered, i.e., some nodes may meet again or a node may be met by several nodes. Therefore, total meetings in time period T results in a very optimistic estimate for $E[N_h(T)]$. In addition to the overlaps of opportunistic contacts, the hop restriction may result in lower $E[N_h(T)]$. In contrast to static networks [1], modelling $E[N_h(T)]$ for general time-evolving networks is not straightforward. Therefore, we derive $E[N_h(T)]$ from

mobility traces and plug it into (4). See also [18] for an analysis of how mobility and node density affect the communication capacity of a mobile opportunistic network.

3.2 Benefit of One Additional Hop

We define the effect of increasing hop count from h to $h+1$ on the search performance as the *added benefit* and calculate it as the difference between $P_h(T)$ and $P_{h+1}(T)$: $\Delta P_{h,h+1} = P_{h+1}(T) - P_h(T)$, where $P_h(T)$ values are either approximated as above or obtained from experiments. Given that users can perceive only significant improvements rather than minimal changes in performance, we are more interested in larger values $\Delta P_{h,h+1}$. Let h_β denote the hop count beyond which the added benefit of one additional hop is lower than β. More formally, h_β is defined as:

$$h_\beta \triangleq \arg\max_h (\Delta P_{h,h+1} \geq \beta) + 1. \quad (5)$$

While $\beta \to 0$ yields the optimal hop count h^* achieving the highest performance, i.e., $h_\beta = h^*$, we search for h values that lead to higher β. Setting $\beta \to 0$, we assess until which hop there is still some gain, albeit minimal, whereas higher β values help discovering the last hop with substantial benefit. We refer to these β values as *any-benefit* and *fair-benefit* hop, respectively.

3.3 Time to Forward Path Completion

In this section, we derive the *forward path completion time* which is the time required for an initiated query to reach one of the content providers. Let us denote by $m_i(t)$ the total number of i-hop nodes at time t. These nodes have received the message via $(i-1)$ relays. Subsequently, we denote the state of a Continuous Time Markov Chain (CTMC) by:

$$S(t) = (m, m_0(t), m_1(t), \ldots, m_i(t), \ldots, m_{h-1}(t), m_h(t))$$

where

- $m = N_h(t) + 1$ is the number of nodes with a copy of the query (n_s and all discovered nodes) and

- $m_i(t)$ nodes are i-hop nodes and $\sum_{i=0}^{h} m_i(t) = m$.

States that have m nodes holding the search query are represented as S_m. The state space consists of all S_m transient states where $m \in \{1, \ldots, N-M\}$ and the absorbing state S_{tagged}, which represents discovery of a tagged node. Hereafter, we drop the time parameter for clarity. From state S_m, three types of events trigger state transitions:

- *Meeting a tagged node*: An arbitrary i-hop node in $\mathcal{N}_h$ where $i < h$ meets with one of the tagged nodes in $\mathcal{M}$. The resulting state is S_{tagged} and the search ends. There is only one such transition from every state.

- *Meeting a node that is undiscovered and not tagged*: An i-hop node meets an undiscovered untagged node. There are $\sum_{i=0}^{h-1} 1_{[m_i>0]}$ such transitions from this state where indicator function $1_{[f(\cdot)]}$ yields 1 if $f(\cdot)$ evaluates to *true*, and the resulting state is $S_{m+1} = (m+1, \ldots, m_{i+1}+1, \ldots)$.

- *Meeting among discovered nodes*: We call a meeting between i-hop and j-hop node an (i, j)-meeting where $i < j$. If $j > i + 1$, N_h does not change but m_j and m_{i+1} change. The new state is $S_m' = (m, \ldots, m_{i+1}+1, \ldots, m_j-1, \ldots)$. The number of such transitions from a state S_m is $\sum_{i=0}^{h-2} 1_{[m_i>0]} \left(\sum_{j=i+2}^{h} 1_{[m_j>0]} \right)$.

We call these three events *Type-tagged*, *Type-1*, and *Type-0* events; the corresponding transition rates are denoted by λ_{tagged}, λ_1, and λ_0, respectively. If the Type-1 event is a meeting with an i-hop node, we denote the respective rate as λ_1^i. Similarly, if a Type-0 event is due to an (i,j)-meeting, the rate is $\lambda_0^{i,j}$. For state $S_m = (m, m_0, m_1, \ldots, m_i, \ldots, m_h)$ the transitions leading to a state change are:

$$S_m \xrightarrow{\lambda_{\text{tagged}}} S_{\text{tagged}} \tag{6}$$

$$S_m \xrightarrow{\lambda_1^i} (m+1, \ldots, m_{i+1}+1, \ldots, m_h) \tag{7}$$

$$S_m \xrightarrow{\lambda_0^{i,j}} (\ldots, m_{i+1}+1, \ldots, m_j-1, \ldots, m_h) \tag{8}$$

and the corresponding transition rates are:

$$\lambda_{\text{tagged}} = \lambda(m - m_h)M \tag{9}$$

$$\lambda_1^i = \lambda m_i (N - M - m) \tag{10}$$

$$\lambda_0^{i,j} = \lambda m_i m_j \tag{11}$$

where λ is the pairwise meeting rate.

Since solving the given Markov model may not be practical due to the state space explosion for large h and N, we approximate T_h and show its high accuracy in Section 4 by comparing it with the results of Markov model. Let $T(m, h)$ denote the remaining time to search completion under h-hop search and when m nodes hold the search query. Under h-hop search, only $m_{h^-} = m - m_h$ nodes are actively searching and can forward the query to their encounters. Assume that m_i are identical for all $i \geqslant 1$. Then, the number of searching nodes m_{h^-} is:

$$m_{h^-} = 1 + (m-1)\left(1 - \frac{1}{h}\right).$$

We calculate $T(m, h)$ as:

$$T(m, h) = \frac{1}{\lambda m_{h^-}} + \frac{\alpha}{\lambda} 0 + \frac{\lambda - \alpha}{\lambda} T(m+1, h). \tag{12}$$

We expand $T(m+1, h)$ similarly and substitute in (12). After a certain number of nodes are searching, the remaining time to search completion converges to zero, i.e., $T(m+k+1, h) \to 0$. Denote $q = (1 - \alpha/\lambda)$. Then, we find:

$$T(m, h) = \sum_{i=0}^{\infty} \frac{q^i}{\lambda(1 + (m+i-1)(1-h^{-1}))}$$

Solving for $m = 1$ gives an approximation for T_h:

$$\tilde{T}_h = \sum_{i=0}^{\infty} \frac{q^i}{\lambda(1 + i(1-h^{-1}))}. \tag{13}$$

4. FORWARD PATH

In this section, we evaluate the performance of hop-limited search (referred to as HOP) while varying (i) content availability, (ii) tolerated waiting time, (iii) network density, and (iv) mobility scenarios. We use $\alpha = \{0.40, 0.15, 0.05\}$ for *high*, *medium*, and *low* content availability, respectively.

4.1 Datasets

In our analysis, we use real traces of both humans and vehicles. For the former, we use the Infocom06 dataset [26] which represents the traces of human contacts during Infocom 2006 conference. For the latter, we use the Cabspotting dataset [22] that stores the GPS records of the cabs in San Francisco. To gain insights about more general network settings, we also analyze a synthetic mobility model that reflects realistic movement patterns in an urban scenario. Below, we overview the basic properties of each trace:

Infocom06: This data set records opportunistic Bluetooth contacts of 78 conference participants who were carrying iMotes and 20 static iMotes for the duration of the conference, i.e., approximately four days. In our analysis, we treated all devices as identical nodes which host content items and initiates search queries. This trace represents a small network in which people move in a closed region.

Cabspotting: This data set records the latitude and longitude information of a cab as well as its occupancy state and time stamp. The trace consists of updates of the 536 cabs moving in a large city area for a duration of 30 days. For our analysis, we focused only on the first three days and a small region of approximately $10\,\text{km}\times10\,\text{km}$ area. 496 cabs appear in this region during the specific time period. The cab information is not updated at regular intervals. Hence, we interpolated the GPS data so as to have an update at every 10 s for each cab. Next, we set transmission range to 40 m to generate contacts among cabs. This trace represents an urban mobility scenario [16, 22].

Helsinki City Scenario (HCS): This setting represents an opportunistic human network in which the walking speed is uniformly distributed in $[0.5, 1.5]\,\text{m/s}$. The nodes move in a closed area of $4.5\,\text{km}\times3.4\,\text{km}$. HCS [19] uses the downtown Helsinki map populated with *points-of-interests* (e.g., shops), between which pedestrians move along shortest path.

4.2 Forward Path Success Ratio

We derive the neighborhood size $N_h(T)$ as an average of 500 samples where each sample represents an independent observation of the network starting at some random time, from an arbitrary node and spanning an observation window equal to the tolerated waiting time. Next, we calculate $P_h(T)$ using (4). We use R [25] for these analysis. In the following, we mostly focus on the more challenging cases such as short T or low α, and report the representative results due to the space limitations.

Fig. 3 illustrates the change in $N_h(T)$ represented as fraction of the network size for Infocom06 for various tolerated waiting time T and content availability α. For each T, we plot $N_h(T)$ and corresponding $P_h(T)$. From Fig. 3(a), we can see the significant growth of $N_h(T)$ at the second hop for all settings. While further hops introduce some improvements, we observe the existence of a *saturation point* [16]. After this point, the change in N_h is marginal either because all nodes are already covered in the neighborhood or higher h cannot help anymore without increasing T.

We present the resulting P_h for low content availability in Fig.3(b). As expected, the second hop provides the highest performance gain compared to the previous hop ($\Delta P_{h,h+1}$) as a reflection of highest $\Delta N_{h,h+1}$. As Infocom06 has good connectivity, almost all queries reach one of the tagged nodes after $h \approx 4$.

We present the effect of content availability for short T in Fig. 3(c). Regarding the effect of content availability, *we observe that search for a rare content item, i.e., low α, benefits more from increasing h compared to highly available content items.* When many nodes are tagged, n_s meets one of these after some time. However, if the probability of meeting a tagged node is fairly low, using additional hops exploiting

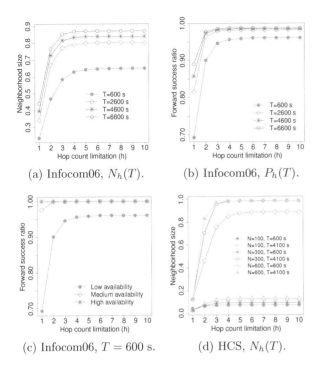

(a) Infocom06, $N_h(T)$.   (b) Infocom06, $P_h(T)$.

(c) Infocom06, $T = 600$ s.   (d) HCS, $N_h(T)$.

Figure 3: (a) Growth of h-hop neighborhood for Infocom06 under various tolerated waiting time (T) and (b) corresponding forward success ratio for $\alpha = 0.05$. (c) Effect of content availability on $P_h(T)$ for Infocom06. (d) Growth of h-hop neighborhood for HCS under various N and T.

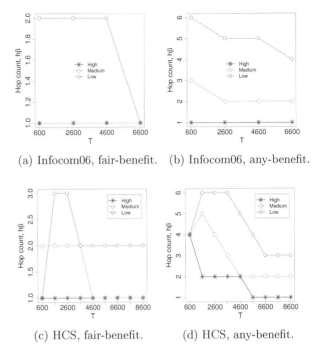

(a) Infocom06, fair-benefit.   (b) Infocom06, any-benefit.

(c) HCS, fair-benefit.   (d) HCS, any-benefit.

Figure 4: Fair- and any-benefit hops.

the mobility of the encountered nodes and spreading the query further is a better way of searching. A smart search algorithm can keep track of the content availability via message exchanges during encounters and can adjust the hop count depending on the observed availability of the content. For low and medium content availability, *the highest benefit is obtained at the second hop*. For a content item which is stored by a significant fraction of nodes, even a single hop search may retrieve the sought content.

Fig. 3(d) illustrates the growth of $N_h(T)$ under various network size N and T. We use our synthetic model HCS by setting $N = \{100, 300, 600\}$ nodes to observe the effect of network density on $N_h(T)$. For this particular setting, the clustering of lines based on T shows that time restriction is more dominant factor in determining $N_h(T)$ compared to N. As expected, $N_h(T)$ is higher for higher N. However, all settings exhibit the same growth trend with increasing h.

4.3 Fair-benefit and Any-benefit Hops

Fig. 4 illustrates the change in h_β with increasing T for $\beta \in \{0.0005, 0.1\}$ which represent any-benefit and fair-benefit hops, respectively. As stated before, Infocom06 has good connectivity among nodes as conference takes place in a closed area and nodes share the same schedule (e.g., coffee breaks and sessions). As a result of this good connectivity, first one or two hops provide almost all the benefits of multi-hop search (Fig. 4(a)). However, Fig.4(b) shows that the optimal hop in terms of the highest P_h is achieved at higher $h \leqslant 6$.

For HCS scenario that represents a network of urban scale, the effect of increasing T is a bit different. Fig. 4(c) shows that short and longer T may have the same operating point in terms of h_β. For low T, the benefit of increasing h diminishes due to the limited number of encounters and the resulting small set of discovered nodes, whereas for long T almost all nodes are discovered without requiring any further hops. The lower h_β with increasing T can also be explained by "*shrinking diameter*" phenomenon, which states that the average distance between two nodes decreases over time as networks grow [20]. Indeed, the diameter of the message search tree gets shorter over time and leads to a smaller hop distance between the searching node and a tagged node. Note the decreasing *any-benefit* hop in Fig. 4(d). For example, searching for a content item with medium availability achieves the highest performance at $h_\beta = 5$ for $T = 1600$ s, while it decreases gradually to $h_\beta = 2$ with increasing T.

4.4 Time to Forward Path Completion

Table 1 shows the search time T_h which is obtained by solving CTMC introduced in Section 3.3 and $\tilde{T}_h$ given by (13). We normalize every value by the maximum search time of each setting. In the table, we also list the approximation errors. First thing to note is the drastic decrease in search time at the second hop. In agreement with our conclusions from P_h, we see that second hop speeds the search significantly resulting in approximately 80% shorter search time for the low availability, 60% for the medium, and 50% decrease for the high availability scenario. As P_h, the most significant improvement in search time occurs for low content availability. Our approximation also exhibits exactly the same behaviour in terms of the change in the search time. As the error row shows, it deviates from the expected search time to some degree: 32% under-estimation to 8% overestimation.

Table 1: Search time and its approximation.

α	Time	$h=1$	$h=2$	$h=3$	$h=4$	$h=5$
Low	T_h	1	0.21	0.13	0.12	0.11
	$\tilde{T}_h$	1	0.14	0.12	0.11	0.11
	Error	0	-0.32	-0.08	-0.03	-0.03
Medium	T_h	1	0.40	0.33	0.31	0.31
	$\tilde{T}_h$	1	0.39	0.35	0.33	0.33
	Error	0	-0.01	0.07	0.06	0.05
High	T_h	1	0.51	0.46	0.45	0.45
	$\tilde{T}_h$	1	0.54	0.49	0.47	0.46
	Error	0	0.05	0.08	0.06	0.04

5. COMPLETE SEARCH

In Sec.4, we show that the first few hops yield the highest benefit in terms of forward path success ratio. In this section, we explore if this trend holds for the whole search, i.e., forward and return path. To this end, we carry out a wide range of simulations to gain insight to the following aspects: (i) the fair-benefit hops for various T and α settings, (ii) average temporal and hop distance to/from content, (iii) characteristics of the return path, and (iv) search cost.

Note that return path also applies hop-limited routing as well as the forward path. We first assume that an oracle stops the dissemination of a completed search immediately, and then relax this assumption in a scheme where nodes are informed about search state via control messages. Using the ONE simulator [19], we design an opportunistic network consisting of $N = 98$ nodes for Infocom06 and $N = 496$ for Cabspotting scenario. 5000 content items are distributed across nodes according to the availability ratios: for example, a content item with $\alpha = 0.4$ is randomly assigned to 40% of the nodes. This assignment is static during the course of the simulation: nodes do not generate new content items and nodes having received a copy during operation will not respond to requests. Every query interval, a random node initiates a query for a uniformly chosen content item. The query generation interval is uniformly distributed in $[10,20]$ s. We simulate the complete system during which approximately 23000 queries are generated.

We use 20 m radio range for Infocom06 and 40 m for Cabspotting, infinite transmission capacity (i.e., all packets can be exchanged at an encounter), and 100 MB of storage capacity; message are 15 KB in size. To obtain an upper performance bound, we implement *epidemic search* (EPID) which does not impose any hop limitations. In the following, we refer to h-hop search as HOP.

5.1 Fair-benefit and Any-benefit Hops

We analyse the effect of h on the search success ratio (P_s, the ratio of queries retrieving a response) and forward path success ratio (P_h). Fig. 5 depicts P_s and P_h for HOP and EPID under various settings: $T = \{3600, 21600, 86400\}$ s, all availabilities, and for Infocom06 and Cabspotting scenarios. Total tolerated search time (i.e., forward and the return path) is set to $2T$.

As Fig. 5 shows, the highest $\Delta P_{h,h+1}$ is at the second hop for all T. However, it takes more hops until HOP achieves the same success ratio as EPID: $h = 5$ for $T = 3600$ s, $h = 4$

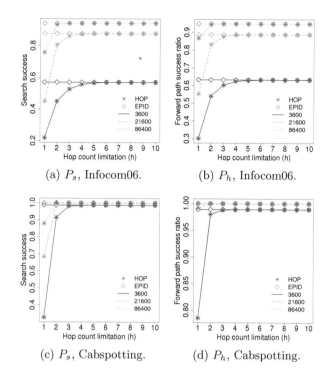

(a) P_s, Infocom06. (b) P_h, Infocom06.

(c) P_s, Cabspotting. (d) P_h, Cabspotting.

Figure 5: Effect of tolerated waiting time, $\alpha = 0.05$.

for $T = 21600$ s, and $h = 3$ for $T = 86400$ s. Cabspotting scenario achieves higher success ratio under the same time limitations compared with Infocom06. Although Infocom06 represents a small area and closed group scenario, we observe more contacts in Cabspotting setting. This may be attributed to higher transmission range as well as higher mobility of the nodes.

If we consider only the forward path as we did previously in Fig. 3(b), we observe in Fig 5(b) that the second hop provides almost all the benefits for longer waiting times. For more strict T, we see that the search success ratio is below 1 meaning that all benefits of multi-hop routing is exploited. Under this setting, the search performance cannot be improved without increasing T. Having visited P_s and P_h figures for Infocom06, we conclude that although the target content is discovered at the second hop with high probability, it does not necessarily ensure that the return path completes in two hops. As such, return path is similar to a search for the content with $\alpha = 1/N$, i.e., a scarce content item. Hence, it may require further hops. For Cabspotting, two to three hops yield the same performance as EPID.

Figs. 6(a) and 6(b) demonstrate the effect of content availability on the whole search success for $T = 600$ s and $T = 21600$ s. As we see in the figures, P_s values are clustered based on T for both Infocom06 and Cabspotting. This behaviour can be interpreted as the tolerated waiting time being more dominant factor in determining the search performance rather than the content availability under the considered settings. Regarding h_β, fair-benefit hops are around 2-3 hops whereas any-benefit hops vary from 2 to 6 hops. Finally, Figs. 6(c) and 6(d) demonstrate the total hop count for the whole search route. In contrary to P_s, we observe a clustering according to content availability in the total search hop counts. While the tolerated waiting time has

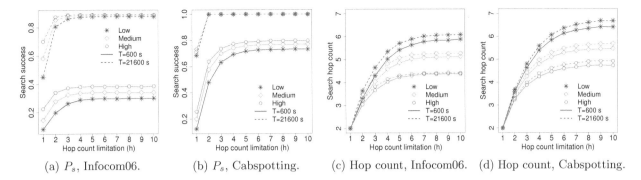

(a) P_s, Infocom06.   (b) P_s, Cabspotting.   (c) Hop count, Infocom06.   (d) Hop count, Cabspotting.

Figure 6: Effect of content availability under $T = 600$ and $T = 21600$ s.

some effect on the average search path length, the effect of content availability is the dominating factor. Low availability content items are retrieved from more far-away nodes whereas items with higher availability are retrieved from closer nodes. Nevertheless, the total path lengths are much shorter than the imposed limit, which means that content is typically retrieved from "nearby" nodes.

5.2 Effective Distance to/from Content

In the previous section, we presented experiment results for different tolerated waiting time settings and referred to them as *short* or *long* T. In fact, temporal dynamics of the network (e.g, average inter-contact time) determine whether a T value is short or not. In this section, we aim to provide insights about the distance to content both in terms of number of hops and time. To this end, we focus on the forward paths under EPID and remove the time restriction (i.e., $T = \infty$). In general, the performance of an opportunistic network is governed by the routing protocol and the node mobility (among other factors). We eliminate the effect of the algorithm by using EPID. This allows us finding the average hop distance between a searching node and a tagged node. Similarly, as we avoid any routing effects, we obtain the shortest time it takes to reach a tagged node from a searching node. We refer to this time as *temporal distance* to content. Let us define *effective distance to content* as the maximum distance, be it hops or time, which ensures that 90% of the paths between a searching node and a tagged node is lower than this distance [20]. We define *effective distance from content* similarly for the return path.

In Fig. 7, we plot the effective hop and temporal distances for both the forward and return paths under different content availabilities for Infocom06 and Cabspotting. While the effective distance to content (i.e., forward path length) is inversely proportional to content availability, the effective distance from content (i.e., return path length) is only slightly affected by content availability. It is also noteworthy that the response hop distance is longer than the query distance for all settings. Regarding temporal distances in Fig. 7 (second row), Cabspotting has much shorter temporal distance compared to Infocom06. This difference explains higher success ratios achieved in Cabspotting compared with Infocom06 under the same T in Fig. 5(c) vs. Fig. 5(a). In Fig. 7 (bottom-left), effective temporal distance is shorter for the responses as opposed to higher hop counts observed in Fig. 7 (top-left). However, as we do not preserve the coupling between the query and response paths of the search,

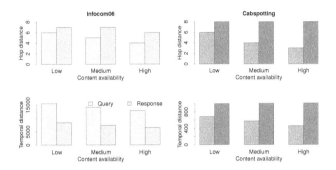

Figure 7: Effective hop and temporal distance for query and return path for Infocom06 and Cabspotting. Left bars: query, right bars: response.

this result does not necessarily contradict with our claim that response path takes longer and is more challenging. In fact, responses that are still looking for the searching node are not accounted for, which may in turn lead to the shorter effective distance. Effective temporal distance is paramount for unveiling the conditions of feasibility of search. For example, setting $T = 600$ s lead to very poor search performance for Infocom06 as shown in Fig. 6(a) because the network evolves slower than this time.

5.3 Characteristics of the Return Path

In the previous sections, we analyzed the query and response paths separately. One arising question is the relation between the forward and return paths: whether the latter depends on the former. In this section, we present the analysis of the query and response paths where query and response path coupling is preserved. We simulate EPID with a restriction on the search time. Using the completed queries, we calculate the Pearson correlation coefficient between the query and response hop (ρ_{hop}) as well as the query and response time (ρ_{temp}). We also find the ratio of the response hop to the query hop (γ_{hop}) as well as the ratio of response temporal path length to query temporal path length (γ_{temp}) to explore how challenging the return path is compared to the forward path.

Table 2 summarises this analysis for Infocom06, which also agrees with the analysis for Cabspotting scenario. First, we do not observe any strong correlation between return and forward path lengths for any of the settings (i.e., ρ_{hop} and

Table 2: Correlation between forward and return paths, Infocom06.

T	α	ρ_{hop}	ρ_{temp}	γ_{hop}	γ_{temp}	P_h	P_s
	Low	0.30	0.36	1.47	2.23	0.35	0.30
600	Med.	0.29	0.34	1.72	3.09	0.42	0.34
	High	0.27	0.32	1.97	4.02	0.48	0.38
	Low	0.35	0.43	1.4	2.18	0.63	0.57
3600	Med.	0.35	0.38	1.61	2.98	0.67	0.61
	High	0.33	0.32	1.85	4.13	0.70	0.65
	Low	0.33	0.13	1.39	2.60	0.95	0.94
86400	Med.	0.35	0.13	1.62	3.52	0.95	0.94
	High	0.35	0.12	1.86	4.50	0.95	0.95

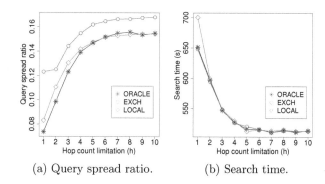

(a) Query spread ratio. (b) Search time.

Figure 8: Hop count vs. search cost and time for Infocom06 (α=0.15, T =600 s).

ρ_{temp} are around 0.1–0.4). This result may be conflicting with the intuition that the information found in nearby/far-away will also be routed back quickly/slowly. However, search process is more complicated due to the intertwined effects of mobility and restrictions on the total search time. For example, consider a forward path with a very large number of hops. Due to the remaining short time before the tolerated waiting time expires, search can only go a few hops towards the searching node. This leads to a long forward path with a very short return path which challenges the above-mentioned intuition. With higher content availability, the required number of forward hops decreases whereas the return path length seems to be barely affected. Hence, the corresponding γ_{hop} and γ_{temp} increase. For all scenarios, return path is on the average longer than the forward path. Using this observation, a tagged node receiving a query can set the time-to-live field of its response message longer than the received query's forward path time.

5.4 Cost of Search

Obviously, increasing hop count increases the neighborhood which in turn increases the chance of finding the sought content. However, the larger neighborhood should also be interpreted as larger number of replication, i.e., higher search cost. In fact, the neighborhood size represents the upper bound of number of replications for a search message if no other search stopping algorithm is in effect. In this section, we evaluate the cost of search considering two simple mechanisms that aim to keep replication much below the upper bound set by $N_h(T)$.

We consider three cases: (i) ORACLE: there is a central entity from which a node retrieves the global state of a message in its buffer and can ignore it if outdated, e.g. a completed search or a query already reaching a tagged node, (ii) EXCH: upon encounter, nodes exchange their local knowledge about search activities in the network, (iii) LOCAL: nodes exchange their knowledge *only* on the shared messages. Note that an ORACLE can be an entity in the cellular network and nodes can access it via a control channel. In fact, this communication with the cellular network is more costly (e.g., energy) compared to the opportunistic communication. Nevertheless, this scenario serves as an optimal benchmark to assess the performance of the other scenarios. EXCH pro-actively spreads information about existing queries to all nodes opportunistically, which may be considered as leaking information to nodes not involved in search. LOCAL circumvents this by only using its local knowledge

and sharing information with peers only about queries that the other node has already seen.[2]

Fig. 8 shows *query spread ratio* which is defined as i.e., the fraction of nodes that have seen this query, and search time. First, we should note that the resulting search success (not plotted) is almost the same under all schemes. Second, note the non-increasing query spread ratio for $h > 5$. This result confirms that the network is a small-world network where all nodes get informed quickly about the search status and drop the outdated messages timely. Hence, even for larger h, nodes detect the outdated messages via local and shared knowledge. In Fig. 8(a), we observe that EXCH maintains the same performance as ORACLE, whereas LOCAL results in more replication as fewer nodes are informed about the completed queries/responses. Nevertheless, because of the small network diameter, a higher h does not result in an explosion of query spread in the network. Regarding search time, we observe substantial decrease in search time also for $h > 2$ and $h < 5$ in contrast to the vanishing benefits after second hop derived from our analytical model (Table 1). Search time tends to stabilise after $h \geqslant 5$. Hence, although several hops are sufficient in terms of search success, further hops (e.g., $h \approx 4$) can be considered for faster search.

5.5 Discussion

Our analysis shows that the two factors affecting the optimal hop count are the content availability (α) and the product of meeting rate and tolerated waiting time (λT). The latter is the number of meetings before tolerated waiting time expires where λ depends on network density and mobility model. If both α and λT are low (scarce content and very few contacts due to network sparsity or short search time), search performance is expected to be low. However, it increases with increase in either of these factors. If one of these factors is large, it is sufficient to have a low hop count limit (e.g., two or three) to obtain good performance. That is, when $\alpha \lambda T$ is large relative to the expected number of tagged nodes met during the search time, limiting the search to a few hops still achieves good results. As $\alpha \lambda T$ decreases, the required hop limit to maintain good search performance is larger. This allows devising adaptation when

---
[2]This is easy to implement even without cryptographic methods by using a two-stage protocol, in which nodes first forward the queries they are carrying and then share information about those queries they received from their peer.

issuing search queries. Nodes can monitor the request and response rate for certain (types of) content items and thus infer popularity and availability in their area.[3] They can also assess the regional node density and meeting rate λ and thus determine the required hop count h given T or vice versa. Moreover, nodes can monitor search performance and determine how well their (region in a) network operates. To improve performance, nodes can decide to increase the availability of selected contents via active replication of the scarce content, obviously trading off storage capacity and link capacity for availability. Such decision could be based entirely upon local observations, but could also consider limited information exchange with other nodes.

We believe that with the guidance of our analysis, a node can decide on the best hop count depending on the network density and the content availability that can both be derived from past observations by the node. Although we show that search cost stops increasing after a few hops, keeping h low may be desirable if we interpret it as a measure of the social relation between two nodes (e.g., one hop as friends; two hop as friend-of-friend). In other words, lower h can be interpreted as more *trustworthy* operation. Moreover, protocols involving lower number of relays are more scalable and energy-efficient [11].

6. RELATED WORK

While the DTN literature has many proposals for message dissemination, which exploit the information about the network such as (estimated) pairwise node contact rates, node centrality, communities, and social ties, efficient mechanisms for content search remain largely unexplored. In a sense, this is reasonable as search can be considered as a two-step message delivery: query routing on the forward path and the response routing on the return path. The forward path is less certain as the content providers are unknown. In this regard, the return path is less challenging as the target node (and a recent path to reach it) is already known. However, routing the response looks for a particular node, whereas the forward search is for a *subset of nodes* whose cardinality is proportional to the content availability. Thus, search requires special treatment rather than being an extension of the message dissemination.

Two questions for an efficient search are (i) which nodes may have the content [3] and (ii) when to stop a search [23]. The former question requires assessment of each node in terms of its potential of being a provider for the sought content. For example, *seeker assisted search* (SAS) [3] estimates the nodes in the same community to have higher likelihood of holding the content as people in the same community might have already retrieved the content. Given that people sharing a common interest come together at a certain "space" (e.g., office, gyms), [11] defines *geo-community* concept and matches each query with a particular geo-community. Hence, the first question boils down to selecting relays with high probability of visiting the target geo-community. As [11] aims to keep the search cost minimal, searching node employs two-hop routing and determines the relays, which thereby reduces the issue of when to stop the search. Deciding when to stop search is nontrivial as the search follows several paths and whether the searching node has already discovered a re-

---

[3]If nodes cache response contents opportunistically [21], availability would grow with popularity.

sponse is not known by the relaying nodes. Hyytiä *et al.* [17] model the expected search utility with increasing hop count and then finds the optimal hop, while [23] estimates the number of nodes having received a query and possible responses by using the node degrees. In our work, we showed that simple schemes via information sharing can stop search timely and maintain similar performance to that of an oracle due to the small world nature of the studied networks.

Different from all these above works, main focus of our paper is more on a fundamental question: *how does the hop limitation affect the search performance?* While this question has been explored in general networking context, content-centricity and the time constraints require a better understanding of flooding in the context of search. Therefore, we first provided insights on search on a simplified setting and next analyzed the effect of various parameters, e.g., time and real mobility traces, via extensive simulations.

In the literature, several works focus on two-hop forwarding in which the source node replicates the message to any relay and the relays can deliver the message only to the final destination [2, 7, 14]. Grossglauser *et al.* in their seminal work [14] show that two hops are sufficient to achieve the maximum throughput capacity in an ideal network with nodes moving randomly. The capacity increase is facilitated by the reduced interference on the links from source to relay and relay to the destination. Chaintreau *et al.* [7] assess this two-hop forwarding scheme in a DTN scenario with power-law inter-contact times and employ an *oblivious forwarding algorithm* (e.g., memoryless routers that do not use any context information such as contact history). Similarly, [6] focuses on a DTN with power-law distributed inter-contact times and derives the conditions (i.e. range of Pareto shape parameter) under which message delivery has a finite delay bound for both two-hop and multi-hop oblivious algorithms. The authors show that "*as long as the convergence of message delivery delay is the only concern, paths longer than two-hops do not help convergence*" as two hops are sufficient to explore the relaying diversity of the network [6]. Another work supporting two-hop schemes is [11] which shows that two-hop search is favourable for opportunistic networks – a resource-scarce setting, as "*one-hop neighbors are able to cover the most of the network in a reasonable time*" in a network with *sufficiently many* mobile nodes. In our work, we include those cases when longer paths still yield (some) performance improvement. Finally, our work supports the conclusion of [8], which theoretically proves the *small-world* in human mobile networks.

Our work is closely related to the k-hop flooding [27] which models the spread of flooded messages in a random graph. Unlike [27], we focus on content search in a realistic setting, and using real mobility traces (both a human contact network and a vehicular network) we provide insights on the effect of increasing hop count on the search success, delay, and cost under various content availability and tolerated waiting time settings. Despite the differences, it is worthwhile noting that our results agree with the basic conclusions of [27].

7. CONCLUSIONS

Given the volume of the content created, downloaded, and stored in the mobile devices, efficient opportunistic search is paramount to make the remote content accessible to a mobile user. Current schemes mostly rely on routing based on hop limitations. To provide insights about the basics of such a generic search scheme, we focused on a hop-limited search in mobile opportunistic networks. First, by modelling only the forward path, we showed that (i) the second hop and following few hops bring the highest gains in terms of forward path success ratio and (ii) compared to single-hop delivery, increase in hop count leads to shorter search time and after a few hops search time tends to stabilize. Next, we revisited these findings via simulations of the entire search process. While simulations validated our claim for the forward path, we observed that return path on average requires longer time and more hops. Moreover, our results do not indicate strong correlation between the return and forward paths. Finally, we showed that search completes in less than five hops in most cases. This is attributed to the small diameter of the human contact network which has also a positive impact on search cost; nodes are informed about search state quickly and stop propagation of obsolete messages. Our simulations validated that increasing hop count to several hops accelerates the search and later search completion time stabilizes.

As future work, we will design a search scheme that adapts the hop count of query and response paths based on the observed content availability and popularity. Moreover, we believe that content-centric approaches should be paid more attention to implement efficient search schemes in mobile opportunistic networks.

Acknowledgements

This work was supported by the Academy of Finland in the PDP project (grant no. 260014).

8. REFERENCES

[1] L. A. Adamic, R. M. Lukose, and B. A. Huberman. Local search in unstructured networks. *Handbook of graphs and networks*, 2006.

[2] A. Al Hanbali, P. Nain, and E. Altman. Performance of ad hoc networks with two-hop relay routing and limited packet lifetime. *Performance Evaluation*, 65(6):463–483, 2008.

[3] S. Bayhan, E. Hyytiä, J. Kangasharju, and J. Ott. Seeker-assisted information search in mobile clouds. In *ACM SIGCOMM workshop on Mobile cloud computing*, 2013.

[4] S. Bayhan, E. Hyytiä, J. Kangasharju, and J. Ott. Analysis of hop limit in opportunistic networks by static and time-aggregated graphs. In *IEEE ICC*, 2015.

[5] S. Bayhan, E. Hyytiä, J. Kangasharju, and J. Ott. Two hops or more: On hop-limited search in opportunistic networks. Technical report, University of Helsinki, Finland, Aug. 2015.

[6] C. Boldrini, M. Conti, and A. Passarella. Less is more: long paths do not help the convergence of social-oblivious forwarding in opportunistic networks. In *ACM Int. workshop on Mobile Opportunistic Networks*, 2012.

[7] A. Chaintreau, P. Hui, J. Crowcroft, C. Diot, R. Gass, and J. Scott. Impact of human mobility on opportunistic forwarding algorithms. *IEEE Trans. on Mobile Comp.*, 6(6):606–620, 2007.

[8] A. Chaintreau, A. Mtibaa, L. Massoulie, and C. Diot. The diameter of opportunistic mobile networks. In *ACM CoNEXT*, 2007.

[9] K. Fall. A delay-tolerant network architecture for challenged internets. In *ACM SIGCOMM*, 2003.

[10] M. Faloutsos, P. Faloutsos, and C. Faloutsos. On power-law relationships of the Internet topology. In *ACM SIGCOMM Computer Communication Review*, volume 29, pages 251–262, 1999.

[11] J. Fan, J. Chen, Y. Du, P. Wang, and Y. Sun. Delque: A socially aware delegation query scheme in delay-tolerant networks. *IEEE Transactions on Vehicular Technology*, 60(5):2181–2193, Jun 2011.

[12] W. Gao, Q. Li, and G. Cao. Forwarding redundancy in opportunistic mobile networks: Investigation, elimination, and exploitation. *IEEE Transactions on Mobile Computing*, 2014.

[13] P. Gill, M. Arlitt, Z. Li, and A. Mahanti. Youtube traffic characterization: a view from the edge. In *ACM SIGCOMM Conf. on Internet measurement*, 2007.

[14] M. Grossglauser and D. Tse. Mobility increases the capacity of ad hoc wireless networks. *IEEE/ACM Trans. on Networking*, 10(4):477–486, Aug 2002.

[15] R. Guérin and A. Orda. Computing shortest paths for any number of hops. *IEEE/ACM Transactions on Networking (TON)*, 10(5):613–620, 2002.

[16] M. A. Hoque, X. Hong, and B. Dixon. Efficient multi-hop connectivity analysis in urban vehicular networks. *Vehicular Comm.*, 1(2):78–90, April 2014.

[17] E. Hyytiä, S. Bayhan, J. Ott, and J. Kangasharju. Searching a needle in (linear) opportunistic networks. In *ACM MSWiM*, 2014.

[18] E. Hyytiä and J. Ott. Criticality of large delay tolerant networks via directed continuum percolation in space-time. In *IEEE INFOCOM*, 2013.

[19] A. Keränen, J. Ott, and T. Kärkkäinen. The ONE Simulator for DTN Protocol Evaluation. In *Proc. of Int. Conf. on Simulation Tools and Techniques*, 2009.

[20] J. Leskovec, J. Kleinberg, and C. Faloutsos. Graphs over time: densification laws, shrinking diameters and possible explanations. In *ACM KDD*, 2005.

[21] J. Ott and M. Pitkänen. DTN-based Content Storage and Retrieval. In *The First IEEE WoWMoM Workshop on Autonomic and Opportunistic Communications (AOC)*, June 2007.

[22] M. Piorkowski, N. Sarafijanovic-Djukic, and M. Grossglauser. CRAWDAD data set epfl/mobility (v. 2009-02-24), Feb. 2009. Downloaded from http://crawdad.org/epfl/mobility/.

[23] M. Pitkänen, T. Kärkkäinen, J. Greifenberg, and J. Ott. Searching for content in mobile DTNs. In *IEEE PerCom*, 2009.

[24] F. Qian, K. S. Quah, J. Huang, J. Erman, A. Gerber, Z. Mao, S. Sen, and O. Spatscheck. Web caching on smartphones: ideal vs. reality. In *ACM MobiSys*, 2012.

[25] R Core Team. *R: A Language and Environment for Statistical Computing*. R Foundation for Statistical Computing, Vienna, Austria, 2013.

[26] J. Scott, R. Gass, J. Crowcroft, P. Hui, C. Diot, and A. Chaintreau. CRAWDAD data set cambridge/haggle (v. 2006-01-31). http://crawdad.org/cambridge/haggle/, Jan. 2006.

[27] M. Vojnovic and A. Proutiere. Hop limited flooding over dynamic networks. In *IEEE INFOCOM*, 2011.

Modeling and Analysis of Opportunistic Routing in Low Duty-Cycle Underwater Sensor Networks

Rodolfo W. L. Coutinho[1,2], Azzedine Boukerche[2], Luiz F. M. Vieira[1],
Antonio A. F. Loureiro[1]

[1]Federal University of Minas Gerais, Belo Horizonte, MG, Brazil
{rwlc, lfvieira, loureiro}@dcc.ufmg.br
[2]University of Ottawa, Ottawa, ON, Canada
{rlimaco2, boukerch}@site.uottawa.ca

ABSTRACT

The problem of reliable data delivery at low energy cost arises as one of the most challenging research topics in underwater wireless sensor networks (UWSNs). Reliable data delivery is demanding because of the acoustic channel impairments and channel fading. Moreover, it is energy hungry given the high cost of acoustic communication. In wireless ad hoc & sensor networks, separately, opportunistic routing has been employed to improve data delivery whereas duty cycled operation mode has been adopted to achieve energy efficiency and prolonging network lifetime. In this paper, we investigate the benefits and drawbacks of *collision* between opportunistic routing paradigm and duty cycle techniques in UWSNs. We propose an analytical model to study and evaluate the performance of opportunistic routing protocols under duty cycled settings designed from three mainly paradigms: simple asynchronous, strobed preamble and receiver initiated; and different network densities and traffic loads. The results show that while duty cycle reduces the energy consumption, it affects negatively in the opportunistic routing performance, increasing the delay and the expected number of transmissions to deliver a packet. The simple duty cycled approach is shown to be suitable for applications that require long-lived network and can tolerate some degree of packet losses. Our results indicate that strobed preamble-based duty cycle is the most effective approach to be integrated with opportunistic routing, when high fidelity monitoring is required, even having not the best performance in terms of energy savings.

Categories and Subject Descriptors

C.2.1 [**Computer-Communication Networks**]: Network Architecture and Design—*Wireless communication*; C.2.2 [**Computer-Communication Networks**]: Network Protocols—*Routing protocols*

MSWiM'15, November 2–6, 2015, Cancun, Mexico.
ⓒ 2015 ACM. ISBN 978-1-4503-3762-5/15/11 ...$15.00.
DOI: http://dx.doi.org/10.1145/2811587.2811608

Keywords

Energy-efficiency; underwater wireless sensor networks; opportunistic routing; asynchronous duty cycling

1. INTRODUCTION

Underwater wireless sensor networks (UWSNs) are creating a new era of underwater monitoring and exploration. In those applications, underwater sensor nodes are capable of communicating with each other wirelessly through underwater acoustic communication. Underwater acoustic links are characterized by having long propagation delays, low bandwidth, time-varying multipath propagation, low and variable speed of sound, ambient and site-specific noises, Doppler spreading, and shadowing zones [2, 21, 11]. Because of the aforementioned characteristics, reliable data delivery is an important requirement in some real-time applications such as oil spill and marine biology monitoring.

Using underwater acoustic communication technology, a link between neighbors can perform poorly or even be down temporarily, which increases packet error rate, packet collisions and retransmissions, delay, and energy consumption. Hence, the geographic and opportunistic routing (OR) paradigm has been adopted in designing routing protocols for UWSNs [27, 28, 14, 6, 8]. OR protocols leverage the broadcast nature of wireless links and select a set of next-hop forwarding candidates, instead of only a unique next-hop node, as in the traditional multihop routing. The selected candidates forward the data packets toward the destination in a prioritized way, such that a node transmits the packet only if all the high priority candidates failed to do so. Thus, a packet should be retransmitted only if none of the candidates receives it, which helps to reduce the energy consumption and packet collision.

On the other hand, energy efficiency is a well-known challenging problem when designing wireless ad hoc & sensor networks. In those networks, each sensor node has a finite power source supplied by batteries with a limited energy budget. Commonly, battery replacement is impossible since nodes are deployed in harsh and inhospitable environments. Thus, each sensor node should perform the designated tasks using efficiently its energy supply, aiming to extend the network lifetime as much as possible to fulfill the application requirements. Several methodologies have been studied to design energy-efficient network topologies and networking protocols. One prominent methodology is duty cycling, where nodes periodically alternate their communication radio between active and sleep modes. The motivation to put nodes at sleep mode come from the fact that wireless sensor networks usually have very infrequent transmissions. For instance, in underwater sensor networks, a transmission could happen once a week or less [12]. This behavior leads nodes to remain in idle listening during most part of the time, wasting energy. By putting the node to sleep, part of the radio circuitry is shut down, mitigating the energy consumption of idle listening.

Duty cycle protocols can be categorized into *synchronized* and *asynchronous* approaches [3, 22, 16]. In synchronized approaches, nodes negotiate a schedule in order to align their active or sleep periods. Thus, the sender node knows when its neighbors are awake and able to receive data packets. Synchronized approach is unfeasible in UWSNs because of the overhead for clock synchronization and schedule exchanging. In asynchronous approaches, the nodes' duty cycle schedules are decoupled. Thus, at an arbitrary instant, only a subset of the nodes are in active mode, providing network services. This approach is suitable for UWSNs as it is simple and does not require periodic overhead. However, it can incur in high delays, as the sender should wait until the next-hop node be active. Roughly, there are three main designs guiding the proposals of asynchronous duty cycle protocols:

- **Simple asynchronous:** Node changes between active and sleep time periodically. When it has data packet to send, it simply transmits the packet addressing to the next-hop node.

- **Low-power listening:** When a node has a data packet to send, it starts sending a preamble as long as the sleep time of the intended next-hop neighbor node. The next-hop node when wakes up and detects the preamble transmission, stays awake to receive the data packet that will be sent after the preamble transmission. A variant approach is named of *strobed preamble*, where short preambles are transmitted followed by a silent period, in order to avoid energy expenditures by sending long preambles.

- **Receiver initiated:** Each node transmits a short beacon when wakes up, to inform the neighborhood about its active status, and stay awake for a short interval enough to receive data packets. When a node has data packet to send, it remains awake waiting the beacon of the intended next-hop node. After receiving the beacon, the sender node transmits the data packet.

Each asynchronous duty-cycle principle design has advantages and disadvantages that are more impactful in UWSNs. For instance, the simple asynchronous approach does not employ any overhead. However, there is no guarantee that the next-hop is awake to receive the packet. Low power listening can discharge sender nodes quickly as they must transmit preambles before data packets. Moreover, depending on the length of the preamble, it is more efficient to have the radio always on since the transmission cost is dominating in underwater acoustic communication. The receiver

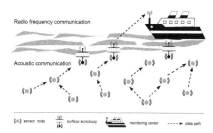

Figure 1: Underwater sensor network architecture.

initiated approach may result in unnecessary energy expenditure mainly for very low traffic generation rate since awaking nodes must send a beacon, even when there is no traffic load.

In this paper, we propose an analytical model to study and evaluate the performance of opportunistic routing protocols under duty cycled settings designed from the following three paradigms: simple asynchronous, strobed preamble and receiver initiated; and different network densities and traffic loads. Our proposed model considers the underwater acoustic communication characteristics, network density and traffic load as well as the peculiarities of opportunistic routing and duty cycle. Preliminary, we have conducted some simulation experiments using the Depth-based Routing protocol (DBR) [28] since the majority of OR protocols designed for UWSNs use the depth pressure metric for candidate set selection, proposed in DBR.

The results show that while duty cycle reduces the energy consumption, it affects negatively in the opportunistic routing performance, increasing the delay and the expected number of transmissions to deliver a packet. Our results indicate that the simple duty cycled approach is suitable for applications requiring long-lived networks that can tolerate some degree of packet losses. Strobed preamble-based duty cycle is shown to be effective to be integrated with opportunistic routing in UWSNs when high fidelity monitoring is required, even having not the best performance in terms of energy savings.

The remaining of this paper is organized as follows. Section 2 provides the background of our proposed model. Section 3 describes our opportunistic routing meeting duty cycle model. Section 4 presents the preliminary results of a duty cycled underwater sensor network running the DBR opportunistic routing protocol [28]. Finally, Section 5 presents our final remarks and future work.

2. PRELIMINARIES
2.1 Network Model
We consider an underwater wireless sensor network architecture comprised of sensor nodes deployed underwater, scattered by surface sonobuoys (sinks), as showed in Fig. 1. All nodes freely drift with water current enabling time and space monitoring. Each sensor node monitors surrounding variables and periodically report the collected data to some sonobuoy through multihop acoustic communication. Each sonobuoy has both a radio frequency-based and an acoustic transceiver allowing it to collect data from nodes through underwater acoustic communication and send the collected data to a monitoring center though radio frequency links.

We model the topology as a graph $\mathcal{G}(t) = (\mathcal{V}, \mathcal{E}(t))$, where $\mathcal{V} = \{V_n \cup V_s\}$ is the set of sensor nodes (N_n) and sonobuoys (N_s); and $\mathcal{E}(t)$ is the finite set of links between them, at time t. Two nodes i and $j \in \mathcal{V}$ are *neighbors* at time t if they can communicate directly, mutually, and consistently over an acoustic link, that is, $e_{i,j} \in \mathcal{E}(t)$. Due to the channel fading, there is a packet delivery probability $p(d_{i,j}, m)$ (please refer to Eq. 6) associated with each link $e_{i,j}$ as a function of the distance $d_{i,j}$ between the nodes and the packet size of m bits to be transmitted through the link. We define $\Omega(i)$ as the set of n_i's neighbors with $n_i \notin \Omega(i)$. Each node can know its neighborhood along the time through periodic beacons dissemination.

2.2 Packet Delivery Probability Estimation

The most suitable way to determine the packet delivery probability of a link, at a given time instant, is by measuring the link quality. Herein, due to the analytical nature of the proposed model, we derive the packet delivery probability from the underwater wireless acoustic channel model. We use the attenuation model proposed by Urick [25] to capture the underwater acoustic signal attenuation. Whereas more realistic models to predict acoustic attenuation can be found in the literature, such as Rogers' model [18] and Bellhop software [1], Urick's model is simple to evaluate analytically and can provide a useful approximation when its parameters are properly chosen, as showed in [24].

Using Urick's model, we review the packet delivery probability estimation presented in [2, 7, 14, 20]. The overall path loss is $A(d, f) = d^k a(f)^d$, where d is the transmission distance, f is the frequency, $a(f)$ is the absorption coefficient and k models the spreading loss with usual values between 1 (cylindrical spreading) an 2 (spherical spreading). The parameter k is equal to 1.5 for a practical scenario. The absorption coefficient $a(f)$, in dB/km for f in kHz, is described by the Thorp's formula [2] given by:

$$10 \log a(f) = \frac{0.11 \times f^2}{1 + f^2} + \frac{44 \times f^2}{4100 + f} + 2.75 \times 10^{-4} f^2 + 0.003. \tag{1}$$

The average Signal-to-Noise Ratio (SNR) over distance d is given as:

$$\Gamma(d) = \frac{E_b / A(d, f)}{N_0} = \frac{E_b}{N_0 d^k a(f)^d}, \tag{2}$$

where E_b and N_0 are constants that represent the average transmission energy per bit and noise power density in a non-fading additive white Gaussian noise (AWGN) channel. Similar to the studies in [4] and [19], we use Rayleigh fading to model small scale fading where SNR has the following probability distribution:

$$p_d(X) = \int_0^\infty \frac{1}{\Gamma(d)} e^{-\frac{X}{\Gamma(d)}}. \tag{3}$$

The probability of error can be evaluated as:

$$p_e(d) = \int_0^\infty p_e(X) p_d(X) dX, \tag{4}$$

where $p_e(X)$ is the probability of error for an arbitrary modulation at a specific value of SNR X. We use the binary phase shift keying (BPSK) modulation as it is widely used in the state-of-the-art acoustic modem [10]. Each symbol carries a bit in BPSK. In [17], the probability of the bit error over distance d is given as:

$$p_e(d) = \frac{1}{2} \left(1 - \sqrt{\frac{\Gamma(d)}{1 + \Gamma(d)}} \right). \tag{5}$$

For any pair of nodes i and $j \in \mathcal{V}$ distant $d_{i,j}$ meters, the delivery probability of a packet of m bits is simply given by:

$$p(d_{i,j}, m) = (1 - p_e(d_{i,j}))^m. \tag{6}$$

In throughout this paper, we shortly abbreviate the above notation as p_{ij}.

2.3 Opportunistic Routing

Wireless links are known to be unreliable due to the channel fading effects. To cope with this problem, opportunistic routing (OR) protocols have been proposed in different wireless ad hoc & sensor network scenarios. OR has been proved to have an important role in UWSNs [26]. Some proposals for UWSNs can be found in [6, 14, 27, 28]. OR improves wireless link reliability by exploiting the broadcast nature and spatial diversity of the wireless medium [29]. In traditional wireless multihop routing, data packets are forwarded from the current sender to one pre-selected neighbor node. These packets may be lost if the link quality between the nodes is not good enough. In opportunistic routing, a set of next-hop forwarding candidates is selected to help relaying the packet. The nodes that successfully received the packet will forward it in a prioritized way. Thus, packet retransmission takes place only if no candidate received it. As multiple candidates are able to continue forwarding the packet, the probability of at least one of them receive the packet increases as compared to the traditional single next-hop routing, improving the bandwidth utilization, reducing the overhead, collisions and saving energy.

In general, opportunistic routing protocols consist of two main building blocks: the *candidate set selection* and *candidates transmission coordination* as described in the following. The candidate set selection procedures are responsible for determining the set of forwarder nodes. First, this procedure verifies which nodes are able to continue forwarding the packet, according to some metric, for instance, the neighbors advancing the packet toward the sea surface in DBR. After, a subset $\mathcal{F}$ of the aforementioned able nodes is chosen as candidate nodes. The candidates in the set $\mathcal{F}$ are ordered according to their priorities as $n_1 > n_2 > \ldots > n_k$. In DBR, the candidate set $\mathcal{F}$ is composed of nodes with depth difference higher than a determined threshold Δ, as compared to the current sender.

The candidate transmission coordination procedures are responsible for coordinating the candidates transmission according to their priorities. Upon receiving the data packet, a candidate node will hold the packet for a time before forwarding it. The holding time is set according to the candidate priority. The higher the priority, the lower the holding time. During the holding time, if the candidate receives the same packet coming from a high priority node, it suppresses its transmission and discards the packet. Ideally, only one transmission must be performed by a candidate set to avoid redundant packets and unnecessary waste of resources. DBR prioritizes the candidates transmission by having a holding time proportionally to the proximity of the node to the sea surface.

3. MODELING OF OPPORTUNISTIC ROUTING IN DUTY CYCLED UWSN

In this paper, we focus on the problem of improving wireless link reliability whereas the mobile UWSNs' lifetime is prolonged. We propose an analytical model to evaluate the OR performance when running in a low duty cycle mobile UWSNs. In modeling OR meeting duty cycled settings, we made the following assumptions:

1. Each underwater sensor node i periodically generates data packets and reports them toward a surface sonobuoy. Data packet generation is modeled according to a Poisson process with mean λ_i.

2. In spite of beaconing being an important process for neighborhood discovery in mobile UWSNs, it is neglected in the model. Actually, a new trend in designing OR protocol has been devoted to investigate beaconless approach, where the candidate set selection is made locally at the receivers (receiver side-based candidate set selection) as in DBR routing [28] protocol.

3. Acknowledge packet transmissions are not considered, since it is not employed at several OR protocols.

4. There is a perfect coordination between nodes, so that, there is no redundant packet transmissions. Besides, it is a quite unrealistic assumption and is commonly done to maintain the model simple and tractable, as in [9, 13]. Accordingly, from the i's candidate set $\mathcal{F}(i)$, $|\mathcal{F}(i)| = m$, and $j \in \mathcal{F}(i)$, the neighbor j will continue forwarding the i's data packet with probability:

$$P_f^{ij} = \left[p_{ij} \prod_{k=1}^{j-1} (1 - p_{ik}) \right] / \left[1 - \prod_{k=1}^{m} (1 - p_{ik}) \right]. \quad (7)$$

In Eq. 7, the term p_{ab} refers to the packet delivery probability from node a to b given by Eq. 6; the term $\prod_{k=1}^{j-1}(1 - p_{ik})$ calculates the probability of candidates with higher priority than j fail in receiving the packet.

3.1 Always-On Communication Radio

In this section, we model the scenario where duty cycle is not employed, that is, nodes are always with radio turned on. In this setting, the outgoing traffic rate of a sensor node i is determined by both its generated data packet traffic and the traffic received from its neighbor, that it carried out. Mathematically, the outgoing traffic rate can be computed as:

$$\Theta_i = \underbrace{\lambda_i}_{\text{Term 1}} + \underbrace{\sum_{\forall j \in \Omega(i) \,\wedge\, i \in \mathcal{F}(j)} \lambda_j \cdot P_f^{ij}}_{\text{Term 2}}, \quad (8)$$

where P_f^{ij} is the probability of the node i to forward data packets received from node j, given by Eq. 7. In Eq. 8, Term 1 computes the traffic generated by the node. Term 2

computes the carried traffic by the node, which was received from its neighbors.

Due to the broadcast nature of the wireless communication medium, the incoming traffic rate at a sensor node i, relative to the reception of intended and unintended neighborhood generated data packets, is:

$$I_i = \sum_{k \in \Omega(i)} \lambda_k. \quad (9)$$

From the data packet transmissions, we can estimate the energy consumption rate at node i as:

$$E_i = \Theta_i \cdot \left(\frac{L_d}{\alpha B} \right) \cdot e_T + I_i \cdot \left(\frac{L_d}{\alpha B} \right) \cdot e_R + \tau \cdot e_I, \quad (10)$$

where τ is the time of a cycle, L_d is the data packet size, α is the channel efficiency, B is the data rate transmission, and e_T, e_R and e_I refers to the electric power in transmission, reception and to keep the radio on, respectively.

Let $P_{i \rightsquigarrow s}$ be the opportunistic routing path from node i until some sonobuoy s. In a scenario where the radio is always on network, the expected number of transmissions to deliver data packets from i to s is recurrently given as [15]:

$$N_i = \frac{1 + \sum_{j=1}^{m} p_{ij} \prod_{k=1}^{j-1} (1 - p_{ik}) \cdot N_j}{1 - \prod_{j=1}^{m} (1 - p_{ij})}, \quad (11)$$

where $N_s, \forall s \in V_s$ is 0.

In OR protocols, the one-hop delay depends not only on the transmission and propagation packet time, but also on the time the forwarder holds the packet before transmitting it. We consider the lower bound of the one-hop delay, which is the packet propagation delay as $H_i = R/v$ where R is the communication range and v is the sound propagation speed. The expected end-to-end data packet delay from node i can be estimated recursively by:

$$D_i = \frac{H_i + \sum_{j=1}^{m} p_{ij} \prod_{k=1}^{j-1} (1 - p_{ij}) \cdot D_j}{1 - \prod_{j=1}^{m} (1 - p_{ij})}, \quad (12)$$

where $D_s, \forall s \in V_s$ is 0.

3.2 Simple Asynchronous-based Duty Cycle

In this setting, each node independently and periodically switches its radio between active and sleep operation modes. During the awake period, the node is able to receive incoming packets from current neighbors' transmissions and to transmit its scheduled data packets.

Fig. 2a shows an example of opportunistic routing over simple asynchronous duty cycle scenario. At the current sender node S, opportunistic routing protocol determines the candidate set and the priority of each node in the set, as in the always radio on network topology. After that, the node broadcasts the data packet. Each awake neighbor that successfully received the data packet will verify if it is in the candidate set and which is its priority. From those nodes, each candidate will schedule the packet transmission according to its priority. During the holding time, the packet transmission will be suppressed if the node receives the same packet coming from a high priority node.

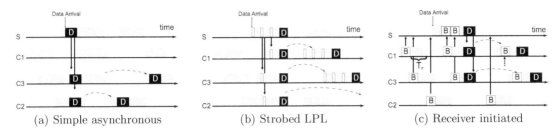

|(a) Simple asynchronous|(b) Strobed LPL|(c) Receiver initiated|

Figure 2: Three duty cycling design principles

The radio transition between the active and sleep operation modes in this setting can be purely stochastic. Accordingly, the time periods of each node on each radio state mode is modeled according to an exponential distributed random variable with the same means value μ_a and μ_s to the active and sleep states, respectively. At any time, the probability of having a node i in active mode is $p_a = \mu_a/(\mu_a + \mu_s)$ and in sleep mode is $p_s = \mu_s/(\mu_a + \mu_s)$.

Using simple duty cycle approach, we can estimate the nodal energy consumption rate as:

$$E_i^S = \underbrace{\Theta_i^S \cdot \left(\frac{L_d}{\alpha B}\right) \cdot e_T}_{\text{Term 1}} + \underbrace{I_i^S \cdot \left(\frac{L_d}{\alpha B}\right) \cdot e_R}_{\text{Term 2}} + \underbrace{\frac{1}{\tau \mu_s} \cdot \mu_a \cdot e_I}_{\text{Term 3}},$$
(13)

where $\Theta_i^S = p_s \lambda_i + p_a \Theta_i$ is the outgoing traffic rate since the node will send its generated data traffic at rate λ_i and the neighbors data traffic received when it is awake and $I_i^S = p_a I_i$ is the incoming traffic rate.

In Eq. 13, Term 3 estimates the amount of energy consumed when the node's radio is on. We determine the average number of awake intervals during the time τ, from the relationship between exponential and Poisson distributions. Accordingly, we can view exponential random variables with mean value $1/\lambda$ as waiting times between events modeled as Poisson process with mean value λ. Let the time between awake states be exponentially distributed with mean value μ_s seconds. Thus, the number of active states can be modeled as a Poisson process with mean $1/\tau\mu_s$ per second.

The expected number of transmissions to deliver a data packet from the node i to some sonobuoy, in duty cycled underwater nodes using simple asynchronous duty cycle approach is:

$$N_i^S = \frac{1 + \sum_{j=1}^m p_a p_{ij} \prod_{k=1}^{j-1}[p_s + p_a(1 - p_{ij})] \cdot N_j^S}{1 - \prod_{j=1}^m [p_s + p_a(1 - p_{ij})]}, \quad (14)$$

where N_s, $\forall s \in V_s$ is 0.

Finally, we estimate the expected end-to-end data packet delay from node i can be estimated recursively by:

$$D_i^S = \frac{H_i + \sum_{j=1}^m p_a p_{ij} \prod_{k=1}^{j-1}[p_s + p_a(1 - p_{ij})] \cdot D_j^S}{1 - \prod_{j=1}^m [p_s + p_a(1 - p_{ij})]}. \quad (15)$$

where D_s^S, $\forall s \in V_s$ is 0.

3.3 Strobed Preamble-based Duty Cycle

The strobed preamble duty cycle approach is an optimized technique of asynchronous *low power listening* (LPL)-based duty cycle. In the LPL technique, the sender transmits a preamble before the packet transmission. The duration of the preamble is equal to the sleep time of the receiver. When the receiver wakes up, it detects the preamble transmission and remains awake to receive the data packet. The main disadvantage of the LPL technique is the long preamble transmissions that cause excessive energy consumption at the sender and non-target receivers, mainly in underwater network scenarios as the transmission cost is of the order of dozen Watts.

In strobed preamble (Fig. 2b), instead of a long preamble transmission, short preambles are sent followed by silent periods. This increases the energy efficiency and can reduce the waiting time, as data packets are sent after the node receives an acknowledgement packet transmitted by the neighbor hearing the short preamble. Here, as we use opportunistic routing to deal with channel fading and keep the link reliability, data packets are only transmitted after successive short preambles transmissions during the maximum sleep interval of the candidate nodes. Therefore, we have to guarantee that all candidates are awake prior to the data packet transmission.

The nodal energy consumption rate at node i can be estimated as:

$$E_i^{SB} = \Theta_i \cdot \left[\frac{\max_{l \in \mathcal{F}_i}\{T_s^l\}}{T_{sp} + T_p} \cdot T_{sp} + \frac{L_d}{\alpha B}\right] \cdot e_T$$
$$+ I_i \cdot \left(\frac{T_s^k/2}{T_{sp} + T_p} \cdot T_{sp} + \frac{L_d}{\alpha B}\right) \cdot e_R + N_r^i \cdot T_a^i \cdot e_I, \quad (16)$$

where T_s^l (T_a^l) is the sleep (active) interval of the node l, $T_{sp} = L_{sp}/\alpha B$ is the short preamble time transmission, and $N_r^i = (T_a^i + T_s^i)/\tau$ is the number of rounds during the cycle.

The expected end-to-end data packet delay from node i can be estimated recursively by:

$$D_i^{SB} = \frac{\frac{\max_{l \in \mathcal{F}_i}\{T_s^l\}}{2} + H_i + \sum_{j=1}^m p_{ij} \prod_{k=1}^{j-1}(1 - p_{ij}) \cdot D_j^{SB}}{1 - \prod_{j=1}^m (1 - p_{ij})}.$$
(17)

where D_s^{SB}, $\forall s \in V_s$ is 0.

As during the data packet transmission all neighbor nodes are awake, the expected number of transmissions to deliver data packets is the same as given by Eq. 11.

3.4 Receiver Initiated-based Duty Cycle

In this paradigm, each node wakes up periodically to interact with potential senders (Fig. 2c). In the beginning of the active period, the node sends out a beacon to inform its neighborhood that it is awake. Then, the node checks the channel activity for T_r time for incoming data packets. If a data packet is received, it schedules the packet to be forwarded according to its priority. Otherwise, it goes back to sleep for T_s time. At the sender, when a data packet is ready to be transmitted, the node remains awake waiting the beacon packets from its neighbor.

Receive initiated-based MAC protocols aim to reduce the energy consumption of the long preamble transmissions of low power listening-based MAC protocols. Moreover, this technique is devoted to reduce the delay since pending packets at neighbors should wait until the medium becomes unoccupied, which may be much longer than a simple data transmission because of the preamble transmission.

Herein, we can estimate the energy consumption rate of a node i using receiver initiated-based duty cycle protocol in underwater sensor network as:

$$
E_i^{RI} = \left[\left(\lambda_i + \sum_{\substack{\forall j \in \Omega(i) \\ i \in \mathcal{F}(j)}} \lambda_j / \tau \cdot T_a \cdot P_f^{ij} \right) \frac{L_d}{\alpha B} + (N_r T_b) \right] \cdot e_T
$$

$$
+ \left[(\mid \Omega(i) \mid \cdot \sigma \cdot T_b \cdot N_r) + \left(\sum_{\substack{\forall j \in \Omega(i) \\ i \in \mathcal{F}(j)}} \lambda_j / \tau \cdot T_a \right) \left(\frac{L_d}{\alpha B} \right) \right] \cdot e_R
$$

$$
+ N_r \cdot T_a \cdot e_I, \quad (18)
$$

where $\lambda_j / \tau \cdot T_a$ is the normalized traffic generation rate of the node j to the active interval T_a of node i, $N_r = (T_a + T_s)/\tau$ is the number of cycles at an interval, T_b is the time duration to transmit a beacon packet and σ is the probability of the node being active, that is $\sigma = T_a/(T_a + T_s)$. The term $\mid \Omega(i) \mid \cdot \sigma \cdot T_b \cdot N_r$ estimates the number of beacon packets received at an interval.

The expected number of transmissions and end-to-end delay are given by Eq. 19 and Eq. 20, respectively. In Eq. 20, as the node transmits the packet only after it receives a beacon, it should wait, in average, $\frac{\min_{l \in \mathcal{F}_i} \{T_s^l\}}{2}$ before sending the data packet. In Eq. 19 and Eq. 20, N_s^{RI}, $\forall s \in V_s$ is 0, and D_s^{RI}, $\forall s \in V_s$ is 0, respectively.

$$
N_i^{RI} = \frac{1 + \sum_{j=1}^{m} \sigma p_{ij} \prod_{k=1}^{j-1} [(1 - \sigma) + \sigma(1 - p_{ij})] \cdot N_j^{RI}}{1 - \prod_{j=1}^{m} [(1 - \sigma) + \sigma(1 - p_{ij})]}. \quad (19)
$$

4. PERFORMANCE EVALUATION

To assess the UWSN performance under different configurations of duty-cycle techniques, simulations have been conducted using MATLAB. We set the number of rounds as $\tau = 60\,\mathrm{s}$, and the time of a cycle as $T_a + T_s = 20\,\mathrm{s}$. We have varied σ in the interval 0.05, 0.1, 0.15, 0.2, 0.25, 0.3 and determined the active and sleep times as $T_a = \sigma(T_a + T_s)$ and $T_s = (1 - \sigma)(T_a + T_s)$, respectively. We randomly deployed 250 and 450 sensor nodes in a 3D region of size

Param.	Value	Param.	Value
B	18700 bps	L_d	150, 350 bytes
α	1	L_b, L_{sp}	4 bytes
$[e_T, e_R, e_I]$	[18, 0.8, 0.08]W	λ	0.2 pkt/min
f	14 kHz	Δ_{DBR}	500 m

Table 1: Simulation parameters

$10\,\mathrm{km} \times 10\,\mathrm{km} \times 10\,\mathrm{km}$. We divided the surface area in a grid with 25 squares with side equals to 2000 m. We continuously deployed one sonobuoy, randomly, at each cell of the grid, until all 64 sonobuoys are completely deployed. The transmission power of the nodes is set to 190 dB μ re Pa. In our scenario, sensor nodes drift freely according to ocean currents. We used the extended 3D version of the meandering current mobility to simulate that movement. The mobility model considers the effects of meandering sub-surface currents (or jet streams) and vortices. The values' parameters of the MCM model are the same of [5]. Due to the mobility, nodes would move beyond of the initial deployment region. The remaining model and network parameters are summarized in Table 1. These values are based on the Telesonar SM-75 SMART modem by Teledyne Benthos [23]. In our simulations, each run lasts 1 h. We compute the performance metrics at each 1 min interval considering the current topology in order to capture the nodes' mobility effects. At the end, we calculate the average value for each configuration to determine the rate per time interval. The results correspond to an average value of 50 runs of the mean value of sensor nodes, with 95 % confidence interval.

Fig. 3a and 3b show the results we have obtained for the average energy consumption rate by node at each time interval. For comparison purposes, the energy consumption rate when the nodes' radio are always on is showed in Table 2. The plots show that duty cycle approaches effectively reduce the energy consumption. This decrement was more significant for simple asynchronous duty cycle settings. The reason of that is that there is no control packet transmissions (strobed preambles and beacons). Another observed trend in the plots is that the effect of increasing the percentage of active time increases the energy consumption rate in all duty cycle strategies. This trend is already expected, as the higher the active time is, the higher the number of received packets transmitted from neighbors.

Figs. 3c and 3d portray the results we have obtained for the average end-to-end data packet delay for the network scenarios of 250 and 450 nodes, respectively. As already expected, the usage of duty cycle increased the delay for delivering a packet. This increment is more significant for the scenario of 250 nodes (Fig. 3c) since the reduced number of next-hops in the candidate set. The results also show that a long packet size leads to the worst performance in terms of delay. In both figures, the receiver initiated-based duty cycle scenario has

Number of nodes	Data packet size	
	150 bytes	350 bytes
250 nodes	4.8871 J	5.0077 J
450 nodes	4.9171 J	5.0794 J

Table 2: Average energy consumption rate for always on nodes' radio configuration

$$D_i^{RI} = \frac{\frac{\min_{l \in \mathcal{F}_i}\{T_s^l\}}{2} + H_i + \sum_{j=1}^{m} \sigma p_{ij} \prod_{k=1}^{j-1}[(1-\sigma) + \sigma(1-p_{ij})]D_j^{RI}}{1 - \prod_{j=1}^{m}[(1-\sigma) + \sigma(1-p_{ij})]}. \qquad (20)$$

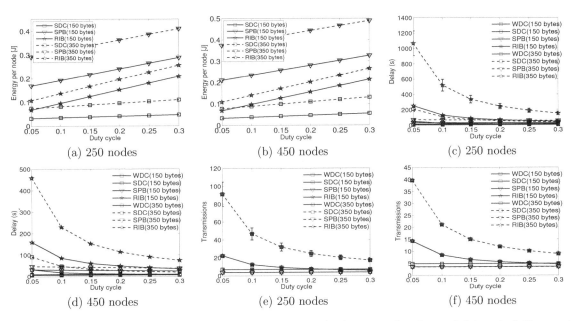

Figure 3: Simulation results. (a-b) Energy cost per node per time. (c-d) Expected end-to-end delay. (e-f) Expected number of transmissions. **Legend: WDC** (always-on radio), **SDC** (simple duty cycle), **SPB** (strobed preamble-based duty cycle) and **RIB** (receiver initiated-based duty cycle).

the worst performance because of two main reasons. First, the sender node should wait until it receives a beacon packet of a candidate, which is an indicative that the neighbor is awake and can continues forwarding the packet. Second, during the packet transmission, only a few candidate nodes (or even only a single node) may be awake, which reduces the probability of receiving the packet. Strobed-preamble duty cycle approach had a performance close to the always on communication radio. The slight increment on the delay is due to the wait time until the neighbors wake up.

Figs. 3e and 3f show the results we have obtained for the average of the expected number of transmissions to deliver the packet. The plots show that increasing the number of nodes decrease the expected number of transmissions. The packet size also impacts the average number of transmissions in low density scenarios. It is interesting noting that both simple duty cycle and received initiated duty cycle approaches have the same performance in high density scenarios (please refer to Fig. 3f). This happens because the high number of candidates result in, at least, one of them to be awake, when the source desires to transmit a packet. In the plots, we can see that the simple asynchronous duty cycle approach and the receiver initiated-based duty cycle approach have the worst performance, mainly due to the low fraction of active time. This happens because there is no guarantee that the neighbors are awake during the packet transmission. Even with a neighbor in active mode, they cannot be in enough number to have a reliable transmission dealing with channel fading. For instance, in receiver-based approach, the opportunistic routing protocol, at some time instances, shall be

working as in traditional routing, transmitting the packet for a single awake node. When the fraction of active time increases, the expected number of transmissions decreases. This happens because it is more likely to have enough nodes help forwarding the packet opportunistically. This result provides important insights and should be carefully considered during the design of duty cycle protocols for underwater sensor networks running opportunistic routing. If the application requires a high packet delivery ratio, the energy saving of the duty cycle operation cannot be reached since more transmissions will be necessary to deliver the packet.

4.1 Discussion

Our results indicate that if the application requires long-lived UWSNs and may tolerate some degree of packet loss (e.g., salinity and temperature monitoring), the simple duty cycle is the most adequate strategy. Considering the scenario of 250 nodes and the packet size of 150 bytes, the simple duty cycle strategy decreases the energy consumption rate in approximately 86% and 80%, when compared against the energy consumption rate when using strobed preamble and receiver initiated duty cycle strategies, respectively.

When a high fidelity of collected data is required (e.g., oil spill, seismic activities and marine biology monitoring applications), the strobed preamble LPL duty cycle strategy is the most adequate. In spite of wasting more energy than the simple duty cycle strategy, our results indicate that the strobed preamble LPL can reduce the expected number of transmissions up to 75% when compared with the required number of transmissions to deliver data packets using simple duty cycle approach. This reduction is important since the energy consumption due to additional transmissions trying to deliver the packet may lose the energy savings of the duty cycle.

5. CONCLUSIONS AND FUTURE WORK

In this paper, we proposed an analytical model to evaluate the energy cost, expected number of transmissions and end-to-end delay in duty cycled UWSN scenarios running OR protocols. Preliminary results showed that duty cycle approaches effectively reduce the energy consumption of the nodes. However, the increment of the expected number of transmissions to deliver the packets may diminish the energy savings of the duty cycle in scenarios where high packet delivery ratio is required. As future work, we plan to extend the proposed model to consider scenarios of event-driven, where we will have different traffic loads along the parts of the network, and study the performance of each node individually. Moreover, we plan to investigate the network performance when depth-based routing variant protocols are used since they change the forwarder candidate set.

6. ACKNOWLEDGMENTS

This work was partially supported by the NSERC Strategic Project Program and NSERC DIVA Network Research Program, ORF/MRI Program, Canada Research Chairs program, CNPq, CAPES, and FAPEMIG Brazilian research support agencies.

7. REFERENCES

[1] Bellhop - Ocean Acoustics Library. http://oalib.hlsresearch.com/Rays/, 2015.

[2] L. M. Brekhovskikh and Y. Lysanov. *Fundamentals of Ocean Acoustics*. Springer, 2003.

[3] M. Buettner, G. V. Yee, E. Anderson, and R. Han. X-MAC: a short preamble mac protocol for duty-cycled wireless sensor networks. In *ACM SenSys*, pg. 307–320, 2006.

[4] C. Carbonelli and U. Mitra. Cooperative multihop communication for underwater acoustic networks. In *WUWNet*, pg. 97–100, 2006.

[5] A. Caruso et al. The meandering current mobility model and its impact on underwater mobile sensor networks. In *IEEE INFOCOM*, 2008.

[6] R. W. L. Coutinho, A. Boukerche, L. F. M. Vieira, and A. A. Loureiro. GEDAR: geographic and opportunistic routing protocol with depth adjustment for mobile underwater sensor networks. In *IEEE ICC*, 2014.

[7] R. W. L. Coutinho, A. Boukerche, L. F. M. Vieira, and A. A. F. Loureiro. Local maximum routing recovery in underwater sensor networks: Performance and trade-offs. In *IEEE MASCOTS*, pg. 112–119, 2014.

[8] R. W. L. Coutinho, A. Boukerche, L. F. M. Vieira, and A. A. F. Loureiro. A novel void node recovery paradigm for long-term underwater sensor networks. *Ad Hoc Networks*, 2015.

[9] A. Darehshoorzadeh, M. Sanchez, and A. Boukerche. Modeling and analysis of opportunistic routing in multi-hop wireless networks. In *IEEE MASCOTS*, pg. 337–344, 2014.

[10] L. Freitag, M. Grund, S. Singh, J. Partan, P. Koski, and K. Ball. The WHOI micro-modem: An acoustic communcations and navigation system for multiple platforms. In *MTS/IEEE Oceans*, 2005.

[11] J. Heidemann, M. Stojanovic, and M. Zorzi. Underwater sensor networks: applications, advances and challenges. *Philosophical Transactions of the Royal Society A: Mathematical, Physical and Engineering Sciences*, 370(1958):158–175, 2012.

[12] J. Heidemann, W. Ye, J. Wills, A. Syed, and Y. Li. Research challenges and applications for underwater sensor networking. In *IEEE WCNC*, pg. 228–235, 2006.

[13] W. Hu, J. Xie, and Z. Zhang. Practical opportunistic routing in high-speed multi-rate wireless mesh networks. In *ACM MobiHoc*, pg. 127–136, 2013.

[14] U. Lee et al. Pressure routing for underwater sensor networks. In *IEEE INFOCOM*, pg. 1–9, 2010.

[15] Y. Li, W. Chen, and Z.-L. Zhang. Optimal forwarder list selection in opportunistic routing. In *IEEE MASS*, pg. 670–675, 2009.

[16] Z. Li, M. Li, and Y. Liu. Towards energy-fairness in asynchronous duty-cycling sensor networks. *ACM Trans. Sen. Netw.*, 10(3):38:1–38:26, 2014.

[17] T. Rappaport. *Wireless Communications: Principles and Practice*. Prentice Hall, 2002.

[18] P. H. Rogers. *Onboard Prediction of Propagation Loss in Shallow Water*. Washington DC: Naval Research Lab Defense Technical Information Center, 1981.

[19] M. Stojanovic. Recent advances in high-speed underwater acoustic communications. *IEEE J. Oceanic Eng.*, pg. 125–136, 1996.

[20] M. Stojanovic. On the relationship between capacity and distance in an underwater acoustic commun. channel. In *WUWNet*, pg. 41–47, 2006.

[21] M. Stojanovic and J. Preisig. Underwater acoustic communication channels: Propagation models and statistical characterization. *IEEE Commun. Mag.*, 47(1):84–89, 2009.

[22] Y. Sun, O. Gurewitz, and D. B. Johnson. RI-MAC: a receiver-initiated asynchronous duty cycle mac protocol for dynamic traffic loads in wireless sensor networks. In *ACM SenSys*, pg. 1–14, 2008.

[23] Teledyne-Benthos. http://www.benthos.com, 2015.

[24] G. Toso, P. Casari, and M. Zorzi. The effect of different attenuation models on the performance of routing in shallow-water networks. In *IEEE UComms*, pg. 1–5, 2014.

[25] J. R. Urick. *Principles of Underwater Sound*. McGraw-Hill, 1983.

[26] L. F. M. Vieira. Performance and trade-offs of opportunistic routing in underwater networks. In *IEEE WCNC*, pg. 2911–2915, 2012.

[27] P. Xie, J. hong Cui, and L. Lao. VBF: vector-based forwarding protocol for underwater sensor networks. In *IFIP-TC6 NETWORKING*, pg. 1216–1221, 2006.

[28] H. Yan, Z. J. Shi, and J.-H. Cui. DBR: depth-based routing for underwater sensor networks. In *IFIP-TC6 NETWORKING*, pg. 72–86, 2008.

[29] K. Zeng, W. Lou, and H. Zhai. Capacity of opportunistic routing in multi-rate and multi-hop wireless networks. *IEEE Transactions on Wireless Communications*, 7(12), pg. 5118–5128, 2008.

Autoregressive Integrated Model for Time Synchronization in Wireless Sensor Networks

Wasif Masood
Wasif.Masood@aau.at

Jorge F. Schmidt
Jorge.Schmidt@aau.at

Institute of Networked and Embedded Systems,
University of Klagenfurt, Austria.

ABSTRACT

Time synchronization is challenging in wireless sensor networks due to the use of low-precision oscillators and the limited computational capacity of resources limited sensor nodes. While several schemes exist, the performance analysis of a majority of them is based on simulations and fail to capture key features of real world deployments. This paper explores the use of autoregressive integrated moving average models to provide a general clock model for sensor nodes with low precision oscillators and limited computational power. Based on measurements with off-the-shelf sensor devices Z1, an autoregressive integrated model for time synchronization is proposed. We derive a synchronization scheme (ARI-Sync) based on this model and compare it against the well known Flooding Time Synchronization Protocol (FTSP) observing significantly improved accuracy, roughly doubling the resynchronization period of Z1 nodes for a typical wireless sensor network application.

1. INTRODUCTION

Wireless Sensor Networks (WSN) have been in focus of research for more than two decades now, because of their unprecedented range of potential applications [30]. The limited computing power, energy and storage size of sensor nodes have curtailed the performance of the underlying services necessary for the realization of applications. Time synchronization is one among many such services. Time synchronization is a must in applications like habitat monitoring [20], multimedia data streaming [4], scheduling of duty cycles for MAC protocols [19] and many more [26].

The problem of time synchronization is non-trivial [14]. In budget efficient wireless devices like sensor nodes, the behavior of underlying oscillators is the major contributor to this non-trivia. Harsh environmental conditions concerning temperature and humidity add further dimensions to this problem. Considering the limited computing capability of sensor nodes, several solutions have been proposed for time synchronization in WSNs [31]. These solutions can be broadly

categorized as *sender-receiver* and *receiver-receiver* based synchronization. In the former case, each sender-receiver pair is synchronized with the exchange of timestamped messages [15]. In the latter case, receivers exchange messages to estimate the offset with their common sender [13]. This paper focuses on the former alternative (sender-receiver synchronization).

The pioneering work in [24] proposed a linear programming approach to exploit the exchanged information to estimate clock offset, but the results are limited in terms of synchronization accuracy[1]. The convex hull optimization approach proposed in [33] improves the synchronization accuracy, but its high computational cost is not practical for resource-constrained sensor nodes.

There exist also several contributions that resort to the Kalman filter (KF) because of its ability to recursively update the drift prediction from noisy measurements and in this way maintain synchronization. This approach has been considered for clock tracking in both steady and temperature varying environments. In [5,7,18], schemes for packet networks synchronization are derived following this approach. Unfortunately, these are not well suited for resource-limited sensor nodes because they result in a too large resource effort for just obtaining time synchronization. In [16], a KF solution with reduced complexity is used to track time varying clock drifts. However, online complexity might still be high for low-cost nodes. On the other hand, the solutions proposed in [21] and [13] are simple enough to be implemented on low-cost sensor nodes but do not provide enough accuracy to meet the increasing synchronization demands.

Finally, other reported schemes like the Network Time Protocol (NTP) [22], its extension [23] and the Precision Time Protocol [1], drafted in IEEE 1588 standards for synchronization of network measurement and control systems, are all based on customized hardware not available for low-cost sensor nodes of interest.

In this paper, we propose a novel approach for time synchronization that is based on *autoregressive integrated moving average* (ARIMA) models [8] widely used in time series analysis. The strength of ARIMA models resides in their ability to remove non-stationarity from a time series and their well-established model building process. To assess the behavior of a practical clock, off-the-shelf sensor devices, namely Zolertia (Z1) [34] are used, which are equipped with low precision 32 kHz crystal oscillators. While we present

MSWiM'15, November 02–06, 2015, Cancun, Mexico.
© 2015 ACM. ISBN 978-1-4503-3762-5/15/11 ... $15.00.
DOI: http://dx.doi.org/10.1145/2811587.2811591.

[1]Accuracy is defined as the time offset between a group of synchronized devices and a reference clock, and is the natural performance metric for sender-receiver schemes.

results for the specific Z1 nodes, we normalize synchronization accuracy in terms of clock ticks. This measure directly relates the synchronization efficiency of the protocol to the maximum measurable efficiency of the underlying platform, allowing a direct comparison of results on different sensor platforms.

Experiments are performed in an indoor office environment using 25 distinct Z1 sensor nodes. The post analysis of the experimental data is performed using the general ARIMA model building process that leads to an autoregressive integrated, ARI$(1,1)$ model for the considered scenario. We show that a time synchronization scheme built on this model (ARI-Sync) can be implemented in Contiki–2.7 on Z1 platform, obtaining an outstanding accuracy at a very low online complexity, outperforming previous solutions of comparable online cost. In particular, the synchronization accuracy obtained for all pairs of nodes, is measured to be below 1 tick (1 tick of 32 kHz oscillator = 30.52 μs). This performance makes it a promising candidate for applications with stringent time synchronization demands like WirelessHART [28] and IEEE802.15.4e [17], where ARI-Sync has doubled the resynchronization period as compared to the similar complexity schemes.

The rest of the paper is organized as follows. Section 2 presents a general clock modeling problem together with a brief introduction to ARIMA models, describes the ARIMA model identification process and details how it boils down to ARI$(1,1)$ for the nodes under consideration. In section 3, the ARI-Sync scheme is derived from that model and section 4 explains the two other protocols that are compared with ARI-Sync. An analysis of the computational complexity of the considered protocols is provided in section 5. The experimental evaluation of ARI-Sync and its comparison with the other considered schemes is presented in section 6. Finally, our conclusions are drawn in section 7.

2. CLOCK MODELING

In cost efficient, low power devices like sensor nodes, electronic oscillators are used to measure time. An oscillator is characterized by the frequency of its output signal, which is counted by a hardware register to give the notion of *clock* or *local time* of the device. Due to slight variations in the manufacturing process, supply voltage, and aging of an oscillator, variations in nominal frequency of oscillators are significant. Such variations are termed *frequency drift* and *phase noise* and result in a frequency offset between devices. The frequency offset causes the clocks to drift from the nominal time while phase noise further adds *jitters* to this drift. The smallest unit of time measured by a clock is called the *clock resolution* or *tick* e.g., the resolution of a 32 kHz oscillator is 30.52 μs and for a 921.6 kHz oscillator, the resolution is 1.08 μs. Throughout this paper, we focus on clock ticks to assess the quality of a time synchronization scheme.

Clock offsets exist due to the different bootup times of the devices. Irrespective to the approach used, the problem of time synchronization is concerned with the estimation of the offset between clocks that varies over time due to frequency offsets between oscillators. In order to estimate this offset, a model that captures the key characteristics of the clock has to be identified.

Let the evolution of the local time of a node be denoted by the function $c(t)$ which we refer to as "the clock" of the node. Note that $c(t)$ represents an actual clock value whose

behavior is affected by the imperfections of the electronic oscillators described above. The relative clock offset between nodes A and B, at a certain time instant t can be written as $\Delta_{A,B}(t) = c_A(t) - c_B(t)$. With the instantaneous sampling period $\tau(t)$, the instantaneous clock drift between A and B is defined as

$$\alpha_{A,B}(t) = \frac{d\Delta_{A,B}(t)}{dt} \approx \frac{\Delta_{A,B}(t) - \Delta_{A,B}(t-\tau(t))}{\tau(t)}. \quad (1)$$

In practice, a discrete clock model $c[k]$ is desirable[2]. Let $c_n = \{c[1], c[2], c[3], \cdots, c[n]\}$, with $n \in \mathbb{N}$ be the univariate discrete time series representation of the clock $c(t)$ that corresponds to the time of reception of packets between a unique sender-receiver pair. Using a recursive representation with uniform sampling, $\tau(t) = \tau$, the discretized clock offset and drift become

$$\Delta_{A,B}[k] = c_{A,B}[k] \quad (2)$$
$$\alpha_{A,B}[k] = \Delta_{A,B}[k] - \Delta_{A,B}[k-1], \quad (3)$$

where $c_{A,B}[k]$ is the time of reception of the k-th packet from A at B. From these definitions, the clock offset can be written as

$$\Delta_{A,B}[k] = \Delta_{A,B}[k-1] + \alpha_{A,B}[k]. \quad (4)$$

The concept of time series analysis can be used to model (4) since this theory provides a variety of techniques to describe the dependence between consecutive observations. The following subsections explain our choice of the time series model and its relevance to the problem at hand.

2.1 ARIMA Modeling

Stochastic models are used to forecast the behavior of a time series in probabilistic terms and are therefore, well suited to model the time series representing a node clock. ARIMA models [8] are a family of stochastic models that have been extensively used to extract local level (offset) and trend information (clock drift) from non-stationary time series [2, 10, 32]. These models are very flexible, having the capability to capture the behavior of different types of time series. One main feature that is of particular interest in the context of time synchronization for WSN is that they are able to remove non-stationarity from a time series. This allows to apply standard *autoregressive moving average* (ARMA) process for the modeling of the resulting time series.

The general form of ARIMA (p, d, q) model of autoregressive (AR), difference and moving average (MA) orders p, d and q respectively, for the discrete time series representation of a clock is given by

$$\phi(B)\nabla^d c[k] = \alpha_0 + \theta(B)\epsilon[k], \quad (5)$$

where B is the back-shift operator ($B^m c[k] = c[k-m]$), α_0 and ϵ are the deterministic linear trend and white noise respectively. $\nabla = c[k] - c[k-1]$ is the difference operator, where the difference order d represents the difference required to achieve stationarity. Finally, the polynomials representing the AR and MA terms of (5) are respectively given by

$$\phi(B) = 1 - \phi_1 B - \phi_2 B^2 - \cdots - \phi_p B^p, \quad (6)$$

---

[2]This is because typically in a practical setup timestamped messages are employed as time references, where timestamps are discrete samples of a continuous clock

$$\theta(B) = 1 - \theta_1 B - \theta_2 B^2 - \cdots - \theta_q B^q. \qquad (7)$$

2.2 Model Identification Process

The first step in ARIMA (p, d, q) modeling is about identifying the orders p, d and q. This identification is done by studying the autocorrelation (ACF) and partial-auto-correlation (PACF) of the time series [9].

Note that c_n represents the evolution of the local time of a node and is therefore non-stationary. Taking this into account, the first step is to find the difference level d for which the series become stationary. ACF of nonstationary series falls off slowly and very nearly linear. The difference d for which ACF "die out" quickly gives the stationary form of c_n [12]. Once the stationarity of a time series is confirmed, the ACF and PACF functions are further used to identify the lags of the AR and MA components in (5). Briefly, the ACF of an AR (p) process tails off, whereas its PACF cuts off after lag p. On contrary, the ACF of a MA (q) process has a cut off after lag q while its PACF tails off. If both ACF and PACF tails off, presence of both AR and MA terms are suggested. The procedure of model identification, estimation and hypothesis testing of ARIMA is explained in details in [9, Chp. 6].

In practice, no two oscillators exhibit exact behavior. Therefore, we have used real sensor devices for our experiments. In particular, we have performed experiments on Z1 sensor nodes which are one among the many low-cost off-the-shelf sensor nodes that employ low-precision oscillators [25]. To empirically test the statistical significance of the model, 25 Z1 nodes are used. From this number of nodes, $\binom{25}{2} = 300$ time series are generated where each series corresponds to a unique sender-receiver pair of Z1 nodes. The experiments were preformed in an indoor office environment with steady room temperature of 23°C, and a constant transmission period of $\tau = 2\,\mathrm{s}$.

Post analysis of all c_n confirmed the absence of MA terms in (5) – using the aforementioned ACF and PACF analysis. The difference level, $d = 1$, is obtained using the Dickey-Fuller unit-root test [11]. This reduces the search to ARIMA $(p, d = 1, q = 0)$ or alternatively ARI $(p, d = 1)$ processes, where p is yet to be identified (ARI because of absence of MA terms).

Table 1: Model order comparison of ARI $(p,1)$

Model	AIC	BIC
ARI $(1,1)$	2.2829	1.3610
ARI $(3,1)$	1.9951	1.0732
ARI $(8,1)$	1.6397	0.7179
ARI $(50,1)$	-3.5447	-4.4666

The Akaike's Information Criterion [3] (AIC) and Bayesian Information Criterion [27] (BIC) provides a measure for the goodness of fit of a model for a given number of parameters in it. The value of p yielding minimum AIC and BIC specifies the best model. The AIC and BIC of different ARI $(p,1)$ models are compared in Table 1 where an improvement in synchronization accuracy is observed with increasing AR order. However, considering the limited computational power of the considered Z1 sensor nodes, our final choice rests with **ARI (1,1)**. As will be shown later on (section 6.1) that this model already achieves the accuracy of below one clock tick.

3. ARI-SYNC TIME SYNCHRONIZATION

Having identified ARI $(1,1)$ as the clock model for sensor nodes, we next focus on the derivation of the clock offset estimator and forecast horizon supported by this model. First, the estimation of the model parameters from the data series is presented. Then, using the estimated parameters, the expression for the propagation of error in offset forecast is derived. Rewriting (4) in the form of ARI $(1,1)$ we have

$$w[k] = \phi\, w[k-1] + \alpha_0 + \epsilon[k], \qquad (8)$$

where $w[k] = \nabla^{d=1} c[k] = c[k] - c[k-1]$ represents the stationary form of c_n and ϕ is the AR (1) coefficient. Writing (8) in terms of $c[k]$, we can further express

$$c[k] = c[k-1] + \phi\, c[k-1] - \phi\, c[k-2] + \alpha_0 + \epsilon[k]. \qquad (9)$$

Note that samples $c[k]$ are generated by the exchange of timestamped messages and give the discrete representation of the continuous clock of a receiver. Since $\epsilon[k]$ is mainly caused by observation and measurement noise, it is reasonable to assume it samples to be independent with variance σ_ϵ^2.

Jitters exists in clock drift due to phase noise in oscillator frequency. The choice of the transmission period τ is critical in capturing the effect of jitters. The smaller the transmission period is, the more visible the jitters are since more information becomes available within the same observation window. On the other hand, with relatively long transmission periods, the granularity of the system is not detailed enough to capture such effects even though they still are accumulated and become effective over the course of time. The correlations in a time series are modeled by the AR terms of ARIMA models [8]. Since the errors accumulated due to jitters in the drift are highly correlated therefore, AR terms in (9) are used to cater them and hence α_0 is modeled as a constant linear drift under steady temperature conditions. This allows (8) to be modeled as an open loop system and avoids the extra cost to calculate $\alpha(t)$ from (1) after every new sample. Since for environments with steady temperature conditions like indoor offices and houses, clock drift over-powers all other uncertainties [6], therefore (9) is enough for long forecast intervals as well. The choice of the sampling period τ will be further discussed in section 6.2.

This model can be used to synchronize nodes of the network with a primary reference clock. The synchronized nodes can then be used to synchronize the two-hop neighbors of the primary source. This procedure can be repeated until all multihop neighbors in the network are synchronized.

3.1 Parameter Estimation

Assuming $\epsilon[k]$ normal iid, the log-likelihood (ll) of (8) is

$$ll\left(\phi, \mu, \sigma_\epsilon^2\right) = f(\phi, \mu) - n \ln \sigma_\epsilon - \frac{S(\phi, \mu)}{2\sigma_\epsilon^2}, \qquad (10)$$

where $S(\phi, \mu)$ is the unconditional sum-of-squares given by

$$S(\phi, \mu) = \sum_{k=1}^{n} \left(\epsilon[k] \,\Big|\, \phi, \mu, w[k]\right), \qquad (11)$$

and $f(\phi, \mu)$ is a prior density on the parameters. The log-likelihood in (10) is dominated by $S(\phi, \mu)$ and $n \ln \sigma_\epsilon$, since $f(\phi, \mu)$ has weightage only for small values of n. Hence for practical purposes, we can ignore the first observation, after which (11) takes the form of conditional sum-of-squares

$$S_c(\phi, \mu) = \sum_{k=2}^{n} [(w[k] - \mu) - \phi(w[k-1] - \mu)]^2. \quad (12)$$

Approximating μ as $\bar{w} = \sum_{k=1}^{n} w[k]/n$ and substituting it in (12), we can minimize $S_c(\mu, \phi)$ and solve for the estimates of ϕ and α_0 as

$$\hat{\phi} = \frac{\sum_{k=2}^{n} (w[k] - \bar{w})(w[k-1] - \bar{w})}{\sum_{k=2}^{n} (w[k-1] - \bar{w})^2},$$

$$\hat{\alpha}_0 = \bar{w}\left(1 - \hat{\phi}\right).$$

The estimation error for a series of length n is then,

$$e_n = c_n - \hat{c}_n, \quad (13)$$

where c_n is the observed time series and $\hat{c}_n$ is the estimate obtained using (9)

$$\hat{c}[k] = c[k-1] + \hat{\phi} c[k-1] - \hat{\phi} c[k-2] + \hat{\alpha}_0. \quad (14)$$

3.2 Error Propagation

Since ARI-Sync model the present only in terms of independent past inputs, it entails an interesting prospect for forecasting the clock offsets as well. Specifically, we are interested in forecasting the value c_{n+l}, for lead time $l \geq 1$, from sample n. Let us define the forecast error $e_n[l]$ from propagating $\hat{c}_n[l]$ until lead time l as

$$e_n[l] = c_{n+l} - \hat{c}_n[l], \quad (15)$$

where $\hat{c}_n[l]$ is the linear forecast function recursively calculated from origin n using (9) as

$$\hat{c}_n[l] = \hat{c}_n[l-1] + \hat{\phi}\hat{c}_n[l-1] - \hat{\phi}\hat{c}_n[l-2] + \hat{\alpha}_0. \quad (16)$$

For $l = 1$, we have $c_n[0]$ and $c_n[-1]$, which corresponds to the observed values of c_n and c_{n-1}, respectively. For an unbiased forecast, $\mathrm{E}[e_n[l]|e_{1:n-1}] = 0$, and the l steps ahead propagation error in (15) becomes the true error ϵ_{n+l}

$$e_n[l] = c_{n+l} - \hat{c}_n[l] = \epsilon_{n+l}. \quad (17)$$

Although the optimal forecast errors for $l = 1$, will be uncorrelated but the errors for some longer lead time t will be correlated. One consequence of this is that there will often be a tendency of (16) to lie either wholly above or below the actual series when it eventually come to hand.

Note that (15) accounts for an "open loop" propagation of the sensor clock. While by definition this scheme is not able to outperform the "closed loop" propagation that can be accomplished using a KF formulation, the accuracy of the proposed model guarantees a propagation error below a typical error threshold over a significant period of time. This allows to trade the tracking accuracy of a KF formulation for a reduced online complexity as no compensation gain is employed.

4. COMPARISON PROTOCOLS

Two other time synchronization methods for WSNs are compared against the proposed ARI-Sync scheme. They are the Flooding Time Synchronization Protocol (FTSP) [21] and the Adaptive Clock Estimation and Synchronization (ACES) [16]. Both FTSP and ACES as well as ARI-Sync provides network-wide time synchronization with respect to some primary source in the network. FTSP is considered because time estimation is based on simple linear regression of complexity comparable to that of ARI-Sync. ACES on the other hand is based on a KF formulation that is more sophisticated in terms of tracking (at a higher computational cost) and attains a better accuracy which serves as a performance reference for closed loop synchronization schemes. ACES, like ARI-Sync and FTSP, also uses MAC layer timestamping, and thereby exploits the ad-hoc structure of the network for global time information dissemination. The aforementioned characteristics of FTSP make it an adequate contender for ARI-Sync while the comparison against ACES highlights the accuracy penalty incurred by our low complexity open loop design.

4.1 FTSP

In FTSP, each message from the primary source is timestamped before transmission and broadcasted over the network to assist time synchronization of the nearby nodes. Receivers estimate their own offsets from the primary source after receiving the message. Consequently, each message provides a synchronization point which allows to relate primary and local time as

$$y_n = \theta_0 + \alpha_0 x_n, \quad (18)$$

where y_n is the primary time and x_n the receiver time. θ_0 is the time offset between y_n and x_n and α_0 is the clock drift. Offset and drift are estimated using simple linear regression within a window of received timestamps. In contrast with ARI-Sync, the simple model used in FTSP is not capable of removing nonstationarity from the observed sequence which results in increased error variance as will be shown later in section 6.

4.2 ACES

ACES is an effective algorithm for time synchronization in moderately resource-limited WSNs. It is based on a simple clock model, but relies on a KF recursion to compensate for the model mismatch. According to [16], the true clock offset $\tilde{\theta}[k]$ is given by

$$\tilde{\theta}[k] = \sum_{i=1}^{k} \alpha[i]\,\tau[i] + \theta_0, \quad (19)$$

where $\alpha[i]$ is the instantaneous clock drift given as

$$\alpha[k] = p\,\alpha[k-1] + \eta[k]. \quad (20)$$

where $\eta[k]$ is the model noise with zero mean and variance $\sigma_\eta^2 = (1 - p^2)\sigma_\alpha^2$ and p is a positive number chosen close to 1 that models the correlation among consecutive samples. Based on the above model, the state space representation is given as

$$\boldsymbol{x}[k] = \boldsymbol{A}\,\boldsymbol{x}[k-1] + \boldsymbol{u}[k], \quad (21)$$

where the state vector, transition matrix and input vector are respectively defined as

$$\boldsymbol{x}[k] = \begin{bmatrix} \tilde{\theta}[k] \\ \alpha[k] \end{bmatrix}, \quad \boldsymbol{A} = \begin{bmatrix} 1 & \tau \\ 0 & \rho \end{bmatrix}, \quad \boldsymbol{u}[k] = \begin{bmatrix} 0 \\ \eta[k] \end{bmatrix}. \quad (22)$$

The noisy observation of the offset is given by

$$\theta[k] = \tilde{\theta}[k] + v[k] = \boldsymbol{b}^T \boldsymbol{x}[k] + v[k], \quad (23)$$

where $b^T = \begin{bmatrix} 1 & 0 \end{bmatrix}$. More details on how the KF is derived from these equations can be found in [16].

A direct comparison of (8) and (20) gives a useful insight on the different modeling approach proposed in this paper. ACES measures the instantaneous drift in clocks and relies on the KF recursion to compensate for model imperfections. On the other hand, ARI-Sync models clock drift as a constant but uses autoregressive terms to compensate for any jitters in the drift. This allows ARI-Sync to perform an open loop forecast of the primary time over a practical time window.

5. COMPUTATIONAL COMPLEXITY

In this section, the computational complexity, of the three protocols discussed, is compared in terms of the model parameter estimation and the online offset forecast recursion. We consider these two tasks separately since parameter estimation is performed at the design stage[3] and does not affect the implementation complexity, while offset forecast is updated online at each iteration comprising most of the implementation cost. The complexity comparison of both tasks for all three protocols is summarized in Table 2.

Let's first focus on the parameter estimation complexity. Equations (8) and (18) from ARI-Sync and FTSP respectively represent a linear regression model for which the ordinary least square complexity is given by $\mathcal{O}(nr^2)$, being n is the sample size and r is the number of parameters, with $r = 2$ in both schemes. Regarding ACES, the key model parameter is p, which is chosen to be close to 1 but is not explicitly estimated. Therefore, we consider no complexity at the design stage of ACES.

Turning now to the online forecast complexity, we have that since the offset forecasts of ARI-Sync and FTSP do not involve parameter updates, their prediction computational cost scales to a constant $\mathcal{O}(1)$. For the ACES on the other hand, the complexity of the associated KF scales as $\mathcal{O}(nm^3)$ in both computation and memory requirements, where $m = 2$ being the state dimension.

Table 2: Computational complexity comparison

	Parameter estimation	Prediction iterations
FTSP	$\mathcal{O}(nr^2)$	$\mathcal{O}(1)$
ARI-Sync	$\mathcal{O}(nr^2)$	$\mathcal{O}(1)$
ACES	-	$\mathcal{O}(nm^3)$

6. EXPERIMENTAL RESULTS

In order to asses the accuracy of ARI-Sync and the comparing protocols, 25 Z1 nodes are used (same nodes as used in section 2.2), out of which $\binom{25}{2} = 300$ unique time series are generated. Each sender-receiver pair of Z1 nodes generates a time series by exchange of 100 packets. Measurements are repeated three times for each series. Consequently, $3 \times \binom{25}{2} = 900$ series are obtained in the end. Each series is measured using a 32 kHz timer with a granularity of 30.52 µs. These time series are collected at a desktop workstation connected to all sensor nodes with USB cables and

---

[3]While in practice, model parameters may be reestimated with a certain periodicity, its impact on the implementation cost is still marginal.

statistical analysis software R is used for post-processing. All experiments are performed in our advanced networking lab where temperature was approximately 23 °C during the whole course of experiments. In all cases, accuracy results are measured in clock ticks.

6.1 Model Accuracy

In the first set of experiments, the goodness of fit of ARI-Sync is evaluated on real Z1 nodes. This is done for all different sensor pairs and then averaged to obtain the mean behavior. Parameter estimation is performed on increasing number of samples form $n = 10$ to 100. The standardized residuals with absolute value of greater than 2.5σ are treated as outliers and are removed. Figure 1 shows the quantile-quantile plot for several values of n. It can be noted that the residuals follow a normal distribution except in the tails. The overlap of residuals observed in figure 1 confirms the significance of ARI-Sync for all the node pairs considered in this experiment.

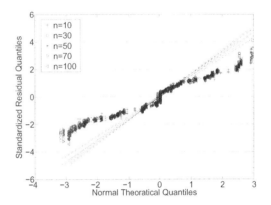

Figure 1: Normal quantile-quantile plot comparing the residuals of ARI-Sync for different n with standard normal distribution on abscissa. Dash lines correspond to the theoretical normal distribution of each n.

Figure 2 focuses on the influence of different n values on synchronization accuracy of ARI-Sync defined in (13). Each bar represents 5% and 95%-quantiles of the results. For the proposed scheme to be effective, enough samples should be considered for which lag one correlations become significant. In this study, ARI-Sync exhibits roughly the same accuracy for all the sample sizes above 10, which can also be validated from figure 1. This confirms that as few as 10 samples are sufficient for parameter estimation, which is a very practical feature considering memory limited sensor nodes.

As a final test, the model accuracy of ARI-Sync is compared with that of FTSP in figure 3, again in terms of the sample size n. In this case, mean absolute deviation (MAD) is used to measure the consistency in accuracy

$$\text{MAD} = \frac{1}{n} \sum_{i=1}^{n} |e[i] - \bar{e}|. \quad (24)$$

For samples with relatively large variations, MAD is a better measure of dispersion than standard deviation because absolute difference in MAD give smaller values than the square of the differences in σ. In figure 3, ARI-Sync shows, on average, a MAD of 7.4 µs which is significantly

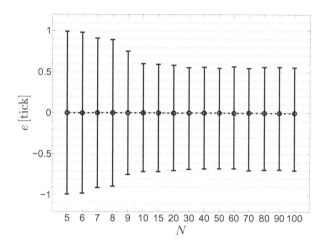

Figure 2: **Model accuracy of ARI-Sync for varying sample sizes. Each bar represents 5% and 95%-quantiles of the results.**

better than that of FTSP[4]. ACES is not plotted in this comparison since it does not propose any parameter estimation technique and chooses the value of its parameter p rather arbitrarily.

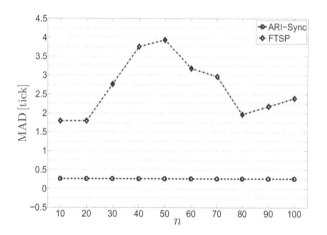

Figure 3: **Model accuracy for ARI-Sync and FTSP.**

6.2 Effect of sampling period on accuracy

When performing these experiments, the measurement results showed that synchronization accuracy was best for series where a drift was observed in every sample. Therefore, we discuss below the impact of the sampling period on model accuracy. Having a drift at every sample implies that

$$\epsilon = \big| w[k] - w[k-1] \big| > 0, \qquad (25)$$

with ϵ being the observable instantaneous clock drift with respect to τ. In this case, AR (1) parameter has equal significance for every sample. However, since the drift is different in each clock, $\epsilon > 0$ may happen for terms beyond lag one.

---

[4]Note in this figure that the results of FTSP presented in this paper differ from those appearing in the initial study [21] mainly because of the different frequency of the employed oscillators.

This affects the estimation of AR (1) parameter since correlation becomes stronger between samples where the drift is observed compared to the samples in between. In the following paragraphs we sketch how the sampling period can be adjusted such that a clock drift occurs after nearly every sample as stated in (25).

Let $\tilde{c}_{\frac{n}{\ell-1}}$ be a new series complying to (25), generated from c_n such that

$$\epsilon(\ell) = \big| w[k] - w[k - \ell] \big| > 0, \qquad (26)$$

where ℓ is an integer ($\ell > 0$). Since τ is fixed before the experiment and drift is relative to τ, there is no single value of ℓ for which (26) is satisfied for the whole series. Specifically, the probability that (26) holds is given as

$$P_\ell = Pr\{\epsilon(\ell)\} > 0\} = 1 - \frac{\sum_{i=\ell}^{n} \big(|w[i] - w[i - \ell]| \big)}{\kappa\,n}, \quad (27)$$

where κ is a normalization factor corresponding to the maximum observable clock drift with respect to τ.

Taking into account this probability, $\tilde{c}_{\frac{n}{\ell-1}}$ is decimated from c_n with a resulting sampling period of $\tilde{\tau} = \tau + (\ell - 1)$, and the value of ℓ for which P_ℓ is highest, is selected. Table 3 shows P_ℓ measured using 100 samples on an arbitrary time series, selected from the available test data.

Table 3: **With $\kappa = 1, P_\ell$ is measured on 100 samples.**

ℓ	1	2	3	4	5	6	7	8	9
P_ℓ	0.61	0.63	0.63	0.63	0.87	0.73	0.62	0.63	0.62

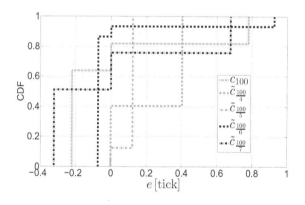

Figure 4: **Cumulative accuracy error with different sampling rates. Series $\tilde{c}_{\frac{100}{4}}$ and $\tilde{c}_{\frac{100}{5}}$ for which P_ℓ is highest show minimal commutative error.**

Figure 4 compares the estimation error for different choices of ℓ. The $\tilde{c}_{\frac{n}{\ell-1}}$ for ℓ with highest P_ℓ, has smallest cumulative error. Note that while τ is predetermined depending upon the application settings and is network-wide constant, $\tilde{\tau}$ on the other hand, can be considered as the sampling rate of the receiver. Since $\tilde{\tau} \geq \tau$, adjusting $\tilde{\tau}$ means that estimation is performed on samples of c_n that are ℓ lags apart. This results a practical approach since decisions are made on each receiver locally without changing the global τ.

Note also that $\tilde{\tau}$ gives the sampling period for which the probability of error occurrences as extreme as $\epsilon(\ell)$ is minimal, but it does not change the value of $\epsilon(\ell)$ which rather depends upon τ. The more distant the samples are, the more extreme $\epsilon(\ell)$ will be. Too small τ will give redundant information on $\epsilon(\ell)$ and also increase network traffic. Therefore, a moderate τ is required to be defined before hand [29]. In our study, where an average drift rate of 3 ppm (parts-per-million) is observed, $\tau = 2$ s resulted adequate enough to keep $\epsilon(\ell)$ below one tick. This can be observed in figures 2 and 3 where the error never exceeded one tick.

6.3 Error propagation performance

In this final section, the forecast accuracy of ARI-Sync is evaluated and compared against ACES and FTSP. This will help identify the resynchronization demand of ARI-Sync. A sender-receiver pair of Z1 nodes is arbitrary selected and a time series is generated with the exchange of 43200 packets with $\tau = 2$ s. The first 10 packets are used for parameter estimation and forecast is performed from $n = 11$. For ACES, $p = 1 - 2 \cdot 10^{-6}$ from [16] is used.

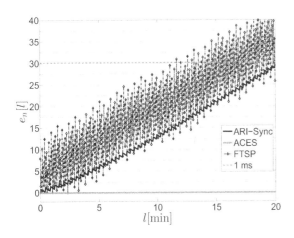

Figure 5: Error propagation performance of ARI-Sync, ACES and FTSP. A guard interval of 1 ms [17] is shown for reference to help measure the resynchronization demand of compared protocols.

Figure 5 shows the error propagation over time for the three protocols. A guard interval of 1 ms accuracy is also shown for reference. Guard intervals are defined to compensate for unaccounted errors in synchronization schemes when tested in real environment. For example, a guard interval of 1 ms exits between the consecutive time slots allocated for channel hoping in IEEE802.15.4e MAC. It determines the time extent to which a certain synchronization is accurate, therefore sets the re-synchronization period.

For ARI-Sync, the error is measured using (15) and (16). Due to the recursive nature of forecasts, errors accumulate over time and form the linear trend in figure 5 as explained in section 3.2. The sawtooth pattern arises from the correlations in $e_n[l]$ and $e_n[l + t]$. FTPS, on the other hand, gives very unstable results because of the strong correlations remaining in the residuals of (18). Finally, as expected, ACES performs the best due to the KF employed to predict one-step ahead forecast at the expense of significantly higher computational cost. From results shown in figure 5, ARI-Sync requires a resynchronization after approximately every 20 minutes that is roughly twice than FTSP at a comparable computation cost.

7. CONCLUSIONS AND FUTURE WORK

Considering the limited computational power of sensor nod-es, an autoregressive integrated model based time synchronization scheme (ARI-Sync) is proposed. The performance of ARI-Sync is assessed on low-cost off-the-shelf Z1 sensor nodes, in an indoor office environment. A synchronization accuracy below one clock tick (30.52 µs) is observed, when tested over 25 unique Z1 nodes. ARI-Sync is compared with the Flooding Time Synchronization Protocol (FTSP) [21] where a remarkably steady behavior in the performance of ARI-Sync is observed, allowing to roughly double the resynchronization period than FTSP.

The error propagation performance is also compared against the Kalman filter based approach from [16] to highlight the trade off between accuracy and complexity of ARI-Sync. The improved model considered in the proposed scheme allows to keep open loop synchronization for up to 20 minutes at a very low computational cost.

Future work along this line includes considering the affect of temperature in clock drift. Furthermore, we intend to explore different state space formulations of ARIMA models to be used with Kalman filter contemplating low computational cost.

8. ACKNOWLEDGMENTS

This work was partly supported by Lakeside Labs GmbH, Klagenfurt, Austria, and funding from the ERDF, KWF, and BABEG under grant 20214/23794/35530.

9. REFERENCES

[1] IEEE std. 1588 - 2002. IEEE standard for a precision clock synchronization protocol for networked measurement and control systems. *IEEE Std 1588-2002*, pages i–144, 2002.

[2] L. Abdullah. ARIMA Model for Gold Bullion Coin Selling Prices Forecasting. *International Journal of Advances in Applied Sciences*, 1(4):153–158, 2012.

[3] H. Akaike. A new look at the statistical model identification. *IEEE Trans. on Automatic Control*, 19(6):716–723, 1974.

[4] I. F. Akyildiz, T. Melodia, and K. R. Chowdhury. A survey on wireless multimedia sensor networks. *Computer Networks*, 51(4):921–960, 2007.

[5] L. Auler and R. d'Amore. Adaptive Kalman Filter for Time Synchronization over Packet-Switched Networks: An Heuristic Approach. In *ACM Proc. on Communication Systems Software and Middleware (COMSWARE)*, pages 1–7, 2007.

[6] J. A. Barnes. The measurement of linear frequency drift in oscillators. In *NRL Proc. on Precise Time and Time Interval (PTTI) Appl. and Planning Meeting*, pages 551–582, 1985.

[7] A. Bletsas. Evaluation of Kalman filtering for network time keeping. *IEEE Trans. on Ultrasonics, Ferroelectrics, and Frequency Control*, 52(9):1452–1460, 2005.

[8] G. E. Box and G. M. Jenkins. Times series analysis. *Forecasting and Control, Holda-Day*, 1970.

[9] G. E. P. Box, G. Jenkins, and G. C. Reinsel. *Time Series Analysis: Forecasting and Control*. Probability and Statistics. Wiley, July 2008.

[10] J. Contreras, R. Espinola, F. J. Nogales, and A. J. Conejo. ARIMA models to predict next-day electricity prices. *IEEE Trans. on Power Systems*, 18(3):1014–1020, 2003.

[11] D. A. Dickey and W. A. Fuller. Distribution of the estimators for autoregressive time series with a unit root. *Journal of the American Statistical Association*, 74(366):427–431, 1979.

[12] G. Elliott, T. J. Rothenberg, and J. H. Stock. Efficient tests for an autoregressive unit root. *Econometrica*, 64(4):813–836, 1996.

[13] J. Elson, L. Girod, and D. Estrin. Fine-grained network time synchronization using reference broadcasts. *ACM SIGOPS Operating Systems Review*, 36(SI):147–163, 2002.

[14] N. M. Freris and P. Kumar. Fundamental limits on synchronization of affine clocks in networks. In *IEEE Proc. on Decision and Control (CDC)*, pages 921–926, 2007.

[15] S. Ganeriwal, R. Kumar, and M. B. Srivastava. Timing-sync protocol for sensor networks. In *ACM Proc. on Embedded Networked Sensor Systems (SenSys)*, pages 138–149, 2003.

[16] B. R. Hamilton, X. Ma, Q. Zhao, and J. Xu. ACES: adaptive clock estimation and synchronization using Kalman filtering. In *ACM Proc. on Mobile Computing and Networking (MobiCom)*, pages 152–162, 2008.

[17] 802.15.4e-2012: IEEE Standard for local and metropolitan area networks–Part 15.4: Low-Rate Wireless Personal Area Networks (LR-WPANs) Amendment 1: MAC sublayer, April 2012.

[18] K. S. Kim and B. G. Lee. Kalp: A Kalman filter-based adaptive clock method with low-pass prefiltering for packet networks use. *IEEE Trans. on Communications*, 48(7):1217–1225, 2000.

[19] G. Lu, N. Sadagopan, B. Krishnamachari, and A. Goel. Delay efficient sleep scheduling in wireless sensor networks. In *IEEE Proc. on Computer and Communications Societies (INFOCOM)*, pages 2470–2481, 2005.

[20] A. Mainwaring, D. Culler, J. Polastre, R. Szewczyk, and J. Anderson. Wireless sensor networks for habitat monitoring. In *ACM Workshop on Wireless Sensor Networks and Applications (WSNA)*, pages 88–97, 2002.

[21] M. Maróti, B. Kusy, G. Simon, and A. Lédeczi. The flooding time synchronization protocol. In *ACM Proc. on Embedded Networked Sensor Systems (SenSys)*, pages 39–49, 2004.

[22] D. L. Mills. Internet Time Synchronization: the Network Time Protocol. *IEEE Trans. on Communications*, 39:1482–1493, 1991.

[23] D. L. Mills. Improved algorithms for synchronizing computer network clocks. *IEEE/ACM Trans. on Networking*, 3(3):245–254, 1995.

[24] S. B. Moon, P. Skelly, and D. Towsley. Estimation and removal of clock skew from network delay measurements. In *IEEE Proc. on Computer and Communications Societies (INFOCOM)*, volume 1, pages 227–234, 1999.

[25] MSP430 32-kHz Crystal Oscillators. Texas Instrument, Application Report : SLAA322B-August 2006, Revised April 2009.

[26] L. Paladina, M. Scarpa, and A. Puliafito. Advantages in synchronization for wireless sensor networks. In *IEEE Symp. on Wireless Pervasive Computing (ISWPC)*, pages 160–164, 2008.

[27] G. Schwarz. Estimating the dimension of a model. *The Annals of Statistics*, 6(2):461–464, 1978.

[28] J. Song, S. Han, A. K. Mok, D. Chen, M. Lucas, and M. Nixon. WirelessHART: Applying wireless technology in real-time industrial process control. In *IEEE Symp. on Real-Time and Embedded Technology and Applications (RTAS)*, pages 377–386, 2008.

[29] D. Stanislowski, X. Vilajosana, Q. Wang, T. Watteyne, and K. S. Pister. Adaptive synchronization in IEEE802.15.4e networks. *IEEE Trans. on Industrial Informatics*, 10(1):795–802, 2014.

[30] J. A. Stankovic, A. D. Wood, and T. He. Realistic applications for wireless sensor networks. In *Theoretical Aspects of Distributed Computing in Sensor Networks*, pages 835–863. Springer, 2011.

[31] B. Sundararaman, U. Buy, and A. D. Kshemkalyani. Clock synchronization for wireless sensor networks: a survey. *Ad Hoc Networks*, 3(3):281–323, 2005.

[32] F.-M. Tseng, G.-H. Tzeng, H.-C. Yu, and B. J. Yuan. Fuzzy ARIMA model for forecasting the foreign exchange market. *Fuzzy Sets and Systems*, 118(1):9–19, 2001.

[33] L. Zhang, Z. Liu, and C. Honghui Xia. Clock synchronization algorithms for network measurements. In *IEEE Proc. on Computer and Communications Societies (INFOCOM)*, volume 1, pages 160–169, 2002.

[34] Zolertia WSN platform, Z1 Datasheet. http://zolertia.com/sites/default/files/Zolertia-Z1-Datasheet.pdf.

Design and Evaluation of an RPL-based Multi-Sink Routing Protocol for Low-Power and Lossy Networks

Kevin Andrea
George Mason University
4400 University Drive
Fairfax, Virginia 22030
kandrea@masonlive.gmu.edu

Robert Simon
George Mason University
4400 University Drive
Fairfax, Virginia 22030
simon@gmu.edu

ABSTRACT

Due to the energy and resource constraints of the embedded Wireless Sensor Networking (WSN) devices that form Low-Power and Lossy Networks (LLNs), efficient support for mobile data sinks is essential. Further, such support should be fully compatible with the broad class of networking mechanisms now defined for LLN support, such as the routing protocol RPL. This paper describes the Hierarchical network of Observable devices with Itinerant Sinks Transporting data (HOIST) protocol. HOIST is designed to service LLNs using an RPL-friendly three-tier hybrid cluster-tree architecture to support sensor nodes deployed over geographically segregated areas. The mobile aspects of HOIST allow for collection from such remote fields without the need for long-distance wireless transfers, which would result in a higher level of energy drain. HOIST supports both real-time data capture and collected data retrieval. We have implemented and field-tested HOIST in a working physical system, as well as in simulation, with results indicating viability for both sparse and dense deployments of nodes under multiple, geographically constrained, uncontrolled mobility models.

Categories and Subject Descriptors

C.2.1 [**Network Architecture and Design**]: Wireless Communication

General Terms

Wireless Sensor Networking

Keywords

Wireless Sensor Network; LLN

1. INTRODUCTION

Wireless Sensor Networks (WSNs) consist of autonomous nodes, which are deployed across potentially large areas according to topological constraints and data collection needs.

MSWiM'15, November 2–6, 2015, Cancun, Mexico.
© 2015 ACM. ISBN 978-1-4503-3762-5/15/11 ...$15.00.
DOI: http://dx.doi.org/10.1145/2811587.2811614.

These nodes collect information about their environment from attached sensors. As WSN nodes are typically powered either by batteries or through energy-harvesting, these devices are power-limited, necessitating the use of resource-constrained, embedded systems. These devices operate over a type of network called Low-Power and Lossy Networks (LLNs), which feature high loss rates, instability, and low data rate transfers[1]. Such WSNs are presently used in precision agriculture[2], disaster management[3], and industrial monitoring[4], where they are expected to operate for extended periods of time without the ability of network operators to perform routine maintenance.

This paper describes Hierarchical network of Observable devices with Itinerant Sinks Transporting data (HOIST) protocol and architecture. The underlying design philosophy of HOIST it to be fully compatible and inter-operable with existing LLN networking standards. It is widely recognized that resource constrained LLNs requiring convergecast routing (a characteristic of our targeted application class) gradient routing techniques are particularly effective [5]. In recognition of this fact, the IETF has standardized the *Routing Protocol for Low Power and Lossy Networks* (RPL) protocol [6]. HOIST is designed as an application layer control plane semi-reliable protocol to be used with off-the-shelf RPL implementations.

HOIST provides a means for data collection from WSNs in a manner that is able to handle such high loss rates, network instability, and low data rate transfers as is expected with LLNs. Building upon basic research in mobile sink support via hierarchical topological methods [7, 8], HOIST is a hybrid tree-cluster, three-tier hierarchical architecture that coordinates both data relay and data sink collections from multiple, geographically segregated WSN deployments. We implemented HOIST with both physical devices and in simulation, and we have analyzed control message timings for enhancing initial deployments. One of the most difficult challenges in supporting mobile sinks is to reduce the amount of time for the sink to establish stable multi-hop routing paths in the networks being visited. As will be seen, a primary focus of our work is to precisely quantify, in our experimental prototype, the time required to establish such routes.

HOIST utilizes uncontrolled mobility to support motivating applications such as precision agriculture[2]. In this application, there can be multiple, geographically segregated fields that are covered with WSN devices. Using mobility, HOIST enables mobile data relays to move between fields to collect stored sensor data. When this data relay arrives at each field, it can follow geographically constrained pathways as dictated by the terrain and WSN field applications themselves. This data relay may also be deployed on aerial vehicles that are able to enter and hold an orbit around each field for the duration of the data collection.

At network startup, the lower-tier of HOIST sensing devices begin their collection from the environment. These nodes will locally store their data in non-volatile memory, without any data transmissions during this normal state of operations. The middle-tier devices are local sinks that are manually placed in a linear topological formation, throughout the center of the node deployment area, and act as cluster-heads for the lower-tier nodes. These middle-tier sinks provide routine node control and network maintenance functionality while awaiting the arrival of one, or both, of the mobile sinks to the area.

The upper-tier devices consist of mobile sinks in either a data relay or a data sink role. This allows both retrieval of collected data from each field, as well as an immediate assessment of the field by performing a spot-check, without interrupting either current or future retrieval operations. When a mobile sink enters range of any middle-tier sink, it will initiate the creation of a tree-like backbone connecting each of the local sinks. Once this is formed, the local sinks coordinate their subordinate nodes to transmit their data. For the mobile data relay, nodes send a number of messages based on network conditions before seeking verification of data delivery. Once this verification is complete, the nodes will continue their broadcast until data transmission is complete. Each of these transmission processes is such that each sink is only coordinating a single sensor device transmission at a time. This reduces network flooding, allowing for sensor device scaling with a logarithmic order of growth in message traffic, as concurrent data transmissions scale linearly with the middle-tier sinks, not lower-tier collectors.

2. RELATED WORK

The aim of HOIST is to provide a means of collecting data from geographically segregated fields of sensing nodes. Topological approaches for mobile sink support have been very heavily studied in wireless networking literature [7, 8]. For instance, there has been much work showing the benefits of both cluster and hierarchical based architectures. Cluster-based architectures[9, 10] divide nodes into virtual groups that limit hop-count for data transmissions and either reduce the overhead of node control messages or the overhead of data forwarding. These approaches designate certain devices as cluster heads, whose responsibility includes the coordination of data transfers and overall management of subordinate devices. Hierarchical-based architectures[11, 12] provide scalable data dissemination through multiple tiers of routers, often using a backbone line, to reduce the number of query and data transmissions between a node and the data sink.

We now describe in detail several relevant architectural approaches. Hierarchical Cluster-based Data Dissemination (HCDD)[12] is an architecture that leverages the benefits of clustering with a hierarchical model by designating certain nodes as routing agents. Sensor nodes first send their data to the local routing agent, which then forwards the data through the interconnection of routing agents towards the sink. HOIST makes use of a similar model by using a middle-tier of local sinks to act as routing agents. Using RPL as our routing interface, each sink is the root of its own DODAG; by placing these sinks in a linear topological formation across the center of the deployment area, we enjoy the benefit of clustering through lower hop count DAGs.

The Hierarchical Role-based Data Dissemination (HRDD) [11] architecture alleviates energy drain problems through mobility, while likewise using clustering and a data dissemination backbone to send data to the sink. The primary achievement of HRDD was alleviating energy-usage problems, reducing the quantity of data and query transmissions, and accelerating the data delivery. One key feature with HRDD is that nodes only forward metadata about events of interest. If the sink desires the full report, it will send a query down for the full data. In HOIST, middle-layer sinks provide all of the route maintenance and coordination functions, similar to the cluster heads. When the mobile data relay arrives, it sends an announcement of arrival to the middle-tier sinks, which form a backbone and begin coordinating with each of their subordinate sensor nodes to send their full data. Each middle-tier sink coordinates the transfer of each node, one at a time, to prevent undue flooding of the network.

A multiple-tiered model with ferrying sinks has been implemented by [13]. Their Mobile Ubiquitous LAN Extension (MULE) approach is designed for sparse sensor networks that enable data to be locally collected and stored before being transmitted to its middle-tier wandering sink devices. HOIST differs in that our sensor nodes form a static network within the middle-tier, maintaining a routing network before the mobile sink arrives. Once any of the mobile sinks arrive, nodes send data through pre-existing routes, removing the need for dynamic routing on the lower-tier in response to any mobility.

[14] describes a three-layer system in an approach called Load Balanced Clustering and Dual Data Uploading (LBC-DDU). In this approach, a clustering algorithm elects cluster heads from amongst the collectors, such that the collectors are all one-hop from a cluster head. The cluster heads coordinate data with the top layer, which is a mobile sink called a SenCar that plans a route to directly collect data from each cluster head. Mobile sinks in HOIST only have to be within range of any of the middle-tier sink devices to communicate with the entire network. In many cases, such as in an agricultural deployment, terrain may prevent direct connection with each cluster head, so HOIST allows mobile devices to skirt along the region and manage communications from the perimeter.

Data sink primary networks for spot-checking conditions without interrupting existing applications have also been described in use. [15] describes how WSNs may be used in urban environments with the ability for emergency responders to connect and view current building sensor information. As each firefighter arrives on scene, their local devices connect with the building and begin receiving sensor information. HOIST employs a mobile data sink for a similar purpose, enabling any end-user to view current conditions in a deployment area.

[3] uses a large WSN deployment to provide an alert service to first responders for fire outbreaks in cultural heritage areas. Their technique focuses on redundancy by sending data to multiple sinks. In HOIST, multiple sinks are used in a similarly hierarchical manner to increase the scale of the deployment while still retaining the ability of the mobile sink

to reply directly to any node in the network. This ability to reply enables data assurance, allowing nodes to retransmit data until delivery is acknowledged, mitigating the need for such redundancy.

Further, mobility models for mobile data collection has also received much interest [7]. Mobility can either be controlled, in which the network moves sinks predictably according to a known process, or uncontrolled[16], with processes beyond the control of the network driving the movement of the sinks. Mobility is also used to reduce the energy cost of networks by either moving directly adjacent to cluster heads [13], or by more evenly distributing the transmission load on a convergecast routed network. In convergecast, devices closest to the sink have to retransmit a disproportionately large number of messages, expending more energy in a phenomena known as the hot spot problem[17]. Mobility addresses this problem by allowing sinks to move about the network, more evenly distributing the power expenditures. As mentioned above, HOIST assumes the most general purpose uncontrolled mobility model.

Finally, due to its importance in practical network settings, RPL support for mobile applications has recently received much attention [18, 19, 20]. However, to the best of our knowledge, HOIST represents the first evaluation of an implemented hierarchical approach for mobile sink support that is fully compatible with standard RPL.

3. ARCHITECTURAL DESIGN

In HOIST, we designed a three-tier architecture to implement a hybrid tree-cluster design, using uncontrolled mobility and the common RPL protocol to provide routing support. HOIST was designed to be used in either sparse or dense networked environments, without any direct lines of communication to a fixed collection center. We utilize specially designated mobile sink devices in the two primary roles for remote data collection: data sink and data relay. The data sink fills the traditional model wherein sensor devices send their information directly to a sink, as the data is collected. A data relay, however, serves the role of moving between the WSN fields to collect data. Not only does this mitigate problems pertaining to energy drain, which would result from trying to relay data from distant fields, but it also enables us to have multiple, independent and geographically segregated fields of deployments in simultaneous operation.

HOIST is an application-layer protocol that governs the coordination and data transfers between the devices at each tier. For the data forwarding between each of the devices, we rely on the RPL protocol. RPL creates and manages routing for the network by using its own ICMPv6 control messages. Messages in HOIST are transmitted as data under the UDP transport protocol; however, these HOIST control and data forwarding messages also use RPL options at the IP layer, which allows RPL to govern the forwarding. RPL specifies this forwarding through the use of the RPL Instance identifier, which itself addresses the root of a collection of DODAGs. HOIST uses three such RPL Instance identifiers for routing; as these identifiers are single-byte fields, we have elected to assign them mnemonically using single ASCII-encoded characters. These identifiers are introduced along with the HOIST sinks below.

The fundamental feature of HOIST is this hierarchical design, as shown in Figure 1, using three tiers of nodes. At the lower-tier, sensor devices known as *Collectors* sense fea-

tures of their environment and store such data locally for later retrieval. The middle-tier nodes, known as *Bridges*, are the local sink devices that perform the role of cluster-heads. These Bridges are each sinks within RPL Instance identifier 'B', opening themselves up for Collectors to join them. Collectors are able to switch between Bridges as network conditions suggest. The Collectors are completely insulated from any network changes made by any higher-tier mobile sinks, reducing the time necessary to update the network topology following mobility to the Bridge sinks only.

The final, upper-tier of HOIST consists of two discrete Instances. Instance 'M' is created by a mobile data relay sink called the *Messenger*, whose objective is to travel to each of the remote WSN deployment fields, retrieve the collected data, and return such data for processing. When the Messenger arrives at a deployment site, RPL will initiate its own route creation by sending a DODAG Information Object (DIO) message, which HOIST uses to indicate mobile sink arrival. When this DIO is received by a Bridge, it is rebroadcast to cause all of the Bridges to create a multi-hop DODAG. Once connected, the Bridges coordinate with each of their descendants, one at a time, and act as the relay to send their data to the Messenger. The total number of Collectors sending data is limited to the number of Bridges, reducing the network load. As a Collector finishes its data transmission, it immediately resumes collecting data.

The second Instance supported by this upper-tier is Instance 'O', which is created by a mobile data sink called the *Observer*. Like the Messenger, this sink can enter the deployment area at any time, causing all of the Bridge devices to join to that Instance. Once connected, however, the Bridges signal each of their Collectors to send the Observer a copy of their latest data. The Collectors will then send a copy of each new piece of data, as it is collected. In this manner, the Observer is able to perform a spot-check on the network.

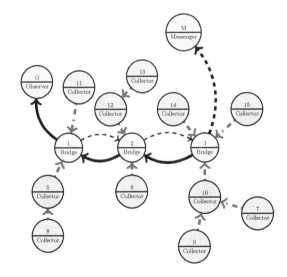

Figure 1: HOIST Overview

In HOIST, Collectors are deployed statically as needed to monitor the local area; they are not affected by any network topological changes stemming from mobility. Once the Collector deployment is completed, Bridge devices are introduced to act as coordinating cluster-heads for the Collectors.

This deployment is done manually by placing them in a linear topological formation such that the Collectors each have a valid multi-hop route to least one Bridge, and that the Bridges are able to evenly distribute the load of Collectors.

The Bridges are all sinks for RPL Instance 'B', which is the collection wrapper for all Bridge DODAGs that RPL uses for its routing. Aside from this function, the Bridges do not collect any data themselves. HOIST uses a link-quality aware Objective Function (OF) with hysteresis for these RPL DODAGs to promote stable, efficient routing. This does not need to be the OF used for either of the mobile sinks; they may use their own custom objective functions as best fits their mobility models.

3.1 HOIST Protocol

HOIST introduces several message types to facilitate coordination and data transmission between the myriad tiers. These messages are sent as application data in UDP packets, routed using IPv6 and RPL. These are separate from the ICMPv6 network control messages used by RPL. The primary messages HOIST introduces are described below.

SYN Sent by Bridges to determine when bi-directional routing is established with the Messenger, which sends a SYN in reply to the originating Bridge.

START Sent by Bridges to coordinate Collectors to begin data transmissions.

DATA Sent by Collectors and relayed by Bridges to send data to the mobile sinks.

CHECK Sent by Collectors to query the Messenger for the last expected message.

ACK Sent by the Messengers in reply to CHECK.

FIN Sent by Collectors to inform their Bridge their data transmission is complete.

TERM Sent by Bridges to inform their Collectors a mobile sink has left.

These messages are sent as application data, carried by UDP, using RPL for its routing. The HOIST data frame is depicted below. *Type* refers to the HOIST message types above. *Bridge ID* is used by the Bridge to record the last octet of its IPv6 address. *Collector ID* is the originating Collector's last octet of its IPv6 address, which is used by the Messenger for data storage purposes. *SR* is the send rate of the Collector and *DC* is the number of data fields in this message. *Starting Index* provides the starting index of the data from the Collector, which is used by the Messenger for data assurance. *Data[x]* refers to the 2-byte data fields that follow.

0	8	16	24	31
HOIST Type	Bridge ID	Collector ID	SR	DC
Starting Index		Data[0]...		

One of the primary factors of HOIST is data assurance for the Messenger device. We have elected to implement a hierarchical network capable of enabling the Collectors to request the next data message expected by the Messenger. This enables the Collector to confirm delivery receipt and schedule any repeated messages as needed to assure complete data reception by the Messenger. HOIST presently performs verification for contiguously received data, which means a Collector will need to resend data beginning with the first message that was not received by the Messenger. The number of messages a Collector may send between these verifications is autonomously adjustable through HOIST.

Communication begins once the initial RPL configuration message (DIO) for Instance 'M', formed by the mobile collection sink, is received by a Bridge as shown in Figure 2. Once this occurs, the receiving Bridge will generate a SYN message for the Messenger. The naive problem with immediately coordinating data transfers is that, for more distant Bridges, the RPL routing table construction messages will not have had ample opportunity to propagate back to the Messenger, leaving the Bridge unroutable. To prevent this cold-start routing miss, a simple SYN handshake takes place. Once the Bridge receives a reply, it begins data coordination. It is normal for this SYN message to timeout on several attempts prior to the first successful reply.

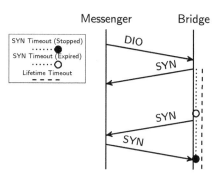

Figure 2: Arrival Handshake - With Timeout

As shown in Figure 2, there are two timeout mechanisms governing this process. The first enables the Bridge to send another SYN packet to the Messenger. The second is a lifetime timeout. This concept of lifetime, described in section 3.2 below, is an enhancement we made to our RPL implementation to signal HOIST that a mobile sink is gone. Should a mobile sink leave (or cease functioning) during the initial SYN process, the Bridge will cease attempts and resume normal operations.

Once the reply SYN message is received, a START timeout period is started and the Bridge begins by sending a message to the first Collector in its downward routing table. That Collector replies with the same message in acknowledgment, after which the Bridge begins waiting for data traffic to relay. If a Collector is unreachable, the timeout will occur, supporting up to N attempts at communications before moving to the next device in the list. Once a Collector receives the START message, it will begin sending its data in packets, maximizing payload data without fragmentation, as shown in Figure 3.

Once a Collector has received this message, it sends blocks of messages to the Bridge using RPL Instance 'B' for addressing, starting a timeout on the Collector. When a Bridge receives a data packet, it sends it using RPL Instance 'M' for addressing. Upon receipt by the Messenger, the data is examined to determine if it is the expected next block. If so, it adds the data to persistent flash memory for later retrieval and updates its next expected block information.

A Collector will always send at least one block of data towards the mobile sink during its transmission operation.

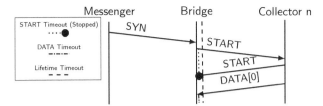

Figure 3: Data Initiation Handshake

HOIST enables Collectors to adjust the number of data blocks they are able to send in response to link quality information, by timeouts encountered, or through hardcoding, as desired. When a Collector has either sent all of its data, or has sent the maximum number of unconfirmed blocks, it will send a CHECK message to the Bridge. The Bridge forwards this to the Messenger, which will immediately reply back with an ACK message containing the next expected message. If the next expected message matches the next message to send, then the Collector will proceed with either finishing the connection, or it will begin sending the next set. This process is depicted in Figure 4.

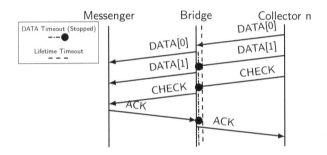

Figure 4: Data Transfer

If the Collector receives no response from the CHECK message, it will continue to resend CHECK packets. HOIST uses two different timing values for this CHECK message retransmission. For the first set of failures, HOIST uses a short duration timer for resending these messages. This is done to account for dropped packets that occur with any LLN communications. After the first set of failures, the Collector operates on the assumption that the Messenger is out of range and routing needs to be rebuilt. At this point, the Collector uses a longer timer, which is designed to give RPL the time to rebuild routing to the Messengers new location. Once an ACK is received, the Collector resumes data transmission operations. Should the Messenger leave communications range long enough that lifetime expires, then the Bridge sends TERM to the current Collector, as shown in Figure 5. When received, the Collector resumes collection operations, marking the last successfully transmitted data segment so it may later resume where it left off.

When the Collector has sent all of its data and has received the ACK message with the proper confirmation, then it will issue a FIN message the the Bridge. Upon receipt, the Bridge will reply with a FIN message back to the Collector and then send a START message to the next Collector in its downward routing table. This process will continue until either all Collectors have finished, or until the Messenger leaves the area and its lifetime expires, at which point the ac-

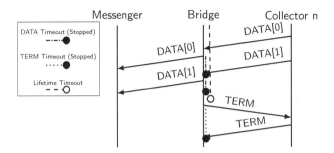

Figure 5: Data Transfer - Lifetime Timeout

tive Collector will be terminated and the Bridge will resume normal operations. All Collectors not actively in sending data to the Messenger will be in normal collection operations and will send their data to the Observer, if present.

The Observer is implemented similarly to the Messenger, albeit without any message delivery assurance. HOIST makes this distinction for the primary reasons that the Observer is a traditional data sink that is interested in the current state of the devices in the local area. Any lost messages will be replaced when a Collector sends following its next collection event. The secondary reason for the lack of delivery assurance is to reduce the need for additional HOIST control message overhead. As the Observer may be present along with the Messenger, adding CHECK and ACK messages would contribute to the flooding on the order of the number of Collectors. As the network operates on the order of the number of Bridges for Messenger operations, this would tremendously increase the flooding of the network; as such, the Observer operates without data assurance.

When the first DIO for Instance 'O' is received by a Bridge, it forms a multi-hop DODAG with the other Bridges, with the Observer as root. Each Bridge then sends START to each Collector. The first messages to the Observer will occur directly after receiving START, consisting of the most recent data collected by the Collector. After this, when a Collector normally collects data on the environment, in addition to storing the data in its own internal array, it will also send a copy through the Bridge to the Observer. This process will continue until the Observer leaves the network, at which point the Bridge will send TERM to each Collector. The Collectors then will continue normal operations.

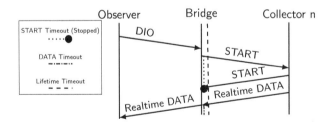

Figure 6: Data Initiation Handshake (Observer)

In the case that both the Observer and Messenger are in range simultaneously, the network will operate as it would for either independent event, with one exception. While a Collector is sending its archived data to the Messenger, it will not be collecting any new data; this means that no messages will be sent to the Observer from that Collector.

Once the data send terminates and the next Collector in the same DODAG begins sending to the Messenger, then the previous Collector will resume collection operations and will send to the Observer.

3.2 RPL Protocol Enhancements

HOIST specifies the mobility, topological, and messaging designs, however, it interfaces with the Routing Protocol for Low-Power and Lossy Networks (RPL)[?], the IETF standard for LLN routing, to handle lower-level message forwarding between the various devices in the network. HOIST uses RPL to create, manage, and provide inter-device routing for HOIST messages. RPL manages routing through a tree-like Destination-Oriented Directed Acyclic Graph (DODAG) structure, which HOIST uses for all of its message forwarding.

As RPL is an IP layer extension, its primary role is to provide routing support for IPv6 message delivery. The primary concern with respect to HOIST is that RPL does not have any inherent support for mobility, leading to network partitioning when the mobile sinks move, while RPL works to identify and correct its routing. While RPL has no control message parameters to notify arrival or departure of a device to a network, it does send the DIO control message from the mobile sinks to initiate DODAG construction. HOIST uses the arrival of a new DIO message as its indicator that a mobile sink has arrived.

While HOIST is able to extract arrival information, RPL has no support for determining departure of a sink from the area. RPL does have a lifetime field governing its instances, however, the lifetime on an Instance only affects routing to that Instance. Once this mechanism is exhausted, the Instance remains active and DIO messages continue to be generated concerning this Instance, which continue to propagate out-of-date information. With no means of knowing if this Instance is alive or not, the Bridges are unable to inform the Collectors of departure and therefore no means for them to resume normal collections.

We enhanced the lifetime mechanism of RPL to extend it for Instance lifetime governance. DIO configuration messages in RPL contain specifications for the routing lifetime of the instance. We elected to use this lifetime information from the mobile sinks as an Instance lifetime counter, which is locally stored on the Instance structure. When a DIO is received, the lifetime is read from the configuration option and a timer is started. When that counter reaches zero, the Instance is purged from the device, which HOIST uses as the indicator that the mobile sink has left the area. When a Bridge propagates a DIO message from a mobile sink to other Bridges – a continual routing maintenance function of RPL – it will send its own current lifetime for the Instance, not the default initial lifetime. This has the advantage of equalizing the lifetimes of the network of Bridges amongst each other. Once a mobile sink either leaves range, or dies, the Bridges will continually decrement their lifetime values for that sink's Instance until it reaches zero, at which point every Bridge simultaneously removes the Instance. This prevents out-of-date information from propagating across the network and makes the Bridge ready for the next mobile sink to arrive.

The second enhancement we made was necessary to support the hierarchical nature of HOIST. In RPL, any DIO received by a node will be accepted as an Instance and joined. This would pose severe problems in situations where

a node might attempt to join the 'M' or 'O' Instances directly, should these devices be active in range of a Collector when it comes online. To prevent this, we implemented both a Whitelist and a Blacklist system in RPL, which are configurable in the code for each of these device types. In HOIST, Collectors have only one authorized Instance in their Whitelist: Instance 'B'. Bridges, on the other hand have Instances 'O' and 'M' in their Whitelist. We implemented this system in the algorithm processing DIO arrival messages. Upon arrival, if either Whitelist or Blacklist constraints are defined, the Instance ID is compared and the DIO is either rejected or accepted as specified.

4. HOIST IMPLEMENTATION

We have implemented HOIST under the Contiki 2.7 Operating System, modified to support multiple RPL Instance routing, Instance whitelisting and blacklisting, and communally balanced RPL Instance lifetimes. While HOIST is easily implementable at the application level, our modifications to RPL needed to be modified within the operating system networking core. As the Contiki operating system provides a base implementation of RPL, we also needed to make some minor changes to complete their implementation. RPL, as implemented by the Contiki operating system, only supports single-Instance RPL networks. We provided significant modifications to the core networking code to enable multi-Instance networks to form. The first modification was to extend the `rpl_dag` table to support storing DODAG-centric metric information for parent selection. Previously, this was a global table that stored one `rank` for each neighbor, regardless of Instances; this prevented all possibilities of operating in a multi-Instance environment. Compounding this, several functions, which were written with the innate assumption that only one Instance or DODAG would ever be in existence at a time, had to be modified.

The core routing decision code also needed to be modified. In Contiki, a four step decision process is executed to determine the proper next hop for the message. For upward routing towards the root, this meant that, regardless of the message's stated Instance ID, all messages destined for non-neighbor sinks would be routed to the default Instance's preferred parent only. This default Instance, however, is set by incoming DIOs, meaning this was like sending a message on a raft down a river that changes directions arbitrarily. While this technique is sufficient for single-Instance routing, any attempt at routing within a multiple-Instance environment will result in failure.

We modified this by adding a step immediately after checking the downward routing table, which is shown as the italicized step 4 in the following list. This additional step checks the RPL Instance ID on the message received and then uses that Instance's preferred parent for routing instead. This modification additionally involved writing many functions to perform such checks. This is a new type of forwarding to facilitate proper routing in a multiple RPL Instance environment.

1. Determine if the destination address is multicast. If the address is a multicast address, send the message.

2. Otherwise, check if the destination address is in the neighbors table. If so, send the message as addressed.

3. Otherwise, check if the destination address is in the

downward routing table. If so, send the message to the next-hop address as listed in the table.

4. *Otherwise, check the destination RPL Instance ID on the message. Send the message to the preferred-parent of the Instance specified on the message.*

5. If there is no RPL header, or if the Instance is unknown, send the message to the preferred-parent of the default Instance.

In this extension to the RPL implementation, the message will be routed as addressed in the event that it is not an adjacent destination. If the Instance is not known, then the message will still be sent along the local device's default Instance to continue to make progress in the understanding that the next device may have a viable route. Messages with no RPL headers are also assessed in this stage to see if their destination address matches a known RPL Instance sink. If so, an RPL header is added to more rapidly facilitate proper routing.

One of our choices in HOIST utilizes the ability to select a custom objective function for each RPL Instance. The current implementation environment on Contiki required a minor modification to enable each device to recognize the full gamut of possible objective functions. We are presently assessing different objective functions at each level for various platforms of mobility. We have tested HOIST using an Unmanned Aerial System (UAS) as the platform for our mobile sinks and discovered that using a hop count based objective function for the mobile sinks was effective when the UAV orbited the entire field, frequently entering and leaving the radio range of each Bridge.

5. HOIST TESTING

We have designed these tests to validate HOIST through the analysis of several factors, and their responses. The primary factors of interest in developing baseline settings for HOIST are the DIO minimum send rate, the maximum DIO send rate doublings, the data transmission send rates, and the number of Collectors in the network. We are interested in these values particularly as they govern the timing for sending RPL's DODAG formation and maintenance control messages. These messages also affect the responsiveness of RPL to mobility. If too few messages are sent, then hysteresis on the Bridges will prevent them from adopting the new routes of a sink after it has moved; however, if they are too frequent, then the network may be inundated with messages that do not offer any new information. As mobility is present in this network, we have designed the tests to ensure these DIO related factors are examined in situations that include network partitioning and reformation. Only by ascertaining a baseline for RPL timings relating to message routing, can we better assess efficacy of HOIST under multiple scenarios.

5.1 Physical Validation

We conducted the first physical validation on nine Zolertia Z1 motes using one Messenger, three Bridges, and five Collectors. A close-up showing a representative set of these devices is shown in Figure 7.

For this implementation in Figure 7, we initialized each Collector with 30 data samples, necessitating each to transfer two data packets to the Messenger data relay, by way of the Bridges. The network formation is visible through LED

Figure 7: Subset of Physical Implementation

codes on the devices. As each node receives its initial DIO, the green LED illuminates. As each Collector finishes its data transmission following the final successful ACK reply, they illuminate their red LED. This trivial demonstration shows HOIST operational on physical Zolertia Z1 devices.

5.2 Simulation Testing

We have used the Cooja simulator to perform baseline analysis on HOIST, with the aim of ascertaining initial settings and suitability for future collection operations. The first round of testing uses 8 Collector and 4 Bridge devices to determine ideal settings for the DIO transmission rates to optimize building and maintaining the HOIST network. For this testing, the Bridges are deployed linearly, with each placed at a distance of 70% of the maximum transmission range, with an offset equal to a random value, sampled from the Gaussian distribution (generated using the Box-Muller method[21]) with a variance of 5% of the maximum transmission range to ensure only its adjacent neighbors are in range. The Collectors are generated after the Bridges and are placed at a distance equal to 70% of the maximum transmission range of an existing device, with an offset equal to a Gaussian random value with a variance of 5% of the maximum transmission range. The angle of placement from the center of the existing device is sampled uniformly.

5.2.1 Simulation Mobility Model

For the first mobility model, we used a geographically constrained path to a point adjacent to the farthest Bridge in the linear formation. The Messenger sink (M) begins at a distance of 150% maximum transmission range away from the first Bridge (B2). Following 30 seconds, the Messenger begins moving at 1.3 m/s and progresses until it is directly adjacent to the last Bridge (B5), where it halts and remains until the end of the simulation. This test is designed to ensure the Bridges form an initial network through B2 and begin data transmissions, that the radio connection between M and B2 breaks due to exceeding the maximum transmission range, and the network has to ultimately reform once M stops. These initial positions and this movement are depicted in Figure 8.

The second mobility model is used for the orbit tests to emulate an Unmanned Aerial System (UAS) in flight, orbiting around a field of deployed devices. In this model, the Messenger sink begins in the same manner, however, once it has entered the field, it moves at a pace of 5 m/s along a geographically constrained path between the first and last Bridges, simulating an orbiting vehicle. This test is designed to force rapid routing changes to continue data transmissions.

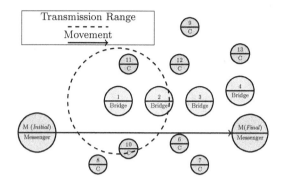

Figure 8: Mobility for Validation

5.2.2 Analysis of DIO Settings

For the first tests of HOIST, we seeded each of the 8 Collectors with 30 data points and set their node collection rate to 120 seconds. The Messenger begins moving at 30 seconds and ceases its movement when it is adjacent to the last Bridge. We ran 30 simulations for each combination of settings for the DIO transmission rates. We selected minimum times for DIO transmission to 2^{11} ms, 2^{12} ms, and 2^{13} ms, and tested each with 4, 5, and 6 doublings of the Trickle algorithm[22].

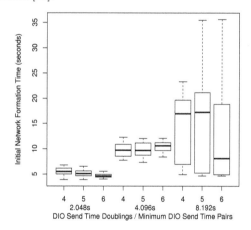

Figure 9: Initial Formation Time Analysis

The collected data for the initial formation time of the 'M' Instance is shown in Figure 9. Using two-factor ANOVA analysis with replication, we calculated that, with a 95% confidence level, using a minimum DIO send time of 2.048 seconds was statistically better at reducing initial formation time, whereas the number of doublings in send rate, through the Trickle algorithm, had negligible effects. There were no statistical interactions between the two factors.

With respect to the duration of the data transfer, we performed two-factor ANOVA analysis with replication, shown in table 2. Looking at the data transfer duration, we did not observe any statistical difference in data transfer times

Source	F-Statistic	F-Critical	P-Value
DIO Minimum	10.34589	3.89546	0.001547
DIO Doublings	1.6970	3.0479	0.1863
Interaction	1.7137	3.0479	0.1832

Table 1: Two-Factor ANOVA on Formation Time

due to the minimum DIO send time, however, the number of doublings was significant at a 95% confidence level. This is as expected insofar as these simulations partition completely all routes to the Messenger early in the transfer of data. Reducing the maximum number of doublings causes the Messenger to send more DIO messages, which help to break hysteresis and enable Bridges to directly connect and restore routing.

Source	F-Statistic	F-Critical	P-Value
DIO Minimum	0.00098	3.8955	0.9751
DIO Doublings	3.2270	3.0479	0.0421
Interaction	9.1561	3.0479	0.00017

Table 2: Two-Factor ANOVA on Transfer Duration

Source	F-Statistic	F-Critical	P-Value
DIO Minimum	2.3747	3.0304	0.0951
DIO Doublings	3.8977	3.0304	0.0215
Interaction	1.5993	2.4062	0.1749

Table 3: Two-Factor ANOVA on Route Reforming

Examining the data collected, we found a great variance on the data transfer times, which appear to have more to do with the placement of the devices than the settings used. We further saw the time it takes to reform the network after initial partitioning was quite similar in that, under RPL, the number of runs where the routing failed to fully reform as of the 600s end of the simulation varied greatly.

For this analysis, as seen in Table 3, we see that while the results vary greatly, the minimum DIO send time did have a statistically significant impact; however, both 2.048s and 8.192s, for these scenarios, yielded similar results with respect to both reform duration and in the number of reform completions. The final assessment performed was on the number of repeated packets necessary to ensure full delivery. Combining the data on the myriad assessments, we have opted to select a minimum DIO send time of 2.048s and 6 doublings as the baseline for our data collection in the presence of a mobile sink.

5.2.3 Analysis of Send Rates

We next worked to establish a baseline for selecting the send rate of the Collectors. This rate governs only the data transmissions, however, this factor is important to properly tune to ensure prompt, but reliable message delivery in increasing network densities.

For these tests, we used the same configuration for the Bridges, however, the Collectors will now vary in size between 8 and 12 devices to increase load on each Bridge. To focus only on the contribution from the Collectors to this analysis, we now stop Messenger mobility when it is adjacent to the first Bridge to prevent network partitioning. For these runs, each combination was repeated 30 times, using a DIO minimum send time of 2.048s and a maximum of 6 doublings.

The first test of significance is to explore the relationship between the send rate and the number of Collectors in the network. We performed two-factor ANOVA analysis results for every combination of 8, 10, and 12 Collectors under 2, 3, and 4 second send rates. With respect to the number of Collectors, we found there was a statistical significance, at a 95% confidence level, with a p-value of 0.0813, that the chosen send rate did affect the data transmission times. This warrants further testing under larger networks of devices; however, it shows that even in the presence of increasing local density, a smaller send rate still provided benefits overall.

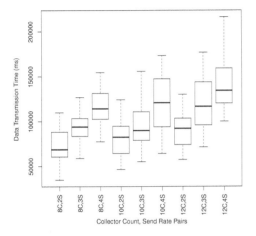

Figure 10: Send Rate Analysis

5.2.4 *Orbit Mobility Analysis*

Our final validation testing was conducted using the Messenger sink aboard an Unmanned Aerial System (UAS), flying in an orbit around a HOIST deployment field. We conducted an initial test using Zolertia Z1 sensor devices aboard an Aurora Flight Sciences Skate UAS[23]. Our integration with the Skate UAS is shown in the cut-away of the payload bay in Figure 11. Our initial testing was conducted with the top two tiers of HOIST only, to establish multi-hop connectivity with RPL using the MRHOF objective function.

We performed initial validation using a simple program that broadcast UDP packets and recorded signal strength received. We programmed the Skate to fly in a 15m orbit at 30m, 23m, and 18m altitude above the ground. The wind for this flight was 4kts with gusts to 10kts, which caused the aircraft to fly in a highly irregular orbit. Despite this, we received approximately 80% of the messages sent from the UAS at the lowest altitude, which we used to fly all subsequent tests.

Our main validation flight tested multi-hop routing between the upper two tiers of HOIST, with three bridges statically deployed on the ground and the Messenger carried aboard the UAS. Our deployment of three Bridges resulted in an initial DODAG formation time of 22 seconds, with full data relay completion within 180 seconds of formation. This implementation demonstrates HOIST operating in an environment with uncontrolled mobility and frequent loss of communications between the Bridges and the Messenger.

Further validation testing was completed by simulation.

Figure 11: Payload Bay on Skate UAS

We modified the simulation in Cooja by increasing the Collector size to 32, with 8 Bridges. Our mobility model brings the Messenger within range after 30 seconds of simulation time. The Messenger transits, back and forth, between the two end Bridges for the duration of the simulation, at a speed of 5.0 m/s. Over 60 simulations, we found that using a hop-count based objective function was more effective at this rate of mobility for an orbiting mobile sink. Future work will be done analyzing efficacy using UAS platforms.

5.3 Data Analysis Conclusion

After looking at the results of the data analysis, we have selected to use a minimum DIO send time of 2.048 s, with 6 doublings, and a 2 second send rate for future implementation testing. These timings, while relating particularly to the RPL routing protocol, enable us to effectively assess HOIST under various conditions. These assessments of HOIST operating under various terrestrial and aerial mobility models provided validation that HOIST is both effective at retrieving data from remote field and is tenable when increasing the size of the number of Bridge and Collector devices.

6. CONCLUDING REMARKS

This is an initial proposal and a basic implementation that is not without discovered limitations on the proposed architecture. We seek to continue our work and aim to refine and present a fully operational HOIST for consideration as a viable mobility-aware, hierarchical solution that can run on off-the-shelf hardware, using a common routing protocol and a simple application-level implementation. These factors allow HOIST to handle high loss rates, instability, and low data rate transfers through both data retrieval from geographically segregated fields and local field, spot-checking operations.

While we are continuing to enhance our implementation of HOIST as described in this paper, our current focus is on using HOIST as a platform for exploring mobility in WSNs. One aspect of this is working with mobility-awareness within the RPL routing protocol. In our work, we have explored timings for RPL route maintenance messages and we are using RPL's Instance structure to provide HOIST with information concerning the presence of the mobile sinks; however, RPL has difficulty in modifying routing in response to mobility, once a route is formed. We are continuing to explore the underlying factors so that we may improve our response to mobility.

HOIST has the ability to adjust the number of data blocks

to send before requesting confirmation; we are working with extending this component to also react to the particular model of mobility in use. An orbiting aerial data relay will have different optimal data transmission patterns than a small autonomous ground vehicle that is able to stop until all data transfers are complete. As we have seen in flight testing, even when the mobility profile is known, external factors, such as high wind conditions, can prevent the expected behavior. Mobility assessment and prediction can enable HOIST, or even RPL, to adjust by changing objective functions, proactively changing routing assignments, or even invalidating the entire network, prompting a global rebuilding.

This paper presents several motivating desires and provides the HOIST architecture to address those needs. HOIST addresses issues with disproportionate energy-drain and managing geographically segregated deployment areas by leveraging the innate benefits of a hierarchical network model. HOIST also uses basic mobility-aware systems, such as the modified lifetime, in order to responsively react to the presence of both Messenger and Observer sinks.

7. ACKNOWLEDGEMENT

This material is based upon work supported by the National Science Foundation under Grant No. CNS-1116122 and CNS-1205453.

8. REFERENCES

[1] T. Winter et al., *RPL: IPv6 Routing Protocol for Low-Power and Lossy Networks*, RFC 6550 (Proposed Standard), Internet Engineering Task Force Std. 6550, Mar. 2012.

[2] J. Valente et al., "An air-ground wireless sensor network for crop monitoring," *Sensors*, vol. 11, no. 6, pp. 6088–6108, 2011.

[3] N. Grammalidis et al., "A multi-sensor network for the protection of cultural heritage," in *19th European Signal Processing Conference, 2011*, Aug 2011, pp. 889–893.

[4] A. Somova et al., "Deployment and evaluation of a wireless sensor network for methane leak detection," *Sensors and Actuators A: Physical*, vol. 202, pp. 217–225, Nov. 2013.

[5] T. Watteyne et al., "From manet to ietf roll standardization: A paradigm shift in wsn routing protocols," *Communications Surveys Tutorials, IEEE*, vol. 13, no. 4, pp. 688–707, Fourth 2011.

[6] E. Ancillotti, R. Bruno, and M. Conti, "Reliable data delivery with the ietf routing protocol for low-power and lossy networks," *IEEE Transactions on Industrial Informatics*, vol. 10, no. 3, pp. 1864–1877, Aug 2014.

[7] M. Di Francesco, S. K. Das, and G. Anastasi, "Data collection in wireless sensor networks with mobile elements: A survey," *ACM Trans. Sen. Netw.*, vol. 8, no. 1, pp. 7:1–7:31, Aug. 2011.

[8] Y. Gu, F. Ren, Y. Ji, and J. Li, "The evolution of sink mobility management in wireless sensor networks: A survey," *IEEE Communications Surveys Tutorials*, vol. PP, no. 99, pp. 1–1, 2015.

[9] J. Lloret et al., "A cluster-based architecture to structure the topology of parallel wireless sensor networks," *Sensors*, vol. 9, no. 12, p. 10513, 2009.

[10] P. Ding, J. Holliday, and A. Celik, "Distributed energy-efficient hierarchical clustering for wireless sensor networks," in *Proceedings of the First IEEE International Conference on Distributed Computing in Sensor Systems*, ser. DCOSS'05. Berlin, Heidelberg: Springer-Verlag, 2005, pp. 322–339.

[11] C.-C. Huang et al., "Hierarchical role-based data dissemination in wireless sensor networks," *The Journal of Supercomputing*, vol. 66, no. 1, pp. 35–56, 2013.

[12] C.-J. Lin, P.-L. Chou, and C.-F. Chou, "Hcdd: Hierarchical cluster-based data dissemination in wireless sensor networks with mobile sink," in *Proceedings of the 2006 International Conference on Wireless Communications and Mobile Computing*, ser. IWCMC '06. New York, NY, USA: ACM, 2006, pp. 1189–1194.

[13] R. Shah et al., "Data MULEs: modeling a three-tier architecture for sparse sensor networks," in *Proceedings of the First IEEE International Workshop on Sensor Network Protocols and Applications, 2003.*, May 2003, pp. 30–41.

[14] M. Zhao and Y. Yang, "A framework for mobile data gathering with load balanced clustering and mimo uploading," in *INFOCOM, 2011 Proceedings IEEE*, April 2011, pp. 2759–2767.

[15] Y. Yang et al., "Opportunities for wsn for facilitating fire emergency response," in *5th International Conference on Information and Automation for Sustainability (ICIAFs), 2010*, Dec 2010.

[16] S. Basagni, A. Carosi, and C. Petrioli, "Controlled vs. uncontrolled mobility in wireless sensor networks: Some performance insights," in *IEEE 66th Vehicular Technology Conference, 2007. VTC-2007 Fall.*, Sept 2007, pp. 269–273.

[17] M. Perillo, Z. Cheng, and W. Heinzelman, "An analysis of strategies for mitigating the sensor network hot spot problem," in *The Second Annual International Conference on Mobile and Ubiquitous Systems: Networking and Services, 2005. MobiQuitous 2005.*, July 2005, pp. 474–478.

[18] D. Carels et al., "Support of multiple sinks via a virtual root for the rpl routing protocol," *EURASIP Journal on Wireless Communications and Networking*, vol. 2014, no. 1, 2014.

[19] O. Gaddour et al., "Co-rpl: Rpl routing for mobile low power wireless sensor networks using corona mechanism," in *9th IEEE International Symposium on Industrial Embedded Systems (SIES), 2014*, June 2014, pp. 200–209.

[20] V. Safdar et al., "A hybrid routing protocol for wireless sensor networks with mobile sinks," in *7th International Symposium on Wireless and Pervasive Computing (ISWPC), 2012*, July 2012, pp. 1–5.

[21] G. E. P. Box and M. E. Muller, "A note on the generation of random normal deviates," *Ann. Math. Statist.*, vol. 29, no. 2, pp. 610–611, 06 1958.

[22] P. Levis et al., *The Trickle Algorithm*, RFC 6206 (Standards Track), Internet Engineering Task Force Std. 6206, Mar. 2011.

[23] "Skate." [Online]. Available: http://www.aurora.aero/products/skate.aspx

An Efficient Burst Transmission Scheme for Wireless Sensor Networks

Zeeshan Ansar, Jianjun Wen, Eyuel Debebe Ayele, Waltenegus Dargie
Chair for Computer Networks, Faculty of Computer Science, Technical University of Dresden
01062 Dresden, Germany
{zeeshan.ansar, jianjun.wen, eyuel.ayele, waltenegus.dargie}@tu-dresden.de

ABSTRACT

This paper addresses link quality fluctuation and its impact on the packet delivery capacity of wireless sensor networks. Independent studies have previously confirmed that link quality fluctuates even in a static deployment and understanding stable durations, good and bad alike, can contribute to the efficient transmission of packets. We propose a two stage Markov model to characterise link quality fluctuation and to determine when and for how long nodes should transmit packets in burst. Both to develop and test our model, we deployed a wireless sensor network consisting of 14 nodes in a garden and transmitted more than 120,000 packets with different links. The experiment results confirm that our approach improved the packet delivery capacity of the links by up to 40% when compared with a baseline and by up to 25% when compared with a scheme that employs conditional distribution functions.

Keywords

Burst transmission; link quality estimation; link quality fluctuation; wireless link

1. INTRODUCTION

In many wireless sensor networks the nodes are deployed on the objects or embedded into the processes they monitor, which considerably influence the quality of communication between nodes. For example, in structural health monitoring, the oscillation of a bridge, in water quality monitoring, the water and the movement of water, in healthcare applications the movement of people, in precision agriculture the movement and the shadow of plants affect the quality of an established link. Fluctuation of link quality in turn has a negative impact on successful packet delivery for applications which require high goodput and for most relay nodes which should aggregate and forward packets towards a base station. Furthermore, repeated retransmission of lost packets increases not only latency at all levels of communication but also energy consumption which may reduce the

MSWiM'15 November 02-06, 2015, Cancun, Mexico
© 2015 ACM.ISBN 978-1-4503-3762-5/15/11...$15.00
DOI: http://dx.doi.org/10.1145/2811587.2811622

lifetime of the entire network. Hence, efficient transmission schemes that take channel characteristics (statistics) into account are critical to improve the reliability and lifetime of the networks.

At present, the duty of dealing with link quality fluctuation mainly rests on the physical layer components, which employ strategies such as dynamic rate adaptation, dynamic channel allocation, or dynamic transmission power adjustment to maintain link quality. These strategies, however, have a limited scope because they can deal only with short-term fluctuations. For example, a node may increase its transmission power to deal with link quality fluctuation; by doing so, however, it affects other nearby nodes which may also increase their transmission power to deal with the new change. The same can be said of dynamic channel allocation. To the best of our knowledge, existing transceivers complying with the IEEE 802.15.4 do not support dynamic rate adaptation. Alternatively, the MAC layer can deal with link quality fluctuation by providing efficient packet transmission schemes that have middle- to long-term scope. One of these schemes can be *burst transmission*, even though it was first proposed to address a different concern, namely, achieving high throughput [2]. The idea is as follows: Instead of making nodes compete for winning a channel for each packet they transmit (as is done with IEEE 802.11 and IEEE 802.15.4 contention-based medium access specifications), nodes are permitted to transmit multiple packets in burst once they win a medium. This scheme disregards short-term fairness but experiment results suggest that it can significantly increase overall network throughput. This same approach can be used to deal with link quality fluctuation. Since wireless sensor networks are deployed for a long time, sufficient statistics can be collected to reason about channel characteristics and from this statistics, it is possible to determine the probability of successfully transmitting n number of packets in succession.

In this paper we propose a two-stage Markov model to deal with link quality fluctuations. The model first classifies link quality into different clusters (or states) and determines the transition probability between the states. Secondly, it estimate the average duration of a link staying in a state and the optimal number of packets that can be transmitted in this state. As a summary, the contributions of the paper are the following: (1) Using data collected from our sensor network, we study the temporal characteristic of channel state variations. (2) Using discrete Markov models, we establish a relationship between a state and the optimal number of packets that can be transmitted in burst. (3) We quantitatively compare the throughput of our model with two approaches, namely, (a) a baseline burst transmission in which no scheme is used to determine the number of packets that should be transmitted in succession and (b) a previous approach which uses Bayesian Estimation [10] to determine the optimal burst size. The rest of this paper is organized as follows: In Section 2, we review work on link quality fluctuation and link quality characterisation in detail. In Section 3, we introduce our approach and the three steps required to develop our transmission scheme. In Section 4, we provide quantitative evaluation of our model and compare it with existing approaches. Finally in Section 5, we provide concluding remarks and future work.

2. RELATED WORK

Link quality fluctuation and its impact on the energy-efficiency and the quality of service of wireless sensor networks is an active research area, particularly in the context of 802.15.4 standard. Different approaches and metrics have been employed to characterise the quality of wireless links. Experimental observations suggest that link quality can be broadly categorised into perfect, intermediate, or poor. They also suggest that it exhibits bursty characteristic [9]. Dealing or copping with these aspects is of paramount importance to deploy and use reliable networks. One approach adopted by the research community is setting in place packet transmission schemes at the MAC layer which take knowledge of link quality fluctuation into consideration. In [6], the authors use the SNR values of RTS/CTS control messages to learn about the current state of a link and to decide whether data packets should be transmitted or withheld. The decision is made by employing a Markov decision process (MDP). In [3], the authors propose cooperative communication between sensor nodes to take advantage of diversity gain to overcome the effect of fading channels. Liu et al. [4] propose a data transmission algorithm that uses a Hidden Markov Model. It delays packet transmissions to overcome periods of poor channel quality and high interference while ensuring that the throughput requirement of an application is met. Srinivasan et al. [9] propose a β metric to compute the burstiness of a link. The β factor of a link is a measure of approximation to an ideal link. A value of $\beta = 1$ and $\beta = 0$ represents a perfectly correlated link and an uncorrelated link, respectively. The β metric is calculated by evaluating the distance between a conditional probability delivery function (CPDF) of a given link and an ideal link. The CPDF is a measure of the probability of successful reception of the next packet after n consecutive successes or failures. The authors propose a transmission control scheme as a performance measure of the β metric. This scheme is intended to increase the packet reception ratio by transmitting packets in bursts until a failure is encountered. When a failure occurs, transmission is halted for 500 ms. The limitation of this approach is the requirement of a large amount of data to predict the success of the next packet. Wen et al. [10] propose an offline scheme that uses the conditional probability distribution function of SNR fluctuation to estimate the expected consecutive success and consecutive failure of packet transmission and to adapt the number of packets that can be transmitted in burst followed by a period of pause.

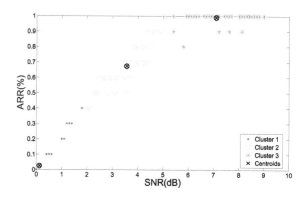

Figure 1: A summary of relationship between the SNR and ARR of a wireless link. SNR is computed as the difference between RSSI and background noise power.

In contrast to the proposed approaches, we aim to provide a middle- to long-term solution for dealing with link quality fluctuation. Our approach extends the idea of burst transmission both to increase network throughput and to gather sufficient statistics pertaining to link quality fluctuation and to use this knowledge for determining when and for how long nodes should transmit packet in burst.

3. LINK QUALITY MODEL

Most existing off-the-shelf transceivers make link quality indicator metrics available to higher layer services including received signal strength indicator (RSSI), link quality indicator (LQI), and background noise level. Unfortunately, it is not possible to establish deterministic relationships between these metrics and successful packet delivery. Packets can be successfully transmitted with a certain probability even when the metrics indicate that the link is bad; and lost even when they indicate that it is good. One of the metrics used to characterise link quality fluctuation is Acknowledgement Reception Ratio (ARR), which summarises the relationship between successful packet delivery and signal-to-noise ratio (SNR). The metric is computed as follows: First, a sequence of packets are divided into a set of subsequence. Each subsequence is transmitted in succession and each packet in a subsequence is acknowledged when it is successfully received. Then for that subsequence, the ARR is the ratio of the number of successfully received acknowledgement packets to the total number of transmitted packets. The SNR of that subsequence is the average of the successfully received ACK packets. Likewise, all the set of subsequence is transmitted, the ARR is produced for each subsequence, and the corresponding SNR is computed. Then a 2-dimensional graph of ARR vs. SNR is plotted to summarise the relationship between the two quantities (as shown in Figure 1). The merit of this approach is that the quality of a link can be evaluated independent of the distance of separation between the transmitter and the receiver and physical layer parameters such as the transmission power and the specific channel allocated. The weakness of the approach is that for a short duration, the channel's characteristic is assumed to be both symmetrical and correlated to account for the SNR of lost packets. We adopt this approach to evaluate the effect of link quality fluctuation on successful packet delivery.

3.1 Clustering

In most practical settings, the quality of a link does not stay at a certain level for so long; instead it fluctuates between different levels. For tractability, these levels can be categorised into a few countable and non-overlapping regions and the average ARR of these regions can be considered to characterise link quality. Previously, different authors have classified these regions into good ($ARR \approx 1$), intermediate ($0.9 \leq ARR \leq 0.1$) and poor ($ARR < 0.1$) states [1, 9]. However, a strict classification of link quality into fixed regions is not realistic, because physical links have individual characteristics. Unlike previous approaches, we use K-mean clustering to determine the optimal number of clusters that best describe the distinct states of a link.

For $n >> 1$, let A_n be a discrete sequence of successfully acknowledged (1) and lost (0) packets. From this sequence, it is possible to establish the (ARR, SNR) pairs for this sequence. For example, Figure 1 displays the (ARR, SNR) distribution for one of the links we considered in our experiment (of which we shall give a detail account in Section 4). The K-mean clustering algorithm [5] can be applied on this vector with the goal of partitioning it into k mutually independent clusters, each cluster with its centroid representing a link quality state. The K-means treats each value of (ARR, SNR) pair as an object. Hence, similar objects are located close to each other, thus forming a cluster. To determine the optimal number of clusters for a given link, we employed the *silhouette method* [8], which iteratively compares the average distance between points within a cluster and across clusters to determine the number of clusters that can distinctly categorise a dataset. We begin with 2 clusters and increase the number of clusters until we obtain an optimal measure of distinctness.

3.2 State Transition Probabilities

After clustering, the next step is determining the probability of transitions between the clusters (signifying link quality fluctuation) during a continuous transmission of packets. This can be done using a first order Markov chain [7]. In this approach, time is divided into discrete slots and packets are transmitted in burst in each slot (for our case, we set the burst size to 10). Using the acknowledgement packets in each slot, the ARR, the average SNR, and the link quality state (cluster) are determined as discussed above. After a sufficiently large number of packets are transmitted and the ARR, SNR, and link quality state of subsequent slots are estimated likewise, the fluctuation in link quality is described by a state transition probability, which is computed as follows:

$$a_{ij} = P(S_j | S_i) = \frac{N_{i \to j}}{\sum_{m=1}^{M} N_{i \to m}} \qquad (1)$$

where M is the total number of states and N is the number of transitions. An interesting aspect of Equation 1 is the possibility of asking (and answering) the following question: Given the channel is in a known state in the beginning of slot τ, what is the probability that it stays in the same state for the next d slots (as expressed by Equation 1). This is an important question because it directly addresses the question of link stability.

$$o = \left\{ \begin{array}{ccccc} S_n, & S_n, & S_n & S_n, & S_m \\ 1 & 2 & 3 \ \cdots\cdots & d & d+1 \end{array} \neq S_n \right\} \qquad (2)$$

The question can be answered using the following expression:

$$P_n(d) = (a_{nn})^d (1 - a_{nn}) \qquad (3)$$

Where a_{nn} is the probability that the link quality is in state n and remains in the same state in the next time slot. Note that the plot of $P_n(d)$ for all d gives the probability mass function for state n, from which it is possible to determine the expected number of slots the link quality stays in state n:

$$\bar{d}_n = \sum_{d=1}^{\infty} d P_n(d) = \frac{1}{1 - a_{nn}} \qquad (4)$$

3.3 Slot Scheduling

The long-term link quality fluctuation can be estimated using Equations 1 and 4. In the beginning c packets are transmitted in burst and based on the ARR of that slot, the state of the link quality is estimated. Then using Equation 4, the expected number of slots in which the link quality remains in the same state is estimated. Once the expected number of slots are utilised, the next state is estimated using Equation 1 and then the same process is repeated all over again. This approach however has two limitations. Firstly, because the transition between states is a probabilistic quantity, the approach will always choose the transition with the highest probability. However, a state transition with a low probability does not mean the transition does not occur. Secondly, once a wrong transition is chosen, the subsequent $\bar{d}_n$ slots computed by Equation 4 for that state do not reflect the actual link quality state. To deal with these problems we introduced two correction factors. Firstly, to correct the error that occurs due to wrong transitions, the transmission schemes takes periodic measurement and reestimate the channel states; if there is a discrepancy between the latest estimated state and the state determined by the transition probability, then the latest state is taken as the present channel state. Secondly, to enable transition into states with low transition probabilities, we randomised the transition process as follows: $randomselect(S, A)$, where $S = (S_j, S_k, ..., S_n)$ and $A = (a_{ij}, a_{ik}, ..., a_{in})$.

3.4 Burst Size Determination

After the state sequence is determined, the next step is determining the number of packets that should be transmitted in burst in each state. The goal is minimising the number of lost packets. Once again we employ a first order Markov chain for this step but this time we fix the number of states to two, success (1) and failure (0). The sequence of received acknowledgement packets during a test phase is used to determine the state transition probabilities. Consider Figure 2 in which after 10 packets are transmitted in burst, the sequence of acknowledgement packets is given. From the sequence of acknowledgement packets, it can be seen that there are altogether 9 transitions: once from 0 to 0, twice from 0 to 1, twice from 1 to 0 and four times from 1 to 1. Hence the state transitions probabilities, in respective order, are: $a_{00} = \frac{1}{9}, a_{01} = \frac{2}{9}, a_{10} = \frac{2}{9}, a_{11} = \frac{4}{9}$. Once the state transition probabilities are determined, the expected number of burst size can be calculated once again by applying Equation 4. It must be noted that the sequence obtained in Figure 2 is not sufficient to produce reliable statistics. In reality, repeated experiments are conducted to obtain the state transition probabilities.

Figure 2: Sequence of acknowledgement packets signifying successful or failed packets transmission and the determination of state transition probabilities.

Table 1: A summary of physical land link layer parameters used to establish 6 links.

	link1	link2	link3	link4	link5	link6
Nodes	(2,11)	(4,9)	(2,12)	(3,7)	(5,10)	(1,4)
d (m)	27	19	35	8	23	15
p (dBm)	-10	-3	-15	-3	-15	-10

4. EVALUATION

To gather statistics pertaining to link quality fluctuation and to evaluate our scheme, we deployed a wireless sensor network consisting of 14 TelosB sensor nodes in a garden (Figure 3). The distance between the nodes was chosen arbitrarily and varied from 8 to 35 m. The nodes established direct links with each other to communicate packets. We selected 6 of these links and transmitted more than 120,000 packets. Table 1 summarises the links we selected for our evaluation and the transmission parameters for each link. Figure 4 displays the packet loss for all the links during a burst transmission of 2000 packets, to demonstrates how link quality fluctuation of even a static deployment impacts packet delivery (packet loss varied between 20 and 70%). Even though packets were transmitted in burst, we set the inter packet interval (IPI) duration to 20 ms, so that each node has sufficient time to receive packets and to store link quality metrics locally. With the statistics we obtained, we determined offline (1) the number of distinct link quality states for each link using the K-mean clustering algorithm, (2) the link quality state transition probabilities, (3) the expected duration a link remains in the same state, and (3) the expected number of packets that can be transmitted in burst for each state. We compared our strategy with (a) a base line in which packets are transmitted in burst without taking knowledge of link quality fluctuation into account and (b) a model we proposed previously [10] and uses the conditional probability distribution function to estimate the expected stable duration of a link, where stability is defined as the link quality staying above a set threshold.

4.1 Cluster Size

As we already mentioned above, previous studies suggest that link quality can be categorised into three fixed states, namely, good (perfect), intermediate (bursty) and bad. While this is a plausible classification, it may not apply for all types of links. In our investigation, we considered different values of k and measured the packet delivery capacity of the links. Figure 5 compares our packet transmission scheme for different values of k with the baseline. The measurement was obtained by transmitting 1000 packets for each test case and for each of the links. For our scheme we considered cluster sizes of 2, 3, and 4. As can be seen from the figure, our transmission scheme improved packet delivery, regardless of

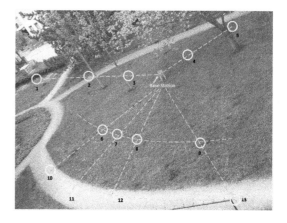

Figure 3: A wireless sensor network deployed in a garden to investigate the fluctuation of link quality over time (circles are added to highlight the position of the nodes). TelosB sensor platforms integrating CC2420 radio were used to establish the network.

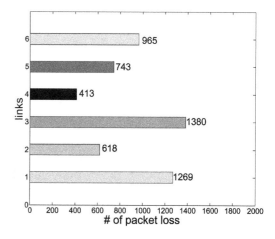

Figure 4: Number of packet lost in different links during burst transmission.

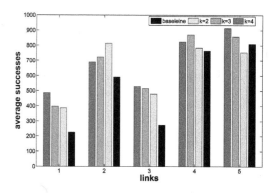

Figure 5: Comparison of the packet delivery capacity of different links with different values for k.

the value of k. Nevertheless, for link 1, 3, and 5, the value of k that resulted in the highest packet delivery was 4, whereas for link 2, it was 2, and for link 3 it was 3. This clearly indicates that the cluster size depends on the specific nature of a link.

4.2 Packet Delivery Capacity

After we determined the optimal cluster size for each link, we compared our transmission scheme with both the baseline and our previous transmission scheme. To test the reproducibility of our scheme, we varied the number of packets we transmitted in burst as follows: 500, 1000, 2000, 3000, 4000, 5000, and 10000. In the present transmission scheme, burst transmission takes place within a single state followed by a pause before a state transition takes place, which means, the maximum burst size within a state is bound by the expected duration of the state whereas in the previous scheme there is no notion of state and a burst can have any size. Figure 6 compares the performance of our transmission scheme with the baseline and with our previous scheme. For this particular case, we transmitted 1000 packets. Both schemes produced appreciable gain compared to the baseline (confirming to the importance of efficient transmission scheme at the MAC layer) but the present scheme outperformed the previous one in almost all the test cases.

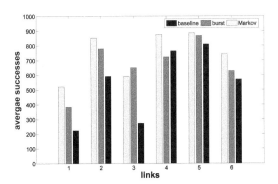

Figure 6: Comparison of the packet delivery capacity of our transmission scheme with the baseline and a previous scheme based on conditional CDFs of SNR.

5. CONCLUSION

In this paper we studied link quality fluctuation in a static deployment and proposed a two-stage Markov model to predict stable durations to schedule packet transmission in these durations only. Our approach is realised in three steps: First the link quality fluctuation is divided into countable regions using a K-mean clustering algorithm. We employed the *silhouette method* to identify the optimal number of regions that sufficiently characterise link quality fluctuation. We considered these regions as states to model link quality fluctuation as a discrete Markov process. Second, we used statistics from ARR vs. SNR relationship to determine off-line the state transition probabilities. Using state transition probabilities, we computed the expected duration a link stays in a given state. Third, for each state, we estimated the number of packets that can be transmitted in burst by applying a discrete Markov process on the binary sequence we constructed from received acknowledgement packages. We

tested our approaches using an outdoor deployment consisting of on 14 TelosB nodes. The experiments results confirm that our approach improves the packet delivery capacity of wireless links. Altogether, we transmitted more than 50,000 packets to obtain sufficient statistics for our model and more than 70,000 packets to evaluate the model. Our approach improved the packet delivery capacity of the links by up to 40% when compared with the baseline approach and by up to 25% when compared with the scheme that employs conditional CDF.

6. ACKNOWLEDGMENTS

This work has been partially funded by the German Research Foundation (DFG) under project agreement: DA 1211/5-1.

7. REFERENCES

[1] M. H. Alizai, O. Landsiedel, J. Á. B. Link, S. Götz, and K. Wehrle. Bursty traffic over bursty links. In *Proceedings of the 7th International Conference on Embedded Networked Sensor Systems, SenSys 2009, Berkeley, California, USA, November 4-6, 2009*, pages 71–84, 2009.

[2] S. Duquennoy, F. Österlind, and A. Dunkels. Lossy links, low power, high throughput. In *Proceedings of the 9th ACM Conference on Embedded Networked Sensor Systems*, SenSys '11, pages 12–25, New York, NY, USA, 2011. ACM.

[3] W. Fang, Q. Zhou, Z. Wang, and Q. Liu. An adaptive transmission scheme for wireless sensor networks. *International Journal of Future Generation Communication & Networking*, 6(1), 2013.

[4] S. Liu, R. Srivastava, C. E. Koksal, and P. Sinha. Pushback: A hidden markov model based scheme for energy efficient data transmission in sensor networks. *Ad Hoc Networks*, 7(5):973 – 986, 2009.

[5] S. P. Lloyd. Least squares quantization in PCM. *IEEE Transactions on Information Theory*, 28(2):129–136, 1982.

[6] C. V. Phan, Y. Park, H. Choi, J. Cho, and J. G. Kim. An energy-efficient transmission strategy for wireless sensor networks. *Consumer Electronics, IEEE Transactions on*, 56(2):597–605, May 2010.

[7] L. R. Rabiner. A tutorial on hidden markov models and selected applications in speech recognition. In *PROCEEDINGS OF THE IEEE*, pages 257–286, 1989.

[8] P. Rousseeuw. Silhouettes: A graphical aid to the interpretation and validation of cluster analysis. *J. Comput. Appl. Math.*, 20(1):53–65, Nov. 1987.

[9] K. Srinivasan, M. A. Kazandjieva, S. Agarwal, and P. Levis. The beta-factor: measuring wireless link burstiness. In *Proceedings of the 6th International Conference on Embedded Networked Sensor Systems, SenSys 2008, Raleigh, NC, USA, November 5-7, 2008*, pages 29–42, 2008.

[10] J. Wen, Z. Ansar, and W. Dargie. A link quality estimation model for energy-efficient wireless sensor networks. In *IEEE,International Conference on Communications, ICC 2015, London, England, June 8-12, 2015*, 2015.

Connected P-Percent Coverage in Wireless Sensor Networks based on Degree Constraint Dominating Set Approach

Habib Mostafaei
Department of Computer
Engineering
Urmia Branch, Islamic Azad
University, Urmia, Iran
h.mostafaei@iaurmia.ac.ir

Morshed U. Chowdhury
School of Information
Technology,
Deakin University, Melbourne,
Australia
muc@deakin.edu.au

Rafiqul Islam
School of Computing and
Mathematics
Charles Sturt University-
Australia
mislam@csu.edu.au

Hojjat Gholizadeh
Department of Computer
Engineering and IT, Amirkabir
University of Technology,
Tehran,Iran
h.gholizadeh@aut.ac.ir

ABSTRACT

In this paper, we propose an algorithm for connected p-percent coverage problem in Wireless Sensor Networks(WSNs) to improve the overall network life time. In this work, we investigate the p-percent coverage problem(PCP) in WSNs which requires p% of an area should be monitored correctly and to find out any additional requirements of the connected p-percent coverage problem. We propose pDCDS algorithm which is a learning automaton based algorithm for PCP. pDCDS is a Degree-constrained Connected Dominating Set based algorithm which detect the minimum number of nodes to monitor an area. The simulation results demonstrate that pDCDS can remarkably improve the network lifetime.

Categories and Subject Descriptors

C.2 [**Computer-Communication Networks**]: Miscellaneous; C.2.1 [**Network Architecture and Design**]: Wireless communication

General Terms

Theory

Keywords

Connected P-percent Coverage; Degree-constrained Connected Dominating Set; Learning Automata(LA); Wireless Sensor Networks(WSNs);

MSWiM'15, November 2–6, 2015, Cancun, Mexico.
ⓒ 2015 ACM. ISBN 978-1-4503-3762-5/15/11 ...$15.00.
DOI: http://dx.doi.org/10.1145/2811587.2811624.

1. INTRODUCTION

Wireless Sensor Networks (WSNs) have found many attractions in various applications during recent years. These networks are constructed from a set of tiny sensor nodes which have many resource constraints and they used for different applications such as border surveillance and etc. Therefore, preserving the network resource is a key factor. Increasing network life time is the most important concerns in many applications. To reach to this goal one of the common approaches is to turn off some deployed nodes in networks and then activate later. This task is done by scheduling algorithms in WSNs. Coverage is one of the essential requirements of WSNs. In this study we need to monitor an area of interest or an event by sensors. In full coverage applications of WSNs, it is necessary to monitor all regions of a network. On the other hand, in some other applications of WSNs, special percentage of network need to be monitored. Therefore, we focus on p-percent of coverage area instead of full coverage. In this problem p% of network area is required to be monitored by sensor nodes and in addition the connectivity between nodes is also mandatory. In recent years, several algorithms have been proposed by literatures to improve network life time in WSNs for many coverage problems such as *full area coverage*, *target coverage*, and *barrier coverage*. But, there are a few works have been done to address the Connected p-Percent Coverage problem.

The idea of connected dominating set (CDS) has recently emerged as a new solution to solve the energy-efficient coverage in WSNs. In this study, we propose an algorithm based on degree- constrained connected dominating set and learning automaton to prolong network lifetime and maintain the network connectivity of the Connected p-Percent Coverage. The proposed algorithm is called p-Degree Constrained Connected Dominating Set (pDCDS). The main contributions of this study are: 1) proposed algorithm can select small number of sensor nodes to monitor the network requirements. 2)It uses a low time complexity to find the number of required nodes compared with similar methods.

2. RELATED WORKS

Coverage problem is widely studied in WSNs during recent years. This problem can be classified into three categories, *target coverage*, *area coverage*, and *barrier coverage*. Wang [13] surveyed coverage problems in WSNs. First, target coverage problem which is the main objective to monitor a set of targets with sensor nodes. In contrast to p-percent coverage, in target coverage all deployed targets should be monitored [6, 9, 7]. However the full coverage goal is to detect full network area instead of known targets with deployed sensor nodes in WSNs. Some recent literature in the field of area coverage can be found in [1]. In barrier coverage, the network's barrier should be monitored by selected nodes [5, 8, 12]. There are many works in the area of full coverage problem in WSNs but according to our knowledge a limited number of works have been done in the area of connected p-percent coverage. In [4] authors devised two methods to preserve p-percent coverage in WSNs. One of their algorithms is centralized and the other one is a distributed approach. Their algorithms can guarantee both coverage and connectivity requirements but failed to achieve low time complexity. Wu et al. [14] also presented two algorithms for addressing this problem. The first algorithm is named pPCA and it is a greedy based manner to solve p-percent coverage problem. The second one is called CpPCA-CDS which is a distributed approach. The main drawback of this work is that it's performance depends on DFS search. Therefore, time complexity of their algorithm increases with applying DFS search to find the solutions. A probabilistic way to find redundant sensor nodes in network while preserving partial coverage requirements is proposed in [3]. However the proposed algorithm does not guarantee the connectivity of sensor nodes.

In this study, we focus on connected p-percent coverage problem in WSNs and to assure connectivity in scattered network by using connected dominating set mode. We use from the attributes of degree-constrained connected dominating set (DCDS) to our algorithm. Our algorithm uses small number of sensor nodes in any given time of network to monitor the network area.

3. PRELIMINARIES AND PROBLEM DEFINITION

In this section we outline basic definitions for p-percent coverage and connected p-percent coverage. We first define required definitions to explain more about Connected p-Percent Coverage problem in a WSN and then we state the problem.

Definition1: p-Percent Coverage problem given an area Ω and N sensors in which Ω is covered p% by a subset of deployed sensors.

Here, a subset of sensors may not be connected, therefore, we define connected p-percent coverage problem.

Definition2: Connected p-Percent Coverage problem given an area and discover a connected p-percent cover set with minimum number of required nodes.

Definition3: A wireless sensor network, suppose a two-dimensional area Ω with N nodes and two sensors are deployed at the same location. It is not required to cover 100% of network area and we assume that only p% of network should be covered.

Definition4: Working nodes ratio $\phi = {}^{n}/_{N}$ where n is the number of active sensors which are responsible to cover p% of network area and N is the overall number of deployed sensors.

Definition5: coverage graph of a network modeled by a weighted, connected, and undirected graph $<V,E,W>$ where V is a set of sensor $V = \{S_1, S_2, ..., S_n\}$ and E is communications link between sensors in network and W. Where W is weights that are in associated with each node. In this work we use Euclidean distance of nodes to determine the value of W in the graph.

Definition6: A CDS (connected dominating set) is a connected subset of the graph nodes such that every node of the graph can be in the set or in the adjacent to at least one node of the set. Let us assume that $G = (V,E)$ is an *undirected* graph, a subset $D(D \subseteq V)$ is a CDS of G if for each node $u \in V$, u is either in D or there exists a node $v \in D$ such that $uv \in E$ and the sub-graph induced by D, i.e., $G(V)$, is connected.

Definition7: A degree-constrained minimum-weight CDS (DCDS) seeks the CDS with the minimum weight subject to a degree-constraint d. A DCDS is a CDS in which no node has a degree greater than a predefined degree-constraint [5].

Problem: How to schedule the nodes in such a way that the network area covered p-percent by minimum number of nodes while the network is connected.

4. LEARNING AUTOMATON

Learning Automaton (LA) has a finite number of actions that can operate in unknown random environment (RE). After selecting an action by an automaton it applies the selected action to a random environment. The RE generates a signal to applied action and gives a grade to the chosen action of automaton. The generated reply from RE is used by automaton to update the vector of action probability. By running this procedure, the automaton learns to choose an optimal action among action set. The environment can be described by the triple $E = \{\alpha, \beta, c\}$ where $\alpha = \{\alpha_1, \alpha_2, ..., \alpha_n\}$ indicates a finite input set or actions, $\beta = \{\beta_1, \beta_2, ..., \beta_n\}$ indicates the output set that can be given by reinforcement signals, and $c = \{c_1, c_2, ..., c_r\}$ indicates a set of penalty probabilities, where each element c_i of c corresponds to one input of action α_i. The environment can be categorized into three models based on reinforcement signals: P-model, Q-model, and S-model. In P-model environment β can choose only two binary values 0 or 1. In Q-model environment β can take value in the interval (0, 1). The reinforcement signal situates in the interval [a, b] in S-model environments. Learning automata (LA) are classified into fixed-structure and variable-structure stochastic. Here, we consider only variable-structure automata [10] in our algorithm. A learning algorithm can be defined as follows $p(n + 1) = T[p(n), \alpha(n), \beta(n)]$. Let us assume that $\alpha(k)$ denotes the chosen action and also p(k) indicates the action probability vector of chosen action by LA at instant k. A linear learning algorithm updates the action probability vector of p by eq(1). Let $\alpha_1(k)$ be the action chosen by the automaton at instant k.

$$p_i(n + 1) = p_i(n) + a(1 - p_i(n))$$
$$p_j(n + 1) = (1 - a)p_j(n) \quad \forall j, j \neq i \tag{1}$$

when the action taken is rewarded by the environment and

$$p_i(n+1) = (1-b)p_i(n))$$
$$p_j(n+1) = \frac{b}{r-1}(1-b)p_j(n) \quad \forall j, j \neq i \qquad (2)$$

where a and b indicate the reward and penalty parameters and r is the number of actions that occur. For the case of $a = b$, the learning algorithm is called the Linear Reward-Inaction(L_{R-I})algorithm, for the case of b<<a, it is called the "Linear Reward epsilon Penalty($L_{R-\varepsilon P}$)" algorithm, and for the case of $b = 0$, it is called the "Linear Reward–Penalty(L_{R-P})" algorithm. In [6, 7, 5, 8, 1] a number of applications of LA in wireless sensor networks are introduced.

5. PDCDS ALGORITHM

In this section we describe pDCDS algorithm to address connected p-percent coverage problem in WSNs by modelling with degree-constrained minimum-weight CDS (DCDS) the degree-constrained minimum-weight CDS (DCDS) detects a CDS with the minimum weight where the weight associated with each sensor node is defined as the sum of its neighbours residual energy level. The subject of DCDS is to put a degree-constraint d on CDS. pDCDS aims at constructing the long-lived energy-efficient network while keeping the network covered. We assign a learning automaton to each deployed node in a network and LA of each node for a set of action. Sensor S_i sends an ACTION message for discovering its neighbors and also to create the action-set of learning automaton Ai. This node initially sends the ACTION message with the maximum transmission range. Every neighbor receiving the ACTION message and replies it. Sensor node S_i waits for a specific period of time to receive the replies. Action set of each node is modelled by $\alpha_i = \{\alpha_1, \alpha_2, \ldots, \alpha_r\}$ for i = (1, 2, ..., r). The initial value for action probability vector of each sensor is defined as follow.

$$p_i^j(k) = \frac{1}{|\alpha_i(k)|} \; ; \; \forall \alpha_i^j \in \alpha_i \text{ and k = 0} \qquad (3)$$

where $|\alpha_i(k)|$ indicates the action-set count at stage k, which is equal to the number of neighbours nodes N_i in this stage and p_i^j shows the choice probability of actionα_j, and selecting action α_j means that the working node is selected. At first, we randomly select a node and name it as current node to construct a DCDS and add this node to φ_k. All sensor nodes in φ_k form a CDS in our proposed algorithm. This node randomly selects one of its action. Choosing an action by LA of this node is equal to selecting one node in its neighbour's list. The other neighbours of current node add to ψ_k set. At this stage each dominator acts as follows. If $E_i < E_{avg}$ and $d_i > \lambda$ LA of dominator penalize the selected action otherwise the selected action will reward. Here, E_i and E_{avg} denotes residual energy of dominator i at stage k and average energy of neighbours' node respectively. Also, d_i indicates degree of dominator i. The value of this parameter shows a number of neighbour's node of each selected dominator by pDCDS method. In the DCDS approach we use degree parameter to give reward/penalty to chosen action by learning automaton. This process continues until $\varphi_k + \psi_k = N$. This means that each node in network is known about its status after this process end. After this phase, each sensor node belongs either to φ_k or ψ_k set. To find a proper subset of nodes to monitor p-percent coverage we repeat this operation k times. Here, we assume that k parameter shows the number of learning steps in pDCDS algorithm. After constructing a degree-constrained minimum-weight CDS by our algorithm. The pDCDS algorithm examines that p-percent coverage requirements is met or not. If p is satisfied, then it is done. Otherwise, each node in φ_k selects a dominate neighbour and updates the p percentage. This procedure stops when p percentage is satisfied. The selected nodes by LA of each node will be active to do p-percent coverage operations and other nodes will be selected on the next rounds of pDCDS algorithm.

THEOREM 1. *The obtained set from pDCDS is connected and can p-percent cover the whole area.*

PROOF. To prove this theorem, firstly, we build a degree-constrained minimum-weight CDS. According to the property of a CDS, each sensor which is not in φ_k must have a neighbour in φ_k and φ_k is connected. Therefore, each node that want to add to φ_k keep φ_k connected. Additionally, added dominate neighbors to φ_k guarantee p-percent coverage of whole area. □

5.1 Time Complexity analysis

In this section, we analyse on time complexity of pDCDS algorithm. Let us assume that V and E be the number of deployed nodes and the number of edge, respectively. Therefore, the average node degree is $O(\chi) = (^E/_V)$. In pDCDS, the main time complexity lies in the learning phase. The other phase of pDCDS can be accomplished in time complexity of O(V). As mentioned earlier the number of actions that each node can take is equal to the number of edge, therefore this phase needs$O(\chi) \times O(V) = O(E)$. Learning automata of each node needs O(E) to select its action. Therefore, each node in learning phase can select one of its edge. Let us assume that iteration number of learning phase is k. As claimed above, the overall time complexity of pDCDS approach is O(KE).

6. EXPERIMENTS

We conducted a number of computer simulation experiments to analyse the performance of pDCDS algorithm. The results of pDCDS approach have been compared with modified CDS method in [2]. A wireless sensor network nodes are randomly scattered in $400m * 400m$ area. We assume that the sensing ranges of all sensor nodes are equal. We set also the value of λ to 7 [1].

In the first experiment, we evaluate the performance of pDCDS algorithm in term of working node ratio and investigate how much lower working node ratio can gain by increasing the sensing range of sensor nodes in deployed network. Here we assume the value of p is 60%. Figure 1.a illustrates the working node ratio of each algorithm. It can be seen from the figure that in proportion as we increase the sensing range of each node, the working node ratio decrease in both approaches. We repeat this experiment to investigate the performance of pDCDS algorithm for different sensor nodes in the deployed network region. In this experiment, we set the sensing of nodes to 50 meter and the value of p to 80%. The outcome of experiment is shown in Figure 1.b. It is evident from the figure that as we increase the number of sensor nodes, the working node ratio decrease in both approaches and our approach pDCDS is performed better in

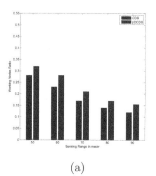 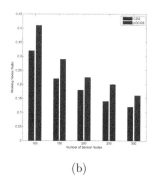 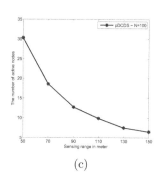 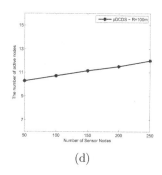

| (a) | (b) | (c) | (d) |

Figure 1: The performance of pDCDS

comparison with CDS approach in term of working nodes ratio. We assess the performance of pDCDS algorithm in term of number of selected active nodes in each subset with fixed number of deployed nodes. To do this, we set the sensing range of each node to 100(m) and p to 80. The result of this experiment is shown in Figure 1.c.We also assess the performance of our proposed algorithm with various sensing range on the number of obtained active nodes in each subset. Figure 1.d shows the obtained result of this experiment with 100 nodes and p to 80 percent. It can be seen from the figure that as much as we increase the sensing range of deployed nodes, the number of selected active nodes by pDCDS sharply decrease. This is due to the following reasons. First, with increasing the sensing range of nodes, the overlaps between sensor nodes are greater and we need small number of nodes required to monitor the network area. Second, with increasing the sensing range learning automaton of each node has better chance to select the proper nodes which has high area coverage contribution. The area coverage contribution is the amount of area which each deployed node in network can sense.

7. CONCLUSION

In this study, we investigate connected p-percent problem in WSNs and devise a degree-constrained minimum-weight connected dominating set to solve the problem. We propose pDCDS algorithm to find nodes to monitor p-percent coverage in deployed network. The proposed approach uses learning automaton to select best dominator and dominatee sensor nodes to cover p-percent coverage. A number of simulation experiments are conducted to study the performance of pDCDS algorithm. The simulations results showed that our pDCDS algorithm performed significantly better than existing similar algorithms.

8. REFERENCES

[1] J. Akbari Torkestani. An adaptive energy-efficient area coverage algorithm for wireless sensor networks. *Ad Hoc Networks*, 11(6):1655–1666, 2013.

[2] K. Donghyun, W. Yiwei, L. Yingshu, Z. Feng, and D. Ding-Zhu. Constructing minimum connected dominating sets with bounded diameters in wireless networks. *Parallel and Distributed Systems, IEEE Transactions on*, 20(2):147–157, 2009.

[3] H. P. Gupta, S. V. Rao, and T. Venkatesh. Sleep scheduling for partial coverage in heterogeneous

wireless sensor networks. In *Communication Systems and Networks (COMSNETS), 2013 Fifth International Conference on*, pages 1–10.

[4] Y. Li, C. Ai, Z. Cai, and R. Beyah. Sensor scheduling for p-percent coverage in wireless sensor networks. *Cluster Computing*, 14(1):27–40, 2011.

[5] H. Mostafaei. Stochastic barrier coverage in wireless sensor networks based on distributed learning automata. *Computer Communications*, 55(1):51–61, 2015.

[6] H. Mostafaei, M. Esnaashari, and M. Meybodi. A coverage monitoring algorithm based on learning automata for wireless sensor networks. *Appl. Math. Inf. Sci.*, 9(3):1317–1325, 2015.

[7] H. Mostafaei and M. Meybodi. Maximizing lifetime of target coverage in wireless sensor networks using learning automata. *Wireless Personal Communications*, 71(2), 2013.

[8] H. Mostafaei and M. Meybodi. An energy efficient barrier coverage algorithm for wireless sensor networks. *Wireless Personal Communications*, 77(3):2099–2115, 2014.

[9] H. Mostafaei and M. Shojafar. A new meta-heuristic algorithm for maximizing lifetime of wireless sensor networks. *Wireless Personal Communications*, 82(2):723–742, 2015.

[10] K. S. Narendra and M. A. L. Thathachar. *Learning automata: An introduction*. Prentice Hall, 1989.

[11] Y. Qianqian, H. Shibo, L. Junkun, C. Jiming, and S. Youxian. Energy-efficient probabilistic area coverage in wireless sensor networks. *Vehicular Technology, IEEE Transactions on*, 64(1):367–377, 2015.

[12] H. Shibo, G. Xiaowen, Z. Junshan, C. Jiming, and S. Youxian. Curve-based deployment for barrier coverage in wireless sensor networks. *Wireless Communications, IEEE Transactions on*, 13(2):724–735, 2014.

[13] B. Wang. Coverage problems in sensor networks: A survey. *ACM Comput. Surv.*, 43(4):1–53, 2011.

[14] Y. Wu, C. Ai, S. Gao, and Y. Li. *p-Percent Coverage in Wireless Sensor Networks*, volume 5258 of *Lecture Notes in Computer Science*, book section 21, pages 200–211. Springer Berlin Heidelberg, 2008.

Minimizing Access Delay for M2M Traffic in Multi-RAT HetNets

Prajwal Osti
Aalto University, Finland
prajwal.osti@aalto.fi

Samuli Aalto
Aalto University, Finland
samuli.aalto@aalto.fi

Pasi Lassila
Aalto University, Finland
pasi.lassila@aalto.fi

ABSTRACT

We study the cell selection techniques for M2M traffic between an LTE macrocell and WLAN femtocells in a heterogeneous network deployment scenario. With the dense deployment of femtocells (operating in WLAN), M2M traffic can primarily be served by them while the macrocell (operating in LTE) can be used by the machines in case of congestion in their own femtocell. We study various load balancing strategies that aid the machines to select a proper cell in such a multi-RAT heterogeneous network deployment scenario so that the access delay for the M2M traffic is minimized. In particular, we derive the optimal static policy of choosing between the WLAN femtocell and the LTE macrocell. In addition, we develop dynamic policies based on the information about the arrivals and the number of backlogged users, and compare their performance against each other and with the optimal static policy. Our results indicate that the potential gains from the dynamic policies can be significant. Moreover, simple backlog-based heuristics perform close to or better than the optimal static policy.

Categories and Subject Descriptors

C.2.1 [**Computer-Communications Networks**]: Network Architecture and Design—*Wireless communication*; C.4 [**Performance of systems**]: Modeling techniques; G.1.6 [**Numerical Analysis**]: Optimization; G.3 [**Probability and Statistics**]: Markov Processes, Queueing Theory

Keywords

CSMA; HetNet; Load Balancing; LTE; M2M; Markov Decision Processes; Random Access; Slotted Aloha; WLAN

1. INTRODUCTION

The dense deployment of wireless devices capable of autonomous communications is expected to put a heavy strain on the network resources. The traditional network may not effectively handle the injection of a massive amount of machine-to-machine (M2M) traffic coming from sensors as they have been designed with the more traditional human-to-human traffic in mind. This problem (and its possible workarounds) has been actively studied in, e.g., [26, 10, 14]. Even the standardizing bodies, such as 3GPP, have been cognizant of this shift in wireless traffic pattern and have been progressively including provisions in the next generation cellular wireless technology, LTE, that aid in M2M communications [1].

The machines are expected to exist in huge numbers and their joint resource demand can easily overwhelm the network, even as early as at the random access (RA) stage [13, 17]. One of the most promising approaches to get around this problem is to deploy the so-called heterogeneous networks [7], in which the large coverage area of a macrocell is overlaid with small femtocells where the traffic demand is high. When densely deployed, the femtos can serve as the primary service providers and the excess traffic is diverted to the macro [16].

In HetNets, the radio access technologies (RAT) at the macro and the femto stations can either be the same (e.g., LTE) or different (WLAN femtos inside LTE macro in a multi-RAT deployment scenario). It has been suggested that the licensed-band operating technologies like LTE offer a significant performance gain over WLANs, which operate in the unlicensed band [19] in femtocells. However, when the issues like mobility and handover are not taken into account and newer versions of WLANs are considered, the performance gain may not be so significant for the LTE femtocells. Moreover, the advent of multimode base stations that can provide both WLAN and LTE coverage makes WLANs a viable and cost-effective alternative for femtocell deployment and some efforts, e.g., [20, 3], are already underway so that the two forms of technologies can smoothly coexist in a multi-RAT HetNet deployment.

In this paper, we study the cell selection problem when the femto stations are operated by WLAN and the macrocell uses LTE. For the macro, we focus just on the first step of the RA procedure that is based on the multichannel Slotted Aloha (MCSA) protocol where each preamble corresponds to an Aloha channel. Thus, a Markov model can be constructed for the macro's backlog [12, 8, 21, 24, 18], similarly as done recently in [23, 9, 16, 2] specifically for the RA of LTE, ignoring the later stages of the RA procedure. For the femtos, we assume that they are based on the CSMA algorithm which is the case with, e.g., IEEE 802.11 WLANs. As in [4, 6, 5], we use a Markov model for femto's backlog. Our

MSWiM'15, November 2–6, 2015, Cancun, Mexico.
© 2015 ACM. ISBN 978-1-4503-3762-5/15/11 ...$15.00.
DOI: http://dx.doi.org/10.1145/2811587.2811602.

objective is to select a proper cell for a new user so that the average access delay is minimized.

We aim to devise optimal or near-to-optimal cell-selection policies, similar to what we have done in [16], where the macro and the femtos are homogeneous from technology point of view, i.e., both of them use MCSA for the access as in LTE. The novelty of the present paper is that we attempt to balance access loads between two technologically heterogeneous systems that operate in discrete time (LTE) and continuous time (CSMA), respectively. With *static policies*, a fixed fraction of femto traffic is assigned to the macro. We are able to explicitly characterize the *optimal static policy* that minimizes the access delay by reducing a complex multidimensional problem to a simpler one-dimensional problem and then iteratively obtain the optimal fractions for each cell. To seek further improvements over the optimal static policy, we use simulations to experiment with different simple *dynamic policies*, inspired by join the shortest queue (JSQ) heuristic. Finally, using the policy iteration algorithm from the theory of Markov Decision Processes that utilizes all the available system state information, we aim at studying the maximal gain from the dynamic policies over the optimal static one.

Our results indicate that it is possible to get better performance using dynamic policies and the amount of gain depends on the system and traffic parameters. They also reveal that the gain using JSQ-based policies can be as high as 30% over the optimal static policies. Furthermore, they show that the gain obtained from the policy iteration approach is even higher. Thus, simple JSQ-based heuristics are not able to provide all the potential gain in such a system.

The paper is organized as follows: Section 2 describes in detail and analyzes the MCSA and CSMA models we use. Then we formulate our cell selection problem in Section 3 and introduce the cell selection policies. This is followed by extensive numerical experiments for various parameter combinations in Section 4. Finally we present our conclusions in Section 5. The characterization of the optimal static policy is provided in Appendix.

2. SYSTEM MODEL AND ANALYSIS

We consider a single LTE macrocell with m WLAN femtocells inside its coverage area. We assume that these femtocells are WLAN Access Points, independent from the macrocell and having their own radio resources.

Our M2M traffic scenario consists of a large population of M2M devices which are asynchronously generating requests to the system. In this case, the arrival of the requests can be well modelled by a Poisson process. More specifically, we assume that each femtocell $i = 1, \ldots, m$, is receiving new connection requests according to a Poisson process at rate λ_i. These requests can be served either by femtocell i or the macrocell (indexed with 0), in case the femtocell is congested. The macrocell has additionally a dedicated flow of requests arriving according to a Poisson process at rate λ_0 that can only be handled by the macrocell (requests from outside the coverage of any femtocell). The assignment of the request between the macrocell and the femtocell is referred to as the cell selection problem. The objective is to balance the access load in order to minimize the mean access delay. Thus we refer to cell selection and access load balancing interchangeably.

The random access in the LTE macrocell takes over PRACH. It consists of $K = 54$ preambles, which the user randomly selects and transmits for initiating a connection to the system. So, PRACH is effectively an MCSA system with 54 channels. On the other hand, each IEEE 802.11 WLAN femtocell uses the CSMA algorithm for the random access. We assume that the femtocells are homogeneous with respect to their service capacities. Below we describe separately our models for the LTE macrocell and for each WLAN femtocell.

2.1 MCSA model for the LTE macrocell

For the LTE macrocell, we utilize the same discrete time Markov chain model as in [16]. Below we describe the model and give the essential results from its analysis presented in [16]. Later on, when considering the cell selection problem, we need to add some details to take into account the access delay within one timeslot.

Consider a multichannel slotted Aloha system with K parallel channels (i.e., preambles in the LTE terminology) and timeslot of $\tau = 1$ (ms). Let n denote the time index. In continuous time, timeslot n refers to the interval $[n, n+1)$. Let X_n, $n = 0, 1, \ldots$, denote the backlog of unsuccessful requests in the beginning of timeslot n, i.e., at time $t = n$, with $X_0 = 0$. Assume that new random access requests arrive (in continuous time) according to a Poisson process with rate λ. Let A_n, $n = 1, 2, \ldots$, denote the total number of requests that arrive in the interval $(n-1, n]$. Thus, A_n is Poisson distributed with mean $\lambda\tau$. We assume that any new request chooses the channel, i.e., the preamble, independently and randomly so that any channel is chosen with the same probability $1/K$. In addition, we assume that any backlogged request makes a retrial in timeslot n independently with probability r_n. If such a retrial attempt is made, the channel is chosen independently and randomly with uniform probabilities $1/K$.[1] A new request or a retrial attempt is *successful* if there are no other new requests or retrial attempts in the same channel. Let D_n, $n = 1, 2, \ldots$, denote the total number of successful new requests and retrial attempts in timeslot n. Based on these assumptions, (X_n) is a Markov chain for which

$$X_{n+1} = X_n + A_n - D_n. \qquad (1)$$

It is well-known that the Markov chain model (1) is unstable for *any* $\lambda > 0$ if the retrial probability r_n remains *constant* [21, 24, 18]. One option to stabilize the system is to let r_n vary dynamically depending on the state of the system so that $r_n = r(X_n)$. The total throughput is maximized by retrial probabilities

$$r(x) = \min\left\{\frac{K - \lambda\tau}{x - \lambda\tau/K}, 1\right\}. \qquad (2)$$

These optimal state-dependent retrial probabilities result in a stable system whenever

$$\lambda < K/(\tau e). \qquad (3)$$

In this paper, we assume that the Markov chain model (1) for the macrocell is stabilized by the optimal dynamic retrial probabilities given by (2). The transition probabilities p_{xy}

---

[1]Thus, new requests are treated differently from the backlogged ones. In the literature, such a model is called *Immediate-First-Transmission* (IFT) [25].

of this Markov chain are given by

$$p_{xy} = \sum_{a=0}^{K+y-x} \frac{(\lambda\tau)^a}{a!} e^{-\lambda\tau} q(x, a, x + a - y), \qquad (4)$$

where the conditional probabilities $q(x, a, d)$ are given by

$$q(x, a, d) = \sum_{\ell=0}^{x} p(K, a + \ell, d) \binom{x}{\ell} r(x)^\ell (1 - r(x))^{x-\ell}, \quad (5)$$

and $p(K, n, k)$ refers to the classical probability to assign n balls into K boxes so that k boxes have exactly one ball,

$$p(K, n, k) = \frac{(-1)^k n! K!}{k! K^n} \sum_{i=k}^{\min\{K,n\}} \frac{(-1)^i (K-i)^{n-i}}{(i-k)!(K-i)!(n-i)!}. \quad (6)$$

Let π_x denote the corresponding steady-state probabilities, satisfying the balance equations $\pi_y = \sum_x \pi_x p_{xy}$. The mean steady-state backlog in discrete time is given by

$$\bar{X} = \sum_{x=1}^{\infty} x \pi_x. \qquad (7)$$

2.2 CSMA model for the WLAN femtocells

For the WLAN femtocells, we use the following continuous time Markov process model. Consider a CSMA random access system. New access requests (i.e., packets) arrive according to a Poisson process with rate λ.[2] If the channel is sensed idle upon the arrival, the access request is served immediately and the transmission of the packet starts. We assume that the packet transmission times are exponentially distributed with mean $1/\mu$. But if the the channel is already busy when the new request arrives, it will be backlogged and an exponential backoff timer with mean $1/\alpha$ is started. If the channel is sensed idle upon the expiration of the backoff timer, the backlogged request is served immediately and the transmission of the packet starts. Otherwise, the request remains in the backlog and its backoff timer is restarted. We also assume that sensing is perfect, which implies that there are never collisions. This is realistic when all devices are reasonably close to the femtocell base station.

Let $X(t) \geq 0$ denote the total number of requests in the system at time t (including both the backlogged ones and the one in transmission if such a request exists). In addition, let $B(t) \in \{0, 1\}$ denote whether the channel is busy (1) or not (0). Based on the assumptions given above, it is easy to see that the pair $(X(t), B(t))$ constitutes a (jump) Markov process in continuous time with transition rates given by

$$\begin{aligned}
q((0,0), (1,1)) &= \lambda, \\
q((x,1), (x-1,0)) &= \mu, \quad x \geq 1, \\
q((x,0), (x,1)) &= x\alpha, \quad x \geq 1, \\
q((x,b), (x+1,1)) &= \lambda, \quad x \geq 1, b \in \{0, 1\}.
\end{aligned} \qquad (8)$$

Let $\pi(x, b)$ denote the corresponding steady-state probabilities. By solving the balance equations, we deduce that the system is stable whenever

$$\lambda < \mu, \qquad (9)$$

and, under this stability condition, we have for any $x \geq 1$ and $b \in \{0, 1\}$,

$$\pi(x, b) = \pi(0, 0) \left(\frac{\lambda}{\mu}\right)^x \prod_{y=1}^{x-1} \left(1 + \frac{\lambda}{y\alpha}\right) \left(\frac{\lambda}{x\alpha}\right)^{1-b}, \quad (10)$$

---

[2]In this section, we use generic notation λ for the arrival rate of new access requests in both models.

where

$$\pi(0, 0) = \left(1 - \frac{\lambda}{\mu}\right)^{1+\frac{\lambda}{\alpha}}. \qquad (11)$$

The mean steady-state number of requests in continuous time is given by

$$\bar{X} = \sum_{x=1}^{\infty} x(\pi(x, 0) + \pi(x, 1)) = \frac{\lambda\left(1 + \frac{\lambda}{\alpha}\right)}{\mu - \lambda}. \qquad (12)$$

2.3 Stability

Recall that in our access load balancing scenario, the system consists of the macrocell receiving requests at rate λ_0 and each femtocell i receiving requests at rate λ_i. In our model, requests can only be routed from a femtocell to the macrocell but not vice versa. For stability, it is required that all cells be stable. Recalling that all femtocells are homogeneous with respect to their service rate μ, by (3) and (9), the maximal stability condition for the whole system is clearly given by

$$\lambda_0 + \sum_{i=1}^{m} \max\{\lambda_i - \mu, 0\} < K/(\tau e). \qquad (13)$$

Our aim is now to optimize the performance of the system under this stability condition by considering different policies for balancing the access load between the femtocells and the macrocell.

3. ACCESS LOAD BALANCING PROBLEM

The access load balancing problem in this system consisting of an LTE macrocell and m WLAN femtocells is the following continuous time stochastic optimization problem. Upon the arrival of a new access request in one of the femtocells, say i, a decision must be made whether the request is served by the femtocell itself or by the macrocell so that the mean long-run access delay is minimized. The *access delay* is defined as the interval between the arrival of the request and the beginning of its service. In the femtocell, the service starts when the transmission of the corresponding packet starts, while, in the macrocell, the starting time refers to the beginning of the timeslot where the request is successful. Note that in both systems the arrival time of the request is considered in continuous time. Thus, when developing the dynamic policies the additional delays due to the discrete nature of the MCSA system must be appropriately accounted for, compared with the continuous-time behavior of the CSMA-based femtocell.

In this section, we first derive the optimal static load balancing policy, which minimizes the mean access delay with the knowledge of just the arrival rates of new requests. We also develop robust dynamic policies (JSQ, JSQ-μ and JSQ-I) that do not rely on the estimates of the arrival rates but utilize the information of current backlogs. Finally, by utilizing the theory of Markov decision processes, we develop a dynamic policy (FPI) that utilizes information both on the arrival rates and the current backlogs. It builds on the optimal static policy and improves its performance. It also gives an indication about the maximal performance gain achievable with dynamic policies when compared to the optimal static policy.

3.1 Optimal static policy

A *static* load balancing policy is defined by giving a vector of probabilities $\mathbf{p} = (p_1, \ldots, p_m)$, where $p_i \in [0, 1]$. In this policy, the decision is based on a random (i.i.d.) experiment so that an arriving request in femtocell i is assigned to the femtocell itself with probability p_i and to the macrocell with probability $1 - p_i$. Under a static policy $\mathbf{p}$, the total arrival rate in the macrocell is equal to $\lambda_0 + \sum_{i=1}^{m}(1 - p_i)\lambda_i$, and in any femtocell i, it is equal to $p_i\lambda_i$. Thus, policy $\mathbf{p}$ is stable if

$$\lambda_0 + \sum_{i=1}^{m}(1 - p_i)\lambda_i < \frac{K}{\tau e}, \quad p_i\lambda_i < \mu, \ i = 1, \ldots, m. \quad (14)$$

The *optimal static* policy is defined by the vector $\mathbf{p}^* = (p_1^*, \ldots, p_m^*)$ that minimizes the mean long-run access delay. Let λ_0^* and λ_i^* denote the corresponding optimal arrival rates in the macrocell and the femtocell i, respectively,

$$\lambda_0^* = \lambda_0 + \sum_{i=1}^{m}(1 - p_i^*)\lambda_i, \quad \lambda_i^* = p_i^*\lambda_i, \ i = 1, \ldots, m. \quad (15)$$

Due to Little's formula, we may, as well, consider the minimization of the mean steady-state total number of backlogged requests. For the macrocell, the mean steady-state total number of backlogged requests (in continuous time) under a stable static policy $\mathbf{p}$ is given by

$$\bar{X}_0^{\mathrm{b}}(\mathbf{p}) = \bar{X}_0 + \frac{1}{2}\left(\lambda_0 + \sum_{i=1}^{m}(1 - p_i)\lambda_i\right)\tau, \quad (16)$$

where $\bar{X}_0$ is calculated from (7) with arrival rate $\lambda = \lambda_0 + \sum_{i=1}^{m}(1 - p_i)\lambda_i$, and the latter term corresponds to the mean number of new arrivals during one timeslot (which should be included due to our continuous-time considerations). For a femtocell i, we have

$$\bar{X}_i^{\mathrm{b}}(\mathbf{p}) = \bar{X}_i - \frac{p_i\lambda_i}{\mu}, \quad (17)$$

where $\bar{X}_i$ is calculated from (12) with arrival rate $\lambda = p_i\lambda_i$, and the latter term corresponds to the mean number of requests in service (which should be excluded from the backlog according to our definition for the access delay). By (12), we even get an explicit expression for the mean backlog,

$$\bar{X}_i^{\mathrm{b}}(\mathbf{p}) = \frac{p_i\lambda_i\left(1 + \frac{p_i\lambda_i}{\alpha}\right)}{\mu - p_i\lambda_i} - \frac{p_i\lambda_i}{\mu} = \frac{(p_i\lambda_i)^2(\alpha + \mu)}{\alpha\mu(\mu - p_i\lambda_i)}, \quad (18)$$

Formally, the optimization problem is as follows:

$$\begin{aligned} \mathbf{p}^* &= \arg\min_{\mathbf{p}}\left\{\bar{X}_0^{\mathrm{b}}(\mathbf{p}) + \sum_{i=1}^{m}\bar{X}_i^{\mathrm{b}}(\mathbf{p})\right\} \\ \text{s.t.} \quad &\lambda_0 + \sum_{i=1}^{m}(1 - p_i)\lambda_i < K/(\tau e); \\ &p_i\lambda_i < \mu, \ i = 1, \ldots, m; \\ &0 \le p_i \le 1, \ i = 1, \ldots, m. \end{aligned} \quad (19)$$

In Appendix, we give a chracterization of the optimal static policy. In particular, we show that the original complex multi-dimensional problem reduces to an elementary one-dimensional optimization problem. Essentially the simplification follows from the assumption that the femtocells are all homogeneous with respect to their service rates μ. This allows to separate the optimization problem to one of just determining the optimal total amount of overflow traffic from the femtocells to the macro. In the optimization, for a given amount of overflow traffic the corresponding optimal routing probabilities are obtained by balancing the loads starting from the highest loaded femtocell as much as possible until the given amount of overflow traffic has been moved.

3.2 JSQ policies

Our first dynamic policy that does not rely on the estimates of the arrival rates but solely utilizes the information of current backlogs is called *Join-Shortest-Queue* (JSQ). Its origin is in task assignment problems for parallel server systems where it is shown to be optimal in the symmetric setting with equal service capacity in each server, see, e.g., [11].

In our application of the JSQ policy, the new request arriving at time t in femtocell i is assigned to the femtocell itself if and only if

$$X_i^{\mathrm{b}}(t) \le X_0^{\mathrm{b}}(t), \quad (20)$$

where $X_i^{\mathrm{b}}(t)$ and $X_0^{\mathrm{b}}(t)$ refer to the current backlog in femtocell i and in the macrocell, respectively. Note that we break the ties favoring the femtocell. At least in the light traffic, this makes sense, since the femtocell can be accessed immediately while in the macrocell, there is always a random access delay until the beginning of the next timeslot.

However, there may be a remarkable difference in the service capacities of the two systems. If, for example, $\mu \gg K/(\tau e)$, then the access delay in the femtocell is much smaller than in the macrocell unless the femtocell is already operating near its stability limit μ. Thus, we also propose a *modified JSQ* (JSQ-μ) policy, in which the new request arriving at time t in femtocell i is assigned to the femtocell itself if and only if

$$\frac{X_i^{\mathrm{b}}(t)}{\mu} \le \frac{X_0^{\mathrm{b}}(t)\tau e}{K}. \quad (21)$$

We note that JSQ-μ is similar to the minimum expected delay (MED) task assignment policy introduced in [15].

Moreover we also propose another variant of the JSQ policy called JSQ-I, in which a newly arriving request to the femto stays at the femto if it is idle, i.e., $B_i(t) = 0$ and according to our model, the transmission begins immediately. If the femto is busy, it is assigned to the femto only if (20) is satisfied.

Note that by keeping the ratio between the backlogs roughly constant, the JSQ policies are inherently maximally stable.

3.3 FPI policy

The final dynamic policy that we study in this paper is called *First-Policy-Iteration* (FPI). The FPI policy is based on the theory of Markov decision processes utilizing the so-called policy iteration step (see, for example, [22]) to improve the optimal static policy discussed earlier. The key observation is that the behavior of the system operated with the optimal static policy can be characterized by parallel *independent* systems. It follows that the effect of a single decision related to a new request in femtocell i can be evaluated separately in the two systems (femtocell i and the macrocell).

Consider an arrival of a new request at time t in femtocell i during timeslot $n - 1$ (so that $n - 1 < t < n$). Assume that the current backlog in the macrocell is equal to $X_0^{\mathrm{b}}(t) = x_0 + a_0$ including x_0 requests that were unsuccessful in the current timeslot together with a_0 new requests already assigned to the macrocell during the current timeslot in the interval $(n - 1, t)$. The expected difference in the future access delay costs when compared to the average costs

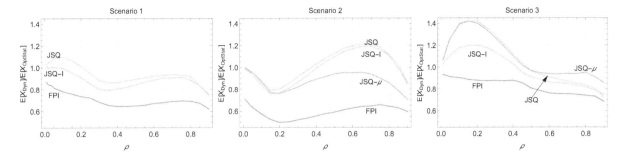

Figure 1: Ratio of total backlog length using the dynamic policy to backlog length using the optimal static policy for Scenario 1 (left), Scenario 2 (center) and Scenario 3 (right).

is given by

$$v_0(x_0, a_0) = \left(x_0 + a_0 + \frac{\lambda_0^*(n-t)}{2} - \bar{X}_0^{\mathrm{b}}(\mathbf{p}^*)\right)(n-t)$$

$$+ \sum_{a=0}^{\infty} \frac{(\lambda_0^*(n-t))^a}{a!} e^{-\lambda_0^*(n-t)} \sum_{d=0}^{\min\{x_0+a_0+a,K\}} q(x_0, a_0 + a, d) \times \quad (22)$$

$$\left[\left(x_0 + a_0 + a - d + \frac{\lambda_0^* \tau}{2} - \bar{X}_0^{\mathrm{b}}(\mathbf{p}^*)\right)\tau\right.$$

$$\left. + v_0(x_0 + a_0 + a - d)\right],$$

where the so-called value function $v_0(x)$ is solved from the following system of equations ($x \geq 0$):

$$v_0(x) = \sum_{a=0}^{\infty} \frac{(\lambda_0^* \tau)^a}{a!} e^{-\lambda_0^* \tau} \sum_{d=0}^{\min\{x+a,K\}} q(x, a, d) \times \quad (23)$$

$$\left[\left(x + a - d + \frac{\lambda_0^* \tau}{2} - \bar{X}_0^{\mathrm{b}}(\mathbf{p}^*)\right)\tau + v_0(x + a - d)\right]$$

and $q(x, a, d)$ is given in (5) when applied with arrival rate $\lambda = \lambda_0^*$. In (22), the first term accounts for the difference in the cost during the interval $[t, n]$ and the mean cost $\bar{X}_0^{\mathrm{b}}(\mathbf{p}^*)$. With the knowledge of the state information x_0 and a_0 and conditioning on the number of random arrivals a during the interval $[t, n]$ (first summation), the number of users attempting access in time slot n equals $x_0 + a_0 + a$. By then conditioning also on the number of departures in time slot n (second summation), the first term on the second last line of (22) gives the difference in the cost in time slot n to the mean cost $\bar{X}_0^{\mathrm{b}}(\mathbf{p}^*)$. After time slot n, the relative values just depend on the backlog ($x_0 + a_0 + a - d$) at the beginning of time slot $n + 1$.

On the other hand, if the current backlog in the femtocell i is equal to $X_i^{\mathrm{b}}(t) = x_i$ and the channel state is $B_i(t) = b_i$ (so that the total number of requests equals $X_i(t) = x_i + b_i$), the expected difference in the future access delay costs when compared to the average costs is given by the value function $v_i(x_i, b_i)$, which satisfies the following system of equations ($x \geq 0$):

$$v_i(x, 0) = \frac{x - \bar{X}_i^{\mathrm{b}}(\mathbf{p}^*) + \lambda_i^* v_i(x,1) + x\alpha v_i(x-1,1)}{\lambda_i^* + x\alpha},$$

$$v_i(x, 1) = \frac{x - \bar{X}_i^{\mathrm{b}}(\mathbf{p}^*) + \lambda_i^* v_i(x+1,1) + \mu v_i(x,0)}{\lambda_i^* + \mu}. \quad (24)$$

Under the FPI policy, the new request arriving at time t in femtocell i is assigned to the femtocell itself if and only if

$$v_0(x_0, a_0) + v_i(x_i + b_i, 1) \leq v_0(x_0, a_0 + 1) + v_i(x_i, b_i). \quad (25)$$

The FPI policy is always guaranteed to improve the performance compared with the initial policy, i.e., the optimal static policy. In principle, by continuing the policy iteration method one would eventually arrive at the optimal policy. In our case, this is infeasible since continuing the iteration would require the joint modeling of the discrete time LTE macrocell and the continuous time CSMA femtocells. However, typically already the first iteration gives the largest relative improvement and we use the results of the FPI policy as an indication of the maximal gains.

4. NUMERICAL RESULTS

We use simulations to explore the behavior of our model under different policies. Due to computational limitations, which affects the calculation of the optimal static policy when number of preambles is high, we consider an MCSA system with $K = 20$ channels which, nonetheless, gives a good indication about the behavior of random access channel of LTE which usually has $K = 54$ preambles. Furthermore, we construct six scenarios by varying m, μ, λ_0 and α (Table 1). We take *Scenario 1* as the baseline with $m = 2$, $\mu = K/(\tau e)$, $\lambda_0 = 0$ and $\alpha = \mu$, from which other scenarios are constructed by changing the value of one parameter at a time. Note that in the baseline scenario, the service completion rate of the femtos, μ, is equal to the maximum service rate for the macro in MCSA, $K/(\tau e)$ requests per second. The service completion rate of the femtos is halved ($\mu = K/(2\tau e)$) in *Scenario 2*, while it is doubled ($\mu = 2K/(\tau e)$) in *Scenario 3*. *Scenario 4* has four femtos ($m = 4$). In *Scenario 5*, the backlogged users in the femtos retransmit less aggressively ($\alpha = \mu/5$). Finally in *Scenario 6*, the macro has dedicated traffic with rate $\lambda_0 = K/(2\tau e)$, which is exactly half of the maximum arrival it can support. In all the scenarios, the femtos have the same arrival rate, i.e., $\lambda_1 = \cdots = \lambda_m$.

The performance is measured as the ratio of the sum of average backlog in all cells using various dynamic policies to the same using the optimal static policy. This ratio, by Little's formula, is the same as the ratio of access delays in the respective cases. In Figs. 1–4, this quantity and other measures of performance are plotted as a function of ρ, a fraction of the maximum arrival rate of a femto station that satisfies the stability condition (13).

As the MDP-based policy iteration algorithm is known to converge rapidly to the optimal solution, we can speculate that FPI is giving near-optimal performance. This is supported by Figs. 1–4 where FPI is conspicuously outper-

Table 1: A summary of the parameters for different scenarios.

Scenario	m	μ	λ_0	α
1	2	$K/(\tau e)$	0	μ
2	2	$K/(2\tau e)$	0	μ
3	2	$2K/(\tau e)$	0	μ
4	4	$K/(\tau e)$	0	μ
5	2	$K/(\tau e)$	0	$\mu/5$
6	2	$K/(\tau e)$	$K/(2\tau e)$	μ

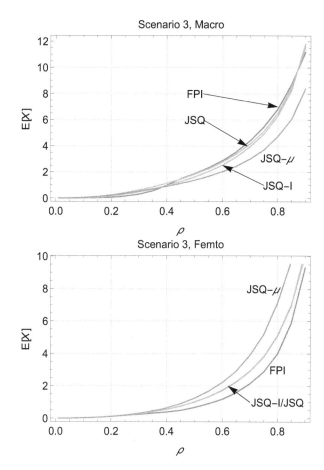

Figure 2: Cell specific backlog length for Scenario 3. The upper panel show the backlog length of the macro while the lower panel shows the backlog length of the femto.

forming all the other dynamic policies and even providing a gain of up to 50% over the optimal static policy. Therefore, in what follows we focus on the performance characteristics of the JSQ-based policies, which are simpler and require less state information.

When the service rates of the femtos are equal to that of the macro as in Scenario 1, Figure 1 (left panel) shows that, except at very low loads, it is always possible to improve the performance (as much as by 30%) over the optimal static policy by using a dynamic policy. When the service completion rate of the femto is halved (Scenario 2), we get performance gain either at very low loads or at very high loads (Figure 1, center panel). Among the JSQ-based policies, JSQ-μ is consistently outperforming the other two and the optimal static policy throughout the load range.

Meanwhile, when we double the service rate of the femto (Scenario 3), we observe from Figure 1 (right panel) that gain is obtained only for high values of the load ($\rho > 0.5$) and JSQ-I is the best-performing JSQ-based policy. Surprisingly it is performing better than the service-completion-rate-aware JSQ-μ. The reason becomes apparent from Figure 2 where we show the mean backlogs in macro (upper panel) and femto (lower panel) separately: JSQ-μ tends to keep the users in the femto whereby the performance of the femtos, and consequently that of the whole system suffers. Thus, considering only the service rates of the cells to account for their heterogeneity, as in JSQ-μ, is not sufficient and could even turn out to be counterproductive. However, JSQ-I, that uses knowledge of femto channel state is systematically performing better than pure JSQ.

As also seen in Figure 2, at low loads there are only few users in the system and performance is good for all policies. Thus, from a practical point of view, the behavior of the gain at low loads is not that significant.

In Scenario 4, with $m = 4$, JSQ-I is the better performing JSQ-based dynamic policy and works better than the optimal static policy when the load is not very small (Figure 3, upper panel). When the backlogged users in the femtos do not retransmist aggressively (Scenario 5, Figure 3 lower panel), we observe that JSQ-I is outperforming JSQ by a fairly good margin.

Finally, from the upper panel of Figure 4 we observe that in Scenario 6, for $\rho \leq 0.4$, a dynamic policy gives either very little or no gain. The reason becomes obvious if we look at the optimal static assignment probabilities at the femto (Figure 4, lower panel), which indicates that for these values of arrival rates, it is always optimal to stay in the femto as macro already has enough users. However, at higher values of the arrival rate, FPI performs much better than the optimal static policy, and even the JSQ-based policies outperform the optimal static policy by a good margin. Simi-

lar results are obtained in Scenarios 2–5 as well if we take $\lambda_0 = K/(2\tau e)$. However, due to space limitations, we omit the plots here.

5. CONCLUSIONS

We study the cell selection problem for M2M devices in a heterogeneous network run by the same operator or in a deployment scenario where information exchange between the cells is possible. The machines can either attach themselves to the femtocell or go to the macrocell in the starting phase of data transmission so that the access delay is minimized. We formulate the problem as minimizing the backlog in a system that consists of both WLANs and LTE. CSMA in WLAN and MCSA in LTE are described as Markov models in continuous time and discrete time, respectively. We devise cell selection policies to operate these disparate systems that reduce the access delay and thereby even the data transfer delay for machines with small data. We have an explicit characterization of the optimal static policy and then we also study dynamic policies which are typically better than the optimal static policy.

The main insight from the study is that it is possible to reduce the access delay in most of the cases but the amount of reduction is highly dependent on various system parame-

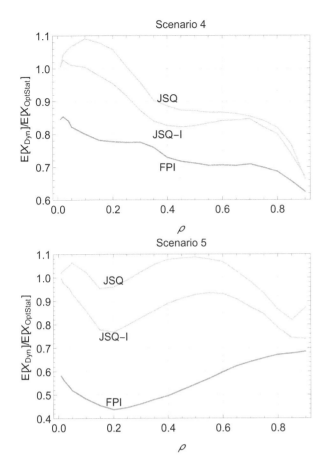

Figure 3: Ratio of total backlog length using dynamic policies to backlog length using the optimal static policy for Scenario 4 (upper panel) and Scenario 5 (lower panel).

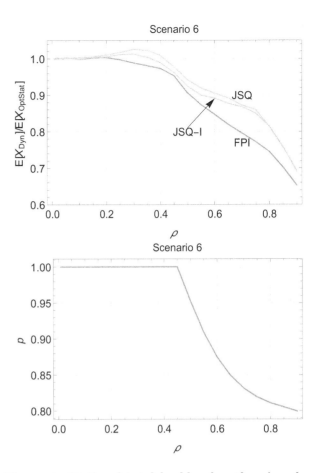

Figure 4: Ratio of total backlog length using dynamic policies to backlog length using the optimal static policy for Scenario 6 (upper panel) and the probability of staying in the femto with the optimal static policy.

ters, the traffic load, and the policy used. We generally have more gains at higher loads. Furthermore, certain dynamic policies give very good performance, typically as good as or better than the optimal static policy. We note that the optimal static policy itself improves performance of the system, if possible, by exploiting the complete knowledge of the system and traffic parameters. However, the proposed JSQ and JSQ-I policies do not depend on such parameters but, instead, rely only on limited instantaneous information (backlogs and channel state) and adapt dynamically to changing loads. Thus, they are robust and provide good performance. On the other hand, these simple JSQ-based rules do not generally extract all the potential performance gain from the system as done by the near-optimal FPI policy, which uses the knowledge of all the system and traffic parameters and the instantaneous state of the system.

6. ACKNOWLEDGMENT

This work was partially supported by TEKES as part of the Internet of Things program of DIGILE (Finnish Strategic Centre for Science, Technology and Innovation in the field of ICT and digital business) and the EIT ICT Labs under the EXAM project.

7. REFERENCES

[1] 3GPP. System improvements for Machine-Type Communications (MTC). TR 23.888, 3rd Generation Partnership Project (3GPP), 2011. V1.6.0 (2011-11).

[2] A. M. Ahmadian, O. Galinina, S. Andreev, and Y. Koucheryavy. Modeling contention-based M2M transmissions over 3GPP LTE cellular networks. In *Communications Workshops (ICC), 2014 IEEE International Conference on*, pages 441–447. IEEE, 2014.

[3] S. Andreev, M. Gerasimenko, O. Galinina, Y. Koucheryavy, N. Himayat, S.-P. Yeh, and S. Talwar. Intelligent access network selection in converged multi-radio heterogeneous networks. *Wireless Communications, IEEE*, 21(6):86–96, December 2014.

[4] G. Bianchi. Performance analysis of the IEEE 802.11 distributed coordination function. *Selected Areas in Communications, IEEE Journal on*, 18(3):535–547, 2000.

[5] T. Bonald and M. Feuillet. On the stability of flow-aware CSMA. *Performance Evaluation*, 67(11):1219 – 1229, 2010.

[6] T. Bonald, A. Ibrahim, and J. Roberts. The impact of association on the capacity of WLANs. In *Modeling and Optimization in Mobile, Ad Hoc, and Wireless Networks, 2009. WiOPT 2009. 7th International Symposium on*, pages 1–10. IEEE, 2009.

[7] A. Damnjanovic, J. Montojo, Y. Wei, T. Ji, T. Luo, M. Vajapeyam, T. Yoo, O. Song, and D. Malladi. A survey on 3GPP heterogeneous networks. *Wireless Communications, IEEE*, 18(3):10–21, 2011.

[8] G. Fayolle, E. Gelenbe, and J. Labetoulle. Stability and optimal control of the packet switching broadcast channel. *J. ACM*, 24(3):375–386, July 1977.

[9] O. Galinina, A. Turlikov, S. Andreev, and Y. Koucheryavy. Stabilizing multi-channel slotted aloha for machine-type communications. In *Information Theory Proceedings (ISIT), 2013 IEEE International Symposium on*, pages 2119–2123, 2013.

[10] A. G. Gotsis, A. S. Lioumpas, and A. Alexiou. M2M scheduling over LTE: Challenges and new perspectives. *Vehicular Technology Magazine, IEEE*, 7(3):34–39, 2012.

[11] M. Harchol-Balter. *Performance Modeling and Design of Computer Systems*. Cambridge University Press, 2013.

[12] L. Kleinrock and S. Lam. Packet switching in a multiaccess broadcast channel: Performance evaluation. *Communications, IEEE Transactions on*, 23(4):410–423, 1975.

[13] A. Larmo and R. Susitaival. RAN overload control for Machine Type Communications in LTE. In *GLOBECOM Workshops (GC Wkshps), 2012 IEEE*, Dec. 2012.

[14] A. Laya, L. Alonso, and J. Alonso-Zarate. Is the random access channel of LTE and LTE-A suitable for M2M communications? a survey of alternatives. *Communications Surveys Tutorials, IEEE*, 16(1):4–16, 2014.

[15] J. Lui, R. R. Muntz, and D. Towsley. Bounding the mean response time of the minimum expected delay routing policy: an algorithmic approach. *Computers, IEEE Transactions on*, 44(12):1371–1382, Dec 1995.

[16] P. Osti, S. Aalto, and P. Lassila. Load balancing for M2M random access in LTE HetNets. In *Modeling, Analysis Simulation of Computer and Telecommunication Systems (MASCOTS), 2014 IEEE 22nd International Symposium on*, pages 132–141, Sep 2014.

[17] P. Osti, P. Lassila, S. Aalto, A. Larmo, and T. Tirronen. Analysis of PDCCH performance for M2M traffic in LTE. *Vehicular Technology, IEEE Transactions on*, 63(9):4357–4371, 2014.

[18] I. E. Pountourakis and E. D. Sykas. Analysis, stability and optimization of Aloha-type protocols for multichannel networks. *Computer Communications*, 15(10):619–629, 1992.

[19] Qualcomm. A comparison of LTE advanced hetnets and Wi-Fi. Technical report, Qualcomm, 2011.

[20] S. Rayment and J. Bergström. Achieving carrier-grade Wi-Fi in the 3GPP world. *Ericsson Review*, 2012.

[21] W. Rosenkrantz and D. Towsley. On the instability of slotted ALOHA multiaccess algorithm. *Automatic Control, IEEE Transactions on*, 28(10):994–996, 1983.

[22] S. M. Ross. *Applied Probability Models with Optimization Applications*. Holden-Day, 1970.

[23] J.-B. Seo and V. Leung. Design and analysis of backoff algorithms for random access channels in UMTS-LTE and IEEE 802.16 systems. *IEEE Transactions on Vehicular Technology*, 60(8):3975–3989, 2011.

[24] W. Szpankowski. Packet switching in multiple radio channels: Analysis and stability of a random access system. *Computer Networks (1976)*, 7(1):17 – 26, 1983.

[25] W. Yue. The effect of capture on performance of multichannel slotted aloha systems. *Communications, IEEE Transactions on*, 39(6):818–822, 1991.

[26] K. Zheng, F. Hu, W. Wang, W. Xiang, and M. Dohler. Radio resource allocation in LTE-advanced cellular networks with M2M communications. *Communications Magazine, IEEE*, 50(7):184–192, July 2012.

Appendix: On the optimal static policy

In this appendix, we give a characterization of the optimal static access load balancing policy $\mathbf{p}^*$. In particular, we show that the original complex multi-dimensional problem reduces to an elementary one-dimensional optimization problem. This is based on the observation that the mean backlogs $\bar{X}_0^b$ and $\bar{X}_i^b$ are convex functions of the corresponding arrival rates. Our results are formulated as Propositions 1 and 2 below. The proof of Proposition 1 utilizes the following elementary lemma.

LEMMA 1. *Assume that $f(x)$ is a convex function. Then, for any $x_1 \leq x_2$ and $0 \leq \Delta \leq x_2 - x_1$,*

$$f(x_1) + f(x_2) \geq f(x_1 + \Delta) + f(x_2 - \Delta). \quad (26)$$

Let $0 \leq x \leq \sum_{i=1}^m \lambda_i$. Consider a vector $\mathbf{p}(x) = (p_1, \ldots, p_m)$ such that

$$\sum_{i=1}^m \lambda_i (1 - p_i) = x.$$

Thus, x is equal to the total arrival rate of the overflow traffic for routing vector $\mathbf{p}(x)$. Let

$$c(\mathbf{p}(x)) = f(\lambda_0 + x) + \sum_{i=1}^m g(\lambda_i p_i),$$

where $f(y)$ and $g(y)$ are positive, twice continuously differentiable and strictly convex functions. Let $f'(y)$, $g'(y)$, $f''(y)$, $g''(y)$ denote their first and second derivatives, respectively.

In addition, define

$$n^*(x) = \min \left\{ n \geq 1 : \frac{1}{n} \left(\sum_{i=1}^n \lambda_i - x \right) \geq \lambda_{n+1} \right\},$$
$$\lambda^*(x) = \frac{1}{n^*(x)} \left(\sum_{i=1}^{n^*(x)} \lambda_i - x \right),$$

where we have defined $\lambda_{m+1} = 0$. It follows from the definition that $n^*(x)$ is an increasing function of x with the property that

$$n^*(x) \leq n \quad \Longleftrightarrow \quad x \leq x_n^*,$$

where x_n^* is an increasing sequence of n defined by

$$x_n^* = \sum_{i=1}^n \lambda_i - n\lambda_{n+1}.$$

The monotonicity of the sequence follows readily from our assumption that $\lambda_1 \geq \ldots \geq \lambda_m > \lambda_{m+1} = 0$. It also implies that

$$\lambda_{n^*(x)} \geq \lambda^*(x) \geq \lambda_{n^*(x)+1}.$$

Consider now a vector $\mathbf{p}^*(x) = (p_1^*, \ldots, p_m^*)$ such that, for any $i \in \{1, \ldots, m\}$,

$$\lambda_i p_i^* = \min\{\lambda^*(x), \lambda_i\}.$$

Note that $p_1^* \leq \ldots \leq p_{n^*(x)}^* \leq 1$, and $p_n^* = 1$ for any $n \geq n^*(x) + 1$. In addition, we have

$$\sum_{i=1}^m \lambda_i (1 - p_i^*) = \sum_{i=1}^{n^*(x)} \lambda_i - n^*(x)\lambda^*(x) = x.$$

Thus, x is also equal to the total arrival rate of the overflow traffic for routing vector $\mathbf{p}^*(x)$. Thus,

$$c(\mathbf{p}^*(x)) = f(\lambda_0 + x) + \sum_{i=1}^m g(\lambda_i p_i^*).$$

PROPOSITION 1.

$$c(\mathbf{p}^*(x)) \leq c(\mathbf{p}(x)). \tag{27}$$

PROOF. The result is proved below by induction.
$1°$ Let $k = 0$, and define, for all $n = 1, \ldots, m$,

$$y_n^{(0)} = \lambda_n p_n.$$

In addition, let $I^{(0)} = \{i \in \{1, \ldots, m\} : y_i^{(0)} > \lambda_i p_i^*\}$ and $J^{(0)} = \{j \in \{1, \ldots, m\} : y_j^{(0)} < \lambda_j p_j^*\}$. Note that, since the amount of overflow traffic is equal to x for both routing vectors $\mathbf{p}(x)$ and $\mathbf{p}^*(x)$, we have

$$\sum_{i \in I^{(0)}} (y_i^{(0)} - \lambda_i p_i^*) = \sum_{j \in J^{(0)}} (\lambda_j p_j^* - y_j^{(0)}).$$

Furthermore,

$$c(\mathbf{p}(x)) = f(\lambda_0 + x) + \sum_{n=1}^m g(y_n^{(0)}).$$

$2°$ Consider now any $k > 0$ such that $I^{(k-1)} \neq \emptyset$ and $J^{(k-1)} \neq \emptyset$. We make two induction assumptions that

$$\sum_{i \in I^{(k-1)}} (y_i^{(k-1)} - \lambda_i p_i^*) = \sum_{j \in J^{(k-1)}} (\lambda_j p_j^* - y_j^{(k-1)})$$

and

$$\sum_{n=1}^m g(y_n^{(k-1)}) \leq \sum_{n=1}^m g(y_n^{(0)}),$$

both of which are clearly true for $k = 1$ by $1°$.
In addition we give the following recursive definitions. Let $i = \min I^{(k-1)}$, $j = \min J^{(k-1)}$, and

$$\Delta = \min\{y_i^{(k-1)} - \lambda_i p_i^*, \lambda_j p_j^* - y_j^{(k-1)}\}.$$

Now, for all $n = 1, \ldots, m$, let

$$y_n^{(k)} = \begin{cases} y_n^{(k-1)} - \Delta, & \text{for } n = i, \\ y_n^{(k-1)} + \Delta, & \text{for } n = j, \\ y_n^{(k-1)} & \text{otherwise.} \end{cases}$$

In addition, let $I^{(k)} = \{i \in \{1, \ldots, m\} : y_i^{(k)} > \lambda_i p_i^*\}$ and $J^{(k)} = \{j \in \{1, \ldots, m\} : y_j^{(k)} < \lambda_j p_j^*\}$. Note that, by our construction, we have

$$\sum_{i \in I^{(k)}} (y_i^{(k)} - \lambda_i p_i^*) - \sum_{j \in J^{(k)}} (\lambda_j p_j^* - y_j^{(k)})$$
$$= \sum_{i \in I^{(k-1)}} (y_i^{(k-1)} - \lambda_i p_i^*) - \sum_{j \in J^{(k-1)}} (\lambda_j p_j^* - y_j^{(k-1)})$$
$$= 0,$$

where the last equation follows from the first induction assumption. Since $0 < \Delta \leq y_i^{(k-1)} - y_j^{(k-1)}$, it follows from Lemma 1 that

$$g(y_i^{(k)}) + g(y_j^{(k)}) \leq g(y_i^{(k-1)}) + g(y_j^{(k-1)}).$$

Thus,

$$\sum_{n=1}^m g(y_n^{(k)}) \leq \sum_{n=1}^m g(y_n^{(k-1)}) \leq \sum_{n=1}^m g(y_n^{(0)}),$$

where the latter inequality follows from the second induction assumption.
$3°$ Let k' be the lowest index for which $I^{(k')} = \emptyset$ or $J^{(k')} = \emptyset$. From $2°$, we deduce that

$$\sum_{i \in I^{(k')}} (y_i^{(k')} - \lambda_i p_i^*) = \sum_{j \in J^{(k')}} (\lambda_j p_j^* - y_j^{(k')}),$$

which implies that both $I^{(k')} = \emptyset$ and $J^{(k')} = \emptyset$. Thus, for all $n = 1, \ldots, m$,

$$y_n^{(k')} = \lambda_n p_n^*.$$

In addition, it follows from $2°$ that

$$\sum_{n=1}^m g(y_n^{(k')}) \leq \sum_{n=1}^m g(y_n^{(0)}).$$

Thus, we conclude that

$$c(\mathbf{p}^*(x)) = f(\lambda_0 + x) + \sum_{n=1}^m g(y_n^{(k')})$$
$$\leq f(\lambda_0 + x) + \sum_{n=1}^m g(y_n^{(0)}) = c(\mathbf{p}(x)),$$

which completes the proof. $\square$

The next step is to optimize the amount of the overflow traffic, x. As shown below in Proposition 2, the optimal value is characterized as follows:

$$x^* = \begin{cases} 0, \\ \quad \text{if } f'(\lambda_0 + x) > g'(\lambda^*(x)) \text{ for all } 0 < x < \sum_{i=1}^m \lambda_i; \\ \sum_{i=1}^m \lambda_i, \\ \quad \text{if } f'(\lambda_0 + x) < g'(\lambda^*(x)) \text{ for all } 0 < x < \sum_{i=1}^m \lambda_i; \\ \inf\{x \geq 0 : f'(\lambda_0 + x) = g'(\lambda^*(x))\}, \\ \quad \text{otherwise.} \end{cases}$$

PROPOSITION 2.

$$c(\mathbf{p}^*(x^*)) \leq c(\mathbf{p}^*(x)). \tag{28}$$

PROOF. For any $0 \leq x \leq \sum_{i=1}^m \lambda_i$, define $h(x)$ by

$$h(x) = c(\mathbf{p}^*(x)) = f(\lambda_0 + x) + \sum_{i=1}^m g(\lambda_i p_i^*).$$

It follows that

$$h(x) = f(\lambda_0 + x) + n^*(x)g(\lambda^*(x)) + \sum_{i=n^*(x)+1}^m g(\lambda_i).$$

$1°$ Fix $n \in \{1, \ldots, m\}$, for a while, and let $x \in (x_{n-1}^*, x_n^*)$. Thus, there is $\delta > 0$ such that $n^*(y) = n$ for any $y \in (x - \delta, x + \delta)$. In addition, we have, for any $y \in (x - \delta, x + \delta)$,

$$h(y) = f(\lambda_0 + y) + ng(\lambda^*(y)) + \sum_{i=n+1}^m g(\lambda_i),$$
$$\lambda^*(y) = \frac{1}{n}\left(\sum_{i=1}^n \lambda_i - y\right).$$

Thus, $(\lambda^*)'(x) = -1/n$ and

$$h'(x) = f'(\lambda_0 + x) - g'(\lambda^*(x)).$$

Furthermore, we have

$$h''(x) = f''(\lambda_0 + x) + \frac{1}{n}g''(\lambda^*(x)) > 0,$$

where the inequality follows from the strict convexity of functions f and g.
$2°$ Fix $n \in \{1, \ldots, m-1\}$, for a while, and let $x = x_n^*$. Thus, there is $\delta > 0$ such that $n^*(y) = n$ for any $y \in (x - \delta, x]$

and $n^*(y) = n + 1$ for any $y \in (x, x + \delta)$. In addition, we have, for any $y \in (x - \delta, x]$,

$$h(y) = f(\lambda_0 + y) + ng(\lambda^*(y)) + \sum_{i=n+1}^{m} g(\lambda_i),$$
$$\lambda^*(y) = \frac{1}{n} \left(\sum_{i=1}^{n} \lambda_i - y \right).$$

and, for any $y \in (x, x + \delta)$,

$$h(y) = f(\lambda_0 + y) + (n + 1)g(\lambda^*(y)) + \sum_{i=n+2}^{m} g(\lambda_i),$$
$$\lambda^*(y) = \frac{1}{n+1} \left(\sum_{i=1}^{n+1} \lambda_i - y \right).$$

Thus, $(\lambda^*)'(x-) = -1/n$ and $(\lambda^*)'(x+) = -1/(n + 1)$ implying that

$$h'(x) = h'(x-) = h'(x+) = f'(\lambda_0 + x) - g'(\lambda^*(x)).$$

Furthermore, we have

$$h''(x-) = f''(\lambda_0 + x) + \tfrac{1}{n}g''(\lambda^*(x))/n > 0,$$
$$h''(x+) = f''(\lambda_0 + x) + \tfrac{1}{n+1}g''(\lambda^*(x))/n > 0,$$

where the inequalities follow from the strict convexity of functions f and g.

$3°$ It follows from $1°$ and $2°$ that $h(x)$ is continuously differentiable and strictly convex for any $0 < x < \sum_{i=1}^{m} \lambda_i$, which justifies the claim. $\square$

On the Design and Evaluation of Producer Mobility Management Schemes in Named Data Networks

Hesham Farahat
ECE Department
Queen's University
Kingston, ON, Canada
h.farahat@queensu.ca

Hossam Hassanein
School of Computing
Queen's University
Kingston, ON, Canada
hossam@cs.queensu.ca

ABSTRACT

Information-centric Networks (ICNs) offer a promising paradigm for the future Internet to cope with an ever increasing growth in data and shifts in access models. Different architectures of ICNs, including Named Data Networks (NDNs) are designed around content distribution, where data is the core entity in the network instead of hosts. One of the main challenges in NDNs is handling mobile content providers and maintaining seamless operation. Accordingly, attempts at handling mobility in NDNs have been proposed in the literature are mostly studied under simplistic and/or special cases. There is a lack of benchmarking tools to analyze and compare such schemes. This paper introduces a comprehensive assessment framework for mobility management schemes in NDNs, under varying topologies, heterogeneous producers and consumers, and different mobility models. We develop a generic and modular simulation environment in ns-3 that is made available for NDN researchers to evaluate their mobility management proposals. We implement and compare the performance of three mainstream Producer mobility management schemes, namely, the Mobility Anchor, Location Resolution and Hybrid approaches in NDNs. We demonstrate how mobility impacts NDN operation, specifically in terms of latency and delivery ratio. We also argue for the superior operation of the hybrid approach to handling mobility in NDNs, yet highlight its high control overhead.

Categories and Subject Descriptors

C.2.m [**Computer-Communication Networks**]: Miscellaneous; C.4 [**Performance of Systems**]: Design studies

Keywords

Information-Centric Networks; Named Data Networks; Seamless Mobility Management; ndnSIM; ns-3; Simulation Framework

MSWiM'15, November 2–6, 2015, Cancun, Mexico.
© 2015 ACM. ISBN 978-1-4503-3762-5/15/11 ...$15.00.
DOI: http://dx.doi.org/10.1145/2811587.2811616.

1. INTRODUCTION

The evolution of social networking, mobile applications and media streaming caused a shift in how the Internet operates. While the Internet was built on a host-to-host model, current usage trends are exhausting network resources in maintaining scalable operation. Consistent attempts at patching up Internet operation to cater for increasing content are bound to fail under the projected increases in data traffic [23]. This includes attempts at supporting Content Distribution Network (CDN) and Peer-to-peer (P2P) overlays on the IP network. In retrospect, the Internet was designed for a mostly client-server architecture. Users, thus, assumed either roles in most scenarios. With an expanding use of the Internet, CISCO's Visual Networking Index (VNI) [1] projects a 2.5 fold increase in global traffic, to reach 132.8 Exabytes per month by 2018 compared to 2013.

Recently, research efforts were directed at developing a paradigm for the future Internet based on content rather than hosts. A promising paradigm, namely Information-centric Networks (ICNs), was presented [5] to address growing challenges with content oriented communication. While considering the strengths and weaknesses of the current Internet design, ICNs are being developed in concerted efforts, and several potential architectures have been proposed. The commonality between all ICN designs is that content is identified by unique names and be cached anywhere in the network. While most of the attention has been directed at addressing challenges such as: routing, naming, and caching [21], while other important challenges remain seldom tackled.

A core property of any future Internet architecture is supporting mobility as a networking primitive. This is exacerbated with a projected increase in mobile entities amounting to 50% of all devices and connections by 2018 [1]. Supporting seamless operation where users can move in the network without service interruptions is core to ICN. This challenge is gaining attention as researchers are attempting to incorporate mobility support in ICN architectures. In the current Internet, the challenge of delivering traffic from or to mobile devices is in how to find the moving hosts in the network. Whereas in ICNs, the challenge is in how to find and track the data [24].

Named Data Network (NDN), formerly known as Content-centric Network (CCN), is one of the pioneering ICN architectures. An implicit assumption of intrinsic mobility "support" inherent to NDN design is realistically impractical due to the late coupling between data and hosts. While recent research efforts addressed mobility challenges in ICNs generally, and NDNs specifically, there remain significant challenges in analyzing the impact of these solutions on the resulting Quality of Service (QoS) and latency measures. We remark that the performance evaluation of mobility management schemes proposed in the literature are mostly performed under simplistic configurations/operations conditions that do not reflect realistic ICN environments. Indeed, there is a lack of comprehensive analysis of the design factors that yield seamless mobility management, and a benchmarking tool to contrast and evaluate mobility management schemes.

In this paper, we address mobility challenges in NDN, as a fundamental functionality in ICNs. Specifically, our contributions are:

1. A detailed analysis of mainstream mobility management scheme in NDN, with insights on design factors that yield seamless mobility.

2. A modular mobility assessment framework, developed within ns-3, to evaluate the performance of mobility management schemes under varying topologies, heterogeneous producers and consumers, and access profiles; to be released for NDN research.

3. An implementation of the three mainstream mobility management schemes in NDN, with contrasted performance evaluation.

Our goal is to provide the means (assessment framework) and design parameters for researchers in NDN mobility to evaluate the performance of their frameworks, and to benchmark against the already developed and tested schemes.

The remainder of the paper is organized as follows. In Section 2, an overview of the mobility problem in NDN is introduced. Mainstream NDN mobility management schemes are detailed in Section 3, highlighting their design parameters, and an analysis of design factors that aid seamless mobility (in light of these schemes) is presented in Section 4. The assessment framework is explained in detail in Section 5. We detail our experiments with these approaches in Section 6, and comment on the performance of each under the presented performance metrics. We conclude our findings in Section 7 and present insights into future directions in NDN mobility support.

2. MOBILITY MANAGEMENT IN NAMED DATA NETWORKS

The Named Data Network (NDN) [23] is one of the main ICN architectures that has potential to be the future Internet. Similar to other ICN architectures, content is named in the network. Hence, information can be requested without the need for location information (such as an IP in the current Internet). Additionally, data can be cached in any NDN node, this would decrease the time it takes to request content. A hierarchical *naming* prefix is used in NDN, which makes routing and forwarding process relatively simpler than other architectures.

NDN is designed to be a *Consumer*-driven network, where in order the users to communicate, the requester (referred here as *Consumer*) will send requests packets (*Interests*) for specific data from content provider (referred here as *Producer*) [21,23]. The *Interest* will be forwarded to the nearest copy of the content, and then the *Data* packet holding the content is generated and sent back to the *Consumer*. This process needs three *Data* structures: Forwarding Information Base (FIB), Pending Interest Table (PIT) and Content

Store (CS) [23]. Particularly, FIB is used to forward *Interest*s to the nearest content location. PITs are used to keep track of the forwarded *Interest*s and requested user, so when the *Data* is available, it can be sent to the *Consumer*. Finally, CS is storage for cached data in an NDN node. Moreover, in case of failures, *Consumer*s retransmit *Interest*s that have not been satisfied for a specific period

In typical NDN, user mobility can be classified to *Consumer* mobility and *Producer* mobility. *Consumer* mobility is handled as if there is a failure in the network where unsatisfied *Interest*s will be retransmitted. Consequently, during this process the *Consumer* will experience a long delay to retrieve the data which may affect the QoS of real-time applications [3].

With regards to *Producer* mobility, NDN uses late binding where content is matched to a location in the forwarding process [21]. Consequently, this design complicates *Producer* mobility compared to *Consumer* mobility. When a *Producer* changes its location, the routing tables should be updated with the new location of the *Producer*. However, updating the FIBs is not a scalable solution since the delay of routing convergence will increase with larger networks. Without using any *Producer* mobility management scheme, *Consumer*s will not be able to reach the moving *Producer* until the routing protocol updates the routing state with the new location, affecting the *Producer*'s availability and *Consumer*'s Quality of Experience (QoE). The authors in [3, 17] have conducted simulations to study the capability of NDN in handling simple mobility events. The results have shown that NDN with its typical architecture fails to provide seamless mobility; thus the use of an effective mobility management scheme is necessary. *Producer* mobility is the focus of this work, since the schemes proposed in the literature is target this type of mobility.

3. MAINSTREAM NDN MOBILITY MANAGEMENT SCHEMES

In this section, we investigate several proposed schemes designed to handle *Producer* mobility in the NDN architecture. Re-applied ideas from current protocols in the Internet such as Mobile IP [6] and Domain Name System (DNS) were at the core of these schemes. We categorize the mainstream NDN mobility management schemes into: Mobility Anchor, Location Resolution and Hybrid approaches. One management scheme from each approach is selected to be a representative scheme, which will be explained and evaluated using the introduced Assessment Framework in Section 5.

3.1 Mobility Anchor Approach

Schemes in this class are based on the Mobile IP protocol [6], which is a proposed standard in the Internet Engineering Task Force (IETF) to support host's mobility in IP networks. In particular, Mobile IP uses fixed nodes called Home Agents that keep track of the location of all mobile hosts originally registered in the home network. While a mobile host is roaming outside of its home network, packets addressed to mobile hosts are tunneled through the Home Agent. Schemes proposed in [11, 12, 16, 18, 19] fall into this category with different designs. Generally, the schemes select an anchor node similar to the Home Agent in Mobile IP The methodology used in [16] is based on tunneling. The access router in the home network called "Home Content Router" (CR_h), is the anchor in this scheme. While the *Producer* is roaming, CR_h will forward any *Interest* directed to the former, to the new location. Once the *Data* is received by the CR_h, it will be forwarded to the *Consumer*. The operation of the scheme can be summarized in three steps: 1. *Movement indication*: Once the mobile *Producer* starts the handover it decides on a tentative name prefix that should be unique in the new domain. 2. *Path redirect configuration*: The mobile *Producer* sends a path update (PU) packet to the router to update CR_h with the new location. The router updates the mobile source record in its routing table, and replies with a path update acknowledgment (PACK). The PU and PACK are handled as normal *Interest* and *Data*. 3. *Interest* redirection: When an *Interest* reaches CR_h, it will be encapsulated by a new *Interest* (tunneled *Interest*) and forwards it to the *Producer* using the location information from Step 2. The *Producer* will send the tunneled *Data* back to CR_h, which will extract the *Data* and send it tp the *Consumer*.

3.2 Location Resolution Approach

The approach in Location Resolution schemes is similar to the one used in DNS, where the *Consumer* queries the location of the *Producer* before sending *Interests*. Location Resolution Servers (LRS) are used to resolve location queries, the servers then should be always aware of the current location of each node. Examples of schemes that use this approach are presented in [4,13,25]. NDN uses late content-to-location binding technique, where the content is matched to a location in the forwarding stage. However, Location Resolution schemes require early binding techniques similar to Data-Oriented Network Architecture (DONA) [14]. This technique will affect content naming used in NDN and will require extra overhead to maintain and query locations.

Kim, et. al have proposed in [13] a mobility management scheme that uses Location Resolution Servers. The operation for both *Consumer* and *Producer* is as follows: 1. *Producer* side: once a handover has occurred, the *Producer* will update its prefix to match the new location (e.g. *Producer* named: /prefix_1 moves from access point 1 (AP_1) to access point 2 (AP_2), the *Producer*'s name will change from /AP_1/prefix_1 to /AP_2/prefix_1). This new prefix is then sent to the LRS to update its records. 2. *Consumer side*: a new timeout period L_h is introduced to detect *Producer* mobility. When the *Data* takes longer than L_h to reach the *Consumer*, the latter will query the LRS for the current location of the *Producer*. Once the new prefix reaches the *Consumer*, it will resend all pending *Interests* with the updated location.

3.3 Hybrid Approach

This approach is considered to be a combination of both Mobility Anchor and Location Resolution approaches, thus it is refereed to as *Hybrid* [20]. The mobile nodes in the Hybrid approach should have a name following this format: *PoA/uniqueID*, where PoA is the Point of Attachment (Access router) that the *Consumer* is directly connected to. A Control Plane is proposed to handle active sessions between a *Consumer* and a mobile *Producer*. The Control Plane has the following components: 1. *Proxy Agent (PA)*: The agent that handles mobility at the point of attachment (Anchor in Mobility Anchor Schemes) 2. *Mobile Agent (MA)*: The

agent that handles mobility at the *Consumer* side 3. *Mobility Controller*: Manages the mapping between the client ID and its location in the network (Location Resolution Server)

All communications pass through the domain's PA, which keeps track of all mobile nodes using the Register and Deregister messages sent by the moving node. Furthermore, the Controller will be updated with the new node's location. When the *Consumer* wants to communicate with the *Producer*, first it asks the Controller for the prefix name and appends it to the *Interest* packet. The *Producer*'s PA receives all the *Interests* (acting as the anchor) and will manage the *Interest* forwarding to the *Producer* by issuing new *Interest* packets.

4. DESIGN OF NDN MOBILITY MANAGEMENT SCHEMES

The three schemes share the same concept where mapping of location to data is needed to support seamless mobility. Specifically, the mapping in Mobility Anchor schemes occurs in the Home Router of the *Producer*; such routers will require extra logic to be added. However, Location Resolution and Hybrid schemes need a new entity (LRS) to handle the mapping. Additionally, these two schemes require the name of the *Producer* (i.e. prefix) to change after the handover to match its current location. Consequently, the same *Data* will be stored in the caches with different names which waste the available resources. In the Mobility Anchor Scheme the change in name should not affect the *Consumer* since the Home Agent will handle the tunneling. On the contrary, the *Consumers* in Location Resolution Schemes should be aware of the change, thus LRS queries should be sent. As a result, the advantage of late binding strategy proposed in the original NDN will no longer be in use with Location Resolution and Hybrid approaches, which could affect other NDN functionalities such as forwarding and routing.

Typically, the tunneling technique used in Mobility Anchor schemes will cause longer delays, since *Data* packets will take longer paths to reach the *Consumer*. However at the same time, this technique will minimize *Interests* being dropped during handover. In Location Resolution schemes some *Interests* will be dropped before querying the LRS but the *Data* packet will take the shortest path to the *Consumer*. The Hybrid scheme takes advantage of both techniques. In particular, regular *Data* will always be sent using the shortest path, while *Data* during handover will be tunneled and will not be dropped.

All schemes will require control packets to be sent in order to support seamless mobility. Such control packets are considered as overhead traffic on the network. In particular, the Mobility Anchor scheme will require a pair of *Interest/Data* (prefix update) to be sent for every mobility event to update the Home Agent. On the other hand, Location Resolution Scheme will require two types of overhead. First, prefix update packets which are similar to the mobility Anchor Scheme but will be directed to the LRS. Second, a prefix fetch pair will be requested by the *Consumer* once a timeout period is expired. However, this timeout can occur as result of other events, unrelated to mobility, in the network such as congestion, which will cause the scheme to send unnecessary packets. Since the Hybrid scheme uses both techniques, causing the overhead to be higher than the other two schemes.

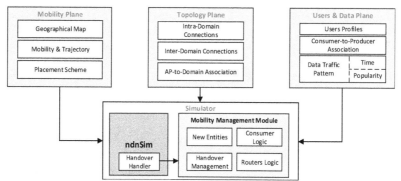
Figure 1: The main components of the Assessment Framework

5. ASSESSMENT FRAMEWORK

The proposed framework is designed to be a benchmarking tool for existing and future mobility management schemes. Hence, the tool will be used to evaluate and compare the schemes using selected performance metrics. The inputs to the Assessment Framework will be varied to study the performance of the mobility management schemes under different scenarios. The components of the framework are shown in Figure 1 and are explained below. The simulator used in the assessment framework is ndnSIM [2] which is an NDN simulator for Network Simulator 3 (ns-3).

5.1 Topology Plane

This component generates various network topologies to be used in the Assessment Framework. The topologies are designed to be hierarchal with multiple domains such as Transit-stub topologies [22], and will allow Intra-domain and Inter-domain communications. Moreover, with hierarchal topologies two different mobility scenarios will be investigated: moving to a new Access Point (AP) within the same domain (Intra-domain mobility) and moving to another domain (Inter-domain mobility). Studying both scenarios will emphasize the advantage of data caching during mobility events, since the effect of Intra-domain mobility are reduced by the available caches in the domain.

The Topology Plane will generate the network in three steps. First, the domains will be generated based on the number of routers and number of distinct domains required. Second, the domains will be connected to form the transit network. Third, the APs will be associated with the different domains.

Once the user leaves the communication range of one AP and enters another, a handover event occurs. Specifically, the user will dissociate from the current AP and associate with the new AP. With this in mind, APs that are geographically neighbors, are not necessarily neighbors in the network topology (i.e. within the same domain).

5.2 Mobility Plane

The positions and movements of users on the map are the outputs of this component. The map may consist of streets, sidewalks and/or buildings. An example of a geographical map that can be used is urban areas which are characterized by having higher densities of users and Wi-Fi APs. This component will also place the APs on the map in addition to the fixed users such as PCs and servers.

Users' trajectory can be generated using analytical ran-

dom mobility models, simulation models or real mobility traces. Random Waypoint, Random Walk and Gauss-Markov are examples of analytical models that use mathematical calculations to determine the next position of a node. Simulation models such as traffic simulators provide more realistic user movements within a given map. Simulation of Urban MObility (SUMO) [15] is widely used to generate such trajectories for vehicles and pedestrians moving at various speeds. Mobility traces of real user's movements can be captured and used in the Assessment Framework similar to the dataset published in [8].

5.3 Users and Data Plane

This component determines the traffic profile of each user, what data the *Producers* can generate and what (and when) the user requests data. Specifically, *Consumers' Interest* patterns are generated which will include the time of request, the *Producer*'s name and the data name. To create realistic request patterns, data will be requested with different popularity (i.e. some data are requested more frequently than others). To model data popularity, distributions such as the Zipf's law [10] can be used. The distribution is controlled by parameter α, where lower values give more uniform-like distributions (i.e. if $\alpha = 0$ then all data has the same probability).

5.4 Mobility Management Schemes Implementation in ndnSIM

The existing ndnSIM (and ns-3) does not provide Wi-Fi handover between access points, nor a mobility management scheme. Therefore, two main updates are done to the current ndnSIM: AP handover handler and a base for mobility management schemes. A new class called `HandoverHanlder` is created and added to the Mobility Module of ns-3. For each mobile node, an object of this class will be instantiated and aggregated to class Node. The handler is responsible for detecting the handover event based on the power received from the AP or the AP-to-user distance. Specifically, it will dissociate the mobile node from the old serving AP and associate it to the new AP. The class will trigger two events in the mobility management scheme by calling the function `PreHandover` before dissociating from the old AP and `PostHandover` after associating with new AP.

`MobilityManagement` is a base class for any mobility management scheme to be implemented in ndnSIM. This abstract class contains two pure virtual functions (the derived class required to implement this function) `PreHandover` and `PostHandover`. In particular, these functions will implement

Table 1: Simulation Parameters

	Parameter	Value
General	Simulation Duration	1000s
	Transit Period	80s
	Map size	$1400m \times 1400m$
	Number of Blocks	7×7
	Number of Users	100
	Producers	50
	Consumers	50
Application	*Interest* Rate	50-80 I/s
	Zipf α	0.2
	Content per *Producer*	$1000 \times 1KB$
Topology	APs	49
	AP Range	200m
	Number of Routers	40
	Core router's links	10Mbps
	Access router's links	5Mbps
	Propagation delay	10ms
Mobility	Model	Manhattan
	Handover delay	0.5s
	Speed	70 km/h
NDN	Forwarding Scheme	BestRoute
	Cache replacement	LRU
	Cache Size	1000 objects

the required actions to be done by the mobile node before and after the handover. Moreover, the class may include any extra logic to be added to the *Consumer*s, routers and/or new entities. For example, Location Resolution Schemes need a new timeout period to be added to the *Consumer* application and the logic of the LRS. `MobilityManagmentHelper` is a class that will be used to aggregate the `MobilityManagement` on all nodes for handling *Producer* mobility. The source code of our modules in ndnSIM is available for the public [9].

5.5 Performance Metrics

In order to provide a seamless experience during mobility in NDN, the management scheme needs to keep the delay experienced by the *Consumer* maintained, avoid *Interest* retransmissions and minimize the overhead. Measuring the following metrics will provide a complete picture of the scheme's performance which covers the effect on both the user and network:

1. *Consumer* Delay (CD) is the total delay the *Consumer* experiences to request an *Interest* and receive the corresponding *Data*. Specifically, it is the time difference between the first attempt of sending the *Interest* and receiving the *Data*. This includes the total timeout and the delay of retransmitted *Interest* and *Data* packets

2. Delivery Ratio (DR) is the proportion of successful *Data* packets received by the *Consumer* to the total number of *Interest*s sent. This metric is a measure of how successful is the scheme in avoiding both *Interest*s and *Data* drops.

3. Scheme Overhead (OH) is the total number of control messages sent by the scheme for the purpose of supporting mobility. For example, in Location Resolution schemes, the overhead includes the prefix update and prefix query packets.

6. EXPERIMENTS, RESULTS AND DISCUSSION

In this section, we present one instance of the Assessment Framework, where the aforementioned mobility management schemes are implemented and tested. The details of the experiments and select results are shown and discussed.

6.1 Experimental Setup

Table 1 summarizes the simulation parameters used for

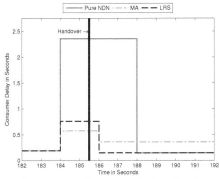

Figure 2: Delay for one *Consumer* during *Producer* mobility event at time=185.5s

this experiment. The topology used is Transit-stub network that consists of 40 core routers and 5 domains. Core routers are connected with links of 10Mbps capacity, while access routers are connected to the core routers with 5Mbps links, and the propagation delay in all links is 10ms.

The map where the users will move on is assumed to be a street grid plan (e.g. Manhattan) where users are either pedestrians on sidewalks or riding vehicles (private cars or public transit). Moreover, a Wi-Fi AP will be installed at every intersection to provide Internet access within its communication range which is assumed to be 200m. Wi-Fi 802.11g is used as a standard for the wireless medium. The handover delay (AP dissociating and associating) is assumed to be 0.5s.

Each *Producer* provides 1000 unique *Data* objects (1KB each), and content popularity is modeled using Zipf's law distribution with $\alpha = 0.2$. *Consumer*s request *Data* by sending *Interest*s (frequency = 50-80 *Interest*/s) with random inter-*Interest* gap that follows exponential distribution with $mean = 1/frequency$.

The main functionalities of NDN are assumed to have the default values in ndnSIM. In particular, ndnSIM uses an opportunistic scheme named as "Cache Everything Everywhere" for object caching [7]. NDN nodes using this scheme will cache any *Data* passing through it. In case of full cache, Least Recently Used (LRU) replacement policy is used. The cache size in the simulation environment is designed to be 2% of the total content in the network, therefore the cache size = 50 (*Producers*) $\times$ 1000 (content per *Producer*) $\times$ 2% = 1000 *Data* objects. Best Route is used as the forwarding strategy in ndnSIM where the next hop is decided on the best-calculated metrics such as number of hops, delay and congestion.

The experiments were executed for 28 runs on 7 different topologies where different random seeds are used in every run. Accordingly, the averages of the performance metrics were calculated to be used in the evaluation. For every metric, the same simulation parameters are used to evaluate pure NDN with no mobility management scheme and NDN with the aforementioned three schemes.

6.2 Impact on a One Consumer

Figure 2 shows the effect of *Producer* mobility on the delay experienced by one *Consumer* using no mobility management scheme (pure NDN), Mobility Anchor scheme and Location Resolution scheme. The *Consumer* Delay (y-axis) is measured for every *Interest* sent by the *Consumer* (x-axis ordered by *Interest* sending time) with handover event

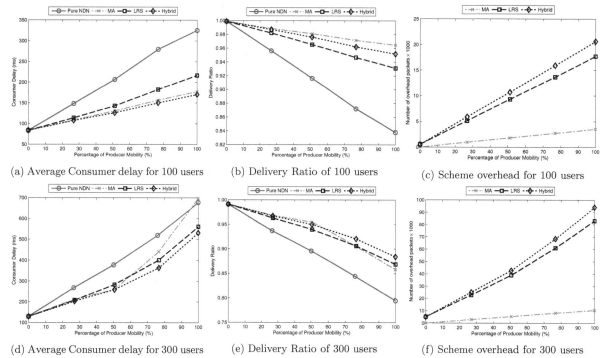

(a) Average Consumer delay for 100 users (b) Delivery Ratio of 100 users (c) Scheme overhead for 100 users

(d) Average Consumer delay for 300 users (e) Delivery Ratio of 300 users (f) Scheme overhead for 300 users

Figure 3: Comparison between the four schemes in two scenarios: 100 and 300 users, using the three performance metrics

occurred at time 185.5s. As shown in the figure, the *Consumer* experiences long delays with pure NDN more than a network with a mobility management scheme. Moreover, the affected period in which the *Interests* could not reach the *Producer* is longer (approximately 4s compared to 2s). During the handover, the CD reached 2.35s from time 184s to 188s, and once the routing protocol finished updating the FIBs at time 188s, CD was back 0.15s. Using a mobility management scheme mitigated this delay problem. In particular, the two schemes have shortened the affected period, and a shorter delay is experienced. Mobility Anchor scheme had less delay during the handover compared to the Location Resolution scheme. However, the delay after the handover in Mobility Anchor scheme is higher than the other scheme and pure NDN due to the tunneling process in which *Interest-Data* path becomes longer.

6.3 Varying Percentage of Producer Mobility

In able to study the effect of mobility on the performance metrics mentioned above, the number of mobile *Producers* is varied from 0% (no mobility) to 100% (all *Producers* are mobile).

6.3.1 Consumer Delay

For 100 users, the average *Consumer* delay of the different schemes as a function of the number of mobile *Producers* is shown in Figure 3a. In pure NDN, the average *Consumer* delay in case of full mobility is 4 times longer than no mobility scenarios. This increase is avoided with the use of a mobility management scheme which will reduce the *Consumer* delay by at least 33%. As for comparing the schemes, the Hybrid approach outperformed the other two schemes just after 25% mobility. This is the result of avoiding *Interest* drops using the Anchors, in addition to the path update using the Location Resolution server. Moreover, the delay in

MA is lower than LRS. This is due to the longer *Data* paths in Mobility Anchor after the handover (a relatively small delay but occurs for all *Interest*). On the other hand, the delay in Location Resolution scheme is due to the value of L_h (location change detection period) and the time needed to query the LRS (a long delay but for short periods just after the handover).

To clarify, Figure 4 shows the Cumulative Distribution Function (CDF) for full mobility scenario (100% *Producer* mobility) for all the schemes. From the figure, we see that the Mobility Anchor scheme has the longest delay (300ms) upon all schemes in 92% of total *Interests*. Furthermore, the delay in this scheme is longer than Location Resolution scheme 95% of total *Interests*, after that the latter's delay exceeds with larger values. To illustrate this, Figure 5 shows the standard deviation (SD) of the *Consumer* delay of each scheme. The SD of Location Resolution scheme reached 0.6, while the SD of Mobility Anchor is maintained below 0.2 which confirms that the variance in delay in Location Resolution scheme is larger than the Mobility Anchor.

To analyze the performance of the schemes in a dense user environment, the number of users is increased to 300 (150 *Producers* and 150 *Consumers*). As shown in Figure 3d, the delay of the schemes increased 4 times where it was 2.5 times in case of 100 users. More interestingly, the delay in Mobility Anchor scheme increases much faster and bypasses the delay in the Location Resolution scheme after 60%. This is due to the increase of number of events requests which will take longer paths.

6.3.2 Delivery Ratio

Figure 3b shows the average delivery ratio of *Consumers* as a function of mobility percentage. The delivery ratio decreased from 100% to 85% without any mobility manage-

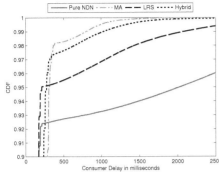

Figure 4: CDF of Delay in 100% *Producer* mobility

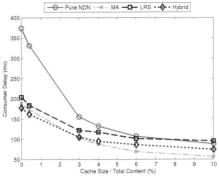

Figure 6: Effect of Cache size with 50% *Producer* Mobility

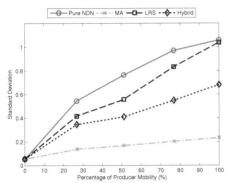

Figure 5: Standard Deviation of *Consumer* Delay

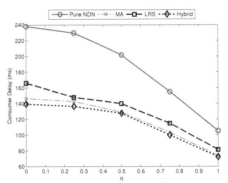

Figure 7: Effect of popularity with 50% *Producer* mobility

ment scheme. This is a result of *Interests* retransmissions and packets drops. On the other hand, using a mobility management scheme will reduce this drop to 95%. In particular, Mobility Anchor scheme has the best delivery ratio among other schemes due to the anchors which forward *Interests* to the new location of the *Producer*, thus no *Interest* dropping occurs.

The result of 300 users scenario is shown in Figure 3e. The same performance degradation of the Mobility Anchor scheme happened after 60%.

6.3.3 Scheme Overhead

To support seamless mobility, schemes need to send control messages to different entities in the network. This overhead is shown in Figure 3c and 3f . Mobility Anchor scheme has very low overhead compared to the two other schemes, since the *Consumers* in the Location Resolution scheme query the LRS. The Hybrid approach has the worst overhead since it needs both types of control messages as discussed in Section 4. Nonetheless, this control overhead is found to be lower than the amount of FIB update messages for all mobility events. For instance, the number of FIB update packets sent is 22 times more than the control overhead of the Hybrid scheme in 100% mobility. Notice that the Location Resolution and the Hybrid schemes has a significant overhead (1000 to 5000 packets) with 0% of *Producer* mobility. This is due that the *Consumers* will query the LRS after the timeout period L_h even though there are no mobility events.

Increasing the number of users was found to have no effect on the trend of overhead. However, the total number of packets is increased by 250% in Mobility Anchor scheme and 450% in the other two schemes.

6.4 Impact of the Cache Size and Content Popularity

To study the effect of caching on the schemes, another experiment was conducted where the cache size varies from 0 (no caching) to 5000 objects (10% from the total content of all *Producers*) and the mobility ratio is fixed to 50%. The results are shown in Figure 6. Generally, the *Consumer* delay is decreasing with the increase of cache size. Notice that Mobility Anchor is the best scheme to utilize large cache sizes. Specifically, any cache size larger than 4%, Mobility Anchor scheme outperforms all other schemes. As a matter of fact, with larger cache sizes Location Resolution scheme has a very close performance level to pure NDN. The reason behind this is the renaming process in Location Resolution schemes (and Hybrid). For instance, after a mobility event of a *Producer*, it will provide the same content but with a different name, which makes the content with the old name stored in the caches obsolete.

Finally, we investigate the effect of content popularity on *Producer* mobility. As mentioned in Section 5, the Zipf distribution can be used to model the popularity of data requests. To test different content popularities, the parameter α is varied while fixing *Producer* mobility to 50% as shown in Figure 7. Starting with $\alpha = 0$, which means all content has the same popularity, and ending with $\alpha = 1$ (The larger α is, the more popular is some content). As shown in the figure, the delay decreases with the increase of content popularity. This is because the caches in the network will store more popular content. It has the same effect of increasing the cache size.

7. CONCLUSION

Supporting seamless mobility in NDN is a challenge. As shown in this study, and several others, that the development of a mobility management scheme for NDN is inevitable. There are existing *Producer* mobility management schemes in the literature that claim to support seamless mobility, but never investigated or compared to one another. Therefore, we designed and implemented a novel Assessment Framework to be used as a benchmark tool and made available to NDN researchers to investigate existing and future mobility management schemes. The framework was used to compare three main classes of *Producer* mobility management schemes; Mobility Anchor, Location Resolution and Hybrid approaches.

Simulations results show that in the case of low mobility, the three schemes have close *Consumer* delay. However, with mid to high mobility, the Hybrid approach has lower delay than other schemes but at a cost of extra overhead. Mobility Anchor approach has a close *Consumer* Delay and higher Delivery Ratio compared to the Hybrid approach. However, with dense user environments the Mobility Anchor scheme has lower performance than all other schemes. Investigating the effect of cache size on mobility has shown that with larger cache sizes the Mobility Anchor scheme has a shorter *Consumer* delay than the Hybrid approach. Finally, the experiments have shown that the Location Resolution scheme has the lowest performance in all metrics; thus it cannot be used without combining it with another scheme.

Our next step is to design an optimal mobility management scheme to be used as a benchmark solution in the Assessment Framework. In addition to extending the framework to evaluate and compare *Consumer* mobility management schemes.

8. ACKNOWLEDGMENT

This research is funded by a grant from the Ontario Ministry of Economic Development and Innovation under the Ontario Research Fund-Research Excellence (ORF-RE) program.

9. REFERENCES

[1] Cisco visual networking index: Forecast and methodology, 2013–2018. White Paper, Cisco, Jun. 2014.

[2] A. Afanasyev, I. Moiseenko, and L. Zhang. ndnSIM: NDN simulator for NS-3. Technical Report NDN-0005, NDN, October 2012.

[3] A. Azgin, R. Ravindran, and G. Wang. Mobility study for named data networking in wireless access networks. In *IEEE International Conference on Communications (ICC)*, pages 3252–3257, Sydney, Australia, June 2014.

[4] A. Azgin, R. Ravindran, and G. Wang. A scalable mobility-centric architecture for named data networking. *CoRR*, abs/1406.7049, 2014.

[5] G. M. Brito, P. B. Velloso, and I. M. Moraes. *Information Centric Networks: A New Paradigm for the Internet.* Wiley, 2013.

[6] E. C. Perkins. IP mobility support for IPv4, revised. RFC 5944, 2010.

[7] A. Dabirmoghaddam, M. M. Barijough, and J. Garcia-Luna-Aceves. Understanding optimal caching and opportunistic caching at "the edge" of information-centric networks. In *Proceedings of the International Conference on Information-centric Networking*, pages 47–56, Paris, France, 2014. ACM.

[8] N. Eagle and A. S. Pentland. CRAWDAD data set mit/reality (v. 2005-07-01). Downloaded from http://crawdad.org/mit/reality/, July 2005.

[9] H. Farahat. Mobility assessment framework. http://mobman.queenstrl.ca, 2015. Accessed on September 15, 2015.

[10] C. Fricker, P. Robert, J. Roberts, and N. Sbihi. Impact of traffic mix on caching performance in a content-centric network. In *IEEE Conference on Computer Communications Workshops (INFOCOM WKSHPS)*, pages 310–315, Orlando, FL, USA, March 2012.

[11] D. Han, M. Lee, K. Cho, T. Kwon, and Y. Choi. Publisher mobility support in content centric networks. In *International Conference on Information Networking (ICOIN)*, pages 214–219, Phuket, Thailand, Feb 2014.

[12] F. Hermans, E. Ngai, and P. Gunningberg. Global source mobility in the content-centric networking architecture. In *Proceedings of the ACM workshop on Emerging Name-Oriented Mobile Networking Design - Architecture, Algorithms, and Applications*, pages 13–18, Hilton Head, South Carolina, USA, 2012.

[13] D.-h. Kim, J.-h. Kim, Y.-s. Kim, H.-s. Yoon, and I. Yeom. End-to-end mobility support in content centric networks. *International Journal of Communication Systems*, 28(6):1151–1167, 2015.

[14] T. Koponen, M. Chawla, B.-G. Chun, A. Ermolinskiy, K. H. Kim, S. Shenker, and I. Stoica. A data-oriented (and beyond) network architecture. *SIGCOMM Computing Communication Review*, 37(4):181–192, 2007.

[15] D. Krajzewicz, J. Erdmann, M. Behrisch, and L. Bieker. Recent development and applications of SUMO - Simulation of Urban MObility. *International Journal of Advances in Systems and Measurements*, 5(3&4):128–138, Dec. 2012.

[16] J. Lee, S. Cho, and D. Kim. Device mobility management in content-centric networking. *IEEE Communications Magazine*, 50(12):28–34, 2012.

[17] Z. Liu, Y. Wu, E. Yuepeng, J. Ge, and T. Li. Experimental evaluation of consumer mobility on named data networking. In *International Conf on Ubiquitous and Future Networks (ICUFN)*, pages 472–476, Shanghai, China, July 2014.

[18] Y. Rao, H. Luo, D. Gao, H. Zhou, and H. Zhang. Lbma: A novel locator based mobility support approach in named data networking. *China Communications*, 11(4):111–120, April 2014.

[19] Y. Rao, H. Zhou, D. Gao, H. Luo, and Y. Liu. Proactive caching for enhancing user-side mobility support in named data networking. In *International Conference on Innovative Mobile and Internet Services in Ubiquitous Computing (IMIS)*, pages 37–42, Taichung, Taiwan, July 2013.

[20] R. Ravindran, S. Lo, X. Zhang, and G. Wang. Supporting seamless mobility in named data networking. In *IEEE International Conference on Communications (ICC)*, pages 5854–5869, Ottawa, Canada, 2012.

[21] G. Tyson, N. Sastry, I. Rimac, R. Cuevas, and A. Mauthe. A survey of mobility in information-centric networks: challenges and research directions. In *Proceedings of the ACM workshop on Emerging Name-Oriented Mobile Networking Design - Architecture, Algorithms, and Applications*, pages 1–6, Hilton Head, South Carolina, USA, 2012.

[22] E. Zegura, K. Calvert, and S. Bhattacharjee. How to model an internetwork. In *Proceedings of IEEE INFOCOM*, volume 2, pages 594–602, San Francisco, CA, USA, Mar 1996.

[23] L. Zhang, A. Afanasyev, J. Burke, V. Jacobson, K. Claffy, P. Crowley, C. Papadopoulos, L. Wang, and B. Zhang. Named data networking. *SIGCOMM Computing Communication Review*, 44(3):66–73, July 2014.

[24] Y. Zhang, H. Zhang, and L. Zhang. Kite: A mobility support scheme for ndn. In *Proceedings of the International Conference on Information-centric Networking*, pages 179–180, Paris, France, 2014.

[25] Z. Zhu, A. Afanasyeva, and L. Zhang. A new perspective on mobility support. Technical Report NDN-0013, NDN, 2013.

Stochastic Geometry Modeling of Cellular Networks: Analysis, Simulation and Experimental Validation

Wei Lu
Paris-Saclay University
Laboratory of Signals and Systems (UMR-8506)
CNRS-CentraleSupelec-University Paris-Sud XI
3, rue Joliot-Curie
91192 Gif-sur-Yvette (Paris), France
wei.lu@l2s.centralesupelec.fr

Marco Di Renzo
Paris-Saclay University
Laboratory of Signals and Systems (UMR-8506)
CNRS-CentraleSupelec-University Paris-Sud XI
3, rue Joliot-Curie
91192 Gif-sur-Yvette (Paris), France
marco.direnzo@l2s.centralesupelec.fr

ABSTRACT

Due to the increasing heterogeneity and deployment density of emerging cellular networks, new flexible and scalable approaches for their modeling, simulation, analysis and optimization are needed. Recently, a new approach has been proposed: it is based on the theory of point processes and it leverages tools from stochastic geometry for tractable system-level modeling, performance evaluation and optimization. In this paper, we investigate the accuracy of this emerging abstraction for modeling cellular networks, by explicitly taking realistic base station locations, building footprints, spatial blockages and antenna radiation patterns into account. More specifically, the base station locations and the building footprints are taken from two publicly available databases from the United Kingdom. Our study confirms that the abstraction model based on stochastic geometry is capable of accurately modeling the communication performance of cellular networks in dense urban environments.

Categories and Subject Descriptors

C.2.1 [**Network Architecture and Design**]: Wireless communication; C.4 [**Performance of Systems**]: Modeling techniques; G.3 [**Probability and Statistics**]: Stochastic processes; I.6.4 [**Simulation and Modeling**]: Model Validation and Analysis; I.6.5 [**Simulation and Modeling**]: Model Development.

Keywords

Cellular networks, stochastic geometry, point processes.

1. INTRODUCTION

Heterogeneous ultra-dense cellular networks constitute an enabling architecture for achieving the disruptive capabilities that the fifth generation (5G) of cellular networks is expected to provide [1]. Modeling, simulating, analyzing and

optimizing such networks is, however, a non-trivial problem. This is due to the large number of access points that are expected to be deployed and their dissimilar characteristics, which encompass deployment density, transmit power, access technology, etc. Motivated by these considerations, several researchers are investigating different options for modeling, simulating, mathematically analyzing and optimizing these networks. The general consensus is, in fact, that the methods used in the past for modeling cellular networks, e.g., the hexagonal grid-based model [2], are not sufficiently scalable and flexible for taking the ultra-dense and irregular deployments of emerging cellular topologies into account.

Recently, a new approach for overcoming these limitations has been proposed. It is based on the theory of point processes (PP) and leverages tools from stochastic geometry for system-level modeling, performance evaluation and optimization of cellular networks [3]. In this paper, it is referred to as the PP-based model. Unlike its grid-based counterpart, the locations of the base stations (BSs) are not assumed to be regularly deployed, but they are assumed to be randomly distributed according to a PP. This approach, due to its mathematical flexibility for modeling heterogeneous ultra-dense cellular deployments, has been extensively used in the last few years and it is gaining exponential prominence in the scientific community. The interested reader is referred to [4]-[8] for the latest achievements in this field of research.

Despite that, the experimental validation of the PP-based abstraction for modeling cellular networks has remained elusive to date. This is especially true for modeling macro cellular BSs, whose deployment is, usually, not totally random. A few researchers have tried to justify the PP-based model by using empirical data for the locations of the BSs, e.g., [3], [9], [10]. These studies have confirmed the potential accuracy and the usefulness of the PP-based model. They, however, are based on a small set of data and on simplifying modeling assumptions. Notably, they do not account for the footprints of the buildings and rely on simplified channel models, where line-of-sight (LOS) and non-line-of-sight (NLOS) propagation conditions that originate from the presence of buildings are neglected. This is mostly due to the inherent difficulties of obtaining accurate data related to the locations of the BSs and of the buildings in urban areas [11]. The importance of modeling LOS and NLOS propagation conditions, however, has recently been emphasized in several papers, e.g., [12] and references therein.

In this paper, we investigate the accuracy of the PP-based abstraction for modeling cellular networks with the aid of experimental data. We explicitly take realistic BS locations, building footprints, LOS/NLOS channel conditions and antenna radiation patterns into account. More specifically: i) the locations of the BSs are taken from a large database made available by OFCOM, the independent regulator and competition authority for the United Kingdom (UK) communications industries [13]; and ii) the footprints of the buildings are taken from a large database made available by Ordnance Survey, the Britain's mapping agency offering the most up-to-date and accurate maps of the UK [14]. Our extensive study highlights that the PP-based model is capable of accurately predicting the performance of cellular networks in dense urban environments. It also shows, however, that their performance highly depends on the channel models and the antenna radiation patterns being used.

In addition, this paper provides another important contribution: we introduce tractable approximations for modeling empirical LOS/NLOS conditions due to blockages and practical antenna radiation patterns, which facilitate the system-level simulation and the mathematical modeling of cellular networks. The relevance of the proposed approximations is twofold: i) simulation, analysis and optimization of ultra-dense cellular networks turn out to be easier, since neither the actual building footprints nor the actual antenna radiation patterns are needed and, more importantly, ii) they offer a transparent interface between telecommunication operators/manufactures and governmental agencies on one side, as well as academic and research organizations on the other side, since accurate data about the locations of the BSs and the footprints of the buildings, which often constitutes sensible and confidential information, does not need to be explicitly provided. By using the proposed approximations, this data can be provided in a modified format, which allows the former organizations not to unveil sensible and confidential information on actual network and city deployments. In this paper, we prove that the proposed approximations are accurate enough for modeling cellular networks. In a companion paper, we have recently verified that the proposed approximations are suitable for mathematical modeling and for computing tractable utility functions for system-level optimization as well. Even though a detailed discussion of mathematical modeling is outside the scope of this paper, the interested reader may find preliminary results in [15].

The remainder of this paper is organized as follows. In Section 2, the system model is introduced. In Section 3, the proposed approximations for facilitating system-level simulations and mathematical analysis are presented. In Section 4, the accuracy of the PP-based abstraction model and of the proposed approximations is substantiated with the aid of experimental data. Also, main findings and takeaway messages are discussed. Finally, Section 5 concludes this paper.

2. SYSTEM MODEL

2.1 Base Stations Modeling

In order to test the accuracy of the PP-based model for the locations of the BSs, we use experimental data from two actual deployments of BSs that correspond to the cities of London and Manchester in the UK. As mentioned in Section 1, this data is obtained from OFCOM [13]. More specifically, we consider the BSs of two telecommunication operators: O2

Table 1: BS statistics from OFCOM - The city of London ($\mathcal{A} = 4\,\mathrm{km}^2$).

	O2+Vod.	O2	Vod.
Number of BSs	319	183	136
Number of rooftop BSs	95	62	33
Number of outdoor BSs	224	121	103
Average cell radius (m)	63.1771	83.4122	96.7577

Table 2: BS statistics from OFCOM - The city of Manchester ($\mathcal{A} = 1.8\,\mathrm{km}^2$).

	O2+Vod.	O2	Vod.
Number of BSs	37	16	22
Number of rooftop BSs	25	12	14
Number of outdoor BSs	12	4	8
Average cell radius (m)	125.925	191.492	163.305

and Vodafone. The empirical data is summarized in Tables 1 and 2 for London and Manchester, respectively. The following terminology and notation are used: i) "rooftop BSs" is referred to the BSs that lay inside a geographical region (polygon) where a building is located; ii) "outdoor BSs" is referred to the BSs that lay in a geographical region where no buildings are located. Information about the locations of the buildings is provided in Section 2.2; and iii) $\mathcal{A}$ denotes the area of the geographical region under analysis. From the number of BSs ($\mathcal{N}$) and $\mathcal{A}$, the density of BSs is obtained as $\lambda_{\mathrm{BS}} = \mathcal{N}/\mathcal{A}$. Accordingly, the average cell radius shown in the tables is computed as $R_c = \sqrt{1/(\pi \lambda_{\mathrm{BS}})}$ [15]. It is worth mentioning that O2 and Vodafone share one BS in the considered region of the city of Manchester. As expected, the data in Tables 1 and 2 confirms that a denser deployment of BSs is available in London.

To study the impact of network densification and the potential gains of sharing the BSs between telecommunication operators, two scenarios are investigated. In the first scenario, the BSs of O2 and Vodafone operate at different frequencies, thus they do not interfere with each other. This is equivalent to having just one telecommunication operator in the region of interest. Hence, only the BSs of one telecommunication operator are accessible to the typical mobile terminal (MT). In the second scenario, O2 and Vodafone share the BSs and they operate at the same frequency. So, a denser deployment of BSs is available in the region of interest and the BSs of both telecommunication operators are accessible to the typical MT. Furthermore, full frequency reuse for the BSs of the same telecommunication operator and a saturated load traffic model are assumed. This implies that, with the exception of the serving BS, all the accessible BSs at a given frequency act as interferers for the probe MT.

As for the PP-based model for the locations of the BSs, we assume that the BSs are distributed according to a Poisson PP (PPP). It is known, in fact, that the PPP results in a pure random deployment and that it is more mathematically tractable than any other PPs available in the literature [16]. In other words, it corresponds to a worst case scenario for testing the accuracy of the PP-based model.

2.2 Buildings Modeling

To take realistic blockages into account, i.e., LOS and NLOS propagation conditions due to the locations and the shapes of buildings (see also Section 2.3), we use experimental data corresponding to the actual deployments of buildings in the cities of London and Manchester. As mentioned

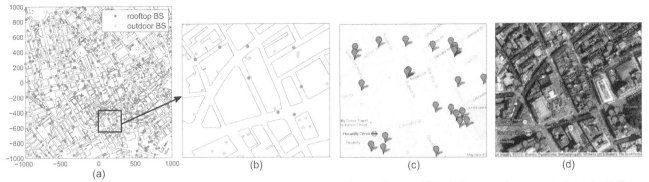

Figure 1: London case study. Dense urban environment, where the 55.9% of the area is occupied by buildings. Horizontal and vertical axis provide distances expressed in meters. (a) Entire region under analysis. (b) Magnification of a smaller region. (c) Google map view of (b). (d) Satellite view of (b).

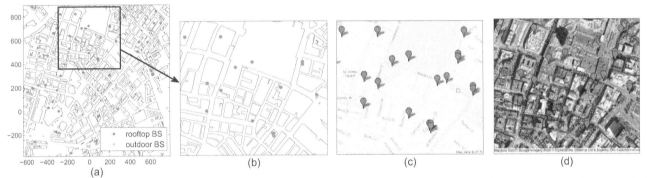

Figure 2: Manchester case study. Dense urban environment, where the 44.46% of the area is occupied by buildings. Horizontal and vertical axis provide distances expressed in meters. (a) Entire region under analysis. (b) Magnification of a smaller region. (c) Google map view of (b). (d) Satellite view of (b).

in Section 1, this data is obtained from OS [14]. In particular, the same geographical regions as those of the locations of the BSs in Section 2.1 are considered. To make sure that the data obtained from the two independent websites of OF-COM and OS can be merged together, we have verified their consistency with the aid of Google maps for the same areas. Figures 1 and 2 provide a graphical representation of the geographical areas under analysis, by merging the data from OFCOM and OS. As far as the buildings are concerned, their elevation is not considered, since this data is not available in the database. Therefore, the analysis of its impact is postponed to a future research study.

2.3 Blockages Modeling

The presence of buildings in dense urban environments constitute an inherent source of blockages, which results in LOS and NLOS links. Modeling LOS and NLOS propagation conditions constitute an important requirement for assessing the physical layer performance of transmission schemes within the 3rd generation partnership project (3GPP) [17]. As far as the PP-based modeling of cellular networks is concerned, however, this is often overlooked due to the mathematical intractability of modeling links having multiple states. Only recently, in fact, some attempts to take LOS and NLOS links into account have been made, e.g., [15] and references therein. In this paper, three approaches for modeling blockages are investigated and compared against each other.

2.3.1 Empirical-Based Model

Based on the locations of the BSs and on the locations and the shapes of the buildings described in Sections 2.1 and 2.2, respectively, LOS and NLOS propagation conditions can be empirically taken into account. In this paper, LOS and NLOS links are identified as follows. Let a generic "outdoor BS" and a generic MT in the region of interest. The related link is in LOS if no building is intersected by connecting the BS and the MT with a straight line. Otherwise, the link is in NLOS. Let a generic "rooftop BS", the BS-to-MT links are assumed to be in NLOS. This is a simplifying assumption used in other papers as well [18], which seems acceptable if no information on the elevation of the buildings is available.

2.3.2 3GPP-Based Model

The 3GPP provides a statistical model for identifying LOS and NLOS links in several scenarios. More specifically, the approach is probabilistic and it does not need any empirical information about the locations of the BSs and of the buildings: a BS-to-MT link is assumed to be in LOS or NLOS with some probability that depends on the BS-to-MT distance. In this paper, we focus our attention only on the MTs that are located outdoors. This is because differentiating between outdoor and indoor propagation would require to introduce different channel parameters. This generalization is postponed to future research. As a case study, hence, we consider the LOS/NLOS model for outdoor MTs in a urban micro-cell scenario, which provides a good representation of the geographical regions considered for London and

Manchester in Tables 1, 2 and Figures 1, 2. In mathematical terms, the probability that a link of length r, i.e., the BS-to-MT distance is r, is in LOS is [17]:

$$p^{(\text{LOS})}(r) = \min\{18/r, 1\}\left(1 - e^{\left(-\frac{r}{36}\right)}\right) + e^{\left(-\frac{r}{36}\right)} \quad (1)$$

where $\min\{\cdot, \cdot\}$ denotes the minimum function. The probability that the link is in NLOS is $p^{(\text{NLOS})}(r) = 1 - p^{(\text{LOS})}(r)$.

2.3.3 1-State Model

As mentioned in Section 2.3, LOS and NLOS propagation conditions are often neglected and all links are assumed to be either in LOS or NLOS. This case study is considered in this paper as well, to better understand the differences between 1-state and 2-state blockage models. For example, if all the BS-to-MT links are assumed to be in NLOS, $p^{(\text{NLOS})}(r) = 1$ and $p^{(\text{LOS})}(r) = 0$ regardless of the link length r.

2.4 Channel Modeling

In addition to modeling blockages, we consider a practical channel model. In particular, path-loss, shadowing and fast-fading are considered. Let a generic BS denoted by BS_i and a generic outdoor MT denoted by MT_k.

As for the path-loss, we consider the physical-based bounded model $l^{(S)}(r_{i,k}) = \kappa^{(S)}(\max\{r_0, r_{i,k}\})^{\alpha^{(S)}}$, where $r_{i,k}$ denotes the BS-to-MT distance, $S = \text{LOS}$ or $S = \text{NLOS}$ if the BS-to-MT link is in LOS or in NLOS, $\kappa^{(S)}$ denotes the path-loss constant, $\alpha^{(S)}$ denotes the path-loss exponent, and r_0 is a positive constant that avoids the singularity of the path-loss model for $r_{i,k} \to 0$.

As for the shadowing, we consider that it is distributed according to log-normal random variable with mean and standard deviation (in dB) equal to $\mu^{(S)}$ and to $\sigma^{(S)}$, respectively. In this paper, shadowing is denoted by $X_{i,k}^{(S)}$.

As for the fast-fading, we consider that the envelope of the links in LOS and in NLOS is distributed according to a Nakagami-m (with $m > 1$) and a Rayleigh random variable with mean power Ω, respectively. In this paper, the envelope of the fast-fading is denoted by $h_{i,k}^{(S)}$. Fast-fading and shadowing are assumed to be independently distributed.

Thus, the received power at MT_k can be formulated as:

$$P_R = \frac{P_T G_{i,k} h_{i,k}^{(S)} X_{i,k}^{(S)}}{\kappa^{(S)}(\max\{r_0, r_{i,k}\})^{\alpha^{(S)}}} \quad (2)$$

where P_T is the transmit power of BS_i and $G_{i,k}$ is the antenna gain of the BS_i-to-MT_k link. If BS_i is the intended BS of MT_k, we assume $G_{i,k} = 1$. If, on the other hand, BS_i is an interfering BS for MT_k, the antenna radiation patterns of BS_i and MT_k are assumed to be randomly oriented with respect to each other and to be uniformly distributed in $[-\pi, \pi)$. In this case, we have $G_{i,k} = g_{\text{BS}}(\theta_i) g_{\text{MT}}(\theta_k)$, where $g_{\text{BS}}(\cdot)$, $g_{\text{MT}}(\cdot)$ are the antenna radiation patterns of BSs and MTs, respectively, and θ_i, θ_k are the angle off the boresight directions of BSs and MTs, respectively. In this paper, we assume $g(\theta) = g_{\text{BS}}(\theta) = g_{\text{MT}}(\theta) \leq 1$ for every θ. Further details about $g(\cdot)$ are provied in Section 2.5.

2.5 Antenna Radiation Pattern

In cellular networks, directional antennas are typically used for enhancing the received power of the intended link and, simultaneously, for reducing the other-cell interference.

In this paper, we are interested in understanding their impact on the accuracy of the PP-based model for cellular networks. Two antenna radiation patterns are considered.

2.5.1 Omni-Directional Model

The omni-directional model constitutes the baseline for comparing any other antenna radiation patterns. In particular, $g(\cdot)$ can be formulated as follows:

$$g(\theta) = 1 \quad \forall \theta \in [-\pi, \pi) \quad (3)$$

2.5.2 3GPP-Based Model

The 3GPP provides a reference antenna radiation pattern for system-level simulations, which is formulated as [19]:

$$g(\theta) = \begin{cases} 10^{-\frac{3}{10}\left(\frac{2\theta}{\theta^{(3\text{dB})}}\right)^2} & \text{if} \quad |\theta| \leq \varphi \\ 10^{-\frac{g^{(\min)}}{10}} & \text{if} \quad \varphi < |\theta| \leq \pi \end{cases} \quad (4)$$

where $\theta_q^{(3\text{dB})}$ denotes the 3 dB beamwidth, $g^{(\min)}$ denotes the minimum gain, and $\varphi = \theta^{(3\text{dB})}\sqrt{g^{(\min)}/12}$ denotes the angle that corresponds to the main lobe [19].

2.6 Cell Association Modeling

The typical (probe) MT is assumed to be served by any accessible BS that provides the highest average received power to it. Thus, path-loss and shadowing are both taken into account for cell association. Fast-fading, on the other hand, is averaged out and neglected. This is, in fact, the typical operating condition based on 3GPP specifications [17].

Let MT_k be the typical MT and the probe link be identified by the subscript "0". Let $C_{0,k}^{(S)}$ be defined as follows:

$$C_{0,k}^{(S)} = \min_{i \in \Phi_{\text{BS}}^{(S)}} \left\{ C_{i,k}^{(S)} = \frac{\kappa^{(S)}(\max\{r_0, r_{i,k}\})^{\alpha^{(S)}}}{X_{i,k}^{(S)}} \right\} \quad (5)$$

where $\max\{\cdot, \cdot\}$ is the maximum function, $\Phi_{\text{BS}}^{(S)}$ is the PP of the BSs in state S, and $1/C_{0,k}^{(S)}$ is the highest average received power at MT_k from any accessible BS whose BS-to-MT_k link is in LOS if $S = \text{LOS}$ or in NLOS if $S = \text{NLOS}$.

From (5), the serving BS of MT_k is that corresponding to the inverse average received power defined as $C_{0,k} = \min\left\{C_{0,k}^{(\text{LOS})}, C_{0,k}^{(\text{NLOS})}\right\}$, since it provides the best link.

2.7 Problem Statement

Let BS_0 be the serving BS of MT_k. Based on (2) and (5), the signal-to-interference-plus-noise-ratio (SINR) at the typical MT, MT_k, can be formulated as follows:

$$\text{SINR} = \frac{P_T G_{0,k} h_{0,k}^{(S_0)}/C_{0,k}^{(S_0)}}{\sigma_N^2 + \sum_{S \in \{\text{LOS}, \text{NLOS}\}} \sum_{i \in \Phi_{\text{BS}}^{(S)} \backslash \text{BS}_0} \mathcal{I}_{i,k}^{(S,S_0)}} \quad (6)$$

where $\mathcal{I}_{i,k}^{(S,S_0)} = (P_T G_{i,k} h_{i,k}^{(S)}/C_{i,k}^{(S)})\mathbf{1}\left(C_{i,k}^{(S)} > C_{0,k}^{(S_0)}\right)$ denotes the generic interfering term, $\mathbf{1}(\cdot)$ denotes the indicator function that originates from the cell association, $S_0 \in \{\text{LOS}, \text{NLOS}\}$ refers to the LOS/NLOS state of the BS_0-to-MT_k link, σ_N^2 denotes the noise power, and the antenna gain of the BS_0-to-MT_k link is $G_{0,k} = 1$ for both omni-directional and 3GPP-based antenna radiation patterns.

In this paper, the performance metric for quantifying the accuracy of the PP-based model is the complementary cumulative distribution function of the SINR, since it provides complete information on its distribution. In addition, it corresponds to the coverage probability of a typical MT as a function of the link reliability threshold. Let T be this threshold, it can be formulated as follows:

$$P_{\text{cov}}(T) = \Pr\{\text{SINR} > T\} \quad (7)$$

3. TRACTABLE SIMULATION AND MATHEMATICAL MODELING

As mentioned in Section 1, the PP-based model of cellular networks has been shown to be tractable under simplifying assumptions for the blockages, the path-loss functions and the antenna radiation patterns [12], [15], [18]. In this section, we introduce some approximations for incorporating realistic models for the blockages and for the antenna radiation patterns in a PP-based modeling framework. To introduce and justify the proposed methodology, in particular, we assume that the BSs are distributed according to a PPP. The accuracy of the PP-based model is assessed in Section 4. The main focus of this section is, in fact, on proposing tractable approximations for modeling LOS and NLOS links that originate from realistic deployments of buildings, and for modeling practical antenna radiation patterns under the assumption that the BSs constitute a PPP.

3.1 Tractable Modeling of Blockages

Due to the presence of blockages (i.e., buildings), a generic BS-to-MT link may be either in LOS or in NLOS with a probability that depends on the BS-to-MT distance, the locations of the BSs, as well as the locations and the shapes of the buildings. This dependence on the distance and on the network topology makes the simulation and the analysis of cellular networks based on the PP-based model less tractable and more time-consuming. In this section, we introduce a piece-wise approximation for taking LOS and NLOS probabilities into account. The proposed approximation is optimized from the point of view of the typical MT and, thus, the spatial deployments of the BSs and of the buildings are explicitly taken into account. This makes it suitable for system-level performance evaluation and optimization. In this paper, it is referred to as the "multi-ball approximation" of blockages.

3.1.1 The Multi-Ball Model

The idea behind the multi-ball approximation lies in replacing the actual LOS/NLOS probability of a typical MT with an approximated function, which still depends on the BS-to-MT distance r but is piece-wise constant as a function of r. In particular, we split the BS-to-MT distance in $N+1$ regions, which correspond to N balls whose center is at the MT. Let the radii of the N balls be $d_1 < d_2 < \ldots, < d_N$. Since r is generic, i.e., $r \in [0, +\infty)$, we have $d_1 \geq 0$ and $d_N < +\infty$. The multi-ball approximation for the LOS/NLOS probability can be formulated as follows:

$$p^{(S)}(r) = \sum_{n=1}^{N+1} q_{[d_{n-1},d_n]}^{(S)} \mathbf{1}_{[d_{n-1},d_n]}(r) \quad (8)$$

where $S \in \{\text{LOS}, \text{NLOS}\}$, $d_0 = 0$, $d_{N+1} = +\infty$, $\mathbf{1}_{[a,b]}(\cdot)$ is the generalized indicator function defined as $\mathbf{1}_{[a,b]}(r) = 1$ if $r \in [a, b)$ and $\mathbf{1}_{[a,b]}(r) = 0$ if $r \notin [a, b)$, and $q_{[a,b]}^{(S)} \geq 0$ denotes the probability that a link of length $r \in [a, b)$ is in

state S. Since a link can be either in LOS or in NLOS, the following constraint need to be satisfied:

$$\sum_{S \in \{\text{LOS}, \text{NLOS}\}} q_{[d_0,d_1]}^{(S)} = \cdots = \sum_{S \in \{\text{LOS}, \text{NLOS}\}} q_{[d_N,d_{N+1}]}^{(S)} = 1 \quad (9)$$

From (8), it is apparent that the larger the number of balls N is, the better the multi-ball approximation is. Simulation and mathematical complexity, however, increase as N increases. In the next sections, we introduce a methodology for estimating N, $d_1 < d_2 <, \ldots, < d_N$, and $q_{[d_{n-1},d_n]}^{(S)}$ for $n = 1, 2, \ldots, N$ and $S \in \{\text{LOS}, \text{NLOS}\}$ in order to find a good trade-off between complexity and accuracy.

3.1.2 Path-Loss Intensity Matching

The proposed approach for computing the parameters in (8) is based on matching the intensities of the path-losses of the actual blockage model of interest and of the approximating blockage model in (8). More specifically, the proposed approach leverages the displacement theorem of PPPs [20].

Let $r_{i,k}$ be the link distance from a generic BS, BS_i, to the probe MT, MT_k. From Section 2.4, the path-loss is $l^{(S)}(r_{i,k}) = \kappa^{(S)}(\max\{r_0, r_{i,k}\})^{\alpha^{(S)}}$ for $S \in \{\text{LOS}, \text{NLOS}\}$. By assuming that the BSs are distributed according to a PPP of density λ_{BS}, it can be proved that the PP of the path-losses $\{\kappa^{(S)}(\max\{r_0, r_{i,k}\})^{\alpha^{(S)}}, i \in \Phi_{\text{BS}}^{(S)}\}$ is still a PPP, whose intensity measure can be formulated as follows:

$$\Lambda_{\text{PL}}([0, x)) = 2\pi\lambda_{\text{BS}} \sum_{S \in \{\text{LOS}, \text{NLOS}\}} \Lambda_{\text{PL}}^{(S)}([0, x)) \quad (10)$$

$$\begin{aligned}\Lambda_{\text{PL}}^{(S)}([0, x)) &= \int_0^{+\infty} \Pr\{l^{(S)}(r) \leq x\} p^{(S)}(r) r dr \\ &= \int_0^{+\infty} \Pr\{\kappa^{(S)}(\max\{r_0, r\})^{\alpha^{(S)}} \leq x\} p^{(S)}(r) r dr\end{aligned} \quad (11)$$

Equation (10) is a direct application of the displacement theorem of PPPs. Further details are available in [20].

The intensity measure in (10) is uniquely determined by the probabilities $p^{(\text{LOS})}(\cdot)$ and $p^{(\text{NLOS})}(\cdot)$ as a function of the link distance r. Let $\Lambda_{\text{PL}}^{(\text{actual})}([\cdot, \cdot))$ be the intensity measure that corresponds to the actual probabilities of LOS and NLOS. For example, it can be obtained by using the empirical- and the 3GPP-based blockage models in Sections 2.3.1 and 2.3.2. Let $\Lambda_{\text{PL}}^{(\text{approx})}([\cdot, \cdot))$ be the intensity measure that corresponds to the multi-ball approximation in (10). We propose to estimate N, $d_1 < d_2 <, \ldots, < d_N$, and $q_{[d_{n-1},d_n]}^{(S)}$ for $n = 1, 2, \ldots, N$ and $S \in \{\text{LOS}, \text{NLOS}\}$ in (10) by minimizing the following utility error function:

$$\left\| \ln\left(\Lambda_{\text{PL}}^{(\text{actual})}([0, x_M))\right) - \ln\left(\Lambda_{\text{PL}}^{(\text{approx})}([0, x_M))\right) \right\|_F^2 \quad (12)$$

where $\|\cdot\|_F$ denotes the Frobenius norm and x_M is chosen in order to capture the main body of $\Lambda_{\text{PL}}^{(\text{actual})}([\cdot, \cdot))$, i.e., it is close to zero for $x > x_M$. The rationale of (12) originates from the fact that, from the point of view of a typical MT, the impact of blockages is almost the same if the intensity measures are close to each other. The logarithm in (12) is used to make the approximation more accurate.

In practice, the optimization problem in (12) can be solved by using, e.g., the function lsqcurvefit, which is built-in in Matlab. We have verified that the solution is quite stable

$$\Lambda_{\text{PL}}^{(\text{LOS,3GPP})}\left([0,x)\right) = \mathcal{H}\left(x - \kappa_{\text{LOS}} r_0^{\alpha_{\text{LOS}}}\right) \left[(1/2)(x/\kappa_{\text{LOS}})^{2/\alpha_{\text{LOS}}} \overline{\mathcal{H}}\left(x - \kappa_{\text{LOS}} 18^{\alpha_{\text{LOS}}}\right) \right.$$

$$+ \left(624.064 - 36\exp\left(-(x/\kappa_{\text{LOS}})^{1/\alpha_{\text{LOS}}}/36\right)\left(18 + (x/\kappa_{\text{LOS}})^{1/\alpha_{\text{LOS}}}\right) + 18(x/\kappa_{\text{LOS}})^{1/\alpha_{\text{LOS}}}\right)\mathcal{H}\left(x - \kappa_{\text{LOS}} 18^{\alpha_{\text{LOS}}}\right) \Big]$$

$$\Lambda_{\text{PL}}^{(\text{NLOS,3GPP})}\left([0,x)\right) = \mathcal{H}\left(x - \kappa_{\text{NLOS}} 18^{\alpha_{\text{NLOS}}}\right)\left[(1/2)\left((x/\kappa_{\text{NLOS}})^{1/\alpha_{\text{NLOS}}} - 18\right)^2 - 786.064 \right.$$

$$\left. + 36\exp\left(-(1/36)(x/\kappa_{\text{NLOS}})^{1/\alpha_{\text{NLOS}}}\right)\left(18 + (x/\kappa_{\text{NLOS}})^{1/\alpha_{\text{NLOS}}}\right)\right] \tag{13}$$

$$\Lambda_{\text{PL}}^{(S,\text{MultiBall})}\left([0,x)\right) = (1/2)q_{[0,d_1]}^{(S)}\left(x/\kappa^{(S)}\right)^{2/\alpha^{(S)}}\mathcal{H}\left(x - \kappa^{(S)} r_0^{\alpha^{(S)}}\right)\overline{\mathcal{H}}\left(x - \kappa^{(S)} d_1^{\alpha^{(S)}}\right)$$

$$+ (1/2)q_{[0,d_1]}^{(S)} d_1^2 \mathcal{H}\left(x - \kappa^{(S)} d_1^{\alpha^{(S)}}\right) + (1/2)q_{[d_N,\infty]}^{(S)}\left(\left(x/\kappa^{(S)}\right)^{2/\alpha^{(S)}} - d_N^2\right)\mathcal{H}\left(x - \kappa^{(S)} d_N^{\alpha^{(S)}}\right)$$

$$+ (1/2)\sum_{n=2}^{N} q_{[d_{n-1},d_n]}^{(S)}\left(\left(x/\kappa^{(S)}\right)^{2/\alpha^{(S)}} - d_{n-1}^2\right)\mathcal{H}\left(x - \kappa^{(S)} d_{n-1}^{\alpha^{(S)}}\right)\overline{\mathcal{H}}\left(x - \kappa^{(S)} d_n^{\alpha^{(S)}}\right)$$

$$+ (1/2)\sum_{n=2}^{N} q_{[d_{n-1},d_n]}^{(S)}\left(d_n^2 - d_{n-1}^2\right)\mathcal{H}\left(x - \kappa^{(S)} d_n^{\alpha^{(S)}}\right) \tag{14}$$

with respect to the choice of the initial point of the search, which, then, can be chosen at random. The computation of (12), however, requires the closed-form expressions of the intensity measures $\Lambda_{\text{PL}}^{(\text{actual})}\left([\cdot,\cdot)\right)$ and $\Lambda_{\text{PL}}^{(\text{approx})}\left([\cdot,\cdot)\right)$. They are provided in what follows for relevant case studies.

Empirical-Based Model.

The intensity measure is computed based on the actual footprints of the buildings, according to Section 2.3.1. Since LOS and NLOS probabilities are not available in closed-form in this case, (11) cannot be directly applied and the intensity measure cannot be formulated in closed-form. For ease of description, the procedure for computing it is in Section 4.

3GPP-Based Model.

The intensity measure is computed by assuming the LOS and NLOS probabilities in Section 2.3.2. More specifically, by inserting (1) in (11) and computing the integrals, the intensity measure in (13) is obtained, where $\mathcal{H}(\cdot)$ is the Heaviside function and $\overline{\mathcal{H}}(x) = 1 - \mathcal{H}(x)$. The result in (13) holds under the assumption $r_0 < 18$ meters, which is usually satisfied for typical setups.

Multi-Ball Model.

Similar to the 3GPP-based model, the intensity measure can be formulated in closed-form by inserting (8) in (11) and by computing the resulting integrals. The result is available in (14) for $r_0 < d_1$, which usually holds for typical setups.

1-State Model.

The 1-state model can be viewed as a special case of the multi-ball model, where $N = 0$, $d_0 = 0$, $d_1 = \infty$, as well as $q_{[0,\infty]}^{(\text{LOS})} = 1$ and $q_{[0,\infty]}^{(\text{NLOS})} = 0$ or $q_{[0,\infty]}^{(\text{LOS})} = 0$ and $q_{[0,\infty]}^{(\text{NLOS})} = 1$. Thus, the intensity measure follows from (14), and it can be formulated as ($S = \text{LOS}$ or $S = \text{NLOS}$):

$$\Lambda_{\text{PL}}^{(\text{1state})}\left([0,x)\right) = \pi\lambda_{\text{BS}}\left(x/\kappa^{(S)}\right)^{2/\alpha^{(S)}}\mathcal{H}\left(x - \kappa^{(S)} r_0^{\alpha^{(S)}}\right) \tag{15}$$

3.2 Tractable Modeling of Radiation Patterns

The antenna radiation pattern plays an important role for system-level performance evaluation. Incorporating practical antenna radiation patterns in system-level simulations and mathematical analysis may, however, not be straightforward, as it usually entails a loss of tractability. This is the reason why the omni-directional radiation pattern in Section 2.5.1 is usually adopted for system-level analysis. In this section, we introduce a tractable approximation for modeling arbitrary antenna radiation patterns, which can be readily used for system-level analysis and simulation.

Let $g^{(\text{actual})}(\cdot)$ be the actual antenna radiation pattern of interest. We propose to approximate it by using a multi-lobe antenna radiation pattern, where the antenna gain is constant in each lobe. In this paper, it is referred to as "multi-lobe approximation". In mathematical terms, the approximating antenna radiation pattern can be formulated as $g^{(\text{approx})}(\theta) = g^{(\text{MultiLobe})}(\theta)$, where:

$$g^{(\text{MultiLobe})}(\theta) = \begin{cases} g^{(1)} & \text{if } |\theta| \leq \theta^{(1)} \\ g^{(2)} & \text{if } \theta^{(1)} < |\theta| \leq \theta^{(2)} \\ \vdots & \vdots \\ g^{(K)} & \text{if } \theta^{(K-1)} < |\theta| \leq \pi \end{cases} \tag{16}$$

with K denoting the number of lobes and $0 < \theta^{(1)} < \ldots < \theta^{(K-1)} < \pi$ being the angles that correspond to the K lobes.

Similar to (12), the parameters of the multi-lobe approximation in (16), i.e., K and $0 < \theta^{(1)} < \ldots < \theta^{(K-1)} < \pi$, are computed by minimizing the following utility error function:

$$\left\| \log_{10}\left(g^{(\text{actual})}(\theta)\right) - \log_{10}\left(g^{(\text{approx})}(\theta)\right) \right\|_F^2 \tag{17}$$

Similar to (12), the logarithm is used for guaranteeing a better approximation. Since the antenna radiation pattern is usually measured in dB, $\log_{10}(\cdot)$ instead of $\ln(\cdot)$ is used. It is apparent from (16) that the larger the number of lobes K is, the better the approximation is. The numerical complexity increases, however, as K increases. In Section 4, numerical examples confirm that a good accuracy can be obtained even by using a small number of lobes.

Table 3: 3-ball approximation of empirical and 3GPP blockage models obtained as the solution of (12).

	d_1 (meters)	d_2 (meters)	d_3 (meters)	$q_{[0,d_1]}^{(LOS)}$	$q_{[d_1,d_2]}^{(LOS)}$	$q_{[d_2,d_3]}^{(LOS)}$	$q_{[d_3,\infty]}^{(LOS)}$
London	15.1335	56.5978	195.7149	0.7948	0.3818	0.0939	0
Manchester	13.2076	57.8840	213.3940	0.7866	0.4981	0.1015	0.0001
3GPP	47.7989	215.9387	1874.442	0.9446	0.2142	0.0243	0.0021

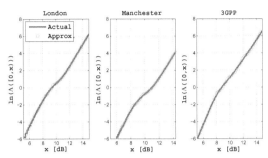

Figure 3: Comparison of the intensity measures of empirical- and 3GPP-based models against their multi-ball ($N = 3$) approximation counterpart.

4. NUMERICAL RESULTS: EXPERIMENTAL VALIDATION

In this section, we illustrate several numerical examples in order to validate the accuracy of the PP-based abstraction for modeling cellular networks, as well as to confirm the tightness of the proposed multi-ball and multi-lobe approximations for simplifying the simulation and for enabling the mathematical modeling of cellular networks.

Simulation Setup.

Unless otherwise stated, the following simulation setup, which is in agreement with the long term evolution advanced (LTE-A) standard, is assumed. The transmit power of the BSs is $P_T = 30$ dBm; the noise power is $\sigma_N^2 = -174 + 10\log_{10}(B_W) + \mathcal{F}_{dB}$, where $B_W = 20$ MHz is the transmission bandwidth and $\mathcal{F}_{dB} = 10$ dB is the noise figure; $\kappa^{(LOS)} = \kappa^{(NLOS)} = (4\pi/\nu)^2$ is the free space path-loss at a distance of 1 meter from the transmitter, where $\upsilon = c/f_c$ is the signal wavelength, $c \approx 3 \times 10^8$ meters/sec is the speed of light, and $f_c = 2.1$ GHz is the signal frequency; $r_0 = 1$ meter; the path-loss exponents of LOS and NLOS links are $\alpha^{(LOS)} = 2.5$ and $\alpha^{(NLOS)} = 3.5$; the mean and standard deviation of the shadowing are $\mu^{(LOS)} = \mu^{(NLOS)} = 0$ dB, $\sigma^{(LOS)} = 5.8$ dB, and $\sigma^{(NLOS)} = 8.7$ dB; the fast-fading envelope of LOS links follows a Nakagami-m distribution with parameters $m = 2$ and $\Omega^{(LOS)} = 1$; the fast-fading envelope of NLOS links follows a Rayleigh distribution with parameter $\Omega^{(NLOS)} = 1$. Used notation: "O2" means that only the BSs from O2 are accessible; "Vodafone" means that only the BSs from Vodafone are accessible; and "O2+Vodafone" means that all BSs from O2 and Vodafone are accessible.

Multi-Ball Approximation of the Blockages.

In Fig. 3, we study the accuracy of the proposed multi-ball approximation for modeling spatial blockages, under the assumption that the BSs are distributed according to a PPP. More specifically, Fig. 3 compares the intensity measure of the empirical-based and of the 3GPP-based models against their multi-ball approximations, which are obtained by solving the optimization in (12). The solution of the optimiza-

tion is provided in Table 3 assuming $N = 3$, which yields a good matching accuracy while still keeping the computational complexity at a low level. The intensity measure of the empirical-based model of the blockages is obtained by using the following procedure based on the actual locations and shapes of the buildings obtained from the OS database.

Step 1: The geographical regions illustrated in Figs. 1 and 2 for London and Manchester are considered. As discussed in Section 2.2, this data is obtained from OS. The BSs are generated according to a PPP of density λ_{BS}, which is chosen according to the data in Tables 1 and 2. Outdoor and rooftop BSs are identified.

Step 2: In the same areas, the MTs are generated according to another PPP of density $\lambda_{MT} = 10\lambda_{BS}$. This choice of λ_{MT} guarantees saturated traffic conditions, i.e., all the BSs have at least one MT to serve based on the cell association in Section 2.6. Among all the MTs, one MT among those that do not lay in a building (outdoor MTs) is randomly chosen as the typical MT.

Step 3: Let the probe (typical) MT, its distance r and link state (LOS or NLOS) with respect to any accessible BSs are computed according to Section 2.3.1.

Step 4: Step 2 and Step 3 are repeated several thousands of times in order to get sufficient statistical data. From this data, two vectors are obtained: a vector containing the distances whose links are in LOS and a vector containing the distances whose links are in NLOS.

Step 5: From the vectors computed in Step 4, $p^{(LOS)}(r)$ and $p^{(NLOS)}(r)$ are estimated by using, e.g., the hist function of Matlab. To this end, a resolution step equal to $\Delta r = 1$ meter and $M_t = 2000$ discrete distances are considered. Thus, the LOS and NLOS probabilities are available for the set of distances r_t for $t = 1, 2, \ldots, M_t$, where $\Delta r = r_t - r_{t-1} = 1$ meter. The corresponding LOS and NLOS probabilities are $p^{(LOS)}(r_t)$ and $p^{(NLOS)}(r_t)$ for $t = 1, 2, \ldots, M_t$.

Step 6: Finally the intensity measure of the path-losses is computed by using (10) and the following discrete (empirical) approximation of (11) (for $S = \{LOS, NLOS\}$):

$$\Lambda_{PL}^{(S)}([0, x))$$
$$\approx \Delta r \sum_{t=1}^{M_t} \Pr\left\{\kappa^{(S)}\left(\max\{r_0, r_t\}\right)^{\alpha^{(S)}} \leq x\right\} p^{(S)}(r_t) r_t \quad (18)$$

The empirical intensity measure in (18) constitute the "actual" intensity for the left and middle plots in Fig. 3. The right plot is obtained by assuming (13) as the "actual" intensity. All in all, a good accuracy is obtained.

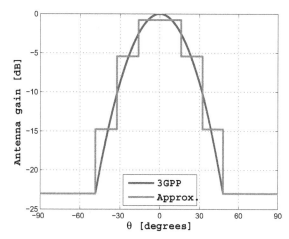

Figure 4: 3GPP-based antenna radiation pattern in (4) and its multi-lobe approximation obtained by using (16) and (17). The multi-lobe approximation is obtained for $K = 4$ and the solution of (17) is $g^{(1)} = 0.8341$, $g^{(2)} = 0.2865$, $g^{(3)} = 0.0334$, $g^{(4)} = 0.005$, $\theta^{(1)} = 16.152°$, $\theta^{(2)} = 32.304°$, and $\theta^{(3)} = 48.455°$.

Multi-Lobe Approximation of the Antenna Radiation Patterns.

In Fig. 4, we study the accuracy of the proposed multi-lobe approximation for modeling realistic antenna radiation patterns. In particular, we test the multi-lobe approximation for modeling the 3GPP-based antenna radiation pattern in (4). The figure shows that a good accuracy is obtained even though $K = 4$. The approximation error can be reduced by increasing K. In what follows, we show, however, that the 4-lobe approximation in Fig. 4 is sufficiently accurate for system-level performance analysis, while offering a low computational complexity.

PP-Based Modeling of the BSs.

In Figs. 5-7, we study the accuracy of the PP-based abstraction for modeling cellular networks, by either considering or not the multi-ball and the multi-lobe approximations for modeling blockages and antenna radiation patterns, respectively. As discussed in Sections 2.1 and 2.2, the empirical coverage probability is obtained by using the locations of the BSs and the footprints of the buildings from the OFCOM and OS databases, respectively. The following procedure for computing the empirical coverage probability is used.

Step 1: The geographical regions illustrated in Figs. 1 and 2 for London and Manchester are considered. As discussed in Section 2.2, this data is obtained from OS. Two case studies for the locations of the BSs are considered. 1) The BSs are distributed according to their actual locations obtained from OFCOM (Figs. 1, 2, Tables 1, 2). 2) The BSs are distributed according to a PPP whose density is the same as that of Tables 1, 2. In both cases, outdoor and rooftop BSs are identified.

Step 2: In the same areas, the MTs are generated according to another PPP of density $\lambda_{MT} = 10\lambda_{BS}$. This choice of λ_{MT} guarantees saturated traffic conditions, i.e., all the BSs have at least one MT to serve based on the cell association in Section 2.6. Among all the MTs, one MT among those that do not lay in a building (outdoor MTs) is randomly chosen as the typical MT.

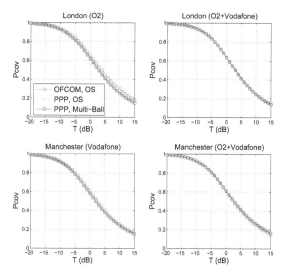

Figure 5: Coverage probability by assuming an omni-directional antenna radiation pattern. Three case studies are analyzed. 1) "OFCOM, OS": the BSs are obtained from the OFCOM database and the buildings from the OS database. 2) "PPP, OS": the BSs are distributed according to a PPP and the buildings are obtained from the OS database. 3) "PPP, Multi-Ball": the BSs are distributed according to a PPP and the multi-ball approximation in Table 3 (London and Manchester) is used.

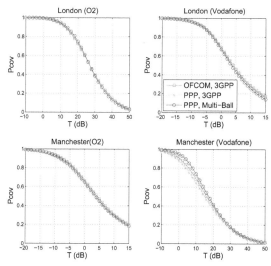

Figure 6: Coverage probability by assuming an omni-directional antenna radiation pattern. Three case studies are analyzed. 1) "OFCOM, 3GPP": the BSs are obtained from the OFCOM database and the LOS/NLOS link states are obtained from (1). 2) "PPP, 3GPP": the BSs are distributed according to a PPP and the LOS/NLOS link states are obtained from (1). 3) "PPP, Multi-Ball": the BSs are distributed according to a PPP and the multi-ball approximation in Table 3 (3GPP) is used.

Step 3: Let the probe (typical) MT, its distance r and link state (LOS or NLOS) with respect to any accessible BSs are computed according to Section 2.3.1.

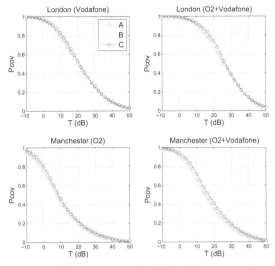

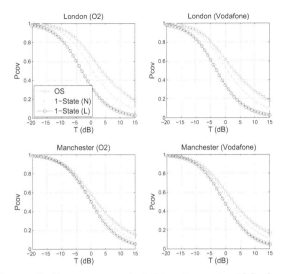

Figure 7: Coverage probability by assuming the 3GPP antenna radiation pattern in (4). Three case studies are analyzed. 1) "A": the BSs are obtained from the OFCOM database and the buildings from the OS database. 2) "B": the BSs are distributed according to a PPP and the buildings are obtained from the OS database. 3) "C": the BSs are distributed according to a PPP, the multi-ball approximation in Table 3 (London and Manchester) is used, and the 3GPP antenna radiation pattern is replaced by its multi-lobe approximation in Fig. 4.

Step 4: For each link between the probe MT and the accessible BSs, path-loss, shadowing and fast-fading gains are generated according to Section 2.4.

Step 5: Let the probe MT and the accessible BSs, its serving BS is identified by using (5) in Section 2.6.

Step 6: The antenna gain of the probe link is set equal to one, while the antenna gains of all the other links are generated as described in Sections 2.4 and 2.5.

Step 7: The SINR and its associated coverage probability are computed by using (6) and (7), respectively.

Step 8: Steps 1-7 are repeated 10^6 times in order to get sufficient statistical data. The final coverage probability is computed as the empirical mean of the obtained 10^6 realizations for each target reliability threshold.

If the LOS and NLOS probabilities are computed based on the 3GPP-based blockage model in Section 2.3.2, the same procedure is used. The only difference is that the actual locations of the buildings are ignored and each link state (LOS vs. NLOS) is identified, according to (1), only based on the distance between the probe MT and each accessible BS. The same comment applies to the 1-state model in Section 2.3.3. In this case, all the links are assumed to be, a priori, either in LOS or NLOS.

All in all, Figs. 5-7 confirm the accuracy of the PP-based abstraction model, and the tightness of the proposed multi-ball and multi-lobe approximations in practical scenarios.

Figure 8: Coverage probability: impact of blockages (omni-directional antennas). Three case studies are analyzed. 1) "OS": the buildings are obtained from the OS database. 2) "1-State (N)": all links are in NLOS. 3) "1-State (L)": all links are in LOS.

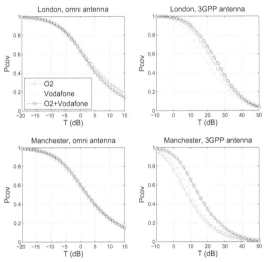

Figure 9: Coverage probability: impact of the antenna radiation pattern (the buildings are obtained from the OS database, i.e., empirical-based blockages are considered). Three case studies are analyzed. 1) "O2": only the BSs from O2 are accessible. 2) "Vodafone": only the BSs from Vodafone are accessible. 3) "O2+Vodafone": all BSs from O2 and Vodafone are accessible.

Achievable Performance: Impact of Blockages and Antenna Radiation Patterns.

In Fig. 8, we study the impact of the blockage model on the coverage probability. This figure highlights the importance of accurately modeling blockages. More specifically, the widespread used 1-state model provides different results from the more accurate and realistic LOS/NLOS blockage model, which accounts for the locations of buildings. Figure 8 points out that the coverage probability may be better than that predicted by using the 1-state model, since the links in LOS result in good probe links while the links in NLOS result in less interference. The proposed multi-ball approximation turns out to be a useful tool for taking LOS/NLOS propagation conditions into account at an affordable complexity, eventually leading to the mathematical analysis and optimization of cellular networks.

In Fig. 9, we study the impact of the antenna radiation pattern on the coverage probability. This figure highlights the importance of accurately modeling the antenna radiation pattern. In particular, it shows that sharing the infrastructure between telecommunication operators may not result in any improvements of the coverage probability if omni-directional antennas are used. If, on the other hand, practical (i.e., directional) antennas are used, e.g., based on 3GPP recommendations (see (4)), the coverage probability may be better due to the denser deployment of BSs. This is due to the fact that directional antennas have the inherent capability of reducing the impact of interference, which is desirable in interference-limited cellular networks.

5. CONCLUSION

With the aid of experimental data for the actual locations of BSs and for the actual locations and shapes of buildings, we have studied the accuracy of the PP-based abstraction for modeling cellular networks. This study has highlighted that the PP-based model is sufficiently accurate for modeling dense urban environments of major metropolitan areas. We have observed that accurate models for the blockages and for the antenna radiation patterns are needed for obtaining reliable estimates of the coverage probability of cellular networks. Finally, we have proposed flexible approximations for incorporating realistic blockage and antenna models into the PP-based abstraction of cellular networks, and have validated their accuracy in relevant scenarios. Based on these findings, the PP-based model seems to be sufficiently accurate and tractable for enabling the mathematical analysis and optimization of emerging ultra-dense cellular networks, which use advanced wireless access transmission schemes.

For further information, the interested readers are invited to watch the companion video recorded at ICC'15 [21].

6. ACKNOWLEDGMENT

This work was supported in part by the European Commission through the CROSSFIRE Project under Grant 317126 and through the 5Gwireless Project under Grant 641985.

7. REFERENCES

[1] 5G-PPP, "5G Vision - The 5G Infrastructure Public Private Partnership: The next generation of communication networks and services", Available: http://5g-ppp.eu/wp-content/uploads/2015/02/5G-Vision-Brochure-v1.pdf.

[2] D. H. Ring and W. R. Young, "The hexagonal cells concept", *Bell Labs Technical Journal*, Dec. 1947.

[3] J. G. Andrews, F. Baccelli, and R. K. Ganti, "A tractable approach to coverage and rate in cellular networks", *IEEE Trans. Commun.*, vol. 59, no. 11, pp. 3122–3134, Nov. 2011.

[4] M. Di Renzo, A. Guidotti, and G. E. Corazza, "Average rate of downlink heterogeneous cellular networks over generalized fading channels – A stochastic geometry approach", *IEEE Trans. Commun.*, vol. 61, no. 7, pp. 3050–3071, July 2013.

[5] M. Di Renzo and W. Lu, "The equivalent-in-distribution (EiD)-based approach: On the analysis of

cellular networks using stochastic geometry", *IEEE Commun. Lett.*, vol. 18, no. 5, pp. 761–764, May 2014.

[6] M. Di Renzo and P. Guan, "A mathematical framework to the computation of the error probability of downlink MIMO cellular networks by using stochastic geometry", *IEEE Trans. Commun.*, vol. 62, no. 8, pp. 2860–2879, July 2014.

[7] M. Di Renzo, P. Guan, "Stochastic geometry modeling of coverage and rate of cellular networks using the Gil-Pelaez inversion theorem", *IEEE Commun. Lett.*, vol. 18, no. 9, pp. 1575–1578, Sep. 2014.

[8] M. Di Renzo and W. Lu, "Stochastic geometry modeling and performance evaluation of MIMO cellular networks using the equivalent-in-distribution (EiD)-based approach", *IEEE Trans. Commun.*, vol. 63, no. 3, pp. 977–996, Mar. 2015.

[9] C.-H. Lee, C.-Y. Shihet, and Y.-S. Chen, "Stochastic geometry based models for modeling cellular networks in urban areas", *Springer Wireless Netw.*, Oct. 2012.

[10] A. Guo and M. Haenggi, "Spatial stochastic models and metrics for the structure of base stations in cellular networks", *IEEE Trans. Wireless Commun.*, vol. 12, no. 11, pp. 5800–5821, Nov. 2013.

[11] T. Bai, R. Vaze, and R. W. Heath Jr., "Analysis of blockage effects on urban cellular networks", *IEEE Trans. Wireless Commun.*, vol. 13, no. 9, pp. 5070–5083, Sep. 2014.

[12] M. Ding, P. Wang, D. Lopez-Perez, G. Mao, and Z. Lin, "Performance impact of LOS and NLOS transmissions in small cell networks", Available: http://arxiv.org/pdf/1503.04251.pdf.

[13] OFCOM, "Sitefinder database", http://stakeholders.ofcom.org.uk/sitefinder/sitefinder-dataset/.

[14] Ordnance Survey: Britain's mapping agency, "OS Open Data", https://www.ordnancesurvey.co.uk/opendatadownload/products.html.

[15] M. Di Renzo, "Stochastic geometry modeling and analysis of multi-tier millimeter wave cellular networks", *IEEE Trans. Wireless Commun.*, to appear. Available: IEEE Early Access.

[16] Y. J. Chun, M. O. Hasna, A. Ghrayeb, and M. Di Renzo, "On modeling heterogeneous wireless networks using non-Poisson point processes", submitted. Available: http://arxiv.org/pdf/1506.06296.pdf.

[17] 3GPP - Technical Specification Group Radio Access Network, "Evolved Universal Terrestrial Radio Access (E-UTRA). Further advancements for E-UTRA physical layer aspects", *TR 36.814 V9.0.0*.

[18] M. N. Kulkarni, S. Singh, and J. G. Andrews, "Coverage and rate trends in dense urban mmWave cellular networks", *IEEE Global Commun. Conf.*, pp. 1–6, Dec. 2014.

[19] 3GPP - Technical Specification Group Radio Access Network, "Spatial channel model for multiple input multiple output simulations", *TR 25.996 V9.0.0*.

[20] B. Blaszczyszyn, M. K. Karray, and H. P. Keeler, "Using Poisson processes to model lattice cellular networks", *IEEE INFOCOM*, pp. 773–781, Apr. 2013.

[21] M. Di Renzo, "Tutorial at 2015 IEEE ICC", Available: https://youtu.be/MB8IvOYYvB0.

SDN Based Control Plane Extensions for Mobility Management Improvement in Next Generation ETArch Networks

Felipe S. Dantas Silva
Federal Institute of Education,
Science and Technology of
Rio Grande do Norte
Natal, Brazil
felipe.dsilva@ifrn.edu.br

Augusto J. V. Neto
Federal University of Rio
Grande do Norte
Natal, Brazil
augusto@dimap.ufrn.br

Douglas Braz Maciel
Federal University of Rio
Grande do Norte
Natal, Brazil
braz@lcc.ufrn.br

Jose Castillo-Lema
University of São Paulo
Sao Paulo, Brazil
josecastillo@usp.br

Flávio de Oliveira Silva
Federal University of
Uberlândia
Uberlandia, Brazil
flavio@ufu.br

Pedro Frosi Rosa
Federal University of
Uberlândia
Uberlandia, Brazil
pfrosi@ufu.br

ABSTRACT

Mobility support is a requirement in next generation networks. The entity Title Architecture (ETArch) is a clean-slate network architecture that uses a naming and addressing scheme based on the Title and has a natural match with Software Defined Networking (SDN) paradigm. ETArch aims at satisfying applications requirements such as mobility. On a previous work, we demonstrated the use of ETArch in order to keep ongoing sessions during handover with no packet loss. The initial approach however, performed the handover without taking into account QoS guarantees during the selection of new Point of Attachments (PoAs). This work proposes an extension to the legacy ETArch Mobility Manager, called *Quality-oriented Mobility Management Approach* (QoMMA), to support a quality-oriented handover management. This extension enables a network-initiated mobility control that improves resources allocation and execute a quality-oriented access point selection. The QoMMA also performs a mobility load balancing in order to maximize admissions of mobile sessions in conditions of congestion. The evaluations were carried out on a testbed that considered real events, and provided evidence that the proposal outperforms legacy ETArch mobility control functionalities.

Categories and Subject Descriptors

C.2.1 [**Computer Communication Networks**]: Network Architecture and Design—*Wireless communication*

MSWiM'15, November 2–6, 2015, Cancun, Mexico.
© 2015 ACM. ISBN 978-1-4503-3762-5/15/11 ...$15.00.
DOI: http://dx.doi.org/10.1145/2811587.2811632.

Keywords

ETArch network; Quality of Service; Load Balancing; Mobility Management; Software Defined Networking

1. INTRODUCTION

Mobility support is a key requirement to applications and in most scenarios, users are carrying a device equipped with multiple network interfaces and has available an ubiquitous high speed access.

The *Entity Title Architecture* (ETArch) [1] is clean-slate network architecture that uses a naming and addressing schemes that are based on a topology-independent designation that uniquely identifies an entity, called Title, and on the definition of a channel that gathers multiple communication entities, called Workspace that supports mobile group-communication. On a first deployment, the mobility mechanisms of ETArch [2] were based of *best effort* approach.

In order to improve *Quality of Service* (QoS) support, a recent work by our research group [3] extend ETArch components. However, the ETArch mobility management model is absolutely user-centric, which means that the user is responsible for making an explicit request for a move to another *Point of Attachment* (PoA).

For this reason, this paper proposes making an extension to the legacy ETArch Mobility Manager, called *Quality-oriented Mobility Management Approach* (QoMMA), to support network-initiated quality-oriented handover management. Moreover, the Mobility Manager operates together with the QoS Manager in order to deploy mobility-based load balancing, and allows the admission of sessions affected by mobility patterns to be maximized by means of moving sessions in the demanding PoA to others with a greater capacity for accommodation. The proposal makes contributions in the following areas: *(i)* network-initiated mobility prediction; *(ii)* quality-oriented PoA selection; *(iii)* mobility load balancing; *(iv)* IEEE 802.21 compliant infrastructured handover control. The evaluation was carried out in a real testbed scenario consisting of OpenFlow/802.11 access points that consider real events.

The remainder of the document is structured as follows: Section II presents the background for this work, highlighting not only the supporting technologies, but also other related approaches. Section III provides an overview of the QoMMA proposal. Section IV outlines the basic operations of QoMMA. Section V shows the results of the evaluations in the control plane. Finally, Section VI offers some concluding remarks and makes suggestions for future work.

2. BACKGROUND

The Entity Title Architecture is a clean-slate network architecture, that can be distinguished from other Future Internet initiatives by its topology-independent naming, called Title, and addresses a semantically-driven designation scheme, that identifies each single entity, and by the defining of a channel that gathers multiple communication entities, called Workspace.

ETArch has a natural match with *Software Defined Networking* (SDN) abstractions and a key component of ETArch is the *Domain Title Service* (DTS), which deals with all control aspects of the network. The DTS is composed by *Domain Title Service Agents* (DTSAs) that are responsible for workspace creation and maintenance upon requests of registered entities. DTSA uses the OpenFlow protocol [4] and IEEE 802.21 Media Independent Handover (MIH) Protocol [5] thus providing a common control to wired and wireless underlying infrastructure that provides mobility across of the workspace with no packet loss [2] between different PoAs.

The ETArch mobility process is managed by the Mobility Manager, which makes use of the IEEE 802.21 protocol, and allows the entities to communicate. Moreover, it goes beyond OpenFlow, from the MIH protocol, and enables other entities to become acquainted with the mobile networks that are detected by *Mobile Node* (MN), as well as their characteristics (capacities and conditions): this information that is of the utmost importance when attempting to improve the handover process in the network.

Although it is able to operate independently of the underlying access technology (wired or wireless), the ETArch Mobility Manager mechanism currently does not take into account the conditions of the candidate networks such as the principle of mobility decision, which is made solely on account of the *Received Signal Strength* (RSS) of candidate PoA.

To obtain a quality-oriented mobility, it is necessary to incorporate mechanisms that support it in an infrastructured manner, so that this process can be managed by the network and no longer by the MN.

2.1 Related Work

The popularity of wireless networks requires the development of mobility control mechanisms to support the different traffic characteristics and needs of mobile users in various infrastructural conditions [6]. The increasing demand for real-time content and services require the wireless networks management systems to provide mechanisms that support different traffic features at different levels of quality [7]. In essence, the mobility management process consists of ensuring the mobile user is *Always Best Connected* (ABC), and

is responsible for offering connectivity alternatives that is more suitable to the user's needs.

A number of strategies have been proposed as solutions to improve the mobility management and to support the growing requirements of mobile users. On a previous work [6] we analyzed and compared several of theses strategies and proposed the *Extended Elitism for Best Selection* (E2BS), a handover decision method inspired by the Elitist Selection Strategy [8] to enable efficient quality-oriented mobility decisions. Its main goal is to meet both the quality requirements of active mobile session flows and to match the current quality standards of neighboring PoA candidates.

In the next session, we provide an overview of the proposed solution, by describing the new features and their relationship with the others components of the ETArch framework.

3. QOMMA PROPOSAL OVERVIEW

The architecture outlined in Figure 1 represents the set of proposed extensions to the ETArch Mobility Manager, called *Quality-oriented Mobility Management Approach* (QoMMA).

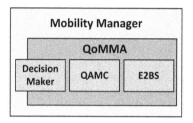

Figure 1: QoMMA architecture

The QoMMA proposal is composed by three main components: Decision Maker, QAMC and E2BS. The proposed extensions were developed and integrated into the DTSA, which acts as the SDN Controller, and thus enables mobility procedures to be managed on the network. The following subsections detail its subcomponents.

3.1 Decision Maker

This is the central core element of the decision-making mechanism. It is responsible for mediating the different requests to the other sub-components, such as: *(i)* changing the status of the monitoring and data collection system (QAMC) (within predefined limits), increasing efficiency (in critical situations), in processing the data collected, such as the MN moving; *(ii)* mapping the *Class of Service* (CoS) to which a particular session belongs and, as a result, determining the importance of the values (weights) of the attributes, through the *Multiple Attribute Decision Making Analytical Hierarchy Process* (MADM AHP) method [9], and where necessary using the E2BS subcomponent; *(iii)* sending the information with the decision of the new network to the MIH function, in cases where the handover is needed.

3.2 QAMC

The *Quality Attribute Monitoring and Collector* (QAMC) is responsible for monitoring and collecting the parameters that trigger: *(i)* the occurrence or need for mobility, loss or reduction of RSS (which show that the MN is moving) and; *(ii)* network quality level, through the QoS parameters. The collected data will be used by the E2BS network selection mechanism, which is outlined in the following section.

The QAMC monitoring interval is adjusted to the system status, defined by the Decision Maker using two different modes: regular and alert.

The regular monitoring is the default mode. In this case, the collecting is performed every 15 seconds, to obtain the network quality parameters and every 5 seconds, to obtain the RSS between the PoA and the MN. If the RSS between a PoA and MN exceeds the threshold that has been previously configured, the system runs in alert mode, which leads to an imminent disconnection of the MN. Thus, the data collecting interval will be reduced, and this will allow the decision-making system to immediately identify alternatives (selection of a new PoA), if these limits are exceeded again, which indicates the sudden need for mobility.

3.3 E2BS

The elitist strategy employed by E2BS is based on a multi-attribute evaluation of the QoS candidate networks. In our model, the population is represented by a set of PoAs and their attributes. This technique is used to select the PoA which offers the best criteria for connection. Assessing the QoS offered by the various PoA to select the best one is carried out by measuring the similarity [10] between the attributes of the elite individual, represented by the reference PoA, and the other candidates. The reference PoA is considered to be the one that has the ideal values, (i.e. attributes like delay and jitter should have values close to zero). E2BS was designed to deal with the attribute importance (i.e. weight) of diverse applications by means of different traffic classes with distinct requirements [11].

In [6] we carried out a performance evaluation of E2BS which confirmed that the capacity of the proposed solution was superior to that of the alternative methods currently available.

4. QOMMA BASIC OPERATION

This section provides a detailed account of the interaction between ETArch features and the new proposed operations supported by the Mobility Manager that makes use of the QoMMA functionalities.

4.1 System bootstrap

The system bootstrap is designed to boot the system with oversized network resources. In this case, the PoAs are configured with over-reservation resources, and this information is recorded in the state table of DTSA. Since this information will be available in advance, the Mobility Manager will be able to make admission decisions in several sessions without any signaling events either for consultation or to set up a ground of resources in the PoA.

In case there is any change in the network topology caused by the entry of a new PoA, the system bootstrap mechanism is triggered for this device. In this way, the QoS Manager sends an OpenFlow message to the new PoA, and sets the CoS over-provisioning patterns, in a way that is compatible with the underlying QoS approach (for instance, by configuring the priorities for packet scheduling).

At this stage, with the support of QAMC, the Mobility Manager will be able to identify the conditions (available bandwidth per CoS, delay, jitter, loss, RSS etc.) of each registered PoA. This information will be used by the E2BS to give priority to the candidate PoA classification.

4.2 Mobile session setup

This process is triggered whenever: *(i)* the DTSA receives a request from a MN to be attached to a PoA or when; *(ii)* the Mobility Manager detects the need for the mobility of a MN owing to the loss or reduction of RSS, which is mainly caused by its movement.

If the first case occurs, the requester MN must register itself at DTSA, by stating the communication requirements (required bandwidth, delay/jitter/loss tolerance etc.). If this process was triggered because of the need for mobility (which is identified by the Mobility Manager), this information will be available in advance at the DTSA state table (in this case, the MN is already registered in the DTSA).

On the basis of this information, the QoS Manager will use the admission control mechanism to check whether the candidate PoA has capacity to accommodate the requester MN session at the desired CoS. If not, new over-reservation patterns will be applied to meet the MN request.

Figure 2 shows a generic scenario, from the system bootstrap to the requester MN handover setup in a new PoA, that displays the events and their respective signaling messages. Due space constraints we will focus on the Mobility Manager. The QAMC sends a *qualityAtributeMonitoring.request*(3) that requests information and monitors the Mobile Node (MN) conditions. By analyzing these parameters using E2BS model and networking conditions and interacting with the QoS Manager that provides the necessary resources to the target PoA. Finally, the QoMMA module sends the *MIH_Net_HO_commit.request message* in order to instruct the MN to perform the handover to the selected network.

4.3 Mobility load balancing

If the admission possibilities provided by the over-reservation mechanism are not sufficient to accommodate new mobile sessions, and shows a lack of resources in the PoA, the Mobility Manager will release resources through a mobility load balancing operation, that reduces the effects of this scarcity, and as a result, the rejection of new mobile session requests.

This process consists of moving already associated MNs to another feasible PoA that is within its coverage area and that offers available resources. Through this operation, it is possible to maximize admissions to the network, by always keeping the MNs well connected.

On receiving a request from a MN that wishes to be associated with a PoA where the CoS does not have sufficient resources to carry out the over-reservation procedures, the Mobility Manager will identify other MNs that are already connected to this PoA that can be moved. Hence, there will be a release of sufficient resources for the admission of the requester mobile session. This operation uses the E2BS decision method is conducted by the Mobility Manager.

If the mobility load balancing operation cannot release the necessary resources to accommodate the requester mobile session, it will be rejected.

5. PERFORMANCE EVALUATION

In seeking to evaluate the feasibility of our proposal, we extended the ETArch Mobility Manager implementation with the QoMMA architecture in accordance with the guidelines

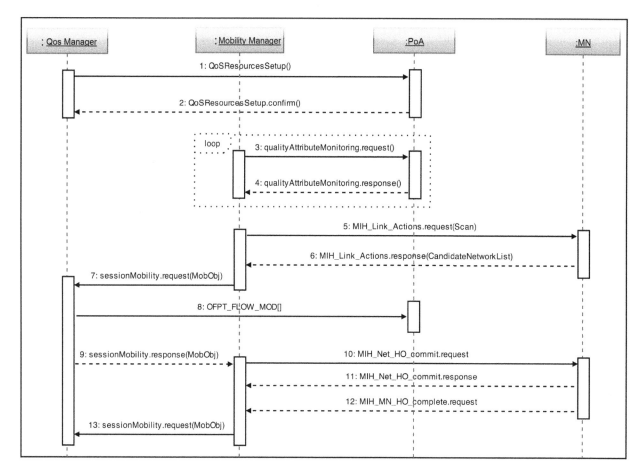

Figure 2: Generic mobility scenario

outlined in Section 3. The aim of this evaluation was to compare the performance of the ETArch admission control strategy (without QoMMA) and QoMMA-enabled Mobility Manager, with load balancing functionalities by means of the network admission capacity of mobile sessions.

5.1 Evaluation Scenario

The experiments were carried out in a real testbed composed by three TP-Link TLWR1043ND routers embedding EDOBRA Switch Configuration [12], to support both IEEE 802.21 and QoS-aided OpenFlow v1.0 (queuing control) facilities. The wireless configuration of EDOBRA switches were set at in 802.11g mode. A Network Server hosts the DTSA OpenFlow Controller by implementing ETArch features with the facilities provided by the new Mobility Manager extensions. The testbed described above was used to perform the evaluation in the control plane, and a wide range of mobile sessions requests were considered with varying constant bit-rate requirements of 450, 350 and 250 kbps [13], linked to three CoS (A, B and C), respectively.

In this scenario, we initialized each CoS over-reservation with 20% of total bandwidth, i.e., 10.8 Mbps. After the system bootstrap, all the session requests were triggered to the same AP, namely AP1.

At this point the AP1 is no longer capable of accommodating new mobile session requests in CoS A until the mobility load balancing procedure has been executed, and new resources released.

As can be seen in Figure 3, new mobile session requests were admitted through the mobility load balancing procedure until it reached the full capacity of the available resources of the network devices. The sessions accommodated in the CoS A of AP1 before, were transferred to AP2 and AP3, and resources in AP1 released by using the load balancing process. So that new mobile sessions could be received. The same occurred with the sessions accommodated in the CoS C of AP1.

The results of Figure 3 reveal the maximization of the admissions of the mobile sessions which could be obtained from the facilities provided by the QoMMA proposal. It is well-know that after the QoMMA mobility procedures, it was possible to reconfigure the network, and thus, to some extent, avoid the rejection of new mobile sessions. In total, there were made 172 requests for an association to AP1, and 107 of them were rejected by the approach without QoMMA and only 1 by QoMMA.

The numerical analysis confirms this behavior, and shows that QoMMA increased the mobile session admission optimization at a rate of approximately 163%, for this scenario, compared with the previous admission control strategy.

6. CONCLUSION AND FUTURE WORK

This work presented an enhancement for the ETArch mobility mechanisms, by adding the Quality-oriented Mobility Management Approach (QoMMA). The QoMMA uses

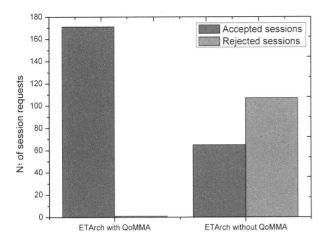

Figure 3: Admission rate with QoMMA and without QoMMA

an always best connected principle in order to keep MNs session with higher QoS guarantees even during handover. The QoMMA allows a dynamic control and a preemptive reconfiguration of the networking by conducting a network initiated handover in order to maximize mobile session admission. The results of our evaluation demonstrated that ETArch with QoMMA enabled the successful admission of new sessions and decreased the rejection of new ones when compared withe the legacy Mobility Manager. This maximization was done while the MN already connected kept their ongoing sessions.

The next stage of this work is to evaluate the extensions of the proposal in a data plane and also estimate the benefits of the application perspective through different benchmarks. The objective is to confirm all the QoMMA capabilities in terms of QoS and *Quality of Experience* (QoE).

Acknowledgment

This work has been developed under the SMART project under grant agreement n.457051/2014-0 (CNPQ/Universal 14/2014). Authors also thanks to CAPES, CNPq and IFRN. Experiments were carried out at NPITI/UPLab of Instituto Metropole Digital (IMD).

7. REFERENCES

[1] F. Silva, M. Goncalves, J. Pereira, R. Pasquini, P. Rosa, and S. Kofuji, "On the analysis of multicast traffic over the entity title architecture," in *Networks (ICON), 2012 18th IEEE International Conference on*, pp. 30–35, 2012.

[2] C. Guimaraes, D. Corujo, F. Silva, P. Frosi, A. Neto, and R. Aguiar, "IEEE 802.21-enabled Entity Title Architecture for handover optimization," in *2014 IEEE Wireless Communications and Networking Conference (WCNC)*, pp. 2671–2676, Apr. 2014.

[3] J. Castillo-Lema, F. Silva, F. Silva, P. R. Rosa, C. G. Guimarães, D. Corujo, and R. L. Aguiar, "Evolving future internet clean-slate entity title architecture with quality-oriented control plane extensions," in *Advanced International Conference on Telecommunications (AICT 2014)*, pp. 161–167, July 2014.

[4] N. McKeown, T. Anderson, H. Balakrishnan, G. Parulkar, L. Peterson, J. Rexford, S. Shenker, and J. Turner, "Openflow: enabling innovation in campus networks," *SIGCOMM Comput. Commun. Rev.*, vol. 38, pp. 69–74, Mar. 2008.

[5] D. Corujo, C. Guimãraes, B. Santos, and R. L. Aguiar, "Using an open-source ieee 802.21 implementation for network-based localized mobility management.," *IEEE Communications Magazine*, vol. 49, no. 9, pp. 114–123, 2011.

[6] F. Silva, J. Castillo-Lema, A. Neto, F. Silva, P. Rosa, D. Corujo, C. Guimaraes, and R. Aguiar, "Entity title architecture extensions towards advanced quality-oriented mobility control capabilities," in *Computers and Communication (ISCC), 2014 IEEE Symposium on*, pp. 1–6, June 2014.

[7] J. Sen, "Mobility and handoff management in wireless networks," in *Trends in Telecommunications Technologies*, 2010.

[8] A. P. Engelbrecht, *Computational Intelligence: An Introduction*. Wiley Publishing, 2nd ed., 2007.

[9] S. Dhar, R. Bera, and A. Ray, "Design and simulation of vertical handover algorithm for vehicular communication," *International Journal of Engineering Science and Technology*, vol. 2, no. 10, pp. 5509–5525, 2010.

[10] Z. Tang, Y. Zhu, G. Wei, and J. Zhu, "An elitist selection adaptive genetic algorithm for resource allocation in multiuser packet-based ofdm systems.," *JCM*, vol. 3, no. 3, pp. 27–32, 2008.

[11] 3GPP, *QoS Concepts and Architecture: TS 23.107, 3rd Generation Partneship Project (3GPP)*. 2009.

[12] EDOBRA, "Edobra switch os - odtone openwrt," 2013. Available at: `https://github.com/ATNoG/odtone-openwrt`. Acessed 4 December 2014.

[13] Microsoft, "Lync server 2013 network bandwidth requirements for media traffic," 2013. Available at: `https://technet.microsoft.com/en-us/library/jj688118.aspx`. Acessed 14 May 2015.

Multiple Access Class Barring factors Algorithm for M2M communications in LTE-Advanced Networks

Meriam Bouzouita
University of Rennes, Rennes, France
SUP'COM, Ariana, Tunisia
mariem.bouzouita@supcom.tn

Yassine Hadjadj-Aoul
University of Rennes, Rennes, France
yhadjadj@irisa.fr

Nawel Zangar
Faculty of science of Tunis, University of el Manar, Tunisia
SUP'COM, Tunisia
nawel.zangar@insat.rnu.tn

Gerardo Rubino
INRIA, Rennes
Gerardo.Rubino@inria.fr

Sami Tabbane
SUP'COM, Tunisia
Sami.Tabbane@insat.rnu.tn

ABSTRACT

The forecast dramatic growth, of the number of Machine-to-Machine (M2M) communications, challenges the traditional networks of Mobile Network Operators (MNO). In fact, a large number of devices may attempt simultaneously to access the base station, which may result in severe congestions at the random-access channel (RACH) level. To alleviate such congestion while regulating the M2M devices' opportunities to transmit, the Access Class Barring (ACB) process was proposed. In this article, we propose a novel implementation of the ACB mechanism in the context of multiple M2M traffic classes. Based on a scheduling algorithm, we have applied a PID controller to adjust dynamically multiple ACB factors related to each class category, guaranteeing a number of devices around an optimal value that maximizes the Random Access (RA) success probability. The obtained results demonstrate the efficiency of the proposed mechanism by increasing the success probability and minimizing radio resources' underutilization with respect to each class priority.

Keywords

M2M; MTC; Access Class Barring; Congestion; Random Access.

1. INTRODUCTION

Machine Type Communications (MTC) or Machine-to-Machine (M2M) communications are nowadays gaining a huge interest from the stakeholders, and particularly the Mobile Network Operators (MNO), and their customers. In fact, M2M communications are seen as one of the most important opportunities to face the revenue's cuts for mobile operators while providing a plethora of services to the customers. These services can be declined in a wide range of

automated applications covering a large number of domains [4][10].

The huge number of M2M devices, which may attempt, at the same time, to access the base station, may result in severe congestions at the random-access channel (RACH) level [7]. In fact, a large number of devices may be triggered simultaneously and attempt to perform the Random Access (RA) in order to request for uplink radio resources. This congestion is even more aggravated when considering the class of event-driven communications, in which a large number of devices is activated during a very short period of time. These devices contend for a limited number of resources, called preambles. Indeed, if two or more MTC equipments choose the same preamble, the Evolved Node B (eNB) will be unable to identify the initiator of the RA and a collision will happen [2]. This may reduce the success access probability and may result in a performance degradation for MNO.

In this paper, our main concern is to design an efficient mechanism to maximize the wireless resources' utilization while guaranteeing the access priorities that may exist between the different class of applications. Another important concern consists in protecting the M2M event-driven communications by prioritizing their access to the channel while adapting rapidly the ACB factors to absorb this type of traffic. To achieve this objective, we proposed both: (1) a Proportional Integral Derivative (PID) controller to make the number of M2M devices attempting the access procedure converge to the optimal one, and (2) a scheduling algorithm to ensure a weighted proportional fairness among M2M devices of the different classes except the class of event-driven devices, which is prioritized.

The remainder of this article is organized as follows. Section 2 is dedicated to the description of the proposed mechanism. Section 3 portrays the simulation setup and discusses the obtained results. Finally, the paper concludes in Section 4 with a summary recapping the main advantages and achievements of the proposed scheme.

2. MULTIPLE ACCESS CLASS BARRING ALGORITHM

Many ACB-based algorithms were proposed in the literature [1]. However, most of them do not consider multi-class M2M devices. Thus, the obtained ACB factor is applied to all classes of M2M devices, which might be harmful for MNO networks. The originality of our approach resides, first, in considering devices belonging to different classes. Second, in opposition to existing works, we propose to find out the optimal number of devices and devising, then, an efficient controller to make the number of devices attempting the RA converge to the optimal one.

2.1 System Model

In this paper, we consider the classical architecture described in [4]. We propose, in the following, to model the RA process, as described in [2]. Our model for M2M devices' random access with multiple ACB factors (i.e. one factor per class) is influenced by the single-class system model that we proposed in [6]. The model is a fluid one: the involved quantities, the whole numbers, are seen here as real quantities. The parameters used in the proposed system model are listed below:

- $x_{1,i}(t)$: the number of backlogged MTC devices from class i at time t, where $i \in \{1, 2, \ldots, k\}$. The constant k represents the number of considered classes.

- $x_2(t)$: the number of MTC devices that pass the ACB check and wait to start RA attempt at time t.

- $x_3(t)$: the number of MTC devices that succeed RA procedure at time t.

- λ_i: the arrival rate of MTC devices from class $i \in \{1, 2, \ldots, k\}$. Different traffic patterns will be considered in the following, depending on the type of M2M application.

- $\theta_{1,i}(x_{1,i})$: the rate of ACB failure for class $i \in \{1, 2, \ldots, k\}$.

- $\theta_2(x_2)$: the rate of RA failures (i.e. collision and re-transmission).

- $\mu(x_3)$: the rate of MTC departure after performing the RA successfully.

- $p_i(x_{1,i})$: the ACB factor for class $i \in \{1, 2, \ldots, k\}$.

- N: indicates the total number of radio resources (preambles) available during one time slot. It is a constant value.

- $R_s(x_2)$: denotes the number of MTC devices that transmitted their preambles successfully.

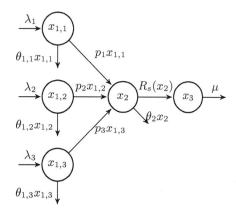

Figure 1: System description for $k = 3$

Now we are ready to describe the evolution of the states $x_{1,i}$ with $i \in \{1, 2, \ldots, k\}$, x_2 and x_3 based on the model described in Fig. 1. Let first define $\mathbb{C} = \{1, 2, \ldots, k\}$ as the set of classes. The system's dynamics is described by the following system of differential equations:

$$
\begin{cases}
\dfrac{dx_{1,i}}{dt} = \lambda_i - p_i x_{1,i} - \theta_{1,i} x_{1,i}, & \text{for all } i \in \mathbb{C}, \\
\dfrac{dx_2}{dt} = \displaystyle\sum_{i=1}^{k} p_i x_{1,i} - R_s(x_2) - \theta_2 x_2, \\
\dfrac{dx_3}{dt} = R_s(x_2) - \mu x_3,
\end{cases}
\tag{1}
$$

with the constraints that for all $i \in \mathbb{C}$, $x_{1,i}$, x_2 and x_3 should be nonnegative.

The function $R_s(x_2)$ is represented by the expected number of MTC devices succeeding in the access process. This number represents the number of preambles with only one device.

Let's define P_s as the probability that a given preamble is chosen by one MTC device (i.e. probability of success). To that purpose, we suppose that there are N available preambles in each RA opportunity and x_2 MTC devices contending for these resources. This is a typical "balls into bins" problem", in which P_s is given by:

$$
P_s = \frac{x_2}{N} \left(1 - \frac{1}{N}\right)^{x_2 - 1}.
\tag{2}
$$

For a large N, this can be approximated by:

$$
P_s = \frac{x_2}{N} e^{-\frac{x_2 - 1}{N}}.
\tag{3}
$$

Therefore,

$$
R_s(x_2) = x_2 e^{-\frac{x_2 - 1}{N}}.
\tag{4}
$$

The collision probability P_c can be derived using (3) and the idle probability (i.e. no user chooses a given preamble):

$$
P_c = 1 - \frac{x_2}{N} e^{-\frac{x_2 - 1}{N}} - e^{-\frac{x_2}{N}}.
\tag{5}
$$

2.2 Optimal number of M2M devices

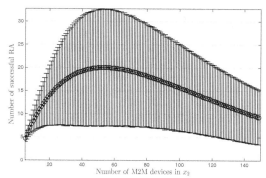

Figure 2: Successful RA

The main idea, in this section, is to derive an optimal number of contending M2M devices x_2 in a way to be used by the proposed controller as an objective to achieve (i.e. targeted number of M2M devices).

All devices that have passed successfully the ACB test, will contend for the same radio resources (N) as a way to access the network. The optimal value of devices, performing RA at the same time (i.e. x_2^{ref}) and maximizing the success probability, is obtained based on Monte-Carlo simulations.

For the simulations, we vary the number of M2M devices between 1 and 150 devices. We evaluated the average and the variance on the number of successful RA. To validate the obtained results, many seeds were tested and the results, obtained in Fig. 2, were similar. The results, depicted in Fig. 2, show that the maximum number of successful RA is obtained when the number of M2M devices in x_2 is equal to $(N-3)$. This number will be adopted as the optimal value (i.e. the targeted value) to generate the appropriate ACB factor in our scheduling algorithm.

2.3 PID feedback control on the access probability

In the proposed approach, the dynamic adjustment of the ACB factor (i.e. access probability) is achieved using a discrete Proportional Integral Derivative (PID) regulator [5]. The main idea, behind, is to make the total number of MTC devices, contending for the access, converges to the targeted value, which is defined in the previous subsection.

The discrete PID regulator can be described by the following equation [5]:

$$P_{acb}(n) = K_p e(n) + K_i \sum_{k=0}^{n} e(k) + K_d(e(n) - e(n-1)) \quad (6)$$

where n, P_{acb}, e, K_p, K_i and K_d represent respectively the instant, the controller output, the difference between the measured value and the set point value (i.e. the targeted value), the proportional gain, the integral gain and the derivative gain. In order to get the ideal response of the system, we considered the Ziegler-Nichols method [5] for the tuning of PID parameters.

As P_{acb} is a probability, a saturation block[1] is added to bind the values within the interval $[0,1]$. The probability calculated in (6) is general and do not concern a particular class of traffic. Thus, the probability P_{acb}^i for each class of service $i \in \mathbb{C}$ is derived from this value, as described in the next section. These values are broadcasted through a signaling channel to the different classes of M2M applications.

2.4 Proposed algorithm

In this subsection, we describe in details the proposed algorithm, which is illustrated in the figure below, to compute multiple ACB factors for the different classes of applications.

After a phase of initialization (at phase 1), the eNB estimates the error (i.e. e) to be used thereafter in the PID regulator (at phase 2). The error reflects the difference between the obtained value of the number of contending devices x_2 at step n and the targeted value x_2^{ref}. Therefore, the eNB estimates the number of successful ACB tests $\hat{x}_2$ by estimating the states $x_{1,i}$, for all $i \in \mathbb{C}$ (i.e. $\hat{x}_{1,i}$, for all $i \in \mathbb{C}$). These estimates can be easily obtained by a per-class counting of the number of devices that have passed successfully the ACB test and by averaging these obtained values using an Exponentially Weighted Moving Average (EWMA).

After that (at phase 3), the eNB uses the PID controller to adjust the ACB factor (i.e. P_{acb}) enabling to converge to-

[1] A component imposing higher and lower bounds.

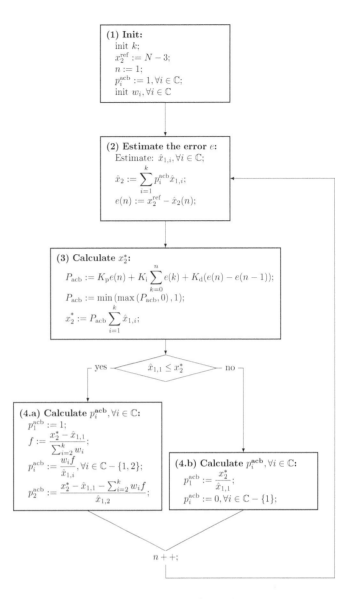

Figure 3: Scheduling Algorithm

wards the targeted number of contending devices (i.e. x_2^{ref}). As the output of the PID controller should be a probability, in spite of considering P_{acb}, we consider only values within the interval $[0,1]$ by applying the: $\min(\max(P_{acb},0),1)$. The computation of the blocking probability P_{acb} allows generating an optimal number of equipments that should pass successfully the ACB process (i.e. x_2^*) based on the estimated $\hat{x}_{1,i}$, for all $i \in \mathbb{C}$ (see phase 3).

In the proposed algorithm, we considered the first class as the most prioritized by using an absolute priority access, as it is the case for some M2M applications such as emergency services. The access probabilities of the devices belonging to other classes are balanced using a weight factor w_i, for all $i \in \mathbb{C}$. Depending on the availability of preambles for the first class, we pass by phase (4.a) or (4.b). Phase (4.b) is executed when there are not enough preambles to grant the access to all the devices of the first class (i.e. x_2^* is smaller than $\hat{x}_{1,1}$). In this case the blocking probability for class 1 is calculated to have an optimal number of contending devices for this class $p_{acb}^1 = \frac{x_2^*}{\hat{x}_{1,1}}$. The devices from the other classes are blocked. When there are enough preambles to grant the access for all the devices in class 1, phase (4.a) is executed. In this case, p_{acb}^1 is equal to one (i.e. all the devices from the class are accepted), and the access is shared fairly between the other classes depending on the weight of each class (i.e. weighted fairness).

Once the ACB factors generation process is finished, it is broadcasted through a signaling channel to all the equipments, which should update their access probability and start ACB check. Then, the operation is repeated from phase 2, after incrementing the step variable n.

Note that the broadcasting of the access probabilities is repeated for each frame, which represents a delay of 10ms. Other delays might be considered for a less important accuracy and reactivity. The considered delay is short but represents a negligible overhead.

3. PERFORMANCE EVALUATION

3.1 Simulation parameters

Having described the details of the proposed algorithm to calculate a per-class ACB factor for heterogeneous M2M devices, we direct now our focus on evaluating its performance using the "Network Simulator (ns3)" environment [8]. The proposed model supports an unlimited and configurable number of types of M2M applications. However, for the simulations, we considered only the following classes:

- *Emergency and prioritized applications (class 1)*: this category of applications must be processed with the highest rate of successful accesses. Emergency applications' arrival follows a Beta-based traffic model [3].

- *Applications for remote control and surveillance (class 2)*: this category represents M2M application with a good level of priority and continuous data transmission [9]. The model of arrival of corresponds here to a uniform process.

- *Smart-grid-related applications (class 3)*: in this category a reasonably large amount of data is periodically transferred to eNB and, thus, causing RAN overload. Such applications have a very low priority of access with delay-tolerance and can be rejected in case of congestion. The periodic arrival of smart-grid related devices is also modeled with a uniform-based process.

The parameters' settings are listed in Table 1. The duration of the simulation corresponds to the distribution period of the traffic of most critical traffic. More details on the traffic patterns can be found in [3].

3.2 Simulation results

To validate the proposed model defined in Figure 1, we present, in this subsection, the analytical values of success and collision probabilities against the ones obtained using simulation. Then, we will give the number of successful ACB tests compared with the targeted value (i.e. optimal value as found in section 2.2) to demonstrate the effectiveness of our proposal. Finally, we show the efficiency of the proposed solution in prioritizing the different M2M applications.

Figures 4 and 5 show the simulation results obtained respectively for the success probability and the collision probability against those obtained theoretically. It can be seen

Table 1: Simulation parameters

Parameters	Values
Simulation duration	10s
Total number of preambles	54
Cell bandwidth	5MHz
Max. # of preamble retransmissions	10
ac-BarringTime	4s
Total number of MTC devices	10000
# of devices in classes (1,2,3)	(1000,3000,6000)
Beta distribution time	10s
Beta function parameters	$\alpha = 3; \beta = 4$

that the simulation results match very well the theoretical values, which allow validating the proposal model.

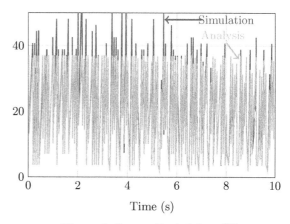

Figure 4: Success Probability (%)

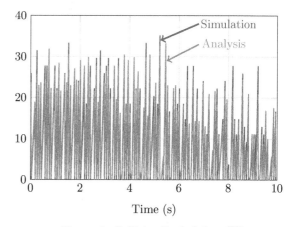

Figure 5: Collision Probability (%)

Figure 6 illustrates the instantaneous and the average (i.e. EWMA) number of successful ACB tests. We can easily see that even if the instantaneous values oscillate between 30 and 70, the average values remain very close to the targeted value (i.e. 51), which is the objective of our mechanism. This, clearly, demonstrates the effectiveness of the PID controller as it helps in regulating the ACB factor dynamically according to the congestion level and the M2M application classes.

Note that values smaller than the target may lead to resources' underutilization, while values bigger than the target

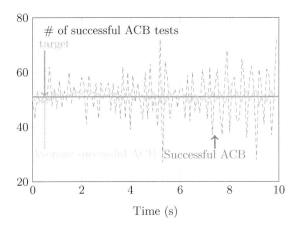

Figure 6: Total successful ACB tests vs Setpoint

may lead to excessive collisions, which also lead to resources' underutilization.

To see the efficiency of the proposed algorithm in prioritizing different classes of M2M applications, let see the results obtained in Fig. 7. Figure 7 depicts the cumulative number of successful ACB tests for each class of M2M applications in figures (B) compared with the cumulative number of arrivals for each class in figures (A). It can be easily seen that the number of arrivals for class 1 is nearly equal to the number of successful ACB tests, which is in a complete conformance with the absolute constraint requirements for this category of traffic.

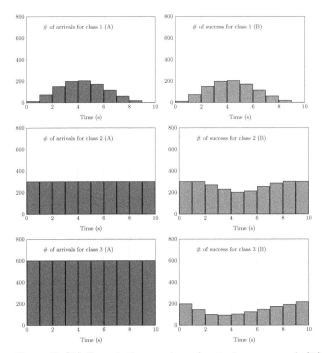

Figure 7: (A) Cumulative number of arrivals per second, (B) Cumulative number of successful ACB tests per second

Another important observation, in Fig. 7, is that when the congestion is at its maximum (between seconds 2 and 8) the traffic of class 2 suffers from some degradation as some of the traffic is blocked. However, the blocking probability of this traffic class, which has a weight bigger than class 3, is low. This has direct consequences on the large number of

successful ACB tests for this class. On the other hand, the less prioritized class (i.e. class 3) suffer from the beginning from blocked traffic. The phenomenon is exacerbated when the congestion is at its peak, as it can be seen in Fig. 7. In fact, given that devices of class 3 have the lowest priority, they will be blocked in case of congestion, i.e. when arrivals of class 1 and class 2 are more important. Consequently, it results in reducing collision probability as it is observed in figure 5.

4. CONCLUSION

In this paper, the RAN overload issue caused by MTC in LTE-Advanced networks has been addressed. We have proposed a novel mechanism as a way to alleviate RAN congestion by efficiently managing the M2M devices' random accesses. Using Monte-Carlo simulations, we find out the optimal number of the MTC devices that should compete for the random access to maximize the number of devices succeeding in the ACB procedure. After that, in order to regulate adaptively the ACB factor guaranteeing a total number of devices around the targeted value, we used a discrete PID controller. Then, we applied a scheduling algorithm as a way to schedule different M2M traffic classes. Simulation results show that the proposed mechanism can accurately predict congestion situations while significantly reducing the collision probability.

5. REFERENCES

[1] 3GPP. Evolved universal terrestrial radio access (e-utra); radio resource control (rrc). Technical report, TS 36.331 V10.2.0, 06 2011.

[2] 3GPP. Medium access control (mac) protocol specification. Technical report, TS 36.321 V10.2.0, 06 2011.

[3] 3GPP. Study on ran improvements for machine-type communications (release 11). Technical report, TR 37.868 V11.0.0, 09 2011.

[4] 3GPP. System improvements for machine-type communications, technical specification group services and system aspects (release 11). Technical report, TR 23.888 V1.6.0, 2011.

[5] K. J. Åström and T. Hägglund. Advanced PID control. ISA-The Instrumentation, Systems, and Automation Society, Research Triangle Park, NC, 2006.

[6] M. Bouzouita, Y. Hadjadj-Aoul, N. Zangar, S. Tabbane, and C. Viho. A random access model for M2M communications in LTE-advanced mobile networks. In Modeling and Simulation of Computer Networks and Systems, pages 577 – 599. Morgan Kaufmann, 2015.

[7] A. Ksentini, Y. Hadjadj-Aoul, and T. Taleb. Cellular-based machine-to-machine: overload control. Network, IEEE, 26(6):54–60, November 2012.

[8] ns3. http://www.nsnam.org/, 2015.

[9] I. Petiz, P. Salvador, and A. N. Nogueira. Characterization and modeling of m2m video surveillance traffic. In IARIA Int. Conf. on Advances in Future Internet - AFIN, August 2012.

[10] G. Wu, S. Talwar, K. Johnsson, N. Himayat, and N. D. Johnson. M2M: from mobile to embedded internet. IEEE Communications Magazine, 49(4):36–43, 2011.

COExiST: Revisiting Transmission Count for Cognitive Radio Networks

Guillaume Artero Gallardo
University of Toulouse - IRIT
TéSA - Rockwell Collins France
Toulouse, France
garterog@alumni.enseeiht.fr

Jean-Gabriel Krieg
University of Toulouse - IRIT
Toulouse, France
jeangabriel.krieg@enseeiht.fr

Gentian Jakllari
University of Toulouse - IRIT
TéSA, Toulouse, France
jakllari@enseeiht.fr

Lucile Canourgues
Rockwell Collins France
Blagnac, France
lucile.canourgues@rockwellcollins.com

André-Luc Beylot
University of Toulouse - IRIT
TéSA, Toulouse, France
beylot@enseeiht.fr

ABSTRACT

Transmission count, the number of transmissions required for delivering a data packet over a link, is part of almost all state-of-the-art routing metrics for wireless networks. In traditional networks, peer-to-peer interference and channel errors are what define its value for the most part. In cognitive radio networks, however, there is a third culprit that can impact the transmission count: primary user interference. It may be tempting to think of primary user interference as no different than interference caused by other peers. However, unlike peers, primary users do not follow the same protocol and have strict channel access priority over the secondary users. Motivated by this observation, we carry out an empirical study on a USRP testbed for analyzing the impact of primary users. Our measurements show that a primary user has a distinct impact on the transmission count, which the de facto standard approach, ETX, designed for traditional networks, fails to capture. To resolve this, we present COExiST (for COgnitive radio EXpected transmISsion counT): a link metric that accurately captures the expected transmission count over a wireless link subject to primary user interference. Extensive experiments on a five-node USRP testbed demonstrate that COExiST accurately captures the actual transmission count in the presence of primary users – the $80th$ percentile of the error is less than 20%.

Categories and Subject Descriptors

C.2.1 [**Computer-Communication Networks**]: Network Architecture and Design—*Wireless communication*; D.2.8 [**Software Engineering**]: Metrics—*Performance measures*; C.4 [**Performance of Systems**]: Modeling techniques

MSWiM'15, November 2–6, 2015, Cancun, Mexico.
Copyright is held by the owner/author(s). Publication rights licensed to ACM.
ACM 978-1-4503-3762-5/15/11 ...$15.00.
DOI: http://dx.doi.org/10.1145/2811587.2811605.

Keywords

Cognitive Radio Networks; Transmission Count; Link Quality; Routing; USRP

1. INTRODUCTION

Estimating transmission count – the number of transmissions required for delivering a packet over a link – as a mean to identifying the best links in wireless networks was pioneered by De Couto et al. [8]. Their approach, ETX, has been modified (mostly augmented) many times to include other features, e.g. the physical bit-rate [10]. Its effectiveness and ease of implementation - the broadcast probes remain the most effective and practical solution for a measurement-based link quality estimation – have made it a building block for most modern routing protocols. It has been applied to contexts far beyond the original, including the sensor networks [12], backpressure routing [18], opportunistic routing [11, 16], network coding [14], etc. Nevertheless, despite the diversity of the contexts in which ETX has been applied so far, one thing has always been the same: the link quality has been mostly a function of channel errors and peer-to-peer[1] interference.

In cognitive radio networks there is a third culprit that can impact the link quality, as perceived by the secondary users: the primary user primacy. Sensing the spectrum [4, 15] to avoid causing harm to primary users is an essential requirement for secondary users, leading to two potential scenarios of throughput loss. One, the spectrum sensing accurately predicts the primary user activity. In this case, secondary users will defer from transmitting, leading to throughput loss[2]. However, the broadcast probes can be queued and released as soon as the primary user ceases transmitting. If the primary user activity lasts less than the size of the moving window ETX uses to estimate loss, say for half of it, all the broadcast probes may end up being delivered by the time the next estimation is performed, making the ETX

---

[1]We use the terms peer and secondary user interchangeably.
[2]Channel switching can alleviate the effect of PU interference. However, it does not come free – secondary nodes will have to switch to a new frequency, if one is available, and reconstitute the networks, a process that takes time and coordination. Thus, in many cases simply deferring and waiting the PU out can be a better strategy.

value of the link perfect. Clearly, this is wrong as only half the channel capacity is available. Ideally, a link metric should penalize this link the same way it does a PU free link where, because of channel errors, two transmissions are required to deliver a data packet. The second scenario of throughput loss occurs when the sensing fails to predict the PU activity. It may be tempting to think of primary user interference in this case as no different than interference caused by other peers. However, there are reasons to believe this may not be the case. For example, with 802.11, a packet transmission is followed by a back-off, which can limit the damage a particular hidden peer interferer can cause, as well as shape how the pattern of losses is perceived by the secondary transmitter. Obviously, primary users do not necessarily use 802.11.

Motivated by these observations, we carry out an empirical study on a five-node USRP testbed network. Our measurements show that when the interferer is a peer node, ETX is pretty adept at approximating the actual transmission count on a particular link. However, keeping everything the same and simply replacing the peer interferer with a primary user leads to significant gaps between ETX and the actual transmission count. Clearly, the primary user is having an adverse and distinct effect on the capability of two secondary nodes to communicate, which the traditional way of estimating transmission count fails to capture.

We present COExiST[3], an approach for estimating transmission count over wireless links subject to primary user interference. Its design is driven by our empirical study where we have identified the parameters that best capture the impact of primary user interference on link throughput. In short, COExiST also quantifies the loss of throughput when secondary users are deferring to primary users by calculating the transmission count as if a secondary user transmits instead of deferring and the transmissions result in failure. COExiST can be used as a stand-alone metric for identifying good links or optimal paths in terms of transmission count, or be combined with other parameters, such as the physical bit-rate, for optimizing other performance metrics.

Throughout this paper we make the following contributions:

- In Section 2, we use an USRP N210 testbed to carry out an empirical study on the primary user impact on transmission count. Our data shows that primary users have indeed a distinct effect – something ETX, the de facto standard approach for computing transmission count, fails to capture.
- In Section 3, we use the lessons learnt from the empirical study to design COExiST, an approach for estimating transmission count in cognitive radio networks. Despite the involved computation, COExiST is shown to have a simple, closed-form expression. Furthermore, we show that COExiST coupled with hop-by-hop Dijkstra-based routing satisfies the optimality, consistency and loop-freeness property.
- In Section 4, we describe the development of our prototype testbed using the USRP N210 radio platform and IRIS [21]. We describe our own CSMA/CA implementation and an implementation of COExiST for OLSR.
- In Section 5, we evaluate the performance of COExiST on our USRP testbed. We show that COExiST is very

---
[3]COgnitive radio EXpected transmISsion counT.

Figure 1: All our experiments are carried out on a five-node USRP N210 testbed.

accurate in estimating the transmission count over links subject to primary user interference – 80% of the time the error compared to the actual transmission count is less than 20%. Furthermore, we show that when using COExiST, OLSR selects higher throughput paths than when using ETX as well as two metrics proposed for cognitive radio networks [19, 23].

2. PRIMARY USER IMPACT ON TRANS-MISSION COUNT

We present an empirical study on the impact of primary user interference on transmission count. Our measurements show that primary users present a distinct challenge when it comes to estimating the transmission count – something ETX, the de facto standard approach of estimating transmission count, fails to capture. We explore the reasons why and provide pointers to potential solutions.

2.1 Experimental Setup

Hardware: Our testbed consists of five USRP N210 [3] software defined radios coupled with SBX daughterboards providing a 400-4400MHz frequency range. The SBX daughterboad is equipped with two front-ends: one TX/RX used for secondary user communications, and one RX2 dedicated to spectrum sensing. Each USRP is connected to 64-bit host computers running the Ubuntu 12.04 LTS system (Fig. 1).

Software: We use IRIS [21], an open source LGPLv3 software defined radio architecture. Unlike the GNURadio, IRIS is designed specifically to support maximum reconfigurability while the radio is running, a capability that better fits our needs for a cognitive radio testbed. IRIS does not come with a MAC protocol implementation so we augmented its architecture to allow for carrier sensing and implemented the DCF part of the 802.11 MAC. At the routing layer we use OLSR with an ETX implementation. The complete details of the software architecture can be found in Section 4.

Emulating Primary Users: We model the primary user activity by transmitting packets using a high power level, thus interfering with SU communications. To shape the ON/OFF periods we vary the burst duration according to typical continuous time distributions such as the exponential or uniform [15]. Figure 2 shows a typical primary user behavior as utilized in our experiments.

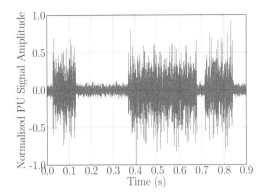

Figure 2: A 1-second sampling of the primary user activity, as utilized in our experiments.

2.2 Impact of Primary Users on Transmission Count

To study the potential impact of primary users, we set up a simple 2-node link – a third node acts as interferer and switches roles between being a peer and a primary user. UDP packets are sent as fast as possible over the link and we collect the actual transmission count as well as ETX, as reported by the OLSR implementation. We repeat the experiment for a variety of PU levels, 0.2 to 0.7, and link reliabilities (counting only channel attenuation), 0.5 to 1.

Figure 3(a) shows ETX and actual transmission count when the interferer is a peer. Here, the peer is running the same CSMA protocol as the other two nodes and the transmission count is mostly due to channel errors, something ETX estimates fairly well. When we replace the peer interferer with a primary user, things change: Figure 3(b) shows ETX performing poorly. This is due to the fact that ETX estimates the channel quality by sending (broadcast) packets on a regular basis and assumes the transmission failures are independent. However, when failures are due to primary user activity there is a high correlation between them, and the transmission count will highly depend on things like how active the primary users are, the pattern of their activity, etc.

2.3 Capturing the Impact of Primary Users

Having shown that ETX fails to capture the full impact of primary users on transmission count, we turn our attention to exploring alternative ways that will. Intuition says that, while the probe packets ETX uses may miss a good chunk of the primary user activity, the time a particular node spends to successfully transmit unicast packets could be a good indication of the PU activity.

To verify our intuition, we perform the following experiment. We use the same 3-node topology as before, with two USRP nodes functioning as the secondary network while the third as a primary user. One of the secondary nodes transmits UDP packets to its peer as fast as possible for 50 seconds. The primary node is silent for the first 25 seconds and is activated for the last 25. During the experiment, at the routing layer we collect the ETX values computed by OLSR, while at the MAC layer, the time between a successful transmission and the next attempt, T_t, and the time between two retransmissions, T_r.

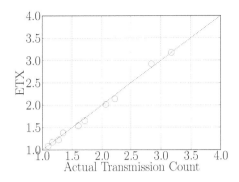

(a) **Interferer is a Peer.** There is a data point for every value of channel reliability considered.

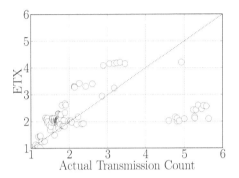

(b) **Interferer is a Primary User.** There is a data point for every combination of channel reliability and primary user activity.

Figure 3: **Primary Users Present a Distinct Challenge when Estimating Transmission Count: The de facto standard approach, ETX, captures well the transmission count when the interferer is a peer (a) but fails to do so when we replace the peer interferer with a primary user (b).**

Figure 4 shows the observed values for ETX (Fig. 4(a)) and the normalized values for T_t, T_r (Fig. 4(a)), as function of the experiment time. The data shows that, while ETX shows a poor correlation to PU activity, T_t and T_r show a strong correlation to it. This is due to the fact that the moving window ETX uses to estimate link losses is larger than the average PU ON period, leading to almost all broadcast probes being delivered. On the other hand, the time spent deferring to the primary users is well captured by T_t and T_r.

2.4 Would a Straightforward Solution Work?

When presented to the challenge of estimating the impact of a primary user on transmission count, the straightforward solution that may cross one's mind is to treat the primary user as yet another probabilistic source of error, use history to estimate the ratio of time a primary user is active, and simply multiply ETX by this value. Figure 5 shows that this would not work. The data collected using the 3-node topology, with one node acting as a primary user, shows that for the same ratio of PU activity, different values of ON periods have a different impact on the packet delivery ratio.

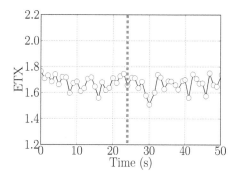

(a) PU becomes active at time 25s and its activity duration is shorter than the moving window ETX uses to estimate loss, leading the latter to completely miss the PU existence.

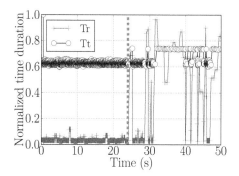

(b) PU activity starts at time 25s. T_t and T_r are averages over 10 samples.

Figure 4: Capturing Primary User Activity: ETX shows a poor correlation to PU activity. However, the time between two transmissions, T_t, and the time between two retransmissions, T_r, show a strong correlation to it.

2.5 Summary

The above empirical study shows the following:

- Primary users present a distinct factor impacting the transmission count.

- The traditional way of computing the transmission count, ETX, is well adept at capturing peer interference and channel errors but fails when it comes to Primary User interference.

- The straightforward solution of multiplying ETX by the primary user availability can perform poorly.

- A cross-layer approach using MAC layer information can significantly improve our capability to capture the impact of primary users.

3. COEXIST

In this section, we present the design and computation of COExiST. As suggested by the empirical study in Section 2, to account for the impact of primary users on transmission

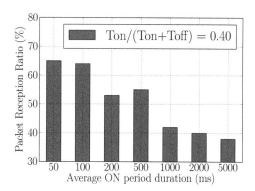

Figure 5: Not all PU Availabilities are Created Equal: All points represent experiments with the same ratio of PU availability; what changes are the absolute values of ON and OFF. Higher values of ON and OFF lead to lower packet reception ratios, and consequently, higher transmission count.

count, COExiST utilizes the perceived primary user activity, the time between a successful transmission and the next attempt, T_t, and the time between two retransmissions, T_r.

3.1 Model & Preliminaries

We derive the COExiST of a given link using the network model defined in Figure 6. We use u to denote the Primary User duty cycle [17] and $\bar{T}_{on}$, $\bar{T}_{off}$ to denote average primary user ON/OFF period durations, respectively. These quantities are related by the formula $u = \bar{T}_{on}/(\bar{T}_{on} + \bar{T}_{off})$ [13, 15]. We model the distributions of the primary activity/non-activity periods using exponential distributions with parameters $\bar{T}_{on}$ and $\bar{T}_{off}$. In practice, such period durations are not always exponentially distributed and depend on the primary network characteristics. Nevertheless, as pointed out in [17], the exponential distribution is shown to be a suitable fit for the empirical distributions observed for commercial systems, such as cellular networks. To keep the computation tractable, the same approximation is also used for T_r and T_t. COExiST, utilizes the probability of successfully transmitting a packet during the OFF period, p_s^{off}, to account for the effect of channel errors and SU-SU interference. Finally, similar to ETX [8], our model assumes an unlimited number of transmission attempts at the MAC layer.

3.2 Analytical Computation

Let $N \in \mathbb{N}^*$ be the total number of MAC layer attempts required to successfully transmit a packet over the link. COExiST estimates $\mathbb{E}[N]$ by resolving an absorbing discrete-time Markov Chain.

Definition 1. *We model the Cognitive Radio MAC layer retransmission scheme using an absorbing discrete-time Markov chain, with the states defined as follows:*

- I_0: *The last packet has been successfully transmitted during the OFF state in the Primary channel. The first transmission attempt of the current packet is pending during the OFF state for which the Primary channel is considered Idle.* **(initial state)**
- B_0: *The last packet has been successfully transmitted during the OFF state in the Primary channel. The first trans-*

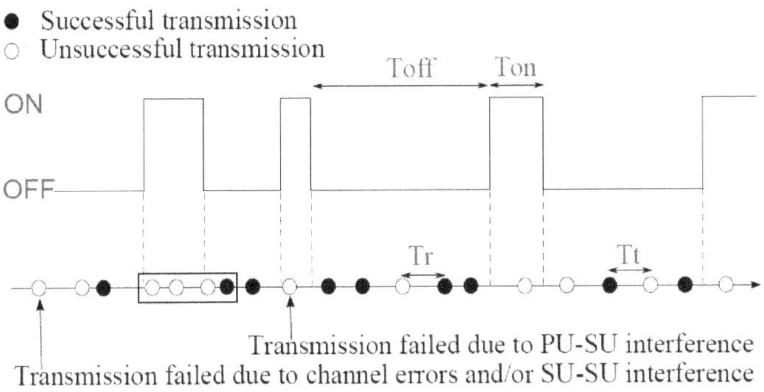

● Successful transmission
○ Unsuccessful transmission

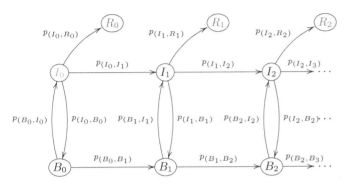

Transmission failed due to PU-SU interference
Transmission failed due to channel errors and/or SU-SU interference

Figure 6: PU and SU networks operating simultaneously. The primary user activity is modeled as an alternative ON/OFF process.

Figure 7: The absorbing discrete-time Markov chain for computing COExiST.

mission attempt of the current packet is pending during the ON state for which the Primary channel is considered Busy. **(transient state)**
- I_k, $k \in \mathbb{N}^*$: The packet has been transmitted k times without any success. The retransmission is pending during the OFF period for which the Primary channel is considered Idle. **(transient state)**
- B_k, $k \in \mathbb{N}^*$: The packet has been transmitted k times without any success. The retransmission is pending during the ON period for which the Primary channel is considered Busy. **(transient state)**
- R_k, $k \in \mathbb{N}$: The packet has been successfully transmitted with a total of k retransmissions **(absorbing state)**

The corresponding Markov Chain, illustrated in Figure 7, has an infinite number of states. It converges probabilistically to one of the absorbing state, R_k, where k represents the number of retransmission attempts performed for successfully transmitting a particular packet over the link. The transition probabilities are defined $\forall k \in \mathbb{N}$ as follows:

- $p_{(I_k, R_k)}$ = Probability that the $(k+1)^{th}$ transmission attempt is successful **and** takes place before the end of the current OFF period,
- $p_{(I_k, I_{k+1})}$ = Probability that the $(k+1)^{th}$ transmission attempt is unsuccessful **and** takes place before the end of the current OFF period,
- $p_{(I_k, B_k)}$ = Probability that the $(k+1)^{th}$ transmission attempt takes place after the end of the current OFF period,

- $p_{(B_k, I_k)}$ = Probability that the $(k+1)^{th}$ transmission attempt takes place after the end of the current ON period,
- $p_{(B_k, B_{k+1})}$ = Probability that the $(k+1)^{th}$ transmission attempt takes place before the end of the current ON period.

The above transition probabilities depend on the modeling parameters: the success probability p_s^{off}, the duty cycle u, the average ON/OFF period durations $\bar{T}_{on}$ and $\bar{T}_{off}$, as well as the average MAC layer durations $\bar{T}_r$ and $\bar{T}_t$. These transition probabilities, for the most part, do not depend on the rank of the transmission attempt. For the case of $k = 0$, they depend on $\bar{T}_t$ but not $\bar{T}_r$. For the case of $k \neq 0$, they are identically expressed except that $\bar{T}_t$ is replaced with $\bar{T}_r$. Therefore, the Markov chain is composed of two homogeneous regions. One is composed of the states I_0 and B_0 while the other of all the remaining states. As a result, the Markov chain can be partially solved on both regions for computing COExiST.

Lemma 1. *The Markov chain transition probabilities satisfy the following relations:*

- $p_{(B_k, B_{k+1})} = 1 - p_{(B_k, I_k)}$

- $p_{(I_k, I_{k+1})} = (1 - p_s^{off}) \times (1 - p_{(I_k, B_k)})$

- $p_{(I_k, R_k)} = p_s^{off} \times (1 - p_{(I_k, B_k)})$

Denoting by $f_{(I_0, R_k)}$ the probabilities of reaching the absorbing state R_k, $k \in \mathbb{N}$ when starting from the initial state I_0, the expected transmission count equals

$$\mathbb{E}[N] = \sum_{k=0}^{+\infty} (k+1) f_{(I_0, R_k)} \qquad (1)$$

This requires the calculation of the Markov chain transition probabilities as well as the reaching probabilities $f_{(I_0, R_k)}$.

1) Transition probabilities: Denoting by $\hat{T}_{on}$ the residual time in the ON period and applying the memoryless property of the exponential distribution, we have $\hat{T}_{on}$ distributed identically with T_{on}, that is, $\hat{T}_{on} \sim \mathcal{E}xp(1/\bar{T}_{on})$. Exactly the same analysis can be done with T_r, for which $\hat{T}_r$ represents the residual time before the next retransmission takes place. With these, the computation of the transition probability $p_{(B_k, B_{k+1})}$ is as follows:

$$p_{(B_k, B_{k+1})} = \int_{t=0}^{+\infty} \mathbb{P}[\hat{T}_r < t] \, f_{\hat{T}_{on}}(t) \mathrm{d}t$$
$$= \int_{t=0}^{+\infty} \mathbb{P}[T_r < t] \, f_{T_{on}}(t) \mathrm{d}t = \frac{1}{1 + \bar{T}_r / \bar{T}_{on}}$$

Using the relations from Lemma 1 and introducing the variable ρ_r such that $\rho_r = \bar{T}_r / (\bar{T}_{on} + \bar{T}_{off})$ we have:

$$p_{(B_k, B_{k+1})} = \frac{u}{u + \rho_r} \qquad \text{and} \qquad p_{(B_k, I_k)} = \frac{\rho_r}{u + \rho_r}$$

Similarly, for the three remaining transition probabilities:

$$p_{(I_k, B_k)} = \frac{\rho_r}{1 - u + \rho_r} \qquad p_{(I_k, R_k)} = \frac{p_s^{off}(1 - u)}{1 - u + \rho_r}$$

$$p_{(I_k, I_{k+1})} = \frac{(1 - p_s^{off})(1 - u)}{1 - u + \rho_r}$$

For the expressions of the transition probabilities involving states I_0 and B_0, ρ_r is replaced with $\rho_t = \bar{T}_t/(\bar{T}_{on} + \bar{T}_{off})$.

2) Reaching probabilities: Computing the reaching probabilities in an absorbing discrete-time Markov chain can be done by applying the reachability equation, whose definition is repeated below:

Definition 2 (REACHABILITY EQUATION). *The probability of reaching state j starting from state i can be computed as:*

$$f_{(i,j)} = p_{(i,j)} + \sum_{\forall k \neq j} p_{(i,k)} \times f_{(k,j)} \quad (2)$$

Theorem 1 (COEXIST). *The expected transmission count over a link subject to primary user interference is:*

$$\mathbb{E}[N] = \frac{1}{p_s^{off}(1-u)} + \frac{u}{\bar{T}_r} \times \frac{\bar{T}_t - \bar{T}_r}{\bar{T}_t/\bar{T}_{on} + 1 - u} \quad (3)$$

PROOF. Applying the reachability equation on the first region of the Markov chain leads to:

$$f_{(I_0,R_0)} = \frac{p_{(I_0,R_0)}}{1 - p_{(I_0,B_0)}p_{(B_0,I_0)}}$$

and for $k \in \mathbb{N}^*$:

$$f_{(I_0,R_k)} = \frac{p_{(I_0,I_1)}f_{(I_1,R_k)} + p_{(I_0,B_0)}p_{(B_0,B_1)}f_{(B_1,R_k)}}{1 - p_{(I_0,B_0)}p_{(B_0,I_0)}}$$

Since:

$$\mathbb{E}[N] = \sum_{k=0}^{+\infty}(k+1)f_{(I_0,R_k)} = \underbrace{\sum_{k=0}^{+\infty}f_{(I_0,R_k)}}_{=1} + \sum_{k=0}^{+\infty}kf_{(I_0,R_k)}$$

the desired result follows from applying Lemma 2. $\square$

Lemma 2. *Computing the analytical expressions of the reaching probabilities leads to the following equations:*

$$\sum_{k=1}^{+\infty}kf_{(I_1,R_k)} = \frac{1}{p_s^{off}(1-u)} \quad (4)$$

$$\sum_{k=1}^{+\infty}kf_{(B_1,R_k)} = \frac{1}{p_s^{off}(1-u)} + \frac{u}{\rho_r} \quad (5)$$

PROOF. Applying recursively the reachability equation, starting from states I_1 and B_1, and performing some linear combinations on the resulting equations leads to recursive expressions of the desired reaching probabilities, as given for $k \in \mathbb{N}^*$ by Equations 6 and 7. Therefore, these reaching probabilities satisfy the same linear second-order recurrence equations. However, they differ on their first terms, making the obtained probability values entirely different for the remaining terms of both sequences.

Each linear second-order recurrence equation can be solved for $k > 1$ using the following well-known method:

1. *Compute the roots r_1 and r_2 of the characteristic polynomial Q given in Equation 8.*

2. *Compute $f_{(I_1,R_1)}$ and $f_{(I_1,R_2)}$ (respectively $f_{(B_1,R_1)}$ and $f_{(B_1,R_2)}$ for the second equation)*

3. *Compute λ_I and μ_I (respectively λ_B and μ_B for the second equation) such that*

$$\begin{cases} \lambda_I + \mu_I & = f_{(I_1,R_1)} \\ \lambda_I r_1 + \mu_I r_2 & = f_{(I_1,R_2)} \end{cases}$$

4. *Finally, combine the results: $f_{(I_1,R_k)} = \lambda_I r_1^{k-1} + \mu_I r_2^{k-1}$*

Applying this method is straightforward in principle but it presents challenging calculations due to the dependence of the variables on three different parameters: u, p_s^{off} and ρ_r. The algebraic expressions for r_1, r_2, λ_I (respectively λ_B) and μ_I (respectively μ_B) are long and complex. They can be computed, however, with the help of a mathematical tool, such as the open source calculation software *Maxima* [2]. Due to the space constraints, we omit these calculations from the analysis.

After checking the convergence requirements, we get:

$$\sum_{k=1}^{+\infty}k \times f_{(I_1,R_k)} = \lambda_I \sum_{k=1}^{+\infty}k \times r_1^{k-1} + \mu_I \sum_{k=1}^{+\infty}k \times r_2^{k-1}$$

$$= \frac{\lambda_I}{(1-r_1)^2} + \frac{\mu_I}{(1-r_2)^2}$$

which simplifies to $1/[p_s^{off}(1-u)]$. Similarly, for the second equation, we get:

$$\sum_{k=1}^{+\infty}k \times f_{(B_1,R_k)} = \frac{\lambda_B}{(1-r_1)^2} + \frac{\mu_B}{(1-r_2)^2}$$

which simplifies to $1/[p_s^{off}(1-u)] + u/\rho_r$. $\square$

Theorem 2 (COEXIST AS A FUNCTION OF ETX). *When the probing packets used for computing ETX are transmitted independently of the primary users activity pattern, COEXIST can be expressed as the following function of ETX:*

$$\mathbb{E}[N] = ETX + \frac{u}{\bar{T}_r} \times \frac{\bar{T}_t - \bar{T}_r}{\bar{T}_t/\bar{T}_{on} + 1 - u} \quad (9)$$

PROOF. The probing packets can be periodically sent in broadcast mode with a higher priority than unicast packets. As per 802.11, the probing packets are neither acknowledged nor retransmitted in case of errors. If every probing packet used for computing ETX is transmitted independently of the primary users activity pattern, the probability for such a probe to be successfully received is:

$$\overbrace{\mathbb{P}[\text{tx ok}|\text{tx during OFF period}]}^{=p_s^{off}}\overbrace{\mathbb{P}[\text{tx during OFF period}]}^{=1-u \text{ by indep.}}$$
$$+ \underbrace{\mathbb{P}[\text{tx ok}|\text{tx during ON period}]}_{=0}\mathbb{P}[\text{tx during ON period}]$$

which is equivalent to PRR $= p_s^{off}(1-u)$. As $1/\text{PRR} = $ ETX, that concludes the proof. $\square$

The value of Theorem 2 is twofold. It shows that ETX is a special case of COEXIST for $u = 0$ and/or $\bar{T}_t = \bar{T}_r$. And more important, in conjunction with Theorem 3 below, it paves the way for leveraging popular ETX implementations to quickly deploy COEXIST. It is the approach we use in Section 4.

$$f_{(I_1,R_{k+2})} = \left(\frac{p_{(I_k,I_{k+1})} + p_{(B_k,B_{k+1})}}{1 - p_{(I_k,B_k)}p_{(B_k,I_k)}}\right) f_{(I_1,R_{k+1})} - \left(\frac{p_{(I_k,I_{k+1})}p_{(B_k,B_{k+1})}}{1 - p_{(I_k,B_k)}p_{(B_k,I_k)}}\right) f_{(I_1,R_k)} \qquad (6)$$

$$f_{(B_1,R_{k+2})} = \left(\frac{p_{(I_k,I_{k+1})} + p_{(B_k,B_{k+1})}}{1 - p_{(I_k,B_k)}p_{(B_k,I_k)}}\right) f_{(B_1,R_{k+1})} - \left(\frac{p_{(I_k,I_{k+1})}p_{(B_k,B_{k+1})}}{1 - p_{(I_k,B_k)}p_{(B_k,I_k)}}\right) f_{(B_1,R_k)} \qquad (7)$$

$$Q(X) = X^2 - \left(\frac{p_{(I_k,I_{k+1})} + p_{(B_k,B_{k+1})}}{1 - p_{(I_k,B_k)}p_{(B_k,I_k)}}\right) X + \left(\frac{p_{(I_k,I_{k+1})}p_{(B_k,B_{k+1})}}{1 - p_{(I_k,B_k)}p_{(B_k,I_k)}}\right) \qquad (8)$$

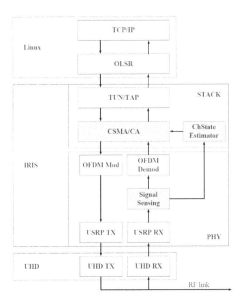

Figure 8: Software Architecture.

Theorem 3 (ROUTING WITH COExiST). *COExiST coupled with hop-by-hop Dijkstra-based routing satisfies the optimality, consistency and loop-freeness properties.*

PROOF. According to [22], establishing the proof is equivalent to demonstrating that the path weight metric is right-monotonic and right-isotonic. As COExiST is additive, it suffices to show that the metric is non-negative – this is straightforward from Eq. (1). □

4. IMPLEMENTATION

To evaluate COExiST, we have used the USRP N210 radio platform and the IRIS[4] software package. We have made significant additions to IRIS that were necessary to run our experiments. Where possible, we used open-source libraries, such as OLSR with ETX, and when not, we added our own implementations, including a CSMA/CA MAC, a primary user model, described in Section 2, and COExiST. Figure 8 shows the architecture of the software running on our testbed.

4.1 CSMA/CA Implementation

IRIS does not yet include a MAC layer component nor any mechanisms that would easily allow running IP applications

---

[4]IRIS is a component-based application whose architecture and parameters are fully reconfigurable. Such reconfiguration, used for instance for tuning the transmission frequency to another vacant channel, can be performed in real-time, something currently not possible with the GNURadio.

over USRP radios. To rectify this, we have implemented the DCF (CSMA/CA) part of 802.11.

A main challenge in implementing a CSMA MAC on USRP radios is implementing carrier sensing. We developed our own solution consisting of a *Signal Sensing* component that computes the complex signal recovered by the UHD driver and estimates the power of the received signal or RSSI. The value, coded in 16 bits, is then passed onto the *Channel State Estimator* component at the frequency of once per physical frame received. The *Channel State Estimator* module estimates the current channel state by comparing to a threshold value. For the simple case of a single threshold mechanism, the activity threshold must be calibrated by calculating the noise-floor and adding 10 dB, as recommended by the IEEE 802.11 standard. If the channel state changes, it sends a *Sensing Change* message to the main CSMA/CA component, the equivalent of the Clear Channel Assessment (CCA) in 802.11.

We use the Google protocol buffers to define the structure of the CSMA/CA and leverage the boost library to synchronize the transmission and reception threads inside the main CSMA/CA component. Finally, we interface our MAC layer to the linux IP stack using the Tun/Tap component provided in IRIS.

4.2 COExiST Implementation

We use Eq. 9 from Section 3 to implement COExiST in OLSR. We use OLSRd, an open-source implementation that also includes an implementation of ETX. As Eq. 9 shows, we can leverage the ETX value and add the second term, which is solely a function of T_{on}, T_r and T_t. Our MAC implementation collects these values and passes them on to OLSR, where a simple modification allows replacing ETX with COExiST. As it does with ETX, OLSR updates COExiST at the default rate of 1/sec. Note that T_r and T_t are based on unicast traffic. For bootstrapping the computation and for the cases where there is no unicast traffic, we use the minimum possible values based on the channel access parameters.

5. PERFORMANCE EVALUATION

In this section we evaluate the performance of COExiST and compare it with ETX [8], SAMER [19], STOD-RP [23] and the actual transmission count.

In summary, we make the following main observations:

1. In Section 5.2, we show that COExiST is a very good approximation of the actual transmission count – 80% of the time the error is less than 20%. In contrast, the 80th percentile error of ETX is 60% and of SAMER, 160%.

2. In Section 5.3, we show that COExiST continues to provide a very good approximation of the actual transmission

count even when the estimation of the primary user activity is erroneous.

3. In Section 5.4, we show that with COExiST, OLSR computes higher throughput paths than with either of the ETX, SAMER or STOD-RP metrics.

5.1 Experimental Setup

Unless otherwise specified, the experimental setup is as follows. The testbed and primary user activity are as described in Section 2.1 while the software architecture as described in Section 4. We carry out two groups of experiments. The first (Sections 5.2 and 5.3) is aimed at evaluating the accuracy of COExiST at estimating the transmission count over a link. For this, three USRP radios are deployed – with two of them representing the secondary network and the third the primary user.

The second group (Sections 5.4) of experiments is aimed at showing the impact COExiST could have on the performance of routing protocols. For this, we use all five USRP radios – with four of them creating a multi-hop secondary network, and the fifth utilized to create up to two primary users. For this group of experiments we connect the USRP radios via RF cables to an RF switch matrix. This enables us to create a multi-hop topology using licensed frequencies and create two primary users using a single USRP.

In all experiments we use Iperf [1] to generate UDP traffic. The radios are configured to send packets at 1Mbps and the data packet size is set to 1500 Bytes. A single experiment runs for 5 mins and the data presented is an average over 3 runs.

Basis for Comparison: We compare COExiST with ETX, the actual transmission count as well as two metrics proposed as part of two routing protocols designed for cognitive radio networks, namely SAMER [19] and STOD-RP [23]. SAMER essentially multiplies the packet reception ratio by the fraction of time with no primary users activity. STOD-RP combines link quality with spectrum availability by dividing ETT [10] by the time duration of the link.

5.2 Accuracy of COExiST

To measure the accuracy of COExiST we carry a series of experiments using three nodes, with two nodes representing the secondary network and the third the primary user. Between every experiment we change the placement of all nodes as well as the PU activity pattern. In every experiment we measure the actual transmission count and collect the transmission counts computed by COExiST, ETX and SAMER[5].

Fig. 9(a) shows that COExiST matches the actual transmission count fairly closely in all the experiments. On the other hand, ETX and SAMER end up either overestimating or underestimating it over a significant number of experiments. More specifically, Fig. 9(b) shows that the 80th percentile error of COExiST is 20%, of ETX is 60% and of SAMER is 160%.

5.3 Sensitivity of COExiST to Input Errors

Next, we evaluate the performance of COExiST in the presence of erroneous estimates about the primary user ac-

---

[5]STOD-RP is not included in this experiment as it does not compute the transmission count but rather the transmission time for a successful packet transmission.

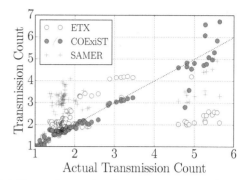

(a) Every data point is an average over three 5-minute experiments.

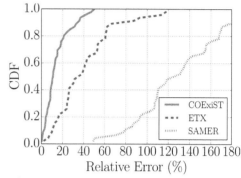

(b) The CDF of errors for the data from (a).

Figure 9: Accuracy of COExiST: For COExiST, 80% of the time the relative error is less than 20%, while for ETX and SAMER is 60% and 160%, respectively.

tivity. To induce a particular amount of errors, we simply modify the OLSR-COExiST implementation to artificially add errors to the parameters of primary user activity coming from the lower layers. We do this to simulate a real-life scenario where estimation errors are to be expected. Figure 10 shows that despite the significant errors, COExiST maintains its accuracy.

5.4 Transmission Count & Throughput

Finally, we evaluate the impact of an accurate transmission count on throughput. For this we carry out two experiments.

5.4.1 Throughput on Single-Hop Paths

In this experiment we use the three node topology and, to overcome the limitation due to the limited number of USRP radios we possess, we try to create in time the equivalent of several links on a multi-hop topology. To do this, we carry multiple experiments where we have a single source transmitting as fast as possible to a single destination while a primary user is interfering and vary the node placement and the PU level of activity from one experiment to another. During each experiment we collect the COExiST and ETX values as well as the realized UDP throughput. Figure 11 shows the collected values for COExiST (y-axis) and ETX (x-axis) for every experiment. For two experiments we show the respective UDP throughput ranges observed (208 to 221 Kbps for one, 239 to 257 Kbps for the other). ETX is smallest for the experiment where the smaller throughput was realized

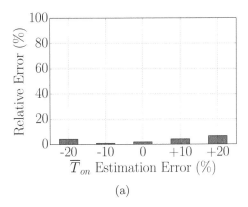

(a)

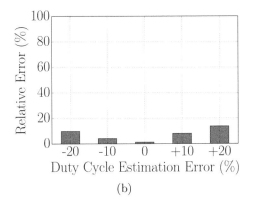

(b)

Figure 10: COExiST remains accurate even when it is given erroneous information about the primary user activity.

– 2.0 for 208 to 221 Kbps, 2.2 for 239 to 257 Kbps – while the opposite is observed with COExiST. The difference observed is obviously due to the time dimension – in a larger network the difference would be due to the space dimension. Either or, a routing protocol minimizing COExiST would select higher throughput links.

5.4.2 Throughput on Multi-Hop Paths

In this experiment, we evaluate the performance of all metrics on the multi-hop topology. In addition to the performance measurements, we also show in Figure 12 the state of the network at the time of the experiment, including the level of channel errors and primary user activity. Note that, as mentioned above, for this experiment, we use an RF switch matrix which allows us to control the channel errors and the level of primary user activity on every link. In the deployed topology, the primary users are hidden to USRP 1.

Figure 12 shows that COExiST is the only metric that identifies the highest throughput path, 1-2-4. This is due to the fact that SAMER considers primary users as a new source of independent channel errors. However, as we have shown in Theorem 2, the packet reception ratio computed by sending broadcast probes is already impacted by the primary user activity. Therefore, multiplying the packet reception ratio by the fraction of time with no primary user activity cannot suffice to capture the actual effect of primary users activity on the transmission count and, ultimately, the realized throughput. On the other hand, STOD-RP adopts

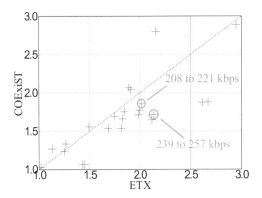

Figure 11: Every data point corresponds to a separate experiment. For two experiments we show the ranges of UDP throughput realized in addition to the respective transmission counts computed by COExiST and ETX in these experiments. COExiST is smallest for the point with the higher throughput, while the opposite happens with ETX.

a different strategy by considering the absolute time a link is available so as to favor links with less PU activity. However, the absolute time a link is free of PU activity does not tell the whole story – a link can be free of PU activity for a while only with the PU becoming suddenly active. STOD-RP is slow in penalizing such link.

6. RELATED WORK

Estimating the transmission count was pioneered by De Couto et al. [8]. It has been modified many times to include other features, e.g., the physical bit-rate [10], and it has been applied to contexts far beyond the original, including to sensor networks [12], backpressure routing [18], opportunistic routing [11, 16], network coding [14], etc.

Nevertheless, ETX was not designed to quantify the impact of primary users on transmission count, as evidenced by its poor performance in our empirical study in Section 2.

In cognitive radio networks, reflecting the unsettled nature of the field, there have been several proposed approaches to routing. Some have advocated for complete system solutions that address joint route-spectrum selection, protection to primary users [9], [7], [20], QoS provisioning [6]. We believe COExiST is complementary to these approaches. No matter how good the sensing and spectrum assignment are, they cannot guarantee PU free networking. COExiST can be leveraged for improving routing once the spectrum assignment converges, and it can be used as part of the spectrum assignment decision by quantifying the impact of primary users on performance. Furthermore, combining COExiST with traditional routing approaches, as we did with OLSR in this work, can allow for backward compatible solutions that can help the market penetration of cognitive radio networks. Routing metrics for cognitive networks have been proposed in [5, 19, 23]. The works in [19, 23], are built on basically multiplying ETX with a factor characterizing the primary user activity level. However, this approach was shown to perform poorly in our performance evaluation study. OPERA [5] focuses exclusively on delay.

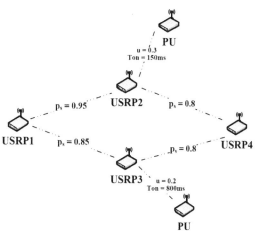

Path	ETX	SAMER	STOD-RP	COExiST	Throughput (kbps)
1-2-4	3.51	5.01	0.12	**3.48**	**165.24**
1-3-4	**3.21**	**4.01**	**0.01**	3.67	141.12

Figure 12: COExiST correctly estimates that 1-2-4 is the best path.

7. CONCLUSIONS AND FUTURE WORK

This paper presents COExiST, an approach for estimating transmission count in multi-hop cognitive radio networks. COExiST can be used as a stand-alone metric for quantifying link qualities and computing transmission-count optimal paths, or be combined with other parameters for creating more sophisticated routing metrics, depending on the particular needs. COExiST is measurement-driven, in that, all its inputs are collected at run-time. Using measurements on a five-node USRP N210 testbed, we show that COExiST accurately captures the transmission count for a variety of primary user activity levels and channel errors.

There are several interesting future directions that we are in the process of pursuing. First, it is important to evaluate COExiST on a larger scale testbed and for this we intend to augment the size of our testbed. Second, it will be interesting to explore how COExiST could be used as a building block for creating more sophisticated routing metrics customized for multi-hop cognitive radio networks.

8. REFERENCES

[1] Iperf-tool, http://dast.nlanr.net/projects/iperf/.
[2] Maxima, a computer algebra system. v5.30.0, 2013.
[3] Ettus Research, A National Instruments Company, http://www.ettus.com/, 2015.
[4] P. Bahl, R. Chandra, T. Moscibroda, R. Murty, and M. Welsh. White space networking with wi-fi like connectivity. In *ACM SIGCOMM*, pages 27–38, 2009.
[5] M. Caleffi, I. F. Akyildiz, and L. Paura. OPERA: Optimal Routing Metric for Cognitive Radio Ad Hoc Networks. *IEEE Transactions on Wireless Communications*, 11(8):2884–2894, 2012.
[6] K. R. Chowdhury and I. Akyildiz. CRP: A Routing Protocol for Cognitive Radio Ad Hoc Networks. *IEEE Journal on Selected Areas in Communications*, 29(4):794–804, april 2011.
[7] K. R. Chowdhury and M. D. Felice. Search: A routing protocol for mobile cognitive radio ad-hoc networks. *Computer Communications*, 32(18):1983–1997, 2009.

[8] D. S. J. De Couto, D. Aguayo, J. C. Bicket, and R. Morris. A high-throughput path metric for multi-hop wireless routing. In *ACM MOBICOM*, pages 134–146, 2003.
[9] L. Ding, T. Melodia, S. N. Batalama, and M. J. Medley. Rosa: distributed joint routing and dynamic spectrum allocation in cognitive radio ad hoc networks. In *ACM MSWiM*, pages 13–20, 2009.
[10] R. Draves, J. Padhye, and B. Zill. Routing in multi-radio, multi-hop wireless mesh networks. In *ACM MOBICOM*, pages 114–128, 2004.
[11] H. Dubois-Ferrière, M. Grossglauser, and M. Vetterli. Valuable detours: Least-cost anypath routing. *IEEE/ACM Transactions on Networking*, 19(2):333–346, April 2011.
[12] O. Gnawali, R. Fonseca, K. Jamieson, D. Moss, and P. Levis. Collection tree protocol. In *ACM SenSys*, pages 1–14, 2009.
[13] C. Jiang, Y. Chen, K. J. R. Liu, and Y. Ren. Renewal-theoretical dynamic spectrum access in cognitive radio network with unknown primary behavior. *IEEE Journal on Selected Areas in Communications*, 31(3):406–416, 2013.
[14] S. Katti, H. Rahul, W. Hu, D. Katabi, M. Médard, and J. Crowcroft. Xors in the air: practical wireless network coding. *IEEE/ACM Transactions on Networking*, 16(3):497–510, 2008.
[15] H. Kim and K. G. Shin. Efficient Discovery of Spectrum Opportunities with MAC-Layer Sensing in Cognitive Radio Networks. *IEEE Transactions on Mobile Computing*, 7(5):533–545, May 2008.
[16] R. P. Laufer, H. Dubois-Ferrière, and L. Kleinrock. Polynomial-time algorithms for multirate anypath routing in wireless multihop networks. *IEEE/ACM Transactions on Networking*, 20(3):742–755, 2012.
[17] M. López-Benítez and F. Casadevall. Time-Dimension Models of Spectrum Usage for the Analysis, Design, and Simulation of Cognitive Radio Networks. *IEEE Transactions on Vehicular Technology*, 62(5):2091–2104, 2013.
[18] S. Moeller, A. Sridharan, B. Krishnamachari, and O. Gnawali. Routing without routes: the backpressure collection protocol. In *ACM/IEEE IPSN*, pages 279–290, 2010.
[19] I. Pefkianakis, S. H. Y. Wong, and S. Lu. SAMER: Spectrum Aware Mesh Routing in Cognitive Radio Networks. *IEEE DySPAN*, pages 1–5, 2008.
[20] A. Sampath, L. Yang, L. Cao, H. Zheng, and B. Y. Zhao. High Throughput Spectrum-aware Routing for Cognitive Radio Networks. In *CROWNCOM*, 2007.
[21] P. D. Sutton, J. Lotze, H. Lahlou, S. A. Fahmy, K. E. Nolan, B. Özgül, T. W. Rondeau, J. Noguera, and L. Doyle. Iris: an architecture for cognitive radio networking testbeds. *IEEE Communications Magazine*, 48(9):114–122, 2010.
[22] Y. Yang and J. Wang. Design Guidelines for Routing Metrics in Multihop Wireless Networks. In *IEEE INFOCOM*, pages 1615–1623, 2008.
[23] G.-M. Zhu, I. F. Akyildiz, and G.-S. Kuo. STOD-RP: A Spectrum-Tree Based On-Demand Routing Protocol for Multi-Hop Cognitive Radio Networks. In *IEEE GLOBECOM*, pages 3086–3090, 2008.

Communication and Block Game in Cognitive Radio Networks

Haosen Pu
Tsinghua University
Beijing, P.R. China
phs199205@gmail.com

Zhaoquan Gu
Tsinghua University
Beijing, P.R. China
demin456@gmail.com

Qiang-Sheng Hua[*]
Huazhong University of
Science and Technology
Wuhan, P.R. China
qshua@hust.edu.cn

Hai Jin
Huazhong University of
Science and Technology
Wuhan, P.R. China
hjin@hust.edu.cn

ABSTRACT

In this paper, we initiate the Communication and Block Game between two unlicensed users and an adversary in Cognitive Radio Networks (CRNs). In each time slot, the two unlicensed users can successfully communicate on the common available channel if it is not blocked by the adversary. In the communication and block game, the two unlicensed users aim to maximize their communication load, denoted as the number of time slots of their successful communications, while the adversary aims to minimize it. We propose efficient algorithms for both users and the adversary and we prove the proposed algorithms will lead a Nash Equilibrium, i.e. the users can achieve the maximum communication load against any adversary's blocking strategy, while the adversary can minimize the users' communication load against any users' channel accessing strategy. We also present efficient algorithms for both users and adversary for the multiple channels scenario where the users and the adversary are equipped with multiple radios. These algorithms also guarantee high communication load for the users, while the adversary can also block a considerable number of users' communications. Our simulations validate the theoretical analyses.

Categories and Subject Descriptors

C.2.1 [**Network Architecture and Design**]: Wireless communication

Keywords

Cognitive Radio Networks; Rendezvous; Game Theory

---

*Corresponding Author

MSWiM'15, November 2–6, 2015, Cancun, Mexico.
ⓒ 2015 ACM. ISBN 978-1-4503-3762-5/15/11 ...$15.00.
DOI: http://dx.doi.org/10.1145/2811587.2811599.

1. INTRODUCTION

Due to the increasing numbers of wireless devices and large amount of wireless service, the unlicensed spectrum has been overutilized while the utilization of licensed spectrum is pretty low [1]. Cognitive Radio Networks (CRNs) are thus proposed to alleviate the spectrum scarcity problem where the unlicensed users are equipped with cognitive radios to exploit and access the portion of the licensed spectrum that is not occupied by any nearby licensed users. Unless otherwise specified, 'users' mentioned in the paper refers to the unlicensed users.

In constructing a CRN, *rendezvous* is the fundamental process to construct a communication link on some licensed channel [12,20]. Technically speaking, the licensed spectrum is assumed to be divided into n non-overlapping channels, and time is assumed to be divided into slots of equal length. In each time slot, the user can access one *available* channel that is not occupied by the licensed users, and two neighboring users achieve rendezvous if they choose the same channel in the same time slot. The state-of-the-art results guarantee rendezvous in $O(n^2)$ time slots [8].

When two users rendezvous on some channel, they can establish a communication link and exchange information through it. However, if an adversary exists in the network who can listen and block the channel in each time slot [7,11,14,15,17], the communication link is disrupted if the adversary blocks the rendezvous channel. Therefore, the users should choose the other available channels for further communication. Correspondingly, when the users are able to construct communication links on different available channels, the adversary also desires to block the communication between two users in as many time slots as possible.

In this paper, we study the communication and block game between two users and an adversary, where the users can communicate through a common available channel if it is not blocked by the adversary. Generally, we assume an adversary joins the network after two users find out the common available channels via the first rendezvous. The adversary is not aware of the users' available channels, but it can listen or block one channel in each time slot. The users are able to establish communication links on different common available channels in different time slots, but the link could not work if the channel is blocked by the adversary meantime. Therefore, the users in the problem aim to maximize the communication load, which is defined to be the number of successful communication time slots against the adversary; and the adversary aims to block the users' communication in as many time slots as possible, i.e. to minimize the users' communication load. In addition, we also extend the problem to the multiple channels scenarios, where the users and the adversary are equipped with multiple radios to sense and access (or to block) multiple channels in one time slot.

In tackling the problem, we face many challenges. First, even though the users are aware of the set of common available channels, they cannot communicate through a predefined channel accessing sequence based on the set, because once the adversary finds out the sequence they can never communicate. Second, when the adversary successfully blocks one time slot's communication between the users, it is a hard choice to block the same channel or the other channels in the next time slot, since the users would also make the same intellectual decision. Third, the users and the adversary cannot be aware of the other's strategy, and thus the designed algorithms for the users (or the adversary) should work efficiently for any adversary's (or the users') strategies. Fourth, when the users or the adversary can access or can block multiple channels, the communication and block game is much harder, especially for the adversary who has to block all possible communication channels.

In this paper, we propose both algorithms for the users and the adversary that would be a Nash Equilibrium for them. Moreover, we also propose efficient algorithms for the multiple channels scenario that achieve more communication load for users and behave more stable for the adversary. The contributions of the paper are summarized as follows:

- We design an efficient algorithm for the users against any adversary's strategy such that in a long run of T time slots, two users can achieve communication load no less than $\frac{1}{4}T$ when there is only one common available channel, and can achieve communication load no less than $(1 - \frac{1}{M})T$ when there are M common available channels;

- We introduce an efficient algorithm for the adversary against any users' strategy. We show that the algorithm works best against the proposed algorithm for the users such that the users' communication load matches the above mentioned lower bound ($\frac{1}{4}T$ and $(1 - \frac{1}{M})T$ when there is only one common available channel and there are M ($M > 1$) common available channels, respectively);

- We show that the proposed algorithms for the users and the adversary would be a Nash Equilibrium when $M \geq 2$, i.e. the users can achieve the maximum communication load against any adversary's blocking strategy, while the adversary can minimize the users' communication load against any users' channel accessing strategy;

- We also present efficient algorithms for both users and adversary for the multiple channels scenario, which guarantees high communication load for the users, while the adversary can also block a considerable number of users' communications.

The rest of the paper is organized as follows. We introduce some related works in the next section and the preliminaries are provided in Section 3. In Section 4, we introduce the algorithm for the users which work efficiently against any adversary's blocking strategy, and we present the algorithm for the adversary in Section 5. Then we show the proposed algorithms are a Nash Equilibrium in Section 6. Moreover, we present the proposed algorithms under the multiple channels scenario in Section 7. In Section 8, we conduct simulations to evaluate our proposed algorithms and the paper is concluded in Section 9.

2. RELATED WORKS

Though many elegant algorithms for the rendezvous problem in constructing a CRN [4,8] have been proposed, to the best of our knowledge, no existing works have considered the problem of maximizing the communication load after rendezvous happens and an adversary may exist in the network. Some works aim to maximize the rendezvous diversity such that the users may achieve rendezvous on all available channels [3], while some works study how an adversary or a jammer could influence the rendezvous process [11,15], but none of them considered the communication and block game in this paper.

In order to simplify the rendezvous process, some rendezvous algorithms employ a central controller or a dedicated common control channel(CCC) through which the users can make agreement on the schedule of the channels. But these methods suffer from several issues: vulnerable to attack, expensive for establishment as well as low flexibility. Therefore, many distributed rendezvous algorithms have been proposed, where the users generate a hopping sequence of the available channels and access the channels by the sequence.

There are two types of such channel hopping based rendezvous algorithms. If the users construct the same hopping sequences based on all channels, we call it global sequence (GS) based algorithms [8,13,18], otherwise, the algorithms constructing hopping sequences on the basis of the users' local information are referred to as local sequence (LS) based algorithms [4,5,9].

There are three state-of-the-art GS based algorithms: The Channel Rendezvous Sequence (CRSEQ) [18] algorithm constructs the hopping sequence based on triangle number and modular operation; the Jump-Stay(JS) algorithm [13] designs both jump frames and stay frames to guarantee rendezvous; and the Disjoint Relaxed Different Set (DRDS) algorithm constructs the hopping sequence by showing its equivalence to the carefully designed disjoint relaxed different set. These algorithms could guarantee rendezvous in $O(n^2)$ time slots if there are n channels in total.

Different from GS based algorithms, LS based algorithms construct the hopping sequences based on the users' available channels and their distinct identifiers (IDs). Alternate Hop-and-Wait (AHW) [5], Modified Local Sequence (MLS) [9] and Conversion Based Hopping (CBH) [10] convert the users' IDs to facilitate the design of different hopping sequences of different users. Another efficient algorithm without using the users' ID is proposed in [4], which constructs the hopping sequences based on graph coloring and the design of Catalan strings. However, all these algorithms only focus on the first time they rendezvous, none of them study the communication process against an adversary after rendezvous.

If an adversary exists in the network, some works have analyzed its impact on rendezvous. In [15], an adversary who can sense and block a channel in each time slot exists when two users try to achieve rendezvous using the JS algorithm. By letting the adversary estimate the hopping sequence in the first jumping stage, Channel Detecting Jamming Attacks (CDJAs) proposed in [15] reduces the successful rendezvous rate of users from 100% to 20% . And in [7], Multi-Radio Channel Detecting Jamming Attack (MRCDJA) is proposed to generalize CDJAs into multiple channel cases(the adversary can access multiple channels simultaneously), which can figure out the hopping sequence in $O(\frac{M}{n})$ expected time which is n times better than that in [15].

In [11,14,17], algorithms of users based on quorum-system are proposed to maximize the probability two users successfully rendezvous. In [11], Frequency Quorum Rendezvous (FQR) is presented based on quorum system to establish a common key for future communication under jamming attack, which works about 40% better than random hopping(RH) and Pseudo-random Frequency Hopping (PFH) [19]. In [14], the authors point out that FQR algorithms are still vulnerable against some smart adversary. An efficient adversary is presented in [14], which decreases the success rate of FQR to 35%, moreover they design Role-based Frequency Rendezvous (RFR) scheme based on different roles of users to achieve steady result of more than 90%. In [17], a game between users and a jammer is proposed and several pure strategies are introduced. The authors also show that the rendezvous performance also depends on whether the receiver and adversary are synchronized, and whether they have a common guess for the sender's strategy.

In our work, we consider the number of successful rendezvous time slots in a long run, and we call it communication load. In previous works, all adversaries are aware of the rendezvous algorithms of the users, and the users adopt the same algorithm or use the common key after they have achieved rendezvous. However, in our work, the adversary only has the knowledge of n channels, and two users may play different strategies as soon as they rendezvous.

3. PRELIMINARIES

3.1 System Model

We divide the licensed spectrum into n channels that don't overlap with each other and denote them as $U = \{1, 2, \cdots, n\}$. Due to the appearance of the licensed users, the unlicensed users cannot access all of n channels, and we denote the channels not occupied by the licensed users as *available*. Therefore, both users can find out the set of available channels after taking a short sensing stage.

Suppose t_m is the minimum time that is sufficient for the users to establish a link and exchange messages when they access the same channel. We divide time into slots of length $2t_m$. Similar to some previous works [15], we assume two users in this paper take different roles: one is sender (denote as user S) who would send messages through a channel (or the constructed link) in each time slot, while the other is receiver (denote as user R), who would listen through a channel in each time slot, and send messages only upon having received the sender's messages. When the sender is sending messages through certain channel and the receiver is listen-

ing at the same one simultaneously, communication can be established and the process is referred as rendezvous [3,8,15].

We assume that two users are able to know their common available channels once they achieve first rendezvous on some channel. In previous works, two users would stay at the common channel and keep communication through it. However in our work, we assume an adversary (denote as A) could also join the network at any time after the users' first rendezvous. In each time slot, the adversary can choose one of all n channels to sense and block. If the sender is sending messages on that channel simultaneously, the adversary could learn that and block the messages from sending to the receiver. Under the attack of an adversary, the traditional strategy of staying at a certain channel for communication is vulnerable. Therefore in this paper, the task of two users is to keep communication and increase communication load (the number of time slots that the users can communicate successfully) in a long run, while the adversary aims to prevent users from communicating.

3.2 Problem Definition

Denote the available channels of the sender and the receiver as C_s, C_r respectively, and $C_g = C_s \bigcap C_r$ as common channels of them. Assuming the sender, receiver and adversary would access channels $f(C_s, t), h(C_r, t), g(t)$ in time slot t respectively, where t is the time slots elapsed when the adversary joins the network.

We say that two users communicate successfully or they can rendezvous in certain time slot t when they choose the same channel j but the adversary doesn't block the channel. We use $I(t)$ to indicate whether two users communicate successfully in time slot t, then $I(t) = 1$ when $f(C_s, t) = h(C_r, t) \neq g(t)$, otherwise $I(t) = 0$. We define the *communication load* as follows:

Communication load: Given the strategies of the users and the adversary $f(C_s, t), h(C_r, t), g(t)$, communication load $CL(f, h, g)$ in a long run T is defined as:

$$CL(f, h, g) = \sum_{t=1}^{T} I(t)$$

Moreover, we define *communication load ratio* $\lambda(f, h, g) = \frac{CL(f,h,g)}{T}$ as the fraction of time slots that the users communicate successfully in T time slots. We define the communication and block game from both the users' and the adversary's aspects.

PROBLEM 1. *(Communication problem for the users):* *Design strategy f, h for the sender and the receiver to maximize $\min_{\forall g} \lambda(f, h, g)$.*

PROBLEM 2. *(Block Problem for the adversary):* Denote converge time CT as the time slots the adversary costs to acquire information of the users to block communication regularly in a long run. The problem is to design strategy g for the adversary to minimize $\max_{\forall f,h} \lambda(f, h, g)$ in a reasonable converge time CT.

3.3 Multiple Channels Scenario

Due to the rapid development of wireless technology, the users as well as the adversary may have the ability to access more than one channel in each time slot. In our work, we assume both the sender and the receiver can access $m \geq 1$

Table 1: Notations

Notation	Definition
CL	communication load
CT	convergence time
WL	the worst communication load against any adversary
$C_s(C_r)$	available channel for the sender (the receiver)
C_g	The common channels set of the users
M	$M = |C_g|$
$\mathcal{S}_u(\mathcal{S}_a)$	the strategy sets for the users (the adversary)
$s_u(s_a)$	the strategies that the users (the adversary) adopted
$\mathcal{U}_u(\mathcal{U}_a)$	the utility of the users (the adversary)
$m(k)$	the number of channels the users (the adversary) can sense in each time slot
U_0	the strategy of the users that they stay on a certain channel to keep communication once they first achieve rendezvous
U_1	the strategy of the users that they change and keep communication on another channel when the users are blocked
U_2	the strategy of the users adopting Alg. 1
A_0	the strategy of the adversary that it continues to block the channel on which it firstly blocks the communication successfully
A_1	the strategy of the adversary adopting Alg. 2

channels in each time slot, and the adversary can sense and block $k \geq 1$ channels.

Supposing that $m \leq \min\{|C_r|, |C_s|\}$ and $k \leq n$, the sender and the receiver would choose a set of m available channels to attempt communication in each time slot, while the adversary can block and sense a set of k channels in all n channels. Denote the sets the sender, the receiver and the adversary choose as P_s, P_r, P_a respectively, then the users can communicate successfully if and only if $|P_r \bigcap P_s \setminus P_a| \geq 1$.

In this scenario, the task of the users is also to maximize the communication load against any adversary's strategy (similar to Problem 1), while the adversary aims to minimize the users' communication load for any strategies the users may adopt (similar to Problem 2).

3.4 Other Definitions and Facts

In this subsection, we introduce some definitions and facts that will be used in this paper.

Denote the strategy sets for the users and the adversary as $\mathcal{S}_u, \mathcal{S}_a$ respectively. We call certain strategy (s_u, s_a) a Nash equilibrium if and only if:

$$\mathcal{U}_u(s_u, s_a) \geq \mathcal{U}_u(s'_u, s_a), \forall s'_u \subseteq \mathcal{S}_u$$
$$\mathcal{U}_a(s_u, s_a) \geq \mathcal{U}_a(s_u, s'_a), \forall s'_a \subseteq \mathcal{S}_a$$

where $s_u \in \mathcal{S}_u$, $s_a \in \mathcal{S}_a$, and $\mathcal{U}_u, \mathcal{U}_a$ is the utility of the users and the adversary respectively. In game theory, utility represents the satisfaction or the reward the player gains through the game [2]. In our work, if the sender, the receiver, and the adversary adopt strategy f, h, g respectively, we denote $\mathcal{U}_u = \lambda(f, h, g)$ and $\mathcal{U}_a = 1 - \lambda(f, h, g)$.

We also use some basic facts and inequalities, due to the page limit, we put them in the full version [16].

The notations used in this paper is listed in Table 1.

4. COMMUNICATION ALGORITHM FOR THE USERS

In previous works, two users would stay on a certain channel to keep communication once they first achieve rendezvous, and we denote the strategy for the users as U_0. However, it's vulnerable to the adversary. Suppose the adversary senses each of n channels in a round-robin pattern, once the adversary blocks the communication between two users successfully on certain channel, it keeps blocking the same channel in the following time slots, and we denote the strategy as A_0. Obviously, under the attack of the adversary, the users' strategy U_0 is inefficient since the adversary can find the channel after at most n time slots and the communication between the users would be blocked afterwards. In this section, we introduce an efficient algorithm for the sender and the receiver to increase communication load under the attack of any adversary's strategy.

4.1 Jumping Algorithm for The Users

Algorithm 1 Jumping Algorithm for the Users

1: **if** The user is sender **then**
2:     Generate random bits sequence l
3: **end if**
4: When achieve rendezvous the first time sender sends available channel sets C_s and random bits l to the receiver, upon receiving this, receiver sends C_r back.
5: Both the sender and the receiver learn the tripe (C_s, C_r, l). All the random choices made in the rest parts of this algorithm is based on l.
6: $C_g = C_s \bigcap C_r, M = |C_g|, S = C_g$
7: **if** $M = 1$ **then**
8:     Choose channel i in $C_s \setminus S$ uniformly at random , $S = S \bigcup \{i\}$
9: **end if**
10: **while** The users keep communicating **do**
11:     Choose channel j in S uniformly at random and access that channel, if $j \notin C_r$, the receiver choose any channel to replace j at that time slot.
12: **end while**

The idea of this algorithm is to randomly choose channels in the common channel set in each time slot. If there is only one common channel, the users choose another channel sacrificing some chance of communication to avoid being blocked easily by the adversary. In the algorithm, l is the sequence of random bits generated by the sender, then it is sent to the receiver along with set C_s when two users first achieve rendezvous. All random choices made by two users are then based on l, thus both users have the full knowledge of each other including the random choices. C_g is the set of common channels set between two users and denote M as the number of common channels. Both users choose channel j in set S in each time slot uniformly at random, where S equals to C_g when $M > 1$, or S contains the unique common channel as well as another random chosen channel in C_s.

4.2 Efficiency Against Adversary's Strategies

We show that our algorithm can achieve high communication load under *any* strategy adopted by the adversary who has the ability to sense and block one channel in each time slot.

Algorithm 2 Try-and-evaluate Algorithm for the Adversary

1: Initialize $E = (1, 1, \cdots 1)$
2: **while** The users keep communicating **do**
3:     Randomly choose a channel j. For each channel i,
       $Pr(j = i) = \frac{E_i}{\sum_{k=1}^{n} E_k}$, sense and block channel j
4:     **if** The adversary blocks the messages successfully
       then
5:         $\alpha = \min\{\frac{E_j}{\sum_{k \neq i, 1 \leq k \leq n} E_k}, 1\}$
6:         $l_1 = \max\{E_1, E_2, \cdots E_n\}, l_2 = \max\{E_j + 1, E_j *$
           $2^\alpha\}, E_j = \max\{l_1, l_2\}$
7:     **else**
8:         $E_j = \frac{E_j}{2}$
9:     **end if**
10: **end while**

THEOREM 1. *No matter what algorithm the adversary adopts, Alg. 1 can achieve communication load ratio $\lambda \geq \frac{1}{4}$ if $M = 1$; and $\lambda \geq 1 - \frac{1}{M}$ if $M \geq 2$.*

The proof of Theorem 1 can be found in the full version [16]. In addition, when $M > 1$, even if the adversary has the ability to **explore more information** (for example it knows C_r or C_s), our algorithm can still achieve $\lambda \geq 1 - \frac{1}{M}$ unless the adversary knows the sequence l of the random bits, since the algorithm works on the basis of l.

5. BLOCK ALGORITHM FOR THE ADVERSARY

If two users know the existence of the adversary, they may adopt different strategies to keep communication. Although the adversary's strategy A_0 (sense all channels and stay blocking the same channel when the first blocking happens) works quite well for some users' strategies (for example U_0 defined in Section 4), it is inefficient against most strategies of the users. For example, considering a trivial strategy of the users: the users' behavior is the same as U_0 until the communication is first blocked, then the users choose another common channel and keep communication (denote this strategy as U_1). It's obvious that the adversary's strategy A_0 can only block U_1 once, which turns out to be a bad result. In this section, we introduce an efficient algorithm for the adversary to find and block the common channels of users. The intuition of this algorithm is to restore a number for each channel which reflects the frequency the sender using that channel. Then the adversary blocks channels according to the evaluation of their frequencies, thus the adversary would block a channel that is accessed more often by the sender. We call this algorithm "try-and-evaluate" algorithm.

5.1 Try-and-Evaluate Algorithm for Adversary

In this algorithm, E is a vector of length n. For each $1 \leq j \leq n$, E_j is used to reflect the frequency that the sender sends message through the channel. This value in E would take a "half-reduce,slow-increase,fast-recovery" pattern. In each time slot, the adversary chooses to block a channel j, if the sender is not using channel j, E_j would be reduced by half; if the adversary successfully blocks a message through it, we divide it into 3 cases according to the value of E_j: in most cases E_j is slowly increased by 1; but E_j increases

faster when it gets larger, and this method helps the adversary converge faster; and if E_j is smaller than some other E_i ($i \neq j$), we would recover it back to E_i and this is what we called "fast recovery" to compensate some underestimated channels in the process of "half-reduce".

5.2 Efficiency Against Users' Strategies

We show the efficiency of Alg. 2 from two aspects: 1) The converge time of Alg. 2 is ($O(n \log n)$) against the users' strategy U_0; 2) Alg. 2 can achieve the smallest communication load of the users in Theorem 1 against the users' strategy (Alg. 1).

THEOREM 2. *The adversary running Alg. 2 would block the common channel with high probability after $t = O(n \log n)$ time slots.*

THEOREM 3. *Alg. 2 achieves the best utility for the adversary in Theorem 1 if the users run Alg. 1.*

We omit the proof of Theorems 2 and 3 which are can be found in the full version [16]. Theorem 2 and Theorem 3 show the efficiency of Alg. 2 against both trivial users' strategy and our proposed strategy (Alg. 1). It is obvious that it also works well for the users' strategy U_1. Actually, it is an efficient algorithm for the adversary against almost all users' strategies, since it modifies the probability of blocking each channel dynamically according to the behavior of the users.

6. OPTIMALITY OF OUR ALGORITHMS

In this section, we do some further analysis for the algorithms for both the users and the adversary (Alg. 1-2), showing that our algorithms are optimal to some extant. For simplicity, we denote the set for all possible users' strategies of pattern $(p_1, p_2, \cdots, p_n)$ as $\mathcal{S}_u$, where the users access channel j with probability p_j in each time slot independently. Denote $WL(f, h)$ as the worst communication load in a long run T against any adversary's strategy if the sender and the receiver run strategy f, h respectively.

THEOREM 4. *Our users' algorithm (Alg. 1) can achieve best WL.*

We omit the proof of Theorem 4 which can be found in the full version [16].

Similar to the notation of $\mathcal{S}_u$, we define the strategy set for the adversary as: $\mathcal{S}_a = \{s_a | s_a = (q_1, q_2 \cdots q_n)\}$, where q_j is the probability that the adversary blocks channel j in each time slot (note that, the choices are also independent for different time slots).

THEOREM 5. *If $M \geq 2$, the users adopting strategy $s_u = \{p_1, p_2, \cdots, p_n\}$ and the adversary adopting strategy $s_a = \{q_1, q_2, \cdots, q_n\}$ would be a Nash Equilibrium if for any $j (1 \leq j \leq n)$, $p_j = q_j = \frac{1}{M}$ when $j \in C_g$ and $p_j = q_j = 0$ when $j \notin C_g$.*

The proof of Theorem 5 can be found in the full version [16].

Notice that, when $M > 2$, our algorithms for the users and the adversary actually do the same as the strategy in Theorem 5. Thus by adopting our algorithms, neither of the users and the adversary could gain more utility by changing their strategies. So the users can achieve the best utility as well as the adversary does simultaneously.

7. ALGORITHMS FOR MULTIPLE CHANNELS SCENARIO

Due to the rapid development of wireless technology, both the users and the adversary could sense or block more than one channel in each time slot. Considering the multi-channel setting, we propose algorithms for the users as well as the adversary in this section, where the users can sense m channels in each time slot and the adversary can block k channels simultaneously. Moreover we briefly analyze the performance of the algorithms.

7.1 Algorithm for the Users

Algorithm 3 Algorithm for the Users in Multiple Channels Scenario

---
1: Run the first 7 lines of Alg. 1, the notation of C_g, M, l is the same as Alg. 1
2: $t = |C_s|$
3: **while** The users keep communicating **do**
4:     $P = 4n^2 \log n, p = q = 0$
5:     $\delta = 0.4 + 0.5 * \frac{M}{M+30}$
6:     Choose $t - M$ channels in $C_s \backslash C_g$ uniformly at random, denote them as $c_{M+1} \cdots c_t$, and $S = S \bigcup \{c_{M+1} \cdots c_t\}$
7:     Generate channel sets sequence seq with $P * M$ channels such that each $seq_{ij}(1 \le i \le P, 1 \le j \le m)$ is chosen from S uniformly at random independently
8:     **for** $i = 1$ to P **do**
9:         In time slot i of this round, Access channels seq_{i1} to seq_{im}. For the receiver, for any $seq_{ij} \notin C_r (1 \le j \le M)$, choose any available channel $c \in C_r$ to replace it.
10:         **for** $j = 1$ to m **do**
11:             **if** $seq_{ij} \in C_g$ **then**
12:                 $p = p + 1$
13:                 **if** Messages through channel seq_{ij} is not blocked **then**
14:                     $q = q + 1$
15:                 **end if**
16:             **end if**
17:         **end for**
18:     **end for**
19:     $X = q/p$
20:     **if** $X > \delta$ and $t > \max\{m, M\}$ **then**
21:         $t = t - 1$
22:     **end if**
23: **end while**

The algorithm for the users in multi-channel scenario is similar to that of single channel scenario, and we describe it in Alg. 3. In each time slot, the users choose m channels uniformly at random from t channels, where t is the number of available channels. We take $P = 4n^2 \log n$ time slots as a round, and we use p, q to calculate how frequently the communication through channels in C_g is not blocked in each round. If p/q is larger than some constant δ, we reduce t by 1 to achieve a better communication load.

7.2 Algorithm for the Adversary

We present our algorithm for the adversary in the multi-channel scenario in Alg. 4, where in each time slot the adversary uses one of k channels (Denote as c_1) to calculate the frequency that the sender accesses each channel. We

---
Algorithm 4 Algorithm for the adversary in Multiple Channels Scenario

---
1: $P_{pr} = P_n = (0, 0, \cdots, 0)$
2: Construct vector E the same as Alg. 2.
3: $\varepsilon = \frac{1}{100}, P = 4n^2 \log n$
4: **while** The users keep communicating **do**
5:     $D = F = (0, 0, \cdots, 0), bo = false$
6:     **for** $i = 1$ to P **do**
7:         Choose c_1 uniformly from n channels
8:         **if** bo **then**
9:             choose c_j ($2 \le j \le k$) independently , and $Pr(c_j = r) = \frac{P_{pr}(r)}{\sum_{1 \le q \le n} P_{pr}(q)}$
10:         **else**
11:             choose c_j ($2 \le j \le k$) independently according to E as Alg. 2.
12:         **end if**
13:         Sense and block channels $c_1, c_2 \cdots, c_k$.
14:         Update E_{c_1} to E_{c_k} according to Alg. 2.
15:         $D_{c_1} = D_{c_1} + 1$
16:         **if** The sender is using channel c_1 **then**
17:             $F_{c_1} = F_{c_1} + 1$
18:         **end if**
19:         $P_n(i) = F_i/D_i, 1 \le i \le n$
20:         $bo = true$ if and only if for all $1 \le i \le n$, $|P_n(i) - P_{pr}(i)| \le \varepsilon$
21:         $P_{pr} = P_n$
22:     **end for**
23: **end while**

---

also divide time slots into rounds where each round contains $P = 4n^2 \log n$ time slots. P_{pr}, P_n are vectors of length n to evaluate the probability that the sender uses each channel in the previous round and in this round respectively. D, F are length n vectors to calculate P_n. If P_n is close to P_{pr}, we regard that the users are in a stable state, and thus we block each channel j with probability $P_n(j)$ in the next round, otherwise we choose each of $k - 1$ channels independently according to Alg. 2. Compared with the simple strategy that the adversary chooses k channels to block by adopting Alg. 2 separately, our proposed algorithm (Alg. 4) for the multi-channel scenario can reduce the fluctuation value in a long run.

More analyses for Alg. 3 and Alg. 4 are presented in the full version [16].

8. SIMULATION RESULTS

In this section, we conduct extensive simulations to evaluate the performance of our algorithms for the users and the adversary under both single channel scenario and multi-channels scenario. We conduct the simulations for 100 separate times and take the average value as the simulation result. Denote Alg. 1 for the users as U_2, and Alg. 2 for the adversary as A_1.

8.1 Single Channel Scenario

To verify the efficiency of our algorithms for the users and the adversary, we first compare the performance of U_1 and U_0 against the adversary's strategy A_0. Moreover, the performance of A_1 is also compared with A_0 against U_0 and U_1. We depict the curves describing the relationship between time T and communication load ratio λ. In addition,

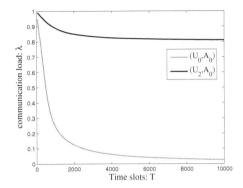

Figure 1: λ **vs.** T **against** A_0

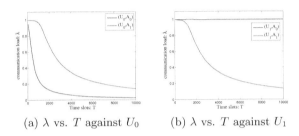

(a) λ vs. T against U_0 (b) λ vs. T against U_1

Figure 2: λ **for** A_0 **and** A_1 **against** U_0 **and** U_1 **when** T **ranging from** 50 **to** 10000

Table 2: The Convergence Time of Alg. 2

n	CT	$CT/n\log n$
100	214	1.07
500	1209	0.8959
1000	2863.1	0.954
2000	5568.37	0.843
5000	14964.8	0.809
10000	31473.6	0.788

Remarks: 1) The number of common channels $M = 5$; 2) CT is the converge time define as follows: denote j as the channel the users stay on, CT is the expected time cost until $E_j \geq \sum_{i \neq j} E_i$

Table 3: The Convergence Time of Alg. 2

M	λ	ε
1	0.2711	0.0211
2	0.50905	0.00905
3	0.67376	0.0071
4	0.755378	0.005378
5	0.804	0.004
8	0.879426	0.004426
10	0.902696	0.002696
100	0.990374	0.000374

Remarks: 1) The number of channels $n = 1000$; 2) λ is the proportion of successful communication time slots during enough long time $T = 500000$; 3) ε is the deviation of simulation results from our theoretical analysis

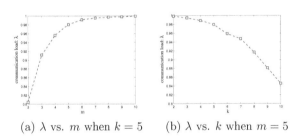

(a) λ vs. m when $k = 5$ (b) λ vs. k when $m = 5$

Figure 3: λ **vs.** m **and** k **when** $N = 1000, M = 10$

we list the converge time CT of A_1 against U_0 for different n values as well as λ of A_1 against U_2 when $n = 1000$ and M varies.

In Fig. 1, λ of both U_0 and U_2 against A_0 are shown in the figure when $n = 1000$, $M = 5$ and T ranges from 0 to 10000. As depicted, U_0 almost cannot communicate after about 10000 time slots, this is because: once the adversary adopting A_0 finds the channel that the users communicate on, they can never communicate again. In contrast, U_2 achieves a better result and it can achieve the communication load of about $0.8T$ in a long run of T time slots, which also verifies the efficiency of Alg. 1.

Fig. 2 shows the performance of A_0 and A_1 against U_0 and U_1. We choose $n = 1000$, $M = 5$ and T ranges from 0 to 10000. From the curves, we know that A_0 blocks almost all communication between the users if they adopt strategy U_0 after a short converge time. However, when A_0 encounters U_1, the adversary can block few proportion of the communication, this is because A_0 always blocks the channel on which it blocks communication successfully for the first time, but the users could then turn to another channel for further communication after the channel is blocked. However A_1 works equally well for the users, though the converge time is larger against U_0 when compared with A_0, but the time is still acceptable.

Table 2 lists the converge time CT of A_1 against U_0 when n varies from 100 to 10000. We set $M = 5$ and define the converge time as the time slot cost until $E_j \geq \sum_{i \neq j} E_i$. It is shown that $CT/n\log n$ is almost monotone decreasing except for $n = 500$; and when $n \geq 500$, $CT/n\log n \leq 1$. The results corroborate our theoretical analysis that Alg. 2 would converge in $O(n\log n)$ times slots, and the shortest

possible converge time would be $O(n)$ since it takes $O(n)$ time slots to find the channel that the users adopt at first.

The communication load ratio λ of U_2 against A_1 is listed in Table 3, where the number of common channels M ranges from 1 to 100 and we set $n = 1000$. ε is the difference between the simulation results and our theoretical analysis. From Table 3, ε is less than 0.01 when $M \geq 2$, and it becomes smaller when M is larger, thus the results also corroborate our analysis in Section 5.

8.2 Multiple Channels Scenario

For the multiple channels scenario, we set $n = 1000$, $M = 10$, and try to find out how the communication load ratio λ changes when m and k vary respectively. Here m, k are the number of channels that the users and the adversary can sense in each time slot respectively.

Fig. 3(a) shows how λ changes when $k = 5$ and m ranges from 2 to 10, and Fig. 3(b) shows the change of λ when $m = 5$ and k varies from 2 to 10. As shown in the figures,

λ is monotone increasing when m increases and it is monotone decreasing when k increase. Compared with the result in single channel scenario, when $M = 10$, $\lambda = 0.9$; while as depicted in Fig. 3, when $m = k = 5$, $\lambda \approx 0.98$. Thus, the users can communicate successfully in more time slots for the multi-channel scenario. This is because the adversary has to block all m channels that the sender is using for communication. Moreover, λ is more sensitive if $m < k$, because the users can communicate successfully nearly all the time when $m \geq k$. Moreover, when $k - m$ gets larger, λ becomes more sensitive. This means that if the adversary can sense more channels in each time slot than that of the users, acquiring the ability to access more channels would be useful for the users (or the adversary) to increase (or decrease) the communication load.

Combining the simulation results for both single channel scenario and multi-channel scenario, our proposed algorithms for the users and the adversary can achieve good performance that corroborates our analyses.

9. CONCLUSION

In this paper, we introduce the Communication and Block Game between two users and an adversary in Cognitive Radio Networks (CRNs). In this game, the users aim to maximize their communication load in a long run of T time slots, while the adversary aims to minimize it. We design efficient algorithms for the users and the adversary. The algorithm for the users guarantee two users can achieve communication load no less than $\frac{1}{4}T$ when there is only one common available channel, and can achieve communication load no less than $(1 - \frac{1}{M})T$ when there are M ($M > 1$) common available channels against *any* possible adversary. In addition, the algorithm for the adversary works best against the proposed algorithm for the users such that the users' communication load matches their lower bound. We further show that the introduced algorithms for the users and the adversary would become a Nash Equilibrium when $M \geq 2$, which means they can achieve their best utilities simultaneously. We also present algorithms for the users and the adversary in the multiple channels scenario (both equipped with multiple radios), which achieves better communication load for the users and a nontrivial utility for the adversary by blocking a considerable number of users' communications.

Since the proposed Nash Equilibrium considers only a subset of all possible strategies, in the future, we aim to generalize our results into all strategies. We will also try to propose more efficient algorithms and present more refined theoretical analyses in the multiple channels scenario.

10. ACKNOWLEDGMENTS

This work was supported in part by the National Basic Research Program of China Grant 2011CBA00300, 2011CBA00301, the National Natural Science Foundation of China Grant 61103186, 61033001, 61361136003.

11. REFERENCES

[1] I. Akyildiz, W. Lee, M. Vuran, and S. Mohanty. NeXt Generation Dynamic Spectrum Access Cognitive Radio Wireless Networks: A Survey. *Computer Networks*, 50(13): 2127-2159, 2006.

[2] R.J. Aumann(2008). "Game Theory" Introduction, The New Palgrave Dictionary of Economics, 2nd Edition.

[3] K. Bian, J.-M. Park. Maximizing Rendezvous Diversity in Rendezvous Protocols for Decentralized Cognitive Radio Networks. *IEEE Trans. on Mobile Computing*, 12(7):1294-1307, 2013.

[4] S. Chen, A. Russell, A. Samanta, and R. Sundaram. Deterministic Blind Rendezvous in Cognitive Radio networks. In *ICDCS*, 2014.

[5] I. Chuang, H.-Y. Wu, K.-R. Lee. and Y.-H. Kuo. Alternate Hop-and-Wait Channel Rendezvous Method for Cognitive Radio Networks. In *INFOCOM*, 2013.

[6] L. DaSilva, and I. Guerreiro. Sequence-Based Rendezvous for Dynamic Spectrum Access. In *DySPAN*, 2008.

[7] Y. Gao, Z. Gu, Q.-S. Hua and H. Jin. Multi-Radio Channel Detecting Jamming Attack Against Enhanced Jump-Stay Based Rendezvous in Cognitive Radio Networks. In *COCOON*, 2015.

[8] Z. Gu, Q.-S. Hua, Y. Wang, and F. C.M. Lau. Nearly Optimal Asynchronous Blind Rendezvous Algorithm for Cognitive Radio Networks. In *SECON*, 2013.

[9] Z. Gu, Q.-S. Hua, and W. Dai. Local Sequence Based Rendezvous Algorithms for Cognitive Radio Networks. In *SECON*, 2014.

[10] Z. Gu, Q.-S. Hua, and W. Dai. Fully Distributed Algorithms for Blind Rendezvous in Cognitive Radio Networks. In *MOBIHOC*, 2014.

[11] E. Lee, S. Oh and M. Gerla. Frequency Quorum Rendezvousfor Fast and Resilient Key Establishment under Jamming Attack. In *Mobicom Poster*, 2010.

[12] G. Li, Z. Gu, X. Lin, H. Pu, and Q.-S. Hua. Deterministic Distributed Rendezvous Algorithms for Multi-Radio Cognitive Radio Networks. In *MSWiM*, 2014.

[13] H. Liu, Z. Lin, X. Chu, and Y.-W. Leung. Jump-Stay Rendezvous Algorithm for Cognitive Radio Networks. *IEEE Trans. on Parallel and Distributed Systems*, 23(10):1867-1881, 2012.

[14] Y. Oh and D. Thuente. Limitations of Quorum-based Rendezvous and key establishment schemes against sophisticated jamming attacks. In *MILCOM*, 2012.

[15] Y. Oh and D. Thuente. Channel Detecting Jamming Attacks Against Jump-Stay Based Channel Hopping Rendezvous Algorithm for Cognitive Radio Networks. In *ICCCN*, 2013.

[16] H. Pu, Z. Gu, Q.-S. Hua, H. Jin. Communication and Block Game in Cognitive Radio Networks. http://grid.hust.edu.cn/qshua/mswim15full.pdf

[17] M. Rahamn and M. Krunz. Game-theoretic Quorum-based Frequency Hopping for Anti-jamming Rendezvous in DSA Networks. In *DySPAN*, 2014.

[18] P. Shin, D. Yang, and C. Kim. A Channel Rendezvous Scheme for Cognitive Radio Networks. *IEEE Communications Letters*, 14(10):954-956, 2010.

[19] M. Strasser, C. Popper and S. Capkun. Efficient uncoordianted fhss anti-jamming communication. In *MOBIHOC*, 2009.

[20] N. Tadayon, and S. Aissa. Multi-Channel Cognitive Radio Networks: Modeling, Analysis and Synthesis. *IEEE Journal on Selected Areas in Communications*, 2014.

Protecting Location Information in Collaborative Sensing of Cognitive Radio Networks

Yunlong Mao
State Key Laboratory for Novel
Software Technology
Nanjing University
Nanjing 210023, China
njucsmyl@163.com

Tingting Chen
California State Polytechnic
University
Pomona, CA 91768
tingtingchen@cpp.edu

Yuan Zhang
State Key Laboratory for Novel
Software Technology
Nanjing University
Nanjing 210023, China
zhangyuan@nju.edu.cn

Tiancong Wang
State Key Laboratory for Novel
Software Technology
Nanjing University
Nanjing 210023, China
go.tcwang@gmail.com

Sheng Zhong
State Key Laboratory for Novel
Software Technology
Nanjing University
Nanjing 210023, China
zhongsheng@nju.edu.cn

ABSTRACT

Collaborative sensing has become increasingly popular in cognitive radio networks to enable unlicensed secondary users to coexist with the licensed primary users and share spectrum without interference. Despite its promise in performance enhancement, collaborative sensing is still facing a lot of security challenges. The problem of revealing secondary users' location information through sensing reports has been reported recently. Unlike any existing work, in this paper we not only address the location privacy issues in the collaborative sensing process against semi-honest adversaries, but also take the malicious adversaries into consideration. We propose efficient schemes to protect secondary users' report from being revealed in the report aggregation process at the fusion center. We rigorously prove that our privacy-preserving collaborative sensing schemes are secure against the fusion center and the secondary users in semi-honest model. We also evaluate our scheme extensively and verify its efficiency.

Categories and Subject Descriptors

C.2.m [**Computer-Communication Networks**]: Miscellaneous

Keywords

Location Privacy; Privacy Preserving; Collaborative Sensing; Cognitive Radio

*This work was supported in part by NSFC-61321491, NSFC-61425024, NSFC-61300235, and NSFC-61402223.

1. INTRODUCTION

With the development of wireless communication and the proliferation of mobile devices in recent years, dynamic spectrum allocation is considered an effective way to remedy the problem of spectrum shortage. Cognitive radio networks in particular have been proposed to enable dynamic spectrum allocation and increase the efficiency of resource utilization. In cognitive radio networks, unlicensed (secondary) users can sense the spectrum and tune their transmitters to the available channel, under the prerequisite that their communication does not introduce interference to the users with licenses (primary users) [10]. For the reason that the primary user has no obligation to help secondary users allocate the channels, secondary users need to cognitively sense the spectrum to avoid interference with existing primary users.

In order to effectively avoid interference in cognitive radio networks, collaborative sensing has been leveraged to detect the existing communication of primary users [18]. In particular, each unlicensed user measures the received signal strength (RSS). Then it either forwards the RSS to a centralized fusion center as a report, or sends its local decision on whether the licensed communication exists to the fusion center after analyzing the RSS. The fusion center collects all the reports from participating secondary users and draws a joint conclusion. If the spectrum is idle, the fusion center coordinates the secondary users to access the available channels. In this way, the white space not being used by the primary users can be fully utilized.

While collaborative sensing has become increasingly popular, some security concerns in this process have been raised. For example, if the reports sent by secondary users are caught and altered by an attacker, it may lead to a wrong sensing result at the fusion center and thus an interference. Even more seriously, collaborative sensing is facing the challenge that secondary users can be malicious and deliberately submit fake or invalid sensing reports. To address these issues, many research works have been proposed [5,7–9,24,25]. Recently, a new privacy issue, i.e., location privacy for secondary users in collaborative radio networks, has attracted people's attention. Related work (e.g., [11,16]) has shown

Table 1: guarantee and assumption of attackers in different schemes

scheme	Zhaoyu's	Shuai's	Ours
can be malicious?	No	Yes	Yes
can collude with FC?	No	Yes	Yes
can FC be malicious?	No	No	Yes

that in the sensing process, the secondary user's location information is highly correlated to the reported signal strength after the propagation from the primary user to the secondary user. Hence the attackers can utilize the reports to explore the location information of the secondary users. As the first remedy of the location privacy issue, [16] proposes a cryptographic scheme to enable the secondary user to conceal its sensing reports in the aggregation process at the fusion center. After that, a very similar privacy issue has been studied by [12, 13]. In their work, secondary users query a central database to obtain spectrum availability information for places around his location, then attackers can infer user's location by finding the overlapping area of spectrum the user has used.

However, the existing solutions for protecting location privacy in collaborative sensing have only considered limited attack scenarios and models. For example, in [16] it is assumed that the fusion center cannot be more than curious, i.e., it must faithfully perform sensing report aggregation although it may try to reveal secondary users' privacy. And according to [13] the solution should be performed in normalized cognitive radio networks with trusted central databases. The difference between our scheme and these solutions is shown in the Table.1. As shown in the table, Shuai's scheme is more relevant to ours. But our scheme is much more efficient. We will discuss the comparing in Section 5.

In this paper, we aim to provide complete privacy protection against the semi-honest adversaries, and then extend it against malicious adversaries (assuming that secondary users and the fusion center can deviate from the sensing protocol). In particular, in our scheme, we leverage an efficient and novel cryptographic scheme as a building block, and carefully design the scheme for each step of the collaborative sensing. Our scheme secures the report information against the attacks by the fusion center or by other secondary users. Compared with other existing works based on public-key schemes, one advantage of our work is that it is more efficient and more flexible. In particular, the scheme enables us to use randomly generated public key to encrypt sensing reports in each round, instead of using and managing the same key pair. To summarize, the contributions of this paper are as follows.

- We study the location privacy issues in collaborative sensing process both in the semi-honest model and in the malicious model. We propose efficient schemes to protect secondary users' report from being revealed in the report aggregation process at the fusion center.

- We show that our privacy-preserving collaborative sensing schemes are secure against the fusion center and the secondary users, in the semi-honest model and in the malicious attack model.

- We extensively evaluate the performance of our schemes and verify their efficiency.

After this introduction, the rest of this paper is structured as follows. In Section 2, we provide a general introduction of all system models and cryptography tools we use. In Section 3 we propose our scheme and provide both security analysis and complexity analysis. In Section 4 we propose an approach in an entirely malicious model as the extension of our scheme. In Section 5 we describe the two-part simulation experiment we performed to verify our scheme's feasibility and efficiency. We conclude the paper in Section 6.

2. PRELIMINARY

In this section, we will have a brief review of the collaborative sensing model. Aiming at existing privacy problems, we use a classical and essential collaborative sensing model, and then based on this model, our secure models consisting of a semi-honest model and a restricted malicious model. The attack scenarios under each model will be introduced. The last subsection is an introduction of a novel cryptographic technique that we use in our scheme.

2.1 Collaborative Sensing

We use a centralized cognitive radio model [19], which has a central control unit, known as Fusion Center (FC), to coordinate the work of each secondary user (SU) in the network and holds the right to make the decision of each affair. Generally, the FC launches one round of sensing, to determine SUs' numbers and coordinate all of them. The whole working process can be considered consisting of two parts, collaborative sensing and spectrum allocation. Our works just focus on the first part, so we put the details of spectrum allocation aside.

Here is the cognitive radio network (CRN) that we consider. Each node (including the FC and SUs) in CRN has a set of fully functional radio equipment and every two nodes can establish direct communication. No node has motility. In this CRN, SU set U_s consists of n users $U_s = \{s_1, s_2, \ldots, s_n\}$. There is only one primary user (PU) U_p concerned, and the channels set $C = \{c_1, c_2, \ldots, c_m\}$ consists of all channels that U_p occupies. The FC is denoted by F. SU s_i's local sensing result in U_p's channel $c_j, j \in [1, m]$ is denoted by r_i^j, and if we just look at a certain channel every time, we can just use r_i instead. Finally, we use R to denote global sensing result the FC gives in the end of collaborative sensing.

Now we define a round of collaborative sensing (which will be omitted to round in the rest). The FC confirms participating SUs and assigns the target channel c_j. Once a new round begins, all participants sense the channel c_j, and send their sensing report r_i^j containing the received signal strength (RSS) of the PU to the FC. When the sensing process completes, the FC must give a final global sensing result R^j based on SUs' reports aggregation. Various methods are available to detect the PU's signal [2]. Generally, we choose the method based on RSS, which follows the distribution below [17]:

$$r_i^j \sim \begin{cases} N(n_0, \frac{n_0^2}{M}), & H_0 \\ N(p_i^j + n_0, \frac{(p_i^j + n_0)^2}{M}), & H_1 \end{cases} \quad (1)$$

In the formula above, we denote SU s_i's sensing report by r_i^j and n_0 is the additive white Gaussian noise (AWGN). p_i

stands for the s_i's received signal power from the primary transmitter on channel c_j. M is the signal sample number. Let H_0 be channel's idle state, and H_1 be channel's busy state. Final result that the FC gives can be described as:

$$R^j = \sum_{i=1}^{n} \omega_i r_i^j, \qquad (2)$$

In the formula above, ω_i is the weight of SU s_i's sensing result. We just use equal gain combination (EGC), setting all weights as 1 [17]. And R^j is the statistical result of the channel c_j.

2.2 Attack Model

Firstly we design our scheme to be effective in both a semi-honest model and a restricted malicious model. Then in section 4, we will extend our scheme to a malicious model. All the parties in the semi-honest model must follow the protocol of collaborative sensing and our scheme, but they can keep their own intermediate results, and in this model, honest users are the majority [15]. In other words, SUs and the FC must honestly do coin flipping and send their result whether they are semi-honest or not. In the restricted malicious model, loosely speaking, only SUs can be malicious, who can behave beyond prescribed protocol and nobody can predict their next move. And malicious users may submit arbitrary reports to disturb collaborative sensing result. Our goal is that our scheme is still secure with the number of malicious users which is smaller than that of half of the SUs. The FC is probably operated and maintained by an untrusted organization.

Because the main difference between the semi-honest model and the restricted malicious model is that SUs can be malicious, to be succinct, we use the semi-honest model as the default setting if no additional statement is attached. And we will have a separate discussion for the restricted malicious model.

Our attention focuses on user's location privacy. The *attacker* we called is the one who wants to acquire SU's location information. Any party in the network including SUs and the FC can be an attacker. We allow attackers to collude in our scheme. That means a semi-honest SU can collude with other semi-honest SU or semi-honest FC. The only assumption of our scheme is that if the FC is an attacker, it cannot collude with the Helper (which is to be introduced at the beginning of section 3), and neither of them could be malicious in the semi-honest model and the restricted malicious model. And this assumption can be removed in the extension of our scheme.

We consider attackers to use the same method as in [16] to get user's location information that we briefly describe here. Generally, we consider one attacker s_a in the set of U_s, who casts covetous eyes on location information of $s_d (\in U_s)$. First of all, s_a collects as much as possible sample locations' information. Then, s_a classifies the RSS sample data of each region into m classes using the input from two channels, and obtains each cluster's central value. Finally, s_a eavesdrop on s_d's sensing reports in the two channels, and calculates their distance with each cluster's central value. If s_a finds that s_d's distance with cluster k is the minimum distance, s_a can regard s_d's location the same as cluster k's.

2.3 Problem Formulation

Now we take care in defining proper notions of security for our problem. Our security is defined in the semi-honest model firstly, and then we will discuss the security in malicious model in Section 4. Intuitively, we want SUs to know nothing from our protocol, and the FC to know only a random permutation of all SUs' sensing results. We formalize the above idea using standard cryptographic terms as follows. Let $I = \{1, \ldots, n\}$ be the index set of the SUs and $\mathbf{r} = (r_1, \ldots, r_n)$ denotes the sensing results from all SUs. Let $\rho(\mathbf{r})$ be a uniformly random permutation of $\mathbf{r}$.

DEFINITION 1. *(Security against secondary users) We say a collaborative sensing scheme (CSS) is* secure against all SUs *in the sense that it reveals* **nothing other than the total number of SUs** *to all SUs if, given any R and a security parameter t, for each $i \in \{1, \ldots, n\}$, there exists a probabilistic polynomial-time simulator S_i such that for every probability*

$$\{S_i(r_i, n, t)\} \stackrel{c}{\equiv} \{CSS\_View_{s_i}(R, t)\},$$

where $CSS\_View_{s_i}(R, t)$ denotes the view of SU i while it *runs the sensing scheme with R being all SUs' sensing results.*

Here, a user's view consists of its own coin flips and all messages from other participants that it sees in the scheme. The notation $\stackrel{c}{\equiv}$ denotes *computational indistinguishability* (please refer to [14] for a precise definition) of two *probability ensembles* [14]. Intuitively, this definition states that what a SU sees from the scheme can be efficiently simulated by a simulator given this user's private input, the total number of SUs and a public security parameter as the only inputs. Therefore, we can conclude that the CSS reveals nothing to all SUs.

Similarly, we can define the security against the FC as follows.

DEFINITION 2. *(Security against the fusion center) We say a collaborative sensing scheme is* secure against all SUs *in the sense that it reveals only* **a random permutation of all SUs' sensing results** *if, given any R and a security parameter t, there exists a probabilistic polynomial-time simulator S_{FC} such that for every probability*

$$\{S_{FC}(\rho(R), t)\} \stackrel{c}{\equiv} \{CSS\_View_{FC}(R, t)\},$$

where $CSS\_View_{FC}(R, t)$ denotes the view of the FC in the *scheme.*

2.4 Derivative ElGamal encryption

ElGamal encryption algorithm is a classic asymmetric key encryption algorithm. Its encryption result is determined by not only plain text and public key, but also a random integer from encoder. In our scheme, we use a derivative algorithm of ElGamal encryption [27]. In addition, we modify it to apply to multiple parties. Choose a big prime with form of $p = 2q + 1$, where q is another big prime. Denote a quadratic residues generator in Z_p^* by g, $g \neq 1$. In this scheme, considering that every node in the network including the FC may be untrusted, we separate receiver party's private key into two parts x_1 and x_2. Both of them are chosen from Z_q randomly, and kept by the receiver. Combine x_1, x_2 to get keys by calculating $x \equiv x_1 + x_2 \, mod \, q$ and $y = g^x \, mod \, p$.

Now, we have (p, g, y) as the public key, and (p, g, x) as the private key. Anyone who wants to send a message m with encryption can randomly choose an integer k from Z_q, encrypt plain text m into (g^k, my^k), then send it to the receiver. The receiver firstly decrypts the cipher text with one part of private key x_1 by calculating $my^k g^{-kx_1}$, and then it can get the original message from calculating $my^k g^{-kx_1} g^{-kx_2}$ in another part.

3. PROPOSED SCHEME

The goal of our scheme is to ensure that SUs will not expose their location privacy during the process of collaborative sensing in CRNs. SUs' sensing reports are original input data, and we want to get the final collaborative sensing result as output with location privacy preserved. But, considering the FC may be an attacker, a preprocessing is needed to protect original data before the FC's aggregation. SUs should anonymize their reports, so that the FC cannot match each report's source. SUs could do this by self-organizing or a trusted third-party.

In order to be more efficient and avoid involving a trusted third-party as much as possible, a SU will be selected to be an assistance Helper to prevent the attack from the FC. The Helper, a new role in our scheme, can be played by any SU. In other words, the Helper is a special SU who assists the FC with the perception of the PU's signal. Except that, the Helper has the same equipment with any SU. We can use many existing methods to select a SU as the Helper [6] [2], such as a voting algorithm. Besides, a novel encryption tool is used to protect sensing report. Since a SU will cost more energy to do computation as the Helper, this role can be played in turn. Many incentive schemes developed for CRNs [1, 21] can be easily applied to compensate for the energy cost, which is out of our concern.

As for the location attacks based on physical layer, it is beyond our discussion. Since this type of attack can be widely found in various kinds of networks instead of just aimed at cognitive radio's location privacy, it deserves separate research, and there are many effective methods to defeat it, such as [23].

3.1 Procedure Of Our Scheme

Our scheme consists of four steps, initializing, reports encrypting, the Helper's decrypting and the FC's decrypting. Generally, we randomly choose a SU as the Helper for one round before the sensing starts. Since the Helper can also be untrusted, to avoid the situations where the Helper is watched or is adversary itself, we re-randomize permuting the combination of users' sensing reports. However, this will not cause any effect on the final aggregating result. This involves our scheme's correctness, and we will prove it later in the end of this subsection.

We use the encryption tool in the following way. The receiver's two parts in derivative algorithm are the FC and the Helper, both of which hold part of the private key respectively. All SUs who want to submit sensing report in a sensing round need to encrypt his report with the public key. Then reports are sent to the Helper who will decrypt reports with his part of the private key and re-randomize permuting the match of reports and sources. The FC will get anonymous sensing data by decrypting report with his part of the private key. Our algorithm's specific flow is shown in Alg.1.

Algorithm 1: procedure of our scheme

F, H:
randomly pick p, q, $p = 2q + 1$, p is l-bit length;
choose one generator of Z_p^* as g ;
H randomly chooses x_1 in Z_q, F randomly chooses x_2 in Z_q;
$x \equiv x_1 + x_2 \ (mod\ q)$;
$y = g^x \ mod\ p$, $y_1 = g^{x_1} \ mod\ p$, $y_2 = g^{x_2} \ mod\ p$;

---

s_i:
foreach $i \in U_s$ **do**
    randomly chooses k_i in Z_q;
    $\bar{r_i} \leftarrow (g^{k_i} \ mod\ p, r_i y^{k_i} \ mod\ p)$;
    s_i sends $\bar{r_i}$ to H;
end

H:
re-randomized permuting $(\bar{r_1}, \bar{r_2}, \ldots, \bar{r_n}) \rightarrow (\hat{r_1}, \hat{r_2}, \ldots, \hat{r_n})$;
foreach $\hat{r_i} = (r_{\hat{i},1}, \ r_{\hat{i},2})$ **do**
    $r_{\tilde{i},2} \leftarrow \frac{r_{\hat{i},2}}{(r_{\hat{i},1})^{x_1}} \ mod\ p$;
end
H sends $((r_{\hat{1},1}, r_{\tilde{1},2}), (r_{\hat{2},1}, r_{\tilde{2},2}), \ldots, (r_{\hat{n},1}, r_{\tilde{n},2}))$ to F;

F:
foreach $i \in [1, n]$ **do**
    $r'_i \leftarrow \frac{r_{\tilde{i},2}}{(r_{\hat{i},1})^{x_2}} \ mod\ p$;
end
F aggregates all of the r'_i to get the final sensing result R.

Here are some explanations of the procedure. First of all, a secure length parameter l should be determined, and it can be set with firmware. Then a pair of primes p, q are generated, and the length of q is l-bit while $p = 2q + 1$. A generator g of Z_p^* is randomly chosen. The Helper and FC respectively generate random integer x_1, $x_2 \in Z_q$, x_1 and x_2 can not be exposed to others. Then let the Helper and FC work together to get x, $x \equiv x_1 + x_2 \ (mod\ q)$ [1] and y, y_1, y_2, $y = g^x \ mod\ p$, $y_1 = g^{x_1} \ mod\ p$, $y_2 = g^{x_2} \ mod\ p$, the public key can be sent to all SUs through broadcasting. Once a SU s_i finishes local sensing, s_i encrypts the sensing report with the public key (p, g, y), and sends the encrypted report to the Helper instead of directly to the FC. The Helper re-randomizes permuting sensing reports received, decrypts reports with its part of the private key x_1 and sends result to the FC. The FC decrypts reports from the Helper with another part private key x_2 to get the original sensing report, do the final aggregation work and announce global collaborative sensing result R.

In the semi-honest model, an SU attacker can obtain nothing about other SU's location even if he colludes with the FC or the Helper. Similarly, if the FC or the Helper is attacker, he cannot obtain anything about any SU's location except those he colluded with. To keep our statement coherent, we put all these proofs in Theorem.5-7. As for the restricted malicious model, the information malicious SUs can obtain is no more than when they are semi-honest, and the security can be guaranteed by Theorem.5.

---

[1] we recommend to obtain x by introducing a trusted third party. However if the trusted third party is not available, we can still obtain x with cryptographic protocols easily.

THEOREM 3. *Our scheme keeps the correctness of sensing result in both semi-honest model and restricted malicious model.*

PROOF. Recall that the FC receives SUs' reports and give aggregation by $F(\mathbf{r})$. Let $A(\mathbf{r})$ denote our scheme algorithm execution. If we can prove that $F(\mathbf{r}) = F(A(\mathbf{r}))$, we can ensure the correctness. We use the same symbols in our scheme's procedure. The Helper has $r_i = (g^{k_i} \mod p, r_i y^{k_i} \mod p)$, $\forall r_i \in \mathbf{r}$, then after randomly permuting, we assume that $\hat{r}_j = \bar{r}_i = (r_{i,1}, r_{i,2})$. Then the Helper partially decrypts $\hat{r}_j$ by $r_{\tilde{j},2} = \frac{r_{i,2}}{(r_{i,1})^{x_1}} \mod p$. Now we have $(r_{i,1}, r_{\tilde{j},2})$ as input for the FC. Finally, the FC calculates $r_i' = \frac{r_{\tilde{j},2}}{(r_{i,1})^{x_2}} \pmod{p} = \frac{r_{i,2}}{(r_{i,1})^{x_1+x_2}} \pmod{p}$, where $x_1+x_2 = x \pmod{q}$, and $r_{i,1} = g^{k_i} \pmod{p}, r_{i,2} = r_i y^{k_i} \pmod{p}$, then $r_{i,1}^x = y^{k_i} \pmod{p}$, $r_i' = \frac{r_i y^{k_i}}{y^{k_i}} \pmod{p} = r_i$. $\mathbf{r}'$, the set of r_i' is exactly the same set as $\mathbf{r}$. And the FC can give the same result because the aggregation is unrelated to the permutation of reports [20].

Unlike semi-honest SU, a malicious SU may falsify his sensing report r_m in uncertain ways. But no matter what content is in r_m, the FC can still give the same result as long as the number of malicious SU's false reports is below the aggregation's threshold which is usually set as half the number of SUs [20]. Therefore, if less than half SUs are malicious, our scheme's correctness can be kept. □

3.2 Security Analysis

Here we formally prove the security of our scheme. After the Helper is introduced, we should take a new attack scenario into consideration, a SU attacker colluding with the Helper. First of all, we define the security requirement for the Helper similarly to the security requirements for SUs and the FC in Section 2.3.

DEFINITION 4. *(Security against the Helper) We say a collaborative sensing scheme is secure against the Helper in the sense that it reveals **nothing other than the total number of SUs** to the Helper if, given any R and a security parameter t, there exists a probabilistic polynomial-time simulator S_H such that for every probability*

$$\{S_H(n,t)\} \stackrel{c}{\equiv} \{CSS\_View_H(R,t)\},$$

where $CSS\_View_H(R,t)$ denotes the view of the Helper in the scheme.

THEOREM 5. *Our scheme is secure against secondary users.*

PROOF. Recall that our security definition against SUs states what a SU sees from the scheme can be efficiently simulated by a simulator given only the total number of SUs and its own sensing result as the inputs. According to our scheme, a SU s_i's view consists of three parts: s_i's internal coin flips cfs, the encrypted sensing results $(\bar{r}_j)_{j \in I \setminus \{i\}}$ sent from other users to the Helper (user i could know these by eavesdropping the communication between other users and the Helper), and the half-decryption results $((r_{\hat{j},1}, r_{\tilde{j},2}))_{j \in I}$ sent from the Helper to the FC (s_i could know these by eavesdropping the communication between the Helper and the FC). Now we construct a simulator S_i as follows.

Given inputs n, t, S_i runs our scheme alone and uses the coin flips cfs^* to simulate cfs. Also, S_i computes $\bar{r}_j^*$ ($j \in$ $I \setminus \{i\}$) by running the key generation algorithm of Elgamal with security parameter t to generate a random encryption key and uses it to encrypt 1. In addition, S_i uses $(\bar{r}_j^*)_{j \in I \setminus \{i\}}$ to simulate $(\bar{r}_j)_{j \in I \setminus \{i\}}$. Similarly, S_i computes n random encryptions of 1 (denoted by $((r_{\hat{j},1}^*, r_{\tilde{j},2}^*))_{j \in I}$) and uses them to simulate $((r_{\hat{j},1}, r_{\tilde{j},2}))_{j \in I}$.

Clearly, distributions of cfs^* and cfs are the same. Also, due to the multi-messages indistinguishability [14] of Elgamal encryption, $(\bar{r}_j)_{j \in I \setminus \{i\}}$ and $(\bar{r}_j^*)_{j \in I \setminus \{i\}}$ are computationally indistinguishable. In addition, it is easy to verify that $((r_{\hat{j},1}, r_{\tilde{j},2}))_{j \in I}$ are n Elgamal encryptions using encryption key y_2, thus $((r_{\hat{j},1}^*, r_{\tilde{j},2}^*))_{j \in I}$ and $((r_{\hat{j},1}, r_{\tilde{j},2}))_{j \in I}$ are computationally indistinguishable according to the multi-messages indistinguishability of Elgamal encryption.

It is easy to see: 1)cfs is independent from $(\bar{r}_j)_{j \in I \setminus \{i\}}$ and $((r_{\hat{j},1}, r_{\tilde{j},2}))_{j \in I}$. 2)$cfs^*$, $(\bar{r}_j^*)_{j \in I \setminus \{i\}}$ and $((r_{\hat{j},1}^*, r_{\tilde{j},2}^*))_{j \in I}$ are pairwise independent. Due to the uniformly random permutation and re-randomization on the ciphertexts performed by the Helper, it can be proved that $((r_{\hat{j},1}, r_{\tilde{j},2}))_{j \in I}$ are random encryptions of a random permutation of all users' sensing results and are independent of $(\bar{r}_j)_{j \in I \setminus \{i\}}$. Therefore, we know cfs, $(\bar{r}_j)_{j \in I \setminus \{i\}}$ and $((r_{\hat{j},1}, r_{\tilde{j},2}))_{j \in I}$ are pairwise independent, and the two ensemble distributions of $(cfs, (\bar{r}_j)_{j \in I \setminus \{i\}}, ((r_{\hat{j},1}, r_{\tilde{j},2}))_{j \in I})$ and $(cfs^*, (\bar{r}_j^*)_{j \in I \setminus \{i\}}, ((r_{\hat{j},1}^*, r_{\tilde{j},2}^*))_{j \in I})$ are computationally indistinguishable. □

THEOREM 6. *Our scheme is secure against the Helper.*

PROOF. Recall our security definition against the Helper requires that the Helper knows nothing other than the total number of SUs. We prove this by constructing a simulator S_H as follows.

According to our scheme, the Helper's view consists of two parts: its internal coin flips cfs and the encrypted sensing results $(\bar{r}_j)_{j \in I}$. Given inputs n, t, S_H runs our scheme alone and uses the internal coin flips cfs^* to simulate cfs. It is easy to see that the two distribution ensembles are the same. Also, S_H simulates each $\bar{r}_j$ with a random encryption of 1 generated by running the key generation algorithm of Elgamal with security parameter t to generate a random encryption key and using it to encrypt 1. Due to the multi-messages indistinguishability of Elgamal, the joint distribution of n random encryptions of 1 is indistinguishable with $(\bar{r}_j)_{j \in I}$. In addition, it is easy to see that the distribution of coin flips and distribution of the encryption results are independent. Therefore, we can conclude that the ensemble of the coin flips and encryptions generated by S_H are computationally indistinguishable to the Helper's view. □

THEOREM 7. *Our scheme is secure against the fusion center.*

PROOF. Recall our security definition against the FC requires that the FC knows nothing other a random permutation of all users' sensing results. We prove this by constructing a simulator S_{FC} as follows.

According to our scheme, the FC's view consists of two parts: the encrypted sensing results $(\bar{r}_j)_{j \in I}$ sent from other users to the Helper (the FC can know these by eavesdropping the communication between SUs and the Helper), and the half-decryption results $((r_{\hat{j},1}, r_{\tilde{j},2}))_{j \in I}$ sent from the Helper to the FC. Now we construct a simulator S_{FC} as follows.

Given a random permutation $\rho(R)$, S_{FC} generates $(\bar{r}_j^*)_{j \in I}$, $|\rho(R)|$ random encryptions of 1, to simulate $(\bar{r}_j)_{j \in I}$ similarly as S_i simulates $(\bar{r}_j)_{j \in I \setminus i}$. Again, the computationally indistinguishability follows from the multi-message indistinguishability of Elgamal encryption. To simulate $((r_{\hat{j},1}, r_{\tilde{j},2}))_{j \in I}$, S_{FC} computes $((r_{\hat{j},1}{}^*, r_{\tilde{j},2}{}^*))_{j \in I}$ by encrypting $\rho(R)$ using encryption key y_2. The computationally indistinguishability between $((r_{\hat{j},1}, r_{\tilde{j},2}))_{j \in I}$ and $((r_{\hat{j},1}{}^*, r_{\tilde{j},2}{}^*))_{j \in I}$ follows from the uniformly randomness of the permutation performed by the Helper.

Clearly $(\bar{r_j}^*)_{j \in I}$ and $((r_{\hat{j},1}{}^*, r_{\tilde{j},2}{}^*))_{j \in I}$ are independent. Same as what we have showed in the proof of the security against users, $(\bar{r_j})_{j \in I}$ and $((r_{\hat{j},1}, r_{\tilde{j},2}))_{j \in I}$ are indpendent. Therefore, $\{(\bar{r_j}^*)_{j \in I}, ((r_{\hat{j},1}{}^*, r_{\tilde{j},2}{}^*))_{j \in I}\}$ and $\{(\bar{r_j})_{j \in I}, ((r_{\hat{j},1}, r_{\tilde{j},2}))_{j \in I}\}$ are computationally indistinguishable. $\square$

3.3 Complexity Analysis

In CRNs, in order to guarantee that SU's dynamic access will not have any influence on the transmission of PU, the shorter the time collaborative sensing cost is, the better. If the sensing process spends more time than the limitation, it may cause the sensing result to be invalid. So it is necessary to analyse the time complexity of our algorithm. In the first part of algorithm, where the Helper and the FC generate the encrypting model cooperatively, the process can be finished in an invariable time $O(k_1)$. As for SUs' encryption process, every user can do the encryption individually. Besides, some fast algorithms of exponent arithmetic can ensure that user's process finishes in another invariable time $O(k_2)$. In the Helper's part, the total time of re-randomize permuting process and partly decrypting can be equivalent to $O(n)$. Similarly, in the FC's part, decrypting time and aggregating time can be equivalent to $O(n)$. It is evident that our algorithm's overhead depends on the amount of network users. Normally, a cognitive radio network can not contain so many SUs to result in an unacceptable overhead. With our proposed scheme, the Helper can assist the FC to coordinate SUs' sensing process, users can send reports to the Helper without worrying about exposing location information, and the FC can give the same aggregated result with the past. Also, our scheme's overhead is acceptable.

4. THE EXTENSION OF OUR SCHEME

In our work described above, we consider a semi-honest model and a restricted malicious model. The malicious user's effect can be wiped off by voting or statistics. Under the condition where the Helper and the FC keep the rule of the whole scheme, though attackers try to peek at other user's privacy, their attempts will be in vain for SUs without both x_1 and x_2, the Helper without x_2, and the FC without re-permutation clues.

However, if we take a look at an entirely malicious model, where anyone, including the Helper and the FC, can turn into a malicious attacker, our scheme will probably be disrupted. For example, a malicious Helper simply drops all reports from SUs and sends a mess to the FC, then the sensing process cannot finish as expected. Moreover, if a malicious Helper broadcasts part-decrypted reports with re-permutation clues, the FC can easily obtain user's privacy.

In the aim of the hope of extending our scheme to be more general and robust, we want to find an effective way to solve the problems emerged in the situation with malicious Helper. In fact, here we are faced with two questions: how can the FC verify the Helper's identity, and how can the FC trust that the reports the Helper sends are faithfully recorded instead of arbitrarily records. But after all,

we should remember that the FC may be untrusted, so we cannot reveal any information of the Helper in the communication. Thus, we should let the FC obtain no knowledge about both the Helper's and SU's privacy except the part already included in encrypted and re-permuted reports.

In another view, we think about a special situation where a vicious user (denoted by V) may fake other users' message, including the Helper's message. V does not care about his own interest. The only purpose he holds is to obstruct sensing process by falsifying other user's report with mess bits. In the cognitive radio network with the protection of our scheme, all of the sensing reports have been transmitted twice, from SU to the Helper, and from the Helper to the FC. When V falsifies a SU's report, this report will be dropped off and cannot affect the final result on the FC, because the aggregation rule will ignore this noise. So, if V wants to exert some serious effects, his best and only choice is to fake or falsify the Helper's message to the FC.

In order to solve the two questions we proposed above, we need to introduce Fiat-Shamir heuristic [4], a paradigm of non-interactive zero-knowledge proof, into our scheme. The core idea is letting the Helper prove that he has private key x_1 and the reports he sends are not arbitrary to the FC, using non-interactive zero-knowledge proof. The proof flow can be illustrated as in Fig.1.

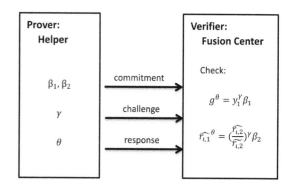

Figure 1: non-interactive zero-knowledge proof flow

As prover, the Helper should prove $\log_{r_{\hat{i},1}} \frac{r_{\hat{i},2}}{r_{\tilde{i},2}} = \log_g y_1$ to the verifier, the FC. The Helper needs to pick α uniformly random from the quadratic residue in Z_p^*, then the Helper gets $\beta_1 = g^\alpha$, $\beta_2 = r_{\hat{r},1}$ as the commitment in standard zero-knowledge proof (ZKP) [22]. A hash function H modeled as a random oracle is needed, and H is a cryptographic hash function whose range is Z_q. So that the Helper can get $\gamma = H(g, y_1, r_{\hat{i},1}, r_{\tilde{i},1}, \beta_1, \beta_2)$, as challenge in ZKP. The last step is to get $\theta = \gamma x_1 + \alpha$ as response. Then the Helper sends $(\beta_1, \beta_2, \gamma, \theta)$ to the FC, who checks whether the following equations hold:

$$g^\theta = y_i^\gamma \beta_1 \qquad (3)$$

$$r_{\hat{i},1}{}^\theta = (\frac{r_{\hat{i},2}}{r_{\tilde{i},2}})^\gamma \beta_2. \qquad (4)$$

if these two equations hold, then the FC accepts the proof of the Helper.

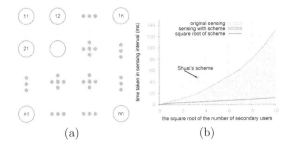

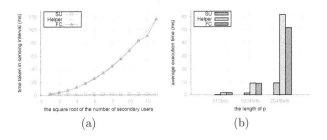

Figure 2: a) SUs' locations in CRN; b) sensing procedure time taken during the sensing interval.

Figure 3: a) average execution time of each party; b) average execution time with different l.

5. EVALUATION

Since our scheme's security has been proved and the overhead of the sensing procedure is crucial [26], we perform a series of simulation experiments to evaluate our scheme's efficiency. We first evaluate the overhead carried by our scheme. Then we examine the overhead carried by each party of our scheme, so that we can analyze where the bottleneck is.

The environment we used for evaluation is an Ubuntu 14.10 64-bit distribution. The CPU is an intel i3-4130 clocked at 3.40GHz, and the installed RAM is 2GB. We implement our scheme with the help of CRE-NS3 [3], which is a cognitive radio extension of ns-3. CRE-NS3 has provided models including spectrum sensing, decision, mobility and sharing. Since our work focuses on location privacy during collaborative sensing process, we ignore other cognitive radio's models in the simulation except necessary components. We modify CRE-NS3, and add our scheme mainly to the spectrum sensing and decision models.

5.1 Setup

All SUs are deployed in grid in an open area. Each of the SUs has 802.11g standard wifi MAC with a rate of 54 Mbps. Every SU can establish direct communication with each other and is able to switch channels by himself. We assume that there are 11 channels that the PU and SUs and occupy. And according to the research of optimal sensing interval [26], we set the sensing interval to be 150ms. All of our simulating timer starts at the beginning of sensing and ends at the end of sensing decision.

Before an attacker seeks SU's location, necessary preparation is the collection of sample locations' information. Generally, we assume that every SU's location is sampled by the attacker. In order to be scalable for more SUs. We deploy SUs in grid and keep them equidistant. SUs' locations can be illustrated as in Fig.2(a).

Sample positions' location information is recorded and associated with signal strength. In each position, the attacker records the results of 20 rounds collaborative sensing on two channels of PU. Then the attacker binds the central values with positions' labels. The central values of sample positions in two dimensions on channels are recorded for further use.

5.2 Efficiency of Our Scheme

After the implementation of our scheme in CRE-NS3, we have measured execution time of collaborative sensing for different scales of SUs. Every time, we enlarge the SU set and add enough SUs on grid in a square area. We get every

scale's average time to generate Fig.2(b) to compare with the time taken by original sensing process in CRE-NS3.

Since the abscissa is the square root of the number of SUs, time taken by our scheme is linearly increasing in fact. And its slope is about 1. Even when the number of SUs is around 100, our scheme can still work with feasible overhead, which is about 100ms, much less than 150ms interval.

Recall that there are three parties in our CRN, i.e. SU, the Helper, and the FC. Sometimes, just one party is to be concerned, so we measure average time on each party in our simulation. We record all SUs' execution time in a round, and calculate the average for each scale. As for the Helper and the FC, we record executing time of every round and get their average values for 100 rounds. From Fig.3(a), it is obvious that the Helper costs most time and has a great proportion on the total execution time. And it is reasonable that the Helper's and the FC's execution time grows linearly due to the increasing number of SUs, with abscissa being the square root of the number of SUs. In fact the slope of this increase is as small as about 1. The comparing result preliminary shows that when the scheme is applied to the network, a large portion of execution time depends on the Helper's efficiency. So if a high-performance node was selected to be the Helper, the total execution time it spends would decrease sensibly.

In the experiments above, we use 1024 bits as default set of the length of l, which is the security parameter of our scheme. To be comprehensive, we measure execution time of different lengths of l. In this situation, we set number of SUs as 10. As shown in Fig.3(b), our scheme is feasible for commonly used lengths of p.

In Shuai's work, when the security parameter has 1024 bits and the CRN has 10 SUs, the total computation time is roughly 48ms for one aggregation [16]. But with our scheme, the average computation time is about 20ms in the same setting. The comparing can be found in Fig.2(b). And it is obvious that our scheme can be more feasible in the massive users environment.

6. CONCLUSION

As the research of cognitive radio continues to improve, and with its outstanding dynamic spectrum accessing, it may well replace the traditional radio in the future. This paper studies the location privacy existed in collaborative sensing process of cognitive radio networks. We formalize privacy issue in both semi-honest model and malicious model. We take a series of simulating experiments to prove our scheme's validity and we discuss its feasibility by analysing the operating results. Our scheme gets robust when there may be malicious users behaving against the rules. Our scheme is proven to be feasible both in theory and simulation. In future work, we will consider the location privacy issue and malicious users who may cause false alarm problems to achieve a more complete protection scheme.

7. REFERENCES

[1] M. Abdelraheem, M. El-Nainay, and S. Midkiff. Spectrum occupancy analysis of cooperative relaying technique for cognitive radio networks. In *Computing, Networking and Communications (ICNC), 2015 International Conference on*, pages 237–241, Feb 2015.

[2] I. F. Akyildiz, W.-Y. Lee, M. C. Vuran, and S. Mohanty. Next generation/dynamic spectrum access/cognitive radio wireless networks: A survey. *Comput. Netw.*, 50(13):2127–2159, Sept. 2006.

[3] A. Al-Ali and K. Chowdhury. Simulating dynamic spectrum access using ns-3 for wireless networks in smart environments. In *Sensing, Communication, and Networking Workshops (SECON Workshops), 2014 Eleventh Annual IEEE International Conference on*, pages 28–33, June 2014.

[4] A. S. Amos Fiat. How to prove yourself: Practical solutions to identification and signature problems. *Advances in Cryptology âĂŤ CRYPTO âĂŹ86, Lecture Notes in Computer Science*, 263:186–194, 1986.

[5] K. Arshad. Malicious users detection in collaborative spectrum sensing using statistical tests. In *Ubiquitous and Future Networks (ICUFN), 2012 Fourth International Conference on*, pages 109–113, 2012.

[6] D. Cabric, S. M. Mishra, D. Willkomm, R. Brodersen, and A. Wolisz. A cognitive radio approach for usage of virtual unlicensed spectrum. In *In Proc. of 14th IST Mobile Wireless Communications Summit 2005*, 2005.

[7] R. Chen and J.-M. Park. Ensuring trustworthy spectrum sensing in cognitive radio networks. In *Networking Technologies for Software Defined Radio Networks, 2006. SDR '06.1st IEEE Workshop on*, pages 110–119, 2006.

[8] R. Chen, J.-M. Park, and J. Reed. Defense against primary user emulation attacks in cognitive radio networks. *Selected Areas in Communications, IEEE Journal on*, 26(1):25–37, 2008.

[9] L. Duan, A. Min, J. Huang, and K. Shin. Attack prevention for collaborative spectrum sensing in cognitive radio networks. *Selected Areas in Communications, IEEE Journal on*, 30(9):1658–1665, 2012.

[10] FCC. Spectrum inventory table. http://www.fcc.gov/oet/info/database/ spectrum/. website.

[11] Z. Gao, H. Zhu, S. Li, S. Du, and X. Li. Security and privacy of collaborative spectrum sensing in cognitive radio networks. *Wireless Communications, IEEE*, 19(6):106–112, 2012.

[12] Z. Gao, H. Zhu, Y. Liu, M. Li, and Z. Cao. Location privacy leaking from spectrum utilization information in database-driven cognitive radio network. In *Proceedings of the 2012 ACM conference on Computer and communications security*, CCS '12, pages 1025–1027. ACM, 2012.

[13] Z. Gao, H. Zhu, Y. Liu, M. Li, and C. Zhenfu. Location privacy in database-driven cognitive radio networks: Attacks and countermeasures. In *INFOCOM, 2013 Proceedings IEEE*, pages 2751–2759, April 2013.

[14] O. Goldreich. *The Foundations of Cryptography - Volume 2, Basic Applications.* Cambridge University Press, 2004.

[15] O. Goldreich, S. Micali, and A. Wigderson. How to play any mental game. In *Proceedings of the nineteenth annual ACM symposium on Theory of computing*, STOC '87, pages 218–229, New York, NY, USA, 1987. ACM.

[16] S. Li, H. Zhu, Z. Gao, X. Guan, K. Xing, and X. Shen. Location privacy preservation in collaborative spectrum sensing. In *INFOCOM, 2012 Proceedings IEEE*, pages 729–737, 2012.

[17] A. Min, K. Shin, and X. Hu. Secure cooperative sensing in ieee 802.22 wrans using shadow fading correlation. *Mobile Computing, IEEE Transactions on*, 10(10):1434–1447, 2011.

[18] S. Mishra, A. Sahai, and R. Brodersen. Cooperative sensing among cognitive radios. In *Communications, 2006. ICC '06. IEEE International Conference on*, volume 4, pages 1658–1663, 2006.

[19] H. Rifa-Pous and J. Rifa. Spectrum sharing models in cognitive radio networks. In *Cyber-Enabled Distributed Computing and Knowledge Discovery (CyberC), 2011 International Conference on*, pages 503–510, 2011.

[20] D. Teguig, B. Scheers, and V. Le Nir. Data fusion schemes for cooperative spectrum sensing in cognitive radio networks. pages 1–7, Oct 2012.

[21] N. Tran, D. Tran, L. B. Le, Z. Han, and C. S. Hong. Load balancing and pricing for spectrum access control in cognitive radio networks. In *Global Communications Conference (GLOBECOM), 2014 IEEE*, pages 1035–1040, Dec 2014.

[22] A. S. Uriel Feige, Amos Fiat. Zero-knowledge proofs of identity. *Journal of Cryptology*, 1:77–94, 1988.

[23] T. Wang and Y. Yang. Location privacy protection from rss localization system using antenna pattern synthesis. In *INFOCOM, 2011 Proceedings IEEE*, pages 2408–2416, 2011.

[24] W. Wang, H. Li, Y. Sun, and Z. Han. Attack-proof collaborative spectrum sensing in cognitive radio networks. In *Information Sciences and Systems, 2009. CISS 2009. 43rd Annual Conference on*, pages 130–134, 2009.

[25] W. Wang, H. Li, Y. Sun, and Z. Han. Catchit: Detect malicious nodes in collaborative spectrum sensing. In *Global Telecommunications Conference, 2009. GLOBECOM 2009. IEEE*, pages 1–6, 2009.

[26] X. Xing, T. Jing, H. Li, Y. Huo, X. Cheng, and T. Znati. Optimal spectrum sensing interval in cognitive radio networks. *IEEE Transactions on Parallel and Distributed Systems*, 25(9):2408–2417, 2014.

[27] S. Zhong. *Privacy, Integrity, and Incentive-Compatibility in Computations with Untrusted Parties.* PhD thesis, Yale University, 11 2004.

Rethinking the Importance of Accurately Simulating the Runtimes of Firmware used in Wireless Sensor Networks

Georg Möstl
georg.moestl@jku.at
Institute for Integrated Circuits
Johannes Kepler University Linz, Austria

Andreas Springer
a.springer@nthfs.jku.at
Institute for Communications Engineering and
RF-Systems
Johannes Kepler University Linz, Austria

ABSTRACT

In a wireless sensor network, the energy consumption of the nodes continues to impose a tight constraint. Researchers have therefore proposed several MAC protocols to decrease the energy consumption of the radio transceiver, which has increased the complexity of the firmware running on the nodes. In this paper, we show the consequences of ignoring runtimes of state-of-the-art MAC protocols, as proposed by some simulators. The quantitative discussion is based on a comparison between hardware measurements and simulations. We ported the Contiki operating system to STEAM-Sim, a recently developed simulator. With this setup it is possible to omit runtimes of firmware in a stepwise manner. We further used STEAM-Sim to accurately evaluate the X-MAC, Low Power Probing, and ContikiMAC radio duty-cycling protocols. The energy consumption profiles of hardware modules thus generated give interesting insights into the protocols. Scalability comparisons to the state-of-the-art simulator COOJA/MSPSim show that scalable and time-accurate simulation of WSNs in the nanosecond range is possible.

Categories and Subject Descriptors

C.2.1 [**Computer-Communication Networks**]: Network Architecture and Design—*Wireless communication*; I.6.3 [**Simulation and Modeling**]: Applications; I.6.8 [**Simulation and Modeling**]: Types of Simulation—*Discrete event*

General Terms

Design, Verification

Keywords

Hardware/software/network co-simulation; wireless sensor networks; real-life code; firmware runtimes; measurements; STEAM-Sim

MSWiM'15, November 2–6, 2015, Cancun, Mexico.
Copyright is held by the owner/author(s). Publication rights licensed to ACM.
ACM 978-1-4503-3762-5/15/11 ...$15.00.
DOI: http://dx.doi.org/10.1145/2811587.2811588.

1. INTRODUCTION

In an increasingly wireless world, wireless sensor networks (WSN) are heavily utilized, for example, in industry, agriculture, forestry, and home automation. A WSN comprises several resource-constrained, tiny sensing devices - the sensor nodes. A sensor node can monitor any kind of environmental condition, such as tension, pressure, sound, temperature, and acceleration, and communicate by means of wireless transmission of electromagnetic waves. The most important property of a WSN is the energy consumption, as the battery-powered nodes should achieve lifetimes of several years. The radio module of a node is the dominant energy consumer and should therefore be switched off by the firmware as often as possible, for which several duty-cycling MAC protocols have been proposed ([6], [2], [17]). Consequently, the ratio between energy consumed by the microcontroller and energy consumed by the radio has decreased, and the energy consumption of the microcontroller is no longer negligible. These microcontrollers are limited in terms of clock frequency (e.g., 8 MHz), databus width (8 bit, 16 bit), and size of working and program memory (several kilobytes). Therefore, the local processing times of the protocols which have an impact on the duty cycles of the radio must be taken into account.

MAC protocols are typically evaluated using simulations. Compared to testbeds, simulators provide a cost-effective way of generating reproducible results in a controllable and observeable environment. Further, simulators scale better and support mobility and debugging in a non-intrusive way. However, care has to be taken to accurately model and simulate WSNs so that the results can reasonably be compared to reality. State-of-the-art simulators such as COOJA [19] concentrate on the duty cycle of the radio. However, this limits the development of WSNs. For example, new protocols such as that introduced in [12] use adaptive transmission power control so that the transmission power of the radio is increased, decreased, or left unaltered by the firmware, depending on the current quality of the channel. Further, energy harvesting techniques are ideal for use in WSNs, as they can prolong the lifetimes of nodes. To avoid worst-case analysis and to efficiently design a power management system located between the harvesting source and the load (i.e., the node), the energy consumption patterns should be known a priori [11].

STEAM-Sim[1] [16] is a recently published simulator which allows firmware, hardware, and network functionality to be

---

[1]downloadable at http://sourceforge.net/projects/steamsim

simulated at nanosecond resolution. STEAM-Sim enables the construction of accurate and detailed energy consumption profiles for every hardware module present in the network. These profiles reveal subtle details of the processed algorithms and protocols and therefore support a better understanding at the node level. However, protocols can easily be compared also at the network level. For our investigations it was important that STEAM-Sim allows omitting the runtimes of parts of the firmware. As STEAM-Sim was originally developed to simulate proprietary firmware, we first ported the Contiki [5] operating system to STEAM-Sim to enable the investigation of well-established MAC protocols implemented in Contiki.

On the basis of our STEAM-Sim simulations, we discuss the following points in our paper: First, we analyze quantitatively the consequences of ignoring the runtimes of firmware running state-of-the-art MAC protocols, namely X-MAC [2], Low Power Probing [17], and ContikiMAC [6]. This discussion is based on real-world measurements and additionally evaluates the accuracy of STEAM-Sim simulating complex firmware. Second, we evaluate the three protocols at the network level using a multi-hop application built upon Contiki. We then zoom in further to the node level, revealing subtle details of the X-MAC protocol. Finally, we compare the scalability of STEAM-Sim to the state-of-the-art simulator COOJA/MSPSim [9] and show that a scalable yet accurate simulator generating detailed energy profiles for WSNs can be built.

The remainder of this paper is organized as follows: Section 2 gives a comprehensive overview of related work. We present a brief description of STEAM-Sim and the porting of Contiki in section 3. The results presented in section 4 corroborate our hypothesis that firmware runtimes should not be ignored and that scalable, meaningful, and accurate simulation of WSNs in the nanosecond range is possible. Section 5 concludes this paper.

2. RELATED WORK

Several tools ([4], [18]) exist for simulating WSNs, but only a few consider the energy consumption of nodes.

Castalia [1] is a highly scalable and energy-aware simulator based on OMNeT++ [24]. It provides realistic channel models based on empirically measured data and temporal variations of the signal strength. As Castalia focuses on the early phase of protocol design, it lacks inclusion of firmware code, detailed modeling of hardware state transitions, and interrupt processing functionality.

Another framework based on OMNeT++ is PAWiS [26], which concentrates on a realistic power model by establishing a hierarchy of power providers and consumers that influence each other depending on particular electrical characteristics. Further, PAWiS allows WSNs to be investigated both at the network level (throughput, reliability, etc) and at the node level. However, it lacks the integration of firmware into the simulation.

PowerTOSSIM [20] is an extension of the TOSSIM simulator and is therefore limited to simulating applications written in NesC and built upon the TinyOS [15] operating system. The high level of abstraction enables good scalability but neglects timing effects of the node, such as interrupt processing, and can lead to inaccurate energy consumption predictions [23].

AEON [14] is a cycle-accurate instruction-level simulator based on Avrora [22]. With AEON it is possible to simulate the timing and energy consumption behavior of AVR-based microcontrollers provided by Atmel. The efficient synchronization of Avrora and the structure of AEON are closely related to TinyOS and to the Mica2 hardware. Further, in [14] the scalability in terms of simulation runtimes and size of energy log files was not described.

Eriksson et al. [9] presented a heterogeneous simulator consisting of the COOJA [19] network simulator, the MSP-Sim [8] instruction level emulator for MSP430 microcontrollers, and a power profiler integrated into the Contiki [5] operating system. External hardware components such as a radio module are modeled using three states (idle, send, receive) and pre-measured current draws. Firmware simulation is cycle-accurate. The scalability of this simulation approach has, however, not been evaluated.

Another heterogeneous simulator is sQualNet [25], which comprises a discrete event network simulator and an emulator for an embedded operating system such as TinyOS or SOS [10]. sQualNet provides good scalability, accurate battery models, and also models the clock drift of nodes. However, sQualNet builds upon the commercially available QualNet [21] simulator.

Landsiedel et al. [13] made a strong case for including application code in the simulation, as the complexity of firmware used in modern WSNs is increasing. However, to the best of our knowledge, we are the first showing the impact in terms of energy consumption of ignoring firmware runtimes in WSN simulations. The quantitative discussion is based on hardware measurements.

3. IMPLEMENTATION

In this section we give a brief description of our simulation setup including the STEAM-Sim [16] simulator. STEAM-Sim enables *software/hardware/network* co-simulation of WSNs building upon the PAWiS [26] framework.

The software (i.e., the firmware), includes the application logic, network stacks, and low-level drivers, and is typically written in the C language. In a first step, this firmware is compiled and linked for the target architecture (i.e., the microcontroller), using a cross-compiler such as *gcc*. The resulting executable is disassembled, combined with a proper timing model, and further processed. As a result, timing information in terms of cycle counts corresponding to each line of C code is gathered. In a subsequent build process, the firmware without low-level drivers is processed by the same cross-compiler, and binary code targeting the x86 CPU, i.e., the CPU where the simulation will be executed, is built. Runtimes differ between microcontroller and x86 CPU. Therefore, while parsing the C code, the *annotation engine* uses the gathered timing information and annotates the source code with the cycle counts of the microcontroller. These cycle counts are treated as delays and are used as synchronization points during simulation. Low-level drivers have to be replaced with code that targets the simulator.

STEAM-Sim provides models which accurately model the timing and electrical behavior of hardware, such as a CC2500 radio transceiver. Depending on the impact of the hardware module on the functionality of the WSN, hardware is modeled at a higher or lower level of abstraction. For example, a serial interface is modeled as a simple delay element, whereas the radio module is modeled in greater detail, including state machines, configuration registers, power levels, etc. This helps to reduce simulation runtimes.

Transmissions of packets are modeled at the byte level and above, which ensures efficient yet accurate simulation. A packet typically comprises preamble, synchronization, length, address, payload, and CRC bytes. Radio propagation is based on the signal-to-noise ratio (SNR). The SNR combined with probability density functions is used to derive bit error rates.

We used the open and flexible structure of STEAM-Sim to port the Contiki [5] embedded operating system by means of re-writing the low-level drivers, for instance, real-time timers, clock module, and serial interface. Further, we combined the Contiki build process with that provided by STEAM-Sim, which is somewhat intuitive as both frameworks build on *GNU make*. In fact, STEAM-Sim is treated like another platform to which Contiki is ported. Notice that the main core of the Contiki operating system stays untouched and is automatically processed and annotated with timing information by the simulator. We had to change only the macro sending command strobes to the radio transceiver. This change required five lines of code, compared to several thousand lines of unchanged code contained in the Contiki core files. Contiki supports multiple microcontrollers and transceivers. We decided to evaluate the behavior of Contiki running on an MSP430F5438 microcontroller and using a CC2420 radio transceiver from Texas Instruments. To this end, we developed and implemented corresponding hardware models within the STEAM-Sim framework.

4. EXPERIMENTS AND RESULTS

In this section, we first evaluate the accurate simulation of runtimes of firmware provided by STEAM-Sim [16]. Decreasing the coverage of the timing annotation given by STEAM-Sim in a stepwise manner and thus omitting runtimes of firmware, we compare the simulated energy consumption with hardware measurements. We evaluate state-of-the-art MAC protocols revealing subtle details at the node level and the overall energy consumption behavior at the network scale. Finally, the scalability of STEAM-Sim is compared to the state-of-the-art network simulator COOJA/MSPSim [9].

For energy consumption measurements, a non-intrusive high-resolution DC Power Analyzer N6705B provided by Agilent was used. The integrated data logger enables long-running measurements. Timing measurements were conducted using an Infiniium 54832D oscilloscope with passive probes. A Keithley 2602A SourceMeter was used to provide a stable power supply to the nodes. The hardware setup comprised MSP430F5438 Experimenter Boards provided by Texas Instruments and equipped with a MSP430F5438A and a CC2420 radio transceiver module.

4.1 Timing Fidelity of Complex Algorithms

To demonstrate that STEAM-Sim can accurately simulate the runtimes of firmware, we evaluated three commonly used and relatively complex algorithms. Input data were generated randomly at startup of the microcontroller application, and input data size was subsequently increased to investigate the accuracy for longer runtimes and to reveal inaccuracies in specific sections of the algorithms. For example, the encryption algorithm can be split into a key generation phase (initialization phase) and an encryption phase. The run-

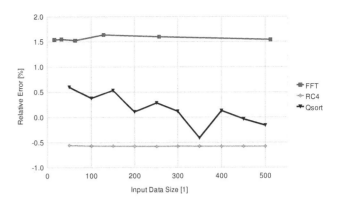

Figure 1: Mismatch between simulated and measured execution times for a sorting algorithm (QSort), an encryption algorithm (RC4), and a digital signal processing algorithm (FFT) for increasing problem size.

times of the algorithms were measured in simulation using log-file analysis, and compared to hardware measurements using pin toggling of dedicated I/O pins of the microcontroller. Results are given in Figure 1, which illustrates the mismatch between simulation and measurements in terms of the relative error.

As a first example, the *Quicksort* sorting algorithm was tested. As can be seen in Figure 1, the maximum error is bounded below +0.6% and slightly decreases for an increasing number of bytes to be sorted. Next, we decided to evaluate the *Fast Fourier Transform (FFT)* algorithm as a representative of digital signal processing algorithms. The FFT is a relatively complex algorithm that makes heavy use of mathematical library routines. However, as Figure 1 shows, STEAM-Sim achieves over 98.3% timing accuracy. The last test case addresses sensor network security, which is a research topic of major interest. We evaluated the *RC4* encryption algorithm for an increasing number of bytes to be encrypted. As can be seen in Figure 1, the error remains constant with respect to the size of input data and is bounded below -0.58%.

Underestimation of execution times is related to pipeline stalls, for example, structural hazards, which cannot be addressed statically (i.e., at compile time). Overestimation is related to the annotation of *switch* instructions in the C language. Breaking down a *switch* instruction to the assembler level reveals several conditional jumps corresponding to the *case* instructions contained in the body of the *switch* instruction. STEAM-Sim makes worst-case assumptions, for example, that every condition has to be evaluated before the correct *case* branch is executed. Generally, the clock generation within a microcontroller depends on electrical effects such as a fluctuating voltage supply or environmental temperature, which are not considered in the simulation.

4.2 Consequences of Ignoring Firmware Runtimes

To gain meaningful results showing the consequences of ignoring firmware runtimes in WSN simulations, we evaluate three state-of-the-art duty-cycling MAC protocols, namely ContikiMAC[6], X-MAC [2], and Low Power Probing (LPP) [17], implemented within the embedded operating system

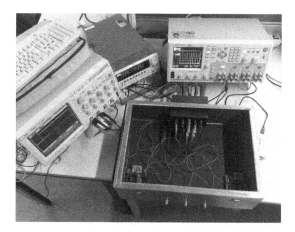

Figure 2: The measurement setup comprised (from left to right) an oscilloscope measuring startup times of nodes, a sourcemeter as stable power supply, a data logger for long-running power measurements, and two nodes placed in a workbench faraday cage to exclude interference caused by, e.g., WiFi.

Table 1: Power model measured for the **MSP430F5438** Experimenter Board equipped with a CC2420 evaluation module. The board was provided with a **3 V** power supply, and the CPU was clocked with **8 MHz**.

Module	Mode	Current [mA]
CPU	active	2.53
	sleep LPM0	0.607
	sleep LPM3	0.0045
LED	on	2.2
Radio	idle	0.39
	calibrate	5.8
	Tx (-5 dBm)	13.9
	listening	18.5
	receiving	18.2

Contiki [5]. We ported Contiki to the STEAM-Sim simulator.

The firmware running on nodes comprises the application logic, the core of Contiki, and low-level drivers. The application logic used in our experiments is related to the Contiki best-effort single-hop unicast example implemented in the Rime network stack. The unicast represents a fundamental networking operation used in WSNs and is therefore a relatively simple yet expressive operation. In our setup, the data source sends a data packet comprising 5 bytes of payload every second to the data sink. As shown in Figure 2, we placed the two nodes into a workbench faraday cage [3] (WBFC, with open cover) to exclude interference caused, for example, by WiFi and to ensure deterministic conditions. Inside the WBFC, we addressed small-scale fading effects related to multipath propagation by determining node positions with good signal-to-noise ratio. To ensure comparable results, we measured the difference in startup times of the nodes by means of an oscilloscope, and used the data to configure simulation runs accordingly.

From our measurements we derived a power model of the microcontroller and the radio module, the specs of which are listed in Table 1. This model was employed to configure our simulation runs, where the microcontroller used sleep mode LPM0.

Table 2 summarizes the measured and simulated energy consumptions of the sensor node, i.e., the data source, for observation times of 1, 60, and 120 seconds. Values of the microcontroller comprise the CPU, serial interfaces, and LED. Since STEAM-Sim makes it possible to decrease the coverage of timing annotation, we evaluated three scenarios: (i) without annotation, which means ignoring runtimes of firmware, (ii) considering only the runtimes of low-level drivers, and (iii) considering all firmware runtimes. Note that delay loops implemented in software such as Contiki's `clock_delay()` are always annotated. As can be seen, STEAM-Sim is able to accurately simulate the energy consumption behavior of the MAC protocols, resulting in a mismatch below 3.7% when runtimes of firmware are considered.

Decreasing the coverage of timing annotation, which means that timing information of more parts of the firmware is omitted, generally reduced the accuracy of energy consumption predictions. Interestingly, ignoring timing information has a greater impact on predictions of the radio's than the microcontroller's energy consumption. For example, simulating the X-MAC protocol for 120 seconds without timing information results in an error of -3.396% for the microcontroller and +43.262% for the radio. The most important finding in Table 2 is that the impact of timing inaccuracies when simulating WSNs heavily depends on the application. Therefore, using an inaccurate simulator does not allow relative comparisons to be made. For example, simulating the energy consumption of the radio with the LPP and the ContikiMAC protocols for 120 seconds without firmware runtimes gives errors of 34.761% and 341.811%, respectively. Clearly, the first result is bad but somewhat reasonable, whereas the ContikiMAC simulation is completely meaningless. The same can be seen when comparing the X-MAC and the ContikiMAC protocol with annotated low-level drivers. Here the error in the energy consumed by the radio for 120 seconds is -1.080% for the X-MAC and +99.419% for the ContikiMAC. The ContikiMAC is the most recently developed MAC protocol and uses many timeouts, such as the fast sleep optimizations, to turn off the radio as often as possible. These optimizations are implemented as timeouts processed in the firmware. It can be concluded that modern protocols used in WSNs require a detailed and accurate simulation of the firmware running on the nodes.

4.3 Evaluation of MAC protocols

In our final case study we evaluate a state-of-the-art multi-hop data collection protocol for WSNs. The Contiki Collect protocol [7] is an address-free protocol implemented on top of the Contiki Rime stack. It enables nodes to send data towards a sink somewhere in the network. Contiki Collect first builds a tree rooted at the sink by exchanging messages that include the expected number of transmissions (ETX) to reach the sink. Every node outside the neighborhood of the sink sends its packets to the neighbor with the lowest ETX routing costs.

Table 2: Simulated and measured energy consumption of the data source running the Contiki unicast application and utilizing different MAC protocols. Values in millijoules are given for the microcontroller (comprising CPU, serial interfaces, and LED) and the radio. Simulation was carried out (i) without timing annotation, i.e., ignoring execution times of firmware, (ii) including execution times of low-level drivers, and (iii) including all firmware runtimes. The observation period was set to 1, 60, and 120 seconds.

Benchmark	Sim	Meas	f [%]	Sim	Meas	f [%]	Sim	Meas	f [%]
microcontroller									
no annotation	*1 second*			*60 seconds*			*120 seconds*		
X-MAC	2.4845	2.5972	-4.337	149.04	154.28	-3.399	298.12	308.60	**-3.396**
Low Power Probing	1.8825	2.1269	-11.490	112.87	126.75	-10.946	225.78	253.45	**-10.916**
ContikiMAC	4.6932	2.0247	131.795	201.75	122.08	65.257	376.76	244.61	**54.026**
driver annotated	*1 second*			*60 seconds*			*120 seconds*		
X-MAC	2.5324	2.5972	-2.492	151.03	154.28	-2.104	302.09	308.60	-2.108
Low Power Probing	1.9760	2.1269	-7.092	119.17	126.75	-5.975	238.16	253.45	-6.034
ContikiMAC	2.3124	2.0247	14.209	145.82	122.08	19.444	291.49	244.61	19.167
full annotation	*1 second*			*60 seconds*			*120 seconds*		
X-MAC	2.5747	2.5972	-0.865	155.34	154.28	0.687	310.69	308.60	**0.677**
Low Power Probing	2.1258	2.1269	-0.050	127.55	126.75	0.633	255.11	253.45	**0.656**
ContikiMAC	2.0996	2.0247	3.698	125.48	122.08	2.785	250.96	244.61	**2.598**
radio									
no annotation	*1 second*			*60 seconds*			*120 seconds*		
X-MAC	4.5403	3.2552	39.481	274.31	191.40	43.319	548.36	382.77	**43.262**
Low Power Probing	4.1213	3.5076	17.495	282.57	210.52	34.228	567.42	421.06	**34.761**
ContikiMAC	11.1903	1.2005	832.145	475.91	73.03	551.671	649.18	146.94	**341.811**
driver annotated	*1 second*			*60 seconds*			*120 seconds*		
X-MAC	3.1864	3.2552	-2.113	189.23	191.40	-1.131	378.63	382.77	-1.080
Low Power Probing	4.2328	3.5076	20.676	291.71	210.52	38.566	585.84	421.06	39.135
ContikiMAC	4.8609	1.2005	304.913	148.83	73.03	103.793	293.02	146.94	99.419
full annotation	*1 second*			*60 seconds*			*120 seconds*		
X-MAC	3.2434	3.2552	-0.362	190.15	191.40	-0.649	380.31	382.77	**-0.642**
Low Power Probing	3.4942	3.5076	-0.383	209.65	210.52	-0.413	419.30	421.06	**-0.418**
ContikiMAC	1.2446	1.2005	3.677	74.53	73.03	2.055	149.53	146.94	**1.767**

4.3.1 Node Level

In the first step, we evaluated the fidelity, i.e., capturing of subtle timing interactions at the node level, of STEAM-Sim employing the X-MAC [2] radio transceiver duty-cycling algorithm available in Contiki. Figure 3 plots the power consumption of the radio transceiver during the final milliseconds of a unicast transmission with 0 dBm running the Contiki Collect application. As can be seen, an X-MAC sender transmits short preamble packets containing an identifier of the target node in a strobed fashion. This approach avoids a long preamble and thus tackles the overhearing problem, where receivers that are not the target of the sender must stay awake for long periods before they can check addresses. Short preamble strobes are interleaved with listening periods. After wake-up, a node listens until a short preamble is received. If the ID of the node matches the identifier given in the preamble (i.e., the node is the receiver of this packet),

the node sends an acknowledgement (ACK) to the sender and switches back to receive mode. At the sender, the ACK is processed by the MAC layer running on the microcontroller, and afterwards the data is sent. During processing of the ACK, the radio transceiver of the sender is put into idle mode to save energy. Switching between power modes (sending, listening, receiving, calibrating, etc.) of the radio typically takes only a few milli- or micro-seconds and is difficult to measure because capacitor buffers are used on printed circuit boards to smooth out current spikes. However, an accurate simulator such as STEAM-Sim makes such subtle details visible to the user.

4.3.2 Network Level

We investigated the behavior of Contiki Collect in terms of the energy consumed at the network level. Contiki Collect was configured to utilize the X-MAC, LPP, and the Contiki-

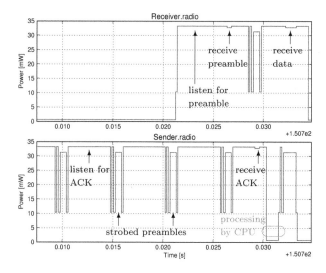

Figure 3: Given the power consumption of the radio transceiver, STEAM-Sim reveals subtle details of the Contiki X-MAC protocol. Processing times of packets and state changes of the radio lasting for a few microseconds are accurately simulated.

MAC radio duty-cycling protocols. The simulated results comprise the energy needed by the radio transceiver and the microcontroller of each node in the network. Therefore, the performance of these protocols for varying channel check rates can be assessed quantitatively. Further, since the energy consumption of the microcontroller is determined, the processing complexity of the Contiki operating system, the Rime network stack, and the Contiki Collect protocol are revealed. The simulated network comprised 10 nodes randomly distributed in a $50\text{x}50\,\text{m}^2$ area. A series of simulation runs was conducted with varying node positions which ensures expressiveness of the simulated MAC protocol behavior. Once the tree has been built, nodes send a data packet towards the sink every 30 seconds for a simulated time of 400 seconds. Packets can get lost due to collisions and fading effects of the wireless channel. The path loss model used is proportional to the square of the distance between sender and receiver.

As Figure 4 illustrates, the LPP and X-MAC protocols show a steep increase in energy consumption of the radio for wake-up frequencies greater than 4 Hz. The poor performance of LPP especially for increased wake-up frequencies is consistent with the design goal of permille duty cycles, as stated in [17]. ContikiMAC achieves the best performance, and for 8 Hz it consumes only 4,056 mJ, which corresponds to one quarter and one third of the consumption of LPP (17,847 mJ) and X-MAC (12,212 mJ), respectively. Investigation of the energy consumption of the microcontroller utilizing sleep mode LPM3 showed that LPP performs worst, consuming 7,742 mJ for a channel check rate of 32 Hz. This is nearly three times the consumption of ContikiMAC (2,755 mJ) and X-MAC (2,831 mJ). Another important finding is that the development of recent energy-efficient protocols such as ContikiMAC has altered the energy consumption ratio between a node's radio and microcontroller. For example, given a channel check rate of 16 Hz, the radio consumes only 2.5 times more energy than the mi-

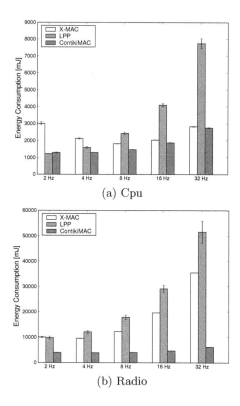

(a) Cpu

(b) Radio

Figure 4: Summed energy consumption of a network running the Contiki Collect protocol for varying channel check rates. Three different MAC protocols were evaluated in terms of the energy consumption of the CPU (8 MHz) and the radio (CC2420, 0 dBm transmit power). The simulated network comprised 10 nodes and was simulated for 400 seconds (note the different scales for the y-axis).

crocontroller running the ContikiMAC protocol. Running the older X-MAC and LPP protocols, the radio consumes 9.6 and 7.1 times more energy than the CPU. Therefore the energy consumption of the microcontroller can no longer be neglected.

4.3.3 Scalability

Accurate simulation of WSNs requires detailed simulation at the node level, which typically increases runtimes and results in poor scalability. We therefore investigated the scalability of STEAM-Sim simulating the Contiki Collect application and compared the results to the COOJA/MSPSim simulation environment included in the release of the Contiki v2.6 operating system. Care has to be taken to ensure a comparable measurement setup in terms of Contiki configuration, positioning of nodes, channel model, and startup times of nodes. Runtimes of simulations were measured utilizing the Linux *time* command and running the simulators in batch mode on an Intel Core 2 Duo processor with 2.66 GHz and 3.2 GByte RAM.

Results in terms of realtime seconds per simulated second are plotted in Figure 5 for an increasing number of nodes in the network and a simulated time of 400 seconds. The Contiki Collect application used the X-MAC, LPP, and ContikiMAC radio duty-cycling protocols, respectively.

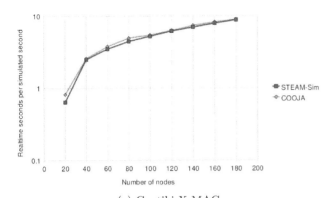

(a) Contiki X-MAC

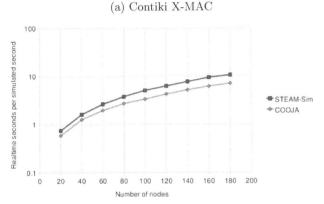

(b) Contiki Low Power Probing (LPP)

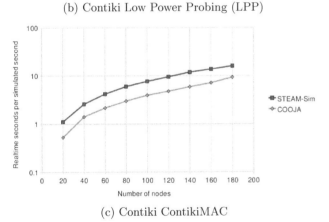

(c) Contiki ContikiMAC

Figure 5: Runtime ratios for 400 simulated seconds of the Contiki Collect protocol utilizing three different MAC protocols (note the log-scale of the y-axis). Compared to the COOJA/MSPSim network simulator, STEAM-Sim is at most 1.51 (LPP) and 2.09 (ContikiMAC) times slower. For the X-MAC protocol STEAM-Sim outperforms COOJA/MSPSim. However, STEAM-Sim provides nanosecond resolution, whereas COOJA/MSPSim is limited to microsecond resolution. Further, STEAM-Sim determines the energy consumption of every hardware module in the network, whereas COOJA/MSPSim provides only duty cycles of the radio modules.

As shown in Figure 5, STEAM-Sim outperforms the COOJA/MSPSim setup for the X-MAC protocol, whereas COOJA/MSPSim is faster for the LPP and the Contiki-MAC protocols. The runtime ratios where STEAM-Sim performs worst compared to COOJA/MSPSim are 0.98 (180 nodes), 1.51 (160 nodes), and 2.09 (20 nodes) for the X-MAC, LPP, and ContikiMAC protocols. As can be seen the two simulators show the same runtime behavior. Further investigations of the COOJA/MSPSim setup revealed that hardware events such as timer interrupts and packet receptions/transmissions are limited to a time resolution of one microsecond. This does not present a limitation to STEAM-Sim, as it builds upon OMNeT++. Scalability results were gathered at a time resolution of one nanosecond, (i.e., 1000 times higher). Further, the energy logging of STEAM-Sim was enabled. Therefore, a detailed energy consumption profile of every hardware module (CPU, timer, etc.) present in the network was generated and saved in a log file. The default COOJA/MSPSim setup used in the experiment and available for download only provides a duty cycle of every radio module present in the network.

As energy log files produced by STEAM-Sim can grow to large sizes for long-running simulations or simulations of large networks, we conducted further experiments. Results show, that the size of log files increases linearly with the number of nodes. The energy log file simulating a ContikiMAC network comprising 180 has a size of 13.79 GByte, which is manageable by modern computer systems. Therefore, determining detailed energy consumption profiles for large sensor networks within the nanosecond range is possible.

5. CONCLUSIONS

In this paper we have presented a quantitative discussion of the consequences of ignoring firmware runtimes as proposed by some state-of-the-art simulators. Results based on hardware measurements show that ignoring runtimes can lead to errors in energy consumption predictions for the microcontroller of up to 54%. The situation is even more serious for the radio module, where errors amount to up to 341%, obviously rendering the simulation results useless. Comparing three different MAC protocols revealed that, given an inaccurate simulator, relative comparison is also impossible. For example, the error when predicting the energy consumption of the microcontroller varied between -3.396% and +54.026%. In contrast, published simulators such as STEAM-Sim provide accurate simulation. We used STEAM-Sim to evaluate the X-MAC, Low Power Probing, and ContikiMAC radio duty-cycling protocols at the network level, and showed that ContikiMAC is the most efficient protocol in terms of radio module and microcontroller energy consumption. Finally, we compared STEAM-Sim and COOJA/MSPSim in terms of scalability. Our results show that accurate and scalable simulations of WSNs at nanosecond resolution are possible.

Acknowledgements

This work has been supported by the Linz Center of Mechatronics in the framework of the Austrian COMET-K2 programme.

6. REFERENCES

[1] A. Boulis. Demo Abstract: Castalia: Revealing Pitfalls in Designing Distributed Algorithms in WSN. In *Proceedings of the 5th International Conference on Embedded Networked Sensor Systems (Sensys)*, 2007.

[2] M. Buettner, G. Yee, E. Anderson, and R. Han. X-MAC: A Short Preamble MAC Protocol for Duty-Cycled Wireless Sensor Networks. In *Proceedings of the International Conference on Embedded Networked Sensor Systems (SenSys)*, 2006.

[3] I. E. Commission. *IEC 61967-5: Integrated Circuits, Measurement of electromagnetic emissions, 150 kHz - 1 GHz*, iec-61967-5 cdv edition, May 2001.

[4] W. Du, D. Navarro, F. Mieyeville, and F. Gaffiot. Towards a Taxonomy of Simulation Tools for Wireless Sensor Networks. In *Proceedings of 3rd International ICST Conference on Simulation Tools and Techniques*, 2010.

[5] A. Dunkels, B. Gronvall, and T. Voigt. Contiki - a Lightweight and Flexible Operating System for Tiny Networked Sensors. In *29th Annual IEEE International Conference on Local Computer Networks*, 2004.

[6] A. Dunkels, L. Mottola, N. Tsiftes, F. Österlind, J. Eriksson, and N. Finne. The Announcement Layer: Beacon Coordination for the Sensornet Stack. In *Proceedings of the European Conference on Wireless Sensor Networks (EWSN)*, 2011.

[7] A. Dunkels, F. Österlind, and Z. He. An Adaptive Communication Architecture for Wireless Sensor Networks. In *Proceedings of the International Conference on Embedded Networked Sensor Systems (SenSys)*, 2007.

[8] J. Eriksson, A. Dunkels, N. Finne, F. Österlind, and T. Voigt. MSPSim - an Extensible Simulator for MSP430-equipped Sensor Boards. In *Proceedings of the European Conference on Wireless Sensor Networks (EWSN), Poster/Demo session*, 2007.

[9] J. Eriksson, F. Österlind, N. Finne, A. Dunkels, N. Tsiftes, and T. Voigt. Accurate Network-Scale Power Profiling for Sensor Network Simulators. In *Proceedings of the 6th European Conference on Wireless Sensor Networks (EWSN)*, 2009.

[10] C.-C. Han, R. Kumar, R. Shea, E. Kohler, and M. Srivastava. A Dynamic Operating System for Sensor Nodes. In *Proceedings of the 3rd International Conference on Mobile Systems, Applications, and Services (MobiSys)*, 2005.

[11] A. Kansal, J. Hsu, S. Zahedi, and M. Srivastava. Power Management in Energy Harvesting Sensor Networks. In *ACM Transactions on Embedded Computing Systems*, 2007.

[12] I. Khemapech, I. Duncan, and A. Miller. Energy Preservation in Environmental Monitoring WSN. In *Proceedings of the IEEE International Conference on Sensor Networks, Ubiquitous, and Trustworthy Computing*, 2010.

[13] O. Landsiedel, H. Alizai, and K. Wehrle. When Timing Matters: Enabling Time Accurate and Scalable Simulation of Sensor Network Applications. In *International Conference on Information Processing in Sensor Networks (IPSN)*, 2008.

[14] O. Landsiedel, K. Wehrle, and S. Gotz. Accurate Prediction of Power Consumption in Sensor Networks. In *2nd IEEE Workshop on Embedded Networked Sensors (EmNetS)*, 2005.

[15] P. Levis, S. Madden, D. Gay, J. Polastre, R. Szewczyk, A. Woo, E. Brewer, and D. Culler. The Emergence of Networking Abstractions and Techniques in TinyOS. In *Proceedings of the 1st Symposium on Networked Systems Design and Implementation (NSDI)*, 2004.

[16] G. Möstl, R. Hagelauer, G. Müller, and A. Springer. STEAM-Sim: Filling the Gap Between Time Accuracy and Scalability in Simulation of Wireless Sensor Networks. In *Proceedings of the 8th ACM Workshop on Performance Monitoring and Measurement of Heterogeneous Wireless and Wired Networks (PM2HW2N)*, 2013.

[17] R. Musaloiu-E., C.-J. M. Liang, and A. Terzis. Koala: Ultra-Low Power Data Retrieval in Wireless Sensor Networks. In *Proceedings of the 7th International Conference on Information Processing in Sensor Networks*, 2008.

[18] B. Musznicki and P. Zwierzykowski. Survey of Simulators for Wireless Sensor Networks. In *Proceedings of the IEICE Wireless Networks Workshop*, 2013.

[19] F. Österlind, A. Dunkels, J. Eriksson, N. Finne, and T. Voigt. Cross-Level Sensor Network Simulation with COOJA. In *Proceedings of the 31st IEEE Conference on Local Computer Networks*, 2006.

[20] V. Shnayder, M. Hempstead, B.-r. Chen, G. W. Allen, and M. Welsh. Simulating the Power Consumption of Large-Scale Sensor Network Applications. In *Proceedings of the 2nd International Conference on Embedded Networked Sensor Systems (SenSys)*, 2004.

[21] S. N. Technologies. QualNet, 2010.

[22] B. Titzer, D. Lee, and J. Palsberg. Avrora: Scalable Sensor Network Simulation With Precise Timing. In *4th International Symposium on Information Processing in Sensor Networks (IPSN)*, 2005.

[23] T. Trathnigg, J. Moser, and R. Weiss. A Low-Cost Energy Measurement Setup and Improving the Accuracy of Energy Simulators for Wireless Sensor Networks. In *Proceedings of the 2008 Workshop on Real-World Wireless Sensor Networks*, 2008.

[24] A. Varga. The OMNeT++ Discrete Event Simulation System. *Proceedings of the European Simulation Multiconference (ESM)*, 2001.

[25] M. Varshney, D. Xu, M. Srivastava, and R. Bagrodia. sQualNet: A Scalable Simulation and Emulation Environment for Sensor Networks. In *Proceedings of the International Conference on Information Processing in Sensor Networks (IPSN)*, 2007.

[26] D. Weber, J. Glaser, and S. Mahlknecht. Discrete Event Simulation Framework for Power Aware Wireless Sensor Networks. In *5th IEEE International Conference on Industrial Informatics*, 2007.

The Effect of Emerging Traffic Patterns on High Speed Wireless LANs

Emma Fitzgerald
Emma.Fitzgerald@eit.lth.se

Bjorn Landfeldt
Bjorn.Landfeldt@eit.lth.se

*School of Electrical and Information Technology
Lund University
SE-221 00 Lund
Sweden

ABSTRACT

As average packet sizes in wireless networks shrink and data rates increase, the fundamental CSMA mechanism in the 802.11 protocol family is put under stress. With the emerging 802.11ax standard, the carrier sensing mechanism is lowering the efficiency of the protocol to the level of random access (ALOHA), and as future-generation 802.11 standards emerge, CSMA-based protocols will fall below this level. In this paper we make two main contributions to the literature. First, we will extend previous analysis to examine more closely the quality of the information obtained from channel sensing, in particular the probability of this information being incorrect and the correlation between true and sensed channel state. Second, we examine how to use this analysis to improve existing CSMA-based protocols, in particular the 802.11 protocol family.

Keywords

CSMA; 802.11; 802.11ax; wireless LAN; MAC

1. INTRODUCTION

The landscape for unlicensed spectrum wireless networks appears very different today than when carrier-sense multiple access was first developed, and these changes can potentially have a large impact on the effectiveness of carrier sensing, the central mechanism in CSMA. Two main trends affect the performance: increased raw data rates, leading to shorter frame transmission times; and an increased number of short packets, which incur higher proportional overhead.

As carrier-sensing is vulnerable to collisions whenever a node senses the channel state within one propagation delay of the beginning of another node's transmission, these trends together increase the vulnerability of the network to collisions. We have previously presented analysis demonstrating that under these circumstances, the performance of CSMA degrades to the point of no longer being any more useful than pure random access [11]. In this paper we make two main contributions to the literature. First, we will extend this analysis to examine more closely the quality of the information obtained from channel sensing, in particular the probability of this information being incorrect and the correlation between true and sensed channel state. Second, we examine how to use this analysis to improve existing CSMA-based protocols, in particular the 802.11 protocol family, under these new operating conditions.

The new 802.11ax standard aims to achieve at least a four times increase in data rate over 802.11 ac [1]. An examination of the protocol overheads, however, reveals that many require constant time independent of the data rate and thus are more detrimental to efficiency at higher data rates. Inter-frame spaces, time spent transmitting acknowledgements and management traffic, as well as headers all detract from the channel capacity available to transmit data from higher layer applications [6, 15, 25, 30]. In addition, the contention window mechanism — employed when a node wishes to transmit but cannot because the channel is already busy — also affects the maximum achievable throughput [6, 7, 26]. A poorly chosen contention window can result in either idle time, when all nodes are waiting for their randomly selected transmission slots and no node is actually transmitting, or collision, if two or more nodes choose the same slot.

Slot times, which are the basis for inter-frame spacing and backoff times, are based not on data transmission times but rather on the propagation delay [14]. Thus as data rates go up, in particular with the use of new, higher rate modulation and coding schemes, a higher proportion of the channel time is devoted to these overheads rather than to transmitting useful data. Some mechanisms have been developed to mitigate this problem, in particular frame aggregation [16, 22, 28, 29], so that more data is sent in between each instance of header, acknowledgement, inter-frame spacing and backoff. Nonetheless, trends in the traffic patterns in wireless LANs and in how these networks are used show that simply moving to larger and larger frames is not a comprehensive answer to the problems of inefficiencies in CSMA protocols.

Many of today's applications generate a high number of small packets [18], and this carries through to lower layers,

*This work was partially sponsored by the EC FP7 Marie Curie IAPP Project 324515, "MeshWise"

with a large proportion of packets smaller than 300 bytes being transmitted [20]. Moreover, usage patterns in wireless LANs are changing, with increases in uplink traffic from many different nodes; real-time, delay-sensitive traffic; and low-frequency sensor traffic such as that needed for smart homes and the Internet of Things [3, 4, 12, 13, 18, 23]. These traffic types are not well suited to frame aggregation.

As our results show, CSMA is inherently unsuited to networks in which packet transmission times are short. Instead, new MAC protocol strategies are needed in order to improve the reliability of nodes' information about the channel state and when they should transmit. This can be achieved through greater coordination and information sharing between nodes, provided we do not unduly increase overhead or introduce incompatibility with existing protocols.

2. RELATED WORK

There exists a large body of work addressing various aspects of CSMA performance under many different conditions and assumptions. Bianchi's model [5] has been particularly influential, with numerous further extensions [8, 9, 19, 21, 27]. However, there are some limitations of the Bianchi model that make it unsuitable for our purposes. The model captures the behaviour of CSMA when the network is at saturation, i.e. when every node always has a packet queued to send. This makes certain simplifications possible. In particular, there is no notion of packet transmission time, since the packet arrival rate does not need to be considered. Collisions are also only modelled when nodes choose the same backoff counter value, not when nodes sense the channel during one propagation delay after the beginning of a packet. This makes sense under saturation conditions where no packet will arrive during this vulnerable period as all nodes already have a packet waiting at all times. There have been some extensions of this work to non-saturated conditions (e.g. [9, 10, 19]), however one or more of these limitations still remain in each case.

We wish to study the combined effect of increasing data rates and short packets and as such, we need to explicitly model packet transmission time. As our results demonstrate collisions due to sensing during a vulnerable period are also a significant factor under these circumstances and they cannot be neglected. Further, we seek to examine network behaviour not just under saturation conditions but also under lighter loads, and in particular how quickly the system is pushed into saturation under increasing loads.

In order to investigate the effects of high data rates, small packets and non-saturation conditions, we instead take as our starting point the model developed by Kleinrock and Tobagi [17]. This model incorporates explicit modelling of packet transmission time relative to the propagation delay and varying offered load. While it focuses on p-persistent CSMA and its variants, rather than 802.11, its results are nonetheless applicable to any CSMA protocol, particularly for the aspects we will consider. In the next section we give a more detailed explanation of this model.

A number of simplifying assumptions are made in the model in order to make the analysis tractable. In particular a common packet size and propagation delay across all nodes is used, and the network consists of an infinite number of nodes collectively forming a Poisson-distributed packet arrival process. These assumptions will of course not hold in any realistic network, however they are reason-

able for examining the theoretical throughput achievable in CSMA. In particular, realistic traffic models following the bursty, self-similar traffic patterns characteristic of Internet traffic are likely to exacerbate the problem of collisions due to channel sensing during vulnerable periods, so the Poisson model represents an upper performance bound for this work. Analysis using a finite number of nodes is developed in [24], however an infinite population model is a reasonable approximation for a large number of nodes and we are particularly interested in high-density networks such as those targeted by 802.11ax. Hence the increased complexity resulting from using a finite population model is unwarranted.

In this paper we also examine the optimisation of the 802.11 contention window parameters. While previous work has been performed in this area (e.g. [6, 7, 26]), here we address the effects of changing operating conditions by taking into account the propagation delay and packet transmission time.

3. KLEINROCK AND TOBAGI CSMA ANALYSIS

Kleinrock and Tobagi [17] analyse the throughput and delay characteristics of a number of CSMA variations, along with ALOHA and slotted ALOHA [2]. In this paper, we will focus on their p-persistent CSMA analysis as it is the most similar to the 802.11 protocols in widespread use today.

We first introduce some notation used in [17], which is necessary in order to understand and discuss our analysis based on this model. Kleinrock and Tobagi characterise MAC protocols in terms of throughput, denoted by S. In this model, all packets are considered to be of the same length and as such, time is normalised to the packet transmission time T. $S \in [0, 1]$ is then the number of packets transmitted per packet transmission time. If packets were perfectly scheduled with no collisions and no idle time between transmissions (which is not actually achievable with the protocols considered), S would thus be equal to 1. Further, the offered load, denoted by G ($G \geq S$), represents the number of packets that nodes collectively attempt to transmit on the channel per packet transmission time, including retransmissions.

A particularly important parameter for our work is a, the ratio of the propagation delay to the packet transmission time. Since in this model time is normalised to the packet transmission time, a is then simply the propagation delay expressed in units of T. Lastly we have p, the persistence parameter. A node which senses the channel busy will first wait until the end of the current transmission, and then attempt to transmit with probability p, or wait one slot time (equal to a) with probability $1 - p$. This is then repeated for every slot until the node transmits its packet, either successfully or unsuccessfully (i.e. resulting in a collision).

The p-persistent CSMA protocol as described in [17] follows a cycle consisting of an idle period followed by a busy period (see Figure 1). During an idle period, no packets are transmitted on the channel and no nodes have packets queued to send. An idle period ends when a packet arrives at a node ready to be transmitted. The system then enters a busy period. Note that during a busy period, the channel itself is not constantly busy, that is, a signal is not present on the channel the entire time. This is because some of the

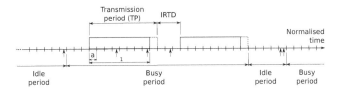

Figure 1: *p*-persistent CSMA cycle as described in [17]. Vertical arrows indicate packet arrivals.

time is spent with nodes waiting to transmit, according to the persistence scheme.

The node (or potentially more than one node, each with its own packet to transmit) where this packet is queued then follows the *p*-persistence protocol to determine a slot in which to start the actual transmission of the packet. This transmission is referred to as a transmission period (TP) and ends one propagation delay (*a*) after the node has completed transmitting the packet. The transmission can either be successful, if no other node attempts to transmit at the same time, or result in a collision, if two or more nodes transmit at once. In the latter case, the colliding packets are then rescheduled for retransmission.

If any packets arrive (at any node) during the TP, the nodes with packets queued perform the *p*-persistence scheme to determine, at each slot, whether they will attempt to transmit. The system then experiences an initial random transmission delay (IRTD) of zero or more slot times, during which the channel is idle. It is possible for more packets to arrive during this time, in which case these nodes will also use the persistence scheme to decide when to attempt transmission. Once at least one node begins a new transmission in a slot, a new TP occurs (which, again, may be successful or result in collision). This process continues until such time as there are no nodes with packets queued for transmission at the end of a TP. The system then enters the next idle period — and thus the start of the next cycle — one propagation delay after the end of the last TP.

The average length of a busy period is denoted by $\bar{B}$ and the average length of an idle period by $\bar{I}$. The total average length of a cycle is then $\bar{B} + \bar{I}$. The average number of slots in an IRTD is denoted $\bar{t}$. Expressions for these values are derived in [17]. Lastly, we will denote average number of TPs in a busy period by $\bar{m}$ (not used in [17]).

4. ANALYSIS OF LARGE *a* VALUES

In [17], only results for relatively small values of *a* are presented, as these were values that were reasonable for the data rates and traffic patterns in use at the time of publication. We developed a software implementation of the model from [17] and now present analysis for larger values of *a*.

Figures 2 and 3 show throughput vs offered load for the various MAC protocols included in the analysis with decreasing *a* values. A value of $p = 0.1$ is shown for *p*-persistent CSMA but the results were similar for other *p* values. As can be seen in the figures, as *a* grows larger, throughput decreases dramatically, eventually to the point that the CSMA protocols perform worse than slotted ALOHA — that is, we eventually gain nothing by sensing the channel and can do no better than pure random access.

To understand why this is the case, we can consider the probability that there will be a collision when a node at-

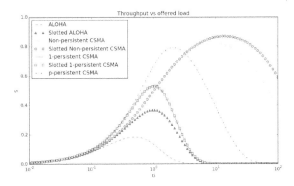

Figure 2: Throughput vs offered load for various wireless MAC protocols, $a = 0.01$

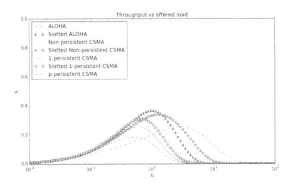

Figure 3: Throughput vs offered load for various wireless MAC protocols, $a = 0.5$

tempts to transmit a packet. As discussed in [17], the probability of a successful transmission is given by $\frac{S}{G}$ and hence the collision probability is $1 - \frac{S}{G}$. Figures 4 and 5 show the collision probability as a function of offered load for the same values of *a* as in Figures 2 and 3, again with $p = 0.1$.

We see that the probability that a packet will encounter a collision using CSMA increases as *a* increases, eventually becoming greater than that for slotted ALOHA. More time is thus wasted transmitting interfering packets that do not result in data being received successfully, reducing the channel utilisation.

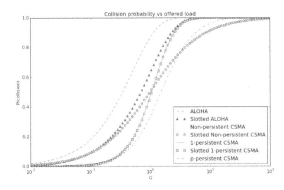

Figure 4: Collision probability for various wireless MAC protocols, $a = 0.01$

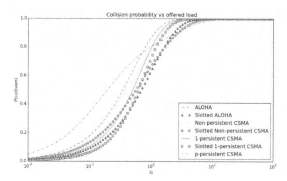

Figure 5: Collision probability for various wireless MAC protocols, $a = 0.5$

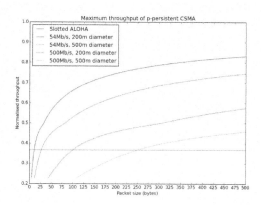

Figure 6: Maximum throughput of p-persistent CSMA for different data rates, network diameters and packet sizes

4.1 Discussion

That the collision probability increases as a increases is a direct consequence of the reason for encountering collisions in CSMA. We first need to distinguish between the two types of collisions possible using CSMA protocols. The first occurs when two nodes are in a backoff state after sensing that the channel is busy, and then choose to retry transmission at the same time. This type of collision can be a large source of overhead if many nodes are waiting to transmit and we are using a small p value (or small contention window size in 802.11). However, the rate of these collisions does not depend on a; it is instead a function of p (or contention window size). Hence these collisions do not account for the rise in collision probability with increasing a.

The second type of collision occurs when a node senses the channel within one propagation delay of another node starting a transmission. During this vulnerable period, the signal from the transmitting node has not yet reached the sensing node and thus goes undetected. The sensing node sees the channel as free even though it is actually busy. These vulnerable periods occur only at the beginning of packet transmissions and as a increases, they account for a higher proportion of the time the channel is busy. Thus the likelihood of sensing the channel during a vulnerable period increases, resulting in an increased collision probability.

Although the Kleinrock and Tobagi model deals with p-persistent CSMA, this problem applies just as much, if not more, to actual CSMA protocols in use today such as the 802.11 family of protocols. The primary difference between the 802.11 DCF and p-persistent CSMA lies in the behaviour of nodes after they have already sensed the channel busy — a probabilistic back-off per slot versus a random number of back-off slots. However, the issue we have explored happens not once the node is in back-off having already ascertained that the channel is busy, but earlier, at the point of determining the channel state through channel sensing. The 802.11 DCF utilises the same channel-sensing mechanism to determine whether the channel is free to transmit and thus is equally vulnerable.

Moreover, the values of a at which the failure of CSMA occurs are realistic in wireless LANs today or in the near future. Figure 6 shows the maximum (normalised) throughput of p-persistent CSMA, according to the model in [17], for a variety of network diameters, packet sizes and data rates. Each of these parameters contribute to the value of a in a real network: the data rate and packet size together deter-

mine the time taken to transmit a packet, while the network diameter determines the maximum propagation delay between any pair of nodes. Today, with 802.11ac, a data rate of 500Mb/s is achievable and as can be seen in the figure, the maximum achievable throughput is poor — even below slotted ALOHA — at small packet sizes.

5. UTILITY OF CHANNEL SENSING

The primary aim of CSMA-based MAC protocols is to attempt to separate transmissions in time such that a node will, ideally, only transmit when no other node is transmitting. Each node, when it has a packet queued to send, attempts to determine when the channel is free for transmission and we can characterise these MAC protocols in terms of the accuracy with which nodes are able to do this. There are two possible types of errors a node can make when attempting to determine when to transmit. It can either incorrectly perceive the channel to be available when it is not, leading to a collision as two nodes attempt to transmit at once, or else it can incorrectly perceive the channel as busy when it is in fact available, leading to wasted time as the channel lies idle even though there are nodes with packets queued for transmission. In ALOHA, only the first type of error is possible since nodes never check whether the channel is busy but simply assume it to be available at any time, and only discover in retrospect (due to lack of acknowledgement) that this was not the case.

The goal of CSMA is to use channel sensing to gather more information about the channel state before transmitting. However, the information gathered is not perfect — it does not exactly match the true channel state at any given time. Sensing will lag behind the true channel state by the amount of time it takes a signal to propagate from a transmitting node to a sensing node. The network diameter, that is, the maximum distance between any two nodes, gives an upper bound on the propagation delay. In [17], all pairs of nodes are considered to have the same propagation delay. This simplifies the analysis and will result in conservative estimates of the information gained from channel sensing.

We can consider CSMA in terms of two random variables: the true channel state and the state as sensed by a node. To determine the accuracy — and hence usefulness — of the

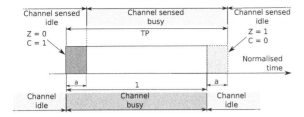

Figure 7: Sensed and true channel states

information obtained through channel sensing, we can take the correlation between the sensed channel state and the true channel state. Throughout this section, we will discuss p-persistent CSMA, however, 1-persistent CSMA and non-persistent CSMA are special cases of this protocol for $p = 1$ and $p = 0$ respectively.

Given random variables X and Y with expected values μ_X and μ_Y, and standard deviations σ_X and σ_Y respectively, the correlation of X and Y is defined as

$$\operatorname{corr}(X, Y) = \frac{E\left[(X - \mu_X)(Y - \mu_Y)\right]}{\sigma_X \sigma_Y}$$

Let the true channel state be denoted C and the channel state as sensed by a node be denoted Z. Each of these variables can take two possible values: busy or idle. C will be busy whenever any node in the network is transmitting, even if this transmission has not yet reached any other node, and idle otherwise. Z is node-dependent and will be busy whenever the signal strength received at a node is above the threshold for the channel to be considered busy, and idle otherwise. Here we will neglect effects such as channel noise, multipath propagation, etc. and assume an ideal channel. Let 1 represent a busy state and 0 represent an idle state (for either variable). Since Z is actually the same process as C, just one propagation delay behind, we have $Z(t) = C(t-a)$, and in steady state, then, $\mu_Z = \mu_C = \mu$ and $\sigma_Z = \sigma_C = \sigma$.

We can take the correlation of C and Z.

$$\operatorname{corr}(C, Z) = \frac{\sum_{c \in \{0,1\}, z \in \{0,1\}} (c - \mu)(z - \mu) P(C = c, Z = z)}{\sigma^2}$$
$$(1)$$

This is equivalent to the autocorrelation of C with a time delay equal to the propagation delay, however when deriving the probabilities to satisfy Equation 1 it is helpful to consider Z and C separately.

In order to derive an expression for $\operatorname{corr}(C, Z)$, we need to find the following: μ, σ, $P(C = 1, Z = 1)$: the probability that the channel is busy and is sensed as busy, $P(C = 0, Z = 1)$: the probability that the channel is idle but is sensed as busy, $P(C = 1 | Z = 0)$: the probability that the channel is busy but is sensed as idle, and $P(C = 0, Z = 0)$: the probability that the channel is idle and is sensed as idle.

To determine these values, we can consider the cycle of busy and idle periods that the channel goes through under p-persistent CSMA, depicted in Figure 1. (See Section 3 for a more detailed explanation of this protocol.) A busy period consists of m transmission periods (TPs), each of which may result in either a successful packet transmission or a collision. The average times spent in busy and idle periods are derived in [17] and denoted by $\bar{B}$ and $\bar{I}$ respectively. Note that as with all other time expressions, these are normalised to the

packet transmission time.

$$\bar{B} = a\bar{t}' + \frac{a\bar{t}(1 - \pi_0) + 1 + a}{\pi_0} \tag{2}$$

$$\bar{I} = \frac{a}{1 - e^{-g}} \tag{3}$$

Expressions for terms not defined here can be found in [17]. The probability that the number of TPs in a busy period is equal to m is $\pi_0 (1 - \pi_0)^{m-1}$, for $m \in \mathbb{Z}_{>0}$ [17], and so we can find $\bar{m}$ by taking the average over this distribution.

$$\bar{m} = \sum_{m=1}^{\infty} m \pi_0 (1 - \pi_0)^{m-1} \tag{4}$$

As a busy period must have at least one TP, m is always at least 1. This is an arithmetico-geometric series and so we can compute this sum:

$$\bar{m} = \pi_0 \left(\frac{1}{1 - (1 - \pi_0)} \right) + \frac{(1 - \pi_0) \times 1}{(1 - (1 - \pi_0))^2}$$
$$= \pi_0 \left(\frac{\pi_0 + 1 - \pi_0}{\pi_0^2} \right)$$
$$= \frac{1}{\pi_0}. \tag{5}$$

When sensing the channel, the probability that it is sensed busy or idle will be equal to the probability of the channel actually being busy or idle, since the sensed channel state is simply the channel state one propagation delay earlier. Thus if we sensed the channel constantly, the proportions of time we would sense busy and idle states is equal to the proportions of time the channel actually spends busy and idle. Hence $P(Z = 1) = P(C = 1)$ and $P(Z = 0) = P(C = 0)$.

The channel is in a busy state only during a TP (excluding the final propagation delay after transmission ends), with $\bar{m}$ TPs per cycle on average. Hence the proportion of time the channel is busy (or, equivalently, the probability that the channel is busy in steady state) is

$$P(C = 1) = \frac{\bar{m}}{\bar{B} + \bar{I}}. \tag{6}$$

The probability that the channel is idle is then

$$P(C = 0) = 1 - P(C = 1)$$
$$= 1 - \frac{\bar{m}}{\bar{B} + \bar{I}}. \tag{7}$$

Next we will derive the conditional probabilities for the channel state given a particular sensed state (see Figure 7). First consider the case that the channel is sensed busy, i.e. $Z = 1$. The channel is sensed busy during a TP after the initial propagation delay. The duration of a TP is $1 + a$ and since we are subtracting one propagation delay from the beginning, we are left with a duration of 1. Of this time, the channel is only actually busy during the transmission itself, whereas during the propagation delay (of length a) at the end, the channel is actually idle. Hence we have

$$P(C = 1 | Z = 1) = 1 - a \tag{8}$$
$$P(C = 0 | Z = 1) = a. \tag{9}$$

To determine the channel state probabilities conditioned on the channel being sensed idle, we must first determine the total time the channel could be sensed as idle. This can either occur within one propagation delay of the beginning of a TP, or whilst the channel is idle and it has been longer than a propagation delay since the end of a TP. The first case occurs on average $\bar{m}$ times per cycle, and is of length a each time, giving a total time of $a\bar{m}$. The second case can occur either during an idle period, of length $\bar{I}$ (note that an idle period does not begin until one propagation delay after the last TP of a busy period), or during a busy period while nodes waiting to transmit are in backoff. The average length of the backoff time is $a\bar{t}$ ($\bar{t}$ slots of length a each) and this occurs $\bar{m} - 1$ times per cycle (between each pair of consecutive TPs). Hence the total time a constantly sensing node would see the channel as idle per cycle is

$$\text{Sensed idle time} = \bar{I} + (\bar{m} - 1]a\bar{t} + a\bar{m}. \quad (10)$$

Of this time, the channel is actually busy during the vulnerable periods ($a\bar{m}$) and idle otherwise. Hence

$$P(C = 1 | Z = 0) = \frac{a\bar{m}}{\bar{I} + (\bar{m} - 1]a\bar{t} + a\bar{m}} \quad (11)$$

and

$$P(C = 0 | Z = 0) = \frac{\bar{I} + (\bar{m} - 1]a\bar{t}}{\bar{I} + (\bar{m} - 1]a\bar{t} + a\bar{m}}. \quad (12)$$

We can now determine the joint probability distribution of C and Z. The joint probabilities are:

$$\begin{aligned} P(C = 0, Z = 0) &= P(C = 0 | Z = 0)P(Z = 0) \\ &= \frac{\bar{I} + (\bar{m} - 1]a\bar{t}}{\bar{I} + (\bar{m} - 1]a\bar{t} + a\bar{m}} \left(1 - \frac{\bar{m}}{\bar{B} + \bar{I}}\right) \end{aligned} \quad (13)$$

$$\begin{aligned} P(C = 1, Z = 0) &= P(C = 1 | Z = 0)P(Z = 0) \\ &= \frac{a\bar{m}}{\bar{I} + (\bar{m} - 1]a\bar{t} + a\bar{m}} \left(1 - \frac{\bar{m}}{\bar{B} + \bar{I}}\right) \end{aligned} \quad (14)$$

$$\begin{aligned} P(C = 0, Z = 1) &= P(C = 0 | Z = 1)P(Z = 1) \\ &= a\frac{\bar{m}}{\bar{B} + \bar{I}} \end{aligned} \quad (15)$$

$$\begin{aligned} P(C = 1, Z = 1) &= P(C = 1 | Z = 1)P(Z = 1) \\ &= (1 - a)\frac{\bar{m}}{\bar{B} + \bar{I}}. \end{aligned} \quad (16)$$

Channel sensing will provide a node with incorrect information about the channel state whenever $Z \neq C$, which occurs with probability $P(C = 0, Z = 1) + P(C = 1, Z = 0)$. We used our software implementation of the model of p-persistent CSMA from [17] to calculate this probability as a function of the propagation delay and offered load. Figure 8 shows the results for $p = 0.1$ (results were similar for other values of p). At low offered loads, the probability of obtaining incorrect information from channel sensing remains low even with a high propagation delay, since the channel is idle almost all the time. When a is small, the probability of incorrect information from sensing also remains low regardless of offered load since sensing provides accurate information nearly all the time. However, once we have even a moderate offered load, the chances of sensing an incorrect channel state increase with the propagation delay to packet transmission time ratio. Note that at high offered loads,

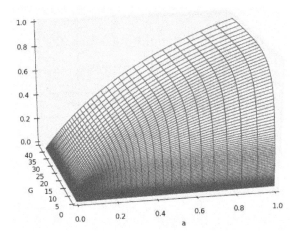

Figure 8: Probability of obtaining incorrect information from channel sensing

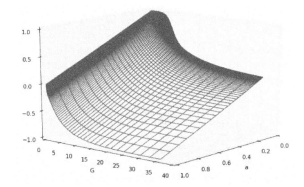

Figure 9: Correlation between true and sensed channel state

the channel state is not actually busy all the time, since the channel will be idle for some number of slots (depending on the persistence value) between transmissions.

To find the correlation between sensed channel state and true channel state, we also need expressions for μ and σ.

$$\begin{aligned} \mu &= E[C] \\ &= 0 \times P(C = 0) + 1 \times P(C = 1) \\ &= P(C = 1) \\ &= \frac{\bar{m}}{\bar{B} + \bar{I}} \end{aligned} \quad (17)$$

$$\begin{aligned} \sigma &= \sqrt{E[C^2] - (E[C])^2} \\ &= \sqrt{E[C] - (E[C])^2} \quad \text{(since C takes values in \{0, 1\})} \\ &= \sqrt{\mu(1 - \mu)} \\ &= \sqrt{\left(\frac{\bar{m}}{\bar{B} + \bar{I}}\right)\left(1 - \frac{\bar{m}}{\bar{B} + \bar{I}}\right)} \end{aligned} \quad (18)$$

The correlation of C and Z is then given by

$$\text{corr}(C, Z) = \frac{\sum_{c \in \{0,1\}, z \in \{0,1\}} (c - \mu)(z - \mu) P(C = c, Z = z)}{\sigma^2}$$

$$= \frac{\begin{array}{l} (0 - \mu)(0 - \mu) P(C = 0, Z = 0) \\ + (0 - \mu)(1 - \mu) P(C = 1, Z = 0) \\ + (1 - \mu)(0 - \mu) P(C = 0, Z = 1) \\ + (1 - \mu)(1 - \mu) P(C = 1, Z = 1) \end{array}}{\sigma^2} \quad (19)$$

where the individual terms are as given in Equations 13–18.

Figure 9 shows a plot of $\text{corr}(C, Z)$ as a function of propagation delay and offered load. We can consider this as a measure of the utility of performing channel sensing. For small a, channel sensing is of high utility (although this decreases as the offered load increases, forcing the channel into a saturated state). As the packet transmission time decreases relative to the propagation delay, i.e. a increases, we are looking further back into the past when performing channel sensing, relative to the timescale at which data is being transmitted. Channel sensing then becomes of no or even negative utility; nodes begin obtaining incorrect information and would instead achieve better performance by transmitting based solely on random access as in ALOHA.

6. OPTIMISING 802.11

In the long term, addressing the problem of increasingly poor quality information obtained through channel sensing will require new approaches to medium access control in wireless networks. However, given the large existing user-base of devices operating on CSMA-based protocols, in particular the 802.11 protocol family, it is worth considering what we can do to mitigate the problem without drastically changing the current protocols, as an interim solution while new protocols are developed and standardised.

To that end, we will now look at optimising 802.11 for networks in which the value of a is large. In the following section we will explore the dependence of the achievable throughput on the parameter p, that is, the persistence probability, for a given a and offered load G. Since our analysis concerns p-persistent CSMA, rather than 802.11, we also need to translate our results to apply to the 802.11 DCF contention window mechanism instead.

6.1 Optimal p

Figure 10 shows the value of p for which the highest maximum throughput is achieved for each combination of a and G. We will refer to this as the optimal p value. As can be seen in the figure, at high offered load, the optimal p value is very low regardless of a, since with a large amount of traffic that nodes are attempting to send, we need to spread the transmissions out widely in time in order to avoid collisions. Conversely, at low G, we see very high optimal p values, as there is so little traffic that the probability of collision is very low, and the best strategy is for nodes to simply transmit as soon as they have data available.

However, if we wish to replicate this behaviour using the contention window in the 802.11 DCF, both very high and very low values of p will be problematic. This is because the contention window values, unlike p, are discrete, A contention window size of 1 is equivalent to a p-value of 1, since both represent nodes sending immediately in the next

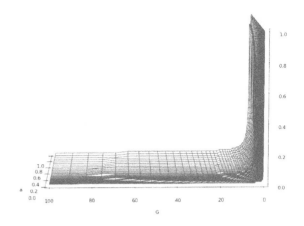

Figure 10: p value that yields the highest maximum throughput

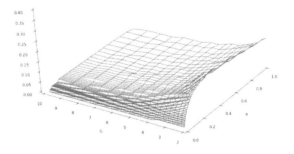

Figure 11: p value that yields the highest maximum throughput, for moderate offered load

slot after the previous transmission, with no back-off. However, while p can be reduced while still retaining near-certain transmission, the contention window must take a significant increase (up to 2) for its next possible value. This already corresponds to a relatively low p value of 0.5 (approximately half the nodes will attempt to send in the first slot after the previous transmission) and thus does not allow for fine tuning the network performance in situations of low offered load.

At the other end of the spectrum of node behaviour, to achieve back-off with the DCF that is similar to that seen with very low p-values, we require extremely large contention window values. In fact, in order to match the performance achievable with p-persistent CSMA, we would need to allow the contention window to grow without bound.

However, if we focus on situations with a moderate offered load, we are able to achieve some performance gains by fine-tuning the contention window size according to both the offered window size and the value of a. Figure 11 again shows the optimal p value as a function of a and G, but restricted to moderate offered loads. Here the dependence on a becomes more apparent and we will exploit this in order to improve the performance of the 802.11 DCF.

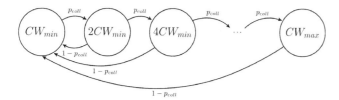

Figure 12: Markov chain for contention window size in 802.11

6.2 802.11 contention window parameters

The primary difference between p-persistent CSMA as described in [17] and the 802.11 DCF lies in the back-off behaviour. In both cases, nodes wait a random number of slots after the previous transmission before attempting a new transmission, however the distribution of this randomly selected number of slots varies. With p-persistent CSMA, we have a geometric distribution over the entire set of natural numbers, whereas with the DCF, we instead have uniformly distributed values over $[1, CW]$, where CW is the current contention window size of the node.

However, we can equate the means of the two distributions as a first-order approximation. We then need to find contention window parameters — the minimum and maximum allowed contention window values — that correspond to a given p value. To do this, we first use the relationship between p and $E[CW]$ obtained in [7] (Lemma 2). After some rearrangement of the expressions given in [7], this yields

$$E[CW] = \frac{2-p}{p} \tag{20}$$

We then need to obtain the correct minimum (CW_{min}) and maximum (CW_{max}) values that will result in the desired average contention window size $E[CW]$, given an optimal p value obtained from our analysis above.

A node executing the DCF doubles its contention window size when it experiences a collision, and drops it back to CW_{min} again after a successful transmission. Given a collision probability p_{coll}, we can then model the contention window size with a Markov chain (Figure 12). Note that here we have a dependence on the collision probability, which we can derive from a and G as shown in Figures 4 and 5.

The number of states N in the Markov chain is dependent on CW_{min} and CW_{max}. The relationship between these is given by

$$N \geq \log_2 CW_{max} - \log_2 CW_{min} \tag{21}$$

We can then derive equations for p_i, the equilibrium probabilities of the Markov chain, by considering the flows across the boundaries between each pair of states.

$$p_{coll}p_0 = (1-p_{coll})p_1 + (1-p_{coll})p_2 + \cdots + (1-p_{coll})p_N$$
$$p_{coll}p_1 = (1-p_{coll})p_2 + (1-p_{coll})p_3 + \cdots + (1-p_{coll})p_N$$
$$\cdots$$
$$p_{coll}p_{N-1} = (1-p_{coll})p_N$$

To simplify the notation, we define α

$$\alpha = \frac{1-p_{coll}}{p_{coll}} \tag{22}$$

and can then re-write the equilibrium equations in terms of α: $p_0 = \alpha \sum_{i=1}^{N} p_i$, $p_1 = \alpha \sum_{i=2}^{N} p_i$, ..., $p_{N-2} = \alpha(p_{N-1} +$

p_N), $p_{N-1} = \alpha p_N$. We also have the normalising condition

$$\sum_{i=0}^{N} p_i = 1 \tag{23}$$

By combining Equation 23 and the first flow equation above, we obtain the following expression for p_0.

$$p_0 = \alpha \sum_{i=1}^{N} p_i = \alpha(1-p_0)$$
$$p_0 = \frac{\alpha}{1+\alpha} \tag{24}$$

Similarly, we can express each p_i in terms of p_{i-1} and hence recursively in terms of p_0 and thus α.

$$p_i = \frac{p_0}{(1+\alpha)^i}$$
$$= \frac{\alpha}{(1+\alpha)^{i+1}} \quad \forall i \tag{25}$$

Once we have the above expressions for the p_i, we can then directly find $E[CW]$ by computing the mean.

$$E[CW] = \sum_{i=0}^{N} CW_i p_i$$
$$= \sum_{i=0}^{N} 2^i CW_{min} p_i$$
$$= CW_{min} \sum_{i=0}^{N} 2^i \frac{\alpha}{(1+\alpha)^{i+1}}$$
$$= \frac{\alpha}{1+\alpha} CW_{min} \sum_{i=0}^{N} \left(\frac{2}{1+\alpha}\right)^{i+1}$$
$$= \frac{\alpha}{1+\alpha} CW_{min} \frac{1-\left(\frac{2}{1+\alpha}\right)^{N+1}}{1-\frac{2}{1+\alpha}} \tag{26}$$

We have three unknowns, CW_{min}, CW_{max}, and N. However, any two of these completely determine the third according to Equation 21. Thus in order to find contention window parameters to use for a given desired $E[CW]$, we can fix either CW_{min} or CW_{max} and solve for the other. For instance, solving for CW_{min} gives

$$CW_{min} \geq \frac{CW_{max}}{2^N} \tag{27}$$

Substituting this into Equation 26, after some rearrangement, yields the inequality in Equation 28.

6.3 Discussion

There are some limitations to this approach. Firstly, we have some quantisation error due to the discrete nature of the contention window size: we cannot match an arbitrary $E[CW]$ perfectly. In addition, if the collision probability becomes too high, $E[CW]$ will also become too high to achieve with our chosen CW_{max}. However, we can get quite good agreement between our desired $E[CW]$ and the actual value of $E[CW]$ achieved even for relatively high values of p_{coll}.

To test this, we conducted a simulation of the Markov chain for the contention window size for a CW_{max} of 512. Figure 13 shows the desired (calculated) $E[CW]$ versus the actual measured average contention window size for a variety of different values of p_{coll}. The quantisation error is most

$$(1+\alpha)\left(1-\frac{2}{1+\alpha}\right)E[CW] = \alpha CW_{min}\left(1-\left(\frac{2}{1+\alpha}\right)^{N+1}\right)$$

$$(1+\alpha)\left(1-\frac{2}{1+\alpha}\right)E[CW] = \alpha CW_{min} - 2^N CW_{min}\frac{2\alpha}{(1+\alpha)^{N+1}}$$

$$2^N CW_{min}\frac{2\alpha}{(1+\alpha)^{N+1}} = \alpha CW_{min} - (1+\alpha)\left(1-\frac{2}{1+\alpha}\right)E[CW]$$

$$CW_{max}\frac{2\alpha}{(1+\alpha)^{N+1}} \leq \alpha CW_{min} - (1+\alpha)\left(1-\frac{2}{1+\alpha}\right)E[CW]$$

$$CW_{min} \geq CW_{max}\frac{2}{(1+\alpha)^{N+1}} + \frac{1+\alpha}{\alpha}\left(1-\frac{2}{1+\alpha}\right)E[CW] \qquad (28)$$

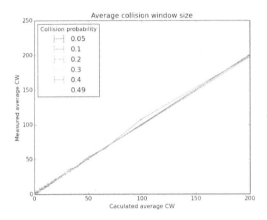

Figure 13: Calculated average contention window vs measured average

evident at small values of $E[CW]$, however for higher $E[CW]$ the simulated results agree well with the analysis up to a collision probability of 0.49. (Note that $p_{coll} = 0.5$ is a special case as then the final term in Equation 28 becomes zero, removing the dependence on $E[CW]$).

This approach allows us to use the analysis presented in the previous sections to fine-tune the 802.11 DCF contention window parameters in order to obtain the best performance. However, as data rates increase and with the trend of decreasing packet sizes in wireless LANs, eventually new approaches to medium access control will be needed.

7. CONCLUSION

In this paper we have analysed the utility of performing channel sensing in terms of the probability of obtaining incorrect information about the channel state and shown that this probability increases dramatically as the ratio of the propagation delay to the packet transmission time increases. We have also determined the correlation between true and sensed channel states and found a similar disconnect between the two at high values of this ratio

We have also applied this analysis to fine-tuning the 802.11 DCF contention window parameters. This allows us to find the parameters that will give the best performance for a given set of operating conditions: offered load and ratio of propagation delay to packet transmission time.

With the continued push for higher raw data rates in 802.11 and changing traffic patterns towards a greater proportion of real-time and uplink traffic, we are reaching the limits of carrier sensing as a means for medium access control in wireless LANs. As we have shown in this paper, these changes result in information obtained through channel sensing that is old and not reliable. This has further implications for the use of new physical-layer technologies such as MIMO and OFDM. Our results indicate that the focus for the use of these techniques in future protocol designs should lie in parallelisation of users — for example with multi-user MIMO, or by assigning sets of subcarriers to different users in OFDM — rather than in further increasing data rates for a single user.

Increasing the reliability can be achieved in two ways: through sampling and prediction using signal processing and machine learning strategies, or by increasing coordination and information exchange among the nodes. The effectiveness of each strategy will depend on the predictability of the frame generation process. A highly regular process will lend itself to learning strategies as they impose no overhead and no coordination. As the uncertainty increases coordination becomes more effective but it comes at a price of overhead and lost flexibility. In the future, we need a new approach to wireless MAC protocols, exploring this landscape of possible strategies and the trade-offs between them.

8. REFERENCES

[1] 802.11ax proposed project authorization request. https://mentor.ieee.org/802.11/dcn/14/11-14-0165-01-0hew-802-11-hew-sg-proposed-par.docx. Accessed 2014-06-18.

[2] N. Abramson. The ALOHA system: another alternative for computer communications. In *Proceedings of the November 17-19, 1970, fall joint computer conference*, pages 281–285. ACM, 1970.

[3] M. Afanasyev, T. Chen, G. M. Voelker, and A. C. Snoeren. Usage patterns in an urban WiFi network. *Networking, IEEE/ACM Transactions on*, 18(5):1359–1372, 2010.

[4] L. Atzori, A. Iera, and G. Morabito. The internet of things: A survey. *Computer networks*, 54(15):2787–2805, 2010.

[5] G. Bianchi. Performance analysis of the IEEE 802.11 distributed coordination function. *Selected Areas in Communications, IEEE Journal on*, 18(3):535–547, 2000.

[6] F. Cali, M. Conti, and E. Gregori. Ieee 802.11 wireless LAN: capacity analysis and protocol enhancement. In *INFOCOM'98. Seventeenth Annual Joint Conference of the IEEE Computer and Communications Societies. Proceedings. IEEE*, volume 1, pages 142–149. IEEE, 1998.

[7] F. Calì, M. Conti, and E. Gregori. Dynamic tuning of the IEEE 802.11 protocol to achieve a theoretical throughput limit. *IEEE/ACM Transactions on Networking (ToN)*, 8(6):785–799, 2000.

[8] P. Chatzimisios, V. Vitsas, and A. C. Boucouvalas. Throughput and delay analysis of IEEE 802.11 protocol. In *Networked Appliances, 2002. Liverpool. Proceedings. 2002 IEEE 5th International Workshop on*, pages 168–174. IEEE, 2002.

[9] N. T. Dao and R. A. Malaney. A new markov model for non-saturated 802.11 networks. In *Consumer Communications and Networking Conference, 2008. CCNC 2008. 5th IEEE*, pages 420–424. IEEE, 2008.

[10] K. Duffy, D. Malone, and D. J. Leith. Modeling the 802.11 distributed coordination function in non-saturated conditions. *IEEE Communications Letters*, 9(8):715–717, 2005.

[11] E. Fitzgerald and B. Landfeldt. The failure of CSMA in emerging wireless network scenarios. In *Wireless Days*, pages 1–4, 2014.

[12] E. Halepovic, C. Williamson, and M. Ghaderi. Wireless data traffic: a decade of change. *Network, IEEE*, 23(2):20–26, 2009.

[13] T. Henderson, D. Kotz, and I. Abyzov. The changing usage of a mature campus-wide wireless network. *Computer Networks*, 52(14):2690–2712, 2008.

[14] IEEE Standards Association et al. 802.11-2012-IEEE standard for information technology–telecommunications and information exchange between systems local and metropolitan area networks–specific requirements part 11: Wireless LAN medium access control (MAC) and physical layer (PHY) specifications, 2012.

[15] J. Jun, P. Peddabachagari, and M. Sichitiu. Theoretical maximum throughput of IEEE 802.11 and its applications. In *Network Computing and Applications, 2003. NCA 2003. Second IEEE International Symposium on*, pages 249–256. IEEE, 2003.

[16] Y. Kim, S. Choi, K. Jang, and H. Hwang. Throughput enhancement of IEEE 802.11 WLAN via frame aggregation. In *Vehicular technology conference, 2004. VTC2004-Fall. 2004 IEEE 60th*, volume 4, pages 3030–3034. IEEE, 2004.

[17] L. Kleinrock and F. A. Tobagi. Packet switching in radio channels: Part i–carrier sense multiple-access modes and their throughput-delay characteristics. *Communications, IEEE Transactions on*, 23(12):1400–1416, 1975.

[18] F. Liu, X. Wu, W. Li, and X. Liu. The packet size distribution patterns of the typical internet applications. In *Network Infrastructure and Digital Content (IC-NIDC)*, pages 325–332, 2012.

[19] D. Malone, K. Duffy, and D. Leith. Modeling the 802.11 distributed coordination function in nonsaturated heterogeneous conditions. *Networking, IEEE/ACM Transactions on*, 15(1):159–172, 2007.

[20] Packet measurements around Boulder, CO. https://mentor.ieee.org/802.11/dcn/14/11-14-0546-01-00ax-packet-traffic-measurements-around-boulder-colorado.ppt. Accessed 2014-06-26.

[21] J. W. Robinson and T. S. Randhawa. Saturation throughput analysis of IEEE 802.11 e enhanced distributed coordination function. *Selected Areas in Communications, IEEE Journal on*, 22(5):917–928, 2004.

[22] D. Skordoulis, Q. Ni, H.-H. Chen, A. P. Stephens, C. Liu, and A. Jamalipour. IEEE 802.11 n MAC frame aggregation mechanisms for next-generation high-throughput WLANs. *Wireless Communications, IEEE*, 15(1):40–47, 2008.

[23] M. Starsinic. System architecture challenges in the home M2M network. In *Applications and Technology Conference (LISAT), 2010 Long Island Systems*, pages 1–7. IEEE, 2010.

[24] H. Takagi and L. Kleinrock. Throughput analysis for persistent CSMA systems. *Communications, IEEE Transactions on*, 33(7):627–638, 1985.

[25] K. Tan, J. Fang, Y. Zhang, S. Chen, L. Shi, J. Zhang, and Y. Zhang. Fine-grained channel access in wireless lan. *ACM SIGCOMM Computer Communication Review*, 41(4):147–158, 2011.

[26] Y. Tay and K. C. Chua. A capacity analysis for the IEEE 802.11 MAC protocol. *Wireless networks*, 7(2):159–171, 2001.

[27] H. Wu, Y. Peng, K. Long, S. Cheng, and J. Ma. Performance of reliable transport protocol over IEEE 802.11 wireless LAN: analysis and enhancement. In *INFOCOM 2002. Twenty-First Annual Joint Conference of the IEEE Computer and Communications Societies. Proceedings. IEEE*, volume 2, pages 599–607. IEEE, 2002.

[28] Y. Xiao. Packing mechanisms for the IEEE 802.11 n wireless LANs. In *Global Telecommunications Conference, 2004. GLOBECOM'04. IEEE*, volume 5, pages 3275–3279. IEEE, 2004.

[29] Y. Xiao. IEEE 802.11 n: enhancements for higher throughput in wireless LANs. *Wireless Communications, IEEE*, 12(6):82–91, 2005.

[30] Y. Xiao and J. Rosdahl. Throughput and delay limits of IEEE 802.11. *Communications Letters, IEEE*, 6(8):355–357, 2002.

Phase-based Ranging of RFID Tags with Applications to Shopping Cart Localization

Jihoon Ryoo and Samir R. Das
Computer Science Department
Stony Brook University
Stony Brook, NY 11794 U.S.A.
{jiryoo,samir}@cs.stonybrook.edu

ABSTRACT

In this work, we investigate the problem of localizing RFID tags using a ranging method used in frequency-modulated radars. The idea is to exploit the phase change of the tag response due to frequency changes that normally happen as the RFID reader frequency hops. We demonstrate the general feasibility of this technique in ranging standard RFID tags using commodity readers. We then use it for a localization application – localizing shopping carts in supermarket aisles. We show that the ranging and localization accuracies are very good (median errors 5 cm and 10 cm respectively) even at distances over 4 m making the technique competitive with existing techniques that require more complex set up.

Categories and Subject Descriptors

C.3 [**Special-purpose and application-based systems (J.7)**]: Real-time and embedded systems, Signal processing systems; I.5.3 [**Pattern recognition**]: Clustering—*Similarity measures*

General Terms

Design

Keywords

RFID; localization; phase difference of arrival (PDOA); shopping cart tracking

1. INTRODUCTION AND RELATED WORK

RFID (Radio Frequency Identification) technology has matured over the years as a means for automatic, low-cost identification of objects at short ranges. RFID has been playing an increasingly bigger role in inventory management, logistics and access control. Typically, the RFID system consists of one or more readers and numerous tags attached to objects to be identified. Tags communicate with the reader using backscatter communications. Backscattering works by

modulating a continuous wave (CW) RF signal emitted by the reader and incident on the antenna of tag. The modulation is achieved simply by changing impedance levels seen by the antenna, thereby changing its reflection coefficient. The minimal intelligence needed to achieve this requires very little power and this power is supplied by the RF signal itself (in the case of so-called 'passive' tags). The reader is also able to interpret the modulated signal backscattered by the tag and can issue specific instructions to the tag about how to respond via standards-compliant protocols such as Class 1 Gen2.

Most applications of RFID can benefit tremendously from an ability to accurately localize the RFID tags attached to objects. related to the "Internet of Things." However, limited capability on the part of the RFID tags themselves limit the range of techniques that can be used and their accuracy. Much of the work so far has targeted using received signal strength (RSS) for localization either directly or indirectly (e.g., [10, 14]). However, use of RSS is notoriously unreliable as the tag orientation, antenna gain or multipath can influence the RSS significantly. Use of 'reference' tags [17] in the vicinity alleviates this issue to some extent, but this increases deployment effort and may not always be practical. Similar issues arise in using parameters that are indirectly related to RSS, such as read rate (fraction of tag read attempts that are successful). Recent efforts have thus focused on using other radio features such as angle-of-arrival (AoA) [2] or signal phase [15, 16, 4, 7, 11] for localization. Though these techniques tackle the orientation and gain problem for the most part and achieve a high degree of accuracy, multipath may still be an issue. The most serious limitation of these techniques is that they require complex set up, such as dense and carefully positioned antennas and/or profiling studies; but still provide limited read ranges.

In this work, we develop a localization technique that addresses the above limitations using a ranging method based on basic radar principles. The idea is to use *phase difference of signals in the frequency domain* to determine the distance between the reader antenna and the tag. Once ranging is done, the actual localization is straightforward and can use well-known trilateration principles using multiple antennas/readers. The ranging uses principles of frequency-modulated radar. Reflected CW signals from the tag at different frequencies will produce a phase differences depending on the difference between the frequencies (Δf, known) and the intervening distance (d, unknown). The distance d can be calculated by knowing the phase difference ($\Delta\phi$, measured). This technique is invariant to the orientation of the tags and immune to multipath for the most part. The basic principles do not depend on the orientation or RSS so long as the RSS is strong enough for the reader to successfully receive the signal from the tag. So long as a line-of-sight (LOS) is present, multipath is mitigated as frequency diversity is used.

While the above ranging principle (sometimes refered to as *frequency-domain phase-difference of arrival or FD-PDOA*) has been known for some time [11], thus far it was not practical to apply this technique to localize RFID tags using commercially available readers. But this bottleneck is removed now due to two key enablers. First, popularly used standards-compliant Class 1 Gen 2 tags use frequency diversity by default. Thus, many randomly chosen frequency channels (out of 50 possible) are enabled during the interrogation phase making application of FD-PDOA realistic in common deployments. By the FCC, regulation each channel must be used equally and channel occupancy is limited to 400 ms in any 10 second window. Second, current generation readers (e.g., ImpinJ's Speedway series, Motorola's FX series [6, 9]) allow reading of low level signal details (e.g., phase of the backscattered response) using standard API support [5] such as LLRP and customized protocols. Thus, measuring of phase no longer requires specialized equipments.

We specifically use the above ranging technique for a targeted problem – localizing shopping carts in a supermarket. Shopping cart localization is deemed important to track customers to assess their interests and also to deliver targeted ads.

In contrast with related approaches of shopping cart localization where active devices are used on the cart (such as RFID reader [18, 8] or Zigbee devices [3, 1]), the proposed method approach is significantly cost-effective. This is because the cart carries one or more passive tags only and thus does not need to use any battery. We believe that the proposed approach is useful in large supermarkets such as Walmart [13, 12] where significant RFID deployments are planned.

In the rest of this paper is organized as follows. In Section 2, we describe the preliminaries. In Section 3 we describe the experimental details and evaluation. Section 4 concludes the paper.

2. PRELIMINARIES

In this section, we describe the preliminaries of the FD-PDOA technique. See Figure 1. Assume, the transmitted CW from the reader has frequency f ($= \frac{c}{\lambda}$, where c is speed of light and λ is the wavelength). The distance between the reader and the tag is d. Then the phase of the received signal ϕ with respected to the transmitted signal is given by

$$\phi = \frac{2\pi}{\lambda} \times 2d = \frac{2\pi f}{c} \times 2d. \quad (1)$$

Sampling the phase at two different frequencies (f_1 and f_2) provides

$$\phi_1 - \phi_2 = \frac{4\pi}{c} d(f_1 - f_2). \quad (2)$$

Finally, solving for d gives

$$d = \frac{\Delta\phi}{\Delta f} \frac{c}{4\pi}. \quad (3)$$

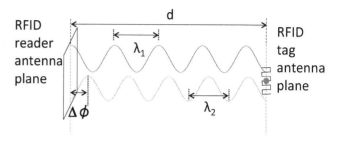

Figure 1: Bakscatter communication illustrating the phase difference-based ranging method.

Note that d is proportional to $\frac{\Delta\phi}{\Delta f}$. In commercial readers and standards compliant Class 1 Gen 2 tag environment, the *phase-frequency slope* $\frac{\Delta\phi}{\Delta f}$ can be constructed during the tag interrogation phase as the reader frequency hops in a random fashion, staying at each frequency for 400ms.

We have observed that due to experimental errors and phase uncertainties introduced by non-negligible antenna cable lengths a calibration factor α is needed for Equation 3. This calibration is done experimentally using the specific reader set up to be used:

$$d = \alpha \frac{\Delta\phi}{\Delta f} \frac{c}{4\pi}. \quad (4)$$

3. EXPERIMENTAL DETAILS AND EVALUATION

3.1 System Details

one or two linearly polarized directional antennas with beam-width approximately 120° for all experiments. The tags used are typical off-the-shelf Class 1 Gen 2. The reader works in the frequency band $902 - 928$ MHz, that is split into 50 channels of width 500 kHz, hopping between them randomly with a dwell time of shorter than 400 ms at each channel. Per FCC requirement each channel must be used in equal proportion.

Some experiments use a multi-reader environment. A tag can independently be interrogated by and respond to two different readers using standard anti-collision mechanisms to avoid conflict (e.g., use of orthogonal channels). Even if it is just being interrogated by only one reader, another in the vicinity can simply be in 'listen' mode and collect measurement samples. This provides more samples and improves localization efficiency noticeably. *Software:* The software runs on a Windows PC using C#. It connects to the RFID reader using the LLRP (Low Level Reader Protocol) protocol. Java/C/C++, No due to ImpinJ's

(a) Lab environment with shopping cart

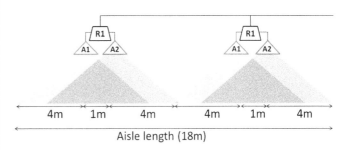

(b) Reader deployment

Figure 2: System setup for evaluation.

System Setup: The reader is mounted at the ceiling at the height of 3.75m with the antenna directed vertically downwards. A shopping aisle is simulated in the lab with wooden and metal shelves on the side. The tags are placed at an horizontal orientation (so that they receive the maximum possible signal) mounted on a shopping cart (height about 1m). See Figure 2(a). Note that this orientation is enough for testing as shopping carts can only rotate along a vertical axis in a normal use.

We have independently verified that the experimental results are invariant to the actual orientation of the tag so long as it remains horizontal facing the antenna. Otherwise, while the FD-PDOA technique does not fundamentally depend on the actual tag orientation, the tags may fail to respond in many channels when the incident RF signal is received at a slanted angle on the tag antenna. This is simply because the received signal at the tag may not be sufficient to 'wake up' the tag or the reflected signal is not strong enough for the reader to receive correctly. If many channels fail to respond, it introduces significant measurement noise and makes the slope calculation prone to error.

For the ranging experiments reported momentarily one reader with one antenna is sufficient. For the localization experiments reported at the end, we have used two readers each with two antennas mounted in a linear fashion along the center of the aisle. See Figure 2(b).

Note that we deal with two different but related distances. One is the actual reader-to-tag distance (d), measured from the center of the tag to the center of the reader antenna. The other is the 'floor-level distance,' which is the same distance, but projected horizontally on the floor. The floor distance is of practical use in our application, though the distance d is what is directly estimated.

3.2 Ranging by Estimating Phase-Frequency Slope

As a demonstration of the power of the technique we first show how the phase-frequency slope $\frac{\Delta\phi}{\Delta f}$ behaves at a specific distance d. For this demonstration, d is fixed such that the floor level tag-reader distance is 2 m. The tag is interrogated at each channel 1,000 times. The statistic of RSS and phase values recorded at the reader at different frequencies

are shown in Figure 3 with error bars showing the min-max range. (The two colors in the phase plot actually corresponds to the values seen at two different antennas that are separated by 1m.) Note the significant variations of RSS at different channels as well as variations within the same channel due to fading, for example. On the other hand, the phase is reasonably stable. Further note that the linearity of the $\frac{\Delta\phi}{\Delta f}$ relationship evident from the plot (Figure 3(b)). The slope of this line has a straightforward relationship to distance (Equation 3).

Note also that the $\frac{\Delta\phi}{\Delta f}$ line is in fact segmented. The segments repeat as half cycles in interval $[0, \pi]$ are completed as the frequency is increased.[1] Ideally, these line segments should be perfectly parallel. Any difference in slopes in the experimental data is solely due to measurement errors or impact of stray multipath, where a NLOS (Non-line-of-sight) path may dominate for certain frequencies. However, so long as a majority of the frequencies report the LOS path, the influence of the NLOS paths in the final estimate can be overridden (see below).

To determine the $\frac{\Delta\phi}{\Delta f}$ slope from the experimental data we use a sequence of simple data processing steps:

1. The median phase value of each frequency (channel) is chosen among those reported as representative.[2]

2. The phase-frequency values are clustered to identify the segments. Segments are then numbered 0, 1, 2, etc. with increasing frequency values.

3. All frequency values are 'translated' so that a *single* line is formed (as if aligning all the segments in a single line). This is done simply by adding $k\pi$ from the chosen phase value at step 1 for each frequency belonging to the k-th segment.

4. Finally, linear regression is used to determine the slope of this line. This slope determines the distance d per Equation 4.

9[1]The phase ϕ is assumed to vary between 0 and π only, as this is the way the reader reports the phase information. Phase values larger than π is reported as $2\pi - \phi$.

9[2]We experimented with other statistical measures, but median works quite well.

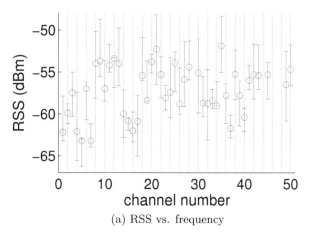

(a) RSS vs. frequency

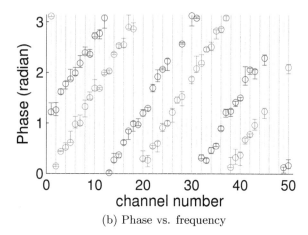

(b) Phase vs. frequency

Figure 3: RSS and phase (in radian) for the 50 channels for a specific (2 m) floor-level distance between the reader and the tag.

There are a few practical issues to consider. While the plots in Figure 3 use all channels, this may not be realistic always. Also, sometimes responses from specific channels may not be available (due to fading etc) even when these channels are scanned. From experience we have found that responses from at least 5 different channels are needed to establish a reasonable level of confidence on the value of the slope, though clearly more channels provide a higher degree of confidence in the slope estimation. For brevity, this analysis is not shown. Since channel dwell time is 400 ms, the tag (shopping cart) must be stationary for at least ($\approx$ 2s) for 5 different channels to be sampled. The need for accurate localization is the highest when the cart is stationary for a longer periods time, e.g., several seconds or longer. We believe that the 2s bound is acceptable for the application at hand. Furthermore, the dwell time can be shorten to increase the frequency of channel hopping, which results in faster decision on localization.

The above experiment is repeated at different floor-level distances. For each distance, different position of the cart is used. The phase-frequency slope (as determined above) is used to estimate first the reader-tag distance which in turn determines the floor-level distance. The CDF of the estimation error is shown in Figure 4. Note the median error is limited to about 5cm with 90-percentile error to about 15cm. This is competitive or better than the errors using other phase-based mechanisms recently reported in literature (e.g., recent work in [7]), while they require more complex set up and also provide limited range (up to only about 1m).

3.3 Motion Filtering

It is clear that when the shopping cart is in continuous motion, the phase responses will not form a straight line due to continuously changing location. The responses could be somewhat random. We have developed a simple heuristic to ignore these periods of motion so that all localizations concentrate on brief stationary periods when linear phase-frequency plots are possible. This 'motion filtering' continuously tracks the standard deviation of recently reported phase values for each frequency. When the average standard deviation falls within a threshold for at least 5 frequencies,

the distance is estimated and is continuously refined as more samples are collected.

3.4 Localization Performance

Finally, we employ the ranging technique described above to localize a shopping cart using the set up described in Figure 2. The two reader antennas for each reader makes independent range measurements and these measurements are combined using trilateration to localize the tag (shopping cart). Since the current set up is limited to only two readers, trilateration is possible only if the cart moved on a straight line along the center of the aisle. This is a limitation of our current setup and is not a limitation of the technique.

The results are shown in Figure 5, where five sets of tests are done at $0 - 4$m floor-level distances at 1m intervals (the actual reader-tag distance is higher as noted in the figure). The estimated distance d is plotted across actual distance. The error bars show the range (min-max) of errors for 100 tests performed for each distance. The median error is separately shown which is only about 10cm again demonstrating excellent localization performance.

4. CONCLUSIONS

While phase-based methods of localizing RFID tags have recently gained popularity, they all require careful and dense deployment of antennas or additional complex set up. We have demonstrated that a standard RFID set up can exploit phase to perform very accurate ranging just by using a single antenna by exploiting FM radar principles. The accuracy is competitive or better with better operating ranges seen in literature while requiring a straightforward set up. We have experimentally demonstrated median ranging accuracy of about 5 cm and localization accuracy of about 10 cm at distances over 4 m. Our ongoing work is focusing on deployment and refinement of the proposed method in realistic environments beyond the lab set up presented here.

5. ACKNOWLEDGMENTS

The authors acknowledge Akshay Athalye for discussions and technical help. The work is partially supported by NSF grants CNS-1354614 and CNS-1405740.

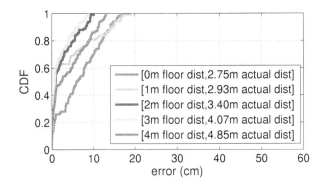

Figure 4: CDF of distance estimation error for different distances.

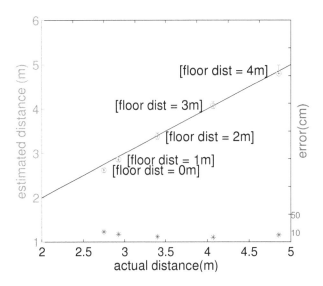

Figure 5: Localization performance at 5 different floor distances as shown.

6. REFERENCES

[1] T. Alhmiedat, G. Samara, and A. O. A. Salem. An indoor fingerprinting localization approach for zigbee wireless sensor networks. *CoRR*, abs/1308.1809, 2013.

[2] S. Azzouzi, M. Cremer, U. Dettmar, R. Kronberger, and T. Knie. New measurement results for the localization of UHF RFID transponders using an Angle of Arrival (AoA) approach. In *RFID (RFID), 2011 IEEE International Conference on*, pages 91–97, April 2011.

[3] S. Gai, E.-J. Jung, and B.-J. Yi. Localization algorithm based on zigbee wireless sensor network with application to an active shopping cart. In *Intelligent Robots and Systems (IROS 2014), 2014 IEEE/RSJ International Conference on*, pages 4571–4576, Sept 2014.

[4] C. Hekimian-Williams, B. Grant, X. Liu, Z. Zhang, and P. Kumar. Accurate localization of RFID tags using phase difference. In *RFID, 2010 IEEE International Conference on*, pages 89–96, April 2010.

[5] Impinj Corporation. SDK for RFID.

[6] Impinj Corporation. Speedway RFID reader series.

[7] T. Liu, L. Yang, Q. Lin, Y. Guo, and Y. Liu. Anchor-free Backscatter Positioning for RFID Tags with High Accuracy. In *INFOCOM*. IEEE, 2014.

[8] X. Lu, L. Xie, Y. Yin, W. Wang, B. Ye, and S. Lu. Efficient localization based on imprecise anchors in RFID system. In *Communications (ICC), 2014 IEEE International Conference on*, pages 142–147, June 2014.

[9] Motorola Solutions. FX RFID reader series.

[10] L. M. Ni, Y. Liu, Y. C. Lau, and A. P. Patil. LANDMARC: indoor location sensing using active RFID. In *Pervasive Computing and Communications, 2003. (PerCom 2003). Proceedings of the First IEEE International Conference on*, volume 0, pages 407–415, Los Alamitos, CA, USA, Mar. 2003. IEEE.

[11] P. Nikitin, R. Martinez, S. Ramamurthy, H. Leland, G. Spiess, and K. V. S. Rao. Phase based spatial identification of UHF RFID tags. In *RFID, 2010 IEEE International Conference on*, pages 102–109, April 2010.

[12] M. C. O'Connor. Can RFID save brick-and-mortar retailers after all? Fortune magazine, April 2014.

[13] P. Rosenblum. How walmart could solve its inventory problem and improve earnings. Forbes magazine, May 2014.

[14] L. Shangguan, Z. Li, Z. Yang, M. Li, and Y. Liu. OTrack: Order tracking for luggage in mobile RFID systems. In *INFOCOM*, pages 3066–3074. IEEE, 2013.

[15] J. Wang, F. Adib, R. Knepper, D. Katabi, and D. Rus. RF-compass: Robot Object Manipulation Using RFIDs. In *Proceedings of the 19th Annual International Conference on Mobile Computing & Networking*, MobiCom '13, pages 3–14, New York, NY, USA, 2013. ACM.

[16] J. Wang and D. Katabi. Dude, Where's My Card?: RFID Positioning That Works with Multipath and Non-line of Sight. In *Proceedings of the ACM SIGCOMM 2013 Conference on SIGCOMM*, SIGCOMM '13, pages 51–62, New York, NY, USA, 2013. ACM.

[17] Y. Zhao, Y. Liu, and L. M. Ni. VIRE: Active RFID-based localization using virtual reference elimination. In *Parallel Processing, 2007. ICPP 2007. International Conference on*, pages 56–56. IEEE, 2007.

[18] W. Zhu, J. Cao, Y. Xu, L. Yang, and J. Kong. Fault-Tolerant RFID Reader Localization Based on Passive RFID Tags. *Parallel and Distributed Systems, IEEE Transactions on*, 25(8):2065–2076, Aug 2014.

EasiPCC: Popularity-aware Collaborative Caching for Web Requests in Low-Duty-Cycle Sensor Networks *

Chenda Hou
Institute of Computing
Technology, Chinese Academy
of Sciences, Beijing 100190,
China
University of Chinese
Academy of Sciences, Beijing
100190, China
houchenda@ict.ac.cn

Dong Li
Institute of Computing
Technology, Chinese Academy
of Sciences, Beijing 100190,
China
lidong@ict.ac.cn

Li Cui
Institute of Computing
Technology, Chinese Academy
of Sciences, Beijing 100190,
China
lcui@ict.ac.cn

ABSTRACT

The lightweight RESTful protocols, such as CoAP, have been proposed to provide web service on resource constrained devices. However, these devices normally operate in battery and work in sleeping mode most time to prolong lifetime. Consequently it is difficult to maintain persistent end-to-end connection and leads to the high access delay for web requests. In this paper, we propose a collaborative caching scheme to solve this problem. Initially we define sleep probability based on the feature of low-duty-cycle networks to decide what data to cache. Then we introduce the definition of node popularity, which focuses nodes that are on the request forwarding public paths and forward most web requests. A centralized algorithm is presented based on the theory of gravity center to find which nodes to cache. Finally, we propose a cache discovery method. Experiments show that our caching scheme significantly improves the performance of web data access in low-duty-cycle sensor networks.

Categories and Subject Descriptors

C.2.1 [**Computer-Communication Networks**]: Network Architecture and Design—*Wireless Communication*

General Terms

Algorithms, Performance, Design.

Keywords

Node Popularity; Web of Things; Low-Duty-Cycle Networks

*This work is supported by the Strategic Priority Research Program of the Chinese Academy of Sciences under Grant No.XDA06010403, the International Science and Technology Cooperation Program of China under Grant No. 2013D-FA10690, and CCF-Tencent Open Research Fund.

MSWiM'15, November 02-06, 2015, Cancun, Mexico
Copyright 2015 ACM. ISBN 978-1-4503-3762-5/15/11 ...$15.00
DOI: http://dx.doi.org/10.1145/2811587.2811626 .

1. INTRODUCTION

Recent advances in Wireless Sensor Network (WSN) technology and the use of the traditional Internet protocols in resource constrained devices have radically expanded the Internet application to cyber-physical area. This revolution builds on the basis of 6LoWPAN and RPL standard, which are used as the networking technology for integrating embedded devices and systems into the Internet. Networking alone, however, does not make the Internet useful. Applications today depend on the Representational State Transfer (REST) architecture style to create Web service. Thus Web-based Sensor Networks (WbSN) or Web of Things (WoT)[1][2] is proposed to apply traditional web service to resource-constrained devices and networks. The Constrained Application Protocol (CoAP) [3] was proposed for building an efficient RESTful web application in resource constrained environments. SeaHTTP [4] extended HTTP with the new methods of BRANCH and COMBINE to support group communication in WbSN.

However, the use of web service in resource-constrained networks is not straightforward as a consequence of the differences between Internet applications and WbSN systems. There is still one critical problem that constrained devices are generally powered by battery. To prolong lifetime, these devices need to work in low-duty-cycle mode for most time. Once devices are in sleeping state, it is difficult to maintain persistent end-to-end connection. Web users will suffer high access delay actually. Therefore it is greatly essential to improve the performance of data accessibility and reduce the web request-response latency in WbSN.

In this paper, we propose the cooperative caching scheme to promote the web access performance. Firstly we define the sleep probability of next time based on the model of low-duty-cycle networks to decide what data to cache. Furthermore we cache data at nodes that are on the request forwarding public paths and forward most web requests while these nodes will not enter dormant state immediately based on the computation of sleep probability. To find those nodes with the highest popularity, a centralized algorithm is presented based on the theory of gravity center. We also provide a three-level cache discovery method, including local, neighbor and path cache discovery. Our experiments show that our approach greatly improves the performance of data access and reduce the access delay.

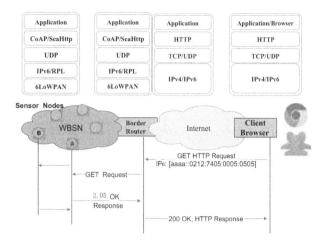

Figure 1: The protocol stacks of Web-based Sensor Networks.

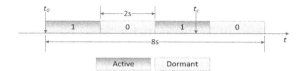

Figure 2: A low-duty-cycle network model.

2. WBSN SYSTEM OVERVIEW

To implement a complete WbSN system, compaction IP protocols, such as 6LoWPAN[5], have been presented to offer IPv6 adapt layer to enable IPv6 connectivity in resource-constrained devices. Moreover, IETF proposes IPv6 Routing Protocol for LLNs (RPL)[6]. Because Transmission Control Protocol (TCP) is heavy and complicate, it is not applicable in resource-constrained devices. So WbSN adopts UDP as the transport protocol generally. In the application layer, some RESTful protocols, such as CoAP and SeaHttp, are presented to implement lightweight HTTP. The protocol stacks of WbSN system are illustrated in Figure 1.

As shown in Figure 1, web users can send a HTTP request with a browser to the URL on one sensor node, and receive a response message with sensing data. In this way, the traditional sensor network is integrated into the Internet seamlessly. Thus web users not only can derive the information on the Internet, but also be aware of the physical information in the real world. However, because it is difficult to maintain persistent end to end connections, WbSN systems cannot work normally with the limit of the performance in data access, such as high access delay. Considering this, we give our caching solution in following parts.

3. CACHING SCHEME

3.1 Low-duty-cycle Model

Before illustrating our caching scheme in detail, we introduce the network model and assumptions used in this work. Especially, we concentrate on the low-duty-cycle model for resource-constrained networks.

Suppose there is a web-based sensor network of N sensor nodes, which is running on the top of 6LoWPAN and RPL portocols. Each sensor node has two possible states: an active state and a dormant state. An active node is able to acquire sensing data, transmit a packet or receive a packet. A dormant node turns all its function modules off except a timer to wake itself up. We assume that all nodes have their own working schedules, which are shared with neighboring nodes. Thus a node can transmit a packet at any time, but can only receive a packet when it is active.

Our low-duty-cycle model is based on the work [7]. Firstly, suppose T is the working period of the whole network. If different nodes have different working period, T can be multiple of the periods of all nodes. Then the cycle time T can be divided into a number of time units of length τ where τ is appropriate for a round-trip transmission time. Then each node picks one or more time units as its active state. We use '1' represents the active state and '0' is the dormant states respectively. The ith node's working schedule can then be represented as $< w_i, \tau >$ where w_i is a string of '1's and '0's denoting the schedule and τ is the length of each time unit. For example, $<1010, 2s>$ where T is 8s and is divided into 4 time units, each of which is 2s long. A node with schedule $<1010, 2s>$ is active during the first 2s and third 2s, dormant during the second 2s and the fourth 2s.

With this model, the sleep probability of next time can be computed and represented by the number of time units. We define P_s as the sleep probability of next time. The definition of P_s is $P_s = (t_w - t_m)/T$, where t_m is the relative time $tm = (t_c - t_0) \bmod T$, t_c is the current time and t_0 is the initial time. So t_m represents the relative time in one period T. As shown in the example in Figure 2, $<1010, 2s>$ where T is 8s and is divided into 4 time units, each of which is 2s long. In the example t_0=3s and t_c=16.7s, so $t_m = (t_c - t_0) \bmod T$=(16.7-3)mod 8=5.7s. The next dormant time t_w is 6s, then $P_s = (t_w - t_m)/T = (6-5.7)/8=3.75\%$. Therefore P_s represents the sleep probability of next time and the larger P_s is, the faster the node will not be active and go into dormant state quickly.

The sleep probability of next time is the key factor to decide what data to cache and where to cache. Intuitively the more likely one node will be dormant, it is more necessary that the sensing data in this node is stored in other nodes to implement collaborative caching. On the contrary, if one node will be in dormant state quickly, the node should not be selected as the caching location. In next part, we propose our method of selecting caching locations based on the sleep probability of next time P_s.

3.2 Caching Locations

How to identify suitable caching locations is also a critical problem in the caching scheme. In traditional web systems, data can be cached everywhere because each node can maintain online state. But sensing data had better to be cached in specific nodes due to the unstable state of nodes in WbSN. Furthermore, given that different data items have different popularity and each node has limited space for caching, we only cache data at nodes that are on the request public forwarding paths and forward many common requests.

3.2.1 Node Popularity

In WbSN the routing protocol is generally based on RPL protocol, which is organized by one dynamic tree topology. Based on the tree topology, we define node connectivity as

C_i, which is equal to the number of the nodes in the node i's child tree. The meaning of C_i illustrates that the more child nodes the node i has, the greater the likelihood the node i forwards requests to its child nodes. In addition, C_i may be affected by the distance between the node i and the border-router. Intuitively, the system can be benefit in the performance of access delay from caching data in those nodes near the border-router.

Also we use F_i to represent the number of forwarding requests for node i in the request history. F_i reflects the popularity of the node i in the network according to the users' interest. Therefore, we define *Node Popularity* as $H_i(n)$ with C_i and F_i in Equation (1):

$$H_i(n) = \begin{cases} C_i & n = 0 \\ \left(\frac{C_i}{H_i(n-1)}\right)^{F_i(n)+1} \cdot \lambda^{F_i(n)} \cdot H_i(n-1) + & \\ (1 - \lambda^{F_i(n)+1}) \cdot F_i(n) & n > 0 \end{cases}$$
(1)

Where C_i is the node i connectivity, $F_i(n)$ is the number of forwarding requests across node i in the nth cycle, λ is a weighing factor which ranges from 0 to 1. When $F_i(n)$ approaches a big number or infinity , $\lambda^{F_i(n)}$ approaches 0. So $H_i(n)=F_i(n)$ and $H_i(n)$ is determined by $F_i(n)$. In other words, the number of forwarding requests is much more crucial when the node i forwards many requests in the cycle. On the other hand, if $F_i(n)$ approaches 0, $\lambda^{F_i(n)}$ approaches 1. So $H_i(n)=C_i$ and $H_i(n)$ comes back to the value of C_i. When there is no any request across the node i, the node popularity is based on the node connectivity.

Now we have the definition of node popularity H_i by considering both the node connectivity and forwarding frequency over a history of request arrivals. Since constrained networks have to be operated at a very-low-duty-cycle to prolong device lifetimes, the computation of the node popularity should be combined with the sleep probability of next time P_s. This is because that some nodes will be in dormant state immediately and these nodes should not be responsible for caching data. In Section 3.1, we have built the model of low-duty-cycle networks and define the value P_s: the sleep probability of next time. So we combine the value P_s and H_n for the computation of the final node popularity H_e, as shown in Equation (2).

$$H_e = \alpha \cdot \frac{1}{P_s} + \beta \cdot H_i$$
(2)

where α and β are weighted coefficients and meet the condition $\alpha \geq 0$, $\beta \geq 0$, $\alpha + \beta = 1$. α and β are also empirical values, where we set $\alpha = \beta = 0.5$. Thus according to the definition of H_e , it reveals that the node popularity is negatively associated with the sleep probability of next time, which illustrates that if one node will be in dormant state quickly, the node should not be selected as the caching location.

3.2.2 The Center of Nodes' Popularity

Based on nodes' popularity, we can select some specific nodes as the network centers to cache data. These center nodes should be easily accessed by other nodes and significantly popular for users' web requests. The cache locations should be selected based on the node popularity defined in Subsection 3.2.1. Intuitively the actual cache locations had better to be close to the nodes with relatively high node

popularity. This observation is similar to the character of gravity center, since the gravity center is close to the regions with high gravity and far away to the regions with low gravity. Therefore our basic idea is inspired by the theory of computing the center of gravity. We think the value of node popularity as one node's gravity and the general popularity distribution of the network can be reflected by H_i. Let x_i and y_i be the coordinates of node i's position. Therefore the center of nodes' popularity H_e is computed as the average of nodes' position weighted by their own popularity H_i using the classic computing Equation (3).

$$H_e = (Hx_e, Hy_e) \Leftrightarrow x_e = \frac{\sum h_i x_i}{\sum h_i}, y_e = \frac{\sum h_i y_i}{\sum h_i}$$
(3)

When we obtain the center of nodes' popularity, such as the node e, we can use the nearest node i for node e as the first center node to cache data. Then the node i will be not included in next computation. The centralized algorithm is illustrated in Algorithm 1.

Algorithm 1 Popularity-based Caching Location Selection Algorithm

---

Input: All nodes' popularity H_i and position coordinates (x_i, y_i)
Output: The center nodes on popularity: P_j, $j = 1, 2, \ldots, k$
1: Initialize variables H_{xs}, H_{ys}, H_s
2: Each node collects its own popularity information in the first cycle
3: At the end of the first cycle, all nodes send its own popularity H_i and position coordinates (x_i, y_i) to the border-router
4: Compute k nodes of $H_e(x_e, y_e)$ in border-router
5: **for** $j=1$ to k **do**
6:    **for all** each node i in set U **do**
7:       $H_{xs} = H_{xs} + H_i \times x_i$
8:       $H_{ys} = H_{ys} + H_i \times y_i$
9:       $H_s = H_s + H_i$
10:    **end for**
11:    $H_{xe}=H_{xs}/H_s$, $H_{ye}=H_{ys}/H_s$
12:    Compute the nearest distance from node i to node e, mark the node i as one center node P_j
13:    Remove node i from the node set U
14: **end for**
15: **return** The center nodes set $P = P_j, j = 1, 2, \ldots, k$

3.3 Cache Discovery

This subsection introduces the process of cache discovery, which is based on three cache tables: local cache table, neighbor cache table and path cache table. To start with users send a web request to the target server node and the request packets are forwarded along the RPL routing paths. When the request arrives at the some hop, it first looks for the data item in its own cache. If there is a local cache miss, it checks if the data item is cached in the neighbor nodes from the neighbor nodes. When one node receives the request and has the data item in its local cache, it will send a response to the requester to acknowledge that it has the data item. In case of a neighbor cache miss, the request is forwarded to the neighbor along the routing path. Before forwarding a request, each node along the path searches the

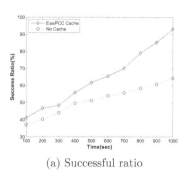
(a) Successful ratio

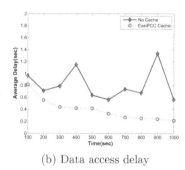
(b) Data access delay

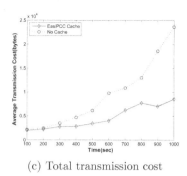
(c) Total transmission cost

Figure 3: Performance of data access with different experiment duration

item in its local cache or neighbors as described above. If the data item is not found on the nodes along the routing path, the request finally reaches the original server nodes and the data source sends back the requested data.

4. PERFORMANCE EVALUATION

In this section, we provide the simulation results to evaluate the performance of our EasiPCC Caching scheme, which is compared with NoCache scheme. NoCache scheme does not make use of any caching technique and each request is only responded by data source node. We concentrate on the following metrics for evaluations:(i)Successful ratio, the ratio of requests being satisfied with the response data.(ii)Data access delay, the average delay for obtaining responses to requests.(iii)Total transmission cost, the total transmission cost in the network. Each experiment is iterated multiple times with randomly generated data and requests for statistical convergence.

We implement the EasiPCC Caching scheme with the Contiki Operating System and Cooja simulation tool in Sky platform. Sky is a typical example of a low-cost sensor node used in resource-constrained networks. Our proposed EasiPCC Caching scheme is built on CoAP protocol, while NoCache scheme is the standard CoAP implementation in Contiki. Both of two caching scheme use UDP as transport layer protocol and UIP with 6LoWPAN as networking layer protocol. In the simulations, we build a 5-hop network using IEEE 802.15.4 in Cooja. The duty cycle is set by the channel check rate in ContikiMac. In this experiment, we set channel check rate is 4Hz, which is about 2% of the duty cycle ratio. One CoAP client sends one request every 5 second and the payload size of one request is 80 bytes.

Figure 3 shows the performance of data access with different experiment duration. As we increase the experiment time from 100s to 1,000s, the success ratio of both schemes is improved, because the network has built the stable routing tree and the number of retransmission is reduced in Figure 3(a). However, the improved ratio is increased at a significantly faster rate (130.45%) in EasiPCC scheme than in No-Cache scheme. The reason is that EasiPCC scheme caches data at popular nodes close to the border-router, resulting in a higher hit rate and lower latency. Similarly, EasiPCC scheme reduces the average access delay by 48.6% than NoCache scheme as illustrated in Figure 3(b). In NoCache scheme, each requests need to be routed to the data source nodes, which adds delivery and forwarding delay. EasiPCC scheme can eliminate many of the delays from the No-

Cache scheme with intermediate caching nodes along the common forwarding paths. Finally, in Figure 3(c), NoCache scheme suffers a very high transmission cost. Web requests in NoCache scheme traverses many hops, resulting in a large amount of forwarding packets, while EasiPCC scheme uses intermediate nodes for caching, thus shortening requests forwarding paths and lowering the overall transmission cost.

5. CONCLUSIONS

We propose EasiPCC, a popularity-aware collaborative caching scheme in low-duty-cycle sensor networks to improve performance of data access. Our caching scheme is built on top of node popularity. Considering low-duty-cycle networks, the sleep probability is proposed to make node popularity more reasonable and accuracy. Then the centralized algorithm is presented based on the theory of gravity center for the caching location selection. Finally, we propose a cache discovery method. Experiments show that our caching scheme significantly improves the performance of web data access in low-duty-cycle sensor networks.

6. REFERENCES

[1] W. S. Jang, W. M. Healy, and M. J. Skibniewski. Wireless sensor networks as part of a web-based building environmental monitoring system. *Automation in Construction*, 17(6), 729-736, 2008.

[2] D. Guinard, V. Trifa, E. Wilde. A resource oriented architecture for the Web of Things. *In Proc. of IEEE Internet of Things 2010*, pages 1-8, 2010.

[3] C. Bormann, A. P. Castellani, Z. Shelby. CoAP: An application protocol for billions of tiny Internet nodes. *Internet Computing*, 16(2): 62-67, 2012.

[4] C. D. Hou, D. Li, J. F. Qiu, H. L. Shi, and L. Cui. SeaHttp: A Resource-Oriented Protocol to Extend REST Style for Web of Things. *Journal of Computer Science and Technology*, 29(2), 205-215, 2014.

[5] G.Mulligan. The 6LoWPAN architecture. *Proc. of the 4th workshop on Embedded networked sensors*. 78-82, 2007.

[6] T. Winter, P. Thubert, A. Brandt, J. Hui, R. Kelsey, P. Levis, K. Pister, R. Struik, and J. Vasseur, RPL: IPv6 Routing Protocol for Low power and Lossy Networks, *Internet Draft, draftietf-roll-rpl-19*, 2011.

[7] Y. Gu and T. He. Data Forwarding in Extremely Low Duty-Cycle Sensor Networks with Unreliable Communication Links. In *SenSys'07*, 2007.

Anticipatory Admission Control and Resource Allocation for Media Streaming in Mobile Networks

Nicola Bui[12], Ilaria Malanchini[3], Joerg Widmer[1]
[1]IMDEA Networks Institute, Leganes (Madrid), Spain
[2]UC3M, Leganes (Madrid), Spain
[3]Bell Labs, Alcatel-Lucent (Stuttgart), Germany

ABSTRACT

The exponential growth of media streaming traffic will have a strong impact on the bandwidth consumption of the future wireless infrastructure. One key challenge is to deliver services taking into account the stringent requirements of mobile video streaming, e.g., the users' expected Quality-of-Service. Admission control and resource allocation can strongly benefit from the use of anticipatory information such as the prediction of future user's demand and expected channel gain. In this paper, we use this information to formulate an optimal admission control scheme that maximizes the number of accepted users into the system with the constraint that not only the current but also the expected demand of all users must be satisfied. Together with the optimal set of accepted users, the optimal resource scheduling is derived. In order to have a solution that can be computed in a reasonable time, we propose a low complexity heuristic. Numerical results show the performance of the proposed scheme with respect to the state of the art.

Categories and Subject Descriptors

C.2.3 [**Computer Systems Organization**]: Networks—*Network management*

General Terms

Prediction, Resource Allocation, Admission Control, Mobile Networks

Keywords

Anticipatory networking; Optimization; Multi-user

1. INTRODUCTION

Many factors contribute to the exponential growth of mobile traffic and multimedia contents will be the dominant component among the causes of this growth, e.g. [1,28]. In this paper we investigate prediction based media streaming

in mobile networks and we discuss admission control and resource allocation.

The quality of a media stream is characterized by the following key performance indicators (KPIs) [10]: (i) streaming continuity and (ii) average stream quality. The former is assumed to have higher priority, since in general interruptions may jeopardize the comprehension of the content and therefore are perceived as the worst quality degradation. The latter is optimized with lower priority, since, even if it has a weaker impact on user's perception, users appreciate when a certain agreed quality-of-service (QoS) is guaranteed. In this paper we consider it to be directly proportional to the stream bitrate [19].

An additional characteristic of prediction based optimization is that the prediction reliability varies in time and, usually, decreases as the prediction horizon length grows [7]. Therefore, anticipatory optimization schemes should consider this either explicitly in the problem formulation [18] or evaluate the impact of prediction error a posteriori [3]. Here we focus on joint admission control and resource allocation with perfect system state prediction to obtain upper bounds on the achievable gains. The extension to imperfect knowledge (e.g. [9]) is left for future work.

We follow a lexicographic approach where, first, we maximize the number of users that are served with guaranteed QoS for the whole duration of the media stream, minimizing the total interruption time, and maximizing the streaming quality. Thus, the streaming requests that cannot be scheduled with guaranteed quality must wait for the system to have enough resources for them to start streaming. Furthermore, we assume that it is always preferable to admit a new user in the system than increasing the quality of a user who is already admitted and the streaming continuity is always preferred to extra quality.

The contributions of our work are the following:

- mixed integer linear program (MILP) formulation of the joint admission control and resource allocation problem;

- online algorithm based on linear programming (LP) and binary search that allows for a very fast solution computation;

- trace-based simulation discussing optimality and complexity of the proposed approach as well as the system performance.

We validate our approach using trace based simulation obtained from real measurement data collected by the MOMENTUM project [13] in Berlin. We show that our online solution closely approximates the results achieved by the MILP formulation and dramatically reduces the computational time.

The rest of the paper is structured as follows: section 2 reviews the state of the art on anticipatory networking solutions, section 3 introduces the mathematical notation and the optimization problem, section 4 describes our proposed approximate solution, section 5 illustrates our evaluation campaign, and section 6 provides our conclusions.

2. RELATED WORKS

Anticipatory optimization techniques are motivated by a series of seminal papers, such as [23, 26], which discuss the predictability of human mobility patterns and the link between mobility and communication. Shafiq et al. [26] studied mobile network traffic and its spatio-temporal correlation with mobility patterns. Similarly, Ahmed et al. [4] studied network user habits in terms of content: the study links content requests and user categories, aiming to their prediction.

The predictability of network capacity and the achievable rate of mobile users have been extensively studied in the literature. These studies range from short term prediction using filtering techniques [24, 25], to medium and long term forecasting solutions [12, 20] accounting for position and trajectory estimates. We contributed to the literature with a general model [7] for predicted rates in mobile networks accounting for prediction uncertainties, and we use the model to devise single user optimal resource allocation policies [9].

For what concerns the state of the art on prediction based network optimization, in what follows we review a few of the papers that are more closely related to our current work.

Majid et al. [17] and Koutsakis et al. [16] exploited medium-long term average prediction of the users' achievable rate to devise call admission control and resource allocation techniques, respectively. While the former is more focused on DiffServ system [6], the latter addressed specifically multimedia traffic in broadband mobile networks. The present work differs from these early papers as well as more recent approaches [27], since we exploit rate fluctuations on a shorter time scale instead of using averages.

More recently, Dräxler and Karl [11] tackled multimedia traffic optimization by devising a different problem formulation that considered an objective function that combined stream interruption time and average quality. The proposed schemes choose when to download a given content segment and at which quality among a discrete set of qualities. In this paper we obtain a simpler formulation by considering continuous quality and by means of approximations. This allows us to include in our objective function both admission control and resource allocation.

Abou-zeid et al. [2, 3] develop a MILP formulation of a similar problem to obtain an optimal resource allocation and to increase energy efficiency. As other prior work, these papers do not consider admission control and thus they cannot enforce Quality-of-Service in the system.

A different approach is taken in [15] and [8], which study different algorithms to solve the resource allocation problem. These approaches aim at finding practical solutions that do not require commercial solvers and can execute in real-time even with non-linear objective functions. In addition, complete solutions, such as [18], integrate prediction techniques and optimization algorithms to solve the resource allocation

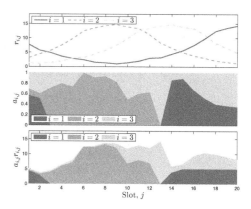

Figure 1: An example of achievable rates $r_{i,j}$ (top), assignments $a_{i,j}$ (center) and obtained rates $a_{i,j}r_{i,j}$ (bottom) in a 3-user scenario.

problem or study optimal video transcoding [5] for admission control and scheduling.

Compared to the aforementioned solutions, this paper proposes a different perspective of the network optimization problem as we enforce QoS by means of admission control. In addition, we propose low-complexity solutions that can be used for online optimization, which require the output to be updated within a short time.

3. PROBLEM DEFINITION

The admission control and resource allocation problem can be modeled as a centralized decision making problem, where a set $\mathcal{N}$ of N users share a given quantity of network resources. Prediction is assumed to be perfect over a set $\mathcal{T}$ of T time slots. In the following, we consider slot duration $t = 1$, thus data rate and download size can be used interchangeably. In the rest of the paper we use the following assumptions: (a) the future knowledge is perfect and (b) the average video bitrate is continuous between 0 and q_M (e.g., by averaging over segments of different quality [22]).

We consider the following input parameters, all of which defined for each user $i \in \mathcal{N}$ and slot $j \in \mathcal{T}$:
• Predicted achievable download rate $r_{i,j} \in [0, r_M]$ is the prediction of the rate a user would achieve if no other user is scheduled. r_M is the maximum achievable data rate.
• Minimum requirement $d_{i,j} \in [0, q_M]$ is the minimum amount of bytes needed in a given slot to stream the content at the minimum bitrate with no interruptions.
• Maximum extra video bitrate $u_{i,j} \in [0, q_M]$, is the maximum amount of additional bytes that can be used in a given slot to obtain the maximum content bitrate.

The problem is characterized by the following variables:
• Resource assignment $a_{i,j} \in [0, 1]$ represents the average fraction of resources assigned to user i in slot j. In each slot, each user can be assigned at most the total available rate, $0 \leq a_{i,j} \leq 1$, and the sum cannot exceed the total available resources, $0 \leq \sum_{i \in \mathcal{N}} a_{i,j} \leq 1$. Figure 1 shows an example with $N = 3$ and $T = 20$. In the top graph the achievable rates are plotted independently. In the center plot, a possible resource assignment is visualized by stacking the fraction of resources assigned to each of the users $a_{i,j}$ on top of each other. In the bottom graph, the cell capacity variation is addressed by stacking the product of the achievable rate and the fraction of assigned resources $a_{i,j}r_{i,j}$.

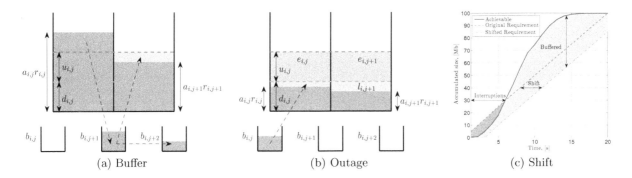

| (a) Buffer | (b) Outage | (c) Shift |

Figure 2: Three examples of the system quantities: 2(a) exemplifies the buffer usage over two subsequent slots; 2(b) shows lateness and extra quality outage examples; 2(c) illustrates the impact of pre-buffering.

- Buffer state $b_{i,j} \in [0, b_M]$ tracks the amount of bytes stored in the buffer and b_M is the buffer size in bytes.
- Pre-buffering time (or waiting time) $w_{i,k} \in \{0,1\}$ with $k \in \{1, \ldots, T+1\}$ defines when the actual playing of the content starts: there must be a single starting point ($\sum_{k=1}^{T+1} w_{i,k} = 1, \forall i \in \mathcal{N}$). Thus user i will wait for $W_i = (\text{argmax}_k w_{i,k}) - 1$ slots where she can only fill the buffer. This waiting implies the requirement sequence has to be shifted to later slots. Thus, in slot j user i is obtaining the rate $a_{i,j} r_{i,j}$ and should satisfy the shifted requirements $\overrightarrow{d_{i,j}} = \sum_{k=1}^{T+1} D_{i,j,k} w_{i,k}$ and $\overrightarrow{u_{i,j}} = \sum_{k=1}^{T+1} U_{i,j,k} w_{i,k}$, where D and U are $N \times T \times T+1$ matrices whose vectors $\mathbf{d_{i,k}} = \{\mathbf{0_{k-1}}, d_{i,1}, \ldots, d_{i,T-k}\}$ and $\mathbf{u_{i,k}} = \{\mathbf{0_{k-1}}, u_{i,1}, \ldots, d_{i,T-k}\}$ are shifted versions of the original requirements, where we used bold fonts to identify vectors and $\mathbf{0_k}$ is a null vector of size k.
- Interruption time[1] (or lateness) $l_{i,j} \in [0, q_M]$ is the missing data to fulfill the minimum content requirement $\overrightarrow{d_{i,j}}$:

$$l_{i,j} = [\overrightarrow{d_{i,j}} - b_{i,j} - a_{i,j} r_{i,j}]_0^{\overrightarrow{d_{i,j}}} \tag{1}$$

where $[x]_a^b = \min\{\max\{x, a\}, b\}$ is a bounding operator that forces the undelivered quantity to be greater than zero and smaller than the requirement in the slot.

- Extra quality outage $e_{i,j} \in [0, q_M]$ is the amount of data missing to obtain the content at the maximum bitrate $\overrightarrow{u_{i,j}}$,

$$e_{i,j} = [\overrightarrow{u_{i,j}} + \overrightarrow{d_{i,j}} - l_{i,j} - b_{i,j} - a_{i,j} r_{i,j}]_0^{\overrightarrow{u_{i,j}}}. \tag{2}$$

Figure 2(a) provides a graphical example of the buffer usage for a single user over two subsequent slots. Starting from an empty buffer, the obtained rate $a_{i,j} r_{i,j}$ is used to satisfy the current requirements and to buffer content for the next slot. The light area of the second slot highlights the fraction of content that has been previously buffered. Whether the buffer contains data to guarantee continuous streaming or extra quality is a key decision in the system and plays a critical role in the following optimization.

Figure 2(b) shows a two slot example where the user does not obtain a rate sufficient to satisfy the requirements: in the first slot this is compensated by the buffer, but this is not possible in the second slot resulting in an interruption of the streaming. Thus, the figure shows in light red the quality

outage and in light green the missing minimum requirements in the second slot.

Figure 2(c) shows the cumulative download size and requirements according to the second user of the example of Figure 1: a waiting time $w_2 = 3$ moves the original requirements (red dashed line) towards the right by 3 slots (green dot-dashed line), avoiding streaming interruptions in the first six slots (red area between the original requirements and the obtained rates, blue solid line). Since content duration can be longer than T, a non-empty buffer is required at the end of the optimization window: in particular, we require the buffer to contain the minimum between the initial amount and the remaining size of the content.

In each slot j user i receives $a_{i,j} r_{i,j}$, which can be used either to satisfy the requirements in the current slot or to fill the buffer for later use. Thus we can write the following equation that describes the next buffer state:

$$b_{i,j+1} = b_{i,j} + a_{i,j} r_{i,j} - \overrightarrow{d_{i,j}} + l_{i,j} - \overrightarrow{u_{i,j}} + e_{i,j} \tag{3}$$

which means the buffer of user i in slot $j+1$ is obtained from the previous buffer $b_{j,i}$ by adding the received data $a_{i,j} r_{i,j}$ and subtracting the minimum requirements $\overrightarrow{d_{i,j}} - l_{i,j}$ and the extra quality $\overrightarrow{u_{i,j}} - e_{i,j}$[2]. Finally, we define $b_{i,0}$ as the initial status of the buffer of user i.

In addition, we introduce two KPIs that we will use to build the objective function for our problem. Namely, we define the fraction of continuous streaming time $\lambda_i \in [0,1]$ and the fraction of the extra quality obtained $\theta_i \in [0,1]$ as:

$$\lambda_i = \frac{1}{T} \sum_{k \in \mathcal{T}} \left(1 - l_{i,k} \overrightarrow{d'_{i,k}} \right) \tag{4}$$

$$\theta_i = \frac{1}{T} \sum_{k \in \mathcal{T}} \left(1 - e_{i,k} \overrightarrow{u'_{i,k}} \right), \tag{5}$$

where

$$\overrightarrow{d'_{i,j}} = \begin{cases} 1/\overrightarrow{d_{i,j}} & \overrightarrow{d_{i,j}} > 0 \\ 0 & \overrightarrow{d_{i,j}} = 0 \end{cases}$$

$$\overrightarrow{u'_{i,j}} = \begin{cases} 1/\overrightarrow{u_{i,j}} & \overrightarrow{u_{i,j}} > 0 \\ 0 & \overrightarrow{u_{i,j}} = 0 \end{cases}. \tag{6}$$

---

[1]Since receiving less data than the minimum requirement causes an interruption in the streaming, we use the effect instead of the cause to define this quantity. However, the actual interruption time is the ratio between missing and minimum requirement in a slot.

[2]Normalization between rates in a slot and amount of data is not required, because we assumed the slot length $t = 1$.

Note that when $\overrightarrow{d_{i,j}} = 0$ $(\overrightarrow{u'_{i,j}} = 0)$ the interruption time $l_{i,j}$ (the extra quality outage $e_{i,j}$) is necessarily equal to 0, hence the substitutions of Eq. (6) are consistent.

In order to guarantee a given QoS we consider two constraints, the minimum continuous play time λ_i^* and the minimum average quality θ_i^*, defined so that $\lambda_i \geq (T - W_i)\lambda_i^*/T$ and $\theta_i \geq (T - W_i)\theta_i^*/T$.

These constraints can be seen as contractual agreements that must be enforced while the content is being streamed and they change the optimization problem from a best effort resource allocation solutions where the KPIs are maximized to a joint admission control and resource allocation approach where quality of service can be guaranteed.

Finally, we build our objective function to, in order of decreasing importance, (i) minimize the aggregate waiting time of the system $(\sum_{k \in \mathcal{N}} W_k)$, (ii) maximize the total continuous streaming time $(\sum_{k \in \mathcal{N}} \lambda_k)$ and (iii) maximize the total extra quality $(\sum_{k \in \mathcal{N}} \theta_k)$. Consequently, we obtain the following **MILP formulation**:

$$\underset{A,B,L,E,W}{\text{maximize}} \quad \sum_{k \in \mathcal{N}} (K(\lambda_k - W_k) + \theta_k) \qquad (7)$$

$$\text{subject to:} \quad a_{i,j} \geq 0; \quad \sum_{k \in \mathcal{N}} a_{k,j} \leq 1$$

$$\lambda_i \geq (T - W_i)\lambda_i^*/T; \quad \theta_i \geq (T - W_i)\theta_i^*/T$$

$$l_{i,j} \geq 0; \quad e_{i,j} \geq 0; \quad b_{i,j} \leq b_M$$

$$l_{i,j} \geq \overrightarrow{d_{i,j}} - a_{i,j}r_{i,j} - b_{i,j}$$

$$e_{i,j} \geq \overrightarrow{u_{i,j}} - a_{i,j}r_{i,j} - b_{i,j} + \overrightarrow{d_{i,j}} - l_{i,j}$$

$$\forall i \in \mathcal{N}; j \in \mathcal{T}$$

Eqns. (3), (4) and (5).

Eqns. (1-2) have been properly replaced by linear form. Note that the objective function is a linear combination of three components: $W_k \in \{0, 1, \ldots, T\}$, $\lambda_k \in [0, 1]$ and $\theta_k \in [0, 1]$, of which the first two are multiplied by $K > 1$. Since $\sum_{k \in \mathcal{N}} W_k \in \{0, \ldots, NT\}$, while $\sum_{k \in \mathcal{N}} \lambda_k \in [0, 1]$ and $\sum_{k \in \mathcal{N}} \theta_k \in [0, 1]$, the minimization of the waiting time is always addressed first in the problem.

Thus, the solver assign resources so that as many users as possible obtain the required λ_i^* and θ_i^*. The weight K ensures that the solver's second priority is the continuous streaming time: ideally for $K \to \infty$ the solution would never choose quality over continuous streaming, but in practice it is sufficient to set $K \gg 1$ as $\max\{\lambda_i\} = \max\{\theta_i\} = 1$.

Having the three quantities in the objective function accommodates all possible scenarios: for instance, if the sum of the achievable rates is very large compared to the sum of requirements, the solution is likely to obtain no waiting time and continuous streaming for all users and the objective function will assign resources to maximize the extra quality.

When all users need some pre-buffering, the objective function will first use resources to reduce the waiting time and then to improve the continuous streaming.

The granularity of the waiting times W_i may leave unused resources between the best solution and the next, unfeasible, value of the objective function. These saved resources can be used to either improve users' λ or θ, whereas they cannot decrease the total waiting time.

4. ONLINE ALGORITHM

A few preliminary tests showed that the MILP formulation of Eq. (7) is too complex (i.e. solvers need too much time) for online operations. The reasons are mainly two: MILP formulations are inherently combinatorial and the dimensionality of the problem is proportional to T^2N due to the three-dimensional matrices D and U, introduced to account for requirements shift. In this section we reduce the formulation complexity in two steps:

- first, we decrease the problem dimensionality from T^2N to TN by replacing waiting times with admission control variables;
- subsequently, to remove the combinatorial aspect of the MILP formulation, we approximate it with a simpler LP approach;
- finally, we perform a binary search over a sorted list of the users to find the largest set of users for which the LP formulation is feasible.

Reduced MILP formulation: to reduce the dimensionality of the problem caused by shifting the requirement sequences according to the waiting time W_i, we introduce a binary variable s_i, representing whether a user is admitted or not in the current optimization windows: $s_i \in \{0, 1\}$, $i \in \mathcal{N}$, where $s_i = 1$ if user i is admitted. Users who are admitted start streaming the content immediately (i.e. $W_i = 0$) and must fulfill both QoS conditions (λ_i^* and θ_i^*) for the whole content duration. Users that are not immediately admitted can only pre-buffer data if resources are still available. We obtain the following reduced MILP formulation:

$$\underset{A,B,L,E,S}{\text{maximize}} \quad \sum_{k \in \mathcal{N}} (K(\lambda_k + s_k) + \theta_k) \qquad (8)$$

$$\text{subject to:} \quad a_{i,j} \geq 0; \quad \sum_{k \in \mathcal{N}} a_{k,j} \leq 1$$

$$\lambda_i \geq \lambda_i^* s_i; \quad \theta_i \geq \theta_i^* s_i$$

$$l_{i,j} \geq 0; \quad e_{i,j} \geq 0; \quad b_{i,j} \leq b_M$$

$$l_{i,j} \geq d_{i,j} - a_{i,j}r_{i,j} - b_{i,j}$$

$$e_{i,j} \geq u_{i,j} - a_{i,j}r_{i,j} - b_{i,j} + d_{i,j} - l_{i,j}$$

$$\forall i \in \mathcal{N}; j \in \mathcal{T}$$

Eqns. (3), (4) and (5),

where we replaced the shifted requirements with the original ones (Eq. (3-5) should be modified accordingly). We observe that the constraints on λ_i and θ_i are only activated if $s_i = 1$. In fact, if user i is not admitted ($s_i = 0$) the constraint becomes $\lambda_i \geq \lambda_i^* - (1 - s_i) = 0$, thus the problem accepts any value for λ_i, which means users that are not admitted can still obtain resources, but they can only pre-buffer data without playing the actual content.

In addition, the term $\lambda_k + s_k$ in the objective function has a discontinuity in $\lambda_k = \lambda_k^*$, as $\lambda_k \in [0, 1]$ varies continuously, while $s_k \in \{0, 1\}$ is discrete. Thus the solver will try to have as many admitted users as possible first ($\lambda_k > \lambda_k^*$). Then, after the largest set of users is admitted with guaranteed QoS, the remaining resources are distributed to either improve the QoS for already admitted users or to other users according to what requires fewer resources.

This allows us to estimate the time a non-admitted user has to wait before starting consuming the requested content:

$$W_i = T - \left\lfloor \frac{\sum_{k \in \mathcal{T}} a_{i,k}r_{i,k}}{\lambda_i^* \sum_{k \in \mathcal{T}} d_{i,k} + \theta_i^* \sum_{k \in \mathcal{T}} u_{i,k}} \right\rfloor, \qquad (9)$$

where the ratio between the total rate obtained $\sum_{k \in \mathcal{T}} a_{i,k} r_{i,k}$ and the needed rate to meet the requirements $\lambda_i^* \sum_{k \in \mathcal{T}} d_{i,k} + \theta_i^* \sum_{k \in \mathcal{T}} u_{i,k}$ approximates the number of slots where the content could be streamed at the agreed quality. After this time, a user is not immediately admitted into the system, but the solution is computed again to consider the impact of (*i*) requirement shift and (*ii*) prediction update.

In addition, since non-admitted users might start with a larger buffer state than new users, they will be required to maintain the same buffer state at the end of the optimization window (if the media is longer) or the remaining content size (if this is smaller than the starting buffer). Conserving the buffer between consecutive optimization windows is particularly useful when the content duration is longer than the optimization window and it is thus not possible to guarantee the QoS over its whole duration. Instead, the buffer conservation takes care of maintaining the quantity of resources that were lacking in the first round of optimization.

LP formulation: starting from the reduced MILP formulation and fixing the set of admitted users $\tilde{\mathcal{N}}$ for which $\tilde{s}_i = I(i \in \tilde{\mathcal{N}})$, a LP formulation is obtained from Eq. (8) setting $s_i = \tilde{s}_i$ and replacing the objective function with:

$$\underset{A,B,L,E}{\text{maximize}} \sum_{k \in \mathcal{N}} (K\lambda_k + \theta_k), \qquad (10)$$

where $I(x)$ is the indicator function and is 1 if x is true and 0 otherwise. This formulation requires all users in $\tilde{\mathcal{N}}$ to satisfy the quality constraints. However, the set of admitted users is given as a parameter. The selection of such set is critical, since it may also lead to unfeasible problems.

Admission and Resource Control (ARC): Hereafter we propose a binary search to approximate the best feasible set of admitted users. To evaluate the set of admitted users we propose a greedy utility function to sort the users and then we define the set of admitted users of size $\tilde{N} = |\tilde{\mathcal{N}}|$ as the set composed of the first $\tilde{N}$ users. By means of a binary search over the size of the admitted set $\tilde{N}$, we find the largest size $\tilde{N}$ for which the problem of Eq. (10) is feasible.

The sorting function has to weight how efficiently resources are used to satisfy users' requirements. This efficiency depends on almost all the input parameters of our problem and, in particular, it is related to the sequence of achievable rates: high rates in the early slots allow a user to fill its buffer and avoid to use low rates slots, but a high rate in a slot where many users have high rates means that many users will try to use resources in the same slots.

Since evaluating all these parameters for every combination of users would be as complex as solving the original problem, we follow an indirect approach: we compute the schedule that maximizes $\sum_{k \in \mathcal{N}} (K\lambda_k + \theta_k)$ if no QoS is enforced ($\tilde{\mathcal{N}} = \emptyset$). In such a case, no user is required to meet any condition on the QoS and resources are assigned, first, to maximize the overall continuous streaming time and, then, the average quality. Thus, the solution of Eq. (10) is certainly feasible and obtains the resource allocation $\tilde{A}$.

According to the scheduling $\tilde{A}$, each user i is characterized by the two KPIs $\tilde{\lambda}_i$ and $\tilde{\theta}_i$. Consequently, the least efficient user i is the one that has the lowest $\tilde{\lambda}_i$. In case of equal $\tilde{\lambda}_i$ we choose over $\tilde{\theta}_i$. In case of both equal $\tilde{\lambda}_i$ and $\tilde{\theta}_i$, we consider the amount of used resources. Therefore, we propose the

---

Algorithm 1 Admission and Resource Control (ARC)

Input: $R, D, U, b_M, \lambda_i^*, \theta_i^*$.
Output: $\tilde{A}, \tilde{\mathcal{N}}$.
  $N_{\min} = 0, N_{\max} = N$
  Compute A, from Eq. (10) with $\tilde{N} = N_{\max}$
  if Problem feasible **then**
    $\tilde{a}_{i,j} = a_{i,j}, \tilde{\mathcal{N}} = \mathcal{N}$
  else
    Compute $\tilde{A}, \tilde{\lambda}_i, \tilde{\theta}_i$, from Eq. (10) with $\tilde{\mathcal{N}} = \emptyset$
    Compute ϕ_i from Eq. (11) $\forall i \in \mathcal{N}$
    Sort $\mathcal{N}$ in descending order of ϕ_i
    while $(N_{\max} - N_{\min}) > 1$ **do**
      $\tilde{N} = (N_{\max} + N_{\min})/2$
      Solve Eq. (10) with $\tilde{\mathcal{N}} = \{i \in \mathcal{N} | i \leq \lfloor \tilde{N} \rfloor\}$
      if Problem feasible **then**
        $N_{\min} = \tilde{N}$
      else
        $N_{\max} = \tilde{N}$
      end if
    end while
    $\tilde{a}_{i,j} = a_{i,j}$
  end if

---

following sorting function:

$$\phi_i = \frac{T(K\tilde{\lambda}_i + \tilde{\theta}_i)}{\sum_{k \in \mathcal{T}} \tilde{a}_{i,k}}, \qquad (11)$$

where $\sum_{k \in \mathcal{T}} \tilde{a}_{i,k}/T$ is the total fraction of resources used.

Once that the sorting function has been defined, we can apply a binary search over the size of the set of admitted users. We call the algorithm Admission and Resource Control and its pseudocode is given in Algorithm 1. The convergence of the binary search is ensured by the sorting of the users: in fact any given set $\tilde{\mathcal{N}}$ always includes all the elements of the smaller sets, thus, if it makes the problem unfeasible, no larger sets can be feasible.

In what follows we provide a few **practical considerations** about its realization in cellular networks. With reference to current LTE, Fig. 3 shows a high level diagram of an eNodeB where only the relevant functionalities are drawn. The prediction and context information functionalities are drawn outside the eNodeB as they contain network wide information that are not specific to any eNodeB. However, it is possible to cache locally in the eNodeB the information that is more frequently used. Also, while the mobility prediction may be computed outside the eNodeB, the short term achievable rate variation might be computed internally as well. The input parameters of the problem ($r_{i,j}$, $d_{i,j}$, $u_{i,j}$) are obtained by combining prediction, context information and admission control functionalities. The contractual agreement function governs the constraints of the problem and defines λ_i^* and θ_i^* for all users.

The admission control function is placed in parallel to the scheduler in order for the former to provide input to the latter without changing the main scheduling logic. These two functions operate at different time granularity: while the scheduler makes decisions every few milliseconds, the admission control time slots are in the order of seconds. The admission control should be able to modulate the user weights used by the scheduler. This allows the system to enforce admission control indirectly: the weight of a user which is

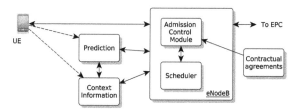

Figure 3: eNodeB high level diagram highlighting the relationship among the different modules.

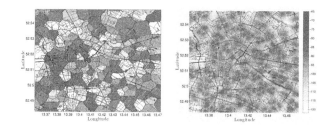

Figure 4: Coverage and pathloss maps of Berlin as measured by the MOMENTUM project [13].

not admitted in the current admission time slot is set to zero, while admitted users receive weights proportional to the fraction of resources assigned by the admission control.

In practice, whenever the admission control solution is re-evaluated, the admitted status of users that still have to complete their stream should be preserved. This can be achieved using an additional equality constraint requiring s_i to be larger or equal than the value obtained in the previous evaluation. New user arrivals can be managed either synchronously if the admission control time slots are smaller than 1 second or asynchronously if longer. In this last case, the users already admitted must preserve their condition.

5. SIMULATION RESULTS

This section presents the results of our evaluation campaign, which can be grouped in three parts: (i) the first part analyzes the computational complexity; (ii) the second evaluates how far the solution obtained by our approximation is from the original problem; (iii) the third part discusses the benefits of the combined admission control and resource allocation technique with respect to the baseline solution and an anticipatory technique that does not enforce QoS.

In particular we consider the following problems:
- *Original*: problem formulation of Eq. (7),
- *Simple*: mixed integer linear formulation of Eq. (8),
- *ARC*: online iterative approach of Algorithm 1,
- *RA*: anticipatory resource allocation without QoS (e.g. [8]),
- *Baseline*: plain proportionally fair scheduling.

Our evaluation campaign considers an LTE network scenario based on the pathloss data provided by the MOMENTUM project [13]. For each evaluation round we generate a random mobility trace in a 12×6 square kilometer area of Berlin (centered at latitude $52.52°$ North and longitude $13.42°$ East). Fig. 4 shows a map of the cell topology (left) in the considered area. From the mobility trace, we generate a pathloss trace computed on the pathloss map (right). Finally, we account for fast fading as in the model discussed in [21] to obtain the achievable rates and we average results over 200 repetitions of 5-minute scenarios.

The requirement traces are constant and equal for all the users to simplify the discussions of the results. However, all the formulations support any type of requirements. In particular, we set $d_{i,j} = 0.4$ Mbps and $u_{i,j} = 4.6$ Mbps to represent the different qualities available for video streams of resolution ranging from 360p (~ 400 Kbps) to 1080p (~ 5 Mbps). Unless specified otherwise, $\lambda_i^* = \lambda^* = 1$ for all users. This means that in all the following results it is required for the streaming to have no interruption. To prioritize continu-

ous streaming time over extra quality we chase $K = 100TN$ for all the simulations.

The first tests aim to understanding which of the three formulations can be used to implement a real-time admission control and resource allocation mechanism based on system state prediction. The main challenge of such a module is to obtain a solution within the validity time of the prediction. To this end, we evaluate the three formulations over repeated instances with varying problem size, i.e., number of optimization variables involved in the specific instance.

Eq. (7) has dimensionality proportional to $T^2 N$, while the simpler formulation of Eq. (8) has a size proportional to TN. However both include integer variable, while Algorithm 1 consists of at most $\log_2 N$ iterations of a simple LP program of size proportional to TN.

In our evaluation we explore the following parameters: users $N \in [10, 50]$, slots $T \in [10, 50]$, quality requirements $\theta_i^* = \theta^* \in [0.5, 1], \forall i$ and we compare the average computational time[3] obtained by the three formulations using GUROBI [14]. In Fig. 5(a) we fix the number of slots $T = 30$ and we plot a solid curve for ARC, dashed ($\theta^* = 1$) and dot-dashed ($\theta^* = 0.7$) curves for Simple and a dotted curve for the Original approach for $N = [10, 50]$[4].

We do not plot curves for different θ^* for the original and ARC formulation as this parameter has minimal impact on the computation time. Instead, we plot two curves for the simple formulation for $\theta^* = 1$ and $\theta^* = 0.7$, because we observe that if the system does not require the full quality to be delivered, the resource allocation has more degree of freedom and decreases the solution speed.

The original formulation becomes too slow very rapidly, while the simple formulation can be computed in less than 10 seconds if $\theta^* = 1$. However, for lower θ^* the simple formulation is affordable for very small problem instances only. This is due to the fact that for small problem instances the solution becomes trivial as almost all users can be admitted. Finally, ARC obtains a solution in an affordable time for all the problem sizes.

In the second set of results we compare the solutions obtained by the simple MILP and the ARC approaches. In particular, we evaluate the number of admitted users $\hat{N}$ (MILP) and $\tilde{N}$ (ARC) and the average waiting time $\hat{W} = \sum_{k \in \mathcal{N}} \hat{w}_k (N - \hat{N})$ (MILP) and $\tilde{W} = \sum_{k \in \mathcal{N}} \tilde{w}_k / (N - \tilde{N})$ (ARC) computed with Eq. (9). We choose $N = 25$ and $T = 50$ and we vary $\theta^* \in \{1, 0.9, 0.8, 0.5\}$. Finally, for each repetition we compute $\delta_N = (\hat{N} - \tilde{N})/N$ and $\delta_W = \hat{W} - \tilde{W}$.

---

[3]In all cases we stop the computation after 100 seconds.
[4]We do not report the curves obtained for a fixed N varying the number of slots, because they show a similar trend.

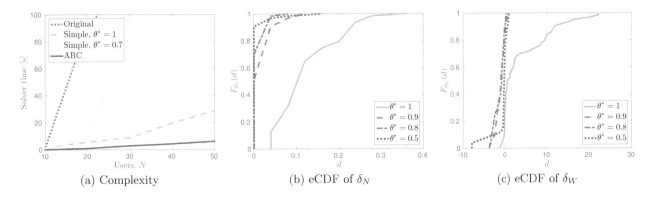

| | (a) Complexity | (b) eCDF of δ_N | (c) eCDF of δ_W |

Figure 5: Evaluation of the computational time and the optimality of the different approaches.

Fig. 5(b) and Fig. 5(c) plot the empirical cumulative distribution function (eCDF) of δ_N and δ_W respectively. Different constraints $\theta^* \in \{1, 0.9, 0.8, 0.5\}$ are plotted with solid, dashed, dash-dotted and dotted lines respectively. The former figure illustrates that the ARC approach closely approximates the number of admited users with respect to the MILP formulation for all but $\theta^* = 1$. In this case, the exact solution of the problem requires the maximum quality to be delivered in every slot to admit a user. Thus, the approximate formulation is less likely to find the exact combination of users. Similarly, Fig. 5(c) shows that for the average waiting time ARC obtains a good approximation. While in the previous figure the domain of the eCDF was limited to positive values, here δ_W can assume negative values, too: in fact, by admitting less user in the system, more resources remains for the non-scheduled users that can start the streaming earlier.

The final set of results compares Baseline (red dashed line), RA (green dash-dotted line) and ARC (solid lines from darker to lighter shade of blue representing $\theta^* \in \{1, 0.9, 0.7, 0.4\}$) to investigate the improvements offered by our proposal over existing solutions. The results for RA is obtained using the formulation of Eq. (10) with no admitted users, hence no QoS is enforced. In this set of graphs we vary both $N \in [5, 50]$ and $\theta^* \in [0.1, 1]$.

Fig. 6(a) shows the average fraction of continuous streaming obtained by the three approaches. Baseline does not leverage prediction and thus cannot avoid streaming interruption. As the number of users increases, the average interruption time reaches 15%. Both RA and ARC show almost no interruptions for any number of user. They only differ if $N > 30$ for which ARC drops a few users to enforce QoS.

Fig. 6(b) shows the average fraction of obtained quality (1 means that all the streams obtain the maximum quality in every slot) for the three approaches. The overall quality obtained decreases with the number of users for all approaches to different degrees. RA and ARC always deliver higher quality than Baseline. In addition, we plot 4 curves for different quality constraints for ARC. The two predictive approaches, ARC and RA obtain the same quality as long as the number of users is small enough to sustain the required QoS, then RA starts violating the constraint, while ARC reduce the set of admitted users.

Finally, Fig. 6(c) shows the average fraction of admitted users $\tilde{N}/N$ for ARC. The comparison between the last three figures highlights the tradeoff intrinsic to our solution: the

joint admission control and resource allocation is able to tradeoff the number of admitted users and the guaranteed QoS. For instance, to obtain a stream with no interruption at 40% of the maximum quality, only 30 of the 50 requesting users can be admitted at once.

6. CONCLUSIONS

In this paper we presented an admission control and resource allocation solution for multimedia streaming in mobile networks. The proposed solution exploits system state prediction to derive the set of users that can be admitted into the system with guaranteed Quality-of-Service and specifies the resource allocation for all users. Starting from a very general MILP formulation, we reduced the approach complexity by means of a simpler LP formulation and binary search and we obtained a very fast approximation with small performance degradation. Not only does our approach improve the state-of-the-art by combining guaranteed QoS and resource allocation, but also achieves this result within a short time. These two features make our proposed solution a good candidate for the realization of online admission control modules that, in coordination with the scheduler, will be able to enforce QoS in base stations. Although these results have been obtained with perfect prediction, we intend to extend the solution to imperfect forecast.

Acknowledgments

The authors thank Dr. Stefan Valentin for the fruitful discussions. The research leading to these results was partially supported by the PhD@Bell Labs Internship program, the Madrid Regional Government through the TIGRE5-CM program (S2013/ICE-2919), the Ramon y Cajal grant from the Spanish Ministry of Economy and Competitiveness RYC-2012-10788 and grant TEC2014-55713-R, and from the European Union H2020-ICT grant 653449.

7. REFERENCES

[1] Cisco Visual Networking Index: Global Mobile Data Traffic Forecast Update, 2014.

[2] H. Abou-zeid, H. Hassanein, and S. Valentin. Optimal predictive resource allocation: Exploiting mobility patterns and radio maps. In *Proc. IEEE GLOBECOM*, 2013.

[3] H. Abou-zeid, H. Hassanein, and S. Valentin. Energy-efficient adaptive video transmission:

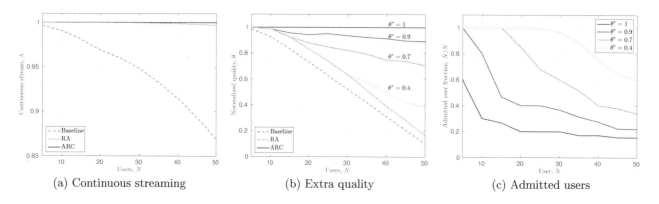

(a) Continuous streaming   (b) Extra quality   (c) Admitted users

Figure 6: Evaluation of the performance of the joint admission control and resource allocation solution.

Exploiting rate predictions in wireless networks. *IEEE Transactions on Vehicular Technology*, 63(5):2013–2026, June 2014.

[4] M. Ahmed, S. Spagna, F. Huici, and S. Niccolini. A peek into the future: predicting the evolution of popularity in user generated content. In *Proc. ACM WSDM*, 2013.

[5] A. Ashraf, F. Jokhio, T. Deneke, S. Lafond, I. Porres, and J. Lilius. Stream-based admission control and scheduling for video transcoding in cloud computing. In *Proc. IEEE/ACM CCGrid*, 2013.

[6] T. Braun, C. Castelluccia, G. Stattenberger, and I. Aad. An analysis of the diffserv approach in mobile environments. In *Proc. IQWiM-Workshop*, 1999.

[7] N. Bui, F. Michelinakis, and J. Widmer. A model for throughput prediction for mobile users. In *European Wireless*, 2014.

[8] N. Bui, S. Valentin, and J. Widmer. Anticipatory quality-resource allocation for multi-user mobile video streaming. In *Proc. IEEE CNTCV*, 2015.

[9] N. Bui and J. Widmer. Mobile network resource optimization under imperfect prediction. In *Proc. IEEE WoWMoM*, 2015.

[10] F. Dobrian, V. Sekar, A. Awan, I. Stoica, D. Joseph, A. Ganjam, J. Zhan, and H. Zhang. Understanding the impact of video quality on user engagement. *ACM SIGCOMM Computer Communication Review*, 41(4):362–373, 2011.

[11] M. Dräxler and H. Karl. Cross-layer scheduling for multi-quality video streaming in cellular wireless networks. In *Proc. IEEE IWCMC*, 2013.

[12] J. Froehlich and J. Krumm. Route prediction from trip observations. *SAE SP*, 2193:53, 2008.

[13] H.-F. Geerdes, E. Lamers, P. Lourenço, E. Meijerink, U. Türke, S. Verwijmeren, and T. Kürner. Evaluation of reference and public scenarios. Technical Report D5.3, IST-2000-28088 MOMENTUM, 2003.

[14] Gurobi Optimization, Inc. Gurobi optimizer reference manual, 2015.

[15] V. Joseph and G. de Veciana. NOVA: QoE-driven optimization of DASH-based video delivery in networks. In *Proc. IEEE INFOCOM*, 2014.

[16] P. Koutsakis, M. Vafiadis, and H. Papadakis. Prediction-based resource allocation for multimedia traffic over high-speed wireless networks. *AEU-International Journal of Electronics and Communications*, 2006.

[17] G. Majid, J. Capka, and R. Boutaba. Prediction-based admission control for DiffServ wireless internet. In *Proc. IEEE VTC-Fall*, 2003.

[18] R. Margolies, A. Sridharan, V. Aggarwal, R. Jana, N. Shankaranarayanan, V. A. Vaishampayan, and G. Zussman. Exploiting mobility in proportional fair cellular scheduling: Measurements and algorithms. In *Proc. IEEE INFOCOM*, 2014.

[19] A. K. Moorthy, L. K. Choi, A. C. Bovik, and G. De Veciana. Video quality assessment on mobile devices: Subjective, behavioral and objective studies. *IEEE J-STSP*, 6(6):652–671, 2012.

[20] A. J. Nicholson and B. D. Noble. Breadcrumbs: forecasting mobile connectivity. In *ACM MobiCom*, 2008.

[21] O. Østerbø. Scheduling and capacity estimation in LTE. In *Proc. IEEE ITC*, 2011.

[22] R. Pantos and W. May. HTTP live streaming. *IETF Draft, June*, 2010.

[23] U. Paul, A. P. Subramanian, M. M. Buddhikot, and S. R. Das. Understanding traffic dynamics in cellular data networks. In *Proc. IEEE INFOCOM*, 2011.

[24] Y. Qiao, J. Skicewicz, and P. Dinda. An empirical study of the multiscale predictability of network traffic. In *Proc. IEEE HDPC*, 2004.

[25] N. Sadek and A. Khotanzad. Multi-scale high-speed network traffic prediction using k-factor Gegenbauer ARMA model. In *IEEE ICC*, 2004.

[26] M. Z. Shafiq, L. Ji, A. X. Liu, and J. Wang. Characterizing and modeling internet traffic dynamics of cellular devices. In *Proc. ACM SIGMETRICS*, 2011.

[27] T. Taleb and A. Ksentini. QoS/QoE predictions-based admission control for femto communications. In *Proc. IEEE ICC*, 2012.

[28] S. Wang, Y. Xin, S. Chen, W. Zhang, and C. Wang. Enhancing spectral efficiency for LTE-advanced and beyond cellular networks [Guest Editorial]. *IEEE Wireless Communications*, 21(2):8–9, April 2014.

Potential Game based Energy Efficient Resource Allocation in HeNB Networks *

Ying Wang, Xiangming Dai, Jason Min Wang, Brahim Bensaou
Department of Computer Science and Engineering
The Hong Kong University of Science and Technology
ywangbf@cse.ust.hk, xdai@cse.ust.hk, jasonwangm@cse.ust.hk, brahim@cse.ust.hk

ABSTRACT

Powering an individual LTE femtocell base station, or Home eN-odeB (HeNB) in the LTE jargon, requires relatively very little energy. It is only when HeNBs are deployed massively, as has happened in the past few years, that energy efficiency becomes an important issue. With large numbers of co-located HeNBs and the increased inter-cell interference resource utilization becomes highly inefficient resulting in a high unnecessary energy consumption. To tackle this problem, coordination techniques could be invoked by the network operator to consolidate the offered workload to the network on as few HeNBs as possible and power down idle ones. Recognizing, however, that such techniques usually impair user-perceived quality of service (QoS), especially with bursty traffic, more sophisticated methods need to be investigated to also consider QoS. Despite the volume of prior work, the key issue – viz. simultaneously reducing energy waste, increasing bandwidth utilization while guaranteeing user-perceived QoS – has not been properly considered so far. In this paper, we model the trade-off between energy efficiency and QoS preservation by manipulating user equipment (UE) association and OFDMA scheduling in controlled networks of HeNBs. The problem being NP-hard, we propose two distributed learning algorithms, within a potential game-based framework, to obtain good and fast solutions to the problem. We demonstrate via numerical results the effectiveness of the proposed algorithms in achieving better performance in terms of utility, power, energy efficiency, convergence speed, and complexity compared to other alternatives.

Categories and Subject Descriptors

C.2.1 [**Network Architecture and Design**]: Wireless communication

Keywords

Energy efficiency; OFDMA scheduling; Home eNodeB; Potential game

*This work is supported in part under Grants: GRF610411 and FSGRF13EG14

1. INTRODUCTION

Deploying LTE HeNBs has recently become highly popular with network operators as an effective and economic way to improving data rates, widening network coverage and reducing the stress on macro-cell base stations. According to a recent report from the Smallcell Forum [1], the number of HeNBs will grow to 47 million by 2017. The rapid growth in the number of deployed HeNBs has led to a significant increase in energy consumption. By 2017, the total amount of HeNB energy consumption will reach 4.1×10^{11} KWH per year, producing million tonnes of carbon dioxide. Knowing that most HeNBs are often always powered yet underutilized, energy-frugal designs for HeNBs become of utmost importance.

Many techniques have been developed to reduce such energy consumption by totally offloading under-loaded base stations and putting them into sleep mode [6, 12, 5]. Nevertheless, these techniques address the energy saving issue, implicitly at the price of impairing user experience (e.g., data rate, delay, and so on). This contradicts the very intention of deploying HeNBs (providing better service). Therefore, we propose to take a fresher look at the issue by considering energy consumption in conjunction with quality of service (QoS). Specifically, in LTE, QoS is negotiated between the network and the user equipment (UE) in terms of *bearers* that characterize end-to-end flows between the UE and the packet data network gateway (P-GW). Several bearers are defined in LTE, each being associated with some predefined requirements such as bandwidth, delay, or loss rate, and so on.

Much recent work has been dedicated to considering both energy saving and QoS in the context of both cellular networks and HeNB networks [19, 13, 9]. For example, in [19] a greedy UE association scheme, to minimize the number of active BSs while satisfying the UE rate requirement, is proposed. The work in [13] studied the trade-off between energy saving and QoS preservation in HeNB networks via a centralized Markov decision process, which is impractical for self-organized HeNB networks. In [9], the joint problem of orthogonal frequency division multiple access (OFDMA) scheduling, power allocation, and UE association was investigated in HeNB networks with elastic traffic. Despite the depth of some of these previous works, several issues that need to be addressed still exist:

- Inter-HeNB interference: Most previous work ignore the existence of interference (e.g., [6, 19, 12]). Thus the results therein are not representative of real HeNB networks. Interference causes unnecessary energy and bandwidth waste, therefore it must be taken into account in the design of energy efficient solutions.

- QoS requirements of heterogeneous radio bearers: In HeNB networks, we focus on the QoS of *radio bearers* that span the wireless link between a HeNB and a UE. Bearers are classified into two categories: guaranteed bit rate (GBR) bearers applied to real-time traffic and non-guaranteed bit rate (Non-GBR) bearers applied to elastic traffic. Previous work, only considered either GBR or Non-GBR traffic [19, 9, 16], and therefore failed to provide solutions for networks with heterogeneous QoS requirements.

• The mismatch between fast OFDMA scheduling and X-2 coordination latency: Distributed protocols with fine-grained OFDMA scheduling in the millisecond time scale result in a high inter-HeNB coordination traffic overhead on the X-2 interface due to incompatible latency levels (e.g, [9]). Therefore, a practical MAC protocol with low coordination overhead is desirable.

Taking into account these three aspects simultaneously, we study the problem of bandwidth and energy efficiency maximization in HeNB networks. The bandwidth efficiency is characterized by the utility of the throughput obtained by the UE relative to their heterogeneous QoS requirements. Calculation of the UE throughput considers the link-level inter-HeNB interference. The energy efficiency is captured by the power consumption of the HeNBs on operation and transmission. As bandwidth and energy utilization maximizations are inconsistent metrics, we opt for a weight parameter to balance them. Our target is achieved by jointly optimizing UE association and OFDMA scheduling: 1) UE association control is adopted to manipulate the sleep/active states of the HeNBs, which in turn affects the bandwidth sharing and power consumption; 2) MAC layer OFDMA scheduling requires low coordination overhead on the X-2 interfaces.

In our recent previous work [17], we have proposed two greedy algorithms to approximately solve the above problem with guaranteed convergence. Specifically, the first algorithm improves the global optimization objective iteratively by local decision update. The second speeds up the convergence by invoking a distributed colouring algorithm on top of the first. Although the proposed algorithms achieved considerable improvements compared to alternative approaches, they are not sufficiently good as: 1) bad local optimal solutions may be reached; 2) the convergence rate may be slow, as only one UE or a subset of UEs is allowed to update its decision(s) in each iteration; this in turn requires coordination among the UEs.

To overcome such problems, in this paper, we further propose two novel iterative algorithms with guaranteed convergence within a game theoretic framework. Specifically, in these two algorithms, 1) UEs update their decisions intelligently by *exploiting historical information* instead of calculating the immediate payoff from the last iteration; 2) *all the UEs* may update their decisions in the same iteration, which can further accelerate the convergence rate considerably.

We have conducted substantial numerical experiments to evaluate the proposed algorithms and the results show that these new algorithms further improve the performance over our previous methods as well as alternative benchmarks on various metrics, such as convergence rate, utility, power consumption, energy efficiency, GBR rejection ratio, and Non-GBR utility.

In summary this paper's contributions are as follows:
• We model the efficient bandwidth and energy utilization in QoS-constrained LTE HeNB networks as an optimization problem and show it is NP hard.
• We propose two game-based distributed algorithms to improve bandwidth utilization and energy efficiency in such networks. The algorithms enable the scheduler to learn from historical data what are the good strategies to choose and speed up convergence rate by allowing all UEs to update their decisions simultaneously.
• We demonstrate via numerical studies that considerable improvements can be achieved by the proposed algorithms compared to

our previous work as well as other benchmarks on multiple performance metrics.

The rest of the paper is organized as follows. In Section 2, we present the system model and problem formulation, and show that the problem is NP hard. In Section 3, we elaborate on the proposed algorithms. In Section 4, we evaluate the performance of our algorithms via numerical experiments. Finally, we draw our conclusions in Section 5.

2. SYSTEM MODEL

Network scenario. Consider a HeNB network that consists of a collection of HeNBs within range of an eNB. We focus on downlink traffic served by this set of HeNBs denoted as B. Typically designed for home users, HeNBs are often randomly deployed (unplanned) resulting in coverage areas that often mutually overlap. We denote U the set of home UEs who own the HeNBs. Furthermore, we assume the HeNBs to be configured to provide open-access (under the control of the network operator), and can provide data service for any UE in U if the UE is in the range of the HeNB. The eNB is always on and is designated as backup to serve mobile UEs not in possession of any HeNB or home UEs that are located outside the coverage area of the HeNB network. The frequency spectrum is orthogonally split between the HeNB network and the eNB to avoid eNB-to-HeNB interference. The UE set U is partitioned along the QoS classes into set U_G for UEs requiring guaranteed bitrate and U_N for those requiring elastic service. Without loss of generality, each UE is associated with only one bearer. Specifically, UE $u \in U_G$ associated with a GBR bearer should be guaranteed a rate of at least d_u, whereas a UE $u \in U_N$ associated with a Non-GBR bearer should obtain an elastic rate that is upper bounded by c_u [14] as specified in the LTE standard.

UE association. As HeNBs' coverage areas may overlap with each other, each UE may have multiple eligible HeNBs to obtain its service. Energy efficiency can be reached by associating UEs to HeNBs with lower energy cost and inter-HeNB interference. HeNBs with no associated UEs can be turned into sleep mode to save energy. We define $I_{b,u}$ to indicate the association of UE u with HeNB b: $I_{b,u} = \{0, 1\}, b \in B, u \in U$.

OFDMA scheduling. In LTE MAC layer, the smallest allocation unit is an OFDMA "tile". Dynamic OFDMA tile scheduling (e.g., [9]) requires millisecond level latency in the coordination among HeNBs on the X-2 interface. Scheduling a large number of OFDMA tiles could also result in a large computational overhead. To overcome these issues, we design a probabilistic channel access protocol with low coordination and computation overhead. Similar to the protocol in [10], each HeNB allocates each OFDMA tile to its associated UE u according to a preassigned channel access probability p_u. Since the allocation intra-HeNB is collision free we forcefully have: $0 \le p_u \le 1, u \in U$

Such access protocol could be viewed as a slotted ALOHA protocol where the scheduling unit (i.e., the time slot) is instantiated to the two-dimensional OFDMA tile. Fig. 1 illustrates UE association and OFDMA tile scheduling in a simple network scenario.

Bandwidth efficiency. We characterize bandwidth efficiency by the satisfaction of the user with respect to the obtained throughput. We denote by r_u the throughput of UE u, and define utility function $\mathcal{F}_G(r_u, d_u)$ to reflect the satisfaction of a GBR bearer UE:

$$\mathcal{F}_G(r_u, d_u) = \begin{cases} 0, r_u < d_u \\ \mathcal{C}_1, r_u \ge d_u \end{cases} \quad (1)$$

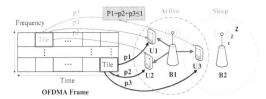

Figure 1: UE association and OFDMA scheduling: Three UEs associated with B1 (idle B2 goes to sleep); Each OFDMA tile is shared probabilistically using distribution $\{p_1, p_2, p_3\}$.

where d_u is the strict rate requirement of the GBR bearer. Zero satisfaction is achieved when $r_u < d_u$, while $\mathcal{C}_1$ is a constant utility obtained when $r_u \geq d_u$.

Similarly, we define $\mathcal{F}_N(r_u, c_u)$ to express the satisfaction of a Non-GBR bearer UE:

$$\mathcal{F}_N(r_u, c_u) = \begin{cases} \mathcal{C}_2 \frac{\log(r_u+1)}{\log(c_u+1)}, r_u < c_u \\ \mathcal{C}_2, r_u \geq c_u \end{cases} \quad (2)$$

where c_u is the upper bound imposed on Non-GBR bearer UE by the LTE standard, and $\mathcal{F}_N(r_u, c_u)$ is crafted such that: when $r_u < c_u$, the utility increases logarithmically with r_u to ensure proportional fairness among elastic traffic bearers; and once a bearer's rate reaches the upper bound or exceeds it ($r_u \geq c_u$), the utility remains constant at $\mathcal{C}_2$. Typically $\mathcal{F}_N(r_u, c_u)$, embodies the diminishing return principle to ensure fairness yet deprives Non-GBR bearers from any incentive of obtaining more than the upper bound even when bandwidth is abundant. To prioritize UEs with GBR bearers over UEs with Non-GBR bearers, we set $\mathcal{C}_1 > \mathcal{C}_2$.

The throughput r_u of UE u equals the product of the nominal data rate R and the expected successful transmission probability, or:

$$r_u = Rp_u \prod_{\substack{b:u \in N_b, \\ I_{b,u}=0}} (1 - P_b), u \in U \quad (3)$$

where N_b is the set of UEs that can be served by HeNB b, and $P_b = \sum_{u \in N_b} p_u I_{b,u}$ is the sum of the transmission probabilities of UEs associated with b.

Energy efficiency. We represent the energy efficiency by the total power consumption of the HeNBs. The power consumption E_b of HeNB b comprises three parts: 1) constant power E_1 for transceiver idling in both active and sleep mode; 2) extra constant power E_2 for computation, backhaul communication, and power supply in active mode; and 3) transmission power, proportional to the transmission probability P_b and the maximum transmission power E_3; or: $E_b = E_1 + E_2 M_b + E_3 P_b, b \in B$, where $M_b = \max_{u \in U}\{I_{b,u}\}$ indicates whether HeNB b is in active mode or otherwise, assuming a HeNB is in sleep mode if no UE is associated with it.

Objective formulation. Using these definitions, from the perspective of an operator, the objective is to simultaneously maximize bandwidth utilization and energy efficiency by jointly optimizing UE associations and channel access probabilities. A non-negative power weight parameter ω is adopted to strike a balance between the two objectives leading to:

$$\max_{\{I_{b,u}, p_u\}} \sum_{u \in U_G} \mathcal{F}_G(r_u, d_u) + \sum_{u \in U_N} \mathcal{F}_N(r_u, c_u) - \omega \sum_{b \in B} E_b \quad (4)$$

Constraints. Each UE needs to be associated with one and only one HeNB, which writes:

$$\sum_{b:u \in N_b} I_{b,u} - 1 = 0, \forall u \in U. \quad (5)$$

Also, probability P_b should not exceed 1 since each OFDMA tile can be assigned to at most one UE under the same HeNB each time:

$$P_b - 1 \leq 0, \forall b \in B. \quad (6)$$

NP-hardness. Consider a simplified version of our problem, with no-interference where each HeNB provides full data rate R. Assume such network contains only GBR UEs and suppose the total capacity of all HeNBs is sufficient to accommodate all UEs. The objective then becomes to minimize only the energy. By setting E_3 small enough compared to E_2, we ensure all active HeNB have equal power consumption. Thus, the resulting problem becomes how to pack UEs with different demands in the smallest number of HeNBs of capacity R each. This problem can be identified to be a bin-packing problem, which proves the NP-hardness of our problem.

3. PROPOSED ALGORITHMS

3.1 Potential Game Model

In problem (4), the integer variables could be relaxed to possibly solve the problem approximately, however the non-concavity of the objective function and non-convexity of the constraints still make it impossible to devise an approximation methods via traditional non-linear optimization techniques. In addition, the distributed nature of HeNB-based networks makes the problem even more challenging. Therefore, we propose to use a game theoretic model [4] to obtain approximate UE association and OFDMA scheduling solutions.

To fit the problem into a game model, we first discretize its decision variables and then remove the constraints. Specifically, continuous variables p_u are transformed into a new discrete variable q_u chosen from a size$-n$ discrete set $\mathcal{Q} = \{0, \frac{1}{n-1}, ..., \frac{n-2}{n-1}, 1\}$. Then each UE u's decision vector becomes $s_u = (I_{1,u}, ..., I_{b,u}, ..., I_{|B|,u}, q_u)$, selected from a finite decision set $\mathcal{S}_u = \{s_u | \sum_{b:u \in N_b} I_{b,u} = 1, I_{b,u} \in \{0, 1\}, q_u \in \mathcal{Q}\}$, where constraint (5) is involved. Next, we remove constraints (6) and replace them by adding a distance based static penalty function $\mathcal{H}(\cdot)$ [15] to the original objective:

$$\mathcal{H}(x) = \begin{cases} \mathcal{C}_3 x, x < 0, \\ 0, x \geq 0 \end{cases} \quad (7)$$

where constant $\mathcal{C}_3$ is a penalty ratio, imposed for violating the constraint (in the extreme case $\mathcal{C}_3 = \infty$). As a result the new discrete and unconstrained problem becomes:

$$\max_{\{s_u\}} \sum_{u \in U_G} \mathcal{F}_G(r_u, d_u) + \sum_{u \in U_N} \mathcal{F}_N(r_u, c_u)$$
$$- \omega \sum_{b \in B} E_b + \sum_{b \in B} \mathcal{H}(1 - P_b) \quad (8)$$
$$s.t. \quad s_u \in \mathcal{S}_u, \forall u \in U$$

Next, we model the new problem (8) as a game, which shall be proved later to be a potential game. First, we define a strategic game $G = (U, \langle \mathcal{S}_u \rangle, \langle \theta_u \rangle)$, where each UE u is modelled as a player u (we use UE and player interchangeably hereinafter), whose strategy is decision vector s_u selected from the strategy space $\mathcal{S}_u$. Player u is associated with payoff function θ_u. Intuitively, since each player in choosing its strategy may affect nearby players whom it interferes with, therefore instead of simply defining θ_u as the player's own profit, we define a specific payoff θ_u, that considers both the profit of the player itself and the profits of the players it may affect, so that improving the local payoff function will not decrease the overall objective, as proven in Lemma 1. As a result:

$$
\begin{aligned}
\theta_u = \sum_{u \in \alpha_u \cap U_G} \mathcal{F}_G(r_u, d_u) + \sum_{u \in \alpha_u \cap U_N} \mathcal{F}_N(r_u, c_u) \\
- \omega \sum_{b:u \in N_b} E_b + \sum_{b:u \in N_b} \mathcal{H}(1 - P_b)
\end{aligned}
\tag{9}
$$

Obviously, θ_u is composed of three parts: 1) The sum of utilities of the GBR and Non-GBR UEs in neighbourhood set $\alpha_u = \{\cup_b N_b | u \in N_b\}$, which contains UEs covered by the transmission range of HeNBs that are able to serve u ($u \in \alpha_u$). Clearly, u's utility is influenced by the strategies of UEs in set α_u, and u's strategy may also influence the utilities of UEs in set α_u. 2) The sum of power consumptions of HeNBs that are able to serve u. 3) The sum of penalties due to violating constraints that are coupled with u. To evaluate θ_u, we only need the joint strategy $\boldsymbol{s}_{\alpha_u^{(2)}}$ of a two-tier neighbourhood set $\alpha_u^{(2)} = \{\cup_v \alpha_v | v \in \alpha_u\}$, which includes the neighbours of the neighbour set α_u. Note that in (9), calculating the utility part requires strategies of $\alpha_u^{(2)}$, whereas calculating the power and penalty parts only requires strategies of α_u ($\alpha_u \subseteq \alpha_u^{(2)}$).

LEMMA 1. *The defined game G is an exact potential game.*

PROOF. Define the objective in (8) as function $\mathcal{P}(\boldsymbol{s}_U)$: $\prod_{u \in U} \mathcal{S}_u \to \mathbb{R}$, which maps the joint strategy $\boldsymbol{s}_U$ to a real number. For any player $u \in U$, the local payoff θ_u captures the effect of strategy s_u on the global objective. When player u switches from one strategy s_u to another strategy s'_u, the change in the objective $\mathcal{P}(\boldsymbol{s}_U)$ equals the change in the payoff function θ_u:

$$
\begin{aligned}
\mathcal{P}(s'_u, \boldsymbol{s}_{U \setminus \{u\}}) - \mathcal{P}(s_u, \boldsymbol{s}_{U \setminus \{u\}}) = \\
\theta_u(s'_u, \boldsymbol{s}_{\alpha_u^2 \setminus \{u\}}) - \theta_u(s_u, \boldsymbol{s}_{\alpha_u^2 \setminus \{u\}}), \forall s_u \in \mathcal{S}_u, \forall s'_u \in \mathcal{S}_u
\end{aligned}
\tag{10}
$$

As property (10) holds for all players, game G is proved to be an exact potential game [11]. $\square$

3.2 Strategy Update Algorithms

In [17], we have proposed two iterative strategy update algorithms that guarantee convergence: the so-called Iterative Greedy (IG) algorithm and the Fast Iterative Greedy (FIG) algorithm. In each iteration of IG algorithm, only one UE may be selected to update its strategy, in an effort to maximize its immediate payoff while the states of other UEs remain unchanged. FIG algorithm is similar to IG, except that it relies on a graph colouring algorithm to enable simultaneous updates by several UEs to speed up convergence.

Despite the considerable improvements achieved by IG and FIG algorithms compared to other benchmarks, several issues can be found in the algorithms: 1) each UE greedily maximizes its immediate payoff based on its neighbour UEs' strategy of the last iteration. Therefore, the quality of the solution is highly sensitive to the UE update sequence; many such sample paths may lead to bad local optima. 2) To ensure convergence, in each iteration, only one UE or a subset of UEs is allowed to update the strategy. This may lead to a long converge time and requires critical coordination among UEs.

To address these issues, in this work, we propose two new strategy update algorithms with guaranteed convergence, the so-called Regret Learning based (RL) algorithm and the Fictitious Play based

(FP) algorithm. Compared to IG and FIG, RL and FP make more intelligent decisions on strategy updates by exploiting historical information. Most importantly, they allow all the UEs to update their strategies simultaneously in each iteration, which helps convergence speed considerably.

3.2.1 Regret Learning based Algorithm

We first propose a *Regret Learning based Algorithm* under the game theoretic framework. In regret learning [7], each UE values a strategy by the "regret of not having played it in the past", which is calculated based on historical observations. This is different from IG and FIG, where each UE greedily chooses the strategy with the largest immediate payoff.

Specifically, to better address our problem, we improve the regret estimation proposed in [18] with the help of inter-HeNB coordination. The regret calculation is as follows.

For any two distinct strategies s_u and s'_u in $\mathcal{S}_u$, the regret of having used s'_u instead of s_u in iteration t is denoted by $\widehat{Q}_u^{(t)}(s'_u, s_u)$ and is given by:

$$
\widehat{Q}_u^{(t)}(s'_u, s_u) = \max\{Q_u^{(t)}(s'_u, s_u), 0\}, s_u \neq s'_u
\tag{11}
$$

where $Q_u^{(t)}(s'_u, s_u)$ is defined as the average payoff increase by replacing strategy s'_u in the past t iterations with s_u:

$$
Q_u^{(t)}(s'_u, s_u) = \frac{1}{t} \sum_{\substack{\tau = 1, \ldots, t: \\ s_u^{(\tau)} = s'_u}} \left(\theta_u(s_u, \boldsymbol{s}_{\alpha_u^{(2)} \setminus \{u\}}^{(\tau)}) - \theta_u(\boldsymbol{s}_{\alpha_u^{(2)}}^{(\tau)}) \right)
\tag{12}
$$

In (12), $\theta_u(s_u, \boldsymbol{s}_{\alpha_u^{(2)} \setminus u}^{(\tau)})$ is the payoff that should be received in iteration τ if we replace UE u's strategy s'_u by s_u while keeping the strategies of all other neighbour UEs in $\alpha_u^{(2)} \setminus \{u\}$ the same. $\theta_u(\boldsymbol{s}_{\alpha_u^{(2)}}^{(\tau)})$ is the original payoff received by UE u in iteration τ. Note that for UE u, maintaining regret $Q_u^{(t)}(s'_u, s_u)$ requires the joint strategy $\boldsymbol{s}_{\alpha_u^{(2)} \setminus u}^{(\tau)}$ at the end of each iteration $\tau < t$, which can be obtained via inter-HeNB coordination. We will further explain the coordination issue at the end of Section 3.

Next, we elaborate the procedure of RL. In the first iteration, all UEs are allocated with initial strategies (no association and zero access probability). Then, in each iteration $t \geq 2$, all UEs update their strategies simultaneously. Each UE u chooses a strategy $s_u \in \mathcal{S}_u$ according to the probability distribution $\gamma_u^{(t)}(s_u)$, which is linearly proportional to the regret value:

$$
\gamma_u^{(t)}(s_u) =
\begin{cases}
(1 - \delta) \frac{1}{\mu} \widehat{Q}_u^{(t-1)}(s_u^{(t-1)}, s_u) + \delta \frac{1}{|\mathcal{S}_u|}, \\
\quad s_u \neq s_u^{(t-1)} \\
1 - \sum_{\substack{s'_u \neq s_u^{(t-1)}, \\ s'_u \in \mathcal{S}_u}} \gamma_u^{(t)}(s'_u), \quad s_u = s_u^{(t-1)}
\end{cases}
\tag{13}
$$

where 1) δ is a trade-off parameter; 2) $1/|\mathcal{S}_u|$ ensures the progression of the game by allowing every possible strategy to have an equal probability of being chosen; 3) constant μ is a normalization parameter to guarantee $\gamma_u^{(t)}(s_u)$ is a probability distribution[1] ($\sum_{s_u \in \mathcal{S}_u} \gamma_u^{(t)}(s_u) = 1, \gamma_u^{(t)}(s_u) \geq 0$).

The RL algorithm for a UE u is summarized in Algorithm 1. A correlated equilibrium is achieved in regret learning based games when each player realizes that the best option is to choose a strategy by following probability distribution $\gamma_u^{(t)}(s_u)$, on the condition

---

[1]Constant μ is set to $2\theta_u^{max}(|\mathcal{S}_u| - 1)$, where θ_u^{max} is the maximum payoff of UE u.

that all the other players do the same. RL converges to a correlated ε-equilibrium [7]. The complexity of RL in each iteration is $O(n^2|B|^2)$, where n is the size of the discrete set $\mathcal{Q}$, and $|B|$ is the number of HeNBs.

Algorithm 1: Regret Learning based Algorithm

Set initial strategy $s_u^{(1)} = \mathbf{0}$; $t \leftarrow 1$;
repeat
 Obtain strategy $\boldsymbol{s}_{\alpha_u^{(2)}\backslash\{u\}}^{(t-1)}$ of set $\alpha_u^{(2)}\backslash\{u\}$ in $(t-1)^{th}$
 iteration;
 Update the regret matrix $\widehat{Q}_u^{(t)}(s'_u, s_u)$ by (11) and (12);
 Evaluate distribution $\gamma_u^{(t)}(s_u), s_u \in \mathcal{S}_u$ by (13);
 Notify strategy $s_u^{(t)}$ to UEs in $\alpha_u^{(2)}\backslash\{u\}$;
 $t \leftarrow t+1$;
until *Convergence*;

3.2.2 *Fictitious Play based Algorithm*

Under the same game framework, we further propose the *Fictitious Play based Algorithm* [8]. In both FP and RL, the UE learns from historical information how to update its strategy. As opposed to RL, in FP, each player chooses its strategy assuming that its opponents are playing stationary mixed strategies according to the empirical frequencies. The algorithm is called fictitious since the actual play does not follow the forecast.

Similar to RL, FP proceeds iteratively. In the first iteration, each UE is allocated with an initial strategy (no association and zero access probability). Then, in each iteration $t \geq 2$, all UEs update their strategies simultaneously until convergence, which shall be proved later. Specifically, in the tth iteration, UE u chooses strategy s_u probabilistically according to distribution $\gamma_u^{(t)}(s_u)$, which is produced by mapping the expected payoff $\vartheta_u^{(t-1)}(s_u)$ at the $(t-1)^{th}$ iteration through a multinomial logit function (i.e., Boltzmann distribution):

$$\gamma_u^{(t)}(s_u) = \frac{e^{\vartheta_u^{(t-1)}(s_u)/\mathcal{T}}}{\sum\limits_{s'_u \in \mathcal{S}_u} e^{\vartheta_u^{(t-1)}(s'_u)/\mathcal{T}}}, \forall s_u \in \mathcal{S}_u \qquad (14)$$

where $\mathcal{T}$ is a constant temperature parameter. The expected payoff $\vartheta_u^{(t)}(s_u)$ is defined as:

$$\vartheta_u^{(t)}(s_u) = \sum_{\boldsymbol{s}_{\alpha_u^{(2)}\backslash\{u\}}} f_u^{(t)}(\boldsymbol{s}_{\alpha_u^{(2)}\backslash\{u\}})\theta_u(s_u, \boldsymbol{s}_{\alpha_u^{(2)}\backslash\{u\}}), \forall s_u \in \mathcal{S}_u$$

$$(15)$$

where $f_u^{(t)}(\boldsymbol{s}_{\alpha_u^{(2)}\backslash\{u\}})$ is the empirical frequency of the joint strategy $\boldsymbol{s}_{\alpha_u^{(2)}\backslash\{u\}}$ of the neighbour set $\alpha_u^{(2)}\backslash\{u\}$ in the past t iterations. The main steps of FP algorithm for a UE u are summarized in Algorithm 2, where u only needs the joint strategy $\boldsymbol{s}_{\alpha_u^{(2)}\backslash\{u\}}^{(t)}$ of its neighbour set in each iteration t. It is known that fictitious play with multinomial logit strategy update rule in potential games converges probabilistically to the set of Nash equilibrium points [8]. Since game G is a potential game, we can prove that Alg. 2 converges probabilistically to a Nash equilibrium. The complexity of FP in each iteration is $O(n|B|)$, where n is the size of the discrete set $\mathcal{Q}$, and $|B|$ is the number of HeNBs.

Algorithm 2: Fictitious Play based Algorithm

Set initial strategy $s_u^{(1)} = \mathbf{0}$; $t \leftarrow 1$;
repeat
 Obtain strategy $\boldsymbol{s}_{\alpha_u^{(2)}\backslash\{u\}}^{(t-1)}$ of set $\alpha_u^{(2)}\backslash\{u\}$ in $(t-1)^{th}$
 iteration;
 Update expected payoff $\vartheta_u^{(t)}(s_u)$ by (15);
 Evaluate distribution $\gamma_u^{(t)}(s_u), s_u \in \mathcal{S}_u$ by (14);
 Notify strategy $s_u^{(t)}$ to UEs in $\alpha_u^{(2)}\backslash\{u\}$;
 $t \leftarrow t+1$;
until *Convergence*;

---

4. PERFORMANCE EVALUATION

4.1 Benchmark Algorithms

For comparison purpose, we adopt the distributed *load-aware algorithm* (LA) proposed in [19] as a benchmark. To the best of our knowledge, the LA algorithm is the closest to our work except that it assumes interference is mitigated in advance by other means. To ensure fair comparison, the interference mitigation method for OFDMA random access in [10] (similar to the one used in our model) is added on top of the original LA algorithm, with differentiation of priorities of GBR and Non-GBR UEs. In addition, we also consider the performance of our two previously proposed IG and FIG algorithms described in [17].

Finally we use a *Simulated Annealing Algorithm* (SA) [3] to provide an upper bound benchmark. In SA, each UE updates its strategy iteratively according to a probability distribution with logarithmic cooling schedule. SA converges to a global optimum probabilistically when time goes to infinity.

4.2 Experiment Setup

We evaluate the performance of RL, FP, IG, FIG, SA, and LA using numerical experiments. The experiment setup is as follows.

The transmission range of each HeNB is set to 10 meters. Each HeNB provides a full rate of 100 Mbps when no collision happens. There are in total 10 levels of discrete channel access probability ($n = 10$). The rate requirement d_u of each GBR UE equals 10 Mbps, and the maximum rate c_u of each Non-GBR UE equals 20 Mbps. GBR UEs' maximum utility $\mathcal{C}_1$ is set as 100, Non-GBR UEs' maximum utility $\mathcal{C}_2$ is set as 10; this ensures a higher priority for GBR UEs over Non-GBR UEs when maximizing the objective. Constant $\mathcal{C}_3$ is set to 100. According to HeNB hardware power consumption in [2], the constant power E_1 is set to 0.7 Watt (20% of the transceiver power), the extra constant power E_2 is set to 6.7 Watt, and the maximum proportional transmission power E_3 is set to 2.7 Watt. Then, the power consumption of an active HeNB can reach at most 10.2 Watt. For RL, δ is set as 0.001. For FP, constant $\mathcal{T}$ is set as 10. For SA, parameter $\mathcal{T}_0$ is set as 10. For LA, parameter ϵ is set to 0.01 and parameter α is set to 0.

4.3 Convergence Analysis

We first examine the algorithm convergence rate on a topology (simple enough to be understood) with three HeNBs and eleven UEs (numbered from 1 to 11). As shown in Fig. 2(a), UE 1, 3, 6, 9, and 10 are GBR UEs and the others are Non-GBR UEs. Power weight ω is set to 1.0 for RL, FP, IG, FIG, and SA.

Figure 3 shows the convergence of utility, power consumption, and energy efficiency, with the legend shown in Figure 3(d). Utility is the sum of utilities of both GBR and Non-GBR UEs, power consumption is the total power consumed in the network, and energy

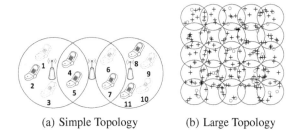

(a) Simple Topology   (b) Large Topology

Figure 2: Topologies (The red nodes are GBR UEs, and the black nodes are Non-GBR UEs)

efficiency is reflected by the ratio of the total utility to the total power consumption (or unit of utility achieved per unit of power consumed). In Figure 3, the samples are averaged over 100 independent test runs with the same initial UE strategies.

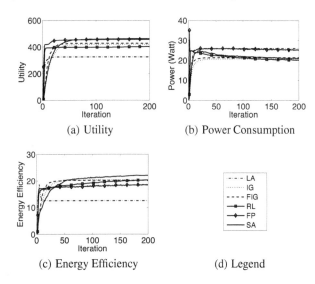

(a) Utility   (b) Power Consumption

(c) Energy Efficiency   (d) Legend

Figure 3: Convergence Analysis

• *Utility.* We can observe from Figure 3(a) that: 1) RL had the highest convergence rate and converged in about 10 iterations. 2) FP and LA converged in less than 20 iterations. 3) Our proposed RL and FP algorithms converged faster than the IG and FIG algorithms (IG converged in 60 iterations, and FIG converged in 30 iterations), thanks to the simultaneous strategy update scheme as well as the exploitation of historical information. 4) SA converged the slowest as it probed an optimal solution probabilistically via a slow cooling schedule. It reached a relatively stable utility in around 100 iterations and kept improving slowly afterwards.

• *Power consumption.* As shown in Figure 3(b), FP had a sudden increase at the second iteration and adjusted to a stable value later on, as in this iteration each UE tried to randomly grab the bandwidth with zero expected payoffs. Also, RL and SA increased in the first tens of iterations and then dropped gradually when the relative benefit of power saving became greater than utility increase. Unlike IG and FIG, RL, FP, and SA decreased slowly after reaching a relatively stable value thanks to their probabilistic strategy update.

• *Energy efficiency.* As shown in Figure 3(c), energy efficiency of RL, FP, and SA increased slowly as power consumption decreased. Our proposed RL and FP reached a good efficiency in less than 10 iterations, while IG, FIG, and SA became stable with a slower

rate compared to RL and FP. LA increased abruptly, followed by a sudden drop, which was caused by the fast increasing power consumption.

Our RL and FP algorithms did not show superior performance on the above three metrics compared to others. For example, FP achieved slightly lower energy efficiency than our previous algorithm IG and FIG, however results of one simple topology are insufficient to draw conclusions. Therefore, in the next subsection, we will evaluate the performance of our algorithms on utility, power, energy efficiency, and other two metrics in larger randomly deployed network scenarios.

4.4 Larger Random Topologies

We consider now larger topologies consisting of twenty-five HeNBs placed on a five-by-five grid, as shown in Figure 2(b). In this scenario, each circle represents the transmission range of a HeNB. Each HeNB was located at the center of each circle. The HeNBs overlapped with one another leading to inter-HeNB interference. In each circle, eight UEs are randomly distributed in the circle's inscribed square resulting in 25 HeNBs and 200 UEs. Black crosses represents Non-GBR UEs, while red circles represent GBR UEs.

Five performance metrics were considered: GBR reject ratio, Non-GBR utility, total utility, power consumption, and energy efficiency. Specifically, GBR reject ratio and Non-GBR utility were designed to evaluate the separate benefit of GBR and Non-GBR UEs. The GBR reject ratio is defined as the percentage of unsatisfied GBR UEs that should be rejected by the HeNBs (as they would obtain less than their required bandwidth), while Non-GBR utility is defined as the sum of utilities of the Non-GBR UEs.

Metric Comparison. Figure 4 and Figure 5 show the results under two topologies with different UE composition: 1) In Figure 4, two GBR UEs and six Non-GBR UEs were located randomly within every other circle, with 26 GBR UEs and 174 Non-GBR UEs in total. 2) In Figure 5, four GBR UEs and four Non-GBR UEs were located randomly within every other circle, with 52 GBR UEs and 148 Non-GBR UEs in total. The results shown in the figures were averaged over 100 random UE distributions with standard deviation. For LA, IG, and FIG, the results were captured after convergence. For RL, FP, and SA, whose UE strategies were updated probabilistically, the metric values were averaged over 100 iterations to eliminate oscillation. To ensure fairness, the 100 iterations are selected right after the convergence of IG and FIG.

From Figure 4 and 5, we have the following observations in both topologies:

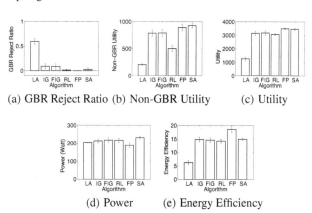

(a) GBR Reject Ratio   (b) Non-GBR Utility   (c) Utility

(d) Power   (e) Energy Efficiency

Figure 4: Large Topology with 26 GBR and 174 Non-GBR UEs

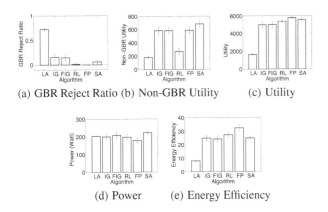

(a) GBR Reject Ratio (b) Non-GBR Utility (c) Utility

(d) Power (e) Energy Efficiency

Figure 5: Large Topology with 52 GBR and 148 Non-GBR UEs

- *GBR reject ratio.* The GBR reject ratio of FP is 0%, the lowest one, meaning all GBR UEs are satisfied in FP. RL also had a low GBR reject ratio compared to others (e.g., 2% of LA, 14% of IG and FIG, and 50% of SA as shown in Figure 4(a)). FP and RL had strong abilities of satisfying GBR UEs thanks to the high bandwidth efficiency obtained by intelligent learning from historical information. Finally, LA has the highest GBR reject ratio.

- *Non-GBR utility.* FP achieved similarly good Non-GBR utility as SA, and higher than the others (e.g., 300% higher than LA, 76% higher than RL, and 13% higher than IG and FIG, as shown in Figure 4(b)). RL achieved higher Non-GBR utility compared to LA, and lower than IG and FIG (e.g., 146% higher than LA, and 35% lower than IG and FIG, as shown in Figure 4(b)). The reason RL favoured GBR UEs over Non-GBR UEs might be: in RL, the probability of choosing a strategy is directly affected by its last iteration strategy, while in FP, strategy update is determined by the expected payoff, which is less sensitive to the last iteration strategy. Therefore, in RL, when a UE has chosen a GBR-beneficial strategy, it is less possible to change to another Non-GBR-beneficial strategy in the next iteration compared to FP. We will conduct further study on this observation in the future.

- *Utility.* FP obtained similarly good utility as SA, and higher than the others (e.g., 176% higher than LA, 13% higher than RL, and 11% higher than IG and FIG, as shown in Figure 4(c)). RL achieved similar utility as IG and FIG, and higher than LA (e.g., 142% higher than LA, as shown in Figure 4(c)). Besides, the standard deviations of IG and FIG are larger than RL, FP, and SA, because different greedy solution search sequences could result in different results. Finally, LA achieved the lowest utility because it tried to reduce interference when all the HeNBs are turned on, which may have resulted in unnecessary waste of bandwidth.

- *Power consumption.* FP consumed the least power (e.g., 19% less than SA, and 13% less than RL, as shown in Figure 4(d)). LA, RL, IG, and FIG consumed similar power, which was less than SA.

- *Energy efficiency.* FP obtained the highest energy efficiency (e.g., 200% higher than LA, and 24% higher than SA, as shown in Figure 4(e)). RL, IG, and FIG had similar energy efficiencies as SA.

Impact of Power Weight. As stated before, maximizing the bandwidth utilization is at odds with minimizing the gross energy consumption. Therefore, we introduced power weight ω as a tuning parameter to balance between utility maximization and power minimization. Below, we investigate how ω affects the performance of RL, FP, IG, FIG, and SA, respectively.

Specifically, we studied ω at five different values: 0.0, 0.5, 1.0, 1.5, and 2.0. We only consider values of ω such that satisfying

GBR UEs always has higher priority than reducing power. The results for power consumption, utility, energy efficiency, GBR reject ratio, and Non-GBR utility are listed in Tables 1 to 5, respectively. Performance of LA is not listed since it is irrelevant to the power weight [2]. Each entry in the tables was averaged over 100 random UE distributions. Similar to the previous experiment, results of IG and FIG were captured after convergence, while for RL, FP, and SA, the results were averaged over 100 iterations due to probabilistic oscillation. The table entries are accurate to two decimal places and unless otherwise stated, they also show the standard deviation (STD) between parentheses.

- *Power consumption.* We observe from Table 1 that overall, the larger the power weight, the lower the power consumption. For instance, when ω increased from 0.0 to 2.0, the power consumption of RL, FP, and SA decreased by less than 15%, whereas the power consumption of both IG and FIG decreased by 38%. This shows that IG and FIG were more sensitive to power weight variation compared to the others in terms of power consumption.

Table 1: Power (STD) in Watt as a function of ω

Alg. ω	IG	FIG	RL	FP	SA
0	225.27 (9.64)	225.08 (11.92)	224.85 (7.95)	191.89 (12.41)	238.09 (5.58)
0.5	216.54 (11.29)	220.49 (12.99)	219.75 (9.26)	191.26 (13.52)	235.44 (6.39)
1.0	213.12 (11.71)	217.90 (13.33)	216.32 (10.93)	189.47 (13.79)	231.94 (7.95)
1.5	140.57 (6.74)	140.30 (6.89)	197.67 (12.99)	179.86 (11.89)	224.96 (9.61)
2.0	140.55 (6.77)	140.34 (6.91)	187.75 (14.54)	174.15 (12.68)	209.98 (12.39)

- *Utility.* As listed in Table 2, in general, the larger the power weight ω, the smaller the utility. The reason is that the algorithms tend to sacrifice some utility to save energy when ω become large.

Table 2: Utility (STD) as a function of ω

Alg. ω	IG	FIG	RL	FP	SA
0	3144.6 (149.0)	3194.7 (175.0)	3015.1 (62.9)	3489.2 (56.5)	3463.7 (76.0)
0.5	3154.5 (148.1)	3186.9 (172.9)	3049.0 (63.1)	3492.1 (60.8)	3466.9 (88.5)
1.0	3152.5 (151.3)	3171.3 (171.6)	3069.3 (70.2)	3489.6 (58.4)	3456.8 (184.9)
1.5	2970.8 (148.6)	2982.7 (167.1)	2996.1 (71.6)	3461.8 (50.3)	3434.0 (105.8)
2.0	2977.1 (150.9)	2986.9 (166.5)	2977.1 (73.7)	3370.6 (58.7)	3408.4 (110.0)

- *Energy efficiency.* We can see that the larger the power weight ω, the better the energy efficiency, as shown in Table 3. In particular, when ω equals 0, 0.5, and 1.0, FP achieved the highest energy efficiency, and RL, IG, FIG, and SA achieved similar energy efficiency. For example, when ω equals 0, FP obtained about 30% better energy efficiency than the others. When ω is above 1.0, IG and FIG are more energy efficient than the others as the power consumption dropped considerably.

Table 3: Energy Efficiency (STD) as a function of ω

Alg. ω	IG	FIG	RL	FP	SA
0	13.98 (0.71)	14.23 (0.81)	13.43 (0.47)	18.25 (1.04)	14.56 (0.45)
0.5	14.59 (0.76)	14.48 (0.80)	13.90 (0.60)	18.34 (1.12)	14.73 (0.40)
1.0	14.82 (0.84)	14.59 (0.85)	14.22 (0.72)	18.50 (1.18)	14.92 (0.48)
1.5	21.15 (0.86)	21.27 (0.95)	15.22 (1.02)	19.33 (1.14)	15.28 (0.56)
2.0	21.20 (0.85)	21.30 (0.96)	15.95 (1.17)	19.45 (1.26)	16.27 (0.83)

- *GBR reject ratio.* From the 100 test cases we used to derive the results, we observed the distribution of the reject ratio to be

---

[2]For reference, the averaged metric values of LA are: power: 203.76 Watt; utility: 1263.80; energy efficiency: 6.2018; GBR reject ratio: 59.31%; Non-GBR utility: 205.77.

269

highly skewed, as a result we present here in addition to the mean reject ratio, the median as it carries more information about the distribution than the standard deviation. We can observe from Table 4 that the GBR reject ratios of all the algorithms remained stable with respect to ω, because satisfying GBR UEs always has higher priority than saving power.

Table 4: Average GBR Reject Ratio (median) in percentage (%) as a function of ω

Alg. ω	IG	FIG	RL	FP	SA
0	8.79 (7.69)	8.08 (7.69)	1.52 (0.91)	0.00 (0.00)	2.11 (0.00)
0.5	8.92 (7.69)	7.92 (7.69)	1.36 (0.76)	0.00 (0.00)	2.13 (0.00)
1.0	9.00 (7.69)	8.42 (7.69)	1.36 (0.86)	0.00 (0.00)	2.68 (3.85)
1.5	7.00 (7.69)	6.54 (3.84)	1.38 (0.36)	0.00 (0.00)	3.55 (3.85)
2.0	6.77 (3.84)	6.46 (3.84)	1.37 (0.51)	0.00 (0.00)	3.48 (3.85)

- *Non-GBR utility.* We can see that it decreased as ω increased, as reducing the power consumption was becoming more important in the objective than increasing the Non-GBR utility.

Table 5: Non-GBR Utility (STD) as a function of ω

Alg. ω	IG	FIG	RL	FP	SA
0	772.88 (55.57)	804.73 (60.51)	454.69 (50.26)	889.25 (56.44)	918.56 (40.89)
0.5	786.48 (57.50)	792.88 (61.56)	484.41 (50.28)	892.09 (60.83)	922.33 (43.83)
1.0	786.51 (59.14)	790.29 (65.31)	504.59 (53.89)	889.61 (58.42)	926.43 (44.38)
1.5	552.77 (36.50)	552.71 (38.60)	432.08 (57.88)	861.84 (50.27)	926.34 (45.91)
2.0	553.11 (37.18)	554.87 (38.64)	412.78 (57.24)	770.63 (58.74)	898.88 (50.43)

Summary. Finally, we summarize the performance of the different algorithms in Table 6 in terms of several qualitative attributes, such as optimal objectives of strategy update, strategy update rules, requirements on simultaneous update, obtained solution qualities, convergence rate, and time complexities in each iteration. Overall, FP turns out to be the best among all the algorithms.

5. CONCLUSION

In this paper, we studied the problem of improving both bandwidth efficiency and energy efficiency in LTE femtocell (HeNB) networks by taking into consideration interference mitigation and heterogeneous QoS requirements. The problem is formulated as a joint optimization of UE association and OFDMA scheduling under a practical MAC protocol. Two distributed algorithms based on historical information are proposed to approximately solve the problem. Extensive numerical results highlight the considerable improvements achieved by our algorithms compared to the benchmarks on various performance metrics.

Table 6: Summary on all Algorithms

Alg. Property	LA	IG	FIG	RL	FP	SA
Optimal Objective	—	immediate payoff	immediate payoff	averaged regret	expected payoff	immediate payoff
Update Rule	—	argmax	argmax	linear probabilistic	multinominal logistic probabilistic	multinominal logistic probabilistic
Simultaneous Update	one UE	one UE	a subset of UEs	**all UEs**	**all UEs**	one UE
Solution Quality	low	medium	medium	medium	**high**	**high**
Convergence Rate	**fast**	medium	medium	**fast**	**fast**	slow
Complexity	$O(|B|)$	$O(n|B|)$	$O(n|B|)$	$O(n^2|B|^2)$	$O(n|B|)$	$O(n|B|)$

6. REFERENCES

[1] Informa Telecoms & Media, Small cell market status. Feb. 2013. Online: http://www.informatandm.com/white-papers-download-small-cell-market-status-february-2013/ (access on Apr, 2014).

[2] I. Ashraf, F. Boccardi, and L. Ho. Sleep mode techniques for small cell deployments. *Communications Magazine, IEEE*, 49(8):72–79, 2011.

[3] S. C. Borst, M. G. Markakis, and I. Saniee. Nonconcave utility maximization in locally coupled systems, with applications to wireless and wireline networks. *Networking, IEEE/ACM Transactions on*, 22(2):674–687, 2014.

[4] A. C. Chapman, A. Rogers, and N. R. Jennings. Benchmarking hybrid algorithms for distributed constraint optimisation games. *Autonomous Agents and Multi-Agent Systems*, 22(3):385–414, 2011.

[5] H. Claussen, I. Ashraf, and L. T. Ho. Dynamic idle mode procedures for femtocells. *Bell Labs Technical Journal*, 15(2):95–116, 2010.

[6] A. Conte, A. Feki, L. Chiaraviglio, D. Ciullo, M. Meo, and M. A. Marsan. Cell wilting and blossoming for energy efficiency. *Wireless Communications, IEEE*, 18(5):50–57, 2011.

[7] S. Hart and A. Mas-Colell. *A reinforcement procedure leading to correlated equilibrium.* Springer, 2001.

[8] J. Hofbauer and W. H. Sandholm. On the global convergence of stochastic fictitious play. *Econometrica*, 70(6):2265–2294, 2002.

[9] I.-H. Hou and C. S. Chen. An energy-aware protocol for self-organizing heterogeneous LTE systems. *Selected Areas in Communications, IEEE Journal on*, 31(5):937–946, 2013.

[10] I.-H. Hou and P. Gupta. Proportionally fair distributed resource allocation in multiband wireless systems. *Networking, IEEE/ACM Transactions on*, 22(6):1819–1830, Dec. 2014.

[11] D. Monderer and L. S. Shapley. Potential games. *Games and economic behavior*, 14(1):124–143, 1996.

[12] C. Peng, S.-B. Lee, S. Lu, and H. Luo. GreenBSN: Enabling energy-proportional cellular base station networks. *Mobile Computing, IEEE Transactions on*, 13(11):2537–2551, Nov 2014.

[13] L. Saker, S.-E. Elayoubi, R. Combes, and T. Chahed. Optimal control of wake up mechanisms of femtocells in heterogeneous networks. *Selected Areas in Communications, IEEE Journal on*, 30(3):664–672, 2012.

[14] S. Sesia, I. Toufik, and M. Baker. *LTE: The UMTS Long Term Evolution, From Theory to Practice.* Wiley, 2009.

[15] A. Smith, A. E. Smith, D. W. Coit, T. Baeck, D. Fogel, and Z. Michalewicz. *Penalty functions.* Citeseer, 1997.

[16] K. Son, H. Kim, Y. Yi, and B. Krishnamachari. Base station operation and user association mechanisms for energy-delay tradeoffs in green cellular networks. *Selected Areas in Communications, IEEE Journal on*, 29(8):1525–1536, 2011.

[17] Y. Wang, X. Dai, J. M. Wang, and B. Bensaou. Energy efficient medium access with interference mitigation in lte femtocell networks. *CoRR*, arXiv:1508.01454, 2015.

[18] Y. Wang, J. M. Wang, and B. Bensaou. Regret-based learning for medium access in lte femtocell networks. In *Proceedings of the 17th ACM international conference on Modeling, analysis and simulation of wireless and mobile systems*, pages 145–152. ACM, 2014.

[19] S. Zhou, J. Gong, Z. Yang, Z. Niu, and P. Yang. Green mobile access network with dynamic base station energy saving. In *The Annual International Conference on Mobile Computing and Networking (Workshop)*, volume 9, pages 10–12. ACM, 2009.

Game-theoretic Analysis of Computation Offloading for Cloudlet-based Mobile Cloud Computing

Xiao Ma
Tsinghua National Laboratory
for Information Science and
Technology
Tsinghua University
maxiao13@mails.
tsinghua.edu.cn

Chuang Lin
Tsinghua National Laboratory
for Information Science and
Technology
Tsinghua University
chlin@
tsinghua.edu.cn

Xudong Xiang
University of Science and
Technology Beijing
xudong.xiang@csnet1.
cs.tsinghua.edu.cn

Congjie Chen
Tsinghua National Laboratory
for Information Science and
Technology
Tsinghua University
ccjguangzhou@gmail.com

ABSTRACT

Mobile cloud computing (MC2) is emerging as a promising computing paradigm which helps alleviate the conflict between resource-constrained mobile devices and resource-consuming mobile applications through computation offloading. In this paper, we analyze the computation offloading problem in cloudlet-based mobile cloud computing. Different from most of the previous works which are either from the perspective of a single user or under the setting of a single wireless access point (AP), we research the computation offloading strategy of multiple users via multiple wireless APs. With the widespread deployment of WLAN, offloading via multiple wireless APs will obtain extensive application. Taking energy consumption and delay (including computing and transmission delay) into account, we present a game-theoretic analysis of the computation offloading problem while mimicking the selfish nature of the individuals. In the case of homogeneous mobile users, conditions of Nash equilibrium are analyzed, and an algorithm that admits a Nash equilibrium is proposed. For heterogeneous users, we prove the existence of Nash equilibrium by introducing the definition of exact potential game and design a distributed computation offloading algorithm to help mobile users choose proper offloading strategies. Numerical extensive simulations have been conducted and results demonstrate that the proposed algorithm can achieve desired system performance.

Categories and Subject Descriptors

C.2.4 [**Distributed Systems**]: Client/server

General Terms

Algorithms; Performance; Design; Theory

Keywords

Computation offloading strategy; Game theory; Algorithm

1. INTRODUCTION

In recent years a type of mobile applications, such as augmented reality, natural language processing and face recognition, are gaining huge popularity [24]. These applications generally requires intensive computation and as a result consume enormous energy. Nonetheless, mobile devices are usually constrained in processing capabilities and battery life. The conflict between the resource-consuming applications and the resource-constrained mobile devices induces the emergence of mobile cloud computing (MC2)[5, 6, 7, 8, 13, 22, 29, 3, 18]. The main idea of MC2 is to integrate cloud computing into mobile devices by shifting computation or storage tasks from mobile devices to the cloud. Although mobile cloud computing is considered as a promising computation paradigm, it faces several challenges. First, moving computation and storage tasks to the cloud consumes considerable energy. Energy shortage has been an inherent issue of mobile computing. And the extra energy consumption will hinder the development of MC2. Second, moving computation or storage tasks from mobile devices to the remote cloud can incur delay and jitters. The delay and jitters are generally uncontrolled at WAN scale, which adversely impacts the performance of mobile cloud computing. To overcome these challenges, cloudlet-based mobile cloud computing is proposed in [23]. A cloudlet is a resource-rich multi-core computer or a cluster of computers that is close to the mobile devices and well-connected to the Internet.

MSWiM'15, November 2–6, 2015, Cancun, Mexico.
© 2015 ACM. ISBN 978-1-4503-3762-5/15/11 ... $15.00.
DOI: http://dx.doi.org/10.1145/2811587.2811598.

Due to the physical proximity, offloading the computation from the mobile devices to the cloudlet bypasses the uncontrolled delay and jitters. In this paper, we focus on the cloudlet-based computation offloading problem.

With the widespread deployment of WLAN, mobile users can usually connect to the Internet via multiple wireless APs. Most previous works analyze mobile cloud computation offloading strategy either from the perspective of a single mobile user or at the setting of a single wireless AP. In this paper, we analyze the strategy of multiple mobile users via multiple wireless APs. In other words, each user chooses a proper wireless AP among the multiple APs to offload the computation task or executes the computation task locally based on his own interest.

The computation offloading problem of multiple users via multiple wireless APs is challenging in the following aspects:

- Mobile devices are owned by different individuals who pursue diverse interests. Coordinating the offloading strategies of different mobile users so as to obtain the desired global system performance and simultaneously satisfy the diverse demands of mobile users is challenging.

- Performance of WLAN APs is a vital factor that influences both the global system performance and interests of individuals. Without coordination among mobile users, load of wireless APs can be unbalanced. Overloaded APs can cause serious interference among mobile users under the same wireless coverage. Coordinating computation offloading decisions of mobile users via multiple wireless APs is more complex than via a single AP. When considering a single AP, mobile users merely need to decide whether or not to offload. When it comes to multiple APs, apart from deciding whether to offload or not, they are also required to choose a proper AP from multiple APs according to the wireless conditions.

To overcome these challenges, we introduce the tool of game theory. Game theory is usually used to analyze systems consisting of multiple rational individuals [17, 15]. The contributions of this paper are summarized as follows:

- We study the computation offloading problem of multiple mobile users via multiple APs. We give a game-theoretic analysis of the computation offloading problem to minimize delay and energy consumption of mobile users.

- In the case of homogeneous mobile users, we present the conditions of Nash equilibrium and propose a computation offloading algorithm that always admits a Nash equilibrium.

- In the case of heterogeneous users, we prove the existence of Nash equilibrium by introducing the definition of exact potential game and design a distributed computation offloading algorithm.

- Numerical extensive simulations are conducted, and results demonstrate that the proposed algorithms can achieve desired system performance.

The rest of this paper is organized as follows. In section 2 we discuss the related work. In section 3 we provide the system model of the cloudlet-based mobile cloud computing. In section 4 we analyze computation offloading strategy of homogeneous mobile users. In section 5 we analyze the case of heterogeneous users. In section 6 we conduct extensive simulations of the proposed algorithms and analyze the results. Finally in section 7 we conclude the paper.

2. RELATED WORK

Many efforts have been devoted to the computation offloading strategy design for a single mobile user [25, 11, 18, 12, 9, 21, 10, 27, 26, 19]. Wen et al. in [25] proposed an energy-efficient computation offloading mechanism by optimally configuring the clock frequency for mobile execution and scheduling the data transmission. Huang et al. in [9] presented a computation offloading algorithm based on Lyapunov optimization to save energy within delay limits. Huerta-Cícnepa and Lee in [10] designed an adaptable application offloading mechanism based on the execution history of the applications and current state of the environment and mobile device. Xian et al. in [27] developed an computation offloading method to save energy by optimizing the timeout. In [19], Rahimi et al. designed a hybrid tiered architecture to optimize performance and scalability of applications by leveraging local and public clouds.

A few researchers have dealt with the computation offloading problem of multiple users. Yang et al. in [28] proposed a framework which allows multiple users to share the computation instances of the cloud and the wireless network to optimize the performance of the mobile cloud system. Rahimi et al. in [20] proposed a framework which translates user mobility to mobile service usage patterns. They proposed a heuristic algorithm to map mobile applications to tiered mobile cloud resources. Barbarossa et al. in [2] proposed a method to allocate both computation and communication resources among multiple mobile users, aiming at minimizing the energy consumption under latency constraints. Chen et al. in [4] proposed a game-theoretic approach to analyze the problem of computation offloading via a single wireless AP for homogeneous and heterogeneous mobile users. They formulate the computation offloading problem among multiple mobile users as a decentralized offloading decision game and design computation offloading strategy for mobile users.

Different from most of the previous work which is either from the perspective of a single user or under the setting of a single wireless access point (AP), we focus on the distributed computation offloading strategy of multiple users via multiple APs. With the widespread deployment of WLAN, offloading computation tasks of multiple users via multiple wireless APs will obtain extensive application.

3. SYSTEM MODEL

Computation offloading is a potential solution to energy saving, but not all mobile applications are more energy-efficient than executed locally [12]. Based on the wireless environment and property of the mobile applications (such as calculation and amounts of transmission), each mobile user makes the computation offloading decision before execution of the computation task. In this section, we introduce the system model of the cloudlet-based computation offloading problem.

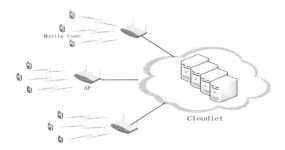

Figure 1: Cloudlet-based mobile cloud computing

3.1 System model of cloudlet-based computation offloading

The case of cloudlet-based computation offloading of multiple mobile users via multiple wireless APs is shown in Figure 1. As shown in Figure 1, $\Upsilon = \{1, 2, ..., K\}$ denotes a set of mobile users, each of which has a computation task $M_k \triangleq \{D_k, L_k\}$. Here D_k denotes the amount of transmission data when the computation task of user k is offloaded, and L_k denotes the amount of CPU cycles to complete the computation task. Mobile users can connect to the cloudlet through a set of wireless APs denoted as $\Lambda = \{1, 2, ..., I\}$. Denote Γ as the decision set, $\Gamma = \{0, 1, 2, ..., I\}$. $s_k(s_k \in \Gamma)$ denotes the computation offloading decision of user k. Specifically, $s_k = 0$ if user k decides to execute the task locally, and $s_k = i$ if user k offloads the computation task to the cloudlet via wireless AP i. We denote the computation offloading decisions of the K players as $S = \{s_1, s_2, ..., s_K\}$

3.2 Energy model

In this section, we analyze the energy consumption of the computation tasks when executed both locally on the mobile devices and offloaded to the cloudlet.

3.2.1 Local energy

When a user executes the computation task locally, the energy consumption

$$E_k^0 = v_k \cdot L_k$$

where v_k denotes the energy consumption per CPU cycle. According to [25], v_k is approximately linearly proportional to the Square of frequency. So E_k^0 can be denoted as

$$E_k^0 = aF_k^2 L_k \tag{1}$$

where F_k denotes the number of CPU cycles/second of mobile device k. According to [14], we set $a = 2.5 \times 10^{-9}$.

3.2.2 Offloading energy

The energy consumption of mobile users in the offloading process is the transmission energy. We compute the transmission energy based on the measurement study presented in [1]. Let E_k denote the energy consumption of user k

$$E_k = E_k^s + E_k^t + E_k^m \tag{2}$$

As Eq.(2) shows, E_k is composed of three parts: 1)E_k^s: scanning energy, which is the energy consumed when scanning available wireless APs. 2)E_k^t: transmission energy, which is the energy consumed during transmission. Denote r_k as transmission rate and p_k^t as transmission power of user k in wireless network, the transmission energy can be denoted

as $E_k^t = P_k^t * D_k/r_k$. 3)E_k^m: maintaining energy, which is the energy consumed to keep the interface on during transmission. Let P_k^m denote the maintaining power, we have $E_k^m = P_k^m * D_k/r_k$. Thus, energy consumption of user k when the computation task is offloaded can be shown as

$$E_k = E_k^s + (P_k^t + P_k^m) * \frac{D_k}{r_k} \tag{3}$$

According to [1], $E_k^s = 5.9J$, $P_k^t = 0.4W$, $P_k^m = 0.05W$.

3.3 Cost function

As analyzed in Section 1, delay and energy are two critical factors of the computation offloading problem. We denote the cost function of user k via wireless AP i as the following

$$C_k^i = E_k^i + a_k * T_k^i \tag{4}$$

where E_k^i and T_k^i denote the energy and delay respectively. a_k is a constant which expresses the relative weight assigned by user k to the energy consumption and delay parameters. Its value can range from 0 to infinity. Each user can assign the value of a_k according to his own interest.

3.3.1 Local cost

We let $i = 0$ when user k executes the computation task locally. The computing time can be denoted as

$$T_k^0 = L_k/F_k$$

and the cost function

$$C_k^0 = aF_k^2 L_k + a_k * \frac{L_k}{F_k} \tag{5}$$

3.3.2 Offloading cost

When offloaded to the cloudlet, the delay of a computation task is composed of two parts: transmission delay and computing delay, which can be denoted as

$$T_k^i = \frac{D_k}{r_k^i} + \frac{L_k}{F_k^{cloudlet}}$$

where $F_k^{cloudlet}$ denotes the CPU cycles/second of the cloudlet allocated to user k. Substitute Eq.3 into Eq.4, the cost function of offloading is shown as

$$C_k^i = \{E_k^s + (P_k^t + P_k^m) * \frac{D_k}{r_k^i}\} + a_k * (\frac{D_k}{r_k^i} + \frac{L_k}{F_k^{cloudlet}}) \tag{6}$$

4. OFFLOADING STRATEGY FOR HOMOGENEOUS USERS

Prior to executing the computation task, each mobile user needs to make a decision of whether or not to offload and via which wireless AP to offload. In this section, we analyze the computation offloading strategy in the case of homogeneous users. Here homogeneity means that the users use the same type of mobile devices and execute identical computation tasks.

4.1 Computation offloading game

We propose a game-theoretic solution to the computation offloading problem. The players are all the mobile users who have computation tasks. s_{-k} denotes the offloading decisions of all the other users apart from user k, $s_{-k} = \{s_1, s_2, ...s_{k-1}, s_{k+1}, ..., s_K\}$. So the cost function of user k can be denoted as $C_k(s_k, s_{-k})$.

Definition 1 A strategy of $S^* = \{s_1^*, s_2^*, ..., s_K^*\}$ is a Nash equilibrium of the computation offloading game if for any $k \in \Upsilon$, we have

$$C_k(s_k^*, s_{-k}) \le C_k(s_k, s_{-k})$$

for any $s_k \in \Gamma$

In other words, when the computation offloading game reaches a Nash equilibrium, no user can reduce his cost by deviating from the current computation offloading strategy.

4.2 Conditions of Nash equilibrium

In this section, we present the conditions of Nash equilibrium in the case of homogeneous mobile users. We assume that the bandwidth of a wireless AP is equally allocated to all users connecting to it and the computation resource of the cloudlet is fairly allocated to all users offloading the computation.

Let n_i denote the number of users connecting to AP i including user k (n_0 denotes the number of users deciding to compute locally). So we have $\sum_{i=0}^{I} n_i = K$, and the bandwidth allocated to user k by AP i can be denoted as $r_k^i = B_i/n_i$. Let F denote the total CPU cycles/second of the cloudlet, and the cloudlet computation resource allocated to user k is

$$F_k^{cloudlet} = \frac{F}{\sum_{i=1}^{I} n_i} = \frac{F}{(K - n_0)}$$

The cost function of Eq.(6) can be derived as

$$C_k^i = A_k * \frac{n_i}{B_i} - G_k * n_0 + H_k \qquad (7)$$

where

$$A_k = (P_k^t + P_k^m + a_k)D_k$$

,

$$G_k = \frac{a_k L_k}{F}$$

and

$$H_k = E_k^s + \frac{a_k L_k K}{F}$$

From Eq. 7, we can see that apart from the number of users connecting to access point i, C_k^i is also related to the number of users deciding to compute locally. For the homogeneous mobile users, $C_k^0 = C, A_k = A, G_k = G, H_k = H$.

Based on Definition 1, we derive the conditions of Nash equilibrium for homogeneous mobile device users as

Condition 1 $s_k = 0$ if for any $i \in \Lambda$, there is

$$A * \frac{n_i}{B_i} - G * n_0 \ge C - H$$

Condition 2 $s_k = i(i \in \Lambda)$ if for any $j \in \Lambda \backslash \{i\}$

$$\frac{n_i}{B_i} - \frac{n_j}{B_j} \le \frac{\theta}{A}$$

and

$$A * \frac{n_i}{B_i} - G * n_0 \le C - H$$

Specifically, if user k decides to compute locally, to avoid switching from 0(computing locally) to wireless AP $i(i \in \Lambda$, Λ is the wireless AP set), there should be $C_k^0 \le C_k^i$. Based on Eq.5 and 7, we derive Condition 1.

In the real-life situation, handover from one wireless AP to another experiences the process of disconnecting and reconnecting. So the switching process incurs extra energy consumption and latency which are denoted as e_k and t_k respectively. In the case of homogeneous mobile users, if user k changes its connection from AP i to j $(i, j \in \Lambda)$, the cost function of AP j should be modified on the basis of Eq.(7) as

$$C_k^j = A * \frac{n_i}{B_i} - G * n_0 + J \qquad (8)$$

where

$$J = H + \theta$$

For homogeneous mobile users,

$$\theta_k = e_k + a_k * t_k = \theta$$

If mobile user k decides to offload the computation task via wireless AP i, to avoid changing the computation offloading strategy, there should be $C_k^i \le C_k^j$ for any $j \in \Gamma \backslash \{i\}$($\Gamma$ is the decision set including computing locally). Based on Eq. 5, 7 and 8, we derive Definition 2.

4.3 Distributed computation offloading algorithm

Above analysis shows the stable profile of mobile users' decisions when Nash equilibrium is attained. However, how to attain a Nash equilibrium while guaranteeing the profits of mobile users? In this section, we propose a distributed computation offloading algorithm (Algorithm 1) for homogeneous mobile users which mimics the selfish greedy nature of the users. Proof of Nash equilibrium of the algorithm is shown afterwards.

Algorithm 1 Offloading strategy for homogeneous mobile device users

---

1: **for** each user with a computation task **do**
2:     calculate the cost of computing locally on the mobile device based on Eq.5;
3:     collect the current load and bandwidth information of all wireless APs;
4:     calculates the cost of computation offloading via all wireless APs based on Eq.7;
5:     choose the proper wireless AP to offload or compute locally to minimize the cost;
6: **end for**

Note that Algorithm 1 will not cause much extra overhead for mobile users due to the simple calculation, small amount of transmission data and proximity of mobile users to the cloudlet.

Theorem 1 A strategy profile resulting from Algorithm 1 is a Nash equilibrium.

Proof: Consider a computation offloading decision profile of mobile users resulting from Algorithm 1. Assume the profile is not a Nash equilibrium. Then, when all users complete the computation offloading decisions at time t, there must exist a pair of access points i and j$(i, j \in \Gamma)$, given the computation offloading decisions of the other players, that the condition of Nash equilibrium cannot be satisfied. We will analyze the problem in the following two situations.

A. If one user decides to compute locally based on the above algorithm, but the condition of Nash equilibrium(condition 1) isn't satisfied. Then there exists an access point $i \in \Gamma$,

$$A * \frac{n_i^t}{B_i} - G * n_0^t < C - H \qquad (9)$$

where n_i^t denotes the number of players connected to access point i at time t. Let mobile user k be the last player to decide to compute locally. Denote the time when user k makes the computation offloading decision as $t^*(t^* \leq t)$. According to Algorithm 1, user k chooses the computation offloading strategy that minimizes the cost. So at time t^*, we have $C_k^0 \leq C_k^i$ for any $i \in \Lambda$. Based on Eq. 5 and 7, we can derive

$$A * \frac{n_i^{t^*}}{B_i} - G * n_0^{t^*} \geq C - H \qquad (10)$$

As user k is the last player to decide to compute locally and we assume that no user leaves the system while the other users are making decisions, there is

$$n_0^t = n_0^{t^*}$$

and

$$n_i^{t^*} \leq n_i^t$$

Eq.9 and 10 contradict with each other. Thus, if a user decides to compute locally according to Algorithm 1, he will reach a Nash equilibrium.

B. If one user decides to offload the computation task via AP $i(i \in \Lambda)$ based on Algorithm 1, but the condition of Nash equilibrium (condition 2) isn't satisfied, that is

$$A * \frac{n_i^t}{B_i} - G * n_0^t > C - H$$

or there exists $j \in \Lambda \setminus \{i\}$,

$$\frac{n_i}{B_i} - \frac{n_j}{B_j} > \frac{\theta}{A} \qquad (11)$$

Let mobile user k be the last player to decide to offload the computation task via access point i. Denote the time when user k makes the computation offloading decision as $t^*(t^* \leq t)$. Then at time t^*, user k chooses the computation offloading strategy that minimizes the cost based on the Algorithm 1. Thus at time t^*,

$$C_k^i(t^*) \leq C_k^0(t^*)$$

and for any $j \in \Lambda \setminus \{i\}$,

$$C_k^i(t^*) \leq C_k^j(t^*)$$

Based on Eq.5, 7 and 8, we can derive

$$A * \frac{n_i^{t^*}}{B_i} - G * n_0^{t^*} \leq C - H$$

and for any $j \in \Lambda \setminus \{i\}$,

$$\frac{n_i^{t^*}}{B_i} - \frac{n_j^{t^*}}{B_j} \leq 0 \qquad (12)$$

As mobile user k is the last to decide to offload via AP i and we assume that no user leaves the system while the other users are making decisions, there is

$$n_i^t = n_i^{t^*}$$

$$n_0^{t^*} \leq n_0^t$$

and for any $j \in \Lambda \setminus \{i\}$

$$n_j^{t^*} \leq n_j^t$$

Eq.11 and 12 contradict with each other. So if a user decides to offload the computation via AP i according to Algorithm1, he will reach a Nash equilibrium.

From the above analysis, we verify the irrationality of the assumption that the strategy profile resulting from Algorithm 1 is not a Nash equilibrium. Thus Theorem 1 is proved.

5. OFFLOADING STRATEGY FOR DIVERSE USERS

Analysis in section 4 assumes that all users are identical. However, in the real-life situation, mobile users usually get diverse computation tasks, computation capabilities, energy consumption etc. In this section, we will analyze computation offloading strategy in the case of heterogeneous mobile users.

For one user who decides to offload the computation via wireless AP $i(i \in \Lambda)$ or compute locally (i=0), the cost should be smaller than any other access points(or compute locally),

$$C_k^i \leq C_k^j \ for \ any \ j \in \Gamma \setminus \{i\}$$

In other words,

$$C_k^i \leq \min_{j \in \Gamma \setminus \{i\}} C_k^j$$

Denote Δ_k as smallest difference of user k,

$$\Delta_k \triangleq \min_{j \in \Gamma \setminus \{i\}} (C_k^j - C_k^i)$$

It is intuitive that the mobile user with smaller Δ is more likely to change his computation offloading decision. Let K_i denote the set of users deciding to offload the computation via AP i ($i \in \Gamma$). With new players choosing to offload via AP i, k^* will be the first to change the offloading decision, where

$$k^* = argmin_{k \in K_i} \Delta_k$$

A mobile user k is motivated to change its computation offloading decision only when a new user with larger Δ chooses the same AP as k. The user k chooses a new AP j and in return may motivate the users with larger Δ connecting to j to change their offloading decisions. As the number of the players is finite, the computation offloading game will attain a Nash equilibrium after finite update iterations when finally the player with the largest Δ chooses the proper wireless AP.

5.1 Existence of Nash equilibrium

We prove the existence of Nash equilibrium in the case of heterogeneous users by introducing the exact potential game.

Definition 2 A game is called an exact potential game when it admits a potential function P(s), for every $k \in \Upsilon$ and every $s_{-k} \in \Pi_{i \in \Gamma \setminus k} S_i$,

$$C_k(s_k^*, s_{-k}) - C_k(s_k, s_{-k}) = P(s_k^*, s_{-k}) - P(s_k, s_{-k}) \quad (13)$$

for every $s_k^*, s_k \in S_k$

Dov Monderer and Lloyd S. Shapley have proved at [16] that every finite exact potential game has a Nash equilibrium.

Algorithm 2 Distributed computation offloading strategy for heterogeneous mobile device users

Initialization:

    Each mobile user $k(k \in \Upsilon)$ initially chooses to compute locally, $s_k^0 = 0$

    Every mobile user k $(k \in \Upsilon)$ is allowed to update the computation decisions, $update_k^0 = 1$

    The update set $\phi(0) = \Upsilon$.

Iteration:

1: **for** each iteration t **do**
2:   **for** each user $k \in \phi(t-1)$ **do**
3:     obtain the load $n_i^{t-1}(i \in \Gamma)$ of all the wireless access points according to s_{-k}^{t-1} ;
4:     compute the better update set μ_k^t and choose the access point i_k^* that minimizes the cost, so the best update decision $b_k^t = i_k^*$;
5:   **end for**
6:   **if** the better update set $\mu^t \neq \varnothing$ **then**
7:     each user k that satisfies $\mu_k^t \neq \varnothing$ contends for the update opportunity;
8:     **if** user k win the contention **then**
9:       Update the offloading decision $s_k^t = i_k^*$;
10:       $update_k^t = 0$;
11:     **else**
12:       $s_k^t = s_k^{t-1}$;
13:     **end if**
14:   **else**
15:     break;
16:   **end if**
17:   **if** the update set $\phi(t) = \varnothing$ **then**
18:     break;
19:   **end if**
20: **end for**

    Note that the update set $\Phi \triangleq \{k : update_k = 1\}$, the better update set of user k, $\mu_k \triangleq \{s_k^* : C_k(s_k^*, s_{-k}) < C_k(s_k, s_{-k})\}$, and the better update set $\mu = \Pi_{k \in \Upsilon}\mu_k$.

Theorem 2 The computation offloading game in the case of heterogeneous mobile users is a finite exact potential game and the potential function P(s),

$$P(s) = \sum_{i=1}^{I}\{\sum_{k=1}^{K}\frac{A_k}{B_i}f(s_k = i) * \sum_{m=1}^{K}f(s_m = i)$$

$$- \sum_{k=1}^{K}G_k f(s_k = i)\sum_{m=1}^{K}f(s_m = 0)\}$$

$$+ \sum_{k=1}^{K}(aF_k^2 L_k + a_k * \frac{L_k}{F_k} - H_k)f(s_k = 0) \quad (14)$$

Here $f(s_k = i) = 1$ if $s_k = i$, else $f(s_k = i) = 0$.

The proof is given in Appendix A

We take advantage of the finite improvement property of the computation offloading game and design the computation offloading decision update algorithm(Algorithm 2) for heterogeneous mobile users.

6. NUMERICAL RESULTS AND ANALYSIS

In this section, we conduct numerical extensive simulations to evaluate the performance of our proposed algorithms. We consider a scenario that n mobile users located

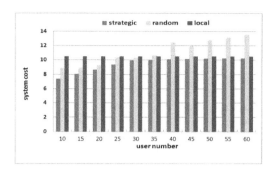

Figure 2: System cost of different computation offloading algorithms(homogeneous)

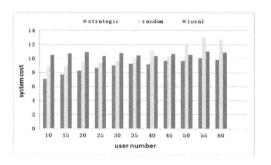

Figure 3: System cost of different computation offloading algorithms(heterogeneous)

in a building with 10 APs accessible. A Cloudlet whose computational capability is $F = 100GHz$ provides service for this building. We set the face recognition application in [24] as the example of computation tasks, of which the transmission block is $L_k = 420KB$. We set the calculation requirement $M_k = 3000Megacycles$. The bandwidth of the APs obeys normal distribution with the expectation μ_{bw} of 5MHz and standard deviation of $0.2 * \mu_{bw}$.

We compare the performance of our proposed algorithms with two other computation offloading strategies. 1)**Local Computation**: all mobile users execute their computation tasks locally on their mobile devices. 2)**Random Selection**: mobile users either randomly choose one of the wireless APs to offload their computation tasks or execute their tasks locally.

We evaluate the performance of each algorithm by using system cost which is denoted as

$$C_{system} = \frac{\sum_{k=1}^{K}C_k^{s_k}}{K} \quad (15)$$

We first evaluate the performance and the impact of user numbers on performance of Algorithm 1 in the case of homogeneous mobile users. The computational capability of each mobile user is $F_k = 1GHz$. As shown in Figure 2, the performance of Algorithm 1 outperforms **Local Computation** and **Random Selection**. When the user number is 10, Algorithm 1 can improve the system cost by up to 20% compared with the other two algorithms. With the increasing number of mobile users, the system cost of Algorithm 1 is getting closer to that of Local Computation while the system cost of Random Select grows much faster than that of Algorithm 1 and Local Computation. This is because

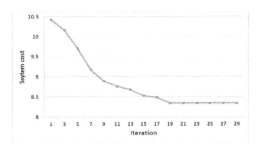

Figure 4: Dynamics of system cost by Algorithm2

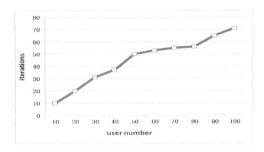

Figure 5: Number of iterations by Algorithm2

as the number of mobile users increases, the bandwidth resources of the APs and the computation resources of the cloudlet become scarcer. By Algorithm 1, more mobile users choose to execute their tasks locally on the mobile devices to avoid competition for the bandwidth and computation resources. However, by Random Select algorithm, many users still choose to offload the computation tasks even though executing the computation tasks locally is more beneficial.

To evaluate the performance of Algorithm 2, we conduct a similar simulation as the first one. The difference is that mobile users are diverse in the the computational capability of their mobile devices. We generate the computational capability of different mobile devices by applying a normal distribution with the mean μ_{comp} of 1GHz and standard deviation of $0.2 * \mu_{comp}$. Figure 3 depicts the results and shows similar trends as Figure 2. When the number of users is 10, our algorithm can reduce the system cost by 25% compared with the other two algorithms.

To verify the convergence of algorithm 2, we run a simulation with 20 mobile users. As shown in Figure 4, algorithm 2 can keep the system cost decreasing and after 19 iterations converge to a low and stable state, which is a Nash equilibrium.

Scalability of a computation offloading algorithm is also an important metric. We evaluate the scalability of Algorithm 2 by calculating the number of iterations before attaining a Nash equilibrium. We record the the number of iterations, which changes with the number of mobile users. As shown in Figure 5, the number of iterations increases weak-linearly with the increasing number of mobile users. Thus we conclude that Algorithm 2 scales well with the number of mobile users.

7. CONCLUSION

Computation offloading is an effective solution to relieving the burden of mobile devices in MC2. With the widespread deployment of WLAN, offloading via multiple wireless APs

will obtain extensive application. In this paper, we take energy and delay into account and analyze the cloudlet-based computation offloading strategy via multiple wireless APs in the case of multiple homogeneous and heterogeneous mobile users. We formulate the problem as a computation offloading game and design computation offloading algorithms for homogeneous and heterogeneous mobile users. Extensive simulations of the algorithms are conducted and demonstrate that our algorithms can effectively improve the system cost while scaling well with the number of mobile users. In our future work, we will consider the influence of user mobility on the computation offloading strategy of the other mobile users.

8. ACKNOWLEDGMENTS

This work is funded by the National Natural Science Foundation of China(NO.61472199,NO.61163050) and Tsinghua University Initiative Scientific Research Program(NO.20121087999).

9. REFERENCES

[1] N. Balasubramanian, A. Balasubramanian, and A. Venkataramani. Energy consumption in mobile phones: a measurement study and implications for network applications. In *Proceedings of the 9th ACM SIGCOMM conference on Internet measurement conference*, pages 280–293. ACM, 2009.

[2] S. Barbarossa, S. Sardellitti, and P. Di Lorenzo. Joint allocation of computation and communication resources in multiuser mobile cloud computing. In *Signal Processing Advances in Wireless Communications (SPAWC), 2013 IEEE 14th Workshop on*, pages 26–30. IEEE, 2013.

[3] M. V. Barbera, S. Kosta, A. Mei, and J. Stefa. To offload or not to offload? the bandwidth and energy costs of mobile cloud computing. In *INFOCOM, 2013 Proceedings IEEE*, pages 1285–1293. IEEE, 2013.

[4] X. Chen. Decentralized computation offloading game for mobile cloud computing. *Parallel and Distributed Systems, IEEE Transactions on*, 26(4):974–983, 2015.

[5] B.-G. Chun, S. Ihm, P. Maniatis, M. Naik, and A. Patti. Clonecloud: elastic execution between mobile device and cloud. In *Proceedings of the sixth conference on Computer systems*, pages 301–314. ACM, 2011.

[6] E. Cuervo, A. Balasubramanian, D.-k. Cho, A. Wolman, S. Saroiu, R. Chandra, and P. Bahl. Maui: making smartphones last longer with code offload. In *Proceedings of the 8th international conference on Mobile systems, applications, and services*, pages 49–62. ACM, 2010.

[7] H. T. Dinh, C. Lee, D. Niyato, and P. Wang. A survey of mobile cloud computing: architecture, applications, and approaches. *Wireless communications and mobile computing*, 13(18):1587–1611, 2013.

[8] N. Fernando, S. W. Loke, and W. Rahayu. Mobile cloud computing: A survey. *Future Generation Computer Systems*, 29(1):84–106, 2013.

[9] D. Huang, P. Wang, and D. Niyato. A dynamic offloading algorithm for mobile computing. *Wireless Communications, IEEE Transactions on*, 11(6):1991–1995, 2012.

[10] G. Huerta-Canepa and D. Lee. An adaptable application offloading scheme based on application behavior. In *Advanced Information Networking and Applications-Workshops, 2008. AINAW 2008. 22nd International Conference on*, pages 387–392. IEEE, 2008.

[11] K. Kumar, J. Liu, Y.-H. Lu, and B. Bhargava. A survey of computation offloading for mobile systems. *Mobile Networks and Applications*, 18(1):129–140, 2013.

[12] K. Kumar and Y.-H. Lu. Cloud computing for mobile users: Can offloading computation save energy? *Computer*, (4):51–56, 2010.

[13] V. C. Leung, M. Chen, M. Guizani, and B. Vucetic. Cloud-assisted mobile computing and pervasive services [guest editorial]. *Network, IEEE*, 27(5):4–5, 2013.

[14] A. P. Miettinen and J. K. Nurminen. Energy efficiency of mobile clients in cloud computing. In *Proceedings of the 2nd USENIX conference on Hot topics in cloud computing*, pages 4–4. USENIX Association, 2010.

[15] K. Mittal, E. M. Belding, and S. Suri. A game-theoretic analysis of wireless access point selection by mobile users. *Computer Communications*, 31(10):2049–2062, 2008.

[16] D. Monderer and L. S. Shapley. Potential games. *Games and economic behavior*, 14(1):124–143, 1996.

[17] M. J. Osborne and A. Rubinstein. *A course in game theory*. MIT press, 1994.

[18] M. R. Rahimi, J. Ren, C. H. Liu, A. V. Vasilakos, and N. Venkatasubramanian. Mobile cloud computing: A survey, state of art and future directions. *Mobile Networks and Applications*, 19(2):133–143, 2014.

[19] M. R. Rahimi, N. Venkatasubramanian, S. Mehrotra, and A. V. Vasilakos. Mapcloud: mobile applications on an elastic and scalable 2-tier cloud architecture. In *Proceedings of the 2012 IEEE/ACM Fifth International Conference on Utility and Cloud Computing*, pages 83–90. IEEE Computer Society, 2012.

[20] M. R. Rahimi, N. Venkatasubramanian, and A. V. Vasilakos. Music: Mobility-aware optimal service allocation in mobile cloud computing. In *Cloud Computing (CLOUD), 2013 IEEE Sixth International Conference on*, pages 75–82. IEEE, 2013.

[21] A. Rudenko, P. Reiher, G. J. Popek, and G. H. Kuenning. Saving portable computer battery power through remote process execution. *ACM SIGMOBILE Mobile Computing and Communications Review*, 2(1):19–26, 1998.

[22] Z. Sanaei, S. Abolfazli, A. Gani, and R. Buyya. Heterogeneity in mobile cloud computing: taxonomy and open challenges. *Communications Surveys & Tutorials, IEEE*, 16(1):369–392, 2014.

[23] M. Satyanarayanan, P. Bahl, R. Caceres, and N. Davies. The case for vm-based cloudlets in mobile computing. *Pervasive Computing, IEEE*, 8(4):14–23, 2009.

[24] T. Soyata, R. Muraleedharan, C. Funai, M. Kwon, and W. Heinzelman. Cloud-vision: Real-time face recognition using a mobile-cloudlet-cloud acceleration architecture. In *Computers and Communications (ISCC), 2012 IEEE Symposium on*, pages 000059–000066. IEEE, 2012.

[25] Y. Wen, W. Zhang, and H. Luo. Energy-optimal mobile application execution: Taming resource-poor mobile devices with cloud clones. In *INFOCOM, 2012 Proceedings IEEE*, pages 2716–2720. IEEE, 2012.

[26] R. Wolski, S. Gurun, C. Krintz, and D. Nurmi. Using bandwidth data to make computation offloading decisions. In *Parallel and Distributed Processing, 2008. IPDPS 2008. IEEE International Symposium on*, pages 1–8. IEEE, 2008.

[27] C. Xian, Y.-H. Lu, and Z. Li. Adaptive computation offloading for energy conservation on battery-powered systems. In *Parallel and Distributed Systems, 2007 International Conference on*, volume 2, pages 1–8. IEEE, 2007.

[28] L. Yang, J. Cao, Y. Yuan, T. Li, A. Han, and A. Chan. A framework for partitioning and execution of data stream applications in mobile cloud computing. *ACM SIGMETRICS Performance Evaluation Review*, 40(4):23–32, 2013.

[29] X. Zhang, A. Kunjithapatham, S. Jeong, and S. Gibbs. Towards an elastic application model for augmenting the computing capabilities of mobile devices with cloud computing. *Mobile Networks and Applications*, 16(3):270–284, 2011.

APPENDIX

A. PROOF OF THEOREM2

For each user $k \in \Upsilon$, for every $s_{-k} \in \Pi_{i \in \Gamma \setminus \{k\}} S_i$, we prove Theorem2 in the following two situations:

I. for each $i, j \in \Lambda$(user k decides to offload the computation via AP i or j)

$$P(i, s_{-k}) - P(j, s_{-k}) = [\frac{A_k}{B_i} * \sum_{m=1}^{K} f(s_m = i)]$$

$$-[\frac{A_k}{B_j} * \sum_{m=1}^{K} f(s_m = j)] = C_k(i, s_{-k}) - C_k(j, s_{-k})$$

II. for $i = 0, j \in \Lambda$(user k decides to compute locally or offload the computation via AP j)

$$P(0, s_{-k}) - P(j, s_{-k}) = (a F_k^2 L_k + a_k * \frac{L_k}{F_k} - H_k)$$

$$-[\frac{A_k}{B_j} * \sum_{m=1}^{K} f(s_m = j) - G_k * \sum_{m=1}^{K} f(s_k = 0)]$$

$$= C_k(0, s_{-k}) - C_k(j, s_{-k})$$

So for any $i, j \in \Gamma$

$$P(i, s_{-k}) - P(j, s_{-k}) = C_k(i, s_{-k}) - C_k(j, s_{-k})$$

According to Definition 2, the computation offloading game is a finite exact potential game

Energy-Efficient Model for Overlay Cognitive Communications

Salvador Perez-Salgado and Enrique Rodriguez-Colina
Department of Electrical Engineering
Metropolitan Autonomous University, Campus Iztapalapa
Mexico City, Mexico
{csps,erod}@xanum.uam.mx

ABSTRACT

Current approaches regarding energy-efficient cognitive radio networks found in the literature aim to optimize the functionalities met by cognitive systems. This is done in order to improve the number of transmitted bits per energy unit and to increase the network lifetime of cognitive devices when they have limited power resources. However, many of these approaches may not fit together when designing a full cognitive radio system. For this reason, a five-layer network model for energy-efficient overlay-based cognitive radio is proposed in this paper. This model includes a set of functionalities necessary to achieve energy-efficiency. We show, by means of simulations, that these functionalities may reduce the number of secondary transmissions by improving the exploitation of primary channels. We also found that, under certain scenarios, the number of transmissions necessary to achieve successful communications can be reduced to the half when the primary network is loaded at 60% of its maximum capacity, when transmissions with low E_b/N_0 are combined with adaptive bandwidth channels.

Categories and Subject Descriptors

C.2.1 [**Network Architecture and Design**]: Wireless communication – *Energy-efficient Cognitive radio*

Keywords

Energy-efficiency communications; overlay cognitive radio

1. INTRODUCTION

Cognitive radio (CR) emerged to efficiently exploit the spectrum, by reducing its waste and congestion [1]. Even when it aims for spectral-efficiency using Dynamic Spectrum Access (DSA), i.e., the opportunistic utilization of the spectrum; energy-efficiency is also desirable. Hence, we define energy-efficient CR as *a device that dynamically access the spectrum minimizing interference caused to the users licensed to use the spectrum*, also called primary users (PU), *and the energy consumption of the cognitive devices*, also called secondary users (SU); *while maximizing the throughput and spectral usage of the secondary transmissions*.

Even when research on CR is not new and has been around for more than two decades, energy-efficiency is still an open issue that requires further analysis. To the best of our knowledge, there

MSWiM'15, November 02-06, 2015, Cancun, Mexico
© 2015 ACM. ISBN 978-1-4503-3762-5/15/11...$15.00
DOI: http://dx.doi.org/10.1145/2811587.2811629

is not yet an integral model of CR that proposes nor analyzes the functionalities required for energy-efficiency. In this paper, we propose an integral model for energy-efficient overlay-based [2] cognitive radio network, and describe the functionalities required at every layer of a five-layer model, similar to the model presented in [3]. Here, the primary networks (PN) –networks of licensed or primary users– are assumed heterogeneous; which implies that the total bandwidth used, the amount of spectral resources assigned to each primary user, and the communication parameters are different. It is also assumed that the secondary networks (SN) –networks of cognitive or secondary users– are capable of identifying whether a primary transmission is being carried out or not. The rest of this paper is organized as follows: Section 2 describes the proposed model and each of its layers. Computer simulation analysis is presented in Section 3. Finally, Section 4 concludes the paper.

2. A MODEL FOR ENERGY-EFFICIENT COGNITIVE NETWORKS

A layered network model separates the different tasks required to communicate nodes in a network, and allows the protocols used in each layer to be substituted at any moment without redesigning the whole system. Each of the proposed layers is analyzed below.

2.1. Energy-efficient Physical Layer

Many characteristics of the PUs are known a priori by the SUs in overlay SNs, like the bandwidth, modulation and coding schemes, and the minimum *signal to noise ratio* (SNR) required for a PU in order to decode messages. Yet, this does not imply that the SUs have to exploit the primary bands as the PUs do. The SUs can consider the primary bands just as spectral resources. Even when the decision on how the spectral resources are exploited is mainly defined in the upper layers, the physical layer must ensure that the available spectral resources can be utilized independently of how the transmissions are carried on, by handling hardware capabilities of CRs and by abstracting them to the upper layers. The proposed Energy-Efficient Physical Layer (E^2PHY) introduces five energy-efficient functionalities, which are presented below.

2.1.1. Adaptive Bandwidth Channels

It can be assumed that the spectral holes left by the PUs are not necessarily of the same bandwidth. So, it is desirable that the SUs can adapt their transmissions to variable-bandwidth channels in order to maximize their channel capacity [4]. This adaptation can improve their throughput and eventually reduce the number of transmissions. Similarly, the SUs may be capable of adaptively merging adjacent fixed-bandwidth channels. When the available white spaces are non-adjacent, multi-carrier approaches can be used. In terms of energy-efficiency, a reduced number of transmissions can reduce overall energy consumption.

2.1.2. Adaptive Power Control

Adaptive power control is a common approach to energy-efficient communications. Transmission power has to be maintained between two thresholds, an upper bound that sets the transmission power as low as possible to avoid energy waste and a lower bound that keeps a *signal to interference plus noise ratio* (SINR) large enough to understand the transmitted data. Yet, the transmitted signals must be powerful enough to overcome adverse channel conditions, like fading and path-loss. An adaptive power control mechanism is required in order to improve the throughput of the SUs while reducing the amount of consumed energy.

2.1.3. Adaptive Channel Switching

One ability required for DSA is adaptive channel switching. This ability allows the SUs resuming their communications in other channels when the arrival of a PU is detected or expected, in some cases it is achieved without performing additional sensing by means of a dynamic selection of backup channels [5]. From an energy-efficient perspective, adaptive channel switching reduces consumption when the throughput of the SN is increased and the interference with the PNs is reduced.

2.1.4. Adaptive Coding and Modulation

Channel coding schemes can be utilized by the SUs in order to reduce retransmissions provoked by adverse channel conditions like noise or interference. Adaptive coding can increase energy-efficiency of the SN by reducing the number of retransmissions and the length of the bit streams, because the most adequate coding scheme can be selected according to the conditions of the available primary channels. In addition, the SUs can employ adaptive modulation to exploit channels with different gains, bandwidth and noise levels.

2.1.5. Sleep Capability

Some approaches in the literature consider that the SUs can switch between sleep and awake states to reduce energy consumption during idle periods [6]. In other words, a SU can choose to turn their transceiver off when a PU is detected present, because no secondary transmissions are allowed during that period.

2.2. Energy-Efficient Link Layer

Energy-efficiency functionalities of the link layer have been aimed in the literature as cross-layered designs involving physical and link layers functionalities. Specifically, power and spectrum allocation, and sensing and transmission duration are approached. Here, we propose an Energy-Efficient Link Layer (E²LNK).

2.2.1. Adaptive Media Access Control

The E²LNK uses an *adaptive media access control* that considers three actions: *1)* spectrum sensing, *2)* transmissions (data, control and sensing outcomes), and *3)* idle periods. The time required to sense and to cooperatively determine the channel states has to be optimally determined so it can minimize energy consumption, and maximize the transmission time and throughput of the SUs, and the protection of the PUs. The spectrum sensing duration has to be enough to accurately identify the status of the primary channels, because an elevated number of false detections leads to collisions and retransmissions, which in turn wastes energy. When a channel is sensed idle, the outcome has to be compared with other nodes to discard shadowing. During the reporting phase, the SUs exchange one or more control frames to confirm the idle state. Finally, if the channel is confirmed idle, the SUs may transmit; otherwise, they should remain idle, enter to sleep mode or try a different channel.

2.2.2. Adaptive Frame Size

There are two types of frames needed by almost every MAC protocol found in the literature: control frames and data frames. The E²LNK has to be capable of adapting the structure of control and data frames in order to exploit the available primary channels. The payload size of the frames determine the maximum transfer unit of the SN. Furthermore, cognitive data can be included in the frame header to manage the SNs.

2.2.3. Access Scheduling with Collision Avoidance

The maximization of throughput and energy-efficiency can be approached from the point of view of a single SU instead of considering the whole SN. When a SN is considered, fairness can improve energy savings because it avoids the starvation problem of the SUs, i.e., the energy invested sensing the primary channels does not go to waste if a fair opportunity to perform transmissions is assured. As for collision avoidance, it is of critical importance that SUs minimize collisions among themselves and with the PUs. Collisions damage the throughput and energy-efficiency of the SN because the energy consumed during the sensing and transmission periods is wasted when a retransmission is necessary.

2.2.4. Local flow and error control

Data integrity in the network can be improved if the E²LNK provides mechanisms to identify transmission errors. Additional energy consumptions caused by retransmissions are justified for *non-delay-sensitive* applications as their main concern is to deliver error-free data. Otherwise, retransmissions must be avoided for *delay-sensitive* applications as long as the number of delivered transmissions is enough to understand data.

2.3. Energy-Efficient Network Layer

When the SN covers wider areas, communications are severely damaged by fading and other effects of wireless channels. Cognitive Access Points (CAPs) can be utilized to create local links (scope of the link layer), and unite local clusters of SUs creating multi-hop networks (scope of the network layer). The proposed Energy-Efficient Network Layer (E²NET) adds one functionality.

2.3.1. Energy Aware Routing

The selection of the best route for energy-efficient SNs has to swiftly recover transmissions from route failures and congestion without route rediscovering, in order to reduce energy waste. The selection of the best route to perform secondary transmissions does not only affect delay, but throughput and energy-efficiency, because communications often use different channels at each CAP.

2.4. Energy-Efficient Transport Layer

Applications determine if the transport layer requires connection-oriented or connectionless communications. Hence, the Energy-Efficient Transport Layer (E²TRA) has to be capable of providing both without any special consideration. The proposed E²TRA considers two functionalities.

2.4.1. Adaptive Acknowledgments

An adaptive acknowledgment mechanism can be employed by the SUs to reduce the number of control transmissions in connection-oriented communications. The frequency of the acknowledgment messages (ACK) can be determined by a trust mechanism which avoid ACK messages when the received segments are trustworthy.

2.4.2. Adaptive Flow an Error Control

Flow an error control in the E²TRA considers retransmissions not only from local SUs, but from source and destination nodes, which in a SN can introduce additional delays. The MTU defined at the link layer and the size of the buffers in the CAPs determine how many data can be transfer in each segment, in order to avoid buffer overruns. Yet, these conditions may change over time in SNs due to the DSA. Therefore, the E²TRA has to dynamically control the data flow between sender and receiver. An adequate flow control and the minimization of retransmissions caused by corrupted data during communications improve energy-efficiency.

2.5. Energy-Efficient Application Layer

This layer defines whether the data that have to be transmitted are *delay-sensitive* or *non-delay-sensitive*. Two functionalities are considered in the Energy-Efficient Application Layer (E²APP).

2.5.1. Adaptive Data Relinquishment

Multimedia applications, e.g., video streaming, reduce delay by sacrificing part of their data. These systems adaptively choose the best quality of their contents to maintain better user experiences from their transmissions. Energy-efficient SNs can exploit this practice by selectively dropping out data in order to adapt their transmissions to the conditions of the PNs and SNs. When the conditions reported by the lower layers aim higher payloads, the E²APP can allow higher quality as long as the energy consumption does not exceed permissible thresholds.

2.5.2. Adaptive Load Partitioning

Due to energy constraints, applications may employ an adaptive load partitioning scheme between the SUs and CAPs. Most of the power intensive processing can be performed in the CAP, while the SUs can play the role of intelligent terminals that display the received data [7]. Hence, energy-efficient communications have to adaptively distribute the network load and data processing regarding specific applications between the SUs and the CAP, considering not only their speed and computational power, but also their energy capabilities.

3. SIMULATION RESULTS

In this section, some energy-efficient functionalities are analyzed by means of computer simulations. We focus our analysis on the *adaptive bandwidth channel* (E²PHY) and the *adaptive media access control* (E²LNK) functionalities.

For the first simulation scenario let us assume a time-slotted system that can transmit opportunistically on one o more primary channels N: $\{x_i = \{0, 1\}, i = 1, \dots, N\}$, with $x_i = 0$ when idle and $x_i = 1$ when busy. All the primary channels were assumed with the same bandwidth. We also assumed that a single SU has data to transmit in its buffer. The amount of these data (d) is reduced at every transmission. When all the primary channels are occupied, a SU cannot transmit and waits for the next time slot, keeping the same amount of data in its buffer. For this scenario, two cases were analyzed: *1) nonadaptive bandwidth channels*, i.e., a SU uses any fixed-bandwidth channel available to transmit its data; and *2) adaptive bandwidth channels*, i.e., a SU identifies the maximum number of adjacent channels during the present time slot, once found these channels are joined as a new channel of bandwidth of χ times the fixed-bandwidth channel. The SU transmits using the maximum bit rate achievable considering different *energy per bit to noise power spectral density ratios* (E_b/N_0), which in turn, imply different SNR and bitrates. The maximum bitrate for each case corresponds with the Shannon's

Channel Capacity of the selected or merged channels, considering Rayleigh fading channels (C_{Ray}) [8] for each SNR. C_{Ray} is shown in (1), where e is the base of the natural logarithm and E is the Euler's gamma constant ($E \approx 0.577215665$).

$$C_{Ray} \approx B \log_2(e) e^{-1/\text{SNR}} \left(-E + \ln(\text{SNR}) + \frac{1}{\text{SNR}} \right) \quad (1)$$

The simulation ran for $n = 100$ time slots and was iterated $L = 250$ times per each primary activity probability $p(\text{PU}^{\text{ON}})$ in $[0.1 - 0.9]$, in order to obtain the mean transmissions required for emptying the buffer of the SU. Other numerical values considered for the simulation were $t_S = 2.4$ ms (about 50% of the time slot used in the GSM standard); $N = 10$ adjacent primary channels of bandwidth $B = 2$ MHz, and a fixed amount of data $d = 100$ MB, initially stored in the buffer of the SU (the amount of stored data is reduced with every successful transmission). Figure 1 shows the reduction in the number of transmissions needed by the SU in order to empty its buffer.

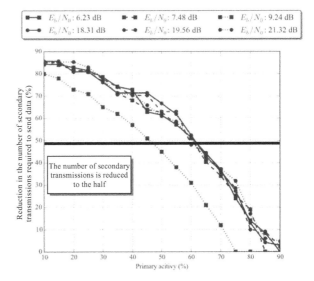

Figure 1. The *Adaptive Channel Bandwidth* functionality of the E²PHY reduces the number of transmissions of the SUs by joining adjacent primary channels.

The reduction in the number of transmissions was computed as the ratio of the nonadaptive and the adaptive transmissions required to empty the buffer of the SU. Under low primary activity, higher reductions occur; but when $p(\text{PU}^{\text{ON}})$ increases, the adaptive and nonadaptive approaches have the same performance, i.e., there is no reduction. This is expected because it is more difficult finding adjacent channels when the PN is heavily loaded. Furthermore, the number of transmissions can be reduced to half when primary activity is 60%. The E_b/N_0 values shown in the figure were obtained from Table 1. The variable k represents an arbitrary fraction of C_{Ray}.

Table 1. **Values used to compute E_b/N_0 in Figure 1.**

k	C_{Ray} (kb/s)	SNR (dB)	B (MHz)	E_b/N_0 (dB)
0.50				9.24
0.75	4 765	10.0		7.48
1.00			2	6.23
0.50				21.32
0.75	16 580	27.5		19.56
1.00				18.31

For the second simulation scenario we assume that the SUs act as hidden receivers overhearing the primary channels. We defined a sensing mechanism called *spectral eavesdropping* as a listening period performed by the SUs, with the aim of identifying idle and busy channels. A MAC divided in: *1)* eavesdropping, *2)* reporting and decision, and *3)* data transmission was assumed, the layout of the access policy is depicted in Figure 2. Also, M SUs and N primary channels were considered. In this scenario, the primary channels need to be eavesdropped during certain time (τ) to determine if they are being utilized. Once this task has finished, each SU reports its sensing outcomes to a CAP using *time division multiple access* (TDMA). Once the results are gathered, a fusion rule is applied at the CAP to determine if the sensed channel is idle or busy. Then, the last transmission slot of the reporting phase is employed to broadcast the fusion result; this allows all nodes being aware of the current status of N, the full reporting and decision phase takes γ ms. Even when the reporting and decision phases prevent collisions, they reduce the time that the SN can exploit a primary channel for transmitting data ($t_{TX}= T - \tau - \gamma$).

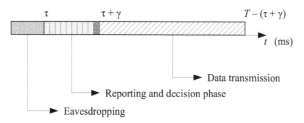

Figure 2. Layout of the simulated access policy.

Based on the simulation results, Figure 3 shows the portion of a time slot that can be utilized for data transmissions after the eavesdropping and reporting phases finished. This is presented as a function of the *eavesdropping ratio* (n), i.e., the percentage of the primary bitstream that has to be eavesdropped to identify an idle channel, and the number of primary channels available. For the simulated scenario, we found that n cannot exceed 5% of the primary frames length, because the eavesdropping and reporting phases would not leave enough time for data transmission during

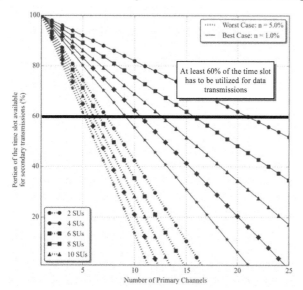

Figure 3. The *Adaptive Access Policy* functionality can increase the amount of time available for secondary transmissions after the spectrum eavesdropping and the reporting phases.

the time slot under certain N and M combinations. For the worst case scenario ($n = 5\%$), up to seven primary channels can be exploited when the minimum portion of the time slot required for data transmissions is over 60% despite the number of SUs connected to the same CAP. For the best case scenario ($n = 1\%$), the number of SUs determines the number of exploitable primary channels. Energy spent in eavesdropping and reporting phases is wasted when no secondary transmissions are performed, but it is necessary to avoid interfering the PUs.

4. CONCLUSIONS

A five-layer network model and the functionalities necessary to achieve energy-efficient overlay cognitive radio were proposed. It is shown by means of simulations that these functionalities can reduce the number of secondary transmissions necessary to carry on a fixed amount of data. We found that the transmissions required to empty the buffer of a secondary user can be reduced to the half for primary network loads under 60%. We also conclude that an *adaptive media access control* is required to maximize the time available for data transmissions after sensing and sharing the results in the secondary network.

ACKNOWLEDGMENTS

This project is supported under the grants awarded by the **prodep** program of the Mexican Secretary of Public Education and by the Council of Science and Technology of Mexico (CONACyT).

REFERENCES

[1]   Simon Haykin, "Cognitive radio: brain-empowered wireless communications," *IEEE J. Sel. Areas Commun.*, vol. 23, no. 2, pp. 201–220, Feb. 2005, DOI=http://dx.doi.org/10.1109/JSAC.2004.839380.

[2]   Andrea Goldsmith, Syed Ali Jafar, Ivana Marić, and Sudhir Srinivasa, "Breaking Spectrum Gridlock With Cognitive Radios: An Information Theoretic Perspective," *Proc. IEEE*, vol. 97, no. 5, pp. 894–914, May 2009, DOI=http://dx.doi.org/10.1109/JPROC.2009.2015717.

[3]   Andrew S. Tanenbaum and David Wetherall, "Reference Models," in *Computer Networks*, 5th ed., Pearson Prentice Hall, 2011, p. 48.

[4]   Claude E. Shannon, "Communication in the Presence of Noise," *Proc. IRE*, vol. 37, no. 1, pp. 10–21, Jan. 1949, DOI=http://dx.doi.org/10.1109/JRPROC.1949.232969.

[5]   Jesús Hernandez-Guillen, Enrique Rodriguez-Colina, Ricardo Marcelin-Jimenez, and Michael Pascoe-Chalke, "CRUAM-MAC: A novel cognitive radio MAC protocol for dynamic spectrum access," in *IEEE LatinCom*, Cuenca, Ecuador, November 2012, pp. 1–6, DOI=http://dx.doi.org/10.1109/LATINCOM.2012.6505997

[6]   Kun Zheng and Husheng Li, "Achieving Energy Efficiency via Drowsy Transmission in Cognitive Radio," in *IEEE GlobeCom*, Miami, FL, December 2010, pp. 1–6, DOI=http://dx.doi.org/10.1109/GLOCOM.2010.5683355.

[7]   Christine E. Jones, Krishna M. Sivalingam, Prathima Agrawal, and Jyh Cheng Chen, "A Survey of Energy Efficient Network Protocols for Wireless Networks," *Wirel. Netw.*, vol. 7, no. 4, pp. 343–358, Jul. 2001, DOI=http://dx.doi.org/10.1023/A:1016627727877.

[8]   William C. Y. Lee, "Estimate of channel capacity in Rayleigh fading environment," *IEEE Trans. Veh. Technol.*, vol. 39, no. 3, pp. 187–189, Aug. 1990, DOI=http://dx.doi.org/10.1109/25.130999.

5G MmWave Module for the ns-3 Network Simulator

Marco Mezzavilla, Sourjya Dutta, Menglei Zhang,
Mustafa Riza Akdeniz, Sundeep Rangan
NYU WIRELESS, 2 MetroTech Center, 11211, Brooklyn, New York
{mezzavilla,sdutta,menglei,akdeniz,srangan}@nyu.edu

ABSTRACT

The increasing demand of data, along with the spectrum scarcity, are motivating a urgent shift towards exploiting new bands. This is the main reason behind identifying mmWaves as the key disruptive enabling technology for 5G cellular networks. Indeed, utilizing new bands means facing new challenges; in this context, they are mainly related to the radio propagation, which is shorter in range and more sensitive to obstacles. The resulting key aspects that need to be taken into account when designing mmWave cellular systems are *directionality* and *link intermittency*. The lack of network level results motivated this work, which aims at providing the first of a kind open source mmWave framework, based on the network simulator ns-3. The main focus of this work is the modeling of customizable channel, physical (PHY) and medium access control (MAC) layers for mmWave systems. The overall design and architecture of the model are discussed in details. Finally, the validity of our proposed framework is corroborated through the simulation of a simple scenario.

Categories and Subject Descriptors

I.6.5 [**Simulation and Modeling**]: Model Development—*Modeling methodolgies*; I.6.7 [**Simulation and Modeling**]: Simulation Support Systems—*Environments*

General Terms

Simulation; Modeling; Architecture; Design; Performance; Cellular; Wireless.

Keywords

mmWave; 5G; Cellular; Channel; Propagation; PHY; MAC.

1. INTRODUCTION

The ever increasing demand of wireless cellular data has motivated researchers to investigate the potentials of mil-

MSWiM'15, November 2–6, 2015, Cancun, Mexico.
© 2015 ACM. ISBN 978-1-4503-3762-5/15/11 ...$15.00.
DOI: http://dx.doi.org/10.1145/2811587.2811619.

limeter wave communication for the 5th generation of cellular technology. A substantial body of literature is currently available discussing physical measurements and formulations for millimeter wave channels [1], [2]. As a logical next step, we aim at studying how the upper layers of the communication network stack work over millimeter wave physical channels. In this work we aim to develop the first millimeter wave module for the ns-3 network simulator [3] that can be used to quantitatively analyze the performance of transport and application layer protocols over millimeter wave last-mile links.

The ns-3 network simulator currently implements a wide range of network protocols across various layers of the communication network. Due to this it is a valuable tool for researchers working on cross-layer design. The ns-3 simulator already hosts modules for the simulation of WiFi, WiMAX and 3GPP-LTE networks. In this paper we propose the first ns-3 module for the simulation of millimeter wave based communication systems.

The simulation module described in this paper is designed to be a fully customizable model where the user can plug in various parameters, like carrier frequency, bandwidth, frame structure, etc., describing the behavior of the millimeter wave channel and devices. In fact, the aim of this work is to enable researchers to flexibly use this module for various scenarios without the need of altering the source code.

The rest of the article is organized as follows. In Section 2, we discuss the architecture of the mmW module. Section 3 discusses the modeling of the physical layer. Section 4 follows with a discussion on the medium access control (MAC) layer for our module. The interfacing of the various modules is discussed in Section 5. In Section 6, we show the results obtained for a simple simulation scenario. Finally, we list our future work items and conclude the paper in Section 7.

2. MMWAVE FRAMEWORK

Our framework includes a basic implementation of mmWave devices, which comprises the propagation and channel model, the physical (PHY) layer, and the MAC layer. The module completely is developed in C++. The design of this module is inspired by the ns-3 Lena module which, in our opinion, has a very robust architecture. **Fig. 1** gives the UML diagram of the most important classes in our mmWave module. We will provide details about the various classes and their interoperation in the following sections.

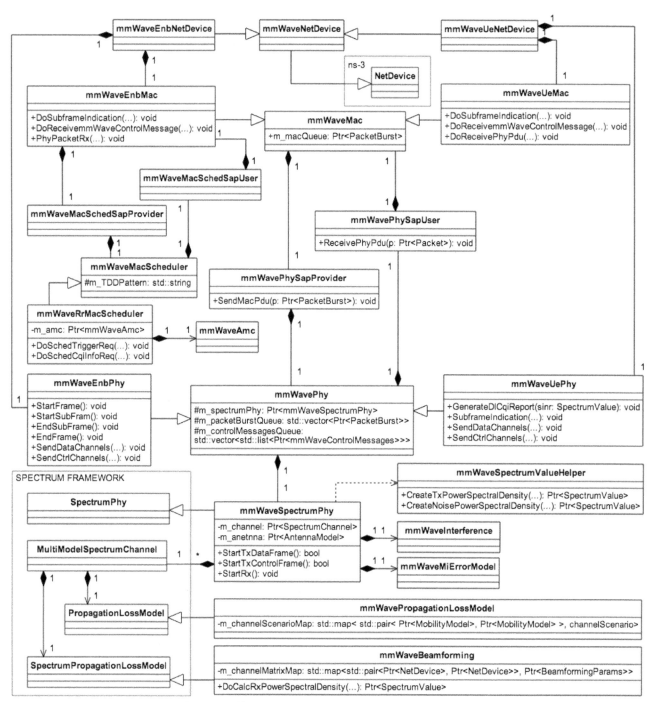

Figure 1: **Class diagram for the mmWave module.**

3. PHY LAYER

The salient features of the mmWave PHY layer are: (i) a fully customizable time division duplex (TDD) frame structure, (ii) a radio characterization that includes small and large scale channel variations, along with supporting multiple input multiple output (MIMO) techniques such as beamforming, (iii) a decoding error model at the receiver, (iv) an interference model, and (v) a feedback loop for channel adaptation. The following parts give a detailed outline of the implementation specifics of the PHY layer for the mmWave module.

3.1 Frame Structure

The authors in [4] and [5] contend that in order to reduce the latency over the air interface, the 5G mmWave systems will be targeted towards TDD operation. The ns-3 module for mmWave implements a customizable TDD frame structure. Each frame is subdivided into a number of subframes of fixed length specified by the user. Each subframe in turn is split into a number of slots of a fixed duration. Each slot comprises a specified number of OFDM symbols. A slot can be either **control** or **data**, assigned for either **uplink** (UL) or **downlink** (DL).

Fig. 2 shows an example of the TDD frame structure based on the work in [6]. Each frame of length 10ms is split in time into 10 subframes each of duration 1ms. Each subframe is further divided into 8 slots where each slot is of length $125\mu s$ representing 30 orthogonal frequency division multiplexing (OFDM) symbols of length approximately $4.16\mu s$. The first two slots are assigned for control in the downlink and in the uplink direction respectively. Slots 3 to 5 are allocated for downlink and slots 5 to 8 for uplink data transmission. A switching gap of $1\mu s$ is introduced each time the allocated direction changes from uplink to downlink or vice versa. In the frequency domain the entire bandwidth of 1GHz is divided into 4 resource blocks (RBs). Each RB is subdivided into 18 sub-bands each of width 13.89 MHz making a total of 72 sub-bands for the entire bandwidth. Each of these sub-bands is composed of 48 sub-carriers. In this case, the total number of resource elements for one slot would be: $N_{RE} = 30 \times (48 \times 72) = 103680$.

3.1.1 Parameter configuration

The frame structure is completely customizable by the user. A common object of the *mmwavePhyMacCommon* class stores the user specified values of all the parameters used by the simulator. The parameters used to customize the frame structure are specified in Table 1.

The value of the Transmission Time Interval (TTI), which in our model is the duration of one slot, can be derived from the parameters in Table 1 as,

$$\text{TTI} = SymbolPerSlot \times SymbolLength.$$

This is implemented by the function *mmwavePhyMacCommon::GetTTI()*.

Similarly we can compute the bandwidth of one RB as,

$$B_{RB} = SubbandsPerRB \times SubbandWidth.$$

This is implemented by the function *mmwavePhyMacCommon::GetRBWidth()*. The total system bandwidth can thus be computed as,

$$B_{system} = B_{RB} \times NumResourceBlock.$$

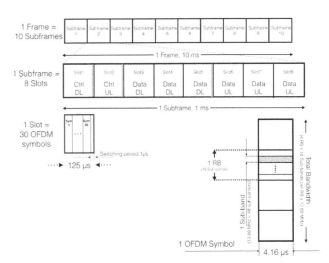

Figure 2: **Example of mmWave frame structure.**

This is implemented by the function *mmwavePhyMacCommon::GetSystemBandwidth()*.

3.1.2 Transmission schemes

The *mmWaveEnbPhy* and the *mmWaveUePhy* models the physical layer for the base station and the user device respectively. Broadly the physical layer (i) handles the transmission and reception of signals, (ii) simulate the start and the end of frames, subframes, and slots, (iii) deliver data packets and control messages received over the channel to the MAC layer, (iv) model the decoding error for the received signal and calculate the metrics like the signal to interference and noise ratio (SINR).

The physical layer contains one instance of the *mmWaveSpectrumPhy* class. The transmission procedure for data frames is performed by the *StartTxDataFrames*. For control messages the *StartTxControlFrames* is invoked. The reception procedure is performed by *StartRx* method. The functionality of the *StartRx* is further subdivided into *StartRxData* and *StartRxControl*. Based on the total band of frequency available for transmission, the PHY computes the transmission power spectral density using the *mmWaveSpectrumValueHelper* component and uses this value for the signal transmission.

After the reception of the data packets, the PHY layer calculates the SINR of the received signal taking into account the MIMO beamforming gains. The physical layer at the user device maps the calculated SINR into a Channel Quality Indicator (CQI), which is fed-back to the base station for the resource allocation. Control signals are assumed to be ideally transmitted. As discussed in Section 3.3, the PHY layer also incorporates the error model where a probabilistic approach is used to determine whether a packet should be dropped by the receiver. The correctly received packets are sent to the MAC layer using the service access point (SAP) discussed in Section 5.

The physical layer handles the start and the end of frames, subframes and slots based on the TTI derived from the user specified configurations. Based on the resource allocation scheme decided by the *mmWaveEnbMac*, as described in Section 4.2.2, the PHY decides the nature of the communication for a particular slot (data/control) and the direction of the message to transfer (uplink/downlink). At the beginning

Parameter Name	Default Value	Description
SymbolPerSlot	30	Number of OFDM symbols per slot
SymbolLength	$4.16\mu s$	Length of one OFDM symbol in μs
SlotsPerSubframe	8	Number of slots in one subframe
SubframePerFrame	10	Number of subframes in one frame
NumReferenceSymbols	6	The number of reference OFDM symbols per slot
TDDControlDataPattern	"ccdddddd"	The control (c) and data(d) pattern
SubcarriersPerSubband	48	Number of subcarriers in each sub-band
SubbandsPerRB	18	Number of sub-bands in one resource block
SubbandWidth	13.89e6	The width of one sub-band in Hz
NumResourceBlock	4	Number of resource blocks in one slot
CenterFreq	28e9	The carrier frequency in Hz

Table 1: **Parameters for configuring the mmWave frame structure.**

of each slot the eNodeB PHY sends a *SubframeIndication* to the MAC. The subframe indication for the first slot triggers the scheduling and resource allocation functions. The data packets and the control messages received from the MAC are stored in the *PacketBurstQueue* and the *ControlMessage-Queue*, respectively, and are transmitted to the connected device in the allocated slots.

3.2 Channel Modeling

As illustrated in Fig. 3, we need to take into account a number of procedures to capture characteristics of the mmWave propagation. The key contribution here relates to the computation of the multi-antenna gains, which is particularly critical for mmWave communications.

The link budget for the mmWave propagation channel is given by,

$$P_{RX} = P_{TX} + G_{BF} - PL - SW, \qquad (1)$$

where P_{RX} is the total received power in dBm, P_{TX} is the total transmit power, G_{BF} is the beamforming gain, and finally PL and SW represent the pathloss and shadowing, respectively.

3.2.1 mmWave Propagation Loss Model

The mmWave pathloss model can be modeled with 3 states, as reported in [2], line of sight(LOS), non-line of sight (NLOS) and outage. For each link, the channel is determined through the following procedure:

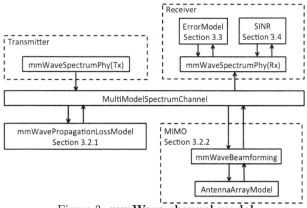

Figure 3: **mmWave channel model.**

- based on the distance between the UE and the eNB, determine the probability of the link being in each of the three states using the model in [2] ($P_{LoS}, P_{NLoS}, P_{out}$);

- uniformly pick a reference value (P_{REF}) between 0 and 1 and compare with the probability associated with each channel state;

- *if* $P_{REF} \leq P_{LOS}$, pick LOS channel;

  else if $P_{LOS} < P_{REF} \leq P_{LOS} + p_{NLOS}$, pick NLOS channel;

  otherwise pick outage.

For each link, on determining the channel state, the pathloss and shadowing is obtained by,

$$PL(d)[dB] = \alpha + \beta 10 log_{10}(d) + \xi, \quad \xi \sim N(0, \sigma^2), \qquad (2)$$

where ξ represent shadowing, parameter d represents the distance from receiver to transmitter, the values of parameter α, β, and σ for each channel scenario are given in [2].

3.2.2 MIMO

Due to the high pathloss, multiple antenna with beam forming is essential to ensure acceptable range of communication in mmWave systems. We briefly discuss the associated concepts of channel matrices and beam forming in this respect.

Channel matrix: We model the mmWave channel as a combination of clusters, each composed of several subpaths.[1] The channel matrix is described by the following:

$$H(t,f) = \sum_{k=1}^{K} \sum_{l=1}^{L_k} g_{kl}(t,f) \mathbf{u}_{rx}(\theta_{kl}^{rx}, \phi_{kl}^{rx}) \mathbf{u}_{tx}^{*}(\theta_{kl}^{tx}, \phi_{kl}^{tx}) \qquad (3)$$

where, K is the number of clusters, L_k the number of subpaths in cluster k, $g_{kl}(t,f)$ the small-scale fading over frequency and time; $\mathbf{u_{rx}}(\cdot)$ is the spatial signature of the receiver, $\mathbf{u_{tx}}(\cdot)$ the spatial signature of the transmitter.

The small-scale fading is generated based on the number of clusters, number of subpaths per cluster, Doppler shift, power spread, delay spread and angle of arrival (AoA) as given in [2] by,

$$g_{kl}(t,f) = \sqrt{P_{lk}} e^{2\pi i f_d cos(\omega_{kl})t - 2\pi i \tau_{kl} f} \qquad (4)$$

where, P_{kl} is the power spread; f_d is the maximum Doppler shift; ω_{kl} is the AoA of the subpath relative to the direction

---

[1]See [2] for a long term statistical characterization of the mmWave channel.

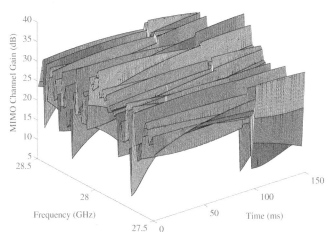

Figure 4: **MIMO channel gain over frequency and time.**

of motion; τ_{kl} gives the delay spread, and f is the carrier frequency.

Beamforming: In order to support phased-array antennas, a new *AntennaArrayModel* class is developed, which contains a complex beamforming vector. For both transmitter and receiver, based on the channel matrices, the beamforming vectors are computed using the power algorithm.

The beamforming gain from transmitter i to receiver j is given as,

$$G(t,f)_{ij} = |\mathbf{w}_{rx_{ij}}^* \mathbf{H}(t,f)_{ij} \mathbf{w}_{tx_{ij}}|^2 \qquad (5)$$

where, $\mathbf{H}(t,f)_{ij}$ is the channel matrix of ij^{th} link, $\mathbf{w}_{tx_{ij}}$ is the beamforming vector of transmitter i, when transmitting to receiver j and $\mathbf{w}_{rx_{ij}}$ the beamforming vector of receiver j, when receiving from transmitter i.

3.2.3 Channel Configuration

To reduce the computational complexity, the channel matrices and beamforming vectors are pre-generated in MATLAB®.

Load Files: At the beginning of each simulation we load 100 instances of the spatial signature matrices, along with the beamforming vectors. Then, a channel matrix instance per UE-eNodeB pair is randomly picked to characterize the radio link. As we will discuss later, we simulate the long term fading by randomly picking an instance of the channel form the pre-generated files.

Link Initialization and Channel Matrix Updates: In the *mmWaveBeamForming* class we define the a member *m_channelMatrixMap* (**Fig.** 1) to map the channel matrix instance to each radio link. During the simulation, the small-scale fading is calculated at every slot, based on Eq.4. The speed of the user is obtained directly from the mobility model. The remaining parameters are only subject to the environmental conditions , rural, urban etc., and therefore assumed constant over the entire simulation time. The reference values for different environments were recorded during the our mmWave channel propagation measurement campaign reported in [7]. On the other hand, for the large-scale fading, the spatial signature matrices are periodically updated with customizable interval, say 100 ms, to simulate a sudden change of the perceived channel.

Beamforming Vector: When configuring each radio link, the beamforming vector is stored in the antenna ar-

ray model of both base station and user side; the former will store the beamforming vectors of all the UEs, the latter will only store the beamforming vectors of the base stations within range.

The beamforming parameters are defined using following structures:

```
struct BeamFormingParams
{
    complexVector_t    m_txW;
    complexVector_t    m_rxW;
    ChannelMatrix      m_channelMatrix;
}
struct ChannelMatrix
{
    complex2DVector_t    m_txSpatialMatrix;
    complex2DVector_t    m_rxSpatialMatrix;
}
```

We can observe in **Fig.** 4 the channel gain trend obtained in a scenario where the number of antennas at the base station and mobile device is 64 and 16, respectively, and the user is moving at a speed of 36 km/h. The beamforming gain with small-scale fading is calculated using on Eq. 5. The small-scale fading includes two components, frequency selective fading and time selective fading, caused by multipath effect and Doppler effect, respectively. The spatial signatures and beamforming vectors are periodically updated with larger interval to capture the effects of long term fading which cause the sudden drop of beamforming gain around 100 ms.

3.3 Error Model

Similar to ns-3 Lena module, our mmWave module includes a error model for data packets according to the standard link-to-system mapping (LSM) techniques. By utilizing the LSM and the Mutual Information Based Effective SINR (MIESM) [8], the receiver computes the error probability for each transport block (TB) and determines whether the packet can be decoded or not. The TB can be composed of multiple codeblocks (CB) and its size depends on the channel capacity. The block error probability (BLER) of each CB depends on its size and associated MCS:

$$C_{BLER,i}(\gamma_i) = \frac{1}{2}\left[1 - \text{erf}\left(\frac{\gamma_i - b_{C_{SIZE},MCS}}{\sqrt{2}c_{C_{SIZE},MCS}}\right)\right], \qquad (6)$$

where γ_i is the mean mutual information per coded bit (MMIB) of the codeblock i, $b_{C_{SIZE},MCS}$ and $c_{C_{SIZE},MCS}$ corresponds to the mean and standard deviation of the Gaussian cumulative distribution, respectively. Now we can compute the TB block error rate:

$$T_{BLER} = 1 - \prod_{i=1}^{C}(1 - C_{BLER,i}(\gamma_i)). \qquad (7)$$

In case of failure, the PHY layer does not forward the incoming packet to the upper layers and, at the same time, triggers a retransmission process.[2]

3.4 Interference

Albeit being presumably less threating in the mmWave regime, because of the directionality of the multiantenna

---

[2]This can be a TCP retransmission, or an hybrid automatic repeat request (HARQ), which is part of our future work.

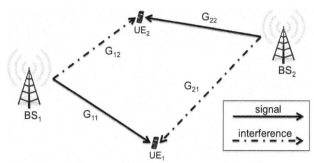

Figure 5: **Interference model.**

propagation, interference computation is still pretty relevant in terms of system level simulations. In fact, there might be some special spatial cases where interference is non negligible. Therefore, we propose an interference computation scheme that takes into account the beamforming directions associated with each link.

We will use **Fig. 5** as a reference. As an example, we compute the SINR between BS_1 and UE_1. To do so, we first need to obtain the channel gains associated with both the desired and interfering signals. Following Eq. 5, we get

$$G_{11} = |\mathbf{w}^*_{rx_{11}} H(t,f)_{11} \mathbf{w}_{tx_{11}}|^2,$$
$$G_{21} = |\mathbf{w}^*_{rx_{11}} H(t,f)_{21} \mathbf{w}_{tx_{22}}|^2. \quad (8)$$

We can now compute the SINR:

$$SINR_{11} = \frac{\frac{P_{Tx,11}}{PL_{11}} G_{11}}{\frac{P_{Tx,22}}{PL_{21}} G_{21} + BW \times N_0}, \quad (9)$$

where $P_{Tx,11}$ is the transmit power of BS_1, PL_{11} is the pathloss between between BS_1 and UE_1, and $BW \times N_0$ is the thermal noise.

3.5 CQI Feedbacks

In order to ensure reliable communication over a variable channel, feedback mechanisms are key in mostly all cellular communication systems. Similar to LTE we utilize the CQI feedback scheme for our module. The downlink CQI feedback message is generated by the *mmWaveUePhy*. In our simulator the UE computes the CQI based on the SINR of the signal received in a particular data slot. The computation of CQI is the same as that for LTE as given in [9] and [10].

4. MAC LAYER

The MAC layer is developed using the class *mmWaveMac* which is the base class for the *mmWaveEnbMac* for the eNodeB and the *mmWaveUeMac* for the user. The chief function of this layer is to deliver data packets coming from the upper layers (the net device in this case) to the physical layer and vice-versa. In fact this layer is designed for the synchronous delivery of upper layer data packets to the PHY layer which is key for proper data transfer in TDD mode.

The eNodeB MAC layer is connected to the scheduler module using the MAC-SCHED service access point (Sec. 5.2). The relationship between the PHY, MAC and the scheduler module for the eNodeB is depicted in Fig. 6. Thus the MAC layer communicates the scheduling and the resource allocation decision to the PHY layer. The scheduler

hosts the adaptive modulation and coding (AMC) module. The following sub-sections discuss these features in depth.

4.1 Adaptive Modulation and Coding

The working of the AMC is similar to that for LTE. The user measures the CQI for each downlink data slots it is allocated. The CQI information is then forwarded to the eNodeB using the *mmWaveCqiReport* control message. The eNodeB scheduler uses this information to compute the most suitable modulation and coding scheme for the communication link.

The AMC is implemented by the eNodeB MAC schedulers. During resource allocation, for the current frame work, the wide band CQI is used to generate the modulation and coding scheme (MCS) to be used and the transport block (TB) size that can be transmitted over the physical layer. The AMC module provides this frame work for the unique mapping of the CQI, the MCS, spectral efficiency and the TB size. The TB size is calculated based on the values of the total number of subcarriers per resource block derived from the user customized configuration, the number of symbols per slot and the number of reference symbols per slot. A cyclic redundancy code (CRC) length of 24 bits is used.

4.2 Scheduler

Following the design strategy for the ns-3 LTE module [10], the virtual class *mmWaveMacScheduler* defines the interface for the implementation of MAC scheduling techniques. The scheduler performs the scheduling and resource allocation for a subframe with both downlink and uplink slots.

4.2.1 TDD scheme

The TDD scheme enforced by the scheduler module is based on the user specified parameter *"TDDControlDataPattern"* given in Table 1. The slots specified for control are assigned alternately for downlink and uplink control channels. The data slots are equally divided between downlink and uplink slots with the first $n/2$ data slots allocated to downlink data and rest for uplink, where n is the total number of data slots. This scheme minimizes the switching time between uplink and downlink data transmissions.

The scheme described in Fig. 2 is an example of the implementation of the above algorithm with the default control data pattern. This module will be further enhanced in future to incorporate more advanced features like dynamic TDD.

4.2.2 Resource Allocation

Using the *mmWavePhyMacCommon* object, the division of resources in the frequency domain can be customized as given in Table 1.

The MAC scheduler currently implements a simple round robin algorithm to allocate uplink and downlink data slots to the connected users. All the frequency elements in a particular slot are assigned to the same user. The control slots are not allocated to any particular user. Any or all user can receive from and transmit to the base station in the control slots.

For the case of the round robin scheduler the use of the CQI is limited to the determination of the transport block size. In future the CQI information will be used to actively control the scheduling decisions.

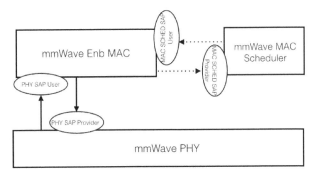

Figure 6: **PHY, MAC and scheduler modules with the associated SAPs.**

5. SERVICE ACCESS POINTS

The interface between the PHY and the MAC and the MAC and the scheduler are defined as service access points (SAPs) as given in [9]. The relationship between the PHY, MAC and the scheduler through their associated SAPs are shown in **Fig. 6**. The relationship between modules connected through SAPs can be viewed as that of service providers and users. The SAP provider caters to the requirement of the SAP user based on certain requests received from the user.

5.1 PHY–MAC

The communication between the MAC and the PHY layer using the MAC-PHY SAP is through the following processes:

i **Subframe Indication**: The subframe indication is sent by the PHY layer to the MAC at the beginning of each slot (unlike LTE where it is sent every subframe). The subframe indication for slot 1 for a particular subframe triggers the scheduling procedure for the eNodeB MAC. The subsequent indications are required for proper delivery of upper layer data.

ii **Data transmission**: The eNodeB MAC maintains data queues for each of the connected UE and just one such queue is sufficient for the user device. Based on the scheduling scheme and the allocated resources, the MAC layer will send the scheduled number of packets (given by the transport block size) to the PHY layer for transmission over the radio link.

iii **Scheduling and allocation notifications**: The scheduling and resource allocation decision received by the eNodeB MAC from the scheduler is relayed to the PHY layer using the *mmWaveResourceAllocation* message. The PHY of the base station in turn transmits this message to all the connected users notifying all the attached devices of the scheduling decision.

iv **CQI notification**: Based on the SINR of the received data slots, the UE PHY calculate the CQI and transmits it to the base station in the next uplink control slot. The eNodeB PHY on receiving the *mmWaveCqiReport* control message, relays it to the MAC.

5.2 MAC–SCHED

The eNodeB MAC uses the service provided by the scheduler by the following processes:

i **Trigger Request and Configuration Indication**: On receiving the Subframe Indication for slot 1 of a particular subframe, the MAC sends a *Scheduling Trigger Request* to the scheduler for the $(subframeNum + delay)^{th}$ subframe, where the delay is specified by the user using the parameter *L1L2ControlLatency*. The scheduler returns the scheduling and allocation decisions in the *Scheduling Configuration Indication* in response to the trigger.

ii **CQI notification**: The eNodeB MAC on receiving the CQI information from the PHY, sends it to the scheduler. The scheduler needs this information for future scheduling decisions.

6. SIMULATION RESULTS

We validate our framework through a simple simulation scenario, where we consider one eNodeB and one UE. The user is at an initial distance of 40m from the base station and moves towards the cell-edge with a constant velocity of 20 m/s. The simulation configuration settings correspond to the default values shown in Table 1. On top of that, the eNB has a transmit power of 30 dBm and a receiver noise figure of 5dB. Simulations are executed twice to capture the difference between the line of sight (LoS) and the non line of sight (NLoS) scenario.

The simulation results are reported in **Fig. 7** . On the one hand, **Figs. 7a** and **7b** show the variation of the downlink SINR with both time and frequency for the LoS and NLoS case, respectively. On the other hand, in **Figs. 7d** and **7c** we can observe the decrease in downlink data rate and average downlink SINR with the increasing distance between the UE and the base station, for both LoS and NLoS links.

7. CONCLUSIONS & FUTURE WORK

In this paper, a novel module for the simulation of mmWave cellular systems has been presented. The module, which is publicly available at [11], is highly customizable to facilitate researchers to use it flexibly and analyze different scenarios using varying configurations. A basic implementation of mmWave devices, MAC layer, PHY layer and channel models are developed. As part of our future work, we aim at introducing several enhancements, which include the *integration* of (i) higher layer modules for end-to-end performance analysis, (ii) a HARQ module, (iii) uplink power control, (iv) ns-3 based channel matrix generation and beamforming computation, (v) more sophisticated MAC algorithms, (vi) relay devices and the *evaluation* of (i) multiple access strategies and (ii) Transmission Control Protocol (TCP) performance over mmWave cellular networks.

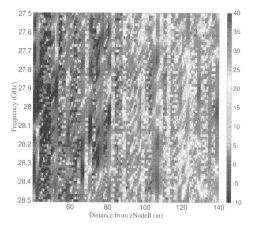
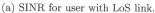
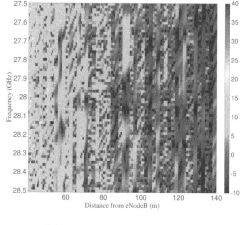

(a) SINR for user with LoS link.

(b) SINR for user with NLoS link.

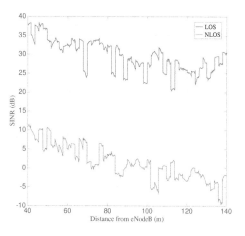
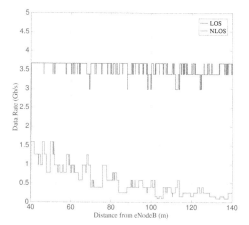

(c) Average SINR estimated by the users.

(d) Data rate for users with LoS and NLoS links.

Figure 7: **Simulation results**

8. REFERENCES

[1] S. Rangan, T. S. Rappaport, and E. Erkip, Millimeter-wave cellular wireless networks: potentials and challenges, *Proc. IEEE*, 102(3):366-385, Mar. 2014.

[2] M. R. Akdeniz, Y. Liu, M. K. Samimi, S. Sun, S. Rangan, T. S. Rappaport, and E. Erkip, mmWave channel modeling and cellular capacity evaluation, *IEEE J. Sel. Areas Commun.*, 32(6): 1164-1179, Jun. 2014.

[3] ns-3 Network Simulator; https://www.nsnam.org/

[4] A. Ghosh, T.A. Thomas, M.C. Cudak, R. Ratasuk, P. Moorut, F.W. Vook, T.S. Rappaport, G.R. MacCartney, S. Sun, and S. Nie, mmWave enhanced local area systems: A high data rate approach for future wireless networks, *IEEE J. Sel. Areas Commun.*, 1152 - 1163, June 2014.

[5] T. Levanen, J. Pirskanen, and M. Valkama, Radio Interface Design for Ultra-Low Latency Millimeter-Wave Communications in 5G Era, *IEEE GLOBECOM*, Dec. 2014.

[6] F. Khan, and J. Pi, mmWave mobile broadband: unleashing the 3-300GHz spectrum, presented at *IEEE Wireless Commun. Netw. Conf.*, Mar. 2011.

[7] T. S. Rappaport, S. Sun, R. Mazius, and H. Zhao, Y. Azar, K. Wang, G. N. Wong, J. K. Schulz, M. K. Samimi, and F. Gutierrez, Jr., Millimeter Wave Mobile Communications for 5G Cellular: It Will Work!, *IEEE Access*, (1): 335-349, 2013.

[8] M. Mezzavilla, M. Miozzo, M. Rossi, N. Baldo and M. Zorzi, A Lightweight and Accurate Link Abstraction Model for the Simulation of LTE Networks in ns-3, *IEEE MSWiM*, Oct. 2012.

[9] FemtoForum, LTE MAC Scheduler Interface Specification v1.11, Oct. 2010.

[10] G. Piro, N. Baldo, and M. Miozzo, An LTE module for ns-3 network simulator, *Proc. of Int. ICST Conf. on Simulation Tools and Techniques*, Mar. 2011.

[11] mmWave module for ns-3; https://github.com/mmezzavilla/ns3-mmwave

Data Dependency based
Parallel Simulation of Wireless Networks

Mirko Stoffers*, Torsten Sehy*, James Gross‡, Klaus Wehrle*
*Communication and Distributed Systems, RWTH Aachen University
‡School of Electrical Engineering, KTH Royal Institute of Technology
stoffers@comsys.rwth-aachen.de

ABSTRACT

Simulation of wireless systems is highly complex and can only be efficient if the simulation is executed in parallel. To this end, independent events have to be identified to enable their simultaneous execution. Hence, the number of events identified as independent needs to be maximized in order to increase the level of parallelism. Traditionally, dependencies are determined only by time and location of events: If two events take place on the same simulation entity, they must be simulated in timestamp order. Our approach to overcome this limitation is to also investigate data-dependencies between events. This enables event reordering and parallelization even for events at the same simulation entity. To this end, we design the simulation language PSimLa, which aids this process. In this paper, we discuss the PSimLa design and compiler as well as our data-dependency analysis approach in detail and present case studies of wireless network models, speeded up by a factor of 10 on 12 cores where time-based parallelization only achieves a 1.6x speedup.

Categories and Subject Descriptors

I.6.2 [**Simulation and Modeling**]: Simulation Languages

General Terms

Languages, Performance, Algorithms

Keywords

Parallel simulation; Static code analysis; Data dependencies

1. INTRODUCTION

Simulation is an essential methodology in the design and development of wireless communication systems. However, wireless simulation models are particularly complex, as they need to reflect sophisticated physical processes in software. Hence, parallelization is necessary to retrieve results in time.

All traditional parallelization approaches base on the local causality constraint, fulfilled "if and only if each Logical Process (LP) processes events in nondecreasing timestamp order" [9, p. 32]. However, we argue that this constraint is not a necessary condition, but two events can be independent even if their re-ordering poses a causal violation. By analyzing data-dependencies at compile time it can be determined if the two events do actually not access a data item in a conflicting manner. Since the only existing approach by Chen et al. [4, 5] does not incorporate the challenging yet essential part of analyzing data access by pointers or references we propose in [18] a novel approach to data-dependency analysis for parallelizing network simulation. We suggest to develop a Domain-Specific Language (DSL) for data-dependency based parallel simulation, but keep it close to C++ to maintain a flat learning curve for model developers. However, to avoid problems rendering data access tracking infeasible, like the unsolved problem of pointer analysis [2, 10], our language differs from C++, but does not remove a feature without providing proper alternatives. We allow using C++ and our language in a single model to enable smooth transition for existing code. In this paper we make the following contributions:

1. We discuss PSimLa, a language similar and compatible to C++, but replacing features of C++ by alternative concepts to increase static analyzability of model code.

2. We discuss the details of our data-dependency analysis approach. This shows, that in fact structured languages can be analyzed by tracking data access, increasing the amount of events recognized as independent and enhancing the degree of parallelism of otherwise hard-to-parallelize simulation models.

We integrate our approaches into OMNeT++ and the parallelization framework Horizon [13, 14]. OMNeT++ is one of the most commonly used open-source simulation frameworks. The shared-memory architecture of Horizon maximizes the applicability of the analysis results due to the possibility to efficiently determine the events currently being processed. We perform a detailed evaluation of this approach and discuss its general applicability. Our evaluation shows that certain previously hard-to-parallelize wireless simulation models achieve almost linear speedup when data-dependency information is exploited. On a 12-core machine our approach is more than 3 times faster than time-based parallelization for a wireless mesh case study, and more than 6 times for an LTE simulation.

The remainder of this paper is structured as follows: After analyzing the problem (Sec. 2), we discuss the design of PSimLa (Sec. 3) in more detail. We show the feasibility of static analysis by introducing a data-dependency analysis algorithm (Sec. 4). We discuss important issues (Sec. 5) before we analyze evaluation results (Sec. 6). Finally, we compare our approach to existing simulation languages and analysis approaches (Sec. 7) before our conclusion (Sec. 8).

2. PROBLEM ANALYSIS

Static code analysis has been commonly used to investigate different properties of computer programs in many languages [2]. However, certain properties of the languages render the analysis easier, harder, or infeasible. The absence of side effects in functional programs, e.g., enables trivial detection of function in- and output. On the other hand, pointer analysis is still considered unsolved [2, 10], hence reliably tracking data access in pointer-based languages like C++ has to be considered infeasible. Though smart pointers and unique pointers mitigate the problems, this still holds for recent C++ standards, especially because raw pointers are still available and necessary. Since most wireless simulation models are written in structured languages and many model developers are not familiar with functional programming, limiting data-dependency based parallel simulation to functional languages is not an option. Instead, we investigate the applicability on structured programming languages.

The infeasibility of pointer analysis excludes languages which heavily rely on pointers. Global variables are considered harmful in parallel programs: in shared-memory systems where they might induce race conditions and in distributed systems, whose entities cannot share the state of a global variable. Since today's wide-spread languages do not adhere to these constraints, we decided to modify a well-established language to support data-dependency analysis. Many model developers are familiar with C++ as the most commonly used network simulators OMNeT++ and ns-3 base on C++. However, to support data-dependency analysis, global variables and pointer support have to be removed and a proper alternative for pointers needs to be provided to avoid rendering the language useless.

Data-dependency analysis has been extensively studied in the compiler construction domain to enable automatic parallelization of arbitrary programs. However, these approaches do not incorporate the notion of simulation time and discrete events into their analysis, hence they would not exploit the full potential in this scope. Instead, we develop an approach that applies similar analyses, but as well accounts for the peculiarities of discrete event simulation.

3. THE PSimLa LANGUAGE

PSimLa is designed according to the goals elaborated [18]. It is a Turing complete language with particular emphasize on static analyzability for data-dependencies. Similarity and compatibility to C++ ensures that existing models can be smoothly translated and the learning curve is kept as flat as possible. In the following, we describe the compilation process and introduce the building blocks of PSimLa in detail.

3.1 Compilation Process

PSimLa is based on C++ and the simulation elements of OMNeT++. Code-to-code translation to C++ enables flexible linking of PSimLa modules with both C++ code and C++-compatible libraries. The compilation runs in 5 steps (cf. Fig. 1). The developer (1) creates code in PSimLa and/or C++ and the configuration in the OMNeT++ NED-, MSG-, and INI-format. Our parser checks the syntax of the PSimLa code and creates an internal representation similar to an abstract syntax tree (2). The static code analysis (see Sec. 4 for more details) can then use this representation to identify event dependencies and independencies (3). The abstract syntax tree is then serialized into C++ code

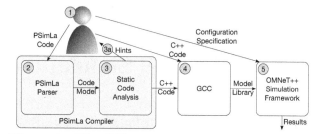

Figure 1: The PSimLa compilation process. The developer implements the model (1), triggers translation of PSimLa code into C++ code (2, 3), triggers compilation of C++ code (4), and executes the simulation using OMNeT++ (5).

effectively resulting in a code-to-code translation of PSimLa into C++. Additionally, the analysis yields C++ code representing the gained dependency information that can be used during runtime for parallelization. If it detects event dependencies, which the developer might be able to resolve manually, it provides hints to the modeler (3a) that can be used to improve upon the model in a next iteration. The final result of step 3 together with the C++ code and configuration specification of the developer poses a simulation model complying with the OMNeT++ specification. This model can be compiled (4) and executed by OMNeT++ (5). A modified version of OMNeT++ (see Sec. 4.6) uses the results of the static analysis to improve the parallelization.

3.2 PSimLa Building Blocks

In [18], we describe the basic building blocks of PSimLa, which correspond to those of OMNeT++. A PSimLa *Module*, corresponding to an OMNeT++ Simple Module, can be specified either in PSimLa or – to maintain compatibility with existing code – in C++. Modules can be connected into Compound Modules or a Network by OMNeT++ NED-files. Data can only be exchanged between Modules by Messages (OMNeT++ MSG-format). Modelers cannot create global variables. Classes can be used to define complex data types and are specified in PSimLa or C++. In the following, we discuss each building block in more detail.

Modules: A Module is defined similar to a C++ class, but with the keyword `module`. In the body, developers include both behavior implementation and parameter and gate specification. The syntax of parameter and gate specification is adopted from OMNeT++. Like a Simple Module in OMNeT++ a PSimLa Module needs to implement an event handler and can implement initialization and teardown functions. From the Module code, the compiler generates an OMNeT++ NED-file as well as C++ code and header files.

Data Types: Like C++, we provide primitive data types and enumerations, and developers can create classes. We also provide container formats from the C++ standard library as language built-ins to increase analyzability due to the possibility to exploit the container semantics in the analysis algorithm. We include the containers `vector` (dynamically resized array) and `queue` (FIFO queue) with the option to include more into the compiler implementation.

Memory Management: To increase the level of analyzability, the memory management is handled by the compiler rather than the developer. Hence, the developer is only provided references to objects. Like Java, we hand object references to functions (call-by-reference). To monitor an object's life cycle, we use reference counting and delete objects as soon as the reference count reaches zero, i. e., no more references to the object persist. Additionally, only one reference must exist to data items included in a message to ensure that no two independent events can access the same data item concurrently. To avoid that reference loops prevent correct cleanup, we adopt the weak pointer concept.

Our prototype implementation of the PSimLa compiler chooses the storage location (dynamic or automatic memory, usually implemented as heap and stack) similar to Java. Local variables of primitive data types are placed in automatic memory, objects and arrays are dynamically allocated. This decreases performance compared to optimized C++ code (see Sec. 6.1), hence future compiler implementations should improve the algorithm to select the best location. However, this does not affect the question how well data-dependency analysis is suited for speeding up parallel simulation.

Libraries: Due to our compatibility with C++, existing libraries with C++ bindings (like the C++ standard library) can be linked with PSimLa models. Nevertheless, PSimLa built-in data types (like FIFO queues) should be preferred over external libraries to increase the code analyzability.

Code Elements: The syntax of PSimLa functions is basically similar to the C++ syntax, except that – as discussed above – the memory is not managed by the user, hence the user cannot use pointers. We provide the well-known `include` directive to include C++ header files to bind existing C++ code. Inside any PSimLa function, inline C++ code blocks can be created. To ease model development, we provide language built-ins for simulation related operations like message transmission or random number generation.

4. ANALYSIS TECHNIQUES

In this section we show the feasibility of static code analysis of PSimLa by discussing our data-dependency analysis approach in detail. We sketched the idea shortly in [18].

To this end, our analysis approach targets three goals:

Maximize Recognition Rate: Our primary goal is to successfully detect as many independent events as possible since this increases the parallelization gain.

Minimize Runtime Overhead: While our static code analysis determines the event dependencies at compile time, the gained knowledge has to be applied during runtime. To this end, it is necessary to determine whether it is safe to execute events in parallel by querying the dependency information. While we cannot completely avoid runtime overhead, we aim at preparing as much as possible at compile time.

Maintain Correctness: The analysis must not recognize two dependent events as independent to avoid false simulation results. Our approach must compute the same results as sequential execution of the code. However, we allow a relaxation to this constraint that can be activated or deactivated by the user: If two events draw a random number from the same Random Number Generator (RNG) stream, there is in fact a dependence between the two events. By executing those events in reverse order the random numbers provided to the events are swapped. Nevertheless, both numbers stem from the same distribution. Hence, if the model only expects a random number following a certain distribution (rather than the next random number from a certain RNG stream), the events could be executed out-of-order (or in parallel if the RNG source is thread-safe or locked). If we waive the guarantee of assigning the same random number to the same event in every execution, we still obtain valid results, but lose repeatability. Consequently, this relaxation switch allows the user to trade repeatability for performance.

In the following we first introduce the analysis approach in general before we discuss the details of each part.

4.1 General Approach

To elaborate promising analysis approaches, we post a simple formalism for parallel simulation. The focus hereby is to determine whether two events are independent or not. We assume that the simulation can be decomposed into a set of partitions which communicate with each other only by message passing. These partitions comply with LPs in distributed simulations. In PSimLa, every Module can be a partition since Modules can only communicate via messages.

We define an event as a 3-tuple, such that the set of all possible events is $E := (T \times P \times D)$. T is the time domain, P the set of partitions, and elements in D denote the data access pattern of an event, i. e., which data element is accessed how. The exact definition of D is provided in Sec. 4.3. Let $s \subseteq (E \times E)$ be the scheduling relation with $(e_1, e_2) \in s$ iff e_2 is created by e_1. The reflexive, transitive closure s^* yields all directly and transitively created events and the event itself.

To formalize independence, we define the operator $\perp \subseteq (E \times E)$ with $e_1 \perp e_2$ denoting that e_1 and e_2 are independent.

In traditional Parallel Discrete Event Simulation (PDES) the approaches differ in the way they predict whether two events on *different* partitions eventually induce a dependency. However, for two events on the *same* partition they all check the local causality constraint [9], i. e., those events are always assumed to depend on each other. Hence, for two events $e_1 = (t_1, p_1, d_1) \in E, e_2 = (t_2, p_2, d_2) \in E$ traditional PDES assumes: $p_1 = p_2 \Rightarrow e_1 \not\perp e_2$.

However, while this assumption is safe, it is not true in general. In fact, the events can still be independent if the effects of e_1 do not influence e_2 and vice versa. We introduce the operator $\succ \subseteq (D \times E)$ with $d \succ e$ indicating that the behavior of e is influenced by a write operation in d.

We can then derive the following additional method to determine independence of e_1 and e_2. Without loss of generality we assume $t_1 \leq t_2$. If first, e_2 is neither affected by e_1 nor any event created by e_1, and second, none of those events (e_1 and the events created by e_1) is influenced by e_2, then e_1 and e_2 are in fact independent: $(\forall (e_1, e') = (e_1, (t', \_, d')) \in s^* : t' \leq t_2 \wedge d' \not\succ e_2 \wedge d_2 \not\succ e') \Rightarrow e_1 \perp e_2$.

Hence, to determine the independence of two events it is crucial to analyze not only time and location of each event, but also its scheduling behavior and data access pattern.

To this end, our approach is to analyze the event handler code in order to categorize event types and identify conflicts with other types based on the data accessed. In the following, we discuss the five steps of our analysis in detail.

4.2 Identifying Event Types

In a first step, at compile time we identify different types of events in the provided simulation model. This allows us to specify dependency rules on an event type basis. At runtime we then only need to determine the type of an event in order to be able to investigate the dependency rules.

The common programming model in OMNeT++ is to provide a single message handler per module and branch upon different attributes of the message delivered to that handler. For example, an event handler at a router might branch upon the message kind (routing message, data packet) and one or more of the branches might branch again upon the receiving

```
1  void handleMessage (Message msg) {
2    if (msg.getKind()==1)
3      myInt=0;
4    if (msg.getKind()==2)
5      myInt=myFn(myInt);
6    sendDelayed(msg,0,"myOutputGate");
7  }
```

Figure 2: Event handler of example PSimLa Module MyMod. Excerpt from our example introduced in [18].

interface (i.e., distinguish packets from the upper layer from packets from the lower layer).

Our event type classification algorithm starts with a single event type per module. We then analyze the event handler code of each module for any branch solely based on a message attribute. The first conditional encountered results in splitting the event type into two different types, one with the condition being fulfilled and one for the opposite. Similarly, a switch statement results in multiple event types, one for each case of the switch statement. For each branch we repeat this procedure possibly splitting the corresponding event type again until no more message attribute based branches are detected. Hence, the branches form a tree and each leaf of that tree corresponds to exactly one event type.

We extend our formalism by the notion of event types. We define Θ as the set of all detected event types and the function $\tau : E \to \Theta$ assigning each event instance its type.

There are three types identified for each instance of the module MyMod in the example in Fig. 2: One for message kind 1, one for message kind 2, and one for message kind being neither 1 nor 2. Note that at compile time we do not know how many instances will be created of each module. Hence, the set Θ is rather a theoretic set that is not exactly known to the analysis algorithm. Instead the analysis only stores the criteria to distinguish event types. For the example, we assume that there is only one instance of MyMod, called mymod, and the output of that instance is connected to its input. Hence, we only have three event types in the simulation. In the following, we refer to those types as $\vartheta_{\text{mymod1}}$ to $\vartheta_{\text{mymod3}}$, respectively.

4.3 Tracking Data Access

For every event type, we first determine which code blocks the program flow passes if an event of this type is executed. This includes any code outside of conditionals, as well as either of the two (potentially empty) blocks of a conditional. For conditionals not branching upon message attributes and therefore not resulting in different event types, we consider both blocks, i.e., we assume the worst case here. This is necessary since not every condition can be evaluated at compile time. Hence, we apply a conservative simplification here. Similarly, we assume that loops are always executed at least once even though the loop termination condition might already be false before the loop is entered for the first time.

In the example, $\vartheta_{\text{mymod1}}$ passes lines 3 and 6, $\vartheta_{\text{mymod2}}$ passes lines 5 and 6, and $\vartheta_{\text{mymod3}}$ passes line 6 only.

For every code block passed by the program flow of each event type, we determine which data items are accessed. Since PSimLa does not provide global variables, data items can only be accessed by two means: First, they can be an element of the current module or (directly or indirectly) referred to by a reference in the module. Second, data items can be an element of the message. Local variables cannot cause conflicts with concurrently running events since they

cannot be accessed by the concurrent event. Since messages must not reference to data items that are still referenced from somewhere else, all items of a message can be treated as local variables. Hence, we only need to investigate items accessed via module members. Additionally, if a reference is copied into a local variable, we have to treat this local variable like the original reference.

For each event type $\vartheta \in \Theta$, we can now create a list L_ϑ of accessed data items by parsing the code line by line and performing the following actions for certain statements.

- On a *function call* we retrieve the code of the called function and parse that code as well.
- On *creating a local reference variable R_l*, we create an initially empty list $\pi(R_l)$ of possible locations this variable might point to. Although during program execution a reference can only point to a single location at any point in time, we need a list of potential locations since we cannot evaluate every conditional, hence there might be more than one option.
- On *copying a reference R_m referred to by a module variable* to a local reference R_l, we add R_m to $\pi(R_l)$.
- On *copying a local reference R_1 to another local reference R_2* we append $\pi(R_1)$ to $\pi(R_2)$.
- If a *local variable of primitive data type* is accessed, we do nothing since this can never cause a conflict.
- If an *object referenced by a local reference variable R_l* is accessed, we append $\pi(R_l)$ to L_ϑ. Note that references are also special cases of objects. Reading or modifying a member variable of a module is as well a relevant operation if this member variable is a reference.
- If an *object referenced by the module* is accessed, we append this object to L_ϑ.

During this procedure we do not only track which objects are accessed, but also how they are accessed. To this end, we distinguish between references, primitive data types, arrays, and certain special data items for language built-ins.

For *references* we track the following two operations:

Dereferencing: If a reference is dereferenced in order to find an object, the reference itself is read.

Update: If a reference is modified, this poses a write operation on the reference itself.

For *primitive data items*, we distinguish between:

Read: The variable value is read, but not modified.

Write: The value is modified in any way but the following.

Increment: The value is incremented or decremented by one of the operators ++, --, +=, or -=. Such accesses are modifications, but can be re-ordered without changing the final result if performed in a thread-safe manner.

Since it is not generally possible to determine the index used to access an element of an *array* (as well as similar index-accessible containers) during compile time, we do not treat each item of an array separately, but treat the whole array as a single item. Hence, we distinguish between read and write operations on the array.

Our analysis recognizes two *language built-ins* that are handled as special data items: RNGs and queues. This list can be extended by adding further objects as language built-ins to PSimLa and implementing the corresponding analysis passes according to the semantics of these objects. For *RNGs* there is only a single operation: drawing a random number. This is treated according to the relaxation switch discussed in the analysis goals. With strict RNG ordering, RNG accesses need to be treated like write operations. With relaxed ordering, the OMNeT++ RNGs are locked and accesses are handled like read-only operations.

For *queues*, we distinguish between:

Enqueue: Appending at the end of the queue.

Dequeue: Retrieving and removing the first item.

Query Size: Determine the size of the queue. This also includes special cases like emptiness checks (size=0).

Now, for each event type we maintain a list of objects accessed and for each access the operation performed.

We now specify the data access pattern set D previously introduced in Sec. 4.1 as $D := \mathcal{P}(\Delta \times A)$ with Δ being the set of all data items in the simulation and A the set of all access operations discussed above. While d is the actual data access pattern of $e = (\_, \_, d) \in E$, we introduce d'_ϑ as a conservative over-estimation of data accesses by events of type ϑ. This reflects the inability of exactly predicting every data access in a Turing-complete programming language at compile time. For every event type ϑ our analysis then determines a set d'_ϑ such that $\forall e = (\_, \_, d) \in E : (\tau(e) = \vartheta \Rightarrow d'_\vartheta \supseteq d)$.

For convenience, we define $r \widehat{=}$ "read primitive data type" and $w \widehat{=}$ "write primitive data type". For the provided example our analysis determines $d'_{\vartheta_{\mathrm{mymod1}}} := \{(\mathrm{myInt}, w)\}$, $d'_{\vartheta_{\mathrm{mymod2}}} := \{(\mathrm{myInt}, r), (\mathrm{myInt}, w), (\mathrm{myParam}, r)\}$, and for the third event type $d'_{\vartheta_{\mathrm{mymod3}}} := \emptyset$.

4.4 Determining Scheduling Relations

For the independence criterion derived in Sec. 4.1 we need to additionally determine the scheduling relation s. Like d, we cannot determine s exactly due to the inability to analyze every property of any Turing-computable function. Instead, we define the relation $s' \subseteq (\Theta \times \Theta)$ with the requirement $(e_1, e_2) \in s \Rightarrow (\tau(e_1), \tau(e_2)) \in s'$. However, the opposite does not necessarily need to be true. This means, s' is a conservative over-estimation of s on event type basis.

In order to derive the scheduling relations, we follow a similar procedure as to derive the data access patterns (see Sec. 4.3). For every event type, we search the reachable code blocks for calls to scheduling built-ins of PSimLa. On occurance of such a built-in, we need to determine the type of the newly created event. Since this type depends on the attributes of the message (see Sec. 4.2), we need to investigate which attributes might be set. This can be an easy task if the attributes are set closely to the scheduling without conditionals that cannot be evaluated during compile time. However, it is not always possible to exactly determine the value of a message property at compile time in a Turing-complete language. Hence, we allow wildcards for message properties. If the message handler of the receiving module branches on a property that contains a wildcard, we have to consider both event types as potential options.

In our simple example, all three event types create a new event by the code in line 6. Since the incoming message is sent unmodified, the type of the newly created event is identical to the type of the incoming event. Hence, $s' = \{(\vartheta_{\mathrm{mymod1}}, \vartheta_{\mathrm{mymod1}}), (\vartheta_{\mathrm{mymod2}}, \vartheta_{\mathrm{mymod2}}), (\vartheta_{\mathrm{mymod3}}, \vartheta_{\mathrm{mymod3}})\}$.

4.5 Inferring Event Dependencies

This step combines the information gathered during the previous steps into a set of dependency information. We defined the relation $\succ$ for this purpose in Sec. 4.1. Again, we define a conservative over-estimation on event type basis $\succ' \subseteq (\Theta \times \Theta)$, such that for every two events $e_1 = (t_1, p_1, d_1)$,

$e_2 = (t_2, p_2, d_2) \in E$ with $t_1 \leq t_2$ the following condition must be fulfilled: $d_1 \succ e_2 \Rightarrow \tau(e_1) \succ' \tau(e_2)$.

Additionally, we define the relation $\succ_{\mathrm{A}} \subseteq (A \times A)$, such that $a_1 \succ_{\mathrm{A}} a_2$ denotes that if in sequential execution the operation a_1 is executed prior to a_2 on the same data item, those operations must not be re-ordered. In particular, this relation holds the following items:

References: If the data item is a reference and either or both of the operations are update operations, the operations must not be re-ordered. Hence, $a_1 \succ_{\mathrm{A}} a_2$ if either a_1 or a_2 is a reference update operation.

Primitive Data Types: If either or both of the operations are write operations, they depend on each other. If both operations are increment operations, we rewrite these accesses by using atomic operations such that they can still be executed independently of each other. However, a read operation and an increment operation yield a dependency since the result of the read operation is changed by the incrementation.

Arrays: If either or both of the operations are write operations, they depend on each other.

RNGs: As discussed in Sec. 3 the user can trade repeatability for performance by allowing re-ordering of RNG calls. Hence, depending on the user's choice, for $a \widehat{=}$ "draw random number" $a \succ_{\mathrm{A}} a$ or $a \nsucc_{\mathrm{A}} a$.

Queues: In general, only read-only operations on a queue can be parallelized. However, we apply special handling of queues to increase the level of parallelism: To every element enqueued, we assign the timestamp of the event that performed the enqueuing operation. This allows us to correct an out-of-order enqueuing operation, by not enqueuing the element to the queue's end, but shifting it to a position, such that the queue elements are ordered according to their timestamps.

A size query then still depends on a previous enqueuing operation: If the size is queried by an event $e_2 = (5\,\mathrm{s}, \_, \_)$, but e_2 is executed prior to $e_1 = (4\,\mathrm{s}, \_, \_)$ and e_1 potentially includes an enqueuing operation, the size query cannot determine how many elements the queue will contain at $t = 5\,\mathrm{s}$ since this depends on the behavior of e_1. However, an enqueuing operation does not depend on a previous size query: An enqueuing operation by e_2 can be executed before a size query by e_1, and e_1 can still determine the size at $t = 4\,\mathrm{s}$ by ignoring any element in the queue with a timestamp greater than $4\,\mathrm{s}$.

Nevertheless, a dequeuing operation must not be re-ordered with neither operation since by removing an element from the queue we lose the necessary information. This could only be solved by keeping information of deleted elements. Since this causes additional overhead, it is not part of our analysis approach.

We use this relation $\succ_{\mathrm{A}}$ and the sets d'_ϑ determined in Sec. 4.3 to determine $\succ'$. A pair of event types is in this relation if we find a conflicting data access: $\exists \alpha_1 = (\delta_1, a_1) \in d'_{\vartheta_1}, \alpha_2 = (\delta_2, a_2) \in d'_{\vartheta_2}$ such that $\delta_1 = \delta_2$ and $a_1 \succ_{\mathrm{A}} a_2$, then $\vartheta_1 \succ' \vartheta_2$. To reduce the runtime overhead, we store for every event type a list C_ϑ with "conflicting" event types, i.e., $\vartheta' \in C_\vartheta \Leftrightarrow \vartheta' \succ' \vartheta$.

For the provided example, we determine the following sets: $C_{\vartheta_{\mathrm{mymod1}}} = \{\vartheta_{\mathrm{mymod1}}, \vartheta_{\mathrm{mymod2}}\}$ for the first event type, $C_{\vartheta_{\mathrm{mymod2}}} = \{\vartheta_{\mathrm{mymod1}}, \vartheta_{\mathrm{mymod2}}\}$ for the second type, and for the third type $C_{\vartheta_{\mathrm{mymod3}}} = \emptyset$.

4.6 Runtime Component

The static code analysis provides the event dependencies in a representation that enables efficient dependency lookups during runtime. We integrate a runtime component into Horizon [13, 14] which exploits this information.

When the conservative synchronization algorithm of Horizon prevents offloading the next event e_N for parallelization, we hand e_N to the runtime component. This first determines the type $\tau(e_N)$ and derives the dependency list $C_{\tau(e_N)}$. We apply a shortcut for the case that this list is empty. In this situation, e_N does not depend on any other event in the simulation, hence we can offload it immediately for parallel execution without any further investigation.

However, if $C_{\tau(e_N)}$ is not empty, we need to determine whether the type of one of the events that are currently executed by a worker thread occurs in $C_{\tau(e_N)}$. We name the set of the currently executed events $O \subseteq E$. If $\exists e \in O : \tau(e) \in C_{\tau(e_N)}$, then e_N depends on e and cannot be executed in parallel with e. Hence, we need to wait for e to complete, before we can check for independence again.

If such an e does not exist, we need to investigate the transitive closure of the scheduling relation of every event in O. To this end, let s'^+ be the transitive closure of s'. During runtime, we establish the set $s'_O := \{\vartheta | s'^+(\tau(e), \vartheta), e \in O\}$ and search for a $\vartheta' \in s'_O$. If we find such an element, e_N cannot safely be executed immediately. If we determine that $s'_O \cap C_{\tau(e_N)} = \emptyset$, then we can safely offload e_N immediately to a worker thread for parallel execution.

5. DISCUSSION

We discuss aspects regarding the investment required by modelers to benefit from our solution as well as the underlying assumptions and general applicability of our approach.

5.1 Manual Effort

With the introduction of a new simulation language we pose a rather high entry barrier for modelers to adapt our solution. To lower this barrier, we decided to 1. keep the syntax as close to C++ as possible to reduce the learning effort, and 2. maintain compatibility with C++-based OMNeT++ models to allow partial translations.

Hence, for existing models we recommend a smooth transition by translating one module after the other. By translating the modules which pose the most severe parallelization bottlenecks, modelers can already expect some speedup from our analysis. Further translation can then be performed at a later point in time or omitted if the gain already suffices.

New simulation models can be implemented from scratch in PSimLa. The similarity to C++ reduces the effort to understand the concepts. Furthermore, existing libraries can still be used within PSimLa models.

We argue that while we cannot completely eliminate the entry barrier, we kept it as low as possible.

5.2 General Applicability

Our analysis bases on two assumptions: 1. Each data item is only accessible from a single module at a time. 2. Global knowledge about the current simulation state exists.

An assumption similar to the first one has to be posed for every parallel simulation approach since multiple processing units cannot access the same data item at the same time. While we decided to scope this on a module level, our approaches can be easily adapted to fit other scopes as well.

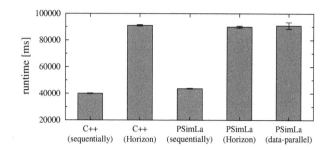

Figure 3: Overhead of the different configurations measured by the Null-Model. Less is better.

However, the second assumption limits applicability of our analysis approach to distributed simulation. An empty condition list still allows immediate execution of any event of such type in distributed simulation as the state of a remote LP does not matter. If, however, the event interferes with other events which might arrive from a remote LP later, the runtime component cannot work in a distributed simulation like described above. Hence, the runtime component has to be adapted by applying different means to determine which event types might arrive at the LP. This needs to be investigated in more detail in future research efforts. Nevertheless, we argue that the design of PSimLa – aiming at a high level of analyzability – as well supports analysis approaches better suited for distributed simulation.

Alternatively, by simply ignoring the state of remote LPs events can be speculatively executed on the local LP. The data-dependency analysis then reduces the number of rollbacks by determining if an event arriving out-of-order does actually not violate the correctness of the simulation.

6. EVALUATION

We evaluate our approaches in terms of both overhead and speedup. Additionally, we conduct two case studies to quantify the impact on existing simulation models. All measurements are conducted on a compute server with two 6-core Opteron CPUs and a total of 32 GB of RAM running Ubuntu 12.04. We repeat every experiment at least 5 times, the plots depict the average and the 95 % confidence interval for each configuration. Note, that some confidence intervals are particularly small, thus hard to recognize.

6.1 Overhead Evaluation

There are two sources of overhead in our approaches: First, suboptimal translation of PSimLa into C++ code can decrease performance. Second, the runtime component of the analysis tool introduces overhead to yield decisions.

To quantify this overhead, we use three different models: First, we verify that the overhead is negligible if we use a "Null-Model" [14], i.e., a model that only handles events without actually performing computations. In this case, the only overhead stems from the fact that the OMNeT++ message pointer that is handled to the event handler, needs to be cast into a smart pointer to activate reference counting. Second, we estimate the code-translation overhead by analyzing the overhead of the most severe data type in our prototype implementation of the PSimLa compiler: multi-dimensional arrays. Third, we measure the decision overhead of the runtime component by feeding it with decision problems of varying levels of complexity.

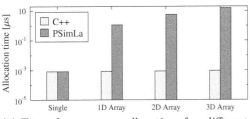

(a) Time for memory allocation for different data types.

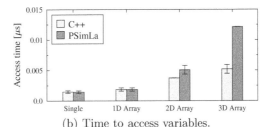

(b) Time to access variables.

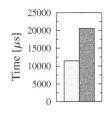

(c) Real-world example: fading model [20].

Figure 4: Code translation overhead. Time needed for different operations. Less is better.

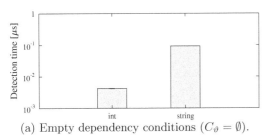

(a) Empty dependency conditions ($C_\vartheta = \emptyset$).

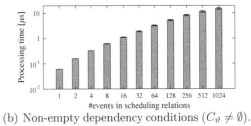

(b) Non-empty dependency conditions ($C_\vartheta \neq \emptyset$).

Figure 5: Decision overhead. Time needed for yielding an offloading decision. Less is better.

Null-Model.

The Null-Model [14] only evaluates overhead by not performing any computations. It consists of 110 modules with an event handler only repetitively rescheduling an event.

We implemented this model in C++ as well as PSimLa to compare the overhead of the two languages. We ran the model 1. sequentially, 2. with the parallelization architecture Horizon [13, 14], and 3. with additional activation of our analysis approaches. The third option can only be applied on the PSimLa model. Fig. 3 depicts the runtimes of these 5 different configurations. Comparing the sequential executions, we observe a slight but negligible additional overhead of PSimLa caused by pointer casts and reference counting. Activating the parallelization architecture Horizon significantly raises the overhead as discussed in [14]. In this case the overhead introduced by the translation of PSimLa is no longer observable. Activating the analysis does not increase the overhead either. We conclude that the overhead of PSimLa and our analysis is negligible if the event handlers of the model are simple. Any additional overhead stems from suboptimal translation of event handler code and complicated offloading decisions as discussed in the following.

Code-Translation Overhead.

As discussed in Sec. 3.2, our prototype implementation does not automatically choose the best storage location for arrays, but always allocates them dynamically. While C++ developers can decide to place an array in automatic memory with virtually no allocation time, our PSimLa compiler allocates dynamic memory even if the array is only required locally. Since this is the primary source for code translation overhead, we decided to quantify this overhead as a worst-case example. We investigated primitive data types as well as 1-, 2-, and 3-dimensional arrays. We measured performance of allocation as well as element access by performing only such an operation in a loop.

The results are displayed in Fig. 4. While *allocation* in automatic memory consumes virtually no time, dynamic allocation in PSimLa is considerable and grows with the number of dimensions. This is not a surprising result and con-

firms that future efforts need to investigate better placement strategies. However, *access* to array elements only poses a small amount of overhead caused by better cache-locality in automatic memory. We also observe that this overhead super-linearly grows with the number of dimensions.

We as well considered a real world fading model [20] heavily using multi-dimensional arrays. For this example, we observe a factor 2 slowdown in the fading computation function due to allocation and access overhead. We hence recommend to use the opportunity of PSimLa to implement parts of the model in C++ for such kind of code and only realize the remaining parts in PSimLa. Nevertheless, the PSimLa compiler needs to deal with this issue in future versions.

Decision Overhead.

When the runtime component has to decide whether to offload the next event immediately for parallel execution, it determines the event type and then determines the scheduling relations only if the next event generally depends on other events. Hence, for the overhead evaluation we investigate two questions: 1. How long does it take to identify the event type ϑ, determine that there are no dependencies ($C_\vartheta = \emptyset$), and return the result? 2. How long does it take to yield a decision if the scheduling relations need to be investigated (since $C_\vartheta \neq \emptyset$)?

For the first question, we measure the decision time for events whose event type is classified by either an integer or a string (14 characters on average). Hence, determining the event type is either an integer-based branch or a string comparison. The results are depicted in Fig. 5(a). The integer-based type classification and decision yielding takes only a few processor cycles (4 ns), the string comparison takes about 100 ns. Hence, on event types with no data-dependencies the decision is yielded highly efficiently, especially if the classification does not involve string comparisons.

If the event has dependencies on other events, we need to determine the scheduling relation for the currently offloaded events s'_O and search it for conflicts. We therefore investigate the overhead for different sizes of s'_O (see Fig. 5(b)). For $|s'_O| = 1$ we need 60 ns to determine the event types, con-

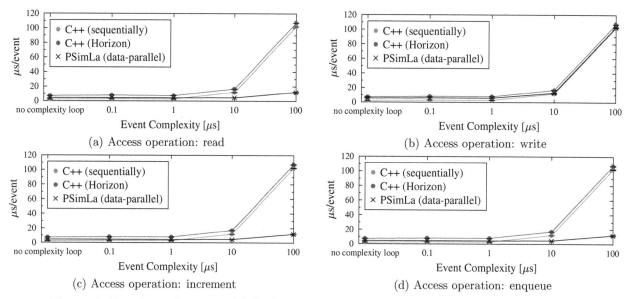

(a) Access operation: read   (b) Access operation: write

(c) Access operation: increment   (d) Access operation: enqueue

Figure 6: Runtime of events with basic operations and a complexity loop. Less is better.

struct s'_O, and yield the decision. With increasing size of s'_O the decision overhead grows almost linearly up to 15 µs for 1024 event types. Hence, the runtime component is more efficient if the scheduling relations are smaller. However, since the number of different event types in a simulation is typically rather low, we expect also the scheduling relation set to be rather small in typical simulations.

6.2 Speedup Evaluation

We evaluate the gain of our analysis approaches in simple cases. We only use one of the basic operations that our analysis should detect (see Sec. 4.3). We create events that only use this basic operation followed by a loop simulating different workloads of the event. Due to the overhead introduced by the parallelization engine the loop needs to maintain a certain complexity until parallelization can pay off. In our experiments, we vary the complexity between 1 µs and 100 µs and run an additional experiment without the loop. We investigate four operations: reading of a primitive data type, writing to a primitive data type, incrementing a primitive data type, enqueuing to a queue.

Fig. 6 depicts the results. Observing the results with no or low complexity again shows the overhead introduced by the parallelization engine Horizon (which cannot run events in parallel since the timestamps do not yield independent events). Our analysis already improves upon this situation by yielding positive parallelization decisions which allow parallelizing the overhead. For a complexity of 10 µs we observe that the parallelization gains significant boosts for read, increment, and enqueuing. We also observe that there is no gain for write operations. This means that the analysis correctly identifies conflicting write operations and prevents them from being executed in parallel. Finally, we observe close-to-linear speedup for high event complexities when the analysis can identify independent events. Additionally, we observe that there is no severe impact of neither the increased complexity by using atomic operations for incrementations nor the sorting of the queue.

From these results we derive that the benefit in general not only depends on the simulation model but also on the model implementation. If an event handler issues a write to a variable used by another event, the two events cannot be parallelized. In a worst case scenario (i. e., the affected event types yield by far the most complex events in the model), this eliminates the benefit of our approach. However, our analysis tool provides information on the determined event dependencies. If the gained speedup does not fulfill the expectations, this information can be used to track down and eliminate the bottleneck. For the implementation of wireless models this means that complex channel computations should be separated from modifying the channel state to avoid introducing unnecessary dependencies.

6.3 Case Studies

We conduct two case studies to evaluate the practical impact of our approaches in wireless network simulation, namely a Wireless Mesh Network (WMN) and an LTE model. We implemented both models completely in C++ as well as PSimLa. We also exploit the opportunity to combine both languages in order to mitigate the drawbacks of poor translation in certain cases (see Sec. 3.1).

We execute all three implementations (PSimLa, C++, and combined) 1. sequentially and 2. parallelized by Horizon. Additionally, we execute the two implementations containing PSimLa code parallelized by exploiting the data-dependency knowledge of the code analysis. This yields eight configurations. We measure the speedup of each configuration compared with sequential execution of the C++ model, i. e., the speedup of this case is by definition 1.

For both case studies we verified that in all configurations the simulation results are identical to the results of a sequential execution. We discuss the results in the following.

Wireless Mesh Network.

The first model simulates a 57 node mesh network where data is transmitted from node to node over a wireless channel simulated with an accurate OFDM fading model [20].

The results are depicted in Fig. 7(a). As the overhead evaluation of the OFDM fading code shows (cf. Fig. 4(c)), the fading code is poorly translated from PSimLa to C++ by our prototype compiler. For this reason, sequential execution of a full implementation in PSimLa yields a considerable

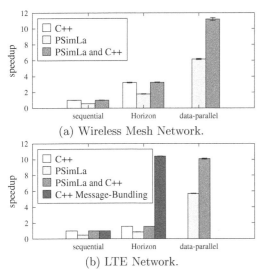

(a) Wireless Mesh Network.

(b) LTE Network.

Figure 7: Case studies: Speedup over sequential execution of the C++ model. More is better.

slowdown over C++ code. Hence, we decided to implement the fading in C++, which yields performance similar to the C++ model if executed sequentially or by Horizon. By additionally exploiting the analysis results the model execution achieves close-to-linear speedup while the C++ model can only be speeded up by a factor of 3.2.

LTE Simulation Model.

Our second case study simulates a 48 cell LTE network with an abstract LTE model as described in [17]. Initially, this model creates separate events if multiple data packets are transmitted in a single Time to Transmit Interval (TTI). Since the parallelizability of these events is not encountered by traditional techniques, this configuration parallelizes poorly (cf. Fig. 7(b)). However, the data-dependency analysis determines the actual independence of those events and achieves close-to-linear speedup.

The results of our code analysis disclosed this bottleneck in the C++ model. We fixed the bottleneck in the C++ model by bundling the events together and achieved a comparable performance. This shows that the analysis has the potential to eliminate performance bottlenecks automatically and avoid the need for manual model adaptations.

7. RELATED WORK

We compare our work with related efforts in the area of DSLs designed for the simulation context as well as approaches to static code analysis of simulation code.

7.1 Simulation Languages

DSLs for simulation have a long tradition. Simula [6] and GPSS [16] have been developed in the 60s and 70s respectively to incorporate the special requirements of simulation in the language design. However, these languages were not designed for PDES. Apostle [22] and Parsec [1] are the most prominent examples of DSLs designed for parallel simulation. Though these languages have been tailored to ease the development of models that can efficiently be executed in parallel, the underlying parallelization concepts only rely on event timestamps in order to derive event dependencies. The languages are not designed with a focus on analyzability.

A more modern approach in this field is Pose [21]. Though Pose is rather a simulation framework than a simulation language, it bases on the DSL Charm++ [11], which is designed for parallel programming in general. The aim of Pose is to make parallelization transparent to the model developer by applying the virtualization scheme of Charm++ providing virtual objects. The framework can map those virtual objects to processors, such that model developers no longer need to cope with efficient partitioning. However, Charm++ is designed to allow developers to create efficient parallel programs, but does not put particular emphasis on analyzability to automatically detect independencies.

Recent efforts include ErlangTW [19], a simulation framework based on the functional programming language Erlang. We already discussed the pros and cons of functional programming languages in Sec. 2. Although we expect static analysis to be easier for functional programs, to the best of our knowledge no approach exists analyzing data-dependencies in ErlangTW. We believe that our analysis approach could be as well applied on ErlangTW with less effort for data access tracking due to the absence of side effects. In this paper, however, we demonstrate the feasibility of data-dependency analysis even for a structured language.

Further modern DSLs are SESSL [7] and DEVS-Ruby [8]. While SESSL focuses on a language to describe simulation experiments, DEVS-Ruby focuses on a specification for models following the DEVS formalism [23]. Neither of those languages incorporates the ability to analyze model code for data-dependencies into the language design. We conclude that a language that actually incorporates this feature can increase the parallelism in simulation models.

7.2 Static Code Analysis

Chen et al. [4, 5] propose a similar approach to analyze data-dependencies for parallel simulation. To this end, they focus on Electronic System Level (ESL) design. As opposed to our approach, the authors did not create a dedicated language, but base their analysis on the language SpecC, commonly used in ESL design. Like C, SpecC supports pointers to address data items in dynamic memory. Similar to our approach, the analysis of Chen et al. checks the model code for conflicts between data accesses. However, since the approach is unable to reliably detect conflicts when data is accessed via a pointer, the authors decided to terminate the analysis on any occurance of a pointer access, and handle the pointer access like a conflicting data access. Hence, only if all items accessed by an event handler are either objects in automatic memory or members of the local module, this analysis can improve performance. While this might be a feasible limitation in the ESL domain, we argue that for a wide area of simulation models, especially wireless networks, this is not a suitable simplification. In order to investigate whether data-dependency analysis is generally feasible for simulation models implemented in a structured programming language, it is necessary to support the basic features of the selected language. In particular, this includes access to data items which are not within the scope of the function, but can only be accessed via a reference or pointer. To circumvent the unsolved problem of pointer analysis [2, 10] without facing this limitation, we decided to create the pointer-less language PSimLa and base our analysis on PSimLa code. This shows the feasibility of detecting data-dependencies even if references are used within the analyzed code.

Further approaches to static code analysis in the area of simulation focus on performance prediction or model testing rather than automatic performance improvements. Cavitt et al. [3] and Kappler et al. [12] use static code analysis to investigate the model and derive performance prediction models. Overstreet [15] showed the usability of static code analysis to verify correctness of simulation models.

We conclude that, while there is an approach using static code analysis to performance improvement of ESL models, there is no general approach to increase the level of parallelism usable in wireless and other simulation models. In this paper, we demonstrate the feasibility of data-dependency analysis for a structured programming language that includes all features necessary for model development.

8. CONCLUSION

This paper discusses the simulation language PSimLa, which is specifically designed for analyzability, as well as an approach exploiting this feature to analyze event dependencies and use this information to increase the level of parallelism. A model can be implemented completely or partially in PSimLa, which is similar to C++. This enables a smooth transition for existing C++ code. The translated parts can then be analyzed at compile time, such that the execution is speeded up by exploiting those information. Our evaluation shows promising results indicating that certain wireless simulation models, which are not well parallelized by traditional approaches, can strongly benefit from this analysis: In two case studies our approach reaches close-to-linear speedup for models which are hardly parallelized by traditional techniques.

Future efforts address three dimensions: language syntax, translation quality, and analysis approaches. The features of PSimLa supported by our prototype implementation of the compiler are sufficient to implement any model. Nevertheless, the feature set needs to be extended to provide all elements of modern high-level languages. The evaluation of the code translation quality has shown certain bottlenecks that need to be eliminated. Especially the allocation of arrays can be improved by smarter concepts to decide whether to allocate dynamic memory or use automatic memory instead. Additional analysis approaches can further improve the degree of parallelism. These should address more sophisticated methods to analyze more complex code, potentially detecting more independent events in situations where our approaches assume dependency due to a too conservative analysis. Furthermore, independence information in a shape better applicable for distributed simulation can improve performance for simulations executed on multiple machines.

Acknowledgments

This work has been co-funded by the German Research Foundation (DFG) within the Collaborative Research Center (CRC) 1053 – MAKI.

9. REFERENCES

[1] R. Bagrodia, R. Meyer, M. Takai, Y.-A. Chen, X. Zeng, J. Martin, and H. Y. Song. Parsec: A Parallel Simulation Environment for Complex Systems. *IEEE Computer*, 31(10):77–85, 1998.

[2] D. Binkley. Source Code Analysis: A Road Map. In *Future of Software Engineering*, 104–119, 2007.

[3] D. B. Cavitt, C. M. Overstreet, and K. J. Maly. A Performance Analysis Model for Distributed Simulations. In *Proc. of the 28th Winter Sim. Conf.*, 629–636, 1996.

[4] W. Chen and R. Dömer. Optimized Out-of-Order Parallel Discrete Event Simulation Using Predictions. In *Proc. of the 2013 Conf. on Design, Autom. & Test in Eur.*, 2013.

[5] W. Chen, X. Han, and R. Dömer. Out-of-Order Parallel Simulation for ESL Design. In *Proc. of the 2012 Conf. on Design, Autom. & Test in Eur.*, 141–146, 2012.

[6] O.-J. Dahl and K. Nygaard. SIMULA: An ALGOL-based Simulation Language. *Communications of the ACM*, 9(9):671–678, 1966.

[7] R. Ewald and A. M. Uhrmacher. SESSL: A Domain-specific Language for Simulation Experiments. *ACM Trans. on Modeling and Computer Sim.*, 24(2):11:1–11:25, 2014.

[8] R. Franceschini, P. Bisgambiglia, and D. Hill. DEVS-Ruby: a Domain Specific Language for DEVS Modeling and Simulation (WIP). In *Proc. of the 2014 Symp. On Theory of Modeling and Sim.*, 15:1–15:6, 2014.

[9] R. Fujimoto. Parallel Discrete Event Simulation. *Communications of the ACM*, 33(10):30–53, 1990.

[10] M. Hind. Pointer Analysis: Haven't We Solved This Problem Yet? In *Proc. of the 2001 ACM SIGPLAN-SIGSOFT Workshop on Program Analysis for Software Tools and Engineering*, 54–61, 2001.

[11] L. V. Kale and S. Krishnan. CHARM++: A Portable Concurrent Object Oriented System Based on C++. In *Proc. of the 8th Conf. on Object-oriented Programming Systems, Languages, and Applications*, 91–108, 1993.

[12] T. Kappler, H. Koziolek, K. Krogmann, and R. Reussner. Towards Automatic Construction of Reusable Prediction Models for Component-Based Performance Engineering. *GI LNI: Software Engineering*, 121:140–154, 2008.

[13] G. Kunz, O. Landsiedel, J. Gross, S. Götz, F. Naghibi, and K. Wehrle. Expanding the Event Horizon in Parallelized Network Simulations. In *Proc. of the 18th Symposium on Modeling, Analysis and Sim. of Computer and Telecommunication Systems*, 172–181, 2010.

[14] G. Kunz, M. Stoffers, J. Gross, and K. Wehrle. Runtime Efficient Event Scheduling in Multi-threaded Network Simulation. In *Proc. of the 4th Conf. on Sim. Tools and Techniques*, 359–366, 2011.

[15] C. Overstreet. Model Testing: Is it only a Special Case of Software Testing? In *Proc. of the 34th Winter Sim. Conf.*, 641–647, 2002.

[16] T. J. Schriber. Simulation using GPSS. Technical report, DTIC Document, 1974.

[17] M. Stoffers, S. Schmerling, G. Kunz, J. Gross, and K. Wehrle. Large-Scale Network Simulation: Leveraging the Strengths of Modern SMP-based Compute Clusters. In *Proc. of the 7th Conf. on Sim. Tools and Techniques*, 2014.

[18] M. Stoffers, T. Sehy, J. Gross, and K. Wehrle. Analyzing Data Dependencies for Increased Parallelism in Discrete Event Simulation. In *Proc. of the 29th ACM SIGSIM Conf. on Principles of Advanced Discrete Sim.*, 2015.

[19] L. Toscano, G. D'Angelo, and M. Marzolla. Parallel Discrete Event Simulation with Erlang. In *Proc. of the 1st ACM SIGPLAN Workshop on Functional High-performance Computing*, 83–92, 2012.

[20] C. Wang, M. Pätzold, and Q. Yao. Stochastic Modeling and Simulation of Frequency-Correlated Wideband Fading Channels. *IEEE Trans. on Vehicular Technology*, 56(3):1050–1063, 2007.

[21] T. Wilmarth and L. Kale. Pose: getting over grainsize in parallel discrete event simulation. In *Proc. of the 2004 Intl. Conf. on Parallel Processing*, 12–19, 2004.

[22] P. Wonnacott and D. Bruce. The APOSTLE Simulation Language: Granularity Control and Performance Data. In *Proc. of the 10th Workshop on Parallel and Distributed Sim.*, 114–123, 1996.

[23] B. P. Zeigler, H. Praehofer, and T. G. Kim. *Theory of Modeling and Simulation: Integrating Discrete Event and Continuous Complex Dynamic Systems*. Academic Press, Waltham, MA, U. S., 2000.

A Computing Profiling Procedure for Mobile Developers to Estimate Energy Cost

Majid Altamimi
EE Department
King Saud University
Riyadh, Saudi Arabia
mtamimi@ksu.edu.sa

Kshirasagar Naik
ECE Department
University of Waterloo
Waterloo, Ontario, Canada
snaik@uwaterloo.ca

ABSTRACT

Mobile devices are constrained by the limited capacities of their small batteries. However, profiling the energy consumed in the task execution is crucial to help the developers to build energy efficient applications. Therefore, the major challenge in the profiling approach is to accurately estimating the energy consumed for an application by the hardware components, such as CPU, memory, storage unit, and network interfaces. In this work, we develop and validate hardware and software profiling models and procedures. We profile smartphone CPU, where we consider multi-core CPUs and the impact of Dynamic Voltage and Frequency Scaling mechanism on the power consumption. In addition, we profile smartphone storage unit by taking into account the writing and reading rate to the unit. Moreover, we experimentally validated these profiles on two diverse smartphones with different versions of operating systems. The experimental results reveal that our profiles are able to estimate the application energy accurately.

Keywords

Mobile devices, Power and energy consumption, CPU, Multi-core CPU, Dynamic Voltage and Frequency Scaling, Application energy.

1. INTRODUCTION

In the span of a decade, mobile devices became popular among users and their number is ever growing. They are essential in the daily life of many people because of their capabilities and functionalities that are beyond just the voice calling. However, the mobility advantage comes from small size and lightweight of devices, to make them handy to be used everywhere. Therefore, manufactures of the devices continually reduce the size and weight while improving the capabilities of the devices. In contrast, battery technology is not making rapid progress in the form of increasing the energy density. As the limited battery capacity is a non-negligible issue, industry and academic researchers

MSWiM'15, November 2–6, 2015, Cancun, Mexico.
© 2015 ACM. ISBN 978-1-4503-3762-5/15/11 ...$15.00.
DOI: http://dx.doi.org/10.1145/2811587.2811627.

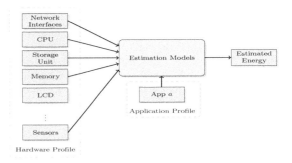

Figure 1: Profiling overview for energy estimation

have been extensively addressing the issue from the hardware level up to the application level [16].

In the recent years, the issue became significant after the emergence of a wide range of applications, many of them being not energy efficient. For instance, some online video streaming and web browser applications are not energy efficient as in the finding of Abogharaf et al. [1] and Albasir et al. [2]. Developing energy aware applications needs information about the energy consumption of the hardware components at the application level [10]. This is achievable by means of developing hardware and application profiles. The hardware profile contains a mathematical description of the power consumption of the hardware components at different operating levels (*e.g.*, idle, standby, and active). On the other hand, the application profile is the mathematical description of the use of hardware components by a given application. In the profiling method, the developers use the hardware profile to estimate the total energy consumed for an application on a given hardware as depicted in Fig. 1.

To profile a mobile device, it is crucial to identify the most hardware components consume energy. In the modern mobile devices, it has been validated that the LCD, networking interfaces, memory, CPU, and data storage unit (*i.e.*, sd-card) are the top energy consumers [5]. The energy consumed by the LCD is linearly proportional to the level of the brightness and the displayed color [15]. The energy consumed by the networking interfaces has a direct relationship to the amount of data transferred by the applications [3]. In fact, the energy consumed by the memory is very small compared to the energy consumed by the CPU, which can be ignored [5].

In this work, we present a procedure to profile the mutlicore CPU and the storage unit of smartphones. We develop the procedure to be applicable to many smartphones. The result of the procedure is mathematical models to profile applications without running additional tests. To summarize, the paper makes the following contributions:

- Profile multi-core CPU where we consider the impact of the *Dynamic Voltage and Frequency Scaling (DVFS)* mechanism and the number of online cores on the CPU profile;

- Model the power consumption of the storage unit as a function of the system clock frequency and the rate of writing and reading to the storage unit.

- Profile an application as a case study to demonstrate the use of hardware profiling; and

- Experimentally validate the profile models and procedures.

The paper is organized as follows. The related works are discussed in Section 2. In Section 3, we explain and develop profiling models and show the profiling procedure that we follow to extract the models parameters. In Section 4, we present a case study for our profiling procedure, and show how to apply the energy estimation models. Some concluding remarks are given in Section 5.

2. RELATED WORK

As the problem of limited energy resource in mobile devices becomes more acute, more research is needed to tackle this problem. Multipurpose systems, like the ones on mobile devices, are very complex; consequently, it is difficult to predict their power consumption. The power profiling approach is a promising one to tackle the problem [17]. In the literature there are two approaches to profiling: post-profiling and pre-profiling. Post-profiling provides information about the power consumption of an application on a given device after running the application. In contrast, pre-profiling predicts the power consumption of an application on a given device before the application is started.

Bugu is a post-profiling approach that drives the relationship between events and power consumption on mobile devices to profile an application [14]. The system consists of two parts: a *Bugu* server and *Bugu* client. The *Bugu* server collects the application power information and provides it to *Bugu* clients after analysing the power and the events from the device. On the other hand, the *Bugu* client monitors the application power consumption. *Bugu* does not breakdown the total power consumption to the power consumed by the hardware components. Moreover, this approach does not consider hardware configurations like online CPU cores and DVFS. *PowerScope* is a post-profiling system that profiles both the hardware components and the application [7]. The energy consumption of the hardware components is measured by external power meters. At the same time of measuring the power, software performs a statistical analysis to the system activities. The hardware profiling is computed offline by combining the statistical analysis with the measure power. To profile an application, *PowerScope* analyzes the application and build mapping from the application structure to the system events that statistically provided from the hardware profiling.

In contrast to *Bugu*, *Devscope* [12] and *PowerBooter* [20] are pre-profiling approaches that profile the hardware components of a mobile device by analyzing the access to the

components and the change in the power state [12]. The power state is provided from the *Battery Monitoring Unit (BMU)*. The output profiles are expressed in the form of lookup tables and equations. The used method would be accurate if it uses an accurate power meter since *BMU* is known to update at a very low rate and provides readings with very low accuracy. It cannot trace very short events that are shorter than *BMU* update rate.

Appscope [19] can profile an application using the models provided by *Devscope*. *Appscope* uses the same concept of *Devscope* by monitoring the system events at the kernel level for the call of the hardware components by the application. Similarly, *pTop* [6] and *Eprof* [18] estimate the energy consumed for an application by tracing system calls for the application. The energy of an application is computed by using the information of the power consumption of the hardware components that the application uses, and the time the application needs these components. *eCalc* [9] and *eLens* [10] use the same approach of *Appscope* but it analyzes the application at the code-level. The application profiles in *eCalc* and in *eLens* show how much of the code uses each hardware component by tracing the code at the development environment. Then, an energy cost function estimates the energy consumed for each type code instructions to profile the hardware components.

In our profiling methods, we use an accurate approach that precisely measures the power consumption at any system event. In addition, we consider the impact of *DVFS*, multi-core CPU, and storage unit of mobile devices. To the best of our knowledge this study is the first study that considers the *DVFS* mechanism for mobile system.

3. PROFILING MODELS

In this section, we present profiling models and procedures for smartphone multi-core CPUs, storage units, and applications.

3.1 CPU profile

To model the energy consumed by the CPU, we should mention to two important facts about the power consumption of a modern CPU in general. First, the power consumption is a function of the CPU clock frequency, and second, the CPU power consumption is proportional to the CPU usage.

First, the total power consumed by a CPU is the sum of the static and the dynamic power [13]. The static power (P_s) is the dissipated power caused by the leak current and the dynamic power (P_d) is the dissipated power caused by the switching activities of transistors. The dymanic power linearly depends on the capacitance (c) being switched inside the CPU chip, the square of the CPU supply voltage (v), and the CPU clock frequency (f) [8] as expressed:

$$P_d = cv^2f. \tag{1}$$

The value of the capacitance is constant for each individual CPU, which depends on the CPU chip design. On the other hand, the values of the supply voltage and the clock frequency have been set up to be constant, but modern CPU technologies adopt to set these values dynamically through a technique called *Dynamic Voltage and Frequency Scaling (DVFS)*. The advantage of adjusting the voltage or the frequency dynamically is to reduce the CPU power consumption. By combining the capacitance and the voltage notations in Eq. (1) into one notation called α, the total power dissipation of the CPU follows the following general equation:

$$
\begin{aligned}
P &= P_d + P_s \\
&= \alpha f + \beta
\end{aligned}
\tag{2}
$$

where β is a constant representing the static power and the power consumed independently of the clock frequency.

In fact, a multi-core CPU acts as a combination of single core CPUs. Hence, the total power consumption of a multi-core CPU denoted by P_{mc}, will also be a combination of the power consumed by each core, as represented in Eq. (3).

$$
P_{mc} = P_b + P_c \times n
\tag{3}
$$

where P_b is the base power to activate a multi-core CPU, P_c is the power consumed in each individual core, and n is the number of active cores. We multiply P_c by n because CPUs are identical cores. Consequently, the multi-core version of Eq. (3) is written as:

$$
P_{mc} = \alpha_b f + \beta_b + [\alpha_c f + \beta_c] \times n
\tag{4}
$$

Another fact concerning power consumption is that the CPU consumes power as a function of the CPU usage (*i.e.,* utilization) [4]. The relationship between the CPU power consumption and the CPU usage is a linear relationship as expressed in Eq. (5).

$$
P_{cpu} = P_{min} + (P_{max} - P_{min}) \times U
\tag{5}
$$

where P_{min} and P_{max} are the power consumed by the CPU at zero and 100% utilization, respectively, and U is the CPU utilization at a given time when the power is calculated.

3.2 Storage unit profile

The storage unit consumes power based on the amount of data written/read on/from the unit, because the unit only activates the cells that are targeted for the writing or reading activity. However, the speed of the bus that activates the cells for writing/reading determines the power consumed by the unit. Usually, this speed takes the value of the CPU frequency of the embedded system, such as modern smartphones. As a result, the power consumption of the storage unit will be a function of the data rate and the system frequency as expressed in the following equation:

$$
P_{su} = \gamma \times R \times f,
\tag{6}
$$

where P_{su} is the average power consumed by the storage unit, R is the data rate of the writing/reading activities, and f is the system frequency. A base power is absent in the equation because the amount of power to activate the unit is negligible.

3.3 Application profile

The aim of application profiling is to model the usage of the hardware components by an application. We profile the application by studying the impact of the application on the CPU and the storage unit. For the impact on the CPU, we need to know how much the application could consume CPU time, which reflects on the CPU utilization and consequently the power consumption expressed in Eq. (5). Moreover, the expected execution time is important to calculate the total

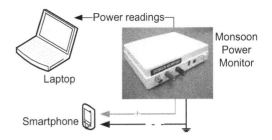

Figure 2: Experiments setup

energy of the application. The expected execution time is calculated as:

$$
T = I \times \frac{cc}{I} \times \frac{1}{f},
\tag{7}
$$

where T is the total execution time, I is the total number of instructions of the application for a given task, cc is the number of CPU cycles, and f is the CPU frequency [11].

On the other hand, the impact of an application on the storage unit can be determined by specifying the application throughput. Here, throughput is the total amount of data read from and written to the storage unit per second by the application. Therefore, the throughput is given by:

$$
R_a = \frac{Data_{read}}{T} + \frac{Data_{write}}{T}
\tag{8}
$$

Substituting T with its value from Eq. (7), we get

$$
R_a = \delta f,
\tag{9}
$$

which represents the throughput as a first degree polynomial function of the frequency, and where δ is the relationship constant.

4. A CASE STUDY

In this section, we validate our developed profiles by conducting experiments on real smartphones and applications. The purpose of the experiments is to evaluate empirically the value of the constants appear in profiling equations Eq. (4) to Eq. (5). In the following subsections, we present and explain the experimental set up, the profiling procedure, and the results.

4.1 Experimental Setup

We set up our experiments as depicted in Fig. 2. In this setup, we use *Samsung Galaxy Note 3* and *Samsung Galaxy Nexus* smartphones. Due to the space limitation, we only present in this paper the profiling for *Samsung Galaxy Note 3*. The power supply simultaneously powers the smartphone and records the power consumption as a time series. The power readings during the experiments are recorded on a separate laptop.

4.2 Experimental Results

In the experiments, we write several scripts that change the system parameter at the kernel level to profile the CPU, the storage unit, and the application. We use the predefined operating points of the system frequency. The scripts initialize the desired frequency to force the CPU to use that frequency. Moreover, we control the number of online cores by our scripts that force the kernel to bring cores online.

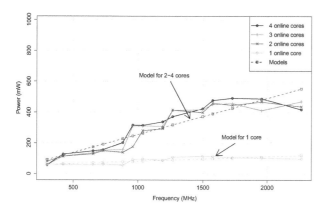

Figure 3: P_{min} **for CPU profiling of Samsung Galaxy Note 3**

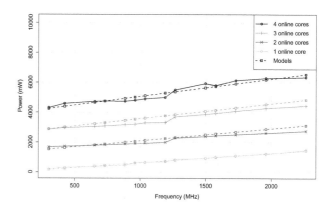

Figure 4: P_{max} **for CPU profiling of Samsung Galaxy Note 3**

4.2.1 CPU profile

In the CPU profiling, the scripts bring a specific core online and adjust its desired frequency. The scripts generate load for the CPU by making its utilization 100%. At this time, the average power consumed by the device is P_{max} in Eq. (5). In the same way, the scripts disable all applications in the user domain and only the *OS* is run on the CPU to minimize the CPU usage and measure P_{min}. At the same time of running the profiling scripts, the power meter records the power readings. These steps are repeated for each operating frequency and different number of online cores.

Figure 3 and 4 show the change in P_{min} and P_{max}, respectively, as a function of CPU frequency. The dotted lines represent the curve fitting that we expressed in Eqs. (10) and (11) as a corresponding to the models in the previous section. We obtain the value of α_b, β_b, α_c, and β_c in Eq. (4) by using curve fitting tools on MATLAB that use linear regression approach and the result values are given for the models in Eqs. (10) and (11).

$$P_{min} = \begin{cases} 0.03f + 51, & n = 1 \\ 0.2f - 30, & n > 1 \end{cases} \quad (10)$$

$$P_{max} = 0.47f - 1340 + [0.175f + 1310] \times n \quad (11)$$

4.2.2 Storage unit profile

In storage unit profiling, we use similar scripts but we add a workload to write and read from the storage unit. We obtain the power consumed by the storage unit by subtracting the power that we know the CPU consumed from the total power consumed by the device. The obtained power is

$$P_{su} = 10^{-3}Rf, \quad (12)$$

where P_{su} is the power consumed by the storage unit in mW, R is the writing/reading rate to the unit in kB, and f is the clock frequency in MHz.

4.2.3 Application profile

In the application profile, we also use scripts to force the system for a specific number of online cores and working frequency. After that, another set of scripts trace the system

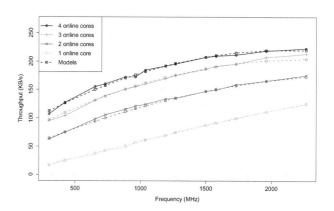

Figure 5: FFmpeg application profiling (KB/s: **Kilo Bytes per second**)

parameters such as CPU usages, writing and read rate to the storage unit, and total execution time. These parameters are used to calculate the total energy consumed by the application using the profiling models. The application that we use in this case study is *FFmpeg* encoding that we use it to encode a *23.97 MB* flv video file into a *20.94 MB* mpeg video file. The same input file and encoding parameters are used for consistency in our experiments. Moreover, the application throughput is shown in Fig. 5, the dotted lines represent the fitting curves that we expressed in Eq. (13). However, the linear fitting does not perfectly match the actual measurement lines because there is a small curvature on the measurement lines in the cases of more than one online core. The curvature increases as the number of online cores increases. For better results, we correct this by adding second-degree terms to the previous equation to give a better match as expressed in Eq. (13).

$$\begin{aligned} R_a = {} & 3 \times 10^{-6}f^2 + 48 \times 10^{-3}f - 22 \\ & + [-7 \times 10^{-6}f^2 + 18 \times 10^{-3}f + 19] \times n \end{aligned} \quad (13)$$

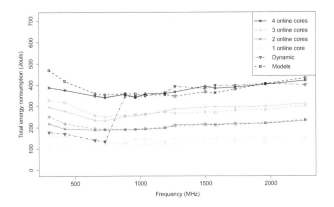

Figure 6: Total application energy consumption Samsung Galaxy Note 3

4.3 Total energy for an application: using of all profiles

In this subsection, we show how the developers use the profiles to calculate the total energy consumed by a smartphone for an application. The total application energy is calculated by multiplying the total power consumption (*i.e.,* CPU and storage unit) by the total execution time. Figure 6 shows the comparison between the energy consumption obtained from the experiments (the solid lines) and from the profile models (dotted lines). This figure further corroborates the fact that for a fixed task the total energy is constant regardless of the CPU frequency [11]. We conducted another set of similar experiments, but we let the *OS* choose the required number of online cores as in the dynamic core selection.

5. CONCLUSIONS

The energy aspect of the mobile devices in many cases has not been addressed well. The problem is that the developers have no clue about the energy consumption of their application on a particular device. In this work, we develop hardware and software profiling models and procedures. These profiles empower mobile developers to estimate the energy consumption of an application on a given device. Moreover, we described how to profile modern multi-core CPUs, storage units, and applications under the *Android* platform. The results of the real experiments on two different smartphones reveal the validation and accuracy of our profiling procedures.

6. REFERENCES

[1] A. Abogharaf and K. Naik. Client-Centric Data Streaming on Smartphones: An Energy Perspective. In *MoWNeT*, pages 36–41, 2013.

[2] A. Albasir, K. Naik, and T. Abdunabi. Smart Mobile Web Browsing. In *iCAST-UMEDIA*, pages 671–679, 2013.

[3] M. Altamimi, A. Abdrabou, K. Naik, and A. Nayak. Energy Cost Models of Smartphones for Task Offloading to the Cloud. *under a second round review for publication in IEEE Transactions on Emerging Topics in Computing (TETC)*, 2014.

[4] L. Barroso and U. Holzle. The Case for Energy-Proportional Computing. *Computer*, 40(12):33–37, Dec 2007.

[5] A. Carroll and G. Heiser. An Analysis of Power Consumption in a Smartphone. In *USENIX ATC*, pages 21–21, 2010.

[6] T. Do, S. Rawshdeh, and W. Shi. pTop: A Process-level Power Profiling Tool. In *HotPower*, 2009.

[7] J. Flinn and M. Satyanarayanan. PowerScope: A Tool for Profiling the Energy Usage of Mobile Applications. In *IEEE WMCSA*, pages 2–9, 1999.

[8] R. Gonzalez, B. Gordon, and M. Horowitz. Supply and threshold voltage scaling for low power CMOS. *IEEE Journal of Solid-State Circuits*, 32(8):1210–1216, Aug 1997.

[9] S. Hao, D. Li, W. Halfond, and R. Govindan. Estimating Android applications' CPU energy usage via bytecode profiling. In *GREENS*, pages 1–7, 2012.

[10] S. Hao, D. Li, W. Halfond, and R. Govindan. Estimating Mobile Application Energy Consumption using Program Analysis. In *ICSE*, pages 92–101, 2013.

[11] J. L. Hennessy and D. A. Patterson. *Computer architecture: a quantitative approach.* Elsevier, 2012.

[12] W. Jung, C. Kang, C. Yoon, D. Kim, and H. Cha. DevScope: A Nonintrusive and Online Power Analysis Tool for Smartphone Hardware Components. In *Proc. CODES/ISSS*, pages 353–362, 2012.

[13] S. Kaxiras and M. Martonosi. *Computer architecture techniques for power-efficiency.* Morgan and Claypool Publishers, 2008.

[14] Y. Li, H. Chen, and W. Shi. Bugu: an Application Level Power Profiler and Analyzer for Mobile Devices. *ACM SIGMOBILE*, 17(3):27–28, 2013.

[15] R. Mittal, A. Kansal, and R. Chandra. Empowering Developers to Estimate App Energy Consumption. In *Mobicom*, pages 317–328, 2012.

[16] K. Naik. A Survey of Software Based Energy Saving Methodologies for Handheld Wireless Communication Devices. Technical Report 2010-13, Dept. of ECE, University of Waterloo, Waterloo, ON, Canada, 2010.

[17] A. Noureddine, R. Rouvoy, and L. Seinturier. A Review of Energy Measurement Approaches. *SIGOPS Oper. Syst. Rev.*, 47(3):42–49, Nov. 2013.

[18] A. Pathak, Y. C. Hu, and M. Zhang. Where is the Energy Spent Inside My App?: Fine Grained Energy Accounting on Smartphones with Eprof. In *ACM EuroSys*, pages 29–42, 2012.

[19] C. Yoon, D. Kim, W. Jung, C. Kang, and H. Cha. AppScope: Application Energy Metering Framework for Android Smartphone Using Kernel Activity Monitoring. In *USENIX ATC*, pages 387–400, 2012.

[20] L. Zhang, B. Tiwana, Z. Qian, Z. Wang, R. P. Dick, Z. M. Mao, and L. Yang. Accurate Online Power Estimation and Automatic Battery Behavior Based Power Model Generation for Smartphones. In *Proc. CODES/ISSS*, pages 105–114, 2010.

Modelling the Bandwidth Allocation Problem in Mobile Service-Oriented Networks

Bo Gao, Ligang He and Chao Chen

Department of Computer Science, University of Warwick, Coventry, CV4 7AL, UK

liganghe@dcs.warwick.ac.uk

ABSTRACT

When the services requested by mobile application workflows are distributed over a network of mobile smart devices, the question arises as to which service should be allocated with how much bandwidth and when in order to satisfy service demands? Furthermore, the mobility of smart mobile devices brings forward the challenge to determine how changes in mobile network conditions affect the bandwidth requirements of interacting services. In this paper, we construct a Network I-O model to describe the bandwidth dependencies in mobile service-oriented networks incorporating and extend on the principles of the Leontief Input-Output model in economics. Various factors such as bandwidth and service demand are accounted for in the model. The network I-O model lays the foundation for future objective developments in ubiquitous mobile computing scenarios. Results from simulation studies are presented to demonstrate the effectiveness of the proposed methods.

Keywords

Mobile service-oriented networks; bandwidth allocation; mobile application workflows

1. INTRODUCTION

Technologies that were once thought to be futuristic like self-driving vehicles and wearable digital assistants are fast becoming a reality. The proliferation of mobile smart devices is radically changing the way applications are delivered. One key characteristic of mobile applications is their unique ability to sense and capture information about the immediate environment its user is in. However, the downside of being in such a dynamic environment is the limited and unreliable wireless network capacity. Therefore allocating the correct amount of bandwidth to the right mobile service on the right device at the right time becomes an important issue.

Consider as an example a wireless network of personal mobile smart devices as shown in Fig. 1. Each service module serves a different purpose to the user and is able to run independently. However, when connected via a network, these services can also be dynamically combined to serve more complex mobile application workflows. For instance, as illustrated in Fig. 1 by the coloured lines, the user can use the tablet to stream a remote video file from the storage service by transcoding it to a format that is readable by the smart TV. At the same time, if the smartphone is also available (has adequate bandwidth) to the network, the tablet can transcode the video file to a voice stream that can be transcribed to a text stream on the smartphone. This text information can then be translated on the tablet to a language chosen by the user and streamed to the smart TV as subtitles.

Observe that the process of service composition is dynamic and non-deterministic. The composition decision may be influenced by many factors such as 1) Network Conditions: the smartphone might not have enough bandwidth therefore the "Voice-to-Text" service on the smartphone cannot receive the voice stream from the "Transcode" service on the tablet; 2) Dynamic Application Information: the film may be in a language which the user can understand, and therefore the "Translation" service is not included in the workflow.

In this paper, we refer to this type of mobile networks as *mobile service-oriented networks* (MSON)s on which a universe of services is distributed, and mobile applications are executed as dynamic compositions of these services. This service-oriented network structure commonly exist among vehicular ad hoc networks (VANETs) [14, 7], urban sensing networks [6, 15], biomedical application workflows [16, 12] and other smart environment applications.

One of the key challenges that comes with the research in MSON is the constrained and unpredictable wireless network connection capacity (e.g., bandwidth). In contrast to desktop based SOA networks [12], focus of the bandwidth allocation problem has shifted from the centre of the network (considered fast in an MSON) to the access points at the edge of the network, which raises the question: *How*

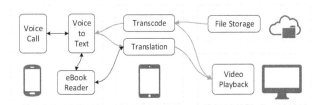

Figure 1: A simple mobile service-oriented network example.

much bandwidth should each service require and when in order to satisfy the desired QoS? Moreover, since the services interact with each other dynamically during workflow executions, it is a non-trivial task to investigate the impact of the changes in service demand (e.g., the arrival rate of workflows) on bandwidth allocations for individual services in order to maintain the QoS. The problem is further complicated by the mobility of the mobile devices. As mobile devices move around, their bandwidth or latency may change, which brings the challenges to adjust the bandwidth allocations for the interacting services.

In this paper, we first discuss the applications of an MSON and related work in the next section. We then extend the Leontief I-O model in economy and formulate the bandwidth dependencies of an MSON with a Network I-O model in section 3. We conduct a series of parametric simulations in section 4 to verify and demonstrate the applicabilities of our network I-O model. We conclude the paper and discuss future directions of this work in section 5.

2. MSON AND RELATED WORK

An MSON infrastructure can be observed from many research areas. In vehicular wireless systems, many applications are built on top of cooperative networks of mobile smart devices installed on smart vehicles. Exemplar applications includes BitTorrent-styled location significant content downloading [14] and vehicle-to-vehicle environment and safety sensing [7]. In biomedical applications, a mobile application workflow is used in [16] to describe a sensor-based biomedical application which includes mobile devices used as both sensors and data processing units. The motivating scenario addressed in [12] describes the benefit of using service composition in a hospital resource scheduling application. In other mobile application areas, a mobile P2P file sharing framework is presented in [10]. A framework for mobile P2P social content sharing is presented in [4]. These studies all share the same underlying MSON infrastructure.

The idea of mobile devices as service hosts is also an active research topic. In [13], an SOA-based approach is presented to support interactions between business applications running on J2ME. In [9], opportunistic composition of sequentially-connected service over a decentralised mobile ad hoc network is proposed. Experiments conducted in [11] demonstrates that this opportunistic communication is viable at scale. A middleware is created in [8] to reduce user perceived latency while accessing remote services on mobiles by pre-fetching and caching data according to a sequence prediction algorithm. The same technique has been shown to reduce battery cost. All these studies are about developing the service-oriented architecture on mobile devices. None of the work discusses the bandwidth requirement of mobile services.

3. NETWORK I-O MODEL

3.1 Input-Output Analysis in Economics

Suppose a nation's economy is divided into n sectors that produce goods or services. Let x_i be the value of goods or services produced by sector i, we then have a *production vector* $\boldsymbol{x} \in \mathbb{R}^n$ to list the output from all sectors of the economy. In order to avoid waste and deficiency, production is planned in accordance to the demand of goods and services

which originates from two channels: ***External demand*** represents consumer demands, exports, planned surplus, etc. from the economy. Let d_i be the external demand of sector i, then $\boldsymbol{d} \in \mathbb{R}^n$, namely the *external demand vector*, lists the external demand (output) of all sectors of the economy. ***Intermediate demand***, represents intra-sector demand of good and services. For instance, assume a small town with two primary industries: a steel plant and a railway. Then in order to produce goods, the steel plant requires services from the railway. To represent the intermediate demand, a square matrix $A \in \mathbb{R}^{n \times n}$, namely the *consumption matrix*, is assumed, in which a_{ij} denotes the production (input) needed from sector i per unit of production (output) by sector j. With this definition, we have that in order to produce x_j units of good or services, sector j will demand $x_j a_{ij}$ units from sector i, that is the intermediate demand by sector j from sector i. When the economy's production balances the total demand for that production exactly, we have:

$$\underbrace{\boldsymbol{x}}_{\text{production}} = \underbrace{A\boldsymbol{x}}_{\text{intermediate demand}} + \underbrace{\boldsymbol{d}}_{\text{external demand}} \qquad (1)$$

which is the cornerstone of the Leontief Input-Output model of economics. This model helps economists understand how changes in one sector affect others, and predict the production level required to balance the demand exactly.

3.2 The Economy of Mobile Service-Oriented Networks

We consider each service as a sector of the network economy. Entailed by the SOA paradigm, services are combined and possibly recombined to create complex applications (workflows) that serve the demand of the end users. This composition of services is a dynamic run-time decision process which adapts to: the fluctuating network conditions (which is especially true for a mobile network), various application-dependent QoS level requirements [17, 2, 1] and dynamic application information (e.g., whether the user requires translation for a video). This means that the exact execution sequence of services is not predefined and therefore the communication demands between services are non-deterministic. This behaviour is similar to that of the common economies analysed by the Leontief I-O model. For instance, consider manufacturing and raw material as two sectors of an economy. Each product of the manufacturing sector has its own bill of materials and may require different amount of input from the raw material sector. Furthermore, a repair service may avoid input from the raw material sector completely if it does not require any replacement parts.

Data as Commodity: Services (sectors) of an MSON economy produce and exchange data to serve the demands of its end users. This data as a commodity may carry information requested by the user (e.g., query services), which may be the product in accordance to user input (e.g., image processing service), or simply be the confirmation from the service that the user's request has been recorded (e.g., flight check-in service).

Bandwidth as Currency: Exchange of data is facilitated by the network. One unit of network bandwidth facilitates the exchange of one unit of data in one unit of time. Similar to the common currency (e.g., one US dollar) used in an economy to measure goods and services of different sectors, one unit of bandwidth is the common currency of an MSON economy.

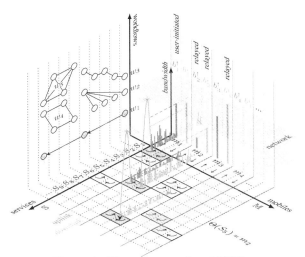

Figure 2: The economy of an MSON

Exchange of Data: Let $\mathbb{S}$ denote the universe of services distributed over the network containing a set $\mathbb{M}$ of mobile devices, according to a mapping scheme $\Theta : \mathbb{S} \to \mathbb{M}$. (In Fig. 2, we have $\Theta(s_1) = m_1, \Theta(s_2) = m_1, \Theta(s_3) = m_3$, and so on.) For each service $s_i \in \mathbb{S}$, assuming that historical data (e.g., collected by filtering logging data) are available [3, 5], and let β_i, measured in units of bandwidth, denote the (average) size of data produced by each run of s_i as an intermediate step of a service composition. The effect of β_i is three-fold:

First, as an intermediate product, β_i needs to be communicated to the next service(s) $s_j \in \mathbb{S}$ as instructed by the service composition (application workflow). If s_j is not located on the same device as s_i, then β_i needs to be sent from its host $\Theta(s_i) \in \mathbb{M}$ over the MSON. We define a co-location indicator

$$\omega_{ij} = \begin{cases} 0 & \text{if } \Theta(s_i) = \Theta(s_j), \\ 1 & \text{otherwise.} \end{cases} \quad (2)$$

so that $\omega_{ij} = 1$ indicates that, if destined to s_j, the task of sending β_i would consume the uplink bandwidth of $\Theta(s_i)$. As illustrated in Fig. 2, when a service workflow w_1 is initiated on m_1, because the next service (s_5) is located on a different device (m_2), m_1 has to first upload the data to the network. We refer to this type of bandwidth cost as *self-initiated cost* later on in this subsection. We assume that a square matrix $P = [p_{ij}]_{|\mathbb{S}|\times|\mathbb{S}|}$, in which p_{ij} denotes the probability that a run of s_i is to be succeed by a call to s_j (β_i is to be sent to s_j), is known through profiling [3, 5]. Together with our co-location indicator ω_{ij}, we define

$$\rho_i = \sum_j p_{ij}\omega_{ij} \quad (3)$$

which gives the probability that each unit product (data) of s_i is to be uploaded to the MSON by $\Theta(s_i)$. Note that $\sum_j p_{ij}$ is not necessarily one, because each run of s_i is not necessarily succeeded by a call to another service.

Second, for a service s_j to receive β_i, the downlink bandwidth of $\Theta(s_j)$ is consumed. In the example illustrated in Fig. 2, this receive action is taken by m_2 which hosts s_5. This creates a dependency between the consumption of the uplink bandwidth of the sender device and the downlink bandwidth

of the receiver device in the MSON economy. We define

$$\eta_{ij} = \frac{p_{ij}\omega_{ij}}{\sum_k p_{ik}\omega_{ik}} , \quad s_k \in \mathbb{S} \quad (4)$$

which gives the probability that a unit of data sent by s_i to the MSON is to be received by s_j. We refer to the cost occurred in this type of process as *relayed cost* later on in this section.

Third, depending on the specification of the application workflow, the service which received β_i may be requested to further communicate with other services. Take for instance the example workflow illustrated in Fig. 2, s_5 is to continue the workflow and communicate with s_9. This action consumes the uplink bandwidth of m_2 and the downlink bandwidth of m_3. As such, following a service workflow, a sequence of services in the service composition would be requested to perform communication tasks. This chain effect exists in every application and is triggered by the execution of the head services of the workflow.

Self-initiated Cost vs. Relayed Cost: Following previous discussion, we discover that the production of data, and thus the cost of bandwidth, in a MSON can also be classified into two classes: ***Self-initiated*** production of data refers to data generated by the head services executed at the start of every application workflow and exhibits the same characteristics as the external demands in Leontief's model. Devices that hosts these head services bear the cost of sending data to subsequent services. These costs are in the form of uplink bandwidth of the sender device, and are initiated solely by the service itself (e.g., triggered by user action). Let λ_i denote the arrival rate of s_i, then the self-initiated cost to the uplink of $\Theta(s_i)$ which we denote $c_i^\uparrow$ is given by

$$c_i^\uparrow = \lambda_i \beta_i \rho_i \quad (5)$$

The other class of data production is in contrast caused by services that executed prior in the application workflow and thus no consequent cost is self-inflicted. We refer to this as ***relayed*** production of data. Bandwidth cost from this class of data production can be in forms of both uplink and downlink bandwidth. We derive the cost function of this class in the proof of Theorem 1.

3.3 Network I-O Model

Given a service $s_i \in \mathbb{S}$, let $x_i = x_i^\uparrow + x_i^\downarrow$ denote its total, uplink and downlink bandwidth costs respectively. We now construct a model that derives these values with the limited information we have about the MSON, i.e., Θ, P, $\boldsymbol{\beta}$ and $\boldsymbol{\lambda}$.

Definition 1. For each pair of services $\{s_i, s_j\} \in \mathbb{S}^2$, the elements of the *uplink consumption coefficient matrix* of $\mathbb{S}$, denoted $A^\uparrow = [a_{ij}^\uparrow]_{|\mathbb{S}|\times|\mathbb{S}|}$ is given by

$$a_{ij}^\uparrow = \frac{1}{\beta_j \rho_j} p_{ji} \beta_i \rho_i \quad (6)$$

THEOREM 1. *Let $\boldsymbol{x}^\uparrow = [x_i^\uparrow]_{|\mathbb{S}|\times 1}$ denote the uplink bandwidth demand vector of $\mathbb{S}$, and $\boldsymbol{c}^\uparrow = [c_i^\uparrow]_{|\mathbb{S}|\times 1}$ denote the self-initiated demand vector of $\mathbb{S}$, then when the network is in equilibrium (meaning that each service is given the amount of bandwidth it requires to run without delay) the following equation holds*

$$\underbrace{\boldsymbol{x}^\uparrow}_{\text{uplink cost}} = \underbrace{A^\uparrow \boldsymbol{x}^\uparrow}_{\text{relayed uplink demand}} + \underbrace{\boldsymbol{c}^\uparrow}_{\text{self-initiated demand}} \quad (7)$$

PROOF. From our earlier discussion in 3.2, we know that the send (uplink) action of a service s_i is triggered by two sources, namely self-initiated and relayed. With $c_i^\uparrow$ defined in (5), let $h_{ji}^\uparrow$ denote the uplink demand that is relayed from s_j to s_i, i.e., when s_j immediately precedes s_i in an application workflow. Therefore

$$x_i^\uparrow = \sum_j h_{ji}^\uparrow + c_i^\uparrow \qquad (8)$$

With (3) we derive that each run of s_j and s_i is to generate data of size $\beta_j \rho_j$ and $\beta_i \rho_i$ respectively. If service s_j were to be allocated an uplink bandwidth of $x_j^\uparrow$, as an equilibrium entails, s_j would execute $x_j^\uparrow / \beta_j \rho_j$ times. From the communication probability matrix P, we know that for every one run of s_j there is a probability p_{ji} a subsequent run of s_i is triggered. Therefore we have

$$h_{ji}^\uparrow = \frac{x_j^\uparrow}{\beta_j \rho_j} p_{ji} \beta_i \rho_i \overset{(8)}{\Rightarrow} x_i^\uparrow = \sum_j \frac{x_j^\uparrow}{\beta_j \rho_j} p_{ji} \beta_i \rho_i + c_i^\uparrow \qquad (9)$$

Consider $i \in \{1, 2, \cdots, |\mathbb{S}|\}$, (9) derives the same set of equations as given by taking (6) into (7). $\square$

Definition 2. For each pair of services $\{s_i, s_j\} \in \mathbb{S}^2$, the elements of the *downlink consumption coefficient matrix* of $\mathbb{S}$, denoted $A^\downarrow = [a_{ij}^\downarrow]_{|\mathbb{S}| \times |\mathbb{S}|}$ is given by

$$a_{ij}^\downarrow = \eta_{ji} = \frac{p_{ji} \omega_{ji}}{\sum_k p_{jk} \omega_{jk}}, \quad s_k \in \mathbb{S} \qquad (10)$$

THEOREM 2. *Let $\boldsymbol{x}^\downarrow = [x_i^\downarrow]_{|\mathbb{S}| \times 1}$ denote the downlink bandwidth demand vector of $\mathbb{S}$, then when the network is in equilibrium (meaning that each service is given the amount of bandwidth it requires to run without delay) the following equation holds*

$$\underbrace{\boldsymbol{x}^\downarrow}_{\text{downlink cost}} = \underbrace{A^\downarrow \boldsymbol{x}^\uparrow}_{\text{relayed downlink demand}} \qquad (11)$$

PROOF. It is easy to understand that within the MSON, the downlink cost is totally dependent on the uplink cost in the sense that no receive action is required if no data was sent, and that all data sent by a service in context of the MSON must be received by another service of the MSON. On this basis, let $h_{ji}^\downarrow$ denote the downlink cost relayed from data sent from s_j to s_i, i.e., the amount of data sent from s_j to s_i, and we have

$$x_i^\downarrow = \sum_j h_{ji}^\downarrow \qquad (12)$$

Recall from (4) that the probability that a unit of data sent by s_i to s_j is given by η_{ij}, we derive

$$h_{ji}^\downarrow = x_j^\uparrow \eta_{ji} \overset{(12)}{\Rightarrow} x_i^\downarrow = \sum_j x_j^\uparrow \frac{p_{ji} \omega_{ji}}{\sum_k p_{jk} \omega_{jk}}, \quad s_k \in \mathbb{S} \qquad (13)$$

Similarly to the proof of theorem 1, by enumerating (13) with $i \in \{1, 2, \cdots, |\mathbb{S}|\}$, we get the same set of equations as given by taking (10) into (11). $\square$

To conclude the network I-O model, we gather the per-service cost from both markets and derive the total bandwidth cost for a host device $m \in \mathbb{M}$ as

$$b_m = b_m^\uparrow + b_m^\downarrow = \sum_i x_i^\uparrow + \sum_i x_i^\downarrow = \sum_i x_i, \quad \Theta(s_i) = m \qquad (14)$$

with b_m, $b_m^\uparrow$ and $b_m^\downarrow$ denote the total, uplink and downlink bandwidth cost of m.

4. SIMULATIONS

In this section, we conduct a series of simulation studies based on two types of service topologies: centralised and chain (illustrated by w_2 and w_3 in Fig. 2) to demonstrate the basic dynamics of the network I-O model. We assume a service-to-mobile allocation scheme given as $\Theta(s_1) = \Theta(s_2) = M_1$, $\Theta(s_3) = \Theta(s_4) = M_2$ and $\Theta(s_5) = M_3$ in both sets of experiments.

Effect of Service Arrival Rate: The service arrival rate is a key QoS metric for mobile application workflows. In this set of simulations, we demonstrate the dynamics of the network I-O model by examining the effect of increase in λ on the bandwidth costs of all services in $\mathbb{S}$. Furthermore, we map each service to a mobile device and examine the effect of the same action on each device's total bandwidth requirement.

In a centralised topology (w_2), we identify s_5 to be the core service and gradually increase λ_5 from 20 to 40. Results as illustrated in the first row of Fig. 3 show that the increased traffic is evenly relayed to the downlink bandwidth cost of the other services (due to the service topology), and because the traffic relayed back from the leaf services are less significant (due to the communication pattern), M_3 which hosts s_5 does not require great increase in downlink capacity.

In a chain topology (w_3), we identify the head service s_1 to be the core service and increase λ_1 to double its initial value. As shown in the second row of Fig. 3, s_1 itself does not demand much extra bandwidth since its succeeding service is located on the same device (M_1). This co-location factor also explains why only $x_2^\uparrow$ and $x_4^\uparrow$ is showing an increase in the first plot and $x_3^\downarrow$ and $x_5^\downarrow$ in the second plot. When these values are summarised per device, b_2 shows the greatest increase because it has to accommodate both the increase in $x_3^\downarrow$ and $x_4^\uparrow$.

Effect of Per Service Data Size: In this set of simulations, we examine the effect of increase in per request data size (i.e., β). In practice, this can be observed when the per frame resolution of a video stream from one user to the other is changed. As shown in the third row of Fig. 3, as we increase β_5, both $x_5^\uparrow$ and $b_5^\uparrow$ increase as they do in the first row of Fig. 3. However, $x_5^\downarrow$ remains unchanged. Furthermore, the uplink bandwidth demand of all other services and their hosts remain unchanged. This is because the increase in β_5 does not affect the relayed uplink bandwidth of the service which is called by s_5, therefore the effect of increase in β is more confined within the MSON than that in λ. The same can be observed from the fourth row of Fig. 3 which illustrates the result from a chain topology (increase in β_1).

Alternative Allocation Scheme: One common bandwidth allocation scheme, as an alternative scheme to our network I-O model, evenly distributes the available bandwidth to the services it hosts. As a result, the service rate of an MSON is prematurely capped by the service which requires the most amount of bandwidth as shown by λ' of Fig. 3 (zoom). It can be seen that the scheme as given by the I-O model, capped at λ'', realise greater potential from the MSON.

5. CONCLUSION

This work extends the existing I-O model in economics to model the service bandwidth allocation problem in mobile service-oriented networks (MSON)s. A network I-O model is

310

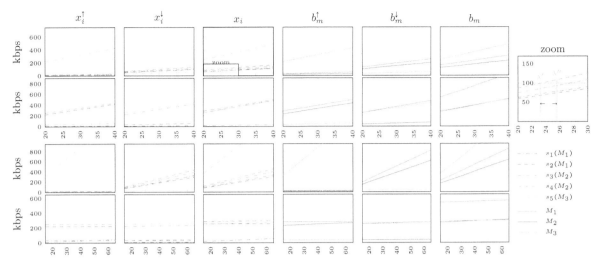

Figure 3: The increases in λ_5 of w_2, λ_1 of w_3, β_5 of w_2 and β_1 of w_3 are projected onto the x-axis of each of the four rows of plots respectively. The effects of these increases including the uplink ($x_i^\uparrow$), downlink ($x_i^\downarrow$) and total (x_i) bandwidth demands of each service (s_1 to s_5 as in plot legends), and the uplink ($b_m^\uparrow$), downlink ($b_m^\downarrow$) and total (b_m) bandwidth demands of each device (M_1 to M_3 as in plot legends) are presented in each of the six columns of plots respectively.

constructed to describes the bandwidth dependency and allocation problem in mobile networks. Elements of an MSON are considered as economic entities with their interdependencies (in terms of bandwidth demand and service QoS) as the underlying structure of the network economy. The network I-O model lays the foundation for future objective developments in ubiquitous mobile computing scenarios. For future work, we would like to extend the application of our network I-O model to include scenarios in which dynamic service allocation schemes are implemented in the network and eliminate the assumption of given service-to-device mappings. The network I-O model presented in this paper would be an essential instrument to optimise the mapping strategies in such scenarios.

Acknowledgement

This work is sponsored by the Research Project Grant of the Leverhulme Trust (Grant No. RPG-101).

6. REFERENCES

[1] ALRIFAI, M., AND RISSE, T. Combining global optimization with local selection for efficient QoS-aware service composition. In *Proceedings of the 18th International Conference on World Wide Web, WWW* (2009).

[2] ARDAGNA, D., AND PERNICI, B. Adaptive service composition in flexible processes. *IEEE Transactions on Software Engineering 33*, 6 (2007), 369–384.

[3] BODÍK, P., MENACHE, I., CHOWDHURY, M., MANI, P., MALTZ, D. A., AND STOICA, I. Surviving failures in bandwidth-constrained datacenters. In *Proceedings of ACM SIGCOMM Conference on Applications, Technologies, Architectures, and Protocols for Computer Communication, SIGCOMM* (2012).

[4] CHANG, C., SRIRAMA, S. N., AND LING, S. An adaptive mediation framework for mobile p2p social content sharing. In *Proceedings of the 10th International Conference on Service-Oriented Computing, ICSOC* (2012).

[5] CHEN, Y., JAIN, S., ADHIKARI, V. K., ZHANG, Z.-L., AND XU, K. A first look at inter-data center traffic characteristics via Yahoo! datasets. In *Proceedings of IEEE INFOCOM* (2011).

[6] CUFF, D., HANSEN, M., AND KANG, J. Urban sensing: Out of the Woods. *Communications of the ACM 51*, 3 (2008).

[7] FERREIRA, M., FERNANDES, R., CONCEIÇÃO, H., VIRIYASITAVAT, W., AND TONGUZ, O. K. Self-organized traffic control. In *Proceedings of the seventh ACM international workshop on VehiculAr InterNETworking, VANET* (2010).

[8] GOB, A., SCHREIBER, D., HAMDI, L., AITENBICHLER, E., AND MUHLHAUSER, M. Reducing user perceived latency with a middleware for mobile SOA access. In *Proceedings of IEEE International Conference on Web Services*, (2009).

[9] GROBA, C., AND CLARKE, S. Opportunistic composition of sequentially-connected services in mobile computing environments. In *Proceedings of IEEE International Conference on Web Services, ICWS* (2011).

[10] HUANG, C.-M., HSU, T.-H., AND HSU, M.-F. Network-aware P2P file sharing over the wireless mobile networks. *IEEE Journal on Selected Areas in Communications 25*, 1 (2007).

[11] LIU, S., AND STRIEGEL, A. D. Exploring the potential in practice for opportunistic networks amongst smart mobile devices. In *Proceedings of 19th International Conference on Mobile Computing & Networking, MobiCom* (2013).

[12] MABROUK, N. B., BEAUCHE, S., KUZNETSOVA, E., AND GEORGANTAS, N. QoS-aware service composition in dynamic service oriented environments. In *Proceedings of ACM/IFIP/USENIX 10th International middleware Conference, Middelware* (2009).

[13] NATCHETOI, Y., WU, H., AND ZHENG, Y. Service-Oriented mobile applications for ad-hoc networks. In *Proceedings of IEEE Conference on Services Computing, SCC* (2008).

[14] PARK, J.-S., LEE, U., OH, S. Y., GERLA, M., AND LUN, D. S. Emergency related video streaming in VANET using network coding. In *Proceedings of the 3rd International Workshop on Vehicular Ad Hoc Networks* (2006).

[15] SHI, J., ZHANG, R., LIU, Y., AND ZHANG, Y. PriSense: Privacy-Preserving Data Aggregation in People-Centric Urban Sensing Systems. In *Proceedings of IEEE INFOCOM* (2010).

[16] VISWANATHAN, H., LEE, E. K., AND POMPILI, D. Enabling real-time in-situ processing of ubiquitous mobile-application workflows. In *Proceedings of IEEE International Conference on Mobile Ad-Hoc and Sensor Systems, MASS* (2013).

[17] YU, T., ZHANG, Y., AND LIN, K.-J. Efficient algorithms for web services selection with end-to-end QoS constraints. *ACM Transactions on the Web 1*, 1 (2007).

Building a Large Dataset for Model-based QoE Prediction in the Mobile Environment

Lamine Amour, Souihi Sami, Said Hoceini and Abdelhamid Mellouk
University of Paris-Est Créteil Val de Marne (UPEC)
Image, Signal and Intelligent Systems Lab-LiSSi and Network & Telecoms Dept, IUT CV
122 rue Paul Armangot, 94400 Vitry sur Seine, France
(lamine.amour, sami.souihi, hoceini, mellouk) @u-pec.fr

ABSTRACT

The tremendous growth in video services, specially in the context of mobile usage, creates new challenges for network service providers : How to enhance the user's Quality of Experience (QoE) in dynamic wireless networks (UMTS, HSPA, LTE/LTE-A). The network operators use different methods to predict the user's QoE. Generally to predict the user's QoE, methods are based on collecting subjective QoE scores given by users. Basically, these approaches need a large dataset to predict a good perceived quality of the service. In this paper, we setup an experimental test based on crowdsourcing approach and we build a large dataset in order to predict the user's QoE in mobile environment in term of Mean Opinion Score (MOS). The main objective of this study is to measure the individual/global impact of QoE Influence Factors (QoE IFs) in a real environment. Based on the collective dataset, we perform 5 testing scenarios to compare 2 estimation methods (SVM and ANFIS) to study the impact of the number of the considered parameters on the estimation. It became clear that using more parameters without any weighing mechanisms can produce bad results.

Keywords

Quality of Experience (QoE); Mobile environment; Crowdsourcing; Mean opinion score; Smartphone; Video.

1. INTRODUCTION

A large growth in Internet based devices (e.g. Smart phone, Tablet, etc.) causes the emergence of multimedia service that changed our daily lives. Our life is increasingly be made of continuous interaction with multimedia services : Email consultation, ticket booking, live games, etc. In this context the use of traditional monitoring networks based only on Quality of Service (QoS) optimization are not sufficient to ensure user's requirements. That is why, system actors (service provider, network operator,...etc.) are investigating a new concept called Quality of Experience (QoE)

MSWiM'15 , November 02-06, 2015, Cancun, Mexico
Copyright 2015 ACM. ISBN 978-1-4503-3762-5/15/11 ...$15.00
DOI: http://dx.doi.org/10.1145/2811587.2811631.

or simply User Quality. This new concept affected several areas such as multimedia services and the medical field to evaluate the real quality perceived by users. To pinpoint the problem of user perception, many works were proposed and several community were created such as *Qualinet* in Europe. Although, this concept is still hard to estimate. One reason for this difficulty is the large number of parameters, which overall impact has not been evaluated yet. All these parameters or metrics are called Quality of Experience Influence Factors (QoE IFs)[1]. To try to deal with the QoE IFs impact on the user's estimation, we propose this work to present some recent works (frameworks) using the crowd-sourcing approach to study the QoE issue. The main objective of our proposed testbed is to subjectively evaluate the user's QoE using a video application. In our experimentation, the participants use android devices in mobile environments and evaluate the quality using the Mean Opinion Score (MOS). In our approach, we collect and consider the impact of several factors (QoE IFs). This paper is structured as follows : In section 2, we discuss the state of the art of QoE and some recent frameworks using QoE for multimedia services. In section 3, we present our mobile test campaign (conditions, setup, procedure). Then, we present the dataset collected and evaluate the importance of the impact of each QoE IFs on the user perception in section 4. Finally, we conclude our work by giving some perspectives.

2. RELATED WORKS

Lately we hear the word Quality of experience on the lips of many people. Some of them say it is an objective measure, others say it strongly related to the user, and another category sees it is interdisciplinary domain between social science, psychology science, cognitive science and economics science. So what do people expect from the QoE ? and how was it shown in the multimedia area ?.

Quality of Experience (QoE), or simply User Quality is a measure of the experience of a customer with a service (Web browsing, phone call, broadcast TV, ...etc.). QoE presents a multidisciplinary emerging field based on several areas (social psychology, cognitive science, economics and engineering sciences). The QoE concept has become very important in several areas such as multimedia services, the medical field and marketing. The International Telecommunication Union (*ITU*) defined in 2007, the QoE in [7] as a human subjective experience. This experience is represented as the overall acceptability of an application or service, perceived subjectively by the end user.

Over time, QoE became a topic of interest in recent years.

We will try bellow to expose some of QoE works, in order to present their results and contributions.

In [4], authors present Android application which is able to evaluate and analyze the perceived Quality of Experience (QoE) for YouTube service in wireless terminals ($UMTS$ and $WIFI$). The application has been tested over 17 Android terminals in one month. The added value of this tool is informing the user about potential causes that lead to a low Mean Opinion Score (MOS) as well as provides some hints to improve it. After each YouTube session, the users may optionally qualify the session through an online opinion survey. The main finding of this work are : (i) The experience has shown that the theoretical model (taken from the literature) provides slightly more pessimistic results compared to user feedback. (ii) The use of the heuristic measurement quantification proposed in [8] increases the MOS from the opinion survey in about 20% compared to the theoretical model, which was obtained from wired scenarios.

In [10], the authors conduct two experiments and simulating two different usage contexts. Each experiment was conducted as completely randomized. The authors used two kinds of variables : (i) Independent variables : category (static and dynamic), resolution, and frame rate. (ii) Dependent variables : picture quality, continuity, and overall satisfaction. Smartphone owners can watch videos while they are sitting, walking, or standing in various environments. Diverse settings of encoding elements for digital videos were compared in static and dynamic situation. This research shows a lot of results including a low resolution and present enough continuity for dynamic videos in a sitting condition. Low frame rate and resolution can be used to encode a static video if it is shown in a walking context. A dynamic video would deliver a worse quality than a static video in the same condition.

Finally, Hoβfeld et al[6] elaborate QoE management requirements for two complementary network scenarios (wireless mesh Internet access networks vs. global Internet delivery). The authors provide also a QoE model for YouTube taking into account impairments like initial and stalling delay. They present two YouTube QoE monitoring approaches operating on the network and the end user level. Finally, they demonstrate how QoE can be dynamically optimized in both network scenarios with two exemplary concepts, AquareYoum and FoG, respectively. This study shows many results including : (i) The highly non-linear relationship between technical impairment level (QoE IFs) and quality perception. (ii) The stalling has strong QoE impact and should be avoided by all means, e.g. by increasing initial delay to fill the video buffer. Finally, this study lets us understand how QoE management can truly improve the user experience while at the same time increase the efficiency of network resource allocation, and give an exhaustive list of key Influence Factors on YouTube QoE (QoE IFs).

3. MOBILE TEST CAMPAIGN

Generally, the user's Quality of Experience (QoE) for multimedia services is evaluated by using the two methods : subjective method and the objective method. Subjective method is proposed by the International Telecommunication Union (ITU) Rec. P.800 and the Video Quality Expert Group (VQEG). It consists of a group of people watching distinct video sequences under a specific controlled environment, and rate their quality. The Mean Opinion Score

(MOS) is an example of a subjective measurement method in which users rate the video quality by giving five different point scores from 5 to 1, where 5 is the best and 1 is the worst quality. The second quality evaluation method is the Objective method which uses different models of human expectations and tries to estimate the performance of the video streaming service in an automated manner, without involving humans.

The main objective of our proposed testbed is to evaluate subjectively the user's QoE using an OTT video application, by considering the impact of several factors (QoE IFs). QoE IFs are classified into different categories : network, application, devices, user feedback, etc. The objective of the study is to measure the individual/global impact of each IF category on QoE in order to build a solid correlation QoE IFs/QoE function. The testbed uses various cellular communication networks (HSPA, 3G(UMTS), 4G(LTE)), where the influence of different parameters is examined in the real time environment.

The testbed experiment mainly consists of the following elements :

- A dedicated mobile application has been developed for experimentation.
- The evaluation was performed at different locations.
- Users were trained to perform the test.
- Several types of terminals were used (e.g. smartphones (with different CPU capacities), tablet, TV, HD screen, laptop,... etc.).
- Several types of videos were used (e.g. sport, movie trailer, documentary, news, music,... etc.).

3.1 Testbed overall design

In the experimental setup, users watched videos on different devices such as smartphones, tablets and android TV using different networks HSPA, UMTS and LTE. The experimental setup is shown in Figure 1, where the user uses different devices and networks to watch the desired video contents.

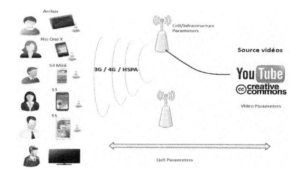

Figure 1: Testbed setup.

Testbed experiment takes place at different locations in an urban cellular environment which is based on crowdsourcing approach. The experimentation was held in the last week of January 2015 in different places in the LiSSi Laboratory and Networks & Telecommunications Department (NTD) (122, Rue Paul Armangot, University of Paris-Est Créteil, 94400, Vitry sur Seine, France). In this testbed, several locations were selected (un-controlled environment). Each one of these locations is characterized by a different RSS (Received Signal Strength). When the video session (a set of videos seen by each user) end, then client provides its quality experience feedback in term of MOS (Mean Opinion Score), which is stored in the remote database.

3.2 Tested conditions

The key goal for crowdsourcing approach is to had a good exploitable data sample. To achieve this objective, we used and collected several QoE IFs (Table 1 gives an overall tested condition used in our testbed). For the tests we selected 40 different video sequences of 240*p* and 360*p* resolution (4 videos for each one of the 10 video categories). The experimentation was made in a totally un-controlled environment, and users give their MOS at the end of each video. In fact, different locations of LiSSI Laboratory and Networks & Telecommunications Department (NTD) were used to study the influence of network coverage in different scenarios.

Parameters	Description
Video	-**10 Types** : News, Cartons,etc. -**Duration** : 60 secondes -**Resolution** : 244p and 360p
Devices	**Samsung 5** : V. 4.2.2, SDK=19 **Samsung 4 Mini** : V. 4.2.2, SDK=19 **Samsung 3** : V. 4.1.2, SDK=16 **HTC X** : V. 4.1.1, SDK=16 **Archos android TV** : V. 4.0.4, SDK=16 **Archos Tablet** : V. 4.1.1, SDK=15
Operator	Orange, Free and Bouygues

Table 1: Overall tested conditions.

We have selected 10 video types' (Figure 2 shows screen shots of some video types used). In each type, we choose 4 videos in YouTube (under Creative Common license).

Figure 2: Screenshots of used videos.

3.3 Tested procedure

In this experimental testbed, each user has tested a set of videos (in one session). All members were students or researchers from different disciplines aged from 17 to 40 years old with a little or no experience of this kind of evaluation. In addition, the participants use smart devices (phone/tablet) with the installed application that starts the experimental video session for the current participant. Each video session provides opportunity to the participant for selecting the desired video content type, and provides the feedback of video's quality in terms of MOS. In fact, the different usage scenarios are considered in order to observe the influence of network performance at different locations (the laboratory, the Department of Networks & Telecoms,...etc.). At the end of each video, the participant provides its quality of perception about the video quality, and additionally answers a few questions that are stored in the database. The questions used in the testbed consist of starting video time, the im-

age and audio synchronization, the image quality, the sound quality and the MOS (1 : very bad/ 5 : very good).

These questions allow us to evaluate the user feedback for each video measure. The answer of each question is between 1 and 5 where 1 indicates that the quality is not acceptable or very bad (time to start very long, lag between picture and audio very high,...etc.) and 5 indicates that the quality is very good (time to start is very fast, no lag between picture and audio,...etc.).

3.4 Results

A total of 63 subjects, 45 men and 18 women, participated in the subjective assessment to construct the dataset. All members were researchers or students from different disciplines aged from 17 to 40 years old with little or no experience of this kind of evaluation. All of them were non-experts in assessing the video quality. The experiment is conducted using the different wireless Internet connections, such as 3G, 4G, HSPA. All the subjects spent at least 5 minutes on watching a session, and 18 of them watched at least plus than 10 videos on one session. Therefore, according to the users' answers, it is reasonable to assume that they are familiar with video-watching applications.

The collected dataset contains 646 samples with 33 several parameters divided on different classes : network, application, devices, user feedback, etc. Figure 3 shows the overall distribution of the MOS by devices and by operators.

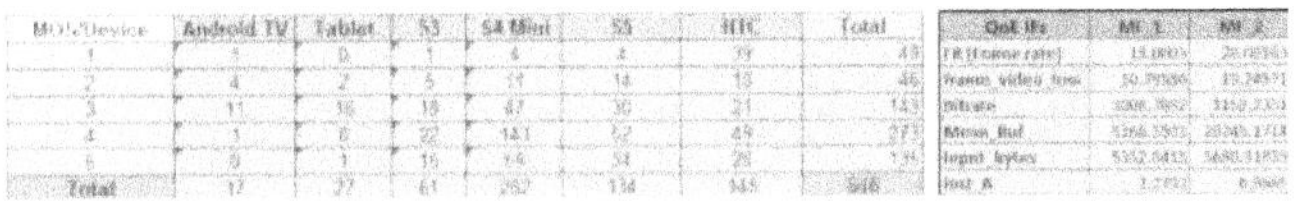

Figure 3: Distribution of the MOS.

4. ANALYSIS

The objective of this section is to conduct a study on application factors that impact the QoE. We start by studying the correlation between these factors in pairs wise. Then, we compare 2 QoE estimation methods to evaluate the impact of number of the considered factors on the estimation.

4.1 Dataset QoE IFs chosen

A large number of volunteers participating in our testbed, and we gather the impact of many QoE IFs. In this paper, we focus on the parameters that have significant impact on the user's QoE. We consider application layer factors (QoA) which we qualified important because : (i) they proved already they influence the user perception. (ii) They want to predict just user perception with application QoA IFs. (iii) They are collected in a non intrusive way (just in the end-user level).

To identify the relationship between these factors (QoA factors) on YouTube QoE, we study the intensity of the connection which may exist between these factors and the user's MOS. To attempt this end, we use the *rcorr* method in *Hmisc* Package *R*[2] to plot Correlation matrix for the QoE IFs chosen (Figure 4).

The main aim of the correlation matrix is to study the intensity of the connection which may exist between these factors and the MOS.

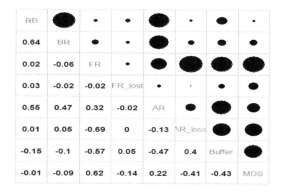

Figure 4: Correlation matrix result.

Table 2 below presents the QoE IFs description.

QoE IF	N	Description
FR (Frame rate)	$f1$	Frames number that are projected or displayed per second.
Buffer	$f2$	The time for one buffering. In fact it's the result of dividing the total buffering duration on the bufferization number.
AR_lost	$f3$	Number of audio bytes that are lost.
AR (Audio rate)	$f4$	Number of audio bytes that are received per second.
FR_loss	$f5$	Number of frames or images that are lost.
BR (Bitrate)	$f6$	Bits number that are conveyed or processed per second.
RB (Read bytes)	$f7$	Total number of video bytes read.

Table 2: Factors description.

The x-axis represents the first value in the compared pair, while the y-axis depicts the second one.

In our crowdsourcing campaign, we focused on quantifying the impact of QoA factors on the QoE perceived on Youtube service using just the factors presented above. In fact, the key influence factors are identified by Pearson's correlation coefficients as described in the correlation matrix (Figure 4). This figure clearly shows that we can categorize the impact of different factors into 3 classes :

- The key factor class : In this class we have the frame rate ($f1$), mean_buffer ($f2$) and loss_audio ($f3$) respectively : 0.62, −0.43 and −0.41 of correlation rate (Pearson correlation). These factors are the most impacting because it was proven by some works in the QoE area that separately they impact on the user perception. For example for the FR, [8] and [9] proved that it plays an essential role in the prediction of the MOS user. Concerning, Mean_buffer, we can cite the work of [12], who measures the QoE of HTTP video streaming.

- The modest factor class : In this class we have : AR Audio byte rate ($f4$), frame lost video($f5$) and input bitrate($f6$) which have respectively 0.22, −0.14 and −0.09 of correlation rate (Pearson correlation). That is can be explained by subjectivity of our dataset. These factors participate to predict QoE, however, in our dataset, their correlation with the user's MOS is limited compared to the first class.

- The no correlation class : In this class we find also the input bytes read. This factor is not on correlation with th user's MOS (r=0.01). This value can be explained by the fact that the read byte number is not very important because it depends on the video compression format (H264, MP4...etc.) and the frame rate[8].

4.2 Methods used

In order to select the best method, we analyze the impact of various parameters on the perceived user's QoE in the mobile video environment. We have designed a comparison of two prediction models (based on the classification), which is implemented on R software [3]. These methods are : SVM Support Vector Machines (SVM)[5] and Adaptive-network-based fuzzy inference system (ANFIS)[11]. For our experimentation in R software [3], we used respectively yhe "e1071" package to test the SVM method and the "FRBS" package for ANFIS method.

4.3 Experimentation

In our experience, we use 6 variables (several scenarios) as inputs from the dataset, which is described in the section 6.1. Further, we perform 5 test scenarios using the SVM and ANFIS to calculate the RMSE (Root Mean System Error).

$$RMSE = \sqrt{\frac{\sum_1^n (f_i - y_i)^2}{n}} \qquad (1)$$

where : f_i is the prediction of MOS, y_i is the true value of the MOS and n is the total number of the considered samples.

In fact, in this experimentation there is 5 scenario types, which are differentiate by the number of QoE IFs, as presented in the next table.

Testbed	QoE IFs
Scenario 1	$\{f1, f2\}$
Scenario 2	$\{f1, f2, f3\}$
Scenario 3	$\{f1, f2, f3, f4\}$
Scenario 4	$\{f1, f2, f3, f4, f5\}$
Scenario 5	$\{f1, f2, f3, f4, f5, f6\}$

Table 3: QoE IFs for each scenario.

In one scenario the procedure works as follows : the data set is divided into 3 sub-samples. The two first parts of dataset are used for training and the third one use for testing. For each method, we use 10-fold cross-validation. In which each fold, the RMSE is calculated. Then, we calculate the scenario Average RMSE.

To run each scenario, we use the R software tool[3]. This tool has produced many outputs, which provide the information about the model prediction using two methods (SVM, ANFIS). Initially, we focus on the RMSE. We compare the error rate between the different models that engender the different QoE prediction model. The results are illustrated in Figure 5. The x-axis represents the different considered scenarios (see the table 3) and the y-axis represents the RMSE prediction performance.

4.3.1 Discussion

In our experimentation, two learning models are trained to calculate the RMSE error rate based on MOS prediction.

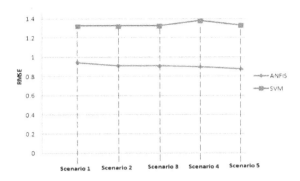

Figure 5: Comparison of RMSE results in of the SVM and ANFIS prediction model.

The ANFIS [11] based model has performed better with an average of 0.85 for the 5 scenarios. For the SVM model [5], it has less prediction performance with an average of 1.35 for the same scenarios (See figure 5).

Both SVM and ANFIS models confirm that using a large number of QoE IFs produces a better user's perception estimation than using a few number. However, due to the interaction between parameters, estimation results may be worse than expected as given in [1]. For example, SVM model performs better using 4 factors ($RMSE = 1.32$) as compared to use 6 factors, which results RMSE equal to 1.385. Concerning the impact of different QoE IFs (QoA factors) and according to the correlation matrix given in section 4.1, we select 3 classes of QoA factors/user's MOS. The first one contains the key factors presented by : Frame rate, time for one buffering and the number of audio bytes lost. The second class contains audio byte rate, frame lost video and input bitrate. Finally, we confirm that the number of bytes is not important because it depends on the video compression format (H264, MP4...etc.) and the frame rate as explained in [8].

5. CONCLUSIONS

In recent years, tremendous growth of video mobile traffic has created a new challenge for network service provider : How to maximize user's Quality of Experience (QoE) in the mobile environment. To deal with this challenge, a subjective evaluation of the user's QoE is required. In this context, we propose a framework based on an android system and Youtube platform to study the impact of several QoE IFs on the perceived quality. The aim of this framework is to build a large dataset for QoE prediction in the dynamic wireless networks (UMTS, HSPA, LTE/LTE-A). Based on the built dataset, we perform an experimentation to study the relationship between QoE IFs and to highlight the most correlated factors. Based on these factors, we compare two estimation methods (SVM and ANFIS) and we highlight the relationship between the number of the considered factors and the estimation accuracy. In fact, our experimentation showed that using a large number of QoE IFs produces a better user's perception estimation than using a small number. However, we must not overlook the interaction between factors. Finally, we find that, ANFIS performance is better than the SVM model. As perspective, this framework can be extended with the introduction of new factors categories such as : QoS (Strength signal, cell load rate,...etc.) or QoA

(CPU, battery,...etc.). In addition, we will continue to work on improving our dataset in order to build a bigger and more consistent dataset by performing tests in different cells and including more users with different profiles and other QoE IFs.

6. ACKNOWLEDGMENTS

This work has been funded by the LiSSi laboratory from the UPEC university in the framework of the French cooperative project PoQEMoN, *Pôle de Compétitivité Systematic* (FUI 16).

7. REFERENCES

[1] L. Amour, S. Souihi, S. Hoceini, and A. Mellouk. A hierarchical classification model of qoe influence factors. *13th International Conference on Wired and Wireless Internet Communications*, May 25-27, 2015.

[2] H. F.E. and C. Dupont. Package 'hmisc'. available at:. `http://cran.r-project.org/web/packages/Hmisc/Hmisc.pdf"`, April, 2015.

[3] I. for Statistics and M. of WU. R software. `http://www.r-project.org/`.

[4] G. Gómez, L. Hortiguela, Q. Pérez, J. Lorca, R. García, and M. C. A. Torres. Youtube qoe evaluation tool for android wireless terminals. *CoRR journal*, 1405-4709, 02 Jun, 2014.

[5] S. Gupta, R. Kambli, S. Wagh, and F. Kazi. Support-vector-machine-based proactive cascade prediction in smart grid using probabilistic framework. *Industrial Electronics, IEEE Transactions on*, 62(4):2478–2486, April 2015.

[6] T. Hoßfeld, F. Liers, R. Schatz, B. Staehle, D. Staehle, T. Volkert, and F. Wamser. *Quality of Experience Management for YouTube: Clouds, FoG and the AquareYoum*, volume 35. 2012.

[7] ITU-T. Report 2007. definition of quality of experience (qoe). *International Telecommunication Union, Liaison Statement*, January 2007.

[8] A. Khan, L. Sun, and E. Ifeachor. Content-based video quality prediction for mpeg4 video streaming over wireless networks. *Journal of Multimedia*, 4(4), 2009.

[9] Menkovski, V., Exarchakos, G., Liotta, A., and A. Sánchez. Measuring quality of experience on a commercial mobile tv platform. In *Advances in Multimedia (MMEDIA), 2010 Second International Conferences on*, June 2010.

[10] H.-I. C. Murat Copcu. The quality of contextual experience of multimedia on the smartphone. *International Journal of Emerging Science and Engineering (IJESE)*, Volume-3 Issue-3:30–33, January 2015.

[11] L. S. Riza, C. Bergmeir, F. Herrera, and J. M. Benitez. Learning from data using the r package" frbs". *Fuzzy Systems (FUZZ-IEEE), 2014 IEEE International Conference on*, pages 2149–2155, 2014.

[12] H. T., S. M., M. Hirth, T. Zinner, P. Tran-Gia, and R. Schatz. Quantification of youtube qoe via crowdsourcing. In *Multimedia (ISM), 2011 IEEE International Symposium on*, pages 494–499, Dec 2011.

A Bloom Filter-Based Algorithm for Routing in Intermittently Connected Mobile Networks

Jairo
Sanchez-Hernandez
Centro de Investigación en
Computación
Instituto Politécnico Nacional
jairojsh@gmail.com

Rolando
Menchaca-Mendez
Centro de Investigación en
Computación
Instituto Politécnico Nacional
rmen@cic.ipn.mx

Ricardo
Menchaca-Mendez
Centro de Investigación en
Computación
Instituto Politécnico Nacional
ric@cic.ipn.mx

Jesus Garcia-Diaz
Centro de Investigación en
Computación
Instituto Politécnico Nacional
jesgadiaz@gmail.com

Mario E. Rivero-Angeles
Centro de Investigación en
Computación
Instituto Politécnico Nacional
erivero@cic.ipn.mx

J.J. Garcia-Luna-Aceves
University of California, Santa
Cruz
jj@soe.ucsc.edu

ABSTRACT

In this paper, we present a new protocol for routing in intermittently connected mobile networks that, by periodically exchanging constant-size Counting Bloom filters, assigns to every node in the network probabilities of reaching any destination. The gradients defined by these probabilities are further used to forward data packets towards any node in the network. The proposed protocol is based on two novel operations defined over the Bloom filters, namely, the unary *degradation* operation that models the loss of topological information as it gets stale or as it is propagated away from the place where it was generated; and the binary *addition* operation that is used to acquire topological information from other nodes. These two operations are used to implement a probabilistic form of soft state that is defined in terms of the content of the Counting Bloom filters. We present a series of experimental results based on extensive detailed simulations that show that the proposed protocol outperforms the Epidemic routing protocol by delivering more data packets with less delay, while inducing less total overhead in both MANET and VANET scenarios.

Keywords

Delay Tolerant Network, MANET, VANET, Routing, Bloom filters

1. INTRODUCTION

Intermittently Connected Networks (ICNs) are a generalization of the mobile ad hoc networks (MANETs) that does not assume the existence of contemporaneous end-to-end paths connecting any pair of nodes in the network. Since

MSWiM'15, November 2–6, 2015, Cancun, Mexico.
© 2015 ACM. ISBN 978-1-4503-3762-5/15/11 ...$15.00.
DOI: http://dx.doi.org/10.1145/2811587.2811609

sources and destinations may be disconnected for arbitrarily long periods of time, applications running on this type of networks must be delay tolerant and hence, they are also referred as Delay Tolerant Networks (DTNs) [22]. Delay tolerant networks (DTNs) are a convenient alternative to provide communication services in situations where installing a communication infrastructure is not practical [9]. Examples of such scenarios are search and rescue missions, networks used to collect migration data of Zebras in Africa [10] and information dissemination in sparse vehicular ad hoc networks (VANETs) [7, 12, 21].

An ICN can be modeled by a time varying directed multigraph where each edge represents a particular type of link with a specific capacity. The latter models situations where two nodes can be joined by different types of network interfaces such as a satellital link or a modem-based telephonic link. In general, the capacity of a link can be seen as a time varying function that takes values from zero capacity when the link is not available, to a predefined maximum capacity that reflects the nature of the link. This way, an edge e_n connecting nodes u, v in the multi-graph indicates that there is a link between nodes u, v in the intermittently connected network. An edge (link) can be defined by $e = ((u, v), c_e(t), d_e(t))$ where $c_e(t)$ is a time varying capacity function, $d_e(t)$ is a time varying delay function and (u, v) is an ordered pair that indicates the direction of the link.

The problem of routing in ICNs can be defined as follows. Given a time-varying multigraph $G(t) = (V(t), E(t))$ and two nodes $o, d \in V(t)$ find a sequence of operations $\gamma_1 \gamma_2 \dots \gamma_n$ that take a packet generated by the origin o to the destination d. The set of γ_i operations are part of the alphabet Γ that is defined as follows.

- Transmission operation denoted by $\gamma_{(u,v)}$: A packet is transmitted from node u to node v

- Storing operation denoted by $\gamma_{store}(u)$: A packet is stored in u's local cache until a condition is met and the packet is either transmitted or deleted.

- Copying operation denoted by $\gamma_{copy}(u)$. Node u creates an exact copy of a data packet.

The problem of routing in intermittently connected networks is known to belong to the class of *NP-Hard* problems

[3], even in the case where both, the history of how nodes contact each other and the traffic load are known ahead of time. The proof proceeds by reducing the problem of Edge-Disjoint Paths to the problem of routing in intermittently connected networks.

In this paper, we present a new protocol for routing in ICNs that assigns to every node in the network a probability of reaching any destination. These probabilities are computed by means of the information stored in a set of Counting Bloom Filters that condense the topological information that nodes have collected as they opportunistically encounter other nodes in the network. We say that the information stored at the filters implements a probabilistic form of soft state because it is gradually lost unless it is constantly refreshed and because it provides probabilistic clues about the likelihood of reaching a destination through any node in the network.

The remaining of this paper is organized as follows. Section 2 presents a small summary of the related work. Section 3 presents the proposed routing protocol which is based on a set of novel operations defined over Counting Bloom Filters [6, 19]. Section 4 shows the results of a detailed simulation-based performance analysis of the proposed protocol. We compare the performance of the proposed protocol against that of the Epidemic dissemination protocol which is a *de facto* baseline for performance comparisons of routing protocols for intermittently connected networks. Lastly, Section 5 presents our concluding remarks.

2. RELATED WORK

We present a small but representative sample of the papers that have addressed the problem of routing in inter-mittently connected networks. Our main propose is to highlight the fact that previous proposal establish individual orderings over the nodes per each of the destinations in the network, and that these orderings are either based on utility functions or probability functions. Unlike these approaches, the proposed protocol simultaneously establishes probability functions for all the destinations using a single constant-size control packet. This property makes the proposed protocol more scalable.

The Epidemic routing algorithm [20] was proposed in 2000 as a simple solution to the problem of routing in delay tolerant networks (DTN). The method used by this algorithm is similar to an infection, where packets represent the disease and the nodes that store a copy of these packets are called "carriers". This way, data packets can spread out very quickly through the connected segments of the network. From this point on, the algorithm exploits the node's mobility to reach other network segments and keep spreading the packets until they reach their intended destination. With this propagation model, packets are almost always delivered, except for the cases in which the destination is located in a completely isolated network component, when packets are discarded at the data queues or when the destination does not even exists. It is important to point out that Epidemic is a brute force algorithm that employs every possible route in the network to reach the destination and hence, is very costly in terms of bandwidth utilization and the memory space needed to store the data packets at the queues. EM-MA [8] is a recently proposed variant of epidemic routing that uses aggregation to reduce overhead, unfortunately, the scalability problems remain.

PRoPHET [13] is a probability based routing protocol for DTNs that take advantage of the repetitive behavioral patterns of the human users. For example, if a node has visited a location many times in the past, there is a high probability that this node will be there in the near future. PRoPHET employs a metric called *delivery probability* $P_{(a,b)} \in [0,1]$ that indicates how probable is that a node u can actually deliver messages to node v. Whenever two nodes come into transmission range, they exchange summaries that contain a list of packets and their delivery probabilities. The information of the summary is then used to request those packets for which the current node is a better forwarder. In [5], the authors propose the space-content adaptive-time routing (SCaTR) framework for DTN MANETs. SCaTR is an extension of traditional on demand routing that takes action when the protocol is unable to establish a connected route. When in DTN mode, SCaTR uses contact values to select the best node that can act as proxy of the destination and store packets at that node until either the destination is discovered, or another node is selected as a better proxy. Contact values are computed based on the past connectivity information that nodes keep in their contact tables. In [18], the authors propose a series of single-copy strategies which are based on utility functions that employ last encounter timers to establish an ordering over the nodes in the network. A data packet is forwarded to a next hop if its priority is larger than that of the current node plus a constant threshold. The authors also propose a hybrid routing protocol, called "Seek and Focus" that first uses randomized forwarding and then utility-based forwarding. In [17] the same authors propose similar multiple-copy strategies for routing in intermittently connected networks. GeoSpray [16] is a routing protocol for Vehicular Delay-Tolerant Networks (VDTN) that employs a hybrid approach of single and multi-copy routing. GeoSpray starts with a multiple-copy approach where a number of copies are spread in order to exploit alternative paths. Then, it switches to a forwarding scheme, where nodes forward data packets to nodes they encounter if they have a better estimated time of delivery.

For a more comprehensive analysis of the large amount of work reporting routing protocols for intermittently connected networks, please refer to the surveys by Benamar et-al [4] and Cao and Sun[7].

Bloom filters or any of their many variants have been used in a large number of applications for distributed systems such as caching, peer-to-peer networks, routing and forwarding, monitoring and measurement and data summarization [19]. Their use as a tool to compute routes, is less extensive, mainly because of the complications introduced by false positives [15]. However, recent proposals such as [14][23] are able ameliorate these complications by either assuming or inducing a tree-like topology. As discussed in Section 3.4, the probability of false positives have no impact on the correctness of the proposed protocol.

3. ROUTING USING COUNTING BLOOM FILTERS

3.1 Overview

The proposed protocol assigns to nodes a probability of reaching every other node in the network. To establish these probabilities throughout the network, nodes periodically exchange counting Bloom filters that condense the topological information they have been able to collect. When a node receives a filter from a neighbor, it uses the *addition* operation to merge its current topological information with the one contained in the received filter. Additionally, nodes use the *degradation* operation to implement a probabilistic form of soft state, in which the information about the destinations is gradually lost as it grows stale and as it is being propagated away from the place where it was generated.

From the filters received from each neighbor, nodes compute a probability of reaching any destination D through that particular neighbor. The gradients defined by these probabilities are further used to disseminate data packets in a store-carry-and-forward fashion to their intended destinations. A given data packet will be forwarded to a neighbor when the probability of reaching its intended destination plus a constant threshold, is larger than the probability of the current node. This way, packets tend to travel only to those regions of the network where it is more likely to find their intended destination. Please note that based on the probabilities assigned to nodes, many other forwarding strategies can be defined.

In the following sections, we present more detailed descriptions of the proposed operators and of the way the probabilities of reaching a destination are computed.

3.2 Filter Operations

A *Counting Bloom Filter* F is an array of m counters that can take values from 0 to c. Given a filter F, $F[x]$ denotes the value of the *x-th* counter (with $x \in 0, ..., m-1$) contained in the filter. We use $\mathcal{F}_m^c$ to denote the set of every filter composed of m counters with capacity c. We also denote the empty filter as F_0, where all counters are set to 0. The three operations defined over the filters are as follows.

The *insert* operation is used to add the identity of a node into a Counting Bloom filter. It takes as parameters a filter F and the identifier $a \in ADDR$ of a node (where $ADDR$ is the space of node identifiers in the network) and returns a new filter that contains the identity a. To insert the identity a in a filter F, denoted as $F + a$, the value of k independent hash functions ($h_i : ADDR \rightarrow \{0 \ldots m-1\}$ with $i \in \{1 \ldots k\}$) is calculated to obtain the indexes of k counters that will be set to the value of c. In this way, the operation defined by $F + a$ results in $F[h_i(a)] \leftarrow c$ with $i \in \{1 \ldots k\}$. Note that this operation is different from the traditional insertion operation defined for Counting Bloom Filters where the counters are incremented in one unit.

The *degradation* operation is an unary operation that consists in decrementing in a single unit the value of each counter with probability $p_{degrade}$. This operation is denoted by $\Delta_{p_{degrade}} : \mathcal{F}_m^c \rightarrow \mathcal{F}_m^c$ and is defined by the Algorithm 1. The degradation operation is used to model situations where some of the information contained in a filter is lost; either because it is growing stale or because it is information that is being propagated away from the place it was generated.

Algorithm 1 $\Delta_{p_{degrade}}(F)$
---
for $i = 0 \rightarrow m - 1$ **do**
    if $F[i] > 0$ **then**
        $F[i] \leftarrow F[i] - 1$; with a probability $p_{degrade}$
    end if
end for

The third operation is the binary *addition* operation which is denoted by $\oplus : \mathcal{F}_m^c \times \mathcal{F}_m^c \rightarrow \mathcal{F}_m^c$. This operation combines the value of two filters F_i and F_j following the Algorithm 2.

Algorithm 2 Addition(F_i, F_j)

F_x is a new filter;
for $l = 0 \rightarrow m - 1$ **do**
    $F_x[l] \leftarrow \max\{F_i[l], F_j[l]\}$
end for
return F_x

3.3 Probabilistic Soft State

Each node i will keep two filters that store its own topological information, namely, F_i^* and F_i^t. F_i^* is constant through time and is defined as $F_0 + i$, whereas F_i^t is time dependent and its content changes because of the updates received from neighboring nodes and from a periodical degradation process. When a node i receives a filter F_j^t from its neighbor j, it updates the value of its own filter F_i^{t+1} according to Eq. (1). Please note that in Eq. (1) the filter received from neighbor j is first degraded to reflect the loss of information and then added to the filter of node i. Additionally, every node i stores in the structure $\mathcal{N}_i$ the latest received filters from all of its neighbors.

$$F_i^{t+1} \leftarrow \Delta_{p_{degrade}}(F_j^t) \oplus F_i^t \qquad (1)$$

The filter F_i^t is periodically degraded according to Eq. (2) as a way to implement a form *probabilistic soft state*. The concept of probabilistic soft state is similar to the concept of *Weak State* proposed in [2] in the sense that both provide probabilistic hints regarding the location of the destinations. Unlike Weak State that is based on geographic information, the probabilistic soft state proposed in this work is strictly based on topological information. Moreover, the probabilistic soft state has a spatial/temporal nature because it captures the fact that information is lost as times goes by, but also as it is disseminated away from the place where it was generated.

$$F_i^{t+1} \leftarrow \Delta_{p_{degrade}}(F_i^t) \oplus F_i^* \qquad (2)$$

The probability of reaching a destination through node i is calculated with Eq. (3). The probability assigned to each node in the network is precisely the one that defines the probabilistic gradient used to reach the destinations. Note that under this scheme, the probability of reaching node i through itself is always 1.

$$pr_i^D \leftarrow \frac{\sum_{\forall x | F_D^*[x] > 0} F_i^t[x]}{kc} \qquad (3)$$

3.4 Protocol Description

Our protocol is defined in terms of a sequence of messages that are exchanged by nodes as they opportunistically meet each other. The messages are as follows.

- BLF: Contains filter F_i^t which condenses the topological information collected by node i.

- SUV: Array of packet identifiers. It is used to publish the set of messages stored at this node.

- REQ: Array of packet identifiers. Set of messages requested by this node.

• DAT: Message that contains a set of data packets.

Every node j broadcasts a hello message m_{BLF} containing his own Bloom filter F_j^t every interval of t_h seconds. As shown in Algorithm 3, upon reception of a message m_{BLF} from node j, node i proceeds to update its own filter by means of Eq. (1) and to compute the new delivery probabilities through node j by means of Eq. (3). Then, node i adds the identifiers of the data packets with destination D, such that the delivery probability at node j is greater than the delivery probability at node i plus a threshold $(pr_j^D \geq pr_i^D + U_e)$, to the list L_{suv} which is sent in a m_{SUV} message to j. This way, the packets listed in L_{suv} are such that their destinations are more likely to be reached through i than through j.

Algorithm 3 Bloom Filter Message

---

when m_{BLF} is received from j **do:**
    $L_{suv} \leftarrow \emptyset$
    $F_i^t \leftarrow F_i^t \oplus F_i^*$
    $F_i^{t+1} \leftarrow \Delta_{p_{degrade}}(F_i^t) \oplus F_i^t$
    for Message m $\in BUFFER_i$ **do**
        $D \leftarrow m.destination$
        $pr_i^D \leftarrow \dfrac{\sum_{\forall x | F_D^*[x]>0} F_i^{t+1}[x]}{km}$
        $pr_j^D \leftarrow \dfrac{\sum_{\forall x | F_D^*[x]>0} F_j^t[x]}{km}$
        if $pr_j^D \geq pr_i^D + U_e \vee pr_j^D = 1$ **then**
            $L_{suv} \leftarrow L_{suv} \cup \{m.id\}$
        end if
    end for
    send(j, L_{suv})
end when

As described by the pseudocode of Algorithm 4, when node i receives the message m_{SUV}, it creates a new list L_{req} that contains the packets listed in L_{suv} that have not been received so far. Then, node i sends a message m_{REQ} back to j requesting the messages in L_{req}.

Algorithm 4 Summary Message

---

when m_{SUV} is received from j **do:**
    $L_{req} \leftarrow \{\emptyset\}$
    for Identifier $m_i \in L_{suv}$ **do**
        if $m_i \notin BUFFER_i$ **then**
            $L_{req} \leftarrow L_{req} \cup \{m_i\}$
        end if
    end for
    send(j, L_{req})
end when

When node j receives the list L_{req}, it sends a message m_{DAT} back to i containing every data packet requested by i. This action can be seen as a series of consecutive $\gamma_{(j,i)}$ operations. Lastly, when node i receives the data packets, it passes to upper layers those packets which are intended to the node itself and stores the others in its internal buffer. This latter action can also be seen as a series of $\gamma_{store}(i)$ operations.

As already mentioned, every node i in the network periodically degrades its own filter F_i^t by means of Eq. (2). This way, node i will eventually lose any state regarding destinations that have move far away or to a different network partition.

It is important to point out that in the presence of false positives, data packets can be disseminated towards regions of the network that do not contain the destination, however, this will not prevent the proposed routing protocol to also disseminate the packets towards the true positive, namely, towards the intended destination. Therefore, while a false positive does increase the cost of delivering a data packet, it does not prevent the data packet from reaching its destination. In the worst case, our proposed protocol will behave like a pure epidemic dissemination protocol but with the extra overhead induced by exchanging the Bloom filters.

4. EXPERIMENTAL RESULTS

In this section, we present the results of a series of simulation experiments comparing the performance of the proposed protocol against that of the Epidemic routing protocol. We selected Epidemic because it has become a *de facto* baseline for performance comparisons of routing protocols for intermittently connected networks and because both are multi-copy protocols that disseminate data packets from sources to destinations. The latter allow us to highlight the performance gains obtained by disseminating data packets only towards those regions of the network where it is likely to find the destination. Both protocols use the same tail drop policy to discard data packets when a data queue has reached its maximum capacity, and the same Hello interval of 1 second. For the proposed protocol, the values used for the degradation interval, the degradation probability $(p_{degrade})$ and the U_e threshold were hand-picked. However, a further sensitivity analysis revealed that the performance of the protocol is fairly insensitive to moderate variations ($\pm 15\%$) of these values. We decided to use relatively small filters (with only 64 counters) to characterize the performance of the proposed protocol under relatively high probabilities of false positives. For all the experiments, we used the NS2 simulator version 2.34 [1].

We designed two set of experiments. The first one is intended to evaluate the performance of the protocols in MANET scenarios where nodes are sparsely spread around a large simulation area and move following the random waypoint mobility model. In the second set of experiments, we evaluate the performance of the protocols in a VANET scenario where nodes move following the street layout of the city of Murcia in Spain which is shown in Figure 1. For the two sets of experiments we use packet delivery ratio, end-to-end delay and total overhead as performance metrics. The results presented in all the figures are the average of 20 independent runs with a confidence level of 95%.

4.1 MANET Scenario

For the MANET scenario, we defined a set of three experiments to assess the impact of different variables over the performance of the proposed protocol. In Experiment 1, we vary the amount of traffic injected into the network to evaluate the effectiveness of the protocols to deliver data packets before they have to be dropped at the data queues. In Experiment 2, we decrease the node density so that the networks become more disconnected, and in Experiment 3, we evaluate the effect of decreasing the node mobility. The objective of Experiment 3 is to evaluate the effectiveness of the proposed algorithm to accurately reflect the topological changes into the counting Bloom filters. The details about the values of the simulation parameters that are fixed across the three experiments are shown in Table 1.

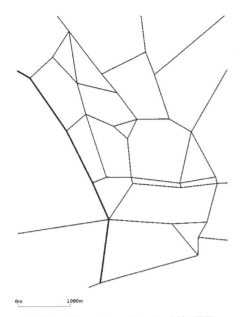

Figure 1: Street layout used in the VANET scenario.

Variable description	Value
Data flows	[1]
Simulation area (square area)	[2]
Pause time	[3]
Mobility model	Random Waypoint
Nodes in the network	100
Node placement	Random
Minimum velocity for nodes	1 m/s
Maximum velocity for nodes	20 m/s
Data flow type	CBR
Packets per data flow	1000
Tx. rate	1 packet/sec
Propagation model	Omni-directional Two-ray ground
Transmission range	250 m
Packet size	128 bytes
Simulation time	5000 seconds
Buffer capacity	2048 packets
U_e Threshold	0.1
Degradation probability ($p_{degrade}$)	0.5
Bloom filter size (m)	64
Counter capacity (c)	32
Number of hash functions (k)	4
Degradation interval	3 seconds
HELLO interval (t_h)	1 second (± 0.25)

Table 1: Simulation environment.

Experiment	Values	Reference value
1	10,15,20 flows	10
2	2000m×2000m 3000m×3000m 4000m×4000m	3000m×3000m
3	10s,20s,40s	0s

Table 2: Specific parameters for each experiment.

Table 2 shows the specific values of the parameters that are varied in each experiment. The column of *reference values* corresponds to the values of the variables that are fixed during a given experiment.

Figures 2, 3 and 4 present the simulation results for the two protocols under the three different scenarios. For all the experiments, the end-points of the data flows were selected at random using a uniform probability distribution. Figure 2 shows the results of Experiment 1, where we increase the amount of traffic injected into the network by increasing the number of concurrent data flows from 10 to 20. Fig. 3 corresponds to the results of Experiment 2, where we decrease the node density by keeping constant the number of nodes and by increasing the simulation area. Lastly, Figure 4 shows the results of Experiment 3, where we reduce the mobility of the nodes by increasing the pause time from 10 seconds to 40 seconds.

Regarding packet delivery ratio, from Figures 2(a), 3(a) and 4(a) we can observe that the proposed protocol clearly outperforms Epidemic by consistently delivering more data packets. The inferior packet delivery ratio attained by Epidemic is caused by a rapid saturation of the buffers of the nodes. On the other hand, the proposed algorithm only propagates packets towards those regions of the network where it is more likely to find the destination and hence it does not waste buffer space of nodes that are located far away from the intended destinations (see Figure 2(a)). For the case of increasing traffic load, the behavior shown by the proposed protocol is as expected. When the traffic increases, the packet delivery ratio is reduced because more packets are being disseminated across the network and hence, more packets have to be dropped at the data queues. On the other hand, when the node density is increased (see Figure 3(a)), nodes tend to meet each other more often and hence, the topological information regarding the destinations percolates faster across the network. Under this situation, the probabilistic gradients are more clearly defined and the dissemination of the packets tends to be more focused towards the destinations. It is also important to point out that when the network becomes more connected, the sequence of SUV-SUV-REQ-DAT messages also becomes more costly. Moreover, we observed the appearance of the broadcast storm problem where many nodes simultaneously engage in SUV-REQ-DAT exchanges with a node transmitting a BLF packet. Lastly, Figure 4(a) shows that the two protocols are fairly insensitive to the different values used for the pause time. These results indicate that under these conditions, the probabilistic soft state used by the proposed protocol is capable of keeping up with the topological changes experienced by the network.

Regarding end-to-end delay, from Figures 2(b), 3(b) and 4(b) we can observe that the proposed protocol clearly outperforms Epidemic by consistently attaining smaller delays. This was also an expected result because Epidemic is a brute force solution that uses all possible paths to reach the intended destinations but that tend to saturate the data queues much faster. Moreover, a detailed analysis of the simulation traces revealed that the delay attained by Epidemic is also due to the fact that most of the packets were delivered to destinations that happened to be relatively close to their corresponding sources. The latter contrast with the proposed protocol that is able to deliver packets to destinations that are located far away from the sources, or in different network partitions.

Lastly, from Figures 2(c), 3(c) and 4(c) we can notice that the extra cost induced by the proposed protocol by periodically transmitting counting Bloom filters is clearly outweighed by the data overhead induced by Epidemic while disseminating data packets towards regions of the network that do not contain the intended destinations.

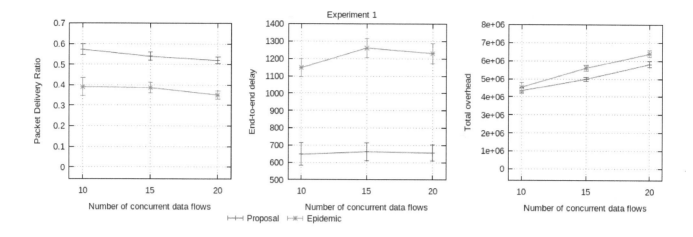

Figure 2: Performance of the protocols in a MANET scenario with increasing traffic load. (a) Packet delivery ratio. (b) End-to-end delay. (c) Total overhead.

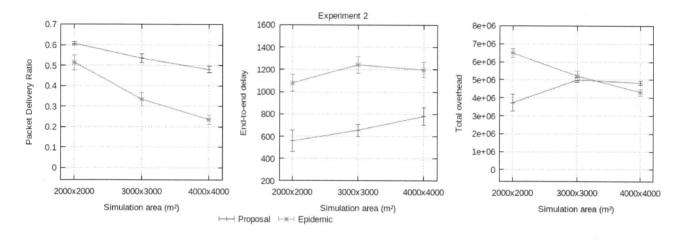

Figure 3: Performance of the protocols in a MANET scenario with decreasing node density. (a) Packet delivery ratio. (b) End-to-end delay. (c) Total overhead.

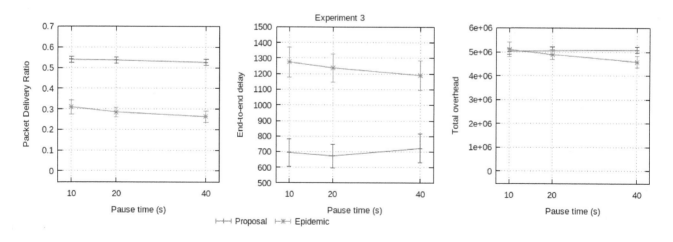

Figure 4: Performance of the protocols in a MANET scenario with decreasing node mobility. (a) Packet delivery ratio. (b) End-to-end delay. (c) Total overhead.

Vehicles entering the scenario every 45s	Flows	Routes	Avg. num. of vehicles
05	25	25	55
15	25	25	155
25	25	25	270
35	35	30	385
45	55	30	520

Table 3: Vehicle flow parameters for the VANET scenario.

Parameter	Value
Data flows	10
Packets per flow	1000
Packet size	512 bytes
Data rate	1 packet/s

Table 4: Parameters for VANET data flows

4.2 VANET Scenario

In this scenario, we evaluate the performance of the protocols when nodes move following the street layout of the city of Murcia, Spain (Figure 1). We used the SUMO simulator of urban mobility [11] to generate mobility traces of two types of vehicles, namely, *cars* and *buses*, which differ only on mobility parameters such as acceleration, maximum speed, and size. For this experiments we use the same set of values for the simulation parameters as described in Table 1, and vary the vehicle density by increasing the number of vehicles entering the simulation area per second as shown in the first column of Table 3. The second column of Table 3 corresponds to the number of different vehicle flows in the scenario. In SUMO, a flow defines the rate at which vehicles enter the scenario, as well as their type (car or bus) and the route they follow. Routes are defined in terms of a sequence of street intersections. The fourth column of Table 3 presents an estimate of the average number of active vehicles in the simulation area. This value is a function of the vehicle arrival rate and, the time vehicles remain active on the simulation, which depends on the length of the routes followed by the vehicles, the behavior of the semaphores, and the traffic congestion of the road network. As in the MANET scenario, the end-points of the CBR data flows are selected uniformly at random from the vehicles currently in the simulation. The details of the vehicle flow parameters are shown in Table 4.

Figure 5 presents the results of these experiments. From Figures 5(a) and (b), we can observe that the proposed algorithm consistently performs similar or better than Epidemic in terms of packet delivery ratio, end-to-end delay and total overhead. Our proposal delivers between 5% and 7% more packets than Epidemic, even in situations where the probability of false positives in the counting Bloom filters is quite high due to the large number of active vehicles in the simulation and the relative small size of the filters (32 counters). Under this situation, our protocol behaves similar to Epidemic because it also tend to disseminate data packets towards regions of the network that do not contain the destination but a false positive. Figure 5(b) shows that in these experiments the end-to-end delay attained by the proposed protocol is slightly better than that of Epidemic. The reason again, is the fact our protocol induces less data overhead, which reduces the waiting times at the data queues.

Lastly, Figure 5(c) shows the total overhead induced by the two protocols. As in the case of the MANET scenario, the proposed protocol incurs in far less overhead because of the reduced cost of disseminating only towards regions of the network where it is likely to find the destinations. This is true even in this scenario where the probability of false positive is high.

5. CONCLUSIONS

In this paper, we proposed a new protocol for routing in intermittently connected mobile networks that uses the concept of *probabilistic soft state* to assign to every node in the network probabilities of reaching any destination. The probabilistic soft state is defined in terms of the content of counting Bloom filters that condense the topological information that nodes have collected from other nodes as they move and that is used to compute the probabilities of reaching the destinations. These probabilities reflect the amount of information nodes have regarding the different destinations. To model the process in which nodes acquire and loss topological information, we defined two novel operations over counting Bloom filters, namely, the binary *addition* operation and the unary *degradation* operation. The addition operation is used to reflect the acquisition of new information, and the unary operation is used to reflect the loss of information, either because it is getting stale or because it is being propagated away from the place where it was generated. Then, nodes use a greedy forwarding strategy that follows the gradients defined by these probabilities to reach the intended destinations.

The proposed scheme has the advantage of establishing probabilistic gradients simultaneously for all the destinations. This contrasts with previous proposals that require the dissemination of control information for every destination node, which is not scalable. In the proposed scheme, nodes periodically exchange constant-size "hello" messages with their one-hop neighbors. Therefore, the protocol's network complexity is constant in terms of the network size. Moreover, the proposed scheme has the advantage that it combines in a simple way the concepts of probability of encounter and hop distance towards the destinations. When the network is connected, the probabilistic gradients are similar to the traditional gradients based on hop distances, but when the network is partitioned, the gradients are similar to those that compute a probability of encounter based on the time nodes last met. This way, the proposed algorithm can work in more general scenarios than previous protocols that exploit the "social behavior" of nodes.

In the presence of false positives in the Bloom filters, data packets can be disseminated towards regions of the network that do not contain the destination, however, this will not prevent the proposed protocol to also disseminate the packets towards the intended destination. We observed this situation in the VANET scenario, where due to the large number of nodes, the probability of false positive is quite high.

The results of a detailed simulation-based performance analysis showed that the proposed algorithm is a viable alternative for routing in both intermittently connected MANETs and VANETs. The proposed protocol consistently outperformed the Epidemic routing protocol in both MANET and VANET scenarios.

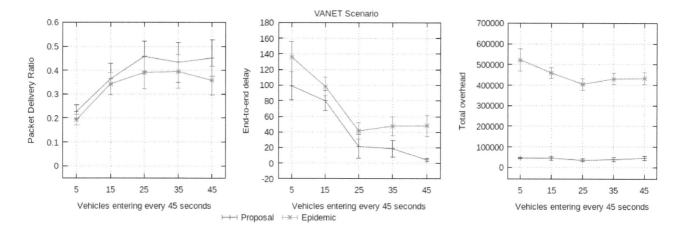

Figure 5: Performance of the protocols in a VANET scenario with increasing node density. (a) Packet delivery ratio. (b) End-to-end delay. (c) Total overhead.

6. ACKNOWLEDGMENTS

Work partially sponsored by the UC MEXUS-CONACyT program, and by the Mexican National Polytechnic Institute (IPN).

7. REFERENCES

[1] The Network Simulator, ns-2.34. http://www.isi.edu/nsnam/ns/.

[2] U. G. Acer, S. Kalyanaraman, and A. A. Abouzeid. Weak state routing for large-scale dynamic networks. *IEEE/ACM Transactions on Networking (TON)*, 18(5):1450–1463, 2010.

[3] A. Balasubramanian, B. Levine, and A. Venkataramani. DTN routing as a resource allocation problem. *SIGCOMM Comput. Commun. Rev.*, 37(4):373–384, Aug. 2007.

[4] N. Benamar, K. D. Singh, M. Benamar, D. El Ouadghiri, and J.-M. Bonnin. Routing protocols in vehicular delay tolerant networks: A comprehensive survey. *Computer Communications*, 48:141–158, 2014.

[5] J. Boice, J. Garcia-Luna-Aceves, and K. Obraczka. Combining on-demand and opportunistic routing for intermittently connected networks. *Ad Hoc Networks*, 7(1):201–218, 2009.

[6] A. Broder and M. Mitzenmacher. Network applications of bloom filters: A survey. *Internet Mathematics*, 1(4):485–509, 2004.

[7] Y. Cao and Z. Sun. Routing in delay/disruption tolerant networks: A taxonomy, survey and challenges. *IEEE Communications Surveys & Tutorials*, 15(2):654–677, 2013.

[8] T. Choksatid and S. Prabhavat. An epidemic routing with low message exchange overhead for delay tolerant networks. In *Progress in Systems Engineering*, pages 429–436. Springer, 2015.

[9] S. Jain, K. Fall, and R. Patra. Routing in a delay tolerant network. In *Proceedings of the 2004 Conference on Applications, Technologies, Architectures, and Protocols for Computer Communications*, SIGCOMM '04, pages 145–158, New York, NY, USA, 2004. ACM.

[10] P. Juang, H. Oki, Y. Wang, M. Martonosi, L. S. Peh, and D. Rubenstein. Energy-efficient computing for wildlife tracking: design tradeoffs and early experiences with zebranet. *SIGOPS Oper. Syst. Rev.*, 36(5):96–107, Oct. 2002.

[11] D. Krajzewicz, J. Erdmann, M. Behrisch, and L. Bieker. Recent development and applications of SUMO - Simulation of Urban MObility. *International Journal On Advances in Systems and Measurements*, 5(3&4):128–138, December 2012.

[12] F. Li and Y. Wang. Routing in vehicular ad hoc networks: A survey. *IEEE Vehicular Technology Magazine*, 2(2):12–22, 2007.

[13] A. Lindgren, A. Doria, and O. Schelén. Probabilistic routing in intermittently connected networks. *SIGMOBILE Mob. Comput. Commun. Rev.*, 7(3):19–20, July 2003.

[14] A. Reinhardt, O. Morar, S. Santini, S. Zöller, and R. Steinmetz. Cbfr: Bloom filter routing with gradual forgetting for tree-structured wireless sensor networks with mobile nodes. In *IEEE International Symposium on a World of Wireless, Mobile and Multimedia Networks (WoWMoM), 2012*, pages 1–9. IEEE, 2012.

[15] M. Sarela, C. E. Rothenberg, T. Aura, A. Zahemszky, P. Nikander, and J. Ott. Forwarding anomalies in bloom filter-based multicast. In *Proceedings of IEEE INFOCOM 2011*, pages 2399–2407. IEEE, 2011.

[16] V. N. Soares, J. J. Rodrigues, and F. Farahmand. Geospray: A geographic routing protocol for vehicular delay-tolerant networks. *Information Fusion*, 15:102–113, 2014.

[17] T. Spyropoulos, K. Psounis, and C. S. Raghavendra. Efficient routing in intermittently connected mobile networks: the multiple-copy case. *IEEE/ACM Transactions on Networking*, 16(1):77–90, 2008.

[18] T. Spyropoulos, K. Psounis, and C. S. Raghavendra. Efficient routing in intermittently connected mobile networks: The single-copy case. *IEEE/ACM Transactions on Networking (TON)*, 16(1):63–76, 2008.

[19] S. Tarkoma, C. E. Rothenberg, and E. Lagerspetz. Theory and practice of bloom filters for distributed systems. *IEEE Communications Surveys & Tutorials*, 14(1):131–155, 2012.

[20] A. Vahdat and D. Becker. Epidemic routing for partially-connected ad hoc networks. Technical report, Duke University, 2000.

[21] N. Wisitpongphan, F. Bai, P. Mudalige, V. Sadekar, and O. Tonguz. Routing in sparse vehicular ad hoc wireless networks. *IEEE Journal on Selected Areas in Communications*, 25(8):1538–1556, 2007.

[22] Z. Zhang. Routing in intermittently connected mobile ad hoc networks and delay tolerant networks: overview and challenges. *IEEE Communications Surveys & Tutorials*, 8(1):24–37, 2006.

[23] H. Zheng and J. Wu. Up-and-down routing in mobile opportunistic social networks with bloom-filter-based hints. In *IEEE 22nd International Symposium of Quality of Service (IWQoS) 2014*, pages 1–10, May 2014.

Swift: A Hybrid Digital-Analog Scheme for Low-Delay Transmission of Mobile Stereo Video

Dongliang He[*]
Univ. of Science and
Technology of China
Hefei, 230027, P.R. China
hedl@mail.ustc.edu.cn

Chong Luo
Microsoft Research Asia
Beijing, 100080, P.R. China
chong.luo@microsoft.com

Feng Wu
Univ. of Science and
Technology of China
Hefei, 230027, P.R. China
fengwu@ustc.edu.cn

Wenjun Zeng
Microsoft Research Asia
Beijing, 100080, P.R. China
wezeng@microsoft.com

ABSTRACT

Efficient and robust wireless stereo video delivery is an enabling technology for various mobile 3D applications. Existing digital solutions have high source coding efficiency but are not robust to channel variations, while analog solutions have the opposite characteristics. In this paper, we design a novel hybrid digital-analog (HDA) solution to embrace the advantages of both solutions and avoid their drawbacks. Basically, in each pair of stereo frames, one frame is digitally encoded to ensure basic quality and the other is analogly processed to opportunistically utilize good channels for better quality. To improve the system efficiency, we design a zigzag coding structure such that both intra-view and inter-view correlations can be explored through prediction in the frames to be analogly coded. A reference selection mechanism is proposed to further improve the coding efficiency. In addition, we address the problem of optimal power and bandwidth allocation between digital and analog streams. We implement a system, named Swift, and perform extensive trace-driven evaluations based on a software-defined radio platform. We show that Swift outperforms an omniscient digital scheme under the same bandwidth and power constraints, or can have around 2x power saving in order to achieve comparable performance. Subjective quality assessment evidences that Swift provides significantly better visual quality than a straightforward HDA extension of SoftCast.

Categories and Subject Descriptors

C.2.0 [**Computer-communication networks**]: General—
Data Communications

[*]This work was done when Dongliang He was a research intern at Microsoft Research Asia.

Figure 1: Left and right views of a stereo image

General Terms

Design, Experimentation, Performance

Keywords

Hybrid digital-analog communication; stereo video; low-delay; binocular suppression; wireless network.

1. INTRODUCTION

Stereo video (or 3D video) has attracted increasing interests in recent years, and there is a trend that a large portion of the stereo videos will be captured and consumed by mobile devices [1]. In particular, several virtual reality (VR) head-mounted displays (HMDs), including Oculus Rift [4], Sony Morpheu [5] and Microsoft Hololens [3], will be available as full products in the early 2016. These HMDs, together with the maturing civilian unmanned aerial vehicles (UAVs) and robots, are capable of providing very exciting immersive first person view (FPV) experiences, either for personal enjoyment or for visual inspection of otherwise inaccessible terrain features. In these fascinating applications, the low-delay transmission of stereo videos over varying wireless channel presents a huge challenge.

The challenges are two-fold. On one hand, a stereo image/video is composed of two views, i.e., a left view and a right view as shown in Fig.1, from which the illusion of depth can be created by binocular vision. The data volume is almost doubled in comparison with the traditional 2D image/video. Therefore, the source coding efficiency is of vital importance to stereo video transmission under the constraint of limited bandwidth. However, there exists a tradeoff between the coding efficiency and low-delay requirements. On the other hand, wireless channel is time-varying and it is well-known that the rate of variation is dependent on the velocity of the mobile device. When the video capturing device, such as a UAV, is in high mobility, it tends to choose a robust modulation scheme and a strong channel code in order to ensure reliable video delivery. This reduces the effective bandwidth and exacerbates the discrepancy between source and transmission rates. As a result, the video quality is sacrificed and the user experience is dramatically degraded.

We intend to increase the perceived quality of stereo videos that are transmitted over a varying wireless channel. Our work is inspired by the recently proposed pseudo-analog video transmission scheme called SoftCast [14]. The basic idea of SoftCast is to skip the quantization and entropy coding in the source encoder and directly transmit the power-scaled DCT coefficients through amplitude modulation. It has been shown that SoftCast overcomes the all-or-nothing behavior of digital transmission and allows the receiver to reconstruct video frames at the quality that is commensurate with its instantaneous channel condition. In other words, pseudo-analog transmission is capable of opportunistically utilizing good channels without suffering from failures in bad channels. However, due to the characteristics of analog transmission, the predicted frames, which are common in digital video coding, are not allowed in SoftCast, otherwise there will be large accumulated errors. Therefore, if SoftCast is directly applied to mobile stereo video transmission, neither the intra-view correlation (temporal correlation within a view) nor the inter-view correlation can be explored, resulting in a very low coding efficiency.

In this work, we propose a novel hybrid digital-analog scheme, named Swift, for low-delay stereo video coding and transmission. We design a zigzag coding structure that significantly improves the coding efficiency while still allows the system to benefit from the robustness and graceful degradation properties of pseudo-analog transmission. In particular, the odd-numbered frames in one view and the even-number frames in the other view are treated as one video sequence, and are encoded with a standard digital codec (e.g. H.264) at basic quality. A robust coding and modulation scheme is adopted to ensure the successful reception of this stream. The rest of the frames are processed using analog methods. When the channel is good, the analog frames will be received with high quality and dominate the perceived visual quality. The crux here is that, for each analogly processed frame, its previous frame in the same view and its matching frame in the other view have both been encoded in digital, and therefore can be used as reference frames. We further propose a reference selection technique for the power-efficient processing of analog frames when references are available. Now that all the analog frames are encoded as predicted frames, and both intra-view and inter-view correlations can be utilized, the overall coding and transmission efficiency is dramatically improved. At the receiver, the digital frames are enhanced by the adjacent high-quality analog frames, both for higher objective quality and more fluent viewing experience.

We implement the proposed Swift system in Matlab 2013a and perform a trace-driven evaluation on a software-defined radio platform SORA [22]. The evaluation confirms that Swift is not only highly robust to channel variations, but also

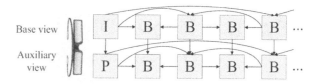

Figure 2: An illustration of Hierarchical-B prediction structure in JMVC

highly efficient in terms of received video quality under given bandwidth and power constraints. Swift is compared with both standard digital solutions and a straightforward HDA extension of SoftCast [14] in trace-driven experiments. Results show that Swift outperforms the straightforward HDA extension of SoftCast by 5dB in average video peak signal-to-noise ratio (PSNR) and achieves 2x power efficiency to obtain a similar video quality as the digital solution. In addition, subjective visual quality evaluation is conducted to confirm that the zigzag coding structure does not introduce zigzag viewing experience of the stereo videos. Compared to a straightforward HDA extension of SoftCast which adopts non-zigzag coding structure, subjective viewing rating of Swift validates that Swift can achieve better perceptual stereo video quality.

The rest of this paper is organized as follows. We provide the background knowledge of stereo video coding and pseudo-analog video transmission in Section 2. Section 3 presents the proposed Swift framework and technical contributions. Implementation and evaluation are described in Section 4. Finally, we summarize in Section 5 and discuss some future work.

2. BACKGROUND

2.1 Digital Video Coding and Transmission

Video compression (coding) is possible because video signals contain strong spatial (intra-frame) and temporal (inter-frame) correlations. In addition to these two types of correlations existing in each view of a stereo video, the corresponding frames (captured at the same time) of the two views also exhibit strong correlations. All three types of correlations should be explored in stereo video compression in order to achieve a high coding efficiency.

The 2D video compression schemes, such as H.264 [24], usually explore the temporal correlations by prediction. Specifically, when encoding a macro-block of the current frame, it searches for a similar block from the already encoded frames and use it as a reference. Depending on whether and how prediction is performed, there are three types of frames, namely I (intra, no prediction), P (predictive) and B (bidirectional) frames, where the latter two only need to encode the residuals between the original and the predicted frames. Spatial correlations are usually explored by the two-dimensional discrete cosine transform (2D-DCT), followed by quantization and entropy coding.

In stereo video compression, inter-view correlations can be explored in a similar way as temporal correlations, i.e. through prediction by motion estimation (ME) and compensation. A multiview video coding extension [23] to H.264 has been standardized for stereo and multiview video compression. In a reference implementation of MVC, named JMVC [8], frames of the auxiliary view can use either base view frames or auxiliary view frames as references for predictive coding, as illustrated in Fig.2. However, it is worth noting that, although a pair of left and right views look very similar, exploiting their correlations does not double the coding efficiency. According to MVC, the reduction in bit rate relative to H.264 is only 20 ∼ 30% on average even when the multi-view video contains up to 8 views. This is because that the intra-view temporal correlation is normally stronger than the inter-view correlation, and merely 20% of the macroblocks are more efficiently predicted from inter-view frames [18].

In stereo video coding, additional coding gain can be achieved by asymmetric coding. According to binocular suppression [17], the perceived stereo video quality is closer to the higher fidelity view, as long as the other view is better than a threshold. Therefore, by encoding auxiliary view with a reduced resolution [12, 19], or coarse quantization [10] or a combination of reduced resolution and coarse quantization [9], the bit rate of stereo video can be significantly reduced and the quality degradation is hardly noticeable.

Generally speaking, the digital video coding efficiency is quite high, although the B-frames should be disabled in a low-delay setting. However, digital transmission in a varying wireless channel is known to have the *thresholding effect* and *saturation effect* [15, 14]. Specifically, the sender decides its coding and modulation scheme based on the estimated channel condition. If the actual channel condition is worse than estimated, the entire stream will be corrupted (thresholding); if the actual condition is better than estimated, no additional gain can be achieved (saturation). In a dramatically varying channel, the sender tends to select a robust modulation scheme and a strong channel code to ensure reliability. However, this significantly reduces the effective bandwidth and as a result the source encoder has to operate at a low target video quality.

2.2 Pseudo-Analog Video Transmission

Recently, pseudo-analog video transmission has attracted much attention for its graceful degradation behavior over varying channel conditions. The pioneering work is SoftCast [14], originally designed for video multicast. SoftCast first decorrelates a group of pictures (GOP) spatially and temporally via 3D-DCT and then divides the DCT coefficients into equal sized chunks. To minimize the received distortion, the chunks are power scaled and then transmitted with amplitude modulation. A linear least square error (LLSE) decoder at the receiver reconstructs the DCT coefficients and the video frames can be reconstructed by inverse DCT. Note that the linear processing in SoftCast allows the decoder to translate different levels of channel noises into corresponding levels of pixel errors. Therefore, it can gracefully adapt to channel variations.

However, the source processing in SoftCast is not very efficient because 3D-DCT without motion alignment cannot fully exploit the temporal correlation. Now the low-delay requirement makes matters worse. To avoid the delay, only 2D-DCT can be used and the temporal correlation is left completely unexplored. A natural question is why not adopt prediction based motion estimation and compensation. The reason is that the encoder and the decoder do not hold the same version of the reference frame. In particular, the en-

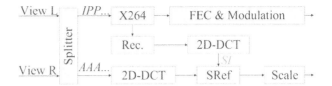

Figure 3: The block diagram of Swift sender

coder does not perform quantization and only has the lossless version of the video frames, while the decoder only has the distorted version. In such a case, performing prediction and only transmitting residuals will accumulate errors at the decoder. The accumulated errors will grow very fast along the prediction path length and dramatically degrade the video quality. For the same reason, the inter-view correlation in stereo videos cannot be explored in analog processing.

For pseudo-analog video transmission, there are some proposals [13, 16] that utilize the temporal correlations through motion-compensated temporal filtering (MCTF). However, MCTF also involves a temporal transform over a GOP and therefore cannot be used in a low-delay setting. The low efficiency in source processing of pseudo-analog transmission may significantly shadow its advantage in handling varying wireless channel.

3. SWIFT DESIGN

3.1 Overview

Swift is a hybrid digital-analog communication system designed for low-delay stereo video transmission. The design is based on the suppression theory of binocular vision [17], which states that the perceived stereo video quality is closer to the higher fidelity view, as long as the other view is better than a threshold. The basic idea behind Swift is that, for each pair of frames, encode one with digital method at basic quality and the other one with analog method. The quality of the analog frame can be gracefully adapted to the channel condition. When the channel is moderately good, the analog frame will be received at a high quality and will dominate the visual quality. Unlike the conventional digital method which encodes the frames into a given quality and runs the risk of receiving a corrupted bit stream in bad channels, Swift simply lets the channel decide how good the visual quality could be.

Fig.3 shows the block diagram of the sender design. Frames from the two views of a stereo video are first divided into two groups, namely the digital coding group and the analog coding group, by a splitter. The splitter alternately chooses the digital frame and the analog frame from the two views. More specifically, the odd frames in the left view and the even frames in the right view are encoded in digital and the rest of the frames are encoded in analog. This zigzag coding structure is shown in Fig.4(b), and the detailed processing of the digital coding and the analog coding are presented in the next subsection.

In a nutshell, frames in the digital coding group are treated as a normal video sequence and are compressed by a standard digital encoder with low delay profile. The output bit stream is protected by a robust forward error correction

(a) A straightforward parallel coding structure   (b) The proposed zigzag coding structure

Figure 4: Comparing the proposed zigzag coding structure with a straightforward design.

(FEC) code and transmitted with standard digital methods. Meanwhile, the reconstructions of the digital frames are used as side information (SI) in analog coding. Specifically, each analog frame is first spatially de-correlated by 2D-DCT, divided into chunks, and then further de-correlated within and between views through chunk-level reference selection technique. The generated analog coefficients are directly transmitted after power scaling. Skipping channel coding and modulation, Swift combines every two analog coefficients into one complex (I,Q) symbol and transmits it through raw orthogonal frequency division multiplexing (OFDM) channel.

The receiver performs the inverse operations. First, it decodes the received digital symbols to obtain the digital bit stream, and then the digital coding frames are reconstructed and chunk level inter-view and intra-view side information is generated. A LLSE decoder [14] will reconstruct the transmitted analog signals. Leveraging the side information, the receiver can then obtain the DCT coefficients and reconstruct the analog frames. Finally, the receiver performs quality enhancement and smoothing for the digital frames.

3.2 Zigzag HDA Coding

The proposed zigzag coding structure is illustrated in Fig.4(b), where I and P denote the digital I-frame and P-frame, and A denotes analog frame. The red dashed arrows illustrate the reference relationship. Comparing with a straightforward parallel coding structure, the proposed zigzag structure significantly increases the number of available SI frames. As a result, the correlations within a stereo video can be better exploited.

Although the digital frames are alternatively drawn from the two views, they are treated as a single video sequence in the source encoder, and are compressed with a standard H.264 encoder with low-delay profile (i.e. IPPP... prediction structure). As mentioned earlier, binocular suppression theory suggests that compressing one frame of the stereoscopic frame pair to a basic quality no lower than a certain threshold will not degrade the stereo visual quality. Subjective quality assessment by Saygili et al. [21] has verified that the threshold PSNR is $31dB$ or $33dB$ depending on the type of displays. Subjective viewing experience rating also shows no significant difference between left- and right-eye-dominant viewers, as has been validated in [11]. Therefore we set the target PSNR of digital frames to 34dB to meet the requirement and allow some small variations.

The digital frames provide the basic quality for binocular vision, and more importantly, they are used as intra-view and inter-view reference to improve the analog coding efficiency. As shown in Fig.4(b), for each analog frame, the previous frame in the same view and the frame in the other view captured at the same time are both digital frames. They are

used as side information in analog coding. Although there exist many ways to utilize the SI, we only consider direct subtraction in this work for its simplicity. Other ways to leverage the SI are left to our future work. Since analog coding does not generate a bit stream, the coding efficiency is reflected in the energy (i.e., the variance) of the resulting coefficients. The lower the energy, the higher the coding efficiency. We will show in the next subsection that, in a communications system with constrained power and bandwidth resources, lower energy of the analog coefficients will result in smaller distortion of the video frame.

Each analog frame is first spatially de-correlated by 2D-DCT. The DCT coefficients are divided into equal-size rectangular shaped chunks. Similar to SoftCast, coefficients in each chunk are treated as instances of a Gaussian variable and the variance can be directly computed. The reference selection technique is proposed to reduce the chunk variances. The motivation behind the reference selection scheme can be explained in the following. Considering two correlated zero-mean random variables A and B, $var\{A - B\}$ equals $var\{A\} + var\{B\} - 2cov\{A, B\}$. If $2cov\{A, B\} < var\{B\}$, taking B as reference, the resulting $var\{A - B\}$ will be even larger than $var\{A\}$. Therefore, only when the correlation level is higher than a threshold, reference subtraction can bring some gains.

Let $X_{a,i}, i = 1, 2, 3...N$ denote the N chunks of an analog frame, $X_{SI,i}^{(Inter)}$ and $X_{SI,i}^{(Intra)}$ represent the corresponding chunks of inter-view and intra-view side information, respectively. The reference selection problem aims at finding the best reference mechanism at the chunk-level granularity among the following three methods: no reference to SI, reference the inter-view SI and reference the intra-view SI. It can be formulated as follows:

$$\min_{I(i),J(i)} min\left\{\lambda_i^{(1)}, \lambda_i^{(2)}\right\}, \ for \ i = 1, 2, ..., N$$

$$\lambda_i^{(1)} = var\left\{X_{a,i} - I(i) \times X_{SI,i}^{(Inter)}\right\}$$

$$\lambda_i^{(2)} = var\left\{X_{a,i} - J(i) \times X_{SI,i}^{(Intra)}\right\} \quad (1)$$

$$I(i), \ J(i) \in \{0, 1\}$$

Define $\lambda_{a,i} = var\{X_{a,i}\}$, $\lambda_{R,i}^{(1)} = var\{X_{a,i} - X_{SI,i}^{(Inter)}\}$ and $\lambda_{R,i}^{(2)} = var\{X_{a,i} - X_{SI,i}^{(Intra)}\}$, the solution is quite straightforward:

$$\begin{cases} I(i) = 0, J(i) = 0, \ if \ \lambda_{a,i} \leq min\{\lambda_{R,i}^{(1)}, \lambda_{R,i}^{(2)}\}; \\ I(i) = 1, J(i) = 0, \ if \ \lambda_{R,i}^{(1)} < min\{\lambda_{a,i}, \lambda_{R,i}^{(2)}\}; \quad (2) \\ I(i) = 0, J(i) = 1, \ otherwise. \end{cases}$$

Note that the masks $I(i)$ and $J(i)$ are entropy encoded and treated as metadata. The output of the reference selection procedure is:

$$X_i = X_{a,i} - I(i) \times X_{SI,i}^{(Inter)} - J(i) \times X_{SI,i}^{(Intra)} \quad (3)$$

X_i's are the analog signals to be transmitted and they can be modeled as zero mean Gaussian sources. Without loss of generality, their variances, denoted as λ_i, are assumed to meet $\lambda_p \geq \lambda_q$ for $\forall p \leq q$.

3.3 Power and Bandwidth Allocation

A communication system is constrained by the power and bandwidth resources. We investigate the problem of optimal resource allocation under the proposed HDA coding and transmission framework. The notations are defined as follows. The total bandwidth can offer M chunks' time slots. The digital bit stream will consume a certain number of time slots which are equivalent to the bandwidth needed for transmitting N_d chunks, then only N_a chunks of coefficients of the analog frame can be transmitted.

$$M = N_a + N_d, \quad N_a \leq N. \quad (4)$$

The total power is constrained by P_t, and the power for digital transmission and analog transmission are denoted by P_d and P_a, respectively.

$$P_t = P_a + P_d. \quad (5)$$

3.3.1 Digital Transmission

To be compliant with existing wireless transmission schemes, the digital bit stream is transmitted following the conventional wireless digital communication framework specified by IEEE standard 802.11a [7]. The stream is scrambled and convolutional encoded, then bit interleaving is applied to resist burst bit errors. Finally, baseband QAM modulation is performed for OFDM transmission.

The digital bit stream must be transmitted without error to guarantee basic visual quality and identical side information at the transmitter and receiver. Therefore, strong protection should be provided to digital transmission. In Swift, rate $1/2$ convolutional code is adopted. We further adopt QPSK modulation with doubled symbol energy for transmission. Note that, BPSK is the most robust modulation scheme, and QPSK could achieve exactly the same bit error rate (BER) performance as BPSK if the per symbol energy is doubled. This could also avoid the bandwidth inefficiency of BPSK since BPSK leaves the Q-axis of the constellation plane unused. For the QPSK symbols used, the average symbol power p_d should meet the following condition to ensure error-free transmission with an extremely high probability:

$$\frac{p_d}{\sigma^2} \geq \gamma. \quad (6)$$

where γ is a threshold and σ^2 is the average power of the constellation noise symbols. For QPSK $1/2$ FEC 802.11a PHY, the threshold SNR of $8dB$ is sufficient to support faithful reception, which has been verified via simulation. To get rid of channel state information feedback from the receiver, Swift is designed based on a relatively low signal-to-noise-ratio(SNR), which is $4dB$, at the sender. In this way, Swift can support a large SNR range and can be readily used for multicast. Suppose the average constellation symbol power is p_t, and note that every (I,Q) symbol conveys 2 analog coefficients, and M chunks' time slots in total means $M/2$

available (I,Q) symbols. We then have

$$p_t = 2P_t/M$$
$$10 \times log_{10} \frac{p_t}{\sigma_m^2} = 4dB \quad (7)$$
$$10 \times log_{10} \frac{p_d}{\sigma_m^2} = 8dB$$

where σ_m^2 denotes the average channel noise power at the target design SNR. The average digital constellation symbol power can be computed from (7).

3.3.2 Analog Transmission

Now that N_d chunks' time slots are used for digital transmission, with average digital (I,Q) symbol energy p_d, the remaining N_a chunks' bandwidth is available for analog transmission. Then

$$P_a = P_t - P_d = P_t - p_d \times \frac{N_d}{2} \quad (8)$$

As has been explained in SoftCast[14], when transmitting the N chunks X_i using N_a chunks' bandwidth and total power P_a over additive white Gaussian noise (AWGN) channels, the chunks with the smallest variances should be dropped and the first N_a chunks are transmitted after power scaling by a factor g_i:

$$g_i = \lambda_i^{-\frac{1}{4}} \cdot \sqrt{\frac{P_a}{\sum_{j=1}^{N_a} \sqrt{\lambda_j}}}, i = 1, 2, ..., N_a \quad (9)$$

So the received signals can be represented as:

$$Y = GX + V \quad (10)$$

where $G = diag(g_1, g_2, ..., g_{N_a})$, $X = [X_1, X_2, ..., X_{N_a}]^T$ and $V \in \mathcal{R}^{N_a \times 1}$ is the additive Gaussian noise whose power is $\sigma^2/2$. The discarded chunks are replaced by their mean value which is zero at the receiver. Let $\widehat{X_i}$ denotes the reconstructed version of X_i, then the distortion can be derived as follows:

$$\begin{aligned} D &= \sum_{i=1}^{N} E\{(\widehat{X_i} - X_i)^2\} \\ &= \sum_{i=1}^{N_a} E\{(\widehat{X_i} - X_i)^2\} + \sum_{i=1+N_a}^{N} E\{X_i^2\} \\ &= \sum_{i=1}^{N_a} \frac{\sigma^2/2}{g_i^2} + \sum_{i=N_a+1}^{N} \lambda_i \\ &= \frac{\sigma^2/2}{P_a} \left(\sum_{i=1}^{N_a} \sqrt{\lambda_i} \right)^2 + \sum_{i=N_a+1}^{N} \lambda_i \end{aligned} \quad (11)$$

Equation (11) proves that the smaller the λ_i, the less distortion, which provides the theoretical support to our selective reference scheme. The assumption above that the first N_a chunks are the ones with the largest variances does not hold in practice. Thus in Swift, the mask of the N_a chunks with the largest variances is also treated as metadata and is entropy encoded and faithfully delivered to the receiver.

3.4 Receiver Quality Enhancement

Some careful readers may have doubt whether the zigzag coding structure introduces unpleasant visual experience although its coding efficiency is high. Actually, this was also the gravest concern in our design of Swift. The problem is illustrated in the following Fig.5. At the receiver side,

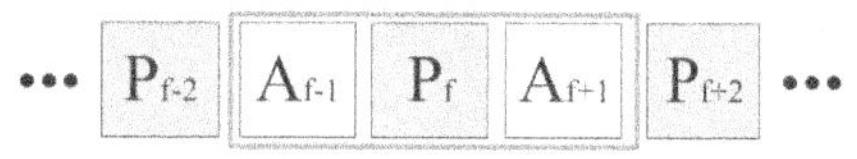

$$\cdots \boxed{P_{f-2}} \boxed{A_{f-1}} \boxed{P_f} \boxed{A_{f+1}} \boxed{P_{f+2}} \cdots$$

Figure 5: The interlacing of digital and analog frames

each view consists of interlaced digitally received low quality frames and analogly received higher quality frames. If a single view is presented, users will definitely experience the twinkling effect. However, if both views are presented, the high quality view (when switching between left and right views) will dominate the visual experience and the twinkling effect is greatly mitigated.

Nevertheless, low-complexity techniques can be adopted at the receiver to further enhance and smooth the visual quality. For each low-quality digital frame, its previous and subsequent frames in the same view as well as the frame in the other view to be displayed at the same time are all high-quality analog frames. The intra-view and inter-view correlations can be utilized to enhance the quality of the digital frames. In our current design, we apply a simple temporal median filter to each low quality digital frame among frames bounded by the green window as shown in Fig.5 for quality enhancement and smoothing. Specifically, the resulting pixel value of the digital frame P_f is

$$P_f(u, v) = median\{A_{f-1}(u, v), P_f(u, v), A_{f+1}(u, v)\} \quad (12)$$

where (u, v) is the coordinate of the pixel and $median\{*\}$ returns the median value.

Our own viewing experience tells that such a low-complexity processing reduces the blocking effects in the digital frames and almost entirely eliminates the twinkling effects. We also invite 15 non-specialists to participate in a subjective quality assessment to confirm our observation. The assessment results are reported in the next section.

4. IMPLEMENTATION AND EVALUATION

We implement a system named Swift based on the proposed techniques. For digital encoding, we use the H.264 reference implementation x264 [6]. The encoding prediction structure is IPPP... and the GOP size is set to 8. Bit-interleaved coded modulation (BICM) for digital transmission is implemented in Matlab 2013a. Swift adopts rate 1/2 convolutional code for FEC and QPSK modulation. In addition, the analog encoder including transform, reference selection, and power scaling and the analog decoder are all implemented in Matlab. In the analog codec, the number of chunks per frame is 256 (16×16). Swift PHY is implemented over OFDM as defined in IEEE 802.11a [7]. To be more specific, the channel is divided into 64 subcarriers of which 48 are used for data transmission. In our implementation, each PLCP frame contains 40 OFDM symbols, which translate to 1920 complex symbols.

To evaluate the performance of Swift, we perform testbed experiments based on the software-defined radio platform SORA [22]. A total of 24 test runs over 802.11a based WLAN are performed. In particular, data generated by

Swift is transmitted in each run, the receiver then records the symbols it receives. The recorded symbols are used to decode the transmitted stereo video for Swift. They are also utilized to extract the channel noise trace by subtracting the exact channel inputs. The noise trace is used to test the references implementations to ensure fairness. In particular, we divide the channel SNR into $2dB$ bins, and all traced data falling into the same bin is averaged for performance computation.

Stereo video sources: We use eight multi-view test video sequences for evaluation. Two nearby viewpoint scenes are taken from each sequence to emulate the left view and the right view. The eight sequences are *dancer, poznanstreet, poznanhall2, kendo, newspaper, breakdancers, ballet, balloons*. The first three videos have a resolution of 1920×1088 and the rest of them have a resolution of 1024×768.

Objective performance metric: The well-known peak signal-to-noise ratio (PSNR) is adopted for objective performance evaluation. It is computed by $PSNR = 10log_{10}\frac{255^2}{MSE}$, where MSE is the mean squared error of all pixels. As Swift compresses digital coded frames to $34dB$ and guarantees their error-free reception when the channel SNR is above $4dB$, only the PSNR of the analog frames, i.e. the dominant P-SNR, is considered in the evaluation. Note that when the average channel SNR is around $4dB$, some packets may experience a worse channel and the digital frames could be received with errors. In such cases, the analog frames which use SI cannot be correctly decoded as well, and the PSNR is calculated by setting all pixel values to 128. The PSNR of analog frames shown in this section is averaged over all the eight test sequences.

4.1 Micro-benchmark Evaluation

Three main technologies utilized in Swift are 1) Reference selection mechanism; 2) zigzag coding structure to provide both inter-view and intra-view side information and 3) temporal median filtering to enhance visual experience as well as the quality of the digitally received low quality frames. We evaluate the gain of each individual component to verify their effectiveness. To illustrate the gain of the first two technologies, we implement two reference systems. Both systems adopt the parallel coding structure as shown in Fig.4(b). The digital view is compressed to 34dB as in Swift, and used as SI for the analog coding. In one reference system, SI is utilized by whole-frame subtraction and in the other reference system, reference selection is enabled. The first reference system is also referred to as a straightforward H-DA extension of SoftCast.

We compare the performance of the three systems under different SNRs and bandwidth ratios ($BW = M/N$). Fig.6 plots the evaluation results. It can be observed that selective reference to SI is a more efficient way to utilize the correlation, and it provides about $1.5dB$ gain in PSNR under different bandwidth settings. The zigzag coding structure provides even larger gains. We can conclude from the figures that the zigzag coding structure outperforms the parallel coding structure by around $3.5dB$ in received video P-SNR. Overall, Swift outperforms the straightforward HDA extension of SoftCast by around $5dB$ under a wide range of SNR and bandwidth settings. Note that there is an obvious quick drop in PSNR when channel SNR is $4.46dB$, which is due to the possible errors in the received digital streams when the channel varies.

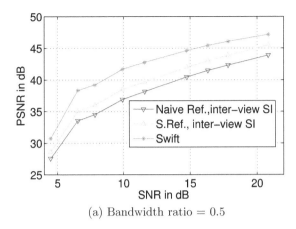

(a) Bandwidth ratio = 0.5

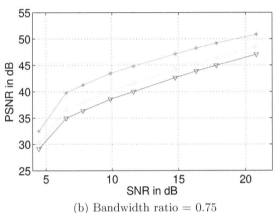

(b) Bandwidth ratio = 0.75

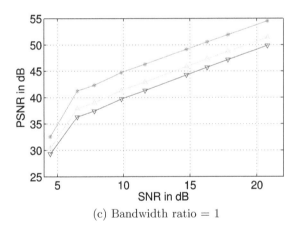

(c) Bandwidth ratio = 1

Figure 6: The average PSNR of the received analog frames of different schemes

The IPPP... compression in the proposed coding structure may not be as efficient as parallel coding structure, for it sacrifices the strong temporal correlations among the encoded frames. To evaluate the compression efficiency loss, we compared the compression performance of zigzag and parallel coding structure (as have been illustrated in Fig.4(b)). By choosing QP for the x264 codec, the left view and the zigzag sequence of stereo videos are compressed to 34dB. The compression rates of them are presented in bit per pixel (bpp). The results for several sequences can be found in Table 1.

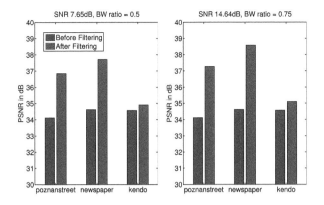

Figure 7: The average PSNR of the digitally received frames before/after temporal median filtering at the receiver.

It suggests that the zigzag coding structure do not degrade the digital encoding efficiency much compared to the parallel coding structure. Although the zigzag coding structure incurs some losses to the digital coding efficiency, the loss will be shadowed by the dramatic increase in analog coding efficiency because both inter-view and intra-view SI can be used.

Table 1: Compression Efficiency Comparison

sequence	Proposed Zigzag		Parallel	
	bpp	PSNR (dB)	bpp	PSNR (dB)
kendo	0.016	34.57	0.012	34.71
ballet	0.021	34.56	0.017	34.47
dancer	0.067	34.49	0.065	34.45
newspaper	0.021	34.61	0.017	34.42

In order to show the benefits of the temporal median filtering process at the receiver side, we evaluated the PSNR of the digitally received frames before and after temporal median filtering at several channel settings using test sequences *poznanstreet*, *newspaper* and *kendo*. SORA trace-driven experiment results are shown in Fig.7. It can be observed clearly that temporal median filtering enhances the quality of the digitally received frames. The better the channel condition is, the better the analogly received frames will be, then the temporal median filtering will result in more enhancement of the digitally received frames. This is because the analogly received frames are of higher quality and the temporal correlation can be leveraged to achieve smooth transition from one frame to the next within each view. In this way, thanks to temporal correlation, the block effect of the digitally encoded frames can be reduced. Note that temporal median filtering is a very simple method for enhancement of digitally received frames , investigation of more effective ones are left for our future work.

4.2 Comparison With Digital Schemes

Traditional digital schemes use separate source coding and channel coding. H.264 [24] is the mostly wide adopted technologies for video source compression. As for stereo video source, multiview video coding schemes are proposed to leverage both inter-view and temporal correlation to improve compression performance. To compare with digital schemes, two reference digital transmission schemes are implemented:

Reference digital transmission schemes: The first digital scheme we implemented is omniscience H.264 simulcast. It compresses the two views individually with IPPP... prediction structure. One view is compressed to low quality with $34dB$ in PSNR. The other view is compressed to meet the bandwidth constraint. We use the JM18.5 [2] reference implementation for source coding and decoding. Omniscience here means the sender knows the exact channel state information(CSI) and can choose an appropriate PHY channel coding and modulation scheme. The other reference digital transmission scheme is omniscience JMVC. The JMVC8.5 [8] reference software is used to compress the stereo videos. Note that, JMVC compresses one view by referring to the other and hierarchical-B prediction structure is used, so the delay of JMVC is a GOP of frames' duration. For efficiency, JMVC first compresses one view with higher quality, and the other view is compressed by referring to the higher quality coded view and is compressed to 34dB. We choose the appropriate QPs for the two views to meet the bandwidth constraint. Note that, digital encoding is more complicated and costly in computational complexity especially when B-frame is enabled. Properties of the Swift and digital schemes are summarized in Table 2.

Table 2: Properties of Swift and digital schemes

	Delay	Complexity	CSI	Channel Adapt.
Swift	low	low	No need	Yes
H264	low	medium	Need	No
JMVC	high	high	Need	No

4.2.1 Stable Environment

We first conduct our experiments on a fairly stable wireless communication environment where the transmitter and the receiver do not move. SORA traces are recorded and then trace-driven evaluations are performed and results are presented in Fig.8. Digital schemes show apparent *cliff effects* duo to the separate source-channel coding. If the transmitter over-estimates the channel condition and chooses a high order modulation, the receiver will experience decoding failure thus get nothing, therefore video quality drops sharply. So conventional digital transmission schemes are not adaptive to the wireless channel variation. On the contrary, Swift can achieve smooth quality scalability in the case of channel variation and can support a large dynamic SNR range. Therefore, Swift can be readily used for stereo video multicast applications. More importantly, PSNR curves of Swift in superior to the envelope of the digital schemes when the bandwidth ratio is 0.5 and 1.

For some applications, bandwidth may not be so critical but energy is quite limited. For example, in stereo aerial photography/filming by micro air vehicle and real time controlling system, power is supplied by battery. In the following experiment, we evaluate the energy efficiency of Swift in comparison with a low delay H.264 digital transmission scheme. We decrease the average per constellation symbol power to 75% and 50% and then evaluate the dominant PSNR of the test stereo video sequences by trace-driven experiment, respectively. From Fig.9 we can conclude that, using Swift for stereo video transmission, half power budget

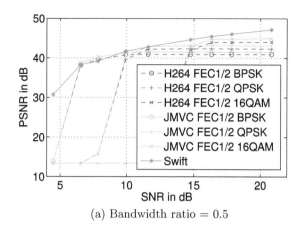

(a) Bandwidth ratio = 0.5

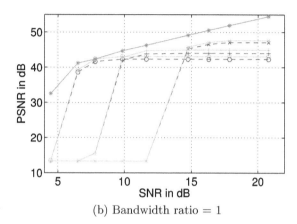

(b) Bandwidth ratio = 1

Figure 8: The comparison of average dominant PSNR of the received stereo videos

can achieve comparable performance as omniscience digital low delay scheme.

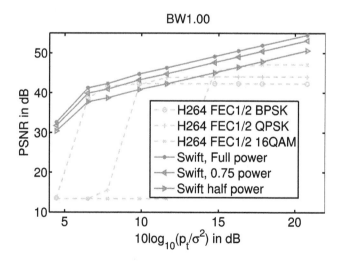

Figure 9: The average dominant PSNR of the received stereo videos of Swift using different power budgets and that of digital transmission scheme using full power budget

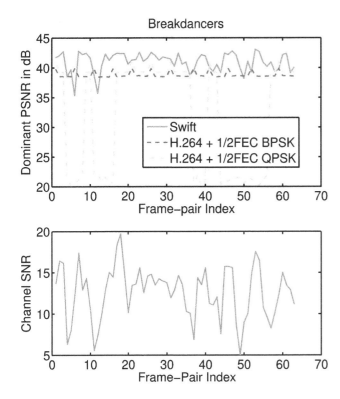

Figure 10: Dominant PSNR of the received stereo frame-pairs over dynamic wireless environment

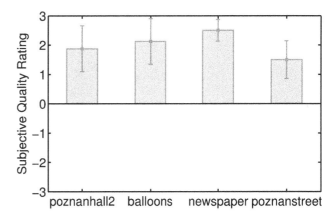

Figure 11: The subjective viewing experience rating

4.2.2 Mobile Environment

To assess the quality scalability over dynamic wireless channel of Swift, we carry out experiments on a mobile receiver. Mobile traces are dumped while moving the antenna of the SORA receiver, then the noise traces are extracted for performance evaluation. In this experiment, the test sequence *breakdancers* is used and the bandwidth ratio is set as 0.5. For every frame-pair of the stereo source video, the dominant PSNR variation along with the dynamic channel environment is shown in Fig.10.

It can be observed that Swift outperforms H.264+1/2 BPSK scheme almost all the time and on average the gain is 2.17dB. The H.264+1/2 BPSK scheme achieves some relatively constant dominant PSNR and can not adapt to the channel variation, so it wastes the channel capacity when the channel condition is better than what the 1/2 BPSK requires. We can also find that, although 1/2 QPSK coding and modulation can achieve higher dominant PSNR than 1/2 BPSK when the channel condition is good, it will degrade sharply if the channel condition gets worse, in which case the digital bits can not be correctly received such that the receiver fails at decoding the following frames in the GOP of the stereo video. We can conclude that Swift scales well over the dynamic wireless channel and provides superior dominant PSNR compared to the digital scheme.

4.3 Comparision with an HDA scheme

A subjective test is performed to compare the performance of Swift with the straightforward HDA extension of Soft-Cast which is also channel adaptive. Actually, the main purpose of the subjective quality assessment is to ensure

that the zigzag coding structure does not introduce zigzag viewing experience. Considering that digital scheme may completely corrupt in highly dynamic channel and is inferior to Swift in terms of dominant PSNR, we do not compare Swift with it. The test is carried out using four stereo video sequences:*poznanstreet, newspaper, poznanhall2* and *balloons*, the first two of which have different object motion level without camera motion while the last two have camera motion as well as median object motion. The frame rate is 30fps. SORA trace-driven testbed transmission is used to obtain the received stereo video signals, the channel bandwidth ratio is 0.5 and channel SNR is 9.82dB. The duration of the test sequences is limited to 10s. In this experiment, an autostereoscopic displayer with resolution of 1600x1200 by SeeReal Technology is used. Fifteen assessors aging from 20 to 30 years old participate in the test. Adjectival categorical judgement of stimulus-comparison method recommended by ITU [20] is adopted for the evaluation. The subjective evaluation score is between -3 and 3, where 3 means the quality is much better and -3 means much worse.

Comparing the visual quality of the stereo video received by the Swift receiver with that of the hybrid-digital-softcast receiver, the subjective quality rating results are shown in Fig.11. The bars show the average score of each sequence and the error bars provide the 95% confidential interval. It is clear that Swift achieves better stereo video visual quality than the hybrid-digital-softcast implementation and the quality improvement is obvious. This also verifies that zigzag asymmetric quality compression together with post temporal median filtering at the receiver is a good choice and will not degrade the stereo video visual experience at all.

5. SUMMARY

In this paper, we present the design of the Swift system for low-delay stereo video transmission over wireless channel. The binocular suppression of human visual system is taken into consideration and both robustness and efficiency are achieved through the proposed technologies. Via trace-driven Sora evaluation and subjective quality assessment, we demonstrated that Swift achieves better objective and subjective performance over conventional schemes. The low delay property and channel adaptation ability make it possible to use Swift in real-time mobile 3D applications such as remote immersive experience and interactive control.

In the current design of Swift, source decorrelation at the encoder is performed by chunk-level selective subtraction, and digital frame enhancement at the decoder is achieved by a simple median filter. In the future, we plan to enhance these two modules for better performance. First, analogous to digital coding, motion estimation and compensation can be used for both intra-view and inter-view decorrelation. Specifically, the motion sensors on the video capture devices can be utilized to perform a fast estimation of the intra-view global motion. Second, we will consider leveraging the matched inter-view analog frame and previous intra-view analog frames for digital frame enhancement at the decoder. Motion compensation should also be considered and the motion vectors transmitted from the encoder could be directly used. Such a design is expected to further improve the performance and reduce the delay. In addition, we also plan to collect and test on stereo videos taken from the air and with drastic motions.

6. REFERENCES

[1] 3d display technology and market forecast report: http://www.displaysearch.com/.

[2] H.264/avc software coordination: http://iphome.hhi.de/suehring/tml/.

[3] Microsoft hololens homepage: https://www.microsoft.com/microsoft-hololens/en-us.

[4] Oculus homepage: https://www.oculus.com/.

[5] Sony morpheus: http://blog.us.playstation.com/2015/03/03/project-morpheus-ps4-vr-upgraded-coming-in-2016/.

[6] Videolan homepage: http://www.videolan.org/developers/x264.html.

[7] *IEEE Wireless LAN Medium Access Control (MAC) and Physical Layer (PHY) Specification 802.11*. Piscataway, NJ, 1997.

[8] *MVC Software Manual: JMVC 8.5*. Joint Video Team of the ISO/IEC MPEG and the ITU-T VCEG, 2011.

[9] P. Aflaki, M. Hannuksela, J. Hakala, J. Hakkinen, and M. Gabbouj. Joint adaptation of spatial resolution and sample value quantization for asymmetric stereoscopic video compression: A subjective study. In *7th International Symposium on Image and Signal Processing and Analysis (ISPA), 2011*, Sept 2011.

[10] P. Aflaki, D. Rusanovskyy, T. Utriainen, E. Pesonen, M. Hannuksela, S. Jumisko-Pyykko, and M. Gabbouj. Study of asymmetric quality between coded views in depth-enhanced multiview video coding. In *2011 International Conference on 3D Imaging (IC3D)*, pages 1–8, Dec 2011.

[11] A. Banitalebi-Dehkordi, M. Pourazad, and P. Nasiopoulos. Effect of eye dominance on the perception of stereoscopic 3d video. In *IEEE International Conference on Image Processing (ICIP), 2014*, pages 3469–3473, Oct 2014.

[12] H. Brust, A. Smolic, K. Mueller, G. Tech, and T. Wiegand. Mixed resolution coding of stereoscopic video for mobile devices. In *3DTV Conference: The True Vision - Capture, Transmission and Display of 3D Video, 2009*, pages 1–4, May 2009.

[13] H. Cui, Z. Song, Z. Yang, C. Luo, R. Xiong, and F. Wu. Cactus: A hybrid digital-analog wireless video communication system. In *Proceedings of the 16th ACM International Conference on Modeling, Analysis and Simulation of Wireless and Mobile Systems*, MSWiM '13, pages 273–278, New York, NY, USA, 2013. ACM.

[14] S. Jakubczak and D. Katabi. A cross-layer design for scalable mobile video. In *Proceedings of the 17th Annual International Conference on Mobile Computing and Networking*, MobiCom '11, pages 289–300. ACM, 2011.

[15] T. Kratochvil and R. Stukavec. Dvb-t digital terrestrial television transmission over fading channels. *Radioengineering*, 17(3), Sep 2008.

[16] X. L. Liu, W. Hu, C. Luo, Q. Pu, F. Wu, and Y. Zhang. Parcast+: Parallel video unicast in mimo-ofdm wlans. *Multimedia, IEEE Transactions on*, 16(7):2038–2051, Nov 2014.

[17] L.Kaufman. *Sight and Mind: An introduction to visual perception*. Oxford University Press,New York, 1974.

[18] P. Merkle, A. Smolic, K. Muller, and T. Wiegand. Efficient prediction structures for multiview video coding. *Circuits and Systems for Video Technology, IEEE Transactions on*, 17(11):1461–1473, Nov 2007.

[19] M. Perkins. Data compression of stereopairs. *Communications, IEEE Transactions on*, 40(4):684–696, Apr 1992.

[20] I.-R. Rec.BT.500-13. *Methodology for the subjective assessment of the quality of television pictures*. International Telecommunication Union, 2012.

[21] G. Saygili, C. Guírler, and A. Tekalp. Quality assessment of asymmetric stereo video coding. In *17th IEEE International Conference on Image Processing (ICIP), 2010*, pages 4009–4012, Sept 2010.

[22] K. Tan, J. Zhang, J. Fang, H. Liu, Y. Ye, S. Wang, Y. Zhang, H. Wu, W. Wang, and G. M. Voelker. Sora: High performance software radio using general purpose multi-core processors. In *Proceedings of the 6th USENIX Symposium on Networked Systems Design and Implementation*, NSDI'09, pages 75–90, 2009.

[23] A. Vetro, T. Wiegand, and G. Sullivan. Overview of the stereo and multiview video coding extensions of the h.264/mpeg-4 avc standard. *Proceedings of the IEEE*, 99(4):626–642, April 2011.

[24] T. Wiegand, G. Sullivan, G. Bjontegaard, and A. Luthra. Overview of the h.264/avc video coding standard. *IEEE Transactions on Circuits and Systems for Video Technology*, 13(7):560–576, July 2003.

An Efficient Transmission Method for Bulk Data Based on Network Coding in Delay Tolerant Network

Wancheng Chen,
YueBin Bai, Jiaojiao Liang,
Wenjia Liu and Rui Wang[*]
School of Computer Science and Engineering,
State Key Laboratory of Software
Development Environment,
Beihang University, China

Xiaoyun Mo
National Laboratory for
Parallel and Distributed
Processing,
School of Computer Science,
National University of Defense
Technology, China

Ziming Luo
College of Computer Science
and Technology,
Harbin Engineering University,
China

ABSTRACT

With nodes in Delay Tolerant Network(DTN) distributing sparsely and moving rapidly, they usually suffer from intermittent connections and communications, thus bringing about limited message forwarding opportunities. All these could lead to inefficient forwarding, low delivery, long latency and limited transmission capacity in performance. In this paper, efficient encoding and decision methods are presented and integrated into the DTN routing strategy. The custody-encoding-forwarding mode is designed by merging the random linear network coding into the DTN routing, together with the replica re-allocation and memory management, and built on that encoding scheme, the intra/inter flow adaptive collaborative network coding is elaborated to implement the fresh custody-decision-encoding-forwarding mode. A decision-making strategy based on Bayesian Network(BN) measures the "degree" in a specific generation in networks by taking comprehensive consideration of current and historical network conditions to enhance the network robustness and self-adaptivity. By evaluating the delivery, delay and overhead performance on ONE and MATLAB platforms, the effectiveness of proposed strategies is validated in the end.

Categories and Subject Descriptors

C.2.1 [**Computer-Communication Networks**]: Network Architecture Design—*wireless communication, store and forward networks*

Keywords

network coding; DTN; Bayesian Network; decision-making; performance

[*]The corresponding author, Email: wangrui@buaa.edu.cn.

1. INTRODUCTION

Since Kevin Fall proposed the concept of Delay Tolerant Networks(DTN) in [4] in 2003, continuous attention has been paid in academic research, industry and application areas. DTN is usually a heterogeneous, self-organized wireless network with no central nodes and regarded as an extremely intermittent ad-hoc network. With its advantages in topology variability, network survivability, node heterogeneity and transmission opportunity, DTN is widely used in extreme environments such as deep space[6], military[10], underwater etc., and obtains sustained attention. Compared with general wireless networks, the DTN topology varies more frequently and connections are unstable or scarce, resulting in large amount of data waiting to transmit. Additionally, high-speed or unregulated motion causes short contact duration and thus nodes cannot transmit all data in one contact. All these could hinder the effective data transmission and form the performance bottleneck in a DTN system. Thus, how to improve network throughput and enhance reliability by designing an efficient data transmission method has become an important research spot in DTN.

Network coding is a data transmission technology in networks proposed by Ahlswede in 2000[1]. It has been widely applied in wired/wireless networks and validated to raise throughput, reduce transmission energy and strengthen network robustness significantly. Network coding is a fine-grained replication technique that one encoded message contains more messages' information, so a message has more replicas with different "appearances". As mentioned, network coding can improve network throughput and reliability and has become an appealing topic in wireless networks in recent years. Li and Koetter proved that the linear network coding[11, 9] can achieve the maximum transmission capacity. After that Jaggi proposed the centralized algorithm of linear network coding with polynomial time[7]. Then the random linear network coding is put forward. It has been very popular recently and belongs to the distributed network coding category.

Features[8] such as intermittent connections, scarce links and short communicating time highlight the significance of inter-node forwarding opportunities. How to transmit data efficiently in DTN is a great challenge for researchers. Network coding offers an effective way theoretically to solve this. For example, Katti firstly introduced network coding into wireless networks. He put forward an opportunity encoding scheme COPE[3] which works well in wireless networks by broadcasting. The scheme reduces coding complexity and improves network throughput. But most studies by directly combining the DTN routing (for example, epidemic routing) and network coding to improve transmission reliability are somewhat straightforward and less innovative. They do not take various network environments into consideration and cannot resolve the adaptability of network coding according to different network limits and application requests.

This paper pays attention to the DTN environment with bulk data in rapid mobility, intermittent connections and short contact duration. An effective routing Spray and Wait is integrated into this paper and two concepts are proposed: the Integrated Encoding scheme based on Random Linear Network Coding(IENC) and the Adaptive Collaborative Network Coding of Intra/Inter Flows(ACNC). The first part describes how an encoded DTN message is delivered to the destination by using the integrated network coding scheme, the effective replica re-allocation strategy and *generation-based* memory management. The latter is a deeper study of the former. It measures the *degree* value per generation in the network coding scheme. Large values could cause the high time cost and computational complexity in encoding and decoding process while small ones could lead to little advantage reflected in network coding, so adaptive degree values will be selected to re-adjust in the network to obtain the performance balance between various application requests and network environments. A Bayesian Network(BN) model will be constructed to guide the degree choices in different conditions. The relative construction process involves the parameter selection, the Bayesian Network construction and the generation of network knowledge base.

The rest of the paper is organized as follows. Related work is introduced in section 2. In section 3, the integrated encoding scheme by merging the spray and wait routing and the random linear network coding is presented and relative issues about replica re-allocation strategy and memory management and DTN routing process are involved. In section 4, the adaptive collaborative encoding of intra/inter flows based on Bayesian Network is elaborated. Section 5 shows simulation results and validates the effectiveness of our proposals by comparing different encoding schemes with classical routings. Conclusions are drawn in section 6.

2. RELATED WORK

To improve the poor reliability and the low transmission efficiency, researchers propose a series of methods. Studies about reliability mainly focus on DTN routing. With reasonable increasing message replicas[2], messages can be delivered to destination nodes with a higher probability and the cost of redundancy. For replicas, one extreme approach is Epidemic routing which spreads the message to the entire network until every node holds one replica or the message is timeout. Epidemic routing decreases delivery delay but increases memory overhead, possibly leading to congestion. Another extreme approach is the single-copy routing, saying that there is only one copy for a message in the whole network. It avoids congestion but may seriously impact delivery rate when forwarding direction has somewhat deviation. Studies about improving the transmission efficiency include: giving priority to the message that has the largest utility to forward; using cluster-based routing[19], in which in-cluster messages are forwarded by general nodes and spread inside a

cluster, out-cluster messages are forwarded by cluster-head nodes and are transmitted to other clusters; adding encoding function to the routing module and then encoding several messages into a combined message to improve the bandwidth utilization.

Network coding is an effective way to improve the wireless network throughput and is mostly suitable for DTN. How to enhance transmission efficiency with the help of network coding has become a hot topic. Main research work involves the network coding built on DTN routing strategies. Authors in [16] combine the network coding with Prophet routing. Intermediate nodes use the linear network coding to encode data before transmitting and simulation results show that this method can increase the delivery. In [17] the network traffic is generated in regular intervals and authors put forward a mathematical model that can analyze data delivery under network coding based Epidemic routing. In [14] authors also propose a method in which the node cache status is set as an variable, and ordinary differential equations are used to analyze data transmission delay. Additionally, a network coding method based Epidemic routing is also proposed in this paper. Based on [14], [13] combines network coding with the Spray and Wait routing and restricts the amount of message replicas. In this scheme, data transmission amount is greatly reduced at the expense of higher delay performance.

But current work mainly focuses on combining network coding schemes with routing strategies without any consideration of DTN particular environments. On one hand, DTN has various application requests which should be dealt with different coding strategies; on the other hand, historical results play a guiding role to current decision-making process but neglected by these studies. How to encode messages efficiently according to current surrounding environments is becoming a new research field in recent years[15]. How does the network coding collaborate with a specific routing to solve problems in DTN scenarios such as intermittent connections, short communicating time, bulk data,etc? This paper mainly will work them out in detail and to achieve that, an efficient integrated encoding method will be introduced firstly.

3. THE INTEGRATED ENCODING BASED ON RANDOM LINEAR NETWORK CODING

As discussed, network coding is a fine-grained replication technique that one encoded message has the equal size with an original one but contains more than one messages' information. In this way, an original message can have more replicas with different appearance and raise message reliability without the expense of replication overhead. In this section, an integrated encoding scheme based on the spray and wait routing and the random linear network coding, denoted as IENC, will be presented for the scenario with rapid mobility, intermittent connections and short transmitting time in which a complete message cannot be forwarded in a contact. Relative issues about replica re-allocation strategy, memory management and forwarding process are complementary with the encoding scheme. Via this, the classical storage-custody-forwarding mode is changed into the optimized storage-custody-encoding-forwarding mode in DTN.

3.1 Assumptions and Limitations

Suppose the number of nodes in the network is N, including M pairs of source-destination nodes ($M < N/2$). Each pair may transmit more than one message flows, so the total number of message flows in the network can be larger than M. Some concepts frequently used in this section are defined. A *source message* is the message generated by a source node. It is usually large and segmented into smaller ones (called *raw messages*) to transmit. An *encoded message* is the combined message encoded by some *raw messages*.

In real networks, due to the various topology and the large network scale, a node obtaining the whole network topology and each node's coding coefficients is too consumed or unrealistic. So T. Ho et al.[5] proposed the random network coding in algebraic framework. Coefficients in this method is chosen from alphabet (Usually a alphabet has a finite field, such as Galois field F_{2^m}. It is validated that when we choose Galois field, the decoding failure probability can be negligible). This encoding method is used in the paper.

The term *generation* restricts what kinds of messages can be encoded to a new encoded one. In this section, messages with the finite combination of raw messages generated by the same source node belong to one generation. The random linear network coding only encodes messages that are in one generation. Ideas about *degree* and *operation mode* are described as follows.

- *Degree*: The number of raw messages combined into an encoded message in this section. This value is critical. The larger it is, the more information it contains but not always the best choice.

- *Operation mode*: The classical *XOR* mode is adopted in this paper to encode raw messages. It is simple and productive, so the encoding and decoding process will be efficient. It is suitable for DTN scenarios where nodes have limited computational capacity.

3.2 Network Coding Mechanism with the Forwarding Process

A source node segments the source message into K smaller raw messages denoted by $m_i (i = 1, 2, ..., K)$. When meeting another node, it transmits the linear combination of K raw messages, denoted by f:

$$f = \vec{a}\vec{M} = \sum_{i=1}^{K} a_i m_i, a_i \in F_q$$

in which f is the encoded message based on raw messages. The source node forwards it to a intermediate (or destination) node. Here $\vec{a}$ is the coding coefficient vector and it constitutes K random numbers a_i selected from the finite field F_q.

The new storage-custody-encoding-forwarding strategy is executed in a intermediate node. It stores the arrived messages in its memory (using the memory management in subsection 3.4) and carries them until it meets another node. If the node has R independent encoded messages, which is to say, its rank is R and these R encoding coefficient vectors constitute an encoding matrix. When two nodes encounter they exchange their encoding matrices and then determine whether the other's encoding matrix could increase its own rank. If so, it will send a request to transmit a random linear combination of all messages (raw or encoded messages)

and vice versa. For example, there are T messages in the other node, denoted as f_1, f_2,..., f_T. We choose a set of coefficients β_1, β_2,..., β_T from the finite field F_q. A new linear combination is defined as follows and the new encoded message is another new linear combination of raw messages m_i:

$$f_{new} = \sum_{j=1}^{T} (\beta_j \sum_{i=1}^{k} a_i m_i) = \sum_{r=1}^{k} c_r m_r, a_i, \beta_j, c_r \in F_q$$

A destination node keeps receiving messages until its rank equals to K, and then it decodes raw messages through matrix inversion. For example, if K independent encoded messages arrived are $\vec{F} = (f_1, ..., f_k)^T$, and raw messages are $\vec{M} = (m_1, ..., m_k)^T$, then $\vec{M} = A^{-1}\vec{F}$. When the destination node decodes all raw messages targeted at it, it restructures the source message and delivers it to upper applications.

3.3 Replica Re-allocation with *Matrix Rank*

Since the integrated encoding scheme is built on the spray and wait(SW) routing, replica re-allocation is related to this routing strategy. It has a limited replica policy called the *forwarding authority*. A source node assigns each generation a replica maximum C called *token*, indicating a message's forwarding authority to the corresponding generation. If C is bigger than 1, it means the message can be sent to other intermediate nodes; otherwise, the message can only be sent to its destination node. With the limited replicas, the network can avoid congestion effectively in most conditions.

When a source node encounters other nodes, it forwards the encoded message as well as the token. The replica re-allocation mainly discusses how the token number C is modified[18] in the forwarding process. Suppose node a forwards a message to node b. The corresponding matrix rank of a is m and that of b is n. The replica number of node a is $token_a$ and that of b is $token_b$. So the re-allocation strategy is as follows:

$$token_b' = \lceil (token_a + token_b) * n/(m+n) \rceil$$

$$token_a' = \lfloor (token_a + token_b) * m/(m+n) \rfloor$$

Here if $token_b'$ is equal to $token_b$, $token_b'$ increases by 1 and $token_a'$ decreases by 1.

3.4 Memory Management based on *Generation*

To utilize the limited memory space in a DTN node efficiently, each generation is set to occupying the equal memory size initially. Suppose the total memory space in a node is P, messages stored in it are classified into Q generations. Each generation is assigned to take up P/Q memory space.

If a node receives a *useful* message (the term *useful* means the message will increase the rank of its corresponding generation matrix), we adopt the following memory management strategy:

- If the receiving node has enough vacant memory space to buffer the message, store it; otherwise continue the next step;

- If the generation the message belongs to should have vacant memory space but it is temporarily occupied by other generations, the receiving node recovers its memory space to buffer the message, otherwise continue the next step. The memory recovery scheme will be shown below;

- Manage its corresponding generation memory and store the message. The memory management scheme will also be shown below.

Memory recovery: release buffer space until enough vacant memory space in the node can store the message. In more detail, choose two records (the selection principle may be FIFO, TTL, Utility-Least, etc.) from the generation that occupies the largest memory space, encode them and store the new encoded one. In this way the node releases some buffer space. If there is only one record, delete it and release the buffer space.

Memory management: release buffer space until enough vacant memory space in its generation can store the message. That is, choose two records (the same selection principle as above) from its generation, encode them and store the new encoded one only. In this way the generation releases some buffer space.

4. THE ADAPTIVE COLLABORATIVE NETWORK CODING OF INTRA/INTER FLOWS BASED ON BAYESIAN NETWORK

As mentioned above, it has been explained why the degree is critical in various DTN environments. How to choose an appropriate value when encoding is a complicated decision-making process. We should consider not only time and computational complexity, but also the historical decision-making results and current network preconditions. Therefore, the concept of Adaptive Collaborative Network Coding of Intra/Inter-Flows based on Bayesian Network(ACNC) is proposed. It can dynamically adjust the degree value by taking consideration of comprehensive network parameters. In the collaborative encoding, the degree means how many small ones to encode a large message should be segmented into (i.e. how much data a Bundle should contain) and how many large messages one generation should cover (i.e. how many segments of different large messages to encode should contain at most). Note that a large message is called a data flow in this section between the source and the destination in this section.

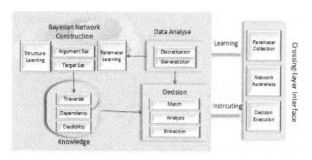

Figure 1: The Structure of Bayesian Network

To achieve this, the basic collaborative encoding model is presented(Figure 1) in this section. There are the following key parts: crossing layer interface, data analyse, Bayesian

Network, knowledge and decision making. The *crossing layer interface* integrates the parameter collection component and the decision execution component into the DTN stack in order to collect network information in each layer and implement cross-layer communication more effectively. The *data analyse* part processes the collected information (for example, discretising continuous variables) and delivers them to the *Bayesian Network construction* part. A Bayesian network[12] is an uncertain knowledge expressing and reasoning model based on probability analysis and graph theory. It is a network graph explaining causal relationships by a directed acyclic graph(DAG). By structure and parameter learning, it builds a weighted DAG used in the *knowledge* part to generalize basic knowledge items. The *decision making* part extracts the useful knowledge and make the best choice to execute.

4.1 Parameter Selection

Different applications and network environments should focus on different network parameter indicators. For example, the quality of service(QoS), is always measured by delay, delivery and overhead; network overhead consists of time and space comsumption; drop ratio embodies the network congestion. It is important to choose suitable parameters in DTN to represent the current environment and to support the network reconfiguration. This paper aims to optimize the network coding performance by choosing the appropriate segment number in one flow and the adaptive flow number in one generation that satisfies application requirements, maximizes gains of network coding and minimizes overhead.

Table 1: Parameter selection

DTN stack	parameter name
application layer	application data size
bundle layer	bundle size, segment number in one flow ($SegNo$), flow number in one generation ($FlowNo$)
transport layer	message delay, delivery, replicas
physical layer	transmission speed($TransSpeed$)

The parameter selection means the data perception and collection process in DTN. Two different types of parameters are considered in this section: *observed* parameters and *controllable* parameters. An observed parameter is used to reflect the current network status which describes the network context and provides support for controllable parameters. A controllable parameter can re-adjust itself in a network and be part of a collaborative encoding policy to improve the encoding performance according to observed parameters. Some parameters are simply selected in the network, such as the transmission speed and the message size while the others are collected by measuring the network performance, including message delay, delivery, overhead and drop ratio. Network parameters in Table 1 are chosen to reflect the current network status and would be the basis of decision-making.

4.2 Bayesian Network Construction

Structure learning is to construct the structure of the Bayesian network between network variables. In this process a search-based scoring method is used to select one structure with the highest score by scoring all the candidates. We adopt a classic algorithm $K2$ which is notable for its high efficiency and accuracy. It is a greedy search algorithm and selects a structure that maximizes the network's posterior probability. It uses the prior nodes' order as inputs. The input order is critical to the network structure because if node i comes prior to node j in the sequence, j cannot be a parent of i. In other words, the potential parent set of node i can only include the nodes that precede it in the input order. In the beginning, the parent set of i is empty. This algorithm visits each node and greedily adds eligible nodes to the parent set of i if this addition increases the score. The score function is defined as follows:

$$P(S, D) = C \prod_{i=1}^{n} \max[\prod_{j=1}^{q_i} \frac{(r_i - 1)!}{(N_{ij} + r_i - 1)!} \prod_{k=1}^{n} N_{ijk}!]$$

where S is the structure to be scored, D is the input data set and $N = \{X_1, X_2, ..., X_n\}$ means the value range of $X_i = \{x_{i1}, x_{i2}, ..., x_{ir_i}\}$. N_{ij} is the total number of relationships between variable X_i and parent X_j, so N_{ijk} is the number of relationships when X_i is x_{ik} and $N_{ij} = \sum_{k=1}^{r_i} N_{ijk}$. q_i is the possible parent number of X_i. It selects the minimum representative subset of the space of the whole network and is a heuristic and hill-climbing algorithm. It stops when any of the following conditions appear:

- The number of parents for a certain node reaches its maximum or no more parents to add;

- The score does not increase any more.

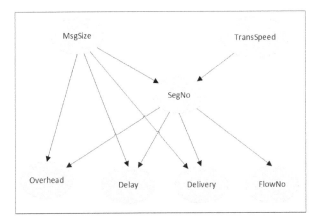

Figure 2: The Structure After Learning

Figure 2 shows the Bayesian network after structure learning, in which the controllable variables are the segment number in one message ($SegNo$) and the flow number in one generation($FlowNo$), and the observed ones includes the message size($MsgSize$), the transmission speed($TransSpeed$), the $Delay$, $Delivery$ and $Overhead$. There exists a dependent relationship if two nodes are connected by an arc form the statistic theory. For example, this figure shows that $Delay$ or $Delivery$ depends on the variable $SegNo$ statistically after the training based on a given data set. Credibility about these dependencies will be measured by parameter learning.

Parameter learning is to compute conditional probabilities of dependent relationships between variables in Figure 2. It is also used to estimate the best set of parents for

each variable. In an application with a given structure, the goal of parameter learning is to find conditional probabilities which maximizes the likelihood function. The normalized log-likelihood L of the data set D is a sum of terms for each node:

$$\max L = \frac{1}{N} \sum_{i=1}^{n} \sum_{D} \log p(X_i | Parent(X_i), D)$$

where p is the conditional probability and $Parent(X_i)$ is the parent set of X_i. p is calculated by

$$p[X_i = x_{ik} | pa_i = X_j] \approx \frac{N_{ijk}}{N_{ij}}$$

where pa_i is the parent of X_i.

4.3 Network Knowledge Base Generation

The construction of knowledge base is to find the optimal configuration parameters in different scenarios to improve the collaborative encoding performance. Knowledge provides support for the *degree* choice. We abstract the graph structure and probabilities in a Bayesian network into knowledge expressing relationships and credibility between observed parameters and controllable parameters. In this paper, the knowledge is defined by the four-triple as follows:

$$\langle precondition, objective, strategy, probability \rangle$$

in which the *precondition* is the current network condition including application requests or network environments, the *objective* usually indicates the network performance indexes (such as delay, delivery, overhead, etc.), the *strategy* means the decision we make to achieve that objective and the *probability* represents the credibility of the expected objective after the corresponding strategy is carried out. Given the Bayesian network structure in Figure 2 and relationships between observed parameters and controllable parameters, elements in the above four triple are represented by:

- precondition element: transmission speed ($TransSpeed$) and message size ($MsgSize$);

- objective element: delay, overhead, delivery;

- strategy element: segment number ($SegNo$) in one message and flow number ($FlowNo$) in one generation.

Table 2 shows part of the knowledge base used in the paper. In this table, the only objective is the delivery and the precondition parameters are the transmission speed and the message size. The strategy lists different combinations of the segment number and the flow number to adapt to different network preconditions. The probability shows the credibility under these strategy combinations. Therefore, the four triple can be denoted as $\langle TransSpeed\&MsgSize, Delivery, SegNo\&FlowNo, probability \rangle$.

In addition, since the knowledge varies dynamically, a management engine is built necessarily to maintain the knowledge base by establishing, updating and even deleting useless or out-of-date knowledge.

5. SIMULATION AND ANALYSIS

In this section we validate the effectiveness of proposed network coding schemes, including integrated encoding scheme based on random linear network coding (section 3) and the adaptive collaborative encoding strategy (section 4) from

Precondition	Objective	Strategy	Probability
TransSpeed=170, MsgSize=500	Delivery=0.85	SegNo=1, FlowNo=3	0.8
TransSpeed=190, MsgSize=900	Delivery=0.95	SegNo=3, FlowNo=1	0.87
TransSpeed=230, MsgSize=900	Delivery=0.85	SegNo=2, FlowNo=2	0.73
TransSpeed=250, MsgSize=1300	Delivery=0.95	SegNo=4, FlowNo=1	0.93

aspects of delivery, delay and overhead. Motion of nodes is assign as the *random waypoint mobility* model and simulation experiments run on *MATLAB* and *ONE*. *MATLAB* is used to analyze data and generate the complete Bayesian network structure. Table 3 lists relative environment settings.

Table 3: Simulation Parameters

Parameter	Value
Scenario size	500m*600m
Simulation time	3600s
Message size	400k-1400k
Message TTL	1800 seconds
Routing protocol	Epidemic, Prophet, SW
Transmission speed	150kBps
Transmission range	14m
Mobility speed	18-36, 45-63, 72-90 km/h
Buffer size	3-30MB
Number of flows	20
Number of nodes	40

5.1 Validation of the Integrated Encoding with Random Linear Network Coding

The integrated encoding scheme based on random linear network coding is proposed in section 3. It is integrated with the Spray and Wait routing in DTN and we will prove its effectiveness in this subsection. For comparison, some classical encoding schemes with Epidemic and Prophet routing in DTN will be simulated. Delivery, delay and overhead of replicas are assigned as performance indexes. Figure 3 shows performance of Epidemic with network coding, Prophet with network coding and the proposed encoding scheme with Spray and Wait routing (denoted as *Epidemic_NC*, *Prophet_NC* and *SW_NC* respectively in the legend of Figure 3).

From the figure, we can see that our proposed encoding scheme performs best and Epidemic with network coding does worst in all indexes not surprisingly. It is because that on one hand, in encoded Epidemic routing, a node sends a copy to every node it meets, which may cause network inefficiency even the congestion; on the other hand, it has to receive a large number of messages, and deletes or updates its limited memory with the encoding operation frequently. All these could lead to the lowest delivery, the highest delay and the most replicas. As for encoded Prophet routing, a node only sends the copy to another which has the highest probability (or at least a higher probability than itself) meeting the destination. Although it seems to lower the redundancy of copies, it would incur a message to take the longer time to deliver to the destination and cause the higher delay. Compared with them, our proposed encoding scheme not only controls the replicas of a message in an ac-

ceptable range by the *token* to avoid the network congestion effectively. With the help of effective encoding and memory management strategy, a node sends messages to its destination nodes in time and thus gets the better performance.

5.2 Validation of the Adaptive Collaborative Network Coding of Intra/Inter Flows

Due to the rapid mobility, intermittent connections and short transmitting time, larger messages (bulk data) possibly cannot be forwarded completely in one contact and have to retransmit the whole message next time even the receiver has successfully accepted most of it. The proposed integrated encoding scheme is proposed to focus on this phenomenon. However, in a network with multiple generations and various lengths of messages, this scheme would cause less satisfactory performance because it cannot re-adjust the *degree* dynamically. Therefore, the adaptive collaborative network coding of intra/inter flows(ACNC) method is put forward in section 4 to solve this problem in a further step. In this subsection, the effectiveness of the adaptive collaborative scheme will be validated while some degree *fixed* integrated encoding schemes will be simulated for comparison. The delivery and delay will be measured in these experiments.

Figure 4 shows the performance of the adaptive collaborative encoding method (denoted as *Adaptive* in the legend) and some *fixed* integrated encoding schemes (denoted as *Fixed* in the legend) with different message sizes. In the subfigure (a) it can be observed that the adaptive method has the overall higher delivery than the other three curves which fluctuate in a larger range. The delivery of the first fixed strategy goes down dramatically as the message size gets larger, which indicates that the larger message needs to be segmented into more smaller ones to get a better performance. But more smaller ones is not always the best choice; it will lead to the low delivery probably (as shown in the fixed strategy with 7 segments of a message less than 600KB). In the simulation, the delivery of the adaptive strategy may be not the highest with all message sizes, but stay stable and vary in a smaller range. From the statistic data, the average delivery of the adaptive method is 15.9%, 2.5% and 3.5% higher respectively than those of the other three fixed strategies. Similar simulation results are observed in the subfigure (b). As the message size gets larger, the delay with less segments increases dramatically. In a scenario with the small message size (for example, less than 600KB), the more segments seems unnecessary and may cause the larger delay performance because destination nodes need to collect more encoded segments to decode the original one. The average delay of the adaptive method is 26%, 4.5% and 6% smaller respectively than those of the other three fixed strategies.

In a scenario with different transmission speed, the performance of the adaptive collaborative encoding method and

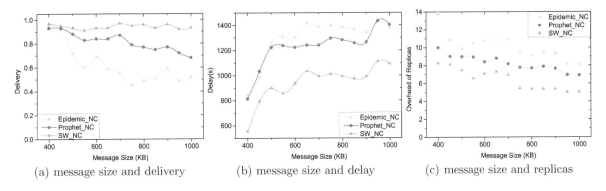

Figure 3: performance of different routing strategies with random linear network coding

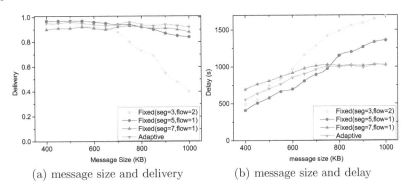

Figure 4: the adaptive collaborative encoding performance with different message sizes

some fixed integrated encoding schemes can be shown in Figure 5. The adaptive method performs better in both message delivery and delay than those of the other three fixed strategies. In these experiments, the delivery gets higher and gaps among these strategies gets smaller as the transmission speed goes up. It is because that more information is forwarded in a contact between nodes with higher transmission speed; that is to say, in this condition, the larger segment of a message will have a much higher probability to be forwarded successfully. That is also the dominant reason why the delivery of a fixed strategy with less segments has a poor performance. It is interesting that more segments, an evident advantage at the small transmission speed, becomes less important when the speed gets higher and turns into the disadvantage even in some cases because too many segments cause the longer delay in collecting more segments to decode the original message. The adaptive method solves this problem effectively by choosing the best decision dynamically it thinks at current scenarios. In a whole, the overall delivery of the adaptive method is 27%, 8.8% and 3.6% respectively than those of the other three fixed strategies, and its average delay is 29%, 10.5% and 6.4% than the others.

With decision-making based on Bayesian networks, the proposed adaptive collaborative encoding method works well in DTN scenarios with multiple generations and various lengths of messages. It can fit different network conditions and improve the DTN performance effectively.

6. CONCLUSION

The DTN scenarios with bulk data, high-speed mobility, intermittent connections and short transmitting time are paid attention to in this paper. In these scenarios, messages forwarded to destination nodes successfully without missing any information is challenging. This paper makes an attempt to work it out. Two concepts are proposed: The Integrated Encoding scheme based on Random Linear Network Coding (IENC) and the Adaptive Collaborative Network Coding strategy of Intra/Inter Flows(ACNC). The former elaborates an encoding scheme involved the spray and wait routing, memory management and replica re-allocation strategy, and the latter focuses on how to select an appropriate *degree* to maximize the advantage of network coding and minimize its overhead. Bayesian Network is utilized to make decisions based on both historical strategy results and current network environments. The custody-coding-forwarding method in the former and the custody-coding-decision-forwarding method in the latter are both implemented. In the end, the effectiveness of the proposed methods is validated by simulation experiments on *MATLAB* and *ONE* in which delivery, delay and overhead are measured.

7. ACKNOWLEDGMENTS

This work is supported by the National Science Foundation of China under Grant *No.*61572062, 61202425 and 61073076, National High Technology Research and Development (863) Program of China under Grant *No.*2012AA010902, State Key Laboratory of Software Development Environment under Grant *No.*SKLSDE-2014ZX-18, and Beihang University Innovation & Practice Fund for Graduate under Grant *No.*YCSJ-02-2015-08.

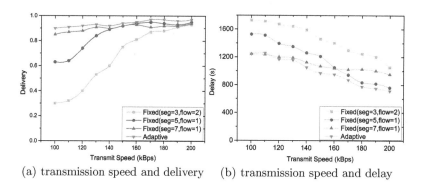

| (a) transmission speed and delivery | (b) transmission speed and delay |

Figure 5: the adaptive collaborative encoding performance with different transmission speed

8. REFERENCES

[1] R. Ahlswede, N. Cai, S.-Y. Li, and R. W. Yeung. Network information flow. *Information Theory, IEEE Transactions on*, 46(4):1204–1216, 2000.

[2] A. Balasubramanian, B. N. Levine, and A. Venkataramani. Replication routing in dtns: a resource allocation approach. *IEEE/ACM Transactions on Networking (TON)*, 18(2):596–609, 2010.

[3] Q. Dong, J. Wu, W. Hu, and J. Crowcroft. Practical network coding in wireless networks. In *Proceedings of the 13th annual ACM international conference on Mobile computing and networking*, pages 306–309. ACM, 2007.

[4] K. Fall. A delay-tolerant network architecture for challenged internets. In *Proceedings of the 2003 conference on Applications, technologies, architectures, and protocols for computer communications*, pages 27–34. ACM, 2003.

[5] T. Ho, M. Médard, J. Shi, M. Effros, and D. R. Karger. On randomized network coding. In *Proceedings of the Annual Allerton Conference on Communication Control and Computing*, volume 41, pages 11–20. The University, 2003.

[6] D. J. Israel, A. J. Hooke, K. Freeman, and J. J. Rush. The nasa space communications data networking architecture. In *SpaceOps 2006 Conference*, 2006.

[7] S. Jaggi, P. Sanders, P. A. Chou, M. Effros, S. Egner, K. Jain, and L. M. Tolhuizen. Polynomial time algorithms for multicast network code construction. *Information Theory, IEEE Transactions on*, 51(6):1973–1982, 2005.

[8] M. J. Khabbaz, C. M. Assi, and W. F. Fawaz. Disruption-tolerant networking: A comprehensive survey on recent developments and persisting challenges. *Communications Surveys & Tutorials, IEEE*, 14(2):607–640, 2012.

[9] R. Koetter and M. Médard. An algebraic approach to network coding. *Networking, IEEE/ACM Transactions on*, 11(5):782–795, 2003.

[10] R. Krishnan, P. Basu, J. M. Mikkelson, C. Small, R. Ramanathan, D. W. Brown, J. R. Burgess, A. L. Caro, M. Condell, N. C. Goffee, et al. The spindle disruption-tolerant networking system. In *Military Communications Conference*, pages 1–7. IEEE, 2007.

[11] S.-Y. Li, R. W. Yeung, and N. Cai. Linear network coding. *Information Theory, IEEE Transactions on*, 49(2):371–381, 2003.

[12] J. Liang, Y. Bai, C. Bi, Z. Sun, C. Yan, and H. Liang. Adaptive routing based on bayesian network and fuzzy decision algorithm in delay-tolerant network. In *High Performance Computing and Communications & 2013 IEEE International Conference on Embedded and Ubiquitous Computing (HPCC_EUC), 2013 IEEE 10th International Conference on*, pages 690–697. IEEE, 2013.

[13] Y. Lin, B. Li, and B. Liang. Efficient network coded data transmissions in disruption tolerant networks. In *INFOCOM 2008. The 27th Conference on Computer Communications. IEEE*. IEEE, 2008.

[14] Y. Lin, B. Liang, and B. Li. Performance modeling of network coding in epidemic routing. In *Proceedings of the 1st international MobiSys workshop on Mobile opportunistic networking*, pages 67–74. ACM, 2007.

[15] M. Radenkovic and S. Zakhary. Flexible and dynamic network coding for adaptive data transmission in dtns. In *Wireless Communications and Mobile Computing Conference (IWCMC), 2012 8th International*, pages 567–573. IEEE, 2012.

[16] J. Widmer and J.-Y. Le Boudec. Network coding for efficient communication in extreme networks. In *Proceedings of the 2005 ACM SIGCOMM workshop on Delay-tolerant networking*, pages 284–291. ACM, 2005.

[17] S.-K. Yoon and Z. J. Haas. Application of linear network coding in delay tolerant networks. In *Ubiquitous and Future Networks (ICUFN), 2010 Second International Conference on*, pages 338–343. IEEE, 2010.

[18] X. Zhang, G. Neglia, J. Kurose, D. Towsley, and H. Wang. Benefits of network coding for unicast application in disruption-tolerant networks. *Networking, IEEE/ACM Transactions on*, 21(5):1407–1420, 2013.

[19] Z. Zhang, M. Ma, and Z. Jin. Ccs-dtn: Efficient routing in social dtns based on clustering and network coding. In *Global Communications Conference (GLOBECOM), 2013 IEEE*, pages 60–64. IEEE, 2013.

Author Index

www.ingramcontent.com/pod-product-compliance
Lightning Source LLC
LaVergne TN
LVHW060134070326
832902LV00018B/2798